PSYCHOLOGY OF RELIGION

CLASSIC AND CONTEMPORARY

Second Edition

PSYCHOLOGY OF RELIGION

Classic and Contemporary

DAVID M. WULFF

Wheaton College
Massachusetts

JOHN WILEY & SONS, INC.

New York • Chichester • Brisbane • Toronto • Singapore • Weinheim

ACQUISITIONS EDITOR   Eric Stano
MARKETING MANAGER   Kimberley Manzi
PRODUCTION EDITOR   Sandra Russell
DESIGN SUPERVISOR   Ann Marie Renzi
MANUFACTURING MANAGER   Dorothy Sinclair
PHOTO RESEARCHER   Hilary Newman
ILLUSTRATION EDITOR   Edward Starr
ILLUSTRATION ASSISTANT   Sandra Rigby

TEXT DESIGN   Lee Goldstein
COVER DESIGN   Carolyn Joseph
COVER ART   Adoring Bodhisattva, a sandstone relief sculpture from one of the twenty-one cave temples of
T'ien-Lung Shan (Heavenly Dragon Mountain) in Shansi province, China, Northern Ch'i dynasty,
550-557 C.E. Courtesy of the Museum of Art, Rhode School of Design, Mary B. Jackson Fund.

This book was set in ITC New Baskerville by Ruttle, Shaw & Wetherill, Inc. and
printed and bound by Hamilton Printing. The cover was printed by Phoenix Color Corporation.

Recognizing the importance of preserving what has been written, it is a policy of John Wiley & Sons, Inc.
to have books of enduring value published in the United States printed on acid-free paper, and we exert our
best efforts to that end.

The paper in this book was manufactured by a mill whose forest management programs include sustained
yield harvesting of its timberlands. Sustained yield harvesting principles ensure that the numbers of trees
cut each year does not exceed the amount of new growth.

Library of Congress Cataloging in Publication Data:
Wulff, David M., 1940-
    Psychology of religion : classic and contemporary / David M.
Wulff. — 2nd ed.
        p.   cm.
    Includes bibliographical references and index.
    ISBN 0-471-03706-0 (cloth : alk. paper)
    1. Psychology, Religious.   2. Psychology, Religious—Study and
teaching—History.   I. Title.
BL53.W77   1997
200′.1′9—dc20   96-43970
                                                        CIP

Printed in the United States of America

10 9 8 7 6 5 4 3 2

PREFACE

*F*or students of religion, these are exceptionally interesting times. At a point in human history when many thought that religion was on its way out, a casualty of science and rationality, we are witnessing a worldwide resurgence of fundamentalism, on the one hand, and a virtual explosion of interest in the "new spirituality" on the other. Evidence of the growing influence of fundamentalism appears in our newspapers almost daily, in reports from around the world on the sometimes violent efforts to reformulate laws and customs in terms of authoritative sacred texts or traditions. The new spirituality has likewise proved to be newsworthy; but as a product of today's religious pluralism, it aspires mainly to personal rather than social transformation. Thus, it is chiefly known from its presence on the best-seller lists and from the multiplicity of self-help groups that appeal to a spiritual dimension. Both fundamentalism and today's eclectic spirituality have become the objects of foundation-supported research. Even federal agencies are funding investigations on spirituality as a possible factor in human well-being.

These are interesting times for students of psychology as well. Throughout much of the twentieth century, the various schools of psychology vied for supremacy, each convinced of its own superiority, each offering a framework for unifying the field. Although today's introductory psychology textbooks give the impression that a consensus is finally emerging, psychology has actually become more diversified and divided. The number of specialized subject areas continues to multiply, and psychologists seem farther away than ever from resolving fundamental conceptual and methodological issues. What does seem to be emerging, however, is a new tolerance born of the postmodern convictions that there is no logical basis for privileging one perspective over another, and that a plurality of views is not only inevitable but also desirable.

Contemporary students of the psychology of religion thus face a double challenge. First, they must conceive of religion in terms sufficiently broad to encompass the diverse expressions of today's religious pluralism. Along with the various fundamentalisms and the "new spirituality," these include more traditional forms of piety as they fitfully evolve in today's increasingly global society. Second, students of the psychology of religion are challenged to draw as broadly and critically as they can on the rich array of perspectives offered by contemporary psychologists. Researchers may choose on pragmatic grounds to operate within a single frame of reference or to employ a limited range of methods. But the field as a whole would be impoverished if a single perspective were to become dominant. Alternate points of view serve to multiply the aspects of religion that we take into account at the same time that they provide critical perspective on the other psychological frameworks. We should be wary of any approach that claims to be sufficient in itself.

The attainment of a pluralistic perspective requires both courage and intellectual maturity. This is especially true in relation to religion, for disinterested examination of it can be deeply disturbing. As young children discover when they learn that "There is no Santa Claus," when we subject an aspect of human culture to self-conscious reflection, the exhilarating moment of insight is often followed by the melancholy realization that the cultural element and our relation to it have been irrevocably changed. Self-awareness robs us of the innocence with which we automatically believed and participated in these once-mysterious cultural forms. As James Carey (1988, p. 11) observes, in the quest for the origins of human society, "each of the ancient cultural practices has been shown to be not in the nature of things, not a representation of the ways of the world, not a mirror of transcendent reality but one more human practice, one more thing we made up along the way to modernity." To recognize the human side of these cultural artefacts, however, can also be enormously emancipating, as advocates of the new spirituality have found.

Attaining a pluralistic perspective in psychology is difficult in part because there are so few exemplars of it. Most psychologists remain committed either to a single point of view or to a limited range of related ones. Even when they set about to characterize alternate perspectives, as today's textbook writers frequently do, they are prone to misrepresenting them and to imposing on them a single, often alien standard of theory construction and assessment. Recent works introducing the pluralistic views of postmodernism and social constructionism into psychology may be harbingers of a new era of mutual respect and understanding.

Embracing a pluralistic perspective, whether in religion or in psychology, also requires a certain level of intellectual maturity. In his classic study of intellectual development in college students, William Perry (1970) found that coming to terms with the complexities of multiple perspectives and the relativistic context in which they exist was the pivotal challenge for his subjects during their four years of college. Growth was not steady but tended to occur in surges, with pauses of waiting or regathering forces. Occasionally some students retreated to an earlier, dualistic position of right and wrong views or escaped by settling into positions without acknowledging their implications for growth. Most, however, eventually found their way into the final stages, of making commitments within the framework of an enduring relativism.

The first edition of this book sought to promote a pluralistic orientation toward both psychology and religion. Because it is mainly a survey of the field as others have conceived of and contributed to it, this work is necessarily limited to the perspectives that the various contributors represent. Collectively, however, their views are remarkably wide-ranging in regard to psychology as well as religion. This revised edition retains the original organization and breadth of coverage. The commitment to the pluralistic standpoint, however, has now been made fully explicit, mainly through a revised introductory chapter that systematically introduces the new pluralisms in religion and psychology. A number of other sections of the book have also been updated through the integration of research findings and reflections derived from more than 350 new references, and portions of the remaining text have been edited to make them more consistently readable.

As readers of this book discover, a comprehensive understanding of the psychology of religion requires systematic knowledge of diverse kinds: of a great variety of psychological theories, principles, and methods as well as essential aspects of neighboring fields such as neurophysiology and sociobiology; of the history of religions along with elements of theology and philosophy; and of the history of the psychology of religion itself, and of the lives of its chief contributors. It also requires acquaintance with a widely scattered literature that, more than 60 years ago, was declared by one of the most knowledgeable psychologists of religion in Europe to be so large that a genuine mastery of it was no longer possible (Gruehn, 1930, p. 891). Yet even if mastery of the field as a whole is out of the question, aspiration to a genuine understanding of religion impels us to draw on insights from every possible quarter.

To help the reader with the various technical vocabularies used in this study, I have included a glossary of more than 550 terms at the back of the book. Every word or expression for which there is a definition in the glossary appears in SMALL CAPITALS at least once in the text, usually on its first occurrence. Because some of these terms appear in the text in two or more variants—for example, ascetic and asceticism—the glossary entry may not correspond exactly to the flagged occurrence. Glossary definitions are necessarily limited to the meanings relevant to the present study. The reader is also encouraged to become well acquainted with the index, which not only offers easy access to various topics in the book but also provides a detailed overview of the diverse subject matter this volume considers.

A more succinct overview of the book's coverage is provided from three different perspectives in Table P.1. The top section of this table employs categories used in introductory surveys of Western psychology. As the reader can see, most of these topic areas are considered in more than one chapter of the book. It is also evident how pervasively the related approaches of developmental, personality, and clinical psychology have contributed to this field. The middle section of the table gives an overview in terms of research methods. Some of these methods are understandably limited to certain theoretical perspectives; others are more widely employed. Read vertically, this table suggests that the German descriptive tradition (Chapter 12), which has been largely overlooked in the English language literature, is the most inclusive in terms of method. The table's bottom section provides an inventory of the book according to the world's major religious traditions (Adams, 1977). The fact that the psychology of religion has been, in the main, the psychology of the *Christian* tradition is here unmistakable. By organizing this book in terms of psychological perspectives rather than such traditional religious phenomena as conversion, I have more easily brought other major traditions into discussion as well. Reading the table vertically once again, we see that the chapters on biological foundations (Chapter 3) and on Jung (Chapter 10) are most inclusive of the religious traditions.

I wish to emphasize that this is a work on the psychology *of* religion. The use of the genitive implies that religion, for better or worse, will be the object of psychological analysis. Some scholars and practitioners interested in both psychology and religion, rather than subordinating one to the other, seek to bring them into mutually respectful dialogue. Still others aspire to an "integration" of the two, with religion usually understood to be a particular Christian theology. The interest in bringing psychology and religion together may also be highly practical. Clinicians may wonder how best to deal with obsessive religious ideation, for example, whereas ministers may seek guidance in deciding when referral to a mental health practitioner is appropriate. These are all legitimate concerns, but they fall outside the

Table P.1 **OVERVIEW OF THE BOOK'S SUBJECT MATTER**

	Book Chapters										
	Objective				Subjective						
	Theory		Method		Psychoanalytic			Jung	Humanistic		
	3	4	5	6	7	8	9	10	11	12	13
Content Areas											
Biological foundations	●										
Perception	●	●							●	●	
States of consciousness	●		●	●		●		●	●		●
Animal behavior		●									
Learning theory		●									
Developmental psychology	●	●		●	●	●	●		●	●	●
Psychometrics			●	●							●
Personality psychology					●	●	●	●		●	●
Clinical psychology	●			●	●	●	●	●			
Social psychology			●	●	●						●
Research Methods											
Experimentation	●	●	●	●							
Questionnaire	●		●	●	●				●		●
Interview			●				●			●	●
Clinical case study	●				●	●	●	●			
Naturalistic observation	●	●					●		●		
Projective techniques						●			●		
Personal documents									●	●	
Phenomenological–interpretive								●	●	●	●
Experimental instrospection									●		
Historical–anthropological	●	●			●	●	●	●	●	●	●
Religious Traditions											
"Primitive"	●	●			●			●		●	
Ancient world							●	●		●	
Native American	●				●						
Hindu	●		●	●		●	●	●	●	●	
Buddhist	●		●	●		●		●		●	●
Jain	●						●				
Jewish					●	●		●	●		●
Christian	●	●	●	●	●		●	●	●		●
Islamic	●			●	●						

focus of this work. It is also legitimate to question the appropriateness of subordinating religion to psychology. Indeed, psychologists of religion from early in the century have themselves reflected on the limits and potential dangers of such an undertaking. Later in this text we will encounter their reflections as well as their critics' responses.

Thus religion is not the exclusive focus of this study; we also critique the psychological perspectives from which we view religion. To bring home the factor of the "personal equation"—the effects of individual personality on scholarly work—we examine in some detail the lives of four prominent contributors: G. Stanley Hall, William James, Sigmund Freud, and C. G. Jung. These four are featured because each is in some way a founder of a major and still-living tradition within this field. Although limitations of space and biographical material have precluded extended treatment of other major figures, brief sketches of their lives are provided wherever possible, in order to situate the psychology of religion in its personal and historical context.

For some readers, I suppose, the often-striking continuities between the founder's personal experience and his later theoretical formulations may suggest that this field is hopelessly contaminated with fallible human subjectivity. It can be argued, however, that every field of human activity is conditioned by personal factors—though psychology may be more so than many others. Beyond serving as case studies in intellectual history, these biographical sketches should suggest to the reader that we are all subject to the personal equation in varying degrees, and that our responses to the material in this book are in some measure testimony to the accumulative effects of our own experience. The study of religion is inevitably an adventure that is both intellectual and personal.

I would like to acknowledge the willingness of various scholars to read and comment on drafted portions of this book, for either the first or the second edition. For reviewing my account of their own work, I am grateful to C. Daniel Batson, Erik H. Erikson, Roland Fischer, James W. Fowler, Hans-Günter Heimbrock, Dirk Hutsebaut, Robert Masters, Kenneth Pargament, M. A. Persinger, B. F. Skinner, and Wilfred Cantwell Smith. Some contributors to this field reviewed not only their own material but also other portions of the book; they include Peter L. Benson, Kurt Gins, Nils G. Holm, Jan M. van der Lans, Paul W. Pruyser, Jack Shand, and Bernard Spilka. Other scholars who commented on one or more chapters include Christopher M. Bache, M. Gerald Bradford, Lowell W. Coutant, Leonard Hassol, Henry S. Levinson, Thomas Parisi, Judy F. Rosenblith, John J. Shea, and Judith van Herik. To Michael Utsch I owe thanks for the opportunity to read a draft of his inaugural dissertation (Utsch, 1995), which provided invaluable leads to recent works in the German literature.

I would also like to express my gratitude to Eric Stano, the psychology editor at Wiley who oversaw the preparation of this new edition, as well as to others at Wiley who contributed significantly to its design and production, including Hilary Newman, Sandra Russell, Ann Marie Renzi, Edward Starr, Sandra Rigby, Dorothy Sinclair, and Kimberley Manzi. Finally, I wish to acknowledge once again my indebtedness to Deborah Moore, the editor of the first edition.

Providence, Rhode Island   *David M. Wulff*
September 1996

CONTENTS

Chapter 3 THE BIOLOGICAL FOUNDATIONS OF RELIGION   49

Chapter 4 **BEHAVIORAL AND COMPARATIVE THEORIES OF RELIGION   117**

Chapter 12 THE GERMAN DESCRIPTIVE TRADITION 524

1

INTRODUCTION:
THE PSYCHOLOGY OF RELIGION
IN A CHANGING WORLD

*W*e live today in a situation of unprecedented crisis. Other ages, to be sure, have suffered no less than ours from massive starvation, social upheaval, and devastating war. Only in our time, however, has the very survival of our species—and of all others as well—been seriously called into question: by the poisoning of air and water, the destruction of vital forests, the irreversible depletion of soil, and the specter of nuclear war. Whether insidious or catastrophic, the end to life on earth looms today as an unthinkable yet growing possibility.[1]

The crisis in the outer world is paralleled by another within. The massive and devastating destruction of World War I left to this century a legacy of disillusionment and self-doubt unprecedented in recorded history (Scheler, 1928). Americans witnessed "a wave of spiritual depression and religious skepticism, widespread and devastating" (W. Horton, quoted in Handy, 1960, p. 6). By mid-century, it had become a truism that the modern world was in the midst of "an age of anxiety," a "time of upheaval of standards and values" and of "painful insecurity" (Rollo May, 1953, p. 7). This anxiety deepened in the next decades, according to the findings of two national surveys of American adults, the first conducted in 1957 and the second, a replication, in 1976 (Veroff, Douvan, and Kulka, 1981). Over the period of a generation, these researchers report, there was a significant increase in worry and symptoms of anxiety, especially among young adults. Moreover, among the sources of unhappiness reported in 1976, "community, national, and world prob-

---

[1] Any reader who doubts the seriousness of this complex crisis should study the most recent assessment of it by the Worldwatch Institute, which publishes its annual report under the title *State of the World* (New York: W. W. Norton, 1984–). Translated into 27 languages and distributed to government officials around the world, this report documents a broad array of environmental, political, and social problems that threaten the planet's future. It also points to possible remedies that must be pursued in earnest throughout the world if unprecedented catastrophe is to be averted.

lems'' were more often mentioned first or second than any other source, a rate nearly double that of 1957 (pp. 57, 528).

In the interval between these two national surveys, another remarkable trend became apparent. For the first time in a history spanning up to two hundred years, most of America's major Protestant churches were losing membership. The substantial growth that these moderate-to-liberal denominations had experienced as recently as the late 1950s was replaced in the following decade by steady and sizable losses that have only recently begun to abate (Bedell, 1996; Jacquet, 1986, pp. 248–249). Parallel if less dramatic shifts in membership occurred in the Roman Catholic and Jewish traditions. This historic decline was reflected in a variety of other indicators as well. Church construction was down, denominational periodicals cut back production, and fewer missionaries were sent abroad (Kelley, 1972; Roof, 1982). Individuals, too, testified to the decline. Between 1965 and 1978, the proportion of Gallup poll respondents who reported that religion was ''very important'' in their lives dropped from 70 to 52 percent. Since then it has hovered in the mid- to upper- 50's (Gallup, 1995, pp. 63–64).

Yet not all Christian denominations have suffered this trend. Some are thriving, including such organizations as the Assemblies of God, the Pentecostal and Holiness groups, the Mormons, the Jehovah's Witnesses, and the Seventh-Day Adventists. Why should these and similar groups prosper, sociologist Dean Kelley (1972) wonders, when they so often violate contemporary standards of reasonableness, relevance, and tolerance? How is it that they, and not the more socially concerned mainline churches, appear to be successfully addressing the contemporary ''malady of meaning''? Is there a connection between the conservative revolution in America of which these trends are a part and the widely documented increase in anti-Semitism and other forms of prejudice, evident especially on college campuses? If so, does today's emerging religious response truly address the crisis we face, or is it in essence a symptom of it or perhaps even a factor in its aggravation? If it is a factor, are we doomed to play the role of helpless observers, or is it possible, by one means or another, to effect a more positive course of events?

Such questions as these lie at the heart of the psychology of religion for many of its proponents. Some, such as Erich Fromm and C. G. Jung, write directly to these questions, and with manifest urgency. Others, like Gordon Allport, approach them more methodically and EMPIRICALLY, patiently seeking clarification through the systematic accumulation of well-specified evidence. We will be challenged to see whether there is an emerging consensus.

These pressing issues are not, however, the whole of the psychology of religion. The field's rich inaugural period preceded the profound disillusionment brought about by World War I, and even some of those who wrote in the midst of it apparently thought of religion as a timeless something that bears no essential relation to current political and social events. Religion is, by its very nature, concerned with a dimension or complex of values that transcends MUNDANE reality. Even in its diverse historical expressions there are constants of MYTHIC and ritual content that seem to persist more or less unchanged in spite of political and social upheaval. The psychology of religion has been and continues to be concerned with these matters, too, as much of the content of this book demonstrates. Indeed, we are always at risk in trying to generalize about a subject matter as diversely conceived as the psychology of religion.

A MISLEADING NAME

Although "the psychology of religion" is the usual way of referring to the field, this expression is misleading in two important respects. First, the definite article suggests a degree of consensus and singularity of view that is far from characteristic of the field. Some psychologists of religion do present their theoretical perspectives or research methods as if everyone agrees on their value. What is apparent to the disinterested observer, however, is the diversity of theories, principles, and approaches, each with its own enthusiastic advocates. Some of these views are truly comprehensive—sufficient, it would seem, to encompass the whole of human piety; others are highly specific, limited to a narrow range of religious expression. Wherever an author refers to *the* psychology of religion, we should remind ourselves of these varieties of psychological perspectives, of which the writer may represent only one.

A Reified Object

The second way in which "the psychology of religion" is misleading is far more serious. The problem lies in the noun *religion,* a satisfactory definition of which has eluded scholars to this day. In a well-documented study, Wilfred Cantwell Smith (1963) demonstrates that the noun *religion* and its plural, along with the nouns that we commonly use to refer to specific religious traditions—Buddhism, Hinduism, Christianity—are not only unnecessary but also inadequate to any genuine understanding. What is worse, they may insidiously undermine the very piety to which they only vaguely refer.

The word "religion" derives from the Latin *religio,* which some scholars say was first used to designate a greater-than-human *power* that requires a person to respond in a certain way to avoid some dire consequence. Other scholars have concluded that *religio* refers to the *feeling* that is present in persons who vividly conceive of and observe such power. The term also came to designate the *ritual acts* carried out at the shrine of a particular god. In every instance *religio* referred to "something that one does, or that one feels deeply about, or that impinges on one's will, exacting obedience or threatening disaster or offering reward or binding one into one's community" (Smith, 1963, pp. 20, 22).

Over the centuries, the meaning of the word "religion" underwent an elaborate evolution. From designating something that one has perceived, felt, or done oneself, the word came to be used with a variety of alternative meanings. "Religion" referred in turn to the alien ritual practices of others, to a universal disposition or an inner piety, to an abstract system of ideas, to the totality of all belief systems, to a peculiar type of feeling, and to an unchanging essence that underlies the diversity of observable, dynamic forms. The general trend was toward reification: religion became in time a fixed, objective entity and each of the traditions a definable system. Understood as personal piety or reverence, "religion" made sense only in the singular; but once it came to refer to the abstracted, depersonalized, and reified systems of others, it could be used in the plural as well.

The concepts of religion and the religions, Smith concludes, are recent derivations of Western and Islamic traditions and far less useful than many assume. It is crucial to note, he says, that these reified religious concepts—including the names of most of the religious traditions—were formulated to serve the practical purposes of outsiders. From within the traditions, such concepts appear as serious distortions. Inherently depreciative, they overlook the dynamic personal quality of religiousness and leave out the crucial factor of TRANSCENDENCE. When these terms are unsuspectingly adopted by insiders as well, they may undermine faith from within. If inadequate for the insider, Smith declares, these concepts must be judged unservicable for the outside observer as well. Thus we are advised to abandon them once and for all.

Tradition and Faith: A New Conceptual Framework

In their place, Smith (1963) proposes that we use two alternatives, CUMULATIVE TRADITION and FAITH. With these two terms, he suggests, we may conceptualize and describe the entirety of the human religious life, as believers or as sceptics, as members of a religious community or as outsiders. The phrase *cumulative tradition,* a human construct offered as a means of making the dynamic flow of human history intelligible without distorting it, refers to all of the observable contents— temples, rituals, scriptures, myths, moral codes, social institutions, and so on—that are accumulated over time and then passed on to succeeding generations (pp. 156– 157). Unlike "religion," which misleadingly suggests an unchanging essence, cumulative tradition and its specific variants—for example, the Christian tradition— make explicit the changing historical contexts that sustain personal faith and that were founded and continue to be nourished by that faith in turn.

In contrast to the perceptible and enormously diverse features of tradition, *faith* is an unobservable and less variable quality of persons. In a monumental work on faith and belief, Smith (1979) defines faith as one's orientation or total response to oneself, others, and the universe. It reflects the human capacity 'to see, to feel, to act in terms of, a transcendent dimension," to perceive meaning that is more than merely mundane. Faith, Smith says, is "an essential human quality" if not "the fundamental human category"; it is certainly the most basic religious one (pp. 12, 141, 7).

Although itself not directly observable, faith is expressed outwardly in a myriad of forms: "in words, both prose and poetry; in patterns of deeds, both ritual and morality; in art, in institutions, in law, in community . . . ; and in still many other ways." Among these expressions, human character stands out. When faith is spontaneously and compellingly embodied in a person's character, says Smith (1963), we realize how "secondary, if not actually irrelevant" other expressions can be (pp. 171, 178). Faith is emphatically not to be equated with belief, which is only one of faith's many expressions and a far from universal one at that.

Of the traditional terms, Smith continues to use the adjective *religious,* for it suggests an attribute of persons, not a reified entity. The abstract noun *religiousness* might be retained on the same grounds, though in this case Smith would have us rehabilitate the venerable term *piety* instead (p. 194). Should we continue to use the remaining expressions—*religion, religions,* and all of the *isms*—they will require constant qualification, first to ourselves and then to our listeners. It would be better, in the light of Smith's argument, to drop them altogether. Old habits die hard, however, especially when succinct alternatives are not ready at hand.

In this book, when it is not obvious which sense of the word is intended, "religion" should be understood as a concise way of referring to both faith and tradition. Except in quotations and the standard expression "the history of religions," the inevitably misleading plural form will be avoided. "Piety" should be understood as a synonym for religiousness and thus as referring to an inner state or process and its outer expressions.

SPIRITUALITY: A CONTEMPORARY ALTERNATIVE

Today many decline to use the noun *religion* and even the adjective *religious*, not because they are aware of the historic process of reification, but because they find the terms *spirituality* and *spiritual* to be more apt. When James Day (1994), for example, interviewed three former participants in an experimental curriculum at the University of California at Irvine, all of them resisted being characterized in traditional religious terms. They were all "at pains to distinguish the 'religious' from the 'spiritual,' to distinguish [themselves] from the former descriptor and to embrace the latter," which they spoke of in "more encompassing, familiar, and positive terms" (p. 162). Most of the hundreds of baby boomers that Wade Clark Roof (1993) and his collaborators interviewed likewise saw a disjunction between the religious and the spiritual, and some of them, too, thought of themselves as being spiritual but not religious. This ascendance of spirituality is also evident in professional publications, including three decades of nursing literature (Emblen, 1992).

The separation of spirituality from religious tradition is a modern development. The word *spirituality* derives from the Latin noun *spiritus,* breath, from *spirare,* to blow or breathe. In Latin translations of the New Testament, the *spiritualis,* or "spiritual" person, is one whose life is ordered or influenced by the Holy Spirit or the Spirit of God. The abstract word *spiritualitas* (spirituality), used at least as early as the fifth century, retained this biblical meaning. By the twelfth century, however, spirituality began to acquire the connotations of a virtual psychological function that was contrasted with corporeality or materiality. Soon yet another meaning emerged, according to which spirituality designated ecclesiastical persons or properties. In the eighteenth and nineteenth centuries the word went into eclipse—perhaps because Voltaire and others had used it disparagingly—only to reappear early in the twentieth century in its original religious or devotional sense. Revived chiefly by French Catholic writers, it has gradually come to be applied to a great diversity of particular forms. Now it is even used to designate a branch of study within theology and the history of religions (Principe, 1983).

The popular understanding today of the words *spirituality* and *spiritual* is clarified in a 1995 national survey of 1713 adult Canadians, 52 percent of whom acknowledged that they had "spiritual needs." When asked to explain what they meant by spirituality, just over half of these respondents used conventional expressions, such as belief in God or Jesus, praying and going to church, and helping others. The rest were less conventional in their responses. They associated the word with the human spirit or soul, with such practices as meditation or reflection, with a sense of wholeness or oneness, and with inner or outer awareness (Bibby, 1995).

An Emergent Model

Writers on contemporary spirituality offer us yet another perspective on the term. In Table 1.1 are 129 nouns that have been modified by the adjective *spiritual* in recent publications. Some of these combinations, such as spiritual director or spiritual perfection, have been in use for centuries; others, like spiritual emergency, are of recent coinage. These terms are grouped into six categories that seem to

Table 1.1 **NOUNS THAT ARE MODIFIED BY THE ADJECTIVE *SPIRITUAL* IN THE CONTEMPORARY LITERATURE ON SPIRITUALITY**

1 The Initial Intimation	2 The Quest	3 The Goal Sought	4 Ways and Means	5 The Goal Attained	6 Pitfalls
Positive:	aim	connection	Persons:	attainment	abuse
concern	aspiration	depths	authority	awakening	authoritarianism
desire	choice	destiny	care	awareness	charlatanism
hope	development	dimension	community	benefits	derailment
hunger	evolution	essence	director	consciousness	disillusionment
inclination	goal	grounding	friend	discernment	exploitation
issue	growth	healing	guide	elite	failure
longing	journey	heights	intervention	emergence	fraudulence
need	progress	home	leader	enlightenment	inauthenticity
potential	quest	knowledge	master	experience	inflation
yearning	seeking	life	teacher	gifts	isolation
	unfolding	mastery		gnosis	malpractice
Negative:	venture	orientation	Resources:	health	materialism
bankruptcy		perfection	beliefs	insight	narcissism
conflict		possibilities	context	integration	pathology
crisis		purification	direction	joy	pride
degeneration		reality	discipline	living	tyranny
deprivation		realm	discourse	maturity	
disorientation		self	exercises	moment	
distress		sensitivity	itinerary	perspective	
doubt		skills	language	rebirth	
emergency		strength	path	sensibility	
emptiness		style	practice	state	
problem		transcendence	system	truth	
suffering		values	techniques	vision	
vacuum		worth	tradition	well-being	
			writings		

accommodate virtually all combinations, excluding references to spiritual beings or entities. Some terms could be placed in more than one category, and those in columns 3 and 5 are to a large degree interchangeable. What is important, however, is the overall impression that the terms in each column give and the process that may be inferred from the essentially chronological sequence of categories.

This array of expressions suggests that commentators on what is touted today as the "new spirituality" employ an emergent model. They think of spirituality as a natural process akin to physical growth or development. Its chief impetus thus comes from within, sometimes in the form of a sensed capacity or yearning, other times out of a deeply negative feeling of emptiness and conflict. Although spiritual growth is occasionally conceived as an unfolding, it is more typically construed in terms of the metaphor of a journey or quest, implying not only an anticipated destination or goal but also a sustained effort extending over a long period of time. The ideal endpoint or goal state entails a radically new outlook, perspective, capacity, or state of consciousness, the potential for which was there at the beginning. The uncertainties and difficulties of this journey are such that the spiritual seeker is expected to need help in various forms from those who have gone before. This help may be given directly, by a spiritual director or the caretaking of a spiritual community, or the seeker may find it in the form of spiritual writings and other resources preserved by the spiritual traditions. There are also dangers or pitfalls, including authoritarianism on the part of the spiritual master and distortions or pathological developments in the individual spirituality that unfolds.

This model of the new spirituality is itself not new, but has deep roots in the historic religious traditions. Indeed, the classic Christian mystics would find every element in the model familiar. Put another way, some of the nouns in Table 1.1 have long been as commonly modified by *religious* as they have by *spiritual,* and virtually all the rest could be conjoined with *religious* as well, albeit with slight shifts in connotation. The preference in the past for the words *spiritual* and *spirituality* can be traced to their simple advantage of denoting more clearly than *religious* and *religion* an inner process or attitude.

What *is* conspicuously new in today's spirituality is the frequent absence of an explicit transcendent object outside of the self. Life is ordered not in relation to the demands of the Holy Spirit or some other divine force, but in reference to the possibilities of the human spirit. Thus Clive Beck (1986), for example, maintains that spirituality is a combination of human qualities that may be possessed by religious and nonreligious people alike. Spiritual persons, he says, are characterized by (1) insight and understanding; (2) a sense of context and perspective; (3) awareness of the interconnectedness of things, of unity within diversity, and of patterns within the whole; (4) integration of body, mind, soul, and spirit, and of the various dimensions and commitments of their lives; (5) a sense of wonder, mystery, and awe, of the transcendent in life; (6) gratitude, gladness, and humility with respect to the good things of life; (7) hopefulness and optimism; (8) a courageous, "spirited" approach to life; (9) energy; (10) detachment; (11) acceptance of the inevitable; (12) love, "the characteristic par excellence of the spiritual person"; and (13) gentleness—a sensitive, thoughtful, caring approach to other people, to oneself, and to the cosmos as a whole. Roof (1993) likewise takes a humanistic view when he writes that spirituality "gives expression to the being that is in us; it has to do with feelings, with the power that comes from within, with knowing our deepest selves and what is sacred to us" (p. 64).

THE NEW RELIGIOUS PLURALISM

There is something else strikingly new in modern spirituality, even for those who subscribe to a conventional religious outlook. The world's diversity of religious traditions, once easily overlooked or dismissed, has come home to us in a quite literal way. In almost every American city, one can now find Hindu and Buddhist temples as well as Muslim mosques, some of them as ornate and imposing as the prototypes in Asia and the Middle East. Throughout the United States one can also find some 60 Jain temples and centers as well as communities of Zoroastrians and Sikhs. This new religious pluralism is similarly evident in England, where there are now more than one million Muslims, 400,000 Hindus, and 400,000 Sikhs. In France, Germany, and Sweden the story is much the same (Eck, 1993, pp. 37–41). The immediate presence of so many people of once-alien traditions has sharply heightened the general awareness of religious pluralism. It is also requiring a degree of accommodation and respect that was earlier unknown.

Consider the situation of teachers at the Lauriston School in Hackney, East London, which enrolls children aged 3 to 11. British law requires state-financed schools to provide religious instruction and daily worship that are "broadly Christian." At Lauriston, 47 percent of the 265 children are members of ethnic minor-

For the ethnically diverse children at Lauriston School in East London, state-mandated Christian religious education has become an introduction to the world's religious traditions.

ities. Thus in addition to Anglicans, Roman Catholics, and evangelical Protestants there are Jews, Hindus, Sikhs, Buddhists, Muslims, Rastafarians, Jehovah's Witnesses, and Greek Orthodox Christians. Moreover, some of the children, like many of the teachers, identify themselves as atheists or agnostics. In trying to follow government requirements, teachers offer what comes down to comparative religious studies. The major holy days in various traditions are observed and discussed as they come along, and values that the world's traditions have in common, such as compassion and sharing, are given primary emphasis (Lyall, 1995).

The sheer presence of people from other traditions in our classrooms and cities is naturally a major contributor to the new realization of religious pluralism. But beyond that is the reality of globalization, the growing sense of a new global social reality or interdependent world-system that, through the influence of modern communication technology, is increasingly becoming the context for all particular cultures. What globalization will mean in the long run for the world's religious traditions is impossible to say, but Peter Beyer (1994), for one, anticipates that for the foreseeable future many if not most people of the world will remain adherents of traditional forms. They will nevertheless be aware of, and affected by, the religious commitments of others to an unprecedented degree.

Such intimate awareness of the faith of other people makes it increasingly difficult to claim superiority for one's own. On the one hand is the dawning realization that the foundations for one's own faith are in large measure an accident of having been born at a particular time and place. On the other is the discovery that the various religious traditions are equally capable of providing life with coherence and meaning. Many people have recoiled from these relativistic implications, thus fueling the spread of fundamentalism around the world (Marty and Appleby, 1991). Others, however, having grown up with many forms of pluralism and the notion that religion is a matter of "preference" or "choice," are deeply committed to pluralism as both a social and a religious reality (Roof, 1993, p. 245).

For many in the post-World War II generation, in the United States and elsewhere, the outcome of the new religious pluralism is a distinctive form of spirituality. Drawing on cross-national evidence, Wade Clark Roof, Jackson Carroll, and David Roozen (1995) identify five prominent characteristics of this new "religious style": (1) an emphasis on individual choice, a "cafeteria" approach that selects religious beliefs and practices as well as moral precepts independent of, and even in opposition to, religious authority; (2) a mixing of codes, the eclectic combining of elements from various religious and quasi-religious traditions—"Eastern spiritual practices, various forms of New Age spirituality, witchcraft, the ecology movement, psychotherapy, feminism, as well as more traditional Judeo-Christian elements"—into a personal form of spirituality; (3) an attraction *either* to new religious movements, in particular the New Age variety, *or* to conservative Protestant traditions, especially Pentecostal or charismatic groups; (4) in either context, a valorizing of religious experience and growth, with an accompanying sense of the nearness of God and the possibilities of personal transformation (the emergent model once again); and (5) an indifference to religious institutions and hierarchies that breeds loyalty to local organizations rather than denominations, but even that only if such organizations address individual needs (pp. 247–253).

Postmodernism

Pluralism and spirituality in their new forms are integral to a broader cultural context that is known as POSTMODERNISM. Lacking any positive core assertions of its own, postmodernism takes its name from its position as successor to the modern world. Those living in the modern age share a confidence that, in spite of the obvious diversity of conflicting beliefs, reality can become progressively known—if not through some religious revelation, then with the aid of human reason and scientific methods. Postmodernism, in contrast, denies the very possibility of knowing reality. All beliefs, religious and scientific alike, are SOCIAL CONSTRUCTIONS, linguistic products of negotiation among persons living at a particular time and place. There are no privileged points of view, no universally accepted methods by which to test one proposition against another, no settled criteria for choosing among options. Thus postmodernism is itself not a single view but comes in almost as many varieties as there are people talking about it.

In the postmodern age, a new polarization has taken shape, a political spectrum resembling the modern era's conservative-through-liberal-to-revolutionary spectrum, yet differing from it in the odd bedfellows it creates. At one extreme are those who are confident that they possess the truth, or at least the means for obtaining it; clustered here, in odd array, are religious fundamentalists, convinced scientists, and a variety of other true believers and objectivists. Near the other extreme are the postmodern constructionists and relativists, who while granting the existence of reality, disclaim any possibility of knowing it. Beyond them, at the far extreme, is the position of SOLIPSISM, the view that reality itself is the individual's invention. While there are probably no true solipsists, the position is the logical outcome of arguments that have been advanced against the convictions of others (Anderson, 1990; Cobb, 1990).

THE NEW PLURALISM IN CONTEMPORARY PSYCHOLOGY

A product of the modern era, psychology is only now beginning to face the implications of postmodernism. From its beginnings late in the nineteenth century, modern psychology has been a pluralistic science. But it has long been an embattled pluralism, with dozens of schools and theories vying with each other for dominance in the field. Through the years, if the protagonists in this struggle agreed on anything it was in their optimistic hope that the field would someday become unified into a coherent and systematically progressive discipline. That achievement, they also concurred, would likely take a long time.

While some today still hold out for a unified science (Staats, 1987), others take the ever-increasing fractionation in psychology as evidence that unification is a hopeless dream. In a book on the conflicts that divide psychology today, Howard Kendler asserted in 1981 that

> The unity of psychology has all but collapsed. Psychology is a multidisciplinary field with different segments employing irreconcilable orientations. As a result, bitter disputes have occurred concerning the proper methodological position that psychology should adopt. . . . These differences are unavoidable considering the fundamental nature of psychology. A choice of competing methodological alternatives cannot be made by purely rational means. . . . The best that can be hoped for within psychology is a mutual understanding of the competing methodological positions and an appreciation of the decisions that led to their adoption (Kendler, 1981, p. 371).

A few years later, after participating in several symposia on the future of psychology, Kendler (1987) decided that his hope for mutual understanding had been too optimistic. "Many psychologists," he said, "are so dominated by ideological commitments that they cannot understand competing conceptions of psychology, much less tolerate them. Consequently, the profession of psychology inevitably will be divided into warring camps that cannot achieve any real peace or even an armistice" (p. 56).

Agreeing with Kendler that contemporary psychology is hopelessly divided, "a jumbled 'hidden-figure' puzzle that contains no figure" (Koch and Leary, 1985, p. 2), Sigmund Koch proposes that we acknowledge this lack of cohesiveness by replacing the term *psychology* with a phrase such as "the psychological studies." Unlike Kendler, however, Koch finds grounds for optimism about this pluralistic field. As he reviewed the 42 papers that he and David Leary (1985) collected for a massive retrospective reassessment of psychology after its first 100 years, he was struck not only by an unprecedented restiveness in the field but also by the changed character of its evident pluralism: in place of the polemics of the early schools was an "undogmatic civility," a "responsible tentativeness." The earlier, once-monolithic scientism, he concludes, is giving way to a "new pluralism," a "pluralism of *search* rather than assertiveness, marked by humility, not hubris" (pp. 940, 938).

Postmodernism in Psychology

In the framework of postmodernism, pluralism is no longer a sign of immaturity but evidence, rather, of health and creativity. Rejecting the positivistic "unity-of-method" thesis of earlier philosophers of science, according to which the natural and social sciences share the same methodological principles, philosopher Paul Roth (1987) advises psychologists and other social scientists to adopt a pluralistic view of rational inquiry, or what he calls methodological pluralism. It is a perspective, he argues, that will encourage research and promote intellectual inquiry.

Because there is no final court of appeal, no higher standard of rationality, our choice of method will come down to a moral decision, he says; we will have to decide how we are going to view our fellow humans and what our purposes will be in studying them (p. 110). Our choice of a frame of reference will finally be made on pragmatic grounds, in accord with our needs and the life we want to live (pp. 245–246).

The profound implications of postmodern thought are only slowly finding their way into psychology. As Steiner Kvale (1992) notes in his introduction to a collection of essays on psychology and postmodernism, there is typically a "time lag" before psychologists take up new ideas being entertained in philosophy and the humanities. The delay may also be accounted for, he suggests, by the fundamental incompatibility of the assumptions of modern psychology and the outlook of postmodern thought. However long it takes, postmodernists believe that the model of inquiry shared by most psychologists throughout the course of the twentieth century will eventually give way to new and more adequate possibilities. Meanwhile, resources for rethinking psychology's agenda within the postmodern framework are steadily accumulating, including works on social constructionism (e.g., Danziger, 1990; Gergen, 1991; Gergen and Davis, 1985; Harré, 1986), narrative psychology (Hermans and Kempen, 1993; Josselson and Lieblich, 1995; Polkinghorne, 1988; Sarbin, 1986; Spence, 1982), hermeneutics (Messer, Sass, and Woolfolk, 1988; Packer and Addison, 1989; Polkinghorne, 1983; Strenger, 1991; Terwee, 1990), metaphor (Leary, 1990; Olds, 1992; Soyland, 1994), and phenomenology (Fuller, 1990; van Manen, 1990).

INTIMATIONS OF A POSTMODERN PSYCHOLOGY OF RELIGION

As the contents of this book testify, the psychology of religion, too, has been highly pluralistic from its beginnings. There is hardly a theory or method in psychology, it seems, that has not been championed by someone for the study of religion. Paralleling developments in the broader field of psychology, this pluralism has at times been contentious, the battling of one perspective against another. For the most part, however, the varying perspectives have developed independent of each other, their proponents ignoring alternative approaches except for occasional dismissive remarks. Complicating matters is disagreement on where the psychology of religion chiefly belongs: Is it a subfield of psychology or is it a specialty within religious studies? It has been fostered in both contexts, in fact, but developments within one setting are often either unknown or inaccessible to workers in the other. Adding still further to the field's contentious pluralism are the diverse understandings of and personal attitudes toward religion among its contributors.

Yet here, too, postmodern thought is gradually creeping in. Paul Watson (1993), for example, points out that the psychology of religion is the product of the Enlightenment mode of thinking and its pretentions to unbiased rationality and objective empiricism, both assumed to transcend the limitations of local or historical knowledge. With the collapse of Enlightenment thought and the subsequent chaotic proliferation of alternative traditions, it has now become apparent that every psychology of religion exists within an "ideological surround." That is, each rests upon certain philosophical and normative assumptions. Far from being value-free, research programs often merely confirm the assumptions with which they start. Watson says that both APOLOGETICS and ETHNOCENTRISM—the defense of one's own position and the prejudicial judgment of the other's—are unavoidable in this work. The solution lies, he suggests, in acknowledging the ideological surround and conceiving of research as a dialogue between the observer and the observed, each balancing in the other the natural tendencies toward apologetics and ethnocentrism.

In a similar vein, Stanton Jones (1994) observes that postmodern philosophy of science reveals to us the human face of all scientific research. Like every other form of human inquiry, it is grounded in prescientific world-views, in foundational presuppositions that are rarely thought out or explicitly acknowledged. Moreover, scientists frequently commit themselves to a theory in advance of collecting and evaluating relevant data, which in any case will never unequivocally support one theory over another. And the complex process of theory evaluation is shaped throughout by the host of values held by the individual scientist. Jones concludes from these postmodern principles, which acknowledge the cultural and human dimensions of the scientific enterprise, that science has much in common with other ways of knowing, including religion.

Historical and Functional Continuities Between Psychology and Religion

Observed commonalities between religion and psychology have prompted some commentators to ascribe to certain forms of psychology the character of a religious movement (e.g., Berman, 1927; Vitz, 1977). With varying degrees of seriousness, they have noted the revering of sacred texts written by charismatic leaders or prophets who help to formulate the dogmas and creeds by which orthodoxy is defined. Evident, too, are objects of veneration—experimental apparatus, psychological tests, electronic computers—and even objects of sacrifice, in the form of laboratory animals. Much like religious devotees, psychologists have sacred places for their various rites, including the conference halls where they gathered periodically to recite their creeds and to testify, as well as the offices and classrooms where they work to win converts. More generally and profoundly, beneath these obvious forms lies a faith that adherence to the teachings of the tradition will in time bring salvation, whether it be in the form of a personal career, the health of a patient, or the transformation of society.

Psychologists unaccustomed to thinking of their commitments and activities as religious in nature will be no less startled by the suggestion that there are continuities between specific religious traditions and particular orientations within psychology. David Bakan (1965), for example, finds various parallels between behaviorism and the Protestant Christian tradition, especially its ethic of mastery. Bakan (1958) has also argued that many of the basic teachings of psychoanalysis are foreshadowed in the literature of the Jewish mystical tradition. In the case of Jung's analytic psychology, which both R. C. Zaehner (1959) and Richard Noll (1994) take to be a religious cult, the prominence of both Western and Eastern religious symbolism, particularly Gnostic (Segal, Singer, and Stein, 1995), is unmistakable. Much of contemporary humanistic psychology is said to be permeated by a religious atmosphere in which religious, philosophical, and psychological matters are mixed together without distinction (Murphy and Kovach, 1972). And transpersonal psychology, which seeks to integrate Eastern religious insights and Western psychology, has been identified by Paul Swartz (1969) as a refinement of the Western prophetic tradition and by Jeremy Carrette (1993–94) as one of the new religious movements.

The historical continuity of religious traditions and contemporary psychological views can also be expressed in terms of the functions they have served. Traditionally, questions about the nature of human existence have been answered within a religious framework. The vital task of ordering and comprehending both personal and social life was accomplished largely through the teachings and ceremonies that form a major part of the world's religious traditions. Today, many of these questions and tasks are directed instead to psychologists. It is they who are now expected to be knowledgeable about human nature, to give counsel to the troubled, and to make meaningful the entire course of life, from birth to death. Not infrequently it is the psychologists who take on the problems of good and evil, of morality and social responsibility. As psychotherapists, they often become in effect both confessors and spiritual directors (Browning, 1987; S. Jones, 1994).

Such continuities do not surprise Bakan (1966b), who believes science and religion pursue the same goal: to make the unmanifest manifest. To Stanton Jones (1994), religion's overlap with clinical psychology in particular suggests the possibility of a more constructive, dialogical relation between religion and psychology, which would pave the way for significant changes in clinical education and practice alike. He also sees implications for psychology as science: rather than viewing religious beliefs as distorting biases to be overcome in the research process, he takes the postmodern view that biases or presuppositions of some kind are a prerequisite for perceiving and understanding anything at all. What is crucial, he says, is recognizing their presence and being aware of the effects they have (p. 197).

OBJECTIONS TO THE PSYCHOLOGY OF RELIGION

Most psychologists, we may assume, continue to view psychology as a strictly scientific undertaking that has nothing in common with religion. Some even view them as antithetical to each other. If the two are to be brought together, it will be in the form of psychology *of* religion—psychology as a disciplined set of procedures and interpretive constructs, on the one hand, and religion as an object for disinterested study on the other. Religion will be treated like any other object of psychological investigation, though there may be some recognition of its enormous complexity and the peculiar difficulties that aspects of it present to scientific investigators.

Yet even to this combination of psychology and religion there is widespread objection. Although a surprising number of the world's most eminent psychologists have contributed to the psychology of religion, the field is commonly overlooked, if not treated with suspicion or contempt. Psychologists are not alone in this attitude; religious people, including scholars in religious studies, often exhibit it as well. Here we will consider the reasons why.

Objections from the Religious Point of View

Some persons, it may be said, seem to find any systematic study of religious experience offensive. When Edwin Starbuck (1937) began circulating his questionnaire on conversion in late 1893, under William James's signature, one critic wrote to James to protest this "moral and spiritual vivisection." Another, a minister, threatened to withdraw his daughter from Smith if she were subjected to such a "spiritual inquisition" (p. 225). Sweeping rejection of this sort may well reflect a fear of the effects on naive belief of any form of self-reflection.

Others have been more selective in their objections. With obvious concern over the growing influence of psychologists of religion in the training of religious educators, professor of education Charles Ellis (1922) identifies and quotes from ten works that appear to be antagonistic to the conservative evangelical Christian outlook, including Sabatier (1897), James (1902), Pratt (1907, 1920), Ames (1910), Leuba (1912), and Coe (1916). A like number were judged to be either "favorable to the fundamentals" or, as in the case of Starbuck (1899), Coe (1900), and Stratton (1911), neutral or ambiguous. J. C. M. Conn (1939), a Presbyterian minister who had studied in England with the psychologist Robert Thouless, seeks in turn to preserve "the Christian religion" by sorting out those in the psychological camp who are enemies of the faith—notably the behaviorists and orthodox psychoanalysts—from a handful of others who seem to be friends.

Reductionism: The objections raised by Ellis and Conn deserve careful reflection and perhaps subtler restatement. The perennial debate over the legitimacy of any social-scientific interpretation of religion has centered chiefly on the issue of REDUCTIONISM, a term designating the explanation of complex phenomena in terms of simpler, underlying processes. In this context, the reductionist view implies, first, that religious phenomena can be adequately understood by applying explanations developed outside the arena of religious studies. Making such a claim, however, also calls into question the very object of religious faith, and thus also the religious person's understanding of the origin and significance of that faith (Pals, 1986).

Max Scheler (1921) states with particular clarity the case against reductionism in the psychology of religion. *Any* explanatory psychology of religion, he observes, finds itself in a unique situation. Whereas all other branches of psychology presuppose the reality of the objects whose effects they investigate, the psychology of religion deals with an object whose reality can be received only in the state of faith. Thus every explanatory psychology of religion is necessarily atheistic, he says, and thus also spurious, for it empties religion of its meaning and intention. A "merely descriptive" psychology of religion *is* possible and meaningful, on the other hand, but only within individual religious systems or communities that share the same psychological states. "There are therefore as many psychologies of religion as there are *separate confessions*" (p. 159).

The case could be stated even more radically. If we concur with Wilfred Smith (1963) that, even within a single tradition, faith is always personal and hence unique, we might rule out the possibility of *any* psychology of religion. Himself more optimistic, Smith maintains that "By the exercise of imaginative sympathy, disciplined by intellectual rigour and checked by elaborate procedures, cross-checked by vigorous criticism, it is not impossible to infer what goes on in another's mind and heart" (p. 188). Yet so to understand the faith of others, Smith (1979) suggests, will require a new comprehension of psychology and the other social sciences.

Reconstructing Complexity: For now, a clearer understanding of existing views may prove to be helpful. According to sociobiologist Edward Wilson (1978), the reduction of observed phenomena to testable principles is "the heart of the scientific method." Yet, he emphasizes, it is only half the process. "The remainder consists of the reconstruction of complexity by an expanding synthesis under the control of laws newly demonstrated by analysis." That is to say, although phenomena at each level of organization are expected to obey the laws of the levels below, "new and unexpected principles" are required to comprehend the increasingly complex phenomena that emerge at each higher level (p. 11). The fear and resentment with which humanists greet the method of reduction, Wilson says, is based on the erroneous equation of the method with the attitude of diminution. Yet that equation, we must add, is not exclusively the error of apprehensive humanists; reductionists in diverse fields have also fallen victim to it.

Psychologists of religion are themselves deeply divided on the issue of reductionism. Some undertake the first half of reductionistic analysis with exceptional fervor and entirely neglect the further challenge of reconstructing complexity. It is they who have won for the psychology of religion the reputation for being "the most irreligious of all the sciences" (Andres, 1944, p. 40). Others, however, oppose all forms of reductionism, insisting that religion is in all essential respects unique and hence irreducible.

Most of the field's proponents lie somewhere in between. Typically, they avoid the more reduction-prone psychology of religious *contents* in favor of the less threatening psychology of religious *persons*. By studying individual differences in attitudes toward God, for example, rather than analyzing the idea of God itself, these scholars appear to leave unchallenged the cherished content of a faith that may also be their own. The implicit desire to preserve that faith is further reflected in the various attitudinal distinctions some of them draw—between, say, mature and immature forms of piety, or intrinsic and extrinsic religious orientations. Curiously enough, such simple discriminations and the questionnaires they have inspired are in their own way reductionistic—though perhaps usefully so.

Intimated here is the wide range of attitudes that can be found within the psychology of religion. That diversity disallows most sweeping generalizations about the field, and it ought also to forestall any generalized opposition to it. The dilemmas that the psychology of religion faces are by and large common to every other scholarly approach to religion; some present themselves to any form of human reflection whatsoever. Such dilemmas should invite thoughtful interest, not escape into the dogmatic certainties to which the religious and irreligious are equally prone.

Objections from the Psychological Point of View

That the religious should feel threatened by the psychology of religion is not difficult to understand. That psychologists should also object to it, however, presents us with a puzzle of a different sort. Because psychologists of religion are sometimes quite open about their own piety, we might assume that the field's critics object chiefly to the mixture of science and faith. Ian Vine (1978) expresses such an attitude: "As long as the area continues to be dominated by researchers who are themselves believers," he writes, "one cannot yet be sure how many findings are objective and reliable" (p. 416). Although the practical religious interests that are common among its proponents may be a factor in the field's failure to thrive, the truth is that most opponents of the psychology of religion know little or nothing of its content. As we will see, the problem seems to lie more with the object of study—religion—than with the field itself.

"In the absence of reliable evidence," writes psychologist Robert MacLeod (1952), "one is inclined to judge the prevailing attitude of psychologists toward religion as one of wary detachment or mild hostility" (p. 263). This attitude was already apparent late in the nineteenth century. When Starbuck approached Hugo Münsterberg for advice relating to the study of religion, the Harvard experimentalist—who otherwise was highly sympathetic to applied psychology and "always meticulously helpful"—proved to be "antagonistic and finally explosive." "He declared that his problems were those of psychology, while mine belonged to theology, and that they had absolutely nothing to do with each other'' (Starbuck, 1937, p. 225).

A Suspicious Neglect: That succeeding generations of psychologists share much the same attitude is often inferred from the virtual absence of religion as a topic in most textbooks of psychology. Early in the 1940s, Gordon Allport (1948) analyzed the treatment accorded religious experience by 50 textbooks of that day. ''About most psychological texts,'' he concluded, ''there is nothing to report excepting that they contain no treatment of the religious sentiment or closely related mental functions'' (p. 83). A series of subsequent surveys reveals that the situation has not fundamentally changed today. Of the texts published in the 1950s and 1970s, most make no reference at all to religion. In the surprising 89.2 percent of textbooks from the 1980s that do mention religion in some form, discussions are most often brief and speculative, commonly featuring research on meditation or the sensational 1978 mass suicide at the People's Temple in Jonestown, Guyana. Although the marked decline in explicitly negative evaluations of religion in the textbooks of the 1970s is still evident in those of the 1980s, religion remains chiefly an incidental source of illustrations, not a subject matter worthy in its own right of sustained discussion (Kirkpatrick and Spilka, 1989; Lehr and Spilka, 1989; Spilka, Comp, and Goldsmith, 1981).

Some psychologists would argue that religion, as a higher-order phenomenon, is properly omitted from textbooks surveying the fundamentals of psychology. With an understanding of more basic topics, such as child development, motivation, attitude formation and change, and psychopathology, students will have learned the principles that are necessary for the comprehension of religion; no separate treatment is necessary. These psychologists might also point out that art, music, and poetry are also ''neglected,'' and for precisely the same reason: they are higher-order or derivative phenomena about which psychologists have little to add. Agreeing that a scientific psychology in search of elementary principles quite naturally leaves the data of religious consciousness out of its account, Charles Shaw (1917) points out that James, the writer of the psychology of religion's one great classic, almost totally ignored the subject in the 1400 pages of his *Principles of Psychology*.

Yet the psychologist's reticence about religion is more profoundly motivated than this argument suggests. We may note first that all introductory psychology textbooks treat phenomena of a higher order in chapters on personality, psychopathology, and social psychology. Second, in accord with Wilson's principle of reconstructing complexity, these phenomena are at least implicitly recognized as requiring novel principles that cannot be derived from a knowledge of lower-order events.

Antipathy Toward Religion: Now and then evidence appears that points to a genuine antagonism toward religion among typical psychologists. The low mean score of a randomly selected group of psychologists who returned Clifford Kirkpatrick and Sarah Stone's (1935) Belief Pattern Scale was said to reveal ''considerable religious hostility'' (p. 580). At about the same time, Leuba (1934) found that the psychologists in his samples of American scientists were less likely to believe in God and immortality than any of the other groups. Several decades later, when Paul Heist and George Yonge (1968) intercorrelated the scales of the Strong Vocational Interest Blank for Men and their own Omnibus Personality Inventory, they found that the more men's interest patterns resembled those of psychologists, the more likely they were to reject conventional religious expressions. No other occupational scale showed this trend to the same degree (p. 36). That this trend is not limited to male psychologists is demonstrated by one of Donald P. Campbell's (1971) findings: on both the men's and the women's Religious Activities scales, psychologists score among the lowest groups. It is thus not surprising that many psychologists treat religion as a taboo topic (Douglas, 1963).

The antipathy that the psychologically oriented apparently feel toward religion is already evident during the student years. In their study of sentiments among Harvard undergraduates, Henry Murray and Christiana Morgan (1945) found a large negative correlation ($-.70$) between a positive attitude toward psychology and a favorable disposition toward religion (p. 205). More recently, Rosalia Paiva and Harold Haley (1971) discovered that, in a national sample of students entering medical school, those who anticipated specializing in psychiatry scored lower than any other group on the Religious scale of the Allport–Vernon–Lindzey Study of Values.

We can only guess at the source of this negativity toward religion. As Allport (1950) suggests, speculation about human nature was long the province of religion and philosophy, and thus only by repudiating these traditions have psychologists thought themselves able to develop new methods and to chart a different course. Moreover, the psychological science that evolved in twentieth-century America was strongly influenced by positivistic philosophy, according to which most if not all religious statements are philosophically meaningless. SALVATION, such as it might be, was no longer considered the concern of religion. Only the new social sciences, in concert with the physical and biological sciences, might hope to deliver human-kind from the fears and suffering that some say inspired the first prayers and magical incantations. It is understandable that these trends in psychology would attract persons who have rejected religion and repel those for whom traditional religious language and forms remain important.[2] It is thus comprehensible why many students, teachers, and practitioners of psychology view religious faith as an outdated and perhaps regrettable phenomenon.

A fuller understanding of the vehement hostility toward religion that some psychologists show would require a careful study of their lives. James Burtchaell (1970) suggests that many of the prominent physical and social scientists who speak disdainfully of religion have in fact "broken free from cloyingly fundamentalist childhoods. Having little or no subsequent contact with any more discriminating forms of faith, they too easily [think] of all religion in terms of the old sawdust trail" (p. 97). Kenneth E. Clark's (1957) study of American psychologists reveals that, in the mid-1950s, as many as one-third of the psychologists in some areas of specialization came from fundamentalist Protestant backgrounds.

As we have already noted, the suspicion or hostility encountered by psychologists of religion is experienced by all scholars of religion. Sociologist Robert Bellah (1970b) observes that "There is no other sphere of human culture which is ex-cluded from sympathetic academic consideration on its own terms on the grounds that such a study endangers science, reason, logic, and the whole heritage of the Enlightenment" (p. 113). The prevalent attitude in American universities, accord-

---

[2] Psychologist Donald T. Campbell (1975) writes that "The recruitment of scholars into psychology and psychiatry . . . may be such as to select persons unusually eager to challenge the cultural orthodoxy. In fact, the social and behavioral sciences do overlap much more in knowledge claims with traditional moral belief systems than do nonhuman biology, chemistry, and physics. It is a prerequisite to a scientific approach in the social sciences that investigators be willing to challenge the cultural orthodoxy. But a science with this entrance requirement may end up recruiting persons who are not only willing to make this challenge but in fact overeager to do so" (pp. 198–199).

ing to Bellah (1970c), is what he calls "enlightenment fundamentalism." "This is the view that science and historical scholarship have effectively disposed of fallacious religious beliefs. If the study of religion has any place in the university at all, which is doubtful to enlightenment fundamentalists, it is to disclose the true reasons why religious believers have been so misguided" (p. 3). That religious traditions and faith can be approached with a scholarly attitude, sympathetically and without preconceptions or prejudgments, is a notion that is apparently foreign to some academic minds, both conservative and liberal, who think of religion only as something that can be preached.

The general inhospitality encountered by the study of religion is undoubtedly responsible for the fact that it is "a grossly 'under-developed area' in our academic life" (Michaelsen, 1964, p. 26). Perhaps the recent upsurge of interest in the world's religious traditions, along with the ever-increasing availability of scholarly publications in this broad field (see Adams, 1977; Eliade, 1987), will gradually ameliorate a situation that ought to disturb every person who cares about the survival of human culture.

A LOOK AHEAD

In the chapters that follow, we explore a wide variety of approaches in the psychology of religion. In the first of these chapters, we trace out the origins of the field, beginning in the nineteenth century and focusing on the most conspicuous trends in the three historic traditions: the Anglo-American, the German, and the French. There, we also briefly consider the situation worldwide today.

Objective Approaches

The remaining chapters may be thought of as forming three clusters, each centering on some basic principle or explanatory construct. The first cluster, consisting of four chapters, is dedicated to objective approaches, so-called because their proponents view human beings from an external perspective; experience, they say, is private and unverifiable and thus unusable in scientific research. They treat religion, then, either as observable behavior or as the outcome of biological processes. Modeled more or less after the physical and biological sciences, the psychologies in this cluster aspire to explain, predict, and control behavior.

Because most contemporary academic psychologists embrace the objective approach, it is often referred to simply as psychology. When objective psychologists wish to distinguish their perspective from others, they employ the adjectives "scientific" or "empirical," terms that for them sum up and valorize the objective, natural-scientific approach. Chapters 3 and 4, the first two in this cluster, represent researchers who have sought a scientific explanation for religion in terms of either biological processes, behavior theory, or cross-species tendencies. The remaining two chapters in this group feature research that is distinguished by its use of objective research methods, often independent of any particular theory. Experimental and quasi-experimental approaches are the ideal, for they allow investigators to test hypotheses about cause and effect. Experimental investigations of religious phenomena, including meditation, mystical experience, and helping behavior, are reviewed in Chapter 5. Where experimentation is not possible, as is usually the case with religion, correlational methods may be employed instead. Their use for exploring the association of religion with various social attitudes and mental health is reviewed in Chapter 6.

Depth-psychological Approaches

The second cluster, likewise composed of four chapters, represents the depth psychologies. Emerging out of the clinical consultation room rather than the research laboratory, these psychologies hold in common the view that dynamic, often irrational unconscious processes play a major role in human experience and conduct. They also ascribe to the experiences of the early childhood years, especially in relation to the parents, a formative influence that persists for the rest of the individual's life. Hereditary and constitutional factors may likewise be assigned a significant place in the psyche's economy. The depth psychologists interest themselves in the feelings and images of conscious experience, but only to the degree that they provide clues to underlying unconscious forces. While thus sharing the humanistic psychologists' subjective orientation, they treat the content of experience as disguised and projected material that invites radical reinterpretation.

The first of the chapters on the depth approach, Chapter 7, considers the orthodox psychoanalytic perspective of Sigmund Freud and his immediate successors, who trace religion chiefly to the Oedipal relationship of the young boy to his father. Chapter 8 explores the interpretations of religion offered by proponents of the revised psychoanalytic approaches known collectively as object-relations theory. Together, they accent the contributions of still earlier experience, especially in relation to the mother, while at the same time casting religion in a more favorable light. The related perspective of ego psychology, as developed by Erik Erikson, is the subject of Chapter 9, where we also encounter the work on religious development of James Fowler. The final chapter in the cluster of depth approaches, Chapter 10, is given over to the analytical psychology of C. G. Jung, whose postulating of a collective unconscious sets him apart from the various psychoanalytic schools. For Jung, religious symbols and rites are the elements that have traditionally facilitated the complex unconscious processes that are directed toward self-realization.

Humanistic Approaches

The final cluster of chapters represents a variety of humanistic approaches. Like the objective psychologists, the humanists conceive of their work as scientific and empirical. Yet for them these words retain their original, broad meaning: *science* is any body of systemically obtained knowledge, regardless of object or method, and *empirical* refers to any approach that is grounded in experience rather than speculation. Thus the humanists pursue what they call the human sciences, which draw on the human capacities for empathy and understanding and thus employ methods and pursue goals rather different from the natural sciences.

Subjective in their orientation like the depth psychologists, the humanistic psychologists differ from them in taking conscious experience to be significant and interesting in its own right. Employing various methodological principles and descriptive typologies, they focus on the subtleties and variations in the personal world, especially of exceptional individuals. If they also posit significant unconscious processes, they side with Jung in ascribing to these processes a highly constructive role. As frequent critics of ordinary piety and traditional religious institutions, they are disposed to valorize some religious forms over others, especially those that promote the achievement of positive human potential.

Chapter 11, the first of the three humanistic chapters, centers on the enduring contributions of William James, who is famous for preferring the more dramatic forms of religious experience. Complementing his views, then, is the work of his student James Pratt, who casts light on more ordinary forms and expressions of piety. In Chapter 12, we meet the chief representatives of the German descriptive tradition, which is noted for its phenomenological and interpretive approaches. This chapter features the classic work on the experience of the holy by Rudolf Otto and the varieties of prayer by Friedrich Heiler, along with the existential–interpretive views of Eduard Spranger, the applications of experimental introspection by Karl Girgensohn and others of the Dorpat School, and more recent research on mystical consciousness and religious development. Chapter 13 rounds out our survey of the humanistic tradition by considering the views of prominent American humanistic psychologists, notably Gordon Allport, Erich Fromm, and Abraham Maslow, along with research that their work has inspired. There, we also take into account transpersonal psychology and the reflections of Rollo May and Victor Frankl. The book concludes with an epilogue that provides a summary schema and final reflections on the relevance of the psychology of religion to the crises that confront the world today.

2

THE FORMAL BEGINNINGS: THREE TRADITIONS

*L*ike psychology itself, the psychological study of religion has emerged out of a shadowy past that long antedates its formal history. The beginnings of the field as a formal discipline are sometimes dated to 1881, when G. Stanley Hall gave a public address in Boston on moral and religious education (Kahoe, 1992). Whether we agree that Hall's report of impressionistic evidence linking conversion and adolescence inaugurated the field, or would prefer to locate its origins rather less definitely, somewhere late in the nineteenth century, we are defining only the latest period of reflection on human piety. Such thinking and speculation, even though sporadic and never widely popular, can be traced back to antiquity.

Two Fundamental Trends

Two trends may be distinguished in these reflections, one descriptive and the other explanatory. Roots of the *descriptive* trend in the psychology of religion can be found in the writings that comprise the scriptures of the great religious traditions; in NONCANONICAL works for spiritual edification, such as Augustine's *Confessions* and the reports of the medieval mystics; and in the writings of certain philosophers and theologians, including Jonathan Edwards (1703–1758), Friedrich Schleiermacher (1768–1834), Søren Kierkegaard (1813–1855), and Albrecht Ritschl (1822–1889).

The *explanatory* trend, prompted by the suspicion that religion is other than what it appears to be, may be found at least as early as the third century B.C.E.,[1] when Euhemerus, along with other Greek rationalists, maintained that the gods are only past rulers and other benefactors of humankind who had come to be

---

[1] Although the expressions B.C.E., "before the common era," and C.E., "common era," have not yet been widely adopted in the place of B.C. (before Christ) and A.D. (*anno Domini*, in the year of the Lord), they are used in this book as a reminder that the silent presuppositions of linguistic usage may distort our perspective on other traditions. For the same reason, "Hebrew Bible" is often to be preferred to "Old Testament," which again is a Christocentric expression appropriate in some contexts but not others.

deified. Two centuries later, Lucretius, the Roman poet and leading expositor of EPICUREANISM, asserted that the gods were born from dream images and from fear of nature's destructive power. Writers of the Enlightenment, including Scottish philosopher David Hume (1757), elaborated the Lucretian dictum into a full-fledged psychology of religion. They concluded that fear, in combination with the wrenching sacrifices demanded by power-hungry priests to placate the raging gods, led to ill temper, inner rage, and ruthless persecution of unbelievers. Moreover, just as religious superstition was said by these eighteenth-century thinkers to be proportionate to how vulnerable people felt, so they argued that such belief declined as the capacity for ABSTRACTION increased (Manuel, 1983). Yet another explanatory thesis appeared in the nineteenth century when Ludwig Feuerbach (1804–1872), writing only a few years before Sigmund Freud was born, argued that the gods are projections of idealized human nature that serve as unconscious means of self-knowledge and self-transcendence.

These two fundamental trends in the psychology of religion—the descriptive and the explanatory, the first portraying religion sympathetically and from within, the second, more critically and from the outside—continue to characterize it to this day. Although it is not impossible for a particular writer to embrace both trends, usually one or the other trend is strongly emphasized. Freud and the behaviorists, for example, have bequeathed to us almost purely explanatory models of religion whereas the phenomenologists have embraced an ideal of pure description. James may serve as a mixed example, for although he is usually identified with the descriptive approach, there is an undercurrent of explanation in his famous reflections on religion.

An accent on one trend or the other is likewise typical of entire literatures. The clearest case in point is the Russian psychology of religion, which has long suffered from both political and linguistic isolation. In the shadow of the former Soviet Union's official policy of promoting atheism, Russian psychologists of religion long devoted themselves to explaining why their fellow citizens were so intransigently religious; they also sought ways to convert them to militant atheism (Kryvelev, 1961; Platonov, 1975). Some contributors followed the classical Marxian view that religion is false because its claims contradict the materialist conception of history, and that as a social force preserving the interests of the ruling class, religion will disappear in a classless society. From this perspective, then, the psychology of religion is called to investigate social conditions and economic relations, not the experience of individuals (Ugrinovich, 1986).

However, observing that religion was not fading away in communist societies, other researchers departed from Marxist doctrine by looking for religion's origins in personal dispositions and universal life circumstances. Acknowledging at least tacitly that religion is animated by phenomena that are not peculiar to class society—such as mental suffering and fear of death, on the negative side, and the need for pleasurable and uplifting experiences on the positive—some investigators proposed instituting a program of aesthetic education designed to meet the needs that have been satisfied in the past by the aesthetic elements of religious tradition (Bukin, 1969; Glassl, 1970; Kolbanovskii, 1969).

The promotion of atheism was secondarily pursued by establishing that, contrary to popular opinion about the famous scientist, Ivan Pavlov was an uncompromising atheist (see Windholz, 1986). Although Pavlov, the son of a Russian Orthodox priest, did indeed deny the existence of a spiritual domain as well as the survival of bodily death in his reply to C. L. Drawbridge's (1932) questionnaire, he also wrote, in English, "My answers do not mean at all that my attitude toward religion is a negative one. Just the opposite. In my incredulity, I do not see my advantage, but a failure comparatively, to believers. . . . I am deeply convinced that the religious sense and disposition are a vital necessity of human existence, at least for the majority" (p. 126). The dissolution in 1991 of the Soviet Union and, with it, the Central Committee's Institute for Scientific Atheism has freed Russian psychologists of religion to share Pavlov's open attitude. The reprinting in 1992 of the 1910 Russian translation of James's *Varieties* (1902) suggests progress in that direction.

The trends in the three major literatures in the psychology of religion—the Anglo–American, the German, and the French—are far more diverse than the Russian and thus less easily characterized. Yet the simple descriptive/explanatory typology provides a useful framework for discussing them as well. Above all, it helps us to understand why today contributors to this field are still at loggerheads on the fundamental questions of methods and goals.

Throughout its brief history, the psychology of religion has been subject to the shifting fashions in Western psychological and religious thought. Commonly viewed with suspicion if not outright hostility by psychologists and theologians alike, and threatened from within by sectarian views of its subject matter and methods, the psychology of religion has lacked the systematic development that might have allowed it to fulfill its original promise. As in the case of psychology itself, most of the early studies in this field have been left behind and forgotten, not because they were found wanting and then surpassed, but because they went out of fashion. The few that managed to survive—including studies by James, Freud, and Jung—have remained to this day the standard and best-known works in the field. Reexamination of some of these classics (e.g., Glock and Hammond, 1973) as well as the recent reprinting, on both sides of the Atlantic Ocean, of other early contributions suggests a renewed effort to assimilate what may be of value in this surprisingly voluminous literature. It is becoming increasingly apparent that every serious student of the contemporary psychology of religion must have some familiarity with the field's erratic development.

In the historical overview that follows, we meet some of the contributors who, because they are still influential today, are featured in subsequent chapters of this book. Briefly encountering them here will allow us to see them more clearly in their historical context. This overview will also introduce proponents whose contributions are much less well known, especially in America. Generally, they are included not only because of their early significance but also because their insights or principles speak to the contemporary debate on the nature of this field.

THE ANGLO–AMERICAN TRADITION

Although elements for a systematic psychology of religion were already abundant in the eighteenth century, formal treatises explicitly applying psychological principles to religion did not begin to appear until a century later, in the mid-1800s. These works were symptomatic of an emerging confluence of intellectual, social, and personal factors that were eventually to give rise to what we know today as the psychology of religion.

A major factor was the remarkable success of the natural sciences in the nineteenth century. Science, as a general attitude and a body of research methods, became widely popular. There was much enthusiasm in particular for its application to human mental life. Psychology, still struggling for independence from philosophy, was one conspicuous outcome; another was the new science of the history of religions, whose widespread acceptance in American universities and seminaries was greatly aided by the ascendant religious LIBERALISM.

In the theological context, among others, the word "liberal" implies an attitude of openness unconstrained by ORTHODOXY, authority, or convention. Although religious liberals may remain associated with some tradition, their chief loyalty is to truth as it becomes known through human experience and subsequent reflection on it. The theological liberalism of the nineteenth century rejected the orthodoxy and RATIONALISM that prevailed early in the century and focused instead on inner experience. Most influential among the nineteenth-century liberal Protestant theologians was Friedrich Schleiermacher (1799), who maintained that religion is not primarily a matter of knowledge or morals, as earlier philosophers of religion had argued, but of attitude. Religion, he said, is a feeling of absolute dependence, which arises naturally in the self-conscious individual.

Schleiermacher's views are prominent, if not always affirmed, in the first works explicitly on psychology and religion: in England, Richard Alliott's *Psychology and Theology: or, Psychology Applied to the Investigation of Questions Relating to Religion, Natural Theology, and Revelation* (1855) and sometime later in America, Duren Ward's *How Religion Arises: A Psychological Study* (1888) as well as Charles Everett's *The Psychological Elements of Religious Faith* (1902), a posthumous work constructed from the notes of his Harvard Divinity School students, including Duren Ward. Drawing critically on both British and continental thinkers, each of these writers analyzed religion in terms of the traditional threefold division of emotion, thought, and will. Because they were writing before psychology had become separated from philosophy, they based their work on armchair reflection, not systematic investigation. Their approach was emphatically from within, for each, like Schleiermacher, saw in religion an essential activity of the human mind.

Francis Galton

The first studies of a more critical and strictly scientific nature were undertaken by Sir Francis Galton (1822–1911), the ingenious English scientist who, in spite of interests that led him far from psychology, was to become the founder of the psychology of individual differences and the first to employ the method of statistical CORRELATION. Undoubtedly best known is his investigation of the objective efficacy of petitionary prayer. Wherever he looked for evidence, Galton (1872) reports, neither leading a prayerful life nor being the object of prayerful concern was associated with any discernible objective advantage. In like manner, his systematic comparison of notable Protestant clergymen with other eminent men yielded no evidence that a life of piety was blessed, on the average, with such tangible gains as health, longevity, or notably influential offspring. If anything, Galton observes, the findings suggest the opposite. That prayer might have subjective gains, on the other hand, Galton had no doubt.

Apparently the first contributor to the correlational psychology of religion, Galton may also have been the first to conceive of a wholly DISINTERESTED experimental approach to religion. In an effort to understand how religious images come to be revered by their worshipers, Galton sought to induce in himself a like attitude toward a cartoon figure of Punch. "I addressed it with much quasi-reverence as possessing a mighty power to reward or punish the behaviour of men towards it, and found little difficulty in ignoring the impossibilities of what I professed. The experiment gradually succeeded; I began to feel, and long retained for the picture

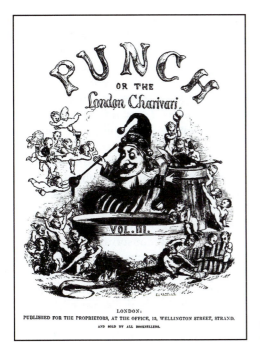

In Galton's experiment, Punch became for him an object of awe and reverence.

a large share of the feelings that a barbarian entertains towards his idol, and learnt to appreciate the enormous potency they might have over him'' (Galton, 1908, p. 277).

Reform in America

In spite of modern psychology's profound indebtedness to Galton and other British and European thinkers, it was in the United States that the psychology of religion first gained momentum. Some European commentators have suggested that America's religious diversity gave the advantage to the psychology of religion in this country. More significant, however, was the spirit of reform that permeated both the social sciences and liberal EVANGELICAL Protestantism. It was the era of PROGRESSIVISM, when many high-minded individuals actively worked to counter the social evils of industrialization. Prominent among the reform efforts that constituted progressivism was the SOCIAL GOSPEL MOVEMENT, which swept through the liberal evangelical churches around the turn of the century. Proponents of the social gospel sought "to align churches, frankly and aggressively, on the side of the downtrodden, the poor, and the working people—in other words, to make Christianity relevant to this world, not the next'' (Link and McCormick, 1983, p. 23). Confident in their moral and spiritual vision and the eventuality of a world won to Christ, the evangelical Protestants found corroboration in the optimistic environmentalist and interventionist assumptions implicit in psychology and the other social sciences, which were themselves animated by pervading ethical concerns. Together they set about to gather and interpret relevant empirical facts and then to apply them toward the end of human betterment (Handy, 1984; Link and McCormick, 1983, p. 24).

Members of the founding generation of the American psychology of religion were committed to both empirical science and the social gospel. George Coe (1937), for example, who had once expected to become, like his father, a Methodist minister, eventually switched from graduate study in theology to philosophy and psychology, in accordance with the gradual but momentous shift in his point of view. His reading of Darwin's controversial *The Origin of Species,* encouraged by a college zoology professor, convinced him that the scientific method could be used to settle both intellectual and spiritual questions. Later influences included the writings of socialist theologian Walter Rauschenbusch and others prominent in the Social Gospel movement; his participation in settlement work and local political reform; and the new social psychology, which he said provided a scientific foundation for his changing perspective. The true function of religion, Coe was to conclude, is the development of personality in the context of relations with others, a view he elaborated in a series of books and articles spanning more than 40 years.

Coe also illustrates the role of more individual and deeply personal experiences in shaping the psychology of religion. Reared in a conservative Methodist home, Coe was troubled as an adolescent by his seeming incapacity to undergo the prescribed experience of conversion. He finally abandoned his quest for the highly touted sense of ASSURANCE late in his college years, affirming instead the importance of the ethical will. Other, similarly pious youth, he soon discovered, also suffered from "religious darkness," and thus it was virtually inevitable, he says, that he would later undertake a formal psychological study of such individual differences. We return to that research in Chapter 3.

The Clark School

G. Stanley Hall, effectively the founder of the American psychology of religion, had likewise started out in theology, opted instead for psychology, and in time proposed using the new discipline as a means of reconstructing religion to accord with the personal and social needs of the modern world. As we see in the next chapter, much of Hall's work, too, shows intimate ties to his own early experience and evolving religious outlook. Hall is distinguished, however, as the founder of America's only "school" of religious psychology, at Clark University where he was president (Vande Kemp, 1992). Among the other members of the famous CLARK SCHOOL, two stand out, James Leuba and Edwin Starbuck, both of whom chose religious CONVERSION as their first topic of research. Of the work by Hall, Starbuck, and Leuba, Starbuck's (1899) is most typical of the Clark school and its legacy. Made available through a German translation in 1909, it was also better known abroad.

Edwin Starbuck: For his 1899 work Starbuck painstakingly analyzed autobiographical questionnaire responses from 192 subjects, the great majority of whom were Protestant Americans; he also obtained 1265 replies to a far briefer questionnaire that were to allow him to demonstrate the coincidence of conversion with the onset of puberty. By means of frequency distributions and percentages as well as brief illustrative quotations from his subjects' reports, Starbuck traced the typical course of conversion and of religious growth more generally. Although the true dawning of the spiritual life proved to occur most commonly during the years of physiological and particularly sexual maturation, Starbuck emphasizes that the latter is merely the occasion, not the cause, of religious awakening. Religion, he says, is nourished by many roots. With time, however, it becomes so far differentiated from its sources—perhaps even opposed to them, as in the sexual sphere— that their connection is no longer apparent. An understanding of these roots is worth pursuing, Starbuck concludes, not because it will give us the key to religion's nature or value, but because it will allow the religious educator to ease the individual's way through the stages of growth into religious maturity. By understanding and promoting the development of the child's character, Starbuck was deeply convinced, one might help to secure world peace and to save humanity (Booth, 1981; Starbuck, 1937, p. 241).

Starbuck's research is representative of the Clark school in several respects. The focus on religious development and conversion reflects not only Hall's leading interests but also those of others of his students. Moreover, Starbuck's commitment to gathering facts in the largest number possible and then to quantifying them in order to reveal general trends became the distinguishing feature both of the Clark school and, to this day, of American psychology of religion. Finally, his concern with religious PEDAGOGY reflects Hall's own, which was clearly expressed in the title of the journal Hall founded in 1904, *The American Journal of Religious Psychology and Education.*

James Henry Leuba: The pedagogical interest of the Clark school was not always in the service of traditional religion. Leuba, unlike his liberally pious colleagues, was convinced that religious experience lacks altogether a transcendent object. Such experience, he insisted, is entirely the result of natural forces. Leuba's challenge to religious tradition was twofold. On the one hand, he sought to demonstrate that mystical experience could be satisfactorily explained in terms of psychophysiological processes. On the other hand, he gathered evidence that scientists who are well informed about such processes and are distinguished in their fields tend not to believe in a personal God or immortality.

Yet Leuba was not a thoroughgoing MATERIALIST insensitive to spiritual values. Indeed, he posited an inborn urge toward a higher moral good, a cosmic trend that he took to be human nature's most fundamental characteristic. Moreover, although he was convinced that traditional religious teachings and institutions have perpetrated momentous evils, he still believed that modified forms of confession, prayer, sacred art, and ceremony could help humanity to realize its ideals. Yet only scientific knowledge, he was quick to add, not naive interpretation of mystical experience, can effectively direct the search for ethical values and transforming inspiration.

William James and the Descriptive Tradition

From the outset there were exceptions to this trend. Best known among them was William James, who is still considered to be America's foremost psychologist. At the beginning of *The Varieties of Religious Experience* (1902), indisputably the one great classic of the psychology of religion, James labels and discredits MEDICAL MATERIALISM, the assumption that identifying the psychophysiological correlates of a religious phenomenon serves to invalidate it. All mental states, he points out, are dependent on bodily states; scientific theories or atheistic convictions are equally conditioned by organic causes. A final evaluation of an idea or experience, he argues, can be made only in the light of its fruitfulness in the individual life.

Although James drew on Starbuck's collection of questionnaire replies, his approach was radically different from the Clark school's. Rather than seeking a representative sample, James chose as his primary subjects the relatively rare cases in which the religious attitude is conspicuous. In place of laborious tabulation and statistical inference, James used his own exceptional capacity for empathic understanding. The few fundamental distinctions he makes are driven home not by the authority of numbers but by compelling individual testimony, provided in lengthy quotations from the PERSONAL DOCUMENTS that James gathered from a variety of sources.

Yet James was more than a disinterested observer who rejected reductive explanation in favor of sympathetic description. The *Varieties* is shaped from start to finish by its author's long-standing concern with the philosophical justification of religious faith. By classifying religious states with similar nonreligious ones, James hoped to demonstrate that what distinguishes these states, beyond the objects they take, is their significance in the lives of the persons who experience them. Furthermore, he sought evidence of a reality corresponding to the "over-beliefs" of the religious person, whose right to affirm such beliefs he cautiously defended in an earlier essay. Although the evidence James was finally to admit is meager by any standards, he affirms unequivocally that religious experience can dramatically transform individual lives, and thus also the world at large.

In spite of widespread criticism—principally for the pathological extremity of its cases—the *Varieties* rapidly became known worldwide as the leading contribution to the field. Its influence was largely general, however, for in it James elaborated neither a specific theory nor a particular method, beyond the judicious use of personal documents. He provided instead the first clear example—albeit perhaps an imperfect one—of the descriptive approach to religious phenomena.

The stimulating influence of James's work is notable especially in the writings of James Pratt, who in 1905 completed a doctoral dissertation under James on the psychology of religion. Pratt's chief work in this field, *The Religious Consciousness* (1920), is a purely descriptive study of a broad range of religious phenomena, including many that, being less striking and more common, had been passed over by James. Furthermore, Pratt was an authority in the HISTORY OF RELIGIONS, especially in the Hindu and Buddhist traditions. Thus he brought to this work a breadth of perspective that is rare in the psychology of religion. Like James, Pratt is associated with no particular methods, apart from personal documents and the employment of a well-furnished mind.

Promise Unfulfilled

Pratt's highly regarded book marks the zenith of the inaugural period of the Anglo–American psychology of religion. The preceding decade had produced several original and provocative works, including Edward S. Ames's *The Psychology of Religious Experience* (1910), a social–psychological study that conceives of religion as the consciousness of the highest social values; George M. Stratton's *The Psychology of the Religious Life* (1911), in which the inner dynamic of conflicting opposites is found reflected in a great variety of sacred writings; and Coe's *The Psychology of Religion* (1916), a work centering in a psychology of personal and social self-realization. The decade following Pratt's book similarly yielded several influential works, notably British psychologist Robert Thouless's psychoanalytically influenced *An Introduction to the Psychology of Religion* (1923) and Leuba's classic *The Psychology of Religious Mysticism* (1925). Yet no other work from this period was as inclusive and balanced as Pratt's, and only James's *Varieties* would exceed it in frequency of reprintings.

The standing of Pratt's book was to be preserved by the field's almost precipitous decline around 1930. Among psychologists, the subject had never achieved widespread popularity, as the failure in 1915 of Hall's erratically appearing journal testifies. Among scholars of religion, on the other hand, the psychology of religion "became so captivating during the first quarter of the twentieth century that it almost eclipsed theology as an academic discipline in some divinity schools'' (Smith, Handy, and Loetscher, 1963, p. 429). Undergraduate courses in the subject area were also commonplace. But between 1923 and 1933, such courses decreased nearly to the vanishing point (Merriam, 1935), and there was so little original research during this period, according to Starbuck (1937, p. 251), that Austrian historian of religion Karl Beth was unable to find enough participants to convene a congress on the psychology of religion at the time of the second world's fair in Chicago (1933–1934).

What had happened to this promising field? Its failure to thrive was the result of a complex of factors. Two major elements were the waning of progressivism after 1917 and the sharp decline of liberal evangelical theology. Their extraordinary confidence had been dealt a heavy blow by the devastating war and the subsequent economic crises and resurgent FUNDAMENTALISM. The postliberal theological mind that emerged under the influence of the DIALECTICAL THEOLOGY of Karl Barth and Emil Brunner emphatically rejected the glorification of human capacities and achievements as well as the emphasis on the religious consciousness that had been promoted by the psychology of religion. The Sovereign God and His revelation in the Bible, not the experiences and judgments of religious individuals, were of paramount concern. Viewed as offensively reductionistic, the psychology of religion was unequivocally rejected by this theocentric outlook as its mortal enemy (Smith, Handy, and Loetscher, 1963, pp. 426–429).

Within the field of psychology, on the other hand, the progression of positivistic science set the stage for the explosive success of the BEHAVIORIST movement in the 1920s. BEHAVIORISM, a deterministic and mechanistic science that limited itself to objectively observable behavior, was naturally inhospitable to the study of religious experience, among other subjective phenomena. Some commentators fault the psychologists of religion themselves for failing in an increasingly scientific era to differentiate their work from the philosophy of religion, theology, and the practical concerns of religious institutions and to accommodate themselves to the new scientific demands (Douglas, 1963). The literature in the field was said to be too speculative and APOLOGETIC, too concerned for the safety of religion, too preoccupied with giving religion a pseudoscientific dignity. At the same time, its proponents were judged to be inadequately trained in scientific theories and methods, to be impatient with the tedious work that must precede the larger conclusions they were drawing, or to be preoccupied with the mere accumulation of facts without a guiding theoretical framework and adequate statistical analysis. Yet given the century-long indifference or even antipathy toward religion among psychologists, it is doubtful that more effort to meet the demands of objective psychology would have forestalled the field's decline.

That decline, it should be emphasized, stopped short of total demise. Although the psychology of religion had largely disappeared from the classroom, it lived on in other settings, in both America and England. The growing enthusiasm for Freud's ideas among pastoral counselors and clinical psychologists was reflected from time to time in articles or books on religion from a psychoanalytic point of view. Like Freud's own writings on religion, some of these works diverged from the predominantly Protestant–Christian preoccupations of the earlier psychologists of religion. Furthermore, in accord with Freud's own contributions, they were frequently critical in attitude. Meanwhile, the older, more positive psychology of religion found shelter in departments of religion and especially in seminaries, where it was typically transmuted into pastoral psychology. The intensely practical orientation of psychology of religion in this setting was expressed in the rise of the clinical pastoral training movement, founded by Anton Boisen (1876–1965), a once-SCHIZOPHRENIC minister who came to view mental illness as an existential and thus religious crisis (Boisen, 1936; Pruyser, 1967). A practical approach to the field is also at the heart of Henry Wieman and Regina Westcott-Wieman's *Normative Psychology of Religion* (1935), a work by a Unitarian theologian and a clinical psychologist, respectively, in which criteria are systematically laid out for evaluating religious living and growth.

The psychology of religion survived, then, as a means of criticizing or even discrediting religion, as in the instance of psychoanalysis, or as an adjunct for educational or pastoral work within a particular theological tradition. The ideal suggested by James and especially Pratt, of an essentially disinterested and scholarly approach founded in systematic description of a wide range of phenomena from diverse traditions, seemed to have become lost. Glimmerings of it reappeared with the revival of interest in the field after 1950, but this potential remains largely unrealized to this day.

THE GERMAN TRADITION

Whereas psychology of religion in America has been advanced primarily by psychologists, in Germany it has always been the province chiefly of philosophers and theologians. At first, as in the work of Schleiermacher and Ritschl, the psychological was subordinated to a particular theological position. Shortly before the beginning of the twentieth century, however, psychology was put forward as a fundamental element in the general theological enterprise, if not also in the study of religion as a whole (RELIGIONSWISSENSCHAFT). In a work on the psychology of faith, Gustav Vorbrodt (1895) characterizes the introduction of an essentially descriptive psychology into historical and systematic theology as both ''beneficial and necessary'' (p. 3). Emil Koch (1896) similarly advocates the introduction of a descriptive psychology into the study of religion, but in contrast to Vorbrodt, he said it must remain wholly independent of all metaphysical or theological discourse. For its data it would rely on the history of religions as well as the scholar's own religious experience.

The growing interest in developing a psychology of religion was given new force and direction with the appearance of the American works, especially the translations of James and Starbuck. The Clark school's questionnaire method was adopted by some in Germany but sharply criticized by others, who considered the technique applicable to a limited number of problems at best. James's method likewise faced a mixed reception, mainly because of its use of extreme, even pathological cases and its neglect of historical and institutional factors. While critical of the methods, many scholars nevertheless praised the Americans for putting forward a psychology of religion conceived as an independent and strictly empirical science of religious facts (Faber, 1913; Koepp, 1920). Consensus on the goals, methods, and limits of the psychology of religion was clearly not close at hand, yet the common interest was sufficient to spark a rapidly growing literature.

Wundt and the Folk Psychology of Religion

Further stimulus came from within German psychology. A singular contribution was made by Wilhelm Wundt (1832–1920), the son of a Lutheran pastor, a physiologist by training, and the reputed founder of experimental psychology. Although a proponent of experimentally controlled self-observation, Wundt argued that the higher mental processes, objectified in such cultural manifestations as language, MYTH, and religion, could be understood only by means of the historical and ethnographic methods of FOLK PSYCHOLOGY. The techniques of individual psychology employed by the Americans struck Wundt as useless for any true psychology of religion. From a randomly selected individual, Wundt (1911) says, one will obtain nothing more than a traditional confession of faith or a solemn report of newly resolved piety. From exceptional instances such as those James selected, one gains at best an interesting case study of religious pathology. Neither approach, he adds, takes into account the religious context of the individual's faith.

Wundt sought to explain religion by laboriously reconstructing its distant past and postulating an evolutionary process originating in elementary and nonreligious subjective events (Wundt, 1905–1909). Myth, he said, is created by the projection of human feelings and desires into objects of the natural world. As the result of this animating process, these objects come to appear as living, personal beings. Associations of various kinds—of one object with another, for example, or of bodily processes with cosmic ones—broaden and elaborate these original creations of imagination. The complex whole that results is myth, which at first cannot be distinguished from religion. As myth evolves, however—and Wundt gives most of his attention to the chief phases of its hypothesized development—religion gradually emerges while yet retaining the mythic form. Religion, Wundt maintains, is the feeling that our world is part of a larger, supernatural one in which the highest goals of human striving are realized. Whereas myth in general is related to everyday experiences in a kind of protoscientific attitude, religious myth seeks to comprehend the meaning—the basis and the goal—of such experience. Even when religious ideas themselves are dark and fleeting, religious feeling may remain strong. Indeed, argues Wundt, it is a unique peculiarity of the religious consciousness that feeling itself may become a symbol.

Other scholars were impressed by the astonishing quantity of material that Wundt had gathered for analysis and the coherence that his standpoint provided, both to this material and to the many theories that came before his. Yet his emphasis on group processes, and the corresponding neglect of individual factors, placed his work outside the mainstream of the German psychology of religion. Furthermore, Wundt's limitation of the folk–psychological approach to the hypothetical stages of religion's evolution that preceded the influence of historical religious personalities led his critics to fault him for leaving out the contemporary and "highest forms" of religion's development. Above all, however, they took exception to his highly speculative efforts to account for religion in terms of its origins (see Faber, 1913; Koepp, 1920).

If the German scholars by and large agreed in their disagreement with Wundt, they remained divided on many other matters. The confusion that reigned during the first decades of this century is particularly evident both in the diverse content of the *Zeitschrift für Religionspsychologie,* first published in 1907 under the editorship of Pastor Vorbrodt and Johannes Bresler, a psychiatrist, and in the fact of this journal's premature demise only six years later. Like its sister journal in America, it had failed to achieve a clearly defined and consistent direction, and it too lacked adequate scholarly support. Meanwhile, the debate over method and purpose continued in other journals.

The Dorpat School

Wundt's experimental psychology of immediate experience, although itself never applied to religion, is indirectly responsible for an alternative approach that is little known outside German-speaking circles. Wundt had limited his introspective science to the search for the elements that compose consciousness, such as images, sensations, and simple feelings, as well as for the laws of their combination. Both his exclusion of the higher mental processes from experimental investigation and his assumption of a "mental chemistry" were eventually challenged by one of his own students, Oswald Külpe. Subsequently, Külpe became famous as the leader of the WÜRZBURG SCHOOL, renowned for its research on imageless thought. Among Külpe's students, in turn, was Karl Girgensohn (1875–1925), a Protestant theologian who adopted the Würzburg school's systematic "experimental" INTROSPECTION to address the long-unresolved debate over the psychological nature of religion.

Girgensohn and his students, collectively known as the DORPAT SCHOOL of religious psychology, presented a series of religious stimuli—most often hymns, poems, or brief but striking sentences—to a variety of subjects. The subjects were asked to report as accurately as possible their experience of these materials. On the basis of the PROTOCOLS provided by his theologically sophisticated subjects, Girgensohn (1921) concluded that religious experience is not simply an inchoate or undefinable feeling, but a combination, rather, of two essential aspects: (1) intuitive thoughts of the divine, vaguely formulated at best, yet recognized or accepted as one's own, and (2) the conviction that the object of these thoughts constitutes an unquestionable reality to which one must make some response.

The prospect of a rigorously empirical psychology sensitive to the nuances of religious experience attracted an international group of scholars to the Külpe-inspired "experimental" approach. When the eclectic *Zeitschrift für Religionspsychologie* ceased publication in 1913, an association of scholars hospitable to the experimental view, the Gesellschaft für Religionspsychologie, immediately established in its place the *Archiv für Religionspsychologie*. Its first editor, Wilhelm Stählin, contributed an experimental study of his own to the inaugural volume of 1914. Students and visiting scholars found their way to Dorpat and, after 1919, to Greifswald and then to Leipzig, in order to work with Girgensohn. Later they gathered in Berlin to study with Werner Gruehn, a student of Girgensohn who, after Girgensohn's untimely death in 1925, became the leader of this school as well as the editor, in 1927, of the *Archiv* (Wulff, 1985a).

Dissent in Vienna: Some scholars, however, were more impressed by the limitations of Girgensohn's work than by his achievements. Beyond criticisms of his particular application of Külpe's experimental techniques, doubts were expressed that anything new or useful might be learned by attempting to re-create religious experience in the laboratory. When Gruehn remained adamant about the superiority of the experimental method, Karl Beth and others formed in 1922 a rival, Vienna-based organization, the Internationale Religionspsychologische Gesellschaft, and established the Vienna Research Institute for the Psychology of Religion.[2] In 1928 they revived the methodologically more diverse *Zeitschrift für Religionspsychologie*.

---

[2] Gruehn and his associates responded by adding *Internationale* to the name of their own organization and appending in parentheses its founding date of 1914, thereby denying the implicit charge of parochialism and asserting their society's priority.

Whereas Girgensohn and Gruehn had pursued a largely descriptive psychology of adult religious experience within the framework of a carefully delimited methodology, Beth (1926) sought to construct a more inclusive developmental psychology of religion using diverse methods sensitive to individual differences. In such a way he hoped to explain the fundamental trends as well as the broad diversity evident in the history of religion, including its modern-day transformations. He assumed that the crucial factors lie below the threshold of consciousness and thus he was receptive in particular to the work of the depth psychologists.

The Psychoanalytic Critique of Religion

The first study of religion from the perspective of modern depth psychology—Freud's brief paper on "Obsessive Actions and Religious Practices"—appeared in the 1907 inaugural issue of the *Zeitschrift für Religionspsychologie,* among whose editorial consultants Freud had agreed to serve. Although he subsequently withdrew from the editorial board, religion remained one of his leading interests. Religious beliefs and practices, he argued in a series of publications, are rooted in the fears and wishes of childhood, especially those that constitute the OEDIPUS COMPLEX. God the father is a re-creation of the omniscient and omnipotent father of infancy, who first inspired the love and fear that characterize the religious devotee's attitude toward the divine. The irrationality of religion's motives and the repression that keeps hidden its all-too-human origins are signaled, Freud argued, by the air of inviolable sanctity that surrounds religious ideas and the compulsive qualities of sacred rites reminiscent of NEUROTIC "ritual."

The psychoanalytic interpretation of religion was pursued for the most part by practicing psychoanalysts, although it found advocates in theological circles as well. Beyond elaborating on Freud's own writings, his followers expanded the range of religious phenomena to which psychoanalysis was applied, in part by drawing more comprehensively on the basic theory. Prototypical in both regards is Harald and Kristian Schjelderup's (1932) study of three fundamental types of religious experience, said to correspond to the first three stages of psychosexual development. The Schjelderups illustrate the three types through a selection of contemporary case studies as well as three examples from the history of religions: Bodhidharma, who carried the Buddha's insight to China; Ramakrishna, the nineteenth-century Hindu mystic; and Protestant Reformation leader Martin Luther.

The disposition of psychoanalysis to reduce religion to infantile or neurotic tendencies rapidly won for it the reputation of being unequivocally hostile and destructive. Some theologians, however, suggested that a more discriminating application of psychoanalytic insights could serve to purify religious faith and practice. Exemplary in this regard was Oskar Pfister (1873–1956), a Swiss pastor and psychoanalyst as well as one of Freud's few lifelong friends. To show how religion can go awry, Pfister undertook a series of studies in "religious pathology"—of the Moravian Count von Zinzendorf, of the cult of the Madonna, of mystic Margarete Ebner, and of GLOSSOLALIA and automatic writing. Drawing as well on his extensive work as pastoral counselor, Pfister developed a comprehensive "hygiene of religion." Neurotic trends in religion, Pfister (1944) maintained, whether on the individual or the group level, lead to an overemphasis on dogma and the replacement of love by hate. Only by returning love to the supreme position, he said, will Christianity regain the spirit of Jesus. We may employ the techniques and insights of psychoanalysis, Pfister adds in a methodological aside, without subscribing to its underlying philosophy or Freud's own views of religion.

Religion as Archetypal Process

Whether in the hands of a Freud or a Pfister, traditional psychoanalysis was mainly disposed to pointing out the weaknesses of religion. Jung's psychology, in contrast, offers a perspective for identifying its strengths. Attributing a fundamentally positive character to the unconscious forces said to underlie religious forms, Jung argued that religion is an essential psychological function. To neglect it, he said, is to risk serious disorder.

Although Jung accepted Freud's idea of an irrational personal unconscious, he also postulated the existence of a deeper-lying region, the COLLECTIVE UNCONSCIOUS, out of whose depths arise the myths and symbols that constitute humanity's religious traditions. Over millennia of time, Jung hypothesizes, recurrent experiences have gradually formed the structural elements of the collective unconscious, the ARCHETYPES, which serve as the basis for recognizing and experiencing anew the persons and situations that compose human reality. In the individual psyche the archetypes are at first wholly unknown and undifferentiated. With time, however, as a result of external events as well as natural inner tendencies, the archetypes are projected into an indefinite variety of corresponding images, among the most important of which are the diverse symbols of religion. By means of these images, the individual gradually differentiates and relates to the archetypes, which represent both dangers and opportunities in his or her life situation. Complementing differentiation is the tendency toward the integration of psychic factors, toward the equilibrium and wholeness that is represented by the archetype of the self through diverse and fascinating images, including the Buddha and Christ.

In the past, says Jung, the process by which the SELF becomes actualized, the INDIVIDUATION process, was directed and promoted chiefly by the religious traditions. To understand the dynamics of this process, therefore, we must become intimately familiar with the traditions' contents. Criticized for treating religion as a source of psychological rather than theological or metaphysical insight, Jung countered by saying that religious teachings reveal to us only the workings of the human psyche. Of a reality independent of our minds, he said, we can know nothing.

To some scholars, accordingly, Jung's ANALYTICAL PSYCHOLOGY seemed to constitute little more than a dogmatic psychologizing of religion that denied any place to METAPHYSICS and theology. For others, however, analytical psychology promised to provide a truly penetrating understanding of the religious life, without reducing it through causal explanation. If a genuinely comprehensive psychology of religion from an analytical view has yet to be attempted, there is no doubt that Jung's thought has inspired many European and American scholars of religion to find new meaning in ancient and often puzzling symbols.

The German Descriptive Tradition

Although depth psychology rapidly won a permanent place in the psychology of religion, a majority of the German scholars committed to this field were advocates, like Girgensohn, of a more strictly descriptive approach. Unlike the Dorpat school's founder, however, most considered a variety of methods more or less equally valid, as long as religious experience remained well in view. Biographies, personal documents of various kinds—confessions, autobiographies, diaries, letters, or poems—as well as interviews, assigned essays, and other such means for eliciting individual

The front face of a stone carved by Jung and placed in the garden of his Tower (see page 418). The evocative Greek inscription reads "Time is a child—playing like a child—playing a board game—the kingdom of the child. This is TELESPHOROS, who roams through the dark regions of this cosmos and glows like a star out of the depths. He points the way to the gates of the sun and to the land of dreams" (Jung, 1963, p. 227).

expressions of religious experience have been employed in this descriptive tradition. The researcher's own religious life has also been considered a vital resource, not only because it provides direct access to the object of study, but also because it constitutes the basis for an empathic understanding of the experience of others.

Only after these materials have been gathered does the descriptive psychologist's real task begin. In place of the statistical evaluation and inference favored by American investigators, the Germans have employed qualitative description, analysis, and classification. The outcome is commonly a schema of "ideal" types, which, by throwing into relief the general character and dynamics of religious experience, serves as a basis for comprehending existing individual forms. Such an understanding, though inevitably imperfect, may be employed in a variety of contexts, from the study of the history of religions to religious education and counseling. As a strictly empirical science, however, the psychology of religion requires no such applications to justify its undertaking, nor, it is argued, should they be permitted to shape its conclusions. Nevertheless, the descriptive psychologists of religion have an obvious sympathy and respect for the religious life. They, of course, would say that such attitudes are required of any scholar who would genuinely understand religion.

Outside German-speaking circles probably the best known of the German descriptive studies are Rudolf Otto's *The Idea of the Holy* (1917) and Friedrich Heiler's *Prayer* (1918). Well before these two works became classics, Wilhelm Koepp (1920) cited them as outstanding examples of the empirical–descriptive approach in the psychology of religion. In *The Idea of the Holy*—"one of the profoundest analyses of religious experience which have ever been made," according to Joachim Wach (1951, p. 217)—Otto undertakes to formulate the NONRATIONAL experience of the holy or the NUMINOUS, as he preferred to call it. Otto's analysis can be briefly summarized in the phrase MYSTERIUM TREMENDUM ET FASCINANS, a formula that underscores the bipolar character of the experience of the "Wholly Other." Frighteningly awesome and overpowering, on the one hand, the *mysterium* is alluring and fascinating on the other. Wherever it is found, says Otto, the experience is incomparable to any other and is thus irreducible.

Heiler's study on prayer examines in a similarly broad historical framework a complex phenomenon that he says lies at the heart of religion and is therefore a decisive measure of piety wherever it is found. Heiler's work provides a TYPOLOGY of the major varieties of prayer—from the nonliterate human being's spontaneous and passionate invocation of the god to the sublime variants of mystical contemplation—as well as a general characterization of prayer's essence. "It is always," says Heiler (1932, p. 355), "a great longing for life, for a more potent, a more blessed life." In its simplest and most spontaneous forms, which Heiler takes to be the most genuine, prayer consists of a living I—THOU RELATION of the individual with the divine personality. It is not self-chosen petition but living communion with God, Heiler concludes, that constitutes the essence of prayer.

In America, where "merely descriptive" psychology attracts far less interest than systematic measurement and causal explanation, the German descriptive psychology of religion has won little serious attention. Works readily available in translation such as Otto's and Heiler's are often cited but hardly ever imitated, much as is true of James's *Varieties*. From the German literature as a whole, only the works of Freud and Jung—an Austrian and a Swiss, respectively—have gained a genuine and sustained hearing from American psychologists of religion.

An Ill-Fated Enterprise

The fate of the German tradition paralleled in certain respects that of the Anglo–American. In each case early proponents failed to sustain a regularly appearing journal dedicated to the psychology of religion, in spite of widespread hope that the field would cast critical new light on perennial theological and pedagogical problems. In both traditions, the waning of liberalism in the 1920s and the ascendancy of Barth's dialectical theology intensified the fear of PSYCHOLOGISM and seriously eroded institutional support. In addition, in both the number of regular contributors remained surprisingly small, so that in its direction and course of development the field was exceptionally vulnerable to personal circumstances and private convictions.

The German tradition is distinguished from the American, however, by the profound disruption it suffered during the course of the two world wars. During these years of unprecedented destruction, research in the psychology of religion was seriously hampered if it could be carried out at all, and publications were either greatly delayed or foreclosed altogether. During the Nazi era, from 1933 to 1945, collaborative scholarly work of any kind was virtually impossible without governmental sanction, and by 1940, both the Vienna Research Institute and the Dorpat school had become defunct. Scholars such as Gruehn and Carl Schneider who did not follow Beth and Freud in fleeing the Nazi flood tide suffered grievous personal losses.

As in England and America, however, the end of World War II was soon followed by notable efforts to reclaim and build on the earlier work. The International Society for the Psychology of Religion that had been founded in 1914 was eventually revived, and issues of its irregularly appearing journal, the *Archiv für Religionspsychologie,* have been published every two or three years since 1962. As we will see in later chapters, a good number of informative studies representing a wide range of approaches has appeared in the more recent German literature.

Yet only a few German scholars have been drawn to the field, and the Society, long dominated by Roman Catholic theologians, has remained small. The appointment in 1995 of Nils G. Holm—a professor of comparative religion at Åbo Akademi University, the Swedish university of Finland, and an active contributor to the psychology of religion (Holm, 1982, 1987a)—to both the presidency of the Society and the editorship of the *Archiv* suggests the possibility of a new era. For now, the center of gravity for international dialogue lies in the loosely organized European Psychologists of Religion, a group that in 1979 began meeting every three years for a formal conference (Belzen and Lans, 1986; Corveleyn and Hutsebaut, 1994; Lans, 1979, 1982).

THE FRENCH TRADITION

Like the Anglo–American and the German traditions, the French psychology of religion has grown out of major intellectual trends in the nineteenth century. Among the most notable of its immediate precursors were Maine de Biran (1766–1824), one of France's most important philosophers, and Auguste Sabatier (1839–1901), a liberal Protestant theologian influenced by Schleiermacher and Ritschl. Biran argued, in opposition to the then-dominant SENSATIONALIST view of the mind, that human knowledge springs from the inner experience of the will's activity, especially as it encounters the resistance of both bodily conditions and the external world. Thus, although he gave priority to careful self-observation of immediate experience, he advocated supplementing it with studies of the physiology of the nervous system, comparative psychology, and psychopathology. In France contemporary psychology is customarily said to begin with Biran (Dwelshauvers, 1920, p. 1).

When Biran (1814–1824) became subject to mystical feelings late in his life, they too became content for introspective study. He wondered, however, if psychology could provide a complete account of their origins. Biran never fully developed his theory of the "third life," the life of the spirit, which he said lies beyond the "sensitive life" of awareness and the "reflective life" of self-contemplation. Nonetheless, his emphasis on inner experience, along with his own acutely sensitive self-observations, prepared the way for an enduring psychology of religious subjectivity (Lacroze, 1970; Voutsinas, 1975).

Whereas Maine de Biran began by laying the foundations of a psychology competent to consider religious experience, Auguste Sabatier started from the other end, seeking to loosen orthodoxy's inflexible grasp on religious doctrine in order to free it for historical and psychological understanding. Religion, according to Sabatier (1897), is first of all a matter of subjective piety, a product of the inner revelation of God. The human imagination spontaneously transforms this piety into a variety of mythic images and forms. The inevitable interpretation of these contents brings conflict and schism in turn. Dogma arises to restore unity to the community and to educate its members. Yet to serve these ends, dogma must be recognized for what it is: a living and changing historical phenomenon, a vital set of symbols that awakens and sets into motion the inner life of piety. By taking these symbols literally, as if they were themselves the objects of religion, or by substituting for them a simpler and more rational content, orthodoxy and rationalism alike have overlooked the psychological origins and nature of the religious life. In so doing, says Sabatier, they have threatened its very existence. Sabatier's theory of CRITICAL

SYMBOLISM dominated theological reflection, both Catholic and Protestant, for more than a generation.[3]

The French Psychopathological Tradition

It was Biran rather than Sabatier who influenced the first and most characteristic studies in the French psychology of religion. In this field as in psychology more generally, France made its chief contribution through work in psychopathology. Although interest in the relation of mental disorder and religion was not absent in the other two major traditions (cf. Cheyne, 1843, and Ideler, 1848–1850), in France it received sustained attention from some of the leading nineteenth-century psychopathologists.

As specialists in mental disease, these medically trained doctors, called *aliénistes* (from *aliéné,* "insane"), were intrigued by the various forms of "religious delirium" that they observed, each of which was found to reflect the peculiarities of the underlying disorder (Dupain, 1888). Furthermore, the numerous parallels between these symptoms and the traditional features of MYSTICAL and other forms of exceptional religious experience did not go unnoticed. Jean Martin Charcot (1825–1893), for example, whose work at the Salpêtrière, the famous neurological clinic in Paris, had made him the leading neurologist of his day, concluded that demoniacal POSSESSION was nothing but a particular form of HYSTERIA. Similarly, he thought that faith healing could be understood in terms of AUTOSUGGESTION and the contagion of mass psychology.

Pierre Janet: Among Charcot's French students and associates, Pierre Janet (1859–1947) is undoubtedly the best-known contributor to the psychology of religion. For a time the dean of French psychology, Janet was strongly influenced by Maine de Biran, indirectly through the midnineteenth-century *aliénistes* and directly through Biran's works (Ellenberger, 1970, p. 402). Although Janet himself undertook the development of a comprehensive theory of religion (see Horton, 1924), his case studies of exceptional religious states are far better known.

Preeminent among these studies is that of "Madeleine," a patient at the Salpêtrière between 1896 and 1904 and Janet's almost daily correspondent for 14 years after that. Madeleine exhibited a remarkable collection of symptoms. Most apparent was her unusual gait, the result of leg muscle contractures that forced her to walk on her toes. She was also subject to a variety of mysticlike states, ranging from ecstatic union with God, during which she remained immobilized in a position of crucifixion, to states of emptiness or even torture, when she felt herself abandoned by God and subject to evil forces. Several times a year Madeleine also exhibited STIGMATA, bleeding wounds corresponding to those ascribed by tradition to the crucified Christ. Through his extensive clinical and experimental investigations of Madeleine—he weighed her, for example, when she thought she was LEVITATING—and by comparing her outpourings with those of the great Christian mystics, especially those of Saint Teresa of Avila, Janet concluded that underneath the shifting states of mystical consciousness lies the disorder of PSYCHASTHENIA, a now-obsolete term for what today is called an obsessive–compulsive disorder (Janet, 1926–1928).

---

[3] James (1902) quotes Sabatier (1897) at length on the nature of religion and prayer, and then adds, "It seems to me that the entire series of our lectures proves the truth of M. Sabatier's contention" (p. 366).

Pierre Janet's patient, Madeleine, in a state of ecstasy.

Theodule Ribot: The identification of mysticism with some form of psychopathology was made by other French investigators as well. Among them is Theodule Ribot (1839–1916), to whom Janet was both pupil and successor. One of the initiators of the POSITIVISTIC movement in French psychology, Ribot (1884, 1896) argued that, of the various forms of emotion, the religious one is peculiarly dependent on physiological conditions. Ecstatic states—which at bottom, he says, are all the same—are most often the spontaneous outcome of individual constitution. Otherwise they may be sought by artificial means, all of which affect bodily conditions. At its extreme, religious passion may pass over into pathology, where, according to Ribot, it will take one of two general forms. In the *depressive,* or melancholic form, the individual becomes obsessed with feelings of guilt and fear; in the more transitory, *exalted* form, the person is overwhelmed by intense feelings of love. The extreme singlemindedness of the ecstatic, says Ribot, signals the annihilation of the will, the first stage of psychic dissolution.

Ernest Murisier: The PATHOLOGICAL METHOD was also employed by Ernest Murisier (1867–1903), a Swiss philosopher–psychologist who completed his theological studies with a thesis on Biran's psychology of religion (Murisier, 1892) and later studied for a year with Ribot in Paris. Murisier is best known for a work (1901) in which, like his famous mentor, he maintains that illness in effect decomposes a complex sentiment and exaggerates its constitutive elements.

The diseases of religious emotion, says Murisier (1901), show two fundamental tendencies corresponding to the individual and social elements in religion, which are ordinarily inseparable. When the *individual* element is isolated and exaggerated, we have the mystic, who seeks relief from severe psychological and physical disturbances by focusing on a single, leading idea. In this way, life is gradually simplified until nothing remains, for the moment, but the pure emotion of ECSTASY or even unconscious RAPTURE. When the *social* element is exaggerated, we have the fanatic. Here the experience of unity is obtained by identifying with a group or community and obediently accepting its teaching and direction. The urgency of the need for stability that is met in this way is reflected in fanaticism's hostility toward dissidents and its energetic quest for converts. From these extremes, then, we gain an understanding of normal piety. It, too, seeks a guiding idea for the evolution of personality, although for the healthy person it is a progressive evolution, not a regressive one. Piety also provides the social stability necessary for individual adaptation as well as the growth and maintenance of culture and morality.

Apologists for the Religious Life

Whether the pathological hypothesis was applied only to exceptional religious types—mainly, the mystic—or was generalized to religion as a whole, some scholars vigorously objected to it. Psychologist Henri Delacroix (1873–1937), for one, argues in his classic study of mysticism that an understanding of what is essential in Christian mysticism requires close study of the great mystics themselves. On the basis of his own investigations of Saint Teresa, Madame Guyon, Saint Francis de Sales, John of the Cross, and Heinrich Suso, Delacroix (1908) concludes that the mystic possesses a peculiar aptitude that is founded in an unusually rich subconscious life. Although undoubtedly subject to exceptional and inescapable physiological and psychological processes, including the AUTOMATISMS and intuitions of the subconscious self, the mystic uses them toward a self-chosen end: the total transformation of the personality. Moreover, far from being instances of impoverishment, DISSOCIATION, or psychosis, the successive stages of the mystic's life represent a new and creative existence. The superior power of the subconscious, shaped and directed by traditional mystical teachings, gradually takes over and simplifies the mystic's life, bringing about a superior and selfless unification.

Even Delacroix's sympathetic and widely praised work, however, was not fully accepted in Roman Catholic circles. A succession of critical works by such scholars as Joseph Maréchal (1924), Jules Pacheu (1911), and Maxime de Montmarand (1920), among others, was published in reply to the diverse psychological studies we have sampled here. These Catholic writers took exception, first of all, to the grouping together of all persons subject to ecstatic or mystical experience. They argued that the great mystics must be carefully distinguished from the inferior ones, the Christian from the non-Christian, even the orthodox Catholic from all others. Underneath apparent similarities may lie profound differences—above all, in the harmony and productivity of individual lives. Furthermore, these critics challenged the adequacy of one or another theoretical explanation, maintaining in the end that psychology cannot hope to comprehend the whole of mystical experience. Room must be left, they argued, for the activity of God, which, they believed, only philosophy and theology are competent to discuss.

The Catholic response to the efforts to develop a psychopathology of religion was not limited to criticism. Long sensitive to the subtleties of the spiritual life, the complications that can distort it, and the difficult task of directing it, Catholic scholars undertook a variety of positive investigations that belong to the psychology of religion. Particularly noteworthy is the series *Études Carmélitaines,* founded in 1911 as a serial and reconstituted in 1936 as a succession of monographs. Most of these publications record the proceedings of a series of conferences on psychology of religion sponsored by the Discalced Carmelites, a religious order founded by

Saint Teresa. With contributions from philosophers, theologians, historians of religion, psychologists, and medical specialists, these volumes explore such themes as stigmatization, mysticism, Satan, contemplation, the boundaries of human capacity, the role of sensation in religious experience, and the relation of liberty and structure (e.g., Jésus-Marie, 1948, 1954). Interrupted during the war, this series of monographs came to an end in 1960 with the retirement of its longtime editor, Father Bruno de Jésus-Marie.[4]

Theodore Flournoy

The interest in exceptional mental states for which the French were famous is also apparent in the work of the eminent Swiss psychologist Theodore Flournoy (1854–1920). Like his friend William James, who considered him a deeply kindred spirit, Flournoy was educated as a physician but never practiced. Instead, he studied with Wundt and eventually was appointed to a chair of experimental psychology that was established at the University of Geneva expressly for him (Le Clair, 1966, pp. xvii, xix). Like James, too, Flournoy had an abiding interest in PARAPSYCHOLOGY, a subject he approached with scientific rigor and exemplary fairness. He carried out detailed studies of mediums in Geneva, including one of "Hélène Smith," who thought herself to be a reincarnation of both a fifteenth-century Indian princess and Marie Antoinette and claimed to have traveled to the planet Mars (Flournoy, 1899). These studies added significantly to the growing understanding of the activity of the unconscious (Ellenberger, 1970, pp. 315–318). It was mainly Flournoy and James, Jung (1954b) remarks, who helped him to understand psychological disturbance in the context of individual lives (p. 55).

Two Principles: Flournoy, who shared James's sympathetic interest in religion, had studied for a semester in the School of Theology at Geneva. He withdrew, however, because theology seemed to him full of unnecessary difficulties (Le Clair, 1966, p. xvii). His religious interest found expression instead in a series of contributions to the psychology of religion. He is particularly well known for identifying two fundamental principles—one negative, the other positive—that provide the foundations for a genuine psychology of religion. According to the PRINCIPLE OF THE EXCLUSION OF THE TRANSCENDENT, psychologists of religion should neither reject nor affirm the independent existence of the religious object, a philosophical matter that lies outside their domain of competence. It is within their province, on the other hand, to acknowledge the *feeling* of transcendence and to observe its nuances and variations with the greatest possible fidelity (Flournoy, 1903a, pp. 38–40, 57).

According to the PRINCIPLE OF BIOLOGICAL INTERPRETATION, the psychology of religion is (1) *physiological* in its seeking out wherever possible the organic conditions of religious phenomena; (2) *genetic* or *evolutionary* in its attentiveness to both internal and external factors in their development; (3) *comparative* in its sensitivity

---

[4] The volumes in the *Études Carmélitaines* reveal a tendency among Catholic psychiatrists and psychologists to retain supernatural causes among their diagnostic categories. Accordingly, unlike Charcot, Ribot, and Janet, they are inclined to distinguish "true" and "false" religious occurrences, including conversion, mystical experience, miraculous cures, and possession (e.g., Lhermitte, 1956). Yet at least a few have been reluctant to employ supernatural explanation, as Paul Siwek (1950), a Jesuit who studied with both Janet and Delacroix, demonstrates in his study of the twentieth-century stigmatist Theresa Neumann of Konnersreuth.

to individual differences; and (4) *dynamic* in its recognition that the religious life is a living and enormously complex process involving the interplay of many factors (pp. 42–45). The names of these two principles are somewhat misleading, for the psychology of religion that Flournoy describes is neither so exclusive of the transcendent nor so thoroughly biological as these phrases suggest. Still, they have served as valuable reminders of the complex agenda that challenges scholars in this field.

Like James once again, Flournoy relied on personal documents in his investigations of religious experience. In the first of his published studies, a collection of six brief religious autobiographies accompanied by his commentary, Flournoy (1903b), too, underscores the diversity of such experience, even in the unexceptional lives he presents.[5] Indeed, he ventures to draw but a single generalization from these cases. The relation between articulate belief and deeper-lying emotional and VOLITIONAL processes, he says, is entirely idiosyncratic. For some people, the personal religious life is fundamentally dependent on the wholesale adoption of traditional beliefs. For others, such beliefs are not only superfluous but also hindrances to the development of the inner life. For these persons, Flournoy remarks, religious growth consists mainly in freeing themselves from the intellectual overlays imposed by education and other environmental influences. By this means, such individuals strive to attain and preserve direct access to inner experience, unfettered by an interpretive framework.

A Modern Mystic: Whereas Flournoy thought psychology and its application should be concerned chiefly with ordinary lives, he himself is best known for his investigations of exceptional cases. Most famous in the psychology of religion is his long and complex case study of "Cécile Vé." The unmarried directress of a Protestant school for girls, Mlle Vé came to Flournoy (1915) in her early fifties with the hope that hypnotic suggestion might promote the healing of a deeply disturbing split in her personality: on the one side, her true self, oriented toward God; on the other, a recurrently intrusive second self, ruled by the demon of sensuality (pp. 24–25). She wanted help, too, in breaking off an intense and morally compromising relation with a married man. A highly intelligent and articulate woman with a rare capacity for introspection, Mlle Vé kept a diary, at Flournoy's suggestion, throughout the years she worked with him. Flournoy's study includes lengthy excerpts from this extraordinarily revealing document, which Leuba (1925, p. 226) says is unequaled in scientific value by any other account of mystical experience.

In the course of her treatment, while feeling desolate after having renounced the troubling liaison, Mlle Vé found herself visited in the moments before sleep by an invisible PRESENCE. A "virile personality," yet neither male nor female, this spiritual friend appeared to her intermittently, a calming presence to whom she could freely pour out her heart (Flournoy, 1915, p. 42). A few months later, she had a still more extraordinary experience: a state of mystical trance in which she felt the overpowering and impersonal presence of the divine. Recurring 31 times during the next 17 months, this frustratingly ineffable experience of "the Life of God" brought home to her how severely limited—"cut and dried"—her

---

[5] In his commentary on the German translation of these case studies, Vorbrodt (1911, p. 36) notes with Flournoy's permission that the fourth document was written by Flournoy's wife Marie, who died in 1909.

conception of divinity had once been (pp. 63, 147). These remarkable experiences were brought to an end, it seemed, by certain inner realizations and outer events. There were continuing effects, however: on the one hand, a depreciation of traditional religious forms; and on the other, a renewed, Christ-centered search for a personal God, "of love and of pity," in the midst of an active life animated by a deeper sense of vitality and interest (pp. 186, 159, 208).

In his commentary on this case, Flournoy identifies several factors that seem to have played a role in Mlle Vé's experience: her unusual tendency toward mental dissociation, most obvious in the oscillation between two opposing states; a strict Protestant upbringing and enduring Christian faith; a deep attachment to her father, a highly cultured schoolmaster of rare moral character; a brutal sexual assault that she suffered as an exceptionally naive 17-year-old, a horrifying occurrence that was engraved in her memory and awakened in her the disturbingly passionate side of her personality; and the suggestions of serenity, courage, and self-control that Flournoy had made, in conversation and hypnotic sessions, in relation to her sexual obsessions. Scrupulously avoiding any simple reduction of Mlle Vé's mystical states to erotic experience, Flournoy concludes that the outcome for her was a personal liberation, an impressive enlargement of personality that was foreshadowed not only in her first descriptions of the experience of the divine, but also in the earlier manifestations of the spiritual friend.

A French Eclectic Tradition

Although his work provided impetus for additional studies of exceptional religious states (e.g., Morel, 1918), Flournoy was also recognized as the "venerable master," "the great and legitimate authority" of an eclectic Protestant tradition mainly concerned with normal expressions of human piety (Bovet, 1951, pp. 19–20). Centered in Geneva, this tradition comprises the work of scholars at both the University of Geneva and the Jean-Jacques Rousseau Institute, a private educational research center with which the eminent developmental psychologist Jean Piaget was long associated. These scholars were particularly influenced by the emerging depth psychologies and the new research on COGNITIVE development, though they drew on the earlier American and French literatures as well.

Georges Berguer: The leading figure in this tradition was Georges Berguer (1873–1945), an intimate friend of Flournoy. Berguer was long the only scholar in the world to occupy a chair in the psychology of religion, first at the school of theology of the Free Church of Geneva and later in the theological faculty of the University. Earlier he had served as a pastor in several parishes in Geneva and France (Godin, 1961, p. 9n; Rochedieu, in Berguer, 1946, p. v).

The advocate of a "scientific theology" as early as 1903, Berguer proposed in his doctoral dissertation an axiom complementary to Flournoy's principle of the exclusion of the transcendent. According to the PRINCIPLE OF PSYCHORELIGIOUS PARALLELISM, a religious phenomenon always possesses two corresponding aspects: a psychological state and an impression of value and objective significance. Neither, Berguer says, is reducible to the other. The psychology of religion is competent to address only the first of these factors, he argues, and thus it cannot account for the religious phenomenon as a whole. Rather, it must be augmented by a theology of faith and moral obligation (Berguer, 1908, pp. 283–284, 350). Thus although conversion—Berguer's case in point—can be understood from the psychological side as the outcome of subliminal forces and concomitant neural processes that yield observable and classifiable phases and types, something yet remains that is accessible only to intuitive and philosophic study: the action of God.

Whereas his thesis on value seems to focus on preserving a domain for "extrascientific theology" (p. 289), Berguer's later writings feature the positive role that the psychology of religion can play. Perhaps the most accessible and interesting of these works is his study of the life of Jesus (Berguer, 1920). Faithful to his principle of psychoreligious parallelism, Berguer emphasizes that the unique and imponderable qualities of Jesus, "perceptible only to the moral sense" and conferring on him "a value, a significance, a place quite apart from that of other human beings," cannot be isolated and analyzed through scientific effort. Just as certainly, however, they will not be injured by a study of the many points of resemblance between Jesus' states of consciousness and our own. Moreover, the insights of dynamic psychology, in making apparent the ends toward which Jesus was striving, may underscore what separates him from the rest of humanity (pp. 14–15).

Much like Jung, Berguer postulates a universal tendency to form representations of divinity and of salvation, "the life with God," that are ever more adequate to the deepest human needs. This "immense task," which engages the polarized subconscious energies and harmonizes all the human capacities, gives rise to a double symbolism: one seeking to represent the attributes of the gods themselves and another providing the means for participating in the divine life, the symbolism of sacred ceremony. Inevitably, humankind has chosen symbols from its own elemental experience, symbols that range from the grossly materialistic to the highly sublimated and spiritualized. Berguer traces this progressive development both in the mystery cults of the Hellenistic period (300 to 100 B.C.E.) and in later Christian developments.

The Christian tradition triumphed, Berguer says, because it centers on the personal life of a being who actually lived through the inner drama of transformation that had been symbolized, but not successfully fostered, by a succession of mythic savior–gods who died and were then reborn. Yet the spiritual victory of Christ, he adds, did not magically transform human nature. To this day, "the Christian struggle consists in a constant effort towards an always more complete SUBLIMATION" of the baser instinctual tendencies, prevalent in the mystery cults, that have regrettably made "a mythical figure of Jesus, a Mystery-god like the others" (pp. 63–64). Through biblical criticism and psychological analysis, Berguer seeks to uncover the psychological truth that underlies the engaging yet falsifying mythic elaborations of the life of Jesus. That life, he concludes, calls a person not to dutiful belief in certain extraordinary historical events but to the profound experience of dying to the self and then returning more fully to life, "the new life of the Spirit" (p. 294).

Like Pfister, then, who was one of his sources, Berguer employs psychology as a means of promoting what he saw as a deeper and truer faith. That same liberal piety is evident in his posthumously published treatise on the psychology of religion (Berguer, 1946), which, like his earlier review and bibliography (Berguer, 1914), shows the strong influence of Flournoy, the early American investigators, especially James, and the European depth psychologists. A similar focus on the psychological value of Christian faith can be found in an early work of Berguer's immediate successor, Edmond Rochedieu (1948).

Pierre Bovet: At the Rousseau Institute, founded in 1912, the best-known contributions to the psychology of religion were made by its longtime director, Pierre Bovet (1878–1965). A disciple of Flournoy who was initiated into psychoanalysis by Pfister, Bovet employed personal documents and a psychodynamic perspective to clarify the course of religious development. The religious sentiment, Bovet (1925) writes, is an extension of the sentiment of filial love, and it is naturally first directed toward the parents. The father and mother, he declares, are the child's first gods, the revered objects of tender love and wondering awe. When experience inevitably proves the parents unworthy of divine attributes, thus precipitating the "first religious crisis," the child spontaneously transfers these qualities to an unseen and wholly spiritual power that is experienced as manifest in the world of nature. In adolescence we meet a second, intellectual and moral crisis, when traditional ideas of an all-powerful and morally perfect God are called into question by scientific knowledge and everyday experience. From a perspective informed both by the Freudian doctrine of emotional ambivalence and by the research of Piaget and others on cognitive development, Bovet concludes that the primary task of religious education is not the inculcation of doctrine but the transmission and evocation of love (p. 138).

Jean Piaget: Piaget (1896–1980) was himself a direct contributor to this French eclectic tradition. Piaget had grown up in a home divided on the matter of religious faith. His kindly but neurotic mother was a devout Protestant, whereas his scholarly father thought conventional piety incompatible with historical criticism. When as a youth Piaget acceded to his mother's wishes that he take a course on Christian doctrine, he was disturbed by the recurring conflict with biology and the weakness of the traditional arguments for the existence of God. It had not occurred to him to doubt God's existence, he says, but it seemed extraordinary to him that persons as intelligent as his pastor took such weak arguments seriously. It was his good luck, Piaget (1952) writes, to discover at this time in his father's library Auguste Sabatier's (1897) influential book, which he "devoured . . . with immense delight." One evening some time later, after his godfather had introduced him to Henri Bergson's *Creative Evolution,* Piaget experienced a profound revelation: "The identification of God with life itself was an idea that stirred me almost to ecstasy," for it suggested to him that biology could explain all things, including the mind itself. The problem of knowing suddenly appeared to him in a new light, and he decided to dedicate his life to "the biological explanation of knowledge" (p. 240). He eventually completed a doctorate in the sciences, and then for three years he studied psychology and philosophy in Zurich and at the Sorbonne.

After Piaget arrived in Geneva in 1921 to become the director of studies at the Rousseau Institute, he and some other members of the Student Christian Association of French Switzerland organized a group for research on the psychology of religion. He presented his own reflections at several of the annual meetings of the association at Sainte-Croix, where Flournoy had earlier been an extraordinarily vivid presence (Piaget, 1922, pp. 42–43). Affirming Flournoy's principles, Piaget acknowledges that psychology cannot render judgment on religious values per se, but it can evaluate whether or not the deduction of a certain value from a particular experience accords with the laws of logic (p. 55), the child's understanding of which he was then researching. Psychology may also help to explain the surprising variety of deductions from more or less the same experience.

In a succession of writings on religious attitudes,[6] Piaget distinguishes two fundamental types, corresponding to two seemingly contradictory qualities attributed to God: TRANSCENDENCE and IMMANENCE. Contrasting notions of causality best distinguish these types. The transcendent God is a God of causes, implicitly divine causes that lie beyond our understanding. By contrast, the immanent God is a God not of causes but of values, a God that lies within us rather than outside the world (Piaget, 1930, pp. 9–10). Piaget reports that the research carried out by his group indicates that, in accord with Bovet's thesis, individuals are inclined toward one or the other of these attitudes by the relation they have had with their parents. People are predisposed toward transcendence and a morality of obedience, he says, when as children they are taught *unilateral respect* for adults, particularly those with authority and prestige. An inclination toward immanence and a morality of autonomy follows, on the other hand, when the attitude is one of *mutual respect,* founded on equality and reciprocity. An entire society and its educational system may be inclined in one direction or the other (Piaget and de la Harpe, 1928, pp. 18–24).

Whereas Flournoy considers transcendence to be a matter about which psychology must remain agnostic, Piaget boldly subjects it to psychological analysis. He judges the transcendent God of classical theology to be no more than a symbol of "the mythological and infantile imagination," and the morality of sin and expiation to be a product of social constraint. Entirely opposed to such MORAL REALISM, he says, is the spirit of Jesus, who offers instead a morality and God of love (pp. 26–29). Troubled by the logic of the hypothesis of transcendence, Piaget opts for immanentism, which, he says, recognizes evil for the mystery it is and reduces revelation to the prescriptions of individual conscience (Piaget and de la Harpe, 1928, p. 37). Berguer (1946), in contrast, maintains that both tendencies reflect essential religious needs and, like liberalism and orthodoxy, are finally reconciled in the figure of Christ (p. 339). Flournoy (1904), too, shared this view. No other religious genius, he once said of Jesus to a Sainte-Croix audience, has so perfectly fused the moral and mystical elements.

A Neglected Literature

Like the Anglo–American and German literatures, the French psychology of religion counts among its earliest contributors several of the century's most eminent psychologists. Yet today none of them retains a position of prominence in this field. When Villiam Grønbaek (1970) surveyed 24 major works on the psychology of religion published in America and Europe between 1950 and 1967, he found that, among the ten most frequently cited names, seven came from the field's inaugural period, including two from the American literature (James and Starbuck) and five from the German (Freud, Gruehn, Jung, Girgensohn, and Otto). Only among the three more recent contributors do we find one from the French literature—André Godin, the Belgian Jesuit psychologist of religion who edited the "Lumen Vitae" series of studies in religious psychology (Godin, 1957–1972). Even in French works of the current revival, the early literature is largely ignored.

---

[6] Copies of these scarce monographs, virtually unknown in America, can be obtained from the Piaget Archives in Geneva. Illuminating discussions of Piaget's writings on religion can be found in a small monograph by Mary Vander Goot (1985), who emphasizes the process of secularization in Piaget's thought by comparing these early works with four much later ones, and in a chapter by Fernando Vidal (1987), who places Piaget's early writings in the context of liberal Protestant thought and the challenge to it of Barthian neo-orthodoxy.

The French tradition, it may be said, did not undergo a sustained development comparable to the other two. It apparently has never had a journal of its own, equivalent to the short-lived *Journal of Religious Psychology* or the similarly ill-fated *Zeitschrift für Religionspsychologie.*[7] Nor, it appears, has it ever been the subject of systematic review and analysis, in a manner akin to Klaas Cremer's (1934) exhaustively comprehensive doctoral dissertation on the German tradition. Even so, in its totality the French literature is surprisingly large, especially if we include the more general works on such topics as belief or doubt (see Berguer, 1914).

THE CONTEMPORARY REVIVAL

Grønbaek's survey suggests that contemporary psychologists of religion are highly dependent on major portions of the early work we have just reviewed. Yet there is much that is new in our own day, both in terms of interpretive frameworks and in methods of research. In addition, new journals, organizations, and centers of graduate study and research activity have been established and internationally recognized. Although the number of scholars actively engaged in this field continues to be relatively small, they now represent a much wider geographic and linguistic range. Given especially the work being carried out in Scandinavia, Belgium, and the Netherlands, among other European countries, we can no longer represent the field's activities in terms of three major traditions.

For English speakers, the international scene today can be most readily accessed by consulting the *International Journal for the Psychology of Religion,* which was founded in 1990, and the collections of papers from the triennial meetings of the European Psychologists of Religion (Belzen and Lans, 1986; Corveleyn and Hutsebaut, 1994; Lans, 1979, 1982). Both of these resources bring together the research and reflections of an international array of psychologists of religion. In addition, the *Journal* provides reviews of books published both in English and in various European languages and offers occasional reviews of the psychology of religion as it has developed in particular countries, including Australia (O'Connor, 1991), Canada (Hunsberger, 1992), Italy (Aletti, 1992), The Netherlands (Belzen, 1994), Poland (Grzymala-Moszczynska, 1991), and Scandinavia (Wikström, 1993; see also Holm, 1987).

As one reads these national overviews, one appreciates anew the difficulties of generalizing about the psychology of religion. In whatever country, however, it is apparent that a variety of political, religious, and intellectual forces have profoundly affected the course of the field's development—if indeed a word implying a progressive unfolding is appropriate here. Such factors remain significant today. Everywhere, moreover, the field has been dependent on the efforts of a small number of people. Some of them have become highly influential, establishing the tone or framework for much subsequent work in their own countries if not abroad as well; other scholars have worked in relative isolation. For some, the psychology of religion is positioned mainly within psychology, academic or clinical, whereas others

---

[7] This conclusion is qualified because of a single citation in Berguer's (1914) bibliography, probably taken from a monograph by L. Perrier, *Le sentiment religieux* (Paris: Fischbacher, 1912), p. 17, in which reference is made to an article by a Monsieur Jœger in the *Revue de la psychologie des religions et des questions médico-théologiques.* No publication of this title is listed in the standard serial catalogues, and Jean-Pierre Deconchy (personal communication, October 8, 1979) reports that the conservatrix of the Bibliothèque Nationale was also unable to find any trace of it.

place it within the history of religions or theology. Some have pursued the psychology of religion as a strictly academic or scientific undertaking aimed at accumulating a body of knowledge or creating an interpretive framework. Others come to it with distinctly practical questions and an expectation that it will be helpful in religious education or pastoral care.

In the chapters ahead, we will see more closely how these various factors and trends have shaped the field. As we proceed, the reader is encouraged to keep in mind Flournoy's two principles: the psychology of religion should avoid making any judgment, one way or the other, about the reality of religious content, and it should be conceived as the comprehensive exploration of the diverse biological and psychological processes governing the development and dynamics of religious phenomena in individual lives. None of the perspectives we consider in this book wholly fulfills these principles. But in combination, these views provide a clear sense of what an adequate psychology of religion should be able to do.

3

THE BIOLOGICAL
FOUNDATIONS OF RELIGION

*I*n this chapter, the first of four representing the objective approach to religion, we systematically explore the implications of the obvious fact that experience and behavior are grounded in bodily conditions. As healthy individuals, we ordinarily take our bodies for granted, giving little thought to how fundamentally they shape our experience. Struck by illness or pain, however, or finding ourselves at the outer limits of our physical capacities, we become sharply aware of our bodies and how they condition our lives. Here we will explore how human embodiment affects religious faith and practice.

BODILY STATES AND RELIGIOUS EXPERIENCE

Although philosophers and scientists are still puzzling over the relation of mind and body, the religious traditions have long recognized the profound influence of bodily conditions on psychological or "spiritual" states. "Spiritual disciplines" often include exercises that operate directly on the body: assuming certain postures, depriving oneself of food or sleep, submitting to various other kinds of bodily discomforts, or controlling the rate of breathing. Each of these techniques manipulates bodily processes as a means of attaining certain desired states of consciousness. Some of these methods are undoubtedly thousands of years old.

Less dramatic but hardly less significant are the normal organic conditions without which there could be no religious experience. There is first of all the prerequisite of a living organism capable of perceiving and responding. Many religious rituals or practices are designed to appeal to the sense organs, especially to the eye and the ear, but also to the nose, the tongue, and the organs of touch. Furthermore, religious rites typically require active bodily participation, ranging from sitting, standing, and kneeling, common in Western traditions, through touching sacred objects and circumambulating holy sites, to dancing, spinning, or falling on one's face. The KINESTHETIC and equilibratory sensations produced by these often highly elaborated movements become closely associated with religious ideas and feelings, which themselves have roots in physiological processes. In various contexts, but especially religious ones, sensations or feelings produced by the internal organs, and by various states of the organism such as hunger or thirst, come to serve as symbols expressing complex attitudes. In sum, it is impossible to find any religious experience or behavior that is not grounded in the fact of embodiment (Girgensohn, 1921; Mudge, 1923; Pöll, 1965; Pruyser, 1968; Starbuck, 1921).

Several of the early advocates of a strictly empirical psychology of religion argued that physiology should be included in its foundations. As early as 1897 James Leuba suggested the possibility of a psychophysiology of ethics, and in 1925 he published his classic work on the psychology of mysticism, which leans heavily on medical and physiological explanations. Gustav Vorbrodt (1904), one of the pioneers of the psychology of religion in Germany, fervently hoped to see the historical theology of his day transformed by the introduction of "psychobiology." The resulting "psychological theology" would recognize human beings as psychophysiological organisms as well as spiritual beings. In the French literature, Theodore Flournoy (1903a) expressed a common sentiment when he declared that whenever possible psychologists of religion should look for a phenomenon's physiological roots.

Hall and the Objective Approach to Religion

The role of bodily processes in religious experience was first scientifically documented by Stanley Hall (1882), who found that most conversion experiences occur around the time of puberty, when the physiological changes of sexual maturation are taking place. In his famous chapter on conversion, Hall (1904, 2) extends that association by delineating a variety of "similarities and covariants" of religion and sexual love, including their common tendency to vacillate between self-assertion and self-abnegation; to become fanatically dedicated to their objects of devotion; to prepare for these objects an ornate place of habitation, or to hallow the sites with which they are associated; to express devotion in rhythmic music and dance; to feel ecstatically and invincibly happy; to engage in elaborate forms of etiquette and ceremony; to become distorted through fetishism or idolatry; and to lend their own enormous vitality to virtually any other act or object. The intimate relation of religion and sexual love is also apparent, Hall notes, in the language and analogies that have been employed over the centuries by religious mystics, theologians, and writers of hymns. Profound differences nevertheless remain, he adds, especially when the transcendent object is not conceived as a being of a particular sex (pp. 295–301).

As the first to gather scientific evidence for the role of physiological processes in religion, and as the author of a developmental theory based on inherited primary impulses, Hall is one of the leading instigators of the biological approach to religion. He was also an early proponent of other aspects of the objective approach. Vehemently opposed to the introspectionism of James's psychology, he championed objective observation, including observation of animals and children, and he put forward principles that were behavioristic in flavor long before the rise of behaviorism (Boring, 1950, p. 523). He offered a course, for example, on "nutritive psychology," in which he explored the great role of hunger and the digestive processes in the economy of all living things. Even religion, whose "primitive gods were mainly eaters, with cruel fangs and enormous mouths and maws" might be defined as a sublimation of the quest for food, "a method of raising the plane of digestion, making the body an ever more fit living temple for the *Biologos*'' (Hall, 1923, pp. 415, 416). Hall also promoted the use of the questionnaire, which today serves as the primary instrument of the correlational psychology of religion.

Whereas Hall bequeathed to the psychology of religion neither an influential theory such as Freud's or Jung's nor a legacy of respect and admiration akin to James's, he did leave to it the general approach that is represented by the next four chapters of this book. To illustrate that even the objective approach cannot escape the influence of the PERSONAL EQUATION, Hall will serve as the subject of the first of four biographical studies in the origins of the psychology of religion. Although the resources for such a study are relatively modest in comparison to what is now available on Freud, Jung, and James, the subjects of the other three studies, they are more adequate than those for other objectively oriented psychologists of religion. Shortly after he retired as president of Clark University, Hall wrote an unusually candid (if not always accurate) autobiography to demonstrate to himself and others "how every item of my psychology and philosophy, whether acquired or original, grew out of my life and my basal and innate traits" (1923, p. 574). Although his mature life seemed to him to be "made up of a series of fads or crazes" (p. 367), including a late-blooming enthusiasm for psychoanalysis, Hall nevertheless found a core of dominant themes with roots deep in his past, suggesting that the principle of continuity inherent in the evolutionary hypothesis was equally applicable to his own life. Invaluably complementing this book-length work and occasional brief memoirs by Hall's students and other associates is Dorothy Ross's (1972) meticulous biography of Hall. Her work underscores the prophetic fervor with which he promoted scientific psychology as the basis for revivifying and transforming education and religion.

THE LIFE OF G. STANLEY HALL

Granville Stanley Hall was born on February 1, 1844, in Ashfield, Massachusetts, a small New England farming community to which Hall was to return again and again throughout his life. His family, says Hall (1923), was extremely conservative, in-

G. Stanley Hall

tensely loyal, and moderately religious. His father, after brief stints as a broom maker, a teacher, and a lumber raftsman, had finally settled down to a lifetime of farming. Gregarious and quick-tempered, he was undemonstrative in his affection and reticent in his religious faith, except as it was expressed through singing in the church choir and teaching a ladies' Sunday school class.

Hall's mother, by contrast, was a patient, sympathetic, and deeply pious woman who for 11 years filled a series of religious diaries with reflections and aspirations as well as feelings of inadequacy. In retrospect, Hall suspected that her piety was in part a sublimation of the close and sympathetic relationship that she had enjoyed with her father, a man far more chivalrous and outwardly affectionate than her husband would prove to be. Both of Hall's parents lived in the shadow of unrealized ambitions and ideals, and both incessantly urged Hall and his younger brother and sister to fulfill these aspirations in their stead. For this incentive Hall was deeply grateful; as his parents had lived their lives for him and his siblings to an exceptional degree, so he came to see his own life as a continuation and realization of theirs.

A Solitary Country Childhood

At least as he remembered it from the perspective of his middle and later years, Hall's childhood was an ideal one. In spite of his parents' personal struggles and disappointments, Hall thought them ideally mated and happily married. Moreover, "that they were poor, humble, and hard up against the stern realities of life" (p. 85) was for Hall a fortunate fact. Wealth, he declared, would have ruined a youth of his temperament. What his family did provide was a surfeit of "excelsior motivations" and a great variety of healthful activities. He always considered it a most happy circumstance that he had spent his early years in the country, far enough from the village to provide a good deal of isolation as well as generous exposure to the awesome and ever-changing face of nature. Childhood, Hall was to write many years later (1900), is "the best period of human life. It is the richest and the largest. It has most sympathies, most delusions, most capacities, most pleasures. . . . In the growing period of life is found almost all that makes life worth living" (p. 186).

Looking back on the pleasures of childhood on a New England farm, Hall best remembers the animals. To his continuing regret he was never allowed to have a dog; of other animals, however, there was always an abundance. The horses, cows, and sheep, individually named and part of Hall's daily responsibilities, provided him with both challenges and opportunities. Together with a variety of wild animals that Hall observed and occasionally captured, they laid the foundations for his persistent interest in animal and COMPARATIVE PSYCHOLOGY.

Hall's relations with these animals foreshadowed not only the directions of his professional interests but also some of his adult personality traits. The extreme mortification he felt in having to drive pigs through the streets of Ashfield, and then to bear a teacher's public reference to this act, gives us a measure, according to Starbuck (1924), of Hall's insistent self-feeling, of his capacity for pride as well as for antipathy toward anyone who threatened his self-regard. Similarly, the contrast between Hall's evident rapport with animals and his childhood passion for hunting, dissecting, and preserving them as trophies is but an early expression of his continuing struggle with two opposing tendencies within himself—on the one hand, a sympathetic love of nature and a dread of all conflict or disharmony, and on the other, a large measure of aggressiveness, first toward his early surroundings and then toward a variety of cultural and intellectual currents.

Hall had said that the principle of evolution "vastly broadened and intensified sympathy with all that lives," for it brought the realization that all animals, including the human species, "are, in a sense, blood relatives." At the same time, however, he considered "the patheticism that agonizes over the sufferings of animals" to be a "morbid extreme" of the trait of sympathy (p. 461). The hunting and domestication of animals, he maintained, are part and parcel of human evolution, elements in the quest to command the powers of nature.

Other themes and experiences of Hall's childhood and adolescence came to figure in his writings as a psychologist: his intense responsiveness to nature, especially to clouds and the moon, but also to trees, fire, water, and snow; his childhood fears—of his heart's stopping or the world coming to an end, of lightning, injury, or inferiority, of the hell preached by the revivalists; and the long and terrifying struggle with adolescent sexuality that left him feeling corrupt and unworthy of association with girls. This struggle, he said, was the principal factor in his religious conversion.

Expanding Horizons

The transition from the relatively simple and familiar world of his childhood to a complex adult life of wide horizons and unusual experience was gradual enough, says Hall, that his life appeared to him to recapitulate the evolutionary history of the human race. Hall's first step away from home came with a year of college preparatory work at a seminary 24 miles from Ashfield. Rudely awakened to his own immaturity, lack of sophistication, and educational backwardness, Hall struggled with strong feelings of inferiority that, in mitigated form, were to haunt him all his life. Sometimes they compelled his best work, other times they inspired him to be unduly critical of people—William James, for example—deserving his respect.

Hard work gained Hall admission to Williams College, where he soon found himself ahead of most of his classmates. His college years were an opportunity to read widely, much of it outside of his courses. He found himself particularly attracted to philosophy—above all, to the empiricist and utilitarian John Stuart Mill. He was profoundly influenced by Darwin and Spencer as well, among others, and he studied closely such writers as Feuerbach and Comte, as well as Emerson, Coleridge, and Tennyson. Among the subjects he eventually taught was the history of philosophy, where he focused on Locke, Berkeley, Hume, and Kant and encouraged all his students to follow intelligently the path toward which they were personally predisposed.

Hall's education was ostensibly pointed toward the ministry, which in his day "was still the chief path open to a young man of philosophical interests and slender means" (Ross, 1972, pp. 29–30). It was also the path that his parents favored. Yet Hall himself had doubts that he was truly suited to this vocation, and, as alternatives, he seriously considered medicine as well as law. Lacking the opportunity for graduate work in the United States or the means for study abroad, Hall finally elected to go to the Union Theological Seminary in New York City.

His theological studies in the midst of a great metropolis constituted an important stage in the "long and laborious process from the rigor of the Puritan faith in which I was reared to complete emancipation from belief in all forms of supernaturalism" (Hall, 1923, p. 422). As an underclassman at Williams, during one of the spring religious revivals that annually swept through the college in that day, Hall had undergone a religious conversion. Although he later described the episode as superficial and inconsequential, his letters from that time (Ross, 1972) reveal some of the hallmarks of typical conversion experiences. By the time Hall was ready to give his trial sermon at Union, however, his views were heretical enough to inspire the president, when Hall consulted him for criticism, to kneel and pray for his soul.

In spite of his unorthodoxy, Hall appeared to be serious in his preparation for a religious vocation. He was employed for a few months by one or another city mission to distribute tracts or to solicit attendance at religious exercises that he also helped to conduct. He sought to broaden his acquaintance with the weekly services of other denominations and traditions as well as the oratory of the great preachers of the day. In addition, as a culmination of his work at Union, he became a preacher for nine or ten weeks in a small town in Pennsylvania.

From Preacher to Worldly Professor

Nevertheless, Hall's years at Union prepared him far more for the calling of psychologist and man of the world than for the ministry. Above all, New York provided him with the first oportunity to indulge an intense interest that persisted throughout the rest of his years: to see at first hand the seamier side of life, in order, he says, "to understand human nature as it is" (p. 580). This almost obsessive interest took him to the scenes of executions and accidents; to police courts, prisons, and morgues; to institutions for the blind, the deaf, the insane, the impoverished; to districts of vice and crime in many American and foreign cities; to prize fights and circus sideshows; to meetings of revivalists and revolutionaries.

Out of his experiences at Union emerged the idea of becoming a professor. Through the sympathetic efforts of Henry Ward Beecher, whose church he had joined, Hall was able to borrow enough money to interrupt his theological education and go to Germany to study philosophy. First in Bonn and then in Berlin, Hall immersed himself in this subject as rapidly as his growing knowledge of the language would allow, and he attended lectures or demonstrations in theology, physiology, anthropology, surgery, physics, and psychopathology.

From his arrival in the summer of 1869 until his return to America late in the fall of 1870, Hall eagerly acquainted himself with a host of people, places, and ideas, reveling in the new freedom that gave him. The "hated Puritan Sunday" that had long been for him a "day of gloom and depression" was transformed into "one of joy and holiday recreation." The inhibitions of teetotalism and sexual repression gave way to love of beer and delight in the company of women. Both signaled a discovery of the joys of carefree association, of frankness and intimate relationship. With two women in particular he finally "realized what love really meant and could do." Germany nearly remade him, he says; more particularly, his discovery of the "charms" of PANTHEISM, AGNOSTICISM, MATERIALISM, POSITIVISM, and above all, EVOLUTIONISM, helped him attain "maturity in his religious consciousness" (Hall, 1923, pp. 219–222).

As he reflected on it long afterward, this influential period in Germany seemed to Hall to have lasted three years, the traditional "triennium" that others spent abroad to study. In actuality, he was forced to return home after a year and a half, when his funds ran out (Ross, 1972, p. 41). Hall completed his degree at Union, served for 16 months as a private tutor to the five children of an eminent Jewish banker in New York, and then, in 1872, accepted a position at Antioch College in Ohio, where he taught philosophy, English, and modern languages and literature, and served as librarian, choir director, and occasionally organist or preacher. Halfway through his four years at Antioch the first volume of Wundt's *Physiological*

Psychology appeared, greatly exciting Hall and helping to convince him "that 'the application of scientific methods in psychology' was among the 'marvelous new developments' in philosophy" (Ross, 1972, p. 59).

Restive in the face of insufficient challenge at a college remaking itself into a school of education, yet unable to find another position, Hall considered returning to Germany to study the new scientific psychology with Wundt. This he was finally to do, but not until after he had spent two years at Harvard, as a tutor in English, a doctoral candidate in philosophy, and James's student in psychology. His work during these years transformed him into a serious scholar; it also won for him the first Ph.D. awarded by Harvard's department of philosophy and the first given in psychology in America (Ross, 1972).

A Pioneer in Psychology

In 1878 Hall sailed once more for Germany in order to pursue his new vision: the possibility of bringing psychology into what he thought of as "the impending physical–chemical explanation of the natural world" (Ross, 1972, p. 83). In Berlin and Leipzig, with such luminaries as Helmholtz, Johannes von Kries, Carl Ludwig, and finally Wundt, Hall studied physics, mathematics, and mathematical electricity; physiology and neuroanatomy; and neuropathology and clinical psychiatry. Abandoning the speculations of traditional philosophy, though still wary of a wholly mechanistic scientific theory, Hall firmly committed himself to a scientific perspective and tried to work out a theory of psychology based on reflex action.

His decision for science, Ross (1972) suggests, reflected Hall's struggle with three personal traits: powerful feelings of dependence, a desire for self-sacrifice, and "aesthetic susceptibilities," all of which he had identified both with the religious sentiment, following Schleiermacher, and with the feminine nature. "Hall's scientific identity reinforced his masculine identification by excluding these 'feminine' concerns from its sphere but only at the price of denying Hall an intellectual outlet for his suppressed feelings and itself assuming a martyred stance" (p. 98). Whatever the motives for his commitment, Hall returned to America in 1880 to become one of the leading figures in intellectual and scientific circles and one of America's foremost psychologists. At the same time, he continued in his efforts to effect a synthesis between his scientific convictions and his persistent religious and philosophical interests. One outcome of these efforts was his work in the psychology of religion.

Hall's academic career, after uncertain beginnings, took him in 1882 to Johns Hopkins University, where he set up a psychological laboratory—the first formally "founded" in America although James had effectively established one at Harvard a few months earlier. He also began publication of the *American Journal of Psychology,* the first psychological journal in America. In 1888 Hall accepted an invitation to help organize and be president of the new Clark University in Worcester, Massachusetts, which was to be for some years exclusively a graduate school, emphasizing research, not instruction. Hall spent the rest of his professional life as Clark's president as well as one of its most influential scholars and teachers. He was to found three more journals: the *Pedagogical Seminary* (today the *Journal of Genetic Psychology*) in 1891, the *American Journal of Religious Psychology and Education* in 1904, and the *Journal of Applied Psychology* in 1915. He collaborated in the founding of the American Psychological Association in 1892, served as its first president, and was elected again in 1924, only a few months before his death that same year. In 1909, on Clark's twentieth anniversary, he brought Sigmund Freud and C. G. Jung to

Participants at the famous Clark University conference of 1909. Hall is in the middle of the front row; Freud and Jung stand immediately to his left and James is the third from his right. Others who are mentioned in this book are William Stern, on James's left, and Ernest Jones, appearing between Hall and Freud.

America to address an audience that included William James (Rosenzweig, 1992). These firsts and foundings, which Hall sometimes tended to exaggerate, and the wide range of subject matter about which he lectured and wrote, mark Hall as *a* pioneer, if not *the* pioneer, in a variety of areas: experimental psychology, developmental psychology (including childhood, adolescence, and old age), human genetics, education, research methodology, and psychology of religion (Starbuck, 1925).

Tragedy and Isolation

Although Hall (1923, p. 595) concluded that his life was, "on the whole, a happy and fortunate one," he also confessed that his scholarly work was "almost literally a life preserver" for him. From the early solitary years in Ashfield to the period of retirement after 31 years as Clark's president, Hall's life was punctuated by an unrelenting series of disappointments, failures, and tragedies. Perhaps most poignant was the death by asphyxiation of his first wife and one of their two children when the gas burner in their home failed to ignite. Hall received the terrible news in Ashfield, where he was recovering from a serious case of diphtheria. Widowed at age 45 after only ten years of marriage, Hall married again a decade later, only to lose his second wife to mental illness after a like period of time.

Not long after his first wife's death, and during his third year as Clark's president, Hall found his dreams suddenly shattered when founder Jonas Clark discovered how much Hall's grandiose plans were costing him and withdrew financial support. Hall's deceptive measures to conceal his patron's decision, with hopes that he would eventually reverse it, as well as his generally autocratic and arbitrary ways, finally cost him two-thirds of his faculty and 70 percent of the students (Ross, 1972, pp. 219–227).

Hall was regularly the object of criticism, not only in his role as Clark's president, but also for his writings on sex and on religion and for asserting that the soul is no less a product of evolution than the body. A sharp, even remorseless critic himself, Hall (1923) complained that every one of his books was criticized with a bitterness that he considered excessive. The "dominantly sad note" of his life, he concluded, was that of isolation (p. 594). Alone from his childhood days and haunted throughout his life by feelings of inferiority, Hall seemed almost incapable of warm and uncomplicated friendship. It is perhaps understandable that he turned to the drama of Jesus' life as an "immunity bath" against abandonment either to optimism or to pessimism, and that he finally claimed for himself the lofty and lonely vision of Jesus and the Buddha (pp. 428, 596). Hall died on April 24, 1924, four years after he retired from being president of Clark.

HALL'S CONTRIBUTIONS TO THE PSYCHOLOGY OF RELIGION

If the honor of having started the psychology of religion can be given to anyone, writes James Pratt (1908), it would have to be awarded to Hall. Not only did he pioneer in this field, but he also served as a guiding influence to graduate students working under him at Clark, several of whom were to become important psychologists of religion. What Pratt calls the Clark school of religious psychology is designated the Hall school by Wilhelm Koepp (1920), among others; W. B. Selbie (1924) prefers the term American school, but he credits Hall no less than Pratt and Koepp do for his pioneering role.

An Ambivalent Sponsor

Two of Hall's leading students seem less certain that Hall deserves this honor. James Leuba (1937) reports that Hall, for whatever reason, was initially "not encouraging" when Leuba proposed doing his dissertation on conversion. Edwin Starbuck (1924) reports that Hall tried hard to dissuade him, too, from pursuing his interest in religion. Starbuck says that he himself had issued two syllabi on the psychology of religion at Harvard in 1894, both of which "were copied almost bodily and without acknowledgment by Clark University." "It is inevitable that the great hungry healthy self of a genius tends to sweep all the men, problems, and

James Leuba

Edwin Starbuck

movements about it into the maw of its own mentality and to regard the output of its digestive functions as products of its own creative energy'' (p. 149).

Although Hall is credited with introducing the questionnaire method in America and is thought to be responsible for its widespread use in the psychology of religion, Starbuck (1924) claims to have been the first to use it to explore religious experience. In the preface to his first book, Starbuck (1899) acknowledges Hall's ''active sympathy and encouragement,'' but in later essays, Starbuck (1924, 1937) says that Hall persistently lacked enthusiasm about his work, even publishing in one of his journals the only entirely antagonistic review of Starbuck's book. Koepp (1920) in fact takes Starbuck, not Hall, as the chief representative of the psychology of religion designated as the Hall school, and he asserts that it was Starbuck's *Psychology of Religion* that first gave the new discipline a definite identity.

If Hall exaggerated his role in the development of the psychology of religion and discouraged the work of others, he nevertheless occupies an important place in the history of this field. Above all, through his own publications and in his position as president of Clark, he lent his considerable prestige to the psychology of religion and gave others the opportunity to pursue it in the context of a leading graduate program in psychology. Furthermore, much of the early research and speculation in this field shows the unmistakable influence of Hall's genetic perspective.

A Genetic Psychology of Religion

During the years between his first paper on the psychology of religion, ''The Moral and Religious Training of Children'' (1882), and the chapter on conversion in his *Adolescence* (1904, 2), Hall espoused a strikingly consistent interpretation of religion that is at once evolutionary and pedagogical. The religious development of the individual, Hall was convinced, follows the religious development of the species. As in embryological development, so in religious: ONTOGENY recapitulates PHYLOGENY. The value of this theory was twofold. On the one hand, it gave direction to his students' research, much of which was aimed at finding statistical evidence for hypothesized trends in religious experience and interests (e.g., Daniels, 1893; Dawson, 1900; Lancaster, 1895; Leuba, 1896; and Starbuck, 1897). On the other hand, the elaboration of this "principle of psychogenesis" offered a new foundation for religious education (Hall, 1900, 1901).

Evolutionary Stages of Religious Development: The presence of religious sentiments in the infant can only be the subject of conjecture. Hall (1882) notes with approval German educator Friedrich Fröbel's remark that "the unconsciousness of a child is rest in God." Other writers of the time had posited a "generic germinal–physical sensation of pure being, a feeling of transcendent happiness or even angelic communion, gradually lapsing into the particular experiences of life." Anticipating Erik Erikson and the object-relations theorists by almost three-quarters of a century, Hall concluded that "fundamental religious sentiments can be cultivated in the earlier months of infancy" through solicitous care of the child's body with an attitude of calmness and tranquillity, avoiding intense stimuli and abrupt sensations or transitions. In such a way, he says, does one encourage the growth of trust, gratitude, dependence, and love, sentiments that are first directed toward the mother and only later toward God (pp. 33–34).

As the child "falls out of" unconsciousness, says Hall, he or she passes through a series of stages of development that are paralleled by various forms of religion: FETISHISM, nature worship, and various others of the "ancient idolatrous stages" (Hall, 1900). Only with the attainment of adolescence is a person ready for the growth into love and ALTRUISM that is the aim of the Christian tradition, for which all other "great but decaying religions" are essential preliminary stages. The task of the missionary, then, is not to destroy other traditions, but to recognize the truth that lies within them and to lead them sympathetically toward completion, just as Jesus did the religion of Moses and David (Hall, 1904, 2, pp. 361–362). Similarly, the difficult challenge to the Sunday school teacher is to shepherd the child through these necessary stages of religious development, neither precipitating premature piety and thus inoculating the individual against a deeper and more profoundly transforming interest, nor delaying natural growth and transformation to a time when it will be more difficult to initiate and complete.

Educating for Religious Maturity: From Hall's perspective, because religious precocity often results in an enduring religious infantilism, it is by far the graver and more common of these dangers. Accordingly, he argues that religious education must be carefully designed in the light of research in child development to coordinate itself with the child's growing interests and capabilities. As the love of nature is the first religion of every race, says Hall (1900), so it should be for the child. The educator's task is to encourage the child's spontaneous responses to nature—feelings of awe, reverence, and dependence—through a study of nature that emphasizes its poetic aspects. Childhood is a time, too, for gifted storytellers to practice their art of stimulating the child's imagination. These stories need not be biblical but may be chosen from among the world's rich supply of fairy tales, myths, legends, or even lives of saints (if reconstructed and naturalized). The emphasis should be on practical morality; doctrine, abstract ideas, and the various methods of "forced feeding" must be carefully avoided.

During the years of preadolescence the emphasis should be placed on the Old Testament, in keeping with the interests that become prominent during this period

(Dawson, 1900). Preadolescence, according to Hall's account, is an age of EXTRA-VERSION and hero worship, dominated by the emotions of fear, anger, jealousy, hate, and revenge. Thus the Old Testament's large repertory of heroic persons and dramatic incidents, its emphasis on law and justice, and its stimulation of the sentiments of awe and reverence are appropriate to this stage.

Not until adolescence, however, is true and deep religious experience possible. In fact, adolescence marks the highpoint of religious development. The years before it are essentially preparatory, and those that follow are centered largely on doctrine, which serves as a substitute and a memorial. Hall's famous statistics on adolescent conversion, along with similar data collected by his students and other researchers, demonstrate that the tumultuous years of sexual maturation are also the years of spiritual transformation. Adolescence, says Hall, is the great turning point from EGOCENTRISM to altruism. The task of religion is to raise to the highest possible level the natural impulses that come alive during these years, while helping the growing individual to steer a safe course amidst the surrounding dangers. Only religion—and perhaps here Hall would have us read only the Christian tradition—is able to develop and elevate the sentiment of love to the fullest. "To love," writes Hall (1900, p. 179), "and to be interested most in those things that are most worthy of love and of interest—that is the end of life." It is also the central point of the New Testament, he states, and thus we are finally to the age when this text should be taught and emphasized. Indeed, Hall (1904, 2) asserts that the Bible in its full sweep, as a record of the evolution of the human soul, is addressed primarily to those who have not yet reached their mid-twenties, the outer boundary of adolescence.

For more mature and cultured young adults, Hall (1901) prescribes a further course of instruction that is both broad and deep. To the more advanced portions of the New Testament—the Pauline letters, for example—he would add the writings of the church fathers and a course on church history; a study of the highest elements in the great religious traditions; and a brief survey of the philosophy of religion, and of ethics and psychology. No place should be given for dogma or orthodoxy, or for the feeling that science and philosophy are opposed to religion. Youth marks the growing point of further evolution and is served, not by reasons, formulas, and routine, but by questions, hints, and inspiration. Yet no matter how far we advance, we retain within, like rudimentary organs, the views of the earlier, indispensable stages. "Probably all of us, even the dogmatist, is at once, despite himself, pagan, pantheist, agnostic, fetishist, and heretic generally, as well as Christian and believer" (Hall, 1904, 2, p. 320). In the end, it is a question of which will prevail.

The Psychological Christ: Hall again took up the evolutionary account of religion in his large, two-volume work *Jesus, the Christ, in the Light of Psychology* (1917), which develops themes on which he had been lecturing over a 20-year period. After surveying the enormous literature on Jesus, including works of scholars evaluating the evidence for his historicity, Hall argues that the establishment of Jesus as a figure in time and space is largely beside the point. Whether his "life be in Judea or in the soul of man" (p. 34), Jesus may be viewed as a product of creative evolution, an incarnation of all the ideal tendencies in the human race.

Psychology's task, according to Hall, is to reveal anew the profoundly transforming meaning of Jesus, in order to bring about a "radical re-evolution and reconstruction in the world" (p. xxiii). In part it can do so by pushing beyond the dogmas of orthodoxy to make fresh contact with "the true facts of inner religious life" (p. 703), which Hall and his students attempted to do with their questionnaires and the study of myths and rituals of other times and traditions. In these ways Hall searched during the last years of his life for the meaning of Christ's death and resurrection, which are the central events for Christian faith. They are, he concludes, projections of the intrapsychic process of transformation, in which lower desires and ends are "put to death" or renounced for higher ones, of which Jesus is the perfect embodiment. More generally, the resurrection "is the most precious and pregnant symbolization of the eternal and inevitable resurgence of the good and true after their opposites have done their worst" (p. xiii).

Hall's book on Jesus, rather than convincing his fellow psychologists to return to the "psychological Christ," only inspired their disdain (Boring, 1950, p. 523). Even though he was unable to overcome American psychology's aversion to religion, Hall succeeded in giving impetus to the objective study of it. The legacy he left includes the ideal of a rigorously scientific approach, the questionnaire method, and the use of statistical analysis. Both objective psychology and psychoanalysis share his rejection of introspection as the sole psychological method, and both concur in his emphasis on religion's rootedness in the human body. Yet the psychologists of religion who employed behaviorism's theories as well as its methods were to take a far more radical and reductionistic stand than Hall had advocated. And virtually none would bring to his analysis the piety (however liberal), the commitment to the Christian tradition, and the theological education that are evident in Hall's writings.

Although best known for providing impetus to the objective approach, Hall seems to have been influential—at least in a general way—among interpretive psychologists as well. Hall's empirical research on concrete religious manifestations is described by psychoanalyst Oskar Pfister (1922, p. 368) as "a huge improvement" over the earlier theological speculations about religion in general. He praises, too, Hall's assumption of a creative unconscious, although Pfister considers the questionnaire method a hindrance to a deeper understanding of its dynamics and development. More specific influences of Hall's ideas are difficult to document, for as Ross (1972) points out, "The psychologists who followed Hall's lead did not always recognize their debt to him, for Hall did not leave a systematic body of ideas behind to be accepted or modified by later psychologists" (p. 422). There is speculation, however, that Hall's (1904, 2, p. 342) positing of *racial* subconscious processes—"wise, benignant, and energetic," and constituting "the larger self" whose messages are experienced as revelations—influenced Jung's later and more elaborate construction of a collective unconscious (Hinkelman and Aderman, 1968). Hall's work is rich in such suggestive detail, though apparently few scholars in recent decades have thought it worthwhile to sift the wheat from the chaff.

Whereas many today would consider the RECAPITULATION THEORY, including the assumption that religious traditions undergo systematic evolution, to be among the chaff (Hilgard, 1987, Küng, 1979), some would still find in it a kernel of truth. In his psychoanalysis of culture, for example, C. R. Badcock (1980) concurs with Hall that the stages of individual psychological development recapitulate the evolutionary course of human culture and of religion in particular. According to educational psychologist Ronald Goldman (1964), "The racial recapitulation theory . . . propounded persuasively by G. Stanley Hall . . . has quietly moved into the field of religious education and taken root over the last fifty years. There is, as we have seen from the research outlined in this book, some truth in this assertion and there is unmistakable evidence that in religious thinking children appear to pass through stages of concepts not unlike those of primitive man" (p. 228).

That Hall's influence, whether subtle or fully explicit, should extend beyond objective psychology reflects his position in the history of psychology. He was a transitional figure who embraced the new ideal of a rigorous psychological science while seeking to preserve traditional human values (Meyer, 1971). For Hall the inner life remained a fundamental reality, from which modern industrialized people were becoming progressively alienated. Religion is, he said, a means for developing the inner life more fully. Scientific psychology seemed to him a way to verify and facilitate this process. The scientific psychologists who came after Hall were unwilling, by and large, to concern themselves with "the inner life," and few if any of them shared his quest for a unified cosmic vision.

BIOLOGICAL INDIVIDUALITY AND RELIGIOUS TYPES

We begin our systematic survey of the biological underpinnings of religion with physical constitution and temperament, two intimately related factors that pervasively condition *all* experience. CONSTITUTION refers to the enduring physical characteristics of the individual taken as a whole, including height, weight, bodily proportions, sexual differentiation, facial features, and so on. TEMPERAMENT denotes the prevailing mood, energy level, and emotional reactivity that together are characteristic of an individual. Evident early in childhood as well as in other animal species, temperament is considered a manifestation of constitution and thus to be largely genetic in origin (Allport, 1961; Strelau, 1983).

The Four Temperaments and Religion

The most durable theory of temperament is the ancient one proposed by the Greek physician Hippocrates and later modified by Galen. They distinguished four basic temperaments: SANGUINE, marked by warmth, cheerfulness, and optimism; MELANCHOLIC, designating a tendency toward sadness or depression; CHOLERIC, said of a person easily aroused to anger; and PHLEGMATIC, characterized by sluggishness and apathy. Although the explanation of these temperamental differences in terms of the relative prominence of four bodily secretions or "humors" has long been abandoned, the four temperaments themselves have retained their intuitive appeal to the present day (Doody and Immerwahr, 1983).

The reverberations of these four enduring dispositions in the religious sphere have interested writers for centuries. In a treatise on "the four complexions," the sixteenth-century mystic Jakob Boehme, himself a rather meek and gentle soul, mercilessly railed against the choleric type as hypocritical, envious, wrathful, violent, and oppressive. This one-side portrait, suggests J. G. Stevenson (1913), is evidently modeled after Boehme's bitterest enemy, a pastor who was "as choleric as he was orthodox" (p. 147) and whose furious accusations of heresy eventually forced Boehme to flee for his life.

In the seventeenth century, Robert Burton undertook an analysis of religious melancholy in his enormously learned and influential book *The Anatomy of Melancholy* (1621). Burton, a melancholic Anglican clergyman whose chief prejudice was against "Papists," provides in essence an encyclopedic survey of the "idolatry and superstition" that he took to be a product of religious melancholy as well as of excessive fasting, solitariness, and meditation. The immediate causes of superstition, he says, are the Devil and the politicians, priests, and imposters who, as the Devil's "infernal Ministers" (p. 888), exploit the ignorance and fears of the common people. Accordingly, the cure of religious melancholy is twofold: restraining the vulgar servants of the Devil by outlawing their meetings and burning their books; and for those distempered by the disease of melancholy or too much fasting or meditation, "The best means to reduce them to a sound mind is to alter their course of life, and with conference, threats, promises, persuasions, to intermix Physick [that is, medical treatment, including medication, diet, bathing, moderate exercise and reading, clean air, and travel abroad, all intended to correct the balance of the four humors]" (p. 924).

From Stevenson's perspective, on the other hand, the melancholic temperament contributes more than the other three to "the ranks of the truly noble," including the prophets of the Hebrew Bible, the Apostle Paul, the extremely AS-CETIC Italian reformer Girolamo Savonarola (1452–1498), and the English Puritan preacher John Bunyan (1628–1688). Yet Stevenson acknowledges that the "basal seriousness" and sensitivity that compel the melancholic toward deeper realities may become morbid in its extremity. He also warns that the occasional barometric or even tidal shifts between the depths of melancholy and the heights of joyous gladness require "alertness, discipline, determination, and prayer" if the highest possibilities of this temperamental type are to be realized (p. 187). Alexander Whyte (1895) and Ole Hallesby (1940) also explore the strengths and weaknesses of the four temperaments in relation to religion, with Hallesby appending for each temperament advice to pastors and spiritual counselors as well as suggestions for self-discipline. These writers unanimously concur with William James (1902) in his ranking of the SICK SOUL, the melancholic type, over the HEALTHY-MINDED, the sanguine, in terms of spiritual profundity and insight.

If virtually opposites in this respect, the melancholic and sanguine temperaments are nevertheless said to have in common the element of *feeling*, in contrast to the action orientation of the choleric type and the thoughtful deliberation of the phlegmatic. In a study of the relation of temperament to religious experience, George Coe (1900) found that individuals who both expected and experienced striking religious transformation were likely to be persons in whom "sensibility"—that is, susceptibility to feeling and emotion—was predominant over intellect and will. Those who did not experience an expected transformation were predominantly intellectual in orientation. Reclassifying his subjects according to the four temperaments, Coe found that persons experiencing an anticipated transformation tended to be sanguine or melancholic types, whereas those whose expectation was not fulfilled were primarily choleric (see Table 3.1; the questions used to determine temperamental disposition can be found in Coe, 1900, Appendix A).

Table 3.1 **RELATION OF STRIKING RELIGIOUS TRANSFORMATION TO TEMPERAMENT**

Subjects Classified According to the Historic Three Mental Faculties		Sensibility	Intellect	Will
Group I:	Expected a transformation and experienced it (N = 17)	12	2	3
Group II:	Expected but did not experience a transformation (N = 12)	2	9	1

Subjects Classified According to the Four Temperaments	Sanguine	Melancholic	Choleric	Phlegmatic
Group I:	8	6	1	2
Group II:	2	3	7	0

Source: Adapted from the tables on page 120 in Coe, 1900.

The Christian tradition, Coe argues, has long been psychologically one-sided. Feeling is emphasized not only in its ideal of sainthood but also in the appeal of Protestant hymns to the melancholic disposition and of popular revival songs to the less profound sanguine temperament. Considering an accent on feeling to be feminine, Coe maintains that the Christian Church has adapted itself primarily to the female nature—hence the disproportionate number of women involved in it. Neglected are "the more masculine, active, or practical qualities of goodness," "the forms of religious life natural to the choleric temperament" (p. 244). "Religion," Coe says, "ought to rest upon and call into exercise all the faculties of the mind, and no superior sanctity should be ascribed to persons whose temperamental make-up is sentimental rather than choleric" (p. 215). The conviction with which Coe addresses this issue attests to his own suffering as a youth unable to experience the feelings prescribed by the Methodist tradition in which he was reared.

Kretschmer's Constitutional Types

While the four-temperament doctrine lives on without the benefits of a viable theory of bodily origin, modern researchers have sought a new understanding of temperament that is more adequately linked to physical constitution. Most influential in this regard is the work of the German psychiatrist Ernst Kretschmer (1888–1964), whose book *Physique and Character* appeared in its first edition in 1921 and in a final revision by the author in 1961; an English translation was published in 1925 and revised in 1936.

Leptosomic–Schizothymic Type: From his study first of mental patients and then of a large number of healthy individuals, Kretschmer identified three basic body types, each of which was found to be correlated with a particular temperamental disposition. The LEPTOSOMIC (asthenic) physique is lean and narrowly built, and the face is long, narrow, and sharply moulded. This body type is associated with the SCHIZOTHYMIC temperament, or, more accurately, class of temperaments. It consists of a complex amalgam of divided tendencies that give the outward appearance of coolness, polite sensitivity, adaptability, and refinement while hidden within may be passionate feelings, rebelliousness, vulgarity, and maliciousness. The inner tendencies may occasionally express themselves in sarcasm or irritability, and on the other hand, when circumstances allow people of this type to feel at home, they can be loving and sympathetic, if in a slightly distant way. The overall impression is one of INTROVERSION, formality, and moral idealism (Kretschmer, 1961).

Pyknic–Cyclothymic Type: The PYKNIC physique is soft, heavy, and rounded, with a short, massive neck and a face that tends to be broad, soft, and rotund. Associated with this type is the CYCLOTHYMIC class of temperaments, named after its tendency to alternate erratically between periods of marked cheerfulness and activity and of sadness and quiescence. Persons of the cyclothymic type are characteristically of a sunny nature—warm, friendly, talkative, and full of good humor. This extravertive type is often resolute and energetically practical, with a corresponding lack of reflectiveness and depth of feeling. Some have a quicksilver temper that suddenly flashes forth and then just as quickly passes away. Those who are subject to depressive episodes remain affable and kindhearted at such times, though quiet and meditative. Unlike the schizothyme, the cyclothyme harbors no suppressed hostility behind the withdrawal, which is marked rather by a certain melancholy, if not also anxiety and feelings of inferiority. Concurring with earlier observations, Kretschmer notes that the more depressive types are frequently religious, manifesting a piety that is heartfelt, full of deep feeling, and conscientiously devout. Tolerant of other views, their piety is also free of bigotry, pedantry, and moralism (p. 181).

Athletic–Viscous Type: The ATHLETIC physique is muscular, broad-shouldered, and tapered, with coarse boning, evident especially in the hands, and a face that is heavily boned, egg-shaped, and elongated, with a projecting, well-moulded chin. Typical of the athletic type is the VISCOUS temperament,[1] characterized by a phlegmatic calm that gives the impression of equanimity and stability. Yet if strongly irritated, some persons of this type—especially the more primitive and uncultured ones—are capable of erupting with explosive anger and massive violence. In many other respects falling between the schizothymic and cyclothymic temperaments, persons of the viscous type tend toward introversion, though they remain sociable in a quiet, passive way. Relatively narrow in their range of interests and typically unimaginative and slow in thought, they show an exceptional tenacity and thoroughness in pursuing whatever engages their energies.

Two Protestant Reformers

Kretschmer offers his abstracted constitutional types as focal points for disclosing natural laws, not as containers for sorting particular individuals (p. x). Yet he does illustrate these types with historical figures whose constitutional endowment is sufficiently distinct to assign them to one type or another. Two of these persons, Martin Luther and John Calvin, will serve to illustrate the implications of Kretschmer's typological work for the psychology of religion.

Martin Luther: The father of the Protestant Reformation, Luther (1483–1546) is famous for the resoluteness and courage with which he opposed the papacy. He is also known for his robust vitality, an earthy sense of humor, momentary outbursts of anger, and his fluent and graphic use of language. Perhaps less familiar are the severe attacks of melancholy that he periodically suffered. Luther often wondered why he was sometimes happy, other times sad, or why his desire to speak would

Martin Luther, who left the impress of his variable but mainly good-natured temperament on the German Reformation.

---

[1] Kretschmer added the viscous temperament to his work after the 1936 revision of the English translation, which thus no longer adequately represents his thinking. Prior to this addition, he considered the temperament of the athletic type to be a nondescript mixture of the other two.

wax and wane. The oppressive episodes of melancholia, he decided, were inflicted on him by God, and he frequently spoke of their religious value. Fortunately, he was in a HYPOMANIC state at the time of his defiant stand at the Diet of Worms in 1521. Looking back on his fearlessness on that famous and often recounted occasion, he wondered later on if he again would be so foolhardy (Grossmann, 1958, p. 10). Thus we see in Luther the basic characteristics of the cyclothymic temperament.

The mature Luther also had a typical pyknic physique, which is evident in the portraits of him by his good friend Lukas Cranach the Elder. As a younger man, however, he was noticeably thinner, and his face more angular. Eberhard Grossmann (1958), a psychiatrist with a doctorate in theology, sees even in the earliest portrait the typical pyknic bone structure. Kretschmer, on the other hand, interprets the youthful tendency toward angularity and a similar trend discernable in Cranach's portraits of Luther's parents (see page 388) as revealing an admixture of schizothymic elements in Luther's inherited disposition. A purely cyclothymic type, he says, would lack the ardor, tenacity, and firmness of character—as well as the hints of fanaticism—that are unmistakably evident in Luther. Nevertheless, it was the cyclothymic character of Luther and the goodnatured pyknic rulers who supported him that was stamped on the early German Reformation (pp. 389–391).

John Calvin: We find a religious reformer of a rather different sort in Calvin (1509–1564), whose doctrine of predestination deeply influenced much of Protestantism and encouraged the rise of capitalism. In marked contrast to Luther, Calvin possessed a leptosomic physique. His face was small and finely chiseled and his nose long. His expression, as Grossmann remarks, reflects the deep earnestness of one who has known human suffering intimately.

Corresponding to this physique and countenance was a schizothymic demeanor. In describing Calvin's "withdrawn and scholarly temperament," William Bouwsma (1988) provides a vivid portrait of Calvin's schizothymia. Calvin was a man driven from within by powerful impulses and haunted throughout life by self-doubt and contradictory tendencies. He was "a singularly anxious man and, as a reformer, fearful and troubled" (p. 32). Feeling constantly threatened by disorder and pollution, he conceived of human existence as a perpetual crisis. Most fearsome

John Calvin, the fanatical and deeply troubled reformer whose schizothymic disposition is mirrored in a wrathful image of God.

of all were death and the final judgment by a God whose terrible wrath and impossible demands forecast inconceivable terrors. Though reticent to an extreme in his deliberate efforts to hide himself from others, Calvin yet reveals to us much of his profound uneasiness—in his theological writings and in the eyes "glazed with fatigue and revulsion" that look out from his later portraits (p. 9).

Although Grossmann sympathetically emphasizes Calvin's self-discipline in the face of shyness and continual fatigue from insomnia and illness, as well as his demonstrated capacity for intimate friendship, Kretschmer compares Calvin to Savonarola and the infamous French revolutionist Robespierre. To all of them he ascribes a triad of schizothymic qualities: idealism, fanaticism, and despotism. Each of them, Kretschmer says, is possessed by an "absolute hatred for reality, for beauty and enjoyment, for all that shows the slightest tendency to laugh, or bloom, or bubble" (p. 393). The ECCLESIASTICAL structure that Calvin left behind, writes Kretschmer, stands as a monument to a great schizothymic organizer who was ethically strict, pure in thought and speech, yet fanatical, impatient, and aggressive, as well as devoid of imagination, laughter, feeling, humor, and conciliation (p. 394).

Religion and Mesomorphy: Are there also influential religious leaders of the athletic–viscous type? When we look through portraits of important figures from the past, observes Kretschmer, we seldom find this type engaged in intellectual or political activities. In contrast to the ardent hypomanic temperament of the pyknic type and the anxious nervousness of the leptosome, the athletic individual lacks the concentrated focus, he says, that is required for a productive use of energy (p. 253).

Leaving aside the element of leadership, we may observe that early authorities associated the athletic type with a less religious outlook. According to Francis Galton (1869, p. 260), "Robustness of constitution is antagonistic, in a very marked degree, to an extremely pious disposition." James (1902, p. 29) makes the same point when he argues that the emotionality, intensity, and love of metaphysics that characterize the "PSYCHOPATHIC" or "neurotic temperament" introduce it to religious realms that the "robust Philistine type of nervous system, forever offering its biceps to be felt, thumping its breast, and thanking Heaven that it hasn't a single morbid fibre in its composition, would be sure to hide forever from its self-satisfied possessors."

Sheldon's Three-Component Model

More recent statistical evidence provides modest support for Galton's and James's thesis. At the foundation of this research is the three-component model of constitutional types proposed by American psychologist-physician William Sheldon (1899–1977). This model, though inductively derived from thousands of photographs of male college students, accords rather closely with Kretschmer's types. In contrast to Kretschmer, however, Sheldon developed a system for specifying the prominence in any individual of all three basic components: ENDOMORPHY, equivalent at its extreme to the pyknic type; MESOMORPHY, the athletic type; and ECTOMORPHY, the leptosomic type. Each component is represented by a number between one and seven, and the three numbers together (e.g., 3–5–2) designate the person's SOMATOTYPE. In addition to delineating these primary components of physique, Sheldon identifies several secondary variables, including GYNANDROMORPHY, the possessing of physical characteristics usually associated with the opposite sex.

Correlated with the three primary components of physique are reported to be three components of temperament: VISCEROTONIA, including such qualities as sociability, love of comfort and eating, and slowness in reaction; SOMATOTONIA, callousness, love of risk and physical adventure, and energetic boldness; and CEREBROTONIA, restrained inhibition, secretiveness, and overquick reactiveness. The correspondence to Kretschmer's temperamental components, we should note, is not so close as to his constitutional components.

An Antisomatotonic Trend: In an earlier work, Sheldon (1936) had argued that Christianity was long a tradition favoring introversion and such female ideals as feeling, warmth, and mystery. Once he had developed his system of somatotyping, Sheldon (1942) documented this "one-sidedness" by applying these techniques to 124 historical paintings of Christ. Averaging the ratings for the large majority of pictures that had been painted before 1900, Sheldon and his students found the following means on the three somatotypic components: endomorphy, 2.2; mesomorphy, 2.6; and ectomorphy, 5.4. With a somatotypic formula of approximately 2–3–5, then, Christ is predominantly represented in these works as an ectomorph. Thus he is an exemplar of "cerebrotonic self-effacement and inhibition of the somatotonic impulse" (Sheldon, 1942, p. 255).

This seeming antisomatotonic trend in the Christian tradition also appears in the research of Juan Cortés and Florence Gatti (1970, 1972). On two separate occasions, they administered the Allport–Vernon–Lindzey Study of Values to well over 100 college students for whom they also had somatotypic ratings. Both times, for men and women, they found that when the second, mesomorphic component was high, the "male" values (Theoretical, Economic, and Political) also tended to be high whereas the "female" values (Aesthetic, Social, and Religious) tended to be low. The other two components of the somatotype showed no significant relation to value scores. In a further study, comparing delinquent and nondelinquent boys, they found that mesomorphy—which was much higher in the delinquents—was again inversely related to the Religious value ($-.23$, $p < .02$, for delinquents). Cortés and Gatti (1972) speculate that mesomorphs, who more than the other types describe themselves as "independent, nonconforming, impetuous, and reckless," are by nature less likely to experience "a feeling of dependence on God, of submission to His commandments" (p. 137). In addition, mesomorphs, assumed by Cortés and Gatti (in contrast to Kretschmer) to be generally extraverted persons, tend to show lower "constitutional conditionability." Thus a given amount of religious conditioning will affect them less than other types.

We must be cautious about such generalizations, however, both within and across religious traditions. Sheldon (1942) found that, of the seven portraits of Christ that were painted after 1915, four yielded mesomorphic ratings of *five* or higher. Taking this finding as evidence that the "ban on somatotonia" was being lifted, Sheldon speculates that "If our grandchildren go to Sunday school they may be shown pictures not of a Christ suffering in cerebrotonic tight-lipped silence on a cross, but of a Christ performing heroic feats of athletic prowess" (p. 268). Sheldon's prediction has proved to be surprisingly prescient: Evangelist Billy Graham maintains that Christ had a perfectly developed physique, and power lifter John Jacobs and other members of his Power Team today evangelize for Christ on stage and television by bending steel bars, ripping telephone books in half, blowing up hot-water bottles until they burst, and smashing piles of bricks. Wearing T-shirts emblazoned with "God made you to win," the Power Team offers a mixture of feats of strength, Gospel singing, inspirational preaching, praying, and personal testifying that is deliberately aimed at suicidal teenagers as well as those involved in heavy-metal music, Satanism, and alcohol or drug abuse (Beale, 1989). Although

Members of the Power Team evangelizing for Christ by assaulting the forces of evil through impressive feats of strength.

mesomorphy may not be quite so dramatically conspicuous among those associated with the Fellowship of Christian Athletes, their number is perhaps a better indicator of American Christianity's growing hospitality to this disposition. Founded in 1954, this organization now has over 22,000 members.

Whereas the Christian tradition may only now be overcoming its historic wariness of the mesomorphic physique and its temperamental potentialities, other traditions long ago found ways to make a place for them. In India, for example, where individual differences are accommodated to an exceptional degree, Hindu mesomorphs of various ages gather at dawn and ritually exercise to honor their divine source of strength, the monkey god Hanuman. And whereas the majority of the devotees of VISHNU choose to worship him in his incarnation as Krishna, the slight and often gynandromorphic cowherd youth whose flirtatious dalliance with the lovely Radha suggests the sweetness of the love of God, many others prefer him in the form of Rama, the distinctly mesomorphic hero of the Indian epic the *Ramayana*. Although Krishna, too, sometimes appears as a warrior–hero who through magical powers slays various personifications of evil, it is only in contemporary "comics" for children that he is endowed with a mesomorphic physique. Altogether these phenomena suggest that constitutional type, rather than disposing individuals toward or against piety in general, may chiefly direct them toward certain forms or expressions of it.

DELIBERATE FACILITATION OF RELIGIOUS EXPERIENCE

Constitution and temperament are largely nature's experiments, lying beyond the individual's control. Within this fundamental emotional climate, however, psychological states can be varied by deliberately manipulating physiological conditions. One great class of these manipulations consists in the diminution or temporary deprivation of certain resources that are ordinarily required for well-being; these practices are frequently carried out in solitude and sometimes lead to ecstatic and even hallucinatory states. A second, contrasting class is made up of diverse practices that heighten bodily movement and sensory stimulation rather than reducing them; the presence of other participants is a virtual prerequisite, and the culmination is frequently a state of nonhallucinatory TRANCE, if not also physical collapse. States of ecstasy can usually be later recalled; states of trance, by contrast, are frequently subject to amnesia. As Gilbert Rouget (1980) points out in drawing this helpful distinction, between the poles of ecstasy and trance lie "an uninterrupted series of possible intermediary states" (p. 11), just as it is possible to combine, over time, any of the practices leading up to them.

Physiological Deprivation and Religious Experience

We begin with practices that entail physiological deprivation: fasting, going without sleep, reducing environmental stimulation, and slowing one's breathing. Sometimes these austerities are self-chosen by exceptional individuals who view them as means of spiritual discipline. Frequently, however, they are prescribed by tradition and faithfully carried out by masses of devotees as acts of religious obedience. We might well anticipate that the effects of these practices would vary considerably, depending on the attitude and expectations of those engaging in them.

Fasting: The most common of these practices is fasting—the partial or complete abstention from food and drink for a specified period of time. Fasting is not ordinarily undertaken with the goal of creating altered states of consciousness, for whatever the motives are, the outcomes sought are generally objective rather than subjective. For example, fasting may be undertaken as an act of mourning. Undoubtedly it is a natural response to grief, but sometimes it is also a means of propitiating or warding off the ghost of the deceased, or of avoiding the food it may have poisoned. Fasting may also be viewed as a way of purifying the body in preparation for certain ritual actions, ceremonies, or festivals. In addition, it may serve as an act of penitence: by undergoing the inconvenience or suffering associated with abstention, the person may hope to gain the pity of higher powers and forestall further punishment. Similarly, abstention has frequently been used as a means of forcing the hand of another, be it a god or another human being, or of gaining magical powers or victorious strength. Whatever the occasion for fasting, individuals undoubtedly recognized that it produced effects that we would call subjective, such as vivid dreams or visions or the diminution of sexual desire. Thus fasting also became a means of seeking prophetic revelations and a technique of spiritual discipline (Heiler, 1961; MacCulloch, 1912).

Variations of Fasting: The task of tracing the effects of fasting is enormously complicated. First of all, the varieties of fasting are so numerous that it is impossible to generalize about them all. To illustrate, we may contrast the practices of the Muslim community and its roughly 350 million members with those of the Ethiopian Orthodox Church, a Christian denomination numbering between 12 and 14 million. Muslims regard fasting as an essential component of their faith: it is one of the Five Pillars of Islam. For one lunar month of each year, all able-bodied Muslims except soldiers, pregnant women, and young children must abstain from all food and drink from sunrise to sunset, after which all may eat and drink in moderation. The Ramadan Fast, according to Gustave von Grünebaum (1951), is regarded by many Muslims as the most important religious act. Although this fast is not a continuous one, the requirement that they abstain from water throughout the day can be extremely difficult when RAMADAN falls during the scorching summer months.

In contrast, the fast required of members of the Ethiopian Orthodox Church disallows all food of animal origin, except fish, and on fast days people may not eat before noon. The total number of fasting days each year for common people is estimated to lie between 110 and 150; for the exceptionally pious, such as priests and old people, fasting days may total 220.

Although fasting is not easy for either group, the Muslims are able to approximate a normal diet at the end of each fast day, whereas the poorer of the Orthodox Christian Ethiopians, unable to afford fish or protein-rich legumes, are likely to suffer from serious malnutrition. This is especially true for pregnant and lactating women, young children, and the severely ill, who often are not aware that they are exempt from the strictly enforced rules. Yet even those who know they can legitimately break the fast may not be able to find foods that are allowed during fasting periods (Knutsson and Selinus, 1970). Morgulis (1923) describes a similar situation in Greek Catholic countries, where fasting is prescribed for nearly one-half of each year. The outcome of such "mass starvation from religious devotion" (p. 14) is a high infant mortality rate, widespread disease, physical and mental underdevelopment, and alcoholism.

Holy Anorexia: Among the anonymous masses of devotees who submit themselves to the sometimes harsh discipline of intermittent fasting, either partial or total, are a remarkable few who extend their virtually total fast for an indefinite period of time. On the one hand are those who deliberately commit suicide for religious reasons. Among the Jains in India, who seek salvation chiefly through ascetic practices, an occasional adherent will voluntarily starve to death as an ultimate expression of AHIMSA (noninjury). On the other hand some rare individuals are said to have survived for years without food and sometimes without water as well. (Ordinarily a person can live only a few days without water, and one to two months without food.) The most celebrated of these include a number of Catholic mystics, some of whom also exhibit stigmata. Catholic physician René Biot (1955) refers to their abstention from food—which for many seems quite involuntary—as a suspension of the nutritive functions, or inedia. Jesuit scholar Herbert Thurston (1952) offers a fuller account of a number of persons who were thought to have lived for years without eating, some of whom gave no religious interpretation to their unusual feat and a few of whom were demonstrably fraudulent. Among the most famous and controversial of these miraculous fasters is Theresa Neumann of Konnersreuth, a simple peasant woman who is supposed to have taken no food or liquid from 1926, the year she received the stigmata, until her death in 1962.

Leuba (1925) associates the prolonged fasts of the great mystics with what Pierre Janet called "hysterial anorexy," or what is today referred to as ANOREXIA NERVOSA, an eating disturbance in which the person manifests a severe loss of appetite and a dread of becoming fat. Sufferers from this disorder have a higher mortality rate than any other group of psychiatric patients. Whatever popular piety may make of the "holy anorexics," as historian Rudolph Bell (1985) calls them, they usually suffered extensive weight loss and an early death. Short of this dire outcome, however, these often hyperactive women—anorexia is overwhelmingly a feminine disorder—found in the diverse austerities and self-tortures they used to obliterate bodily urges the means for attaining spiritual perfection. According to Bell, who found signs of anorexia in the lives of more than half the 170 Italian women saints he investigated, self-starvation was also a way of seeking liberation from highly PATRIARCHAL families and institutions that might have had rather different plans for them.

Carol Bynum (1987) grants that, defined flexibly, the term anorexia nervosa may well be applicable to the behavior of some late medieval women. And she, too, recognizes that fasting did serve as a way of manipulating others, including religious superiors and even God. Yet she finds the key to their fasting in the symbolic meanings of body and food, according to which their suffering had cosmic significance. In whatever era it appears, Bynum emphasizes, anorexia nervosa must be understood within its own cultural context.

The Physiology of Fasting: A second problem in studying the effects of fasting is the extraordinary complexity of the metabolic processes involved in the digestion and absorption of food. We cannot trace out these processes here, except to observe that the brain is nourished exclusively by glucose (simple sugar), which the body cannot store for more than a few hours. During total fasts of even a few days, glycogen, the form in which carbohydrates are stored in the liver for future use, is converted back into glucose. When the relatively modest reserve of glycogen is exhausted, triglycerides (a combination of the trihydric alcohol glycerol and fatty acid) in body fat are broken down, a process that frees the components for use. Finally, when body fat is depleted, muscle protein is broken down into amino acids, most of which can be converted into glucose. In normal individuals, an extended fast will cause mineral and vitamin deficiencies; acidosis, which is an increase in the acid content of the body, altering a variety of bodily functions; and ketosis, which is an accumulation in the blood of ketone bodies, a group of compounds produced in the liver during the metabolism of fatty acids, resulting in less efficient metabolic utilization. The brain can adapt itself to using the ketone bodies, which can provide most of its energy requirements (Bell, Emslie-Smith, and Paterson, 1980; Owen et al., 1967).

Interestingly, these metabolic signs of fasting have proved valuable in throwing light on the phenomenon of "supernatural fasting." In 1927, at the order of her bishop, the chronically ill Theresa Neumann consented to be closely observed by four Franciscan nuns, a task that she and the members of her household made exceedingly difficult. During this brief two-week interval, her urine proved to be high in acetone, one of the ketone bodies, as well as strongly acidic. In contrast, the urine analyzed nine days after the observation period contained no acetone and was alkaline in reaction, characteristics suggesting normal dietary intake. Two years later, when Theresa's family was asked to make samples of her urine regularly available for analysis, they claimed that she had ceased to urinate. A request from

Theresa Neumann of Konnersreuth (1898–1962), a Roman Catholic stigmatist who is supposed to have had nothing to eat or drink for the last 36 years of her life.

the Church in 1937 for new, medically controlled observations was vehemently rejected by Theresa's father. Paul Siwek (1950), in reviewing these curious facts, concludes that Theresa's claim may have been an unconscious fraud. Like others who assert that they eat and drink nothing, she may have taken food while in a somnambulistic or autohypnotic state. It is also possible that she sincerely believed that there was no moral fault in overlooking the "almost nothing" she did eat, if it served to edify the souls of those who were drawn to her and her miracles.

Psychological Effects: The psychological ramifications of the metabolic changes brought about by fasting depend, of course, on how thoroughgoing the fast is and how long it is carried out. Also critical are individual differences, some of which are undoubtedly attributable to the quality of the prefasting diet. Edward Kollar and his associates (1964), for example, report that of their five subjects who fasted from four to six days, one said that he felt "tranquilized and peaceful," whereas the others reported irritability, fatigue, and apathy or depression. The thinking, speech, and actions of all subjects slowed down, and although they were able to mobilize themselves for specific tasks, they were otherwise unable to sustain attention and were prone to make mistakes. These authors conclude that fasting for this period of time—an interval not uncommon in religious contexts—is a stressful experience, bringing their subjects close to the neurotic symptoms reported in the classic study of starvation by Ancel Keys and his associates (1950).

The 36 conscientious objectors who volunteered for Keys's study were subjected to a semistarvation diet (1570 calories, 50 grams of protein, and 30 grams of fat) for a period of 24 weeks. A wide range of abnormal behavior was reported. All subjects suffered from moodiness, depression, and general emotional instability; the drives for activity and sex declined markedly and these men tended instead to become solitary and preoccupied with food. (In contrast to total fasting, semistarvation does not make the sensation of hunger disappear.) Many of them complained of occasional visual disturbances, such as eye aches, an inability to focus, or the presence of "spots" before their eyes. At the same time, there was evidence of a slight increase in auditory acuity. Although there were occasional episodes of elation, lasting from a few hours to several days, these were always succeeded by "low" periods. Subjects reported a decline in the ability to concentrate and in general alertness, yet clinical impressions suggested no change in intellectual capacity. There were significant modifications on several personality tests, indicating increases in social introversion, depression, emotional instability, and nervous tension and decreases in social leadership and self-confidence. Scores on the Minnesota Multiphasic Personality Inventory generally showed an elevation of the "neurotic" end of the profile (HYPOCHONDRIASIS, DEPRESSION, and HYSTERIA), as well as significant increases in PSYCHASTHENIA (a term that Janet used to describe a disorder marked by morbid anxiety and fixed or obsessive ideas) and SCHIZOPHRENIA. These investigators summarize the personality changes during starvation as a diffuse psychoneurosis; for a few individuals there was also evidence of a psychotic reaction.

The findings of these experimental studies cannot be easily generalized to religiously motivated fasting. Advocates of fasting, whether in the name of health or as a spiritual discipline, would rightly distinguish between carefully conducted fasting that is purposefully undertaken with the guidance of specialists who understand its potentialities for benign effects, and fasting that is submitted to merely for scientific purposes and supervised by investigators interested primarily in its negative consequences. The neurotic tendencies exhibited by the subjects in these studies may well constitute unexplored opportunities for learning self-control and self-transcendence. It is also possible that some forms of fasting, especially if undertaken by persons who are prepared to experience positive results, may yield unusually constructive benefits. According to Carl Rahn (1928), these gains may include a heightened clarity or vividness of consciousness—a characteristic of some religious experiences—and an increased capacity for concentration of attention. By making possible the control of bodily desires, fasting serves as a PROPAEDEUTIC to a series of new attitudes and capacities; it "limbers up the mental processes on the one hand, and allays the neuro-muscular tensions on the other," making possible a "new mode of psychophysiological functioning" (p. 184). Describing the results of his own 40-day fast, Sadhu Sundar Singh asserted that the peace and happiness he had known since his conversion to Christianity some eight years earlier grew increasingly intense as his physical strength waned—evidence, he thought, of their divine origin. After the fast he found himself less subject to a variety of temptations, including that of giving up the difficult and uncertain life of an ascetic (Streeter and Appasamy, 1921).

Unfortunately, the systematic research on which most positive claims for fasting are based has been conducted with only one or several subjects in each study (e.g., Glaze, 1928; Langfeld, 1914). Keys and his associates claim that these few subjects "were mostly extreme food faddists or otherwise far from being classifiable as psychologically normal" (p. 778). Nevertheless, these studies, along with the anecdotal evidence of persons like Sundar Singh, suggest that fasting has potentialities that none of the larger research projects has reported.

Unusual dietary conditions that are the occasion of exceptional religious experiences may occur apart from deliberate fasting. For example, the maize diet of the South African Nguni is deficient in niacin or nicotinic acid, a B vitamin necessary for healthy metabolism, as well as in tryptophan, an essential amino acid that is converted into niacin. Gussler (1973) proposes that this diet may be partially responsible for the symptoms of *ukuthwasa,* a spirit possession illness that is treated by initiating and training the sufferer as a diviner. The chronic malnourishment among the Nguni produces in some individuals the syndrome of pellagra, a deficiency disease marked by a variety of physical and mental symptoms, including psychosis. Although not all pellagra victims are thought by the Nguni to be possessed, the similarities in the symptoms of *ukuthwasa* and pellagra suggest to Gussler that malnourishment and the resulting acute malfunctioning are a large factor in the occurrence of the stereotypic and highly institutionalized possession illness. Whatever the cultural presuppositions and the quality of diet, however, it is also possible that certain individuals either are unable to absorb sufficient niacin for normal metabolism or require unusually large amounts of it. Such, at least, seems to be one implication of research suggesting that massive doses of niacin may be helpful in the treatment of schizophrenia (Hawkins and Pauling, 1973). Medical science has only begun to explore the dramatic effects that a change in diet can have on psychological well-being.

Other Modes of Deprivation and Religious Experience: Less common than fasting are three other practices that curtail spontaneous satisfaction of essential bodily needs: sleep deprivation, restricted environmental stimulation, and breath control. Used singly or—as is often the case—in some combination, these techniques can be powerfully effective in precipitating exceptional states.

Sleep Deprivation: Like abstention from food, going without sleep can be elected for periods varying considerably in length, regularity, and severity. Less extended and demanding are occasional vigils through part or the whole of a night as an act of devotion or of PENANCE. Nightlong watches may also be prompted, according to Friedrich Heiler (1961), by a fear of the pollution of sleep and the night. From this point of view, refraining from sleep becomes a necessary preparation for a range of cultic rituals.

Alternatively, abstaining from sleep may be undertaken as a sustained and rigorous ascetic discipline. James (1902) cites the case of Saint Peter of Alcantara, who is supposed to have slept no more than an hour and a half each day for 40 years. He accomplished this MORTIFICATION only by occupying a cell too short to allow him to lie down, and by always standing or kneeling, except when he assumed a sitting position for his short naps. Fourteenth-century Saint Catherine of Siena, an anorexic who, as long as her strength permitted it, flagellated herself with iron chains three times a day for one and a half hours each time, "with great difficulty . . . conquered fatigue and reduced her sleep to as little as thirty minutes every two days on a wooden board (perhaps a forgivable medieval exaggeration here, but the point is clear enough)" (Bell, 1985, p. 43). Some mystics, such as Theresa Neumann, are said to have actually needed no more than two or three hours of sleep a night.

The potentially dramatic effects of sleep loss have been vividly demonstrated by contemporary research. Some subjects who undergo total sleep deprivation will exhibit psychotic symptoms, including delusions and visual or tactile HALLUCINATIONS, after only three or four days. Such striking reactions are likely to occur among persons with a history of psychiatric disorder or those who fall at the extremes of temperamental disposition—as may well be the case with a number of saints or mystics. More nearly inevitable with such a period of sleep loss are fatigue, irritability, lapses in attention, blurred vision, disorientation, and feelings of persecution. Symptoms after only a day or two of sleeplessness are predictably much less dramatic. When deprivation is only partial, as in the cases cited, the sleep cycle will adjust itself in order to maximize the occurrence both of stage four sleep, the deepest and last stage of the sleep cycle, and of rapid eye movement (REM) sleep, a state of heightened brain activity that occurs during stage one and is accompanied by dreaming. Although little research has been done on protracted partial sleep deprivation—and none on religiously motivated varieties of it—we may safely assume that the more severe the partial deprivation, the more obvious will be the symptoms typical of total sleeplessness (Horne, 1988; Kales, 1969).

Much remains unknown about sleep, including its fundamental biological function. The long-entrenched notion that it is a time of general body restoration has been rejected, at least for humans, by sleep researcher James Horne (1988). Horne speculates that it is the brain and particularly the CEREBELLUM that requires sleep-induced relaxation for repair of neural circuits and other forms of cerebral restitution. Clearly, there are individual differences in the need for sleep, varying especially with age but also with mental health. Because many living organisms sleep little or not at all, however, we cannot say categorically that it is essential for life. Yet it has been well demonstrated that deprivation of sleep among some organisms, including human beings, will cause serious physiological and psychological disturbance and can finally lead to death (Kales, 1969).

Restricted Environmental Stimulation: Another requirement for normal psychological equilibrium is an optimal level of sensory stimulation. Too much or too little stimulation can cause a range of pathological symptoms. Of these extremes, stimulus reduction in varying degrees has been used throughout the world by individuals and communities seeking to deepen their religious consciousness. "Solitude," says William Hocking (1912, p. 403), "is the essence of mysticism," and it has been found in a variety of contexts and ways. Spiritual seekers of various traditions commonly retreat to the mountains, the forest, or the desert in order to eliminate all intercourse with other human beings and to reduce the distractions of civilization. Temporary residence in a hollow tree or mountain cave, or perpetual immobility at the top of a pillar or on a branch of a tree, simplifies even further the outer world of reality. Within religious communities, which may themselves be situated in a forest or desert place, tradition has provided several means for reducing sensory stimulation: drab dwellings that are sparsely furnished and in which life is enormously simplified; rules or vows of silence, lasting from hours to a lifetime; periodic seclusion in individual cells; and lengthy periods of contemplation, dedication, and prayer (Cutten, 1908; Hastings, 1908–1926). In the Christian context, some individuals subject themselves to the practice of *inclusio,* in which they have themselves shut up in small, narrow cells, often attached to a convent or church. The well-known fourteenth-century anchoress Julian of Norwich, for example, spent the later years of her life confined to a room in a small dwelling attached to a Norman church. Three windows allowed her to speak to persons seeking her counsel, to communicate with her servants, and to hear Mass and receive communion (Julian of Norwich, 1901; Thouless, 1924).

Systematic experimental study of such "stimulus deprivation," or what Peter Suedfeld (1980) more accurately calls restricted environmental stimulation, was undertaken by psychologist Donald Hebb and his colleagues at McGill University in 1951. Since that time it has become widely known that drastic reduction in environmental input can lead in a matter of hours to a range of dramatic phenomena: depersonalization, disturbances in body image, auditory and visual hallucinations, intellectual deterioration, susceptibility to propaganda, and extreme and variable emotion. So stressful are these effects that some subjects will typically quit by the second day. The production of such experiences generally requires elaborate experimental conditions, which vary considerably from one study to the next. These conditions involve several distinguishable features: minimal levels of stimulation, reduction of stimulus variability, social isolation, and physical confinement.

Remarkably similar conditions are employed among the Shakers of St. Vincent in the rite of "mourning" for one's sins. For a period of 6 to 14 days or even longer and while kept on a restricted diet, the mourner is blindfolded with mourning bands, placed in a supine position, and isolated in a small room, in anticipation of a spiritual journey. Undertaken only after a sign from the Holy Spirit has been received, mourning is recognized as an exceedingly difficult task, one that some aspirants will not be able to complete (Henney, 1974, pp. 53–57).

Such thoroughgoing reduction in stimulation for religious purposes is rare, however. Of the various modes of stimulus deprivation that have been studied experimentally, the one most uniformly characteristic of the religious practices we have reviewed is social isolation. From the reports of Arctic explorers, shipwrecked sailors, prisoners in solitary confinement, and persons traveling alone in small airplanes or boats, it is known that extended social isolation, especially in conjunction with a monotony of environment and routine, can yield effects similar to those reported in experimental studies of restricted stimulation. It can also produce the "sensed presence" of another, often helpful being (Suedfeld and Mocellin, 1987). Thus, even though religious practices only rarely approximate the conditions of these studies, they may entail similar physiological processes.

At present, we have no theory that gives an adequate account of the complex biochemical and physiological correlates of these states. It has been found that the electrical activity of the brain becomes progressively slower as the period of isolation increases, whereas the GALVANIC SKIN RESPONSE, body movements, and subjective reports all reflect increasing activation or arousal. Some fluctuations, including day–night rhythms, as well as marked individual differences, are also evident. Explanatory efforts have focused on the RETICULAR ACTIVATING SYSTEM (RAS) of the brain stem, which controls the state of arousal of the organism. When external sensory input drops markedly, it is postulated, the balance between cortical activity and RAS function is changed in such a way that cortical factors play a larger role, producing the various phenomena observed in stimulus deprivation studies. Much is yet to be learned about the RAS, however, and the presence of individual differences, the role of social influences, and the enigma of slowed brain waves concurrent with autonomic arousal must ultimately be explained as well (Solomon et al., 1961; Zubek, 1969).

Breath Control: Among the fundamental resources of the body that have been systematically limited as part of religious practice is oxygen, without which we ordinarily cannot survive for more than a few minutes. *Rhythmic breathing and holding the breath,* both means of modifying the proportions of oxygen and carbon dioxide in the bloodstream, are techniques less widely practiced than the others we have considered. In the Islamic mystical practice of solitary DHIKR, the worshiper silently and incessantly repeats the name of God while assuming a prescribed posture and adopting a respiratory rhythm corresponding to the rhythm of the mystical syllables. In the Taoist tradition holding the breath for increasingly long periods of time is a technique of "mystical physiology" that is thought to prolong the life of the body indefinitely. And in Hesychasm, an Eastern Christian monastic tradition going back to the twelfth century, breath control is integral to the chief practice of unending repetition of the Prayer of Jesus, "Lord Jesus Christ, have mercy on me!" The worshiper assumes a well-defined posture and speaks in rhythm with the heartbeat and breathing, which is retarded as much as possible or even held (Bloom, 1954; Eliade, 1954; Wunderle, 1947). Breathing also serves as a focus of the attention in Theravada Buddhist and Zen practices, but in these instances no effort is made to modify it.

Nowhere has the art of breath control been more highly developed than in YOGA. Of the eight stages of yogic progression, PRĀNĀYĀMA or "breath-restraint" is the fourth. Adept yogis will practice one or another of the eight varieties of *prānāyāma* four times in the course of 24 hours, including 80 rounds of inhalation, holding, and exhalation in each sitting. Although the ratio of the three parts or "moments" of respiration can vary, the most common among experienced practitioners is 1:4:2. *Prānāyāma* is almost always carried out in one of the meditative postures, with utmost concentration and as deliberately and slowly as possible. Particular emphasis is placed on the holding period, which may last three minutes or longer; during this time both nostrils may be closed with the fingers of the right hand. By refusing to breathe nonrhythmically like the rest of humankind, and by progressively slowing respiration, the yogi seeks to experience in a wakeful condition each of the various states of consciousness (Behanan, 1937; Bernard, 1944; Eliade, 1954).

Breath control undoubtedly influences psychological states in a variety of ways. James Pratt (1920, p. 388) suggests that it allows a measure of control over the "excitement–calm 'dimension' of feeling," or what psychologists today simply call arousal. Just as assuming the posture and facial expression of some emotional state can help to engender that state in actuality (James, 1890; Zuckerman et al., 1981), so breathing slowly and regularly can bring relief to the distressed individual. "In the first days of practice," writes Mircea Eliade (1954, p. 58), "concentration on the vital function of respiration produces an inexpressible sensation of harmony, a rhythmic and melodic plenitude, a leveling of all physiological unevennesses. Later it brings an obscure feeling of presence in one's own body, a calm consciousness of one's own greatness."

These results also reflect chemical changes. On the one hand, some of these breathing exercises entail a far healthier use of the lungs than in normal spontaneous respiration. Inhalation is much deeper, so that a person ventilates the alveoli more fully and tones the breathing muscles, and the extended holding allows for a fuller diffusion of the inspired air (Wood, 1959). On the other hand, although the meditative posture undoubtedly reduces the body's need for oxygen, respiratory practices that place a premium on holding the breath presumably cause HYPOVENTILATION, which produces both hypoxemia (insufficient oxygen in the blood) and carbon dioxide retention. As a chronic condition hypoventilation can have serious consequences (Slonim and Hamilton, 1971); its effects as a temporary state are less clear.

Carbon dioxide acts at many different sites in the body, including the respiratory, circulatory, and nervous systems. In the brain it increases cerebral blood flow and intracranial pressure while reducing the excitability of the neurons, notably those in the reticular activating system. The interplay of these and other effects is exceedingly complex and difficult to understand, though certain gross changes are unmistakable (Nunn, 1987, p. 460). Barry Wyke (1963) reports that the inhalation of increasing concentrations of carbon dioxide will produce symptoms of confusion, irritability, euphoria or depression, dizziness, stupor, and finally coma. Ladislas Meduna (1958) has demonstrated that the inhalation of a mixture of 30 percent carbon dioxide and 70 percent oxygen (compared with 0.03 and 20.95 percent in normal atmospheric air) can produce feelings of cosmic importance and ecstasy. Dreams or sensory hallucinations, some of them horrifying beyond description, have also occurred under these conditions, along with rhythmic movement and seizures. It is rather doubtful, however, that the carbon dioxide concentrations produced by religiously motivated breathing practices approximate the order reported in these studies.

Exceptionally rapid breathing can also produce dramatic effects, as Günter Schüttler (1971) demonstrates in his study of the Tibetan ORACLE–priest he observed in 1970 at Kalimpong, West Bengal. The 45-year-old priest had first shown signs of his special status as a mouthpiece for the divine when he was 13 years old. Restless and easily irritated, he suffered from sleep disturbances, numbness in his hands and feet, diarrhea, and loss of appetite; he also had many dreams. At the direction of a teacher of the Dalai Lama, he undertook an intensive course of meditation, and from age 14 he was able to make prophecies and answer questions placed to him. He had become an oracle–priest.

Occasionally possession would occur spontaneously; in general, however, it was the outcome of an elaborate ritual involving chanted prayers and rhythmic music. For this ceremony the oracle–priest was dressed in colorfully embroidered robes; a round metal mirror was hung from his neck and, once the trance state was underway, an extremely heavy miterlike cap decorated with small silver skulls was placed on his head. Issuing from under the ornate helmet, behind and in front of his ears, were two red bands, which were tied tightly under his chin in such a way

The Tibetan oracle–priest in trance

that the jugular veins were visibly compressed. During the first 15 to 20 minutes of the ritual, after the priest had inhaled smoke from a censer held under his nose, he underwent a series of remarkable changes. His eyes rolled upward, his face turned red, then gray. His initial groaning gave way to shrieks, then to staccato tones, and finally to hissing. His upper torso rocked back and forth, his right arm suddenly shot out as if to ward off some object, and his toes beat a quick, rhythmic cadence on the floor. His skin glistened with sweat, and saliva ran from his mouth. Respiration was rapid and irregular. After 20 minutes, short and hastily spoken words could be heard among the whispered sounds. The possessing spirit was finally ready to speak.

The pattern of HYPERVENTILATION exhibited by the priest, Schüttler observes, would lead to carbon dioxide depletion, blood alkalosis, and constriction of the arteries carrying blood to the central nervous system. In addition, the uptake of oxygen in the blood may have been hindered by the unidentified fumes inhaled from the censer. The priest's paleness, the Parkinsonian-like trembling of the extremities, and the paroxysmal spasms at the close of the ceremony may all be explained, Schüttler says, by the mechanism of hyperventilation TETANY. The reduction in blood circulation, perhaps exacerbated by the apparent constriction of the jugular veins, led inevitably to marked sensations of numbness and of pain. Hyperventilation was almost certainly responsible for the marked alterations in consciousness (pp. 110–111).

Overstimulation and Religious States

The Tibetan ritual introduces us to a group of practices that contrast sharply with the techniques of sensory reduction and indeed with virtually every form of solitary religious observance. The generation of emotional excitement in an assembled group of people, often by greatly increasing stimulation or by appealing to common fears, hopes, or desires, is a typical part of many religious traditions. Some of these "collective ecstasies" (Félice, 1947) are among humankind's most remarkable— and occasionally most regrettable—practices; others of them, though less extraordinary, may nevertheless provide the foundations for individual piety and enduring tradition.

Ecstatic Dance: Probably the most widespread of these expressions are rhythmic music and dance, typically in combination. Heiler (1961) writes that "Dance is of the greatest significance throughout the history of religion; next to sacrifice it is the most important cultic act—indeed, among primitive peoples, it is more important than sacrifice" (pp. 239–240). The oldest meaning of dance, Heiler says, is magical. It is undertaken as a panacea, to provide protection against illness and death, famine, storm and flood, volcanic eruption, eclipse of sun and moon. It is also a defense against demons—hence the wedding dance, the dance of death, and the dance at the coronation of a king. Dance is, moreover, a form of sympathetic magic: one seeks to bring about the desired event—whether a successful hunt, an abundant harvest, a victorious battle, or a life-restoring rain—by engaging in dance movements suggestive of the event. According to Jane Harrison (1927), MIMETIC dances may also serve as a mode of instruction, a way of disclosing the mysteries, especially during initiation rites. Some forms of dance are an expression of religious devotion, a means of honoring the divinity, of making an offering, of embodying an attitude of thankfulness or joy.

Yet the most important meaning of dance, Heiler writes, is the mystical–ecstatic. By overcoming the heaviness of the body, the dancer (who may be a priest, a shaman, or a prophet) soars in "mystical flight" into the spiritual realm. Ecstatic dance—and Gerardus van der Leeuw (1933) says that dance is almost always ecstatic to some degree—transforms the dancer into a godlike being. Indeed, the gods themselves are sometimes represented as dancing. Shiva, the Indian god of creation and destruction, is widely known as the King of Dancers (Naṭarāja). In ancient Greece, the Kouretes, semimythical young men who were initiators, guardians, and child rearers, were depicted as armed and orgiastic dancers. Helios, the sun god, was greeted at dawn with dancing, an imitation of the god's own movement (Harrison, 1927). And in the APOCRYPHAL Acts of Saint John, Christ leads his apostles in an ecstatic dance around him, as he intones a magical hymn of praise (Pulver, 1942).

Shiva as Naṭarāja, the King of Dancers

Although dance is found in religious contexts throughout the world (see Bourguignon, 1968; Hanna, 1988; Wosien, 1974), a few groups have become famous for the preeminence that dance has attained in their practice. Of particular interest are the dancing or whirling dervishes, who form one of the Sufi or Islamic mystical orders, the Mevlevi, which was founded in the thirteenth century by the well-known poet Jalaluddin Rumi (Anderson, 1923; Friedlander, 1975). The members of the Mevlevi Order are particularly famous for their love of music. Helmut Ritter (1933) reports that Muslims consider the music of this order, to which the best of the Turkish composers belong, to be the finest religious music the Islamic world possesses.

The Mevlevis are better known in the West for their elaboration of *dhikr*, "recollection," the spiritual exercises by which the devotee draws near to God. *Dhikr*, Rouget (1980) points out, is of two types. Solitary *dhikr*, or *dhikr* of the privileged, entails progressive ascetic practice, including breath control and silent immobility, and culminates in an ecstatic state of total absorption in the divine. Collective *dhikr*, or *dhikr* of the commoners, requires but one degree of ascetic discipline and through music and dance aspires to trance states that have sometimes included spectacular demonstrations of "fakirism"—bloodlessly piercing the flank with a skewer, walking on burning coals, and swallowing broken glass (p. 263). The first type of *dhikr* clearly belongs among the practices we reviewed under the category of physiological deprivation; the second type concerns us here.

Whereas each of the various dervish brotherhoods has developed its own style and repertoire of music and dance, they all share in common the distinctive way in which they intone the divine name. The ceremony begins with the preparatory chanting of prayers, interspersed with music and songs, while the dervishes sit in a circle around the spiritual leader, the *shaikh*. At a certain point, the *shaikh* signals the swaying participants to rise:

> Still keeping their circular formation, which may be tight or lax, depending upon whether the men are holding each other's hands or shoulders, the participants all join in unison in a rhythmic intonation either of the first part of the profession of faith (*shahada*); *La ilaha illa Allah* ("There is no god but God"), or of the name of Allah, or of such other words as *huwa* (Him) or *hayy* (Living). The words are half-chanted, half-shouted to a very pronounced rhythm, which the men obtain by strongly exaggerating their respiratory movements as they breathe in and out. Produced far back in the throat, the voice used is very raucous. The sound that escapes from their chests as they rise and fall to the rhythm has been described . . . as "a collective rasp". . . . In certain cases, this general and raucous panting is—as the Arabs express it themselves—very similar to the sound of a saw moving back and forth. . . . But perhaps it would be more correct to speak of "roaring" (p. 272).

However it is described, notes Rouget, "this great hubbub has an air of savagery and animality about it. As they roar, the participants sway back and forth or from left to right, with their necks disarticulated and their heads violently hurled about by the movement." At the direction of the *shaikh*, the men accompany their singing and rhythmic recitation with the dance movements for which the dervishes are famous: circular dancing, whirling, and leaping. These components of their rhythmic movements symbolize spiritual realities. The circular dancing represents the spirit of the initiate brought by revelation into the cycle of existing things (the state of the gnostic); the whirling suggests a profounder penetration into the inner nature and being of Allah (the state of the assured one); and the leaping portrays ecstatic transport from the human to the unitive level (Trimingham, 1971, p. 195).

Whirling Dervishes in Konya, Turkey

Idries Shah (1964) asserts that Sufi dance movements are dependent on the mystical intuitive knowledge that only a teaching master can apply, and they have been developed "in accordance with the mentality and temperament of the people of Konia" (p. 329), a Turkish community where the ritual can still be observed (Friedlander, 1975; Ritter, 1962). Attempts to export the practice, Shah says, have yielded nothing but ineffective pantomime.

Ecstatic dance can be found in many other places and times: in the ancient ceremonies of DIONYSUS, the wine god, which were conducted in the night-enshrouded mountains by flickering torchlight amid the wild sounds of thundering drums, clashing cymbals, and deep-toned flutes (Oesterreich, 1921, p. 336); in the dancing epidemics that spread episodically throughout Europe during the Middle Ages (Hecker, 1837); and in the rituals of African tribesmen, such as the !Kung Bushmen, who dance all night around a central fire, the men circling the flames with heavy, rhythmic steps, and the women, sitting shoulder to shoulder in an inner circle, clapping and singing wordless songs (R. B. Lee, 1968). There are also the sacred services of the strongly ascetic Men of God, a Russian sect known by outsiders as Khlysti or Flagellants, which employed frenzied dancing as its principal means for receiving the divine spirit (Grass, 1915); the two Ghost Dance movements that swept through the Indian tribes of the western United States in the late nineteenth century (La Barre, 1972; Miller, 1959); and the rites of the Hasidic Jews of eastern Europe, as well as a contemporary secular adaptation, the hora, the ecstatic circle dance of Israel's pioneers (Bourguignon, 1968).

"Right dancing," says Hall (1904, 1), who explicitly excludes from this category the dance of the modern ballroom, "can cadence the very soul, give nervous poise and control, bring harmony between basal and finer muscles, and also between feeling and intellect, body and mind. It can serve both as an awakener and a test of intelligence, predispose the heart against vice, and turn the springs of character toward virtue" (pp. 214–215). The immediate outcome, however, and often the goal of such exuberant and exhausting dancing is, in some contexts, a state of ecstatic trance or of spirit possession, both of which frequently culminate in physical collapse and a comatose state.

Other Ecstatic Practices: The same outcomes are yielded by a variety of other practices that have in common excessive sensory stimulation or profound emotional arousal. Some of these—such as brandishing weapons, handling or walking on fire, flagellating oneself (or others), or sacrificing animals—sometimes occur in conjunction with dance rituals. Also associated with dance—itself "the aphrodisiac *par excellence*," according to van der Leeuw (1933, p. 374)—is a broad spectrum of erotic manifestations, ranging from the adamant rejection of sexuality of the dancing Skoptsi, a Russian sect akin to the Khlysti except for the astonishing addition of castration (Grass, 1920), to the orgiastic extravagances of the dancers in the cult of Dionysus.

The association of religion and erotic emotion is an intimate one, according to many researchers (Ellis, 1910; Goldberg, 1930; Leuba, 1925; Schubert, 1941). "Early religious rites," says Havelock Ellis, "were largely sexual and orgiastic because they were largely an appeal to the generative forces of Nature to exhibit a beneficial productiveness" (p. 311). The connection between the religious and the sexual emotions is sometimes expressed in concrete symbols, as in the various phallic cults (Elder, 1987; Hartland, 1917; Monick, 1987) or in the ritual use of sexual intercourse in "left-handed" (unorthodox) TANTRIC practice (Bharati, 1965). At other times the erotic element appears more sublime or metaphorical, as in *bhakti*, the Hindu way of affectionate devotion, or in the ecstatic prose of some Christian mystics.

Beyond dance and the more or less obviously erotic are other emotionally charged rites, including several that have been the objects of considerable research in America. These include the religious revival, which particularly interested the early psychologists and sociologists of religion (Davenport, 1905; Dimond, 1926); the handling of snakes, which forms a part of the religious services of some Christian fundamentalists in Southern Appalachia (Gerrard, 1968; Kane, 1987; La Barre, 1962; Schwartz, 1960); and SPEAKING IN TONGUES (glossolalia), a phenomenon

On the tenth day of Moharram, a group of Shiite Muslims in Karachi, Pakistan, inflict cuts on their heads with ritual daggers to mourn the death of Imam Hussein, the grandson of the prophet Muhammad.

commonly observed in religious revivals, snakehandling services, Pentecostal meetings, and other rites around the world (Goodman, 1972; Kildahl, 1972; Malony and Lovekin, 1985; Richardson, 1973; Samarin, 1972).

The extremes to which such practices can lead are vividly described by Hall (1904, 2) in his summary of an account of a weeklong revival at the beginning of the nineteenth century:

> The flickering camp-fires and the darkness of the surrounding forest, the sobs, groans, and shrieks of those in the valley of the shadow of death, the songs and shouts of joy of those who had found eternal joy in Beulah [an idyllic land in Bunyan's *Pilgrim's Progress*], were too much for the excited imagination, and circulation was affected and nerves gave way; in the "falling exercise" many dropped to the ground, cold and still, or with convulsive twitches or clonic contortions of face and limbs. . . . The crowd swarmed all night from preacher to preacher, singing, shouting, laughing, some plunging wildly over stumps and benches into the forest shouting "Lost, lost!" others leaping and bounding about like live fish out of water; others rolling over and over on the ground for hours; others lying on the ground and talking when they could not move; and yet others beating the ground with their heels.
>
> As the excitement increased it grew more morbid and took the form of "jerking," or in others it became the "barking exercise," and in yet others it became the "holy laugh." The jerks began with the head, which was thrown violently from side to side so rapidly that the features were blurred and the hair almost seemed to snap, and when the sufferer struck an obstacle and fell he would bounce about like a ball. . . . Men fancied themselves dogs and gathered about a tree barking and yelping—"treeing the devil." They saw visions and dreamed dreams, and as the revival waned, it left a crop of nervous and hysterical disorders in its wake (pp. 286–287).

Nearly two hundred years later, such an account may strike us as quaintly exaggerated, as a condescending effort, perhaps, to discredit the participants in revival services. Certainly we would not expect to observe such goings-on in modern Western society. In fact, however, the phenomena are neither exaggerated nor passé. A visitor today to one of the frequent services of the Toronto Airport Christian Fellowship (formerly the Airport Vineyard Church) in Toronto, Canada, would witness "uncontrollable laughter, 'drunkenness' in the Spirit, intense weeping, falling to the floor, physical convulsions or 'jerks,' pogoing and bouncing, shouting and roaring" according to Guy Chevreau (1994, p. 27), a Baptist minister associated with the work there. A reporter from a Toronto newspaper describes in these terms the hotel scene of a "catch the fire again" conference sponsored by the church late in 1995:

> The ballroom carpets were littered with fallen bodies, bodies of seemingly straitlaced men and women, who felt themselves moved by the phenomenon they say is the Holy Spirit. So moved, they howled with joy or the release of some long buried pain. They collapsed, some rigid as corpses, some convulsed in hysterial laughter. From room to room come barnyard cries, calls heard only in the wild, grunts so deep women recalled the sounds of childbirth while some men and women adopted the very position of childbirth.
>
> Men did chicken walks. Women jabbed their fingers as if afflicted with nervous disorders. . . . A minister from Syracuse, N.Y., spent hours on his back, at times in repose, at times shaking, at times his legs aloft. A minister from Ireland, doing a Monty Python silly walk, wobbled to the microphone, beaming. "What are you feeling now?" [pastor John] Arnott asked him. The minister . . . shook his head, giggled, and crashed to the floor, legs up. . . .
>
> And around these scenes of bedlam were loving arms to catch the falling, smiling

faces, whispered prayers of encouragement, instructions to release, let go (Scrivener, 1995, p. A2).

Drawing thousands of visitors each week, the so-called Toronto Blessing has become Toronto's chief tourist attraction. Many of those "catching the fire" are bringing it back to their home churches in turn, so that similar phenomena are now appearing around the world (Poloma, 1995).

Toward an Explanation: The task of accounting for the psychological effects of the broad range of complex practices that we have surveyed here in brief is an enormously difficult one. We might reasonably begin by analyzing the effects of particular elements in these rites, such as the music or rhythmic beat. Alan Daniélou (1961) argues, for example, that the frequency ratios in music have a precise effect on the psychophysiology of the listener; through repetition, he says, sounds can "transform our sensibility, our way of thinking, the state of our soul, and even our moral character" (p. 26).

Auditory Driving: A number of researchers have suggested that the loud and rhythmic music and especially the beat of drums that so often accompanies these ecstatic practices may directly affect neural functioning. Andrew Neher (1961, 1962) has demonstrated that rapid and loud drumming can modify the electrical rhythms of the brain, paralleling the well-documented effects of rhythmically flashing light. "Photic driving," as a neural response at the flash frequency is called, can produce a variety of subjective effects, including kinesthetic and cutaneous sensations as well as feelings of fear, disgust, or pleasure; it may also lead to hallucinations and even epileptic seizures. All 12 of Neher's subjects manifested a DRIVING response similar in many respects to photic driving. Half of them—a high proportion in comparison to those in photic driving experiments—also showed involuntary eyeblinking, ordinarily the first sign of a muscle twitching that may spread to other areas and culminate in convulsions. This symptom appeared in those who exhibited the greatest auditory driving.[2]

Using only a gourd rattle, anthropologist Felicitas Goodman (1986) has induced altered states of consciousness in a variety of subjects who are prepared beforehand to expect unusual and positive changes. In less than 15 minutes after the rattling began, most subjects in one series of experiments had dropped to the floor, shivering, trembling, or twitching. "Those on their knees would rock up and down, their faces flushed; some perspired. In some instances, their fingers twitched, others had cold and stiff hands and feet" (p. 88). At the outset of the experiment, these undergraduate volunteers experienced tingling or prickling sensations, and some eventually hallucinated. Coming to after the rattling stopped was reported to be difficult. "The body and head were heavy, eyes would not stay open, and when they finally did, everything was too bright, very luminous or fuzzy, the latter doubtless a result of the dilated pupils" (p. 89). Goodman, too, attributes these results to auditory driving.

Subauditory Components: From his studies of the Ilahita Arapesh in Papua New Guinea, where tropical storms are truly awesome, anthropologist Donald Tuzin (1984) proposes another possible explanation for certain effects of ritual sound. He suggests that drumbeating, deep-voiced chanting, and the eery sound of the

---

[2] Rouget's (1980, pp. 172–176) extended and gratuitously disdainful critique of Neher's research, which he judges to be "valueless," is at various points both misleading and obtuse. Regrettably, one or two of Tuzin's commentators (Tuzin, 1984, p. 590) seem to have read Rouget uncritically.

A woman attending a 1995 conference sponsored by the Toronto Airport Christian Fellowship "catches the fire" and collapses in laughter as those around her pray.

bullroarer, among other ingenious sound-making devices, derive their power to generate religious feelings from the *sub*auditory sound components that they have in common with thunder. With sufficient distance, thunder may be inaudible to the ear and yet deliver powerful infrasonic waves that trigger the brain's reticular activating system without providing sensory clues to their origin. The result, Tuzin suggests, is anxiety-arousing sensations of the uncanny, of the intrinsically mysterious, which humans resolve by attributing the origin of these feelings to the supernatural realm. Thus to re-create this experience of the numinous reality, human beings everywhere incorporate into ritual practice a variety of sound-making devices, including the mighty pipe organ that reverberates in the vaulted spaces of many a great cathedral.

No researcher claims that such sounds alone will produce religious feelings or induce trance states. Neher, for one, "strongly doubt[s] that any one factor such as auditory driving will be shown to be of sole, or even predominant importance in possession states; rather, such states are likely to be caused by a number of interrelated factors, from physiological to cultural, which vary greatly from one setting to another" (quoted in Prince, 1968, p. 135). Goodman (1986) has experimentally investigated one such factor, that of *posture*, in conjunction with the gourd rattling. She found surprisingly consistent differences in her subjects' trance experience when they assumed six different postures derived from the ethnographic literature, including a reclining position represented in the Paleolithic rock painting in Lascaux Cave in France. A neutral posture not associated with religious ritual was experienced by the trance seekers as unpleasant and, while in it, none was successful in attaining a trance state. Goodman's experimental design also takes into account the important factors of expectations and environmental setting.

A Pavlovian Model: Alternatively, we might begin by examining the overall effect of these rites on their participants. We may safely predict that the vigorous and prolonged movement patterns that commonly occur in ecstatic rituals, in combination with the excitement or stress that frequently accompanies them, will increase heart and breathing rates, modify blood chemistry, and sometimes disturb the sense of balance and equilibrium. Often a point of "breakdown" is eventually reached, evidenced by a sudden change in the individual's behavior.

British psychiatrist William Sargant (1957, 1969, 1973) has found the research of the famous Russian physiologist Ivan Pavlov to be particularly useful in explaining this dramatic outcome. Pavlov discovered that when a dog is subjected to stress that exceeds its capacity for habitual response, a form of protective or TRANSMARGINAL INHIBITION will often occur. He observed three stages to this change in cortical brain activity. In the "equivalent" stage the dog will give reactions of the same magnitude to stimuli of varying intensity; in the "paradoxical" stage it will give a livelier response to weak stimuli than to strong ones, for at this point strong stimuli will only increase the protective inhibition; and in the "ultra-paradoxical" stage, positively conditioned responses change to negative ones, and negative ones to positive, so that the dog may attack the master it once loved and become attached to the assistant it formerly hated. Pavlov also found that transmarginal protective inhibition is accompanied by an unusual degree of suggestibility, an exceptional openness to environmental influences.

Pavlov had suggested that these feelings might help to account for various pathological conditions in human beings. For Sargant, they provide a way of understanding the phenomena associated with religious conversion, spirit possession, faith healing, and speaking in tongues. Hellfire preaching, rhythmic music, and frenzied dancing are all means of bringing about transmarginal inhibition and HYPERSUGGESTIBILITY. Furthermore, just as castration or intestinal disorders increased the vulnerability of Pavlov's dogs to this process, so the same or similar conditions, as well as debilitation produced by sleep or food deprivation, can act in human beings to hasten the process of breakdown and relearning.

Pavlov's model also helps to explain why some individuals seem inherently more susceptible to this process than others. Like Pavlov's dogs, human beings can be classified into temperamental types, which reflect differences in "the strength, mobility, and equilibrium of the two opposing processes of excitation and inhibition" in the central nervous system (Gray, 1964, p. 157). Interestingly, Pavlov's types correspond to the classic four temperaments—choleric, sanguine, phlegmatic, and melancholic—which Pavlov calls strong excitatory, lively, calm imperturbable, and weak inhibitory, respectively. Of these, the weak inhibitory (the melancholic) showed the greatest vulnerability to stress, although the other three types also showed the effects of transmarginal inhibition when the stress was sufficiently acute. Furthermore, Pavlov noted the remarkable fact that those dogs least vulnerable to stress—the lively (sanguine) and the calm imperturbable (phlegmatic)— were most likely to hold tenaciously to the new behavior patterns learned after disruption of the nervous system. Persons of "weak character," extrapolates Sargant, are more likely to undergo conversion; but persons of "strong character," once they exhibit a dramatic change in their belief and attitudes, are more likely to retain their new orientation throughout the rest of their lives.

George Stratton (1911) observed that some temperaments are more easily aroused than others by group excitement. Moreover, he added, it is to the type that is resistant to contagion, and that more easily concentrates on the highest when alone, that the truly exceptional experiences and insights are likely to come. "Especially when the intellectual element becomes stronger and the revelation is nobler, the illumination seems more apt to come to the solitary." In agreement with Philippe de Félice (1947), who considers collective ecstasies to be inferior forms of mystical practice, Stratton says that it is "the great leaders of religion [who] are reached in solitude; the followers are more stirred by the company of men" (p. 115).

The Role of Endorphins: Yet another brain mechanism, discovered in the early 1970s, seems to play a role in the remarkable effects of ecstatic religious practices. Although the pain-relieving and euphoria-inducing properties of the opiates have been known since before the common era, only recently have scientists identified specific opiate receptors in the brain. These receptors were found to be concentrated in the areas that mediate pain reception as well as in the LIMBIC SYSTEM, a collection of structures just under the CEREBRAL CORTEX that are the chief regulators of emotional states and are connected to many other parts of the brain. These locations help to explain the capacity of the opiates to blunt pain and to produce euphoria (Snyder, 1986).

But why, researchers wondered, does the brain possess opiate receptors at all? It was a natural next step to infer that corresponding to these receptors is some opiatelike NEUROTRANSMITTER that occurs naturally in the brain. Three families of such substances were subsequently found. Today they are known as ENDORPHINS, a contraction of the phrase "*endo*genous m*orphine*like substances." Thus in certain exceptional circumstances, when pain and fear would likely be maladaptive, the brain activates a mechanism that dramatically reduces them and in some instances produces EUPHORIA and altered states of consciousness instead. Research evidence suggests that endorphins are responsible for the analgesia produced by acupuncture and may also yield the "runner's high." They have been experimentally activated in animals by food deprivation, sexual stimulation, and various stress inductions (Akil et al., 1984). Unlike morphine and other opiates, the natural endorphins are nonaddictive (because they are rapidly degraded) and thus do not show the development of tolerance that forces drug addicts to take increasingly large doses in order to obtain the same effects.

A number of researchers now speculate that endorphins play a major role in trance states and other phenomena associated with ritual. Prolonged physical exertion, as in ritual dance; loud, rhythmic music or other acoustic stimulation; fear-inducing procedures such as handling snakes or fire, whipping or piercing of flesh, or preaching of eternal damnation—such practices as these, especially if joined with extended fasting, thirsting, sleep deprivation, stimulus reduction, or hyperventilation, are thought likely to facilitate the production of endorphins and thereby the achievement of euphoric altered states of consciousness (Jelik, 1982). The first laboratory confirmation of this hypothesis was reported by Goodman (1988, p. 39), who with Ingrid Mueller, a German medical student, monitored a variety of physiological changes in four volunteer subjects after trance had been induced through gourd rattling. The trance state, Goodman reports, was accompanied by an increase in heart rate, a drop in blood pressure, a decrease in the blood of stress-related hormones, and the appearance of endorphins, the level of which remained high for some time after the trance was over.

Raymond Prince (1982) suggests that the organism itself may create "artificial threat situations" in the form of nightmares, delirium, or psychosis, as a means of generating the helpful endorphins. Healers, too, may employ "mock hyperstress" toward the same end. The result is often what Prince calls "the omnipotence maneuver": in the midst of terror a person suddenly flips over into a state of euphoria, which is commonly experienced as resulting from supernatural interven-

Trained through ecstatic dance to enter a controlled trance state, this devotee at the Thaipusam Festival in Kuala Lumpur, Malaysia, honors the Hindu god Murugan by carrying a heavy *kavadi,* the many long needles of which were embedded in the skin after trance was attained. Research suggests the possibility that endorphin immunoreactivity may be elevated at the beginning of the stressful, week-long training. (Simons, Ervin, and Prince, 1988; Ervin, et al., 1988)

tion. As in NEAR-DEATH EXPERIENCES, there may be a residual conviction of a certain invulnerability and a feeling of having been singled out for special favor by God or fate. Noting that religious experiences often occur at times when individuals feel helpless and have little self-esteem, Prince speculates that the omnipotence maneuver is "a kind of psychological analogue of homeostatic physiological mechanisms that function not so much as life preserving as preserving the sense of well-being" (p. 420).

Drugs and Religious Experience

All the methods of hypoarousal and hyperarousal serve to change body chemistry. Their successful application is usually dependent, however, on one or more of several conditions. The seekers must possess a certain predisposition, which tradition and instructions typically augment; they must be willing to make a serious effort and an extended commitment, as in meditative practices; they must consent to suffer discomfort or pain, as in fasting or FLAGELLATION; or they must attend the rituals of a tradition-centered group, as in ecstatic dancing. The use of drugs, either as they occur naturally in plants or after they have been synthesized in the laboratory, seems to entail none of these requirements, yet drug intoxication typically yields remarkably dramatic effects.

The Psychedelic Drugs: Investigators of the drugs used for inducing ecstatic or mystical states have not been able to agree on a generic name for these substances. The U.S. government and most medical researchers call them HALLUCINOGENS because they can produce extraordinarily vivid, hallucinationlike experiences. However, if we define hallucinations strictly as complex false perceptions seen with open eyes and taken as real, these drugs rarely produce them (Barber, 1970, p. 28). Moreover, the label overlooks other, equally remarkable manifestations. Investigators struck by the capacity of these drugs to produce "model psychoses" have called them *psychotomimetic.* Yet this label is also misleading and insufficiently inclusive, for their effects mimic psychoses only to a degree and differ from them in important ways. *Psychoactive* is a more nearly neutral label than the preceding two, especially because it avoids suggesting that the concomitant experiences are pathological and delusional; yet it is so general that it includes both stimulants (such as the amphetamines) and sedatives (the barbituates), neither of

A ritual stone mushroom from Guatemala.

which groups belongs here. The label closest to a neutral and properly delimited one is PSYCHEDELIC, "mind-manifesting," though some still object to it because of its association with the excesses of the drug culture of the 1960s (see Stevens, 1987). The word psychedelic was coined by psychiatrist Humphry Osmond in appreciation of the drugs' capacities to reveal heretofore unknown dimensions and sensitivities in the individual mind (Grinspoon and Bakalar, 1979).

Although these labels are of relatively recent vintage, the drugs themselves have been known from time immemorial. Among the earliest of these substances for which we have some record is SOMA. Simultaneously a god, a plant, and the plant's juice, Soma is the subject of paeans passed down from the Vedic civilization in India several thousand years ago. From the lyric descriptions of the plant–god in the hymns of the *Rig Veda*, Gordon Wasson (1969) argues that Soma is an hallucinogenic mushroom called the fly agaric.[3] This crimson mushroom is known to have played a role in the religious practices of tribes in the northern regions of Siberia. Mushrooms apparently also were used for ritual purposes more than 3500 years ago in Mesoamerica, if we are to judge from the mushroom-shaped stone effigies that have been found there. The Aztecs called these mushrooms *teonanacatl*, God's flesh (Wasson, 1961). According to Robert Graves (1960), concoctions of edible fungi were also known in ancient Greece, where they were called nectar and ambrosia, the food of the Olympic gods. The hemp plant, *Cannabis sativa,* has a similarly long history: it was well known to the Chinese emperor Shen Neng, who mentions it in a work on pharmacy he wrote in the year 737 B.C.E (de Ropp, 1957).

Six Chemical Groups: A full discussion of the ritual use of psychoactive substances would draw our attention to all corners of the globe (Félice, 1936). It would also acquaint us with upwards of 150 plant species that are used for their intoxicating effects, although of these species only 20 or so are of major importance (Schultes and Hofmann, 1980, p. 21). F. C. Brown (1972) classifies the common hallucinogens into six chemically distinct groups.

---

[3] On the basis of Iranian sources rather than the *Rig Veda*, David Flattery and Martin Schwartz (1989) maintain that Soma was most likely derived, not from the fly agaric, but from the psychotropic plant harmel (*Penganum harmala*). Harmaline, the extract of this plant, is a beta-carboline similar in its subjective effects to *yagé*, a substance chiefly used by shamans.

1. The phenylalkylamines, which include mescaline, a constituent of certain species of cactus, the best known of which is the peyote.
2. The lysergic acid derivatives, preeminently lysergic acid diethylamide (LSD–25), originating, like the others, from ergot, a product of a fungus that parasitizes cereal grains.
3. The indoles, which include psilocybin, found in the mushroom *Psilocybe mexicana;* dimethyltryptamine (DMT), one of the most widely distributed hallucinogens and a constituent of an inhalant made in South America from the seeds and pods of two leguminous plants; and the beta-carbolines, which are the active ingredients of a hallucinatory potion called *ayahuasca* or *yagé,* made from the root of a South American tropical forest vine.
4. The cannabinoids, obtained from *Cannabis sativa,* known in its varying grades under several names: marijuana, hashish, charas, ganga, bhang, and so on.
5. The piperidybenzilate esters, derived from the plant family *Solanaceae* and most particularly the genus *Datura,* which have been known as narcotics and poisons since antiquity.
6. A group of minor hallucinogens, including fly agaric (*Amanita muscaria*), nutmeg, and the Polynesian beverage kava, which is made from the pulverized roots of a plant indigenous to many South Pacific islands.

The distribution, psychoactive action, chemical composition, and traditional use of these varied substances have been extensively explored by anthropologists (Aberle, 1966; Furst, 1972; Harner, 1973; La Barre, 1938; Slotkin, 1956), ethnobotanists (Schultes and Hofmann, 1980), enthnopharmacologists (Efron, Holmstedt, and Kline, 1967), and other interdisciplinary specialists (Efron, 1970; Hicks, Fink, and Hammett, 1969; Hoffer and Osmond, 1967). We must necessarily narrow our focus here to some generalizations about the best known of these drugs: mescaline, psilocybin, and LSD.

The Phenomenology of Psychedelic Experience: The subjective states induced by these substances have been described by a large number of investigators, many of whom tried them themselves.[4] The range of experiences these drugs produce is extraordinarily wide, depending on a multitude of factors, including the size of the dosage, the predispositions and expectations of the subject, the occasion of the experience, the atmosphere and aesthetic features of the setting, and the number, personal qualities, and expectations of the others present. For many, the experience is extremely positive; for others, it is nothing less than a purgatory or hell that can lead to enduring psychiatric problems, hospitalization, and, indirectly, death (Barber, 1970; Hicks, Fink, and Hammett, 1969; Snyder, 1986). The rarity of serious emotional disturbances among members of the Native American Church, who eat peyote regularly during religious ceremonies, suggests that the dangers are at a minimum when drug ingestion is carefully institutionalized and ritualized, and when emphasis is placed on the sacredness of the substance, the importance of adherence to societal standards, and the immediate interpersonal world (Bergman, 1971).

Perceptual Changes: Among the first subjective effects to appear after the in-

---

[4] See Aaronson and Osmond, 1970; Barber, 1970; Barr et al., 1972; Clark, 1969; Cohen, 1966; de Ropp, 1957; Grinspoon and Bakalar, 1979; Grof, 1972, 1975, 1985, 1993; Hoffer and Osmond, 1967; Huxley, 1954, 1956; Jordan, 1963; Katz, Waskow, and Olsson, 1968; Masters and Houston, 1966; Metzner, 1968; Stevens, 1987; Terrill, Savage, and Jackson, 1962; K. Thomas, 1971; Unger, 1963; and Watts, 1962.

gestion of moderate doses of LSD, mescaline, or psilocybin is what Havelock Ellis called a "saturnalia" or "orgy" of vision (Unger, 1963). Light and color become greatly intensified, objects seem plastic or alive, and fantastic imagery swirls through the visual field. Dramatic scenes of mythic proportions may unfold in a profuse series of EIDETIC IMAGES. Sensitivity to sounds, tastes, and odors may be increased, though less frequently, and perception through one sensory modality may in some subjects evoke images in another, a phenomenon called SYNESTHESIA. Any object whatsoever, no matter how trivial or unimportant under ordinary circumstances, may become endlessly fascinating and indefinably significant. Time, the medium of these experiences, is also radically transformed. Intervals only minutes long are so full and rich that they seem to last forever. As clock time dissolves into timelessness, eternity may for the first time become an astonishing reality. Space also undergoes transformation: areas and objects change in size and shape; two-dimensional pictures take on a third dimension while faces become two-dimensional; and objects may seem too close or to enlarge too quickly as the subject begins to approach them.

More remarkable, perhaps, is the dissolution of the self, sometimes called DEPERSONALIZATION or derealization. The body image undergoes distortion or alteration, tactile sensitivity is impaired, and the ego becomes progressively detached. The sense of self may fade altogether, so that one no longer seems to be the locus of what one is experiencing. One suddenly *is* the music that shortly before was coming from the other side of the room, and the pain that is ordinarily excruciatingly intimate no longer seems to be one's own.

The awesome experience of union with the surrounding world, the sudden illumination of existence, the "sacramental vision of reality," in Huxley's (1954) phrase—such experiences as these have led some observers to hail the psychedelic drugs as the open sesame of mystical experience. Timothy Leary (1964) asserts that between 40 and 90 percent of subjects ingesting psychedelic drugs can be expected to undergo intense mystical or revelatory experiences. Frequencies ranging from 24 to 83 percent are recorded elsewhere (Weil, Metzner, and Leary, 1965). The lower percentages are generally from studies involving patients in psychotherapy, medical personnel, and others of unknown religious orientation, as well as settings that are neutral. Higher percentages may be expected when the subjects are religious and the setting is at least supportive, if not designed to encourage a religious response.

Death and Rebirth: The religious experiences induced by these drugs are not limited to the benign and blissful moments of cosmic unity. Stanislav Grof (1972, 1975, 1985) describes agonizing encounters with loneliness, hopelessness, guilt, and death, followed by a dramatic death–rebirth struggle that may be accompanied by visions of explosive energy, orgiastic cruelties, and bloody torture and execution. The final stages may entail disgusting encounters with various forms of bodily refuse and putrefaction and then rejuvenation through a purifying fire. This series of exhausting struggles, which are regularly accompanied by dramatic physical symptoms, often include visions of sacrifice and wild ritual reminiscent of ancient religious practices. These visions suggest to Grof that the psychedelic drugs give indirect access to the archetypal layers of the unconscious as postulated by Jung.

Once subjects have "hit the cosmic bottom," they undergo "rebirth." Typical of this culminating stage are experiences of salvation, love, and forgiveness; of union with the cosmos; of enormously enhanced appreciation of natural beauty; of a desire to live simply and harmoniously with nature. Mary Barnard (1963), following others before her, hypothesizes that hallucinogenic plants lie at the origin of the world's myths and theology. Whether or not the ingestion of drugs was in fact the first occasion for profound religious experience, Huston Smith (1964) argues that drug-induced experiences cannot be distinguished phenomenologically from religious experiences occurring under other circumstances.

Accompanying these profound perceptual changes—and reflecting the suggestibility and distractibility of drugged subjects—are frequent and sometimes abrupt fluctuations of mood and affect, ranging from a euphoria bordering on feelings of omnipotence to paranoid suspiciousness, free-floating anxiety, and stark terror. It is chiefly because of the latter possibilities that specialists argue that no one should take these drugs without professional supervision. Persons under the influence of psychedelic drugs tend to be highly sensitive to those around them, giving particular weight to nonverbal cues. They are therefore easily hurt and prone to feel neglected; they are also likely to give a powerful response to the most subtle hints of apprehensiveness, hostility, or manipulation. Used with care, however, these drugs are thought by some to hold much promise in the therapy of neurosis, alcoholism, autism, criminality, and terminal illness. Although there is some evidence that accords with the enthusiastic claims made for the therapeutic application of the psychedelic drugs, more adequately designed studies are clearly needed (Abramson, 1967). Whatever therapeutic value may lie in these substances will eventually have to be weighed against possible psychological and physical side effects, including permanent damage to the nervous system (Henderson and Glass, 1994).

Explaining the Drug Effects: How these drugs affect the nervous system remains largely an enigma. The picture is complicated by the wide range of chemicals involved; by the largely unpredictable differences in response, from person to person and even from one day to the next in the same individual; and by the important role played by factors other than the kind and amount of drug taken. Too much of the research carried out on the hallucinogenic drugs, says F. C. Brown (1972, p. 51), has been designed to evaluate the effects on a single system (e.g., cerebral blood flow, oxygen or glucose utilization, or respiration quotient, on none of which does LSD have a significant effect) or the drug's therapeutic potential and adverse consequences. Relatively little is known about the fundamental mode of action of any of these agents. Theodore Barber (1970) doubts that any broad principle could be formulated today that would adequately cover the complex effects of the psychedelic drugs.

Research on LSD: Some findings about LSD, the most potent of these drugs, may illustrate how complex these matters are. Much of the research with psychedelic drugs has been carried out on laboratory animals, including rats, mice, cats, monkeys, and rabbits. Unfortunately, lack of correspondence in the various experimental designs makes it difficult to compare the wealth of data. Moreover, because enormous differences have been found among these species, it is hard to know which, if any, of the findings may be generalized to human beings. There does seem to be agreement that, in humans, less than 1 percent of the ingested dose of LSD—typically 100 micrograms, or 1/10,000 of a gram, an amount barely visible to the unaided eye—reaches the brain, a finding that demonstrates the extreme sensitivity of some of the brain's receptors. Some researchers claim that even this trace of LSD is gone from the brain by the time the drug begins to take effect, a fact suggesting that LSD "triggers" a relatively enduring reaction. Nicholas Giarman (1967), however, rejects this hypothesis, for it is based on the seven-minute half-life of the drug in mouse blood and brain, not the two- to three-hour half-life in human blood. Concentrations of LSD are found in the lungs, the kidneys, and especially the liver, and traces of it are detectable throughout the body water. (Several writers claim that LSD is blocked by the blood–brain barrier, but Giarman notes that the similarity in amount of LSD in blood and cerebrospinal fluid contradicts this assumption.)

Research with the squirrel monkey has shown that the concentration of LSD in the visual system, especially in the iris, is up to 18 times greater than that in the brain; physiological changes produced by the drug extend from the eyeball through the LATERAL GENICULATE to the OCCIPITAL CORTEX. LSD dilates the pupil, introducing more light and reducing the depth of focus; it partially paralyzes the accommodation mechanism in the ciliary muscle, which adjusts the shape of the lens; it raises the intraocular pressure, which may be the cause of the more vivid presence of phosphenes, the luminous patterns that normal individuals see when their eyes are closed; it alters the activity of the retina, albeit perhaps as the result of feedback from changes at higher levels; and it may enhance sensitivity to the structures within the eyeball itself (entoptic phenomena), which may be the source of the spirallike forms, gratings, tunnels, and so on that are characteristically perceived with psychedelic intoxication (Barber, 1970). Werner Koella (1970) cites evidence that LSD raises the visual THRESHOLD and impairs the transmission of electrical impulses across the SYNAPSES (the points of conjunction between neurons) of the thalamic relay in the lateral geniculate, at the same time that increased excitability appears in the cerebral cortical visual projection area. "One could indeed suggest," he says, "that, in the absence of (or with reduced) visual input to the cortex, the somewhat more excitable visual cortical networks produce their own imagery, independent of what 'meets the eye' " (p. 208).

Like some other psychedelic drugs, LSD is strikingly similar in chemical structure to SEROTONIN, a naturally occurring neurotransmitter that exerts an excitatory function at some brain synapses and an inhibitory one at others. Because of its resemblance to serotonin, LSD interacts in various ways with the brain serotonergic system, though the exact nature and sites of this influential interaction still remain elusive. Barry Jacobs (1984) thinks the primary action is postsynaptic, that is, on the target sites of serotonergic neurons rather than on these neurons themselves. As a general rule, says Jacobs, where serotonin exerts excitatory effects, LSD will act to block them; on the other hand, it leaves serotonin's inhibitory effects unchanged. LSD may itself serve an excitatory function in the serotonergic system. Whereas LSD also interacts with dopaminergic synapses, those acted on by the widely distributed neurotransmitter dopamine, Jacobs thinks this action is not critical for LSD's hallucinogenic effects.

The different regions of the brain vary in their susceptibility to LSD. Researchers have found that minute doses too small to produce behavioral changes can yet inhibit the spontaneous firing of neurons in the midbrain raphe, the cell bodies of which contain serotonin (Aghajanian, Sheard, and Foote, 1970). Although these small doses of LSD hardly affect the reticular formation, also located in the midbrain, other studies suggest that the drug produces electrical activity typical of reticular-activating-system arousal (Hoffer and Osmond, 1967). Dominick Purpura (1967, p. 182) has reviewed a number of studies that suggest LSD has a major effect on brain stem reticular regions. He concludes that this drug, through its synaptic action, is most likely to have its effect within the complex networks of the brain stem—which includes all the brain except the cerebellum and cerebrum. Purpura also cites evidence that LSD disrupts the learning of discriminative motor activity in animals through brief seizurelike episodes in the HIPPOCAMPUS and related structures in the limbic system, which, as we know, is associated with emotional response. This hippocampal activity continues for four to six days after the administration of LSD, or occasionally even longer.

In more recent research on the effects of psychedelic drugs, Aghajanian (1980) has singled out the LOCUS COERULEUS, a small but remarkable nucleus in the brain stem that is connected through its lengthy axons to between a third and a half of the rest of the brain's cells. When the neurons of the locus coeruleus begin to fire in response to emotion-arousing environmental stimulation, they secrete the neurotransmitter NOREPINEPHRINE, which then acts throughout the cerebral cortex to regulate emotional response. Struck by the similarity of rats' behavior when their locus coeruleus is electrically stimulated and when they are given LSD, Aghajanian set about to establish how LSD, among other psychedelic drugs, affects this tiny but influential brain structure.

Aghajanian discovered that LSD markedly increases the responsiveness of locus coeruleus cells to sensory stimulation of every kind, but without causing spontaneous firing in the absence of such stimulation. This effect is apparently achieved indirectly, through an intermediate set of neurons, for application of the drug directly to locus coeruleus neurons does not enhance their responsivity. Aghajanian's finding, Solomon Snyder (1986, p. 203) suggests, helps to explain LSD's subjective effects, including the accentuation of sensory perceptions and the phenomenon of synesthesia, if not also the sense of perceiving higher realities.

Can these provisional findings of research on LSD be broadly generalized to other psychedelic drugs? The fact that LSD, psilocybin, and mescaline have exhibited CROSS TOLERANCE with one another might be interpreted as evidence that they act similarly in the brain. Furthermore, George Aghajanian, Michael Sheard, and Warren Foote (1970) found that mescaline and DMT inhibited midbrain raphe units, just as did LSD, whereas a large variety of other substances, including amphetamine and chlorpromazine, were not inhibitory. Yet cross tolerance can be accounted for in other ways, and mescaline's action on raphe units proved to be far less potent and more selective than that of LSD or DMT. As Giarman (1967) points out, the psychedelic drugs have been grouped by their reported effects in human beings, not by their pharmacological or behavioral action in animals. Thus we must be cautious in generalizing from one of these drugs to any of the others.

CHRONIC BRAIN DISORDERS AND RELIGION

With the exception of constitution and temperament, we have until now been dealing with physiological conditions brought about voluntarily and usually for limited periods of time. Chronic brain disorders can also have implications for religious experience and practice, whether these disturbances be the direct result of brain tumor or disease or a by-product of some other bodily illness that "poisons" the brain through the circulatory system. Unfortunately, the specialists concerned with these disturbances rarely report that religiousness is modified by known changes in brain tissue. Nevertheless, some evidence from chronic disorders again illustrates the rootedness of religious experience in the billions of neurons that compose the human brain.

Graves' Disease

Some abnormal conditions may occasionally be accompanied by exceptional states of religiosity that are still too infrequent to be included among the defining symptoms of these disorders. Willy Hellpach (1907b), for example, discusses a case of *exophthalmic goiter,* also known as GRAVES' DISEASE, that was accompanied by religious eccentricity occasionally bordering on psychosis. Graves' disease is caused by overactivity of the thyroid gland, the secretions of which perform a range of vital functions, including the regulation of oxidation and metabolism, the production of glucose from amino acids, the maintenance of calcium level, and the control of mental and sexual development (Greisheimer and Wiedeman, 1972). Marked overproductivity of the thyroid (hyperthyroidism) is accompanied by an exceptionally high basal metabolism rate, profuse sweating, diarrhea with weight loss, rapid heart action (tachycardia), tremors, insomnia, and emotional excitability. There may also be serious mental disturbance: in one study of 17 patients with thyroid dysfunction, 13 showed profound disruption in psychological functioning (Whybrow, Prange, and Treadway, 1969).

Hellpach's patient, a young Catholic girl earlier undistinguished by her piety, had become obsessively religious following the onset of Graves' disease. She went to Mass every morning, without breakfast and after a cold bath. She also attended every High Mass and every devotion, and she went to confession more often than anyone else. Still unsatisfied, she would stop by the church several times daily simply to pray, typically for hours at a time. At home she was obsessed with religious matters, often claiming in great excitement to have had singularly remarkable experiences. She also reported that, in her dreams, the Blessed Virgin revealed information about the sexual lives of the priests in her congregation. The erotic content of these dreams became progressively crasser. Eventually she dreamed that she herself was the target of the priests' sexual demands, against which she would struggle throughout the night. Several months later, when her physical symptoms began to abate in response to medical treatment, her rigidly obsessive piety also started to relax, and the sexual elements in her dreams faded away.

Hellpach observes that Graves' disease bears no specific relationship to the development of religious delusions. Rather, this disease merely produces a high degree of excitement, which in this case, because of the spiritual nature of the patient's premorbid outlook, took the form of obsessive religiosity. Any other physical disorder that causes excessive emotionality and disturbance in cognitive functioning might likewise be the occasion for an exceptional form of piety—if the victim is religiously predisposed. It is no surprise, therefore, the morbid religiosity is common in mental hospitals.

Mental Retardation

Among the few other chronic disorders associated with a characteristic form of religiousness and linked to disturbances in the brain or the brain's chemical environment is mental retardation. The level of intellectual functioning of a given individual is determined by four factors: genetic endowment; adequacy of nutrition, especially before birth and during the first, critical years when the brain is developing; the occurrence of disease or injury that impairs brain function; and the amount of stimulation and education that the individual receives while growing up. Fortunately, it is not our task to decide the relative importance of each of these factors. What is significant here is that three out of four of them are physiological in nature. Singly or in combination, these four factors are responsible for mental retardation in 2 to 3 percent of the population of the United States and in a similar percentage in Europe (Farber, 1968).

The disabilities of the mentally retarded are inevitably reflected in their religious behavior and experience—unless, of course, the retardation is so severe that all religious conduct is precluded. The mentally retarded, observes Kurt Schneider (1928), are frequently able to memorize Bible verses, prayers, and songs; but there is likely to be little within them that corresponds to these imitative expressions. Those who are educable can be introduced to elements of the religious life, and they will frequently carry out religious rituals with enthusiasm. Yet the shallowness of their religious understanding and its lack of form and coherence make it clear that these religious expressions are heavily dependent on the environment. Because of this dependence, Schneider continues, the mentally retarded are usually prone to conversion in situations set up to encourage it. Moreover, irrelevant factors, such as friendliness or good food, can play a decisive role.

A Comparative Study of Slow Learners: The religious thinking of the mildly retarded has been systematically investigated by Rudolf Pohl (1968), who asked eighth- and ninth-year students, of 13 and 14 years of age, to write explanations for 39 words, most of which had religious connotations. Sixty-six of his subjects were normal students in a regular school; 95 were enrolled in a special school for slow learners and had a median IQ of 78. The responses to the stimulus words provided by the slow learners differed from the normal students' responses in several fundamental ways. The less capable subjects showed a stronger tendency to give nonreligious answers, even to obviously religious words (e.g., Holy Spirit, heaven, Easter). Furthermore, they tended to give literal rather than abstract meanings, for example, characterizing angels as transparent rather than imperceptible. They were more prone to ANTHROPOMORPHIZE, were less likely to doubt or criticize, and were inclined to itemize activities associated with a word rather than to abstract out relations or characteristics. Occasionally they limited their answers to the context in which the word might be used—"One often hears of that in church"—or to a sentence containing the word—"Our teacher tells us about salvation." Some resorted to "folk etymology," associating incorrect meanings to the phonetic elements in the word. Highly subjective or egocentric, sometimes even nonsensical, their answers revealed an incapacity to distinguish essential qualities from accidental and unimportant ones.

The religiousness of the mentally retarded has, in short, the characteristics of the young child's piety, a topic of enduring international interest (e.g., Bovet, 1951; Elkind, 1971; Goldman, 1964; Harms, 1944; Hyde, 1990; Meiler, 1967; Thun, 1959). As Stubblefield and Richard (1965) concluded in their brief study of 22 retarded adolescents and adults, the religious development of the mentally retarded parallels the growth of normal children. It differs by stopping short of normal adult levels, remaining more or less permanently in one of the stages ordinarily outgrown. A healthy nervous system is, of course, no guarantee of religious maturity, however it is conceived; but without normal neurological functioning, spiritual depths will not likely be attainable.

Epilepsy

Mental retardation, like exophthalamic goiter, conditions religiousness without actually serving as its origin. By contrast, another chronic brain disorder, EPILEPSY, has long been thought to have among its symptoms a peculiar type of religiosity. Until recently, most of the evidence was clinical and impressionistic. Yet specialists seem to disagree only on the causal links that lead to it, not on the regularity of its occurrence.

Epilepsy is not itself a disease entity with a single cause, but a disorder of the central nervous system in which consciousness is subject to episodic disturbances; during these episodes, convulsions of varying severity may occur. Electroencephalographic study has revealed the presence of abnormal patterns of electrical activity during these seizures. Although some individuals with epilepsy have other serious disturbances, as well, including psychosis, criminal tendencies, or impaired intelligence, it is now well known that many with this disorder show no additional symptoms and are able, on the contrary, to lead essentially normal, productive lives. Personality disturbance does appear to occur more frequently among persons with a history of epilepsy, or at least among some groups of them. However, the classic "epileptic personality," with its impulsivity, suspiciousness, explosive irritability, egocentrism, excessive religiosity, and viscosity of intellect and emotion, is clearly far from universal among persons with this disorder. With the development of a more satisfactory system for classifying the various forms of epilepsy—each of which may have multiple causes, including an hereditary factor—it may someday become possible to specify the likelihood and kinds of personality disturbance that may be expected with one or another type (Schmidt and Wilder, 1968; Tizard, 1962).

The Sacred Disease: Long thought to have marked some of the world's great spiritual leaders, epilepsy possesses a striking relationship to certain phases of religious experience:

> First, the epileptic attack, preceded by its momentary "aura" or warning, and manifesting itself in violent convulsions, with the loss of consciousness, immediately suggests that a spirit has entered the body. The fact that the attack nearly always does some physical injury to the patient encourages the belief that the spirit is malevolent. On the other hand, the attack may take, so to speak, a substitute form; instead of losing consciousness, the patient suffers what is called an "epileptic equivalent." In these conditions he is just as truly "out of his mind" as in the former; he becomes dissociated, is confused, and often undergoes a tremendous emotional upheaval. Sometimes he . . . passes through a deep, genuine, and profoundly impressive religious experience. This not only sets its mark upon the character of the patient, but may, if the people near by are religiously minded, convince them that a prophet is in truth before them. The association of epilepsy with certain of the more dramatic aspects of religion is therefore not in the least accidental (Murphy, 1928, p. 339).

To be sure, this relationship is far from simple. Although many shamans may be epileptic, there are at least some tribes that distinguish epilepsy from genuine possession (Eliade, 1951). T. K. Oesterreich ((1921) asserts that many instances of possession are produced through autosuggestion, not epilepsy, although epileptic seizures presumably serve as a model for this state. In any case, the association is strong enough to have won for epilepsy the epithet "the sacred disease."

Authorities continue to debate whether or not great religious figures such as Saint Paul or Muhammad were in fact epileptic (see Dewhurst and Beard, 1970; Freemon, 1976; Gruehn, 1960; Holmes, 1929; Landsborough, 1987; Moxon, 1922; Stern, 1957; Temkin, 1971; Weitbrecht, 1948). Whatever the truth may be, there is no doubt that some epileptics have remarkable religious experiences. Not uncommonly, for example, these individuals find themselves caught up into heaven during the epileptic trance. Kurt Schneider (1928) gives an account of a 37-year-old Protestant man who, during the twilight state, would discover himself in heaven, talking to Saint Peter. Told always that it was not yet his time, he still felt as though he were dying. One of James Howden's (1873) nonpsychotic patients, a gardener, was convinced for two days after an attack that he was either dying or in heaven, surrounded by trees, shrubs, and flowers of surpassing beauty. Later he interpreted the vision as sent by God for his conversion. Leuba (1925) cites the case of a priest who would feel himself suddenly transported from the street into heaven just before an epileptic attack; later, after the rapturous state had passed, he would find himself sitting on the curb, aware that he had had a seizure.

Some persons with epilepsy report that the ecstasies accompanying their attacks are the most blissful and overwhelming experiences of their lives. Others, however, are haunted by frightening visions or agonizing emotions. Schneider cites the case of a 21-year-old Protestant who thought before his seizures that the world was perishing. Another patient, a 20-year-old Catholic, found herself regularly visited by the Devil, who appeared to her as a small, brown figure eager to put her in a sack or claiming that her mother was dead. The religious, metaphysical, or mystical character of these states, according to William Boven (1919), reflects an unconscious attempt to come to terms with the mysterious, quasi-supernatural experiences of the epileptic process. This "periodic rendezvous with death" evokes images either mournful or beatific, and it occasionally becomes the nucleus of the basic psychological disorder.

Epileptic Piety: In spite of the common occurrence of religious hallucinations during epileptic attacks, they are not the key to epileptic religiosity according to some early psychologists of religion. Hellpach (1907a), who claims that the sensory delusions accompanying other forms of illness are no less frequently religious, asserts that epilepsy's relationship to religiousness lies rather in a simpleminded and hypocritical religiosity that is easily distinguished from the genuine variety. The piety of epileptic individuals is typically characterized, Hellpach writes, by a predisposition to engage in religious-sounding pomposity, to play a religious role, to become intoxicated with the formalities of religious practice. This interest in the formal and theatrical aspects of religion, Hellpach says, bears no relationship to the conduct, thought, and aspirations of profound piety, which engages the person as a whole. Epileptic religiosity, agrees Hans Weitbrecht (1948), is usually without ethical impulse or consequence, and is often interwoven with cruel and sadistic impulses, disgust, and sexual agitation. Howden (1873) cites the case of a 27-year-old epileptic man whom he describes as "one of the most sincerely pious, as well as one of the most dangerous homicidal, lunatics in Scotland" (p. 485).

In an early study designed to test whether or not persons with epilepsy are unusually religious, Fleck (1935) found that of the 100 epileptic men and women he treated, only 23 showed a religious orientation. Although Fleck observes the stiff formality and listlessness that earlier investigators had attributed to epileptic religiosity, he asserts that piety per se appeared no more frequently among his patients than among normal individuals, if it was not even less common. Religiosity, he concludes, is not an integral feature of epilepsy. When it occurs, it merely reflects the lower intellectual functioning and augmented credulity of the ill, as well as an effort to escape an unfortunate life situation by turning to the religious community (p. 129).

Research carried out some 40 years later with the invaluable aid of the EEG suggests that religiousness may be a concomitant not so much of epilepsy in general as of those cases in which the focus—the region from which the electrical irregularities originate—lies in one of the TEMPORAL LOBES. Kenneth Dewhurst and A. W. Beard (1970), for example, found that out of 69 patients with temporal lobe epilepsy, 26, or 37.7 percent, showed an interest in religion after the onset of their illness, whereas only 8 had earlier manifested such an interest. Six of the 26 had undergone conversion experiences. Norman Geschwind (1983), who until his death in 1984 was a distinguished Harvard neurologist and chief of the Harvard Neurological Unit at Beth Israel Hospital, reports being increasingly impressed during his many years of seeing patients with temporal lobe epilepsy by a particular configuration of personality traits. The most common of these features, he says, is increased concern with philosophical and religious issues; a tendency toward extensive and often emotionally tinged writing, frequently on philosophical or cosmic themes; diminution of sexual activity, if not also some alteration in sexual preference; and increased aggressiveness, though usually not to the point of criminality.

David Bear and Paul Fedio (1977) undertook a systematic study of these and 14 other personality characteristics thought to be associated with epilepsy, including humorlessness, dependency, excessive concern with detail, a sense that events have great personal significance and are under divine guidance, compulsive orderliness and ritualism, a tendency toward repetition, a deepening of all emotions, and tendencies toward guilt and hypermoralism. Using a 100-item questionnaire designed to measure the 18 traits, Bear and Fedio compared self-ratings and observer ratings for 27 epileptic patients known to have temporal lobe foci with the ratings for two control groups, one of normal adults and another of patients with neuromuscular disorders. Statistical analysis revealed significantly higher scores for the epileptic patients on all 18 of these variables; 11 of these differences, including differences in religiosity and philosophical interest, were significant at the .001 level.

Geschwind and his associates (1980) offer a case study illustrating these trends. The patient, a 36-year-old married housewife with two children, was referred to Geschwind's neurological unit because of striking and uncharacteristic changes in her behavior. She had taken to sunbathing in the nude on her front porch, and she reported sexual arousal during Mass, including occasions of orgasm while gazing at the crucifix; she interpreted these experiences as "sexual union with God." Exhibiting a pervasive euphoria, she began writing long letters about her sexual preoccupations and the possible moral consequences of her exhibitionism. Although her increased interest in discussing sexual matters suggests that she was an exception to the usual trend of hyposexuality, we do not know whether actual sexual activity had increased as well.

When she and her husband completed Bear and Fedio's Temporal Lobe Personality Inventory for her, a profile typical of patients with temporal lobe seizures was obtained, including high scores on religiosity, altered sexual interest, and deepened emotions. Although the patient had never experienced major or partial motor seizures, she did report frequent violent headaches that were accompanied by "glassy-eyed" staring; EEG study revealed irregularities suggestive of temporal lobe epilepsy. Subsequent medication produced self-insight as well as dramatic changes in behavior, including a return to more modest dress, fewer religious thoughts, and cessation of letter writing. Interestingly, the peculiar fusion of religious fervor and sexual feelings returned for the brief period when the patient neglected to take her prescribed drugs.

Some authorities on epilepsy have suggested that the putative characteristics of the epileptic personality may be caused by the periodic seizures as well as the anticonvulsant drugs, whereas others attribute them to the psychological stress caused by the illness. Geschwind (1983) argues against all such explanations, however, pointing out that these personality trends are apparent even in patients who have had no seizures or only minor ones, who have never received anticonvulsant medication, and who may not even be aware that they have epilepsy. Moreover, he says, patients suffering from such devastating neurological disorders as amyotrophic lateral sclerosis (Lou Gehrig's disease) do not show similar personality traits. He speculates instead that

> this syndrome is the result of the presence of an intermittent spike focus in the temporal lobe. The presence of the focus leads to an alteration in the responsiveness of the limbic system, so that the patient's emotional responses are altered in characteristic fashion, i.e., there is heightened emotional response to many stimuli, and diminished sexual responsiveness (p. S28).

Paradoxically, because intermittent stimulation can be more potent than very frequent stimulation, anticonvulsant treatment that reduces the frequency of abnormal discharges may actually exacerbate the behavioral changes mediated by the limbic system.

God in the Temporal Lobes: Can these conclusions be generalized beyond persons diagnosed as epileptic? Canadian neuropsychologist Michael Persinger has launched a research program based on the assumption that they can. Persinger (1983, 1987) hypothesizes that, for all individuals, the temporal lobes are the origin of religious or mystical experience. He postulates a continuum of temporal lobe lability, on which people can be arranged according to the frequency and severity of hypothetical "temporal lobe transients" (TLTs), momentary foci of electrical activity, or microseizures, which may occur without causing any observable motor activity or alteration in ongoing cognitive processes. People diagnosed as epileptic will lie at one extreme; in the middle will be individuals who report a variety of essentially normal experiences, including DÉJÀ VU, recurrent vivid dreams, feelings that certain stimuli or events are intensely meaningful, and moments of felt depersonalization. A subject's initial position along this continuum will be determined by a variety of predisposing factors, including heredity and age. Serving to precipitate TLT experiences, then, would be a multitude of culturally conditioned factors, including the various practices discussed earlier in this chapter as well as such life crises as severe illness, accidents, or the death of a loved one. The major neural consequence of the TLTs is thought to be an alteration of the synaptic organization of limbic regions, in a manner similar to but less intense than the changes noted in brains of people with known limbic seizures (see Sutula et al., 1989). These changes in neuronal structure, Persinger hypothesizes, will affect recall of the personal past, experience and beliefs in the present, and plans for the future.

To test these hypotheses, Persinger has developed a 140-item Personal Philosophy Inventory (PPI), which includes clusters of statements intended to measure a variety of "temporal lobe signs," that is, experiences, attitudes, and behavior that have been associated with epileptogenic foci in the temporal lobes. Although a direct test of Persinger's chief hypothesis—that religious or mystical experiences are correlated with concurrent microseizures in the temporal lobes—would be exceedingly difficult to arrange, the PPI allows the assessment of a variety of related propositions. Indeed, the PPI's internal structure itself lends his hypothesis some support. When Persinger and Katherine Makarec (1987) intercorrelated the PPI cluster scores for 414 university students, they found significant positive correlations between the Complex Partial Epileptic Signs (CPES) cluster, which refers to experiences frequently reported by patients with temporal lobe foci (e.g., visions or inexplicable odors) and the three clusters measuring paranormal or mystical experience, sense of presence (of another being), and heightened interest in writing.

More striking were the results of a study in which Makarec and Persinger (1985) correlated PPI scores with EEG measures. In this investigation, two groups of subjects who had earlier taken the PPI were exposed to exotic rhythmic sounds, ranging between seven and ten beats per second, and then to a diffuse light pulsating at a frequency of seven cycles per second; both stimuli were designed to elicit various signs of "epilepticity," including alpha driving. (Alpha waves, of 8 to 13 cycles per second, ordinarily appear in states of relaxation.) During these intervals, EEG measures were taken of temporal lobe activity and, as a control, of occipital lobe activity. Makarec and Persinger found that for both groups of subjects the number of EEG spikes in the temporal lobe correlated significantly with three clusters of the PPI: religious belief or dogma (.67, .76), paranormal or mystical experience (.50, .52), and sense of presence (.49, .50). SPIKE ACTIVITY in the occipital lobe, on the other hand, was unrelated to PPI scores. Measures of alpha activity in the temporal lobes, but not in the occipital lobes, have been found in normal populations to be related to PPI scores (Persinger, personal communication, October 30, 1989). Church attendance, by contrast, has proved to be unrelated to any of the measures.

Persinger, who is now experimenting with the induction of temporal lobe activity by means of a computer-modulated electromagnetic field (DeSano and Persinger, 1987), boldly concludes that "The God Experience is an artifact of transient changes in the temporal lobe" (Persinger, 1987, p. 137). It is, he suggests, an adaptive mechanism that compensates for the human capacity to anticipate future aversive stimuli, above all death. Although helping to preserve the sense of self, he remarks, the God Experience also fosters passivity, and it could easily prompt unreasoned decisions that lead to such results as nuclear disaster. An understanding of the origins of this experience, he argues, will help to reduce its destructive potential at the same time that it may enable us to appropriate and expand its powers to heal bodily ills.

In erecting a neural model of normal religious experience on the foundations of epilepsy research, Persinger is employing a tactic that has a long and distinguished history in psychology. Findings in the field of pathology have frequently added to our understanding of normal processes, especially those in the nervous system. Yet in this case it may be premature to speak of "the religiously inclined temporal lobe," as Tuzin (1984, p. 585) puts it, for two studies using Bear and Fedio's Temporal Lobe Personality Inventory raise important questions regarding the association of temporal lobe epilepsy with religious experience. In the first of these studies, only 4 of the 18 inventory scales significantly distinguished a group of 14 patients with temporal lobe epilepsy from a like-sized group with primary generalized seizures: sense of personal destiny, dependence, paranoia, and philosophical interest (Hermann and Riel, 1981). Thus in this study religion proved *not* to be significantly associated with a temporal lobe focus. In the second study, comparisons of five groups of subjects—three groups with neurobehavioral or psychiatric disorders, only one of which also had temporal lobe epilepsy, and two groups of nonpsychiatric controls—led to the conclusion that psychiatric disorder per se, apart from the additional factor of temporal lobe epilepsy, is sufficient to elevate scores on the Bear–Fedio inventory (Mungas, 1982).

The considerable interest that Bear and Fedio's findings have stimulated assures us that research in this area will continue. For now, it is important for us to realize that the case studies and group data that have been used to describe the epileptic personality in general and epileptic religiosity in particular have come largely from the files of patients under psychiatric care. The individual with epilepsy but no obvious psychiatric problems is largely unrepresented, and the Dostoevskys in the epileptic population are completely ignored. Thus we should be exceedingly cautious in generalizing from any of these studies.

CEREBRAL ASYMMETRY AND RELIGION

The tracing of religious experience to abnormal electrical activity in the temporal lobes implies that such experience is both exceptional and pathological. A rather different approach to localizing religious experience in the brain has been inspired by contemporary research on CEREBRAL LATERALIZATION, the tendency of the two hemispheres of the brain to develop certain specialized functions. From this perspective, religious practice and experience are interpreted as entirely normal capacities of the still-mysterious right hemisphere.

Our current understanding of cerebral lateralization, and particularly of right-hemispheric function, is a relatively recent achievement. The study of brain-injured patients, a major source of knowledge for early neuropsychologists, showed that linguistic functions are most often located in the left hemisphere,[5] where even a small lesion can drastically affect a patient's behavior. Given the importance of language, and the fact that comparable damage to the right hemisphere might produce no serious dysfunction at all, earlier researchers concluded that the left hemisphere is dominant, with the right one subserving only elementary sensory and motor functions. The right hemisphere seemed to be little more than a reserve organ that could play a compensatory role should the other hemisphere become disabled. Gradually, however, observations of the more subtle changes brought about by damage to the right hemisphere convinced specialists that it, too, plays a major role in human functioning (Springer and Deutsch, 1995).

An unprecedented opportunity to study differences in hemispheric functioning presented itself in the 1960s, when certain intractable cases of epilepsy were being treated by severing the thick bundles of nerve fibers that connect the two hemispheres. Although carried out to prevent seizures originating in one hemisphere from spreading to the other, this surgical procedure mysteriously reduced the incidence of seizures at the focal point as well. Because their major interhemispheric communication systems—the corpus callosum and the anterior commissure—had been sectioned, making it also impossible for perception, learning, and memory to be transferred from one hemisphere to the other, these patients allow researchers to assess one hemisphere's functions independently of the other.

To carry out such studies researchers have had to develop special apparatus. The earliest technique involved flashing one image in the right visual field, which communicates with the left cerebral hemisphere, and another image in the left

---

[5] Researchers have inferred from various forms of evidence that virtually all right-handed persons, who make up about 90 percent of the population, have left-hemispheric language dominance. Among left-handed persons, 60 to 70 percent also show left-hemispheric language dominance while the remaining 30 to 40 percent are divided about equally between right dominance and bilateral speech control. Such figures remain imprecise not only because of the difficulty of establishing cerebral dominance, but also because handedness is a *continuous* variable that can be only roughly estimated by writing hand or self-described handedness (Geschwind and Galaburda, 1987).

visual field, corresponding to the right hemisphere, thus making it possible to send separate messages to the two halves of the brain. Touch has also been used toward the same end. An object placed in one hand will be clearly identifiable only to the contralateral hemisphere, as long as the other hemisphere is not given clues either in its half of the visual field or through some distinctive sound. Only the left hemisphere can vocalize a response, however, for in the great majority of cases it alone possesses the speech centers. To communicate with the mute right hemisphere, the investigator must ask it to give its response manually—for example, by selecting through touch an object whose name has been flashed to the left visual field (Gazzaniga, 1967, 1970). To allow more sustained ocular scanning under the guidance of a single hemisphere, Eran Zaidel (1985) has more recently developed a contact lens arrangement that reduces the opportunity for one hemisphere to cue the other.

Lateral Specialization

The left hemisphere, these studies affirmed, is capable of speech and complex language usage, whereas the right one is silent, with a linguistic capacity that is roughly comparable to that of three- to six-year-old children (Zaidel, 1985). In contrast to the left hemisphere's verbal–symbolic superiority is the preeminence of the right hemisphere in visual–spatial matters. The left hand of a split-brain subject is able, for instance, to arrange blocks to match a pictured design or represent the three dimensions of a cube in a drawing, whereas the right hand cannot. Whether or not the nondominant hemisphere of a split brain has a separate consciousness is a matter of speculation, for it cannot express itself through speech or writing. In any case, what keeps the two halves working more or less in concert with each other is the commonality of sensory input as well as the functional harmony built into the brain stem—to which both hemispheres remain connected—and the networks of the spinal cord.

Although the surgery itself may be partially responsible for the effects discovered in split-brain patients, evidence is accumulating that the same lateral specialization is found in normal persons. In one study, for example, EEG-monitored subjects who were writing a letter showed more beta waves—a sign of active information processing—over the left hemisphere and more alpha waves over the "idling" right one. Subjects who were arranging blocks showed the reverse pattern (Ornstein, 1986). The fact of lateralization suggests to some researchers that the specialized functions of the two halves are to some degree antagonistic, so that a nonlateralized brain would be able to develop one set of these functions to a high degree but the other set little or not at all. With the assignment of these functions to separate hemispheres, their simultaneous development for complementary use is presumably optimized, increasing the likelihood of survival for both the individual and the species (Geschwind and Galaburda, 1987; J. Levy, 1974). Lateralization, then, apparently enhances the development of rational thinking, logical analysis, and linguistic and mathematical abilities in the left hemisphere, and visuospatial capacities, musical ability, emotional response, synthetic or holistic perception, and a range of other functions less well identified, in the right one.

The Bicameral Mind

Religion, we said, is thought by some scholars to have its wellsprings in the right hemisphere, and more particularly the right temporal lobe. The most elaborate development of this thesis is offered by research psychologist Julian Jaynes (1976;

Witelson and Kristofferson, 1986), who recasts the whole of humankind's religious history in terms of the interplay of neurophysiology and culture. On the basis of a remarkable synthesis of historical and contemporary evidence, Jaynes argues that self-reflective consciousness arose only as recently as 1000 B.C.E., and that before then, human beings possessed a BICAMERAL MIND whose hallucinatory right-hemispheric processes were experienced by the left hemisphere as helpful messages from the gods.

The bicameral mind itself was dependent on the emergence of language, the primary vehicle for these divine messages and the means by which they could be identified and brought under social control. Like the hallucinations today of the troubled schizophrenic, these commanding voices of the gods occurred at times of stress or crisis. In accord with the demonstrated organizing capacities of the right hemisphere,

> the function of the gods was chiefly the guiding and planning of action in novel situations. The gods size up problems and organize action according to an ongoing pattern or purpose, resulting in intricate bicameral civilizations, fitting all the disparate parts together, planting times, harvest times, the sorting out of commodities, all the vast putting together of things in a grand design, and the giving of the directions to the neurological man in his verbal analytical sanctuary in the left hemisphere (pp. 117–118).

An authoritarian hierarchy of priests was required to sort out the inevitably conflicting admonitory voices, says Jaynes, yielding a precarious THEOCRACY of human and hallucinated authority. The first gods, Jaynes surmises, were the kings whose elaborately buried remains date from at least 9000 B.C.E.; their tombs, furnished as though the kings were still alive and speaking to their subjects, were correspondingly the first god-houses or temples. Also testifying to the bicameral mind, Jaynes suggests, are the enormous numbers and varieties of human effigies that have been found, often with open mouths, exaggerated ears, or prominent, staring eyes. Long a mystery to archaeologists, these figurines may have served as MNEMONIC devices, "reminders to a nonconscious people who could not voluntarily retrieve admonitory experience" (p. 167) if they did not actually help to produce the bicameral voices by which their possessors were ordered about.

What finally led to the breakdown of the bicameral mind? Jaynes proposes seven different factors that undermined this mentality.

1. The advent of writing in the second millennium B.C.E., which, though allowing the gods' orders to be preserved in clay or stone, also robbed them of their commanding auditory immediacy and gave them a controllable location that people could choose to avoid.
2. The expansion of trade with other bicameral cultures inevitably brought the inherently fragile hierarchies of control into situations of conflict, especially if one of the cultures was in crisis and its people were thus hallucinating threatening voices.
3. The "immediate and precipitate cause" was the tremendous social chaos produced by geological catastrophes, mass migrations and invasions, and devastating wars, for which the gods—the overwhelmed right hemisphere—had no consistent or helpful solutions.
4. In the intermingling of peoples that followed, the discovery of often-bewildering differences may have led to the positing in others (but not at first in oneself) of an interior self responsible for these differences.

5. In attempting to meet the new challenges, the right hemisphere developed new capacities, summed up as narratization, for discerning patterns in the stories of past, god-ordained events and codifying them into epics for later recollection.
6. The discovery of the survival value of deceit, in relation to foreign invaders, fostered an "analog 'I' " that harbored inner, revengeful thoughts contradictory to outer, conciliatory behavior.
7. To these six cultural factors Jaynes adds a seventh, biological factor, the possibility of natural selection, which would favor those less bicameral individuals who could resist the increasingly dysfunctional commands of their inner gods.

Lamenting the loss of the intimate voice of divinity, as the temporal lobe areas of the right hemisphere became increasingly inhibited, the dawning conscious mind resorted to a variety of strategies for divining the will of the silent gods: recording omens or portentous sequences of events; casting lots, such as bones, sticks, or stones; reading the entrails of sacrificed animals, or incense smoke, oil or hot wax poured into water, and ashes; and spontaneous divination, which requires no particular medium. The everyday, matter-of-fact relation to divinity was replaced by divine worship and prayer, which first identified and exalted the god, now displaced by consciousness to the celestial realms, before petitioning for divine help or favors.

The shift from the bicameral mind to the subjective conscious one is evident, according to Jaynes, in various of the world's religious scriptures. In some the transition itself is unrecorded. The Hindu tradition, for instance, "hurtles from the bicameral VEDA[S] into the ultra subjective UPANISHADS," whereas the Chinese literature "jumps into subjectivity in the teaching of Confucius with little before it." Jaynes finds the fullest available account of "the birth pangs of our subjective consciousness" in the Hebrew Bible (Jaynes, 1976, pp. 313, 312). "This magnificent collection of history and harangue, of song, sermon, and story is in its grand overall contour the description of the loss of the bicameral mind, and its replacement by subjectivity over the first millennium B.C." (p. 294). To be sure, many of the books of the Hebrew Bible were subject to an extended process of compiling and editing that obscures their origins and age. Yet some of the books are relatively "pure" and datable, and in these Jaynes finds dramatic evidence for his thesis. The book of Amos, dating from the eighth century B.C.E., is "almost pure bicameral speech, heard by an illiterate desert herdsman and dictated to a scribe" (p. 296). The book of Ecclesiastes, written six centuries later, marks the other extreme: filled with reflective subjectivity, it hardly ever mentions God. The process itself by which the bicameral mind broke down and consciousness arose can be found narrated, Jaynes suggests, in the deceit-triggered events of the story of the Fall, in the third chapter of Genesis.

Although the teachings of Jesus would seem to be directed to the conscious rather than the bicameral mind, according to Jaynes, the history of the Christian tradition testifies to the perennial longing for bicameral absolutes. Humankind seems unable to relinquish its

> fascination with some human type of relationship to a greater and wholly other, some *mysterium tremendum* with powers and intelligences beyond all left hemispheric categories, something necessarily indefinite and unclear, to be approached and felt in awe and wonder and almost speechless worship, rather than in clear conception, something that for modern religious people communicates in truths of feeling, rather than in

what can be verbalized by the left hemisphere, and so what in our time can be more truly felt when least named, a patterning of self and numinous other from which, in times of our darkest distress, *none* of us can escape—even as the infinitely milder distress of decision-making brought out that relationship three millennia ago. (p. 318).

What has survived in all of us, Jaynes hypothesizes, is a vestigial neurological structure or pattern of relations that underlies what he calls the *general bicameral paradigm.* This PARADIGM has four aspects: (1) a *belief system,* or "collective cognitive imperative," that defines the phenomenon and specifies the roles to be enacted; (2) a *ritualized induction,* which through the focusing of attention serves to narrow consciousness; (3) the *trance* itself, characterized by greatly diminished consciousness and sense of self and resulting in the assumption of a group-sanctioned role; and (4) the *archaic authorization* for the trance, usually derived from a god but sometimes from an authority identified by the belief system as responsible for the course of events. This paradigm, together with its neurological substratum, still makes possible today a wide range of phenomena, including oracles such as the Tibetan priest, the possession states fostered by Umbanda (an Afro-Brazilian religious tradition popular in Brazil), speaking in tongues, as well as hypnosis. The sheer ineffability of such experiences has suggested to other researchers, too, that the right hemisphere must play a dominant role (Davidson, 1976; Lex, 1979).

Jaynes's provocative thesis possesses considerable explanatory power, especially in accounting for the intimate familiarity with the voice and will of God that was apparently common long ago but that today is experienced only under most exceptional circumstances. Moreover, experimental evidence supports his localization of the sources of this experience in the right temporal lobe. Jaynes cites the famous studies of neurosurgeon Wilder Penfield (1975), whose patients frequently reported hearing hazy voices coming from some strange and unknown place when he stimulated their right temporal lobes with a mild electric current. In another remarkable study, in which patients about to undergo temporal LOBECTOMY were given LSD, removal of the right temporal lobe diminished the drug's effects whereas excision of the left one did not (Serafetinides, 1965). On the other hand, the hypothesis put forward by some researchers that meditation serves either to inhibit the cognitive functions of the left hemisphere or to facilitate right-hemispheric abilities is supported at most only in the early stages of meditation, depending in part on the type of practice engaged in. In later, more advanced stages, it appears that functions in both hemispheres are either automatized or inhibited (Earle, 1981). Persinger is now exploring the mechanisms and implications of these various findings (Persinger, 1993; Persinger, et al., 1994).

A Mystic's Stroke of Misfortune: The case of the eighteenth-century Swedish scientist–mystic Emanuel Swedenborg (1688–1772) offers a unique opportunity to test some of these emerging principles. For much of his life, Swedenborg was an observer, systematizer, and theoretician of the natural world, with a bent toward the sciences, including astronomy, physics, chemistry, physiology, and psychology. In his middle fifties, however, he became subject to angelic voices and remarkable dreams and visions, the substance of which was frequently recorded through automatic handwriting that had a style of its own. He reportedly demonstrated an astounding capacity of CLAIRVOYANCE and claimed to be able to communicate with the souls of the dead (Toksvig, 1948).

About three months before he died, Swedenborg suffered an apoplectic stroke that for three weeks left him in a "trance" or "lethargic state," as contemporary observers described it. As he "came to himself again," he found his body paralyzed

Emanuel Swedenborg (1688–1772), the Swedish scientist and mystic whose visions and voices illustrate the bicameral mind.

on one side and his speech somewhat indistinct; worst by far, his spiritual sight of nearly 30 years was entirely gone. For several days, "He was under the greatest tribulation of mind on that account, calling out, 'O my God! hast thou then at last abandoned thy servant?' " The voices, however, did finally return a few weeks before he died (Tafel, 1877, pp. 545–576).

Although the accounts of Swedenborg's stroke and loss of heavenly voices are frustratingly brief, the rarity of such a combination of events invites speculation about the brain processes that were involved. The big question, it would seem, is which side of his body was paralyzed. If it was the left one, then we could infer that his spiritual voices came from the right hemisphere, in accord with Jaynes's thesis. Unfortunately, his contemporaries failed to anticipate our need for such information, but his handwriting and his reported lament over his useless paralyzed arm together suggest—unfortunately for this thesis—that he was paralyzed on the right side (Robert H. Kirven, personal communication, July 13, 1979).

On the other hand, however, Swedenborg had a lifelong tendency to stammer (Tafel, 1877), a condition that is associated with "nonrighthandedness"—that is, handedness not strongly biased to the right—and thus also with anomalous lateralization (Geschwind and Galaburda, 1987). Hence even if we knew which hand he used in writing, we could not confidently infer his cerebral organization. More telling, then, is the apparent fact that the cerebral accident that deprived him of his spirit voices did not rob him of his own, allowing us to infer after all that these messages originated in his "nondominant" hemisphere. Presumably Swedenborg was neurologically disposed toward such "wakeful ecstacies," which he could deliberately induce by drastically inhibiting his breathing, a technique he had already employed in early childhood while saying his morning and evening prayers. He also reported that the beating of his heart would become "gentler and softer" at such times, to the point that respiration and heartbeat would coincide. Apparently without realizing it, Swedenborg was employing breath control and listening to the heart, techniques of ancient yogic practice (Toksvig, 1948, pp. 218–219).

Swedenborg, we might speculate, had learned how to restore the bicameral mind, much as other mystics apparently have. According to Roger Bastide (1931), most mystics have felt "the impression of a double personality . . . , from St. Teresa who called herself 'divided' to St. John of the Cross who 'declared that within him were two distinct beings' " (p. 233). Curiously enough, C. G. Jung, too, had always thought of himself as two persons, whom he characterized in terms that are highly reminiscent of the descriptions of right and left hemispheric functions. Moreover, the model of the human psyche that he developed is strikingly compatible with lateralization research (Stevens, 1982).

To persons dominated by the rationality of the left half of the brain, as educated persons in the West tend to be, the experiences of Swedenborg and Jung will likely evoke incredulity, or even disdain. Similarly, common religious practices such as the vow of silence, the contemplation of illogical mysteries, and the frenetic participation in ritual song and dance will be taken by such persons as evidence of the irrationality or even madness that underlies civilization's thin veneer. To those with highly developed right-hemispheric functions, however, these actions are valuable means for discovering truths that are far too large for the rationalist's categories. Growing recognition by the scientific world that the nonrational has essentially as large a place in the anatomy and physiology of the brain as does the rational may gradually reduce the tension between these two modes of functioning. A more harmonious and widespread development of these modes may eventually help to minimize the unfortunate and sometimes destructive extravagances that exclusive devotion to one or the other of them can bring.

A CARTOGRAPHY OF ECSTATIC AND MEDITATIVE STATES

Can the disparate phenomena that we have surveyed from a neuropsychological perspective be brought together within a common framework? Roland Fischer (1969, 1971, 1978, 1986), for one, thinks so. He suggests that ecstatic and meditative states can be placed on a circular continuum representing varying states of subcortical arousal (see Figure 3.1). Movement in one direction on the continuum reflects ERGOTROPIC AROUSAL, which is marked by increased activity of the sympathetic nervous system (which mobilizes the body during stress), greater frequency of

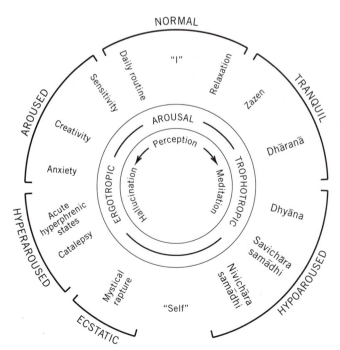

Figure 3.1. Fischer's cartography, which schematizes the two alternate ways to the attainment of the Self. (See the Glossary for definitions of terms.)

saccadic or rapid scanning movements of the eyes, and diffuse cortical excitation. The other direction indicates TROPHOTROPIC AROUSAL, which is hypoarousal or reduced stimulation, and consists of increased parasympathetic discharges, decreased saccadic frequency, reduced cortical activity, and muscular relaxation. According to Fischer, increased ergotropic arousal is characteristic of creative, psychotic, and ecstatic states, whereas trophotropic arousal occurs in conjunction with various forms of meditation, including *zazen* and yoga.

Two Ways to the Self

Although the two ends of this continuum represent opposing physiological processes, they bring about much the same result, as Fischer's circular cartography implies. The farther the person moves in either direction from the normal state of perception, the greater the transformation of the objective time–space world familiar to the experiencing "I." Fischer represents these changes in time and space largely through a description of the ergotropic states produced by psychedelic drugs; analogous changes presumably occur with trophotropic arousal. In either case, the end state is the same: the "Self" that in its experience of oneness with the universe sees and knows beyond the limitations of the physical time–space world.

The circular diagram takes into account another phenomenon, "trophotropic rebound" at the peak of ergotropic arousal, in which the individual passes from ecstasy into SAMĀDHI, the last stage in the yogic progression. Fischer's description of this reaction as a "physiological protective mechanism" is immediately suggestive of Pavlov's transmarginal inhibition, which may be the same thing. Apparently, rebound in the other direction, from *samādhi* to ecstasy, is also possible, according to findings reported by Ernst Gellhorn and William Kiely (1972). They cite startling changes in heart rate and EEG when long-experienced yogis achieve the ecstatic state. James Corby and his associates (1978) also report increased autonomic activation during meditation for experienced yoga meditators.

The processes with which we are concerned are more complicated than Fischer's diagram may immediately suggest. First, as Fischer himself points out, these states do not form a continuum in the sense that a person must pass successively through them to attain the ecstatic "Self." The schizophrenic is not necessarily a candidate for mystical ecstasy, nor is the mystic necessarily a schizophrenic, although both may be subject to "hallucinations." Furthermore, it should not be assumed that the reciprocal ergotropic and trophotropic reactions bear a precisely inverse relationship to each other, so that an increase in one is automatically accompanied by a decrease in the other. The fact that the marked trophotropic arousal that occurs during meditation does not lead to sleep suggests to Gellhorn and Kiely that it is simultaneously counteracted by a partial activation of the ergotropic system (for which they cite evidence that we cannot consider here). They state that the yogi's effort to keep the ergotropic–trophotropic balance to the trophotropic side excites the ergotropic system without increasing muscle tone, until with sufficient training it culminates in the experience of ecstasy.

Higher-Level Interpretation

The effort to account for ecstatic and meditative states in terms of the ergotropic–trophotropic balance is considered unsatisfactory by Gary Mills and Ken Campbell (1974), who argue that such a model cannot explain important differences in the many forms of meditation. Yet it is possible, as Fischer (1971) suggests, that some of these differences represent *cortical interpretations* of subcortical processes. Generalized subcortical arousal, either ergotropic or trophotropic, produces diffuse emotional states that can be variously interpreted at the cortical level. Indeed, advocates of ATTRIBUTION THEORY have argued that the cognitive processes of attaching a label or attributing a cause, in accordance with the immediate context or a person's enduring beliefs, is essential for the transformation of undifferentiated emotional states into well-defined ones—in this case, religious ones (Bowker, 1973; Leys, 1932; Proudfoot and Shaver, 1975; Schachter and Singer, 1962; Spilka, Shaver, and Kirkpatrick, 1985). Fischer (1971) adds that the "freedom" to interpret subcortical activity diminishes as this activity increases, until it finally disappears altogether in the "Self"-state of ecstasy and *samādhi*, which signals the indistinguishable integration of cortical and subcortical activity.

If the theory of ergotropic–trophotropic balance, in combination with attribution theory, cannot account for all the phenomena we have studied here, it surely embraces aspects of many of them, including respiratory and postural exercises, stimulus reduction, blood sugar manipulation, hyperventilation, the use of drugs, Graves' disease, the induction of unpleasant or painful emotions, and individual differences such as those that Pavlov and Sargant explored (Gellhorn and Loofbourrow, 1963). Fischer (1972) speculates further than the closer one approximates to the "Self"—that is, the greater the arousal of either system—the greater the proportion of time one will spend in the right, nonverbal cerebral hemisphere. The rational "I," in other words, consists of propositional thinking specific to the left hemisphere, whereas the ecstatic "Self" is a reflection of the intuitive activity of the right hemisphere. As evidence of this hemispheric shift, Fischer notes that the syntactic structure of language becomes increasingly simplified under rising levels of drug-induced arousal. The loss of freedom to interpret subcortical activity at high arousal levels, he says, may alternatively be viewed as an emancipation from the confining rationality of the left-hemispheric "I." Only at moderate levels of arousal can the "Self" of exalted states and the interpreting "I" come into communication, through the subjective symbols of dreams and hallucinations. It is these symbols, Fischer (1971) asserts, that are the source of art, religion, literature, and science.

The usefulness of Fischer's schema is suggested by the work of anthropologist Barbara Lex (1979), who employs the same model to explain the adaptive function of religious ritual, particularly of the type that conduces to trance states. The purposes of such ritual, she asserts, is to restore the emotional equilibrium among group members who have suffered an imbalance between trophotropic and ergotropic arousal:

> Rituals properly executed promote a feeling of well-being and relief, not only because prolonged or intense stresses are alleviated, but also because the driving techniques employed in rituals are designed to sensitize or "tune" the nervous system and thereby lessen inhibition of the right hemisphere and permit temporary right-hemisphere dominance, as well as mixed trophotropic-ergotropic excitation, to achieve synchronization of cortical rhythms in both hemispheres and evoke trophotropic rebound (pp. 144–145).

Lex suggests that a quality of redundancy in a ritual's driving techniques accommodates the individual differences in trophotropic–ergotropic balance that result from genetic inheritance and life experience.

Lex acknowledges the preliminary character of her analysis and underscores the need for further research on the neurophysiological bases of ritual trance.

Given the accelerating pace of research in neuropsychology and the number of recent discoveries, we may be confident that significant additional evidence bearing not only on ritual but also on most of the other topics treated in this chapter will soon be forthcoming. No other approach in the psychology of religion promises as revolutionary a future as the biological one.

EVALUATION OF THE BIOLOGICAL APPROACH

Neuropsychologists possess at least one advantage over every other explanatory approach represented in this book: no one challenges the reality of the fundamental processes to which they appeal. Whereas the unconscious, for example, will likely always remain a disputable hypothetical construct, nobody doubts the existence and crucial importance of the brain. Moreover, a neuropsychological approach seems particularly appropriate when we are dealing with practices that radically affect bodily states. At issue, then, is not whether neurophysiology plays a role in religious experiences—for presumably all experience is represented somewhere in the brain—but whether referral to brain and other bodily processes is the most appropriate way by which to comprehend them. Important, too, is the question of what we may legitimately deduce about the truth claims of religious experience from knowledge of its biological correlates.

ON THE RELATIVE VALUE OF THE BIOLOGICAL PERSPECTIVE

Let us begin with the question of when a physiological explanation is informative in the psychology of religion. It would be well to acknowledge at the outset that, impressive though the gains in neuroscience have been in recent decades, our understanding of brain processes is still exceedingly limited. Thus even if we agree that a neuropsychological explanation is appropriate for some particular phenomenon, we will be quickly forced into the realm of speculation, as much of this chapter demonstrates. Given the many billions of neurons that make up the brain and their relative inaccessibility in normal, living human beings, this situation is not likely to change dramatically in the foreseeable future.

A glance back over the content of this chapter reminds us that socially deviant expressions of piety, or sudden shifts to extreme states such as trance or physical collapse, most often call forth speculation about biological factors. When individuals show gradually acquired behavior that is normative for their cultural group, ordinary principles of learning seem to suffice. Other explanatory perspectives, however, are also interested in exceptional states, and it may not be easy to decide which explanatory principles are most relevant in any particular case. We may illustrate this point with John Calvin. Whereas Kretschmer focuses exclusively on the contributions of Calvin's leptosomic physique to his anxious and humorless disposition, we could equally well argue that his unhappy childhood played the major role. Calvin's mother died when he was four or five years old, and his father soon remarried; shortly thereafter his father sent him, the youngest of four children, to live with a neighboring family. Bouwsma (1988) suggests that his mother's death and the subsequent eviction from the family household instilled in Calvin "a sense of homelessness" that was deepened in adulthood by exile from his motherland, France, over which he grieved for the rest of his life (p. 11). We might also postulate a causal connection between the paternal rejection that Calvin suffered as a child and his later, wrathful image of God. Luther's disposition might similarly be reexamined in terms of early parental relationships, as we will see in Chapter 9. By ignoring factors other than physique, Kretschmer has understandably exaggerated the role of biological disposition in shaping the character of his subjects, including Luther and Calvin. Although it is reasonable to infer that constitution played some part in their lives, perhaps in combination with other bodily conditions,[6] it is impossible to say how large its contribution was.

The place of biological factors is even more indeterminate in ordinary piety, for which, as James implies, basic principles of habit formation may be all that are needed to account for it. Occasional efforts have been made, however, to introduce neuropsychological principles here as well. It has been proposed, for example, that direction of hemispheric dominance may distinguish different religious groups. Colin Martindale (1978) hypothesizes in particular that Jewish subjects, who tend to score higher on the verbal subtests of the Wechsler intelligence tests than on the performance subtests, have a corresponding tendency toward left-hemispheric dominance. Intelligence test scores suggest a similar if less marked trend for Protestants and a tendency toward hemispheric balance among Catholics. The same ordering in terms of left-hemispheric dominance is suggested by the finding with the Omnibus Personality Inventory that Jewish students tend to be the most intellectually disposed and Catholic students the least, with the Protestants falling in between (Heist and Yonge, 1968). If these intellectual differences do reflect differential development of left-hemispheric functions, they most likely result from differences in acculturation, as Martindale suggests. But then it may be more economical to explain them simply in terms of learning principles, unless there are other kinds of evidence suggesting systematic differences in lateralization. Yet even in fairly well-defined groups, such differences may be difficult to find. In one study employing a large battery of neuropsychological tests, no evidence of differences in lateralization was found when comparing conservative Christians with non-Christians (Dodrill, 1976).

It is well to be reminded that physiological processes are silently at work behind all religious experience and conduct. Yet apart from research on meditation, which we examine in greater detail in Chapter 5, systematic empirical evidence of biological correlates is exceedingly limited. One enormous problem, as we have already suggested, is finding adequate means by which to observe the brain's intricate and still largely mysterious processes without interfering with them. Another, to be explored in Chapter 6, is the assessment of religiosity, including the exceptional states that most invite biological speculation. Probably no reader needs convincing that neurophysiology has a major hand in producing the more dramatic phenomena we have surveyed, but beyond such a generalization, we are hard pressed to say exactly what is happening in the brain at such times.

---

[6] Haile (1980) cites evidence that Luther suffered from uremic poisoning during his last nine years, a result of chronic problems with kidney stones and urine retention. Among the effects of uremic poisoning are irritability, intermittent mental confusion, and difficulties in concentration. Perhaps on this basis we can better understand Luther's regrettable anti-Semitic writings, particularly his rambling and vicious *Against the Jews and Their Lies* (1542). At the time of its writing, the "great Reformer had weakened, his mind was impaired, depths of the personality were revealed painful to contemplate." Haile suggests that these depths had long been there; the brain damage had "only weakened accustomed repressive mechanisms" (p. 292).

ON THE BROADER IMPLICATIONS OF A PHYSIOLOGY OF RELIGION

The ease with which broad generalizations have been made in this area has long troubled psychologists of religion in Germany. Some stand opposed to any effort to account for religious experience in physiological terms. Such an approach, avers Hermann Faber (1913, p. 114), is "useless, unfounded, and extraordinarily dangerous." Citing psychologist Theodor Lipps as his authority, Faber argues that psychology must employ its own terminology, derived from conscious experience, rather than concepts borrowed from the physical or biological sciences. The task of bringing together the findings of biology and psychology, adds Emil Pfennigsdorf (1927), is not the psychologist's, but falls rather to the metaphysician and the philosopher of nature. Werner Gruehn's (1960, p. 540) position is much the same: physiological explanations are not only false, because the inexhaustible richness of the spiritual life cannot be traced to parallel processes in the body, but also dangerously *misleading*, for such explanations can desensitize the uncritical reader to the complex realities of human experience.

Reductionism: Hostile and Friendly

The danger Gruehn warns us against is, in a word, reductionism. Beyond indiscriminately sweeping together the diverse manifestations of religious faith and tracing them to some common set of processes in the nervous system, some investigators conclude that their apparent success demonstrates that religious faith is unfounded. Theodore Flournoy (1903a) had thought to foreclose that conclusion in delineating his two basic principles. Although he urges psychologists of religion to seek out the physiological conditions of religious experience, he also disallows any conclusions regarding the reality of the religious object. James Leuba (1925) disagrees, however, arguing that any religious faith that finds its justification in particular forms of inner experience is called into question when we are able to identify the psychophysiological causes of such experience. A comparative study of trance states produced by drugs and other physical means, he says, leads to the conclusion that these states—"with their impression of unlimited power and of passivity, their excitement and quietude, their hallucinations and exclusion of the world of sense, their absolute certitude and moments of doubt, their harmony and ineffability"— reveal not a god but "the lawful workings of our psychophysiological organisms" (p. 316). Persinger (1987) represents the same position today, though without Leuba's scholarly elaborations.

We could conclude otherwise, however. Just as the visual and auditory systems are set up to represent the physical world, though remaining subject to widely varying individual differences and artificial stimulation, so we could argue that the nervous system is variably attuned to the spiritual realm. Such is the view of Swedenborg (1749), whose remarkable speculations about the brain anticipated a number of later discoveries (Toksvig, 1948). He declares that "The intellectual things of spirits and angels enter by influx into the left side of the head, or brain, whereas what relates to their will enters into the right. . . . But when evil spirits enter, their influx is like an inundation, into the left side of the brain with their phantasies and direful persuasions, and into the right with their lusts" (1749, p. 221).

Although researchers today are rather less inclined to speak of angels and spirits, some clearly view the discovery of intuitive or nonrational functions in the right hemisphere as broadly supportive of at least some traditional religious ideas.

Similarly, neurophysiological correlates of meditation and related states are offered as evidence that these phenomena are in some palpable sense genuine. Although such attitudes would seem to be friendly toward religion, they are still in their own way reductionistic. Indologist Fritz Staal (1975) makes this point in his critique of research on meditation that emphasizes its calming effect. "The Buddha sought the causes of suffering, and its elimination, not a feeling of relaxation. The physiological studies do not throw any light on such larger issues and are not in a position to provide even a first understanding of the phenomena they describe." The bodily changes accompanying meditation, he adds, "are probably side effects of little consequence" (p. 110).

Staal's argument is reminiscent of James's (1902) criticism of medical materialism: religious states may indeed have physiological concomitants, but knowledge of their correlates tells us nothing about their spiritual significance. James was arguing against those who, by tracing physiological origins, sought to discredit religious experience. Today, interestingly, the motives are often reversed: by postulating that half the brain is analogical in character, researchers have given a renewed legitimacy to nonrational phenomena. If the neurophysiologists accomplish nothing more, the recovery of the other half of ourselves is a noteworthy achievement. Yet the final significance of either half, James would remind us, lies far beyond the scientist's instruments.

The Mind-Body Problem

However much progress scientists make in figuring out how the brain works, we will still be left with the seemingly insoluble mystery of how brain and mind are connected. Implicit in much of the speculation of this chapter is the materialistic theory held by most neuroscientists today: conscious experience is merely a by-product of neural activity, with no reciprocal effect of its own. According to the eminent neurobiologist John Eccles, however, this theory accounts for neither the emergence of consciousness out of material substance nor its evolutionary development with the increasing complexity of the brain. According to the principles of biological evolution, Eccles points out, "Mental states and consciousness could have evolved and developed *only if they were causally effective* in bringing about changes in neural happenings in the brain with the consequent changes in behavior" (Eccles and Robinson, 1984, p. 37). Even more problematic, he says, is the illogic of postulating a thoroughgoing physicalistic determinism that reduces cognitive activity—including the theorist's—to self-deception. Eccles opts instead for the dualist-interactionist theory, which posits mind and brain as distinct and independent entities that somehow interact.

Penfield (1975) arrived at the same conclusion after years of proceeding on the monistic assumption that mind is the product of the physical brain. He observed that neither epileptic discharge nor direct electrical stimulation of the brain ever activated the mind. Elaborate recollections and other conscious experiences did occur at such times, but they were either automatic, as in epileptic seizures, or felt to be caused by the surgeon's probes. Given what we know about brain activity, says Penfield, "It is simpler (and far easier to be logical) if one adopts the hypothesis that our being does consist of two fundamental elements," the mind and the brain, each with its own form of energy. The mind is conceived as a "semi-independent element," which is switched on by the "highest brain-mechanism" during wakefulness, to take over control, and then is switched off again during sleep (pp. 80–82). Penfield anticipates that the nature of the mind's energy will someday be discovered. But "Whether there is such a thing as communication between man and God and whether energy can come to the mind of a man from an outside source after his death is for each individual to decide for himself. Science has no such answers" (p. 115).

The dualistic view accords well with certain religious doctrines, such as that of a soul that survives bodily death, but from a scientific perspective it, too, is seriously problematical. János Szentágothai (1984), a distinguished Hungarian neurobiologist and professed Christian, holds out for "an acceptable third way between the essentially reductionist and the dualist interpretations" (p. 9), a natural scientific explanation of the reciprocal relation between ordinary neural functions and "the higher, more global events encompassed by the term 'mind' " (p. 3). Citing evidence that clusters of transplanted neurons have the capacity to organize themselves into systems capable of spontaneous activity, Szentágothai proposes accounting for self-awareness and other higher mental activities in terms of modules of neurons open to energy and information flow from the outside and "connected with one another in a way that allows for reentrance of [internally generated] patterns in an infinite number and variety of loops" (p. 9). Szentágothai acknowledges that, given the current state of knowledge in the neurosciences, others may think it unrealistic to hope for a theory that adequately accounts for higher mental activities.

Most researchers steer clear of the hoary problem of the MIND-BODY RELATION, either limiting themselves to the electrical and chemical activities of the brain or exploring consciousness apart from any reference to neurological processes. That the two factors, conscious mind and physical body, are intimately related is obvious from the material reviewed in this chapter. Although it is easy to see that bodily states profoundly affect the experience and activity we call mind, evidence of various kinds indicates that the relation is reciprocal. Again and again we see that mental activity—whether in the form of intention, expectation, or interpretation—not only affects the experienced outcome of various bodily changes but also yields observable differences in brain activity itself. Even though this unsolved and perhaps insoluble problem will necessarily limit what a physiological psychology of religion can accomplish, the study of the intersection of body and mind in the religious context will surely contribute to whatever solution may lie on the distant horizon.

4

BEHAVIORAL AND COMPARATIVE THEORIES OF RELIGION

*O*rdinary piety, we concluded in Chapter 3, does not lend itself to physiological explanation but may more easily be accounted for in terms of basic learning principles. Others have suggested that certain aspects of religion may reflect a cross-species genetic predisposition, perhaps selected through an evolutionary process. In this chapter we explore these possibilities through a study of two other explanatory approaches within scientific psychology, BEHAVIOR THEORY and COMPARATIVE PSYCHOLOGY, both of which have developed independently of physiological psychology.

Behavior theory and comparative psychology have in common the view that the behavior of human beings can be illuminated through the study of animals. Proponents of this view do not agree, however, on which way to read the continuum between human beings and nonhuman species. Behavior theorists have traditionally denied any role to higher cognitive processes, preferring to account for human behavior by applying mechanistic principles derived from the study of laboratory animals. Humankind is thus seen to be much like the "lower" species. Comparativists, on the other hand, and especially ETHOLOGISTS, who think it crucial to observe animals in their natural habitat, have suggested that other species are more capable of conceptual and symbolic thinking than was earlier thought. Thus animals are seen to possess certain "higher" human qualities, albeit in distinctly limited measure (Hilgard, 1987).

With the notable exception of the social learning theorists, whose ideas we will also consider in this chapter, behavior theorists are in general extreme environmentalists, for they assume that behavior is determined chiefly by stimulus events in the outer world. This stance is in large part a pragmatic one, for genes are much less easily modified than the environment and our knowledge of their role is still imprecise. Yet some behaviorists are also convinced that the role of heredity in determining behavior has been greatly exaggerated. In contrast, the comparativists are more inclined to attribute particular patterns of behavior to inborn genetic predispositions. This view was particularly encouraged by the cross-species studies of the European ethologists.

Globally applied to religion by unsympathetic psychologists, behavior theory reduces human piety to analogues of laboratory animal behavior. Lawrence Casler (1968) illustrates such an approach:

> One's religious convictions may likewise be regarded as nothing more than a complex set of learned responses to a complex set of stimuli. The objection that man is born with a knowledge of and reverence for God receives its strongest rebuttal from the practices of the major religions, whose emphasis on . . . religious instruction seems at odds with such concepts as revelation or innate knowledge. The combination of formal religious training, informal parental inculcation . . . and ubiquitous social pressures . . . makes clear why so many children engage in religious behavior. Whether the mediator in such cases is the learned motive to conform or the learned motive to imitate, religious utterances and other religious activities tend to be positively reinforced. The intense emotionality that so often accompanies or defines the "religious experience" may result from the capacity of religion to satisfy such needs as dependency, affiliation, and (perhaps) erotic gratification, needs that may themselves be products of instrumental learning. Thus, to the extent that religiosity is inferred from behavior, principles of conditioning appear to be sufficient for a complete explanation (p. 133).

Behavior theorists sometimes also conceive of religious traditions as self-serving and destructive systems of behavior control. John B. Watson, who championed the behaviorist movement in America early in the twentieth century, exemplifies this conviction. Although he says very little about religion in his various articles and books, he clearly viewed it as a means of control devised by "medicine men"—his generic term for all religious persons in positions of influence. According to Watson, a "religious habit system" is instilled in the individual through fear and maintained by the attitude of authority:

> Religious philosophical dogmas . . . have long deterred us from making even a decent logical formulation of the way thinking goes on. Throughout the ages churchmen—all medicine men in fact—have kept the public under control by making them believe that whatever goes on the world which can't be easily observed must be mysterious, must be strong medicine, something much more powerful than those things which can be observed. The motive is obvious. It is the only way the medicine man can keep control. Science has almost had to blast its way through this wall of religious protection (J. B. Watson, 1928, pp. 79–80).

Religion is therefore doubly antithetical to science: it fosters dogmas that are unverifiable, such as the belief in a soul that is separate and distinct from the body, and it uses methods—fear and authority—that are anathema to objective scientific research. Among educated persons, Watson claims, religion is being replaced by experimental ethics.

Other behaviorally[1] oriented psychologists, however, have found a surprising harmony between behavior principles and certain traditional religious elements, whether they be Christian (Bufford, 1981), Buddhist (Mikulas, 1981; Silva, 1984),

---

[1] Following English and English (1958), I use BEHAVIORAL to refer to any approach that emphasizes the objective study of behavior, whereas BEHAVIORIST, whether as noun or adjective, designates a person or position that adheres more narrowly to the philosophy and ideology of BEHAVIORISM (see Zuriff, 1985). BEHAVIORISTIC indicates an approach that possesses *some* of the characteristics of behaviorism.

or Hindu (Balodhi and Mishra, 1983). The key to this radical difference in perspective seems to be whether or not behavior theory is applied from within the ideological framework of behaviorism, as it was by Watson. If it is so applied, behavior theory seems inevitably to come into conflict with religion (W. P. King, 1930). But some proponents of the behavioral approach, including a number of conservative Christians, demonstrate that the specific principles can be adopted apart from the philosophy of psychology that gave rise to them. Comparative psychology has proved to be similarly ambiguous in its implications for religion: some proponents sweepingly dismiss human piety by drawing parallels with analogous animal behavior, whereas others construe such parallels as evidence of universal religious propensities. We encounter both views in this chapter.

BEHAVIOR THEORY AND RELIGION

Behavior theory is a general term designating no particular theory; rather, it denotes any approach that considers psychology's task to be the explanation of observable behavior in relation to environmental stimuli (English and English, 1958). Most often based on animal research, the various behavior theories usually employ hypothesized *intervening variables* to account for the relation between stimulus and response. Such mechanisms may be postulated to lie in the nervous system, but there is no requirement that they actually exist. Whatever language or model is employed, its adequacy is judged strictly by how well it serves to explain, predict, and control behavior.

The behavioral approach is grounded in the philosophic view of *empiricism*, which maintains that experience rather than reason is the source of our knowledge. The empiricism of the behavior theorists is of a rather strict variety deriving from such philosophers as Thomas Hobbes, John Locke, and David Hume. In its classic form, it incorporates four theoretical propositions:

> (1) SENSATIONALISM, the hypothesis that all knowledge is derived through sensory experience; (2) REDUCTIONISM, the thesis that all complex ideas are built up out of a basic stock of simple ideas, and that complex ideas are in turn reducible to these simple ideas; (3) ASSOCIATIONISM, the thesis that ideas or mental elements are connected through the operation of association of experiences that occur closely together in time (contiguity), and (4) MECHANISM, the thesis that the mind is like a machine built from simple elements with no mysterious components (Bower and Hilgard, 1981, pp. 2–3).

Behavior theorists are empirical in another sense, for they also embrace *objectivism*, the doctrine that limits the data of science to objectively observable facts. Thus instead of "ideas or mental elements" they refer to units of stimulus and response. In accord with the reductionist hypothesis, and as a safeguard against the reintroduction of introspective evidence, behavior theorists frequently carry out their research with laboratory animals, most often rats specially bred for docility.

EARLY BEHAVIORISTIC FORMULATIONS

The development of the behavioral approach to religion closely follows the general history of psychology. The greatest moment for twentieth-century psychology was Darwin's theory of evolution, which substituted for nineteenth-century associationism the concepts of heredity and individual adaptation, and gave to psychology a strong biological and comparative orientation. In accord with the LAW OF PARSI-MONY, the same principles of explanation were to be applied to both animals and human beings. Religious behavior was initially viewed, therefore, in terms of inherited instinctual propensities and evolutionary value.

Belief as Reflex Arc

The earliest attempt to develop an explicitly behavioristic interpretation of religion was made by Wesley Raymond Wells, first in a doctoral dissertation at Harvard University (Wells, 1917) and then in a series of published articles collected in a book entitled *The Biological Foundations of Belief* (1921). According to Wells, a belief is an organic response, "a system of REFLEX ARCS so integrated that some given assertion or proposition may be responded to positively" (Wells, 1921, pp. 71–72). The biological foundations of religious belief are essentially twofold. On the one hand, religious beliefs rest on the primary INSTINCTS of curiosity, self-abasement, flight, and parental caretaking, and on the parallel emotions of wonder, negative self-feeling, fear, and tenderness. Here Wells follows the British psychologist William McDougall (1908), who later became a vigorous opponent of behaviorism. On the other hand, beliefs possess direct survival value through the subjective effects they have on biological well-being.

Wells illustrates the enormously powerful influence of deeply held beliefs with the phenomenon of sudden death among nonliterate people who learn that they have violated some fundamental taboo. In most instances, however, religious beliefs have proved to have hygienic and moral value. "The universal existence of religious belief among primitive peoples," Wells writes, "is evidence of its survival value" (p. 6), whether or not the belief is true. Wells concludes his small book by advocating the teaching of religion to children and of idealistic philosophy to college students, not because these ideas are true but because they lend "grandeur to the universe, and zest to the moral urgings of the individual life" (p. 119).

Religion as Redintegration

By the time psychologist David Trout (1891–1954) undertook his much larger-scale work, *Religious Behavior* (1931), an anti-instinct movement had swept through American psychology and largely eliminated instinct as an acceptable explanatory construct. Although Trout, who was a churchgoing Protestant, explicitly rejects the mechanistic materialism characteristic of radical behaviorism, he otherwise seeks to remain faithful to a behavioristic point of view. To define religious behavior, Trout begins with the Apostle Paul's criteria of hope, faith, and love, tentatively "the only general experiential differentia which characterize every religious act and at the same time distinguish it from non-religious and irreligious forms of behavior" (p. 27). Behind these experiences or "modes of organismic behavior" are said to lie bodily processes. Hope signifies the experience of a particular dynamic organization of neurons, muscles, and glands. When hope becomes certain the individual experiences faith. "His muscles are highly coordinated, his neurons are organized into a specific pattern, his glands, and other bodily processes are inter-related in a total organization approximate to that which prevails when the expected event is actually occurring" (p. 6). Love is "faith becomes enthusiastic," "the experience of intensification of a response through glandular secretions, neuromuscular facilitation, and the contemporaneous incidence of prepotent stimuli" (p. 388).

Telic Behavior: Defined as a collection of organismic responses, religious behavior has several fundamental qualities. Foremost it is TELIC, that is, it is directed toward a positive goal, whether it be the satisfaction of a biological need or the achievement of some form of life beyond this world. The telic character of reactional organismic behavior is affected by a variety of factors: the frequency of association of stimuli and responses; the intensity and proximity to one another of the stimuli; and the emotional state of the organism during the first as well as subsequent associations.

The element of foresight specifically depends on the process of REDINTEGRA-TION, a concept introduced by the Scottish psychologist Sir William Hamilton, adopted by William James (1890), among others, and systematically developed by Harry Hollingworth (1926). According to the theory of redintegration, a stimulus tends to bring back into consciousness the entire constellation with which it was associated. Any one stimulus in an original set, or even a similar or accidentally contiguous stimulus, may redintegrate the total experience, including any response that may have occurred in the original situation. Thus, for example, a young boy soon learns to withdraw his hand from a candle flame without having to experience again the pain that accompanied his first efforts to grasp it; the mere sight of the flame redintegrates the neural pattern that leads to withdrawal. By the same principle, any of various objects present when he was burned by the candle may later serve to redintegrate the entire incident for him.

The application of the principle of redintegration to religious phenomena is suggested by Hollingworth (1926) himself. "Most of the . . . ceremonials of religious devotion . . . depend for their effectiveness on this redintegrative process. The thrill of piety comes to be aroused by trivial details of the original setting—the cross, the hymn, the candlestick" (p. 93). Trout views religious behavior as a means of completing persistently incomplete redintegrations, or, to put it more generally, of redintegrating goal-reaching responses. Among the most distinctive of religious techniques for redintegration is the making of gods, who become the means of achieving any of a number of goals that seem otherwise unobtainable, for example, dominance, submission, rapport, companionship, food, shelter, rest, or sex. Unfortunately, according to Trout, psychology reveals that many religious conceptions are based on illusions, autistic thinking, or pathological organismic processes. Yet if scientific analysis destroys faith in such techniques of adaptation, it also creates a new faith—that of the scientist. Scientific behavior, then, is also religious, for it, too, is telic in character.

Unabating Intensity: According to Trout, three other qualities, in addition to the telic, characterize religious behavior. First, the religious response is relatively *free of conflict*. Alternative ways of responding, experienced as sin, indecision, or fear, are more or less inhibited. The religious choice seems to be the only right one, the sole means of salvation, and the individual remains relatively insensitive to distracting stimuli. Second, religious behavior shows PERSEVERATION: individuals faithfully pursue the goals they love at the cost of considerable time and energy. Mystics in particular are remarkable for their "perseverative efficiency," the capacity to persist for a period of time in a relatively fixed response that others would find impossibly monotonous. Finally, the religious response has an unusual *intensity* or eagerness for its goal. Intensification facilitates redintegration by maintaining attention and reducing the number of repetitions necessary for developing the redintegrative facility; the outcome is an experience of greater certainty when closure or completion is achieved.

In sum, "That response is most religious which is going forward to positive redintegrative closure with the greatest degree of intensified facility" (p. 388), a response subjectively experienced as hope, faith, or love. In less technical words, "Any mode of behavior which is conceived as contributing in considerable degree to the achievement of the most valued goals one knows is for that individual a religious act" (p. 28).

From Trout's view, then, religious behavior can be found almost everywhere and in nearly all living organisms. "The ant and the chimpanzee, the preliterate and the erudite modern scholar, the parent and the child, the male and the female may respond in different ways to different objects, but all respond positively, perseveratively, with facility and intensity to those things which they respectively foresee as goals" (p. 392). Nonreligious persons or organisms behave automatically and without enthusiasm, show no integrated movement toward the future, and have no expectations or hope.

Although both Wells and Trout undertook their studies from avowedly behavioristic standpoints, no behaviorist today would employ their particular explanatory terms. Instinct, we have noted, was left behind in the empiricist's quest for environmental causes of behavior. Trout's emphasis on "telic" or purposive behavior, even though explained in relatively mechanistic terms, is also inconsistent with the view of that majority of contemporary behaviorists who consider purpose an unverifiable interpretation (Zuriff, 1985, p. 46). Perhaps most discordant today is Trout's extensive use of concepts that are defined largely in terms of introspectively known experience, such as "rapport," "empathy," or "self." Yet Trout does emphasize that he considers such experience to be epiphenomenal, or derivative, "a subjective index of intraorganismic processes" that is "approximately as useful to the scientific student as the symptomatic introspections of the patient are to the physician." Introspective reports, he stresses, are helpful only in accumulating "objectively verifiable data" (pp. vii–viii).

MODERN BEHAVIOR THEORY AND RELIGION

To illustrate the approach of modern behavior theory, we examine religion from three different perspectives: the elegantly simple associationist theory of Edwin Guthrie; the enormously influential operant conditioning theory of B. F. Skinner; and the more cognitively oriented social learning theory that derives from the work of Albert Bandura, among others. Faithful to the empiricist position that human beings have few if any innate behavior patterns, these behavior theorists agree that the key to understanding behavior lies in the process of *learning*—the acquisition, maintenance, and changing of particular responses. They differ, however, in how they account for this process.

Several key issues distinguish the various theories of learning, most of which were developed during the middle third of the twentieth century. The *stimulus–response* theories, in contrast to the *cognitive* theories, tend to share three kinds of preference. They explain learning in terms of peripheral or movement intermediaries, such as "chained" muscular responses in the limbs, rather than in terms of central or ideational intermediaries, such as memories or expectations; they discuss what is learned in terms of "habits" rather than "cognitive structures"; and they depend on past-oriented trial-and-error explanations in analyzing problem solving rather than on present-oriented "insight" explanations.

Unrelated to the conflict between stimulus–response and cognitive theories of learning are several other issues. Can an association between a stimulus (S) and a response (R) be formed simply through CONTIGUITY, or must the simultaneous occurrence of a stimulus and response also be accompanied by reinforcement for an association to be established? Does the EXTINCTION of learned responses merely reflect a change in expectation of reward, or is it the outcome of active inhibitory processes that interfere with the once-rewarded behavior? Is the S–R bond formed in an all-or-none fashion, or is the bond gradually built up through successive associations? Finally, is there only one kind of learning, which can account for all modes of acquiring behavior, simple or complex, or is a multifactor theory needed to explain all possibilities? (See Bower and Hilgard, 1981.)

The various theories of learning have prompted a great number of experimental studies, many of them designed to test hypotheses generated by these controversial issues. Unfortunately, the data yielded by these studies are subject to alternative explanations. Advocates of opposing views are frequently able to advance equally persuasive arguments for their own interpretations. Learning theorists will thus remain divided on these issues for some time to come. Meanwhile, the demand for workable techniques, especially in psychotherapy and education, has prompted many practitioners to begin applying these still-debated principles. Increasingly they are being applied to religion as well.

A Stimulus–Response Theory

The most fully developed application of modern behavior theory to religion was carried out by George Vetter (1894–1978) in his book *Magic and Religion* (1958), which is based on the learning theory of Edwin Guthrie (1952, 1959; Voeks, 1950). Guthrie's is a stimulus–response association psychology, and in terms of the preceding issues he is therefore a peripheralist who uses the concepts of habit and trial-and-error learning. He proposes only one fundamental law of learning: the movement that last occurred in the presence of a combination of stimuli will tend to take place again whenever the stimulus combination recurs. All that is necessary for the formation of an S–R association, Guthrie argues, is *contiguity,* the occurrence together in time. This association gains its full strength the first time the stimulus and response are paired. Rewards are helpful in forming S–R associations, not

George Vetter

because they somehow reinforce the bonds but because they serve to change the stimulus situation. Thus the movement that accompanied the stimulus pattern just before the reward changed it was the last to occur in its presence and hence will be the one most likely to recur when that pattern appears again.

The obvious improvement that occurs with repeated performance of certain complex behaviors, or *acts,* is not evidence of growth in the strength of the S–R bonds. Rather, it is the result of a multiplication of the number of such associations formed between elements, or *cues,* in a stimulus complex and the *movements* that compose the acts. The more movements a particular act requires, and the more cues that must become associated with these movements in order to perform the act effectively and accurately, the more the individual will have to practice the complex behavior. Relearning an act that has been faultily carried out requires gradual replacement of improper movements through the performance of appropriate ones, incompatible with the original movements, in the presence of the associated cues. That is, conditioned responses are "extinguished" only through associated inhibition, the learning of incompatible responses. The same principle accounts for forgetting. The painstaking effort usually necessary in relearning complex acts testifies to the difficulty of locating all the cues associated with the undesired responses. The older the habit, the more cues that will have to be sought out. The situation is further complicated by the fact that not all the cues lie in the environment; many of them are *movement-produced stimuli,* such as kinesthetic sensations. These internal cues bridge the time interval between an external stimulus and an apparently delayed response, or they may even initiate behavior for which there is no apparent environmental stimulus.

In applying contiguity learning theory to religious behavior, Vetter (1958) reflects Guthrie's interest in complex human behavior as well as his insistence on simple and mechanistic principles. Vetter repudiates both instinct and purpose as scientific concepts, instead limiting theorizing to "objectively identifiable entities." "Scientific knowledge must be instrumental," he declares, "it must be useful for prediction or control of the materials or phenomena in question" (p. 27). Accordingly, Vetter rejects the host of ANIMISTIC conceptions that he says have mischievously filled our language with words, especially nouns, that have no objective referent: mind, consciousness, will, soul, experience, and so on. For mentalistic theories Vetter would substitute a "materialistic theory of mind," which "certainly commends itself on the basis of simplicity, as well as on the factual evidence" (p. 125). An objective, scientific theory of behavior, he asserts, ought to apply equally to animal and human, to the simple and the complex, to religious as well as practical behavior.

Fruits of Religious Faith: Abandoning the "fiction of impartiality"—for "it is absolutely impossible for anyone to be impartial about anything" (p. 11)—yet embracing the goal of objectivity, Vetter is frankly unsympathetic to the claims and activities that are typically labeled religious. "One glance at any of the current anthropomorphic deities," he writes, "is sufficient to demonstrate to all but those hopelessly indoctrinated during their helpless infancy, that these gods were created by man when he was not too well informed" (p. 509). A careful look at the behavior of religious leaders, says Vetter, reveals that their wisdom is bounded on all sides by human shortcomings. Rather than lifting human beings above petty and self-serving interests, dogmatic faith has inspired wars of religious bigotry, savageries such as the Inquisition, and resolute opposition to any genuine advance of human knowledge. On any social issue, religious leaders have at best merely reflected the

This engraving from 1723 depicts an auto-da-fé ("act of the faith"), the ceremony by which the Spanish Inquisition judged heretics guilty and then delivered them over to secular authorities to be burned. Estimates of the number of people who were executed during the three and a half centuries that the Spanish Inquisition existed range from a few thousand to more than thirty thousand.

general trend of public opinion. On some issues, such as birth control and abortion, they have stubbornly clung to a morality developed more than two millennia ago by a few barbarous tribes. When some social amelioration has been gained, it has come in spite of the priesthood, not because of it. "The reason that organized religions have been almost completely impotent in providing intelligent and effective moral leadership," Vetter concludes, "is simply that they have had none to give" (p. 520). Yet he also argues that the practice of clerical celibacy has removed, at a cost, some of the most gifted individuals from the biological strain.

The effect of religion on the rank and file of believers is no more impressive, according to Vetter. Research suggests that religious faith bears little or no relationship to moral conduct, whether it be defined positively as kindness or helpfulness, or negatively as the absence of criminal behavior, juvenile delinquency, or deceit. Worse is the repeated evidence that prejudice is *positively* related to orthodoxy and church membership. In a spirit closely akin to Leuba's (1933), Vetter pointedly observes that these are the fruits of an institution that spends enormous sums of money on buildings and publications, provides a focus for an incalculable amount of human energy and time, and retains an influential hold on important social programs, political activities, and much else that occurs in our culture.

A Critique in the Name of Science: The problems we face, says Vetter, demand the careful application of scientific method, which he takes to be profoundly incompatible with dogmatic religious faith. The contradictions between science and religion are revealed not only by logical analysis of their contrasting attitudes but also by various studies that suggest that scientists in general tend to reject religious beliefs and practices.

> Increasing knowledge of the nature of man and his universe makes it more and more difficult to retain or justify the naive anthropomorphic conception of a god or gods that has come to us out of the past. The believer is driven to embrace more and more abstract, attenuated, and incidentally meaningless ideas in order to be able to retain any belief in such a symbol. They are meaningless in the sense that they are incapable of contributing anything to the organization or the understanding of the facts of any part of human behavior or experience. Some hold that such fictions are critically and vitally important to a culture. But one looks in vain for any substantiating evidence for

such assertions. Rare indeed, and then only for limited periods at best, are any fictions superior to any facts (pp. 209–210).

By Vetter's account, the notion of a spiritual world and spiritual beings arises out of widespread misunderstanding of common human activities and experiences. Thinking of ourselves as purposeful agents with nonmaterial souls and free wills, we generally assume that the events occurring around us are, like our own activities, the outcome of animistic agents. More compelling are the pathological states, such as those induced by drugs, fasting, ecstatic dancing, and epileptic seizures, that yield dramatic hallucinatory revelations of "spiritual" realities, which earlier human beings never thought to question. More sophisticated modern individuals reject the products of such suspicious psychological states, but only a few extend their doubt to the entire "spiritual realm," in spite of the total absence, according to Vetter, of supporting empirical evidence.

Vetter finds it curious that there is little or no convergence of the claims about this realm and the rituals that are supposed to relate the individual to it. Moreover, the tendency to make hair-splitting distinctions between what is true and what is false has created hundreds of sects, each confident that it embraces the "true religion." A careful study of religious beliefs and practices, as well as of scholars' definitions of religion, forces us to conclude that the beliefs and practices labeled "religious" have only one thing in common: the beliefs lack any empirical or statistical evidence, and the practices are "regular, habitual, and predictable ways of meeting the unpredictable, the impossible, or the uncontrollable . . . , if [these] are momentous" (p. 213). The question for the psychologist, then, is how such beliefs and practices have evolved. It is at this point that Vetter finds the psychology of habit germane.

Behavior in Unpredictable Situations: Finding itself in a difficult or distressing situation, any animal will try to change that situation or find a way to escape from it. Through a process of trial and error, a solution may eventually be found and learned. Some circumstances, however, allow for no solution, and the frequent result is "superstitious" or stereotypic behavior. Vetter cites two famous animal studies to clarify this point. In the one by B. F. Skinner (1948a), REINFORCEMENT was presented to pigeons in a manner wholly unrelated to the birds' activity. The result was "superstitious" behavior, for whatever response the pigeon happened to be making when the reinforcement appeared tended to be repeated, even though the behavior actually played no role in obtaining the reinforcement. In the second study cited by Vetter, Norman Maier (1949) first taught rats to identify which of two stimulus cards marked the window that would give way when they were forced to jump from a stand onto a food platform. Subsequently, whenever each stimulus card gave way only half the time, the rats began jumping repeatedly to the same window. Even when jumping in the fixated direction was punished every time by a fall into the net, and the other window was left unlocked as a safe alternative, the rats futilely persisted in the stereotyped habit. Skinner's study demonstrates, says Vetter, how a nonfunctional act can become a habitual response to a stimulus situation if this act is occurring when the situation changes fortuitously. Maier's results point to a tendency to adopt rigidly fixated behavior in the face of situations presenting insoluble problems.

Vetter considers these nonfunctional and "irrational" behaviors of pigeons and rats to be prototypes of human religious behavior. Like these less complicated species, human beings tend to respond to unpredictable or uncontrollable situations with ritualistic behaviors. Following Guthrie, Vetter assumes that such behaviors are fixed as habits by fortuitous changes in the stimulus situation, including the emotional and attitudinal states of the individual. Human beings differ from animals in developing articulate beliefs, which Vetter defines as "response tendencies attached to verbal statements either spoken by someone else or by the believer himself" (p. 245). Historically, Vetter asserts, beliefs follow the learning of certain habitual acts in order to provide explanations or rationalizations for them. The less evidence there is for a belief, or the more contradictory the evidence, the greater the tenacity and emotional intensity with which the belief will be professed. When a belief is held with an unusual intensity unrelated to the amount or quality of evidence for it, Vetter identifies it as "faith."

The behaviors that tend to occur in the face of frustratingly insoluble circumstances and subsequently to become fixated are determined by four factors. First, if the situation is in any way similar to other situations for which effective patterns of behavior have previously been learned, the crisis situation may be met with ritualized forms of these behaviors. For example, an adult facing a hopelessly distressing situation may revert to behavior appropriate to a child in the presence of a parent. "That gods are so frequently treated as super parents is no doubt not unrelated to the fact that each of us acquired predictable behavior adjustments toward parents long before coming to grapple with cosmic questions" (p. 218).

A second factor concerns the general character of the behavior. In order for a behavior sequence to become associated with a stimulus complex, it must either act to change these stimuli or be in process when the situation changes for some other reason. Thus activities that are maintained in earnest for long periods of time, without the expenditure of a large amount of energy and perhaps even providing the calm necessary for simultaneous practical efforts, are likely to have the advantage. Alternatively, highly dramatic and exciting activity may help to distract the individual and to pass the time until the emotional stress comes to an end. Accordingly, we find on the one hand behaviors in the nature of "entreaty" or resignation, such as meditation or prayer, and on the other hand behaviors classified as "orgy" or ceremony, which expend great amounts of energy. Both forms of behavior are established by the same learning process.

Vetter provides a detailed analysis in the case of prayer. This form of behavior is generally taught to the individual as a child, for whom it is not only a seeming act of piety but also something of an intellectual accomplishment. In either respect it is likely to win the child warm praise. Social approval, therefore, provides the first step in the conditioning process. Prayer gradually becomes associated with the satisfaction of hunger and relaxation that follow the grace beginning each meal. Similarly, bedtime prayers are usually followed by sleep, which terminates the worry or apprehension that may have given the prayer its content. Countless prayers said under the conditions of want or worry and almost always followed by the termination of the undesirable state gradually establish praying as the predictable response to stressful situations.

> Notice that with few exceptions indeed, the individuals who persist in praying are those who acquired the habit of praying early in life, when they began by praying for the food already there, the sleep that had already effectively "sanded" their eyes. Such an individual, praying under great emotional stress for the unattainable, need only continue such prayers until the . . . stress, by sheer fatigue . . . finally exhausts itself, as all emotional states must in time do. This relief from emotional stress then occurs *while the prayers are still being said.* Hence, when emotional stress recurs the odds favor the

prayers as the most likely reaction since that is what the individual was doing when last the distress was present. The praying persists as a habit simply because that was what was practiced under distress and nothing else. The greater the variety of circumstances under which prayer alone was resorted to the more likely it is that it will be elicited and persisted in. And, on the basis of the processes called by the Russian experimenters "higher order conditioning" (or "secondary reinforcement" by the theorists who assume it is the "reward" that fixates the steps of behavior leading up to it) the activity of praying itself comes to speed up the process of emotional equilibrium formerly completely dependent upon regulatory organic processes alone. In this way, prayers come to have important emotional effects upon those who practice them. By virtue of the conditioning process, the saying of prayers can early induce the emotional states or resignations that once waited upon a favorable turn of events or upon the exhaustion of states of grief or frustration. This is, of necessity, true also of ritual activities other than prayer (p. 226).

Prayer has several distinct advantages over other forms of religious behavior. Verbal cues are in general long-lived and potent conditioners for many kinds of activities and psychological states. Words also have the advantage of requiring little expenditure of energy, especially when they become habitual, and can be thought or spoken simultaneously with other activities, usually with little or no interference. They can also help to create a compelling fantasy life that temporarily blots out the unpleasant realities of the material world. Alternatively, they can even constitute self-provided cues for inducing states of autohypnosis, complex disturbances of normal bodily activities that are felt in this situation as religious or mystical experiences. Moreover, prayer is superior to other rituals in that it is useful even to the solitary individual removed from the complex external cues provided by the sights, sounds, and odors of the religious sanctuary. Like all other religious practices, however, prayer always derives its efficacy from its "autosuggestive or confidence-giving or conflict resolving or merely distracting effect" (p. 200).

Two other factors, less important than the first two, shape the nature of ritual behavior. First, if other things are equal, mimetic behavior that symbolizes or caricatures the problem or the desired outcome is likely to be favored. An example is the sprinkling of water during rain-making ceremonies or the manufacture of wax, clay, or precious-metal images of ailing body parts for presentation at a shrine or altar. Second, a degree of mystery and secrecy surrounding the various procedures is likely to be favored, especially because they preserve a place for the specialists in the religious realm. Vetter gives considerable emphasis to the role of the medicine man, shaman, parson, or priest, about whom he has few positive things to say. Rather than encouraging the problem-oriented and innovative trial-and-error approach of the scientist, the priest self-servingly promotes the methods of entreaty and orgy. Like an opiate, these methods are directed at the human sufferers themselves, not at the material conditions that are the source of frustration. Because humankind has come to "prefer food without blessings to blessings without food when the hunger drive attains to a given intensity" (p. 392), the effective domain of "the world's oldest profession" is rapidly shrinking. With a "sharp eye to the future of their own vested interests," priests have "long maintained a diminishing glory with rear-guard action and will no doubt long continue to do so" (p. 393).

Stages of Secularization: The process of progressive SECULARIZATION, in which more and more problems of living are transferred from the domain of religion to the empirical arena of science, is said by Vetter to be the most striking characteristic of Western civilization. In the dark past of human history, no distinction was made between the realms of religion, magic, and science. As humankind became more familiar with other cultures, people singled out as magic all foreign or outlawed practices thought to be highly potent. The beliefs and practices that were taken to be false or impotent they termed "superstitious." In later stages, which remain incomplete even today, magic is denied all efficacy and is considered to include all activities recognized as incompatible with science. In contrast, all factors or forces thought to be effective and yet to transcend scientific analysis are called religion. In the final stage of "magico-religious belief," religion too is denied any instrumental use, except its efficacy in transforming the human "spirit" and in providing a system of social ethics. This gradual process whereby humanity frees itself from "the tyranny of the past" gives Vetter hope that we will ultimately be able to reassign "the very real energies now spent in praising, adoring, invoking, wheedling, contemplating, or entreating forces of whose existence there is not one shred of scientific evidence" (p. 141).

Vetter advocates more scientific investigation, both of the effects of religion on personality and of the presently unsolved problems to which religion is a response. Rejecting religion's "fiction of complexity" on the one hand, and earlier theories that trace religion to fear, frustration, sex, or some other single origin on the other hand, Vetter asserts that only an associationistic or conditioned–reaction psychology will allow for the prediction and control of religious acts. "Religions are historically a trial-and-error product exactly like every other element in our culture, and as such are proper subjects for objective analysis and study. It is high time they are one and all stripped of their pretenses of having some special, transcendental character. They are but behavior; human, all too human!" (p. 522).

Outlines of a Skinnerian Psychology of Religion

Several themes propounded by Watson and Vetter are also found in the writings of Harvard psychologist B. F. Skinner (1904–1990), who in a 1967 survey was judged to be the world's most influential living psychologist (Seberhagen and Moore, 1969). Like Watson, Skinner views religion primarily as a traditional means of

B. F. Skinner

controlling behavior. Skinner, however, gives this theme more attention and elaboration. Furthermore, like both Watson and Vetter, Skinner suggests that the priests instituted or developed some religious beliefs and practices in order to enhance their own position. For example, according to Skinner (1971), the pharaohs were "convinced of the necessity of an inviolable tomb by priests, who argued to this effect because of the sacerdotal privileges and powers which then came to them" (p. 168). Skinner also shares Watson and Vetter's opposition to the traditional language that refers to subjective human experience. Skinner (1974) suspects that "The exploration of the emotional and motivational life of the mind . . . has been one of the great disasters" (p. 165). The environment and its controlling contingencies of reinforcement were converted into a "fanciful inner world" of experience and of ideas, purposes, and will. Only today, through Skinner's "radical behaviorism," is humankind disabusing itself of the fiction of the autonomous individual and discovering exactly how the environment controls behavior.

Rejecting all the "explanatory fictions" that have been used in the past to account for the relation of persons and their environments, Skinner and the growing number of psychologists who have undertaken the "experimental analysis of behavior" have set about to gather and organize data into a system of behavioral laws. Through the use of complex apparatus and automatic recording devices, they systematically manipulate the environment—primarily of rats and pigeons—in order to derive general principles specifying the relationship between behavior and the consequences that follow it.

The traditional stimulus–response psychologist is concerned mainly with RE-SPONDENT BEHAVIOR, which is elicited by known stimuli. In contrast, Skinner is interested primarily in OPERANT BEHAVIOR, emitted responses that operate on the environment and produce reinforcing effects. If the occurrence of an operant is followed by a reinforcing stimulus, says Skinner (1953), the probability that the operant will recur is increased. If no reinforcement occurs, the rate of the operant behavior will gradually decline. Much of Skinner-inspired research involves the study of response rate as a function of the patterns or CONTINGENCIES OF REINFORCE-MENT, in which the reinforcing stimulus is typically a tiny amount of food. Skinner acknowledges that genetic endowment and personal history are also determinants of behavior, but because these two factors lie outside of the psychologist's control with respect to human beings, they are largely ignored. Skinner suspects, however, that their influence has been exaggerated by psychologists who have not fully appreciated the effects of the immediate environment.

Although Skinner has not undertaken a systematic analysis of religious behavior, he claims to "know of no essentially human feature that has been shown to be beyond the reach of a scientific analysis" (1974, p. 239). That human piety in particular is not to be exempted is indicated by Skinner's brief chapter on religion in *Science and Human Behavior* (1953), as well as by occasional references to it in several others of his books. In piecing together Skinner's psychology of religion in the next two sections, we examine two main themes: the origin of religious behavior and the role of religious institutions in the control of behavior. The second theme receives by far the greater emphasis.

Religion as Operant Behavior: An account of the origins of religious behavior requires no special principles beyond those we have already reviewed, which are examined at greater length by Bower and Hilgard (1981). Religious behaviors occur because they have been followed by reinforcing stimuli. Yet there need be no logical or causal relationship between the emitted behavior and the reinforcement. Lacking such a connection, the reinforcement is described as ADVENTITIOUS, a phenomenon demonstrated in Skinner's (1948a) study of "superstition" in the pigeon. When reinforcement was presented at regular intervals, without regard for what the birds were doing, six out of eight pigeons came to exhibit a variety of clearly defined and rapidly repeated "superstitious" behaviors. One turned in circles, another thrust its head into a corner of the cage, and yet another bowed to the floor without touching it. Once established, these superstitious responses showed a marked tendency to persist, even when reinforced only infrequently. Another study (Morse and Skinner, 1957) shows that such adventitiously reinforced behaviors can be further conditioned to occur (or not to occur) in the presence of an incidental stimulus, such as a light, so that the stimulus gains a discriminative function.

Enough research has been done, Skinner (1974) declares, "to suggest that the same basic processes occur in both animals and men, just as the same kind of nervous system is to be found in both" (p. 227). The repertoire of the human being is, of course, enormously more complex than that of the pigeon, but the principles discovered with simpler species should nevertheless apply to all others. Remarking that it is unlikely that human beings have lost the sensitivity to adventitious reinforcement, Skinner (1971) notes that Saint Paul himself recognized it in his principle that grace (positive reinforcement) is not contingent on works (behavior defined as "pious"). Not all religious behavior is superstitious, however, for religious codes reflect in part the contingencies of reinforcement maintained by social environments.

It is undoubtedly difficult to view one's own traditional rituals as the outcome of accidental conditioning, for once ritualistic behaviors are learned, elaborate myths are invented to explain and perpetuate them (Skinner, 1974, p. 134). Once the individual is transported to another cultural setting, however, the odd gestures of bobbing, bowing, slapping, or circumambulating may suddenly appear foreign and inexplicable—until Skinner's pigeons are recalled. Similarly, the concept of a DISCRIMINATIVE STIMULUS helps to account for the more familiar outpouring of piety in the presence of stained-glass windows, hard benches, and organ music, and its sudden evaporation behind the steering wheel, the credit card, and the hunting rifle.

Skinner reinterprets various traditional religious concepts in terms of his radical behaviorism. *Faith* and *belief*, which he says have long been used to explain behavior, in fact merely tell us how likely it is to occur. They are thus "at best by-products of the behavior in its relation to antecedent events" (1971, p. 93). Faith, the more highly valued of these attitudes, is our customary way of accounting for persistent behavior when we are ignorant of the environmental events that reinforce it (1974, p. 133). A *god*, according to Skinner (1971), is "the archetypal pattern of an explanatory fiction, of a miracle-working mind, of the metaphysical" (p. 201). For a behaviorist it is a useless concept. *Piety, morality, sinfulness,* and other religiously defined internal states are in actuality not inner possessions of individuals or of humankind as a species, but rather labels for forms of behavior shaped by certain social environments (p. 198). A person becomes pious as a result of his or her history of reinforcement. "We call him devout and teach him to call himself devout and report what he feels as 'devotion' " (1971, pp. 116–117). Persons of authority who conduct themselves with *benevolence, devotion,* or *compassion* do so in order to avoid COUNTERCONTROL behaviors that would weaken or destroy their power. Yet countercontrol is not the only reason why people treat each other well, for such behavior is also valuable for the survival of the species and has therefore come to acquire reinforcing value (1974, p. 192).

Religious institutions, like ethical and political ones, are designed to control behavior. The notion of control, Skinner observes, is disturbing only to persons who maintain the fiction of the self-governing, autonomous individual. The question for Skinner is not whether there should be control. Since all behavior is controlled and to liberate persons from one source of control is merely to turn them over to another, it is a matter of who will do the controlling and what means will be used. The problem with religious control, apart from the fictions used to maintain and disguise it, is its dependence on aversive reinforcement or the threat of punishment. The often troublesome control of religious institutions, among others, "is exerted in ways which most effectively reinforce those who exert it, and unfortunately this usually means in ways which either are immediately aversive to those controlled or exploit them in the long run" (1974, p. 190). Skinner has steadfastly opposed all aversive control because of the negative emotions that are its by-products. He observes with satisfaction, therefore, that religious agencies have moved away from aversive measures—such as the threat of hellfire (a tactic Skinner's own grandmother used) and the "sense of sin" that it generates—to nonaversive ones, like the emphasis on God's love.

Religion as Controlling Agency: In some respects religious creeds and laws merely summarize existing patterns of social reinforcement that are designed to reduce selfish, primarily reinforced behavior and to strengthen behavior useful to others. "The formal laws of . . . religious institutions . . . specify contingencies of reinforcement involving the occasions upon which behavior occurs, the behavior itself, and the reinforcing consequences. The contingencies were almost certainly

The trembling supplicant in this Buddhist representation of the Final Judgment faces the prospect of hell for killing another human being, an act recalled for him in the mirror next to the judge's desk. According to the law of karma, Skinner would say, behavior is automatically reinforced or punished depending on its moral character.

Self-flagellation as a form of penance, depicted here in a woodcut by Albrecht Dürer, is still practiced in various religious traditions today. Skinner conceives of it as a means of self-control aimed at avoiding the far more aversive conditions of hell.

in effect long before they were formulated'' (Skinner, 1969, p. 140). The contingencies codified as commandments, laws, or traditions are maintained by specialists, often with the support of rituals and the dramatic art, music, and stories contained in them.

Yet religious control is commonly more stringent than the group practice from which it is derived. Going beyond the restrictions necessary to maintain cooperation in the group and the well-being of its individual members, religious agencies may demand more extreme behaviors, such as chastity, celibacy, vows of poverty, or even mortifications of the flesh and acts of martyrdom. This control is made more effective with the establishment of an extremely powerful "self-control," which results from conditioned aversive stimulation. Flagellants, for example, maintain their self-torturing behavior by reminding themselves of the more aversive prospect of hell. Individuals also exert self-control by manipulating the external stimuli to which they are exposed. By avoiding stimuli that lead to sinful behavior, and by adhering to a restricted diet and a daily routine punctuated by specified "spiritual" exercises and limited personal contact, a person may maximize behaviors thought to be virtuous. Many of the same principles may be applied to others as well, through the censorship of movies and books and the enactment of laws designed to reduce the occasions for sinful behavior (Skinner, 1953). If the control exerted by religious institutions becomes excessive, or if it conflicts with the demands of other controlling agencies, the devotee may finally reject religious orthodoxy, either attacking it directly or turning to some other, less coercive alternative.

A Utopian Vision: The place that Skinner would give to religion were it possible to create a culture *ab novo* is suggested by his utopian novel, *Walden Two*

The gestures of these Amish children express their disapproval of intrusions from the outside world.

(1948b), in which he explores the possibilities of engineering a society to produce happiness for all its members. From Frazier,[2] the experimental psychologist who founded the scientifically designed community, we learn that religion was admitted to Walden Two only when the governing Board of Planners overruled Frazier's opposition "to anything beyond the truth." Its role, however, in no way resembles the place it has in "indoctrinated communities," such as an Amish town in Pennsylvania, a monastery in Sicily, or even a whole nation that, like India, is pervasively religious. These religious cultures, observes Frazier, "have perpetuated themselves for centuries by rearing children to ways of life which seem to us to violate every human instinct. Look at the monasteries, lamaseries, and other forms of unnatural societies" (p. 172). Perpetuated, yes, says Frazier, but at a cost.

> If these communities have survived, it's only because the competition hasn't been keen. It's obvious to everyone that civilization has left them behind. They haven't kept up with human progress, and they will eventually fail in fact as they have already failed in principle. Their weakness is proved by their inability to expand in competition with other forms of society. They have fatal defects, and I submit that the defects have not been seen because of overpropagandizing. . . . In order to make such a culture acceptable it's necessary to suppress some of the most powerful human emotions and

[2] Pauly (1987) indicates that Frazier, who is characterized in the novel as a "conceited, aggressive, tactless, selfish" psychologist, is an amalgam of Skinner and one of his mentors at Harvard, physiologist William Crozier, who in turn was strongly influenced by the mechanistic biologist Jacques Loeb. "Many of Frazier's mannerisms were those of Crozier, and the name was a combination of his own (Frederick) and Crozier's." Regarding the "audacious scene" in which Frazier identifies himself with Jesus Christ, "as a scientific Man of Sorrows and Good Shepherd, bringing his flock to a better life," Pauly notes that "A crozier was the staff carried by shepherds and bishops, and Crozier was Skinner's own initial scientific patron and protector. In dropping out of the academic world, Frazier had found an alternative to the sinecure and social irrelevancy into which Crozier had sunk and Skinner was sinking." In the years following the publication of *Walden Two,* Pauly says, "Skinner came increasingly to proclaim Frazier's positions" (p. 196).

motives. Intellect is stultified or diverted into hypnotic meditations, ritualistic incantations, et cetera. The basic needs are sublimated. False needs are created to absorb the energies. Look at India—do you need any clearer proof of the interchangeability of propaganda and progress? (pp. 173–174).

In Walden Two, according to its MESSIANIC protagonist, both historical tradition and revealed truth are disregarded; only principles that can stand the test of experimentation are acceptable. As a result, religious observance comes to play only a minor part in the life of the community.

> The simple fact is, the religious practices which our members brought to Walden Two have fallen away little by little, like drinking and smoking. . . . Religious faith becomes irrelevant when the fears which nourish it are allayed and the hopes fulfilled—here on earth. We have no need for formal religion, either as ritual or philosophy. But I think we're a devout people in the best sense of that word, and we're far better behaved than any thousand church members taken at random.
>
> We've borrowed some of the practices of organized religion—to inspire group loyalty and strengthen the observance of the Code. I believe I've mentioned our Sunday meetings. There's usually some sort of music, sometimes religious. And a philosophical, poetic, or religious work is read or acted out. We like the effect of this upon the speech of the community. It gives us a common stock of literary allusions. Then there's a brief "lesson"—of the utmost importance in maintaining an observance of the code. Usually items are chosen for discussion which deal with self-control and certain kinds of social articulation.
>
> There's nothing spurious about this—it's not an imitation church service, and our members aren't fooled. The music serves the same purpose as in a church—it makes the service enjoyable and establishes a mood. The weekly lesson is a sort of group therapy. And it seems to be all we need. If the Code is too difficult for someone or doesn't seem to be working to his advantage, he seeks the help of our psychologists. They're our "Priests," if you like. . . .
>
> So much for our services. No ritual, no dalliance with the supernatural. Just an enjoyable experience, in part aesthetic, in part intellectual (pp. 165–166).

Second Thoughts for the Future: Twenty-five years after the publication of *Walden Two,* in an interview with a Catholic priest–psychologist (Kennedy, 1974), Skinner explained that he himself left the Presbyterian Church when he was an adolescent. "Neither my wife nor I are religious. I look to this world for my reinforcers" (p. 143). Skinner nevertheless seems to have found new meaning in some religious practices, especially in the light of his concern for the future.

Religion, he says, has "always reinforced the idea that we need some people who don't expect too much from the present. These are the kind of people who are willing to take vows of poverty and celibacy. Perhaps they are essential because they focus on the future and make us aware of our responsibility for it" (p. 138). Religion may be necessary for ordinary people, Skinner says, for "miracles and sanctions" could be replaced only through an extraordinary management effort. Ritual is important because "it helps us understand the script of life; it helps us understand the mood of our own experience" (p. 143).

To be truly effective, however, churches must replace all the traditional aversive techniques with positive ones. This is a difficult task when their concern for the future is preempted by efforts to survive in the present. The ability to delay gratification in the light of the future, says Skinner, is America's most important problem. "The institutional Churches have always been a great help in this regard because they arrange additional reinforcers that make people look toward the

Lazarus, who before he died ate what fell from the table of the rich man (Dives), now looks down from the bosom of Abraham to see Dives suffering in hell (Luke 16: 19–31); from a German picture Bible.

future while making sacrifices in the present. Religion has always helped people to do that, to be heroic in the present in view of a better future'' (pp. 138–139).

Heaven and Hell in New England Theology: Although Skinner's various suggestions have not yet been amplified into a full-scale psychology of religion, its potential has been tested by several researchers. Illustrative in relation to historical data is a doctoral dissertation completed at Boston College by James Armstrong (1977), whose committee of readers included Skinner himself. Armstrong applied the principles of operant conditioning to the development of Christian ESCHATO-LOGICAL concepts—that is, teachings regarding "the last things," including death, the Final Judgment, heaven, and hell. He was particularly interested in the trends in New England theology as reflected in Congregational funeral sermons between 1672 and 1952.

The reinforcing properties of the concepts of heaven and hell are more complex than the simple rendering of them as reward and punishment would suggest. From the view of operant conditioning, hell serves both as a PUNISHMENT—an aversive stimulus that, if sufficiently threatening, will suppress the occurrence of unwanted behavior—and as a NEGATIVE REINFORCER, for its removal (in one's anticipation) reinforces the positive behavior initiated as a means of avoiding such a fate.[3] Put more succinctly, the threat of hell suppresses undesirable forms of behavior at the same time that it reinforces desirable ones.

By itself, heaven is simply a positive reinforcer, though it may have difficulty competing with earthly rewards that are not so far off on the horizon. In combination with hell, however, heaven becomes a negative reinforcer as well, because attaining it simultaneously extricates the person from hell. Thus heaven's potency as a reinforcer declines when people stop believing in a realm of eternal punishment. Without hell, the individual is also deprived of anticipating the joy of seeing

---

[3] Because negative reinforcement is often confused with punishment, Armstrong thoughtfully proposes renaming it "extrication reinforcement." Rather than burdening the reader with yet another, in this case idiosyncratic term, however, I have elected to remain consistent with Skinner's usage.

his or her malefactors tortured. This rather dubious pleasure is intimated in the New Testament, was openly celebrated by early theologians, and has ever since been evoked with varying degrees of seriousness by religious and political commentators.

The medieval Church's heavy reliance on the threat of postmortem punishment as a means of control was a natural response, says Armstrong, to the catastrophic and rapidly changing conditions in Europe. Yet punishment inevitably elicits responses aimed at countercontrol, which in this instance frequently took the form of passive acquiescence and incipient disbelief. It was also expressed in suggestions that the preachers of doom were themselves destined for hell, as Cranach's antipapal woodcut illustrates. To regain control, various efforts were made to mitigate the harsh doctrine of hell and thus make it more believable. Unbaptized infants were allotted a less dreadful fate, in LIMBO; PURGATORY was established as a place of time-limited suffering; torment was graded according to the seriousness of the individual's sins; and "invincible ignorance" became a legitimate defense. In any form, however, the threat of punishment, especially if it is remote, is never an entirely effective means of suppressing behavior that is positively reinforced in the present.

Armstrong's analysis of the contents of funeral sermons documents a major shift in Protestant New England away from threats of punishment and toward more immediate and richly rewarding reinforcement. By 1850 such expressions as hell, God's wrath, and the Devil had virtually disappeared from the sermons. Moreover, according to Armstrong, the improved worldly circumstances brought about by the rapid industrialization and technological advances of the midnineteenth century accelerated the predictable decline in heaven's power as a reinforcer. To make heaven more competitive as a reinforcer, preachers embellished their descriptions with concrete details, including pearly gates, golden streets, and joyful reunions with friends and family members. Yet when these preachers intimated with increasing frequency that the deceased subjects of their sermon had already gone to heaven, it became more difficult to make such a reward contingent on good behavior. In sermons at the end of the century, references to heaven were brief and exceptionally vague; concern was expressed, rather, over the declining belief in personal immortality. Perhaps most telling of all, by this time funeral sermons were rarely published.

Armstrong interprets the current growth in conservative denominations as an effort, in the face of twentieth-century disillusionment, to restore the long-term contingencies of a final judgment. Such belief simultaneously provides immediate reinforcement in the form of certainty and existential security. Religiously conservative or not, a majority of contemporary Americans do profess belief in heaven and hell. A Gallup poll commissioned in 1988 by *Newsweek* magazine to accompany a major article on current thinking about heaven found that 94 percent of Americans believe in God, 77 percent in heaven, and 58 percent in hell. Of those who believe in heaven, 76 percent think their chances of going there are good or excellent; only 6 percent of believers in hell, on the other hand, anticipate going there themselves. If there is a resurgence of belief in heaven and hell today, it nevertheless remains radically attenuated. Among theologians who still use the terms, heaven and hell are usually not future dwelling places but already-existing characterological states of intimacy with, or alienation from, God. Even conservative and literalistic believers—reluctant as many of them are to condemn their nonbelieving friends to eternal torment—are moderating their conceptions of hell

The forces of hell devour the Pope in this woodcut by Lucas Cranach the Elder; from an antipapal pamphlet entitled *The Passional of Christ and Antichrist* (1521). Imagining one's enemies in hell has been a source of pleasure for centuries.

(Woodward, 1989). Thus we may doubt that heaven and hell will, in America at least, soon regain their former potency as general-purpose reinforcers.

Behavioral Psychology in the Service of Religion: Even apart from their application to religion, the reductionistic language and mechanistic views of behavior theory have long inspired vigorous criticism from religious scholars (e.g., W. King, 1930). It is thus startling to see today a growing hospitality to operant behavior theory among evangelical Christians. Some propose to integrate spirituality with a behavioral perspective, anticipating benefits for both sides. People having difficulty carrying out a spiritual discipline could be taught some behavioral self-control techniques, for example, and behavior therapists would find themselves better able to work with religious clients (Miller and Martin, 1988).

Clinical psychologist Rodger Bufford (1981) finds numerous parallels between operant principles and biblical teachings. Pointing out that one of the consequences of the Fall recorded in the book of Genesis is the requirement that we work in order to eat, Bufford concludes that "God has established a system in which reinforcement principles are an intrinsic part of the created order and of his plan for its operation" (p. 175). Poised to reinforce or punish the Israelites, according to their response to His law, " 'God was the first behaviorist' "—or, more accurately, the first methodological behaviorist, for Bufford rejects on biblical grounds the philosophy of radical behaviorism. He suggests a variety of ways to apply operant principles to Christian education, including the development of programmed religious instruction; the offering of reinforcements—for example, dessert, special outings, or a reduced rate at a summer camp—for learning Bible verses; and from early on in a child's life, daily association between verbal religious expressions (e.g., "God loves us") and positive nonverbal experiences.

Although some may share Bufford's apparent reservations about using "arbitrary" reinforcers such as food rather than "natural" ones—that is, extrinsic instead of intrinsic reinforcers—at least there is evidence that they do work. Philip Captain (1975) found that money was an effective reinforcer of Bible reading among adolescent volunteers from one California church's Sunday school department. Monetary reward also increased positive self-ratings by the subjects in relation to their Bible reading. However, although these more positive attitudes toward themselves persisted two weeks after reinforcement was discontinued, the increase in reading did not. In contrast, verbal praise from parents showed no effects at all, in comparison to the unrewarded control group. Captain thinks this finding may reflect the adolescent struggle for independence from parental attitudes.

Social Learning Theory and Religion

Vetter and Skinner consider piety to be the summation of individual enacted behaviors established by subsequent reward. Others maintain that people become religious chiefly by observing and thinking about the religious individuals around them. This is the view of SOCIAL LEARNING THEORY, "a form of cognitive behaviorism that analyzes the learning, motivation, and reinforcement of social behavior in terms of cognitive events mediating the impact of external events" (Bower and Hilgard, 1981, p. 472). The social learning theorists maintain that complex human behavior cannot be reasonably accounted for in terms of individually reinforced response units. Rather, they argue that much of our learning is carried out more globally, by observing others perform complex acts and then attempting to imitate them.

Young children seem to imitate gestures and simple acts involuntarily. As they grow older, they begin to pick and choose among potential models and behavior patterns, thereby creating their own distinctive repertoire. Mediating this process are various cognitive activities, including remembering observed behavior, anticipating possible outcomes of their own performance of it, and selecting and organizing what they themselves will finally enact. Thus learning generally goes on *vicariously*, without the person's having to experience the enactment directly. Rather than shaping the learning process, then, reinforcement determines whether or not the learned behavior will be carried out.

Albert Bandura (1977), one of the chief proponents of social learning theory, analyzes observational learning in terms of four interrelated processes. *Attentional* processes encompass not only the qualities of the model—how accessible, distinctive, and likeable he or she is—but also certain characteristics of the observer, including perceptual set, sensory capacities, and reinforcement history. *Retention* processes are the means by which a person retains an impression of the observed behavior in the model's absence: mental images, verbal encoding, and symbolic and motor rehearsal. *Motor reproduction* processes entail the actual enactment of the model's behavior; the person's success is determined by his or her general physical capabilities and the skillful acquisition of the component responses through self-observation and other forms of feedback. Finally, *motivational* processes refer to the effects of anticipated reinforcement. The imagined outcomes not only determine whether an act will be performed but also affect the quality of attention given to the model and the effort given to retaining and reproducing the sequence of observed behavior. Unlike the radical behaviorists, Bandura allows for self-reinforcement, carried out on the basis of gradually acquired internal standards that help to provide consistency in behavior. Over a period of several decades, Bandura and his associates have conducted numerous experiments to clarify each of these four processes.

If individual learning theory has an edge in explaining the *origin* of certain

Matthew Strode, in the company of his sister Pepper, shouts threats of damnation and hellfire at passersby outside Eastfield Elementary School in Marion, North Carolina.

religious behaviors, social learning theory would seem to provide a more adequate explanation for its *transmission* from one generation to the next. Though certainly no behaviorist, James Pratt (1920) argued long ago that imitation accounts for the child's thorough acquisition of religious traditions. Furthermore, the impressiveness of the sources from which belief and custom come, and the law of habit "working in connection with social approval and disapproval," lend to these elements the qualities of sacredness and authority. Yet imitation also helps to explain subsequent changes in religious outlook, Pratt says, for it is difficult to resist the "psychological atmosphere" of others who think differently, especially if they possess a measure of prestige. "We are all imitators," Pratt declares; "it is only a question of whom we shall imitate." We are also rational beings, he hastens to add, and thus "most of us, in some slight degree, are also originators" (pp. 86–87).

Holy Terrors: A conspicuous example of imitation's potential for shaping religious behavior can be found in a trio of preaching children who became the focus of national attention in the spring of 1988. Following an incident during which ten-year-old Duffey Strode was roughed up at their Marion, North Carolina, elementary school by three other children, apparently over the Strode family's religious views, Duffey, his brother Matthew, and their sister Pepper, five and six years old, respectively, started appearing an hour before school began, in order to preach hellfire to the others as they arrived. In spite of repeated suspensions for insubordination and violation of school rules, the children continued their preaching—soon, in the presence of a phalanx of reporters and photographers. Asked one morning by the assistant principal to enter the school building, Duffey screamed, "Thou shall not take the name of the Lord thy God in vain. Thou shall not commit adultery! You're guilty! Even your eyes are filled with adultery! Men can't keep their eyes off women and women can't keep their eyes off men. Adulterers shall be put to death and their blood shall be upon them!" Other school administrators and teachers were accosted by Duffey with charges of being "whore-mongers," "queers," and "adulterers." Matthew, who could recite Bible passages before he was able to read, waved a Bible at passersby and shouted at them about adultery, damnation, and hell. When a sheriff's deputy picked him up to carry him to his father, David Strode, Matthew struck the officer in the face. Consistent with the Strodes' belief that only men should preach, Pepper limited her participation to standing next to her brothers with a Bible in her hand (Boston, 1988, pp. 154, 155).

The chief model for the Strode children's unusual behavior was readily accessible. Their father had been arrested in Pennsylvania two years earlier for shouting threats of damnation and hellfire at motorists waiting at traffic lights. Strode, a machinist, had become a street preacher after a dramatic conversion six years before, following a self-described barroom existence. After their move to Marion, he continued his preaching at high school football games and in the shopping district; he sometimes took his sons with him, who thus had repeated opportunities to observe his aggressive style and learn the rhetoric of unbridled hellfire preaching. Unrestrained this preaching surely was. Appearing on a television talk show in the midst of the school controversy, Strode called the Pope a child molester, attacked women preachers, and declared that the show's hostess was going to hell. Although the Strode family members were equally opposed by members of their Baptist church and angry school parents, their behavior was undoubtedly sustained by both mutual and self-reinforcement, if not also by the attention they received from the national news media. In the end, the Strodes decided to withdraw their children from the school and to teach them at home; they vowed that their preaching would continue unabated.

Models of Altruism: Modeling can also sustain more admirable behavior. In a remarkable interview study of more than 700 persons living in Poland, Germany, France, the Netherlands, and several other European countries during the Nazi occupation, Samuel and Pearl Oliner (1988) sought out the characteristics that distinguished "rescuers" from "nonrescuers." The study encompassed 406 verified "rescuers," individuals who heroically risked their own lives by giving shelter or otherwise aiding Jews. The 126 "nonrescuers" consisted of 53 "actives," who said they either were members of resistance groups or had in some other way helped Jews, and 72 "bystanders," who acknowledged that "they had done nothing out of the ordinary during the war either to help other people or resist the Nazis" (p. 4).

Although the rescuers' self-sacrificing efforts might well be viewed as supremely religious acts, scores on standard measures of religiosity turned out to be only weakly related to rescue. Self-ratings of present-day religiosity did significantly distinguish the groups, with a higher proportion of rescuers describing themselves as either "very religious" or "not at all religious," whereas nonrescuers tended to fall in between (see Figure 4.1). But comparisons of retrospective ratings of prewar religiosity as well as of parental religiosity were most often insignificant. Similarly, although the proportion of those attending Protestant parochial schools who later became rescuers was much larger than the proportion attending Catholic ones, a majority of subjects in both groups attended neither.

The principal distinguishing characteristic of the groups was their family background, especially the examples set by their parents. The developmental course that produced the individuals whose universalistic sympathies compelled them to become rescuers

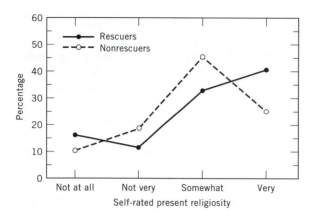

Figure 4.1. The religiosity of rescuers and nonrescuers of Jews. Source: Based on Table 6.6 in Oliner and Oliner, 1988, page 291.

begins in close family relationships in which *parents model caring behavior* and communicate caring values. Parental discipline tends toward leniency; children frequently experience it as almost imperceptible. It includes a heavy dose of reasoning—explanations of why behaviors are inappropriate, often with reference to their consequences for others. Physical punishment is rare. . . .

Simultaneously, however, parents set high standards they expect their children to meet, particularly with regard to caring for others. They implicitly or explicitly communicate the obligation to help others in a spirit of generosity, without concern for external rewards or reciprocity. *Parents themselves model such behaviors, not only in relation to their children but also toward other family members and neighbors.* Because they are expected to care for and about others while simultaneously being cared for, children are encouraged to develop qualities associated with caring. Dependability, responsibility, and self-reliance are valued because they facilitate taking care of oneself as well as others. Failures are regarded as learning experiences, with the presumption of eventual mastery, rather than inherent deficiencies of character, intellect, or skill.

Out of such benevolent experiences, children learn to trust those around them. Securely rooted in their family relationships, they risk forming intimate relationships outside it. Persuaded that attachment rather than status is the source of basic life gratifications, as they mature they choose friends on the basis of affection rather than social class, religion, or ethnicity. In the context of such diverse relationships, they develop new cognitive and social skills as well as sensitivities. They feel more comfortable dealing with people different from themselves and are readier to emphasize the likenesses that bind them to others than the distinctions that separate them. More open to new experiences, they are more successful in meeting challenges. . . .

Because of their solid family relationships, such children tend to internalize their parents' values, increasingly incorporating standards for personal integrity and care within their own value systems (pp. 249–250; emphasis added).

According to the Oliners, individuals of this orientation are more likely to offer help, or be asked for it, when lives of strangers are threatened.

Imitating Saviors and Saints: Religious traditions themselves provide numerous models for adherents to observe and imitate. According to psychiatrist Mortimer Ostow (1958), even a single image can possess considerable efficacy in this regard. Inferring from animal behavior and symptoms of brain disease that there is "a primitive tendency in the human nervous system to imitate others" (p. 715), Ostow suggests, for example, that the serene image of the meditating Buddha induces a state of tranquillity and self-control among those who worship before it.

The value of such images is greatly enhanced by the elaborate stories associated

This Japanese Buddha (Dainichi Nyorai, ca. 950 C.E.) has for centuries offered a model of tranquillity and self-control.

with them. A reading of the voluminous Buddhist scriptures, Pratt (1928) remarks, leaves the impression of a very great personality who perfectly combines calm reason with boundless sympathy and compassion. A person familiar with this literature will bring to the Buddha image a far richer set of positive associations. For Christians, of course, Jesus serves as the great exemplar; *The Imitation of Christ,* the famous devotional work by the fifteenth-century monk Thomas á Kempis, expresses in its very title the calling of every sincere follower of Christ. Yet perhaps in recognition that such lofty models may seem beyond imitation, the traditions have at the same time offered a host of more assuredly human figures—the saints, gurus, and other great souls—whose thoughts and ways are more easily copied.

Religion as Role Taking: According to the influential Swedish psychologist of religion Hjalmar Sundén (1908–1993), the texts that acquaint us with these religious models teach us particular *roles.* The result is a transformation of our perceptual experience, which is selected and shaped at all times by our past experience, present needs, and enduring attitudes. Sundén's concept of role is borrowed from the American pragmatic philosopher George Herbert Mead (1863–1931) and certain sociologists and social psychologists directly influenced by him. According to Sundén (1969), the term "role" refers to an organized model of behavior related to a particular life *situation.* Furthermore, it implies *expectations* of particular *interactions.* In Mead's formulation, "taking the role of other" consists of imagining oneself in the other's place in order to anticipate how the other will respond. Sundén uses the expression "ROLE TAKING" in the stronger sense as well: the actual assuming or appropriating of the role in question, by identifying with the other. The capacity to take the role of other, Sundén (1959) remarks, has its crucial origins in the early identification between child and mother (pp. 8–9).

In a typical situation, then—say, the reading of a long-familiar biblical story that speaks to an individual's present situation—the person identifies with the human subject in the story, and thus assumes his or her role. At the same time, the reader adopts the role of God, in the more limited sense of anticipating God's part of the interaction. The outcome of this dual role-taking, Sundén (1959) says, is a fundamental change in perceptual experience: the person now perceives the events in his or her own life as the result of the action of God (p. 29).

Two implications are clear in Sundén's combination of social and perceptual psychologies. First, religious experience is essentially *relational* in character, for it is the product of interaction between the individual and God. It is relational, too, in that the roles taken by a person are largely determined by the status accorded him or her by intimate associates. Second, religious experience depends on thorough acquaintance with religious texts, which provide the latent roles that can be assumed to fit the occasion. "Without a religious reference system, without religious tradition, without myth and ritual," Sundén declares, "religious experiences are unthinkable" (p. 27). In sharp contrast to William James, Sundén maintains that "what is religious is not the private possession of a person, but something that one has in common with many others" (p. 87). Yet familiarity with the texts is only the first prerequisite for a religious restructuring of experience. Also necessary are a motivational factor and perceived similarity between a person's own situation and the situation of the religious model whose role he or she might assume. Without these elements, there will be no expectation and thus no interaction.

The preaching of the Strode children may serve to demonstrate how Sundén's theory might be systematically applied. Growing up in the home of a Baptist street preacher, these children were not only familiar with the Bible but also able to recite portions of it from memory. Morever, while accompanying their father on his missions, they had the opportunity to become familiar with the "texts" of his hellfire preaching. The associated roles they learned, particularly of biblical prophets railing against unrepentant sinners, would have created a perceptual set to experience their own world in similar terms. What activated this set and thus precipitated the boys' preaching was the school principal's decision to punish Duffey along with the three other children involved in the fight. Seeing himself unjustly reviled and persecuted much like the biblical prophets, Duffey responded by quite literally enacting their roles, just as he had seen his father do. The school yard, formerly an indifferent, secular setting, was now perceived as a religious battleground of good and evil. Five-year-old Matthew, who looked to his older brother for his cue to begin preaching, presumably shared much the same experience. We may speculate that the boys adopted two other roles as well, but in these instances they did so in the more limited sense of anticipating a response: the role of God, who we may assume was imagined to be watching his faithful servants with real satisfaction, and the role of the sinners, who were apparently thought to be not only hard of heart but also hard of hearing. The actual response of the school and the rest of the Marion community eventually confirmed them in their well-rehearsed roles.

Sundén's role theory has had its greatest influence among psychologists of religion in the Nordic countries. Thorvald Källstad (1974) has used it, for example, in conjunction with Leon Festinger's COGNITIVE DISSONANCE theory to account for the religious development of evangelist and founder of Methodism, John Wesley. An intensive reader of the Bible and devotional literature, including Thomas à Kempis's *The Imitation of Christ,* which he translated into English, Wesley took the role of "the radical and abused disciple of Jesus" (p. 287), along with those of other models of faith. Together, these roles allowed him to perceive the unfolding of events in his life as divinely ordained. Dissonance reduction theory helps to clarify several points of conflict along the way, including the contrast between the Anglican model of faith with which he was reared and the Moravian model by which he was later deeply impressed, during his nearly two-year stay among its representatives in America.

Sundén's role theory was also applied on the individual level by Hans Åkerberg (1975), who considers it the key to the dramatic conversion of Nathan Söderblom, a Swedish scholar and archbishop. Söderblom experienced a period of deep crisis that centered on the conflict he experienced between Bible-centered revivalist piety and the revolutionary historico-critical view of the Bible. Seeing parallels between his own situation and that of the Israelites, Söderblom adopted their role along with that of the merciful God. Through the ensuing interaction, he radically restructured his world (p. 309).

Role theory's potential ability to illuminate more general religious phenomena has been pursued by several other scholars, including contributors to a symposium on Sundén's theory published in the *Journal for the Scientific Study of Religion*. Nils Holm (1987b), for instance, interprets glossolalia, or speaking in tongues, as a sign of having taken the "role of baptism in the spirit," which is learned both from the Bible and from the religious communities in which it is practiced. He sides with William Samarin (1972) and others who maintain that speaking in tongues is not dependent on a trance-state, but is rather a pseudo-language learned through imitation and practiced according to linguistic rules (see Malony and Lovekin, 1985, pp. 100–112). Holm focuses on the perceptual process that follows baptism in the spirit: when the expectant individual finally speaks in tongues, his or her taking on of the role of the disciple at the same time that the role of God is actualized leads to a restructuring of the perceptual field. The speech then appears to be a gift from God. The community members whose presence facilitates the emergence of speaking in tongues now confirm the speaker's new perceptions and increase the feeling of the baptism's authenticity.

Jan van der Lans (1987) applies role theory to meditation, which, following Sundén, he views as a technique that activates previously learned religious roles and thus will change an individual's perceptual experience. In sitting in the lotus position and concentrating on a mandala depicting Buddhas and other enlightened beings, the Buddhist meditator takes on the Buddha role, thus effecting a "phase-shift" from a profane frame of reference to a religious one. In an experiment he designed to test such an interpretation, van der Lans found that a four-week course of Zen meditation yielded reports of religious experience from half of the 14 subjects who had a religious frame of reference. None of the 21 subjects who lacked a religious frame of reference or had only a weak one reported such an experience.

Sundén's role theory has also been applied by Owe Wikström to the religious experience of the elderly; by Thorleif Pettersson to the dynamics of ordinary recall of religious experience; by Johan Unger to reports on perceptions of God; and, in America, by Donald Capps to the religious development of John Henry Newman and to petitionary prayer. (For references, see Holm, 1987a.) Related studies have been gathered in a volume of papers dedicated to Sundén on his seventieth birthday (Källstad, 1978). Moving testimony to Sundén's profound influence on European scholars can be found in a more recent, commemorative volume, which was published two years after his death (Holm and Belzen, 1995). There, Sundén's wide-ranging and highly eclectic thought is discussed in conjunction with a variety of contemporary trends, including social constructivism, narrative psychology, symbolic interactionism, attribution theory, and object-relations theory. While providing a more intimate portrait of Sundén and his work, the authors testify to his success in inspiring the next generation of scholars.

COMPARATIVE STUDIES OF RITUAL BEHAVIOR

With the exception of social learning theorists, researchers in the behavioral tradition have relied heavily on laboratory animals for testing their theoretical principles. In the confines of the radically simplified laboratory environment, we would hardly expect to observe anything reminiscent of human religious practices, although the odd behaviors of Maier's "frustrated" rats and Skinner's "superstitious" pigeons are thought by some to resemble religious ritual. Even if we grant these analogies—and of course many of us will not—the fact remains that both patterns of behavior were the product of exceedingly artificial circumstances.

In their natural habitats, however, some species of animals have engaged in activities that have been spontaneously compared to religious observances. The significance of these behaviors to the animals is in some instances highly obscure and thus strictly a matter of speculation. In other cases, however, the behaviors serve an evident natural function, tempting some investigators to assume a similar function for the human analogues. Nearly always, however, there is sufficient ambiguity to allow a range of interpretations.

Speculation regarding religious experience in animals appeared shortly after Darwin published his theory of evolution in 1852. German philosopher Eduard von Hartmann (1882) addresses this possibility at the beginning of his book on the development of religious consciousness in the human race. Accepting the notion of evolution, though adding to it a teleological foundation, Hartmann suggests that animals do indeed possess a religious ANLAGE, or rudimentary religious predisposition. Yet because animals lack the capacity for disinterested observation of the surrounding world, the capacity to experience the religious relationship to a higher power is awakened in them only under exceptional conditions. In contrast, human beings are sometimes able to transcend practical needs and reflect on the remarkable manifestations of the heavens and the earth, finally developing their own religious anlage in relation to the power that lies behind these appearances.

CANINE DEVOTION

According to Hartmann, domestication can awaken the slumbering religious potential in animals by providing them with an appropriate object for religious relation. It is difficult, he says, not to ascribe a religious character to the relationship of intelligent and expressive house pets—notably dogs—to their masters, "for therein we find the animal's love and gratitude joined by a respect elevated to adoration; the slavish fear before a superior power transformed into reverence, the habitual attachment into a lasting and total surrender, into faithfulness unto death; and the obedience of training transmuted into a subordination of the will out of deep devotion" (p. 7). Fortunate is the dog, says Hartmann, who has found a master whose incomparably superior power is balanced by nobility of spirit. Such an animal has the best opportunity to develop a religious relationship.

Although Hartmann assumes a certain continuity between animals and human beings in their common possession of a religious disposition, he argues that the awakening of the animal's religious consciousness, because it depends on human interaction, offers no useful analogy for the comparable process in humans. For zoologist Alister Hardy (1979), however, the dog's devotional relation to humans is more than an analogy; it is evidence, he claims, for the *biological* character of the human relation to God.

The comparison first came to Hardy after reading ethologist Konrad Lorenz's account of the dog–human relation in his book *King Solomon's Ring* (1949). Lorenz identifies two sources for the dog's utter devotion to its master: the wild dog's submissive attachment toward its pack leader, which in the domesticated dog is transferred to the owner; and the preservation of the wild puppy's ardent affection for its mother as a permanent trait in the adult domesticated dog. Such affection, along with certain physical characteristics that were also juvenile features eventually outgrown by the domestic dog's wild ancestors, has by the process of selective breeding been preserved into adulthood—a phenomenon known as NEOTENY.

Human beings, too, Hardy points out, possess certain neotenous qualities, for example, the particular angle of the head in relation to the spinal column and the retarded closure of the sutures between the bones of the skull, which allows an extended period of brain development. Thus, like dogs, humans may retain into adulthood the early tendency to form loving attachments. Furthermore, Hardy wonders whether the dog's sudden "sealing" of the bond of attachment, during a crucial period of susceptibility, is analogous to the human being's peculiar vulnerability to dramatic religious conversion during adolescence.

Human beings resemble dogs in their social development as well. Once humankind departed from the fruit diet they shared with their primate relatives and became carnivores, they too formed cooperative hunting packs with clearly identified leaders. When hunting later gave way to agriculture, the submission and loyalty to the pack leader were redirected to a new, invisible "leader" whose qualities gradually emerged out of the discussions of recurring experiences of a mysterious "something other." Over time, the feelings of loving devotion that originated in the child–parent relation were also gradually incorporated into this new relation. The disposition toward friendliness and mutual aid that sustained the hunting pack provided the foundation for "comradeship and brotherly love."

The implication of this reconstruction, Hardy emphasizes, is not that theistic piety is false or that dog and human are related in some evolutionary sense. Rather, it is that the biological factors shaping the relation of dog to human are also at work in the formation of human images of God. The Bible, Hardy says, is one tradition's record of the transformations that have occurred in such images: "The change from the stern image of a wrathful, jealous God demanding that lambs shall be sacrificed as an appeasement for the people's sins, shown to us in the Old Testament, to that of the loving Father of the New Testament" involves the same principles as those found in "the change of emphasis from a strict obedience to an undisputed pack-leader to that of the more filial-like devotional relationship of the domestic dog to man" (p. 170).

HELIOTROPISM AND RELIGION

The domesticated dog might be considered fundamentally similar to a laboratory animal, for it, too, has been developed through selective breeding, situated in an artificial environment, and subjected to human-determined contingencies of reinforcement. What might we find if we turned to genuinely wild animals instead?

Four baboons, with arms up-raised in adoration, perch atop the altar in the sun sanctuary nearby the Egyptian temple Abu Simbel. This unroofed sanctuary, the most nearly intact of its kind, was so oriented that the rays of the rising sun would strike the two obelisks and then the altar. Housed in the shrine to the right of the altar was a fifth, seated baboon wearing both a crescent and a full moon (considered a double of the sun) and a scarab beetle surmounted by a sun disk (*Ramsès*, 1976). All these images are now in the Egyptian Museum in Cairo.

Perhaps the most striking phenomenon, because it is seemingly inexplicable in other than religious terms, is the sun-oriented ritual that has been witnessed in a certain species of baboon (*Cynocephalus porcarius*) in the wilds of South Africa. Jacques Malan (1932), who observed a company of such baboons for a period of about a month in 1920–1921, describes this remarkable ritual. For the largest part of the day these baboons busied themselves with food gathering, grooming, "phi-landering," and other routine activities.

> But no matter what held their attention, the moment the sun touched . . . the horizon, they left their ground, swarmed over the ridge, and barked themselves into ecstasy at the sinking sun. At such times they seldom busied themselves with anything, but remained in a sort of rapt watching attitude until the sun had gone. Then they returned to their ground—I thought in a chastened and strangely chatterless mood, but that may have been an illusion stimulated by contrast after the din they had just made. In the mornings the rising of the sun was nearly always greeted with the same chorus of barking, and its movement over the rim of the horizon watched with the same peculiar raptness (p. 314).

That this behavior might merit a religious interpretation did not occur to Malan until a year later, when he learned that the natives themselves spoke of the baboons as praying, going to church, or "holding" religion.

Malan reports that similar "solar rituals" have been observed in other species as well, including many of the bigger birds and the South African meercat. Another author's pet mongoose sought out in a daily ritual the rays of the setting sun, until one day "She laboriously climbed up to the thatched roof . . . and gave a long, last look at the sun, then she came down again with great difficulty, and died" (quoted in Malan, p. 316).

Whereas we might interpret these behaviors as forms of sun worship and thus give them a religious cast, Malan classifies them instead as instances of positive HELIOTROPISM, a reflexive tendency found in many living organisms to orient themselves toward the sun. The concept of TROPISM was championed at the end of the nineteenth century by the German-American biologist Jacques Loeb (1859–1924), who anticipated that the physicochemical explanations of tropisms in relatively simply animals would some day also account for the inner life of human beings. "Our wishes and hopes, disappointments and sufferings have their source in instincts which are comparable to the light instinct of the heliotropic animals. . . . For some of these instincts the chemical basis is at least sufficiently indicated to arouse the hope that their analysis, from the mechanistic point of view, is only a question of time" (Loeb, 1912, p. 30). Of the psychologists discussed in this chapter, both John Watson and B. F. Skinner were influenced by Loeb's engineering standpoint, with its singular emphasis on scientific manipulation and control.

Mysticism as Retinal Reflex

Sharing Loeb's point of view, Malan guesses that "at the moment of the sun's setting or rising the vibration frequency of the normal sunray is subtly altered and that the retinal reflex, which in some peculiar way is probably much more sensitive in animals than in man, draws the animal toward the direct light" (p. 316). Whatever the true explanation, says Malan, the chances are that "certain fixed reactions to the sun are firmly rooted in animal behavior by the time human consciousness emerges and that sun-worship is merely an elaboration of a tendency already vaguely formulated in animal consciousness." Here Malan sees nothing but a reflexive reaction to the sun. "Mysticism . . . too, perhaps, needs just that one sure probe into its entrails to slay forever 'the mystic's spiritual divinity' and to lay bare a new maze of shuddering reflexes." The mystic and other persons with a natural aptitude for religion are, then, nothing more than ATAVISTIC biological curiosities, "merely men whose primitive reactions are still more or less functioning and whose animal memory or animal reflexes are still wholly or partially acute" (p. 317).

From Light to Enlightenment

In contrast to Loeb, for Oliver Reiser (1932), the heliotropic theory of religion, and the methods and results of biological psychology in general, may support a religious world-view, albeit perhaps not a traditional one. He suggests that

> religion is a transmutation of the form of response in lower organisms known as *heliotropism,* and that on the side of biological evolution and of religious evolution there is evidence of a movement towards a realization of *vision,* which, starting as an unconscious desire to *see,* is eventually sublimated into the spiritual craving which is the soul's quest for *illumination* (pp. 6–7).

The attitude of worship, Reiser says, is founded in the tendency to respond sympathetically to light, the miraculous agency in the creation of living matter. If light was active in the original synthesis of protoplasm, as Reiser concludes from the evidence, "Is it too fantastic to suppose that living systems have retained a biological memory of a cosmic environment with which they aspire again to communicate?" (p. 8). Perhaps, he continues, "life has preserved an implicit desire to again react in sympathy with the form of radiant energy which cradled it" (p. 9).

Citing Plato's analogy of knowledge and light in the sixth book of the *Republic* and Goethe's assertion in his *Theory of Colors* that the eye developed so that "the light from within may meet the light from without" (p. 13), Reiser rejects Loeb's mechanistic explanation of higher mental processes in terms of compulsive tropisms. Rather, Reiser argues for regarding conscious purpose as biological purpose that has become aware of itself. Evolution is *guided*—by light itself, which is commonly symbolized as a god. Through the evolutionary process, humans have developed into social beings who subordinate selfish impulses to external social realities. Reiser thinks that this tendency "is analogous to, if not derived from, such forced movements as heliotropism" (p. 19). The socially conditioned *symbol* comes to govern the reactions that once occurred directly in response to the formative stimuli. Hence human beings now looked to a heaven above rather than to the sun, and they seek enlightenment rather than light.

Light in Contemporary Research

As Reiser anticipated, in the decades since the publication of his article our understanding of light's profound involvement in diverse biological processes has advanced steadily. Indeed, a new, interdisciplinary field, PHOTOBIOLOGY, has formed around this ramifying theme. Sunlight, beyond tanning the skin and stimulating subcutaneous synthesis of vitamin D, plays a major role in synchronizing fundamental biochemical and hormonal rhythms of the body, affecting both physical and psychological well-being. It has been found, for example, that sunlight or its equivalent facilitates the body's absorption of calcium; it also relieves the depression of those suffering from SAD, seasonal affective disorder. Curiously, sunlight also disposes people to be more helpful to a would-be interviewer and to leave a waitress more generous tips, suggesting the notion of a "sunshine Samaritan" (Cunningham, 1979). Scientists are now pondering the effects of long-term exposure to artificial light, which possesses spectral characteristics strikingly different from those of the sun's direct rays (Wurtman, 1975).

As research on photobiology has accumulated, so also has documentation of the symbolism and experience of light in religious contexts. Reiser's claim that "god is light" is certainly unorthodox from the perspective of the Hebrew Bible, as he notes. Among Eastern traditions, however, light is a typical manifestation of divinity. The ancient Egyptians regarded Re, the sun god, as the supreme creator and sustainer of life. In the *Rig Veda*, the earliest of the Hindu scriptures, the sun is described as "the *atman*—the Self—of all things," "the god of gods." In other texts revered by the Hindus, notably the *Mahabharata* and the *Puranas*, Krishna and Vishnu reveal themselves in streams or flashes of dazzling light. In the yogic tradition, the stages of progression toward illumination are traditionally marked by the appearance of a succession of mystical colored lights (Eliade, 1962, pp. 26–28). Theos Bernard (1944) describes his own experience of these lights during an intensified three-month retreat at the hermitage of a well-trained yogi.

> In the second month the lights made their appearance. In the beginning it was not unlike looking into a kaleidoscope; but this condition soon passed, and single colours, brilliant and radiant, remained. Then came the "white light" that is referred to so frequently. . . . At times it became almost blinding; however it never lasted long. . . . I was eventually able to see this white light with my eyes wide open in the daylight. The mind seemed to be wiped out completely and nothing existed but this brilliant light (pp. 89–90).

In the Buddhist tradition, which began as a reform movement within Hinduism, light is similarly associated with divinity. The Buddha's birth is compared with the rising of the sun, and, as a realized being, he is conceived as having a radiant body, sometimes represented by a flame rising above his head. Other figures sanctified by the Buddhist tradition are depicted in a similar fashion. The well-beloved Amida, the Buddha of Infinite Light, is the central figure of a mystical tradition that ascribes

Flames issuing from his shoulders form a halo around the head of Vaiśravana, an ancient Indian folk god assimilated into the vast Buddhist pantheon of China.

great importance to the experience of the light that signifies encounter with ultimate reality. The symbolism of light is also conspicuous in other traditions, including the Taoist, Zoroastrian, Islamic, Jewish, and Christian (Eliade, 1962).

James (1902, p. 204) remarks that the phenomenon of PHOTISM, as psychologists call these hallucinatory impressions of bright light, "possibly deserves special notice on account of its frequency." Contemporary research suggests that the appearance of light is still a common element in religious experience. In a representative sample of Americans, Andrew Greeley (1975) found that 14 percent of the relatively large number who reported having mystical experience agreed that they felt "bathed in light"; Greeley remarks that "an amazing number of the mystics I have interviewed personally report the light phenomenon" (p. 87). Oxford researcher Alister Hardy (1979) observes that among the first 3000 who responded to their advertised appeal for accounts of religious experience, 135 reported feeling bathed in a glowing light and 264 wrote of seeing some particular pattern of light, sometimes accompanied by deep feelings of emotion (p. 34). Not only is light a recurring feature—if not the hallmark—of ecstatic experiences, but in one form or another, including sunrise and less often sunset, it also frequently serves as their trigger (Laski, 1961).

The experience of light is also associated with stimulus deprivation, the ingestion of psychedelic drugs, near-death experiences, and marked inhibition of breathing, as in the cases of Swedenborg and Bernard. All these circumstances suggest a physiological cause, and, indeed, Leuba (1925) declares that few trance phenomena "are more striking and incontestably wholly physiological in origin" than photism, though he does not himself construct an explanation. Ronald Siegel (1980), on the other hand, attributes these light phenomena to changed electrical activity at various points in the visual system.

No explanation will be convincing, however, that does not take into account three important facts regarding the experience of light (Albrecht, 1958; Arbman, 1963–1970; Benz, 1969; Eliade, 1962; Foster, 1985).

1. The experience occurs in many different forms, most of which are clearly distinguishable from ordinary sensory perception.
2. It is not uncommonly associated with a numinous being of light, or the felt presence of a friendly companion.
3. In the overwhelming majority of cases, whatever the subject's usual world-view, it is experienced in religious terms, inspiring overwhelming feelings of awe and reverence and sometimes bringing about a lasting change in the individual's disposition.

Reflecting back on the sun-greeting ritual of baboons that he, too, had witnessed in Africa, C. G. Jung (1962) writes that "At that time I understood that within the soul from its primordial beginnings there has been a desire for light and an irrepressible urge to rise out of the primal darkness. . . . The longing for light is the longing for consciousness" (p. 269). Over the decades that Jung compared the symbolism of the great mythic traditions with the individual fantasies of his patients, light and especially the sun emerged as pervasive archetypal factors leading toward understanding and wholeness. A striking finding by Greeley supports this association of light and mental health. He found that the experience of being bathed in light, in combination with three other elements identified with classical mystical experience, correlated remarkably highly (.52) with a measure of psychological well-being. It is perhaps no wonder, then, that light is the most common symbol in religious language (Heiler, 1961, p. 65).

RITUAL DANCING IN APES

Dance, another important element in human religious history, has also been observed among primates. It has been proposed, writes phenomenologist James Edie (1987), "that the origin of religious experience antedates the appearance of the human race on earth, since some of the higher anthropoids occasionally seem to perform a kind of ritual dance together and deck themselves with leaves and fruit peels as if in an expression of a religious attitude toward the world and one another. Such leaves and fruit peels would then have been the first liturgical vestments" (p. 59). In a classic study of the intelligence of apes, Köhler (1921) describes such behavior in a group of chimpanzees at the Anthropoid Station in Tenerife. They engaged in a spinning game that is strikingly reminiscent of the dancing of the whirling dervishes of the Sufi tradition.

> Any game of two together was apt to turn into this "spinning-top" play, which appeared to express a climax of friendly and amicable *joie de vivre*. The resemblance to a human dance became truly striking when the rotations were rapid, or when Tschego, for instance, stretched her arms out horizontally as she spun round. Tschego and Chica— whose favourite "fashion" during 1916 was this "spinning"—sometimes combined a

forward movement with the rotations and so they revolved slowly round their own axes and along the playground.

The whole *group* of chimpanzees sometimes combined in more elaborate *motion-patterns*. For instance, two would wrestle and tumble about playing near some post; soon their movements would become more regular and tend to describe a circle round the post as a centre. One after another, the rest of the group approach, join the two, and finally they march in an orderly fashion and in single file round and round the post. The character of their movement changes; they no longer walk, they trot, and as a rule with special emphasis on one foot, while the other steps lightly; thus a rough approximate rhythm develops, and they tend to "keep time" with one another. . . . Often the circular common movement would be varied by individuals spinning round their own axis at the same time. . . .

It seems to me extraordinary that there should arise quite spontaneously, among chimpanzees, anything that so strongly suggests the primitive dancing of some primitive tribes (pp. 314–315).

Köhler comments that self-adornment often occurs in conjunction with this dancing, although it can be observed at other times as well.

Almost daily the animals can be seen walking about with a rope, a bit of rag, a blade of grass or a twig on their shoulders . . . bushes and brambles are often carried about in considerable quantities spread over the whole back. In addition, string and pieces of rag are to be seen hanging in long strings over their shoulders to the ground from both sides of the neck. . . . The trotting-about of the apes with objects hanging round them . . . seems to give them a naive pleasure. . . . It is very likely that primitive adornment like this takes no account of external effect—I do not give the chimpanzees credit for that—but is based entirely on the extraordinary *heightened bodily consciousness of the animal*. It is a feeling of stateliness and pride, feelings, indeed, which occur also in human beings when they decorate themselves with sashes or long tassels knocking against their legs (pp. 91–93).

The meaning of the ape's proclivity to self-ornamentation and to engage in "carnivals" of drumming, dancing, and singing obviously remains a matter of speculation. Adolph Schultz (1969) suggests that through the impressively resounding "morning songs" that occur at sunrise individuals signal their presence to their neighbors or claim territory. Vernon Reynolds (1967) says that "the best answer we could find as to why [the 'carnival' behavior] occurred was that all this excitement was caused when groups of chimpanzees that normally had different ranges met in the same area" (p. 132). Moreover, the calling and drumming usually occurred when food was plentiful and thus may have served "to announce the whereabouts of good food." Yet Reynolds also notes the ape's "tendencies to one or more of these forms of primitive rhythmic expression, from the roots of which stem our human music and dance" (p. 181), indicating that these behaviors may be expressive as well as functional.

Seeing Reality Symbolically

For philosopher Susanne Langer (1942), these rituals require no functional interpretation. On the contrary, she says they express the liberation from practical affairs that marks the beginning of symbolic transformation and abstraction. Ritual, which may antedate language, serves to articulate feelings, to express outwardly a complex attitude.

The chimpanzee's rudimentary capacity for symbolic representation is further illustrated by more individual behaviors. Langer relates the case of Gua, a chimpanzee reared in a human nursery, who was inexplicably terrified by toadstools, as well as by a pair of blue trousers, a pair of gloves, and an old, flat tin can. In contrast, she formed an intense attachment to her master's coveralls, which were an acceptable substitute for him in his absence. Köhler's Tschego wedged a cherished sea-polished stone into a fold between the lower abdomen and the upper thigh, a storage place commonly used by apes for all sorts of objects. To this spot Tschego also pressed the hands of other chimpanzees and even of humans, apparently as a form of greeting. Gua used kissing, a natural expression among chimpanzees, in a ritual of forgiveness that had to be satisfactorily completed before she would settle down again to play.

In these ritual behaviors and symbolic objects, says Langer, we probably have "the first manifestations of the mental function which in man becomes a peculiar 'tendency to see reality symbolically'" (p. 110), a predisposition that gives rise to art, science, and religion. The rituals of Köhler's apes reminds Joseph Campbell (1959), too, of human mythical and religious conduct. He notes in particular the unexpected detail of the central pole, which is reminiscent of the cosmic pillar or world tree, the AXIS MUNDI that connects earth with heaven (see Eliade, 1957; Jung, 1954c).

RITUALIZATION

Ritual animal behaviors of another, more common type have also been compared to human religious rites. Many animal species engage in what ethologists and other students of animal behavior refer to as *display* activities. These activities frequently incorporate instinctual movements that have been displaced from their usual function and then exaggerated or modified in their new role as SOCIAL RELEASERS. In this capacity, they initiate particular reactions in other members of the same species. In birds they communicate a readiness to fly, or in a variety of species, an intention to attack or flee or to engage in reproductive behavior. Triggering a postulated INNATE RELEASING MECHANISM, such display activities typically initiate a complex series of repetitive exchanges that coordinate movement, control aggression, or form a pair bonding.

Konrad Lorenz suggests that human ritual shows many of the characteristics of animal RITUALIZATION.

> All the means ensuring unambiguity of communication are employed exactly as in phylogenetic ritualization. Mimic exaggeration, redundant repetition and typical intensity are clearly marked in most human ceremonies. In particular, "measured" speed, frequency and amplitude are symptoms that mark human ceremonial behaviour. The deans walk into the aula of the university with measured step; the Catholic priest's chanting during mass is strictly regulated in pitch and rhythm by liturgical rules. The riot of form and colour accompanying human ceremonial, all its pomp and pageantry are developed, in cultural history, in the service of the same functions and along lines astonishingly parallel to those seen in phylogenetic ritualization. In both cases it is abundantly clear that the evolution of the stimulus-sending part of the communicatory system is adapted to the special requirements of the receiver: in other words, it is the receiving set which exerts the selective pressure responsible for the evolution of the sending mechanism (in Huxley, 1966, p. 281).

Other scholars have speculated about specific elements in the religious context itself that may act as triggers to innate releasing mechanisms in human beings. Ostow (1958) suggests that, just as certain species disarm an opponent by assuming a vulnerable posture, so common works of Christian art that depict vulnerability or helplessness—the crucifixion, the infant Jesus, the Virgin Mary, or the Pietà—may reduce hostility and aggressiveness among those who gaze at them. In addition, much as animals will exaggerate their body size, exhibit conspicuously colored structures, or make loud, threatening noises during intraspecific fighting, so immense cathedrals, richly embroidered vestments, and awesome ritual sounds may promote submission in human worshipers.

Campbell (1959) also wonders whether the remarkable innate releasing mechanisms that send the newly hatched turtle rushing toward the sea or that compel the baby chick to flee for cover when a hawk flies overhead do not have their parallel in the human response to universal mythic themes. More specifically, he hypothesizes that these themes, including the gods themselves, constitute "supernormal sign stimuli." Such images are even more effective than naturally occurring phenomena in triggering innate releasing mechanisms. If so, "a functioning mythology can be defined as a corpus of culturally maintained sign stimuli fostering the development and activation of a specific type, or constellation of types, of human life" (p. 48).

Although Lorenz maintains that human rituals serve the same function as animal ritualization—communicating, restricting aggression, and increasing pair or group cohesion—he also emphasizes that the rituals of human cultural history have been established by rather different means. Whereas phylogenetic rituals—those of animals—are the slowly evolved product of natural selection and genetic transmission, human rituals are the outcome of a much more rapid process of cultural evolution. Yet human transmission of culture also entails certain phylogenetically evolved mechanisms, including the compulsions of habit and the emotional bond between generations that are essential if an acquired custom is to be faithfully preserved. Such mechanisms, Lorenz maintains, require complementation within the sphere of culture; we should remember, he warns, that "even a partial loss of cultural tradition is very dangerous, and also that it can occur all too easily" (p. 281).

Whether or not ethologists and those inspired by them are justified in drawing the parallels they do, their work has helped to give a new hearing to the concept of instinct after decades of neglect. Around the turn of the century the notion of instinct was widely used in discussing human conduct, preeminently by McDougall (1908), who made instinct the key to understanding all human activity. As we have already seen, it was also used to explain religious behavior—by McDougall himself, who denied the existence of a specifically religious instinct, as well as by others before and after him, who argued for one (Woodburne, 1920). After an intervening period when almost all talk among psychologists was of learned behavior, it has once again become acceptable to speculate about the role of inherited tendencies in human behavior.

SOCIOBIOLOGY AND RELIGION

Prominent among those who are building on the ethologists' findings are the proponents of the recently emergent field of SOCIOBIOLOGY, which also incorporates knowledge from ecology and population genetics. Edward Wilson (1978), one of sociobiology's chief exponents, defines it as "the systematic study of the biological basis of all forms of social behavior, in all kinds of organisms, including man" (p. 16). According to Wilson, sociobiology recasts the very foundations of psychology and the other social sciences in terms of neo-Darwinist evolutionary biology.

Its chief goal is to predict the features of social organization from a knowledge of demography—for example, the size, density, and age distribution of a population—as well as the behavioral constraints that the population's shared genetic constitution imposes.

The Evolution of Altruism

Of the matters addressed by sociobiologists, Wilson emphasizes the problem of altruism, the self-sacrificing dedication to the welfare of others that can be found in varying degrees throughout the animal kingdom. According to the theory of evolution, traits are selected to maximize personal fitness. Accordingly, altruism ought to have died out long ago, for when an organism—whether a honeybee attacking an intruder or a human soldier shielding a comrade—sacrifices itself, it removes its genes from the population pool. The solution to this enigma lies in the principle of KIN SELECTION: self-sacrifice increases the reproductive potential of the organism's relatives, who also carry the altruistic gene. Sociobiologists thus substitute for the classical principle of personal fitness the notion of INCLUSIVE FITNESS, which takes into account the effects on the relatives as well.

Wilson identifies two basic forms of altruism. "Hard-core" altruism, which typifies termites and honeybees, is unilaterally directed at others—most likely the organism's closest relatives—and occurs without expectations of reciprocity or reward. It is likely to have evolved through kin selection. "Soft-core" altruism, in contrast, is consciously calculated and ultimately selfish, carried out in anticipation of receiving something in return. A product of cultural evolution primarily through the selection of individuals, it is shaped and directed by society through elaborate sanctions. Wilson describes hard-core altruism as the enemy of civilization, for it is inflexibly limited to a person's own relatives or social unit. Altruism in human beings, Wilson optimistically suggests, is mainly of the more selfish but also more malleable variety, although it is substantially hard core when directed at relatives, especially children. The outcome, Wilson says, is "a melange of ambivalence, deceit, and guilt that continuously troubles the individual mind" (p. 159).

Persuading individuals to subordinate their own interests to those of the group lies at the heart of religion, according to Wilson. This process, because it is unique to the human species, cannot be understood by any direct application of the principles of behavioral evolution derived from lower animals. Thus "Religion constitutes the greatest challenge to human sociobiology and its most exciting opportunity to progress as a truly original theoretical discipline" (p. 175).

The Adaptive Functions of Religious Traditions

The basic substratum of religious altruism, says Wilson, consists of a universal, powerful, and relatively inflexible emotional disposition that has evolved through genetic selection. On this foundation, then, the religious traditions have built a superstructure by means of three related mechanisms. *Objectification* entails creating a framework of images and definitions for describing reality; examples include "heaven and hell, human life as an arena for the struggle between the forces of good and evil, gods controlling each force of nature, and spirits ready to enforce the taboos" (p. 188). *Commitment* to these ideas, in the form of emotional self-surrender, is facilitated through the elaborate and repetitive ceremonies overseen by shamans and priests. Finally, *myth* provides a rational explanation of the creation and functioning of the natural world and why the tribe possesses a favored place within it. Prominent recurring themes in these narratives include the struggle for supremacy in this world between two supernatural forces, and the eventual resolution with the coming of the apocalypse and the millennium. In combination, these three mechanisms convince self-interested individuals that the quality of their lives in the next world depends on their compassion and generosity in this one. At the same time, the residual of kin-selected, hard-core altruism may be extended through such kinship imagery as being brothers and sisters, the children of the same father–God (Batson, 1983).

Following the principles of genetic advantage and evolutionary change, religious practices adapt themselves to ensure the well-being of their practitioners. To test this general principle, Vernon Reynolds and Ralph Tanner (1983) graded the world's major religious traditions according to whether they encourage reproduction or place more emphasis on limiting it and caring for those who are already living. Among the attitudes they assessed were those toward sex, marital age, divorce, contraception, abortion and infanticide, personal hygiene, and caretaking of others at various stages of life. They hypothesized that the less predictable the environment was perceived to be, the more a tradition would encourage reproduction, in order to replace the children likely to be lost in such crises as flood, famine, or serious illness. As a measure of environmental predictability, Reynolds and Tanner employed two indicators: per capita energy consumption and per capita gross national product. For both variables they found, as predicted, a highly significant ($p < .001$) negative correlation with emphasis on reproduction. The religious traditions, they concluded, "act as culturally phrased biological messages. They arise from the survival strategies of past group members and continue to advise at the present time. As such, a religion is a primary set of 'reproductive rules,' a kind of 'parental investment handbook' " (p. 294). Yet, as they emphasize, this is only one dimension of a religious tradition's adaptive functions.

Another such function is proposed by psychiatrist Marc Galanter (1989), who combines sociobiology with operant conditioning principles to account for the appeal of contemporary "cults," or charismatic groups. Galanter hypothesizes that the tendency to band together into close-knit groups, evident among other primates, has evolved over the millennia according to the principle of inclusive fitness. Although joining such groups may require sacrifices that diminish personal fitness, the traits shared by the group are themselves more likely to survive. The individual is nevertheless directly reinforced for group association by what Galanter calls the *relief effect*: the more closely affiliated with such a group a person is, the greater the reduction in feelings of emotional stress. Dissociation, on the other hand, will be marked by heightened neurotic stress. Evidence does indeed suggest that individuals join such groups as the Unification Church or the Divine Light Mission during times of personal stress and that as a consequence of affiliation they experience immediate relief. The relief effect, Galanter says, continues to operate throughout the period of membership, effectively reinforcing conformity to the group's teachings; it is also correlated with a mistrust of outsiders.

Given these and other advantages that accrue from religious association—from the conferring of identity and the reduction of guilt to the regularizing of relationships and the certification of practices vital to the group's survival—Wilson (1978) wonders whether a neurologically based "readiness to be indoctrinated" (p. 184) has not gradually evolved in human beings. Such a readiness, he suggests, could be selected both at the level of the group, whose survival would be enhanced by a genetic predisposition to conformity, and at the individual, Darwinian level, where self-sacrifice would be rewarded through the benefits of membership in a group perceived as powerful.

Grounded in dispositions that are the product of genetic evolution over un-numbered generations, religious processes are "powerful, ineradicable, and at the center of human social existence" (pp. 206–207). Wilson acknowledges that sci-entific materialism cannot take the place of the religious traditions, for without doctrines of divine privilege and immortality, it cannot draw on religion's biological source of power. Yet in the face of the "loss of moral consensus, [the] greater sense of helplessness about the human condition and [the] shrinking back toward the self and the immediate future" that are the result of the decline of the religious traditions, a decline promoted by sociobiology itself, Wilson optimistically antici-pates that religion's "source of energy . . . can be shifted in new directions when scientific materialism itself is accepted as the more powerful mythology" (pp. 195, 207).

Others are not so confident that religion can be replaced by science. In his widely cited presidential address to the American Psychological Association, social psychologist Donald T. Campbell (1975) intimated that nothing is likely to counter the selfishness selected by biological evolution as successfully as such traditional religious ideas as temptation, original sin, and an afterlife that compensates us for deprivations in this life. Restrictive laws will not work without "strongly supporting internalized, individual, altruistic restraint." Even if scientists could convince everyone of the value of self-control, it would still be in "the rational best interests of single individuals to be 'free-riders' or to cheat on the system" (p. 200). Religious and moral precepts, the uncompromising extremity of which, suggests Campbell, gives a measure of the tendency they oppose, possess a socially adaptive value and a psychological validity that most likely far exceed our present understanding. Campbell urges his fellow behavioral scientists to be humbly cautious in their approach to religion and to assume "an underlying wisdom in the recipes for living with which tradition has supplied us" (p. 198).

Warning psychologists of the risks of undermining the adaptive functions of "well-winnowed traditions," Campbell offers as compelling a defense for conser-vative religious views, and for caution in psychological theorizing, as can be found in the psychology of religion. He also provides another lead on why strict churches are thriving today, especially in comparison to the mainline denominations. He would likely agree with Laurence Iannaccone's (1994) analysis, according to which groups that demand full participation by all members, as well as strict adherence to its beliefs and lifestyle, thereby screen out free riders, whose lack of commitment dilutes the group's resources and thus reduces the benefits of membership for the others. But Campbell would emphasize the character of those benefits, which derive from the very restrictions and sacrifices that outsiders find so hard to comprehend. One need not subscribe to the sociobiological point of view to recognize the reassurances that strict requirements provide for persons who find the world, inside and out, an overwhelming and threatening place (K. M. Brown, 1994; Marty and Appleby, 1991).

EVALUATION OF BEHAVIORAL AND COMPARATIVE THEORIES

The threat of reductionism that is deeply woven into the psychology of religion is nowhere more evident than in the approaches of this chapter. The behaviorist perspective in itself, quite apart from its application to religion, has inspired vig-orous dissent from a variety of scholars because of its reductionistic stance. Representative of the earlier literature is a symposium edited by William King, *Behaviorism: A Battle Line* (1930). Behaviorism, writes one of its contributors, Josiah Morse, "is a natural offshoot of materialistic ontology and cosmology and atheistic theology" (p. 15). "Of all fundamentalists," says Charles Josey, "the Behaviorist is the most narrow" (p. 63). The critical view articulated by the contributors to this volume is well expressed by Rufus Jones.

> We are quite willing to be told that we are curiously carved pieces of the earth's crust, or strange dust-wreath vortexes, if we may add to the account *the something more which we know we are.* The whirling dust-wreaths of the street do not have longings. The bits of earth-crust which we throw about with our shovel do not yearn for what is not and then forthwith construct it. Desires and strivings, visions and ideals, emotions and sentiments, are as much a genuine part of us as are the iron and lime and phosphorus in our bodies. We have insights of what ought to be, appreciations of beauty, convictions of truth, experiences of love, and these things are not part of the earth's crust. They are not physical realities. They are not *results* of masses of matter in motion. They cannot be adequately explained mechanically. They are real for mind and only for mind (quoted in King, p. 21).

Some contemporary philosophers have been equally unsparing in their criticisms of behaviorism, especially as it has been espoused by B. F. Skinner. Charles Scott (1972) has described Skinner's "technology of behavior" as "remarkably insensitive to the subtleties of value inquiry." The Skinnerians are not alone, however, for they represent the perspective of the larger part of our culture. The Skinnerian view "presents vividly the blindness of our culture regarding itself. It tells us about our infatuation with control, our loss of a sense for human spirituality, our values which parade under the name of 'ethical neutrality,' our ignorance of human subjectivity, our love of easily arranged data" (p. 336). Anthony Flew (1973) finds Skinner's proposals "both elitist and authoritarian." Moreover, he identifies the notion that a scientific study of human beings must avoid all anthropomorphic discourse as Skinner's "most fundamental and most catastrophic presupposition" (p. 98). With it, Flew says, he has dehumanized human psychology.

It has long been recognized, however, that we can accept the *methods* and *basic findings* of behaviorism without subscribing to its materialistic philosophy. As Edward van Ormer (1931) points out in his reflections on the value of behavioristic methods for the study of religion, "If handled honestly [they] will contribute much to science no matter who is at the helm" (p. 266). We have seen such selective appropriation in the work of Bufford (1981), who devotes an entire chapter to the systematic application of behavior principles to Christian education. It is also illustrated by the contributors to the volume *Behavior Therapy and Religion* (Miller and Martin, 1988), who offer proposals for integrating behavioral and spiritual perspectives.

Even when divested of its ideological framework, behavior theory has generated little enthusiasm in religious circles. In his examination of recent publications in pastoral counseling, Christian education, and theology, Phillip Huckaby (1975) found that behavioral psychology was either ignored or criticized. It has fared no better among contemporary German scholars seeking to ground religious education in a psychology of learning. Stimulus–response association, positive reinforcement, and especially modeling can be found in the religious realm, acknowledges Hans-Günter Heimbrock (1984). Yet like other religiously liberal scholars, he maintains that behavior theory will require considerable modification and augmentation if it is to represent specifically religious learning processes adequately (p. 145).

Religious learning, Heimbrock argues, is not simply a matter of acquiring specified observable behaviors, such as reciting Bible verses from memory. Rather, it is the development of inner, symbolic representations, which he says are evident even in biblical models of learning. Moreover, an understanding of religious symbols cannot be taught. It can only emerge out of reflection and interpretation based on a person's own experience. Thus the process of religious learning is inevitably centered in the person, and it is correspondingly limited by individual life history as well as intellectual and imaginative capacities. In the light of such views, it is understandable that Heimbrock and his associates find the cognitive-developmental theories of Ronald Goldman (1964), Fritz Oser (1980; Oser and Gmünder, 1984), and above all James Fowler (1981) to be far more helpful in reconceiving religious education than the various behavior theories (Fraas and Heimbrock, 1986).

THE LIMITS OF BEHAVIORISM

The chief criticisms that have been made of the strictly behaviorist approach represented by Vetter and Skinner can be summed up in terms of two broad issues: the reduction of experience to its expressions in publicly observable behavior, and the discounting or neglect of important determinants of such behavior. Although less radical behavioristic psychologies may be interpreted as attempts to overcome these limitations, any psychology that aspires to be an objective science is still faced by them. Unfortunately, proponents of such psychologies do not often take these problems seriously, if they are even aware of them.

Reduction of Experience to Observable Behavior

A psychology that limits itself to objectively observable behavior, say its critics, not only hamstrings itself in understanding the behavior of organisms but also violates its own principles in the very act of carrying out its work. Those who consider the behaviorist perspective inadequate often challenge its advocates to account for *their own* conduct in terms of their theory's sparse principles. Skinner did not hesitate to say that his work as a psychologist was as determined by contingencies of reinforcement as his pigeons' behavior. Yet as Erwin Straus (1956) argues, truly consistent objective psychologists, because they exclude from their science "the very province of communication and mutual understanding" ought to lapse into silence. Of course they do not. Rather, they remain fully engaged in the intersubjective human world that gives meaning to their various undertakings.

> As a matter of fact, objective psychology cannot exist without a black market furnished with contraband from the psychology of living experience. For by its observations, descriptions, and communications it belongs to the human world. The scholar acts and talks, he is pleased or he suffers, he is a man like all other men. While stating his case, he belongs to a world the existence of which he denies in his statements. But his statements make sense only if a locus for his statements is given (pp. 111–112).

Prevented by their presuppositions from undertaking a phenomenological analysis of the everyday world, observes Straus, objective psychologists remain limited to naive concepts of experience even as they seek a radical reduction of them.

Let us consider an illustration of the kind of reduction they propose. Skinner (1971) suggests that the following translations are less ambiguous and more meaningful than the original statements.

> original: ". . . he lacks assurance or feels insecure or is unsure of himself"
> translation: "his behavior is weak and inappropriate"

original: "there is nothing he wants to do or enjoys doing well, he has no feeling of craftsmanship, no sense of leading a purposeful life, no sense of accomplishment" translation: "he is rarely reinforced for doing anything"

original: "he is disappointed in himself or disgusted with himself" translation: "he is no longer reinforced by the admiration of others, and the extinction that follows has emotional effects" (p. 147).

"These translations," write Benjamin and Dorothea Braginsky (1974), "offer not only an inaccurate portrayal of the human situation but a peculiar one as well. Important information is excluded in the shift from words that denote human affairs to words that denote the objective realm of the value system of the observer. Indeed, any professional translator would never think of omitting the amount of information that is lost when one uses behavioristic translations" (pp. 60–61). The "linguistic contortions" to which Skinner is driven by his rejection of "mentalism" leads British historian Arnold Toynbee "to suspect that the traditional language may, after all, come nearer to expressing the truth than the artificial language that, so it is claimed, is required for stating the truth scientifically" (in Wheeler, 1973, p. 116).

At the very least, it has been argued, the behaviorists should recognize that other levels of inquiry or other universes of discourse could equally well be defended as the most appropriate ones. But such an admission would apparently be uncongenial to many of them.

> Many objective psychologists are violently repelled by everything they call animistic or mentalistic. With the same intensity, on the other hand, they are fascinated by the idea of physiological mechanisms. The mentalistic seems to them deceptive, spookish, unreal—a metaphysical abomination. Over and against such principles, mechanism radiates as the true being, absorbing their total interest (Straus, 1956, p. 121).

Agreeing that Skinner's sweeping denigration of everyday language suggests a metaphysical bias, philosopher Max Black concludes that the vocabulary of ordinary life remains indispensable. Such terms as "intention," "goal," and "feeling" cannot be satisfactorily replaced by the behaviorist's curious paraphrases (in Wheeler, pp. 130–131).

Neglect of Important Determinants of Behavior

Surprising as it may seem, the behaviorist paradigm has proved inadequate even for the prediction of the behavior of rats and pigeons. Skinner and other strict behaviorists make two assumptions that research evidence now seriously challenges. First, they assume that the principles uncovered in the Skinner box or other such stark laboratory environments can, with certain elementary modifications in the descriptive terms, be generalized to any other environment. Second, they assume that the findings from laboratory studies of one species can, with similar modifications, be extended to any other species. "The upshot of [these] two assumptions," writes Brian Mackenzie (1977), "is thus that a descriptive schema which proves adequate to characterize the behaviour of rats and pigeons in two different kinds of Skinner boxes is adequate to characterize the behaviour of all organisms in all environments" (p. 161).

Species-Specific Tendencies: The falseness of the assumption of environmental generality is demonstrated by the work of Keller and Marian Breland (1961), students of Skinner who established a business of training animals through operant conditioning for various commercial purposes. When they removed thoroughly trained animals from the conditioning apparatus and placed them in complex situations more nearly resembling their natural environments, the well-established conditioned response chains were consistently displaced by behavior sequences that had not been earlier reinforced by the Brelands. More appropriate to the consuming of food than the obtaining of it, these behavior sequences actually served to prevent the animals from receiving reinforcement. These new behaviors, said to be the result of INSTINCTIVE DRIFT, were highly resistant to extinction. Equally striking is their finding that the conditioning of new behaviors in these more complex environments was impossible. "After 14 years of continuous conditioning and observation of thousands of animals, it is our reluctant conclusion," write the Brelands, "that the behavior of any species cannot be adequately understood, predicted, or controlled without knowledge of its instinctive patterns, evolutionary history, and ecological niche" (p. 684). For the practical task of controlling animal behavior, the Brelands conclude, ethology offers more than laboratory studies of learning.

The assumption of speciational generality is challenged by the evident differences in the behavior of various species even in similar experimental environments. As Mackenzie (1977) notes, it is not difficult to condition a laboratory rat to press a bar in order to avoid shock, but it is nearly impossible to condition a pigeon to peck a key using the same aversive stimulus. Contrary to the behaviorist's assumption that any animal can be conditioned to carry out any behavior of which it is physically capable, it is now evident that each species is disposed to make certain associations and not others, as the Brelands also observed in working with 38 different species. Moreover, instinctive drift occurs even in the laboratory environment. When researchers undertook to replicate Skinner's superstition experiment cited earlier in this chapter, they found that, contrary to what operant theory predicts, the reinforced idiosyncratic behavior became increasingly restricted to earlier parts of the interval between deliveries of food, and pecking became the dominant behavior just before food was given (Roitblat, 1987).

Parallel constraints operate in the human cognitive realm, according to cultural anthropologist Pascal Boyer (1994). Many anthropologists assume that any of a great diversity of religious ideas can be entertained and then passed on to others through ordinary and largely implicit processes of socialization. Arguing to the contrary, Boyer maintains that universal and early-arising cognitive structures in the "human mind-brain" limit what ideas will seem natural to other people and thus succeed in being transmitted. Beyond accounting for why some religious representations are more likely to take root than others, Boyer's postulated universal intuitive principles explain how people may come to share aspects of cultural representations that have not been conveyed to them in any observable way. For example, the Fang people of Cameroon "know much more" about the ghosts, or wandering spirits of the dead, that populate the forest "than is ever transmitted." All of us, he says, possess similar inferential mechanisms that allow us to fill out what we hear and yet restrict us in the range of generalizations we produce (p. 116).

The Human Existential Framework: More obvious processes are likewise neglected when behavior theory is applied in the human realm. Two essential aspects of the human existential framework are overlooked: the capacity for self-reflection, which is manifest in the sense of identity; and the complex social context in which humans live. The capacity for self-reflection, it has been suggested, may serve as the foundation for "conditioning" that is *self*-chosen and executed, thus making individuals less predictable and controllable in their continuing dialogue with the environment (Wheeler, 1973, p. 250). The legend of Siddhartha Gautama, the king's son who became the Buddha, illustrates this point well. Surrounding his son with every worldly pleasure and commanding that he be kept ignorant of sickness, decrepitude, and death, Suddhodana the king was determined that Siddhartha not fulfill the prophecy that he would renounce the household life and become a Buddha. When Siddhartha nevertheless saw in succession the four signs fashioned for him by the gods—an old man, a sick man, a dead man, and a monk—he returned to his palace deeply agitated, finally resolving to retire from the world in search of NIRVANA. After six years of extreme ascetic practice proved futile, tradition says, Siddhartha finally succeeded in his quest by means of various austerities, deep recollections, and inner struggles. At the risk of trivializing this great legend, we may infer from it that even the most elaborate system of behavior control can be rather abruptly subverted by human reflective awareness.

More to this story's point, however, are the inescapable facts of human existence that triggered the future Buddha's reflection and subsequent renunciation. The experience of human vulnerability and mortality unmistakably plays a critical role in all religious traditions. Yet precisely such experience is missing from Skinner's *Walden Two*; the most serious health problem in this ideal community is a broken leg, and no one is elderly or dies. This lack of realism is symptomatic of behavior theory's neglect of the human existential context, apart from which religious conduct as well as any other behavior remains deeply ambiguous or even incomprehensible.

Social Factors and Inner Dynamics: Also neglected by many behaviorists are the complex social factors that are especially important in human behavior. The great bulk of Skinner's research was carried out on individual organisms isolated in greatly simplified environments. Yet as Dennis Pirages points out, "there is a world of difference between pigeons pecking triangles and humans refusing to sell their homes to others of a different race. It is quite easy to make the pigeons peck the triangle on command, but it is not so easy to modify the socially anchored behavior of humans" (in Wheeler, 1973, p. 60). To comprehend human community and institutions, principles other than operant conditioning are most likely required.

Social learning theory attempts to remedy this shortcoming of classic behavior theory by situating the learning process in its natural social context. Furthermore, through its admission of certain cognitive processes it provides an avenue, albeit a somewhat narrow one, for readmitting important inner events. According to Bower and Hilgard (1981), "In broad outline, social learning theory provides the best integrative summary of what modern learning theory has to contribute to the solution of practical problems" (p. 472). Yet it too may be criticized for employing too elementary and mechanistic a formula. Among children, as noted earlier, imitation plays a large role in the acquisition of complex behaviors, and it remains an active mechanism in the lives of many adults. But we may wonder how the behavior being imitated arose in the first place, especially when it is as elaborate as behaviors found in the religious realm.

Other psychologists posit complex inner dynamics that may even be subverted by the disposition to imitate. According to Jung (1935),

Human beings have one faculty which, though it is of the greatest utility for collective purposes, is most pernicious for individuation, and that is the faculty of imitation.

Collective psychology cannot dispense with imitation, for without it all mass organizations, the State and the social order, are impossible. Society is organized, indeed, less by law than by the propensity to imitation, implying equally suggestibility, suggestion, and mental contagion. But we see every day how people use, or rather abuse, the mechanism of imitation for the purpose of personal differentiation: they are content to ape some eminent personality, some striking characteristic or mode of behaviour, thereby achieving an outward distinction from the circle in which they move. . . . As a rule these specious attempts at individual differentiation stiffen into a pose, and the imitator remains at the same level as he always was, only several degrees more sterile than before. To find out what is truly individual in ourselves, profound reflection is needed; and suddenly we realize how uncommonly difficult the discovery of individuality is (p. 155).

According to tradition, the Buddha began his quest by imitating the austerities practiced by countless others before him. In time, however, he saw the futility of such exercises and finally went his own way. Toynbee doubts that "either heredity or environment, or these two forces together, fully account for the behavior of . . . the Buddha," or for the behavior of Zarathustra, Jeremiah, Jesus, Muhammad, and Saint Francis of Assisi. "I believe that these 'great souls' did have the freedom to take spiritual action that has no traceable source. I also believe that there is a spark of this creative spiritual power in every human being" (in Wheeler, 1973, p. 119).

Behavior Theory as a Means of Attacking Religion

The limits of behavior theory for understanding religious lives, especially those of revered exemplars, is implicitly acknowledged by two earlier proponents who wrote books revealing a lifelong and basically sympathetic interest in comparative religion. One, George Stratton (1911, 1923), was a Wundt-trained experimentalist; the other, Knight Dunlap (1946), was a behaviorist best known for his attack on instinct theory. Neither of these objective psychologists brought his theoretical or methodological view to bear on the mass of religious phenomena he systematically surveyed. Wundt explicitly declared his experimental method inadequate for the study of the higher mental processes that play so large a role in myth and religion; to study them he developed a second method, that of folk psychology (see Chapter 2).

Are we justified in concluding that when behavior theorists are genuinely and sympathetically interested in religion, they are likely to find their usual methods and theories inadequate or irrelevant? Furthermore, should we suspect that when behaviorists do apply their conceptual systems to religious phenomena, they are able to do so only because of seriously limited and essentially unsympathetic views of religion? The evidence would seem to point in this direction, at least for the strict behaviorists we have considered in this chapter. We know that both Watson and Skinner grew up in fundamentalist Protestant homes and, as children, had taken seriously the doctrine they were taught (Bakan, 1966a; Creelan, 1974; Skinner, 1976). As adults, both utterly rejected their religious traditions and later attacked them in their professional writings under the broad rubric of "religion." "When one becomes a scientist," writes Morse, "he does not cease to be a human being. He takes his temperament and mental type with him wherever he goes." The range of behavioristic views is testimony, says Morse—using the same phrase that George Vetter had employed in his derogations of religion—that "scientists are 'human, all too human'" (in W. P. King, 1930, p. 15).

Vetter, like Watson and Skinner, reduces religion to a narrow fundamentalism. Within this limited context, he selects out as typical the worst of piety's apparent fruits. He finds the essence of religion in the aspects that most nearly resemble the stereotypic behavior of rats or pigeons when placed in unpredictable experimental situations. He reduces the broad range of religious behavior to the simple dichotomy of entreaty and orgy. His conclusion is that science is inexorably taking over the functions of religion, foremost by reducing the unpredictability of the physical world. Although his analysis contains enough truth to give these generalizations an aura of plausibility, in subsequent chapters we will see how limited they are. For now we can simply note that none of them does justice to the history of religions.

The reduction of the complex meanings of religious symbols to the minimal terms of behavior theory involves two fallacies, says Abraham Roback (1923) in his criticism of the essays of W. R. Wells (1921), cited early in this chapter. The first is the *fallacy of identifying coordinates*: when fact A—say, some organic condition—seems always to accompany fact B—a particular form of religious experience—the two facts are erroneously taken to be identical. The *fallacy of mistaken essentials* then follows: some one coordinated element, most likely a fundamental term in the behaviorist's theory, is taken as *the* essential or identifying element. For Vetter and many other theoretical behaviorists, a theory of learning provides them with the coordinated facts and elements. Yet according to Robert MacLeod (1964), a phenomenologically oriented experimental psychologist,

> To say that an act has been learned is to say nothing more than that it was developed along lines which could not have been predicted in accordance with the classical principles derived from garden peas and fruit flies. Contemporary geneticists, as you know, are refreshingly open-minded about the so-called laws of genetic determination, especially so far as behavior is concerned. The question of what is genetically determined and what is learned is not as simple as it appeared even a few decades ago. If you will pardon me, I suggest that we banish "learning" from psychology as an explanatory construct and substitute some such purely descriptive term as "development," or even "change." Surely we and our animal friends are always undergoing developmental changes, only some of which become explicitly observable and even less frequently reportable (p. 50).

Learning is not likely to be soon abandoned as a psychological construct; even phenomenologists continue to use it. Yet they conceive of it in fundamentally different terms, distinguishing mere acquisition of "information" from genuine learning. Rare, difficult, and ever incomplete, genuine learning precipitates a radical restructuring of some aspect of one's world. Although it is contingent on exposure to situations conducive to learning activity, no particular conditions will guarantee its occurrence. It is thus far less predictable. Unlike mere information acquisition, genuine learning hits learners hard, often surprising them with what they have learned and exacting an existential commitment to it. People choose to live out what they have learned because it proves to be existentially more satisfying than earlier understandings. Unlike acquired information, genuinely learned content is thus unforgettable, as long as the learner continues to inhabit the transformed world (Colaizzi, 1978).

The phenomenological model of learning, being an elaboration of "insight" learning long championed by cognitive theorists, comes much closer to describing the momentous experience of the Buddha than behavior theory can. It also promises far more to those who, like Heimbrock, are reconceiving the process of religious learning. As Colaizzi acknowledges, however, genuine learning is uncommon. Thus a multifactor account of learning would seem to be necessary if we are to encompass the variety of ways in which religious traditions are acquired. The more cognitively oriented social learning theory may in fact describe reasonably well how most people become religious in the context of established tradition.

ON COMPARING HUMAN AND ANIMAL BEHAVIOR

Reduction of Anthropomorphic Language

Just as phenomenologists and others are unwilling to reduce human experience to the spare categories of animal conditioning, so many are reluctant to ascribe to animals the attitudes and cultural possessions of human beings. Critics of behavior theory, ethology, and sociobiology protest in one voice the application of such human terms as ritual, altruism, and communication to a wide range of animal behaviors that only superficially resemble the usual referents of these terms. Howard Kaye (1986), for example, objects to Wilson's use of "altruism" and his implicit assumption that its manifestations are essentially the same whatever the species.

> Although in ordinary usage human actions are judged altruistic according to the actor's *intent*, Wilson defines altruism solely by measuring the *results* of an action in units of genetic fitness. Thus automatic, reflexive, rigidly determined actions of amoebas, insects, birds, and even the evolution of impalatability in certain moths . . . that increase the genetic fitness of "kin" are considered altruistic, whereas a conscious, intended act of kindness by one human being for another that leaves the genetic fitness of each untouched would not be so considered (p. 105).

Such confusing usage, says Kaye, glosses over "fundamental distinctions, such as that between acts of instinct and reflex and acts of consciousness and volition" (p. 106).

Dutch biologist and phenomenologist Frederik Buytendijk (1951) argues in a similar vein that what distinguishes human dance movements from the rhythmic "dancing" of apes is the consciousness with which they are experienced and the playfulness with which they are carried out. Prerequisite to true dance, Buytendijk maintains, is a fundamental ambiguity in the body as it is lived. On the one hand the body is something that I *have,* a peculiarly intimate *that* that mediates feelings and sensations; on the other hand, the body is what I *am,* a part of the world of other human beings. Should the fundamental tension between *having* a body and *being* a body be indistinct, as it is even in the small child, then, says Buytendijk, dance in the true sense is impossible.

According to Langer (1972), the ethologists' use of the terms "ritual" and "ceremony" is legitimate only when they are applied to *expressive*—not practical— movements that have become repetitive and formalized, such as have been observed in some higher primates. Though recognizing in the animal a minimal capacity for symbolic transformation, Langer still affirms the "great shift" of the human species away from the other primates, signaled by the evolution of symbolic activity—above all, by language and the society it makes possible.

Exaggeration of Genetic Factors

Whereas behavior theory has underplayed the role of genetic inheritance, ethology and sociobiology tend to exaggerate it. Such an emphasis is perhaps the inevitable result of studying diverse species. What stands out are the intraspecies regularities, especially among nonhuman animals, rather than the individual differences that strike students of human behavior. Although recent research does suggest that human individual differences also have a genetic component, most of them are thought to be more profoundly influenced by environmental and social factors. Certainly these factors are more important in human beings than in any other species.

Wilson's further assumption that traits are selected according to the principle of inclusive fitness seems difficult to defend in the light of the many human preferences that ultimately serve to diminish a person's genetic fitness. The realm of religion is particularly problematical in this regard, for here, as Kaye (1986) points out, self-sacrifice benefits not the person's kin but the genetically unrelated religious community. John Crook (1980), in a sociobiological analysis of celibacy and monasticism, finds a solution to this problem within a broader framework. The nonviolence, selflessness, and compassion cultivated by monastic orders can spread to the population at large, he suggests, increasing the frequency of reciprocally altruistic acts and thus the inclusive fitness of the monks' own kin. Other practices, however, including martyrdom, may not be so easily explained.

Is there any evidence that religion is in fact under genetic control? Recent research suggests that to some degree it is. As part of their ongoing study of twins, researchers at the University of Minnesota assessed the similarity in religiosity of twin pairs by using five measures, including a fundamentalism scale, three religious interests scales, and the Religious scale from the Allport–Vernon–Lindzey Study of Values (SV). All five scales were administered to 53 identical (monozygotic or MZ) and 31 fraternal (dizygotic or DZ) twin pairs who had been reared apart. Two of the interest scales were also completed by 458 identical and 363 fraternal twin pairs who had grown up together. If the scores of MZ twin pairs, who share the same genetic inheritance, are more highly correlated than the scores of DZ twin pairs, who on the average share only 50 percent of their genes, researchers may conclude that the measured variable has a genetic component. On all five measures of religiosity in this study, the MZ correlations were strikingly higher than the DZ correlations. Among those reared apart, for example, the SV Religious scores correlated $-.08$ for DZ twins whereas they correlated .55 for MZ twins. The results of this study suggest that about 50 percent of the variance in these five measures is accounted for by genetic factors (Waller, Kojetin, Bouchard, Lykken, and Tellegen, 1990). Given the bias of these scales toward conventional piety, however, we cannot estimate the degree to which genetic inheritance contributes to the more striking and original expressions of religiosity. These data do suggest, however, that the speculations of ethologists and sociobiologists regarding human piety are not entirely unfounded.

Doubtful nevertheless that sociobiology will in fact possess the scope and explanatory power that Wilson holds out for it, particularly in the religious and ethical realm, his critics take note of the evident religious quality in his vision of an ideal society. In offering a new faith "appropriate to our needs and times, majestic in its sweep, consistent with our belief in scientific rationality, and restoring a sense of purpose to our activities," Wilson stands "in a long line of missionaries . . . who have preached the gospel of scientific materialism" (Morin, 1980, pp. 304–305). Others in this chapter have expressed a similar faith, though not his view of the power of religion or his inclination to assimilate science—the "evolutionary epic"— to mythology. They do, however, share a certain moral vision that, as Kaye argues in Wilson's case, stands in irreconcilable opposition to their reductive scientific materialism. Either the new intellectual and social order they envisage is nothing more than a mechanistically determined by-product of their own genetic endowments and conditioning histories or their reductionistic views of human beings are wrong.

However worthy their vision may be, Bernard Davis's (1980) conclusion in regard to sociobiology doubtless applies to them all. In spite of advances in the behavioral and biological sciences, Davis observes, "The future of religion seems likely to continue to be pluralistic rather than monolithic, involving different patterns that meet different individual needs rather than a single pattern that achieves thorough consistency with science" (p. 290). The inescapable reality of individual differences, whatever their origins, is one of the great themes explored in the chapters ahead.

5

RELIGION IN THE LABORATORY

As the flood of behaviorism gradually receded from the world of psychology in the middle of the twentieth century, it revealed a landscape dramatically transformed. In place of the earlier introspective fascination with human experience was a commitment to the objective viewpoint and methods that the behaviorists had borrowed from the natural sciences. Whereas behaviorism as a comprehensive explanatory system had retreated into enclaves within academic and clinical psychology, methodological behaviorism—the view that privileges the methods of behaviorism but not its explanatory principles—became the very cornerstone of psychological science. The majority of psychologists are still methodological behaviorists today, even though they may not recognize or employ the label themselves.

Within the broad stream of methodological behaviorism—or what Lee Cronbach (1957) and many others prefer simply to call scientific psychology—flow two major currents, the experimental and the correlational. Both approaches begin with quantitative description—of behavior as it varies from one laboratory situation to another, on the part of the experimentalists; and of attitudes and conduct as they vary from one person to another, on the part of the correlationists. Although their views are not inherently incompatible, the two groups have grown far apart in their technical training and in their research interests and goals. Among psychologists of religion, however, this division is far less sharply drawn, for both approaches have been applied to a common set of problems. Nonetheless, many researchers think that a truly experimental approach to this field is exceedingly difficult, if not impossible. Although the content of this chapter is testimony to what can be accomplished with some ingenuity, the great bulk of objective empirical research is correlational in character.

Experimentalists strive to establish general theories of behavior that apply to all people. Crucial to the attainment of this goal, they say, are laboratory environments that allow them to study the relationships of variables under greatly simplified and highly controlled conditions. By systematically varying these conditions and observing the resulting effects on their subjects' behavior, researchers test out various hypotheses about cause and effect. The eventual outcome, they hope, will be laws that characterize "the generalized, normal, human, adult mind" (Boring, 1950, p. 413).

Whereas experimentalists either minimize individual differences by using highly similar laboratory subjects or dismiss them as unavoidable ERROR VARIANCE, correlationists take such variability as their central problem. Although similarly dedicated to developing an explanatory science, correlationists are chiefly interested in uncovering the origins of individual differences and clarifying their diverse effects on people's lives. Such differences, as the outcome of complex, uncontrolled, and long-term "experiments" of nature, are generally not subject to laboratory investigation. To observe and analyze such individual variation as it naturally occurs, the correlationists have developed a large variety of psychological tests and other assessment procedures. Although more broadly applicable than experimental methods, these correlational techniques do not allow cause-and-effect inferences of comparable power.

Whatever their differences, experimentalists and correlationists agree that every variable they study must be "operationalized," that is, some standard operations must be established for observing and measuring the variable. For example, anxiety may be operationalized in terms of a numerical score on a self-report anxiety questionnaire (a correlational approach) or of a galvanometer reading of the level of skin resistance to a weak electric current (an experimental technique). Such measurement procedures are sometimes said to provide an "operational definition" for a particular concept or term. Given that these procedures do not actually define the associated terms (Leahey, 1980), it is more accurate to say that a concept, once defined by ordinary means, may be operationalized in a variety of ways. Any one of them may serve to identify and measure a variable and thus make it available for either correlational or experimental investigation.

EARLY "EXPERIMENTAL" APPROACHES

The first self-proclaimed experimental psychology of religion was undertaken in Europe by members of the Dorpat school shortly after the turn of the century. As we may recall from Chapter 2, Karl Girgensohn borrowed from the Würzburg school the techniques of "experimental introspection" to explore the fundamental elements and structures of religious experiences. Girgensohn (1921) asked his well-trained subjects to describe their responses to a variety of religious poems and hymns, to answer a series of inquiries designed to reveal the basis of their fundamental religious beliefs, and to discuss with the investigator their understanding of faith. Drawing on the detailed protocols he obtained from his subjects, Girgensohn sought to clarify the nature of religious feelings as well as the place in religious experience of imagination and will.

Whatever the value of the painstaking work of Girgensohn and his associates, we may wonder if it should be called experimental. Georg Wunderle (1922) argues that such a usage essentially changes the true meaning of the word, thus introducing a regrettable ambiguity. The German psychological tradition does in fact distinguish two types of experiment: (1) the highly simplified and controlled variety that serves to uncover causal relationships (the *Kausalexperiment*); and (2) the type employed by the Würzburg school, which functions as a "fact-finder" or "demonstration" (*Darstellungsexperiment*), a means of bringing a phenomenon more clearly into view (Tumarkin, 1929, p. 19). Because Girgensohn's research is much closer to the descriptive psychology of the phenomenological psychologists than to the far more strictly defined experimental psychology advocated by the objective psychologists, we postpone our study of it until Chapter 12.

Some Early American Experiments

In America, the word *experimental* was at first also used rather flexibly. George Coe (1900), for example, says he used "hypnotic experiments" to explore the relation of conversion experience to suggestibility. He divided his subjects into two groups, according to whether or not they reported that their expectations of undergoing striking religious transformation had at some time in the past been fulfilled. When he tried to hypnotize these subjects, 13 of the 14 who said they had experienced transformation proved to be passively suggestible to Coe's hypnotic instructions whereas 9 of the 12 who did not experience transformation showed evidence of spontaneity or originality in their responses. From what is strictly correlational evidence, Coe concludes that passive suggestibility, when combined with temperamental disposition and positive expectation, allows us to predict with considerable confidence that striking transformation will occur.

The experimental procedure used by Goodwin Watson[1] (1929) comes closer to today's conceptual model. Seven carefully prepared worship services were conducted at an interdenominational conference of several hundred adolescent boys. One service, for example, consisted of dramatic readings emphasizing the vastness and complexity of the universe; another was composed of deeply moving music; a third presented a series of readings contrasting common religious principles or ideals with statistics or case studies demonstrating the bitter realities. At the end of each service, the boys were asked to indicate on a seven-point scale the degree to which they found the service worshipful. After the final service, they were asked to rank all seven in order of merit. Individual comments were also solicited after each service. Watson reports that the service of music received the highest ratings, and the one focusing on the quest for meaning in a vast universe, the lowest. In general, the services that emphasized feeling rather than intellectual content tended to be ranked higher. Statistical differences in ratings according to age, denominational affiliation, size of home town, and work experience were largely insignificant.

The effectiveness of particular forms of worship was also the focus of a series of experiments undertaken by Ruth Hill (1933) for a doctoral dissertation in the University of Chicago Divinity School. Hill was interested in the effects of a series of six dramas on attitudes toward other races or ethnic groups as well as toward criminals. Each drama was presented during a worship service of appropriate songs, scriptures, and prayer. The first group of three dramas, presented at regularly scheduled evening worship services, featured the following themes: difficulties in Chinese–American relations; the positive human qualities, struggles, and simple piety of Russian peasants; and the problems facing a group of Jewish immigrants from Poland when they sought entrance to America. The second set of dramas, performed for a young people's group that met just before the Sunday evening service, depicted three themes: the possibility of redeeming criminals by treating them with mercy rather than justice; the evils of capital punishment and the prospect of its abolishment; and the presence of goodness, along with evil, in the lives of typical criminals.

The subjects in this study consisted of 79 members of the acting and production staffs (called "players"), 186 members of the audience, and 101 other members of

---

[1] Goodwin Watson (1899–1976), a professor at Teachers College, Columbia University, as well as an ordained minister of the Methodist Episcopal Church, should not be confused with John B. Watson, the religiously hostile proponent of behaviorism.

the same congregations or of nearby churches who served as the loosely equated CONTROL GROUPS. Players and members of the audience completed appropriate attitude questionnaires before and after participation in these dramatic services of worship; some were also interviewed. Persons in the control groups also completed the questionnaires a second time, after an equivalent interval of time.

Hill reports that both players and audience involved in the first set of dramas showed a greater decline in racial prejudice, on the average, than did their control groups. With the dramas on criminality, however, only the players showed positive changes in attitude, and for them the change appeared on only one of the two attitude measures. Interestingly, in the study as a whole, the largest shifts in attitude were shown by those actively involved in the drama productions—above all, by the actors themselves. Age was a factor as well: the older players tended to record larger changes of attitude than did the younger players of high school age. Hill also provides evidence that the six dramas varied in their effectiveness, with the less obviously didactic and argumentative ones showing an advantage. Interview data suggested that the dramas' effectiveness in changing attitudes was more or less proportional to the emotional response they evoked.

The "experiments" of Coe, Watson, and Hill are much closer in form than Girgensohn's to the contemporary model, but they still fall short of it in precision and control. Although all three investigations lack the sophisticated design expected by today's experimentalists, they do rely on statistical evaluation, which is the hallmark of modern objective research. Furthermore, they contain, at least implicitly, the features of hypothesis testing and comparison groups, which are also characteristics of contemporary experimental design.

The Religious Seeker as Experimentalist

If we take the word "experimental" in its broadest sense, as designating any approach that chooses among alternatives by submitting them to the test of experience, we may observe that the attitude of the religious seeker is itself often an experimental one. In her classic study of mysticism, Evelyn Underhill (1911) urges her readers to adopt just such a practical attitude. She invites them to undertake the following simple experiment as a means of gaining new knowledge of the relation between the human mind and the external world.

> All that is asked is that we shall look for a little time, in a special and undivided manner, at some simple, concrete, and external thing. This object of our contemplation may be almost anything we please: a picture, a statue, a tree, a distant hillside, a growing plant, running water, little living things. . . .
>
> Look, then, at this thing which you have chosen. Wilfully yet tranquilly refuse the messages which countless other aspects of the world are sending; and so concentrate your whole attention on this one act of loving sight that all other objects are excluded from the conscious field. Do not think, but as it were pour out your personality towards it: let your soul be in your eyes. Almost at once, this new method of perception will reveal unsuspected qualities in the external world. First, you will perceive about you a strange and deepening quietness; a slowing down of our feverish mental time. Next, you will become aware of a heightened significance, an intensified existence in the thing at which you look. As you, with all your consciousness, lean out towards it, an answering current will meet yours. It seems as though the barrier between its life and your own, between subject and object, had melted away. You are merged with it, in an act of true communion: and you *know* the secret of its being deeply and unforgettably, yet in a way which you can never hope to express. . . .

The price of this experience has been a stilling of [the] surface-mind, a calling in of all our scattered interests: an entire giving of ourselves to this one activity, without self-consciousness, without reflective thought. To reflect is always to distort: our minds are not good mirrors. The contemplative, on whatever level his faculty may operate, is contented to absorb and be absorbed: and by this humble access he attains to a plane of knowledge which no intellectual process can come near (pp. 301–302).

Although it falls far short of the "transcendental contemplation of the mystic," this elementary experiment brings into play, says Underhill, the same capacities that underlie the mystic's "apprehension of the Invisible Real."

EXPERIMENTAL STUDIES OF PRAYER

The experimental attitude may serve the religious individual in a far more pragmatic way. Prayer in its petitionary forms invites self-interested experimental evaluation, as many children realize. "Occasionally," writes H. G. Wells (1934) in his autobiography, "I would find myself praying—always to God simply. He remained a God spread all over space and time, yet nevertheless he was capable of special response and magic changes in the order of events. I would pray when I was losing a race, or in trouble in an examination room, or frightened. I expected prompt attention" (pp. 70–71). Later on, disturbed by uncertainties about personal immortality, "I would lie quite still in my bed invoking the Unknown to 'Speak now. Give me a sign' " (p. 126). Unfortunately, prompt attention and signs are not often forthcoming, and the resulting cognitive dissonance eventually leads to changed expectations or assumptions. As in the case of Wells and some of Allport's (1950) combat veterans, the outcome may be atheism; others retain their faith by revising their understanding of prayer.

Certain scientists in the early 1870s actually proposed testing the efficacy of prayer through formal experimentation, a suggestion that appalled many ministers and theologians of the day. The idea in particular of "a 'control group' of sick persons, for whom one deliberately does *not* pray [was said to be] so repugnant to the true Christian as to cast doubt on the sanity of the enterprise" (Brush, 1974, p. 562). Although Francis Galton's (1872) correlational study of prayer did appear in the midst of this controversy, it was not until the middle of the twentieth century that experiments of the type proposed were finally carried out (see Francis and Evans, 1995).

As Robert Thouless (1971, p. 93) remarks, Galton's study might better be classified as experimental theology than psychology. The same label would apply to any other studies of the objective efficacy of prayer, such as Randolph Byrd's (1988) experiment on the effects of intercessory prayer. Of the 393 coronary patients who agreed to participate in Byrd's study, half were randomly selected to receive daily prayers from born-again Christians praying outside the hospital. The remaining patients served as the control group. Throughout the study, neither the patients, the hospital staff, nor Byrd himself knew to which group each patient had been assigned. Byrd monitored 26 variables, including medications and other required interventions and the occurrence of such complications as pnemonia. On 6 of these variables the prayer group had significantly more favorable scores; overall ratings of their hospital stays were also significantly higher. Although none of these differences was dramatic, Byrd considers the overall trend sufficient evidence for the efficacy of "intercessory prayer to the Judeo-Christian God."

Although psychologists of religion have showed interest in Byrd's study (e.g., Brown, 1994a), it entails assumptions and variables that fall outside the usual boundaries of the field. It also raises difficult theological questions. More obviously in the domain of psychology are studies of the *subjective* effects of prayer, for when the person praying is the locus of potential effects, the entire chain of cause and effect remains open to psychological analysis.

An Experiment in Prayer Therapy

Formal experiments on prayer's subjective effects are scarcely to be found. One, reported by William Parker and Elaine St. Johns (1957), has been prominently touted in the popular inspirational literature as offering scientific proof for the power of prayer. This claim invites us to take a closer look. Forty-five volunteers suffering from neurotic and psychosomatic disorders were placed in three equal-sized groups. The 15 members of the experimental group received "Prayer Therapy" in weekly two-hour group meetings in the Speech Clinic at the University of Redlands, California; the 15 members of one control group were seen weekly for individual counseling sessions in which no mention of religion or prayer was made; and the remaining 15 individuals formed a second control group, the "Random Prayers," who agreed to pray, in whatever manner they were accustomed, every night before retiring and with the specific aim of overcoming the problem that the experimenter had identified for each individual.

At the beginning of this study all subjects were evaluated with the aid of five assessment devices: the Rorschach Inkblot Test, the Szondi Test, the Thematic Apperception Test (TAT), the Sentence Completion Test, and the Word Association Test. Slightly more than nine months later, these tests were readministered and evaluated by an "impartial tester," who also estimated the amount of improvement demonstrated by each participant. The prayer therapy group is reported to have shown 72 percent improvement in both symptoms and test results, the psychotherapy group 65 percent improvement, and the random prayers, no improvement. "It seemed conclusive," write Parker and St. Johns, "that Prayer Therapy was not only a most effective healing agent but that prayer properly understood might be the single most important tool in the reconstruction of man's personality" (p. 34).

A Failure of Design: Prayer may indeed have such power, but unfortunately, errors in the design of this experiment leave the proposition untested. The first and most serious error was made in the method of placing the participants in the three treatment groups: rather than assigning them randomly, as many experimenters would do, the investigators invited their volunteers to choose the group that most appealed to them. Individual differences in participants were thus allowed to operate in an uncontrolled manner, so that group differences may reflect not the treatment differences, but the differences in personality types attracted to each alternative.

Second, the variations in the treatment groups were insufficiently controlled to allow firm conclusions about the factors responsible for the final outcome. Even if the participants in this study had been randomly assigned to the three treatment groups, the results could be interpreted in a way that makes prayer an irrelevant variable. It could easily be argued, for example, that psychotherapy is the critical factor responsible for the observed improvement, and that group psychotherapy has a slight, if significant, advantage over the individual form of counseling used in this investigation. The "Random Pray*ers*," receiving no therapy at all, understandably showed no improvement. If an even more parsimonious explanation is desired, we may speculate that the critical factor was simply sympathetic human contact. As they stand, however, the results seem to argue *against* the efficacy of prayer, not for it, as these authors conclude.

There are still other problems with the study. We do not learn, for example, whether the "impartial tester" was properly ignorant of an individual's group affiliation at the time the test protocols were evaluated, a precaution that should have been taken to minimize tester bias. Moreover, the tests used are highly controversial and certainly do not allow the confident judgments reported by these authors. Especially in light of the subjectivity inherent in these tests, the reduction of the various observations and test scores to a percent improvement must be a largely arbitrary procedure. It is no wonder, then, that the authors report no tests of statistical significance.

Concluding Thoughts on the Efficacy of Prayer

The absence of compelling scientific evidence for the efficacy of prayer is apparently not a problem for the 88 percent of Americans who report that they pray to God (Poloma and Gallup, 1991, p. 3). In a 1996 poll of 1004 adult Americans, 82 percent said that they believe in "the healing power of personal prayer," 73 percent that "praying for someone else can help cure their illness," and 77 percent that "God sometimes intervenes to cure people who have a serious illness" (C. Wallis, 1996). Many, presumably, base their conviction that prayer is effective on their own personal experience.

That conviction, according to James (1902), lies at "the very core of living religion," and thus religion "must stand or fall by the persuasion that effects of some sort genuinely do occur." If prayer

> be not effective; if it be not a give and take relation; if nothing be really transacted while it lasts; if the world is in no whit different for its having taken place; then prayer, taken in this wide meaning of a sense that *something is transacting*, is of course a feeling of what is illusory, and religion must on the whole be classed, not simply as containing elements of delusion—these undoubtedly everywhere exist—but as being rooted in delusion altogether, just as materialists and atheists have always said it was (pp. 366–367).

Yet the question of efficacy is not as simple as Byrd and others are inclined to treat it. Walter Muelder (1957), writing as dean of the Boston University School of Theology, observes that

> There are obvious differences among physiological, psychological, social, and metaphysical or theological levels of the prayer response and among the kinds of effects which prayers produce. Moreover, we must contrast the special datable acts called praying from the whole life of devotion which may include them. . . . We may expect a significant difference in efficacy between the outbursts of men and women in a crisis, especially if they do not habitually pray, from that of a saintly devotee (p. 35).

There is a great difference, agrees Paul Johnson (1953), between prayer that is treated as a magical, mechanical trick for bypassing the laws of the universe and prayer that is "a dynamic experience of harmony within and without that heals conflict and loneliness in renewing one's sense of belonging to a larger wholeness" (p. 35). No scientific study will ever yield a fraction of the instant primal conviction that comes from this experience.

MEDITATION IN THE LABORATORY

''Prayer,'' as the word is commonly used, suggests a spoken, sometimes formal address to a divinity, one element of which is often heartfelt petition. However, if we define prayer broadly, as James (1902, p. 365) does when he takes it to mean ''every kind of inward communion or conversation with the power recognized as divine,'' we will frequently find it impossible to distinguish prayer and meditation. Some prayers are conceived as meditative in form, yet still possess an implicit petitionary character. Others, such as mystical prayers, are wholly inarticulate, formless, and passive, seeking nothing other than blissful union with the divine (Underhill, 1911; Washburn, 1995). We are unmistakably outside the realm of prayer only when meditative practice is undertaken without any notion of a divine force or power (or at least one lying outside of the individual), as it often seems to be today. Meditation's apparent independence both of theistic belief and of the expectation of divine intervention may be responsible for its popularity among contemporary Western seekers. It may also account for the fact that research on meditation is the most conspicuous application of experimental methods in the psychology of religion.

Varieties of Meditative Practice

Meditation is practiced in a great variety of forms. It may be undertaken in solitude or in concert with hundreds of others. It may be conducted in silence or by chanting aloud a sacred syllable or mystical phrase. It may be practiced in a comfortable seated position or a difficult posture, or it may be performed while walking slowly or engaging in mundane activities. It may last only 15 or 20 minutes, or it may fill

Thai monks engaged in walking meditation in a Buddhist shrine.

most of the individual's waking hours for weeks at a stretch. It may focus upon any of a myriad objects: a "simple, concrete, and external thing," such as Underhill invites us to choose; some part of the body, such as the navel, or a bodily process, such as breathing; vivid images of the repulsive products of death and decomposition, especially of the meditator's own body, or the tortures of hell; momentous events in history; the form, words, or deeds of some revered saint or spiritual director; or the glorious possibilities of heaven. It may seek to become absorbed in, or to understand, some mystery or paradox. Alternatively, it may shun all objects, formulas, or themes, seeking only an empty, formless silence (Conze, 1956; Goleman, 1988; Humphreys, 1935; Kabat–Zinn, 1994; Naranjo and Ornstein, 1971; Nyanaponika Thera, 1962; Reichelt, 1947; J. C. Smith, 1992; Trimingham, 1971; J. White, 1974).

Meditation is sometimes combined with a group practice that produces ergotropic arousal, which is the antithesis of the calm inwardness usually associated with meditation. Karl Reichelt (1947), for example, describes a preliminary exercise undertaken by some Buddhist monks in East Asia for its effect on their breathing. Meditation periods begin with a race about the interior of the spacious meditation hall, during which each monk beats the one in front of him on or below the shoulder blades with wooden slats. "A more fantastic scene . . . could hardly be imagined, especially at night time, when hundreds of men in grey gowns, beneath the dim light of the kerosene lamps, are racing around at high speed with dust whirling about them" (p. 70). We may call to mind, too, the Sufi ritual of *dhikr* or recollection, which the Mevlevi dervishes developed into an elaborate and exhausting dance.

Underlying the diversity and seeming contradictions among meditational practices is a single aim: the withdrawal of the attention from the countless external objects and events that distract it, in preparation for the hard-won achievement of a higher knowing, variously called illumination, enlightenment, or union with the First Principle or Highest Good. For the mystic, then, meditation has always been a preliminary stage. The objects of meditation serve to gather up the scattered threads of conscious life; some of them also remind meditators of the right attitudes and the final goals toward which they are striving. Ultimately, however, these objects, too, must be left behind (Hocking, 1912; West, 1987).

Studies of Yoga

The discovery of the fruits of meditation, and the development of its various techniques, were undoubtedly the outcome of countless trial-and-error "experiments." The subjective empirical attitude implied here is illustrated by Kovoor Behanan (1937) and Theos Bernard (1944), both of whom undertook the discipline themselves in their systematic studies of YOGA. Behanan, a native of India who earned his doctorate at Yale, describes two phases in his breathing exercises. In the first, lasting 15 to 20 minutes, he felt a kind of physical excitement, marked by tingling sensations and sometimes muffled sounds or a rapid succession of color images. In the second stage, excitement gave way to extremely pleasant feelings of tranquillity and relaxation, which marked the beginning of the period of concentration. When concentration was successful, which it increasingly came to be, the object would become vague and ill defined, his own body would fade out of awareness, and he would find himself in a hazy, effortless state of mental vacuity that was at the same time extraordinarily pleasant. When the state suddenly ended, the object of concentration would once more come into focus.

The general outcome of engaging in these practices for a few months, Behanan reports, was an increased power of endurance, fewer headaches, and a previously unknown emotional stability. The half-dozen yogis that he saw daily for more than a year struck Behanan as the happiest persons he had ever known. "The most venerable ascetic system," writes James (1907a, pp. 136–137), "and the one whose results have the most voluminous experimental corroboration, is undoubtedly the Yoga system. . . . The result claimed, and certainly in many cases accorded by impartial judges, is strength of character, personal power, unshakability of soul."

At the time James was writing, "experimental corroboration" could only refer to the personal experiments that aspiring yogis carried out on themselves, with an eye to the effects of these mental exercises on their spiritual condition. As Huston Smith (1991) observes, *raja* ("royal") yoga—"the way to God through psychophysical experiments"—is designed for patient, inner-directed, and undogmatic individuals inclined toward the scientific approach of hypothesis testing. Beyond such a disposition, all that is required is "a strong suspicion that our true selves are more than we now realize and a passion to plumb their full extent" (pp. 41, 42).

It was not until the 1930s that a more objective kind of experimental evidence was sought for yoga's effects. Behanan himself employed a measure of oxygen consumption, the rate at which oxygen is assimilated by the body; it is a function thought to lie outside of voluntary control. His consumption increased 12 to 25 percent, depending on the type of yogic breathing pattern he employed. A detailed accounting of these results was published years later (Miles, 1964). As early as 1935 Thérèse Brosse (1946, 1954, 1963), a French cardiologist, sought to measure the degree to which yogis are able voluntarily to regulate their heart action. One of the electrocardiographic records that she published showed a reduction in heart potential to nearly zero; some yogis, she inferred, are able to bring the heart almost to a halt. A series of follow-up studies by B. K. Bagchi and M. A. Wenger (1957;

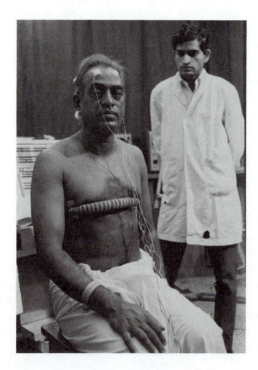

Ramanand Yogi is here prepared for laboratory study of his capacity to reduce his need for oxygen while seated in an airtight box.

Wenger and Bagchi, 1961; Wenger, Bagchi, and Anand, 1961) yielded less impressive findings. Only one of four subjects claiming control over heart and pulse demonstrated a capacity to slow them; none could actually stop them. "Direct voluntary control of autonomic functions," Wenger and Bagchi (1961, p. 322) concluded, "is probably rare among yogis." Yet changes per se in autonomic functions are frequent and marked. In experienced yogis they found faster heart rates, lower finger temperatures, greater conductance in the skin of the palm, and higher blood pressure. These differences suggest that, at least for some subjects, yoga is an active process clearly distinguishable from a state of relaxation. Any other conclusion is uncertain: sudden changes in the various measures were not unusual, and the data as a whole are fragmentary.

Electroencephalographic findings have been more noteworthy. Various researchers have demonstrated that meditation is typically marked by a predominance of alpha waves, brain waves of 8 to 13 cycles per second that accompany states of relaxed wakefulness. As meditation progresses, striking changes may occur. N. N. Das and H. Gastaut (1957) report that during deep meditation their best-trained yogis exhibited fast rhythms (beta waves, typically found with intense concentration or mental agitation) that reached their highest amplitude during the *samādhi* period. Their finding has been confirmed by James Corby and his colleagues (1978) with their experienced tantric yoga meditators. Das and Gastaut also observed that stimuli that ordinarily disrupt ("block") alpha rhythms had no effect on the EEGs of their yogis, an observation reported as well by Bagchi and Wenger (1957). In addition, B. K. Anand, G. S. Chhina, and B. Singh (1961) found that the alpha BLOCKING they observed in yogis who were not meditating did not show the ordinarily predictable adaptation to continuing repetition of the stimulus. These findings confirm the yogis' claim that during deep meditation they are utterly oblivious to events in the surrounding environment. When they are not meditating, they apparently tend to remain unusually sensitive to what is going on around them.

Psychophysiological Correlates of Zen

Zen meditation has also been brought under experimental investigation. Many of these studies were conducted in the meditation halls ordinarily used by the subjects. Others were carried out in the experimenters' laboratories in which special conditions could be more easily arranged. As with the yogis, control observations were sometimes made on the same subjects outside of the meditative state; other times beginners or nonmeditators were used. Sometimes control groups were deemed unnecessary, since normative data are available for most of the measures used in these studies.

Because breath regulation is an important element in Zen practice and is easy to measure, it has been the chief focus of much of this research. Respiratory rate drops dramatically, to an average of four breaths a minute; there is correspondingly a considerable increase in tidal volume (the amount of one expiration). Breathing is typically abdominal rather than thoracic. Oxygen consumption decreases within a minute after the onset of meditation and remains 20 to 30 percent below the normal rate until the end of the session. Accompanying these changes in respiration are decreases in muscle tension and blood alkalinity (Akishige, 1977; Hirai, 1974, 1989).

Changes in the electrical activity of the brain constitute the other major focus of Zen meditation research. According to Akira Kasamatsu and Tomio Hirai (1966; Hirai, 1974), electroencephalographic changes during the meditation period are typically marked by four stages. (1) Within 50 seconds after meditation has begun, alpha waves appear—in spite of opened eyes, a condition that ordinarily suppresses alpha activity. (2) After about five or ten minutes, the ALPHA RHYTHMS increase to an amplitude approximately 50 percent higher than the alpha activity of normal subjects with closed eyes. (3) Some time later the alpha frequency gradually decreases. (4) In some instances a rhythmical theta train will finally appear, a wave pattern that usually marks the onset of sleep and the occurrence of dreamlike images, but that here occurs with the eyes still open and without giving way to even slower, delta waves and "sleep spindles." These researchers also found that changes in EEG patterns correlate with the number of years spent in Zen training as well as with ratings of proficiency by the Zen master. That is, the majority of the disciples who had meditated for five or fewer years, or who had low proficiency ratings, showed only the pattern of stage 1, whereas all the disciples who had more than 20 years of training, or who received high proficiency ratings, showed the patterns of either stage 3 or stage 4.

Comparison with Yoga: A further discovery, apparently yet to be replicated, provides striking evidence of an essential difference between Zen and yoga. When Kasamatsu and Hirai's control subjects, sitting with eyes closed, were subjected to click stimulation every 15 seconds, the amount of alpha blocking with each click rapidly decreased. In other words the control subjects showed the normal process of HABITUATION to a repeated stimulus, such as the city dweller exhibits in response to constant traffic noise. In contrast, Zen masters showed virtually no adaptation: the alpha blocking remained more or less constant throughout the testing period. Queried about their experience, the Zen masters responded that they perceive stimuli more clearly in the meditative state and yet remain unaffected by them. A similar pattern of nonhabituating alpha blocking has been observed in yogis, as we noted earlier, but in their case it was found *outside* the meditative state. During meditation there was no alpha blocking at all. This finding, as Tart (1990, p. 577) has suggested, is consistent with the differences in philosophic outlook of Zen and yoga: yogis seek to disengage themselves as much as possible from the phenomenal world of illusion, whereas the disciples of Zen seek not so much to withdraw from the objects that surround them as to see these objects rightly.

The task of making psychophysiological comparisons between different meditative systems is fraught with difficulties. First, as Abdulhusein Dalal and Theodore Barber (1969) emphasize, it is often difficult to obtain the cooperation of those who best represent a particular system. Dalal says that the yogis who have experienced *samādhi* are likely to view the scientist's efforts as trivial and futile, if not also sacrilegious. When practitioners are willing to serve as subjects in scientific research, it is hard to estimate the degree to which their practice is genuine, and thus, the degree to which the data obtained from them may be generalized to others following the same system. We must be prepared for important differences—within the traditions themselves (e.g., among the different schools of Zen or of yoga) and in individuals within a particular school (see Miike, 1968). Second, meditators frequently report that the presence of the researcher and the attached measuring devices disturb their practice. Crude though these measurements may be—at least in comparison to the complex phenomena they are taken to represent—they are yet highly obtrusive.

A problem that would appear to be more easily resolved still remains: the measures used and the conditions under which they are taken have not been standardized. What is called for is the application of similar experimental conditions to representatives of different meditative systems. The studies carried out thus far allow very few comparisons.

Transcendental Meditation

The problem of obtaining the cooperation of enough meditators with similar training to allow for meaningful generalization would appear to have been solved in the recent research on transcendental meditation (TM). In spite of its roots in ancient Indian scriptures, TM is said to be neither a philosophy nor a religion. Although it possesses elements of both, its practitioners need adopt none of the teachings of Maharishi Mahesh Yogi, the founder and chief promulgator of TM—none, that is, except the simple technique that constitutes TM's core. With hundreds of thousands of persons who have undergone the mandatory six-hour-long training and are now meditating for 20 minutes twice a day, and with an organization that actively seeks corroboration of its claims in the scientific laboratory, TM has become the focus of hundreds of studies worldwide (see Orme-Johnson and Farrow, 1977; Chalmers, et al., 1989; Wallace, Orme-Johnson, and Dillbeck, 1990).

One of the most celebrated studies of TM, and the first in a series similar to the foregoing investigations of yoga and Zen, was carried out as a doctoral dissertation in physiology by Keith Wallace (1970a) at the University of California at Los Angeles. This research was followed up at Harvard's Thorndike Memorial Laboratory of the Boston City Hospital, where Wallace joined a team already investigating TM's effect on blood pressure (Benson, 1975; Wallace, 1970b; Wallace and Benson, 1972; Wallace, Benson, and Wilson, 1971). The subjects in this series of studies were a group of TM practitioners varying in age from 17 to 41 and ranging in meditation experience from less than a month to nine years; 8 were women and 28 were men. Connected to a variety of measuring instruments, each subject was asked to sit quietly for 20 to 30 minutes (an interval that served as the control period), then to meditate for 20 to 30 minutes, and finally to sit again quietly, without meditating, for a third such period of time. The investigators then compared the various measurements recorded during the meditation period with those taken during the control period of nonmeditative rest. Although 36 subjects contributed data to the published reports, some measures were taken on no more than 4 or 5; only one measure was taken on as many as 20. Regrettably, these research reports do not indicate the characteristics of any of these smaller samples, especially the amount of meditation experience. Perhaps some of the differences they report are common only among advanced meditators.

Physiological Changes: A variety of statistically significant changes occurred during meditation. Oxygen consumption dropped 17 percent and carbon dioxide elimination decreased proportionately. Skin resistance, a measure of relaxation, rose sharply during meditation and then dropped nearly to the initial levels afterward. Heart rate decreased on an average of three beats per minute and respiration about two breaths per minute. There was a slight increase in the acidity of the blood (Wallace, Benson, and Wilson, 1971).

For a sample of eight subjects, the concentration of blood lactate, a substance produced in skeletal muscles during exercise, declined precipitously during meditation and continued to fall for the first few minutes of the second rest period. Although it then rose again, it remained considerably below the premeditation level. A more recent experiment involving 42 TM practitioners found a similar decline in blood lactate during meditation but not during a comparable period of relaxed reading (Jevning, Wilson, and O'Halloran, 1982). Given that high blood lactate levels have been associated with anxiety states, Wallace and his colleagues hypothesize that the low levels of lactate in their subjects are partly responsible for the exceptionally relaxed state they experienced. The lactate–anxiety connection has been challenged, however, by other researchers (Ackerman and Sachar, 1974), and thus the significance of the changes in lactate level remains debatable. Nevertheless, it is suggestive that these changes parallel those occurring during normal rest or sleep and yet take place several times faster.

Brain Wave Patterns: ELECTROENCEPHALOGRAPHIC readings were also taken for an unspecified number of these subjects. Prior to meditation, when they were resting with their eyes closed, they showed predictable alpha activity. During meditation these waves increased in regularity and amplitude and typically slowed to eight or nine cycles per second. Five subjects showed occasional trains of five- to seven-cycle theta waves as well. Nonhabituating alpha blocking was observed in some of these meditators.

This pattern of changes appears more clearly and fully in a study undertaken by J. P. Banquet (1973). Using 12 volunteer subjects who had practiced TM daily for periods ranging from nine months to five years and a group of 12 matched controls who were shortly to learn TM (including three persons who were later inducted into the experimental group and therefore served as their own controls), Banquet used a design similar to Wallace's. Subjects were asked to rest for ten minutes, first with their eyes open and then closed. Next, the experimental group was asked to meditate for 30 minutes and the controls to relax with eyes closed for the same period of time. Finally, both groups were instructed to move slowly out of meditation or relaxation, to concentrate on a thought or image for five minutes, and then to open their eyes. A push button allowed subjects to communicate to the experimenter the occurrence of any of five conditions, including the achievement of "transcendence," the deepest point of meditation. The Maharishi teaches that transcendence consists of pure awareness.

EEG changes during the meditation of the experimental group suggested to Banquet a pattern of three continuous stages. (1) The alpha activity that began in the initial rest period showed increasing amplitude and slower frequency, just as Wallace had observed. (2) A dominant theta pattern developed, beginning with short bursts of high-voltage theta waves and usually continuing with longer theta trains of constant frequency. (3) Against a background of slow frequencies, four of Banquet's meditators showed generalized fast frequencies with a dominant beta rhythm, reminiscent of Das and Gastaut's observations of their most proficient yogis. The subjects who reached the third of Banquet's stages indicated their achievement either of deep meditation or of "transcendence" by means of the push button. Remarkably, even in these states meditators were reportedly able to signal the experimenter and—what is yet more startling—to answer questions without altering the brain wave pattern. At the end of the meditation period alpha trains returned, persisting in advanced students into the postmeditation interval when the eyes were again open. Banquet found that blocking usually did not occur in stages one and three; the rhythmic theta activity of stage two did show blocking, but this pattern reasserted itself within a few seconds. If these theta waves had been the product of drowsiness, Banquet points out, the stimulus would have transformed them into alpha activity.

That these EEG patterns are not simply the outcome of resting quietly is suggested by the results of the control group. Four of these subjects, during the period they were sitting relaxed with eyes closed, developed no stable alpha rhythms at all, showing instead mixed frequencies dominated by beta waves. The remaining eight control subjects developed a constant alpha rhythm, evidence of successful relaxation but nothing more. Although four also had slow theta frequencies, the presence of low-voltage delta activity revealed a state of drowsiness, a fact that was confirmed by their subjective reports.

Another of Banquet's findings is given special emphasis by Harold Bloomfield and his associates (1975). The EEG rhythms of the meditators showed a tendency toward coherence, or synchronization. As each new pattern of electrical activity established itself, it tended to spread to other areas of the brain, until the readings at various points on the scalp showed a uniformity of frequency, amplitude, and wave form. Bernard Glueck and Charles Stroebel (1975) report the same pattern of synchronized waves, which spread from the dominant hemisphere to the other one. "Since no single brain-wave form has proven significant in the total physiological response occurring through the practice of TM," conclude Bloomfield and his associates, this synchronization tendency "may be regarded as the critical change in EEG patterns corresponding to the deep rest gained during TM" (pp. 77–78). Later research has shown it to be significantly correlated with rated clarity of "transcendental" experience (Haynes et al., 1977). A more objective marker of coherence—if also more controversial—is "yogic flying," which so far consists of momentary episodes of hopping as much as two feet up and five feet forward while in a sitting position (Travis and Orme-Johnson, 1990). Flying is one of the "sidhis," or powers, that are said to be signs of having attained the state of pure consciousness.

Responses to Stress: TM practitioners are also reported to show exceptional patterns of response to stress. David Orme-Johnson (1973) exposed a group of eight TM meditators and a control group of eight nonmeditators to 100-decibel tones delivered at irregular intervals averaging 53 seconds in length. Using the galvanic skin response (GSR) as a measure of the stress reaction, he found that the meditators took an average of 11.0 trials to habituate (that is, virtually to stop reacting) and the nonmeditators 26.1 trials. Both in this experiment and in a second one, Orme-Johnson found that meditators showed significantly fewer spontaneous GSRs than nonmeditators, which constituted further evidence of greater autonomic stability.

A more obviously stressful stimulus—a 12-minute industrial safety film with three vividly simulated, severe accidents—was employed by Daniel Goleman in his doctoral research at Harvard (Goleman and Schwartz, 1976) to assess more directly the effects of meditation in a stress situation. The subjects were 30 meditators with more than two years' experience with TM and 30 nonmeditators who expressed an interest in meditation or yoga but had not yet practiced either of them. Using both skin conductance and heart rate as measures of stress reactivity, these investigators found that the meditators not only demonstrated a greater decrease in both measures following the view of each accident—a finding consistent with Orme-Johnson's—but also *a greater increase on both measures in anticipation of each accident.* The second finding is puzzling, for it suggests that meditators are more vulnerable to stress, not less. Yet they also recover more rapidly from it. Meditation is adaptive, conclude Goleman and Schwartz, "principally in terms of recovery from stress arousal, not in terms of coping actions while under stress" (p. 464).

In his critical review of the literature on meditation and stress reactivity, David Holmes (1987) cites Goleman's findings as evidence *against* the hypothesis that proficient meditators are less vulnerable to stress than nonmeditators. For Holmes the crucial results are the meditators' greater skin conductance and heart rate under stress, not their significantly more rapid recovery. In any event, he points out that other studies, too, show that meditators tend to be *more*, not less, responsive to stress. Yet another point of view emerges if we cast a wider net, and include not only experimental studies but also the more numerous clinical ones, and if we are more favorably inclined toward meditation than Holmes appears to be. Then we may conclude with Dean Shapiro (1980) that "meditation may be a promising clinical intervention technique for several stress-related dependent variables" (p. 135). What Shapiro and others (e.g., West, 1987) point out, however, is that there is yet no compelling evidence that meditation is superior to other self-regulation strategies.

In Praise of TM: The physiological effects of TM, conclude some of its more enthusiastic researchers, are unlike those of wakefulness, sleep, dreaming, or hypnosis. In comparison to sleep, TM may be more efficiently restful, for during meditation oxygen consumption decreases more rapidly and skin resistance rises more steeply than these functions do during sleep. On the other hand, the physiological changes of TM show its kinship to the more austere practices of the traditional forms of meditation, especially Zen and some forms of yoga. Yet TM achieves the "wakeful hypometabolic physiologic state," a condition of alert and exceptional relaxation, in only a fraction of the time.

Wallace (1970a), who became the charter president of TM's Maharishi International University (renamed the Maharishi University of Management in 1995) in Fairfield, Iowa, points to these data as evidence that TM, "the science of creative intelligence," gives access beyond waking, dreaming, and sleeping to higher stages of consciousness. According to Wallace and other TM proponents, it promises a large number of benefits, ranging from marked reduction in the use of drugs, alcohol, and cigarettes and dramatic relief from anxiety and other symptoms of neurotic and psychosomatic disorders, to improved concentration, increased energy and productivity, enhanced personal relationships, greater creativity and self-actualization and even reversal of biological aging (Bloomfield et al., 1975; Forem, 1974; O'Connell and Alexander, 1994; Wallace, 1986). Lying beyond these apparently measurable and verifiable changes—or perhaps underlying them—are said to be new perceptions of life's meaning and purpose, new insights into the fundamental nature of reality. We need no special measuring devices to document the affectionate devotion to the Maharishi, the profusion of testimonies to changed lives, and the rapidly growing commitment to the "world plan," which seeks "to achieve the spiritual goals of mankind in this generation" (Forem, 1974, p. 10). Clearly, behind the humble technique offered to mitigate the problems of daily life in a technologically advanced society is a dynamic religious movement. Yet it is not religious in the narrow sense of mandatory creeds and exclusive allegiance, a point its advocates wish to emphasize.

Beyond Tradition: Random Mantras and Electronic Gurus: Persons outside the TM movement may give these data a different interpretation. Herbert Benson (1975, 1984, 1987, 1996), a medical researcher impressed by the healing power of faith but suspicious of religious cults, sees TM as just one more way of eliciting the "relaxation response." The obverse of the involuntary "fight-or-flight" reaction that serves many organisms well in time of danger but that predisposes us today to the diseases of arteriosclerosis, heart attacks, and strokes, the relaxation response can be activated by many methods, some ancient, others modern. Benson maintains that these methods share (1) a quiet setting, (2) an object or mental device upon which to dwell, (3) a passive attitude, and (4) a comfortable position. He asserts that TM's individually assigned MANTRA, the secret Sanskrit expression that serves as the meditator's object of attention, is not essential to bring forth the physiological changes found during transcendental meditation. His research indicates that any easily repeated and natural-sounding syllable or phrase can be substituted for it. His own choice is "one," though for patients accustomed to praying he recommends repetitive prayer, such as the Catholic rosary. Prayer of this type, he reports, produces the same physiological changes that he had observed in practitioners of transcendental meditation (Benson, 1996, p. 199).

Lawrence LeShan (1974) also ignores the ancient Indian conviction that sound and essence are intimately bound together, making the sound a person chooses a matter of consequence. Instead, he proposes that a mantra be assembled out of syllables randomly chosen from the pages of a telephone directory. Sharing Benson's conviction that diverse methods, ancient and modern, achieve essentially the same effect, LeShan offers a virtual Baedeker to a number of well-developed techniques, each of them excised from its traditional context and motives and served up for a few weeks' sampling by the Western seeker of self-actualization.

Both Benson and LeShan believe that many of the fruits of meditation can be obtained without the guidance of the traditional director or GURU. Other researchers propose, in effect, that the teacher, who is often difficult to find, be replaced by modified versions of the very devices that have served to monitor the physiological correlates of meditation. By feeding back to the subject a continuous record of alpha and theta activity, muscle tension, skin temperature, and so on, investigators have found that these functions can be placed under limited yet impressive voluntary control in just a few training sessions (B. B. Brown, 1974). These BIO-FEEDBACK techniques yield psychological states reminiscent of those reported by meditators, including pleasurable feelings of tranquillity; changes in body image, even to the point of feeling disembodied or levitated; a "poised non-drowsy reverie," associated with a high percentage of alpha frequencies; and images akin to those sometimes experienced on the edge of sleep (HYPNAGOGIC IMAGES), which have been found to accompany low-frequency alpha waves and theta frequencies (Green and Green, 1986; Green, Green, and Walters, 1970a; Kamiya, 1969). Besides promising relief from anxiety, headaches, hypertension, insomnia, muscular tics, hyperactivity, perhaps also ulcers, epileptic seizures, drug addiction, and even cancer (Karlins and Andrews, 1972), biofeedback may provide the means for "psychophysiological training for creativity" by increasing the occurrence of hypnagogiclike states of reverie (Green, Green, and Walters, 1970b). If feedback techniques do not effectively replace meditation, as the litanies of effects might suggest, they may at least prepare individuals for rapid progression in the more traditional discipline of their choice.

Problems in Meditation Research

The rapidly growing literature on meditation is already enormous: a bibliography covering the years 1931 to 1996 includes more than 1500 published works (Murphy and Donovan, 1996; see also Jarrell, 1985). Yet many fundamental questions remain unresolved, partly because a large portion of the research is conducted by partisans of transcendental meditation. Their critics complain that their almost uniformly positive findings, their sometimes incautious conclusions, and their faithful quoting of the Maharishi belie their use of the disinterested style of scientific research. On the other hand, some of the criticisms of their work may be equally suspected of bias.

On the issue of the mantra, for example, TM proponents Glueck and Stroebel (1975, p. 314) conclude that it is a key factor, but they base their judgment on highly impressionistic findings from "a number of individuals who were doing their own variants of meditation, usually a *mantra*-type meditation." In contrast, Benson (1975, pp. 113–114) concludes that his simplified technique produces results identical to TM's; yet he did not record EEG changes, which, as we have seen, some researchers take to be the most striking of TM's physiological correlates. In neither case are the data sufficient for the conclusions drawn. Furthermore, even if the evidence were adequate, we could still make a case for or against the mantra's unique value. It could be argued, for example, that the mantra is effective because of the mystery and ritual that surround its assignment and use, not because the TM teacher has almost instantly discerned the nature of the individual's character and assigned a consonant mantra. In other words, we could view the mantra as a PLACEBO, which works because its user thinks it should. Alternatively, even if TM proved to have no unique physiological correlates, we could persuasively argue that the mantra's most significant effects lie beyond the physiologist's instruments.

The Confounding of Independent Variables: Apart from the considerable difficulty of finding willing subjects who are similarly advanced in the same meditative system, two major problems haunt meditation research. One is the task of identifying a suitable control group. Ideally, the control subjects should differ significantly from the experimental subjects on only one independent variable: meditation practice. In actuality, they almost always differ on other dimensions as well. Meditators in these experiments may score higher or lower than control subjects because of the kind of persons they are—a kind attracted to meditation, active in seeking it out, and willing to serve as subjects—rather than because of their meditative experience. Raymond Prince, Antoinette Goodwin, and Frank Engelsmann (1976) found, for example, that a high proportion of their subjects who sought TM initiation had experienced an important crisis shortly before and were seeking from TM some kind of relief. Abatement of these crises by the time of the follow-up interviews is cited as a major reason for the diminished levels of stress.

Meditators may also differ because of the placebo effect: the expectations engendered by the TM instructions and ritual undoubtedly differ from the expectations produced by control conditions. In the course of the experiment, it is not uncommon for control subjects to request or to be promised the opportunity to undergo TM training after the study is over. When meditators are used during intervals of nonmeditation as their own controls, in order to eliminate the element of personality differences, the factor of expectation remains. TM's active distribution of reprints and summaries of research reports guarantees that increasing numbers of persons will approach TM with considerable anticipation. The combination of these expectations with a few hours of quiet sitting may be sufficient to produce the sometimes dramatic differences that are reported (J. C. Smith, 1975). Because experimenter expectations can also influence the final outcome of laboratory investigations, a double-blind study, in which neither experimenter nor subject knows to which group the subject belongs, would help considerably in resolving these questions. Whether the investigator will be able to find subjects sufficiently naive and yet adequately motivated for such a study, and then implement a design that is ethically acceptable, is yet another question.

The Measurement of Dependent Variables: The second major problem in the investigation of meditation concerns the physiological and psychological measures that have been used. For example, however impressive the EEG may be, its application in meditation research is roughly akin to using a half-dozen microphones to assess life in New York City. In either case, we can detect trends in general activity—the shift, say, from early evening to early morning—but the subtleties of the innumerable components that make up the global measures still lie beyond the capacities of these instruments. Moreover, even the gross patterns of the EEG remain a matter of dispute. As Peter Fenwick (1987) and Thomas Mulholland (1972) emphasize, any particular EEG-measured brain rhythm may correspond to widely varying brain states. Alpha, for example, is found not only in the relaxed waking state but also in coma just before death (Fenwick, p. 105). The meanings of other physiological indicators are also ambiguous, being subject to varying interpretations.

Psychological measures must also be used with caution. When researchers, for example, seek to assess TM's effects on SELF-ACTUALIZATION, they frequently use Shostrom's (1966) Personal Orientation Inventory (POI) as their measure of the dependent variable. Yet they never seem to acknowledge the POI's limitations (see Chapter 13). Beyond the shortcomings peculiar to the POI are complications shared by all personality inventories. Wes Penner and his associates (1973) found that subjects who were given the Omnibus Personality Inventory before and after an intensive TM course showed elevated scores on the Response Bias scale on the second administration, evidence that they may have been trying to make a good impression. Changes in scores need not indicate corresponding changes in personality; they may simply reveal the subjects' intense desire to appear changed in positive ways, or, as eager volunteers, to demonstrate the efficacy of TM.

As Michael West (1987, p. 21) points out, the selection of dependent variables is often a pragmatic one, governed far less by well-informed hypotheses about meditation than by familiarity with and confidence in the measurement instruments. Noting that thus far the considerable research effort has produced only a modest result and that "many of the most important research questions are still to be asked" (p. 195), West advocates undertaking longitudinal studies that look for longer-term changes that occur apart from the meditative state.

Such an approach is becoming more common in India, where there is a growing body of longitudinal research on yoga as a means of treating certain diseases. Although yoga was not traditionally used as a form of therapy, a large number of yoga ASHRAMS, societies, or institutes scattered throughout India have made elaborate claims about the yogic practices. A study conducted in 1960–1961 by a government-sponsored committee headed by B. K. Anand concluded that the absence of proper records at the 19 institutions they visited made it impossible to evaluate these therapeutic claims (Anand et al., 1962). They recommended that the government sponsor a program for scientific assessment.

Since then a good deal of research has indeed been carried out, much of it akin to what we have already sampled (Funderburk, 1977) but some of it directed to the question of long-term benefits for health. For example, in a study by H. R. Nagendra and R. Nagarathna (1986), 570 patients suffering from bronchial asthma were put through a two- to four-week training program in integrated yoga and then reevaluated 3 to 54 months later. Highly significant improvement was found on most of the variables assessed, allowing reduction or elimination of medication in a majority of the cases. Regular practitioners showed the greatest improvement. R. H. Singh, R. M. Shettiwar, and K. N. Udupa (1982), having conducted their own studies at the Yoga Research Centre of the Institute of Medical Sciences, Banaras Hindu University, report that yoga can yield clinical improvement in chronic cases of diabetes, migraine, bronchial asthma, hypertension, rheumatic diseases, thyrotoxicosis, and gastrointestinal disorders. Most of the earlier research on yoga, they observe, was carried out with insufficient scientific controls, "thus the present status of research on yoga therapy is largely preliminary in nature" (p. 195).

AN EXPERIMENT IN DRUG-INDUCED MYSTICISM

In the early 1960s some researchers looked to the psychedelic drugs for what seemed to be the perfect solution to the problem of experimental controls. Prominent among these investigators was Walter Pahnke (1931–1971), who, with medical and theological degrees already in hand, undertook a study of psychedelic experience for his doctoral dissertation at Harvard in the history and philosophy of religion. Pahnke sought to determine whether the experiences triggered by psychedelic drugs are fundamentally similar to the experiences of acknowledged mystics. He himself took no psychedelic substances, either before or during this study.

Pahnke (1963, 1966) began by delineating the common characteristics of mystical states of consciousness by drawing on the writings of mystics and scholars. He looked especially to the work of philosopher Walter Stace (1960), who claims that all mystics, regardless of era or tradition, experience certain universal elements. Pahnke lists nine features, the first seven of which are taken from Stace.

1. The experience of *unity* or oneness, perceived either outwardly, in the external world, or inwardly, in a state of pure awareness that is free of all distinctions, including the sense of being a separate self.
2. *Transcendence of time and space*, into "eternity" and "infinity."
3. A *deeply felt positive mood*, of utter joy, blessedness, and peace.
4. The *sense of sacredness*, prompting a response of awe and wonder.
5. A conviction of *objectivity and reality*, an intuitively sensed knowledge or illumination of one's finite self as well as of ultimate reality.
6. A quality of *paradoxicality* or logical inconsistency, as in the mystical assertion that the *empty* unity is at the same time *full* and complete.
7. *Alleged ineffability* or indescribableness, in spite of the mystics' continuing efforts to relate what they have experienced.
8. The attribute of *transiency*, a shortness in duration that contrasts with the ongoingness of ordinary experience.
9. *Persisting positive changes in attitude and behavior*, including increased integration of personality, more sensitivity and love toward others, a new, richer appreciation of life and its meaning, and a deeper sense of the value of mystical experience (Pahnke, 1966).

The Experimental Design

With his categories established, Pahnke divided a group of 20 male graduate students from the Andover-Newton Theological Seminary into ten pairs, matched on the basis of religious background, past religious experience, and general psychological makeup. One student from each pair was randomly assigned to the experimental group; the other served as a control. The ten pairs were then organized into five groups of four students each, on the basis of friendship and apparent compatibility. Two leaders who were personally acquainted with the effects, positive and negative, of psychedelic drugs were assigned to each group. None of the students, on the other hand, had taken psychedelic substances before volunteering for this experiment.

All subjects participated in five hours of testing, interviews, and group discussions held to inform them about the design of the experiment and to maximize trust and positive expectation. They and their leaders then met in a suite of rooms in Marsh Chapel at Boston University where they heard a broadcast of a Good Friday service that was being conducted in the main sanctuary. Ninety minutes before the service began, two subjects in each of the five groups had received capsules containing 30 milligrams of psilocybin; one of each pair of leaders had been given 15 milligrams of the same substance. The other students and leaders had received identical-appearing capsules containing 200 milligrams of nicotinic acid, a B vitamin that in this quantity produces transient flushing and tingling sensations. Pahnke carefully employed a double-blind arrangement: neither he nor the participants in his study knew at this point who had received the psilocybin, Moreover, to encourage the recipients of the B vitamin to believe that they had swallowed psilosybin instead, he told everyone that the placebo to be given to half of them would have no side effects. The service, composed of organ music, solos, readings, prayers, and personal meditation, lasted two and one-half hours; most of the subjects remained in the small prayer chapel throughout this period of time.

Assessing the Results

Immediately following the service, individual reactions and group discussions were tape-recorded. At the experimenter's request, each subject wrote an account of his experience as soon after the experiment as he could, and within a week each completed a 147-item questionnaire designed to measure the degree to which each of the nine phenomena in Pahnke's list had been present in the individual's experience. An interview based on this questionnaire followed. Six months later all subjects completed a follow-up questionnaire designed to reevaluate the characteristics of the experience and to identify and measure any enduring changes. Descriptive accounts and other qualitative data were quantified through content analysis carried out by trained judges unacquainted with the particulars of the experiment.

Pahnke converted the scores derived from the content analysis and the two questionnaires into percentages of the maximum possible score. After averaging these three percentages together for each scale, he carried out the statistical comparisons shown in Table 5.1. For all 17 comparisons, the experimental group shows markedly higher scores; 15 of these comparisons are significant at the .02 level or better and the remaining two at the .05 level. As the table suggests, however, and as further examination of the evidence demonstrated, the experimental subjects did not undergo "complete" mystical experiences. That is, they did not experience all the categories in a maximal way. Even so, the reported experiences of those who took psilocybin resembled mystical experience far more than did the experience of the controls, "who had the same expectation and suggestion from the preparation and setting" (Pahnke, 1966, p. 307). Moreover, eight of the ten receiving the psychedelic drug seemed to have had profound and relatively enduring effects in

Table 5.1 **RESULTS OF PAHNKE'S GOOD FRIDAY EXPERIMENT**

Category	Percentage of Maximum Possible Scores for Ten Subjects		p^a
	Experimental	Control	
1. Unity	62	7	.001
A. Internal	70	8	.001
B. External	38	2	.01
2. Transcendence of time and space	84	6	.001
3. Deeply felt positive mood	57	23	.02
A. Joy, blessedness, and peace	51	13	.02
B. Love	57	33	.05
4. Sacredness	53	28	.02
5. Objectivity and reality	63	18	.01
6. Paradoxicality	61	13	.001
7. Alleged ineffability	66	18	.001
8. Transiency	79	8	.001
9. Persisting positive changes in attitude and behavior	51	8	.001
A. Toward self	57	3	.001
B. Toward others	40	20	.002
C. Toward life	54	6	.01
D. Toward the experience	57	31	.05

[a] Probability that the difference between the experimental and control groups was due to chance. These numbers indicate that, for every comparison, the experimental group scored significantly higher than the control group.
Source: Adapted from Table 1 in Pahnke, 1966.

their lives. Noting that the mystical experience appears to be the most difficult of the altered forms of consciousness to facilitate, Pahnke concludes from his findings that "These phenomena are now sufficiently reproducible to allow mysticism to be studied scientifically under laboratory conditions" (Pahnke and Richards, 1966, p. 193).

Walter Clark (1969), who served as one of Pahnke's group leaders, says that he knows of "no experiments . . . in the history of the scientific study of religion better designed or clearer in their conclusions than this one," that it provides "the most cogent single piece of evidence that psychedelic chemicals do, under certain circumstances, release profound religious experience" (p. 77). Pahnke systematically applied the disciplined techniques of experimental research to psychedelic experience, which earlier had been known mainly through the testimonies of persons who took the drugs under haphazard and poorly specified conditions. He composed two groups of persons with similar backgrounds and attitudes, created identical expectations within them and then exposed them to the same environmental conditions. With set and setting carefully controlled, any differences found between the two groups would presumably be the result of the single independent variable, the drug.

A Miracle That Failed

Pahnke's experiment, soon afterward dubbed with evident exaggeration "the miracle of Marsh Chapel," unexpectedly ran into trouble. Whereas the quicker-acting B vitamin at first gave the control subjects the impression that they had received the psilocybin, the drug's powerful effects on the others and the fading of their own symptoms soon made them aware of who the experimental subjects were. As one control subject later recalled,

> After about a half hour I got this burning sensation. . . . And I said to T.B., "Do you feel anything?" and he said, "No, not yet." We kept asking, "Do you feel anything?" I said, "You know, I've got this burning sensation, and it's kind of uncomfortable." And T.B. said, "My God, I don't have it, you got the psilocybin, I don't have it." I thought, "Jeez, at least I was lucky in this trial. . . ." I figured, with my luck, I'd probably get the sugar pill, or whatever it is. . . .
>
> Nothing much more happened and within another 40 minutes . . . everybody was really quiet and sitting there. . . . All of a sudden T.B. says to me, "Those lights are unbelievable." And I said, "What lights?" He says, "Look at the candles." He says, "Can you believe that?" And I looked at the candles, and I thought, "They look like candles." He says, "Can't you see something strange about them?" So I remember squinting and looking. I couldn't see anything strange. And he says, "You know it's just spectacular." And I looked at Y.M. and he was sitting there saying, "Yeah." And I thought, "They got it, I didn't" (Doblin, 1991, pp. 5–6).

Surely no one will deny that psilocybin played a large role in the outcome of this study. Obviously, however, there was also a precipitous drop in the expectations of the controls. Had the control subjects continued throughout the study to think they had received the drug, their scores on Pahnke's questionnaire might have been higher. Yet had they been separated from the experimental subjects, in an effort to maintain their naïveté, some scores may have been diminished. According to Pahnke (1966, p. 306), it was their "observation . . . of the profound experience of the experimentals" that appeared to be the basis of their own experience of love and the persisting changes in their attitudes toward others and toward the Good Friday experience itself that they subsequently reported.

The significance of factors other than the drug is also illustrated by the one experimental subject who was determined from the outset to prove that drugs do *not* produce religious experiences. "He alone made no religious preparation for the experiment, and he was the only one of those who got the drug who reported no evidences of mystical experience" (W. H. Clark, 1969, p. 77). What he finally demonstrated is the importance of the set that the subject brings to an experiment, as well as the difficulty of controlling for unknown factors that can inexplicably distort the results.

A Quarter-Century Follow-Up

Almost 25 years after Pahnke carried out his celebrated study, Rick Doblin (1991) tracked down and interviewed 16 of the 20 subjects, 7 from the experimental group and 9 of the controls. All of them completed again the 100-item questionnaire that Pahnke had used in his six-month reassessment. After a quarter of a century, the two groups showed the same yawning gap in the rated intensity of their experiences, with the experimental subjects giving even higher average ratings than they had at six months. Whereas the control subjects recalled few details of the Good Friday service and reported hardly any positive persisting changes, those in the experimental group had vivid memories of the events and described with evident appreciation the various ways in which they had benefited from the experience. They unanimously agreed that it had had genuinely mystical elements and was more intense and emotionally wide-ranging than any mystical experiences they had later on. Although they recalled having more difficult moments, such as feelings of fear and guilt, than Pahnke had let on in his reports,[2] they nevertheless described the experience as one of the high points of their spiritual lives.

A Second Double-Blind Experiment

Pahnke's subjects took it for granted that the psilosybin had made all the difference. From a scientific perspective, however, the dramatic change in expectation early in the experiment left in doubt the relative contributions of the two varying factors: the drug and the subjects' expectations. In a follow-up study conducted at the Massachusetts Mental Health Center with Carl Salzman and Richard Katz, Pahnke (1967) took additional precautions to maintain throughout the experiment the control subjects' ignorance of their status. This time the experimenters used a "placebo" consisting of either a threshold dose of psilocybin or a combination of dextroamphetamine and sodium amytal, in order to give the control subjects an experience verging on a psychedelic one. Furthermore, all subjects were instructed to remain silent and to recline and relax throughout the six-hour experimental session. In this study, therefore, fewer clues were available to the two controls in each group of four subjects.

Although Pahnke again used a double-blind design, his second study does not replicate the first one: most of the 40 subjects were professionals over 30, and the setting consisted only of candlelight, flowers, pictures of nature scenes, and classical music. Nevertheless, 7 of the 20 subjects receiving moderate doses of psilocybin reported mystical experiences, whereas only 1 of the 20 control subjects did.[3] That a smaller proportion of the experimental subjects in the second study reported mystical experiences than in the first one is not surprising, considering how much more evidently religious the subjects and experimental conditions were in the Good Friday experiment.

Other studies using psychedelic drugs, though less elaborate in design than Pahnke's, have yielded results that also demonstrate the capacity of these drugs to precipitate religious experiences. Investigations summarized by Leary (1964), Leary and Clark (1963), and Clark (1969) provide further evidence that, whether or not the set and setting are obviously religious, at least a third of subjects ingesting psychedelic substances will report that their experiences were religious or mystical. Some of these experiences appear to transform lives, even of chronic alcoholics or maximum-security prison inmates. Unfortunately, none of these studies approximates the degree of experimental control that Pahnke sought to achieve. It is therefore impossible to sort out the individual factors and to draw firm conclusions about cause-and-effect relationships. Stringent federal laws and international treaties now make it difficult to do research with psychedelic drugs, effectively fore-

---

[2] One of Pahnke's subjects was sufficiently distressed during the course of the experiment to require an injection of thorazine, a tranquilizer. He refused to participate in Doblin's follow-up study and is thus not represented in these generalizations.

[3] The criterion for mystical experience was a score on Pahnke's mysticism questionnaire of at least 60 percent of the maximum. Pahnke, who tragically drowned in 1971 while scuba diving, never published a detailed account of this second experiment. The findings reported here are inferred from his brief summary of the combined results of the two studies. Pahnke and his collaborators realized that to achieve statistical significance for a difference of this order, additional trials would have had to be conducted (Carl Salzman, personal communication, December 1, 1976).

closing the further investigations that would help to clarify the complex processes involved.[4]

EXPERIMENTAL MYSTICISM WITHOUT DRUGS

Several researchers have demonstrated that quasi-mystical experiences can be induced in laboratory subjects without violating the law or risking possible physiological side effects from drugs. Moreover, their methods have the advantage—at least with some subjects—of working far more quickly and surely than the techniques of understimulation and overstimulation reviewed in Chapter 3. Like the drugs, these methods require no commitment to any particular tradition.

Hypnotic Alteration of Space and Time

Whereas Pahnke had used Stace's characteristics of mystical states as criteria for establishing which of his subjects had had mystical experiences, research psychologist Bernard Aaronson used them to *induce* mystical states through hypnosis. In a series of investigations involving six male university students (including one, a poor hypnotic subject, who was asked to simulate the experimental conditions instead), Aaronson (1966, 1967, 1968, 1969a, 1969b, 1970) modified his subjects' experience by means of POSTHYPNOTIC SUGGESTION. After preliminary testing, each subject was hypnotized and then "programmed" to experience *post*hypnotically some pervasive perceptual change. These modifications included an increase or decrease in the depth of the visual field, its clarity, the size of objects, and their relative distance; alternation in the speed of time, so that it seemed to move faster or slower, or to stop altogether; and removal or expansion of the time zones of past, present, or future, or some combination of them. Each modification took place on a separate day and with one subject at a time. Amnesia for earlier hypnotic experience was suggested at each session, in order to prevent an accumulative effect over the months that these studies took. Following the hypnotic induction, subjects were observed for a two-hour period and then taken for an automobile ride over a standard course. After they had written an account of the day's experience and had undergone further interviews and testing, they were rehypnotized in order to remove the posthypnotic suggestion. A final interview brought each session to a close.

The changes brought about by the hypnotic inductions ranged from irritability, paranoid hostility, or even catatonic stupor, to self-absorbed rumination, calm happiness, or manic euphoria. Most noteworthy for our purposes were the conditions under which quasi-mystical experiences occurred. *Increased depth* yielded in all subjects except the simulator "a sort of psychedelic experience with mystical overtones." One subject, described as dependent and open, "was transported into an experience of great beauty: sounds, colors, and contours all were enhanced; space seemed almost solid; each object and its placement seemed part of a Divine order."

---

[4] The Multidisciplinary Association for Psychedelic Studies (MAPS), founded by Rick Doblin in 1986, has been working since then to reverse the political suppression of research on psychedelic drugs and to raise funds to support such research where it is possible. The growing openness of the Food and Drug Administration, signaled by its approval of research on the safety of psychedelic drugs, is discussed in the quarterly newsletter of MAPS, all issues of which can be found on the World Wide Web (http://www.maps.org).

This subject "felt he could do no less than spend his life serving God" (Aaronson, 1968, pp. 16–17).

Modifications of temporal experience also yielded seemingly mystical states, at least for one of the two hypnotic subjects employed in the time-zone series. Much as we might expect, the conditions of *no future, expanded present, expanded future,* and *expanded present and future* produced for him a rich, boundless present, akin to the timelessness that Stace and Pahnke observed. These conditions brought with them "a mood of great luminosity," a state that this normally "hypomanic and convivial" subject himself described as mystical. Curiously, at the end of one of the days, the experience suddenly gave way to a manic episode of lighthearted pranks (Aaronson, 1966, 1968). What the induced conditions have in common, concludes Aaronson, is the augmentation of perception. The inductions that diminish it result not in mystical experiences but in psychotic ones, an outcome indicating that these two kinds of experience are in some sense opposites.

Aaronson's studies suggest that quasi-mystical experiences can be produced by inducing posthypnotically some of the perceptual changes reported by acknowledged mystics. This discovery led Aaronson (1969b) to take a somewhat more direct approach, using a far lengthier induction designed to create the egoless experience of emptiness or "the void." Experience of the void is characteristic, according to Stace (1960), of the INTROVERTIVE MYSTICAL EXPERIENCE. A second induction, written to prompt the EXTRAVERTIVE MYSTICAL EXPERIENCE of cosmic unity, was used for comparative purposes. Finally, as in the previous studies, control sessions involving hypnosis but no induction were also scheduled. The subjects, who were four male college students between the ages of 18 and 24, were allowed to experience each condition for a half hour. Each was then brought out of the hypnotic state, interviewed, and asked to write a description of his experience.

At least three, if not all four, of the subjects reported the presence of eight of Pahnke's nine criteria for mystical experience following both the induction of the void and the induction of cosmic unity. The ninth criterion, a direct, intuitive, and authoritative knowledge of ultimate reality, was consistently met in the reports of two of the subjects. In contrast, those in the control condition reported only two of Pahnke's criteria, positive mood and transiency. Although Aaronson's investigation lacks the elaborations and controls of Pahnke's experiments, he concludes on the basis of it that it "opens the possibility for the study of the technology of mysticism and the development of an experimental psychology of religion."

Devices and Games for Inducing Mystical Experience

These possibilities are also suggested in the work of Jean Houston and Robert Masters, a wife-and-husband team whose early interest in psychedelic experience has grown to include a broad range of "subjective realities." Houston and Masters, who established their Foundation for Mind Research in 1964, did not initially focus on religious or mystical experiences. Their work with drugs, however, as well as with the alternatives they were forced to seek out when the new drug laws went into effect, inevitably brought them face to face with what they cautiously described as "religious-type experiences." Today they are actively "enabling" such experiences and boldly developing a nondogmatic system of spiritual guidance.

A Sound-and-Light Show: Among the techniques Houston and Masters have developed is a device called the Audio-Visual Environment (AVE). The AVE consists of a program of 120 to 160 slides of abstract oil paintings and a synchronized soundtrack, most often of electronic music but sometimes of Sufi or Zen chanting.

The subject sits for 30 to 45 minutes in front of an eight-foot semicircular rear-projection screen, so that each painting, as it appears and then dissolves into the next one, fills the subject's field of vision. Responses to the AVE include distortions in perception of time and body image, muscular relaxation, euphoria, anxiety, and even trance states. Religious feelings and images occasionally also occur. Although the AVE program has not yielded any dramatic religious-type experiences, it has at least once produced what Masters and Houston (1973) call an "esthetic mystical experience." Struggling to describe the extremely pleasurable experience, the female subject wrote that "I had the sense that there was only one color—not that I was seeing monochromatically, but the colors were also just color. . . . And it was without any sense of an environment, or it felt as though all the environment was my own body" (p. 105).

A Cradle of Creativity: More spectacular in its effects is the Altered States of Consciousness Induction Device (ASCID), designed by Masters from hints in the literature on witchcraft and possession states and resembling a pendulumlike platform found by anthropologists in Dutch Guiana (Cavander, 1974). The ASCID, which Houston and Masters sometimes refer to as a "cradle of creativity," looks like an up-ended canvas stretcher, attached at the top to a metal framework and ending at the bottom in a triangular metal platform just a few inches off the floor. The subject stands on the platform, blindfolded and held in place by canvas belts; the free-swinging device will sway, rock, or twirl in response to the subject's slightest movements. Within 2 to 20 minutes, a trance state frequently ensues, unfolding spontaneously or in a manner shaped by the experimenter's directions.

When the carefully screened research subjects are left undirected, report Masters and Houston (1973), they tend to experience fantastic subjective realities reminiscent of myths, fairy tales, or science fiction. They may also have experiences of a religious or mystical type. Placed in the ASCID, a young, college-educated woman soon felt herself dying, then reborn as the mythic Prometheus; a "tremendous cosmic life force" surged through her body. As she brought fire to the human world and to particular individuals, for whom it was a symbolic gift of great significance, she had an intense feeling of personal fulfillment. "The whole experience was so positive and profound," she wrote some time later, "that I was in a state of total awe and wonder. . . . I feel myself to be boundlessly happy and at complete acceptance and peace with myself. . . . I feel myself to be in an active connection with the harmony and unity of nature and the cosmos" (p. 90).

Another subject, a theologian, moaned and wept as he described the spontaneous ecstatic vision that he experienced in the ASCID. "It is as if my mind were united to the mind of God," he declared. "I am expanding, expanding . . . and I can read secrets of the universe and glimpse the forms of things . . . beautiful forms, mathematical forms, geometrical forms. They are all alive, colorful and brilliant. This is the Source of the Forms, the World of the Divine Ideas, the Creative Source. It is the *Fons et origo*. . . . the experience of the Unity, the *Nous*, the *Logos* of the soul" (Houston and Masters, 1972, p. 313). The practical results were the dissolution of a long-standing writing block, and—according to the subject's report—improved family relations, better teaching, and continuing growth. The writing that followed was judged by these investigators to be a creative and highly lucid exposition of complex, difficult ideas.

Suggestion increases the ASCID's effectiveness in producing religious-type experiences. In one sequence subjects were told that they would experience their bodies "as breaking down into minute, moving particles," along with everything

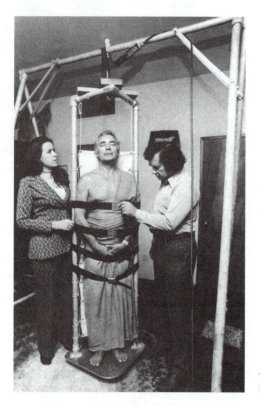

The "cradle of creativity" used by Jean Houston and Robert Masters to facilitate mystical experience.

else in the world. "The world would then consist of a vast sea of particles of matter and the subject[s] would just merge with that sea, losing all sense of [their bodies] and becoming one with the whole." Feeling their bodies dissolved and their egos merged with the "endless sea of being," the deeply entranced subjects would slip out of rapport with the experimenter for a few minutes. During this interval, almost all subjects later reported, they experienced ecstatic or blissful union with "the one." Afterward they felt extremely relaxed and euphoric (p. 316).

The religious-type experiences that Houston and Masters have specifically suggested to their subjects have thus far not been as powerful as the most impressive of the spontaneously occurring ones. This finding is not surprising, for the depth and intensity of the experience have proved to depend largely on the individual's preparation and readiness, much as is true with psychedelic drugs. Yet these researchers hold out the possibility that further refinement of their techniques, including the addition of more specifically religious elements to the setting and instructions, might increase the potency of the directed experiences. "Explored with sufficient dedication," these " 'visionary worlds' . . . might well prove as inexhaustible as those described by a Swedenborg or the medieval Sufi mystics" (p. 321).

Mind Games: Descent into the Self: After years of experimenting with research subjects, with and without the aid of psychedelic drugs, Masters and Houston (1972) have assembled what amounts to a modern-day handbook of spiritual guidance, composed of a progressive series of hypnotic group exercises called *Mind Games.* Their highly eclectic system is adapted from traditional rituals, mythic themes, literary images, psychedelic and mystical experiences, Jungian concepts, guided-imagery therapy, and contemporary research, including the work of Aaronson. The structure of the games is based largely on a "pattern of 'descent' " observed in Masters and Houston's (1966) earlier work with psychedelics, a pattern of four levels hypothesized to correspond to layers of the psyche. These researchers recommend that the games be played by five to eleven players, one of whom serves as the guide. Playing one to three times a week, the participants will need from five months to a year to complete the 64 games.

Mind Games is written for the most part in what Masters and Houston call "subcortical linguistics," a flowing, repetitive form of speech that aids in the achievement of trance or hypnoid states. Urged to seek ever-deeper levels of trance, the subjects are led through a fantastic series of perceptual manipulations, imaginary experiences, and meditative exercises. The first series is designed to develop the ability to enter altered states of consciousness and to introduce subjective transformations that are elaborated in the more advanced games. It starts with exercises in hearing music through all the senses, experiencing gross changes in body image, and imagining oneself to be a cat, a stone, a plant, or another person. Through the use of Aaronson's techniques, the speed of time is altered and depth perception is increased. Familiar objects are seen as if for the first time. These changes, comparable to those that occur early in a psychedelic experience, represent the *sensory* level of transformed consciousness. An empathic relation to objects and other living creatures, signaling a breakdown of subject–object boundaries, may help the individuals to pass on to the deeper *recollective-analytic* level, where they encounter life–historical material. This level is approached directly in another first-cycle game, the reliving of early personal experiences, perhaps as far back as infancy. The first cycle or "book" is concluded by the subjects' meditation on their mirror images and the question "Who am I?"; by a Rite of Liberation from the limitations imposed by persons in the past; and by seeking a symbol of the self, represented by the innermost in a series of concentric circles.

The remaining three cycles or books are intended to induce experiences on the more profound third and fourth levels of transformed consciousness. The *symbolic* level is marked by images that are mythical, ritualistic, historical, or archetypal. The subjects may undergo initiation rites, participate in other ritual observances, or sense their place in the sweep of history. Masters and Houston's games encourage the subjects to reach this level through a number of trance inductions, such as creating and interrogating a "Group Spirit"; undertaking heroic adventures with seemingly impossible challenges; practicing "visionary anthropology," whereby the subjects investigate an alien culture or a larger reality; and sleeping in the sacred confines of an imaginary ancient temple, in order to receive the dream-born healing and tutelage of the gods. The subjects may encounter fantastic THERIOMORPHIC guides—a crocodile in whose belly the subjects descend through the waters of time, an ancient, gem-studded turtle, an enormous, upright, bejeweled black cat, and a trinity of hawk-headed humanoid figures in leather armor; witness wild, elemental rites deep in a jungle, or the singing of monks in a temple high in some Asian mountain; climb to the heights to encounter and learn from the archetypal Wise Old Man; speak ecstatically in tongues; pursue, in a shared trance, knowledge of the Holy Grail, the philosopher's stone, or the pyramids; create together a group work of art expressing a collective consciousness; and mount to the stars, oneself a constellation, and then become a tiny cell in a living organism.

The growing sense of the interrelatedness of all things in the cosmos sets the stage for the fourth and final level of consciousness, the *integral.* Here the subjects are said to undergo integrative illumination, total self-understanding, and positive self-transformation, as they encounter with deep emotion the Ultimate or Fundamental Reality. The mind games prepare the subjects for this culminating experience through solitary periods of fasting, meditating, and keeping watch, largely in the trance state. Gathered together once again, the players continue by spending a night out-of-doors, with inductions to sense the environment in new ways and their rootedness in the earth, to meditate on the fire about which the group will sleep, and then on earth, air, and water as well, and to invoke the heavens and the Spirit of the Moon. They are directed to merge with "a wondrously beautiful white and golden light" and undergoing purification in a column of white fire; to imagine multisensory stimulation that carries the subjects to hitherto-unknown levels of bliss and rapture; and then finally to break through the web of past relationships and events that holds them short of ecstatic freedom in body and mind. Only then is one ready for the final descent down the archetypal stone staircase, the culminating meditation on the question "Who am I?" and the profoundly dramatic experience of death and rebirth as the symbol of the innermost self grows smaller and then disappears.

According to Masters and Houston (1972), these games are designed to help participants "become more imaginative, more creative, more fully able to gain access to their capacities and to use their capacities more productively" (p. 229). At the same time, these exercises will allow the individual "to function more effectively within the reality consensus, in the 'external world,' and according to the legitimate demands of everyday life" (p. 235). During an altered state of consciousness, the subjects are instructed to suspend all reality testing, to accept unquestioningly the "programed-in belief systems" (p. 72); afterward, they are urged to view each element of the trance experience as "only a symbolic form, a psychic construct that is being used . . . to explore some awarenesses and potentials described since ancient times in the writings, religions, and philosophies of some other cultures" (p. 101). The games are emphatically "not the expression of any religion, spiritual discipline, occult or other belief-system, or of any ideology apart from the general aims stated" (p. 237). Indeed, these investigators argue that religious teachings sometimes cut short the ecstatic pleasures of which material beings are capable.

Lacking careful controls and quantified measures of independent and dependent variables, Masters and Houston's investigations may well be thought to lie outside the realm of experimental research. In the broad sense of the word "experimental," however, their work rightly belongs under this rubric. Avowedly phenomenological in orientation, they have sought at the same time to reproduce in their "laboratory" (however unconventional it may be) a host of phenomena that have heretofore been known only in traditional contexts. They have systematically observed the effects of their various procedures and through trial and error have assembled a program of exercises usable by normal adult human beings toward the end of self-actualization (Houston, 1987.) That they have managed to induce the state of credulity or imaginative participation necessary to allow ancient rituals and images to function dramatically in some modern minds is a remarkable achievement.[5] What is still lacking is a thorough report and evaluation of their findings, beyond the few case studies they have presented (Masters, 1974; Masters and Hous-

---

[5] For testimony of what can be accomplished in a mere half hour, see the first-hand report of *Time* magazine researcher Clare Mead ("Mysticism," 1970). Mead reports attaining, in a deeply moving way, a new and ineffable understanding of the problem of injustice.

ton, 1973) and Alice Pempel's (1978) analysis of transcripts from the numerous sessions of three of their most accomplished subjects.

We might also want to weigh the implications of hypnotically producing sacred experiences as "games" for self-improvement, or of seeking to suspend judgments about ontological realities while actively inculcating a world-view and inducing profoundly moving experiences that confirm it. We should remember, too, that both traditional and modern spiritual guides warn of dangers when we court the powers of unknown factors. Whether we locate these factors in the depths of the psyche, as do Jung and Grof, or in the very fabric of the cosmos, their destructive potential must be taken into account. Grof (1988, 1993), who is also inducing psychedelic experiences through nondrug techniques, including hyperventilation, considers knowledge of the psyche's cartography to be essential for effective and safe exploration (1988, p. xvi). Pempel (1978, p. 26) notes that all three of the Masters and Houston subjects she studied sometimes found it hard to integrate the rich and occasionally frightening material they encountered while in altered states of consciousness.

A FIELD STUDY OF THE GOOD SAMARITAN

Some psychologists of religion place mystical experience at the heart of religion and thus feature it in their research and reflections. Yet such subjective states are notoriously difficult to pin down and assess. Moreover, the use of drugs or hypnosis to induce them only multiplies the factors to be evaluated and understood—and undoubtedly also the risks. Many persons, like Jonathan Edwards more than two centuries ago, are more impressed by "behavior or practice in the world" that conforms to religious ideals and constitutes "a business which [one] is chiefly engaged in, and devoted to, and pursues with highest earnestness and diligence . . . to the end of life" (Edwards, 1746, p. 383). In other words, helpful acts by a Good Samaritan provide more reliable evidence of true religiousness than the ineffable

Arrival of the Good Samaritan at the Inn, by Gustave Doré.

sighs of an enraptured ecstatic. They are also much easier for the psychologist to operationalize.

Simulating the Way to Jericho

Continuing a series of studies of the unresponsive bystander, John Darley and Daniel Batson (1973) undertook to observe the Good Samaritan under controlled conditions in order to explore the personal and situational factors that determine such benevolent actions. Forty male students at the Princeton Theological Seminary participated in a study that they were told was "on religious education and vocations." Following an initial testing session, during which they took a religiosity questionnaire, the subjects were sent, one by one, to a nearby building, where they were to give a three- to five-minute talk "to provide . . . a clearer picture of how you think than does the questionnaire material we have gathered thus far" (p. 103). On the way to the office next door, each subject passed through an alley where a "victim" was planted, "sitting slumped in a doorway, head down, eyes closed, not moving. As the subject went by, the victim coughed twice and groaned, keeping his head down." If the subject stopped to ask if he was all right or to offer help, the victim would groggily thank him and then decline his aid, explaining that his breathing difficulties would pass once a pill he had just swallowed took effect.

The victim rated each subject in this study in terms of a six-point "scale of helping behavior," ranging from failing to notice the victim at all (a scale value of zero) to refusing to leave him, perhaps even insisting on taking him somewhere else for refreshment or medical help (a value of five). After giving the scheduled talk, each subject was administered an "exploratory questionnaire on personal and social ethics," which was designed to elicit a report of the incident in the alley as a check on the victim's assessment of the subject's behavior. The subject was then told about the deception, probed for his reactions to the victim, and given an opportunity to discuss the study as a whole.

The degree of help offered by the subjects, the dependent variable of this study, was examined in relation to three independent variables: (1) the urgency with which each was sent next door to give his talk; (2) the subject matter assigned to him for his presentation, either the task-relevant topic of alternative employment for seminary graduates or the helping-relevant theme of the Good Samaritan; and

The "victim" in Darley and Batson's Good Samaritan study.

(3) the type of religiosity of the subject, as measured during the preliminary testing session. Three corresponding hypotheses were presented:

1. Persons in a hurry will be less likely to help than persons not in a hurry.
2. Individuals preoccupied with religious and ethical thoughts (as the priest and the Levite in the New Testament parable presumably were) will be no more likely to offer aid than persons thinking of other things.
3. Persons who are "intrinsically religious," or alternatively, whose religiousness is the expression of a quest for meaning, will more likely be helpful than persons whose religiousness resembles that of the priest or the Levite, for whom, according to Darley and Batson, religion is only a means toward other ends.

Several statistical procedures were used to evaluate the data in the light of these hypotheses, including ANALYSIS OF VARIANCE, MULTIPLE REGRESSION analysis, and rank CORRELATION.

Determinants and Styles of Helping

The urgency with which subjects were sent to give their talks proved to be the most obvious determinant of the degree of helping behavior. Of the subjects in the "high-hurry" condition, who were told that they were late and must hurry, only 10 percent offered help, either by stopping or by reporting the victim's plight to someone else. Of those in the "intermediate hurry" condition, who were merely told that the assistant in the next building was ready for them, 45 percent gave aid. And of the subjects in the "low-hurry" condition, who were led to anticipate a wait of several minutes, 63 percent offered assistance. Statistical analysis demonstrated that these differences are significant at the .05 level.

The subject matter of the individual's talk also seems to have made a difference: 29 percent of those assigned the task-relevant theme offered help, whereas 53 percent of the subjects given the helping-relevant or Good Samaritan topic acted on the victim's behalf. This difference is not great enough, however, given the size of the subject groups, to be considered statistically significant at the minimally acceptable level ($p < .05$). The investigators therefore concluded that the assigned topic did not make a difference in helping behavior. "A person going to speak on the parable of the Good Samaritan is not significantly more likely to stop to help a person by the side of the road than is a person going to talk about possible occupations for seminary graduates." Thus, the second hypothesis, like the first one, is confirmed by these data.[6]

Two Styles of Helpfulness: The subjects' type of religiosity bore the least obvious relationship to helping behavior. Religiousness was assessed by the use of six scales that together appeared to measure three factors: (1) religion as a means to other ends (the EXTRINSIC RELIGIOUS ORIENTATION), (2) religion as an end in itself (the INTRINSIC RELIGIOUS ORIENTATION), and (3) religion as a quest for mean-

---

[6] On the basis of a less conventional, Bayesian analysis of Darley and Batson's data, Anthony Greenwald (1975) challenges the appropriateness of this conclusion. He reports that his alternative hypothesis, that preparation for speaking on the parable of the Good Samaritan increased the likelihood of helping by more than 50 percent, was favored over the NULL HYPOTHESIS (an increase of 50 percent or less) by 4.86 to 1. Acknowledging that these odds are not very large, Greenwald points out that there is nevertheless no question about which hypothesis they favor. In a near-replication of Darley and Batson's experiment, Nancy Radant and her associates (1985) found that subjects receiving "religious prosocial cueing," through the reading of two religious parables, were significantly more helpful.

ing in the personal and social world. None of these three factors showed a relation to the dependent variable, with a single exception. Of the 16 subjects who did offer some kind of help to the victim, those who scored low on the religion-as-quest scale tended to insist on doing something for the victim, despite his protests. Those who scored high on quest, in contrast, tended to be more tentative in their offers of help. (The correlation between the quest and helping scales for subjects offering help was $-.53$, $p < .05$.) Insistent helpers also tended to score high on a doctrinal orthodoxy scale. (Helping and orthodoxy correlated .63, $p < .01$.)

What we may conclude is unclear. Certainly the third hypothesis is not supported, unless we judge that the "super-helpers" acted less appropriately and hence, in effect, less helpfully. Darley and Batson decided in favor of distinguishing two styles of helpfulness—one that was "directed toward the presumed underlying needs of the victim and was little modified by the victim's comments about his own needs," and another that was "more tentative and seemed more responsive to the victim's statements of his need" (p. 107). The first was characteristic of the doctrinally orthodox; the second was characteristic of those for whom religion is an ongoing search.

Darley and Batson feature this stylistic difference rather than helpfulness per se. They suggest that helpfulness is likely to be situationally controlled, in this case by the experimenter's request that the subjects hurry. In their haste the subjects may have failed to notice the situation in the alley, or they may have simply chosen, in the instant, to be helpful to the experimenter rather than the victim. "Conflict, rather than callousness, can explain their failure to stop." Personality variables— here, the type of religiosity—would appear to have determined how the individuals conducted themselves after they decided to help.

Further Studies of Why People Help

Hesitant to be content with this unanticipated and perhaps fortuitous result, Batson undertook a parallel experiment (Batson and Gray, 1981) designed to test two hypotheses: that (1) persons with an intrinsic religious orientation are prompted to help by an internal need to be helpful, whereas (2) persons with a QUEST RELIGIOUS ORIENTATION are impelled into action by a desire to meet the expressed needs of the sufferer. The subjects in this study were 60 female introductory psychology students at the University of Kansas. All had earlier rated themselves as at least moderately religious. Once seated in the laboratory cubicle, each subject was told that the succession of letters that would be given to her were being written by another student, "Janet Armstrong," who by chance had been assigned the role of "communicator" in a written conversation that was part of a study of impression formation. The real subject, as the "listener," was encouraged to respond in whatever way seemed appropriate. She was also asked, while Janet was supposedly writing her first note, to rate herself on 22 personal-trait scales, including two scales assessing self-perceived helpfulness and concern. These two ratings served as indirect measures of an internal need to be helpful. Actual helpfulness was assessed by blind ratings of the third and final response that the subject made to Janet's increasingly detailed admissions of loneliness. For half the subjects ("help wanted condition"), Janet expressly asked that her listener meet with her again for further conversation; for the other half ("help not wanted"), the same expression was followed by the resolve to work out the problem on her own.

The results favor both hypotheses. The self-rated traits of helpfulness and of concern proved to be significantly correlated with the Intrinsic scale (.28 and .35, respectively) but not with the Extrinsic and Quest scales, supporting the hypothesis that persons with an intrinsic religious orientation are distinguished by a greater internal need to be helpful. Furthermore, the intrinsic or end factor showed a weakly positive correlation with helping whether or not Janet wanted it, whereas the quest factor was positively correlated with helping (.37, $p < .05$) only in the help-wanted condition. In the help-not-wanted condition, it was *negatively* correlated with helping (-32, $p < .09$), suggesting that, when Janet withdrew her request for help, offers to help her anyway became less frequent as quest-factor scores went up.[7] Thus the quest orientation proves once again to be associated with greater responsiveness to the expressed desires of the needy person, whereas the intrinsic orientation is linked with insistent helpfulness even in the face of rejection, much as we would expect if an unvarying, pressing need to be helpful were involved.

Perhaps, however, high scorers on the Intrinsic scale are so deeply concerned for needy persons that they are less easily put off by what they may rightly take to be a reluctance to impose on others or a disposition to underestimate the seriousness of their need. Aware of this possibility, Batson and his collaborators undertook several additional studies to clarify the motives underlying the help offered by the intrinsically oriented. In one of these studies, scores on the Intrinsic scale predicted volunteering only when the likelihood of actually being called on to help was perceived as low (Batson, et al., 1989). In another study, the helping of high scorers on the Intrinsic scale was associated with thoughts of the personal rewards of helping rather than with preoccupation with guilt or altruistic concern for the needy person (Batson and Flory, 1990). Thus it appears that prosocial behavior associated with the intrinsic religious orientation is motivated not by compassion for others or a desire to avoid feeling shame or guilt, but by an egoistic need to feel good about oneself and to be perceived by others as kind and caring (Batson, 1990; Batson, Schoenrade, and Ventis, 1993).

What light, we may ask, do these quasi-experimental studies throw on the phenomenon of the Good Samaritan? In the biblical parable from which we derive this term (Luke 10: 29–37), a traveler who had been stripped, beaten, and left half dead by robbers was "passed by on the other side" by a Levite, who served at that time as a religious functionary, as well as by a priest. The Samaritan, a member of a tribe considered by the Jews to be hostile and religiously heretical, not only stopped to give first aid but also took the traveler to an inn, where he gave the innkeeper money for the injured man's care. The parable was intended to provide a model of neighborliness, but it also underscores that there are different forms of piety, that the most conspicuous forms may not be the most genuine, and that the differences among the behaviors they inspire may be profound.

In the first of Batson's studies, variations in religious orientation proved to have little if any effect. In the near-replication of this study carried out by Nancy Radant and her associates (1985), religious orientation similarly showed no relation to helping. We should note, however, that in both studies the range of religiosity scores was limited by the relative homogeneity of the subject groups: Darley and Batson's subjects were all Presbyterian seminarians and Radant's subjects were all conservative Christian students. Without a moderately wide range of religious orientation scores, correlations with other variables will be limited at best. The result

---

[7] Because convention requires a probability level of less than .05, the latter finding is strictly not statistically significant, given the number of subjects involved. It is nevertheless close enough to be suggestive.

will be an emphasis on situational rather than personality factors, just as was found in both of these studies.

An accent on situational determinants is likewise inevitable, according to Peter Benson and his colleagues (1980), whenever helping is operationalized as assistance offered on the spur of the moment in response to an unanticipated need. To assess the role of intrapersonal factors, they argue, we must turn to more deliberate and sustained forms of helping, such as volunteer work in the real world. Using questionnaire data gathered from 113 male and female students at Earlham College, a small Midwestern liberal arts institution associated with the Society of Friends, Benson and his associates found that nonspontaneous helping reported for the previous year was significantly and positively correlated with 10 of their 21 intrapersonal factors, including intrinsic religiousness, rated importance of religion, and church attendance.

Batson's later studies did find significant correlations with religious orientation, perhaps in part because the subjects were religiously more diverse than in the first one. Furthermore, his designs allowed him and his associates to infer his volunteers' motives for offering to help. Likewise advantageous was his measuring of the critical variables by several different means. For example, Batson and Flory (1990) assessed *religious orientation* by questionnaire replies, *motive-relevant cognitions* by latencies in naming the colors in which three sets of motive-related terms were printed (words with special meaning for the subject are said to interfere with the color-naming task, producing longer latencies), and *helping* by the number of hours, if any, that the subjects offered on a brief response form soliciting their help for a student in need. Correlational studies, in contrast, often rely on the same mode of assessment—typically, questionnaire scales—for the significant variables, thus allowing RESPONSE SET, or response style, to inflate the correlations, yielding spuriously significant results (Batson, 1977).

Simulating real-life situations in the laboratory is nevertheless exceedingly difficult if not impossible, especially with religious variables. Moreover, the procedures are enormously time-consuming and require a degree of cooperation from subjects that in many contexts may be difficult to attain. And because laboratory procedures by their very nature accent the role of external influences, they lend themselves more readily to social-psychological research than to investigations of the interrelationships of intrapersonal variables. For these and still other reasons, correlation remains the more popular avenue of research among objectively oriented psychologists, especially those examining religion. The next chapter explores the correlational approach, surveying the techniques, findings, and issues that form a large part of the contemporary psychology of religion. It concludes by reflecting critically on both experimental and correlational methods, especially as they are applied to human piety.

6

THE CORRELATIONAL STUDY OF RELIGION

*P*sychologists of religion have long preferred the more naturalistic approach offered by correlational methods. The earliest American contributors of the modern period, including Stanley Hall, James Leuba, Edwin Starbuck, and George Coe, made extensive use of frequency counts and tabulations of questionnaire replies to discern trends in religious behavior and experience. Starbuck (1899), for example, reports the frequency of conversion by age, sex, and theological background, and then correlates these data with changes in height and weight during the childhood and adolescent years. He tabulates the reported "mental and bodily affections" that characterized the preconversion states of his subjects; the motives and forces that led to conversion; the elements that composed the conversion experience; the feelings that followed the experience; and the character of the postconversion struggle. Starbuck also describes statistically the course of religious belief through the life-span and the relative prominence of religious feelings and ideals in adults of various ages.

Galton and the Efficacy of Prayer

The earliest systematic investigation of religion by correlational techniques, such as they were in the latter half of the nineteenth century, was undertaken by Francis Galton. Charmed by statistics, Galton became convinced of their value in exploring and understanding human variation.

> Some people hate the very name of statistics, but I find them full of beauty and interest. Whenever they are not brutalized, but delicately handled by the higher methods, and are warily interpreted, their power of dealing with complicated phenomena is extraordinary. They are the only tools by which an opening can be cut through the formidable thicket of difficulties that bars the path of those who pursue the Science of man (Galton, 1889, 62–63).

According to Edwin Boring (1950), Galton was the first to work out the method of statistical correlation. He was also a pioneer in the use of questionnaires and rating scales, devices that lie at the heart of the correlational psychology of religion.

Does Prayer Have Objective Effects? Galton's most famous contribution to the psychology of religion is his study of the objective efficacy of petitionary prayer. Rather than involving himself in the difficulties and limitations of an experimental investigation, Galton (1872) chose simply to tabulate the evidence he could find around him. Did public prayers on behalf of the reigning sovereign, for health and longevity, have an evident effect? Apparently not, reports Galton, who cites statistics showing that male members of royal houses, from 1758 to 1843, were the shortest-lived among various affluent classes. The alternative hypothesis that prayers are efficacious in saving royalty from otherwise even shorter life-spans seemed to Galton rather improbable.

Statistics also demonstrated that a prayerful life gave no advantage to members of the clergy, at least the eminent ones. Galton (1869) documents this conclusion in detail in a comparative study of "Divines," based on a four-volume encyclopedia of evangelical biographies (Middleton, 1779–1786) that includes such figures as John Calvin, John Donne, Jonathan Edwards, Martin Luther, Cotton Mather, and John Wycliffe, as well as many others less well known today. From his study of these biographies, Galton draws several conclusions: (1) Divines are not founders of notably influential families, whether on the basis of wealth, social position, or abilities; (2) they tend, if anything, to have fewer children than average; (3) they are slightly less long-lived than the eminent men in Galton's other groups; and (4) they usually have wretched constitutions.

Galton gives special emphasis to the last conclusion. Many of these religious figures were sickly in their youth, a fate for which they compensated, he suggests, by turning to bookish pursuits. As adults they remained infirm, even taking pleasure in dwelling on the morbid details of their suffering. Indeed, says Galton, "There is an air of invalidism about most religious biographies" (p. 256). The majority of the few Divines who possessed vigorous constitutions had, according to Galton, been wild in their youth. Anticipating the findings of James as well as later research results, he concludes that "Robustness of constitution is antagonistic, in a very marked degree, to an extremely pious disposition" (p. 260).

In no observed respect, then, were the clergy that Galton studied exceptionally favored; on the contrary, they were among the less fortunate of the human race. That the exceptionally pious—combining, according to Galton, the unrelated trends of high moral character and instability of disposition—may pass on to their children only one of these traits accounts for the absence of extreme piety, or the presence of notoriously bad behavior, in the next generation. The slight advantage in life-span that *ordinary* clergy had, on the average, over most other professional groups can be explained, says Galton (1872, p. 129), by "the easy country life and family repose."

Galton reports a variety of other findings that likewise suggest that petitionary prayer does not have consistent objective effects. Missionaries, in spite of their worthy objectives, proved not to live longer than other people; Galton reports that many of them died, in fact, shortly after arriving in their host countries. Similarly, Galton found that the newborn children of the "pious classes" were no more likely to survive than children born to parents less inclined to pray for the well-being of their offspring. Compared with other buildings, churches were no less frequently damaged by lightning, fire, earthquakes, or avalanches. Medical doctors and insurance companies, presumably eager to discover the slightest advantage that some factor might give for health or safety, seemed nowhere to take into account the influence of prayer or pious disposition.

A Biased Selection: Both the rather unsympathetic chapter on Divines and the essay on prayer, which Galton published three years later, after it had been rejected three times because of its controversial nature, were sharply criticized (Forrest, 1974, pp. 111, 172). Perhaps his most judicious critic was Karl Pearson (1924), one of Galton's associates and his biographer, who notes the bias in Middleton's selection of men of piety. By limiting himself to Middleton's encyclopedia, Pearson observes, Galton omitted nearly all the founders and many of the central figures of the great religious movements, including Saint Augustine, Saint Thomas Aquinas, Saint Francis, Meister Eckhardt, George Fox, Emanuel Swedenborg, and John Wesley. Entirely excluded, too, are a number of influential women. Middleton's selection includes, Pearson observes, individuals eminent in piety but undistinguished in intellectual ability. During most of the years covered by this collection of biographies, many churchmen became eminent largely because they were politicians or statesmen, not because they were profoundly religious. Galton claims that practical considerations forced him to limit himself largely to persons of English nationality, or at least to persons well known in England. He excluded Roman Catholic Divines because, as celibates, they provided no data for his statistics on heredity. Thus his conclusions about Divines may be generalized strictly to male Protestant Christians who lived at a particular time and were eminent in a particular part of the world.

The Subjective Effects of Prayer: Although many of his contemporaries considered Galton a "flippant freethinker," he was in his own way a religious man: reverent, deeply committed to high ideals, and even subject to mystical intimations (Blacker, 1946). He perceived a unity within all of life and he held that "Men and all other living animals are active workers and sharers in a vastly more extended system of cosmic action than any of ourselves, much less any of them, can possibly comprehend" (Galton, 1869, p. 361). "Man," he wrote elsewhere (1908, p. 323), "is gifted with pity and other kindly feelings; he has also the power of preventing many kinds of suffering. I conceive it to fall well within his province to replace Natural Selection by other processes that are more merciful and not less effective. This is precisely the aim of Eugenics." Galton felt that the principles of EUGENICS should be embraced as though they were religious tenets.

Although prayer may not have strictly objective results within this lawful cosmos, Galton had no doubt that it can yield subjective effects, whether they include "a confident sense of communion with God" or the no less powerful feeling of solidarity with what surrounds us, a world governed by physical laws that include the hereditary ones that so interested Galton. Either outcome can "ennoble the resolves" and "give serenity during the trials of life and in the shadow of approaching death" (Galton, 1872, p. 135). Galton regularly led his own household in prayer, albeit with some reservations, and he "always made it a habit to *pray* before writing anything for publication, that there be no self-seeking in it, and perfect candour together with respect for the feelings of others" (quoted in Pearson, 1930, p. 272). With prayers of aspiration rather than solicitation he clearly had no quarrel.

The Emergence of Modern Correlational Psychology

Since Galton's day correlational psychology has become remarkably more sophisticated. The impetus for developing tests that measure individual differences at the level of complex functions came in particular from two sources: the interest of the French government at the beginning of this century in identifying and educating the mentally retarded; and, a decade or so later, the sudden need of the war-pressed United States Army to classify in short order more than a million recruits. From an initial interest limited largely to intelligence and special abilities, psychological testing grew to encompass an enormous diversity of instruments—some commercially published, many others not—serving education, industry, clinical psychology, and scientific research (Anastasi, 1988).

Over the same period of time, Galton's relatively simple statistical approach evolved into highly complex methods, including such widely used procedures as FACTOR ANALYSIS, ANALYSIS OF VARIANCE, and a variety of other tests for evaluating statistical significance. Advances in the design of electronic computers in the 1950s rapidly made practical the use of the more tediously complex statistical methods, and they spurred on the development of ever more elaborate quantitative theories and procedures. Drawing on these new statistical methods as well as modern principles of test construction and validation, contemporary correlational psychologists have continued Galton's exploration of individual differences, including differences in religiousness.

THE PROBLEM OF MEASURING RELIGION

The first major task of the correlational psychologists of religion is to develop precise and reliable means for assessing individual piety. Research on religious behavior and experience, they maintain, requires an "operational definition" of these events. That is, the researcher must specify precisely the operations or procedures that will be used to observe them. Because a person can be religious to varying degrees, these procedures are typically quantitative, yielding scores that can be correlated statistically with a range of other dimensions. The search among personality characteristics, attitudes, and other variables for correlates of religiousness is the second major task of these correlational investigators (see Hood, Spilka, Hunsberger, and Gorsuch, 1996).

In estimating the piety of a new family in the neighborhood, for example, we would ordinarily resort to a predictable series of observations. Are they members of a religious organization? If so, how often do they attend religious services and other functions? Have they furnished their house with religious pictures, statues, or other sacred objects? Are there religious books or magazines lying about? Do they bow their heads before meals, cross themselves, or engage in other obvious ritual behavior? In asking questions directed at observable and even quantifiable behavior, we are conducting ourselves much like the correlational psychologists, although our observations are likely to be less systematic and precise.

As most social scientists will acknowledge, such indicators of piety are crude at best, no matter how carefully the observations are made. Persons may be active in religious organizations, not primarily as an expression of religious faith, but as a means of gaining friendship, making business contacts, or expressing their socioeconomic status and values. Sacred objects around the house may carry little religious meaning for its occupants, serving rather as sources of aesthetic pleasure or nostalgic links to the past. The books and magazines, some of them perhaps gifts from persons outside the family, may be largely unread. Pious gestures may occur out of sheer habit or to fulfill the expectations of others. The absence of these indicators is likewise ambiguous: some profoundly religious people may exhibit none of them.

Although psychologists and sociologists of religion employ similarly rough-and-ready measures of religiousness (see Argyle and Beit-Hallahmi, 1975), many of these researchers have sought more subtle means of assessment. On the one hand, they recognize the ambiguity of any outward expression and therefore seek to develop questionnaires that also evaluate the less obvious underlying beliefs and attitudes. On the other hand, many are convinced that these indicators are not parallel measures of a single dimension, religiousness, but that they reflect, rather, several dimensions of piety varying more or less independently of each other.

Early Measures of the Beliefs of Scientists

The earliest questionnaires were relatively long and complex, inviting detailed answers that could not easily be quantified (see Lehmann, 1915; Pratt, 1907; Starbuck, 1899). Leuba's (1916, 1934) studies of the beliefs of American scientists are a famous exception. In 1914 and again in 1933, Leuba sent out a brief questionnaire to a large number of scientists chosen at random from the current edition of *American Men of Science* and the directories of the American Sociological Society and the American Psychological Association. Leuba included in his samples a number of "greater" contributors who had been identified as eminent in their fields by a small group of distinguished peers. Recipients of the questionnaire were asked to indicate whether they believed "in a God to whom one may pray in the expectation of receiving an answer. By 'answer' I mean more than the natural, subjective, psychological effect of prayer." As alternatives they were offered "I do not believe in a God as defined above" or "I have no definite belief regarding this question." Three corresponding statements regarding immortality were also presented (Leuba, 1916, p. 223).

Leuba's findings, summarized in Table 6.1, indicate that the probability of belief declines (1) the more knowledge the scientist has about "living matter, society, and the mind," (2) the greater the scientist's peer-rated eminence, and (3) the more recent the response to Leuba's questionnaire. Here is evidence, Leuba (1950) concludes, of a revolution in thought and a readiness for a transformation of the churches into liberal religious societies that recognize natural spiritual forces and promote "spiritual hygiene and culture" (p. 124). A follow-up study carried out more than two decades later by Ronald Mayer (1959), using Leuba's scales

Table 6.1 **PERCENTAGES OF AMERICAN SCIENTISTS AFFIRMING BELIEF IN GOD AND IMMORTALITY, 1914 AND 1933**

	Lesser Scientists		Greater Scientists	
	1914	1933	1914	1933
A. Belief in a God Who Answers Prayer				
Physical scientists	50	43	34	17
Biological scientists	39	31	17	12
Sociologists	29	30	19	13
Psychologists	32	13	13	12
B. Belief in Personal Survival after Death				
Physical scientists	57	46	40	20
Biological scientists	45	32	25	15
Sociologists	52	31	27	10
Psychologists	27	12	9	2

Source: From Leuba, 1934, page 297.

along with two others, confirmed most of the same trends, although Mayer did not find significant differences among disciplines for the eminent scientists.

As we might anticipate, many of Leuba's subjects objected to the limitations imposed by his questions, often adding in marginalia or separate letters the qualifications or alternatives they felt were needed to represent their own views. One wrote, for example, "I do believe in a God and in prayer, but *not as you have outlined it*" (Leuba, 1916, p. 235). Of course, any questionnaire may inspire such dissent. Even the more open-ended set of questions sent by C. L. Drawbridge (1932) and his associates to the fellows of the Royal Society drew its share of protests. A surer way of representing the individual views of scientists was employed by Edward Long (1952), who turned to published works—many of them obscure—for evidence of religious outlook. What he demonstrates, however, is the possibility of finding scientists with conservative religious views, not the validity of his conclusion that among scientists "the lack of pattern is obvious" (p. 145). Having limited himself to scientists who had published their religious views, and then having chosen which of them to include, Long has no basis for generalizing about scientists as a whole.

For such generalizations, a simple device such as Leuba's questionnaire, combined with an appropriate sampling technique, is far more serviceable. Yet it is possible to simplify matters still further. Rather than sending out a questionnaire, Harvey Lehman and Paul Witty (1931) used *American Men of Science* and *Who's Who in America* in combination to establish the frequency and nature of religious affiliation among eminent scientists. They found that these distinguished researchers acknowledged a denominational affiliation half as often as all others listed in *Who's Who* (25 percent as compared with about 50 percent, a figure close to the level of affiliation in the general population of the United States at that time [Argyle, 1958]). More revealing was the discovery that, among these scientists, the liberal denominations, such as the Unitarians, Congregationalists, and Episcopalians, were markedly overrepresented, and the conservative groups, including the Baptists, Lutherans, and above all the Roman Catholics, were strikingly underrepresented. Lehman and Witty speculate that these findings are symptomatic of the conflict between conservative religious doctrine and scientific thought.

The Thurstone Scales of Religious Attitudes

In the late 1920s and early 1930s, as the psychologist's measurement techniques became more sophisticated, so also did the questionnaire of the psychologist of religion. When the eminent University of Chicago psychologist L. L. Thurstone (1887–1955) made his famous adaptation of psychophysical methods—developed for studying the relation of physical stimuli and bodily sensation—to the quantification of social values, he chose as his illustrative case the Scale for Measuring Attitude Toward the Church.

With an initial list of 130 carefully edited statements derived from solicited opinions and published literature, Thurstone and Ernest Chave (1929) asked 341 subjects to sort slips of paper bearing these brief statements according to how appreciative each appeared to be. The subjects were *not* to respond to them in terms of their own opinions about the church. The arrangements of the statements into 11 piles, ranging from "highest appreciation" to "strongest depreciation," gave these researchers an objective means of determining each statement's *ambiguity* (as reflected in the variability of ratings) and its *scale value,* equivalent to the median ranking of the 300 subjects whose sortings appeared to be properly carried out. A second group of 300 subjects was asked to endorse the statements that expressed their own sentiments. Their responses provided a basis for determining the consistency with which each item was answered in relation to the others, a measure that was used to estimate an item's *relevance.*

The final set of 45 items that compose the published questionnaire (reprinted in Chave, 1939) was chosen to minimize ambiguity and irrelevance, as well as to distribute the median rankings of the items more or less uniformly along the entire scale. This elaborate procedure created an attitude scale consisting of "equal-appearing intervals." The questionnaire is scored by calculating the average scale value (or, alternatively, the average rank order) of all the statements an individual has endorsed. Two estimates of the RELIABILITY, calculated by the split-half method (see Anastasi, 1988), yielded values of .92 and .94—satisfactory evidence by any standards that the test's scores are highly consistent. A striking correlation with reported church attendance provides some evidence of the scale's VALIDITY.

Using similar procedures, Chave and Thurstone constructed and published several other scales for use by psychologists of religion. These include five forms of the Scale of Attitude Toward God, which assesses individual conceptions of God, belief in the reality of God, and the degree to which belief in or ideas of God influence conduct, and two forms of the Scale of Attitude Toward the Bible, on which scores may be interpreted in a range from "Strong prejudice against the Bible" to "Strong belief [in] and devotion to the Bible" (Chave, 1939). Two forms of yet another scale, on Sunday observance, were prepared by Charles Wang and Thurstone (reprinted, with the church scale, in Shaw and Wright, 1967). The particular content of these scales was contributed by Thurstone's collaborators, not Thurstone himself, who, though a Lutheran minister's son, was apparently less than enthusiastic about orthodox observance even as a child. His short-lived interest in attitude measurement was itself largely derivative, serving his wish "to introduce some life and interest in psychophysics" (Thurstone, 1952, p. 310). He left it to others to use and evaluate these scales, of which the Attitude Toward the Church scale has been most widely employed.

What advantages do these painstakingly derived tests have over the far simpler indicators that Leuba or Lehman and Witty used? Could the researcher not just as well ask the subjects to rate themselves on a continuum labeled at one end "Strongly favorable to the church" and at the other end, "Strongly against the church," with the midpoint designated "Neutral"? Such is precisely what Thurstone and Chave did. Converting this self-rating line into a simple ten-point scale, they correlated it with their more elaborate measurement device. The outcome, a correlation of .67, indicates that the two measures have approximately 45 percent of their VARIANCE in common (see Nunnally, 1978)—a sizable amount, by the standards of the social sciences, but still less than half. Moreover, from examining individual question-naires, the authors inferred that the subjects tended to evaluate themselves on the self-rating line as more favorably disposed to the church than is indicated by the scale statements they endorse. Thurstone and Chave are properly cautious in interpreting these observations, yet it would seem safe to conclude that the brief measure cannot serve as a substitute for the longer measure without a change in meaning.

Brevity is not necessarily a virtue, of course, as we saw in Leuba's research. Too brief a questionnaire may leave subjects doubtful that their views are properly represented. Too long a questionnaire, on the other hand, runs the risk of losing the subject's sustained cooperation. From a PSYCHOMETRIC perspective, the extended questionnaire is the more valuable one. Other things being equal, the more items a psychological test has, the more reliable it will be (although a point of diminishing returns will soon be reached). A variety of questions also allows a far more adequate sampling of the domain to be measured, and the scores they yield, because they range more widely than those of brief questionnaires, permit finer discriminations among the persons answering them. The broader range of scores correspondingly increases the possibility of finding significant correlations with other measures.

FACTOR ANALYSIS AND THE DIMENSIONALITY OF RELIGION

A longer questionnaire also invites evaluation through FACTOR ANALYSIS, a term that refers to a group of elaborate statistical methods for which we are again indebted to Thurstone, among others. Although itself complex, factor analysis is employed as a means of simplification. It is used to find the few "factors" that account for the pattern of correlation among a large number of variables—in the present case, usually the individual items of a questionnaire.

Factor analysis begins with a matrix of correlation coefficients, which indicate the degree of relationship of every questionnaire item with each of the others. Correlation coefficients range from +1.00, which indicates a perfect *positive* relation between two variables, to −1.00, which designates a perfect *negative* (or inverse) relation. The closer the correlation coefficient is to zero, the more nearly independent of each other the two variables are. Thus if two statements on a questionnaire showed a correlation of .68, we would conclude that respondents who agree with one of these statements are likely to agree with the other. If the correlation were −.68, on the other hand, agreement with one statement would signal the likelihood of disagreement with the other. If the correlation coefficient were close to zero—say, .06—we would conclude that the statements are unrelated to each other.

During the process of factor analysis, the computer scans the table of correlation coefficients and extracts in succession the small number of factors that account for the interrelationships among the items. In a new table, then, the computer indicates the "loading," or correlation, of every questionnaire item with each of the extracted factors. The researcher will note which items load most heavily on each factor and, by studying their content, infer what the factors are. Identifying factors is rarely easy, and coming up with succinct yet accurate labels is likewise a challenge. Also of interest in the table of factor loadings are the numbers indicating how much variance, or variability, in the test scores is accounted for by each of the factors. In every instance of factor analysis, some variance will remain unexplained by any of the factors.

It is routine today to factor-analyze any questionnaire that consists of more than a few questions. Researchers developing complex inventories with multiple scales frequently use factor analysis as a way of checking to be sure that the scales possess the statistical coherence their content suggests they should have. Scale items that do not show an appropriate pattern of factor loadings—relatively high on the factor they are intended to measure and correspondingly low on all the others— can be either rewritten or replaced. It is also common to factor-analyze scales written to measure only one variable, especially if the investigator suspects that the variable has two or more facets and thus is factorially complex. A number of religiosity scales have been factor-analyzed to check out their suspected complexity—and, by extension, the complexity of human piety.

Religion as a Single Factor

Like other researchers, psychologists and sociologists of religion do not agree about the factorial complexity of the object of their study. Some continue to assume that religiousness is a unidimensional quality that can be adequately assessed by any number of indicators. There is some evidence supporting this position, most of it obtained through factor analysis.

The earliest factor-analytic study providing such support was carried out by Thelma Thurstone, who administered 11 of her husband's attitude scales to several hundred university students. She found that the church, God, and Sunday observance scales clustered together on the far end of one factor, a dimension identifiable as either conservatism or as religion (Thurstone, 1934). The scales measuring positive attitudes toward evolution and birth control loaded negative on the same factor, just as they did in investigations by Leonard Ferguson (1939, 1944a).

A variety of studies, drawing on disparate materials, have confirmed these early findings. Each of three factor-analytic evaluations of test items written to represent Eduard Spranger's (1914) six personality types found a single religion-related factor (Brogden, 1952; Gordon, 1972; Lurie, 1937). The longer and more homogeneous scale of attitudes toward the church and religion administered by Adolf Holl and Gerhard Fischer (1968) to a group of Austrian soldiers similarly yielded a single religiosity factor. Two other factors, Distance from the Church as Organization and Social Contact, although correlated with church attendance, were interpreted as nonreligious determinants. Unidimensionality is also confirmed in a series of studies by L. B. Brown (1962, 1966) and A. J. Wearing and Brown (1972), who consistently found a single factor regardless of the combination of measures they employed.

The Case for Multidimensionality

Most psychologists and sociologists of religion favor a multidimensional perspective. So also do other scholars. Well before the advent of factor analysis, the Roman Catholic lay theologian Baron Friedrich von Hügel (1908) identified three "elements of religion," three successively developing modes of apprehension or outlook: (1) the *traditional,* or *historical,* dependent largely on the senses, imagination, and memory, and originating in childhood; (2) the *rational,* or *systematic,* emerging with the capacities for reflection, argument, and abstraction; and (3) the *intuitive* and *volitional,* signaling the maturation of inner experience and outer action. James Pratt (1920) takes a similar approach, although he separates the two aspects composing von Hügel's third element in his own four "typical aspects of religion": the traditional, the rational, the mystical, and the practical or moral. Both von Hügel and Pratt argue that each element or aspect, however much it may be emphasized in a particular case and to whatever degree it may conflict with the others, remains fundamentally bound up with the rest.

Yet another variation on the facets of religion is offered by sociologist Charles Glock (1962), whose *experiential* and *consequential* dimensions closely parallel Pratt's mystical and practical aspects, whereas his *ritualistic, ideological,* and *intellectual* (that is, knowledge) dimensions seem largely to expand von Hügel's and Pratt's traditional category and touch little if at all on the rational (see Table 6.2). Although Glock thinks "it scarcely plausible" that the five dimensions he discerns are wholly independent of one another, he leaves the question of their interrelation to quantitative research.

Religion in Five Dimensions: The task of operationalizing Glock's dimensions

Table 6.2 ASPECTS OF RELIGION ACCORDING TO VON HÜGEL, PRATT, AND GLOCK

von Hügel	Pratt	Glock
1. Traditional (historical)	1. Traditional	⎰ 1. Ideological (belief) ⎨ 2. Ritualistic (practice) ⎱ 3. Intellectual (knowledge)
2. Rational	2. Rational	
3. Intuitive and volitional	⎰ 3. Mystical ⎱ 4. Practical (moral)	4. Experiential (feeling) 5. Consequential (effects)

was taken up by Joseph Faulkner and Gordon DeJong (1966), who painstakingly developed five scales of four or five items each, employing the cumulative scaling technique originated by Louis Guttman (see Nunnally, 1978; Shaw and Wright, 1967). For their subject group as a whole, the intercorrelations among the five scales and thus presumably among the five dimensions ranged from a high of .58 (between the Ideological and Intellectual scales) to a low of .36 (between the Experiential and Consequential scales). When the subject group was broken down by sex, religious affiliation, or parents' church membership, some correlations ranged slightly higher and others considerably lower. These researchers found, for example, that the Ideological and Experiential scales correlated more highly for females than for males (.60 versus .39); that the Jewish students showed the lowest correlation by far between the Ritual and Consequential scales; and that half of the ten correlations among the five scales were statistically insignificant for students whose parents were not church members. Although most of the scale intercorrelations *are* statistically significant for the total group of 375 students, they appear at the same time to be low enough to support the multidimensional position.

The response both to Glock's proposed dimensions and to Faulkner and De-Jong's efforts to measure them might be taken as a case study in the complexities of this area of research. Rodney Stark and Glock (1968) themselves had operationalized a slightly modified set of Glock's dimensions, using a rather different collection of items. Nonetheless, the pattern of intercorrelations they found was "extremely similar" to Faulkner and DeJong's (p. 179). They also discovered that the ideological commitment or Orthodoxy scale, because of its relatively high correlations with the others, is the best single measure of the five. Andrew Weigert and Darwin Thomas (1969), unconvinced by these apparent convergences, argue that the Faulkner–DeJong scales are inadequate measures of Glock's dimensions. Three of the four items constituting the Intellectual or knowledge scale, they point out, actually measure belief, and only one of the five items composing the Experiential scale assesses the individual's own religious emotion. Most of the 23 items might be described as ideological in format, so that the preeminence of the Ideological scale is no surprise. Similar criticisms are made by James Gibbs and Kelly Crader (1970), who fault the Experiential scale on the same grounds as Weigert and Thomas and argue that the items on the Consequential scale are contaminated by the religious context in which they are framed. Yet the data they collected using revised Experiential and Consequential scales "tend to support the pattern of relationships reported by Faulkner and DeJong" (p. 111).

In their reply to Weigert and Thomas, Faulkner and DeJong (1969) emphasize the difficulty of finding items of religious knowledge that form a proper scale, and they remind their critics of the breadth of Glock's original characterization of the experiential side of religion. They do not justify, however, their counting of literal belief in the story of creation or biblical miracles as positive evidence of "an intellectual orientation toward one's faith." Nor do they acknowledge that for only one of their five experiential items does an affirmative answer unequivocally indicate that the respondent has had the experience in question. Whatever their items do assess, they are correct in pointing out that the relatively low intercorrelations are evidence that the five subscales do not measure the same thing.

Challenges to the 5-D Scales: Most criticisms of Glock's dimensions and the Faulkner–DeJong "5-D" scales are based on patterns of statistical relationship rather than on content analysis of questionnaire items. Although some researchers have also found low scale intercorrelations (e.g., Kuhre, 1971; Lehman and Shriver, 1968; Ruppel, 1969), others have discovered intercorrelations sufficiently high to call into question the assumption of multidimensionality (see Cardwell, 1969; Clayton, 1971a; Finner and Gamache, 1969; Gibbs and Crader, 1970; Rohrbaugh and Jessor, 1975). Several factor-analytic studies make the challenge especially clear. Richard Clayton and James Gladden (1974) factor-analyzed the responses of two groups of largely Protestant university students to the 5-D scales and found five and four factors, respectively. In both instances, however, only the first factor—Ideological Commitment—is clearly defined. This factor accounts for an astonishing 78 percent of the common variance in one group of subjects and 83 percent in the other, a finding that demonstrates that it is by far the most important factor. A second-order factor analysis of the factors themselves produced one general factor. "Religiosity," they conclude, "is essentially a single-dimensional phenomenon composed primarily of Ideological Commitment," the strength of which is reflected in experience and practice (p. 141).

Ursula Boos-Nünning's (1972) investigation in West Germany yielded findings that likewise raise doubts about Glock's frequently cited formulation. When Boos-Nünning factor-analyzed the responses of randomly selected Catholics in a large city of the Ruhr Valley to a 78-item questionnaire designed to measure six dimensions of religiosity, including Glock's five, only two of the six appeared as factors in her results: Religious Knowledge and Tie to the Parish. Most of the items representing Glock's ritualistic, ideological, experiential, and consequential dimensions loaded on Boos-Nünning's first factor, called General Religiosity, which accounts for 51 percent of the common variance. The second of her six factors, Tie to the Parish (or Parish Communication and Information, as she came to call it), accounted for 18 percent, and the third, Marital and Sexual Morality, accounted for only 9 percent. The last three—Belief in God, Public Religious Practice, and Religious Knowledge—were responsible for only 7 or 8 percent each.

Glock's dimensions were also put to the test by two other German researchers, Albert Fuchs and Reinhard Oppermann (1975). They factor-analyzed similarity ratings for 16 of the most frequently used religious words in the German language, such as *Glaube* (faith), *Gott* (God), *Engel* (angel), *Predigt* (sermon), and *Gnade* (grace), which were presented to their heterogeneous sample in paired combinations. Their two factors, accounting, respectively, for 53 and 17 percent of the total variance, confirm at best only the ideological and ritualistic dimensions of Glock's schema. Once again, therefore, the evidence argues against the complexity hypothesis. It tends, rather, to support the notion of one major factor, either general in character or ideological in emphasis.

The Multiplicity of Evidence: What, then, are we to make of the numerous factor-analytic studies that report two or more major factors largely independent of each other? William Broen (1967), for example, found that the pattern of responses of 24 religious subjects to 133 statements yielded two factors: Nearness to God, reflecting a sense of "the Deity's loving presence and guidance," and Fundamentalism–Humanitarianism, a bipolar factor emphasizing at the "positive" end humankind's sinfulness and need for a punishing God and at the "negative" end the potential goodness and self-sufficiency of human beings. Broen found a high enough correlation (.32) between these two factors to allow him to combine them as a measure of "general religiosity," yet one sufficiently low to support his argument for multidimensionality.

At the other extreme of factorial complexity is the work of Morton King and Richard Hunt (1969, 1972a, 1972b, 1975a, 1990; King, 1967). Their basic set of items, derived from other researchers' work as well as from interviews and questionnaire replies, was assembled as an instrument for measuring 11 hypothetical dimensions. The responses of members of 27 congregations representing four mainline Protestant denominations in Dallas County, Texas, yielded—in spite of modifications in item composition made for each denomination—a remarkably stable set of ten religious factors: (1) Creedal Assent, (2) Devotionalism, (3) Church Attendance, (4) Organizational Activity, (5) Financial Support, (6) Religious Knowledge, (7) Orientation to Growth and Striving, (8) Extrinsic Orientation, (9) Salience: Behavior (earlier called Talking and Reading about Religion), and (10) Salience: Cognition (indicating the prominence of religion in everyday thoughts and feelings).

Items selected to measure eight of these factors were included, with others, in a questionnaire distributed to a nationwide sample of members of the United Presbyterian Church in the U.S.A. The entire questionnaire was then factor-analyzed (King and Hunt, 1975a). Among the 20 interpretable factors that were found, all eight of the King and Hunt factors reappeared; moreover, their item compositions were almost identical to those found in earlier investigations. Although nearly all the correlations among the King–Hunt scales are statistically significant (King and Hunt, 1972b, p. 119), the relatively low average of these correlations (.37) supports the case for multidimensionality. Group differences on these scales, as well as correlations with other measures, demonstrate the potential usefulness of so complex and thorough a measuring instrument.

Evidence for multidimensionality continues to accumulate. Starting with a new religiosity questionnaire rather more sophisticated than earlier instruments and administering it to both American and German students, DeJong, Faulkner, and Rex Warland (1976) found six familiar dimensions. Yet they also report evidence of "generic religiosity," encompassing belief, experience, and practice. Using the same questionnaire, Dale Hilty and Sue Stockman (1986) replicated five of the six factors as well as the higher-order generic religiosity. Various other scales intended as general measures of religion have upon analysis yielded two or more factors (Cline and Richards, 1965; Himmelfarb, 1975; Maranell, 1968; Shand, 1961; Tapp, 1971).

More specialized scales have proved to be factorially complex as well. Robert Coursey (1974) found six factors in a scale designed to measure the liberal–conservative dimensions among Roman Catholics. Leon Gorlow and Harold Schroeder (1968), Robert Monaghan (1967), and Sam Webb (1965) investigated the motives or needs underlying church attendance or religious activities more generally and report, respectively, seven, three, and eleven factors. In a succession of studies using many of the same adjectives, Bernard Spilka, Philip Armatas, and June Nussbaum

(1964), Richard Gorsuch (1968), and Walter Broughton (1975) found three or more major dimensions in the conceptualization of God, with notable convergence of factors, whereas Godelieve Vercruysse (1972), employing descriptive phrases, found six such factors with his adolescent subjects and four rather different factors with his adults. Finally, Ralph Hood's 32-item Mysticism Scale, which he derived from Stace's (1960) analysis, yielded two factors—General Mysticism and Religious Interpretation—when factor-analyzed by Hood (1975) and three when analyzed by Dale Caird (1988) using college students and also by Duane Reinert and Kenneth Stifler (1993) using three groups of older adults varying widely in religious background and psychiatric status. In both of the latter studies, Hood's second factor split in two: a noetic (Caird) or noetic/ineffability (Reinert and Stifler) factor, accenting the experience of insight if not also the indescribableness of the experience, and a religious factor, emphasizing the sense of the holy.

Support for the multidimensional position can also be garnered from studies reporting relatively low intercorrelations among different measures of religiousness (e.g., Finner, 1970; Fukuyama, 1961; Lenski, 1961; Vernon, 1962). The difficulty here is deciding how small such correlations must be, given the inevitable imperfections of these scales, to argue that they are measuring different dimensions.

With evidence and advocates on both sides of the dimensionality issue, and what may seem to be a blur of factors identified by those in the multidimensional camp, what firm conclusions can we hope to draw? For those who assume that factor analysis of religiosity scales is a way of uncovering an unchanging truth about all human beings, regardless of time or place, the diversity of outcomes may be interpreted as a disheartening yet temporary state of affairs, ultimately resolvable through further refinements in the scales and statistical procedures. For those of a postmodern perspective, on the other hand, the scales, procedures, and factors are all fallible human constructions—useful for certain purposes, no doubt, but not mirrors that reflect a psychological reality unchanged by context or history. What they do reveal is how social scientists think about religion today, and what their subjects make of it as well.

Factor analysis, all will agree, is a sophisticated procedure for discerning a pattern within a particular set of data. What the researcher includes among these data will determine the configuration of factors reported by the computer. If we assemble a questionnaire composed only in part of religious items, all of which express conventional attitudes or practices, and then give this questionnaire to a heterogeneous sample of persons, varying especially in religious background and commitment, we may be fairly confident that the religious items will cluster together to form a single "religious factor." If, by contrast, the questionnaire consists entirely of religious items, varied and subtle in content, and it is given to a relatively homogeneous and religiously sophisticated group of persons—members of the clergy, for example, such as Jack Shand (1961) employed—then we may naturally expect a range of religious factors. That religious "insiders" may provide a more differentiated factor structure than "outsiders" is demonstrated in Gary Maranell and Nevell Razak's (1970) comparison of priests and ministers with college professors.

Religion's Singular Complexity

No one has yet found *the* fundamental dimensions of religiousness—nor will they ever be found. Scales of any kind should be understood as conventional devices that serve the particular needs of the researchers (King and Hunt, 1975b, 1990;

Nunnally, 1978). Although Dittes (1969) argues cogently that the multidimensional approach is likely to be the more fruitful one for the social scientist, he also takes seriously the evidence for a single common factor, suggesting that it "be construed simply as 'religion as seen by the general population' " (p. 618). "The resolution," writes Gorsuch (1984), "could be *both/and* rather than either/or" (p. 232). As he demonstrates by reference to Maranell's (1974) results, a single, general factor of religiosity may relate well to other broadly conceived variables (e.g., age), whereas more specific religious factors may serve best to identify exceptions to these general trends.

The paradox we face here—that religion may be many things and yet one, a *unitas multiplex*—was addressed by von Hügel (1908) long before factor analysis and the dimensionality issue emerged. If religion were a mere multiplicity, a collection of parts without a whole, he says, it would be neither persuasive nor effective; yet if it were a simple unity, a whole without parts, it could not be a source of truth (p. 50). It may be, however, that both von Hügel and contemporary researchers are misled by the word *religion*. As we noted in Chapter 1, this word has become a reified abstraction that misleadingly suggests an unchanging essence, either within each tradition or underlying them all. If we substitute Wilfred Smith's (1963) preferred terms, cumulative tradition and faith, we immediately see that multiplicity is the inescapable fact, overwhelmingly so in the case of the historic traditions but unmistakable, too, in the realm of faith. It is personal faith that researchers aspire to measure, and it will always be expressed in a diversity of individual forms.

No set of scales, however complex, can hope to represent the nuances of personal faith. Every scale is a compromise: its statements must be general enough to be usable by a range of people, yet they must be specific enough to distinguish among the respondents. For example, the statement "I believe in God" would in the United States be too general, for around 95 percent of respondents are likely to agree. On the other hand, the declaration "I am regularly visited by an invisible Presence to whom I can pour out my heart," although crucial for representing the experience of Flournoy's (1915) mystic, would be either too specific for a general questionnaire or too easily reinterpreted to include any vague sense of a spiritual presence.

Some researchers have aspired to develop questionnaires sufficiently broad to be usable across religious traditions (Bhushan, 1970, 1971; Yinger, 1969, 1977); others, daunted by the obvious difficulties of encompassing so wide a range of concepts and practices, propose the development of parallel scales for the various traditions, including in each the specific expressions shared by persons of similar faith (King and Hunt, 1972b). Glock (1962) clearly has a program of this breadth in mind, but only after we have found adequate means for assessing religious commitment in our own culture.

Most existing religiosity scales have been developed for use by Christian subjects. Yet even more broadly conceived questionnaires may not provide sufficient options for thoughtful, imaginative, and religiously complex subjects. Noting that it has long been typical to provide respondents with only two options in relation to creedal statements—literal affirmation and literal disaffirmation—Hunt (1972a) has proposed adding a mythological alternative. For example, to the statement "Jesus was born of the Virgin in a manner different from human beings," a subject may give one of three responses: (1) a literal one: "Agree, since God conceived Jesus in Mary's womb before she had sexual relations with Joseph, her husband"; (2) an antiliteral one: "Disagree, although most religions claim a virgin birth for their founder, we know that such an event is physically impossible"; and (3) a mythological one: "Agree, but only in the sense that this is an ancient mythological way of talking about the Ultimate Reality as manifested in Jesus" (Hunt, 1972a, p. 49).

Although Andrew Greeley (1972) asserts that Hunt's contribution "ought to mark a decisive turning point in religious research," he urges the inclusion of a fourth option, a "HERMENEUTIC dimension," which would more clearly and consistently retain the transcendental referent. Thus on the question of the virgin birth, respondents might agree that "The Ultimate Reality was present in Jesus in a way decisively different from the way It is present in the rest of us." The LAM (Literal, Antiliteral, and Mythological) scales, replies Hunt (1972b), in themselves represent three hermeneutical perspectives; a fourth would increase the options but not exhaust them. It is a question, therefore, of how many and which perspectives to incorporate.

In his research with Hunt's LAM scales, Norman Poythress (1975) did find a sizable group of people—28.2 percent of 234 college undergraduates—who could be classified as mythological types and thus as having a proreligious but nonliteral outlook. But contrary to Hunt's expectations, the Mythological scale did not show a distinctive pattern of relations with personality variables (in this study, intelligence, authoritarianism, and racial prejudice). Using a revised, Dutch version of the scales, in which metaphorical—and thus more clearly symbolical—alternatives were substituted for the mythological ones, Jan van der Lans (1991) found that nursing students who preferred the metaphorical alternatives gave a larger number of associations to a series of photographs and thus have, van der Lans infers, a greater tendency toward imaginative thinking. Associates of van der Lans have prepared an English version of his LAM scales for use with Hindu subjects and a Dutch version for research with Muslims.

The challenge of representing the more sophisticated, symbolic understandings of religion that have emerged in the postmodern world has also been taken up by Dirk Hutsebaut (1996a). Guided primarily by philosopher Paul Ricoeur's notion of the second naïveté—a new, more sophisticated openness to the objects of religious faith that is made possible through prior critical reinterpretation—Hutsebaut and a group of seminar students set about to formulate questionnaire items that measure this religious attitude, along with others represented in the summary schema of this book (see page 635). Factor analysis yielded three dimensions or attitudes, which correspond to the first, third, and fourth quadrants of the schema (the atheistic stance of literal disaffirmation, represented by the second quadrant, did not appear in their data). The attitude of *orthodoxy* is characterized by a predominance of literal thinking, a high level of religious certainty, positive god images, and a tendency toward anxiety and guilt. The *external critique* attitude is marked by religious ambivalence, a preference for the objective certainties of science, and expressions of revolt against God. The attitude of *historical relativism,* finally, recognizes the historically conditioned character of religious statements, interprets the Bible symbolically, and is open to complexity and uncertainty.

THE QUEST FOR THE CORRELATES OF RELIGION

Even as correlational psychologists labor to create more adequate ways of operationalizing religion, they are moving forward with their main task: identifying the psychological, social, and other correlates of religious behaviors, experiences, and attitudes. Initially, the finding of correlates may help to validate the measures of religion being used. Yoshio Fukuyama (1961), for example, found that his measures of four of Glock's dimensions showed meaningful patterns of relation to age, sex, education, socioeconomic status, and selected attitudes. Such correlations provide evidence that his scales are assessing what they are supposed to.

With the validity of their measures reasonably well established, researchers may then proceed to test a variety of hypotheses, some derived from theories about the causal origins of individual piety, others pertaining to its consequences. As we noted in the last chapter, experimental procedures are far superior for establishing causal relations, yet they are difficult to apply in the realm of religion. Thus correlational methods may be cautiously used in their place. Much correlational research, it may be said, has been undertaken without the support of a well-developed theoretical or conceptual framework. Some is carried out with no particular hypothesis or expectation in mind. Although psychological methodologists are frequently disdainful of such DUSTBOWL EMPIRICISM, it can provoke helpful new thinking and research.

The literature making up the correlational approach to religion is today enormous and still growing rapidly. Books taking stock of this literature as it existed around 1970 (Argyle and Beit-Hallahmi, 1975; Scobie, 1975; Strommen, 1971) were already filled with references to research on a large diversity of topics. More recent book-length overviews document what even insiders find to be a bewildering number and variety of research findings, a fair number of which contradict each other (Batson, Schoenrade, and Ventis, 1993; Grom, 1992; Hood, Spilka, Hunsberger, and Gorsuch, 1996; Paloutzian, 1996). Essays on the problems of measuring religion have become more common (Gorsuch, 1984, 1990; Haub, 1992; Williams, 1994) at the same time that literature reviews on specific topics, especially mental health or well-being, have multiplied (e.g., Bergin, 1983; L. B. Brown, 1994b; Corveleyn and Lietaer, 1994; Gartner, Larson, and Allen, 1991; Koenig, 1990, 1993; Payne, Bergin, Bielema, and Jenkins, 1991; Paloutzian and Kirkpatrick, 1995; Schmitz, 1992; Schumaker, 1992; Shafranske, 1996). Such reviews are sufficiently numerous, in fact, to have become themselves the subject of critical analysis (Larson, Sherrill, and Lyons, 1994).

RELIGION AND SOCIAL ATTITUDES

The complications facing correlational psychologists of religion are well illustrated in an area of research that early attracted the attention of social scientists: the relation of piety to social attitudes and behavior. For many, including William James, religion must finally be evaluated by such fruits. Yet according to this criterion, say some of its sharpest critics, religion has been mainly a disaster. Morris Cohen (1946), for instance, in scanning the history of the Christian, Jewish, and Islamic traditions, is struck primarily by the "fierce intolerance," the self-serving disregard for truth, the "pretended certainties" that prevent "needed change and cause tension and violent reaction." In making a "virtue of cruelty" and a "duty of hatred," religion has proved itself "effective for evil," not good. It is a fact, he says, "that there is not a single loathsome human practice that has not at some time or other been regarded as a religious duty" (pp. 351–352).

Philosopher Alfred North Whitehead (1926) is more explicit about some of religion's harmful effects.

History, down to the present day, is a melancholy record of the horrors which can attend religion: human sacrifice, and in particular the slaughter of children, cannibalism, sensual orgies, abject superstition, hatred as between races, the maintenance of degrading customs, hysteria, bigotry, can all be laid at its charge. Religion is the last refuge of human savagery. The uncritical association of religion with goodness is directly negatived by plain facts. Religion can be, and has been, the main instrument for progress. But if we survey the whole race, we must pronounce that generally it has not been so (pp. 37–38).

Religion's Dark Side Today

While it is tempting to assume that the "dark side of religion," as Cohen calls it, is mostly a thing of the past, today's newspapers regularly remind us of its continuing existence. In some cases the effects are dramatic and lethal: in 1978, the suicide of 913 followers of Jim Jones in the jungles of Guyana; in 1990, the death of more than 2000 people when Hindu fundamentalists in Ayodhya, a small town in India, tore down a sixteenth-century mosque that they believed was built on the birthsite of Lord Rama; in 1993, the death of six people and the injury of more than a thousand in the bombing of the World Trade Center in New York City by individuals associated with Islamic fundamentalism; in 1994, the mass suicide-murder of 53 members of the doomsday cult Order of the Solar Temple, located in Switzerland and Canada, and then 16 more, including three children, the following year; in 1995, the gassing of Tokyo subway stations by members of a Buddhist sect, resulting in the death of 11 people and the sickening of 5500 others; in 1997, the mass suicide by all 37 members of a group known as Heaven's Gate, in anticipation of being taken to a higher evolutionary level by a heavenly space craft thought to be following the Hale-Bopp comet; and again and again in the 1990s, the murderous suicide bombings in Israel by dozens of young Palestinians who believed that such acts of "martyrdom" would win for them—and their friends and relatives—unimaginable physical and spiritual bliss in heaven.

Less singularly dramatic expressions of the dark side of religion sometimes also make it into the newspapers, though many times not. There are the recurrent episodes of clergy malfeasance, for example, including a conservatively estimated 400 Roman Catholic priests and brothers charged with sexual abuse since 1982. Long reluctant to acknowlege the problem, the leadership of the Church now faces serious financial problems from the many millions of dollars awarded by the courts to the numerous victims. Yet clergy abuse of congregants is not limited to Roman Catholic circles: various studies have found that it is common in Protestant churches as well, including both conservative and liberal denominations (Shupe, 1995). Adding insult to injury in many cases is the refusal of the church hierarchies to deal appropriately with the abuse and the tendency of many congregants to blame and harass the victims when they make their charges known (Fortune, 1989). Victims of child sexual abuse within their own families often suffer the same callous treatment by church authorities (Imbens and Jonker, 1985).

Deeply troubling, too, are the stories of the resurgence of repressive fundamentalism in various parts of the world. In Afghanistan, for example, more than half the country is now dominated by the Taliban, an Islamic fundamentalist political and military force that, emerging from the chaos of civil war, is abruptly wrenching this country's millions of inhabitants back into a dark past. Women long accustomed to various freedoms are now being forced back into purdah, the Muslim tradition of secluding women in their homes. Allowed only to work in hospitals and clinics, and then only with members of their own sex, women must shroud themselves from head to toe whenever they go out. Girls, told that education is only for boys, have been expelled from schools and colleges. Television sets and stereo systems have been publicly "hanged"and books thought to be tainted by Western influence confiscated. The Koran is harshly interpreted and enforced through modern means: murderers and "enemies" of the Taliban are publicly hanged from cranes, and the hands and arms of convicted thieves are surgically amputated. Remarked one elderly Afghan scholar, "We are ruled now by men who offer us nothing but the Koran, even though many of them cannot read; who call themselves Muslims, and know nothing of the true greatness of our faith. There are no words for such people. We are in despair" (Burns, 1996, p. A8).

A dark side indeed—but might it not be the case, as the Muslim scholar seems to suggest, that what we see here are not genuine forms of religiousness, but aberrations and perversions of it? Or perhaps they reflect a radically different human impulse that insidiously masquerades as piety. Are not most religious people basically good and kind souls, even those who think of themselves as sinful? Might it not be that, when they misstep, it is in spite of their religiousness, not because of it?

An Elusive Search for Humanitarianism

More than a half century ago, social scientists began exploring the relationship of religiousness to a variety of moral and humanitarian concerns. What they uncovered was disturbing, especially to those who were religious themselves. Abraham Franzblau (1934), for example, found a negative relation between acceptance of religious beliefs and all three of his measures of honesty. Furthermore, religious belief bore no relation to his test of character. Among the nearly 2000 associates of the Young Men's Christian Association who responded to Murray Ross's (1950) questionnaire, the agnostics and atheists were more likely than the deeply religious to express willingness to help the needy and to support radical reform. Hirschi and Stark (1969) discovered that children who attended church regularly were no less likely to commit illegal acts, according to their own estimations, and Ronald Smith, Gregory Wheeler, and Edward Diener (1975), in a QUASI-EXPERIMENTAL situation, found that religious college students—including a group of Jesus people—were no less likely to cheat on a multiple-choice test and no more likely to volunteer to help mentally retarded children than atheists and other "nonreligious" persons. The religious subjects in Russell Middleton and Snell Putney's (1962) investigation even reported a *higher* frequency of cheating on examinations than did the skeptics.

In only two areas of moral concern do religious subjects consistently distinguish themselves: drugs and sex. However religiosity is measured, it has proved to be negatively related to the use of illicit drugs (Benson, 1992; Gorsuch, 1995). Similarly, high scorers on religiosity measures are significantly less likely than low ones to approve of or engage in any form of sexual behavior that has traditionally met with social disapproval. Responding to a variety of religiosity scales, unmarried college students have consistently shown themselves to be less permissive concerning premarital sex the more conservative they are religiously (Cardwell, 1969; Clayton, 1971b; Heltsley and Broderick, 1969; Sutker, Sutker, and Kilpatrick, 1970; Woodroof, 1985). Religiousness in married subjects is likewise associated with avoidance of traditionally disapproved practices, such as extramarital sex. Apparently, however, it is not correlated with any other measured dimensions, such as frequency of intercourse or consistency of attaining orgasm (Bell, 1974; Fisher, 1973; Martin and Westbrook, 1973).

Abstention from illicit drugs and disapproved sexual behavior is not paralleled by a corresponding attentiveness to traditional humanitarian ideals. Studies investigating the relation of measures of religiousness to scales labeled "humanitarianism" have consistently found either no relation (Ferguson, 1944b) or a slightly negative one (Defronzo, 1972; Kirkpatrick, 1949). Similarly, Victor Cline and James Richards (1965) report no correlation between their Compassionate Samaritan factor and acceptance of conventional religious teachings, and Bruce Hunsberger and Ellen Platonow (1986) found that higher scorers on a Christian orthodoxy scale were no more likely than lower scorers to volunteer to help charitable groups. Rokeach (1969) found his religious subjects to be preoccupied with personal salvation and relatively indifferent to social inequality and injustice.

The presumed connection between piety and "prosocial behavior" has been equally elusive in the laboratory. Lawrence Annis (1976) found that none of his four measures of religiousness predicted who among his subjects would investigate nearby sounds of a "lady in distress." Similarly, Ralph McKenna (1976) reports that when a "stranded female motorist" claimed to have misdialed in trying to contact her garage, clergymen (or whoever answered their telephones) were no more willing than control subjects to place the needed call.

On the other hand, a few studies do report findings more nearly consistent with religion's traditional image. Warner Wilson and Wallace Kawamura's (1967) student subjects showed a small, positive correlation between measures of religiousness and social responsibility. In L. D. Nelson and Russell Dynes's (1976) study, both devotionalism and church attendance showed low, positive correlations with self-reported helping behavior, both ordinary and emergency, in a city that had earlier been struck by a tornado. Robert Friedrichs (1960) similarly reports a low but positive relation of religiousness to a rating of altruism, but only when piety is measured by belief in God, not by church attendance. In all three studies, however, correlations are so small that religiousness accounts for less than 5 percent of the variability in humanitarian concern.

Upwards to 14 percent of humanitarianism's variance is accounted for by religiosity among the British and American students who participated in Wesley Perkins's (1992) study in 1978–79. But in comparable student samples ten years later, the proportion dropped to 9 and 1 percent, respectively. In the same study, egalitarianism proved to be virtually unrelated to religiosity, which was operationalized as affirming religion as a source of guidance and of answers to a variety of problems.

Religion and Prejudice

The apparent failure of religious involvement to foster a humanitarian outlook has received its closest assessment in research on conservative social attitudes. The overall pattern of findings here is much like the one we have just reviewed. Using a variety of measures of piety—religious affiliation, church attendance, doctrinal orthodoxy, rated importance of religion, and so on—researchers have consistently found positive correlations with ETHNOCENTRISM, AUTHORITARIANISM, dogmatism, social distance, rigidity, intolerance of ambiguity, and specific forms of prejudice, especially against Jews and blacks (Batson and Burris, 1994; Batson, Schoenrade, and Ventis, 1993; Dittes, 1969; Gorsuch, 1988; Gorsuch and Aleshire, 1974; Hunsberger, 1995).

This traditional cross burning by members of the Ku Klux Klan at a 1987 rally led by the group's national leader in Rumford Point, Maine, roused the anger of many local religious and civic leaders. The Klan is well known for its campaigns of hate against Jews, blacks, and Catholics.

There are very occasional exceptions. In an ethnically diverse group of introductory psychology students, Gerald Meredith (1968) found no significant correlation between two measures of religious attitude and a pair of ethnocentrism and dogmatism scales. Dean Hoge and Jackson Carroll (1975) found that, after they statistically removed the effects of other variables, all their religious measures together accounted for only 5 percent of the variance in their index of ANTI-SEMITISM. Similarly controlling for social–psychological factors, Middleton (1973) reduced the common variance between these dimensions to a mere 2 percent. The factor-analytic study of Christopher Bagley, Roger Boshier, and David Nias (1974) yielded two factors, a religious one and a "racialist-punitive" one, which were wholly independent of each other; identical results were found for diverse samples in England, the Netherlands, and New Zealand. In a sample of 652 students in six Southern colleges, Terry Prothro and John Jensen (1950) found a slight but significant correlation between positive attitudes toward the church and toward blacks and Jews.

A Curvilinear Relation: Some of these exceptional studies suggest that, among the subject groups studied thus far, the positive relation of religion and prejudice holds mainly for white Americans. Other studies show a pattern that continues to recur: the positive correlation becomes negative at the upper extreme of piety. Gregory Shinert and Charles Ford (1958), for example, compared a group of daily communicants (a majority of whom were seminarians and nuns) with a group of laypersons at the same Roman Catholic university who did not receive communion daily. The daily communicants proved, on the average, to have significantly *lower* ethnocentrism scores. Similarly, Glenn Wilson and Francis Lillie (1972; Wilson, 1973) found that two groups at the extremes of conventional religiosity—officer cadets of the Salvation Army and members of the Young Humanist Association—both showed exceptionally low levels of racial prejudice.

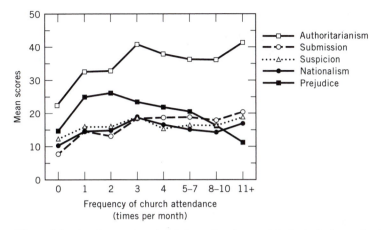

Figure 6.1. Church attendance in relation to four factors of Authoritarianism and to Prejudice. Source: From H. H. Remmers (Ed.), *Anti-Democratic Attitudes in American Schools.* Evanston, Ill.: Northwestern University Press, 1963, page 253.

The CURVILINEAR relation between piety and prejudice is well illustrated in a study by Elmer Struening (1963). Using as his subjects the instructional, administrative, and professional service staffs of a large Midwestern university, Struening sought to explore the relation of several variables to scales of authoritarianism and prejudice. The authoritarianism scale, taken largely from the F SCALE of Theodor Adorno and his associates (1950), was scored for a general factor (in Figure 6.1, Authoritarianism) as well as three specific ones: "authoritarian religious submission" (Submission), "cynical and suspicious view of human environment" (Suspicion), and "aggressive authoritarian nationalism" (NATIONALISM). The prejudice scale, which yielded a single score (Prejudice), contained items assessing both generalized prejudice and discriminatory attitudes toward specific groups. The relation of these five variables to frequency of church attendance is shown in Figure 6.1.

First, let us note the obvious curvilinear relation between church attendance and prejudice. As in other studies, those who report attending church once or twice a month have strikingly higher prejudice scores than those who do not attend at all. As the frequency of attendance rises beyond the twice-monthly point, the level of prejudice falls off, until—at an attendance rate of more than twice a week— it reaches a point slightly lower than the mean prejudice score of those who never attend.

The same general pattern is evident in other studies. Friedrichs (1959) found that New Jersey community residents who said they attended between 31 and 60 religious services in the year 1958 were the most prejudiced, and those reporting 61 or more services, the least prejudiced among his subjects, including those who claimed no attendance at all. The University of Texas subjects of Robert Young, William Benson, and Wayne Holtzman (1960) who attended church weekly were more tolerant of blacks than those reporting attendance once or twice a month, though they remained less tolerant than nonattenders. Hoge and Carroll (1973) found that members of eight Protestant churches showed the curvilinear pattern, though it was somewhat erratic, especially for members of the Southern churches. Dean Kilpatrick, Louis Sutker, and Patricia Sutker (1970) report the curvilinear trend in their Southern university data, but only for the female students.

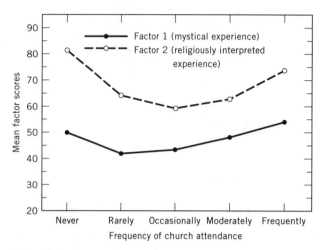

Figure 6.2. Relation of church attendance and mysticism factor scores. (The number of subjects was 34 for each category of attendance; analysis of variance was significant for each factor, $p < .01$.) Source: Based on Table 2 in Hood, 1976, page 1131.

Although the pattern has been found chiefly in studies of prejudice and church attendance, it has also appeared in research on religious belief and experience. In an experimental study of obedience to destructive commands modeled after Stanley Milgram's (1974) classic series of investigations, David Bock and Neil Warren (1972) found that subjects with moderate religious beliefs administered significantly higher levels of electric shock when the experimenter's confederate failed at his task than did the religiously extreme groups. Hood (1976) discovered that, among undergraduates who completed his Mysticism Scale, the more extreme the attendance frequency—high or low—the more likely the report both of mystical experience (Factor I on his scale) and of religiously interpreted experience (Factor II; see Figure 6.2).

Studies on well-being have reported the pattern as well. In a random sample of women who responded to a *Redbook* magazine questionnaire, Phillip Shaver, Michael Lenauer, and Susan Sadd (1980) found that reported physical and mental symptoms as well as overall unhappiness showed a striking curvilinear relation to self-reported degree of religiousness, with the slightly religious reporting the most symptoms and unhappiness; for both variables, the relation is significant at the .001 level (see Figure 6.3). Similarly striking is the curvilinear relation that Anette Dörr (1987, 1992) found between a religious experience scale (consisting of five items from Boos-Nünning's [1972] General Religiosity factor) and self-rated depressivity. Among her 162 subjects, a third of whom were patients being treated for depression, those falling in the middle group on the religious experience scale had the highest average level of depressivity. Those in the highest religiosity group were lowest on the depression scale.

Unfortunately, many studies do not scale the religiosity dimensions finely enough to allow the curvilinear pattern to appear. In addition, when significance tests have been applied to the data, they are usually not sensitive to curvilinearity. Even so, of the 25 studies they reviewed, Richard Gorsuch and Daniel Aleshire (1974) judge that the findings of 20 are consistent with this trend. Evidence is inconclusive on the question of which extreme has the lower prejudice scores.

Had Struening cut off the high extreme of his church-attendance scale at eight

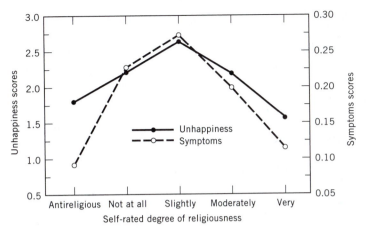

Figure 6.3. Relation of religiousness to unhappiness and symptoms scores. Source: Based on Table 1 and Figure 1 in Shaver, Lenauer, and Sadd, 1980, page 1567. Modifications made in consultation with the first author.

to ten times per month, we would probably conclude that authoritarianism also bears a curvilinear relation to piety. Such a conclusion would have been consistent with the finding of most other researchers that the various measures of conservative social attitudes tend to be highly intercorrelated (Allport and Ross, 1967; Maranell, 1967; O'Neil and Levinson, 1954; Rokeach, 1960; Weima, 1965). Prothro and Jenson (1950) see evidence in these correlations for a general tolerance factor, which Wilson (1973), seeking a more nearly neutral term, argues for calling conservatism. Yet Struening's results, and those of Frank Knöpfelmacher and Douglas Armstrong (1963), suggest that lumping these dimensions together may be premature. Knöpfelmacher and Armstrong discovered that the positive correlation between ethnocentrism and authoritarianism held for all their religious groups of adolescents *except* the Catholics. As in some other studies, the Catholic subjects, on the average, had higher authoritarian scores than any other group. Yet in their responses to the Bogardus Social Distance Scale, they were also significantly less ethnocentric than all other denominational groups. The Catholics in Stark's (1971) study showed a similar trend.

The Role of Acquiescence and Conformity: It is crucial to note that the items on the F Scale are so worded that agreement with them yields a high authoritarian score, and disagreement a low one (see Table 6.3). Such a scale is thereby open to the response set of ACQUIESCENCE, the tendency to answer "true" or "yes" whatever the item content. Indeed, Dean Peabody (1961) found that agreement with items on the F Scale can frequently be attributed to a general set to agree, whereas disagreement seems to be indicative of *anti*authoritarian attitudes. Thus scores on the F Scale might be expected to correlate with those on any other measure that entails a significant element of acquiescence—including, it would appear, most common scales of religiousness (Fisher, 1964) as well as other indicators of conservative attitudes. Struening's subjects who attended church two times a month or less often may have been individuals whose motives for conformity were strong enough to prompt occasional attendance yet insufficient to compel acquiescence to the church's teachings against discrimination. His other subjects may have had greater needs for conformity, leading to elevated F scores, frequent attendance, and relatively low prejudice scores. When the church itself tends to encourage

Table 6.3 SELECTED ITEMS FROM THE CALIFORNIA F SCALE AND THE ROKEACH DOGMATISM SCALE

California F Scale[a]	Rokeach Dogmatism Scale
1. Obedience and respect for authority are the most important virtues children should learn.	1. The United States and Russia have just about nothing in common.
2. Science has its place, but there are many important things that can never possibly be understood by the human mind.	2. Man on his own is a helpless and miserable creature.
3. Every person should have complete faith in some supernatural power whose decisions he obeys without question.	3. I'd like it if I could find someone who would tell me how to solve my personal problems.
4. Homosexuals are hardly better than criminals and ought to be severely punished.	4. It is only natural for a person to be rather fearful of the future.
5. The businessman and the manufacturer are much more important to society than the artist and the professor.	5. There is so much to be done and so little time to do it.
6. When a person has a problem or worry, it is best for him not to think about it, but to keep busy with more cheerful things.	6. Once I get wound up in a heated discussion I just can't stop.
7. Some day it will probably be shown that astrology can explain a lot of things.	7. If given the chance I would do something of great benefit to the world.
8. People can be divided into two distinct classes: the weak and the strong.	8. Of all the different philosophies which exist in this world there is probably only one which is correct.
9. Human nature being what it is, there will always be war and conflict.	9. A group which tolerates too much difference of opinion among its own members cannot exist for long.
10. Most people don't realize how much our lives are controlled by plots hatched in secret places.	10. Most people just don't know what's good for them.

[a] F Scale items are from Forms 40 and 45, containing 30 items, and Dogmatism Scale items are from Form E, containing 40 items. All items on both scales are scored in the positive direction.
Source: California F Scale items from Adorno et al., 1950, pages 255–256; Rokeach Dogmatism Scale items from Rokeach, 1960, pages 73–80.

prejudicial attitudes—a tendency that Glock and Stark (1966; Stark, et al., 1971) argue is inherent in Christian orthodoxy's claim to being the sole possessor of truth—all measures of conformity, including church attendance, would bear a linear relationship to prejudice.

Yet the conformity said to be one of the chief characteristics of the authoritarian personality—whose putative fondness for authority, distrust of other human beings, and inflexible patterns of thinking have long been familiar in the literature of the social sciences—is much more than the simple tendency to acquiesce. In fact, the conformity that is part of this personality syndrome appears to be separable from the acquiescent response set (Kirscht and Dillehay, 1967). Some prejudice is undoubtedly the result of unreflective and "innocent" acquiescence to the opinions of associates. In contrast, the prejudice of the authoritarian personality is thought to be highly motivated, a product of the suspiciousness, even hatred, of all persons who are not part of one's own group. Yet prejudice is not the only response to the feeling of threat and the underlying sense of life's precariousness; churchgoing is one as well (Dittes, 1973b).

A Balanced Authoritarianism Scale: One obvious way to reduce the effects of a response set would be to prepare a new scale with half the items reversed—that is, written in the "contrait" direction—so that on these items agreement would *lower* the total score rather than raise it. Thus a strong tendency to agree would yield moderate rather than extreme scores. Canadian psychologist Bob Altemeyer (1988) took precisely this precaution in painstakingly developing a new 30-item Right-Wing Authoritarianism (RWA) Scale. Doubtful that we really know what the California F Scale measures, or what the Dogmatism Scale (see Table 6.3) that Milton Rokeach (1956) developed as an ideology-free alternative is about, Altemeyer found that the RWA is more internally consistent and unidimensional than these scales. It is also better at predicting other attitudes and behavior.

During 20 years of highly original research with one or another version of the RWA and a variety of measures of religiosity, most of which he also developed, Altemeyer found a rather straightforward pattern of relationships.

> The findings are really rather simple. Authoritarians in my samples tend to be religious persons, and vice versa. High RWAs usually have tightly wound religious ideologies. They appear to be under appreciable pressure to believe truly, and they keep doubts to themselves, split off and tucked away.
>
> One finds other evidence of balkanizing. Vast, complicated religious material such as the Bible is "lined up" to support authoritarian submission, aggression, and conventionalism. Contradictory material exists alongside the selected interpretation but is disconnected. Or Highs may say they agree with Jesus' admonition not to judge and condemn others, but this "agreement" has no apparent effect on their behavior. Their belief system appears self-confirming, enduring, and closed. Really, the beliefs could be anything, and hostilities based on them appear highly resistant to change (pp. 230–231).

Altemeyer emphasizes that not all his religious subjects were high-scoring RWAs, nor was it impossible to find high-scoring atheists. Yet overall these trends were consistent and strong, with the highest intercorrelations appearing with the Christian Orthodoxy Scale—"particularly ironic," he notes, "for the Gospels largely portray Jesus of Nazareth as tolerant, forgiving, and preaching a message of universal love" (p. 201). The highest scorers on the RWA were the Fundamentalists and Mennonites whereas United Church members, Anglicans, and Jews scored lower, with Catholics and Lutherans falling in between. The lowest scorers of all were those with no religious affiliation.

The Authoritarian's Positive Side: Like most other researchers, Altemeyer considers authoritarianism a distinctly undesirable trait. Thus he notes with real concern the more or less steady increase in RWA scores among University of Manitoba students between 1973 and 1987. He has subsequently undertaken studies to see if prejudice among right-wing authoritarians can be reduced through personal-value confrontation (Altemeyer, 1994).

Experimental psychologist and former chaplain A. T. Welford (1971), in contrast, doubts that the authoritarian personality "deserves all the scorn that has been heaped upon it."

> The "authoritarian" has been regarded as an inflexible, unimaginative, intolerant, over-conforming, prejudiced disciplinarian. Yet, if one looks closely at the questionnaire statements used to define him, it seems fair to describe him also as a person who

is prepared to sacrifice some spontaneity for stability, some permissiveness for the sake of order and peace, some immediate pleasure for the pursuit of long-term aims, and some sentimental toleration for the sake of efficiency. He may, of course, go too far in these directions, and may not appear as a gay, interesting person with whom immediate easy friendship is possible. A substantial measure of his qualities is, however, essential for dealing responsibly with the world as it is, and even more for making ideals come true (p. 47).

Two investigations seem to underscore some positive qualities in the authoritarian or dogmatic personality. Employing a modified version of the F Scale as well as the Gough Adjective Check List, Mark Allen (1955) found that the "religious authoritarians" among his Mormon subjects described themselves as cooperative, idealistic, mannerly, praising, submissive, and forgetful; the nonauthoritarians tended to describe themselves as bitter, cold, cynical, egotistical, defensive, outspoken, prejudiced, self-centered, and stern. David Williams and Bruce Kremer (1974) also found that conservative attitudes need not always have negative correlates. To students enrolled in a secular counseling program, on the one hand, or in counseling programs in Roman Catholic or Protestant seminaries, on the other, Williams and Kremer administered three testing instruments: Rokeach's Dogmatism Scale, a measure of acceptance of traditional Christian doctrines, and a portion of a Test of Counselor Attitudes. Although the pastoral counseling students proved to have higher religiosity and dogmatism scores, as might have been predicted, they also showed more nondemanding acceptance of clients described to them than did the secular counselors.

A response set, here in the form of social desirability, may also have contributed to these results. Yet it is also true that what ostensible scales of authoritarianism and dogmatism actually measure is far from clear (Kirscht and Dillehay, 1967; McKinney, 1973). Without doubt these and related scales have yielded predictable results consistent with the theories proposed to explain the origins and dynamics of the personality characteristics in question. As is true of all other isms, however, there is a danger of reification and overgeneralization. No psychological assessment device should be taken at face value. The care with which Altemeyer has developed and critically examined his own authoritarianism scale, while continuing over the years to monitor changes in its psychometric characteristics, is exemplary in this regard.

The Role of Other Nonreligious Factors: Of special importance in interpreting scales measuring authoritarianism, intolerance, or conservatism are the factors of intelligence, education, socioeconomic status, and national region. Correlations (chiefly negative) between each of these variables and conservatism have appeared in disparate contexts and at various times. These factors also happen to be related to measures of religiousness. Thus, when statistical methods have been used to separate out their contribution to the relation between piety and prejudice, the result is frequently a much-reduced correlation. By taking into account education's negative correlation with prejudice, for example, Joe Feagin (1964) reduced religious orthodoxy's correlation with prejudice from .35 to .23 and thus their common variance from 12 to 5 percent. Bagley and Boshier (1975) found that the correlations of .20 between Roman Catholic affiliation and a measure of prejudice dropped to an insignificant .07 when they controlled for social class and affiliation-without-attendance. And Rob Eisinga, Ruben Konig, and Peer Scheepers (1995) found that, for their Dutch subjects, the introduction of such nonreligious variables as age, region, political allegiance, and social class substantially reduced the effects of orthodox religious beliefs on secular anti-Semitism.

The mediating role of intelligence may be more fundamental. Reinterpreting authoritarianism chiefly in cognitive rather than in motivational terms, Chris Brand (1981) maintains that authoritarians are best characterized not by their fondness for authority but by "some simple-minded way in which the world has been divided up for them" (p. 23)—most basically, according to species, race, gender, and age. The conflicting needs of these groups loom large in the lives of authoritarians, whose prejudices naturally favor their own positions and interests. Education, especially in the liberal arts, counteracts so crude a world-view, Brand observes. Thus he attributes the negative correlations between authoritarianism and intelligence test scores (which average around $-.50$) primarily to "crystallized intelligence," the enduring intellective capacity that is shaped by education and experience. The correlation between right-wing authoritarianism and education ($r = -.28$, $p < .01$) reported by Altemeyer and Hunsberger (1992) supports this interpretation.

Religiousness, especially religious orthodoxy, has also been found to be negatively correlated with intelligence and irreligiousness to be positively related with it. Thurstone (1934) found intelligence to be positively correlated with liberal or radical attitudes, including agnostic or atheistic religious views. The same trend is reported by Dean Hoge (1974), who found social and religious liberalism to be positively correlated with verbal scores on the Scholastic Aptitude Test (SAT). The religious skeptics among Poythress's (1975) subjects scored significantly higher than religious believers on both the verbal and the quantitative portions of the SAT, a trend likewise observed by Heist and Yonge (1968). Poythress's skeptics, it should be noted, scored significantly lower on authoritarianism.

Brand speculates that religiousness is related chiefly to "fluid intelligence," the capacity to solve new problems. He observes that piety is consistently linked to age: young children and the elderly, more than other age groups, tend to show high levels of religious belief and involvement (see Argyle and Beit-Hallahmi, 1975). Not coincidentally, says Brand, fluid intelligence shows a mirror-image pattern: it rises through childhood and declines from middle age onward. Thus he concludes that to be religious is to be unable or unwilling to think independently (p. 27). Although fluid and crystallized intelligence are positively correlated, Brand intimates that their relation to one another and to the various facets of authoritarianism and piety is too complex to allow simple generalizations regarding the association of religious and authoritarian trends. Only when the level of fluid intelligence forecloses a liberalizing education and thus sharply limits crystallized intelligence, says Brand, will authoritarianism and religiosity appear to merge.

Two Types of Piety: Intrinsic and Extrinsic

Thought provoking and worthy of testing though Brand's generalizations are, they overlook the fact that people are religious in different ways. It is these differences, some researchers argue, that provide the key to understanding the religion–prejudice connection. Over the last several decades, one distinction in particular has stood out. Theodor Adorno and his associates (1950) reported in their classic study of the authoritarian personality that the conventionally religious—those disposed "to view religion as a means instead of an end" (p. 733) and to attend church in order to be classed with normal or even privileged people—are the ones who show ethnocentric attitudes. In contrast, persons who "take religion seriously," for whom religion is "a system of more internalized, genuine experiences and values" (p. 310), are likely to oppose ethnocentrism.

Measuring the Two Types: Struck by these findings, Allport (1954) at first identified the contrasting religious outlooks as "institutionalized" and "interiorized." Later, Allport (1959) chose the terms *extrinsic* and *intrinsic*, which, in spite of conceptual and psychometric difficulties, have won widespread acceptance. The extrinsic orientation is characteristic of those who

> are disposed to use religion for their own ends. The term is borrowed from axiology, to designate an interest that is held because it serves other, more ultimate interests. Extrinsic values are always instrumental and utilitarian. Persons with this orientation may find religion useful in a variety of ways—to provide security and solace, sociability and distraction, status and self-justification. The embraced creed is lightly held or else selectively shaped to fit more primary needs. In theological terms the extrinsic type turns to God, but without turning away from self.

The intrinsic orientation characterizes those who

> find their master motive in religion. Other needs, strong as they may be, are regarded as of less ultimate significance, and they are, so far as possible, brought into harmony with the religious beliefs and prescriptions. Having embraced a creed the individual endeavors to internalize it and follow it fully. It is in this sense that he *lives* his religion (Allport and Ross, 1967, p. 434).

Allport and his students set about to develop measures of these two orientations. After an initial effort by Cody Wilson (1960), who sought to assess only the extrinsic trend, a new, 21-item scale that included both (see Table 6.4) was prepared. By factor-analyzing the responses to it of a group of Southern Baptists, Feagin (1964) discovered that the two types of items formed separate, virtually unrelated scales. This result disconfirmed Allport's assumption that the two orientations lie at opposite ends of the single dimension. On the basis of the factor loadings, Feagin formed a 12-item Intrinsic/Extrinsic Scale, with six items measuring each orientation. Allport and Michael Ross (1967), apparently considering the longer scale more adequate, used all but one of the original 21 items in their later study. Their 20-item Religious Orientation Scale, which Hood (1971) found to correlate relatively highly (.78) with Feagin's shorter form, is the one most widely employed today.

The Two Types and Social Attitudes: Among his Southern Fundamentalists, Feagin discovered that only the Extrinsic scale correlated consistently with an antiblack scale. For one group alone—the college students—did the pattern reverse itself, with the Intrinsic scale showing the significant relationship. In every case, however, the correlation was in the predicted direction. An extrinsic orientation tended to go along with prejudice, and an intrinsic one with rejection of it. Allport and Ross found much the same pattern in their denominationally more diverse sample. In most instances, those scoring high on the Extrinsic scale were more prejudiced on all five measures than high scorers on the Intrinsic scale. The most prejudiced of all, however, were the "indiscriminately proreligious," who agreed with both intrinsic and extrinsic items. Allport and Ross suggest that this response pattern reflects an undifferentiated cognitive style with roots deep in the personality structure. Such a style would also account for the stereotypy of prejudice.

For the record, it should be observed that in two of Allport and Ross's samples—the 53 Pennsylvania Presbyterians and the 35 Tennessee Methodists—the intrinsic types were *more* antiblack than the extrinsic types. Among the Roman Catholic, Lutheran, and Nazarene subjects, the indiscriminately proreligious appeared to be

Table 6.4 **THE ALLPORT–ROSS RELIGIOUS ORIENTATION SCALE**[a]

Intrinsic Items	Extrinsic Items
2. I try hard to carry my religion over into all my other dealings in life.* (.57/−.03)	1. What religion offers me most is comfort when sorrows and misfortune strike.* (.00/−.72)
7. Quite often I have been keenly aware of the presence of God or the Divine Being. (.36/.17)	3. Religion helps to keep my life balanced and steady in exactly the same way as my citizenship, friendships, and other memberships do.* (−.04/−.64) (Omitted from the Allport and Ross scale)
8. My religious beliefs are what really lie behind my whole approach to life.* (.59/.00)	
9. The prayers I say when I am alone carry as much meaning and personal emotion as those said by me during services.* (.56/−.08)	4. One reason for my being a church member is that such membership helps to establish a person in the community.* (.03/−.49)
13. If not prevented by unavoidable circumstances, I attend Church (a) more than once a week, (b) about once a week, (c) two or three times a month, (d) less than once a month.* (.61/−.03)	5. The purpose of prayer is to secure a happy and peaceful life.* (.03/−.72)
	6. It doesn't matter so much what I believe so long as I lead a moral life. (.10/−.05)
14. If I were to join a church group I would prefer to join (1) a Bible Study group or (2) a social fellowship. (.36/−.08)	10. Although I am a religious person I refuse to let religious considerations influence my everyday affairs. (.21/−.31)
16. Religion is especially important to me because it answers many questions about the meaning of life. (.40/.11)	11. The Church is most important as a place to formulate good social relationships.* (−.21/−.51)
18. I read literature about my faith (or church) (a) frequently, (b) occasionally, (c) rarely, (d) never.* (.68/−.02)	12. Although I believe in my religion, I feel there are many more important things in life. (.03/−.16)
20. It is important to me to spend periods of time in private religious thought and meditation.* (.60/.03)	15. I pray chiefly because I have been taught to pray. (−.14/−.26)
	17. A primary reason for my interest in religion is that my church is a congenial social activity. (.01/−.05)
	19. Occasionally I find it necessary to compromise my religious beliefs in order to protect my social and economic well-being. (.32/.10)
	21. The primary purpose of prayer is to gain relief and protection.* (.10/−.63)

[a] These items, revised by the members of a Harvard University seminar in 1963, are worded according to Allport and Ross (1967), who provided four alternative responses to each statement (see items 13 and 18 for examples). The numbering here follows Feagin (1964). Each item is followed by its loading on Feagin's two factors (intrinsic and extrinsic, respectively). An asterisk indicates that Feagin assigned the item to his corresponding six-item subscale. (See also Hunt and King, 1971.)
Source: Adapted from Table 1 in Feagin, 1964.

slightly *less* prejudiced than the extrinsic type. Unfortunately, it is not unusual for statistical trends inexplicably to reverse themselves. Yet, given the complexity of causation in the social–psychological realm and the relative crudeness of the measures, it is hardly surprising that findings are not always consistent. Buried in every sample, after all, are the anonymous individuals who deviate from the trends that the group shows as a whole. Recurrent patterns are the most the correlationists can hope for, and these abound in research employing the Allport–Ross and Feagin scales.

Because the Intrinsic and Extrinsic scales have proved with most samples to be only slightly (and negatively) correlated with each other (Donahue, 1985), generalizations about the correlates of one scale do not predictably apply in reverse to the other. The Extrinsic scale, but not the Intrinsic, has shown persistent correlation with the conservative attitudes we have been discussing, including prejudice (Amón, 1969; Brannon, 1970; Hoge and Carroll, 1973; Matlock, 1973; Morris, Hood, and Watson, 1989; Ponton and Gorsuch, 1988; and studies cited earlier) dogmatism (Hoge and Carroll, 1973; Kahoe and Dunn, 1975; Strickland and Weddell, 1972; Thompson, 1974); authoritarianism (Kahoe, 1974, 1975); and ethnocentrism (Dicker, 1977).

The Intrinsic scale does occasionally correlate negatively with such social attitudes, as we have already seen, and it has also been found to be positively related to volunteering to help others (Bernt, 1989; Benson, et al., 1980; Hunsberger and Platonow, 1986). Yet in some other studies it has proved to be *positively* related to conservative or prejudicial attitudes. For the Roman Catholics, Protestants, and Jews whom A. Lange (1971) studied in Amsterdam, intrinsic religiosity consistently was correlated positively with authoritarianism, rigidity, and dogmatism (with coefficients ranging from .30 to .46). Similarly, in a group of predominantly Baptist college students, Kahoe (1975) discovered significant positive correlations between the Intrinsic scale and 11 of the 30 items composing the F Scale. Whereas the more numerous F Scale items correlating with the Extrinsic scale were scattered throughout the nine item cateogories of Adorno and his associates (1950), those related to the Intrinsic scale—including foremost items 2 and 3 in Table 6.3—are limited largely to four of these clusters, Conventionalism, Superstition and Stereotypy, Authoritarian Aggression, and, above all, Authoritarian Submission. Correlation with the last two qualities is confirmed by Bock's (1973) discovery that it was the intrinsic subjects, not the extrinsic, who tended to obey the commands of a scientific authority to administer an electric shock to an experimental confederate. And Altemeyer (1988, pp. 210, 218) reports that his Right-Wing Authoritarianism Scale correlated positively with all but one of the 11 Intrinsic scale items, yielding an overall correlation of .36 for students and .41 for their parents. The relation with the items of the Extrinsic scale was much less consistent, with corresponding correlations of $-.10$ and $-.09$.

As Glenn Griffin, Richard Gorsuch, and Andrea Davis (1987) remark on their finding that, among Seventh-Day Adventists on St. Croix, intrinsic religiosity was positively correlated with prejudice against Rastafarians, the relation between religious orientation and social attitudes is mediated by the particular religious norms in terms of which the person is oriented. If a tradition itself tends to foster prejudice against another group, as seemed to be the case on St. Croix, then intrinsically oriented persons within the tradition will likely share this prejudice. An intrinsic orientation in itself is thus no guarantee of positive social attitudes.

Because the Allport–Ross Intrinsic scale tends to correlate positively with orthodox Christian views (e.g., Johnson, George, and Saine, 1993), high scorers tend to share the social attitudes and values traditionally associated with conservative Christian groups. Thus, in comparison to low scorers, those high on the Intrinsic scale are likely to be less sexually permissive (Haerich, 1992; Reed and Meyers, 1991, Wann, 1993; Woodroof, 1985); to prefer nonrevealing clothing (Edmonds and Cahoon, 1993); to express nonfeminist attitudes (McClain, 1979), including, among women respondents, opposition to egalitarianism (Kahoe, 1974b) and an emphasis on family over career (Jones and McNamara, 1991); and to be prejudiced against gay men and lesbians (Herek, 1987). Similarly reflecting traditional Christian values, high Intrinsic scorers tend to score higher on measures of responsibility (Kahoe, 1974a), altruism (Chau, et al., 1990), empathy (Watson, Hood, Morris, and Hall, 1984), and social interest (in the Adlerian sense of feeling connected to others; Leak, 1992). High scorers have also shown a tendency to score higher on Glock's religious practice, feeling, and knowledge dimensions (Dodrill, Bean, and Bostrom, 1973), to report more religious or mystical experiences (Hood, 1970, 1973; Weima, 1986), and, in relation to Lawrence Kohlberg's (1981) levels of moral development, to show "principled" rather than "conventional" moral thinking when the individual's denomination itself operates at the higher level (Ernsberger and Manaster, 1981).[1]

The Indiscriminate Types: A few studies have sought to take into account the numerous subjects who agree with both intrinsic and extrinsic items, the "indiscriminately proreligious," as well as the indeterminate number who disagree across the board, the "indiscriminately antireligious" or "nonreligious" (Allport and Ross, 1967). Andrew Thompson (1974) found that the adolescents in Roman Catholic religious education classes who were *by comparison* indiscriminately antireligious had the lowest dogmatism scores of the four groups, although their scores were not significantly lower than those of the next lowest, the intrinsic category. (If we were certain that the acquiescent response set played a role in these data—and it well may have—this is precisely the ordering we would expect.) The adolescents' parents, on the other hand, gave responses that are consistent with Allport's predictions: the indiscriminately proreligious are the most dogmatic, the extrinsic and indiscriminately antireligious follow, and the intrinsic are the least dogmatic. Sanderson's (1974) study of student subjects yielded results similar to Thompson's. Right-wing political views—including superpatriotism, opposition to civil liberties, ethnic bigotry, and cultural intolerance—were most conspicuous among indiscriminately proreligious subjects, followed by the extrinsic subjects, the intrinsics, and the indiscriminately antireligious. Although intrinsically oriented subjects were third in rank, the Intrinsic scale nevertheless showed a low positive correlation with right-wing attitudes.

In Eugene Tate and Gerald Miller's (1971) study of United Methodist group members, the value Equality—found by Rokeach (1973) to be the one most closely related to racial tolerance of the 36 in his Value Survey—was ranked third in personal importance by the intrinsic group, fifth by the extrinsic, and ninth by the indiscriminately proreligious (Allport's order once again). The indiscriminately antireligious, unrepresented in Allport's data, ranked Equality sixth. The character of the "antireligious" is more clearly expressed in their having given the values Freedom, Mature Love, Self-Respect, Independent, and Intellectual noticeably

---

[1] This relation did not appear with the Unitarian-Universalists, for some of whom the theistic assumptions of the Religious Orientation Scale were undoubtedly problematical. Otherwise, Ernsberger and Manaster's findings cast doubt on Kohlberg's (1981, p. 303) claim that religious association plays no significant role in moral development. Kohlberg's scheme itself is challenged by Evangelical scholar Donald Joy (1983) for its strictly empirical character. Psychologist Carol Gilligan (1982) points out its exclusive emphasis on male development and the impersonal, masculine logic of fairness, which brings with it a corresponding neglect of the logic of relationship that is typical of women. The masculine disposition of the Evangelical Christian tradition is reflected in Joy's agreement with Kohlberg in elevating justice over care.

higher rankings than all the religious groups, and a strikingly lower ranking to Salvation, A World at Peace, Courageous, and Cheerful.

Problems with the Scales and the Typology: Although it is not difficult to find statistically significant relations between the Intrinsic–Extrinsic scales and a variety of other measures, some researchers challenge the import of such findings. Hoge and Carroll (1973) reduced to insignificance the correlation between Feagin's Extrinsic scale and two of three prejudice measures by controlling for social status and dogmatism. Feagin's subscale, they conclude, "lacks a clear definition of what is being measured; we know only that it is not tapping extrinsic religious motivation" (p. 189). The Intrinsic scale has been found in some studies to be positively related to measures of social desirability. Daniel Batson, Stephen Naifeh, and Suzanne Pate (1978) interpret this trend as evidence that correlations between this scale and positive social attitudes may be largely a product of wanting to look good. The findings of Gary Leak and Stanley Fish (1989) suggest that the Intrinsic scale's relation to desirable responding may be attributed to both conscious impression management and unconscious self-deception.

Content analysis of Allport's definitions and his items reveals that both are conceptually more complex than the simple intrinsic–extrinsic distinction would suggest (Hunt and King, 1971). Statistical analyses have led to the same conclusion. Factor analyses of the original Allport–Ross scales and of Spanish, German, and Norwegian versions have yielded as few as two factors and as many as six (Amón and Yela, 1968; Gorsuch and McPherson, 1989; Kaldestad, 1991; Kirkpatrick, 1989; Reed and Meyers, 1991; Zwingmann, et al., 1994). The most common solution consists of three factors, an intrinsic one and two extrinsic ones, which Lee Kirkpatrick (1989) labels Social-Extrinsic and Personal-Extrinsic. Factor analyzed with other questionnaire items, however, the IE scales have proved to be less cohesive. When King and Hunt (1972b) tried to include the intrinsic–extrinsic dimension in their questionnaire, the Extrinsic scale lost some of its items and the Intrinsic scale disappeared altogether, its statements scattered among several other factors. Altemeyer (1988, p. 210), on the other hand, found the Intrinsic scale to be distinctly more coherent and reliable than the Extrinsic scale.

Given that (1) the evidence is overwhelmingly against the notion of a single intrinsic–extrinsic dimension; (2) the two dimensions themselves are complex and inadequately defined in operational terms; and (3) what is being pursued may in reality be on the level of general personality variables that are not religion-specific, Hunt and King (1971) urge the abandonment of the general labels in favor of distinctions and measures of greater specificity. Kirkpatrick and Hood (1990) likewise recommend leaving the simplistic IE framework behind in favor of more sophisticated approaches. Affirming Hunt and King's criticisms, they cite evidence that the Intrinsic scale is little more than a religious commitment scale. The Extrinsic scale, on the other hand, may not be a measure of religion at all, but a reflection of more general cognitive or personality characteristics. Furthermore, because these scales can be used meaningfully only with religious subjects, correlations with other variables are inevitably restricted. As Kirkpatrick and Hood point out, other measures of religion are better predictors, as in the case of Fundamentalism's higher correlation with prejudice than either I or E (McFarland, 1989). Among the other theoretical and methodological problems that Kirkpatrick and Hood note is the implicit, value-ladened distinction between good (intrinsic) and bad (extrinsic) religion. Dittes (1971) earlier addressed the same issue when he observed that the intrinsic–extrinsic typology has served its users' prophetlike concern for the purity of religion far better than the scientist's quest for understanding. In spite of such criticisms, however, the typology and the Allport–Ross scales remain highly popular among contemporary researchers.

The Search for Alternatives

The search for more adequate alternatives also continues. One noteworthy proposal is offered by Bernard Spilka and his associates. In place of the intrinsic–extrinsic distinction, Russell Allen and Spilka (1967) posited two different cognitive orientations, a *committed* one said to be characterized by an abstract, complex, open, and yet coherent and serviceable way of thinking, and a contrasting *consensual* one, which tends to be literal-minded, dualistic, vague, closed, and removed from everyday activities. Subjects who, on the basis of interviews, were classified as *committed* in orientation proved to attend church more frequently and to consider themselves more religious than the *consensual* in orientation. They were also less likely to be prejudiced and more likely to be "worldminded." In their selected sample of relatively religious Protestant students, Allen and Spilka found that church attendance itself bore no significant relation to level of prejudice, nor did Wilson's (1960) extrinsic scale appear related to the committed-consensual distinction. A factor analysis of the Religious Viewpoints Scale issuing out of Allen and Spilka's research largely confirmed its two-factor structure. It was also demonstrated that persons scoring high on Rokeach's Dogmatism Scale were more likely to be consensual in orientation than committed (Raschke, 1973).

Yet because the Religious Viewpoints Scale—a factor-analytic distillation of 38 different measures—incorporates a substantial part of the Allport–Ross Religious Orientation Scale, it is doubtful that it measures something distinctive. The committed and intrinsic subscales have seven items in common, and correlations between them range from .62 to .88. Such an overlap is sufficient to consider them as measures of the same dimension. Similarly, the Consensual and Extrinsic subscales, although they share but one item, correlate around .50 (Minton and Spilka, 1976; Spilka et al., 1977). Thus in their effort to operationalize the two cognitive orientations, these researchers have inadvertently returned to Allport's original distinction, though with labels that may be more accurately descriptive. Had they succeeded in measuring the two points of view, which correspond to the contrasting dualistic and contextual–relativistic frameworks that emerged in William Perry's (1970) study of intellectual development in college students, they would have enriched the literature with a valuable research instrument.

Religion as Quest: Daniel Batson and his associates offer a more distinctive alternative. For his Good Samaritan experiment, recounted in Chapter 5, and in his continuing research on the attitudinal and behavioral correlates of religiosity, Batson fashioned his own questionnaire, the Religious Life Inventory. Two of its three scales were written to augment the Allport–Ross Religious Orientation Scale: the External scale as a measure of the extrinsic, means orientation[2] and the Internal

---

[2] Batson's External scale measures something other than extrinsic orientation. Five of its six items assess the degree to which personal or organizational influences have shaped the respondent's religious outlook rather than the degree of its present utilitarian character. Contrary to Batson's initial assumption that these two variables would be related, the External scale proved to be rather highly correlated with the Intrinsic, Internal, and Orthodoxy scales but not with the Extrinsic scale (Batson, Schoenrade, and Ventis, 1993, p. 172).

scale as a measure of the intrinsic, end orientation. The third, the Quest scale[3]—and the crucial one from Batson's standpoint—was designed to measure the quest orientation, "the degree to which an individual's religion involves an open-ended, responsive dialogue with existential questions raised by the contradictions and tragedies of life" (Batson, Schoenrade, and Ventis, 1993, p. 169). When Batson factor-analyzed the Religious Life Inventory in combination with the Allport–Ross scales and a doctrinal orthodoxy scale patterned after Glock and Stark's (1966), he found three factors: Religion as Means, Religion as End, and Religion as Quest.

Batson, who completed doctoral studies in both theology and psychology, had argued in an earlier, theological work (Batson, Beker, and Clark, 1973) that an experience may be identified as religious, not on the basis of its referent or intentional object (e.g., the divine), as the phenomenologists represented in Chapter 12 maintain, but to the degree it is generated by conflicts that "challenge one's reality at its core, e.g., 'What is the meaning of life, given death?'" (p. 192). Christian experience in particular is said to entail a radical perceptual shift, a fundamental reorientation outward, away from self and toward the needs of others. Furthermore, Christians are called upon to manifest this changed outlook by committing themselves to responsible action, in spite of acknowledged limitations in their view of reality, and by showing a corresponding nondoctrinaire openness to further change in accord with later experience. "The Christian hope," Batson writes, "is not in a given concept or event [e.g., Jesus' incarnation or resurrection] but in a direction, an opening movement outward in loving concern for one's neighbor" (p. 59). Hence Batson's interest in the parable of the Good Samaritan and his valorization of the reflectively critical quest orientation over the other two.

As we saw in the last chapter, Batson concludes from his Good Samaritan data that persons for whom religion is a quest are sensitive to the wishes of persons in need, whereas intrinsically religious persons seemingly act out of an insistent internal need to be helpful, pressing themselves on others even when their aid is not wanted. Similarly, when Batson, Naifeh, and Pate (1978) supplemented the anti-black scale used by Allport and Ross with a more subtle, behavioral measure of prejudice—choosing a black or white interviewer—in an effort to minimize the effects of social desirability, they found that only the Quest factor and scale were consistent in correlating negatively with both measures of prejudice. Although the End factor and Intrinsic scale were also negatively related to the questionnaire measure of prejudice, they proved to be positively (though insignificantly) related to the behavioral measure. Thus on the more subtle indicator of prejudice, the Means and End factors were indistinguishable, whereas the Quest factor correlated significantly more negatively with prejudice than either of the other two orientations. A generalized replication using a different behavioral measure of prejudice produced much the same pattern of results (Batson, Flink, Schoenrade, Fultz, and Pych, 1986).

Seeking more direct validation of their scales, Batson and Lynn Raynor-Prince (1983) found that only the Quest factor showed a significant, positive relation to cognitive complexity in the religious domain, as measured by a paragraph completion test employing sentence stems suggesting existential conflict, for example, "When I consider my own death. . . ." Both the End factor and the related Intrinsic scale showed negative—albeit, again, statistically insignificant—correlations.

---

[3] The Quest scale was originally called the Interactional scale, but for ease of communication, other researchers—and now Batson himself—use the shorter, more meaningful label.

Batson argues that his quest concept reintroduces three aspects of Allport's concept of mature religion that are overlooked by the notion of intrinsic religiosity: complexity, doubt, and tentativeness. He incorporated this way of being religious, he writes, "to tap what I considered a more mature, flexible type of religiosity than the other two" (Batson, 1976, p. 207).[4] Batson has found support for this early conviction in the research that he and his associates have subsequently carried out. The generally well-regarded intrinsic orientation, conclude Batson, Schoenrade, and Ventis (1993), is marked by a freedom from worry and guilt that is bought at the high price of uncritical bondage to one's religious beliefs; by thinking that tends to be simplistic and rigid; and by a self-centered desire to *appear* tolerant, sensitive, and loving. In contrast, the skeptical quest orientation appears to be associated with freedom from the bondage of doctrine but not from existential concerns; with flexible open-mindedness, competent self-reliance, and self-actualization; and, at the crucial level of social consequences, with tolerance of others and sensitivity to their needs. If one were to judge which of these orientations constitutes "true religion," Batson and his associates intimate, it would be quest, not the intrinsic orientation (pp. 375, 198, 288, 364, 189).

Assessing the Quest Orientation: Batson's critics, who are often advocates of the intrinsic orientation, have challenged his work on both methodological and conceptual grounds. They have noted with concern, for example, the low internal consistency of the original, six-item Quest scale. This problem has now been addressed by the development of a more reliable, twelve-item scale, which incorporates five of the original items (see Table 6.5). With an internal-consistency reliability hovering around .80 and a correlation with the original scale of about .86, the new scale appears to be measuring the same thing but much more reliably (Batson and Schoenrade, 1991a, 1991b).

Factor analysis confirms what is apparent from the item content: the Quest scale is not unitary, but consists of two or more factors, including doubt. In one series of analyses, the Doubt factor proved to be negatively correlated with the Intrinsic scale and positively correlated with the Extrinsic scale. It also showed a very slight tendency to be associated with maladjustment (Watson, Morris, and Hood, 1989). Spilka and his associates have found the Quest scale to be related negatively to a standard measure of social desirability and positively related to measures of trait anxiety and religious questioning (designated "religious conflict") (Spilka, Kojetin, and McIntosh, 1985; Kojetin, McIntosh, Bridges, and Spilka, 1987). They infer that high scores on quest reflect personal distress, a conclusion that accords with Mariano Moraleda's (1977) finding that, among Spanish adolescents, religious ambivalence and doubt are associated with higher levels of anxiety.

Doubt is one of the facets of Allport's conceptualization of mature religion that Batson and his colleagues say have been neglected by the Intrinsic scale. Yet as Michael Donahue (1985) notes, Allport ascribes to doubt an interim role in the maturation of the religious sentiment, a factor that gradually fades as increasing commitment and its fruits strengthen the individual's faith. The instability of the

---

[4] Batson and Ventis (1985, p. 400) more recently deny that they represent the quest outlook as more mature. To others, however, their valorization of quest is unmistakable. Derks and Lans (1986) wonder whether "Batson's *psychological* theory of religious attitudes [isn't] essentially a *theological* theory of true Christianity" (p. 204). They identify Batson's theory with social gospel theology, which we know from Chapter 2 was a major factor in the rise of the psychology of religion at the beginning of the twentieth century.

Table 6.5 BATSON'S TWELVE-ITEM QUEST SCALE, ARRANGED ACCORDING TO THE SCALE'S INTENDED THREE FACETS

Complexity

1. I was not very interested in religion until I began to ask questions about the meaning and purpose of my life.
2. *I have been driven to ask religious questions out of a growing awareness of the tensions in my world and in my relation to my world.
3. My life experiences have led me to rethink my religious convictions.
4. *God wasn't very important for me until I began to ask questions about the meaning of my own life.

Doubt

5. *It might be said that I value my religious doubts and uncertainties.
6. For me, doubting is an important part of what it means to be religious.
7. I find religious doubts upsetting. (rating reversed in scoring)
8. *Questions are far more central to my religious experience than are answers.

Tentativeness

9. As I grow and change, I expect my religion also to grow and change.
10. I am constantly questioning my religious beliefs.
11. *I do not expect my religious convictions to change in the next few years. (rating reversed in scoring)
12. There are many religious issues on which my views are still changing.

*Items taken from the six-item Quest scale
Source: Adapted from Table 1 in Batson and Schoenrade, 1991b.

attitude of doubt is underscored in a classic study by Robert Thouless (1935). When Thouless asked subjects to indicate the degree of certainty with which they believed or disbelieved 40 statements on religious and other subjects, he found a marked tendency either to hold or to reject the belief in question with a considerable degree of conviction. This "tendency to certainty" was significantly greater for religious propositions than for nonreligious ones. Doubt or uncertainty, Thouless concludes, is an uncommon or at least a short-lived state for most people. Rarer still, he notes, is the capacity to adopt and sustain the laudable attitudes of tentativeness or of partial assent, which Batson's scale purports to measure but in fact may not.

Hood and Morris (1985) propose that the quest and intrinsic orientations be understood as stages of religious faith. The quest perspective, they say, is characteristic of persons still "in process" whereas the intrinsic orientation describes persons who have found satisfying answers to the existential questions. Consistent with this interpretation, the Quest scores of a group of 205 Presbyterians ranging in age from 11 to 83 tended to decline with age ($r = -.19$, $p < .01$), whereas scores on the Intrinsic scale generally increased ($r = .29$, $p < .001$) (Watson, Howard, Hood, and Morris, 1988). The men in Marvin Acklin's (1985) study showed a similar decline in Quest scores over the years (age and quest correlated $-.30$, $p < .01$; see Figure 6.4). Furthermore, their Quest scores proved to be negatively correlated ($r = -.31$, $p < .01$) with a short version of the Washington University Sentence Completion Test of Ego Development, a measure of emotional and cognitive maturity. The comparable correlations for the women were slightly positive but insignificant. Acklin concludes that Batson's Quest factor measures a "precommitment or transitional religious outlook"; contrary to what Batson had

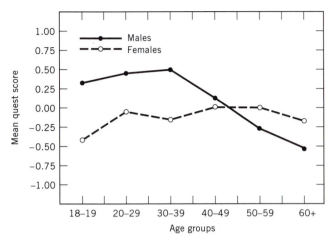

Figure 6.4. Quest factor scores by age group (*N* = 20 for each of the six groups.)

suggested, it "does not appear to be a measure of religious maturity at all" (pp. 53, 60).

There are even doubts that the quest orientation, at least as it is represented by Batson's Quest scale, is properly called religious. As Donahue (1985) points out, the Quest scale tends not to correlate with other measures of religiousness. This is not surprising when such measures are limtied to literal belief and other conventional expressions of faith, as has often been the case. But it is odd that Batson's scale showed no distinctive relation to Hutsebaut's (1996a) historical relativism factor, which is partially defined in terms of quest. And whereas Altemeyer and Hunsberger's (1992) Quest scale shows a high negative correlation (− .79) with their Religious Fundamentalism scale, the Batson Quest scale as augmented by McFarland (1989) yielded a far more modest one (− .36).

Although certainly instances of the quest attitude can be found in the world's religious traditions, by itself it is not likely to foster deep religious experience. We may recall that, of the seven worship services that Goodwin Watson (1929) presented for evaluation by his young subjects, the one that focused on the quest for meaning in a vast universe received the lowest ratings. Without some sense of an objective reality, James Pratt (1920) would say, a worshiper is not likely to experience subjective effects. Nor is the quest orientation likely to inspire the saintly virtues by which James (1902) found religion to be vindicated, as Batson and Raynor-Prince (1983) themselves appear to acknowledge. For Thouless, the attitude of tentativeness is not a religious orientation but an intellectual one, the attainment of which he sees as one of the goals of a liberal education.

Whatever the Quest scale measures, other investigators are likewise combining it with the IE scales to study social attitudes. Their findings are often similar to what Batson and his associates report. In one study, for example, the Quest scale was the only one of the three to be significantly and positively related to level of moral judgment (Sapp and Jones, 1986). In another investigation, which compared rankings on the Rokeach Value Survey with Batson's three ways of being religious, the quest orientation correlated more highly with the ranking of Equality—the value most revealing of racial tolerance and such liberal attitudes as approval of church involvement in social and political issues—than with any of the 17 other terminal values. Neither the means (extrinsic) nor the ends (intrinsic) orientation showed any relation to the ranking of Equality (Luce, Briggs, and Francis, 1987). Of the seven other values to which the quest orientation showed a significant relation, four are reported by Rokeach (1973, p. 101) to be either positively or negatively related to racist attitudes. For all four, the correlation with the quest orientation is in the direction of antiracism. In contrast, two of these four values—Salvation and Family Security—correlate in the racist direction with the intrinsic orientation. Once again, then, a less transparent indicator of tolerance and concern for others proved to be positively related to quest but either unrelated or negatively related to end or intrinsic religiosity.

In a study by Sam McFarland (1989), an augmented Quest scale proved to be a uniquely consistent predictor of nondiscrimination among university undergraduates. McFarland correlated his general measure of discrimination and its four components—against blacks, women, communists, and gay and lesbian persons—with the Extrinsic, Intrinsic, and Quest scales as well as a Fundamentalism scale and the extrinsic subscales identified by Kirkpatrick (1989). He found that for males the extrinsic measures tended to be positively related to discrimination of various kinds and the Intrinsic scale to be unrelated. For females the Intrinsic scale was *positively* related to all forms of discrimination except toward blacks, whereas the extrinsic subscales tended to be *negatively* related. When these correlations were recalculated after removing the specific contribution of Fundamentalism—which was positively related to every form of discrimination—all but one of the intrinsic correlations were reduced to insignificance. The extrinsic correlations remained largely unchanged. The quest measure, on the other hand, was significantly and negatively correlated with all measures of discrimination, for males and females, before and after the effects of Fundamentalism were partialed out. Altemeyer and Hunsberger (1992) found that both McFarland's Quest scale and a 16-item Revised Quest Scale of their own were negatively correlated with right-wing authoritarianism and four measures of prejudice. Fundamentalism, in contrast, was positively associated with all five of these variables.

Concluding Thoughts on Quest: Whatever the present conceptual and psychometric shortcomings of the Batson Quest scale and its relatives, these measures are finally creating a place in the correlational literature for the liberal religious outlook. Nearly half a century ago, Pratt (1950) argued that, for the modern, honest, and thinking individual, worship can only be understood as "an active search," "an ONTOLOGICAL venture"; religion, he said in further anticipation of Batson, "has always to do with the practical question of destiny," of personal and collective fate, and it "almost inevitably gives one a larger horizon than one would otherwise have" as well as "a certain *depth*." Pratt, too, discerns at the heart of Christian experience "the impulse to helpfulness and to service" (pp. 59, 62, 66, 73, 122).

In like spirit, British educator Ronald Goldman (1967) observes that the general temper of our time is one of "search and questioning." Religious education in particular must become an open-ended "exploration of experience in depth" rather than the teaching of infallible truths. It must be an education for uncertainty and personal choice (pp. 7, 14). Goldman's (1964, 1965) own research on religious thinking and his subsequent recommendations for religious education suggest that, as a sustained posture of tentativeness that allows for a life of commitment, the quest orientation is indeed a more mature stage than the settled orthodoxy tapped by the Intrinsic scale. William Perry's (1970) research on the intellectual development of college students and James Fowler's (1981) on the stages of faith development, compel the same conclusion. As Thouless and Fowler found, however, such a posture is rarely attained. We may suspect that it is not well represented by Batson's questionnaire items, none of which suggests the movement toward a goal that is implied in the metaphor of quest (Wulff, 1992). It may be, however, that the ideas of a path and destination are incompatible with today pluralistic religious searching (Woodward, 1994). Clarifying and assessing the quest orientation is surely one of the psychology of religion's most urgent tasks.

RELIGION AND MENTAL HEALTH

The Intrinsic, Extrinsic, and Quest scales were all initially developed to clarify religion's relation to social attitudes. Today they are more commonly used for exploring piety's connection to personal adjustment. This redirection of effort reflects a general shift in the research on the consequences of piety, from an interest in its social correlates to an emphasis on its implications for health, both physical and mental. Physical health is easily defined and assessed, usually in terms of longevity, the absence of disease, or self-ratings of overall health. "Mental health," a widely used borrowing from the medical realm, has a range of connotations that suggest not merely the absence of psychiatric symptoms but also the presence of such positive qualities as self-acceptance, autonomy, personal integration, and self-actualization (Jahoda, 1958). It is correspondingly more difficult to operationalize.

Correlates with Physical Health

Correlational evidence indicating that religiousness in one form or another is related to physical health dates back to the early nineteenth century. The great bulk of this research, however, consists of epidemiological studies in which religiosity was included as just one variable among many and measured by the simplest of indicators, usually religious affiliation. Moreover, significant findings in relation to religion were commonly left undiscussed. Thus until recently these rather numerous findings were largely unknown (Levin and Schiller, 1987).

In their review of well over 200 such studies, Jeffrey Levin and Preston Schiller (1987) report a number of interesting trends. The prevalence of certain diseases varies significantly from one religious group to another, sometimes the result of genetic inheritance or of particular health or dietary practices, such as the vegetarianism of Seventh-Day Adventists. And contrary to Galton's report, various studies of religious professionals show some health advantages for certain classes of them, though at least one study subsequent to Galton's confirms a higher mortality rate for missionaries than for lay people. In some studies but not others, frequency of religious attendance, self-rated religiosity, and other such measures are positively related to self-rated health and decreased mortality from various specific causes.

Levin and Schiller conclude their review of this extremely diverse literature by calling for the development of a paradigm for guiding new, more adequate research on how and why religiousness affects physical health. They also urge the thoughtful adoption of more subtle measures of religiosity, especially indicators of Allport's intrinsic type. To promote such research, Levin and his associates are working to establish a new field that they call the epidemiology of religion (Levin, 1994a; Levin, 1994b; Levin and Vanderpool, 1987). Meanwhile, Herbert Benson (1996) and his associates continue to document the positive effects on physical health of the "faith factor"—the combination of the relaxation response with "remembered wellness," Benson's preferred term for what others call the placebo effect.

Mental Health and Religion: A Complex Relation

Research on religion and mental health, on the other hand, needs no such advocacy, for it is today widely pursued using a variety of measures and research techniques. Given that both variables—mental health as well as religion—are conceived as multidimensional, the possibilities for interrelationship seem virtually inexhaustible. In an early effort to assay the literature on religion and mental health, Bernard Spilka and Paul Werme (1971) conclude that the inconsistencies they found in the empirical findings testify not to the absence of a relationship, as some had inferred, but to a complex association that requires thoughtful redefinition and assessment of each term. They suggest four different ways that religion may be related to mental health: (1) It may become an expressive outlet for existing mental disturbance. (2) It may suppress symptoms and resocialize the individual, encouraging more conventional and socially acceptable forms of thought and behavior. (3) It may provide a refuge or haven from the life stresses that might otherwise precipitate mental disorder. (4) And it may provide resources for the development of broader perspectives and the fuller realization of individual capabilities.

Ecclesiogenic Neuroses

Religious association and teachings may also present hazards, as Spilka and Werme acknowledge. Struck by how many of his patients with sexual disorders came from conservative Christian circles where sex was a forbidden topic surrounded by secrecy, prohibitions, and threats, Berlin gynecologist Eberhard Schaetzing (1955) coined for these disturbances the term "ecclesiogenic neuroses"—that is, church-caused disorders. The term was soon adopted by others, who expanded its meaning to encompass a variety of other disturbances likewise thought to have roots in religious teachings and practices. In his handbook on the prevention of suicide, Berlin physician and theologian Klaus Thomas (1964) estimates that about 10 percent of all neuroses are ecclesiogenic. Judging from his own work with Christian patients, psychoanalyst Heinrich von Knorre (1991) thinks this estimate is rather high, but he does confirm that sexual disorders are common among Christians. Psychiatrist Samuel Pfeifer (1993), on the other hand, objects to the term ecclesiogenic because of the oversimplified causal model he says it suggests. Piety alone, he asserts, does not make anyone sick. In every case of religion-related disorder, he claims, religious elements encounter a "neurotic" personality existing in the broader context of the stresses of human life (p. 110).

Certainly religious elements interact with personal disposition. The unusually high incidence of schizophrenia among the followers of Bratslav Hasidism, for example, reflects in part the appeal that this messianic, ultraorthodox sect in Israel and New York has for isolated and paranoid individuals. But it is participation in the sect's unusual practices, such as praying all night at the tombs of spiritual leaders, that finally brings about the psychotic break (Witzum, Greenberg, and Buchbinder, 1990).

Patriarchal Religion and Child Abuse: The ecclesiogenic label, with its emphasis on pathological influences in religious tradition, may nevertheless be appropriate on occasion, as recent work on religion and child abuse suggests. Historian Philip Greven (1991) documents, through religious books on child discipline and the autobiographies of notable religious personalities, that devoutly Christian parents have long physically abused their children under the conviction that the child's will must be broken if the child is to live in conformity with the superior will of God. Recent research indicates that Fundamentalists above all others are today likely to use corporal punishment (Ellison, 1996; Grasmick, Bursik, and Kimpel, 1991; Wiehe, 1990), and they are also likely to express views on childrearing similar to those of parents with a history of abusing their children (Neufeld, 1979). The apocalyptic religious world-view that is common among those who advocate such corporal punishment may be understood, says Greven, as an expression of "the nuclear core of rage, resentment, and aggression" that remains from their own childhoods of abuse (p. 206). It is perhaps not surprising, then, that a fundamentalist upbringing is a common factor in patients with multiple personality disorder (Bowman, 1989).

It would likewise be inappropriate to ascribe to individual neurosis the stress that countless women have suffered in growing up in religious cultures dominated by patriarchal imagery and relationships. According to an interview study carried out in the Netherlands by Annie Imbens and Ineke Jonker (1985), various elements in the Christian tradition in particular have contributed to the occurrence of child sexual abuse, first serving to justify incestuous acts in the eyes of the perpetrators and then making it difficult for the victims to seek and obtain help. These elements include a stern patriarchal image of God and the presumption by men that they are the ones who are called by God. Women are correspondingly subordinated, derogated, suppressed, and silenced, both in biblical texts and religious practice. Adhering to the norms prescribed for them by the Christian tradition, girls become easy prey for sexual abuse by male family members. They are then blamed for the transgression and held responsible for disrupting the family if the violation becomes known. Traumatized both sexually and religiously, all 19 women in Imbens and Jonker's subject group eventually left the church. The increased risk for sexual abuse that is associated with conservative Christian beliefs and the high rates of religious defection among women who suffer such abuse in childhood have also been observed by others (D. Elliot, 1994; Russell, 1986; Taylor and Fontes, 1995). Growing awareness of these trends is challenging counselors, religious and secular, to find ways to respond effectively to abuse in religious families (Horton and Williamson, 1988).

In many Christian churches today, traditional patriarchal language and values are being gradually rethought and systematically replaced. Meanwhile, women are coping in a variety of ways, commonly by noting improvements over the past or contrasting their situations with less favorable ones in other religious traditions and secular contexts. Their strong emphasis on relational values rather than cognitive and hierarchical ones likewise serves to minimize the effects of inequality (Ozorak, 1996). While seeking a larger role in the functioning of religious organizations, women are also claiming the prerogative of renaming the sacred, which they find not in some distant space but in the palpable realities of everyday life (Gray, 1988). Largely excluded from the interreligious dialogue that has sprung up in the face of the new religious pluralism, as religious leaders and scholars explore ways of maintaining their own cherished traditions while yet respecting those of others, women have undertaken a gender-sensitive dialogue of their own (O'Neill, 1990). And as they work to redefine the issues of spirituality for women, many are leaving the familiar traditions behind in their quest for spiritual resources—including the image of the Goddess—that are powerful and transforming for them (Christ, 1995;

Women ritually share milk and honey at a 1993 conference in Minneapolis dedicated to "re-imagining" traditional Christian concepts in terms of women's experience. Drawing 2000 women from major Protestant denominations, the conference created a furor within the United Methodist and Presbyterian (U.S.A.) churches, some of whose officers were among the conference planners (Steinfels, 1994).

King, 1993; Pirani, 1991). Healing—physical as well as spiritual, including relief from the pain suffered in growing up in a patriarchal world—is assumed in feminist spiritual thought to be needed by all women (Eller, 1993, p. 109).

Conservative Religion and Mental Health: Acting to counter such changes is a worldwide resurgence of militant fundamentalism, a response to perceived threats in modern, secular culture, including the challenges of the feminist movement (Hawley, 1994). There has been a corresponding surge in scholarly investigation, much of it under the sponsorship of The Fundamentalism Project at the University of Chicago (Marty and Appleby, 1991, 1992). Empirical research on fundamentalist and other conservative religious groups is also growing, some of it aimed at the question of the relation of conservative religious views to mental health.

One study, for example, directly tests Schaetzing's claim that "dogmatism of the church" causes neurosis. Hartmut Spring and his associates (1993) assessed the level of religious anxiety and depressivity—the indicators of ecclesiogenic neurosis proposed by Thomas (1964)—in two Catholic congregations, one long situated in a heavily Catholic milieu and the other recently established in an area with a minority of Catholics. The assumption that the first congregation, designated "traditional," was higher in dogmatism of the church than the second, "pluralistic" congregation was supported by the finding of higher mean scores on orthodoxy and authoritarian submissiveness among members of the first group. As predicted, members of the traditional congregation proved to be significantly higher on religious anxiety (e.g., in relation to hell, the Devil, feelings of guilt, punishment from God, and so on) than members of the pluralistic group. Although members of the two congregations did not differ from each other in depressivity, both groups scored distinctly higher in comparison to the normative population. The heightened depressivity scores thus also lend support to the ecclesiogenic hypothesis. On the other hand, as Spring and his colleagues acknowledge, one could account for these data another way: persons already high in depressivity may be drawn to the Church for help.

From his own experience as a former conservative evangelical, the eminent biblical scholar James Barr (1980) affirms a causal relation in accord with the ecclesiogenic hypothesis. He maintains that Fundamentalist sentiments induce in open and happy young people the strained and suspicious outlook of the authoritarian mind. Historian and psychoanalyst Charles Strozier (1994), in contrast, found that all of the Fundamentalists he interviewed had histories of trauma, which they eventually learned to talk about in the rhetoric of literal Christian belief. The "broken narratives" for which they sought healing in born-again experience became for Strozier the defining characteristic of Fundamentalists. Although they found consolation and hope in the dramatic mythic imagery of the anticipated apocalypse, they remained extraordinarily preoccupied with personal guilt and shame. Themes of real or symbolic death were also conspicuous in their thinking, whether they were reflecting on their personal pasts or anticipating the imminent violent destruction that they believed is necessitated by human evil. Life in the present is for them frightening and fragile, a constant struggle.

Strozier maintains that Fundamentalism "can only be understood as a kind of collective illness in our contemporary culture"; there is, he adds, "generally something unsteady" about its followers (p. 3). Yet he declines to describe the lives of Fundamentalists as pathological. Categories of pathology are meaningless, he says, for understanding a mass movement that involves roughly a quarter of the United States population. Of Strozier's respondents, all of whom seemed to be typical members of the churches in which he worked, none was perceived by others as odd or disturbed.

Empirical researchers agree that Fundamentalists do not score higher than other groups on measures of pathology, on the average, as long as the measures are religiously neutral and social class is held constant (Hood, Morris, and Watson, 1986; Stark, 1971). In regard to other measures of mental health, however, the findings are less consistent. On the positive side, for example, Christian, Jewish, and Muslim fundamentalists proved as a group to be much more optimistic than members of more liberal Christian and Jewish groups, in accord with the greater hopefulness of the religious messages they had heard and read (Sethi and Seligman, 1993, 1994). Fundamentalism has also been found to be a positive indicator of marital happiness (Hansen, 1992).

On the negative side, a group of certified family therapists rated Fundamentalist families as significantly less healthy than nonfundamentalist families on three of eight factors on a Family Health Scale and more healthy on only one. Fundamentalist families had clearer expectations of how family members were to behave in relation to each other but they were also less emotionally close, less flexible in dealing with change, less likely to encourage members to assume responsibility and exercise their own judgment, and less likely to show caring without smothering (Denton and Denton, 1992). Fundamentalism has also been identified as a common feature of families with adolescent members exhibiting "conversion," which here refers not to religious conversion but to a disabling physical disorder for which no organic cause can be found (Seltzer, 1984).

Insignificant differences have been found as well. Born-again Christian students in one study were no more likely to report "great stress" than others (Schafer and King, 1990). In another study, Fundamentalists from the Southern Baptist Church proved not to differ in level of ego development from nonfundamentalist members of the United Methodist Church (Weaver, Berry, and Pittel, 1994).

Religious Orientation and Mental Health

As we noted earlier, inconsistencies of this sort are characteristic of the entire literature on religion and mental health. In a meta-analysis of the literature, Allen Bergin (1983) found that 47 percent of the studies he reviewed reported a positive relationship, 23 percent a negative one, and 30 percent no relation at all. In a later review of the literature, John Gartner, Dave Larson, and George Allen (1991; Gartner, 1996) suggest that some of these discrepancies can be accounted for in terms of the types of measures that have been used. Most studies reporting positive associations assess the mental health variables in terms of directly observable behavior (e.g., using or not using drugs). In contrast, the preponderance of studies reporting negative relationships assess mental health by using questionnaires purporting to measure one or another hypothetical intrapsychic construct (e.g., rigidity or self-actualization). These questionnaires, Gartner and his colleagues suggest, are not only less reliable and valid but also more likely to be value biased. Weighing in on the side of behavioral measures, of mental health as well as religion, they conclude that the bulk of the evidence suggests that religion is associated with positive mental health.

Most researchers remain committed to the more subtle and broadly significant constructs, including the dimensions of religiosity. Much of the research today on the mental-health correlates of religion uses the Allport-Ross Religious Orientation Scale, with the expectation that the Intrinsic scale will be positively associated with mental health and the Extrinsic scale negatively associated. Findings have tended to support these predictions. The Intrinsic scale, for example, has proved to be positively associated with life satisfaction (Zwingmann, 1991; Zwingmann, Moosbrugger, and Frank, 1991), psychological adjustment (Watson, Morris, and Hood, 1994), self-control and better personality functioning (Bergin, Masters, and Richards, 1987), self-esteem (Nelson, 1990; Ryan, Rigby, and King, 1993), an internal locus of control (Jackson and Coursey, 1988; Kahoe, 1974a; Stewin, 1976), purpose-in-life scores (Bolt, 1975; Crandall and Rasmussen, 1975), spiritual well-being (Mickley, Soeken, and Belcher, 1992), adjustment and morale in the elderly (Koenig, Kvale, and Ferrel, 1988; Van Haitsma, 1986), but also proneness to guilt (Chau, et al., 1990; Richards, 1991). Negative associations with the Intrinsic scale have been found for anxiety and death anxiety in particular (Bergin, Masters, and Richards, 1987; Powell and Thorson, 1991), neuroticism (Chau et al., 1990), depression (Dörr, 1987, 1992; Genia, 1996; Nelson, 1989), impulsivity (Robinson, 1990), and maladaptive narcissism (Watson, Morris, Hood, and Biderman, 1990). When correlations with the Extrinsic scale are significant, they tend to show the opposite pattern, such as positive correlations with anxiety (Bergin, Masters, and Richards, 1987), depression (Genia and Shaw, 1991), and fear of death (Bolt, 1977; Kraft, Litwin, and Barber, 1987) and negative ones with autonomy (Tisdale, 1966) and internal locus of control (Kahoe, 1974a; Park, Cohen, and Herb, 1990; Strickland and Shaffer, 1971).

The Quest scale is less often used in studies of mental health than the IE scales. It also less frequently yields significant findings. If any trends are emerging, one of

RELIGION AND MENTAL HEALTH

them may be positive correlations with measures of personal distress, a relation we earlier noted in the research of Spilka and his associates. Like these researchers, Vicky Genia (1996) found a significant negative correlation between quest scores and social desirability. Using Batson's 12-item Quest scale, she also found a low positive correlation with depression (.16) and a negative one with a measure of self-esteem (− .16), though both correlations were reduced to insignificance when she controlled for social desirability. Richard Ryan, Scott Rigby, and Kristi King (1993) found comparably low positive correlations between the quest orientation and measures of anxiety and depression, but in their study none was large enough to be statistically significant. Consistently significant and positive correlations have been found, on the other hand, between the quest orientation and fear of death or negative perspectives on death, on the one hand, and with openness and cognitive complexity on the other (Batson, Schoenrade, and Ventis, 1993, pp. 282–285). Yet even these correlations are modest.

Religion as a Way of Coping

While many researchers remain enthusiastic about the IE distinction if not also quest (Gorsuch, 1988), others are developing more complex and potentially fruitful theoretical frameworks. One of the most promising is offered by Kenneth Pargament and his associates (Pargament, 1990, 1996; Pargament and Park, 1995). Rather than conceiving of religion as either a means or an end, as in the traditional IE construction, Pargament (1992) proposes that religion be conceived as "a general disposition to use particular means to attain particular ends in living" (p. 211). A means-*and*-ends analysis of religion, he says, brings out aspects of the religious life that are overlooked in the literature dominated by the three religious orientations, including the social aspects that address the need for intimate association and the diverse feelings, beliefs, and practices that are religion's content. For such an approach, Pargament has adopted the term *coping* as it is used in the clinical and social-psychological literatures. The coping model emphasizes the constructive role that religion can play within the complex, ongoing process by which people try to comprehend and deal with the various personal and situational problems that come into their lives.

Each of the elements in the coping process, says Pargament (1990), requires careful assessment. The problematic event or situation, which may be anything from a minor irritation to a major life change, must be understood according to its subjective meaning for the individual. How a person experiences and appraises a situation, and then estimates his or her own ability to handle it, will naturally play a large role in shaping the outcome. The coping activities themselves may take a variety of forms, some directed at the situation and others aimed at the person's emotional response. Coping efforts may be genuinely constructive and rational, but they can also be ineffective or even self-defeating. Whatever its forms, coping can lead in time to reappraisals of the precipitating event. The possible outcomes of coping are similarly diverse: they may be situational, psychological, social, or physiological in nature; they may be essentially positive or negative, or a mixture of gains and losses; and they may range from immediate or short-term outcomes to much longer-term ones, perhaps of a very different character.

Religion may enter into the coping process in a variety of ways. The *critical event* may itself be religious, such as a conversion or mystical experience or some insight or realization from reading sacred scripture; or the event may be religiously framed, as in the case of an interpersonal experience within one's congregation or a life transition that is marked by a religious ceremony, such as confirmation, bar or bas matzvah, a wedding, or a funeral. *Appraisals* of the situation may also be religious in character. When good or bad things inexplicably happen, they may be interpreted as rewards or punishments from God, or as divinely ordained opportunities for learning certain virtues. They may also be thought to have occurred without God's consent, and to be an occasion of grief in the heavenly realm as well. The *coping activities* set in motion may likewise be religious. One may seek advice or consolation from a member of the clergy or some other religious associate, if not also from God. One may show a variety of cognitive, emotional, and behavioral responses, such as deciding what lesson God intended through this event, having certain feelings toward God, trying to lead a more virtuous life, or promoting justice in the wider world. The *outcomes,* finally, can be religious, including changes in religious beliefs, feelings, and participation if not also in the overall direction of one's spiritual life. Pargament (1990) notes that association with a religious tradition may multiply the number of available resources for coping, but various traditional teachings and practices may also impose serious constraints.

In underscoring the complexity of the process of coping, Pargament's theoretical framework offers a major challenge to other researchers on religion and mental health. In place of the simple correlational procedures that many use, his model calls for the inclusion of multiple variables, including moderating variables that determine when and how the others are related; the use of statistical procedures sensitive to curvilinear relationships; the employment of qualitative techniques for assessing the individual's subjective construction of events and idiosyncratic efforts at coping; and a recognition that the complex outcomes of the coping process may entail tradeoffs, a combination of positive and negative gains. Associations with a strict religious group, for example, may provide feelings of intimacy and self-worth at the same time that it discourages the development of certain skills and fosters intolerance of others' views.

While thus recognizing the dark side of religion, Pargament's coping model is fundamentally a positive one, for coping implies some degree of success in adjusting to life's circumstances. The model has the great virtue of viewing religion within its living context: the ongoing lives of individuals as they search for significance in their day-to-day experiences. Multifaceted as this model is, it provides the foundations for a broad and sustained research program. Like other emerging theoretical frameworks in the psychology of religion, such as the perspectives of attachment theory (Kirkpatrick, 1992, 1995a; Oksanen, 1994) and general attribution theory (Proudfoot and Shaver, 1975; Spilka, Shaver, and Kirkpatrick, 1985; Spilka and McIntosh, 1995), it offers a new focus and impetus for the correlational approach and the prospect of a more vital and dynamic field.

EVALUATION OF THE EXPERIMENTAL AND CORRELATIONAL APPROACHES

Experimental and correlational techniques tend to inspire one or the other of two extreme responses. Some persons, including many of the researchers whose work we have reviewed in the last two chapters, assume that measurement, laboratory controls, and statistical analysis are the only sure means for gaining scientific knowledge of human experience and behavior. They are thus disdainful of the more subjective, interpretive methods used by the humanistic disciplines. Humanistic scholars, on the other hand, are commonly mystified and alienated by the application of quantitative and experimental procedures in the human sphere. Peculiarly sensitive to the nuances and ambiguities of human language and accustomed to using textual and other historical materials, these scholars are deeply skeptical about the reduction of any human experience to rating scales and averages.

Wisdom would seem to lie in a more moderate position. There is no question that correlational and experimental procedures can be—and frequently have been—misused, yielding results that have little meaning or relevance. Thoughtfully applied, however, objective research methods can be highly serviceable. As Marie Jahoda (1977, p. 155) argues, experiments "present the strictest test of assumptions that has yet been devised. With all their pitfalls, for this purpose no better technique exists, as long as the phenomena under investigation are not simplified out of existence by the experimental manipulation." Galton, we read earlier, considered statistics an extraordinarily powerful tool for disentangling complex relationships— as long as these methods are "delicately handled" and "warily interpreted."

CAN RELIGION BE BROUGHT INTO THE LABORATORY?

At various points in the last two chapters we have noted some of the pitfalls and problems of the methods of the objective approach, especially as they are applied to religion. It is always difficult to bring real-world phenomena into the experimental laboratory. Phenomena as delicate and complex as religious ones are even more problematical. The most dramatic success in the laboratory approach to religious experience has been achieved with the use of psychedelic drugs. In addition to the legal and ethical complications, however, there is still the question of how authentic drug-induced experiences are. The debate has been vigorous (see Osmond and Smythies, 1959; H. Smith, 1964; Zaehner, 1957, 1972), but particularly informative are reports from those who have experienced both states. They claim that drug-induced experiences are not as profound and meaningful as those achieved through traditional religious means (Jordan, 1971). Moreover, it is doubtful that, in comparison to religious experiences without drugs, psychedelic states have as much "faith-filled carryover." Indeed, Houston Smith suspects that psychedelic experiences may as readily abort a religious quest as further it (Smith, 1967, p. 144; 1976).

Apart from psychedelic drugs, which obviously raise complex issues and are at any rate almost impossible to obtain under current law, is true experimentation possible in the psychology of religion? Huxley (1961) cites research on fasting and sleep deprivation as evidence that ascetic practices, like drugs, are a means of changing body chemistry toward the production of transformed religious awareness. Might ascetic practices, along with other modes of bodily manipulation, also serve as a means of continuing experimentation? Contrary to Huxley's report, the research findings of Ancel Keys and his colleagues (1950), summarized in Chapter 3, included no "visionary experiences." Yet the Keys study was not designed to elicit them. Given a different set and setting, we can easily imagine a different outcome. It is doubtful, however, that so dangerous and personally costly an experiment would be undertaken for the purposes we are considering.

The hypnotic investigations of Bernard Aaronson and the quasi-hypnotic explorations of Houston and Masters, on the other hand, seem genuinely to offer promising and practical techniques for more carefully controlled experimentation, at least with the minority of subjects capable of "deep trance" phenomena (Gibbons and DeJarnette, 1972). Less dramatic, perhaps, but already more or less in accord with accepted research practice are the numerous laboratory studies of meditation. If there are doubts abroad about experimentation in the psychology of religion, some researchers obviously do not share them.

According to Wilhelm Koepp (1920), a fundamental paradox undermines any experimental approach to religion undertaken for scientific purposes. Religious experience, he argues, can only be called forth for its own sake. When it is asked to serve a scientific aim, it is inevitably transformed. The phenomenon loses its essentially religious character, leaving only aesthetic and other secondary aspects. Virginia Hine (1969) illustrates this principle in her own observations of glossolalia. The strongly positive emotional states usually accompanying the experience of speaking in tongues, and often persisting long after the utterance itself, are likely to be wholly absent when the Pentecostal subject is working with a scientific observer. It is understandable, therefore, that many profoundly religious persons refuse to cooperate with the would-be experimenter. Yet, turning to the "irreligious" is no solution, according to Koepp, for they are incapable of meeting "the first requirement of a religious experiment, actual entry into the religious sphere" (p. 58).

Agreeing that a strictly experimental psychology of religion is impossible, Batson (1977) holds out for quasi-experimental methods such as he himself has employed. The same label is applicable to Harold Burtt and Don Falkenberg's (1941) study, in which they demonstrate the persuasive effect that knowledge of majority or expert opinion can have on religious attitudes and beliefs, as well as to Jean-Pierre Deconchy's (1971, 1980) similarly conceived but more highly elaborated investigations in France. Quasi-experimental techniques do not entail the same degree of control that characterizes the ideal laboratory experiment. Yet they may still elicit the critic's doubts about the genuineness of the religious phenomena under evaluation, the adequacy of the various measures employed, and the ethics of artificial intervention and deception.

CAN RELIGIOUS FAITH BE MEANINGFULLY MEASURED?

Experimental and correlation psychologies of religion are founded on the assumption that fundamental aspects of religious faith are measurable. Those who disagree do not deny that some expressions of faith—attendance at religious services, most obviously—can be quantified. What they do doubt is that an individual's religiousness can be evaluated numerically or categorically without gravely misrepresenting it.

The most common means used to assess piety is the questionnaire. Early forms of this device almost always required respondents to write lengthy answers. The problems were legion. To answer most of the questions adequately required an exceptionally high level of cooperation, memory, introspective capacity, self-knowledge, vocabulary, and precision in description. Ever present were the problems of suggesting answers in the very asking of the questions; the unknown principles by which the subject decided what and how much to include; the tendency to draw on conventional or orthodox expressions; the probability that the formulation of a response produced an artificial clarity and order; the nearly universal fact of selective return; and the fragmentary and superficial quality the results often show as a whole (Coe, 1916; Pratt, 1920; Siegmund, 1942; Spranger, 1924; Stählin, 1912; Uren, 1928).

Today's questionnaire typically requires the respondent merely to indicate agreement or disagreement with a series of statements, or to select one alternative out of a cluster of three or four. The radical standardization and simplification of questionnaire responses greatly facilitate the statistical analyses that are the hallmark of objective psychology. Yet thus far it has proved extraordinarily difficult—some would say impossible—for the researcher to write alternatives that will accommodate all the respondents to their own satisfaction, and then to win the approval of the historian of religion and the psychometrician. Users of these scales have often been appropriately circumspect in their claims for them, and they have made their items and procedures public so that others might judge their adequacy or usefulness for themselves. Nonetheless, the conclusions that are drawn are sometimes subtly but seriously misleading.

Misleading Generalizations

The category of the "nonreligious" will illustrate the point. To be classified as nonreligious, people must either refuse to identify themselves with some traditional religious group or score relatively low on some scale, probably a measure of orthodoxy or ORTHOPRAXY. The "nones" and the "nonreligious" have surprised researchers by consistently proving themselves least prejudiced, least likely to yield to authority, and most likely to report mystical experiences. Gorsuch and Aleshire (1974) recognize that subjects of this type may actually view themselves as "religious." Some may even believe in God and attend church regularly (Vernon, 1968).

Whereas common sense may bring to mind the delinquent or criminal as the most obvious example of the nonreligious type, research has found that the lawbreaker frequently reports a religious affiliation and positive religious attitudes (e.g., Payne, 1972; Yochelson and Samenow, 1976). On the other hand, "Those who break away from religion," declares Cohen (1946, p. 347), "are often among the most high-minded members of the community." "It is a fact," agrees Ignace Lepp (1963, p. 134), "that a number of superior people refuse the Christian religion—and indeed all religion—because they do not find it noble enough, because its ideal does not satisfy them, because its exigencies do not strike them as 'being up to the mark.' " These "atheists in the name of value," however, do not form a homogeneous group that some new scale can be written to identify.

If "nonreligious" is seriously misleading, then the category "indiscriminately antireligious" (Allport and Ross, 1967) surely needs reconsideration too, especially when the subjects included therein—perhaps selected from religious environments, as Andrew Thompson's (1974) were—have only relatively lower scores than the others. The whole enterprise of measuring religion in terms of "objective" referents—beliefs and practices, foremost—as well as conventionally pious sentiments, needs careful rethinking. At the very least, the names applied to these measures—and thus also the generalizations that are based on them—should be replaced with more modest labels commensurate with the character of the questionnaire items. Gorsuch and Aleshire's (1974) use of "Christian faith" instead of "religion," although the term is only relatively more precise, is a clear step forward.

Also potentially misleading are the generalizations regarding trends that have been found through the use of these measurement devices. The many "statistically significant" correlations and group differences that have been reported in this literature are typically rather small. Put in more exact, technical terms, the amount of "explained variance" is rarely more than half the total variance, and frequently much less, and the distribution of scores of various subject groups always overlap considerably. Leaving behind the individuals who make up these groups obscures the fact that many of their scores contradict the "statistically significant" differences finally reported. Moreover, the important but exceedingly difficult question of "How much of a difference makes a difference?" cannot really be answered apart from some specified practical concern. In other words, *statistical* significance does not automatically guarantee *human* significance (Bakan, 1966c). If applied indiscriminately, Ana-Maria Rizzuto (1979, p. 5) warns, the conclusions of the experimental and correlational psychologists may be harmful in the clinical context.

THE EXCLUSION OF SUBJECTIVITY

The problems we have discussed have long been recognized by thoughtful proponents of objective methods. Less often appreciated are the costs of rejecting other methods, particularly those designed to be sensitive to human subjectivity and the holistic patterns of individuality. "Anyone who thinks that he must concentrate and rely on only one type of approach, such as laboratory experiment, for his knowledge of man," writes H. P. Rickman (1979, p. 89) in his study of Dilthey, "is like an observer who peeps through the key-hole when the door is wide open."

Science Through a Keyhole

For objective psychologists of religion, the keyhole is typically a questionnaire, and what they glimpse through it is the personal world of human experience. The doorway is constituted by the investigators' own subjectivity as well as the various expressions—from spontaneous gestures to written documents—by which a person can come to know the subjectivity of others. To state the paradox more directly: though formally denying themselves access to the inner, subjective world, the objective psychologists ask wholly untrained and methodologically naive subjects to plunge into it themselves, but usually under the constraint of an extremely narrow range of possible responses. Then, on so uncertain a foundation, these researchers attempt to build a science that is intended to comprehend that underlying subjectivity. In later chapters we will see what happens when investigators find some means by which to pass through the doorway themselves.

Two Contrasting Lives: A brief example will suggest how a subjective method—in this instance, the case study, based on personal documents and biographical sources—can provide a fuller view of individual piety and its relation to personality trends. Drawing on research from her doctoral dissertation on religion in the lives of well-to-do Colonial Americans, Susan Kwilecki (1986) offers two contrasting examples: Robert Carter (1728–1804), who represents the intrinsic–committed orientation, and John Hancock (1737–1793), who typifies the extrinsic–consensual orientation.

Carter, a recluse interested in law and music but distinctly not in the financial and political responsibilities that fell to persons of his station, was for a time a rationalistic deist. Later, during a period of illness, he became a convert to evangelical Christianity and soon played a major role in promoting the Baptist Church in Virginia. A few years later, after discovering the writings of Emanuel Swedenborg and corresponding with the Baltimore Swedenborgian Society, he moved to Baltimore and became the group's leader. When it later disbanded, he associated himself with a variety of other religious assemblies until his death a few years later. Although the religious and ethical writings he left behind lack sophistication, they reveal a conceptually differentiated outlook well integrated with other areas of life, suggesting the intrinsic–committed orientation.

In contrast, Hancock, a wealthy and charming extravert who had an exceptional need to be in the limelight, rarely referred to religion in his writings. The few, brief allusions are either politically expedient formulas or incidental expressions of early-learned traditional doctrine lacking any real conviction. Even the death of his only son, though the occasion for profound grief, did not inspire any genuine religious feeling. The church to which he was a generous patron was but one more arena in which to be noticed and to exercise power. Hancock, says Kwilecki, is a textbook model of the extrinsic–consensual orientation.

Beyond giving reality and texture to objective psychology's abstractions, these cases illustrate how religious orientation is inextricably bound up with personal disposition and need. Although correlational psychologists have reported a large number of correlations between religion and personality variables, only idiographic case studies bring these variables to life and show their complex interrelations. Yet the relation is reciprocal, for only correlational research, notes Kwilecki, can reveal the generality of the trends that appear so strikingly in these two examples.

Closing the Door to Subjectivity

The exclusion of subjectivity is more radical still in the experiments on meditation that employ physiological measures as the dependent variables and then infer differences in mental states from them. According to Indologist Fritz Staal (1975), "Such methods tell us how meditation affects the body, not how it affects the mind. . . . A balanced study of mental states can only result from fully taking into account not only behavioral and physiological, but also experiential or subjective data" (p. 103). Although Staal finds some physiological investigations—notably those of Thérèse Brosse (1963)—both carefully done and suggestive, he concludes that they tell us little.

> Despite the impressive amount of careful research that has gone into the study of Yoga, and of mysticism generally, through EEG, ECG, and similar methods, one cannot help feeling that it is like studying art through films of the eye movements of art viewers. Even if the results are valid, their significance is minute (p. 104).

In contrast to Brosse's measured conclusions, those of Robert Wallace are judged to be unreflectively dogmatic and largely promotional. "The kind of advertisement for transcendental meditation that Wallace indulges in, and that acts instead on many as a deterrent, throws little light on transcendental meditation, or on meditation in general" (pp. 106–107). Thomas Mulholland (1972) similarly regrets the pseudoscientific "alpha cult" that is another by-product of EEG research. After three decades of research, he says, scientists have found no clearly defined psychological process associated with alpha. Even its physiological origin is a matter of uncertainty.

As meditators themselves, many of these researchers know from first-hand experience that what they gain is not well represented in these physiological measures. One such researcher, Michael West (1987, p. 193), finds his own experience "vastly more fruitful" and the psychological research "vastly more frustrating" in comparison to each other, a discrepancy that he compares to a Zen koan. Why does he keep on meditating when empirical evidence suggests that the practice reduces arousal no more than ordinary rest? "The simple answer would be to say that I trust my experience more than my science. But the more complex anwer is that my reading of the research and theoretical literature in this area has not given me reason to discontinue my practice and has offered some reason for sustaining it (if any more reason beyond my subjective experience were needed)." West might find a solution to his koan if he employed a method that allowed him to take his experience more fully and systematically into account, much as Carl Albrecht (1951) does in his own, phenomenological study of meditative–mystical experience (see Chapter 12). By comparison, the "phenomenological" studies reviewed in West's book hardly deserve the name, for the observers are apparently untrained in phenomenological investigation, and the whole enterprise continues to be framed with assumptions that violate the phenomenological attitude.

In an age that is suspicious or disdainful of the "merely subjective," it is easy to understand why most meditation researchers emphasize objective methods. Advocates of TM realize that many people will take transformed states of consciousness seriously only if they can be shown to be related to palpable physical reality. Yet selling these states on the basis of their calming effect rather misses the point. In its traditional contexts, meditation has always been directed toward some higher state of awareness or illumination, not mere relaxation or reduction of stress. In separating the practice of meditation from this broader purpose and then reducing its significance to objectively observable bodily changes, its modern-day proponents risk trivializing what has been one of the most powerful instruments of the spiritual quest.

THE NEGLECT OF RELIGIOUS CONTENT

The methods employed by the objective psychologists lend themselves far more readily to the study of religious *persons* than to religious *content*. They are thus also distinctly ahistorical. The corresponding neglect of the inexhaustibly rich world of myth, symbol, and ritual is one major reason why many scholars in religious studies are less than enthusiastic about the objective approach. In sharp contrast, the depth psychologies provide a variety of interpretive principles for uncovering the under-lying meaning and coherence of these universal yet highly variable expressions of the religious spirit. There are profound differences among these principles, and they too require critical assessment. Yet they at least have the virtue of addressing religion in its totality.

The investigation of religious content is not utterly foreclosed to objective psychologists, as a study of the ancient Chinese Yin–Yang symbol demonstrates (Craddick, Thumin, and Barclay, 1971). These researchers asked 242 university students in psychology and English classes to rate a projected green-and-blue version of this circular symbol using the SEMANTIC DIFFERENTIAL, a series of 30 seven-point scales defined in terms of bipolar adjective pairs, such as good–bad, sacred–profane, hard–soft, and agitated–quiet. The results show that the Yin–Yang diagram had essentially positive connotations for these students, who tended to perceive it as good, beautiful, kind, pleasant, happy, and clean. Its intended representation of integration and harmony was reflected in relatively high ratings on relaxed and quiet, whereas its potency was also suggested by associations with strong, powerful, deep, and agile. Its ancient association with the conjunction of male and female (among other opposites) was appropriately reflected in a mean rating precisely at the midpoint for the masculine–feminine scale. These researchers conclude that their data confirm the traditional interpretations of this symbol, if not also aspects of Jung's psychology.

Once again, we have a study of a religious element removed from its traditional context. Using subjects who most probably know little if anything about the Taoist tradition, with which this symbol is usually associated, these investigators made no effort to discover its connotative meaning for the Eastern mind. Rather, they sought to explore the "inherent"—thus presumably universal—meanings of the symbol. Although the semantic differential's bipolar structure would seem peculiarly appropriate for studying an abstract symbol that is thought to represent the conjunction of life's basic oppositions, it is impossible to know whether a middle rating reflects the dynamic balance traditionally implied by the symbol or merely a judgment that the symbol's qualities are in that respect indeterminate. Furthermore, even in the few cases in which the *mean* rating does fall close to the midpoint, there is considerable *individual* variation around that mean. If the Yin–Yang symbol does have inherent qualities in line with the Taoist interpretation, it would seem that many Western students do not clearly perceive them. Whereas the harvest from this study is thus rather modest, the undertaking at least suggests the possibility of exploring religious content by objective procedures.

We should be cautious, of course, in concluding that the problems and limitations of any particular study are intrinsic to its method or approach. Objective studies frequently suffer more from inadequate conceptualizing than from the inherent constraints of quantitative techniques (Kirkpatrick, 1995b). As we will see in subsequent chapters, objective procedures can serve a highly useful function in testing out hypotheses issuing out of other psychological perspectives. They are not sufficient in themselves for a comprehensive psychology of religion, but it would seem foolish to reject them out of hand on the basis of what has been accomplished with them thus far. Their potential, we might suspect, is far from fully realized.

7

THE PERSPECTIVE OF SIGMUND FREUD

*A*lthough objective psychology has long criticized psychoanalysis for failing to measure up to scientific standards, the two perspectives actually have much in common. Both reject unaided introspection as a means of gathering fundamental data. Both maintain that human conduct is the outcome of complexly determined causal events that lie outside awareness. Both are the self-conscious products of a positivistic and materialistic world-view dedicated to saving humankind from its deep-rooted delusions and self-defeating ignorance. As a result, both have issued radical challenges to religious faith.

The two perspectives are in other respects fundamentally dissimilar. The most evident difference is the place given to subjectivity. Whereas proponents of objective psychology limit themselves to observable behavior equally accessible to other scientists, psychoanalysts draw their evidence from the private inner world of the individual psyche. In contrast to the objective psychologists, who maintain a stringent detachment from their anonymous and briefly encountered groups of subjects, the psychoanalysts become participant–observers in the lives of their suffering patients. The data of objective psychologists consist of the terse and quantified responses of randomly selected subjects; those of the psychoanalysts are composed of lengthy and intimate case studies of a few exceptional individuals.

Thus although they share the commitment of objective psychologists to the ideal of an empirical science, psychoanalysts agree with the humanists that the complex inner world of the individual must be taken into account. The stance of the psychoanalyst—one foot in the world of objective science, the other in the realm of human subjectivity—reflects the position of the school's founder, Sigmund Freud, who sought to restrain with scientific discipline his own humanistic tendencies. The compromise that he worked out, though unacceptable in varying degrees to both objective and humanistic psychologists, has been singularly consequential for Western civilization. In the psychology of religion it has come to form a major current, broader even than Freud's own well-known contributions.

In this and the next two chapters we survey the voluminous psychoanalytic literature on religion. The present chapter is on Freud and his immediate followers.

We begin with a biographical study of Freud and an overview of orthodox psycho-analytic theory. We then proceed to examine Freud's writings on religion as well as a portion of the literature that elaborates on the broad themes most prominent in his analysis. Our study of Freud concludes with an evaluation of his theories. In Chapters 8 and 9 we consider a much broader range of religious phenomena as we draw on the insights of certain major revisions of psychoanalysis, including object-relations theory, the "new narcissism" of Heinz Kohut, and the ego psy-chology of Erik Erikson. Together, these three chapters demonstrate the remark-able comprehensiveness of the psychoanalytic perspective.

If we cannot agree that psychoanalysis is "the only kind of psychology that can say anything of significance about mystical or religious experience" (Rubinstein, in Havens, 1968, p. 33), we must recognize that it says much that is worth hearing. Yet, the psychoanalyst warns us, to listen will not be easy, for like the patient in analysis, we will be prone to manifest resistance and denial when confronted with matters that violate our conscious sensibilities. From the psychoanalytic point of view, even well-informed and thoughtful incredulity probably has such unconscious resistance among its motives. Valid or not, such an argument well may leave us unconvinced, for its seems to preempt any critical analysis. We must nevertheless acknowledge the human capacity for self-deception and applaud the psychoana-lyst's efforts to minimize its effects on our understanding of what it is to be human. Freud's life was dedicated to that understanding, although, as we will see, his own motives are complex and only partially known.

THE LIFE OF SIGMUND FREUD

The reader who would come to know Sigmund Freud faces a paradox. On the one hand, the amount of published and unpublished material bearing on his life and thought is staggering. Although he twice destroyed most of his own personal pa-pers—once in 1885 and again in 1907—his published writings contain much that is frankly autobiographical, and we now have access to many of his thousands of letters. In addition, there is an extensive biographical literature, including the classic and still authoritative biography of Ernest Jones (1953–1957), Freud's close and faithful disciple who was given access to much unpublished material, including the more than 900 letters that Freud wrote to his fiancée. According to Peter Gay (1988, p. 741), a distinguished historian trained in psychoanalysis and himself the author of a magisterial biography of Freud, "The secondary literature . . . is vast, rapidly growing, almost out of control. Some of this avalanche is revealing, much of it useful, more of it provocative; an astonishing share is malicious or downright absurd." Included in this great outpouring of scholarship and speculation is a separate stream of publications concerned with the nature and consequences of Freud's Jewish identity.

On the other hand, in the midst of this almost unprecedented biographical fascination, Freud remains tantalizingly elusive. Surprisingly candid though he was about his own dreams and hard-won insights into his own psyche, he was carefully circumspect in what he wrote about them. Those close to him have been similarly cautious. Published letters have been edited, others withheld altogether. A good deal of unpublished material, including extensive interviews with his close associ-ates, was placed in the Freud Archives of the Library of Congress in Washington, with the understanding that it would not be made available for 50 to 100 years.

Sigmund Freud

Much of this material will eventually become accessible, if not also published, and undoubtedly in some future day Freud will be better known. It seems most likely, however, that important aspects of Freud's life will remain forever obscure.

A Jewish Childhood in Vienna

"I was born," writes Freud, "on May 6th, 1856, at Freiberg in Moravia, a small town in what is now Czechoslovakia."

> My parents were Jews, and I have remained a Jew myself. I have reason to believe that my father's family were settled for a long time on the Rhine (at Cologne), that, as a result of a persecution of the Jews during the fourteenth or fifteenth century, they fled eastwards, and that, in the course of the nineteenth century, they migrated back from Lithuania through Galacia into German Austria (Freud, 1925a, pp. 7–8).

His father, Jacob Freud, is said to have been a wool merchant, and it may have been the decline in textile manufacture in Freiberg, as well as hostility toward the tiny Jewish minority in this overwhelmingly Roman Catholic town, exacerbated by general economic distress and rising nationalism, that prompted him to relocate his family three years after Sigmund was born (Jones, 1953). They spent a year in Leipzig and then moved on to Vienna, where Freud was to live for almost the rest of his life.

Schlomo Sigismund, as Freud was named, grew up at a time when the Jewish world was rapidly changing. In his father's youth, to be a Jew meant being a member of a highly visible and severely oppressed minority. Emancipation in the middle of the nineteenth century brought dramatic changes for the Jews, although it did not mark the end of anti-Semitism. To illustrate for young Sigmund how much better things had become, Jacob Freud told of an incident in his own past.

> "When I was a young man," he said, "I went for a walk one Saturday in the streets of your birthplace; I was well dressed, and had a new fur cap on my head. A Christian came up to me and with a single blow knocked off my cap into the mud and shouted: 'Jew! get off the pavement!' " "And what did you do?" [Sigmund] asked. "I went into the roadway and picked up my cap," was his quiet reply (Freud, 1900, p. 197).

Appalled by his father's "unheroic conduct," Freud turned for consolation to fantasies of Hannibal, the Semitic general from Carthage who swore eternal hatred for Rome. What for the elder Freud may have been no more than a casual story during an afternoon's walk was to be for the younger one a long-enduring source of resentment—toward his cowardly father and toward the hostile world of the Gentiles.

Freud's early experience brought other complex emotional challenges to his young mind. He was the firstborn of seven children by his father's third wife. Jacob Freud was 40 years of age at the time of Sigmund's birth, his wife Amalia was 20—several years younger than Emanuel Freud, the elder son from Jacob's first marriage. Emanuel's son John, furthermore, was a year old when Sigmund was born. The two boys—nephew and uncle—were to be inseparable companions as well as frequent adversaries. To this early friendship Freud attributes the enduring pattern of all his subsequent relations with contemporaries. He always needed, he writes, an intimate friend and a hated enemy—ideally in the same person, though of course not at the same time (Freud, 1900, pp. 424, 483).

Until he was two and a half, Freud was cared for by a Catholic nanny said by his mother to be "an ugly, elderly, but clever woman." In spite of his nanny's occasional harshness, Freud supposes that he had grown to love her. She spoke with him frequently about God and hell and often took him with her to church. "When you returned home," his mother reported, "you preached and told us all about God Almighty." The sudden dismissal of Freud's nanny, when she was found to have some of his possessions, coincided with the birth of Freud's sister Anna, the second child to threaten Freud's exclusive claim on his mother. The first interloper, his brother Julius, died when the jealous Freud—always "the indisputable favorite of his mother"—was 17 months old. The outcome, he claims, was an enduring germ of guilt (Freud, 1900, pp. 247–248; 1985 [1897], pp. 219–221; Jones, 1953, p. 5).

Jones maintains that these events and odd family circumstances, together with young Sigmund's misconstruing of them, facilitated the greatest of Freud's discoveries, the Oedipus complex. They have also been the object of much recent speculation, especially about Freud's father as well as the nanny, who is thought to have been virtually a second mother to Freud. Both are linked to traumatic experiences in Freud's early life, perhaps even sexual abuse, and Freud's relation to each is thought to have been consequential in his later theorizing—about the psyche in general and human piety in particular (Balmary, 1979; Krüll, 1979; Vitz, 1988). There seems to be a consensus that their contributions to Freud's thinking about religion extends well beyond the specific religious ideas and practices that they may have taught him.

The Decline in Familial Piety

We know little with certainty about the religious climate in Freud's home. Freud says that his father came from a Hasidic background but was estranged from it as a young man. Nevertheless, he continued to revere the Hebrew scriptures, which for him were the only writings worthy of long hours of study. Freud (1925a, p. 8) himself reports a "deep engrossment in the Bible story," beginning shortly after he learned to read. Only much later did he recognize the effect that this fascination had on the direction of his subsequent interests. On Freud's thirty-fifth birthday—the beginning, according to Jewish tradition, of middle age—Jacob presented him with the newly rebound family Bible. The Hebrew inscription that Jacob lovingly wrote inside enjoins his son to draw upon this well of "wisdom, knowledge, and understanding." Whether or not Freud could still read Hebrew at that age remains a moot question (Rice, 1990).

Although Freud's parents apparently did not follow the Jewish dietary laws, they continued to observe major festivals. Years later, one of Freud's nieces was astonished one Seder to hear her grandfather recite the Passover Haggadah from memory. Freud's mother seems to have been far less invested in traditional Jewish observance. Although she was known on several occasions to have invoked God's blessings on behalf of her family, after her husband's death she gathered her family primarily on Christian, not Jewish, holidays. All in all, the family was not notably pious, and Freud emerged from it an avowed atheist (Heller, 1956; Rainey, 1975).

What little we know of Freud's youth underscores his serious disposition, his studiousness, and his privileged circumstances within the Freud household. Alone among the seven children to have his own room, Freud spent long hours in it reading and studying. Friends were received there, amidst the overflowing bookcases, and he would often take his evening meal at his desk, in order to conserve time for his studies. When the sounds of his eight-year-old sister Anna's piano practicing intruded into his sanctuary, he successfully appealed to have the piano removed, thus bringing to an end all musical education in the family. Freud's lifelong aversion to music was also to preclude musical instruction for his own children. So single-minded an interest in scholarly matters put Freud at the head of his class, gained him graduation with highest honors, and richly furnished a mind that would revolutionize the Western world (Bernays, 1940).

The Education of a Neuropathologist

In Vienna at that time, says Jones, the career choice for a Jew of Freud's intellectual bent was effectively twofold: law or medicine. Freud's broader interests in "the riddles of the world" did not fit neatly into either alternative, nor was he particularly interested in becoming a physician. For a while, in accord with childhood political ambitions, he expected to study jurisprudence. In the end his strong attraction to Charles Darwin's theories and—according to Freud's recollection—a chance hearing of the exalted "Fragment upon Nature" ascribed to Goethe (who, with Shakespeare, was one of his intellectual heroes) drew him to the study of the natural sciences and medicine (Wittels, 1931). Even with his matriculation as a medical student at the University of Vienna, however, Freud was to forage well beyond the prescribed course work, in the sciences as well as in philosophy. Among the most stimulating of his teachers was philosopher and psychologist Franz Brentano, the major forerunner of phenomenology and a former priest who challenged Freud to reconsider his atheistic convictions. It took Freud eight years—three more than the required minimum—to earn his MD, which he received not long before his twenty-fifth birthday in 1881 (Gay, 1988).

It was during these years of study that Freud became taken with the philosopher Ludwig Feuerbach, famous for his critique of religion. "Among all philosophers," Freud wrote to a friend in 1875, "I worship and admire this man the most" (quoted in Gay, 1988, p. 28). In his *Essence of Christianity* (1841), Feuerbach argues that human beings, finding their longings frustrated in this world, have created a God and a heaven as a means of fulfilling these wishes. God, he maintains, is a projection of all the excellencies of human nature; divested of these qualities, human beings conceive themselves as corrupt and wicked. Yet in the course of religious history, these qualities are gradually reclaimed, through what are conceived as the actions of God (pp. 174, 27–31). Although Freud later denied that Feuerbach had had lasting effect on his own thinking (Binswanger, 1956, p. 75), the numerous parallels between his own writings on religion and Feuerbach's are sufficiently striking to suggest a direct influence. As Van Harvey (1995) notes, however, Freud's theory comes out different in the end.

Another significant figure in Freud's life was Ernst Brücke, in whose physiology laboratory Freud was to work for six years, including one after he completed his medical studies. Brücke, who Freud (1926b, p. 253) said "carried more weight with me than any one else in my whole life," was a model of scientific discipline and rectitude and a representative of the movement in science known as Helmholtz's School of Medicine. As an exponent of this school, Brücke opposed the Romantic philosophy of nature popularly espoused in the early nineteenth century. He embraced instead an evolutionary physiology exclusively grounded in physical forces. Apparently brought to the door of Brücke's laboratory by the Romantic sentiments expressed in the essay on nature, once inside Freud became for a time a thoroughgoing materialist who kept Mother Nature at a safe distance. Under Brücke's influence, Freud was to acquire the principles that would later serve him in constructing his own distinctive theories (Gay, 1988, p. 26; Jones, 1953, p. 45).

Freud's work at Brücke's Institute seemed to open up for him the possibility of a theoretical career. He had proved himself a competent researcher and had even come close to making important discoveries. He was not, however, an experimentalist at heart. There was in Freud's nature, says Jones (p. 53), a "pronounced passive side," which rejected the active domination of experimentation in favor of the more passive viewing of microscopic investigation. Although he would always remain loyal to the scientist's ideal of intellectual integrity, whatever the cost, he finally grew impatient with the demands of precision and measurement. Long restrained, his speculative tendencies were again to dominate, eventually creating a human context in which he could exercise his penchant for contemplative understanding.

Two immediate motives seem to have impelled Freud's reluctant decision to practice medicine. First, there were no prospects for advancement at the Institute of Physiology, given the seniority of Brücke's two assistants and the upsurge of anti-Semitism in Vienna. Brücke himself had advised him to abandon a career in laboratory research, noting in particular Freud's financial straits. Second, Freud had fallen in love with Martha Bernays and hoped to marry her, once he established himself financially. Thus in spite of considerable inhibitions to practicing medicine, he undertook the three-year residency that would prepare him for a practice in neuropathology, a branch of medicine that was rather ill defined. At the same time he was able to conduct research at the Institute of Cerebral Anatomy. Publications of his laboratory and clinical observations on the physiological origins of nervous diseases won him an appointment as lecturer in neuropathology, a position that carried prestige and some privileges but no salary. A travel grant soon afterward allowed him to go to Paris, where from the autumn of 1885 to the spring of 1886, he was a student with Jean Martin Charcot at the Salpêtrière. Charcot, considered the greatest neurologist of his time, was the most important influence in turning Freud from neurophysiology to psychopathology (Jones, 1953).

The Growth of Freud's Thinking

Besides Brücke and Charcot, two others of Freud's associates played noteworthy roles in the evolution of his thinking. One was Josef Breuer, 14 years Freud's senior and a scientist–physician of considerable reputation and humanity. Freud had come to know Breuer, himself an adherent of the Helmholtz school, at the Institute of Physiology, where they became close personal friends. During Freud's last two years at the Institute, Breuer treated a now-famous patient, Anna O., who showed all the classic symptoms of hysteria, including—to Breuer's horror—a phantom pregnancy in response to his dedicated care. Freud was intrigued by Breuer's case and returned to it again and again as the years passed and his own thinking evolved. With much reluctance, Breuer finally agreed to publish it jointly, in the famous *Studies on Hysteria* (Breuer and Freud, 1895). Breuer was clearly ambivalent about the central role Freud had by now given the sexual life in the etiology of the psychoneuroses, though Breuer's own disturbing experience with Anna O. would seem, if anything, to confirm it. The compromise they effected for this book marked the beginning of the decline of their 20-year relationship, which was the first in a series of Freud's friendships to end in enmity.

Much of what we have come to know about the development of Freud's ideas we owe to the detailed and intimate letters he wrote to yet another associate, Wilhelm Fliess, whom Frank Sulloway (1979, p. 147) says is perhaps the most important of the four associates (including Brücke, Charcot, and Breuer) who influenced Freud's early psychoanalytic thinking. Two years younger than Freud, Fliess had much in common with him. He, too, was a medical specialist (in nose and throat) of Jewish middle-class origins, was solidly grounded in the humanities, and had been brought up in the teachings of the Helmholtz school. The two even shared the fate of suffering from recurrent migraine attacks and severe nasal infections. Brilliant and self-confident, Fliess centered his fanciful, even bizarre, speculations around the themes of bisexuality, periodicity, and numerology. Freud found himself immediately drawn to him, reports Jones, in an attitude of extreme dependency. The 254 letters that he wrote to Fliess between 1887 and 1902, along with the scientific notes and drafts sent occasionally to Fliess for his judgment and admiration, constitute an invaluable record of the gradual evolution of Freud's thinking, as well as the suffering that his struggle for insight cost him.

Freud's Creative Illness

In particular, we learn of Freud's own "very considerable psychoneurosis" (Jones, 1953, p. 304), which consisted primarily in severe attacks of anxiety and extreme changes in mood, as well as his related struggle with addiction to cigar smoking. This anxiety disorder haunted him for the better part of a decade, reaching its height during the years 1897 to 1900, shortly after his father's death. These are also the years during which he began his self-analysis—his most heroic feat, according to Jones—and put foward his most original theories, as he untangled the hidden threads of his own Oedipus complex. Convinced for several years that his patients' memories of childhood sexual seduction by some adult, usually the father, were literally true, he gradually—and seemingly reluctantly—came to view these fantasies, rather, as long-repressed wishes springing out of his patients' infantile sexuality. Through the healing process of his own analysis, he also came to appreciate the vital role of dream interpretation, the subject of his most important book, published in 1900.

His was a creative illness, says Ellenberger (1970), much like that found among shamans and mystics. Fliess played the role of the SHAMAN master or spiritual director, guiding the apprentice through his lonely ordeal until he suddenly emerged, transformed and triumphant in his new truth. Undoubtedly, Freud to some degree shared in the "ecstatic," dream-delivered aspects of shamanistic learning; but Ellenberger's formula may overemphasize Fliess's role in the teaching of the well-established, complex tradition that completes the shaman's education (see Eliade, 1951). In part it is a question of the sources of Freud's ideas. Is there a tradition with which Freud's work is continuous, perhaps one that Fliess shared, or is Freud's system the product of an exceptionally creative and well-furnished mind acting independently upon the puzzling disorder of neurotic symptoms, its own as well as others?

Psychoanalysis and the Jewish Tradition

As David Bakan (1958) points out, Freud's own occasional efforts to trace the origins of psychoanalysis are not particularly satisfying. He credits germinal ideas to persons who later deny having them, ideas that in any case do not account for Freud's elaborations. Alternatively, as in the instance of his dream theory, he unhelpfully credits "insight" that fortuitously fell his way. Jones, among others, would add that Freud's own life circumstances predisposed him to see patterns or to make connections that others had missed. Freud himself subscribes to such an explanation when he remarks in his address to the B'nai B'rith Society that "because I was a Jew I found myself free from many prejudices which restricted others in the use of their intellect; and as a Jew I was prepared to join the Opposition and to do without agreement with the 'compact majority' " (Freud, 1926a, p. 274).

Parallels to Jewish Mysticism: Freud's Jewish identity, which he affirmed again and again throughout his life, is thought by some scholars, often themselves Jewish, to have played a far more definitive role in his work than Freud ever acknowledged. Noting the preponderance of Jews both among patients and among practitioners of psychoanalysis, Abraham Roback (1918, 1929) asserts that Freud's method is "strongly reminiscent" of the symbolism underlying Jewish mystical philosophy, which is called KABBALA. "The stress laid on the male and female elements, the juggling of numbers, the exploitation of all sorts of symbols to suit a particular conjecture, and many other such indications, have their counterpart in psychoanalysis" (1929, p. 161). Roback adds that Jews are "racially inclined" toward introspection and analysis, toward seeking the origins of their experience as well as the "why?" or "whither?"—the question of purpose (pp. 184–185). "Psychoanalysis, on the whole," he concludes, "contains a mystical tendency," though one inclined toward the concrete rather than the abstract and unseen.

Bakan (1958) similarly hypothesizes in a more elaborate work that Freud's opus, though manifestly that of a scientist, is continuous with the Jewish mystical tradition. Bakan points out that many of the fundamental themes of psychoanalysis can be found in the *Zohar* or "Book of Splendor"—which for centuries was the most widely revered of the writings of the Jewish mystical tradition—if not also in the TALMUD, for which the *Zohar* is in large part a commentary. Among these themes are bisexuality and malevolent childhood impulses, an emphasis on family and sexual relationships, and a system of dream interpretation (see also Lorand, 1957). In addition, the psychoanalytic principle that requires therapists-in-training themselves to undergo analysis with experienced psychoanalysts is in keeping with the Kabbalistic tradition of oral transmission, in large part by allusion rather than direct expression.

Fliess's Possible Role: If Freud's psychoanalytic work is genuinely Kabbalistic, as Bakan maintains, is it possible that Henri Ellenberger is correct in taking Wilhelm Fliess to be Freud's master or guide, or at least one of several? Gershom Scholem (1960, p. 1) says that the Kabbala, with its "intricate, introverted symbolism," became "alien and disturbing" to the Jews of western Europe after they had resolutely turned to European culture late in the eighteenth century. Bakan notes, however, that among the Jews trained in the Western tradition of scholarship was a small group, including Vienna's most popular Jewish preacher, who were interested in applying this tradition to Kabbala. Elements in Fliess's theory—the presupposition of bisexuality, the employment of numerology, the notion of a predestined time of death—as well as the general flavor of it suggest that he shared such an interest and was "an even less secularized Kabbalist than Freud" (Bakan, p. 62). We cannot know, of course, precisely what role Fliess played in introducing Freud to Kabbala, if it was not already known to him. In any event, by the time Freud was writing *Moses and Monotheism,* he had apparently obtained a selection of books on Jewish mysticism: Chaim Bloch, a well-known student of Kabbala and Hasidism, claims to have seen in Freud's library a section of Judaica containing Kabbalistic works, including the *Zohar* (Bakan, 1960).

Freud's Objection to the Thesis: Unfortunately, no one has confirmed Bloch's observation, nor have the books in question ever been found. We also have evidence that Freud strongly objected to the thesis as it is briefly stated in Roback's *Jewish Influence in Modern Thought* (1929), which Roback had sent to him. In a "reproachful" letter to the book's author, Freud claims that his father was estranged early on from his Hasidic background and comments that his own "education was so un-Jewish that today I cannot even read your dedication, which is evidently written in Hebrew" (Freud, 1960, [1930], p. 395; Roback, 1957). The day before he wrote this letter, Freud reportedly remarked to Smiley Blanton (1971, pp. 42–43) that Roback's book "is not worth much"; "that psychoanalysis itself is a Jewish product," he added, "seems to me nonsense." To the charge of mysticism, he replied, "I think I am farthest from being a mystic." Yet Freud conceded that "There was a danger that people would consider psychoanalysis as primarily Jewish," as indeed they later did (Diller, 1991).

While vigorously working to dissociate psychoanalysis from Judaism, Freud continued to call attention to his own Jewish identity. In a series of recent studies, scholars have plumbed anew the evidence bearing on Freud's religious background, the depth of his father's learning (especially as reflected in his famous biblical inscription), and the critical importance of Freud's lifelong identity as a "Psychological Jew," in a phrase that Yosef Yerushalmi (1991) borrows from Philip Rieff (1959). Although thoroughly secularized, the Psychological Jew affirms certain traits considered to be quintessentially Jewish: "Intellectuality and independence of mind, the highest ethical and moral standards, concern for social justice, tenacity in the face of persecution," and fierce resistance to any prejudicial effort "to define them against their own wishes" (Yerushalmi, 1991, p. 10). Moshe Gresser (1994) argues that, in shaping a Jewish identity based on a dual allegiance to Jewish ethnicity, on the one hand, and to liberal humanism on the other, Freud offers a model of responsible human identity for our present age.

Other scholars have documented the powerful effects of the pride and sense of unity that issued from the Jewish consciousness of Freud and other psychoanalysts. Although it supported the growth of the movement, it also created tensions within it, alienating many of its non-Jewish members and giving an overall impression of sectarianism (Klein, 1981). It has also been argued that specific elements within the Jewish tradition, including its teachings regarding women and sexuality and the psychodynamics of the Jewish family, profoundly affected various of Freud's theories (Robert, 1974; Roith, 1987).

Given the virulent anti-Semitism in Vienna,[1] observes Bakan (1958), Freud may well have chosen to conceal any Jewish influences consciously known to him. He may also have feared that his borrowing of insights from Kabbala, once recognized, would be mistaken for commitment to a mystical point of view. The "openly horrified glance" that he gave to Viktor von Weizsacker (1954, p. 67), when von Weizsacker awkwardly confessed to being "perhaps something of a mystic on the side," gives us a measure of Freud's feelings about such a possibility. Yet it may be that Freud was "profoundly imbued with the principal conceptions of Judaism and the style of Jewish thought" only on the unconscious level (Fraenkel, 1959, p. 96).

Freud the Psychoanalyst

Whether or not Freud's disturbance truly had the dimensions of a "creative illness" and finally found resolution in a secularized form of Jewish mystical teachings, it left him free enough throughout to look after a family grown large—including six children, his wife Martha, and, from 1896 onward, his wife's sister Minna—as well as to maintain his practice as a specialist in nervous diseases. He had become the leading authority on children's paralyses and had published a book on aphasia, but he was becoming far more interested in the problems presented by his neurotic patients and the task of developing a comprehensive theory for understanding them. Espousing and then abandoning a range of treatment methods, from orthodox electrotherapy to hypnotic suggestion, Freud gradually came upon the method of FREE ASSOCIATION, which some take to be his most important achievement. Used with his patients and in his own self-analysis, this technique aided him in developing his psychology of dream interpretation and the consequential doctrine of infantile sexuality. By the time *The Interpretation of Dreams* was published, in 1900, the essential ground plan of psychoanalysis had been drawn.

Orthodoxy and Dissent: Throughout the decades that followed, Freud continued to work out the details of his theory and demonstrated how it might illuminate various aspects of human culture, including religion, a subject to which he was particularly drawn. Although Freud's ideas were at first greeted with alarm and hostility, when they were not contemptuously ignored, a growing circle of associates gathered around him, providing support and serving as his emissaries to the wider world. There were famous and painful defections from that circle, including Alfred Adler and C. G. Jung, who, with others, were to object to Freud's insistence that his hard-won insights not be compromised. In many ways a man of his own time and class, Freud was unprepared to accept his discovery of infantile sexuality. Yet once he was convinced of its importance, not just in the lives of neurotics but for

---

[1] One of the grounds on which Bakan's thesis is challenged is the claim that Freud greatly exaggerated the intensity of anti-Semitism in Austrian society during his lifetime. Roith (1987, p. 153), however, maintains that "The testimony from some of Freud's contemporaries . . . indicates that, if anything, it has been underestimated." Even if Freud was personally shielded from the evident "canker of anti-Semitism" by the heavily Jewish composition of the Viennese intelligentsia with which he was associated, as Marie Jahoda (1977, p. 7) suggests, he would still have recognized the dangers in wider circles. Scholars who reject Bakan's thesis on the grounds that there is no evidence that Freud was acquainted with the Jewish mystical tradition (e.g., Gay, 1987, pp. 130–131; Rice, 1990, p. 119) are silent about the claim that Kabbalistic works were seen in Freud's library.

The desk at which Sigmund Freud wrote for hours each morning, photographed shortly before he fled Vienna in 1938. The manuscript lying on the desk is thought to be his *Moses and Monotheism.*

all human beings, he was adamant that it be "our shibboleth" (Jones, 1957, p. 15). For the orthodox, it has remained one of the fundamental tenets of psychoanalysis.

The dissension among his followers punctuated an otherwise uneventful existence at Berggasse 19, the address of the apartment and offices in Vienna where Freud lived and worked for nearly half a century. In his professional quarters he surrounded himself with a profusion of books, pictures, rugs, and above all else, antiquities—ancient gods and goddesses, buddhas and BODHISATTVAS, terra-cotta heads, theriomorphic figures in wood or metal, stiffly posed bronze statuettes, funerary objects, oil lamps, vases—most of them from Egypt, Greece, and Rome, but some from the Near and Far East (see Engelman, 1976). These objects, crowding both his study and the consulting room, were silent witnesses to Freud's daily rhythm of patients, consultations, and writing, predictably interrupted with occasional meetings, weekly university lectures (as professor of neurology), and Saturday evenings of tarock, a card game associated with Kabbala. Summers brought long-anticipated opportunities for travel and extended holidays in the country, where Freud could happily satisfy his penchant for mountain walks (M. Freud, 1957; Jones, 1953, 1955).

The Way to Eternal Nothingness: It was the "splendid panorama" of the countryside and a reading of Flaubert's *Temptations of Saint Anthony* that one day in 1883 called up for him "the real riddles of life," "the awareness of our perplexity in the mysteriousness that reigns everywhere" (Jones, 1953, p. 175). That awareness undoubtedly intruded itself with increasing frequency in his last decades, when his writing grew increasingly speculative. Already preoccupied with death, in 1923 Freud was to begin a torturous 16-year struggle with cancer of the jaw, which finally so debilitated him that he requested of his physician a fatal overdose of morphine (Gay, 1988, pp. 651, 739–740). Before the end, however, the no-less-malignant forces of Nazism had burned his books and forced him, in 1938, to flee the city that he had both loved and hated. Resettled in England and resigned to his fate, he died a year later. At last he had found his "way to the longed-for rest, to eternal nothingness" (Freud, 1960 [1929], p. 392).

Freud was a man praised for unfailing honesty and moral courage; for tactful sensitivity and unsolicited generosity; for an enchanting, sometimes ironic sense of humor and an enormous capacity for enjoyment; for broad learning combined with a personal liking for simplicity. He was also said to be surprisingly unsophisticated, even naive, and capable of awkward indiscretion, irritating arbitrariness, and adamant prejudice. He was inclined, says Jones (1955, p. 412), sharply to divide people into liked and disliked. His associates agreed that his intuitive capacity for judging character was paradoxically poor. Among his life-long prejudices was a dislike of religion, or at least the less reflective form of it embraced by the masses, for whom he had profound contempt. It was their demand for consolation, he thought, that drove them to religion's assurances, which he himself refused to the very end.

AN OUTLINE OF PSYCHOANALYTIC THEORY

Freud offers us, says Gardner Murphy (1957, p. 103), "an epic view of human nature," a vision in which "artistic congruity and power are even more important than internal consistency or detailed conformity to fact." Although Freud claims that psychoanalysis is based firmly in observation and that it shares the Spartan world-view of positivistic science, his writings on love and death, and his eloquence on the fate of the individual struggling toward fuller humanity, have less the character of science than that of heroic poetry. Freud's science-as-epic also has elements of tragicomedy. On the one hand is the bondage to primordial and destructive passions, over which civilization's victories are at best temporary. On the other is the rootedness of all culture and individual aspiration in the embarrassingly mundane and muddled preoccupations of early childhood. Heroic indeed is the person who willingly sacrifices impulse gratification and courageously faces the hidden but still-living fantasies of his or her own infancy.

The Psyche's Reluctant Evolution

In the dark and unfathomable depths of the unconscious, postulates Freud, are two fundamental urges or drives (*Triebe*). One, aimed at the formation and preservation of unities, is Eros, or the life impulse; the other, which seeks to sever connections and return life to an inorganic state, is the drive toward death, the impulse of destruction. The first of these drives is responsible for the sexual and sexually derived interests of humankind. The second, when deflected outward by the first, is the source of human aggression. The "concurrent and mutually opposing action of the two basic [drives]," says Freud (1940, p. 149), "gives rise to the whole variegation of the phenomena of life." Yet they are only the first, though also the most fundamental, of the ANTINOMIES that constitute the human drama.

The Pleasure Principle: At birth and for a few months thereafter, the human infant is said to be governed solely by the PLEASURE PRINCIPLE. His[2] world of impressions has little of the order or clarity that he will later take for granted. Rather, his perceptions are limited to vague apprehensions of his general state of excitation. When tensions within increase, he experiences unpleasure; with their decrease

---

[2] The use of the generic 'he' is retained here, not only because avoiding it would require awkward circumlocutions but also because, throughout his account of psychosexual development, it was the male whom Freud had chiefly in mind. The masculine bias of psychoanalysis, about which more will be said, is helpfully analyzed in Strouse's *Women and Analysis* (1974).

comes pleasure. As his experiences gradually take on form and rhythm, the infant is able dimly to imagine the states or objects that will bring him relief, and indeed, their sheer presence in fantasy offers a short-lived consolation. These imaginings inevitably fail, of course, to satisfy his biological needs. Worse, his caretakers perversely refuse to share his conviction that the yet vaguely understood persons and objects in his surrounding world are at his beck and call. Only gradually does he relinquish exclusive obedience to the autistic and illogical laws of the infantile psyche, laws that in their totality Freud calls PRIMARY PROCESS.

Governed by the pleasure principle and primary process "thinking," the infant demands immediate gratification of his wishes. In addition, he is POLYMORPHOUSLY PERVERSE. It matters little to him who or what the object is, as long as it provides gratification. Once such a pleasure-yielding object is found, sexual energy or LIBIDO is invested in it, a process known as CATHEXIS. The child's mother, of course, is usually the first source of gratification. Thus the aspects of her that are represented in the child's experience become objects highly cathected with psychic energy. Parts of his own body, at first hardly distinguished from his mother's, are presumably also highly cathected with libido, a condition called NARCISSISM, after Narcissus, the youth in Greek myth who fell fatally in love with his own reflection.

The Reality Principle: Reality inexorably imposes its limitations on the young child, forcing him to renounce many of his cathexes, if not also the impulses they satisfy. Primary process gives way to SECONDARY PROCESS, the logical form of thinking characteristic of conscious awareness, and the pleasure principle is displaced by the REALITY PRINCIPLE, which will eventually enable the individual to effect a compromise between inner impulses and environmental demands and limitations. These new functions are the achievement of the nascent EGO (the Latin equivalent chosen by a translator for Freud's German *das Ich,* "the I"). The matrix out of which the ego arises and the psychical province that "remains the most important throughout life" (Freud, 1940, p. 145n) is called the ID (*das Es* or "the it," a label suggesting its alien quality). Forever unconscious, the id retains essentially unchanged the character of the infantile psyche. The pleasure principle and the primary process continue to function in it, but now they are monitored by unconscious portions of the ego, whose task it is to decide which impulses may be safely gratified, at what times, and in what objects. When it determines that some urges must be denied expression altogether, it opposes them through the formation of ANTICATHEXES, energy-absorbing mechanisms that block the establishment of cathexes.

Conflict and Defense: The ego, according to Freud, always remains the servant of the id. Its task is to forward the pleasure-seeking interests of the id while avoiding the anxiety that signals imminent danger of unpleasure. It is responsible for the process of SUBLIMATION, the unconscious diverting of illicit impulses into more highly refined and elaborated interests that are socially acceptable but allow partial satisfaction of biological needs. The ego also carries out DREAM WORK, the complex mental operations that transform unconscious thoughts and wishes into well-disguised dream fantasies. These manifest images, whether or not recalled upon waking, represent fulfillment of the latent wishes. Dream interpretation is the process of tracing this series of transformations backward, from manifest dream to latent dream content. By this means the psychoanalyst seeks to bypass the ego's unconscious defensive maneuvers and uncover the repressed mental contents that are the cause of the patient's symptoms. As we will see, the same principles of interpretation have been applied to other psychic manifestations, including religious texts and rituals.

The Psychosexual Stages

The evolution of the infant from an irrational and pleasure-centered organism to a mature, reality-oriented adult who is able, in Freud's famous phrase, "to love and to work," takes the child through several well-defined though overlapping stages. The first three of these "psychosexual stages" are identified in terms of the bodily or EROTOGENIC ZONE that serves as the primary source of "sexual" pleasure. Libido flows in turn toward each of these zones and the pleasure-giving objects associated with them. With time, the impingement of reality forces the child to renounce his undisguised and freely expressed interest in these pleasures and their vicissitudes. Disapproval is often sharp enough that the very memories of such pleasures are highly repressed. According to the psychoanalysts, it is because of this motivated forgetfulness, called INFANTILE AMNESIA, that we are likely to respond to their account of the child's development with skepticism.

The evidence for these stages is not inconsiderable. Some of it comes from observations of young children themselves, though their behavior is often ambiguous and subject to widely diverging interpretations. More commonly, the psychoanalysts have drawn their conclusions from adult patients. The varieties of sexual aberration are cited by Freud (1905) as illustrations of how the complexly structured sexual drive can "come apart" when blocked or fixated, revealing the components ordinarily absorbed into the whole. The behavior of severely regressed PSYCHOTICS has also been cited as evidence for the character of infantile preoccupations, although the legitimacy of generalizing from profoundly disturbed individuals to normal persons has been widely disputed. Especially valuable, therefore, are the reports and associations of adequately functioning adults as they undergo psychoanalysis. We should also not overlook the testimony of ordinary linguistic usage, especially in jokes, derogatory epithets, and obscene expressions, wherein the reference to infantile fantasies and bodily pleasures, though projected onto others, is typically undisguised.

Oral Stage: First to emerge in the developmental sequence is the ORAL STAGE, during which the mouth serves as the chief erotogenic zone. Although oral activity is obviously essential for nourishment of the body, it seems from the beginning to provide something more. "No one," says Freud (1905, p. 182), "who has seen a baby sinking back satiated from the breast and falling asleep with flushed cheeks and a blissful smile can escape the reflection that this picture persists as a prototype of the expression of sexual satisfaction in later life." Such satisfaction eventually comes to be sought apart from the taking of nourishment, especially after the child is forced to give up the mother's breast. In childhood it is achieved through the autoerotic practice of thumb-sucking; in adulthood it may be pursued through a variety of more or less socially acceptable forms of oral stimulation, including cigarette smoking and gum-chewing. The inclusion of biting and chewing signals the appearance of sadistic impulses to find pleasure by inflicting pain upon another. These impulses, more generally associated with the second phase of development, are an instance of the fusion of sexual and destructive urges.

The infant's experience during the oral stage, say the psychoanalysts, may profoundly condition the rest of his years. Deeply satisfying and undisturbed nursing will leave behind vague, unconscious memories of blissful and unbounded union with the mother and will likely predispose an individual to an optimistic outlook on life. Disappointment of oral needs, on the other hand, will incline a person to be consistently apprehensive, to the point that the worst in every situation is expected. Abnormal indulgence may in some individuals lead to an enduring attitude of passive expectation that someone will take care of them, whereas the opposite may breed impatience, a tendency to cling, or an aggressively demanding social attitude. Even one's choice of profession and hobbies may be rooted in oral eroticism (Abraham, 1924).

Anal Stage: In the ANAL STAGE, or sadistic-anal stage, as Freud usually referred to it, the major focus of pleasure and unpleasure moves to the other end of the alimentary canal, which he says is never without considerable erotogenic significance. The retention of fecal matter in the lower bowel, and then the sudden expulsion of it through the anal sphincters, can be the source of intense pleasure, sometimes mixed with pain. Sharing at first neither the adult's disgust with feces and the associated odors and sounds, nor the sense that they are lifeless foreign matter, the child initially sees his feces as a detachable, interesting, and valuable part of his own body. They are as well "his first 'gift': by producing them he can express his active compliance with his environment and, by withholding them, his disobedience" (Freud, 1905, p. 186). Thus the fecal mass may be used both for producing pleasurable sensations in the anal zone and for giving expression to his relations with his caretakers.

The psychoanalysts maintain that the attitudes and experiences associated with the learning of bowel control have far-reaching implications for later tendencies and values. The eliminatory process itself may take on the character of a "SCATO-LOGICAL ceremony," typically a REACTION FORMATION or pattern of behavior opposite in nature to the repressed desires. Broader traits of personality may also stem from events during the anal stage. According to Freud (1908), intense anal eroticism is commonly sublimated in the qualities of miserliness, obstinacy, and orderliness. Other traits, ranging from sadistic cruelty to creative productivity, are also thought to be rooted in this stage of development, much as specific adult interests and occupational choice may be (see Healy, Bronner, and Bowers, 1930).

Phallic Stage: The oral and anal stages entail no inevitable differences in experience or outcome for the two sexes. The third stage, however, marks the point of considerable divergence. The PHALLIC STAGE begins somewhere around the end of the third year, when the developing ego has achieved a measure of integration, and objects, especially the mother, have acquired coherence and stability. At this time the male child's interest turns to his genitals, whose sexual function he surely does not yet understand, though he is inclined vaguely to associate their sensations with his first love object, his mother. At the same time that he comes to desire exclusive claim on her love and attention, he experiences jealousy and rage toward all rivals, especially the father. Struck by the parallels to the Greek legend of Oedipus, who unwittingly murdered his father and married his mother, Freud named this pattern of object relations the *Oedipus complex.* Inverse Oedipal wishes are also possible; it is apparently not uncommon for the child to wish to take the place of the opposite-sexed parent and to enter into an erotic relationship with the parent of the same sex (Freud, 1923a, 1924). Indeed, Charles Brenner (1973, p. 106) asserts that generally the double attitude is held toward both parents.

The Oedipus complex, says Brenner, "is a real love affair," a "tempest of passions of love and hate." For many, he says, it is "the most intense affair of their lives." Inexorably, however, if family pathology does not encourage it, the complex is finally brought to an end by the deeply disquieted ego. On the one hand is the intolerable ambivalence of love and hate toward the same parental object. The father, after all, is cherished and loved protector as well as hated rival, and the desired mother may precipitate jealous anger when she spurns her young suitor's advances in favor of his father. On the other hand is the fear of castration or mutilation, which lies at the core of the CASTRATION COMPLEX.

Three factors converge to convince the young boy of the dreaded possibility of genital mutilation. First, he has already experienced the loss of the mother's breast and his own feces, both of which he once thought were parts of his own body. He may also have been threatened with the loss of his penis, when a parent or some other caretaker discovered him manipulating it. Most compelling of all is his realization that there are human beings who lack his prized organ, not, he thinks, because they are female, but because they too had forbidden desires and were severely punished for them. In the end, the child's narcissistic interest in his sex organ is normally great enough to triumph over "the libidinal cathexis of his parental objects," and thus the ego finally renounces the Oedipal desires (Freud, 1924, p. 176).

The object cathexes sacrificed at the end of the Oedipus complex are replaced by IDENTIFICATION. Instead of aspiring to displace one or the other of his parents, he identifies with their authority and values. In the process he either desexualizes and sublimates the forbidden libidinous trends or inhibits their aim, changing them into harmless impulses of tender affection. In the (probably rare) ideal case, the outcome is the actual abolishment of the Oedipus complex. If on the other hand the complex is only repressed, it will become a pathogenic element in the id (Freud, 1924).

The parental attitudes INTROJECTED into the ego, when the Oedipus complex is more or less successfully abolished, form the nucleus of the third division of the psyche, the SUPEREGO (*das Über-Ich,* "the above-I"), a largely unconscious factor experienced as the conscience. Although this ego ideal takes over the function of parental authority, it is often far more severe than the real parents. Its excessive severity, says Freud (1940, p. 206), "corresponds to the strength of the defence used against the temptation of the Oedipus complex." The superego will normally undergo modification through further identifications in later childhood, adolescence, and even adulthood. Yet its original nucleus "remains always the firmest and most effective part" (Brenner, 1973, p. 119).

The Oedipal conflict, its eventual resolution, and the concurrent establishment of the superego are no less a part of the female Oedipus complex. Like the boy, the young girl starts out with the mother as her strongest object relation. She too is thought to interpret the newly discovered fact of sex differences as idiosyncratic and the result of castration. However, in place of the boy's dread anticipation of a possible event, she experiences an after-the-fact combination of resentment, shame, and envy. Blaming her mother for her insufficient genital endowment, she turns for consolation and restitution to her father. Hopeful of compensation for the lost organ, which through the unconscious logic of primary process is equated with a child, she identifies with her mother and, in her mother's place, wishes to receive the gift of a baby from her father. Even after she abandons this fruitless longing and learns that she shares her fate with the entire female sex, she retains the feeling of inferiority. What was once an explicit *penis envy,* the feminine equivalent of castration anxiety, is displaced into the broader character trait of jealousy.

Although the girl also finds herself in an Oedipal triangle, her experience does not compel her to abandon it as decisively as the boy does. Whether or not her Oedipal attitude remains active, says Freud (1940), is not a matter of great consequence. If it does, however, she is likely to choose a husband resembling her father and to extend to him her father's authority. Her superego—the "heir of the Oedipus complex''—will have a correspondingly different character. Anticipating feminist displeasure and acknowledging his own uncertainties about the female Oedipus complex, Freud (1925b, 1933) suggests that the feminine superego is relatively less strong and more dependent on its emotional origins. Women are therefore likely to "show less sense of justice than men," to be "less ready to submit to the great exigencies of life," and are "more often influenced in their judgements by feelings of affection or hostility." Freud believes too that "the majority of men are also far behind the masculine ideal and that all human individuals, as a result of their bisexual disposition and of cross-inheritance, combine in themselves both masculine and feminine characteristics, so that pure masculinity and femininity remain theoretical constructions of uncertain content" (1925b, pp. 257–258).

For both sexes, the Oedipus and castration complexes are indisputably central to the phallic stage, yet other elements also play a role. Especially noteworthy are the urges to look and to gain knowledge, called SCOPOPHILIA and EPISTEMOPHILIA. Both urges are already "powerfully at work" in the anal stage, says Freud (1916–1917, p. 327), but they are most marked in the phallic stage, when they are directed above all to the parents' sexual life. If the interests in looking and in its counterpart, showing, persist unmodified into adulthood, they are known as voyeurism and exhibitionism. More often the scopophilic and epistemophilic drives are sublimated in a wide range of adult interests, among them philosophy and mysticism (Abraham, 1913). Other sensory modalities, including touching, hearing, tasting, and smelling, which happen to play a larger role in the two pre-Oedipal stages, may express sexual impulses no less than seeing.

With the resolution or at least subsiding of the Oedipal conflict, children of both sexes enter a period of LATENCY, which is relatively free of the crude sexual interests of infancy. Libidinal energy is redirected by means of sublimation or reaction formation into new activities and objects in the environment, many of them in association with the wider world of school and peer relations. Although sexual feelings are not altogether absent during this period, it is said to be marked by no significant further developments in their dynamics.

Genital Stage: The latency period comes to a close with the onset of puberty, when the fourth, genital stage of development is inaugurated. The occurrence of physiological sexual maturation brings with it the challenge of organizing the revivified cathexes of early childhood and subordinating them to the primacy of the genitals. According to Freud (1940, p. 155), some of these cathexes are retained as they originally developed; others serve a subordinate role in the preliminary stages of sexual intercourse; and still others remain outside the organization, either to be wholly SUPPRESSED or to be transformed into character traits or into sublimations with new aims. Given the myriad subtle complexities of human life, even during the first five or six years, it is no surprise that this process is frequently halted or left incomplete. The libido may be *fixated* at one of the earlier stages of development, a precondition for sexual deviation. Alternatively, genital organization may be incompletely attained, leaving intact certain pregenital cathexes to which the individual may *regress* in the absence of genital-stage satisfaction or in the face of certain life difficulties.

When the genital stage is successfully established, it marks the transformation of the individual from a narcissistic, pleasure-seeking infant to a well-socialized and reality-oriented adult who is capable of mature, heterosexual relationships. Where once the interests were only of the crassest and most self-serving variety, there is now a capacity for altruistic love, moral discernment, and cultural appreciation.

These achievements of the ego in its role as mediator among the conflicting demands of id, superego, and external reality are won only through a large measure of impulse renunciation, on which human culture depends. Yet even at its best the victory is only a temporary one, for each generation must begin anew, albeit with the help (or hindrance) of the one that came before. The victory is also incomplete, for the loftiest achievements of wish transformation retain hidden signs of their humble origins in the id's unrelenting demands.

The Enduring Inheritance from the Formative Years

Individuals vary enormously in how successfully they negotiate the danger-infested waters of the psychosexual stages. No one, however, comes through them without an unconscious residue of categories in terms of which, at some deep level, all experiences are interpreted. Other human beings are to some degree likely to be unconsciously perceived and responded to as though they were father, mother, brother, or sister. A wide range of objects or materials may unconsciously call forth a person's early attitudes toward the bodily parts and substances that played leading roles in the drama of infancy. The elemental modes by which the infant relates to the world of objects—such as sucking, biting, retaining, or expelling—may serve to encode any of a variety of individual–world interactions in adulthood. Subtle differences in contemporary states of mind and body may dissolve before primordial categories formed by the infantile experiences of hunger, satiation, anxiety, and guilt. The most abstract search for knowledge may reverberate with the long-forgotten questions and theories of childhood, especially about sex differences and the origins of babies. This residue of early object relations, bodily states, perceptions, fears, and fantasies inevitably colors and shapes, however subtly, the conscious everyday experience of even the most mature and reality-oriented adult.

Disturbance and Psychotherapy: The system of compromises among opposing demands that the ego works out during the years of immaturity continues to function throughout the individual's life. If all goes well, the ego persists in its task of gradually usurping more and more of the territory of the id, thus increasing its own stock of energy for use toward rational, highly sublimated ends. If, however, psychic and environmental circumstances conspire to threaten the ego's dominion, an elaborate system of *defense mechanisms* may be employed to eliminate the danger, including, first of all, REPRESSION and denial, and then in their train, FIXATION, REGRESSION, reaction formation, or PROJECTION, among others. At first, only dreams and the "psychopathology of everyday life"—minor slips of the tongue, puzzling forgetfulness, or small accidents (Freud, 1901)—may reveal this defensive process, although rigidity or constriction of the personality may also give evidence of the new demands on the ego's limited capacities. But when the threat that childhood dangers may be revived becomes too great, any of a large variety of neurotic symptoms may show themselves: anxiety states, physical disorders, obsessive thinking, COMPULSIVE rituals, sexual deviation, drug addiction, and so on. These symptoms may undergo complex secondary elaborations, involving the individual's entire character, and at worst they may culminate in the severe regression of psychosis or the tragically illusory solution of suicide (see Fenichel, 1945).

In the course of psychotherapy, the task of the psychoanalyst is to become an ally of the ego and help it to regain its authority. By means of *free association, dream analysis,* and strategic *interpretation* of the material provided by the patient, including the various forms of resistance offered by the unconscious ego, the analyst seeks to uncover the repressed mental contents responsible for the individual's disturbance.

Central to the success of a full-scale analysis, which generally requires more than a thousand sessions, is the phenomenon of TRANSFERENCE. This "new edition" of the old infantile conflict consists of a reenactment of the Oedipus situation, with the analyst cast in the role of parent. The gradual transformation of this repetition into a recollection is said, to the degree that it is successful, to free the patient from the influences of long-repressed impulses and to restore to the ego's service the libido held captive in the unconscious struggle. It is generally agreed that certain personality types and some kinds of disorder lend themselves to the psychoanalytic process far more readily than others.

A fuller account of psychoanalysis can be found in various booklength surveys (e.g., Bally, 1961; Brenner, 1973; A. Elliott, 1994; Healy, Bronner, and Bowers, 1930; Munroe, 1955; Wyss, 1961). The serious reader should also consult a brief but persuasive work by Bruno Bettelheim (1983), who argues that the English translations of the writings of Freud seriously distort some of his central concepts and misrepresent his humanistic reflections by rendering them in the language of medicine and science. The translations also attribute to Freud more definiteness and certainty than is found in his original German texts. Beyond these problems are the challenges of representing the subtleties of the enormous psychoanalytic literature and of presenting sufficient case material to vivify the theory and demonstrate the remarkable variety of ways in which the same psychic processes play themselves out in individual lives.

FREUD'S PSYCHOLOGY OF RELIGION

The outcome of applying psychoanalytic theory to religious phenomena is dependent above all on the interpreter's fundamental attitude toward religion. If we assume from the outset that religion has no objective validity, that it in no way points to a transcendent reality, we will likely conclude that religious experience, ideas, and rituals are simply a product of human needs and desires. If, instead, we perceive behind the panoply of religious phenomena a reality larger than human invention, we may see psychoanalysis as a means by which to comprehend the extraordinary variety of responses to the transcendent. It could thus become a means for purifying and deepening religious faith.

Freud the Godless Jew

Freud is notorious for his own attitude toward religion. Two of his followers, James Putnam and Oskar Pfister, tried to find in their mentor's unfailing courage and fierce dedication to truth the makings of a religious man or even the best of Christians. Freud himself doggedly insisted that he was a "God forsaken 'incredulous Jew' " who was "profoundly irreligious" (Hale, 1971, p. 105, 195; Jones, 1957, p. 20; Meng and Freud, 1963, p. 63). Yet Freud was no run-of-the-mill unbeliever merely indifferent to religion's claims. Rather, religion seems to have inspired in him an active hatred of it, or at least of Roman Catholicism, the dominant tradition in Freiberg and Vienna. When René Laforgue (1956, p. 344) urged Freud in 1937 to flee the Nazis, Freud is said to have retorted that his "true enemy" was not the Nazis but "Religion, the Roman Catholic Church." Some think that Freud's early experience with his Catholic nanny contributed to his hostility toward Christian doctrines and rites. It would be natural, too, for Freud to associate anti-Semitism with the tradition claimed by the great majority of Vienna's populace, even if certain of its officials had refrained from making "sharp anti-Jewish statements" (Rainey,

1975, p. 68). At any rate, his contempt for human nature was reserved above all for "the Christian Aryan variety" (Meng and Freud, 1963, p. 140).

We should not overestimate the specific character of Freud's antipathy to religion. What he described as his "completely negative attitude to religion, in any form and however attenuated" (Meng and Freud, p. 110) was directed at Jewish religious practice as well. Jones (1953, p. 140) says that Freud, who "detested all ceremonies, especially religious ones," had witnessed the Jewish wedding of a friend of his with "fascinated horror." Two years later, when he himself was about to marry, he briefly played with the idea of changing his government-required "confession" to Protestant, in order to avoid the complicated Jewish ceremonies that Austrian law would otherwise demand of him (Jones, p. 167). In the end, he learned the Hebrew prayers that were his to recite during the marriage rites, which for his sake were kept as simple as possible. Once married, Freud ruthlessly set about to wean his bride from the Jewish orthodoxy in which she had been reared. Their own children were to grow up innocent of any instruction in Jewish practice (Gay, 1988; M. Freud, 1957, p. 14).

God the Exalted Father

Freud was not content simply to banish religious observance from his household. He undertook an analysis of it as well, in the context of his general theory. According to one of his first statements on the matter, religion is at bottom "*nothing but psychology projected into the external world. . . .* One could venture to explain in this way the myths of paradise and the fall of man, of God, of good and evil, of immortality, and so on" (Freud, 1901, pp. 258–259). Precisely what in the psyche is projected Freud makes explicit in his study of Leonardo da Vinci. It should not surprise us, says Freud, that Leonardo, born out of wedlock and apparently fatherless for the first several years of his life, should have given occasion for charges of religious APOSTASY. Having escaped the intimidating presence of a father during early childhood, Leonardo found himself exceptionally free of "the fetters of authority," including those of religion.

Leonardo illustrates the fundamental proposition of Freud's psychology of religion: that religiousness in every form has its deepest roots in the Oedipus complex. Differences in religion reflect differences in the structure and fate of this complex. "A personal God is, psychologically, nothing other than an exalted father," says Freud (1910). "Biologically speaking, religiousness is to be traced to the small human child's long-drawn-out helplessness and need of help; and when at a later date he perceives how truly forlorn and weak he is when confronted with the great forces of life, he feels his condition as he did in childhood, and attempts to deny his own despondency by a regressive revival of the forces which protected his infancy" (p. 123). The "longing for the father," which "constitutes the root of every form of religion" (Freud, 1913, p. 148), inevitably calls up the entanglements of the Oedipus complex, including feelings of fear and guilt. Obedient submission to the OMNIPOTENT father of infancy, introjected as the ego ideal and projected as God, restores the long-lost relationship, although the tension of ambivalence will likely persist. When the relation with the father undergoes an exceptional development, as in Leonardo's case, so also will the individual's religious life.

A Physician's Conversion: The seminal role of the Oedipus complex in religious faith seemed evident to Freud in the case of an American physician who sought to win Freud over to Christian faith through letters and prayer. Learning of Freud's religious indifference through an interview published in 1927, the physician was moved to share with Freud an account of his own conversion experience. His first letter recounts how one afternoon of the year he graduated, he happened by the dissecting room while the body of a "sweet-faced dear old woman" was being carried to the autopsy table. Already troubled with doubts about Christian doctrine, the fledgling physician immediately thought, "There is no God: if there were a God he would not have allowed this dear old woman to be brought into the dissecting-room." Shortly thereafter he decided to stop going to church.

As he thought the matter over, however, an inner voice urged him to "consider the step" he was about to take. He silently said in reply, "If I knew of a certainty that Christianity was truth and the Bible was the Word of God, then I would accept it." In a matter of days, "God made it clear to my soul that the Bible was His Word, that the teachings about Jesus Christ were true, and that Jesus was our only hope. After such a clear revelation I accepted the Bible as God's Word and Jesus Christ as my personal Saviour. Since then God has revealed Himself to me by many infallible proofs." Freud, too, the pious doctor assured him, would discover God's truth if only he would open his mind.

Given the multitude of horrors that God has allowed throughout human history, mused Freud, why did the doctor's indignation toward God happen to break out in response to the dissection room impressions? Freud proposes the following interpretation.

> The sight of a woman's dead body, naked or on the point of being stripped, reminded the young man of his mother. It roused in him a longing for his mother which sprang from his Oedipus complex, and this was immediately completed by a feeling of indignation against his father. His ideas of "father" and "God" had not yet become widely separated; so that his desire to destroy his father could become conscious as doubt in the existence of God and could seek to justify itself in the eyes of reason as indignation about the ill-treatment of a mother-object. It is of course typical for a child to regard what his father does to his mother in sexual intercourse as ill-treatment. The new impulse, which was displaced into the sphere of religion, was only a repetition of the Oedipus situation and consequently soon met with a similar fate. It succumbed to a powerful opposing current. During the actual conflict the level of displacement was not maintained: there is no mention of arguments in justification of God, nor are we told what the infallible signs were by which God proved his existence to the doubter. The conflict seems to have been unfolded in the form of hallucinatory psychosis: inner voices were heard which uttered warnings against resistance to God. But the outcome of the struggle was displayed once again in the sphere of religion and it was of a kind predetermined by the fate of the Oedipus complex: complete submission to the will of God the Father (Freud, 1928, p. 171).

A Judge's Delusions: When the Oedipal disturbance is more serious, the transformation in the religious sphere will likely be more idiosyncratic, even bizarre. For Daniel Paul Schreber, a distinguished jurist in Dresden who wrote an elaborate and still-deluded account of his own psychotic illness, the outcome was an intricate psychotheological system with elements clearly revealing the PARANOID character of his disorder. Schreber believed that the Order of Things had become disrupted when the rays of God—who at times appears as a bumbling, obtuse fool—were attracted to Schreber, only to turn against him in an alliance with Schreber's ill-intentioned physician. This interference with the Order of Things, Schreber was convinced, led inexorably to the destruction of everyone in the world but himself. Thereafter, by becoming "unmanned" at God's behest and cultivating in himself for God's pleasure a constant state of spiritual "voluptuousness," Schreber thought that he would be transformed into God's wife. In this role he would become impregnated by the divine rays, give birth to a new race of human beings, and restore the world to its lost state of bliss.

In the peculiarities of Schreber's delusions, Freud (1911b) finds evidence once again for the infantile attitude of the boy toward his father, who in Schreber's case was an orthopedic physician famous as the founder of therapeutic gymnastics in Germany. Schreber's illness may be traced first of all, says Freud, to an outburst of homosexual libido, directed at the outset toward his doctor. Schreber's strong resistance to this fantasy transformed the physician into his persecutor and replaced him with the figure of God, whose requirement of a feminine attitude for cosmic purposes Schreber could more easily accept. The close association of Schreber's physician with God and their similar roles in Schreber's delusions suggested to Freud that they are duplications of the same important though ambivalent relation—that with his father.

The nature of Schreber's relations with his parents is largely a matter of conjecture. In the widely read books on child rearing authored by his father, however, we have vivid documentation of the Draconian techniques and sadistic orthopedic devices he recommended—and most probably employed on his own children as well—as a means of assuring faultless development and preventing masturbation. Such relentless assults on the bodies and personalities of his hapless children seem clearly to underlie the "divine miracles" by which the deranged Schreber found himself repeatedly and pointlessly tortured (Niederland, 1974).

Schreber's delusional system, says Freud (1911b, p. 56), was "a magnificent victory" won by the infantile sexual urges. Whereas the father had once vigorously sought to suppress young Schreber's sexuality, he now, as God Himself, required of Schreber constant voluptuousness. The paternal threat of castration is finally accepted, even embraced, as the wish to be transformed into a woman. Marriage to God (his father) fulfills his long-repressed inverse Oedipal wishes, and the offspring issuing from their union compensate for the conscious disappointment that he and his wife had no children.

The Origins of the Religious Traditions

Neither Schreber nor the American physician came upon his relgous convictions in a cultural vacuum. Although both had been assailed by doubts before the appearance of their newfound certainties, each had grown up in a society long steeped in religious values. That they were religious was therefore no mystery; what Freud found noteworthy was the content and intensity of their religious experiences and the particular circumstances associated with their occurrence.

Religion as Neurosis: Although as therapist Freud would naturally be interested in the religiousness apparent in individual lives, it was the larger question of religion's origin in the human race that was of consuming interest to him. The bulk of his work in the psychology of religion is directed to this problem. In his first publication on this subject, a paper contributed for the inaugural issue of the *Zeitschrift für Religionspsychologie,* Freud (1907) points to certain parallels between neurotic ceremonials and religious ritual. Both actions, he says, are carried out with scrupulous attention to every detail; they are conducted in isolation from all other activities and brook no interruption; and their neglect is followed by anxiety or guilt. There are also, of course, obvious differences. In contrast to neurotic rituals, sacred rites are performed in concert with other community members. Religious ceremonial is meaningful in every detail, whereas the neurotic's private observances seem utterly senseless. Yet ordinary worshipers, according to Freud, give little thought to the significance of the actions they carry out. They may be as unaware as the neurotic of the motives impelling their participation.

From his clinical practice Freud had concluded that the compulsive rituals of neurotics originate in the repression of a sexual impulse. The ceremonial springs up in part as a defense against the temptation to commit the forbidden act and in part as a protection against the unknown misfortune that the neurotic fearfully anticipates. Obsessive actions are also a compromise, so that they yield to some degree the pleasure they are designed to forestall.

"The formation of a religion, too," says Freud (p. 125), "seems to be based on the suppression, the renunciation, of certain instinctual impulses." In this instance, however, the rejected impulses are not exclusively sexual but include a variety of egoistic and socially harmful ones as well. Nevertheless, the outcome has much in common with neurotic ritual. The religious individual's struggle with temptation and feelings of guilt and the anxious expectation of divine retribution were familiar long before the neuroses were identified. In the religious realm, too, the process of suppression is only temporarily successful, necessitating acts of penance from time to time. Similarly, there is a tendency to displace the original concern onto once-trivial details, so that the minutiae of religious practice become the main thing. In the occasional commission of the forbidden acts in religion's name, even the feature of impulse gratification through compromise can be found. Religion, concludes Freud, may be viewed as a universal OBSESSIONAL NEUROSIS, just as neurosis may be described as a distorted private religion.

A Fateful Patricide: The parallels between neurotic preoccupations and religious or protoreligious conduct soon again became a matter of special interest to Freud. In his book *Totem and Taboo* (1913), he undertook to explain two associated practices of certain "primitive" peoples. The tribe and the members' common ancestry come to be symbolized by means of some object, usually an animal. This totem, as it is called, is treated as sacred and may not ordinarily be killed. And these peoples also established elaborate taboos, including prohibitions designed to prevent sexual relations between members of the same totem clan. Again the resemblance to obsessional neurosis seems apparent. Foremost is the submission to unexplainable prohibitions, with the unshakable conviction that violation of them, however unwitting, will be automatically and severely punished. The chief prohibition of both obsessional neurosis and taboo is against touching—either in a literal sense or in the broadest possible meaning, that of contact in any form. DISPLACEMENT operates in both cases: the prohibition extends from one object to the next, in a form of contagion. And both give rise to ceremonial acts of expiation, penance, or purification, acts that must not be omitted.

The thought patterns underlying all forms of neurosis bear a resemblance to the animistic and magical thinking found among totemic peoples. Neurotics demonstrate a delusion that Freud calls OMNIPOTENCE OF THOUGHTS, the conviction that the mere thinking of some eventuality is sufficient to bring it about. Thus the neurotic who unconsciously wishes for the death of some associate feels a sense of guilt appropriate to actually having carried out these wishes. Omnipotence of thoughts may be traced through three stages in the evolution of human understanding of the universe, says Freud. In the *animistic stage,* which corresponds to the period of narcissism in the young child, human beings ascribe omnipotence to themselves. In the *religious stage,* which parallels the shifting of libido to external objects, above all to the parents, the omnipotence is extended to the gods, though it is also retained as a means of influencing them. In the *scientific stage*, the counterpart of which is the individual's renunciation of the pleasure principle and the attainment of reality-oriented maturity, human omnipotence is largely abandoned, except for the lingering faith in the power of the human mind to understand the laws of reality.

The pattern of similarities between the protoreligious concerns of totemic tribes and the ceremonials and thought patterns of obsessive neurotics led Freud to look for deeper connections. He was struck by the correspondence between the fundamental prohibitions of TOTEMISM—against killing the totem animal and against have sexual intercourse with members of the same totem group—and the two aspects of the Oedipus complex: the desire to eliminate the father and the wish to possess the mother. That the totem does represent the father, argues Freud, is suggested by two findings. The tribe members themselves believe that they are descendants of the totem, and young children occasionally have a PHOBIA of a particular species of animal. Analysis has identified animal phobias as a displacement of the ambivalence felt toward the father. If the totem animal is indeed the father, the two core prohibitions of totemism correspond to childhood's forbidden Oedipal wishes.

What remained to be explained is how totemism first came about. Drawing on other scholars' findings and speculations, some of which were disputed even at that time, Freud postulated the following scenario. (He later qualified this sequence of events as a condensation of what must have happened countless times over thousands of years [Freud, 1939, p. 81].) The setting is the small "horde" or group in which, according to Darwin's conjecture, early human beings lived. The horde was dominated by one powerful and violently jealous male who had seized the women for himself and had driven off or killed all rivals, including his sons.

> One day the brothers who had been driven out came together, killed and devoured their father and so made an end of the patriarchal horde. United, they had the courage to do and succeeded in doing what would have been impossible for them individually. . . . Cannibal savages as they were, it goes without saying that they devoured their victim as well as killing him. The violent primal father had doubtless been the feared and envied model of each one of the company of brothers: and in the act of devouring him they accomplished their identification with him, and each one of them acquired a portion of his strength (Freud, 1913, pp. 141–142).

Their monstrous deed done, the brothers found themselves filled with remorse, for they had loved and admired their father as well. Moreover, with their father's death they had become rivals among themselves for the possession of the women. Burdened by guilt and faced with imminent collapse of their social organization, "They revoked their deed by forbidding the killing of the totem, the substitute for their father; and they renounced its fruits by resigning their claim to the women who had now been set free" (p. 143). Thus were born the two fundamental taboos of totemism.

The momentous and terrible event lived on in the sons' memories and soon came to be commemorated and symbolically repeated in the totem feast. Here Freud is following the controversial hypothesis of W. Robertson Smith (1889). In his classic study of Semitic religion, Smith concluded that, before the emergence of anthropomorphic deities, periodic ritual killing and communal eating of the sacred totem animal had been an important element in totemism, which he thought to be the starting point of all religious traditions. According to Freud's interpretation, the totem meal represents a temporary suspension of remorseful obedience to the father and a renewed effort to appropriate his powers. Thus totem religion preserves the ambivalence implicit in the Oedipus complex.

In Freud's view, the impress of the Oedipus complex remains on all later religious forms and practices, including those of our own day. Freud postulates that each succeeding generation down to the present has inherited the sense of guilt resulting from having killed and devoured the father—or, given the omnipotence of thoughts, from merely having entertained such acts in fantasy. Although Freud acknowledges the grave difficulties of so uncertain and bold a premise, he argues that such a hypothesis is necessary to account for the survival of these traditions over the centuries.

Freud maintains that the Christian doctrine of atonement represents a particularly undisguised acknowledgment of the "guilty primaeval deed." Because humankind was redeemed from its burden of original sin when Christ gave up his own life, we may infer that the sin was murder. That the outcome of Christ's sacrifice was reconciliation with God the Father suggests that the crime to be expiated was PATRICIDE. The son's ambivalence toward the father also plays a role here, for through his offering of atonement Christ himself became God and now replaces the Father as the center of religious devotion. The revival of the ancient totemic meal in the form of the EUCHARIST, the symbolic consumption of the body and blood of Christ, serves both as a means of identifying with the son in his new role and as a "fresh elimination of the father, a repetition of the guilty deed" (p. 155).

Freud's Historical Novel: The criticism that *Totem and Taboo* unleashed seems to have been a major factor in Freud's considerable hesitancy two decades later to publish what would be his last book, *Moses and Monotheism.* Originally entitled "The Man Moses, an Historical Novel," it was a work that Freud never expected to publish, partly because he recognized that the historical evidence for his theory was insufficient. He also feared that Father Wilhelm Schmidt, an ethnologist said to be a confidant of the Pope and influential in Austrian politics, would like his new book no more than he did *Totem and Taboo* and in response would be instrumental in placing a ban on psychoanalysis in Vienna (E. L. Freud, 1970 [1934], pp. 91–92). In addition, Freud anticipated an "onslaught" against it by his fellow Jews (Schur, 1972, p. 520). In spite of these misgivings, Freud published the first two relatively brief sections of the eccentrically constructed book in 1937, and the last, most controversial part after his arrival in England in 1938. The book as a whole appeared in German and English in 1939.

The themes of *Moses and Monotheism* are essentially continuous with those of *Totem and Taboo.* Comparing the life of a people to that of the individual psyche, Freud postulates that totemism, the presumed first stage of all religious traditions, signaled the beginning of a slow "return of the repressed," a gradual developmental process through which the totem animal's place was finally taken by a single anthropomorphic deity. The virtual recovery of the primal father in the form of the deity, after a long period of latency, was marked at first, Freud says, by the experience of awe and rapturous devotion. It was not long, however, before the hostile feelings once again moved to the fore. This process and its consequences for Judaism are the chief concern of *Moses and Monotheism,* though Freud also considers the implications for the Christian tradition and for religion generally.

Freud's account of the development of the Jewish tradition begins with speculation on the origins of its founder, Moses. Noting first that the name Moses is itself Egyptian in origin, Freud draws on Otto Rank's (1909) study of hero myths to argue that the legendary rescue of the infant Moses by an Egyptian princess serves to disguise his true identity. In reality, concludes Freud, Moses was an Egyptian, probably from an aristocratic family and perhaps a high official or a priest.

According to Freud's reconstruction, Moses was a member of the narrow circle of followers of Ikhnaton, the Egyptian pharaoh who zealously promulgated the monotheistic worship of the sun god Aten. When the king died and his alienated people returned to their older religious traditions, Moses turned in disappointment to the Jews, whom he chose as his people and protégés. He instructed them in the Aten religion, introduced among them the Egyptian custom of CIRCUMCISION, and with a retinue of his closest followers (the Levites, according to Freud) led them peacefully out of Egypt.

Unable to tolerate so highly spiritualized a religion, the wandering Jews repeatedly sought to overthrow Moses' tyrannical leadership, until one terrible day they finally murdered him. Several generations later, perhaps, during which time the memory of Moses and his teachings were preserved by the Levites, the Jewish tribes came under the influence of a new religion, centering on the worship of Yahweh, a bloodthirsty and demonic volcano god of local reputation. The mediator in this new religion, the son-in-law of the Midianite priest Jethro, was also named Moses. The outcome was a compromise. The practice of circumcision was retained, Yahweh was credited with the liberation from Egypt (highly dramatized to fit his character), and the Egyptian Moses was substituted for the Midianite one. To make it appear that Yahweh had long been the god of the Jews, the legends of Abraham, Isaac, and Jacob were introduced.

Like repressed childhood traumas, the disavowed facts and ideas that did not fit into the new version of the tradition's origins lived on among the descendants of those who had followed the first Moses out of Egypt. Like repressed events, the religion of the Egyptian Moses gradually returned, until it came once more to dominate. The Jews are indebted to this religion, says Freud, for their grand conception of a single, Almighty God; for the sense of having been chosen by Him for His special favor; and, through the prohibition against making images of God, for their exceptional advances in intellectuality and renunciation of impulses. Yet they also carry the burden of a father murder, which itself harks back to a far earlier one, in the totemic past. Remorse for having killed Moses stimulates the wishful hope for the Messiah, the return of the murdered Father. The Jews' steadfast refusal to recognize Him in Christ, and thus to admit, with Christians, their inherited crime of patricide, leaves them with an insatiable sense of guilt that inspires ever-new raptures of moral asceticism. For their guilt the Christian world continues to make them do penance.

Religion's Precarious Future

Although the history of the Jews has given them an exceptional disposition, they share with all other people the two universal sources of religious ideas: the unconscious racial memories of the slaughter of the primal father and the early childhood experiences of their own parents. The second source, the personal origin of religion, receives renewed emphasis in the most widely read of Freud's writings on religion, *The Future of an Illusion* (1927). In this work, as the title suggests, he raises the question whether humankind might someday do without the consoling "illusions" of religious belief.

In his notorious branding of religion as ILLUSION, Freud did not mean to say that religious persons are necessarily deceived or misled (though he clearly thinks they are). Rather, by means of this epithet he sought to emphasize the preeminent role of human wishes among the motives prompting religious belief and practice. The powerful and enduring nature of religious dogmas, which are supported not through observation and reason but through unchallengeable appeals to the authority of the past, is compelling evidence, he says, that they are illusions, "fulfilments of the oldest, strongest and most urgent wishes of mankind. The secret of their strength lies in the strength of those wishes" (p. 30).

The personal roots of religiousness, Freud reiterates, lie in the infantile past of the individual, in the periods of terrifying helplessness that were relieved by the mother, the first love object, and later by the protective love of the stronger father. The discovery that this helplessness does not end with childhood; that one is endangered throughout life by the powers of nature, by other human beings, and even by forces within oneself; and that death will finally upset life's precarious balance brings back the old anxieties and the desperate longing for the care of the powerful father. In such a manner is born the idea of a benevolent Providence, OMNISCIENT and omnipotent, who protects human beings from the awesome forces of nature, rewards and punishes evil, and promises perfection in life after death.

This irrational origin of religious ideas gives them the character of sanctity and inviolability, which also extends to the laws and institutions that impose the renunciation of impulses on which civilization depends. Unfortunately, both the ascetic demands and the promised consolations of religion have often been insufficient to restrain the majority of persons who have not internalized culture's prohibitions. Even in periods when religious teachings had greater influence than we see today, it is doubtful that people were more content with civilization or less opposed to it. "If the achievements of religion in respect to man's happiness, susceptibility to culture and moral control are no better than this," asserts Freud, "the question cannot but arise whether we are not overrating its necessity for mankind, and whether we do wisely in basing our cultural demands upon it" (p. 38).

The support of civilization's ordinances by means of religious sanctions and rewards has several important implications. Whereas the control of impulses is ideally carried out by the intellect, religion seeks to do it through emotion. The masses have renounced impulse expression not out of reasonableness but out of fear. The aura of sanctity surrounding society's institutions, moreover, leads to a rigidity in them that precludes revision or reinterpretation. Most disturbing of all, obedience depends on acceptance of the dogmas used to justify the cultural prohibition; a decline in religious belief, therefore, can only mean chaos.

Religion, Freud argues, is no less dangerous for individuals than it is for society. Introducing religious dogma before children are spontaneously interested in it or capable of grasping its significance, and then discouraging critical reflection on it, is likely to have but one outcome: dominance by prohibitions of thought and neurotic control of impulses through repression. That acceptance of this "universal neurosis" protects the devout individual from the dangers of certain personal neurotic disorders is surely insufficient compensation for these limitations. As Freud sees it, only the abandonment of religion and its dogmatic teachings about reality will free a society and the individuals who compose it to grow beyond this immature phase of development. "The whole thing is so patently infantile, so foreign to reality," Freud writes with exceptional candor in *Civilization and Its Discontents* (1930, p. 74), "that to anyone with a friendly attitude to humanity it is painful to think that the great majority of mortals will never be able to rise above this view of life."

What does Freud offer in religion's place? Science, not intuition, he says, is the only way we may come to know reality outside ourselves. What science and reason cannot tell us—and the gaps are many—we will have to do without. Persons who have been "sensibly brought up" and educated to reality will leave behind the warm and comfortable home of childhood, facing with courage and resignation the helplessness and insignificance that is their lot. With time, life will become tolerable for everyone and at long last civilization will no longer be oppressive.

Sons and Fathers: Religion's Masculine Roots

Although both sexes experience infantile helplessness, Freud's psychology of religion is otherwise clearly centered in masculine reactivity. It is the *male's* ambivalent relation with his father, both in his own and in the race's childhood, that lies at the core of religion as Freud views it. It is a telling fact that each of Freud's few case studies of individual piety—all but one of them brief and based exclusively on personal or historical documents—is of a male subject: Leonardo, Schreber, and the American physician, whom we have already encountered; the obsessively pious "Wolf Man" who sublimated his masochistic and homosexual impulses in an identification with Christ (Freud, 1918; Gardiner, 1971); and Christoph Haizmann, a seventeenth-century Bavarian painter who thought himself in bondage to the Devil. (The Devil was a duplicate, according to Freud's [1923b] analysis, of the subject's deceased father and a substitute for him [see Vandendriessche, 1965].) Apart from a short and curiously unpsychological paper tracing the continuity of the cult of the goddess Diana with present-day worship of the Virgin Mary (Freud, 1911a; see Le Rider, 1993) as well as a few other passing references to mother–goddesses, Freud overlooks projections in religion of the young child's PRE-OEDIPAL relationship with its mother. That religion may entail reactivation of the even earlier, narcissistic stage of development, before the ego has separated itself from the external world, Freud (1930) does acknowledge in his comments on the objectless "OCEANIC FEELING" associated with mystical states. Yet he considers it a phenomenon adventitiously joined to religion and one difficult to study because of its "almost intangible quantities" (p. 72).

Given Freud's commitment to OVERDETERMINATION, the principle that every behavior and experience has multiple causes, we would not expect so single-minded an emphasis on the Oedipus complex in his discussion of religion's origins. Indeed, Freud (1913, p. 100) assures us that psychoanalysis will not "be tempted to trace the origin of anything so complicated as religion to a single source." When he adds in the same breath that psychoanalysis is "duty bound . . . to lay all the emphasis upon one particular source," he disclaims that it is the only one or even the most important among many. It happens merely to be the one, he seems to imply, that the psychoanalyst is most competent to trace. Other researchers, he says, will have to estimate its relative importance.

Freud's emphasis on the *male* Oedipus complex rests on an assumption that he makes explicit in his essay *The Ego and the Id* (1923a). "The male sex," he writes, "seems to have taken the lead" in the acquisition of "religion, morality, and a social sense—the chief elements in the higher side of man. . . . They seem to have then been transmitted to women by cross-inheritance." The logic is straightforward. The superego, formed by identification with the father, becomes "a substitute for a longing for the father," and thus "it contains the germ from which all religions have evolved" (p. 37). As we observed earlier in this chapter, the girl's castration complex is of such a character that the feminine superego is less well established.

Accordingly, it is less likely than the masculine superego to manifest itself in the religious beliefs and observances that are the focus of Freud's psychology of religion.

FURTHER STUDIES ON THE MODEL OF FREUD

Freud was not the first, of course, to suggest that religion is the projection of human subjectivity or the seeking of compensation in the face of life's disappointments and inequalities. Nor did he originate the critique of religious ideas and experience that finds their origin in human sexuality. His contributions have been extraordinarily influential primarily because of his fame as the founder of psychoanalysis and his spelling out of the specific dynamics that he saw at work in the religious life.

The most immediate response to Freud's psychoanalytic approach to religion came from within his own circle of associates, especially from Ernest Jones, Oskar Pfister, Otto Rank, and Theodor Reik. Also influenced were other analysts or scholars similarly convinced of the value of psychoanalysis, though less intimately associated with Freud, such as the Hungarian anthropologist Géza Róheim. Soon the possibility of casting new light on religion by means of psychoanalysis attracted worldwide interest from contributors of diverse backgrounds and motives. Criticism was also rapidly forthcoming. Today the literature dealing with psychoanalysis and religion, though predictably uneven in quality, consists of many hundreds of books and articles.[3]

Freud's analysis of religion can be characterized in the briefest possible compass by recalling his fundamental explanatory construct, the Oedipus complex; the specific phenomena that engaged his interest, the rites of "primitive" peoples and the development of the Jewish tradition; and his basic attitude toward religion, a negative one. With a few notable exceptions, the earliest contributors to the psychoanalysis of religion essentially followed Freud in all three of these respects. These three features represent much of the literature even today. The following sampling of orthodox psychoanalytic studies is organized in terms of them.

OEDIPAL THEMES IN RELIGION

According to Ernest Jones (1927, p. 195), "the outstanding conclusion" that emerges from the first two decades of psychoanalytic research on religion is that "The religious life represents a dramatization on a cosmic plane of the emotions, fears and longings which arose in the child's relation to his parents." This insight, he says, can help explain five characteristics of religion that other scholars have used to define or epitomize it. (1) The qualities attributed to a *supernatural spiritual order* or to beings of such an order, as well as the emotional attitudes shown toward them, "are all direct reproductions of the child's attitude toward his parents." There is often a trinity of beings—Father, Mother, and Son—though in the Christian Trinity, in which the Mother is replaced by the male Holy Ghost, the Oedipal wishes have been renounced and the Father attachment has been emphasized

---

[3] For bibliographies on psychoanalysis and religion, see Capps, Rambo, and Ransohoff, 1976; A. Cronbach, 1926, 1931–1932, 1946; Grinstein, 1956–1973; Meissner, 1961; Reik, 1921a, 1921b; Spiegel, 1972; and especially Beit-Hallahmi, 1978, 1996, and Nase and Scharfenberg, 1977.

(Jones, 1928). (2) Anxious *concern with death* reflects above all the ambivalence felt by the individual toward loved persons. "Dread of death," says Jones (1927, p. 196), "invariably proves clinically to be the expression of repressed death wishes against loved objects." This anxiety also reflects, he claims, the intimate association in the unconscious between death and castration. (3) The sense of *meaning and supreme values* and (4) the *association with morality* both reveal the strivings of the superego, the desire to accord oneself with the ego ideal in order to be approved by and reconciled with the Father–God. (5) The *feeling of inadequacy*, the conviction of sin and guilt, springs from the child's unsuccessful efforts "to make all his impulses conform with adult moral standards" (p. 197). The "profound Oedipus origin of the sense of sin" accounts both for intense longing after salvation and for the savage depictions of eternal damnation, which "emanate from the infant's lively and unrestrained sadistic phantasies and are of the same nature as his own hostile wishes against his father for which the punishments are (projected) retaliations" (Jones, 1930, p. 204).

A Scrupulous Unitarian

Patristics scholar and lay analyst Robert Casey (1942) illustrates the feelings of guilt that are the legacy of the Oedipus complex and "the stuff of religion" in a brief case report of an elderly, unmarried woman. Throughout her life this woman had embraced the liberal, guilt-minimizing theology of the Unitarians and the sunny optimism of the New England transcendentalists. At the same time, she was markedly ascetic and overscrupulous. She strictly avoided work of any kind on Sundays, gave generously to others but seldom indulged herself, and was prone to self-reproach and exaggerated remorse over trivial matters. At 75, when she developed senile dementia, she became convinced that she had committed an unspecified but unforgivable sin that antedated Christ, Adam, and even God Himself. Subject to fits of profoundly sorrowful weeping and bitter self-recrimination, she saw no hope for expiation.

Casey interprets the woman's DELUSIONS as evidence of long-standing and powerful wishes for the father for whom she felt personally responsible. Before the illness, her liberal theology and optimistic world-view served as unconscious defense mechanisms against her incestuous wishes. Her anxious denial of the traditional pessimistic view of human nature as well as the notion of a severe and exacting God was undergirded by her active interest in biblical criticism. Feelings of guilt over the unrecognized fantasies expressed themselves in exceptional self-denial and SCRUPULOSITY along with exaggerated guilt feelings over matters seemingly unrelated to the repressed wishes.

A Pietist's Sublimations

The case of Count Nicolaus Ludwig von Zinzendorf, the eighteenth-century Moravian leader and theologian whom some of his fellow Lutherans considered insane, illustrates both the potential ramifications of the Oedipal phase and the exceptional forms it can take. Zinzendorf was only a few weeks old when his father, a minister of state in Saxony, died from massive hemorrhaging brought on by pulmonary tuberculosis. At the age of four, when his zealously pietistic mother remarried, he was given over to his grandmother, the Baroness Catherine von Gersdorf, and his aunt Henrietta, 14 years his senior. The baroness was an evangelical scholar of some reputation, and her castle was a frequent meeting place for other eminent Pietists. They and his demanding private tutor, a man of exceptional religious

Count Nicolaus Ludwig von Zinzendorf, German pietist and founder of the Moravian movement.

feeling, were for years the precocious Zinzendorf's primary associates. He was not allowed the company of other children until his unhappy stay at boarding school, between the ages of 10 and 16.

The devotional fervor of the Pietists found a place in Zinzendorf's own heart almost from the beginning. Deprived of his father, of whom his mother frequently spoke, and then of his mother, by a father substitute who made his appearance during the critical Oedipal period, Zinzendorf found consolation and love in the figure of Jesus. "From the earliest years," Arthur Lewis (1962) writes, "Zinzendorf enjoyed an intimate and entirely natural companionship with Jesus Christ" (p. 23). Intimate it clearly was; its naturalness, by Pfister's (1910a) account, is another question altogether. From calling Jesus "the creator" or "pure bridegroom of my soul" Zinzendorf came in his fifth decade to be preoccupied with Jesus' cold sweat, wounds, and blood, with his lifeless corpse, and above all with the wound in his side (see Excerpt 7.1). Zinzendorf's religious libido, says Pfister, was devoted to the "lateral cavity" with a passion that reached orgasmic ecstasy (p. 57). Pfister observes that Zinzendorf unmistakably describes this side wound as the female genitals, in their service both as a passageway of birth and as an organ of sexual relations. Zinzendorf was also fascinated by the circumcision of Jesus, which he made the subject of numerous talks and hymns. Thus to Jesus he attributed both male and female genitalia. It is through Christ, says Zinzendorf, that the word "shame" is abolished in relation to these "dear organs" (p. 83). The representation of Jesus as an ANDROGYNOUS father–bridegroom was paralleled by the transformation of the Holy Ghost into the Mother and the Father–God into a Grandfather or Father-in-Law.

Excerpt 7.1

The fanatical preoccupation with the wounds of Christ that permeated the Moravian Church while under Zinzendorf's domination is reflected in the following hymn. It is one of thousands that they composed to express their love of Christ the Spiritual Bridegroom and to celebrate their redemption through his blood and wounds.

> Our husband's Side-wound is indeed
> The queen of all his wounds;
> On this the little pidgeons feed,
> Whom cross' air surrounds.

There they fly in and out and sing,
Side's blood is seen on every wing.
The bill that picks the Side-hole's floor,
Is red of blood all o'er.

Ye cross'-air birds, swell the notes
Of the sweet Side-hole song,
That fountain's juice will clear your throats,
And help to hold it long.
Each day and year shall higher raise
The Side-hole's glory, love and praise:
Hallelujah! Hallelujah!
To the Side Gloria!

Source:
From *A Collection of Hymns of the Children of God in all Ages . . . designed chiefly for the use of the congregations in union with the Brethren's Church* (London, 1754), no. 460, quoted in J. J. Sessler, *Communal Pietism Among Eearly American Moravians.* New York: Henry Holt, 1933, p. 169.

Zinzendorf's hypersexualization of religion, in the technical language of psychoanalysis, reflects a tremendous displacement onto Jesus of a polymorphously perverse libido that had not undergone the process of reality orientation provided by normal relations with parents and siblings. In his passion for Jesus, which was strongly encouraged by his pietistic family and teachers, Zinzendorf had unwittingly sublimated homosexual, sadistic, MASOCHISTIC, and NECROPHILIC trends that later generations of Moravians were to expunge thoroughly from their literature and hymns. He unconsciously identified the dead and bloodied Jesus with the unknown but deeply revered father, who had been described to him as a young child in similarly graphic terms. Simultaneously, the androgynous Jesus served as the object of desires that might otherwise have been directed toward his mother and the other women who cared for him. It is one of the predictable paradoxes of such psychic trends that Zinzendorf actively promoted the desexualization of marriage (including his own, presumably) as well as the removal of children from their parents at the earliest possible age, so that their love might be wholly concentrated on the Spiritual Bridegroom.

Individual piety does not often reflect so clearly the dynamics of the Oedipus complex nor is it common for the erotic elements to be so evident as in the instance of Zinzendorf or, for another example, in Anton Unternährer, the schizophrenic founder of a Swiss sect. Seeing himself as the second Christ, Unternährer claimed that there is only one sacrament pleasing in the eyes of God: sexual intercourse (Rorschach, 1927). Yet it is plainly true that the family circle—including aunts, uncles, grandparents, and any other influential caretakers—is often re-created in the gods, angels, prophets, and saints of a particular religious tradition (Casey, 1938). Identification with one or another of these figures instead of a parent is not uncommon and may serve, say the psychoanalysts, as a means both for dealing with sexual and aggressive wishes and for developing a positive identity (Arlow, 1964; Lubin, 1958, 1959; Ostow, et al., 1968). Guilt feelings resulting from forbidden wishes and ambivalent feelings in relation to family members, illustrated in the case of the Unitarian woman, are among "the most powerful tools of religion" and may be fostered by the religious traditions when such feelings are insufficient (Ostow and Scharfstein, 1954, p. 42).

ANTHROPOLOGICAL STUDIES

The psychoanalyst's case studies vividly demonstrate the idiosyncratic nature of individual piety, given the possibilities for variation in childhood experiences. Yet a common biological endowment and the near-universality of certain fundamental elements in parent–child relations permit certain generalizations about groups of people, especially when they share the same social milieu. Freud's theoretical concepts, if not also his own writings on primitive rites, have served as a major source for a small number of anthropologists in carrying out their own culture-and-personality studies (La Barre, 1958; Muensterberger, 1969).

Géza Róheim: Religion and the Castration Complex

The introduction of psychoanalysis into anthropological reflection was first undertaken by the psychoanalytically trained anthropologist Géza Róheim. The proponent of an "intransigent and well-nigh Talmudic Freudianism" (La Barre, 1966, p. 275), Róheim considered Freud's *Totem and Taboo* to contain "epoch-making discoveries" that at last made possible a dynamic approach to anthropology. Among Róheim's first major works was a lengthy elaboration and defense of Freud's theory of the primal horde, based on exquisitely detailed armchair explorations of Australian myths and ceremonies (Róheim, 1925, p. 15; see also Jurji, 1974; Robinson, 1969). Particularly notable among Róheim's modifications is the conclusion that the ceremonial eating of the totem animal represents both fundamental tendencies of the Oedipus complex: killing the father and, by means of symbolic displacement upward, incestuous intercourse with the mother. In fact, Róheim took the incestuous element to be the primary one (Róheim, 1925, p. 249; 1945, p. 225).

Elsewhere Róheim (1930) has undertaken a survey of animistic beliefs and rites in cultures throughout the world, focusing his attention on the following elements: death and passage to the other world; magical procedures for killing others, making rain, or gaining another's love; curative practices of medicine men; the king taken to be an incarnation of the deity; and the phenomenon of the scapegoat, who is punished or killed to EXPIATE the sins of the community as a whole. In this great diversity of belief and practice, a single principle emerges: "Supernatural ideas are but the symbolic representation of biological facts" (p. 25). Among these realities, the sexual ones loom largest, along with the fears associated with them. Thus the image of the soul's passing over a precarious and razor-sharp bridge to the next world, the entry to which is guarded by fierce dogs, symbolizes "the seminal fluid passing by means of the male member into the womb" (p. 44). In accord with the principle of condensation, the bridge simultaneously represents the castrating sword or razor, and the dogs give form to the associated anxiety. For Róheim, dread of castration, a possibility said to be symbolized ever anew by the loss of semen in coitus, proves to be the key to this intricate system of ideas and rituals. The castration complex, he concludes, "plays a central part both in neurosis and in the primitive forms of magic and religion" (p. 381).

Weston La Barre: Religion as Shamanism

The Oedipus complex is no less important in the psychoanalytic studies of human piety by American anthropologist Weston La Barre, although he emphasizes somewhat different aspects of it. The *mysterium tremendum* that Otto placed at the heart of religion, the mysterious power that is both frightening and fascinating, springs out of the long-forgotten experience of the father in childhood. "At the base of every relation is the familial experience," "the universally human nuclear family," says La Barre (1972, p. 12), "and all religions consequently contain some basic oedipal story in their myths." With the inevitable variations in the individual Oedipal situation come compelling differences in the conception of God. "Thus arguments about the nature of 'God' are an irrational hurling of individual oedipal convictions at one another; and it is fruitless because each is talking about ontogenetically somewhat different phenomena" (p. 111). Modern theology, La Barre adds, consists of nothing more than disguised clinical autobiographies (p. 605).

Adolescent Conflict and Cultural Crisis: Like Freud and Róheim, La Barre is less concerned with the fate of individual piety than with the very origins of "belief in spiritual beings," which, with British anthropologist Edward Tylor, he takes to be the essence of religion. The first gods, claims La Barre in his major work on religion, *The Ghost Dance* (1972), were the shamans—anguished, creative, if sometimes also psychotic medicine men. Their self-dramatizing quests for an identity vision, typically occurring in adolescence when conflict between individual biology and group culture is at its height, serve at the same time to protect a society in crisis. La Barre asserts that all religious traditions were at first crisis cults, the overdetermined products of political and socioeconomic turmoil or various calamities. The American Indian Ghost Dances of the late nineteenth century, the Indian's last, desperate efforts to save their culture from ruin, become for La Barre the paradigm for every religious movement. "Christianity," for example, "is the still cognitively troubled and imperfectly melded Hellenistic 'ghost dances' of the Hellenic and Semitic peoples crushed by Rome" (p. 254).

Rejecting Freud's notion of inherited unconscious memories of a primal horde and apparently less taken than Róheim by the sheer genitality of primitive religion, La Barre does share with them the conviction that religion, wherever it is found, is firmly rooted in the universal elements of early childhood. Although La Barre's account of the psychodynamics of shamanism is not always lucid, there is no mistaking his conclusion that the shaman, characteristically a TRANSVESTITE, is pathologically locked-in the phallic stage of development, still possessed by fantasies of omnipotence, troubled by fluid ego boundaries, and feminized in his attitude

Snake handling at a church in the southeastern United States.

toward the omnipotent father. The shaman in turn serves as the paranoid father for the frightened and infantilized members of his tribe, on whose behalf he masters the spirits and thereby preserves for the group a measure of psychic equilibrium.

The Handling of Snakes: Similar dynamics are seen to operate in the Southern snake-handling cult, which La Barre (1962) characterizes as a crisis cult of poor whites confronted by changing cultural and economic realities. Frustrated by tantalizing new opportunities that remain out of their reach, these poor industrial workers reaffirm the compulsive and joyless ethos of their past, a repressiveness that finds relief only in the weekly services of handling snakes.

What accounts for this ecstatic courting of danger from poisonous serpents? By means of "psychiatric ethnography," La Barre makes a convincing case for the psychosexual significance of the snake, in whatever culture or time it is found. By various peoples, a range of phallic and urethral qualities are attributed to this creature, which in reality is innocent of them all. If the snake can be transformed by human imagining into a PHALLUS, so too can the phallus be made to mimic the snake. Just as the snake seems to gain immortality by shedding its skin, by sacrificing a part of itself, so too can humankind, through the sacrificial shedding of skin in circumcision. The biblical Hebrews, La Barre speculates, were snake cultists, and Moses was a snake shaman serving a snake god. With time the snake god was displaced by others, but the practice of circumcision survived, serving simultaneously as a memorable castration threat, a sign of membership and loyalty, and a magical means of gaining immortality.

Accordingly, for the rigidly antisexual members of the snake-handling cults, the ecstatic manipulation of serpents, in conjunction with the embracing of other participants and the baiting of authorities, represents a disguised return of the repressed—of dangerous and blameworthy sexual desire. For the cult leader, whom La Barre explores in depth, ministering to a congregation of snake handlers provided "a socially adapted though somewhat mutilated solution of the oedipal problem" (p. 160) in relation to a hysteric mother and a more permissive, if also undemonstrative father who proved to be easily hoodwinked. The psychopathic character that this leader had become found its perfect counterpart in the hysterically repressed women who willingly surrendered their superego control to him, confident that he would provide for them too the "ineffable experience" that "is clearly an induced, if sometimes unwitting, public orgasm" (p. 137). Flouting the strict morality of his childhood and daring the outwitted Father–God to punish him, the cult leader symbolically seduced his own mother—and did so under the very façade, religion, that she provided for him.

ANALYSIS OF THE JEWISH TRADITION

Most anthropologists do not share Róheim and La Barre's conviction that the psychoanalytic perspective enriches anthropological investigation. Many psychoanalysts, on the other hand, give ethnographic evidence a fundamental place in their own studies, especially of religion. The crasser imagery found in ancient and preliterate societies, seemingly less affected by civilization's repressive influences, is thought to provide important evidence of the wishes and fears presumed to underlie the more sublime varieties of religion as well. By employing techniques derived from dream interpretation, the psychoanalyst seeks to reconstruct the process by which the original, often grossly literal ideas and practices were transformed into the religious traditions familiar to us today. The connection made, what remains is to clarify the dynamics of the cruder elements, sometimes with the aid of case studies from clinical practice. That the Jewish tradition is most frequently the object of such analysis is no surprise, given the preponderance of Jews, usually nonobservant, among the psychoanalysts (M. Lubin, 1969) as well as the greater tendency of Jews to seek psychiatric help in times of difficulty (McCann, 1962; Weintraub and Aronson, 1974).

Biblical Exegesis

A large portion of the psychoanalytic literature on religion takes up the problem of interpreting biblical texts, most often of the Hebrew Bible (see Spiegel, 1972). Some of these studies concern themselves with a single passage or a notable biblical character; others seek to comprehend a recurrent theme or a fundamental process, including those culminating in events in the Christian story. Whatever the focus, however, the biblical material is found again and again to provide eloquent testimony to the universality of sexual and aggressive impulses, the profoundly ambivalent emotions of the Oedipus complex, and the rationalizing capabilities of the defensive ego. For the psychoanalyst, the Bible is truly a source of revelation, but of matters far more human than divine.

In assuming that psychic events are complexly overdetermined, the psychoanalyst is prepared to find a multilayered ambiguity beneath the usually coherent surface of biblical stories. Beyond reiterating the long-recognized composite character of much biblical literature, writers of this persuasion maintain that the elements of the Bible, like the events and figures in dreams, have a multiplicity of hidden meanings. Every element has potential significance, and the most trivial of them may provide the key to the whole.

The Story of Paradise: The simple and compelling story of the garden of Eden found in the second and third chapters of Genesis will serve to illustrate psychoanalytical biblical EXEGESIS. The events in Chapter 2 of Genesis (see Excerpt 7.2) include the creation of man, Adam, from the dust of the earth; the planting of the verdant garden in Eden, containing the tree of life and the tree of knowledge of good and evil; and the creation of woman, later called Eve, from one of Adam's ribs as he slept. Chapter 3 begins with Eve's temptation by the cunning serpent, her sharing of the fruit from the forbidden tree with Adam, and Adam and Eve's self-conscious covering of their nakedness with fig leaves. It ends, after God's discovery of their disobedience, with the successive cursing of each of the offenders and the driving of Adam and Eve out of the garden, to prevent their eating from the tree of eternal life as well.

EXCERPT 7.2

From the Book of Genesis, Chapters 2 and 3

2 . . . In the day that the Lord God made the earth and the heavens, when no plant of the field was yet in the earth and no herb of the field had yet sprung up . . . the Lord God formed man of dust from the ground, and breathed into his nostrils the breath of life; and man became a living being. And the Lord God planted a garden in Eden, in the east; and there he put the man whom he had formed. And out of the ground the Lord God made to grow every tree that is pleasant to the sight and good for food, the tree of life also in the midst of the garden, and the tree of the knowledge of good and evil. . . .

The Lord God took the man and put him in the garden of Eden to till it and keep it. And the Lord God commanded the man, saying, "You may freely eat of every tree

The Fall of Man, by Albrecht Dürer.

Expulsion from Eden, by Dürer.

of the garden; but of the tree of the knowledge of good and evil you shall not eat, for in the day that you eat of it you shall die.''

Then the Lord God said, "It is not good that the man should be alone; I will make him a helper fit for him." . . . So the Lord God caused a deep sleep to fall upon the man, and while he slept took one of his ribs and closed up its place with flesh; and the rib which the Lord God had taken from the man he made into a woman and brought her to the man. Then the man said, "This at last is bone of my bones and flesh of my flesh; she shall be called Woman, because she was taken out of Man." . . . And the man and his wife were both naked, and were not ashamed.

3 Now the serpent was more subtle than any other wild creature that the Lord God had made. He said to the woman, "Did God say 'You shall not eat of any tree of the garden'?" And the woman said to the serpent, "We may eat of the fruit of the trees of the garden; but God said, 'You shall not eat of the fruit of the tree which is in the midst of the garden, neither shall you touch it, lest you die.' " But the serpent said to the woman, "You will not die. For God knows that when you eat of it your eyes will be opened, and you will be like God, knowing good and evil." So when the woman saw that the tree was good for food, and that it was a delight to the eyes, and that the tree was to be desired to make one wise, she took of its fruit and ate; and she also gave some to her husband, and he ate. Then the eyes of both were opened, and they knew that they were naked; and they sewed fig leaves together and made themselves aprons.

And they heard the sound of the Lord God walking in the garden in the cool of the day, and the man and his wife hid themselves from the presence of the Lord God among the trees of the garden. But the Lord God called to the man, and said to him, "Where are you?" And he said, "I heard the sound of thee in the garden, and I was afraid, because I was naked; and I hid myself." He said, "Who told you that you were naked? Have you eaten of the tree of which I commanded you not to eat?" The man said, "The woman whom thou gavest to be with me, she gave me the fruit of the tree, and I ate." Then the Lord God said to the woman, "What is this that you have done?" The woman said, "The serpent beguiled me, and I ate." The Lord God said to the serpent, "Because you have done this, cursed are you above all cattle, and above all wild animals; upon your belly you shall go, and dust you shall eat, all the days of your life. I will put enmity between you and the woman, and between your seed and her seed; he shall bruise your head, and you shall bruise his heel." To the woman he said, "I will greatly multiply your pain in childbearing; in pain you shall bring forth children, yet your desire shall be for your husband, and he shall rule over you." And to Adam he said, "Because you have listened to the voice of your wife, and have eaten of the tree of which I commanded you, 'You shall not eat of it,' cursed is the ground because of you; in toil you shall eat of it all the days of your life. . . . In the sweat of your face you shall eat bread till you return to the ground, for out of it you were taken. . . ."

The man called his wife's name Eve, because she was the mother of all living. And the Lord God made for Adam and for his wife garments of skins, and clothed them.

Then the Lord God said, "Behold, the man has become like one of us, knowing good and evil; and now, lest he put forth his hand and take also of the tree of life, and eat, and live for ever"—therefore the Lord God sent him forth from the garden of Eden, to till the ground from which he was taken. He drove out the man; and at the east of the garden of Eden he placed the cherubim, and a flaming sword which turned every way, to guard the way to the tree of life.

Over the centuries the Paradise story has attracted the attention of unnumbered commentators (see McKenzie, 1954; Pagels, 1988). Although the narrative is still widely taken as literal history,[4] today many biblical scholars interpret it as an AETIOLOGICAL MYTH, that is, a story designed to explain origins—in this instance, of the sorrows and painful contradictions of human existence. The account's evident "breaches, seams, and irregularities," far from undermining its validity as they would were it taken literally, are said to give it unfathomable richness and inexhaustible breadth. Its reticence, indirection, and lack of sharp definition lend it a mysterious universality. They also make the exegetical task exceptionally difficult (von Rad, 1972, pp. 99–100). Occasional commentators such as Joseph Coppens (1948), as well as others who wrote long before Freud, have given special place to the few obviously sexual elements in the story. Many others, like Gerhard von Rad, minimize them, emphasizing instead the theme of rebellious separation from God as a result of the human yearning to pass beyond divinely ordained limits. Thus the sin is willful disobedience of God, the result of hubris. Its manifestation in bodily shame is "the sign of a grievous disruption which governs the whole being of man from the lowest level of his corporeality" (von Rad, p. 91).

An Anti-Sexual Narrative: To the vigilant eye of the psychoanalyst, on the other hand, the apparent sexual elements are only the tip of the iceberg. In an early and well-documented study of this narrative, Ludwig Levy (1917) finds it permeated with symbols of sexuality. The word "Eden" itself means "bliss," and the forbidden tree that stands at the center of the garden suggests its specific nature. Traditionally, the tree bore *apples* (the female breast), by the eating of which (coitus) one would *know* (a biblical expression for sexual intercourse) *good and evil* (sexual capacity). Like some other commentators, Levy proposes that the

---

[4] Of the 2100 students at 41 U.S. colleges and universities who responded to Alan Almquist and John Cronin's (1988) questionnaire on human evolution, 38 percent agreed that "The biblical account of creation of life by God as described in Genesis is correct." The percentages by region were East, 15.0; South, 45.9; Midwest, 46.7; Southwest, 52.0; and West, 30.9.

two trees identified by the narrator were originally one. Hence the tree of knowledge is also the tree of life, linking sexuality with death (the outcome of eating from the tree, according to God's words, but also a common association of orgasm) as well as with immortality (the feeling of youthful potency and the creation of new life).

The work of La Barre (1962) and others (e.g., Coppens, 1948; Fortune, 1926; Pfister, 1913), prepares us to see the serpent, too, as an erotic symbol. The snake's conversation with Eve, says Levy, is a profound portrayal of the storm and stress of the maturing sex drive as it battles with feelings of prohibition. Adam and Eve's choice of fig leaves to cover themselves after their fall into sin further emphasizes its sexual nature, for the fig tree itself is an ancient phallic symbol. Even the curses that bring the narration to an end testify to this first, momentous sin: Eve is to suffer in pregnancy and childbirth, and Adam is condemned to plow the field (have intercourse with his wife), but in this new modality, without pleasure. The association of field and woman illuminates as well the condemnation of the serpent–phallus to crawling on its belly and eating dust, but no longer with the woman's ready cooperation. The antisexual position represented by the story of Adam and Eve, says Levy, was necessary to disentangle religion from the fertility rites and the mysteries of the pagan traditions, in the context of which the serpent was revered as divine. Only in this way could ethics be placed at religion's center. With the danger of falling back into the old paganism behind us, Levy concludes, our task now is to free sexuality from this long-associated curse.

A Drama of Incest: Although Coppens (1948) selects Levy's analysis as an example of "radical sexual exegesis," Levy has only underscored what the early church fathers and many biblical scholars since have suspected all along. Other psychoanalysts have probed deeper. The garden, the tree, even the snake are identified as symbols of the mother. Eve, too, is a mother—"the mother of all living," in Adam's words—and thus she is his mother as well. The sin forbidden by the Father–God and responsible for Paradise's end was not simply coitus but more specifically incestuous union with the mother (Róheim, 1940). The creation of Eve from Adam's rib is an instance of disguise by conversion into the opposite. The hidden truth is that Eve gave birth to Adam.

Fodor (1954) suggests that Eve represents the phallic Mother–Goddess of primitive Canaanite religion, the virgin-with-a-penis. It was from her that the rib—that is, the phallus—was taken, in order to create Adam, who became its new possessor. The castration–defeat of the Mother–Goddess is marked as well by the cursing of the earth, the placing of enmity between the woman and the serpent that was once hers, and the demotion of woman to the role of companion to man, whose children she must bear in pain. Paradise before the fall symbolizes the innocent and blissful unity of mother and child. Growth and sexual maturation, however, lead inexorably to the Oedipal crisis and eviction by the father from Paradise, the way back to which is guarded by the castrating sword. Only after a life of toilsome independence will Adam find his wish fulfilled, when he in death returns to the embrace of Mother Earth.

A Primeval Patricide: Have we exhausted the hidden meaning of the Paradise story? Far from it, says Theodor Reik (1957), one of the best known and most authoritative of the psychoanalytic exegetes. The sexual elements in the narrative, he maintains, serve chiefly to disguise the more terrible primeval crime for which they were merely the motivation. Setting aside both Eve and the serpent as elements from another cycle of myths, Reik argues that the core of the Paradise story consists of DEICIDE and THEOPHAGY, the murder and eating of God. More precisely—and here Reik follows Freud, but with an emphasis on the second element—it is the slaying and eating of the father–chief of the primal horde. Observing the widespread phenomenon of the sacred tree, which is the dwelling place of divinity if it is not the god himself, Reik argues that Jahveh was a tree god, the totem substitute for the murdered father. Adam stands in the place of the patricidal brothers. As the sons in the primal horde consumed their father's body to acquire his powerful qualities, so Adam ate of the forbidden tree, the totemistic god, in order to become divine himself. God's words in Genesis 3:22, "Behold, the man is become as one of us," testify to the wished-for outcome.

Other Biblical Stories: Other passages in the Bible are similarly thought to be constructed of the distortions, substitutions, and reversals that the unconscious ego uses to disguise forbidden and dangerous wishes. According to the fourth chapter of Genesis, for example, Cain, tiller of the ground, slew his brother Abel, and then, fearful for his own life, received a mark to protect him. The hidden truth, says the psychoanalyst, is that Cain committed incest with his mother, murdered his father, and then, out of grief and guilt, mutilated his own genitals—a double, virtually, of the Paradise story immediately preceding it (Reik, 1917).

Further on in Genesis we learn how Jacob, at the command and direction of his doting mother, tricked his blind father into giving him the blessing intended for his twin brother Esau, who had earlier sold his birthright to the cunning Jacob for a mess of pottage. Some time later, while waiting at night on the River Jabbok in fearful anticipation of Esau, Jacob wrestled with a man, later identified as God, who injured him in the hollow of his thigh and then, still unvictorious at daybreak, gained freedom from Jacob's grip only by consenting to bless him and by giving him a new name. In this story the psychoanalyst finds parallels to ancient initiation rites and their dynamics. Jacob, once again a pubescent youth, having deceived his father, betrayed his brother, and determined to take a mother substitute to wife, is fallen upon by his father (or brother or father-in-law), who in a more primitive narrative was killed and devoured by Jacob. Once circumcised, Jacob is released, reconciled with the father and free to take on the sexual prerogatives of the adult (Reik, 1919a; Zeligs, 1974).

For a final example, we may recall the events narrated in the Book of Jonah. Ordered to go to the wicked city of Ninevah and proclaim against it, the recalcitrant prophet fled from the Lord by boarding a ship to Tarshish. During a storm stirred up by God's wrath, Jonah is thrown overboard into the sea, where a great fish swallows him up. Three days later he is disgorged, repentant, onto dry land. Here we have a regressive fantasy, according to Hyman Fingert (1954), who identifies Tarshish, the ship's hold, and the fish's belly as symbols of the mother, to whom Jonah flees at a time of emotional crisis. The deeply conflicted feelings represented here are Oedipal ones: intense longings for the beloved mother; anger at the father for his apparent violence toward the mother during intercourse—a seeming destructiveness that is associated by the child with his own sexual impulses and is symbolically represented by the raging sea; and anger, too, at the mother for her rejection of the child's infantile wishes, a maternal "wickedness" projected onto Ninevah. The fate of being swallowed by a fish is an overdetermined one, for it represents not only a return to the safety of the mother's womb but also a TALION PUNISHMENT. That is, the wish to devour the father is met with the corresponding penalty of being devoured by him (Abraham, 1920). Jonah's odd depression and suicidal impulses after saving Ninevah give a measure of what it cost him to renounce his guilty wishes for the mother and for her destruction. It also reveals the degree of his identification with her in the inverse Oedipal situation.

Modern biblical scholars have of course not taken eagerly to psychoanalytic exegesis. Yet even their own work, it is said, contains evidence for the dynamics reported by the analysts. In a study of unconscious factors in biblical interpretation, Reik (1919a) observes the astonishing proclivity of biblical experts to substitute father for mother in the phrase from Genesis 24:67, ''and Isaac was comforted [by his wife Rebecca] after his mother's death.'' Reik finds the reasons provided for making such an alteration to be ''forced and entirely insufficient.'' The unconscious motive for these experts' rationalizations, he speculates, lies in their resistance to the incestuous character of Isaac's love for Rebecca. Ironically, by insisting that it is the father who died, they clear the way for the realization of such incestuous tendencies. Thus even today, according to Reik, the biblical texts remain subject to the processes of wish-fulfilling distortion and defensive rationalization.

Ritual

The various modes of ritual observance that through the ages have been a distinctive expression of the Jewish world-view have challenged the psychoanalysts no less than the Hebrew scriptures. Jewish dietary laws, Sabbath customs, and the objects worn during prayer seem to the analysts to cry out for an analytical interpretation. So, too, do circumcision rites and the celebration of the Day of Atonement, among other festival occasions. Once again, with the aid of clinical case studies and eth-

An elaborately carved case for the *mezuzah*.

A Jewish man touching the *mezuzah* as he leaves a house, detail from the *Rothschild-Miscellany* (Hebrew manuscript), Northern Italy, ca. 1470.

nographic parallels, the psychoanalyst finds testimony to the symbolism of the body and the drama of the nuclear family.

The Mezuzah: Apparent first of all to the alert psychoanalyst are the emblems of male and female sexuality, often found in conjunction. A relatively simple example is the MEZUZAH (literally, "doorpost"), a small scroll of parchment made from animal skin and inscribed with biblical passages that command loving obedience to a potentially angry God. The *mezuzah* is laid in a case with a small aperture and attached at an oblique angle to the right-hand doorpost. The person entering and leaving the house or room touches or kisses it, ostensibly as a reminder of God as fortification against sinning. Said to be "one of the most widely observed ceremonial commandments of Judaism" (Rabinowitz, 1971a, p. 1477), the *mezuzah* has a long, uncertain history, which the psychoanalysts have sought to reconstruct.

Georg Langer (1928), for example, compares the phallic-shaped *mezuzah* to the sometimes more blatantly phallic doorposts that various ancient peoples placed in the front of their houses as protection against evil spirits. According to Langer, the *mezuzah* derives its capacity to avert evil from the father's threatening phallus. This interpretation is suggested by the requirement that the *mezuzah* be covered if coitus is to occur in its presence. Yet it also symbolizes female sexuality, not only because the case is an object of containment but also because it is mounted in the doorway, which is said to be an unconscious symbol of the female genitals (Eder, 1933; Langer, 1928).[5]

Tefillin and Prayer Shawls: A similar though somewhat more complicated dynamic is proposed for the TEFILLIN (phylacteries) and prayer shawls that are worn by Jewish males from age 13 onward. In accord with a literal interpretation of the the four biblical passages that are contained on animal parchment within them, the TEFELLIN consist of two black leather boxes bound by leather thongs to the arm and forehead and worn during services on weekday mornings. The meticulously detailed regulations governing their manufacture and use are said to be observed with remarkable uniformity throughout the Jewish world (Rabinowitz, 1971b). Two garments are donned before laying (putting on) TEFILLIN: a small, four-cornered one that has tassels (ZIZITH, "fringes") applied in an elaborately specified way to its corners and that is worn throughout the day under regular clothing; and a larger one, the TALLITH, a similarly fringed shawl usually made of wool and worn only during prayer. The two garments are said to be derived from a single one, which wrapped the entire body and possessed much longer and more conspicuous *zizith*. The fringes of these garments, like the *tefillin*, are kissed at prescribed moments in the ritual.

Authorities on the Jewish tradition widely maintain that these ritual objects, most likely derived from the protective AMULETS of preliterate peoples, have taken on a new and rather different meaning in the Jewish context. But the psychoanalyst,

---

[5] The phallic interpretation of the *mezuzah* is rather startlingly confirmed in the accompanying fifteenth-century Italian portrait of a Jew touching the *mezuzah*. To any reader of Leo Steinberg (1983), the gathering of the robe grasped in the left hand can only suggest an erect phallus. The numerous representations of Christ that Steinberg collected from about the same time, to illustrate the Renaissance emphasis on Christ's genitalia and thus, it seems, his humanity, include more than a dozen pictures in which the folds of the loincloth strongly suggest phallic tumescence, even after death. Like Langer, Steinberg discerns in this remarkable and perhaps disturbing theme a symbolic representation of power, but in this case power over death itself. Especially for the incredulous, it may be helpful to note that the *mezuzah* and circumcision are associated in the Jewish tradition, for both are obligatory expressions of God's covenant with Israel.

Tefillin and the tallith are here worn during morning prayer by a member of the ultraorthodox Lubavitch movement.

for whom the most important meanings are unconscious, finds the true significance of these objects and rites to be essentially unchanged. Thus it is that the resemblance of the head *tefillah*[6]—especially the earlier cylindrical form of it—to the more clearly phalliclike objects also worn on the head in other cultures convinces Langer (1930) of the *tefillin*'s primary phallic significance. In the Jewish tradition the process of disguise has advanced further, through the introduction of the cubical house shape, which is said to symbolize the female organs of reproduction and thus, in combination, coitus. The nature of the unspecified sin against which the *tefillin* is traditionally a warning is further revealed by self-fettering, which is carried out on one's arm with the leather thongs. This is a symbol, Langer claims, of self-castration. Yet there is ambivalence here, for the objects are made of leather, which is known to have positive erotic meaning.

M. D. Eder's (1933) clinical work with Jewish patients reveals that the kissing of these ritual objects may also express antithetical meanings, corresponding to different psychosexual stages of development. For example, it may be a "love offering," accompanied by erotic sensations, to a parental image. Alternatively, it may be a disguised ORAL-SADISTIC assault on the aggressive father or the frustrating mother. "The function of the phylacteries and ritual ornaments," Eder concludes, "is to preserve the balance between id impulses and superego demands in the Oedipus situation allowing the ego to act more or less harmoniously" (p. 371).

Reik (1919b, 1930) takes a different tack in the search for the meaning of such observances. He discerns in these ritual objects the remnants of a ceremonial animal disguise. The head *tefillah* suggests the horns of a bull and the hand *tefillah*

---

[6] Both Reik and the *Encyclopaedia Judaica* use *tefillah* as the singular of *tefillin*. This usage, however, is apparently far from universal: *tefillin* is often used as both singular and plural.

its hooves; the leather thongs represent its hide. As Abraham (1920) first pointed out, the wool tallith is easily the fleece of a ram, and the *zizith* recall its four legs, the joints represented by the fringes' knots. (That totems evolve makes the coexistence of *tefillin* and *tallith* unproblematical, says Reik.)

The ceremonial donning of these elements harks back, proposes Reik (1930), to the ancient practice of wearing the pelt of the sacrificial animal, in order to take on the totemic animal's sanctity and secure its protection. With time, only parts of the animal's skin came to be used, then artificial substitutes, of like material and similar shape. The ancient function remained the same, however. Once more, then, Reik draws us back to Freud's theory of the primal horde. The deity with whom the wearer of these fragmentary ritual objects identifies is none other than the Father–God of old, the victim of the primal crime.

Yom Kippur: An examination of the Jewish Day of Atonement, Yom Kippur, said to be a "supreme festival" of "unparalleled joy," "the most important day in the liturgical year" (Herr, 1971), adds to the plausibility of Reik's interpretation. From the psychoanalytic view, nearly every element in this celebration seems to point to Oedipal wishes or a totemic past. On the Day of Atonement, as on the Sabbath, all manner of work—that is, any action having an effect on nature, on Mother Earth—is forbidden. This defense against incestuous tendencies, says Erich Fromm (1927) in a paper from his orthodox days, is coupled with a wish for the father's death, the symbolic meaning of the Sabbath's origin: God "rested" on the seventh day, after having presented Eve to Adam. On the Day of Atonement the pious celebrant is specifically enjoined to fast, to abstain from coitus, and to go without shoes. If Sandor Feldman (1941) is correct in interpreting the removal of shoes as a castration symbol, these prohibitions seem designed to prevent a recurrence of the two primal crimes—eating the father and cohabitating with the

Abraham is restrained by an angel from fulfilling the command of God to sacrifice his only son, Isaac (Genesis 22:1–14); by Rembrandt.

mother—while also reminding the unconscious psyche of the terrifying penalty for such wishes. The conscious ego knows only that "danger to life overrides all the prohibitions of the Day of Atonement just as it does those of the Sabbath" (Herr, 1971, p. 1378). Fear of the father's revenge through castration or even death is also represented by the custom of trimming the hair the evening before; by the traditional belief that Yom Kippur was the day of Abraham's circumcision; and by the association of this festival with the day of the Akedah, the binding of Isaac, a frequently recited story of a father's aborted sacrifice of his son. The story of Isaac has been repeatedly analyzed in Oedipal terms and compared to primitive initiation rites (Reik, 1961; Wellisch, 1954; Zeligs, 1974).

"The most beloved ritual of the Day of Atonement," according to Herman Kieval (1971, p. 1166), is the *Kol Nidrei,* a formula of unknown origin that is set to a heart-rending melody and declares null and void all oaths and obligations in the year ahead. Reik (1919b) interpreted the scandalous irresponsibility suggested by this puzzling formula, which a nineteenth-century synod of the Reform movement once sought to expunge from the liturgy, as the return of a deeply repressed wish, akin in dynamics to an obsessional neurosis. The nature of this wish, Karl Abraham (1920) claims, is revealed in two biblical passages read in conjunction with each other on the Day of Atonement: Leviticus 18, which explicitly opposes incest, and the book of Jonah, which, as we know, is interpreted as representing punishment by being devoured by the father. The earlier practice of sacrificing animals on this day, notably bulls and male goats, and the unusual hand gesture of the *tallith*-covered priest, who, holding the fourth and fifth fingers together, spreads them apart from the other three, thus suggesting the cloven hoof, both hint at a still-living totemic past, including the primal crime. As the original vow against repetition of this crime sank deeper into the unconscious, says Reik, it became displaced to all oaths and renunciations generally, which Jews are reputed to observe with exceptional conscientiousness. Similarly, the protective measures against the feared outcome of violating these oaths became displaced and multiplied. The *Kol Nidrei,* then, is a wish to shake free of this intolerable burden and to commit over again the old outrage. Solemnly sung on the eve of the Day of Atonement, the *Kol Nidrei* is followed the next day by elaborate expressions of repentance and renunciation, reestablishing the bond with the father.

Blowing of the Shofar, a woodcut from an old Minḥah book (Amsterdam, 1723).

The sounding of the *shofar,* a primitive instrument that tradition says was first made from the horn of the ram sacrificed in Isaac's place, also expresses this ambivalence (Reik 1919b). On the one hand, its use is a reminder—and thus an aid to mastery—of the temptation to commit the ancient sin, making possible reconciliation through identification with the offended deity. On the other hand, it constitutes the sin's repetition, by symbolically appropriating both phallus and voice, and thus the sexual power, of the totem father. "The deepest meaning of the Day of Atonement," writes Abraham (1920), "is therefore now apparent. The father–god who has been murdered is recognized anew by his sons, and in his turn resumes his obligations towards them" (p. 147).

Dietary Laws

The qualities of Jewish practice that Reik considers obsessional are perhaps nowhere more evident than in the dietary laws, an extraordinarily complex system of rules governing which animals may be eaten, the methods for ritual slaughter, and the process of koshering or preparing the meat (see Rabinowicz, 1971). There are also stringent rules designed to ensure that milk and meat, and the objects they touch, are scrupulously kept separate. According to a guide to the dietary laws, "Separate cooking utensils, dishes and cutlery are an absolute necessary. . . . [and] a kitchen with separate sinks is to be recommended. . . . [But] the main 'battle' between milky and meaty foods and utensils takes place on the cooking range, where the boiling pots are ready to shoot out steam or to overflow at any time. The need for caution is imperative, since even a single drop of milk splashing onto the outside of a hot meaty pot would render the latter unusable!" (quote in Greenberg and Witztum, 1994, p. 215).

In a brief study of these laws, Frieda Fromm-Reichmann (1927) argues that they ultimately derive from totemistic practice. Just as the original totem animal is represented in ceremonial garb and gesture, so it also appears in dietary practices. Yet in this context it undergoes a reversal that is said to be common in unconscious processes. Together with other animals that share its capability to form horns, antlers, or other structures of hornlike substances, and thus its capacity to represent the paternal phallus, the totem animal becomes an object that Jews are permitted— not forbidden—to eat. At the same time, the danger of this act is acknowledged by the innumerable precautions that surround the killing of the animal and its preparation for the table. Because eating meat represents identification with the totem father, to drink (the mother's) milk at the same time symbolizes incest; hence the law against eating meat and milk together and the elaborate separation of the utensils associated with the preparation of each. Fromm-Reichmann finds support for her thesis in two case studies of young Jews, a man and a woman, both of whom experienced unmistakable sexual excitation when they ate forbidden meat. Curiously enough, both also expressed anxiety that their parents would learn of their violation of the dietary laws.

THE ATTACK ON RELIGION

By reducing sacred tradition to sexual and aggressive impulses, especially urges that are peculiarly offensive to contemporary sensibilities, psychoanalysis has inevitably gained the reputation of being fundamentally hostile to religion. Freud's own animosity is well known; that of some of his followers is no less apparent. Ernest Jones's "violent atheism" (Veszy-Wagner, 1966, p. 98), for example, can hardly be missed in his essay "The Madonna's Conception Through the Ear" (1914), in which he relentlessly pursues his repellent but well-argued thesis that a certain genre of paintings of the Annunciation can be explained as a magnificent sublimation of infantile COPROPHILIA conditioned by intense castration wishes and fear. "The Christian myth," Jones says in his conclusion, "is perhaps the most gigantic and revolutionary phantasy in history" (p. 356).

Theodore Schroeder: A Welcomed Amateur

Among the proponents of the psychoanalytic view none has assaulted religion more single-mindedly than has Theodore Schroeder, a civil engineer turned lawyer who himself became a prolific contributor to the psychoanalytic literature on religion (see Ishill, 1940; Sankey-Jones, 1921; Shipley, 1933; Van Teslaar, 1915). The only surviving child of a Catholic mother who was disowned by her parents when she married a Protestant, Schroeder spent much of his adult life fighting every form of censorship. Paradoxically, he himself adamantly opposed novels, operas, and plays, which he considered stimulants of infantile and irrational emotions. Nothing, however, inspired his contempt as much as religion.

At first Schroeder's criticism was limited to the Mormon tradition, the origins of which he placed in the sexual impulses (Schroeder, 1908). After moving from Salt Lake City to New York, he generalized his theory of sexual origin to religion as a whole. His "erotogenetic interpretation of religion" was in the beginning little more than the hypothesis that there is a correlation between sex and religion, the latter explicitly defined in terms of emotional or ecstatic experiences. With his discovery of psychoanalysis, and after his own seven-month analysis with psychiatrist William Alanson White, the superintendent of St. Elizabeths Hospital in Washington, Schroeder became an ardent proponent of psychoanalytic theory as a means of unmasking once and for all what he saw as the insanities of religion. Whereas most psychoanalysts have thought that *some* of the motivating force behind religion is derived from sexuality, Schroeder maintained that *all* of it can be explained in terms of sexual impulses.

Schroeder articulated his elementary theory over and over again in a series of papers spanning more than 25 years and appearing in a number of the leading journals of psychoanalysis and the psychology of religion (see Sankey-Jones, 1934). An organizer of the Free Speech League in 1911, he also dreamed of founding an institute for religious psychology (Vande Kemp, 1985). He was prepared to donate his own time, he declared in his advertisements, if only a generous donor would pay the remaining expenses.

Even a casual reading of Schroeder's papers suggests good reasons for his failure to find his long-sought benefactor. In addition to being a poor writer, a fact that even his staunchest admirers (Ishill, 1940, p. xxiii) acknowledge, Schroeder was a remarkably careless scholar. A long chapter in one of his books on free speech, for example, is characterized by Leonard Levy (1960, p. 157n) as "a combination of prodigious research and wishful thinking." "Endowed with a vivid imagination he read into most passages meanings which they simply do not have and often contradict." His evidence, observes Levy, "in many cases . . . disproves his point."

The tendentious and illogical quality of his writing is also evident in his articles on the psychology of religion. What is more astonishing, given that his articles profess to represent the psychoanalytic perspective (e.g., Schroeder, 1929) and appear in psychoanalytic journals, is their strikingly unpsychoanalytic point of view.

The themes to which we are now well accustomed—infantile sexuality, the Oedipus complex, incest wishes, castration anxiety, the vicissitudes of repression, and the task of symbol interpretation—appear nowhere. Instead, we are given a repetitive mishmash of neologisms and pseudopsychological terminology, some of it apparently borrowed from Alfred Adler's individual psychology.[7] We read of "prenatal psychisms," "psychosexual ecstasy," and "autogenic erotic explosions" (Schroeder, 1922, 1932). Moreover, some of his assumptions—for example, that impulses themselves may mature—contradict fundamental psychoanalytic principles. Virtually the only psychological literature that Schroeder cites is his own, and one suspects he was ill acquainted with that of anyone else. The overall impression is that of a rank amateur set on proving a narrow hypothesis.

Why, then, were his articles accepted for publication and thus given a permanent place in the literature on the psychoanalysis of religion? One answer seems obvious, that his general rhetoric and hostile point of view were in themselves congruent with the perspective of psychoanalysis. Thus the editors—including Schroeder's own analyst, W. A. White, who long edited the *Psychoanalytic Review*—apparently welcomed his pronouncement that

> All religion, at all times, and everywhere, in its differential essence, is only a sex ecstacy, seldom recognized to be that, and therefore, easily and actually misinterpreted as a mysterious and "transcendental," or super-physical, undiscriminating witness to the inerrancy of all those varying and often contradictory doctrines and ceremonies believed to be of super-physical value in the promotion of present material, ecstatic or post-mortem well-being and which, in the mind of the believing person, happen to be associated with and conceived as attached to the feeling-testimony (Schroeder, 1914, p. 148).

Psychoanalytic observations, Schroeder (1929, p. 365) claims, "tend to show that all moral values are merely symptomatic of unwholesome emotional disturbances."

The appearance of one of Schroeder's papers in a contemporary anthology on psychoanalysis and religion (Nase and Scharfenberg, 1977), as well as his inevitable presence in bibliographies on the psychology of religion (Beit-Hallahmi, 1978; Capps et al., 1976; Meissner, 1961; Vande Kemp, 1984), assure him a forum for some time to come. If Reuben Fine (1979, p. 449) is even approximately correct in reporting that "No prominent analyst today could be said to believe that religion has any real value for mankind," we may also anticipate that Schroeder will be heard with sympathy. On the other hand, his failure to represent and develop convincingly a coherent point of view, even a borrowed one, or simply to add illuminating case material to the literature, makes him a poor competitor with more recent contributors to the psychoanalysis of religion. As an outspoken exemplar of psychoanalytic hostility to religion, however, Schroeder is virtually without peer.

EVALUATION OF THE FREUDIAN PSYCHOANALYTIC PERSPECTIVE

Two conspicuous groups of persons apparently deem critical evaluation of psychoanalysis unnecessary: (1) those who consider Freud's thinking to be hopelessly

---

[7] Schroeder is distinctly not an Adlerian, however, and he certainly does not share Adler's view of religion. A nontheistic humanist, Adler interprets the idea of God much like Feuerbach. That is, God represents an ideal of human perfection toward which we strive (see Adler and Jahn, 1933; Ansbacher, 1971; Küng, 1979). Adler's influence has been felt far more in pastoral psychology than in the psychology of religion.

dogmatic and unscientific, an outdated product of nineteenth-century cultural assumptions and values; and (2) certain practitioners of orthodox psychoanalysis who tacitly assume that Freud's ideas are fundamentally true, requiring at most only a degree of fine-tuning and cautious elaboration.

Most commentators fall somewhere between these dogmatic extremes, acknowledging that Freud was a brilliant theoretician and practitioner who has bequeathed to us a rich legacy, yet recognizing that his vision had its limits and was conditioned by its cultural context. In the following review of the critical response to Freud and his orthodox followers, we first consider Freudian psychoanalysis as a general system and then look more closely at its application to religion.

HOW ADEQUATE IS PSYCHOANALYSIS?

Lying as it does on the boundary between objective and subjective psychology, psychoanalysis has inspired a continuing, sometimes acrimonious debate over whether it is science or hermeneutics. Freud himself claimed for it the status of a natural science, and many psychologists today insist on measuring its worth by contemporary scientific standards. Others object to this view, however, branding it as scientistic and arguing that, contrary to Freud's own opinion, psychoanalysis is best conceived as an interpretive discipline that seeks to understand subjective experience rather than to explain it. Therefore, Freud's theories are to be evaluated, not by subjecting them to piecemeal testing by experimental or correlational procedures, but in terms of the criteria we would use to judge the adequacy of narrative: coherence, comprehensiveness, continuity, and the capacity to elicit an aesthetic response (Spence, 1982). Freud's theories are thus seen as guiding metaphors subject to artistic truth, not as hypotheses to be tested according to historical truth.

Still others argue that psychoanalysis is both empirical science and hermeneutics, given a definition of science broad enough to include the individual case study and the subjectivity of the investigator. Proponents of this view underscore the multiple layers of psychoanalysis—some subject to empirical verification, others not—as well as the extraordinary complexity and diversity of the psychological phenomena it strives to encompass (Edelson, 1988; Jahoda, 1977; McIntosh, 1979). The following evaluation of psychoanalytic theory takes into account both scientific and hermeneutical perspectives.

Psychoanalysis as Science

Freud's theories are often said to be largely untestable by scientific means. According to this view, psychoanalytic concepts are too vaguely defined, its hypothesized processes essentially unmeasurable, and the postulated causal relations so elusively complex that no outcome could prove the theory false. In fact, however, hundreds of studies employing a great diversity of methods have been carried out to test Freud's theoretical principles. In their book-length review of this still-growing and increasingly sophisticated literature, Seymour Fisher and Roger Greenberg (1977) report that Freud's predictions are often borne out by empirical research. They conclude, for example, that clusters of traits in both children and adults do indeed correspond to the oral and anal character types depicted by Freud. In addition, there is a modest scattering of evidence that these traits result from certain bodily experiences in childhood. Several aspects of the male Oedipus complex also appear to be confirmed, including rivalry with the father, sexual fantasies in relation to the mother, and—to a greater degree than in females—proneness to anxiety and fear of bodily injury in response to erotic stimuli (the castration complex).

Other ideas proposed by Freud are apparently not supported by empirical findings. Resolution of the boy's conflict with his father, for example, and identification with the father's masculinity and moral values seem to be prompted not by fear, as Freud says, but by the father's warm and nurturant attitude. The resulting superego standards are not dramatically more severe than in the girl's case. Indeed, a number of the sex differences Freud hypothesized remain unconfirmed. Freud's theory of dreams fares little better in these studies. No evidence has been found for his claim that dreams conceal an unacknowledged wish. They do, however, seem to provide an outlet for tension or disturbance, as he had postulated (pp. 392–415). In a more recent review, Ross Levin (1990) likewise concludes that Freud's original model of dreaming is in need of revision, especially given the considerable empirical evidence that dreaming serves to consolidate and integrate affective experience.

Some social scientists are less concerned about gathering empirical evidence for Freud's theories than about finding alternative explanations for the phenomena he described. The Oedipus complex in particular has been the subject of diverse reinterpretations. Anthropologist Marvin Harris (1977), for example, cogently argues that the cause of the "widespread if not universal" occurrence of Oedipal strivings is not human nature, as Freud claims, but a certain cultural configuration, which Harris calls the "male supremacy complex." The conditions for creating hostility between generations in males and penis envy in females are present, he writes,

> in the male monopoly over weaponry and the training of males for bravery and combat roles, in female infanticide and the training of females to be passive rewards for "masculine" performance, in the patrilineal bias, in the prevalence of polygyny, competitive male sports, intense male puberty rituals, ritual uncleanliness of menstruating women, in the bride-price, and in many other male-centered institutions. Obviously, wherever the objective of childrearing is to produce aggressive, "masculine," dominant males and passive, "feminine," subordinate females, there will be something like a castration fear between males in adjacent generations—they will feel insecure about their manliness—and something like penis envy among their sisters, who will be taught to exaggerate the power and significance of the male genitalia (pp. 95–96).

Harris concludes that war causes the Oedipus complex, not the other way around, and that variations in the disposition toward warfare as well as the related differences in sex roles and hierarchies can in turn be understood as responses to the pressures of overpopulation and intensified competition for food.

Bakan (1971) argues somewhat similarly that Oedipal fears may in some measure be a realistic response to infanticidal impulses—including child abuse today— that function to preserve the population-resource balance. The Bible contains many allusions to infanticide, Bakan points out, and among them may be the story of Adam and Eve. If we take the fruit of the tree of "knowledge" to be a baby, as someone once suggested to Bakan, this ancient myth may be interpreted as an injunction to substitute the birth control measure of modesty for that of killing children (p. 84). The putative Oedipal fantasies of Freud's patients may similarly have been expressions of the trauma of real childhood abuse, according to Jeffrey Masson (1984), who charges that Freud suppressed this truth, after briefly recognizing it, in order to escape the professional isolation it was costing him. It is more likely that Freud repressed it, according to the speculation of other commentators, to avoid facing his own early experience of sexual seduction by his father, mother, or nanny (Balmary, 1979; Roith, 1987).[8]

Psychoanalysis as Hermeneutics

If we accept Paul Ricoeur's definition of hermeneutics as "the theory of the rules that preside over . . . the interpretation of a particular text, or of a group of signs that may be viewed as a text" (1965, p. 8), psychoanalysis clearly qualifies as a form of hermeneutics. The group of signs may be literally a text, as in the case of biblical exegesis. More typically, however, the "text" consists of a dream, a neurotic symptom, or a slip of the tongue. Psychoanalysis serves as an interpretive system for uncovering the deeper meaning hidden beneath the surface of manifest content.

The field of hermeneutics, Ricoeur says, is structured by a fundamental opposition. At one pole is a hermeneutics of belief, which aims to restore the meaning of a text, allowing its authentic message to manifest itself anew. At the other pole is a hermeneutics of suspicion, which reduces and demystifies, relentlessly stripping away the illusions and idols that we take for reality. On the face of it, psychoanalysis would seem to be a theory of the second type, a hermeneutics of suspicion intent on destroying fundamental elements of Western culture. Yet by the brilliant application of a hermeneutics of restoration, Ricoeur uncovers a deeper significance that puts Freud's theory in a different light.

A brief summary of Ricoeur's interpretation of the Oedipus complex will illustrate this approach. Psychoanalysis, Ricoeur suggests, is best interpreted as a scientific myth rendered in the language of desire. The Oedipus complex in particular is a "positivistic transposition" (p. 209) of the ancient Greek tragedy after which it is named. The kernel of truth in Freud's libido theory, says Ricoeur, lies in its "intersubjective structure of desire." For Freud, desire always exists in an interpersonal context. It also has a history, which consists of successive encounters with the often-opposing desires of others, especially the desires of authorities. In a formula, "The fundamental meaning of the Oedipus complex is that human desire is a history, that this history involves refusal and hurt, that desire becomes educated to reality through the specific unpleasure inflicted upon it by an opposing desire" (p. 387). The Oedipus complex, Ricoeur observes, is but one among many transitions in the lifelong process of choosing and then having to give up objects of desire.

Thus, in contrast to those who plumb psychoanalytic theory for empirically testable hypotheses, Ricoeur and other reinterpreters of Freud (e.g., Becker, 1973; N. O. Brown, 1959; Homans, 1970; Rieff, 1959) have sought to recast or reconceive his basic propositions, in order to reclaim for our understanding the insights they contain. Yet how are we to know if their interpretations are true? And when interpretations conflict, how are we to choose among them?

Clinician and philosopher Carlo Strenger (1991) lays out three possible responses—apart from dogmatism—to psychoanalysis and any other such interpretive framework. The *skeptical* position starts with the assumptions that there is a truth to be known and that it makes sense to say that theoretical propositions are supported or disconfirmed by empirical data. The skeptic, then, estimates the degree to which a given theory is supported by existing evidence. The *relativist* position,

---

[8] Masson (1984, pp. 138–144) presents evidence that the son of Wilhelm Fliess believed that his father, later described as an ambulatory psychotic, had sexually molested him as a young child. If this is true, Masson points out, Fliess would naturally not have encouraged Freud in his seduction theory, about which he was writing at that very time.

which is hinted at by some authors rather than explicitly endorsed, assumes that contradictory propositions may be equally true, or a single proposition both true and false, depending on one's point of view. Relativists may further assume that if it is not possible to establish one true account of a state of affairs, then there must be no truth to be found. Strenger rejects relativism as an incoherent refuge from rigorous thinking. The *pluralistic* position, finally, maintains that different interests and perspectives use different standards of rightness, leading to alternate versions of human experience and behavior. These descriptions need not contradict or exclude each other, but in any case there are few if any grounds for comparing them.

A proponent of the postmodern pluralistic position, Strenger argues for considering personality theories and related psychotherapeutic systems as alternate conceptual frameworks that—because they employ different methods—operate on different phenomena, which they then organize in divergent ways. Strenger does not rule out the possibility of informative empirical research, but such research, he says, cannot resolve the considerable differences that are a matter of world-view and ethical values. While acknowledging the need of practitioners for a convincing and workable conceptual framework, Strenger urges them to keep their views open to continuing reevaluation. An advocate of "civilized and rational dialogue between opposing views" (p. 183), Strenger believes that the existence of competing approaches is a vital antedote to dogmatic self-satisfaction.

EVALUATING THE FREUDIAN INTERPRETATION OF RELIGION

Freud's psychology of religion consists of two distinct though related theories, one bearing on the rise of individual piety, the ontogenetic theory, and the other on the origin of religion in the human race, the phylogenetic theory. Both, of course, are founded in the dynamics of the Oedipal conflict, but the phylogenetic theory entails considerable historical reconstruction as well. Whereas empirical research is necessarily limited to the testing of aspects of the ontogenetic theory, hermeneutics may concern itself with either.

Empirical Assessment of the Ontogenetic Theory

Freud locates the origin of individual piety in the experience of infantile helplessness and the longing for protection by the omnipotent father. Because the superego becomes a substitute for the father and is supposed to be more severe in the male, men are postulated to play the primary role in the shaping of religion, which they then pass on to women. Religious ritual, we also recall, is thought by Freud to be akin to obsessional neurosis; it is said to be a defensive maneuver against a variety of sexual and egoistic impulses. All these themes invite empirical evaluation.

Does Religion Stem from a Longing for Protection by the Father? In perhaps the earliest study offering evidence bearing on the question whether a longing for protection fostered religion, Kimball Young (1926) reports that, of the 2922 Protestant hymns that he classified, the largest proportion—33 percent—were on the theme of *infantile return* to a powerful and loving protector who shields humankind from all harm. The second most common theme, encompassing another 25 percent of the hymns, was *future reward,* the anticipation of a joyful life in heaven. This theme and most of the ten others he identified, Young points out, are closely related to infantile return. Support for Freud's thesis was not forthcoming, however, in a study James Tennison and William Snyder (1968) carried out years later with college students. These investigators found no significant correlation between a measure of the need for succorance and a composite measure of favorable attitudes toward the church.

Freud's God-as-infantile-father proposition is usually assessed simply by correlating concepts of God with similarly measured concepts of father and mother. In spite of rather wide-ranging individual differences (from − .64 to .89 in Nelson and Jones's 1957 study), this research has consistently found the concept of God to correlate more highly with the mother concept, on the average, than with the father concept. This finding reflects a marked tendency in men and women for God to be more strongly associated with the image of the preferred parent, which for both sexes is more often the mother. When subjects expressed no preference, perhaps indicating a more harmonious family, the God–father and God–mother correlations tended to be equal as well as higher than in the other cases (Godin and Hallez, 1964; Nelson, 1971; Nelson and Jones, 1957; Strunk, 1959a).

Antoine Vergote and his associates found that the God representation of their subjects was composed of two nuclear factors: the maternal one of availability and the paternal one of law and authority. In all six of their cultural groups, however, availability accounted for a much larger proportion of the variance. Thus the representation of God again proved to resemble the mother figure more than the father. Interestingly, the tendency to attribute primarily maternal qualities to God was even more marked in a group of Roman Catholic seminarians and women religious. Concurrent personality assessment revealed that these subjects had a greater attachment to their mothers than laypersons do (Vergote and Tamayo, 1981).

The general assumption that one's *mode of relating* to divinity, however it is conceived, is derived from childhood interactions with the parents was evaluated by Melford Spiro and Roy D'Andrade (1958), using data from 11 diverse societies. They tested three hypotheses.

1. The more individuals are indulged in early childhood, when crying and other signs of need automatically elicit parental nurturance, the more likely that they will later think supernatural help is contingent on the use of *compulsive* rituals. Like crying, such rituals compel the divine agents to satisfy the individuals' desires.

2. If the older, more reality-oriented child is socialized to expect assistance only by actively soliciting parental concern, supernatural nurturance will be taken as contingent on *propitiatory* rituals, through which divinity is coaxed or cajoled into action.

3. If, on the other hand, parents tend to be nurturant even in the absence of solicitation, supernatural reward will later be experienced as *noncontingent*, requiring neither ritual action nor obedience to certain demands.

For all three hypotheses Spiro and D'Andrade found a good measure of support. (1) High initial satisfaction of dependency needs proved to be significantly related to the use of compulsive rituals, though the correlation with the element of contingency did not reach significance. (2) High expectation of having to solicit parental concern correlated significantly with contingent supernatural nurturance but with neither ritual nor propitiation. (3) High parental nurturance even without solicitation correlated, as predicted, with noncontingent supernatural nurturance. For all three hypotheses, it is worth noting, the significant correlations were impressively high, in the .70s and .80s.

Parallel results were found in another cross-cultural study, this one based on ethnographic reports on 62 widely scattered societies. William Lambert, Leigh Triandis, and Margery Wolf (1959) found that nurturant agents in societies in which the gods or other supernatural beings were conceived of as predominantly aggressive were significantly more likely to be described as inflicting pain on male infants than in societies with chiefly benevolent supernatural beings. Although eight other male infancy training variables indicative of indulgence did not yield significant differences, on all but one of these dimensions the societies with benevolent beings were higher. A larger proportion of significant differences were found for the childhood variables. Parents in societies with aggressive spiritual beings were more likely than parents in the other societies to encourage self-reliance and independence in their sons, and to do so more often through punishment than reward. Boys in these societies were rated as significantly more self-reliant and independent, whereas boys in societies with benevolent spiritual beings were rated as more nurturant.

None of these results bears on Freud's claim that God is *nothing but* an exalted father, for testing that hypothesis requires evidence beyond the reach of empirical science. They do support, however, Freud's belief that how a person conceives of and relates to God is profoundly influenced by his or her earliest relationships. Yet Freud is mistaken when he assumes that the father invariably serves as the model for God. Even among persons reared in a strongly patriarchal religious tradition, it seems, God tends to be more maternal than paternal. As we will see, some psychoanalytic revisionists would take much satisfaction in such a finding.

Are Men the Originators of Religion?   A casual glance at the history of religion might tempt us to assume that men are the originators of the religious traditions. Almost all the founders and reformers who come most easily to mind are male: Lao Tzu, Gautama Buddha, Confucius, Jesus Christ, and Muhammad; or later, Augustine, Guru Nanak, Martin Luther, Ramakrishna, and Mahatma Gandhi. If we quickly scan the more anonymous ranks of priests and other religious leaders in virtually any tradition, we again find ourselves overwhelmed by a masculine presence. Yet quite apart from the fact that so fleeting a review of religious history overlooks the times and traditions in which women have played a major role (see Falk and Gross, 1989; Sharma, 1987), we should hesitate to assume that the sex that has wielded more influence or power in the course of religious history is thereby, as a class, the more religious.

For his part, Freud has more ordinary people in mind, and among them women are consistently more religious. In study after study, members of the female sex— young and old—almost always score higher on indicators of religiosity, whether these be measures of belief, attitudes, experience, or participation. Only among Jews and Mormons, both of whose traditions are distinctly male oriented, do men tend to be equally or more religious (Argyle and Beit-Hallahmi, 1975; Vernon and Cardwell, 1972). Similarly contradicting Freud's theory, evidence suggests that females have a somewhat greater tendency to feel guilty (Wright, 1971) and thus to have stronger superegos. In Freud's favor is the argument that, because women feel more vulnerable and anxious than men, they are more likely to seek protection and consolation in the cosmic realm (Argyle and Beit-Hallahmi, 1975, p. 77). They apparently also tend to have a more benevolent image of God than men do, a finding in accord with Freud's theory of an Oedipal origin (Larsen and Knapp, 1964; Wright and Cox, 1967).

Is Religion Akin to Neurosis, a Defense Against or a Substitute for Forbid-

den Impulses? Without question the mentally disturbed are frequently attracted to religion. Those suffering from anxiety and guilt are understandably drawn to resources that promise forgiveness, love, and moral support. If in more serious disorders, such as schizophrenia, the individual feels overwhelmed by normal sensory stimulation, meditative practices may provide relief. And when the world takes on a more ominous PHYSIOGNOMY, threatening the psychotic with nothingness, total destruction, or death, the religious traditions offer images and interpretations that make sense of and perhaps even mitigate these delusional fears. The more serious the impairment, we should note, the more likely the individual will turn to personal religious expression such as prayer, rather than to institutional forms (Lindenthal et al., 1970).

Need the attractiveness of religion to the mentally troubled imply that religion itself is neurotic? More precisely, is religious ritual as compulsive as Freud claims? If so, does this mean that religious ritual serves as a defense against forbidden desires, including sexual impulses? The first of these questions has been systematically addressed by Siri Dulaney and Alan Fiske (1994) on the basis of ethnographic evidence drawn from 20 different cultures. Starting with a list of 25 symptoms of obsessive-compulsive disorder (OCD), Dulaney and Fiske coded the frequency of these symptoms in brief excerpts drawn from anthropological descriptions of rituals associated with life-cycle transitions (birth, initiation, marriage, and death). Using the same sources, they coded a comparable number of descriptions of work. Statistical analysis strongly supported their hypothesis that cultural rituals contain more OCD-like features than episodes of work. Of the thirteen symptoms that appeared in their samplings of cultural rituals, the following seven were strikingly more frequent in ritual: fear that something terrible will happen; fear of causing harm to others or oneself; taking measures to prevent such harm; concern or disgust over bodily wastes or secretions; attending to a threshold or entrance; attributing special significance to colors; and carrying out repetitive actions. Two other symptoms were also far more common in rituals than in work, though their frequency of occurrence was too low for statistical significance: placing things in their proper places, and arranging people or things in some precise spatial configuration. Of the 12 OCD symptoms that happened not to appear in their samplings—for example, repetitive washing—Dulaney and Fiske note that most can easily be found in the literature on ritual.

Whereas one could read these findings as strong support for Freud's view that religious ritual mimics neurotic ritual and thus serves a similar function, Dulaney and Fiske propose reading the relationship the other way around. They posit a universal capacity for ritual, an inborn psychological mechanism by which people mark life transitions, secure social relationships, cope with misfortune, and respond to life's mysteries. Obsessive-compulsive disorder, Dulaney and Fiske suggest, represents a malfunctioning or hyperactivation of this mechanism, an idiosyncratic effort to restore the world to order. Yet lacking the collective legitimation that lends religious ritual its efficacy, the ideas and rituals of OCD are perplexing and embarrassing to the sufferer, who commonly finds that they hinder rather than help.

The second question—Does religious ritual serve as a defense against forbidden desires or impulses?—is better addressed through clinical data. In a study of 23 chronically scrupulous Roman Catholic children between the ages of 10 and 17, Wayne Weisner and Anthony Riffel (1960) concluded that the underlying problem lay in handling aggressive and sexual impulses. The aggression—usually unrecognized by anyone—found expression in extreme competitiveness, marked sibling rivalry, and frequent manipulativeness. Sexual conflict was manifested in incapacitatingly ambivalent preoccupation with sexual matters and in excessive guilt. These children showed typical obsessive-compulsive symptoms, evident both within the religious sphere and outside of it. The possibility that religious scrupulosity is related to sexual impulses was suggested many years earlier in a questionnaire study of Catholic high school girls by Joseph Mullen (1927), who found that the majority of those reporting attacks of scrupulosity were first troubled by them on the threshold or during the early years of adolescence. Elmer Clark's (1929) data on the age of religious awakening, gathered at about the same time, show a remarkably similar pattern, including the peak at the age of 12.

Clinical studies of Muslims in Saudi Arabia (Mahgoub and Abdel-Hafeiz, 1991) and ultraorthodox Jews in Israel (Greenberg and Witztum, 1994) demonstrate that, in the context of religious traditions that are particularly demanding about cleanliness and ritual exactness, OCD symptomatology frequently includes religious content. Yet as these studies report, compulsive religious observances are recognized by both the sufferers and their religious advisers to be unusual and excessive. Furthermore, among the Jewish subjects, the aspects of ritual behavior that were focal in the OCD symptomatology are not central to Jewish practice. Some laws requiring meticulous observance were not implicated at all. The "fit" between obsessive-compulsive disorder and religious observances was clearly far from perfect. Although neither of these studies addresses the dynamics of the symptomatology and thus Freud's thesis, together they do suggest caution in equating the driving forces of neurotic ritual with the motives of religious rites. As Sandor Feldman (1959) points out, for most religious persons, ritual comes to a clear and satisfying conclusion, whereas neurotics are always in doubt, tortured by the unendingness of their compulsive observances. Still, the similarity of much religious ritual to symptoms of OCD, along with recent correlational evidence linking the disorder to religiosity measures (Higgins, Pollard, and Merkel, 1992; Lewis, 1994), suggests that Freud was on to something.

The Interpretive Critique of Freud's Phylogenetic Theory

No other psychological interpretation of religion has inspired as much critical assessment as Freud's. Although his ontogenetic theory has itself provoked a considerable outpouring in the literature—not all of it unfavorable—it is his phylogenetic speculations that have received the harshest criticisms. Many psychoanalysts simply ignore this aspect of his work as well as the controversy it has spawned, but others of Freud's followers have sought to counter the criticisms, sometimes by introducing new evidence or by undergirding his ideas with other theoretical frameworks. The following brief summary of the major criticisms of Freud's theories includes some examples of these later efforts at reclamation.

Reliance on Doubtful Anthropological and Historical Speculation: Both *Totem and Taboo* and *Moses and Monotheism* are founded in a reconstruction of ancient events that most cultural anthropologists and biblical scholars—in Freud's time as well as ours—categorically reject. Such earlier researchers as Wilhelm Schmidt, A. L. Kroeber, and Bronislaw Malinowski labeled as sheer conjecture Freud's notion of a primal horde in which the sons killed and devoured the father. Furthermore, these anthropologists argued, totemism is neither universal nor invariably characterized by some one element (the incest taboo, Freud had said); and where totemism has existed in the past, only rarely did it entail the ritual killing and eating of the totem god.

Freud's bold reconstruction of the story of Moses, selectively based on the highly speculative and widely disputed work of several historians, is also vigorously repudiated. Each of the main elements in his account has been challenged. There are no compelling grounds, his critics have said, for concluding that Moses was an Egyptian, especially one of august stature, whereas there are logical and psychological reasons for arguing against it; the monotheistic views of Ikhnaton and Moses are said to be too distant in character and time for one to have been derived from the other; the figure of a second, Midianite Moses is purely Freud's invention, as he himself admitted; and the putative murder of the Egyptian Moses is based on the entirely conjectural and generally ignored theory of but a single (albeit distinguished) scholar, Ernst Sellin (Banks, 1973; Philp, 1956; Rosmarin, 1939). Having dismissed the core suppositions of the book, scholars are now reexamining this work for its deeper meanings, including evidence bearing on Freud's Jewish identity (Eilberg-Schwartz, 1994; Paul, 1996; Rice, 1990; Yerushalmi, 1991).

Yet Freud's theories were not to be easily refuted. *Totem and Taboo* became "one of the minor gospels of three generations of the Western intelligentsia," according to the eminent historian of religion Mircea Eliade (1967, pp. 24–25), who himself dismisses it as a "wild 'gothic novel.' " More recently, Christopher Badcock (1980, 1986) has drawn on new research on the gelada baboon, the evolutionary principles of sociobiology, and the earlier observations on initiatory rites by Reik and Róheim to argue that Freud's theory is "the most plausible and powerful explanation we possess of the origins of human society, and of culture in general" (1980, p. 2). Gelada baboons, who share striking adaptive features with human beings, reproduce in "one-male groups" precisely reminiscent of Freud's primal horde. They do not, however, avoid incest and suppress aggression toward the paternal generation. These traits gradually emerged in human beings, Badcock hypothesizes, through many thousands of years of natural selection that favored a deep emotional ambivalence: on the one hand, potentially PARRICIDAL aggression promising success in the hunt for food; on the other hand, altruistic submissiveness to the interests and thus the survival of one's own group. Bloody initiation rites, Badcock infers, are the means by which the "civilizing psychological forces that operated in the original parricides" have been kept alive in the succeeding generations (p. 23).

Reliance on Questionable General Assumptions: Apart from the matter of evidence, serious questions have been raised about certain basic presuppositions that undergird Freud's arguments. Prominent in his historical reconstruction are two closely related assumptions: the inheritance of acquired characteristics and the existence of a group psyche. Beyond hypothesizing an oft-repeated primal murder, Freud concludes that the subsequent guilt and remorse have been passed on genetically to the succeeding generations, which then collectively show the symptoms of individual neurosis. But the assumption that modifications occurring in the lifetime of an organism are preserved and passed on by heredity, a view associated with the name of the French biologist Chevalier de Lamarck (1744–1829), is now almost universally rejected.

Although Badcock (1980), too, subscribes to the notion of a group psyche subject to a "collective neurosis" (p. 132), he argues that today the discredited Larmarckian assumption is unnecessary to support Freud's thesis. Rather than conceiving of Freud's "memory traces" as *acquisitions* of an individual lifetime, they may be understood as *mutations* in the genetic code that have been gradually selected according to the sociobiological principle of inclusive fitness (pp. 33–35). Money-Kyrle (1929, p. 193) maintains that neither a mechanism of evolutionary change nor an actual primeval parricide is necessary. Even Freud, he notes, recognized that the totem feast might more simply be accounted for ontogenetically, in terms of the universal "unconscious hatred of fathers." This "more sober version" of the theory, says William Alston (1964, p. 71), allows us to take it more seriously.

The two assumptions under discussion belong to the broader framework of cultural evolutionism, which maintains that all religion develops in terms of a uniform progression. Animism–Totemism–Polytheism–Monotheism is Badcock's formulation. Contemporary scholarship challenges such a dogmatic hypothesis, however, suggesting instead that the various traditions have developed in wholly unsystematic ways, yielding a great plurality of forms (Küng, 1979; E. R. Wallace, 1984).

Like other cultural evolutionists, Freud takes science to be the highest stage of development. He claims it is the only means by which we can come to know reality. Among those who have taken issue with this assumption is Freud's life-long friend Oskar Pfister (1928), whose doubts about Freud's scientific optimism are manifest in the title of his response, "The Illusion of a Future." Both liberal Lutheran pastor and orthodox psychoanalyst, Pfister claims that religion is the source of the most striking ethical advances and the tap root of the greatest art and the noblest aspirations. It satisfies the deep human longings for emancipation from guilt, for a love that transcends life's intolerable uncertainties, for a feeling of at-homeness and peace, for a unifying vision of the world, for mystical union with the divine. Religion, Pfister says, lifts the human spirit to new, ecstatic heights, strengthens the heart, and deepens the value of human existence. To believe that science will make the religious enlargement of life superfluous, concludes Pfister, is itself an illusion.

Paralleling Freud's belief that science is superior to religion is another assumption: the superiority of masculinity over femininity. Judith Van Herik (1982) astutely points out that, together, these presuppositions establish a "hierarchy of religio-cultural attitudes," ordered according to the degree of impulse renunciation. At the bottom of Freud's hierarchy are the naive Christian worshipers who, in a submissive, feminine attitude, seek fulfillment through personal relation with a loving and powerful Father–God. At the second level are the Jewish worshipers who in a more active, masculine manner obey the father's demands for renunciation of wish-fulfillment, thereby instigating various intellectual, cultural, and ethical advances. Beyond this attitude of "normal masculinity"—which, still dominated by a repressed Oedipus complex, borders on the neurotic—lies the highest level, of "ideal masculinity." Here, the Oedipus complex has been dissolved and reality becomes depersonalized; renunciation has finally allowed the emergence of the postreligious, scientific outlook. Thus we see more clearly how fundamentally Freud's negative view of femininity, as well as his treatment of masculinity as the universal norm and ideal, has guided his interpretations of religion. Although naturally declining Freud's pejorative assessment of femininity, feminist theologian Naomi Goldenberg (1979) concludes from Freud that father-centered religion must be overthrown if women are to become independent and thus responsible for their own lives.

One further assumption made by Freud requires our attention. He believed that a naturalistic explanation of religious belief, especially in terms of infantile and neurotic origins, renders such belief unacceptable to rational adults. Alston (1964), who addresses this view at considerable length, concludes that a causal explanation of a theistic belief does not logically falsify it, unless the belief explicitly excludes such an explanation. To argue, more specifically, that theistic belief is unworthy of serious attention because of its roots in neurotic or infantile processes requires independent evidence that a belief so produced is likely to be untrue, or that the persons who hold it are thereby hampered in their adjustment to reality. Evidence summarized by Batson, Schoenrade, and Ventis (1993, p. 255) that points to an inverse relationship between religiosity and serious mental disorder would seem not to support Freud's contention.

Some critics have countered Freud's views by arguing that the posture of atheism is no less susceptible to psychological explanation. Following the leads of other scholars (e.g., Zilboorg, 1962), Edwin Wallace (1984) identifies eight important factors that underlie Freud's general attitude toward religion as well as the specific features of his analysis of it: (1) discomfort with the superstitious, speculative, and even mystical trends within himself; (2) ambivalence toward the Jewish tradition; (3) intense conflict with his own father; (4) extensive exposure to neurotic expressions of piety among his patients; (5) disillusionment with his Catholic nanny; (6) ambivalence toward his infant brother Julius, who died when Freud was nearly two; (7) aversion to dependency, passivity, and submissiveness; and (8) Freud's adoption of psychoanalysis as a world-view. Doubting that Freud encountered much piety at all among his well-educated and secularized Jewish patients, Paul Vintz (1988) features two other factors: (1) Freud's rejection of his father, said to be responsible for his emphasis on the Oedipus complex, his seeming attack on the Jewish tradition, and his personal disbelief in God; and (2) the childhood trauma of "abandonment" by his nanny, a virtual second mother who, Vitz says, unwittingly created in Freud a "Christian complex" or "religious neurosis," which he eventually countered by declaring religion an illusion.

The vehement atheism of Ernest Jones, loyal disciple and biographer of Freud as well as contributor to the psychology of religion, has been traced to the very same pair of roots: an Oedipal struggle with the father and an early-childhood disillusionment with a superstitious nanny (Veszy-Wagner, 1966). Theodore Schroeder's father, it is said, was a severe disciplinarian who beat him with a rubber tube; Shroeder, the only one of three children to survive into adulthood, left home at the age of 16 (Ishill, 1940). Disturbances in childhood and adolescence were exceptionally prevalent among the 325 male[9] members of the American Association for the Advancement of Atheism who responded to George Vetter and Martin Green's (1932) questionnaire. Of those who had separated from their religious tradition by the age of 20, half by that time had lost one or both parents, a mortality rate estimated to be at least twice the average. Of the entire sample, virtually all could readily recall the death of someone "near or dear" to them during their earlier years, and nearly a third reported an unhappy childhood or adolescence, much as did two comparison groups of college radicals. In contrast, among college conservatives none reported an unhappy childhood and only 4 percent an unhappy

---

[9] Of the 350 questionnaires returned (out of 600 sent to a random sample of members), only 25 were from women, a proportion approximately representative of the entire membership. The women's returns were said to show a "preponderance of rather intense and unfortunate emotional experiences . . . with organized religion," and particularly with church deacons and ministers (p. 184).

adolescence. More recently, David Caplovitz and Fred Sherrow (1977) found that, in their sample of college graduates, religion was more likely to be rejected the poorer the reported relations with parents. Again, it must be emphasized, these findings do not themselves invalidate the religious views in question, as both Zilboorg and Vitz would like to think, but they do demonstrate what Freud once said, that psychoanalysis is strictly a neutral instrument, equally employable in the service of religion.

Neglect of the Phenomenology and History of Religion: Pfister's critique points us to what is perhaps the most fundamental weakness in Freud's analysis of religion. He selects certain limited aspects of it—belief in a Father–God and the practice of repetitive ritual observances—and treats them as though they constitute the whole of religion. Although many of his critics grant that Freud "has said absolutely the right thing about certain forms of religiosity" (Schaer, 1946, p. 15), they argue that he has seriously neglected both the diversity of religion's forms and the complexity of its character. They object in particular to his reduction of the cognitive element in religion to the role of secondary rationalization. They agree that religion has deep roots in the affective life, but they argue that the true origin of its speculations lies in the natural human tendency to ask questions about the nature of the universe and our destiny within it. Furthermore, they say, religious teachings frequently refer to indisputable realities in the social and natural worlds (Dalbiez, 1941; Wallace, 1984). Philp (1956, p. 88) adds that the possibility of self-deception is well understood in most religious traditions, as the widespread practices of self-examination and meditation testify.

Freud was undoubtedly more knowledgeable about religion than some of his critics have inferred. Certainly he was aware that the parallels he was drawing between religious phenomena and neurotic tendencies were far from perfect, even at the causal level that interested him most. For example, he carefully distinguishes the ego-debilitating dynamics of *repression,* responsible for neurosis, from the potentially adaptive dynamics of *suppression,* attributed to religious ritual. Although such a distinction could have led to constructive interpretations of the functions of religious ritual, Freud finally chose to ignore the difference (V. P. Gay, 1979).

Freud's inattentiveness to religion on the level of experience is also reflected in his view that, contrary to appearances, religion has undergone no real historical development. Instead, it ceaselessly repeats its own, indestructible origins (Ricoeur, 1965, p. 243). Such critics as Gordon Allport (1950) argue that, whatever the origins of a religious expression may be, its significance or meaning in the present must be viewed independently, allowing for the possibility of fundamental change. If Allport's case for the "functional autonomy of motives" is defensible on the level of individual lives, it would seem to be even more so when origin and significance are separated by unnumbered generations. Thus, even if we can be persuaded that Freud and his followers have in some measure succeeded in uncovering the earliest meanings of certain texts, symbols, or ritual activities, their significance today can only be known through a study of their contemporary appropriations.

Perhaps a simple example will help make the point. Michael Carroll (1987) provocatively suggests that the various elements constituting the Catholic practice of praying the ROSARY—the fingering of beads, the orderliness and repetitiousness of prayer phrases, the seeking of favor from the Holy Mother, and the name's suggestion of the fragrance of roses—make coherent sense if the ritual is understood as a disguised fulfillment of repressed anal-erotic desires.[10] The practice became popular, he notes, in a Germanic culture "overwhelmingly concerned with anal-erotic themes," which found their way into the Lutheran tradition as well (p. 494).

Defensible or not, does such an analysis convey the meaning of the rosary to today's humble devotee? Jesuit psychologist Joseph Maréchal (1924) offers a different perspective.

> Look at this good old woman telling her beads, on a winter evening, in the chimney corner. During the day her attention was dispersed over the small cares of her household, and confined to the limits of a modest village horizon. But see how now, her duties done, she sits down on her shaky chair, draws out her rosary, and after making a great sign of the cross, begins to mutter Hail Marys one after another in a slow rhythm. The monotony of these repetitions clothes the poor old woman with physical peace and recollection; and her soul, already directed on high, almost mechanically, by her habitual gesture of drawing out the rosary, immediately opens out with increasing serenity on unlimited perspectives, felt rather than analyzed, which converge on God (pp. 157–158).

The value of the rosary, Maréchal points out, lies in the attitude of interior devotion that it helps easily distracted individuals to establish and sustain. Surely this is the primary significance of prayer beads in other traditions as well. Although the peculiar qualities of the rosary may be attractive to persons of an "anal" disposition, what is most crucial is the experience that this "artifice of beginners" is able to facilitate. At least for Maréchal's old woman, this experience seems directly accessible to empathic understanding, requiring no appeal to unconscious infantile desires.

About such matters, however, the post-Freudian mind can no longer be entirely confident. Maréchal's portrait is brief and "idealized," descriptive of no particular person and thus lacking the richness of detail typical of a clinical case study. If we had such particulars, we would undoubtedly find ourselves impelled to take a closer look, suspicious that the rosary has other, perhaps less lofty meanings in our subject's life. Certainly it is true that the Freudians too easily overlook the inherent properties of religious objects, as some critics contend—for example, Balaji Mundkur (1983), who takes fear, not doubtful similarity to the phallus, to be the primary determinant of the symbolic significance of the snake. Yet among the lessons we have learned from Freud is the insight that nothing is ever as simple as it first appears. When carefully and patiently observed, psychological phenomena prove again and again to be indefinitely complex, subject to interpretations on a variety of levels.

FREUD'S LEGACY TO THE PSYCHOLOGY OF RELIGION

If Freud's own interpretations of religion do not adequately take into account the complexity of religion, especially its more admirable manifestations, they do have some enduring value. For some commentators, this value is deeply practical, for both individuals and institutions. Ricoeur, for instance, urges his readers to submit

---

[10] This thesis, which offended a number of readers (Capps and Carroll, 1988), is reminiscent of the more broadly framed argument of Ernest Jones (1914), who proposes interpreting baptismal water, the sacred flame, incense, and even speech and music, among many other religious elements, as progressive sublimations of infantile coprophilia.

their faith to the purifying "instruction and harsh schooling" of Freud's teachings on religion. He warns that a person's faith will not emerge intact, but the greater risk lies in avoiding the encounter altogether (1966, p. 71; 1965, p. 551). Although most "unbelievers" will assume that their rejection of religion is merely confirmed by psychoanalysis, it would seem that they, too, might benefit from learning about the childhood origins and continuing dynamics of their particular views. Vetter and Green's atheists, it may be said, were surprisingly oblivious to the possible role played by their childhood exeriences. Most attributed their antireligious outlook to later reading and reflection. The psychoanalysts, of course, would not predict otherwise. Insights into such matters, they say, ordinarily require the help of a trained therapist.

Psychoanalysis is also thought to promise health to religious institutions. The psychoanalytic theory of neurosis, Pfister (1944) maintains, can help to explain why neurotic fear and the means of combatting it have so dominated the history of the Christian tradition. Whereas Christ met fear with an attitude of understanding and love, the emphasis since then, Pfister says, has fallen on guilt and vicarious atonement, encouraging "compulsive formations of a collective-neurotic character" (p. 271). Pfister found this emphasis on guilt and atonement to be particularly prominent in the Catholic tradition. The insights of psychoanalysis, he claims, can help to undo these neurotic trends in dogma and ritual and to foster religious communities that become once more "vessels of Christian love" (p. 572). Roy Lee (1949), a Protestant minister like Pfister, also embraces psychoanalysis as a means of clearing away "the rubbish that clings to Christianity" and of freeing it "to grow to its full strength and maturity" (p. 197). Toward these ends, Lee (1963) prepared a guide to the religious education of children in which, among other things, he recommends the greatest caution in teaching religious doctrine before the Oedipus complex has been resolved. Otherwise, he says, the child's distorted images of the parents will become enduringly associated with the idea of God.

Such practical concerns, of course, have always been part of the psychology of religion. Yet the psychoanalysis of religion has implications beyond them. Recognizing depth psychology's broader potential, Schaer (1946) criticizes Pfister on two counts. He treats psychoanalysis chiefly as a technique of psychotherapy rather than as a method for scientific research; and he writes off as pathological the forms of religion that he, a liberal Protestant, finds alien rather than looking for a deeper interpretation. Himself a Protestant theologian, Schaer prefers Jung's approach to religion for its impartiality and greater breadth of religious interest.

As the next two chapters demonstrate, psychoanalysts of religion have been able to transcend the limits of Freud's personal views without abandoning his fundamental insights. Some have done so by applying certain aspects of Freud's general theory that he overlooked, especially those portions dealing with the pre-Oedipal stages. Others have relied on more recent developments in psychoanalysis, including ego psychology and object-relations theory. In either case, these interpreters have tended to apply their theories to a much wider range of religious phenomena than Freud had considered. They are also more inclined to take a sympathetic stance. Yet they, too, are part of Freud's remarkable legacy, which has forever changed our understanding of religious faith and tradition.

8

OBJECT-RELATIONS THEORY AND RELIGION

*T*hat the Oedipus complex and the relation to the father were not destined to be the whole of the psychoanalytic interpretation of religion Freud himself seemed at moments to recognize. In his essay on Leonardo da Vinci, Freud (1910, p. 123) observed that "The roots of the need for religion are in the parental complex; the almighty and just God, and Kindly Nature, appear to us as grand sublimations of father and *mother,* or rather as revivals and restorations of the young child's ideas of them" (emphasis added). As noted in Chapter 7, Freud (1930) also acknowledged religion's connection with the "oceanic feeling," an unbounded subjective state that harks back, according to the psychoanalysts, to the infantile stage of limitless narcissism, before objects—including the parents—are distinguished from the ego (see Kovel, 1990).

Although Freud himself thus raised the possibility of pre-Oedipal elements in religion, explicitly the maternal and narcissistic elements, his commitment to the centrality of the Oedipus complex ultimately won out, both in his own writings and in those of his immediate followers. In his rare and hesitant reflections on mother–goddesses, the mother IMAGO that stands out is not that of the enfolding mother who nourishes, protects, and consoles ("Kindly Nature"). Rather, it is the mother in the context of the Oedipal crisis, whose son–lover dies an early death and whose priests are castrated for her protection, presumably at the instance of the father (Freud, 1913, p. 152; 1921, p. 135). She is also a jealous but easily placated mother, who accepts worship as a sop for the inevitable slight of being displaced in importance by the father (Freud, 1939, p. 83). Freud also gives short shrift to the more archaic oceanic feeling and the need that it expresses. They play at best, he thought, a secondary role in religion. "I cannot think of any need in childhood," he (1930, p. 72) concludes, "as strong as the need for a father's protection."

It was not long before other psychoanalysts sought to balance Freud's account of religion. Some of them happened to be born into Christian rather than Jewish homes, or as adults lived in the context of still other religious traditions. Like Freud, they found it natural to apply psychoanalytic principles to the familiar though perhaps also puzzling ideas and practices that lay so close at hand. Some discovered that when the net was cast more widely, even if only within the bounds of the Jewish tradition, phenomena were brought to the surface that required a more comprehensive use of psychoanalytic theory if they were to be understood. Finally, as we observed at the end of Chapter 7, some psychoanalysts came to see that Freud's theory could just as readily be employed for interpreting antireligious attitudes as religious ones, or for distinguishing genuine or healthy forms of piety from pathological varieties. Through its critical function psychoanalysis might even prove to be a friend of the religious traditions.

In this chapter we survey this wider psychoanalytic literature. We are concerned here primarily with two related theoretical developments used to interpret religion: British object-relations theory, represented by Ian Suttie, Ronald Fairbairn, Harry Guntrip, and D. W. Winnicott; and the revised perspective on narcissism of Heinz Kohut, which is related closely enough to object-relations theory to be included in the present chapter. In surveying the *pre*-Oedipal themes prominent in this work, we become acquainted at the same time with a much broader range of religious phenomena, including some from India, China, and Japan. Along the way, we see how more orthodox psychoanalysts have viewed these same religious manifestations. The related views of Erik Erikson, which similarly encompass both East and West, are examined separately in Chapter 9. In this chapter and the next, we conclude with an evaluation of the respective approaches.

THREE FORMS OF RELIGIOUS EXPERIENCE

A ground plan for a comprehensive psychoanalysis of religion, encompassing both Oedipal and pre-Oedipal factors as well as a variety of religious traditions, was proposed well before the emergence of the object–relations perspective. This schema was published in 1932 by the Norwegian psychologist Harald Schjelderup and his brother Kristian, a theologian and psychotherapist who had been trained in orthodox psychoanalytic technique by Oskar Pfister. Earlier psychoanalytic writers had noted the importance in certain religious contexts of the mother motif (e.g., Fromm, 1930; Jones, 1923; Pfister, 1910b, 1931, Rank, 1924) and of narcissism (Alexander, 1923; Jones, 1913; Morel, 1918). It was left to the Schjelderups, however, to integrate these themes into a comprehensive schema of psychoanalytically interpreted religious types. Initially derived from a series of individual case studies, this simple typology was eventually tested against the history of religions.

On the basis of both contemporary and historical evidence, the Schjelderups identified three main forms of religious experience. In the first of these types, the preeminent feelings are those of guilt and fear, occurring in conjunction with longings for submission and atonement and occasionally with the experience of conversion. For this type, the relation to the father lies in the foreground. The second type is characterized by deep yearning for the divine, for closeness to or even union with God, for peace and rest in God. For this type the individual's relation to the mother is decisive. The third type is marked by fantasies of being oneself divine, an outcome of narcissistic withdrawal of libido from external objects and corresponding infantile SELF-GRANDIOSITY. The three types—father religion, mother religion, and self religion—thus correspond to three different stages of childhood development. Freud limited himself to religious experience of the first type, in which the father motif is dominant. According to the Schjelderups, however, "the mother motif plays an equally if not even more important role in the religious attitude" (p. 107). The narcissistic self-motif must also be taken into account, they add, although it is not always easily distinguished from the other two types.

THE MOTHER IN RELIGIOUS FAITH AND TRADITION

We need not look far in the history of religions to discover the importance of the mother. Forms of the Mother–Goddess abound, and where the Father–God has displaced her she often reappears in disguise. Students of religion who wish to find still-living examples of goddess worship inevitably turn to India, where today divinity is still generally addressed as mother. Going so far afield for evidence of maternal influence on the religious life is unnecessary, however. According to the psycho-analysts, we may expect to find it everywhere, in individual faith as well as in historical tradition.

A Theology Student's Longings

The dynamic role that the mother can play in individual piety is vividly illustrated by the Schjelderups in a case study of a 22-year-old Protestant student of theology who undertook analysis because he suffered from depression, an inhibition against work, and a variety of other symptoms. For this young man, God was a being of goodness and loving kindness "who welcomes us with open arms." The yearning for nearness to or union with God that lay at the heart of the patient's religious attitude grew especially intense whenever he broke off a love relationship, which for him was always short-lived. Relation to God, he said, is most closely approximated in this life by a loving union in marriage. Lacking such a relation himself, he felt only melancholy and a longing for eternal rest, for nirvana. "The Buddhist religion has always attracted me," he once remarked.

The home in which the patient grew up was a deeply troubled one. The young student's father was a hard, even brutal man who severely mistreated his wife. On occasion, after he had been out drinking, he would even threaten her with a gun. From an early age, the patient found his mother turning to him as her confidant, seeking his consolation. She would take him into bed with her, caress him, and talk about everything imaginable. When she was depressed it was his task to console her. "I was the spiritual advisor of my mother," he said.

As a young adult, the patient found himself almost incessantly preoccupied with his mother, recalling how pleasant it was to be in bed with her, how she had bathed him as a child, and how terribly he had yearned to return home to her when he left at the age of 16. He dreamed about her as well, especially during the years of puberty, when he would find himself again at the breast or undisguisedly engaging in intercourse with her. From time to time he also had anxious dreams of being immovably imprisoned in a tight container, dreams that he immediately associated with his mother and that the Schjelderups take as evidence of severe regressive tendencies, of a desire to return to the maternal womb. From the time he left home, the patient found himself inexorably drawn to visit "perpetually open" Catholic churches, where he was always overcome by a particular mood, one he associated with a catacomb, with "something subterranean, with many caverns and niches." He himself traced this feeling back to his longing for his mother.

He also had incestuous feelings toward his younger sister, expressed at first in childhood play and later in dreams. Again and again he sought the personal characteristics of both mother and sister in other women, but invariably he was unsatisfied. He looked in particular for someone who would "understand" him and with whom he could "cry out his misery." When he spoke with women about "spiritual questions," he would feel himself grow closer to them, physically and emotionally. If their conversation turned to specifically religious matters and he felt himself cast in the role of spiritual director, he would suddenly experience a flare-up of sexual attraction.

In becoming a minister, then, the patient was able not only to devote himself to God, the perfect mother who would console and protect him, but also to continue in the role of advisor that he had fulfilled so perfectly as a child. The Schjelderups conclude that the form of the young child's response to his mother, including specific feelings and thoughts, was carried over essentially unchanged into the young man's total religious outlook. Although longing for the mother appears in this case as the most prominent unconscious motive, the Schjelderups acknowledge that other factors may also play a role.

Sri Ramakrishna: A Simple Child of the Mother

Given a sufficiently receptive milieu, personal longings for the mother can also shape historical religious tradition. Such was the case of Ramakrishna (1836–1886), the famous nineteenth-century Bengali mystic who in the Schjelderups' analysis serves as the historical representative of the mother motif in religion. Like the accounts of other spiritual heroes, those of Ramakrishna—who today is still widely revered as an incarnation (avatar) of God—are filled with tales of childhood precocity, mystical visions, and miraculous events. The possibilities for a genuine case history would thus seem to be severely limited, and indeed, the Schjelderups tell us nothing of his childhood. Yet portions of the biographies of Ramakrishna seem probable enough, and the overall impression underscores the aptness of a devotee's loving characterization of him as "the simple child of the Mother" (Nikhilananda, 1942, p. 20).

A Desperate Search for the Mother: Ramakrishna was the youngest son among five children born to a poor BRAHMIN family in a largely low-caste agricultural village of Bengal. His elderly father, a piously orthodox and deeply respected

Ramakrishna, the nineteenth-century Hindu mystic.

man, died when Ramakrishna was only seven. The young boy "now felt especially drawn towards his mother" (Saradananda, 1911–1918, p. 52), spending more time with her and helping in any way he could with household duties. He was said also to be a source of consolation and delight to others of the village women, whom he would entertain with songs or plays or by imitating to perfection their manner and gestures. He was reportedly their confidant and advisor as well. On occasion he dressed himself as a woman, taking pleasure in his ability to pass in front of men without their suspecting his dissimulation (p. 63). Years later, when he undertook to practice in its turn the traditional MĀDHURYA BHĀVA, the "mood of erotic love" in which one relates to God as woman to her lover, he donned female dress and ornaments, "perfect in all respects" (p. 233). He remained so dressed for six months, during which time he reportedly lost all consciousness of being a man.

At about the age of 17 Ramakrishna was brought to Calcutta by his nearly 50-year-old eldest brother, a teacher and priest who, with little success, undertook to educate his young sibling. Several years later and at first reluctantly, Ramakrishna found himself officiating in the worship of Kali in a new temple outside Calcutta, one that had been founded by a well-to-do but low-caste widow. His elder brother, whom he succeeded in this position, died shortly thereafter.

Ramakrishna now devoted himself with extraordinary fervor to the daily ritual of awaking, bathing, adorning, feeding, and PROPITIATING Kali, the Divine Mother of the Universe. "After the regular forms of worship he would sit there for hours and hours, singing hymns and talking and praying to her as a child to his mother, till he lost all consciousness of the outward world. Sometimes he would weep for hours, and would not be comforted, because he could not see his mother as perfectly as he wished" (Müller, 1898, p. 36). He would spend whole nights meditating in an old burial ground nearby, divested even of his sacred Brahmanical thread, and "returning to his room only in the morning with eyes swollen as though from much weeping." In profound agony, hardly ever eating, the sleepless sufferer would cry out, "Art Thou true, Mother, or is it all fiction—mere poetry without any reality? If Thou dost exist, why do I not see Thee?" (Nikhilananda, 1942, p. 13).

Thought mad by some of those around him, Ramakrishna was taken back to his native village by his mother and brother. Later, seeming much improved, he was joined in marriage to a five-year-old girl who he said was destined to be his wife. His return to the Kali temple outside Calcutta several years later, however, brought only further intensification of his former devotional fervor. "Crowds assembled round him and tried to console him, when the blowing of the conchshells proclaimed the death of another day, and he gave vent to his sorrow, saying, " 'Mother, oh my mother, another day has gone, and still I have not found thee' " (Müller, 1898, pp. 38–39).

One day, "feeling as if my heart were being squeezed like a wet towel" and unable any longer to bear separation from the Mother, Ramakrishna took down the sword kept in Her temple, intent on ending his life.

Suddenly the blessed Mother revealed Herself. The buildings with their different parts, the temple, and everything else vanished from my sight, leaving no trace whatsoever, and in their stead I saw a limitless, infinite, effulgent Ocean of Conciousness. As far as the eye could see, the shining billows were madly rushing at me from all sides with a terrific noise, to swallow me up! I was panting for breath. I was caught in the rush and collapsed, unconscious. What was happening in the outside world I did not know; but within me there was a steady flow of undiluted bliss, altogether new, and I felt the presence of the Divine Mother (Nikhilananda, 1942, p. 14).

As he regained consciousness, he spoke but a single word: "Mother."

In the game of hide-and-seek that the Divine Mother played with Her slight and delicate son, intensifying both his suffering and his joy, She would manifest Herself in various ways. Sometimes, "from a sea of translucent mist he would behold the Mother rising, first Her feet, then Her waist, body, face, and head, finally Her whole person; he would feel Her breath and hear Her voice." On other occasions, "He would see flashes like a swarm of fire-flies floating before his eyes, or a sea of deep mist around him, with luminous waves of molten silver" (p. 14). With time, he came to see the Mother in the people around him, as well as in the temples, the river, and the trees. "Whatever is, is the Mother—isn't that so?" he once said (p. 60). All women, even prostitutes, were for him the Mother; so too his young wife, Sarada Devi, who came to live with him when she was 18. Sharing with him a spiritual relationship that was never physically consummated, she was eventually to be known by Ramakrishna's followers as the Holy Mother.

The Teachings of Ramakrishna: Ramakrishna underwent years of spiritual training, at the hands of two GURUS in particular—one a middle-aged Brahmin nun adept in TANTRIC and VAISHNAVA modes of worship, the other a naked wandering monk who, as a master of the disciplines of ADVAITA VEDANTA, viewed all the world and its deities as illusion. Through this training the nearly illiterate Ramakrishna, an unpretentious man of homely and stammering speech, attained to the highest realization. Sometimes he was the ecstatic devotee of the Divine Mother; other times he found himself blissfully absorbed in BRAHMAN, the undivided and impersonal Supreme Reality. Himself he saw as an incarnation of God, akin to Christ, the Buddha, and Krishna, sent for the benefit of humanity. The truth that he had found, he was sure, is the same truth sought in every other religious tradition. From his own experience, he claimed, he knew that each path to God leads to the same goal. The different, seemingly contradictory systems of philosophy are all means to the same end, representing different yet complementary stages on the way toward Ultimate Reality. In the end, however, thought must be left behind: SAMĀDHI, the full realization of God, can only be felt, not described.

To those who wished to join the religious order that he founded, Ramakrishna emphasized "the steep path of renunciation," the only means, he said, by which their lives could become wholly unblemished. Selecting candidates untouched by "woman and gold," he required of them absolute continence and total avoidance of greed and lust. (Ramakrishna's own deeply fostered aversion to gold, a substance he equated with "filth" [Gupta, 1897–1932, p. 210], is said to have taken the form of a literal allergy, which finally extended to any metal whatsoever.) During their training, the young men who were destined to become monks were kept apart from the married householders. Married men were also welcomed among his disciples, but their family responsibilities required that they undergo an entirely different training in which renunciation was largely mental. Today the teachings of Ramakrishna as recorded by his immediate followers are promulgated by the Ramakrishna Mission, which carries out its impressive educational and philanthropic work through 86 monasteries and mission centers in India. It also operates a number of branches in America and a scattering of other countries.

The enormously popular Hindu goddess Kali, who, terrifying in form and trampling on her consort Shiva, is nevertheless worshiped as "the mother."

The Terrible Mother

Ramakrishna almost always experienced the Divine Mother as being of compassionate and ever-available love, but Her embodiment in the image of Kali powerfully bears witness to another, far-from-benign aspect. A dark, naked, and full-breasted figure with flowing, disheveled hair, a garland of human heads around her neck, and a girdle of severed hands about her waist, Kali is depicted dancing victoriously on the body of Shiva, her consort, who lies prostrate in the middle of the cremation grounds. In one hand she bears a bloody sword and in another, the freshly severed head of a man; with still another hand, in startling contrast, she offers an expression of assurance, and with a fourth the gesture of benediction or the bestowing of boons. Blood courses down her cheeks, framing an open, smiling mouth with protruding tongue and powerful, fanglike teeth. In some representations she wears as earrings yet another set of heads—or the corpses of dead infants. Today young male goats are still sacrificed daily, by decapitation, before this terrifying image. Earlier she was thought to require human victims, a conviction not unknown even in our own day (see Wulff, 1982). The image of Kali, so horrible at first glance to Western eyes, is said by Sister Nivedita (1897, pp. 20–21), one of Ramakrishna's few women disciples, to be "perhaps dearer than any other to the heart of India. . . . Others we admire; others we love; to Her we belong."

The terrifying mien of Kali and the unfathomable sense of belonging to her are not the exclusive possession of India. Although the fearful qualities of the Great Mother are nowhere pushed closer to the outer limits of terror, they have also manifested themselves in a variety of other mother–goddesses found throughout the world. Again and again, the being who gives birth and lovingly sustains life also proves to be the one who devours and destroys. The Terrible Mother is the mother of suffering, death, and destruction, aided by hunger and pestilence and especially by war. She is the phallic snake mother, the possessor of the tooth-studded womb (the VAGINA DENTATA), and "the deadly devouring maw of the underworld" (Neumann, 1955, p. 149). To ensure the process of rebirth and the renewal of fertility, she requires unthinkably cruel and bloody sacrifices marked by castration, beheading, flaying, and dismemberment.

When we assume with the psychoanalysts that concepts of divinity are grounded in childhood relations with the parents, we can easily understand why the loving and succoring mother would be included in the heavenly realm. That she might on occasion appear in this role as an irascible or even a negligent mother is also comprehensible. Whence, however, come these grotesque, terrifying conceptions of a mother so actively and unconscionably cruel that we would expect her to be a figure from a lone psychotic's worst delusions, not a character on the world stage of human piety? How is it possible that she is perceived as loving and kind by the millions who worship her with unstinting devotion? Ian Suttie (1935, p. 189) states that the Great Mother cults are "perhaps the greatest problem for the archaeology of culture and the psychology of religion." Freud, Suttie observes, found them "a mystery as repellent as they are insoluble." Other psychoanalysts, including Suttie himself, have sought a coherent answer to this problem, apparently with some success.

The Oedipus Complex Once Again: The pervasiveness of symbolic if not literal castration in cults of the Great Mother suggests to some Freudians (e.g., Money-Kyrle, 1929; Ray Chaudhuri, 1956) that in a mother religion, too, the phallic stage and the Oedipal crisis are centrally implicated. From this point of view, the Mother–Goddess might be interpreted as a complex and ambivalent condensation of the wishes, fears, and defensive maneuvers associated with the castration complex. Representing the beloved mother as a phallic being, the mother-with-a-penis, avoids the reality of sex differences and thus the child's most compelling evidence for the possibility of castration. Furthermore, declaring the mother a virgin—traditionally signifying lack of attachment, not sexual innocence (Harding, 1935)—denies her relation to the father, thus reducing a cause for jealousy of him, if not eliminating him altogether.

In the representations of Kali, the father is eradicated in yet another way. The mother herself kills him, sometimes by beheading. Her malevolent arms, it would thus seem, are reserved for the father, whom she strikes down in dramatic fulfillment of the son's wishes or in agreement with the young boy's apprehension of cruelty in the act of intercourse. In contrast, with her benign arms she invites her adoring but horrified son to approach her, promising him blissful fulfillment of his deepest wishes. To the various aspects of the castration complex C. D. Daly (1927) adds yet another: the fear of the menstruating woman, who arouses not only castration anxiety but also primordial fear of death.

Pre-Oedipal Contributions: To other psychoanalysts the widespread phenomenon of the terrifying Mother–Goddess testifies to fears and fantasies that arise well before the Oedipus complex is constellated, perhaps during the very first months of life. Freud himself seemed always "to regard the first year of infancy as a dark mystery enshrouding dimly apprehensible excitations rather than active impulses and phantasies" (Jones, 1953, p. 323). Convinced of the importance of the first year or two of life and the child's relation to the mother, some of Freud's followers have sought to bring into focus the fantastic, even monstrous, texture of the child's early imaginings. To the naive reader, these putative fantasies are as unbelievable as they are repugnant. To some analysts, on the other hand, they are commonplace elements, still living in the obsessions and dreams of adult patients.

Psychoanalysts are largely in agreement that the subjective world of the young infant is at first highly fragmentary. Its elements consist chiefly of bodily parts with which it has had contact, especially the breast, as well as the various sensations created by physiological processes and the rhythms of physical care. It is also reported that some of these elements and their emerging combinations, when associated with pleasure, are perceived as inherently "good"; others, accompanied by tension or pain, are "bad." The mother herself, once she emerges as a whole being, may be perceived as two persons rather than one—a "good mother" and a "bad mother" who unpredictably alternate with each other. In the presence of the good mother, life is a blissful, unending paradise; under the reign of the bad mother, one must fear for life itself. Pre-Oedipal foundations for the superego are said to be laid by the child's efforts to transform the bad mother, when she appears, into the good one. Gradually and reluctantly, the child comes to recognize its own mother as a single individual possessing both positive and negative qualities. Still living in the unconscious are the images of the wholly beneficent and the implacably evil mothers, from which are derived the benign fairy godmothers and the wicked witches or cruel stepmothers that have delighted and terrified children since time immemorial (Bettelheim, 1976).

Melanie Klein: The Infant as Monster: Some psychoanalysts, notably the Vienna-born British analyst Melanie Klein (1882–1960) and her followers, add some startling details to this portrait. Emphasizing to an unprecedented degree the early modes of infantile sexuality and the principle of the death impulse, Klein ascribes to the young infant an astonishing precocity, accounted for in part by postulating vague, inborn intimations of both male and female sex organs as well as coitus and childbirth. Klein maintains that the compelling self-destructive impulses that constitute the drive toward death are present virtually from the beginning of life. These impulses, which the infant projects outwardly in self-protection, combine with frustration-derived rage and the pleasures obtained through the mouth's natural functions to transform the infant into a veritable oral-sadistic monster, especially during and after weaning. In fantasy the child launches a series of SADISTIC attacks on the objects that impinge on it, first and foremost the breast that failed to provide sufficient satisfaction, but other parts of the mother's body too, especially the "insides." Modes of bodily activity besides the oral one also come to be employed in this imaginary destructive assault.

> The idea of an infant of from six to twelve months trying to destroy its mother by every method at the disposal of its sadistic trends—with its teeth, nails and excreta and with the whole of its body, transformed in phantasy into all kinds of dangerous weapons— presents a horrifying, not to say an unbelievable picture to our minds.

Klein (1932, p. 130) adds that "The abundance, force and multiplicity of the cruel phantasies which accompany these cravings are displayed before our eyes in early analyses so clearly and forcibly that they leave no room for doubt."

Having projected its own sadistic trends onto the mother, the child expects a similar assault in return, so that "The mother's body becomes a place filled with dangers which give rise to all sorts of terrors" (p. 242). What is perhaps worse, the child's efforts to deal with the object world by introjecting it, both in its good and frightening aspects, lead to the child's being itself filled with the dangerous objects. The child seeks to master its anxiety, says Klein, by fantasies of the destructive omnipotence of its own excreta and by pitting its internalized "good" objects against the "bad" objects. Simultaneously, the internal dangers are projected outward, where they may more easily be faced if not simply disproved.

In Klein's work, then, we have a first, provisional answer to our questions about the origin of and devotion to the terrifying Mother–Goddess. She is the bad mother writ large, to whom is attributed the young infant's own worst sadistic wishes. At the same time she is the good mother, the source of life's bounty, the protectress against all evil. By assuming that it is the evil in the outer world toward which the Mother's wrath is directed, the conscious mind resolves the incompatability between these two aspects.

If, however, the Great Mother is the pre-Oedipal mother, if the sins she inexorably punishes "are *offenses against mothers and against babies, not* precocious sexual jealousy of the father's privileges and rebellion against *his* authority" (Suttie, 1935, p. 106), why does she so often appear as the phallic mother who castrates her devotees? According to Klein (1932, p. 131), the boy's "tremendous fear of his mother as the castrator" stems not only from the mother's being the one who takes away the child's feces, an act signifying dismemberment and castration to the infantile mind (Klein, 1928, p. 190), but also from the unconscious fantasy that the mother's womb retains the father's penis, an object perceived as a dangerous weapon and thus an object of intense hatred and anxiety, which are displaced to the mother's body. In accord with the infantile psyche's equation of part with whole, the penis in the mother's body represents father and mother combined in one person. This combination, according to Klein (1932, p. 132), is regarded as particularly threatening, for it recalls a terrifying combination of murderously sadistic fantasies aimed at the parents as they are joined in intercourse, as well as fantasies of the parents' destroying each other, using their genitals and excrement as weapons.

THE OBJECT-RELATIONS PERSPECTIVE

Acknowledging that, like many other readers, she, too, responded with a "naive repugnance" to Klein's descriptions of the infant's fantasy world, Ruth Munroe (1955, p. 215) claims that the orthodox Freudian objection is not to the characterization per se but to its ascription to so young a child, as well as its emphasis on oral sadism. Klein's work has been hailed as "the real turning point in psychoanalytical theory and therapy within the Freudian movement itself" (Guntrip, 1971, p. 47). In particular, it has been decisive for the recognition of the mother's crucial role in child development and thus, by extension, for the mother's role in religion, which Freud had almost entirely overlooked. Controlled studies of infants and young children, most notably the research of René Spitz (1946), have also underscored the mother's importance, demonstrating that a mother's loving care, apart from the provision of shelter and nourishment, can indeed be a matter of life or death for the very young child.

From Drive to Relation

From a more technical standpoint, Melanie Klein's influential work may be viewed as a transition from the drive-centered theory of Freud to a variety of subsequent approaches that give primacy instead to interpersonal relations, especially the earliest ones. Freud believed that the individual is a closed system of energy in which tensions build up and press for discharge. The goal, according to Freud's CONSTANCY PRINCIPLE, is a return to the pleasant state of quiescence. The objects that happen to serve this function are initially not attached to the underlying drives but are created, over time, out of the infant's particular experiences of satisfaction. Whereas for Freud the source, aim, and impetus are inherent aspects of a drive, the object is not. Rather, it is adventitiously acquired and remains forever subordinate to the aim of reducing tension (Greenberg and Mitchell, 1983).

For Klein, drive and object are inherently linked. Objecting to Freud's notion of PRIMARY NARCISSISM, defined as an objectless state characteristic of the earliest months of infancy and thought to underlie a number of psychic disturbances later in life, Klein argues that the drives are associated from the beginning with certain objects, a priori knowledge of which is a constitutive part of their nature. Although Klein accepts Freud's fundamental schema of sexual and destructive forces, she redefines the very nature of these motivational factors. Because she conceives of these drives as inherently oriented toward and structured in accord with reality, and thus treats them as psychological rather than physical forces, in her system they come to possess many of the properties of the Freudian ego. Thus though retaining the concept of drive, Klein so reconceptualizes it as to place object relations at the center of the emotional life (Greenberg and Mitchell, 1983, pp. 136–146).

In spite of continuing difficulties, Klein attempted to combine an object-relations view with Freud's original theory of organically determined drives. Others, greatly stimulated by her work, abandoned the drive model altogether, placing relations with others, real and imaginary, at the heart of their theories. In addition to Klein, the psychoanalysts most prominently associated with object-relations thinking include Ronald Fairbairn (1889–1964), Harry Guntrip (1901–1975), and Donald Winnicott (1896–1971). Each of these British analysts has written sympathetically of religion. Of the object-relations thinkers, Winnicott has been especially influential among scholars seeking a dynamic interpretation of religion.

Two other analysts who are featured in this book have also been associated with the object-relations perspective: Erik Erikson and Heinz Kohut. Guntrip (1971) states that, although Erikson apparently retained the dualistic Centaur model of id and ego, he had effectively abandoned it, transforming Freud's libido theory into an object-relations view. However, other commentators do not include Erikson among the object-relations theorists. At any rate, his contributions are sufficiently distinctive and influential to require a chapter of their own. Kohut, whose prominence in recent years has been virtually unrivaled, is presented by Greenberg and Mitchell (1983) as the most important of those ''mixed model theorists'' who have attempted to join together the conflicting drive and relationship perspectives. His views and the literature stimulated by his writings are discussed later in this chapter under the subject of narcissism.

Ian Suttie: Religion as Relational Therapy

Fundamental themes of the object-relations perspective first appeared in the oddly neglected work of yet another analyst, Ian Suttie (1889–1935), a British psychiatrist who is a forerunner of Fairbairn (Guntrip, 1971) and is distinguished by his exceptional interest in the history of religions. The first English psychologist to recognize the importance of cultural factors (J. A. C. Brown, 1964, p. 65), Suttie maintains that the patterns of sexual development that Freud had taken to be universal, most notably the Oedipus complex, are largely the outcome of particular constellations of family dynamics and, in turn, of prevailing cultural circumstances. In the place of Freud's notion of a blindly insistent libido, Suttie substitutes an innate need for companionship, combined with undirected curiosity or interest. Rather than accounting for aggression in terms of an independent drive for self-annihilation, Suttie views anger or rage as a response to the denial of love, an effort to preserve the self from isolation and to restore the lost relationship.

Drawing not only on clinical evidence but also on animal behavior and ETH-NOLOGY, Suttie opposes Freud's patriarchal and antifeminist theory by attributing to the mother the social significance that Freud had assigned to the father. It is the mother, Suttie points out, who, by virtue of her bodily functions, is the object of the first emotional relation to emerge out of the initial phase of "infantile SOLIP-SISM," during which there is no discrimination of self and other. Thus it is the mother, not the father, who is primal, and it is around her, as we will see, that all jealousies center. This bond of love is not grounded in sexual longing, Suttie says, but is founded in a natural tenderness and a mental sympathy that are at first *mediated* by caresses and nurtural gratifications. Later objects of interest are not symbolic substitutes for repressed and deflected love for the mother, but emerge out of the world of concern that the child learned to share with her. Suttie (1935, p. 56) hypothesizes that all later social activities, including art, science, and religion, are efforts to restore or to find a substitute for the love of mother that was left behind in infancy.

Of these activities, religion particularly interested Suttie. In interpreting religion in Oedipal terms, Suttie observes, Freud neglected much of religion's variety, including the remarkable mother cults of antiquity. Freud's views of the individual and social functions of religion were correspondingly narrow. Suttie's (1932, 1935) own studies of religion are notable not only for their inclusion of the Mother–Goddess but also for their greater sensitivity to the positive therapeutic value of religion, especially within the Christian tradition.

"Broadly speaking," writes Suttie (1935, p. 104), "*religion,* which, like mental illness, springs from dissatisfactions of development and particularly from the surrender of infancy, is mainly concerned in its higher forms to better our affective relationships with others (i.e. is ethical)." Thus in marked contrast to the self-preoccupation and misery of the mentally ill, religion expresses its concern in the form of social institutions and a body of revered tradition. It is, in effect, a system of psychotherapy. At the same time, appealing as it does to those most in need of help (salvation), it "tends to fall into the hands of neurotics" (p. 120). This vulnerability is particularly evident, according to Suttie, in transitional phases of historical religious development.

Mother Cults and the Cain Jealousy: Elaborating on a major portion of the Schjelderups' schema, Suttie focuses on two sharply contrasting types of religious tradition, one centered on the mother and the other on the father. Each is associated with its own form of culture. *Cults of mother–goddesses,* on the one hand, are situated within societies that are essentially MATRIARCHAL in family organization, affecting both the course of individual development and, in some measure, the structure of the society.[1] Although the Mother–Goddess is viewed primarily as the nurturer and caretaker, when her law is broken she punishes inexorably and fatally. As we have observed earlier, the crimes she punishes are offenses against mothers and babies (that is, younger siblings); her ethical demands seek to avert *regression* rather than sexual precocity.

---

[1] Suttie acknowledges that "a truly matriarchal *society* is an abnormality, or theoretical possibility which hardly, if ever, can exist" (p. 98). Not a single indisputably matriarchal society has been found by anthropologists and archaeologists.

The form of jealousy that must be renounced in the context of mother cults centers around nurtural needs and maternal favors. Of the various jealousies that disturb the family unit, Suttie considers the CAIN JEALOUSY, "the ethical leitmotif of the mother cults," to be "by far the most important in the process of socialization," given its inevitable and early appearance (pp. 87, 90). Cain slew Abel because Abel's offering was more pleasing in the sight of the parent–God; that is, Cain's younger brother—the baby—was apparently better loved. The punishment for this nurtural jealousy came from the mother, who avenged her baby's death by expelling Cain from the home and refusing, as Mother Earth, to yield to him her fruits. The Lord God, the father, who was himself subject to a regressive jealousy of the child's nurtural favors from the mother (LAIUS JEALOUSY, named after the father of Oedipus), sides with his evicted son and acts as his protector, by placing a mark on him that will preserve him from the hostility of others (p. 107).

Sacrifice in the mother cults also centers on the Cain jealousy, the rivalrous struggle among siblings for nurtural favors. The young, innocent victim, sometimes explicitly regarded as Earth's child, is showered during his or her elected reign with all the honors and privileges befitting a god or goddess. At the end of the year, however, the victim must become a bloody sacrifice to the fickle mother, making way for the next child. "By allowing the Earth Mother to have her new baby," writes Suttie, "we have renounced our guilty, regressive Cain jealousy" and regained the mother's nurturing care (p. 108). With renunciation and expiation comes a measure of gratification, for by killing the baby, we satisfy our jealousy of the favors received by this usurper of the privileged position, and by electing another, we become reborn, through identification, as the favored child.

Cults of the Jealous Father: In *cults of father–gods,* both myth and sacrifice are concerned with the rivalry of father and son for the possession of the mother. In the patriarchal cultures associated with these cults, argues Suttie (1932, 1935), a variety of circumstances concur to relax the primary and "vastly more effective" *maternal* repression of the Oedipal wish (1932, p. 82) and thus to bring this complex into prominence: early childbearing, marked age disparity between husband and wife, and the wife's lack of social companionship and reality interests. Under these conditions, women are forced to rely on their children for interest, affection, and self-esteem, thus intensifying and prolonging the mother–child bond.

The jealousy of the father that is correspondingly intensified is both powerful and complex, according to Suttie. Complementing the son's precocious jealousy of the father's privileged position with the mother is the father's "regressive jealousy of the child's nurtural possession of the mother," the Laius jealousy, which is directed toward daughters as well as sons. And complementing the woman's putative jealousy of the male sex organs is ZEUS JEALOUSY,[2] the man's "violent jealousy" of the woman's capacity to bear and suckle children, an envy reflected in widespread initiation rites in which the female functions of menstruation and childbearing are simulated by men (see Bettelheim, 1962, for a detailed account). Thus the father seeks not only to displace the baby in relation to the mother but also to usurp the mother's role in relation to the baby. In patriarchal societies, Suttie notes, the male's jealous and aggressive possessiveness remains unchecked, promoting intensification of his infantile longings *and* his sexual precocity.

Patriarchal myth and ritual, says Suttie, are directed chiefly toward precocity

---

[2] Zeus, the highest of the Olympian gods, gave birth to Athena from his axe-cloven head after having ravished and swallowed the Titaness Metis.

and its repression. The focus of its mythology is the struggle between fathers and sons rather than between siblings; religious interest is prompted by the problem of guilt rather than of nurturance. In sacrifices, the victim is either a criminal or a scapegoat—the sinful, precocious child who is killed chiefly to satisfy the Laius jealousy of the Sky Father. Unconsciously, the jealousies gratified through this sin offering are parricidal rather than infanticidal. "Goodness is now submission to authority, observance of a multitude of taboos, cultivation of a sense of unworthiness and the practice of asceticism, none of which ethical activities were regarded with the least esteem under the matriarchal culture and upbringing" (Suttie, 1935, p. 112). Like the Schjelderups, Suttie sees in matriarchal religious elements the projection of pre-Oedipal wishes, fears, and conflicts, and in the patriarchal tradition, the projection of Oedipal ones.

A Distorted Tradition of Love: Suttie maintains that in Christianity we find an attempt to combine the ethical perspectives and other strengths of the two traditions. To this effort, he adds, we may attribute both its successes and its failures. Viewed psychologically, the Christian tradition reveals two essential and radically innovative features: the promulgation of a social life based on love rather than authority; and an emphasis on good social relationships between persons rather than on individual duty toward God. These principles, remarks Suttie, correspond to a transitional phase in the child's development. Having become reconciled with the once ambivalently perceived parents and with the other children of whom the child was jealous, the now more confident child is ready to enter into a wider fellowship. The attitude of Christ that is expressed in the New Testament stories, parables, and miracles is largely that of the loving, compassionate, and generously nurturant parent who at the same time declines to exercise the power that would meet "the profound infantile craving for the comforting belief in parental omnipotence" (p. 118), a craving that belongs to an earlier stage of maturation. With these themes that are suggestive of the dynamics of the matriarchal cults, Christianity combines another, the patriarchal theme of confidence in God. This seeking of reconciliation with the parent implies that the child is overcoming feelings of guilt and self-denigration and rooting out unconscious fear and hostility toward the parent (p. 121).

Appealing like other psychotherapeutic systems to the immature and neurotic, the Christian tradition rapidly became distorted in the hands of the guiltily anxious and aggressively individualistic persons it was unable to "cure." Among them were Peter, Jesus' closest disciple, and Paul, the fanatical Jew-turned-Christian who was perhaps the most influential of the missionaries to the Gentiles. It is true, Suttie observes, that the Christian tradition also includes the remarkably tolerant Hellenistic strain, which was interested for the most part not in the problem of guilt but "in the meaning of life and the relationship of Creator (parent) and created (child)." Yet on the whole, Suttie (1935, p. 127) claims, the tradition has been marked by a "peculiar tendency . . . to schism, antipathy and intolerance."

Even when the maternal element was restored to the Godhead, through the European cult of the Virgin Mary, the cost was a thoroughgoing desexualization, imposing CELIBACY on its priests—who are, of course, addressed as "father"—and removing every possible sexual association from the Virgin Mother. In thus re-creating the mother imago of early childhood, the Catholic tradition promoted its "avowed ideal of *regression to a sexless infancy* ('Except ye become as little children . . .')." Suttie argues that setting aside the father not only "seriously impaired the repressive and propitiatory value of that portion of the faith that was inherited from Judaism, viz. the Jehovah imago," but also led to several regrettable consequences: glorification of the Pope–father, the accepting expectation of purgatorial suffering, and increasingly violent efforts to convert the heathen and root out the heretics upon whom Christians projected their own Oedipal longings (Suttie, 1932, p. 298).

Real women, on the other hand, were depreciated as a result of the antisexualism and antifeminism that follow inevitably, says Suttie, when faith serves as a neurotic defense. In time and with the resurgence of patriarchal trends, the guiltily antisensual Protestant heresy appeared, as a reaction against the mother cult and the failure of repression for which it was indirectly responsible. Meanwhile the Catholic Church's orthodox scholars reified their own incestuous interests by projecting them into the figure of the witch, who inherited all the attributes of women incompatible with the imago of the virgin mother. Then followed the violent and pornographic attack on women that was condoned and even fostered by the leaders of the medieval church (see Excerpts 8.1 and Alexander and Selesnick, 1966, pp. 66–68).

EXCERPTS 8.1

From the *Malleus Maleficarum* (Witches' Hammer)

> This infamous manual for witch hunters was inspired by a 1484 bull of Pope Innocent VIII and reluctantly approved by the Faculty of Theology of the University of Cologne.

Now the wickedness of women is spoken of in *Ecclesiasticus* xxv: There is no head above the head of a serpent: and there is no wrath above the wrath of a woman. I had rather dwell with a lion and a dragon than to keep house with a wicked woman. And among much which in that place precedes and follows about a wicked woman, he concludes: All wickedness is but little to the wickedness of a woman. Wherefore S. John Chrysostom says on the text, It is not good to marry . . .: What else is woman but a foe to friendship, an unescapable punishment, a necessary evil, a natural temptation, a desirable calamity, a domestic danger, a delectable detriment, an evil of nature, painted with fair colours! . . . (p. 43).

But the natural reason [for woman's greater corruptibility] is that she is more carnal than a man, as is clear from her many carnal abominations. And it should be noted that there was a defect in the formation of the first woman, since she was formed from a bent rib, that is, a rib of the breast, which is bent as it were in a contrary direction to a man. And since through this defect she is an imperfect animal, she always deceives. . . . All this is indicated by the etymology of the word; for *Femina* comes from *Fe* and

The burning of three women as witches at Dernburg in 1555. The poster from which this illustration is taken says that when the fire was lit for one of them, Satan appeared and carried her away (Carus, 1900, pp. 360–362).

Minus,[a] since she is ever weaker to hold and preserve the faith. . . . Therefore a wicked woman is by her nature quicker to waver in her faith, and consequently quicker to abjure the faith, which is the root of witchcraft (p. 44).

All witchcraft comes from carnal lust, which is in women insatiable. . . . Wherefore for the sake of fulfilling their lust they consort even with devils. . . .

Now there are, as it is said in the Papal Bull, seven methods by which they infect with witchcraft the venereal act and the conception of the womb: First, by inclining the minds of men to inordinate passion; second, by obstructing their generative force; third, by removing the members accommodated to that act; fourth by changing men into beasts by the magic art; fifth, by destroying the generative force in women; sixth, by procuring abortion; seventh, by offering children to devils. . . . (p. 47).

The crimes of witches, then, exceed the sins of all others. . . . However much they are penitent and return to the Faith, they must not be punished like other Heretics with lifelong imprisonment, but must suffer the extreme penalty. . . . the confiscation of their goods and decapitation (p. 77).

If after being fittingly tortured [the accused] refuses to confess the truth, [the Judge] should have other engines of torture brought before her, and tell her that she will have to endure these if she does not confess. If then she is not induced by terror to confess, the torture must be continued on the second or third day (p. 226).

---

[a] The authors' misogyny extends even to the creation of false etymologies. According to the work's sympathetic translator, Montague Summers, "female" is actually from *fe-, feu-,* meaning to produce; thus, *fetus* and *fecundus,* fruitful.

Source: From *Malleus Maleficarum,* 1487.

Many features of the Dark and Middle Ages, Suttie proposes, may perhaps be traced back to a disequilibrium between matriarchal and patriarchal factors in development. They even suggest "the possibility that there is everywhere a constant tendency to oscillation between the two extremes of matriarchy and patriarchy, and that this may be an important factor in the evolution and conflicts of cultures" (Suttie, 1932, p. 302). Suttie leaves no doubt that, from the perspective of child rearing, the preferred context is matriarchal. Under such conditions, he says, "the quest for love . . . is directed upon the *real social environment*" rather than to the paradise of early childhood or a precocious Oedipal intimacy. With a reduced need for dependency fantasies as well as for propitiating a wrathful parent, "nurtural deities are less necessary, punitive ones less dreaded than is the case with patriarchal upbringing" (Suttie, 1935, p. 129).

Suttie's tragically early death, just months before his book was published, robbed the psychology of religion of one of its most promising contributors. His general views, including his conviction that, at bottom, religion has to do with personal relations, live on in the work of other object-relations theorists. As we will see, however, none of them shares Suttie's fascination with the history of religion.

Ronald Fairbairn: The Therapist as Exorcist

Apart from Klein herself, the most systematic contributor to object-relations thinking is Ronald Fairbairn. On the face of it, Fairbairn's theory might seem to be little more than an extension of Klein's, given that much of it is cast in the same language. Yet the meaning of the borrowed concepts and terms has in every instance been changed, for his vision was fundamentally different from hers. Abandoning entirely the classic drive theory, Fairbairn argues that the inner object world is wholly derived from real, external objects that have proved unsatisfactory. Thus the creation of an inner world of fantasy, which for Klein is the earliest mental act and a direct and inevitable expression of the basic drives, is for Fairbairn only secondary and compensatory. According to his view, the human psyche is from the beginning oriented toward real people in the external world. And whereas Klein attributes individual pathology and suffering to the basic human endowment, especially the drive toward death and its by-product, aggression. Fairbairn finds their root in maternal deprivation (Greenberg and Mitchell, 1983). Like Suttie, he assumes that aggression derives from the failure of satisfactory relations with external objects.

Fairbairn's interest in the dynamics of religion was apparent even before his own distinctive view emerged. In a paper he wrote on the religious fantasies of a 31-year-old unmarried woman, Fairbairn (1927) concludes that by imagining herself as Christ, or as the Mother or the Bride of Christ, the patient found symbolic fulfillment of Oedipal wishes directed toward a father whose lifelong absence exaggerated the normal infantile image of the awesome and omnipotent father. This conventional Freudian analysis is nevertheless qualified, for Fairbairn remarks that, "Personally I am very far from being one of those who considers that higher values can be accounted for wholly in terms of their psychological origins; and indeed, if it were so, it would be a poor outlook for human culture." Fairbairn is carefully explicit, too, in distinguishing such "unusual and grandiose" imaginings from "the normal religious experience of the devout person orientated in reality" (pp. 188–189).

Apparently, Fairbairn never again undertook an original analysis of religious ideation. Nevertheless, references to it occasionally appear in his later writings, for he recognized that portions of psychodynamic theory have long been implicit in religious concepts, and that, because of its naive spontaneity, religious language can even today serve to give clearer and more vivid expression to psychological insights.

In a paper on the fate of bad objects, for example, Fairbairn (1943) addresses the question of why the child deals with such objects by internalizing and then repressing them, making the objects good and the child bad.

> The cogency of the answer may best be appreciated if the answer is framed in religious terms: for such terms provide the best representation for the adult mind of the situation as it presents itself to the child. Framed in such terms the answer is that it is better to be a sinner in a world ruled by God than to live in a world ruled by the Devil. A sinner in a world ruled by God may be bad: but there is always a certain sense of security to be derived from the fact that the world around is good—"God's in His heaven—All's right with the world!": and in any case there is always a hope of redemption. In a world ruled by the Devil the individual may escape the badness of being a sinner: but he is bad because the world around him is bad. Further, he can have no sense of security and no hope of redemption. The only prospect is one of death and destruction (pp. 331–332).

But could not the child simply *reject* the bad objects? No, says Fairbairn, for, however bad the parents may appear to be, the child cannot do without them; the child "is 'possessed' by them, as if by evil spirits" (p. 332).

The task of psychotherapy, as Fairbairn sees it, is release of bad objects from the unconscious, for they are the origin of all mental disorder. "It may be said of all psychoneurotic and psychotic patients that, if a True Mass is being celebrated in the chancel, a Black Mass is being celebrated in the crypt. It becomes evident, accordingly, that the psychotherapist is the true successor to the exorcist. His business is not to pronounce the forgiveness of sins, but to cast out devils" (p. 333).

In a later paper, Fairbairn (1955) suggests that what the patient seeks in psychotherapy is chiefly *salvation*—"from his past, from bondage to his (internal) bad objects, from the burden of guilt, and from spiritual death. His search thus corresponds in detail to the religious quest" (p. 155). For Fairbairn, remarks Harry Guntrip (1961), the chief historian and interpreter of the British object-relations school, "Religion is an impressive activity and experience of human beings throughout the centuries, and is to be approached not with hostility as a mere nuisance, irrelevance and brake on progress, but with sympathetic insight in order to understand what human beings have actually been seeking and doing in their religious life" (p. 253).

Harry Guntrip: From Salvation to Communion

Guntrip himself most fully expresses the positive attitude of object-relations theory toward the religious life. He argues that psychotherapy and religion are intimately related, for both, he says, seek to promote personal wholeness through satisfactory object relations. The son of a Methodist preacher and himself a Congressional minister for 18 years, Guntrip knew at first hand the costs of bad object relations. He was haunted throughout most of his life by the deeply repressed trauma, at three and a half, of the death of his younger brother and the unsuccessful struggle that followed to get his schizoid and sometimes violent mother to relate to him, her only surviving child (Guntrip, 1975).

Although he was eventually deeply influenced by Fairbairn—through his writings and then, more directly, through a thousand hours of analysis with Fairbairn—Guntrip was also profoundly affected during his studies of philosophy and religion by the " 'personal relations' school of thought." Of particular significance was his teacher John Macmurray (1936), who wrote at that time that "The field of religion is the field of personal relations. . . . Its problem is the problem of communion or community" (p. 23). Turned by emotional and intellectual struggles from " 'theological fundamentalism' to left-wing 'liberal modernism,' " Guntrip (1961) finally concluded that the resources of both philosophy and religion were insufficient to deal with the problems brought to him in his role as minister. Psychoanalysis seemed to offer the key instead (pp. 18–19). Enlisted as a part-time therapist and lecturer in psychology during the war emergency, he finally left the ministry to become a full-time psychotherapist in the Department of Psychiatry at Leeds University. Soon after he underwent analysis with Fairbairn and eventually also with Winnicott.

The Need for Personal Relation: Together with the other object-relations theorists, Guntrip (1969a) assumes that all human beings share "an absolute need to be able to *relate* in fully *personal* terms to *an environment that we feel relates beneficently to us*" (p. 328). In the realm of human relationships, this fundamental need is often inadequately met from the early years onward, fostering a persistent state of anxiety. A common solution lies in a SCHIZOID denial of the basic need itself; by this means the person withdraws as much as possible from actual human relations and is thus thrown back on the inner world of internalized "bad objects." When the person forgoes either schizoid denial or the alternative, depressive reaction to these bad object relationships, psychoneurotic symptoms will appear as defensive maneuvers (Guntrip, 1969b).

Historically, religion has always been the means by which humankind has sought relief from the suffering occasioned by bad object relations. "Religion has always stood for the saving power of the good object relationship," by providing "a God, a Saviour and a Church . . . to whom the anxious soul can fly for refuge and salvation." Psychic healing may be offered through such means as the forgiveness of sins, conversion, or EXORCISM. When misfortune or old age make healing in the deeper layers of the psyche impossible, religion may help to preserve the person's faith and to strengthen resolve and courage (Guntrip, 1956, pp. 131, 142, 192).

As experience and in its most essential form, religion is said to be the same for all persons: a fundamental sense of connectedness to and personal validation by the universe, the ultimate, all-embracing reality (Guntrip, 1969a, p. 332; 1969b, p. 267). The sense of cosmic connection, when it develops, has its earliest roots in the good infant–mother relationship. This foundational experience of being at one with the mother "is the starting point and permanent foundation of ego-identity and ego-strength, a quietness at the centre, a core of personality which must be preserved inviolable, beyond the reaches of external world pressures" (Guntrip, 1969b, p. 270). Evicted in due time from this paradise of infantile dependence, the individual must pass through a series of difficult, transitional relationships to reach full maturity (Guntrip, 1961, pp. 363–364).

Distortions in Religion: Given its intimate association with emotional need and character type, religion is inevitably adulterated by immature or neurotic trends. Persons falling short of maturity, says Guntrip (1956), will have in varying degrees the characteristics of either the schizoid or the depressive personality, which together "represent the ultimate and irreducible ways in which a human being can become psychically crippled and devitalized" (p. 97). The schizoid person, whose devouring need for love feels terrifyingly destructive, renounces all objects and remains suspended, without affect, between the internal and external worlds. Drawn to the impersonal and thus nonthreatening world of scientific analysis, the aloof, schizoid person may simultaneously reject religion, "for religion is pre-eminently about personal and emotional needs and relationships" (p. 102). If religion does find a place in the life of the schizoid, it will be intellectualized, "a philosophy of life, not a passionate, loving devotion" (p. 103).

The depressive reaction may be expected instead when the experience of deprivation occurs somewhat later in childhood, following a period of adequate nurturance. The response to the unsatisfying yet exciting object is in this instance one of rage and aggression. Fearful that this hate or "love made angry" will destroy the object that is needed and loved, the person guiltily represses the anger and turns it inward, toward the self. Thus he or she protects the love object by self-hate and punishment. Yet having preserved the love object by identifying with it, the person ends up attacking it as well. The ambivalent and moody depressive type is correspondingly disposed to a conviction of sin and the saving experiences of repentance and conversion. Ministers given to hellfire preaching, Guntrip suggests, are likely depressed persons themselves, who find relief from self-castigation by attacking the sins of others. The ranks of fanatical crusaders are filled with depressive types, who find relief in being aggressive in someone else's cause (pp. 103–106).

Full-scale depression, it might be added here, frequently brings with it a decline in religiosity. Kurt Schneider (1928) cites the case of a Catholic woman whose states of depression began with the conviction that she was unworthy of receiving the Sacrament and culminated in an incapacity to believe, pray, or confess. The picture of Christ on the wall, seemingly transformed, no longer said anything to her (p. 29). In Günter Hole's (1977) questionnaire and interview study of the faith of 110 depressive patients, a variety of indicators of religious attitudes show the same gradual decline with increasing depth of depression (see Figure 8.1). Interesting in the light of object-relations theory is Hole's finding that 30.8 percent of his subjects reported that their childhoods were largely or thoroughly "difficult," "bad," or "horrible," and another 18.7 percent said that theirs were clouded with stress or difficulties (p. 84). The more negatively the patients characterized their childhoods, the greater the frequency and intensity of their reported feelings of guilt, which they most often associated with failings toward family members. Guntrip's linking of religious conversion to the depressive type is supported by the finding of J. L. Gallemore, W. P. Wilson, and J. M. Rhoads (1969) that 52 percent of their 62 affectively disturbed patients reported conversion experiences whereas only 20 percent of their control group did.

Religious Maturity: Feeling isolated, lonely, and unreal, the troubled individual yearns for *salvation,* which the religious traditions have long sought to provide. In contrast, the fortunate person who has found the way from infantile to mature dependence attains the experience of *communion,* both with others and with the Ultimate. The fullest realization of maturity, says Guntrip (1956, pp. 198–199), involves "an essentially religious way of experiencing life." He considers it a psychological fact that "The religious experience and faith of a mature person gives the most comprehensive and invulnerable security, and the largest scope for self-realization possible." Yet a "sound and enlightened faith" and a measure of religious experience are also possible for even profoundly disturbed individuals, who may be stabilized by these possessions, and in any event will find them the best context for psychotherapy. Guntrip urges religious educators to deepen their own understanding of human emotional needs, in order to teach religion in a manner that, rather than subordinating a person to some authority, will foster growth of the true self. Such an education will also promote a reverent sense of feeling at home in the universe, that larger whole on which human beings are fundamentally dependent. What ultimately matters, says Guntrip (1969a), is not the professing of certain dogmas or the performing of prescribed rituals, but attaining real religious experience.

D. W. Winnicott: Religion as Transitional Phenomenon

Guntrip stands out among the British object-relations theorists for the prominence he gives to religion, but Winnicott is the contributor who has captured the fancy of religious-studies scholars. A pediatrician and a psychoanalyst deeply influenced by Klein, Winnicott is famous for his notion of the TRANSITIONAL OBJECT, a term he coined for the blanket or teddy bear that young children use to sooth and comfort

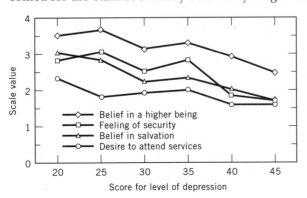

Figure 8.1. Relation of religious attitudes and level of depression in 110 patients. (The scale assessing the desire to attend religious services is a three-point scale; the others have four points.) Source: From Hole, 1977, page 144.

themselves. Religion, he suggests in several somewhat cryptic and provocative asides, is continuous with this consoling object and serves a similar function: the creation of an illusory, intermediate area of experience that helps throughout life to bridge inner and outer realities. Religion shares this role with other cultural forms and creative activities (Winnicott, 1953).

The heart of Winnicott's contribution to psychoanalysis lies in his clarification of the conditions that make possible a child's emerging awareness of being a person separate from others. Of greatest importance, he says, is a devoted mother. In her natural and highly adaptive preoccupation with her baby, such a mother provides a "holding environment" that serves to contain the infant's fragmented world of experience. By presenting her offspring with some need-satisfying object that the excited infant is about to hallucinate (e.g., the breast), she creates a "moment of illusion." The object presents itself as the infant's own creation. This experience of omnipotence, which in its repetition lays the foundations for a healthy sense of capability and power, requires that the mother have both empathic sensitivity and accurate timing. Also vital for the creation of a "perfect environment" is a responsive maternal face that, like a mirror, faithfully reflects back to the child what the selflessly devoted mother sees. Finally, the mother must also provide a "nondemanding presence" that allows the quiescent infant to develop the capacity to experience a state of formless "going-on-being" and thus the capacity to be alone (Greenberg and Mitchell, 1983, pp. 191–193; Winnicott, 1971, pp. 111–113).

Fortunately, the infant's need for this idyllic environment soon declines, at the same time as the mother's other interests reclaim her attention. It is essential that the mother gradually introduce the child to the hard realities of an uncontrollable world, by progressively "failing" in her adaptation to the infant's needs. Supported by the growth of ego functions and an emergent urge toward separateness, the child comes to recognize the reality of objects and learns in due time to communicate a variety of needs through gestures and other expressions (Greenberg and Mitchell, 1983, pp. 193–194).

Transitional Phenomena: The transition from hallucinatory omnipotence to the recognition and acceptance of objective reality—a progression that Winnicott says is impossible without a "good enough 'mother' "—is eased by the transitional object, "the first not-me possession" (Winnicott, 1953, pp. 89, 94). Whether the soft and amorphous blanket that is cathected around six to nine months of age or the cuddly stuffed animal adopted in the second or third year (Hong, 1978), the transitional object occupies a third, intermediate area of experience that parent and child tacitly agree will never be challenged. That is, the child shall have certain rights over the self-chosen object, and no one shall raise questions regarding its nature or source. Thus relatively preserved from the process of disillusionment, the transitional object provides relief from the strain of bringing together the inner and outer worlds. In this capacity, Winnicott says, "The transitional object stands for the breast, or the object of the first relationship" (p. 93). This interpretation is supported by the blanket's being typically transported, at bedtime or in moments of crisis, to the child's mouth or face. Although widely assumed to be symbolic of the mother or what she provides, the transitional object gains an autonomy of its own. Should it be lost, even the mother will not likely be able to console the child (Hong, 1978).

Winnicott (1953) assumes that no one completes once and for all the difficult transition from "primary creativity" to full reality acceptance. Thus all of us require an intermediate area of experience, of illusion and TRANSITIONAL PHENOMENA, which Winnicott says are inherent in the whole of human culture but most notably in art and religion. As long as we do not press others to accept our "illusory experience" as being objectively real, we are free to enjoy it, perhaps even to form a community of persons who possess similar experiences. Should we insistently strain the credulity of others, however, they will likely think us eccentric or mad. Ever reluctant to give examples of transitional phenomena, beyond the specific objects treasured by young children, Winnicott emphasizes the universal, diffuse, and infinitely varied character of these phenomena in the normal adult world.

Paul Pruyser: Illusion Processing in Religion

Winnicott's suggestive clues for a revised psychoanalysis of culture have been more fully elaborated by Paul Pruyser (1916–1987), a Dutch-born clinical psychologist long associated with the Menninger Foundation in Kansas and a leading contributor to the psychology of religion. Although a proponent of the drive model of classical psychoanalysis, Pruyser also incorporated Winnicott's theory of transitional phenomena to cast new light on the visual arts, music, literature, the physical sciences, and religion. All these cultural expressions, he maintains, entail in some essential way the skillful processing of illusion.

Religion as illusion: have Winnicott and Pruyser taken us back to Freud's pejorative perspective? Not at all, says Pruyser, who points out that Freud's use of the term *illusion* reflects in part his own positivistic and antireligious outlook. This term, Pruyser notes, derives from the Latin verb *ludere,* to play. Thus in saying that cultural phenomena are illusionistic, he means to emphasize their derivation from the play of human imagination. Agreeing with Freud that such illusions are wish fulfilling, Pruyser (1974) maintains that they also serve as ideals, for they make evident a person's shortcomings while providing direction and impetus for the attainment of loftier goals (p. 201).

What Winnicott calls the realm of illusion or the intermediate area of experience is in Pruyser's (1983) work termed the ILLUSIONISTIC WORLD. Following Winnicott's lead, Pruyser positions this third world between the private, inner world of AUTISTIC fantasy and the public, outer world of realistic and verifiable sensory perception. In contrast to these two worlds—long the only well-defined alternatives in the psychoanalytic literature—the illusionistic world "is the world of play, of the creative imagination in which feelings are not antagonistic to thinking, in which skills and talents are used to the utmost, and where pleasure is found without categorical abrogation of the reality principle" (Pruyser, 1977, p. 334). The distinctive character of this third world is made evident in Table 8.1, which shows Pruyser's systematic comparison of it with the other two.

Although Winnicott and Pruyser locate much of human culture in this intermediate sphere, religious language seems peculiarly appropriate to describing its contents. As Pruyser (1974) points out, the transitional object of the young child has about it a sacred character. It is most obviously a ritual object, subject to reverent and ceremonial attention from the entire family (pp. 206–207). Yet it is also "the transcendent," for it falls neither in the world of private images nor in the world of ordinary sense perception (p. 111). Moreover, this equation is reversible. Deities, ideal human virtues, and ultimate spiritual states are all "elaborations of the transitional sphere," symbols that, when widely accepted, possess their own consensual validity (pp. 201, 217). It is in the illusionistic world, Pruyser concludes, that religion most appropriately finds itself, for "The transcendent, the holy, and mystery are not recognizable in the external world by plain realistic viewing and hearing, nor

Table 8.1 **PRUYSER'S SCHEME OF THE THREE WORLDS**

Autistic World	Illusionistic World	Realistic World
Untutored fantasy	Tutored fantasy	Sense perception
Omnipotent thinking	Adventurous thinking	Reality testing
Utter whimsicality	Orderly imagination	Hard, undeniable facts
Free associations	Inspired connections	Logical connections
Ineffable images	Verbalizable images	Look-and-see referents
Hallucinatory entities or events	Imaginative entities or events	Actual entities or events
Private needs	Cultural needs	Factual needs
Symptoms	Symbols	Signs, indices
Dreaming	Playing	Working
Sterility	Creativeness	Resourcefulness
Internal object (imago)	Transcendent objects prefigured by the child's transitional object	External object

do they arise directly in the mind as pleasurable fictions. They arise from an intermediate zone of reality that is also an intermediate human activity—neither purely subjective nor purely objective'' (p. 113).

Perhaps because of its intermediate status, the illusionistic world is peculiarly delicate and vulnerable. "Civilization," writes Pruyser (1983), "is a precarious achievement that needs constant nurture and a great deal of vigilance against intrusions from either the autistic or the realistic side" (p. 71). Religion above all is prone to distortion, especially the traditions that offer an anthropomorphic deity and thus invite infantile regression to primitive wishes and modes of relating.[3]

The effects of *autistic* distortion of the illusionistic world are evident both in history and in the psychiatric clinic. In the religious traditions, for example, we find fantastic images of perfectly benign deities, winged angels, and blissful heavenly realms juxtaposed with apocalyptic visions of bloody retribution, horned devils, and eternal suffering. Virtue may be made of surrendering personal agency in slavish obedience to the "Spirit," or of yielding to "paroxysms of impulsive emotionality" (Pruyser, 1977, p. 336). When the autistic factor dominates, Pruyser (1983) says, religious ritual may become a grim and compulsively repetitive performance that brings no satisfaction (p. 172). At the extreme, intrusion of the autistic world will lead to unmistakable delusion and hallucination, such as in the lives of Daniel Paul Schreber, introduced to us by Freud, and of Anton Boisen (1936, 1960), founder of the clinical pastoral training movement whose own experience with psychotic religious delusions convinced him of their potentially healing power.

The dangers of *realistic* distortion are of a different sort. Relentlessly attached to the external world of sense impression and literal meaning, the realistic outlook restages the illusionistic symbols of transcendence in its own theater, reifying them and stripping them of their subtle nuances and mystery. Such a perversion is evident, for example, in the literal adherence to the DOCTRINE OF SCRIPTURAL

---

[3] On balance, Pruyser suggests, having internalized a benevolent anthropomorphic God will foster the capacity to be alone, a prerequisite for a spirited and productive use of the imagination.

INERRANCY and the subsequent CREATIONIST attack on the theory of evolution. How foolish, says Pruyser (1983), to pit the illusionistic perspective and language of the Bible against the realistic outlook and expressions of Darwin, rather than recognizing that each may be true within its own sphere. Realism's heavy hand is evident, too, in the complex historical process of institutionalizing illusionistic ideals. Too often the playfully conceived symbol is transformed into obligatory doctrine and ritual, sustained by an elaborate organizational structure and often pressed on others, sometimes under the threat of death (pp. 167, 177). Ascetic self-torture and ritual sacrifice are other fruits of an all-too-literal translation of symbols.

Sheer physical survival demands, of course, that we take the realistic world into account. Moreover, a healthy measure of realism is necessary, says Pruyser in agreement with the Freudian drive model, "to curb and counteract the boundless and dangerous impulsivity of the autistic world." Yet a thoroughgoing realism will inhibit the play of imagination and thus restrict the growth of human potentialities (p. 176). What is needed is "education toward illusion processing" (p. 71), which begins in the child's play with transitional objects and culminates in "playful" participation in the adult world of human culture. In the religious realm, "One comes to the thought of a Ground of Being, or of a God behind the gods, or of the Holy which is no longer confined to burning bushes, altars, amulets, and fatherly caretakers. The Holy may now be seen in macroscopic as well as microscopic grandeur, in stars and cells, in evolution and in such beautiful conceptions as E = MC^2" (Pruyser, 1974, p. 241). For those deep in the illusionist world of creative play, religion will become, as it was for Albert Einstein, an open-ended *search* in a universe pervaded by mystery, not an incontestable *find* in a realm truncated by dogma.

We may wonder whether most people can find satisfaction in so abstract and spare a world of religious images as Pruyser offers. Whereas Winnicott asks only that objective reality not be demanded for one's illusionistic objects, Pruyser requires that the objects themselves be moderated by the dynamic interplay of the autistic and realistic worlds. Suspecting autistic dominance in proportion to an image's fixity, concreteness, and detail, Pruyser (1974, p. 203) would doubtless look askance, for instance, on the multiple-armed and copulating deities of the tantric Hindu tradition. Winnicott, unlike Pruyser, would presumably view them as legitimate transitional objects—as, indeed, would the Indian sages themselves. From the Hindu perspective, however, the transition is *from* external reality *to* the greater reality of Brahman, the impersonal and irrepresentable ultimate source of being (O'Flaherty, 1984, p. 59).

Ana-Maria Rizzuto: The Representation of God

In East and West, images of divinity are the shared possession of countless people. Underlying these images, emphasizes Ana-Maria Rizzuto (1974, 1979, 1992), are private and highly idiosyncratic representations with still-living roots in the individual's early object relations. Rizzuto, a Boston psychoanalyst born and educated in Argentina and later deeply influenced by Winnicott, maintains that a representative of God is a universally inevitable outcome of the child's relations with parents and other caretakers as well as of the child's burgeoning interest in causal events. Whether or not the individual is prompted to *believe* in that representation, it is said to remain potentially available throughout life.

A Complex Development and Dynamics: Freud was basically correct, says Rizzuto, in tracing the origin of the GOD REPRESENTATION to early parental relations.

Yet he underestimated, she adds, the complexity of this derivation, especially the role of the mother. Of the 20 Christian and Jewish patients whom Rizzuto studied by means of questionnaires, interviews, and drawings of their families and of God, none appeared to have formed the God representation exclusively from one parental imago. Furthermore, the God image was derived equally from the real parents, the wished-for parents, and the feared parents of the subject's own imaginings. Although Rizzuto acknowledges the special importance of the Oedipal period, which Freud had featured exclusively, she reports having found God images belonging to every stage along the developmental way. An individual's representation of God, Rizzuto says, will be marked by the emotional factors that are dominant at the time it is formed (p. 44). The person's subsequent *concept* of God may stand in sharp opposition, creating a situation of disturbing conflict.

If "the birth of the living God" is complex, as the psychoanalytic principle of overdetermination would certainly predict it to be, so also are its modifications and uses throughout an individual's lifetime. Unlike the blanket or teddy bear, which slowly loses its meaning and is then abandoned, the God representation is increasingly cathected during the early years and long after retains its functions, at least potentially, as an illusory transitional object. It ordinarily undergoes transformation in concert with revisions in the intimately related parent and SELF-REPRESENTATIONS, especially at the momentous time of the Oedipal crisis but also in late adolescence, when the maturing individual is challenged to integrate a self-representation sufficiently unified for the life decisions immediately ahead. The growth in cognitive capacities that occurs somewhat earlier, around the time of puberty, and occasionally precipitates a crisis of doubt, may also add new dimensionality to the God representation. "Each new phase in the identity cycle," including the final one of dying, "brings with it its specific religious crisis" (p. 52), and thus the challenge to form a new, more adequate God representation. Frequently, however, the God image remains essentially unchanged, perhaps in time becoming anachronistic and irrelevant. As a transitional object, then, God "shares the unpredictable life of the small child's teddy bear: when needed he is hurriedly pulled from his resting place, hugged or mistreated, and when the storm is over, neglectfully left wherever he may happen to be. There he remains, quietly offering the silent reassurance of an almost imperceptible presence" (p. 203).

We may possess a God representation without also believing in it. To believe in God, Rizzuto (1980) maintains, is to express loyalty to the inner representations of ourselves and of the persons to whom we owe our existence (p. 117). Yet disbelief may also be an expression of fidelity if, say, in an effort to resolve our ambivalent feelings, a negative God representation has come to be placed in opposition to the images of the idealized parents (Rizzuto, 1979, pp. 88–89). Belief or its absence is thus an indicator of "the particular private balance each individual has achieved at a given moment in his relations with primary objects and all other relevant people, whether or not he uses the mediatory services of a transitional object for this process" (p. 202). To illustrate the dynamics of this complex adaptive process, Rizzuto presents in detail four of her case studies, one of which we will briefly review here.

The Birth of a Disapproving God: A 27-year-old married woman with four children, Bernadine Fisher had been admitted to a psychiatric unit following a half-hearted suicide attempt. Conceived out of wedlock by two deeply troubled teenagers who subsequently married and had six more children, Bernadine exemplifies the tragic consequences of inadequate mothering. Both of her parents were lifelong psychiatric patients. Her mother suffered from severe phobias and anxieties, her father from chronic anxiety, depression, and unremitting unhappiness. He was also alcoholic. Both behaved like small, maternally deprived children, the father forever competing with their offspring for the mother's attention, the mother envying them and expecting *them* to satisfy *her* needs. The parents quarreled incessantly, and all the children predictably had serious problems.

Although Bernadine's mother did look after the children's physical needs, she failed to provide the recognition and approval that are essential to adequate care. Instead, she constantly criticized her children and threatened to abandon them because of the problems she said they caused. Only in moments of crisis did she show any concern for Bernadine, and even then she would maintain distance by predicting disastrous results. Bernadine had frequent bitter arguments with her mother, who tried to convince Bernadine that if she would only change her ways, all the family's problems would be solved. Change she would not, but she accepted her mother's judgment that she was a terrible child.

Mitigating such poor primary relations was a close attachment to her maternal grandmother, who became reconciled with her once-rejected daughter when Bernadine was about two. Yet the grandmother "disappeared" the following year; only some time later did Bernadine learn that she had actually died. Sudden death had once before robbed her of an important relationship, when her father accidentally killed her beloved kitten in closing the car door. Her memory of the accident and of her intense sorrow afterward long remained disturbingly vivid. So also did her traumatic hospitalization at the age of five for an emergency appendectomy. She cried constantly, she said, for in painful contrast to the mothers of the other children, hers never came to visit her at all. Memorable from that occasion, too, was her anger at the nurses, who would not allow her to take home the crib toys in which she had found solace.

Yet the worst part of her life, she said, was still to come. Living in a new neighborhood and knowing none of her classmates, Bernadine became an outcast after having been caught stealing in the first grade. "My life from six to eleven was terrible. . . . I was in trouble at the school. I was in trouble every other day. I cried all the time. I hated myself. I hated my family, my teachers. I hated everybody and everything and I was just miserable" (p. 157). At home she had violent temper tantrums, pulling out her hair and destroying her clothes and bedroom furniture. Her behavior finally showed improvement after she began seeing a psychiatrist, to whom she became strongly attached. This therapeutic relation was abruptly terminated, however, when her parents refused to participate in the mental health clinic's family program.

Although neither of her Irish Catholic parents professed belief in God or would go to Mass, they insisted that their children attend regularly and receive the Sacrament. In contrast to the parents, the paternal grandmother, who looked after the children while their mother worked, always carried her rosary with her and spoke frequently of the church and its value. Frightened at the time of her First Communion by her own unforgivable badness, Bernadine was finally able, on the occasion of her confirmation, to have a good experience in church. She felt she belonged, and she liked how she felt during Mass; yet she still did not feel close to God.

Years later, when Rizzuto analyzed Bernadine's God representation, it appeared to have changed very little with the passage of time. God was still a distant, frightening judge who, because of his disapproval, was also her "enemy." This God was strong, loving, helpful—but not toward terrible Bernadine. On rare, solitary occasions, this dominant representation was displaced by another, a nonthreatening "personal" God with whom she felt she could genuinely communicate. A third representation, also existing in isolation, was suggested by her unexpected drawing of God as a sun emanating warm and sustaining rays: "a bright, clean, warm feeling," she wrote in explanation at the bottom of the page.

Each of these representations, says Rizzuto, is totally devoid of elaboration, and none reflects Oedipal experience. The prevailing representational level, she judges, is that of a three- or four-year-old; the SADOMASOCHISTIC involvement suggests the anal-sadistic stage. The absence of Oedipal traits and the lack of synthesis among the three representations can be explained, Rizzuto hypothesizes, by the deep frustration Bernadine experienced as a result of profound maternal deprivation and the jealous competition for mothering she engaged in with her father and younger siblings. "In her need to find some equilibrium she idealized her mother, attributing strength and love to her and explaining the mother's failure to display these traits toward her as the consequence of her own bad character" (p. 170). This idealized image was then displaced, without elaboration or disguise, into the cosmic realm, creating her dominant representation of God and giving the quality of eternity to her guilty feelings of unlovable badness. The second, far less available image is derived, Rizzuto speculates, from the accepting maternal grandmother. Finally, the third, remote but benign representation may constitute a "highly elaborated transformation of infantile wishes for the holding, good mother Bernadine never had" (p. 168)—a safely depersonalized synthesis of generous, nonjudgmental, and physically satisfying elements. Bernadine's representation of God, Rizzuto concludes, is predominantly maternal, although other family members have contributed to it as well. Her representation of the Devil, in contrast, was derived from her frustrating father and her own feelings of badness. Her conscious acceptance of her badness, however, made belief in the Devil psychologically unnecessary. Whether in relation to God or the Devil, the teachings of her paternal grandmother and of the church apparently touched her not at all.

Rizzuto's case study rounds out our survey of the chief representations of the British object-relations school and those directly influenced by it. The summary of their views on religion that is presented in Table 8.2 underscores three common themes: the origin of religious conceptions in early parental relations; the interest of religion in promoting mature object-relations; and the vulnerability of religion to distortion, both in individual lives and historic tradition. Although the object-relations theorists clearly share Freud's view that religion has its primary roots in early parental relationships, they reject not only his exclusive focus on Oedipal factors but also his conviction that religion is always neurotic and immature. Its undeniable and pervasive distortions and immaturities are inevitable, they maintain, given the concern of the religious traditions with the deepest needs of troubled human beings.

NARCISSISM IN RELIGIOUS FAITH AND TRADITION

In Rizzuto's case study of Bernadine Fisher, we find God represented as a totally external factor. "The difference between God and herself," Rizzuto writes, "is so striking and disproportionate that there is nothing of God, nothing godlike, inside her. God has strength, she lacks it; God has rules, she has to obey them; God has the upper hand, she must submit" (p. 168). Contrasting sharply with this attitude

Table 8.2 **SUMMARY OF THE VIEWS ON RELIGION OF THE OBJECT-RELATIONS THEORISTS**

	Orienting Conception of Religion	Focal Concepts
Suttie	Religion seeks to better emotional relations.	*Cults of mother–goddesses:* aimed against regression. *Cults of father–gods:* aimed against sexual precocity. The Christian tradition has become distorted in trying to combine the strengths of both cultic forms.
Fairbairn	Religious concepts give vivid expression to psychological insights.	The therapist acts as an *exorcist* who casts out bad objects. The patient's goal is *salvation*—from the past, bad objects, guilt, and spiritual death.
Guntrip	Religion promotes wholeness through satisfactory object relations.	Religion suffers distortions of two kinds: *schizoid* and *depressive*. Immature individuals yearn for *salvation* from bad object relations. With the attainment of mature dependence, one experiences *communion*—with others and with the Ultimate.
Winnicott	Religion helps to bridge inner and outer realities.	Religion occupies an *intermediate realm* of experience, of "illusion" and *transitional phenomena.* **Pruyser:** The *illusionistic world* of religion is subject to *autistic* and *realistic* distortions. **Rizzuto:** The God *representation* is a dynamic process founded in early parental relations.

is the Schjelderups's (1932) third type of religious experience, which is dominated by the conviction that one is oneself divine. This "narcissistic self-motif" appears in several of their individual case studies, one of which we will review here. It is also apparent, they maintain, in the tradition of Zen Buddhism and its founder, Bodhidharma.

A Quest for Self-Perfection

The patient illustrating for us the self-motif in individual piety was a 24-year-old clerk who felt himself to be strangely "encapsulated," removed from this life and its realities. At the foundation of his existence was a persistent longing for perfection in whatever he did; the slightest mistake would make him feel worthless. In the presence of other people he was tormented by anxiety and feelings of inferiority. At the same time, paradoxically, he fancied himself superior to them all. No one else, he thought, was as directly in contact with God as he was. Religion accordingly seemed to be his private concern; the slightest mention of it would embarrass him, as if he had been referred to personally.

Underlying the subject's longing for perfection and his conviction of greatness, analysis gradually revealed, were repressed childhood fantasies of his own divinity. "Within me," he said, "is an eternal quest for some ideal existence. That desire became intensified to the point of wanting to be God—or in any case a kind of god. An individual should be perfect in every respect." Spontaneously appearing with the feeling that something separated him from ordinary people was the fantasy image of a mountaintop vista, which triggered the thought, "God, who looks out over the earth—omnipotent" (p. 36).

The ANALYSAND was the second oldest of four brothers. His mother was an efficient, unsentimental businesswoman who was wholly disinclined to give or receive tenderness. She dominated the analysand's father, an anxious and vacillating man who played the role of martyr. In sharp contrast to the passivity and compliance that came to characterize the patient as an adult, he had been confident and exceptionally willful as a young child—and the source of constant conflict, chiefly with his mother. Over time, however, that self-confidence gradually eroded; every act of self-assertion seemed to end in undeserved punishment.

Of decisive importance was the issue of cleanliness. Endowed with marked anal tendencies, the child was so frequently punished for failing to comply with his mother's obsessive demands that he came to anticipate punishment whenever a feeling of pleasure arose. The association of pleasure and fear was irreversibly established sometime before his third birthday when his governess, unusually impatient with his old habit of taking "too long" on the chamberpot, caught and broke his leg in the bars of his crib. This acutely painful injury, which the child naturally took to be punishment for sitting too long, came to play an essential role in his later neurosis.

Severe conflict in other areas added to the patient's difficulties. Through analysis he was able to recall the occasion when, with growing curiosity toward the world around him, he attempted to explore his mother's genitals. Her extremely sharp rebuke, he later claimed, disturbed all further development: "I was allowed to take an interest in nothing—must always withdraw—[either] I would be frightened away or the interest would fail to materialize." A series of other traumatic incidents relating to sex strengthened the fear-inspired suppression of sexual interest, an inhibition that soon came to acquire categorical meaning: "As an adult he experienced anxiety as soon as he took an interest in anything at all" (p. 39).

The subject's development was also strongly influenced by severe jealousy of his father and brothers, toward all of whom he recalled having death wishes. The birth of a younger brother was especially fateful, for with it he concluded that he had been replaced as the youngest for having failed to be good enough in his mother's eyes. He became obsessed thereafter with surpassing his younger sibling, in order to regain his former position. Here, say the Schjelderups, is one of the deepest roots of his unbounded wish to excel over all others and to be first in every respect.

What we are not told, surprisingly, is the significance for the patient of the envied brother's death at the age of four. So dramatic a fulfillment of the analysand's death wishes must not only have confirmed the infantile conviction of the omnipotence of thoughts and thus the fantasies of being divine, but also have created in him a deep sense of guilt—the source, perhaps, of the anxiety-filled fantasies of hell that tortured him as a child. We are informed, however, that the patient's "complete transformation of character" had apparently taken place by his sixth or seventh year—not long, it appears, after his brother's death (p. 38).

Thus the slowly emerging childhood fantasies of being God and of attaining perfection would seem to have served a complex function. They offered the child freedom from criticism and punishment and from his guilt-induced fantasies of hell. Once he had satisfied his mother's desire by becoming perfect, she would no longer need anyone else; he could have her all to himself. With this fantasy he felt himself totally isolated from reality, as though he had returned to his mother's body or retreated from the world into an egg. The thought of being God also revived the child's primitive sense of self-grandiosity, note the Schjelderups, and it provided a measure of healing by gratifying the "wishes for greatness" that had been stunted by severe environmental opposition.

Bodhidharma and Zen Buddhism: A Search Within

The Schjelderups's case study may leave us with the impression that the self-motif in religion is merely an aberration in individual lives, the outcome of unusual inner psychic conflict. Yet it also appears in long-established religious traditions, they maintain, the result of particular historical developments. For an "extraordinarily characteristic expression" of the self-motif, the Schjelderups turn to Zen Buddhism and its founder, Bodhidharma, who died around 530 C.E.

Enshrouded as it is by legendary detail, little can be said about the life of Bodhidharma. The twenty-eighth in a series of masters and disciples said to reach back to the Buddha himself, Bodhidharma is known to have traveled from his native India to China and there to have founded, as the First Patriarch, the tradition of Chinese *Ch'an* Buddhism, better known to us by its Japanese equivalent, Zen. Legend has it that in one monastery he sat facing a wall, deep in meditation, for nine uninterrupted years. "Wall-gazing"—suggesting not merely the physical act

A traditional representation of Bodhidharma, the First Patriarch of Chinese *Ch'an* Buddhism, from a fourteenth-century hanging scroll.

but also the suddenness of illumination—became the appropriate term for express-ing the way to enlightenment that is peculiar to Zen (Dumoulin, 1959, pp. 68, 71). Although the Zen tradition may bear the imprint of Bodhidharma and other strong personalities among its patriarchs, as Heinrich Dumoulin suggests (p. 270), the heavy overlay of legendary embellishments forced the Schjelderups to rely instead on later representations of the tradition, in conjuction with personal impressions from Kristian Schjelderup's visit to a Japanese monastery.

Encountering the Buddha Within: It is far from easy, the Schjelderups warn us, to give a clear definition of Zen Buddhism, for the tradition itself resists every attempt at formulation. When one Zen master was asked by a disciple who and what the Buddha really might be, he is said to have replied, "Hold your tongue, the mouth is the refuge of all corruption" (p. 76). According to Zen teachings, neither the Buddha nor anything else in the world can be truly comprehended through a system of intellectual constructs. The challenge, rather, is to achieve a state of mind that transcends our ordinary categories—including the distinction between self and others—and to see the world as it is, without grasping it with thoughts or feelings.

What is most essential in Zen, say the Schjelderups, is the fundamental convic-tion that, to encounter the Buddha, we must look within. James Pratt (1928) makes the same point by quoting from an early Chinese Zen master:

> If you wish to seek the Buddha, you ought to see into your own nature: for this nature is the Buddha himself. If you have not seen into your own nature, what is the use of thinking of the Buddha, reciting the SUTRAS, observing a fast, or keeping the precepts? . . . The Buddha is your own mind: make no mistake to bow to external objects . . . The mind is the Buddha, the Buddha is the way, and the way is Zen. To see directly into one's original nature, this is Zen.

These words, says Pratt, "express the conviction of the whole school through the centuries" (p. 624). "It is," he too emphasizes, "the very heart of Zen. The Uni-versal lies within, and only by immediate inner intuition can one know it. Having known it one knows all" (p. 644).

The Quest for Oneness: To attain such an intuition, Zen NOVITIATES must undergo intensive training over a period of many years. At the heart of this training is the practice of ZAZEN or sitting meditation. With legs crossed in the lotus position, eyes lowered, and respiration slow and regular, Zen monks sit silently for long hours each day in a sparsely furnished meditation hall. Concentrating their atten-tion on their breathing, the monks seek to forget their ordinary preoccupations, to empty their minds of all thoughts and images. At some point in their meditative practice their master may instruct them to focus on an assigned KOAN, a seemingly absurd problem or riddle that may take a monk years to solve. Struggling to find the solution—an answer that may scandalize ordinary reason even more than does the question—helps the aspirant to deepen concentration and perhaps even to attain the long-sought-for inner unity and illumination. Wrong answers to a koan may elicit from the master a loud cry or a deftly aimed blow. A proper answer—which may itself be a wordless gesture, such as a hand thrust or the waving of the sleeve—may well not require the master's verification, for the novitiate will usually be struck by the answer's self-validating power.

The immediate aim of such extraordinary diligence is SATORI, the joyful expe-rience of sudden illumination, Like other forms of mystical experience, *satori* is considered beyond ordinary comprehension. One Zen practitioner described the experience in these terms.

> Ztt! I entered. I lost the boundary of my physical body. I had my skin, of course, but I felt I was standing in the center of the cosmos. I saw people coming toward me, but all were the same man. All were myself. I had never known this world before. I had believed that I was created, but now I must change my opinion: I was never created; I was the cosmos; no individual existed (quoted in H. Smith, 1991, p. 136).

Yet *satori* is not the final goal, Huston Smith points out, but only a point of departure and a recurring sign of progress. The ultimate aim is to experience the ordinary objects and events of this world with similar wonder and delight. With such a perception, the normal dualism of self and other is transcended. All distinctions become inconsequential in an all-enveloping oneness that responds with unwavering equanimity to good and evil, pleasure and pain, life and death (pp. 136–139).

Two Mystical Types: For the psychologist of religion, according to Pratt (1928), Zen is particularly interesting in the ways it differs from other mystical types. Unlike yogic states of consciousness, which may be narrowed to the point of unconscious trance, *satori* represents an intensification of consciousness. In contrast to the most common type of Christian mysticism, which lovingly dwells on the personality of the divine, there is in Zen no consciousness of a numinous object and thus no dualistic longing for communion—not even with the Buddha, whose nature is, after all, one's own. "It is self-realization, not communion," Pratt concludes, "that Zen seeks and finds" (p. 637).

The same point is brought home by the Schjelderups in their distinction, borrowed from Rudolf Otto, of two main types of mysticism. In *union mysticism,* the religious longing is directed toward an object that lies outside oneself; in *self-mysticism,* for which there is no external religious object, the individual turns inward, in quest of self-redemption and self-deification (p. 91). Psychologically speaking, say the Schjelderups, union mysticism's longing for oneness with the divine corresponds to a regression to the mother. Self-mysticism, which includes Zen and yoga but elements in other religious traditions as well, expresses a still-deeper regression, to the narcissistic self-grandiosity of the small child. Thus mystical experience, of the one type or the other, is a frequent manifestation of mother and self religions. Father religion, although it, too, may find mystical expression (e.g., in erotically tinged bride mysticism), is more typically expressed in prophetic piety and in its emphasis on a feared and morally demanding God who must be propitiated.

Returning to the Womb: The pathological dynamics of these mystical tendencies are more fully considered in Kristian Schjelderup's (1928) psychoanalytic study of asceticism. Here he declares that "Narcissism is always *regressive* and induces a retrogressive process," the furthest goal of which may be the neurotic and *pre-*narcissistic fantasy of returning to the mother's body (pp. 199–200). The reversal of the normal developmental process that Buddhist meditative practices supposedly promote is described in detail in Franz Alexander (1923), long the director of the Chicago Institute of Psychoanalysis. Normal libidinous interest in the world is first suppressed, he says, by general ascetic training. Then, through prescribed meditative exercises designed to emphasize the repulsiveness of the body (see Excerpts 8.2), the withdrawn libido is redirected to the individual's body with an attitude that is purely sadistic. The person is temporarily thrown into a state of melancholia over the loss of pleasurable objects.

EXCERPTS 8.2

Distaste for the Body in Buddhist Meditation

Among the goals of the *Sutra on the Applications of Mindfulness* (Satipatthanasutta), which Edward Conze (1956) identifies as "the most important single text" on meditation in the Buddhist CANONICAL scriptures (p. 24), is the development of an active distaste for the human body. The formula pertaining to this aspect of mindfulness reads as follows.

And further, the disciple contemplates this body, from the sole of the foot upwards, and from the top of the head downwards, with a skin stretched over it, and filled with manifold impurities. There are in this body:

   hairs of the head, hairs of the body, nails, teeth, skin;
   muscles, sinews, bones, marrow, kidneys;
   heart, liver, serous membranes, spleen, lungs;
   intestines, mesentery, stomach, excrement, brain;
   bile, digestive juices, pus, blood, grease, fat;
   tears, sweat, spittle, snot, fluid of the joints, urine (p. 95).

Buddhaghosa (ca. 400 C.E.), author of *The Path of Purity*, "one of the great spiritual classics of mankind" and the one book Conze would choose to have on a desert island (p. 25), expands on this passage with such comments as these.

   From the sole of the feet upwards. . . . all one can see are manifold impurities, which consist of hairs of the head, hairs of the body, etc., and which are extremely malodorous, repulsive and unsightly (p. 95).

   After it has reached [the stomach], the food, as long as it is undigested, remains in just that region, which is like an unwashed cesspool, pitch dark, traversed by winds which are scented with various rotten smells, excessively malodorous and loathsome. . . . When it has been disgested by the body's heat, the food is not transformed into something like gold or silver. . . . But, constantly giving off foam and bubbles, it fills, having become excrement, the abdomen, . . . and, having become urine, it fills the bladder (pp. 101, 102).

The Satipatthanasutta continues.

   And further, if the disciple, sees . . . a corpse, thrown on the charnel field, dead for one, two or thee days, swollen, blueish and festering, he draws along his own body for comparison, and thinks: "Verily, also this body of mine is subject to such a law, is going to be like that, and it has not gone beyond this (p. 103).

Buddhaghosa develops this subject by recommending that the decay or progressive destruction of corpses be imagined in ten different ways, each designed to counter a particular form of lust toward the body, for example, a hacked and scattered corpse to free a person from lust after perfection of body build and a worm-eaten corpse to benefit the individual who lusts after his or her own body while thinking "this is mine" (p. 105).

Once further meditation conquers in turn the feeling of disgust, the way is open, says Alexander, for narcissistic regression and the pleasurable flooding of the whole organism with positive libido. The outcome, he claims, is a state comparable to the CATATONIC ecstasy of a schizophrenic. This "narcissistic orgasm of the entire body" (p. 134) is followed by a diminution of pleasure until, reaching the threshold of nirvana, the practitioner attains utter mental emptiness. Akin to the final stage of schizophrenia, nirvana is said to be a recovery at last of the experience of the mother's womb. Thus the Buddhist goal of conquering old age, sickness, and death is attained by the nullification of birth. The Buddha's putative recollection of countless earlier existences, of the creation and decline of prior worlds, suggests to Alexander the possibility of a still-deeper regression, beyond the stages of intrauterine life to the very beginnings of embryonic development.

Christian Speculative Mysticism: The narcissistic trends of self-mysticism have also been observed among Christian mystics, notably by Ferdinand Morel (1918) in a doctoral thesis on "mystical introversion." Morel focuses chiefly on Pseudo-Dionysius the Areopagite, an enormously influential early Christian writer, but takes certain other Christian mystics into account as well. He argues that the marked inclination of the speculative mystics to turn away from the world and to elaborate obscure metaphysical doctrines that deify the ecstatic self reveals an inborn introvertive predisposition and a reduced resistance to deviation fostered by education and other environmental factors. Sickly and timid as children, these mystics were sometimes afflicted with a vague agoraphobia (fear of open spaces) that soon became systematized as a phobia of the opposite sex. Feeling nostalgic for the mother, perhaps for the intrauterine state itself, on the one hand, and threatened by erotic attraction both to the mother and to members of the same sex, on the other, the mystic renounces sexuality and turns inward, regressing to the narcissistic state of mystical unintelligibility.

Thus the *speculative* mystic succumbs to morbid self-aggrandizement (MEGALOMANIA) and has a paranoid disregard for the things of this world. In contrast, the *orthodox* mystic substitutes for a disappointing reality an autistic system that centers on certain erotic relations with imaginary objects or persons (Excerpts 8.3). The speculative, narcissistic type of mystic is almost always a male, says Morel, and the orthodox, autoerotic type is usually female (pp. 293–324). These distinctions and trends find some corroboration in the research of historian Herbert Moller (1965, 1971), who reports that, at least in western Europe, "affective mysticism"—the equivalent of Morel's orthodox type and opposed by both union and self-mysticism—tended to flourish chiefly among women and during periods of heavy male outmigration.

EXCERPTS 8.3

The erotically conceived relation to divinity that Morel says is characteristic of orthodox mysticism is illustrated in the following quotations from three well-known Catholic mystics.

Margarete Ebner (1291–1351), a nun who was a member of the Rhenish mystical society of the Friends of God led by Meister Eckhart, John Tauler, and Henry Suso, and who was said to have telepathic and clairvoyant powers.

I had a great desire, together with my St. Bernard, to receive the kiss from the Lord, and that I would be embraced with the love of his arms and that he would take hold of me with a grip into my heart. And this was fulfilled on me one night. I was given to understand that God wished to accomplish it on me. . . . And then the grip was so powerful that I felt it for a long time, waking and sleeping (quoted in Moller, 1965, p. 263).

Teresa of Avila (1515–1582), the Spanish nun who founded the strict order of Discalced, or Barefoot, Carmelites; was canonized in 1622; and in 1970 became the first woman to be proclaimed a doctor of the church.

In his hands I saw a great golden spear, and at the iron tip there appeared to be a point of fire. This he plunged into my heart several times so that it penetrated to my entrails. When he pulled it out, I felt that he took them with it, and left me utterly consumed by the great love of God. The pain was so severe that it made me utter several moans. The sweetness caused by this intense pain is so extreme that one cannot possibly wish it to cease, nor is one's soul then

*content with anything but God. This is not a physical, but a spiritual pain, though the body
has some share in it—even a considerable share* (quoted in Moller, 1965, p. 263).

Marguerite Marie Alacoque (1647–1690), who was also canonized by the Roman
Catholic Church and is famous for her revelation of the Sacred Heart of Jesus.

*When I have received Jesus, I feel quite done up, but filled with joy so intense that at times for
a quarter of an hour everything is silence within me except for the voice of Him whom I love.*
Once, when she protested the weight of her bridegroom's love, He said,
*Let me do my pleasure. There is a time for everything. Now I want you to be the plaything of
my love, and you must live thus without resistance, surrendered to my desires, allowing me to
gratify myself at your expense* (quoted in Leuba, 1925, pp. 113–114).

Narcissism among Contemporary Christians

We need not turn to other cultures or times to find narcissistic elements in religion.
The responses of 1400 adult Americans to his Value Survey suggested to Milton
Rokeach (1969b) "a portrait of the religious-minded as a person having a self-
centered preoccupation with saving his own soul, an other-worldly orientation
coupled with an indifference toward or even a tacit endorsement of a social system
that would perpetuate social inequality and injustice" (p. 29). The "grand theme"
of salvation, agrees Pruyser (1978), is too often appropriated in ways that are
"blatantly narcissistic." So, too, is the notion of providence, of being preferentially
protected and nurtured by an ever-vigilant heavenly father; or the personal conviction of being among God's elect. Narcissism may also exist on the group level. The
"narcissism of minor differences" is splendidly illustrated, Pruyser suggests, in the
long history of denominational proliferation and conflict. We may similarly suspect
narcissistic motives, he says, in the work of Christian missionaries among people
with well-developed traditions of their own.

Noting as others have the "rising cult of self-centeredness" in contemporary
society, Pruyser finds himself particularly disturbed by "the *blatancy* of narcissistic
strands" in current religious practices. He remarks first on the "instant mysticism"
that is provided by psychedelic drugs, a potentially addictive experience that is
ordinarily sought outside the context of any theology or spiritual discipline and
therefore lacks both object and goal. The sense of "triumphant omnipotence" that
is attained through drug-assisted narcissistic regression is inevitably short-lived, he
says, leaving an enduring "narcissistic nostalgia" until the experience can be repeated.

Narcissistic motives are also implicated in the "collective disinhibitions" that
are engendered by evangelistic revival meetings and similar group actions. Through
the elusive doctrine of spirit possession and insistent appeals to infantile residual
trends, such traditions diminish the sense of personal agency and responsibility
while promoting a dangerous self-inflation. Pruyser is notably suspicious of the
loud, immodest proclamations and intrusive, high-pressure methods of some
"born-again" Christians, behavior suggesting to him the grandiosity and manipulativeness of the narcissistic character. The activities of witnessing and testifying,
says Pruyser, are often beset by "reflective narcissism," the need to have one's own
self-love mirrored back in the affirmation and admiration of others, to be assured
that one's faith is worthwhile. Even liturgical reform may have narcissistic roots,
Pruyser suggests, if it is motivated by sheer boredom and the unconscious resentment over insufficient love or admiration that usually underlies a state of ennui.

Poised to counter such narcissistic trends, Pruyser adds reassuringly, is an abundance of antinarcissistic motifs in the religious traditions. A clear example, he says, is the story of Paradise in the book of Genesis. The theme of becoming like God by eating from the forbidden tree expresses in mythic language the narcissistic longing that resides in every human soul. This story, he maintains, defines the root of sin as arrogant and rebellious striving to become omniscient and omnipotent—that is, to become God. Original sin may thus be understood as the "basic genetic disposition" of primary narcissism, the free expression of which the story resolutely seeks to discourage. In his contribution to a work on biblical interpretation, Werner Kühnholz (1978) elaborates this view by suggesting, for example, that Adam and Eve are mirror images of each other, the one created from a part of the other's body. Their relation is for a time asexual and narcissistic, like that of a brother and a sister. Narcissism is an enduring source of conflict not only in the Hebrew Bible, says Kühnholz, but also in the Christian tradition. Although Christianity opposes narcissism by encouraging humility and self-abasement (and loving relations, Pruyser would add), it yet makes narcissism a virtue by valorizing the fact of being a Christian and by promoting an identification with God, for example, through the Eucharistic introjection of Christ.

A REVISED PERSPECTIVE ON NARCISSISM

According to the classic psychoanalytic view enunciated by Freud (1914), narcissism is an infantile psychic disposition that persists as the lifelong antithesis of reality-oriented object relations. For libido to become invested in external objects, it must be diverted from the supply that is naturally directed inward toward the ego. When such objects are later relinquished, as they are during sleep, the libido will revert once again to its narcissistic form. It is also possible, Freud says in apparent contradiction, for an object choice itself to be narcissistic. That is, he says, some persons choose love objects resembling themselves or their ego ideal in order to feel loved. Whether directed inwardly or outwardly, narcissism is thought to stand in the way of normal object relations and thus is always potentially pathogenic. As used by many psychoanalysts, the adjective narcissistic is unmistakably negative in tone.

Heinz Kohut and the Psychology of the Self

A more positive perspective on narcissism is offered in the increasingly influential work of the Chicago psychoanalyst Heinz Kohut (1913–1981). Greenberg and Mitchell (1983) claim that Kohut is the most important of the theorists who combine classic drive theory and the newer relational model. Unlike Freud, Kohut posits two types of libidinal energy: narcissistic libido and object libido. Whereas *object libido* is invested in persons or things that are experienced as distinctly separate from oneself, *narcissistic libido* is used in the cathexis of objects that are felt to be a part or extension of the self, so-called SELF-OBJECTS. It is thus the cathected object's relation to the self, not object relation per se, that differentiates the two kinds of libido.

Paralleling this distinction are two "separate and largely independent developmental lines." One follows Freud's (1914) original model—from pre-ego autoerotism through ego-directed narcissism to object love—and another leads from autoerotism through ego-directed narcissism to "higher forms and transformations of narcissism" (Kohut, 1971, p. 220). Objecting to the imposition on clinical practice of Western civilization's valorization of altruism, Kohut maintains that transformed narcissism, no less than object love, may contribute to the healthful adaptation and productivity of the mature personality.

Two Configurations of Perfection: When the undifferentiated state of primary narcissism is gradually disturbed by cognitive growth and the unavoidable insufficiencies of parental care, says Kohut, the infant finds consolation by establishing two new and relatively stable systems of perfection, the GRANDIOSE SELF and the IDEALIZED PARENTAL IMAGO, both of which are cathected with narcissistic libido. The grandiose self, an inflated self-image that is manifest in the child's exhibitionistic wish to be looked at and admired, is an adaptive achievement appropriate to this early developmental phase. So, too, is the idealized parental imago, a psychic representation that seeks to preserve the original impression of parental perfection and omnipotence and that yet changes with the growth of the child's cognitive capacities. Of the two narcissistic configurations, the idealized parental imago would seem to represent a more elaborate development. It is invested not only with idealized libido, the appearance of which signals a maturational advance unique to the narcissistic developmental line, but also with object libido, a fact increasingly evident as the imago slowly emerges from the self.

Should the child's parents themselves suffer from narcissistic fixations and thus be "grossly unempathic and unreliable," or—much less crucially—should the child be abruptly separated from a parent or parent substitute or experience profound disappointment in such persons, gradual integration of the two narcissistic forms into the personality will be disturbed, yielding a variety of psychological disorders. Under favorable circumstances, these structures become attenuated and transformed. The grandiose self will yield to a realistic sense of self-esteem and pleasurable engagement in purposeful and goal-directed activity, and the idealized parental imago will gradually become reinternalized as the superego and thus lend emotional support to the maturing individual's values and ideals. These transformations give to the self a bipolar structure—ambitions at one pole, ideals at the other. Between them there is a "tension gradient" that promotes the person's various actions (Kohut, 1966; 1971, pp. 25–28, 64–65; 1977, p. 180).

Cosmic Narcissism: The taming and redirecting of narcissistic cathexes allow the ego to use them for some of its loftiest goals. Kohut (1966) identifies transformed narcissistic components in the creative activity of artists and scientists; in empathic understanding of other minds; in the capacity for humor in its more profound forms; and in the attainment of the broad attitude toward life and the world that is called wisdom. He also finds them in the very considerable achievement of accepting the finiteness of one's own existence. This feat rests, he says, on the creation of a higher and expanded form of narcissism, a COSMIC NARCISSISM that transcends individual boundaries and participates in a "supraindividual and timeless existence." Like the passive and usually fleeting "oceanic feeling," cosmic narcissism is rooted in the primordial experience of identity with the mother. Unlike the oceanic feeling, however, cosmic narcissism is "the enduring, creative result of the steadfast activities of an autonomous ego," an outcome very few might be expected to achieve. Attained, like humor, through the gradual transference of libido from the narcissistic self to self-transcending ideals, cosmic narcissism is marked not by grandiosity and elation but by "quasi-religious solemnity" and "quiet inner triumph," combined with a residual of sadness for the once-cherished self (pp. 264–268).

Narcissism in India

If Kohut's self psychology thus valorizes a rare religious outlook in the name of transformed narcissism, it also provides a framework for interpreting prominent themes in popular piety. Exemplary in this regard are the reflections on certain aspects of Hindu piety by Sudhir Kakar, a New Delhi psychoanalyst trained in West Germany and associated for a time with Erik Erikson at Harvard. In the widespread cult of Shiva, the androgynous god who is paradoxically portrayed as both chaste ascetic and erotic lover, Kakar (1978) finds vivid evidence for the peculiar fate of narcissism among Indian men.

A Fateful Boyhood: A constellation of factors in the psychosocial world of the Indian male, says Kakar, interferes with the successful integration of the grandiose self and the idealized parental imago, leaving the masculine psyche with a peculiar narcissistic vulnerability and emotional self-absorption. First, as Morris Carstairs (1957) and others have also observed, the Indian child enjoys an unusually intense and prolonged relationship with the mother. Until the age of four or five, the child is almost constantly in the presence of the mother, who provides frequent physical contact and is inclined toward unlimited indulgence of the child's wishes and demands. During her occasional absences other members of the extended family minister to the child with similar tolerance and generosity.

Around the fifth year, the male child suffers the shock of an abrupt separation from the mother and the sudden imposition by the males in his family of inflexible demands for obedience and conformity. Following this deeply bewildering "second birth," the Indian boy learns to rely less and less on his mother, replacing his attachment to her with a variety of less intense relationships with other family members. The boy's loss is profound, says Kakar, for it "amounts to a narcissistic injury of the first magnitude." The dual convictions "I am perfect" and "You are perfect but I am part of you" that Kohut attributes to the two chief narcissistic configurations remain relatively unmodified and unintegrated into the personality, Kakar surmises. Indian men are thereby predisposed to "a heightened narcissistic vulnerability, an unconscious tendency to 'submit' to an idealized omnipotent figure, both in the inner world of fantasy and in the outside world of making a living; [and] the lifelong search for someone, a charismatic leader or a *guru*, who will provide mentorship and a guiding world-view, thereby restoring intimacy and authority to individual life" (p. 128).

The injury inflicted by the sudden loss of the "good" mother can be partially healed through the gradual process of identifying with the father—if the father is emotionally available to the son. In India, the father's ambiguous role acts to sustain the male child's narcissistic vulnerability. The dynamics of the large Indian family, according to Kakar, demand of the father a certain aloofness and impartiality. Although Indian fathers are as loving as fathers anywhere else in the world, they act toward their sons with a restraint and perfunctoriness that leaves an unconscious residue of resentful anger.

Devotion to a Phallic God: The resulting narcissistic orientation of Indian males is strikingly illustrated, in Kakar's view, by the images and worship of Shiva, whose popularity among Hindu devotees is second only to Krishna's. Although Shiva is frequently represented in human form—preeminently as a cross-legged ascetic deep in meditation or as four-armed Naṭarāja, the dancing Lord of the universe—his presence in innumerable temples and roadside shrines is almost always symbolized by the LINGA, a stubby column of stone or metal rising up out of

A Shiva *linga* set in the *yoni,* with a snake swimming up the channel that serves as a drain for the water offerings poured on the *linga* by worshipers (Kedāra Ghāṭ, Banaras, India).

In preparation for the evening *āratī,* or service of worship, the *linga* is washed with water and milk and then honored with fragrant sandlewood paste, flowers, and *bilva* leaves.

a pear-shaped base, called the yoni. Worship of Shiva is carried out by pouring a liquid offering—typically holy water or milk from a cow or coconut—over the *linga.* A channel carved in the YONI then delivers the fluid back to the reverent worshiper, who may either drink it or sprinkle it on the head. The *linga* may also be elaborately adorned, using such materials as sandalwood paste, leaves, or flowers.

As early Western visitors to India were shocked to discover, *linga* means "phallus" (but also "characteristic") and *yoni* "vulva." Thus this highly stylized object of fervent devotion represents the conjunction of the male and female sex organs. That the *linga* is literally Shiva's phallus is evinced by the occasional anthropomorphic images representing him as ITHYPHALLIC, with perpetually erect penis, and especially by the episodes of Shiva's castration—reversible, to be sure—in ancient myths accounting for the *linga's* origin. Yet modern Indologists rightly point out that the *linga* is not only a phallic emblem but also a bisexual symbol, incorporating in the form of the *yoni* the female principle, said to be the seat of Shiva's divine energy. Moreover, as Diana Eck (1985) emphasizes, the *linga* is for worshipers today an ANICONIC image, a nonrepresentational sign of the deity that first manifested itself—according to the ancient myth that they prefer—as an immeasurably long and earth-splitting column of fire, out of which Shiva eventually emerges. That the *linga* might be understood as a phallus, says Eck, is consistently appalling to these contemporary devotees (p. 36).

Yet phallic symbol it is, argues Kakar, who sees it and its worship as an institutionalization of the "universal male propensity" to equate the phallus with the totality of masculine virtues. Writes Kakar,

> The symbolic linga of Shiva not only incorporates the little boy's desire and striving for the strength and "agentic" ability of manhood by identifying with the anatomical reality and functional capacity of the erect male genital, it also serves a defensive function, psycho-analytically speaking, in that an identification with the great phallus is a bulwark against the anxiety triggered by the separation from the mother during the time of the second birth (p. 156).

Devastated by the sudden challenge to his indulgence-fostered sense of control and budding self-esteem, the young boy compensates by activating the grandiose self and its convictions "I am perfect" and "I do not need anyone." This attitude finds

Ardhanārīśvara, or Shiva as the lord who is half woman.

mythic embodiment in the image of the solitary Shiva meditating high in the remote Himalayas. As an adult devotee of Shiva, the Indian male identifies with the great god's wondrous phallus, thus taking possession of its legendary attributes and restoring the infantile sense of psychic invulnerability.

Kakar states that situating the *linga* in the *yoni* adds to the reassurance of a grandiose phallus the further consolation of the narcissistic self-sufficiency that issues from the unconscious idea of bisexuality. Such narcissistic bisexuality is also expressed in a popular representation of Shiva that, in both contour and gesture, is half male and half female. The paradox of Shiva's being an ithyphallic ascetic can be resolved, Kakar concludes, by taking the *linga* as a symbol of narcissistic libido rather than object libido, of a "chaste" sexual investment in an autonomous grandiose self rather than an "erotic" one in the threatening world of external "objects" (p. 160).

Kakar regards many of the more recently founded religious cults in India, as well as a number of the new political movements, as similar atempts to restore the infantile narcissistic economy. This narcissism, he says, is increasingly being threatened throughout Indian society by accelerating socioeconomic change. The enduring and deeply felt conviction that "the 'ultimate' reality of the maternal cosmos of infancy" is superior to "the 'worldly' reality of post-maternal childhood" must give way to a more equitable balance of these realities, Kakar warns, if Hindu culture is to remain a living force in a world that greatly needs its insights into human nature (pp. 187–188).

Narcissism and Christian Faith

The potential for applying Kohut's theory in the Christian context is illustrated in the work of German theologian Hans-Günter Heimbrock (1977), who finds in the image of the crucified Christ a symbol of transformed narcissism. Building on the writings of Paul Ricoeur and Jurgen Moltmann, both of whom have developed their theological views in dialogue with psychoanalysis, Heimbrock maintains that the historical development of the biblical image of God has advanced along the very dimensions revealed in Kohut's analysis of narcissism and its transformations (p. 98).

The Symbol of a Powerless God: The omnipotent and moralistic God of the Hebrew Bible, says Ricoeur (1969), is a projection of the Oedipal father, a creation of our own weakness. The progressive freeing of the biblical image of God from these origins culminates for Ricoeur in the crucifixion of Christ, whose death he interprets as the death of God and thus, after Dietrich Bonhoeffer, the powerlessness of God. Because this death is primarily an act of loving self-sacrifice out of compassion for others, rather than an act of murder, it completes the metamorphosis of the archaic father image and thus marks the overcoming of Oedipal wishes.

Moltmann (1973) also sees in the powerlessness of the crucified God a counterimage to the Oedipally derived father idols who inspire continuing rebellion. In place of an all-powerful and protective God is one of more human dimensions, capable of suffering—and thus also of love. Moltmann views the symbol of the cross as a theological reality principle that counters the regressive aversion to suffering and flight from reality that religion has often sustained and embellished. The image of the crucified God thus opens humankind to its own humanity, preparing it to accept its freedom and its mortality. No longer driven to rebel against a guilt-inducing divine father authority but drawn, rather, into sympathetic association with a suffering God, the human being becomes open to suffering and to love, to the possibility of a new spontaneity of the heart.

In the biblical symbols discussed by Ricoeur and Moltmann, Heimbrock finds represented a progressive transformation of narcissistic fantasies. If the death of God signals a renunciation of the Oedipal father, as Ricoeur would have it, so is it also a renunciation of the grandiose self. In humbling Himself by becoming an impotent sufferer, the crucified God frees the individual from the compulsion to shore up the weak self through an omnipotent self-ideal. Furthermore, says Heimbrock, the pathos of God enables the person to empathize with the situation of others, just as the realistic acceptance of personal weaknesses and finitude allows the individual to tolerate and even share in the frailties of others. These capacities, Heimbrock suggests, along with the notion of a compassionate god who chooses to suffer out of love for humankind, represent mature transformations of the primary empathy ascribed by Kohut (1966) to the earliest narcissistic stage.

On the basis of a "psychological hermeneutics," Heimbrock concludes that the central thrust of the Christian tradition is not the promulgation of a theistic ethics—which, psychologically speaking, is rooted in the image of the Oedipal father—but the creative liberation and transformation of narcissistic fantasies. Viewed from the perspective of Kohut's psychology, the symbol of the powerless God is said to provide a general theological criterion for evaluating the products of human fantasy. The critical question, says Heimbrock, is whether the imaginative process "fixes on the illusion of omnipotence, on the divinization of persons and powers (as the archaic self-objects), or whether it inspires one to perceive the suffering of others, to accept one's own finitude, and to act with creative spontaneity toward others" (p. 129)—all of which constitute the ripe fruits of a mature narcissism.

Grandiosity in Christian Faith: In America, pastoral counselor Robert Randall similarly illustrates the potential of Kohut's psychology for a constructive critique of Christianity, both as historic tradition and individual faith. He discerns the contours of the archaic grandiose self, for example, in the "grandiose monistic claims" of Christian sects or denominations that confidently proclaim irrefutable knowledge of God's will and plan for humankind and argue that they alone possess the way to salvation. We may hold fast to what we experience as ultimately meaningful, says Randall, without grandiosely denying human limitations in discerning truth and closing ourselves to insights from other sources, especially psychology (Randall, 1984, pp. 109–110).

In a case study of a 30-year-old HYPOCHONDRIACAL high school teacher, Randall (1976) demonstrates how piety, initially serving to restore a disturbed primary narcissism, may become increasingly mature with the progressive transformation and integration of narcissistic trends. When unspecified factors disturbed the patient's conviction that everything in his life was "just perfect" and that he was uniquely special to God, he began bargaining with God, hoping to forestall a divine plan for doing him in. God's seeming failure to mirror the patient's grandiose self, just as his narcissistic father had failed him years before, eventuated in the patient's retreat to a fantasy of merging with the suffering and dying Christ. This fantasy, Randall says, served to secure the boundaries of the self, reestablish narcissistic relations to God as a self-object, and compensate for the disappointment that the patient had caused his mother. Two years of therapy brought a number of changes, most fundamentally a transmutation of his grandiose self into "healthy self-esteem, internalized goals and values, and a regulation of his drives and impulses" (p. 44). Bargaining with God had ceased, and the patient gained a growing appreciation for religion apart from his narcissistic wishes and needs.

TOWARD AN INTEGRATIVE VIEW

As we might infer from Randall's case study, the narcissistic self-motif in religion may occasionally appear in conjunction with the other two motifs. Acknowledging this possibility, the Schjelderups observe that there is a particularly close relation between mother religion and self religion, for "A maximum regression can be both an expression of an intense longing for the mother and a narcissistic 'withdrawal of libido' " (p. 60). These two pre-Oedipal motifs are unmistakably evident in the piety of Ramakrishna, who alternated between devotion to the Divine Mother and absorption in an undifferentiated Supreme Reality. He thought of himself, we may recall, as an incarnation of God.

Just as we must recognize, therefore, that the Schjelderups's types may not always be easily discriminated, so we may also acknowledge that the distinction between the object-relations perspective and Kohut's view is not nearly as easily drawn as Kohut claims. As Greenberg and Mitchell (1983) point out, much in Kohut's theorizing is reminiscent of the thinking of the object-relations theorists, especially that of Fairbairn and Winnicott. Both Kohut and Winnicott, for example, "see infantile omnipotence as providing the centerpiece for the development of the self; both stress the necessity for a slow, progressive adaptive failure on the part of the parents, allowing the development of durable internal resources" (p. 367). Kohut was himself convinced that his emphasis on the lifelong value of transformed infantile modes of relation sets his theory apart from the others and avoids the "developmental morality" inherent in them. Yet this conviction is based, say Greenberg and Mitchell, on a misinterpretation of both his own and the other theories. Nonetheless, Greenberg and Mitchell acknowledge that Kohut has made distinctive contributions to psychodynamic theorizing, notably in the preeminence he gives to the subjective experience of the self.

Students of the psychology of religion regard Kohut's and Winnicott's views as both compatible and complementary. Psychiatrist Paul Horton (1974), for one, employs both of them in seeking a minimally reductionistic understanding of mystical experience. The mystical state represents, he says, a dramatic "upsurgence of residual primary narcissism," which for Horton includes the intrauterine relational mode. He also discerns narcissism at the heart of the transitional experience described by Winnicott and concludes that mystical experience may itself serve as a transitional phenomenon. For an artistically gifted 20-year-old patient of his, who was struggling with a symbiotic attachment to her mother, recurrent mystical experience resembled typical transitional phenomena in several ways.

1. It blended the experience of inner and outer realities.
2. It provided the patient with a last, inner refuge during periods of overwhelming loneliness, soothing her much as her mother once did.
3. It was unchallengeable, though she did not think so until Horton won her confidence.
4. It became more important than the mother, a more reliable means of relieving anxiety than either mother or therapist.
5. It showed maturational potential, providing both impetus for separation from the mother and valuable resources for more adaptive individuation and integration.

In accord with certain other investigators (e.g., Allison, 1968; Prince and Savage, 1966), Horton concludes that, as a transitional phenomenon, the regressive state of mystical experience can serve an important adaptive function.

THE WIDER INFLUENCE OF THE OBJECT-RELATIONS PERSPECTIVE

To illustrate the diverse implications that scholars of religion are finding in the object-relations perspective, we will bring our survey to a close by briefly reviewing several further studies. John McDargh (1983), whose work has been particularly influenced by Ana-Maria Rizzuto, finds object-relations theory to be a useful complement to theological discussions of faith and has derived six dimensions of faith from the theory. Four are associated with the early stages of self-becoming: (1) the sense of being real, (2) the sense of being in relation to a real and meaningful world, (3) the capacity to be alone, and (4) the capacity to tolerate dependency. The two other dimensions represent the goal of the mature life of faith: (5) the capacity to tolerate ambivalence, in our own feelings and in the world of reality, and (6) the sense of self as available for loving self-donation (self-giving interpersonal intimacy). In addition to addressing the questions of "from whence" (the first four dimensions) and "to where" of faith (the last two), McDargh takes up the question of "how," by discussing the object representation of God. Two case studies serve to illustrate the value of this object-relations perspective on faith.

Diane Jonte-Pace (1987) perceives object-relations theory as a potential resource for a feminist psychology of religion. The groundwork has been laid, she says, in the rediscovery of the maternal–infant matrix of the image of God and of religious experience more generally. Such a realization serves as a vital corrective to the long-standing ANDROCENTRIC bias of the psychology of religion at the same time that it reveals a "feminine underlay" in patriarchal images of God. On these foundations, then, Jonte-Pace proposes to build a Kleinian psychology of religion as a means of illuminating the images of the goddess that represent her as two opposing forces and associate her with hunger, nourishment, and being devoured. Contrary to the Jungian perspective of Erich Neumann (1955), who maintains that the splitting of the goddess represents progressive archetypal differentiation, Jonte-Pace argues that it is a symptom of individual and cultural pathology, corresponding to the splitting of objects into good and bad elements that Klein ascribes to an early stage of development. The same tendency—to divide into idealized and denigrated aspects—has occurred in images of women. From a Kleinian standpoint, says Jonte-Pace, maturity in religion, as in interpersonal relations, entails an integration of diverse aspects—love and care as well as anger and aggression—into a single whole. It also requires tolerance of emotional ambivalence and compassion for our fellow human beings. Given our unprecedented capacity for destruction today, she intimates, such an integration may be essential for our survival.

Just as object-relations theory adds dimension to Freud's understanding of the image of God, so it offers a fuller picture of the significance of ritual, according to Mary Ellen Ross and Cheryl Lynn Ross (1983). Freud's interpretation of ritual, they say, fails to take into account its LIMINAL elements, using anthropologist Victor Turner's phrase: the spontaneous, playful, and even creative aspects of ritual performance. Liminality (from *limen*, "threshold") refers to the ambiguous transitional period in a rite of passage when the ritual subjects enter a state radically different from the past or coming one. The Rosses find that the characteristics of this realm—including the reversal of status hierarchies and other distinctions, the reconciliation of polarities, the sense of comradeship and communion, and the imagining of an ideal order—are developmentally continuous with child's play and Winnicott's still-earlier "potential space" of transitional objects. To illustrate their thesis, they examine the Roman Catholic Mass in terms of pre-Oedipal issues. Although they accept the Freudian view of it as a compromise allowing a measured expression of aggression, the Rosses suggest that it is also "a ritual of mother and infants" (p. 36) directed toward overcoming separation through community, reconciling polarities, and making present what is absent.

While scholars of religion are exploring the implications of the object-relations perspective for their work, others are now looking to it as a resource for pastoral care. Jesuit psychologist Michael Garanzini (1988) places his discussion of the theology of ministry and healing within the framework of what he calls the attachment cycle, the ever-recurring, often painful, yet ultimately valuable process of attachment, separation, loss, and reattachment in relation to other persons (the ASL-R cycle). Even enduring relationships, if they are healthy, progress through such a cycle in their movement toward mature dependence. Though belonging more to pastoral psychology than the psychology of religion, Garanzini's study is noteworthy here for its conviction that object-relations theory and the related, ethology-inspired work on attachment by British researcher John Bowlby (1969–1980) can be directly enlisted in the work of advancing the "kingdom." Together with the symposium on religion and Kohut's psychology edited by George Fitchett (1982), and Lee Kirkpatrick's (1992, 1995) proposal to use attachment theory as an encompassing framework for the psychology of religion, Garanzini's book may be a harbinger of a vigorous new literature, paralleling the literatures inspired by the work of Freud and Jung.

EVALUATION OF THE OBJECT-RELATIONS PERSPECTIVE

Such scholars as these, interested as they are in a dynamic yet positive interpretation of religion, have hailed object-relations theory as a critical new development in psychoanalytic thinking. As we have seen, its emphasis on the earliest interpersonal relations of the individual, and thus on the vicissitudes of pre-Oedipal development, provides a more inclusive framework for the study of the world's religious traditions. Its perspective on religion also seems less reductionistic and more constructive, though it is far from uncritical of religious trends.

Other scholars have misgivings about the object-relations perspective. Some advocates of orthodox psychoanalysis argue that object relations are already thematic in Freud and that classical psychoanalysis is fully competent to deal with pre-Oedipal elements. As we have seen, the Schjelderups and others have demonstrated its capacity to make coherent sense of religious themes that do not fit into Freud's narrowly Oedipal psychology of religion. Still others, recognizing the important influence that the object-relations perspective has had on libido theory, especially in its understanding of BORDERLINE and psychotic states, maintain that an integration is what is ultimately needed. Graeme Taylor (1978), for instance, found that the two perspectives, applied essentially in sequence, finally relieved the symptoms of a woman who felt herself possessed by the Devil.

Although a synthesis would seem to be a reasonable compromise, the two perspectives are actually based on fundamentally different premises. Freud's drive model takes as its basic unit of study the individual mind driven to seek private gratification of its biological needs. In contrast, the relational model takes as its irreducible unit the individual in his or her relational context; fulfillment takes the form of satisfying and enduring relationships with others. Tracing the roots of these two models—one individualistic, the other social—back into the history of Western social and political philosophy, Greenberg and Mitchell (1983, p. 403) suggest that they are no more reconcilable than Hobbes is with Rousseau and Marx. Any combination of them is bound to be unstable.

A REVIEW OF EMPIRICAL EVIDENCE

What the two perspectives do have in common is their founders' conviction that their psychologies are scientific (Fairbairn, 1955, p. 151). In the last chapter we alluded to a considerable body of research bearing on Freud's psychology, a portion of which supports certain of his propositions. How do the views we have examined in this chapter stand in terms of empirical evidence?

On Mystical Experience as Regression to Infancy

Let us begin by examining the claim of orthodox psychoanalysts that mystical experience represents regression to the narcissistic state of the infant. According to some proponents of this interpretation, the putative regression is wholly dysfunctional; others, such as Raymond Prince and Charles Savage (1966), see it as a potentially constructive maneuver serving the ego much like sleep or play. Prince and Savage identify several aspects of mystical experience that suggest a return to an infantile state.

1. General abstraction from the external world and unresponsiveness to immediate external stimulation, as observed both in meditating yogis and in infants having highly pleasant or unpleasant experiences.
2. Vague, distorted, or fragmentary imagery of the type reported by Ramakrishna and thought to be hallucinatory revivals of what the infant experiences while nursing at the breast.
3. An ecstatic feeling of immediate contact with primal reality.
4. The experience of fusion with a greater being and a corresponding disappearance of the sense of self.
5. The incapacity to express these experiences in words.

The closest we can come to adequate empirical evidence bearing on these claims is the testimony of thoughtful mystics themselves. Two have responded directly to Prince and Savage's paper. Claire Owens (1967) suggests that mystical regression, if it be such, is to a collective level that is a resource for transformation in the direction of inner harmony and wholeness. She points out that the mystic's withdrawal from the world is voluntarily chosen as a means of attaining some higher value. Whereas an encounter with "primal reality" leaves the infant immersed in erotic bodily sensations, the mystic is rendered oblivious to bodily feelings and purified of narcissistic tendencies. Acknowledging that mystical experience is itself ineffable, Owens notes that it has produced great works of religious literature, just as intuitive flashes of insight have inspired works of genius in other fields.

The Trappist monk Thomas Merton (1966) grants that regressive features are not uncommon in mystical experience and are even necessary in an early, transitional stage, in which many aspirants become bogged down. But "experiences deep enough to be ecstatic or to be qualified as 'unitive' should . . . be beyond all regressive symptoms" (p. 4). Unitive experience that is "merely regressive and narcissistic would be invalid religiously and mystically." Merton considers psychoanalytic language and the underlying assumption of the superiority of rational, discursive knowledge to be antithetical to comprehending the deeper and more genuine aspects of mystical experience. The nature and fruits of mystical experience is a topic to which we shall return later.

Evidence Bearing on the Object-Relations Perspective in General

The claims of the object-relations theorists are more easily assessed. In her critical evaluation of various psychoanalytic theories of infant development, Sylvia Brody (1982) points out that object-relations theories were not formulated on the basis of systematic studies of infancy. Some of these theorists refer to no specific infant behaviors at all, and the references to infants given by others are most often anecdotal. "One looks for the real infant in these formulations," Brody writes, "only to find a reconstructed one, or none." In pursuing knowlege, these theorists have lost sight of the object of their study (p. 532).

Observational studies have been subsequently carried out by others, particularly to test out Winnicott's notion of the transitional object. Brody's (1980) critical review of this literature suggests the following conclusions.

1. There is no consistent relation of the use of a transitional object either to early experience with the mother or to later object relations and creativity.

2. Frequent maternal encouragement of the use of a transitional object indicates that it should not be viewed as solely the infant's creation; it is, rather, a product of mutual compliance.

3. The cherished blanket is probably best not conceived as the first not-me possession or as the mother's breast but as an extension of the infant's self; periodic contact with it may serve to heighten the experience of body boundaries and thus help to shape and preserve a body ego.

4. In environments that support normal social and cognitive development, the blanket is usually given up by about age three or four.

5. Less adequate mothers tend to allow their children to retain their transitional objects for years, a circumstance frequently associated with symptoms of maladjustment.

6. Teddy bears, dolls, and like objects are not appropriately considered transitional objects in Winnicott's sense, for they serve well into latency as age-appropriate toys for furthering ego integration. They bridge the transitions of time and space in the child's experience and dispel feelings of sadness, loneliness, and fear.

From Brody's Freudian perspective, Winnicott's broadly inclusive concepts of transitional phenomena and a third, intermediate realm of illusory experience are, if anything, even more problematical. Citing philosopher Anthony Flew's rather unsympathetic analysis of Winnicott's notions of illusion and the third world of experience (in Grolnick, Barkin, and Muensterberger, 1978), Brody argues that Winnicott's varying use of these terms not only fails to describe the mental states referred to but also tends to idealize infancy, along with fantasy, thinking, and creativity. To encourage a young child to dwell in a world of private meanings, Brody says, is to risk habituation to a passivity that will exclude the experiences necessary for developing the child's potential.

Flew's and Brody's rejection of Winnicott's third world in the name of Ockham's razor, the principle of economy, must be declined in turn as too parsimonious for an adequate psychology of religion. Flew's apparent inability to conceive of religious dogma in other than literal terms may be contrasted with the spontaneous understanding of the three- and four-year-old children of a correspondent of James Pratt.[4] These children, their mother reported, insistently classified the content of their world in terms of three categories: pretend, real, and real–pretend. The third category, apparently referring to imaginings known not to be literally true but possessing vivid reality feeling, would seem to be equivalent to Winnicott's and Pruyser's third world of illusionistic thinking, but with a label less likely to tempt the rationalistic philosopher and orthodox psychoanalyst to differentiate religious thinking from creative or imaginative activity.

Just as the category "real–pretend" made sense to these children, so also do Winnicott's terms make sense to many of today's psychiatrists and psychologists, including those well acquainted with the research literature. Exemplary in this regard is psychiatric researcher Daniel Stern (1985), who undertakes to "invent" anew the infant's inner world of experience on the basis of current developmental

---

[4] Letter from Margaretta Morris Scott to James B. Pratt, November 28, 1913. James B. Pratt Papers (Box 21, folder 7), Williamsiana Collection, Williams College Archives and Special Collections, Williamstown, Massachusetts.

research. Along the way, he compares this "observed infant" with the "clinical infant" re-created in the course of adult psychotherapy. In contrast to the object-relations theorists, who assume a prolonged period in infancy when self and other remain fused in an undifferentiated state of "we," Stern concludes that the sense of a "core self" and a "core other" arises very early, and that the infant actively constructs and accurately perceives the relation of self with other. Stern also gives close attention to the possible role in self–other interactions of constitutional factors, an area that the object-relations school has neglected more than any other (Greenberg and Mitchell, p. 229). Yet Stern affirms the more fundamental object-relations assumption that the infant's subjective world is deeply social from the beginning, and he subscribes to several of Winnicott's principles, including transitional objects and transitional phenomena.

Evidence Bearing on an Object-Relations Psychology of Religion

Much of the research that bears on the object-relations view of religion has already been cited in the evaluation of Freud's theories. There we saw a consistent trend for the God image to bear closer resemblance to the mother than to the father. This tendency was noted more than half a century ago by Paul Vogel (1936), who employed the methods of the Dorpat school in an intensive study of nine Lutheran children between the ages of 5 and 14. The earliest form of religion, Vogel observes, consists of the preverbal mother–child relation. Family records of certain conversations and spontaneous expressions for the two youngest children allowed Vogel to conclude that mother and God remain closely associated for a matter of years and only gradually become separated.

Yet relations to parents do not exhaust the sources of the God image. As Rizzuto (1979) has emphasized, the individual's highly idiosyncratic and personalized representation of God derives not only from significant object relations but also from evolving self-representations and religious instruction. The contributions of self-representations have been partially assessed by research relating images of God to self-esteem and self-perceptions. In a group of 128 male Catholic high school students, Peter Benson and Bernard Spilka (1973) found self-esteem to be positively correlated with loving and kindly God images and negatively related to controlling, vindictive, and impersonal God images. Fewer correlations were significant in a follow-up study of male and female Catholic high school students, but the trends were similar. For males, lower self-esteem was associated with a wrathful image of God, and for females higher self-esteem was related to loving and kindly images. Self and God ratings in terms of "loving" and "controlling" tended to be similar (Spilka, Addison, and Rosensohn, 1975).

More recently, when John Buri and Rebecca Mueller (1987) correlated the concept of God with parental authority scales and self-esteem in a group of 127 Catholic college students, only the self-esteem variable showed a significant relation (.45). Once again, high self-esteem was associated with a conception of God as loving, patient, and forgiving. Given that self-esteem begins to develop early and remains stable over the years, Buri and Mueller think it likely that self-esteem is the causal antecedent of the God concept, not the other way around, as David Flakoll (1974) earlier hypothesized. It is conceivable, of course, that later teachings about a loving God might serve to mitigate a low level of self-esteem. Yet according to Buri and Mueller, "It appears to be the case that those individuals who are likely in the greatest need of a God image that is gentle, patient, and loving (i.e., those

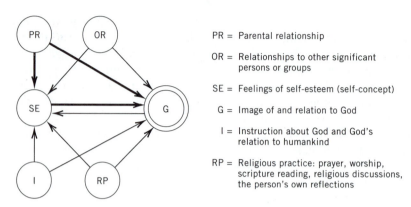

PR = Parental relationship

OR = Relationships to other significant persons or groups

SE = Feelings of self-esteem (self-concept)

G = Image of and relation to God

I = Instruction about God and God's relation to humankind

RP = Religious practice: prayer, worship, scripture reading, religious discussions, the person's own reflections

Figure 8.2. Grom's schema summarizing the relation of the God image to other factors in the individual's life. Source: From Grom, 1981, page 709.

who suffer from low self-esteem) are more apt to view God as stern, critical, and condemning" (p. 8).

These various trends bearing on the representations of God are helpfully summed up by Bernhard Grom (1981, 1986) in the diagram in Figure 8.2. Of the five factors shaping the God image, two stand out: *relations to the parents* and *self-esteem.* Given the evidence that parental relations are also a major influence on a person's feelings of self-worth, we could argue that they are the single most pivotal factor. The powerful effect of parental relationships has also been documented for religious commitment. Loss of religious faith or the giving up of an earlier religious identification is frequently associated with rejection by or alienation from one's parents (Bruder, 1947; Caplovitz and Sherrow, 1977). On the other hand, joining a religious group may be a way of seeking the acceptance and love that were missing in the person's family of origin. This is Alexander Deutsch's (1975) conclusion after finding that negative parental relations and strong inferiority feelings were frequently reported in his interviews with 14 of the devotees of a Hindu-inspired American guru.

Among the 40 religious converts whom Chana Ullman (1989) interviewed, difficulties in relation to the father in particular stood out; nearly 80 percent of the converts reported evidence of having an extremely stressful relationship with the father compared to only 23 percent in the matched group of 30 nonconverts. Fathers were absent, passive to the point of psychological unavailability, or actively rejecting. In the course of her investigation, Ullman was surprised to discover that religious conversion has little to do with an existential quest for truth. Rather, it comes after intense emotional turmoil and culminates in an experience akin to falling in love—most often with a prophet, leader, or mentor who appears as a perfect father. The object of the convert's love may also be a group of lavishly acceptant peers or an unconditionally loving transcendent being with whom the convert can merge. The conspicuousness of the father in these interviews might at first suggest that a traditional Freudian interpretation is warranted. But the relative absence of a sense of guilt in the conversion testimonials, along with the extent to which the self was experienced as inauthentic and empty, reveals the pre-Oedipal dynamics that are addressed by the British object-relations theorists and Kohut's self psychology. Ullman gives particular attention to the narcissistic aspects of conversion, especially the wish for merger.

The claim of the object-relations theorists that religion is concerned primarily with improving relations is compellingly supported in a study of congregational nurture undertaken in the late 1970s by the Lutheran Church in America (Johnson, 1979). In the more than 300 interviews carried out with members of nine participating congregations, traditional religious expressions such as "God," "Christ," or "Grace" proved to be so rare that the theologically sophisticated interviewers thought at first they were doing something wrong. Yet when they directly asked about basic Christian beliefs, conversation would come nearly to a halt. They concluded that an overwhelming majority of the laypersons whom they interviewed "simply did not find the language of belief—including the basic symbols and doctrines of the Christian tradition—to be a comfortable or meaningful way to express their faith" (p. 63). There was a corresponding recognition and tolerance of ideological pluralism, even within the more conservative congregations, and Lutheran doctrine was rated as relatively unimportant when judging sermons or choosing a new congregation.

What did prove to be critical was the factor of *caring*. Again and again, when asked what was important to them in being associated with their congregations, these members told dramatic stories of their pastors' sensitive caring for persons in times of crisis. Caretaking by lay members of the congregation also figured into these stories, and a portrait soon emerged of persons strongly bonded together by mutual care and support. At the same time there was a striking "theological gap." These stories were not linked to any biblical or theological themes, nor was God's presence mentioned as a significant factor. These church members refused to discuss faith in God apart from their experience of caring relations with significant others.

Viewed from the psychoanalytic perspective, these field data reveal a striking shift in the Lutheran tradition. What in Luther's time was a strongly Oedipal institution has become pre-Oedipal in our own day, judging from the emphasis we have seen on availability and care as well as the reported emphasis on God's love and the neglect of God's judgment. Orthodox psychoanalysts would interpret this shift as regressive; the object-relations theorists, though they, too, believe religion plays a compensatory role, would take it to be a sign of institutional health.

The tradition itself has shown concern about where these trends might lead. "Congregations could be converted into human-relations clinics, with the pastor serving as local guru/therapist. Members could become devoted only to their own mutual care and support, devoid of any sense of participation in a transcendent drama that included but was not limited to the dynamics of their own interaction" (p. 11). Allport might say there is a risk here of extrinsic religion replacing the intrinsic. Though considering such an outcome unlikely, given the theological emphasis of the Lutheran tradition, the report's author insists that concern for nurture not be separated from the church's broader theological and ecclesiastical mission.

The findings reported in this study do not, of course, allow us to generalize to religion as a whole, especially to traditions that do not have congregations or formal membership. Yet representative as these data probably are of many other American religious denominations, they do suggest why the object-relations perspective makes sense to so many people today. Without question it stands as an important corrective to the orthodox psychoanalytic interpretation of religion, and it describes important trends in at least some religious contexts. Yet in its singular emphasis on the need for satisfactory relationships, especially as it is shaped by experience with the mother, this perspective, too, risks remaining one-sided in its approach to religion. In the next chapter, on Erik Erikson, we will find the psychoanalytic perspective expanded in yet other ways, making it still more inclusive and thus more adequate for understanding the world's religious traditions. Altogether, the three chapters on the psychoanalytic perspective show why many consider it the most comprehensive psychology of religion we possess today.

9

ERIK H. ERIKSON: RELIGION IN THE HUMAN LIFE CYCLE

*A*mong psychoanalytic revisionists no others have yet achieved the towering presence—both in the technical literatures and in the popular press—of Erik Erikson (1902–1994). No other psychoanalytic innovator, furthermore, has given comparable attention to religious and ethical questions, or received as enthusiastic a reception in the theological and pastoral worlds. Revered by generations of college students who found in his sensitive and highly suggestive writings a deeper understanding of their own struggles and ideals, Erikson gave new clarity and dignity to the lives of their parents and grandparents as well. For the study of religion in particular his contributions remain inestimable. The author of a pervasively influential life span theory of ego development and the architect of modern psychohistory, Erikson laid broad foundations for understanding both personal faith and historic tradition.

FROM BOHEMIAN ARTIST TO WORLD-RENOWNED PSYCHOANALYST

Born in 1902, Erikson grew up in Germany as the son of a Jewish pediatrician. His mother, who was also Jewish, was a native of Denmark. What the young, Nordic-featured Erik did not know—or was supposed not to know—was that the highly respected physician was in reality his stepfather. His true, Danish father had abandoned Erik's mother before he was born. A gifted artist whose large-scale wood-prints were once exhibited in Munich, the youthful Erikson felt disinclined to follow his loving stepfather into medicine. Indeed, by then he had become alienated from all that his middle-class family stood for. After completing, without distinction, a classical education at a humanistic *Gymnasium* (roughly equivalent to completing one year of college in America), he alternated for several years between wandering about Europe and returning home for the formal study of art (Erikson, 1975).

Erikson's valued years as a ''Bohemian'' were brought to a sudden end by a fateful invitation from an old friend, similarly adrift, to join him in Vienna as a teacher in a school set up for the children of Freud's patients, colleagues, and analysts-in-training. Erikson accepted, and before long he was drawn into the circle

Erik Erikson

of Freud's immediate associates. While he taught the children art, he himself became once again a student, in the training institute of the Vienna Psychoanalytic Society and in the Vienna Montessori teachers' association. He was eventually to graduate from both (Coles, 1970).

During his years in Vienna—from 1927 to 1933—Erikson studied with some of the leading proponents of psychoanalysis, including Heinz Hartmann and Ernst Kris, who with Erikson played prominent roles in the development of psychoanalytic ego psychology. Anna Freud, the master's daughter and also a major contributor to ego psychology, was Erikson's analyst. Freud, by then in his seventies and in semiretirement, had been weakened by his battle with cancer and was distracted by the financial problems of the psychoanalytic publishing house. He nevertheless continued to write, including *The Future of an Illusion,* which was published the year Erikson arrived in Vienna (Coles, 1970; Jones, 1957).

By 1933, the rising tide of fascism had forced most of the Jewish analysts in Germany and Austria to flee, many of them to America. Himself born of Jewish parentage—though he was later to become a professing Christian (Kushner, 1993)—Erikson moved to Boston in late 1933 with his Canadian-American wife and their two young sons. A daughter would be born five years later. While serving as the city's only child analyst, he joined in the work of Henry Murray and his associates at the Harvard Psychological Clinic. Though possessing no university degree, he was also appointed at the Harvard Medical School.

During the succeeding years, which brought distinguished positions at Yale, the University of California at Berkeley, the residential Austin Riggs Center in Massachusetts, and then once again Harvard, Erikson became well acquainted with a number of eminent psychologists, sociologists, and anthropologists, including Kurt Lewin, Lawrence Frank, and Margaret Mead. The ideas of these colleagues gave new dimensions to his psychoanalytic thinking, and two of them—Scudder Mekeel and Alfred Kroeber, both psychoanalytically trained anthropologists—took him to observe the American Indian tribes that each had adopted for study: the Sioux in South Dakota, and the Yurok on the Pacific Coast, respectively. Constituting "two of [his] most instructive experiences" (p. 112), these field visits provided memorable illustrations for his classic book *Childhood and Society* (1950), in which he explores the deep and subtle connections between a society's values and norms and the ways they shape the individual's development.

Major themes in this seminal work—the "epigenetic" perspective, the valorization of play, and above all the concept of identity—were soon amplified and further illustrated in a series of additional publications, including nine other books. Three of these volumes are of particular significance for the psychology of religion: *Young Man Luther* (1958), a work reflecting a shift in interest from childhood to youth as well as a change in method, from cultural anthropology to social history; *Gandhi's Truth* (1969), which won both the Pulitzer Prize and the National Book Award; and *Toys and Reasons* (1977), in which Erikson expands on ritualization, a theme he had developed earlier for a symposium at the Royal Society of London (Erikson, 1966). Noteworthy, too, is a lengthy essay on the social and historical significance of the Galilean sayings of Jesus (Erikson, 1981).

AN EPIGENETIC THEORY OF DEVELOPMENT

The foundation stone of Erikson's reconstruction of psychoanalysis is the principle of EPIGENESIS, a term that he borrowed from embryology. The psychological growth of the individual, he suggests, proceeds in a manner analogous to the development of fetal organ systems. Just as each organ has its own time to arise—and *must* arise then, and without disturbance, if it is to develop fully and become part of the functioning whole—so also do the psychological potentialities of the growing individual. And much as the arrest of some one organ can threaten the remaining hierarchy of development, so too can disturbance in the psychological sphere (Erikson, 1982, pp. 27–28). The embryologist, of course, is concerned only with prenatal development; Erikson projected his epigenetic theory of ego development across the entire life span.

In Erikson's famous schema, presented diagrammatically in Table 9.1, each stage is characterized by a specific developmental task or "psychosocial crisis" that must be resolved at its own critical time if an individual is to advance to the next phase. Successful resolution adds to human maturity some fundamental ego quality. Each of the "turning points," the columns in Erikson's diagram suggest, is anticipated and prepared for from the beginning and then consolidated in the stages that follow; every ego quality exists in some form virtually from the beginning. Read horizontally, the table implies that each task and the potential fruits of its resolution have connotative significance for all the other stages, earlier as well as later. Starting at whatever point one wishes, every line of the chart must be related developmentally to every other line. The process represented is a progressive differentiation of coexisting and intimately related psychic parts (Erikson, 1950, pp. 269–273; 1982, p. 59).

The principle of epigenesis also serves as a reminder, Erikson (1982) says, that the body in its hierarchical organization is a vital component of human existence. Any comprehensive psychology must take it into account. Two other organizational processes are essential in the individual's life: the psychic organization of personal experience and the cultural organization of human interdependence. All three of these complementary processes—the somatic, the psychological, and the communal—must be reckoned with to understand any human event (pp. 25–26). To start with any one of these processes will lead automatically to the other two.

All three processes are explicit in Erikson's developmental schema. The childhood or pregenital stages correspond to Freud's own, each grounded in particular somatic experience. Erikson, however, gives a much larger role in each phase to ego and societal factors. The ego, he points out, serves not only to reduce unwanted

Table 9.1 **ERIKSON'S EPIGENETIC DIAGRAM OF EIGHT DEVELOPMENTAL STAGES**

	1	2	3	4	5	6	7	8
VIII Old Age								Ego Integrity vs. Despair
VII Adulthood							Generativity vs. Stagnation	
VI Young Adulthood						Intimacy vs. Isolation		
V Adolescence					Identity vs. Identity Confusion			
IV School Age				Industry vs. Inferiority				
III Play Age			Initiative vs. Guilt					
II Early Childhood		Autonomy vs. Shame, Doubt						
I Infancy	Basic Trust vs. Mistrust							

Source: Modified from pages 56–57 in Erikson, 1982.

stimulation from inner libidinous wishes or outer reality demands but also to guard the unity of the person and to allow active mastery of the external world (Erikson, 1964, p. 148). To accommodate this larger agenda, Erikson extended his schema of ego development to encompass the entire life span.

In further contrast to Freud but much like the object-relations theorists, Erikson postulates that the individual comes into the world prepared for an average "expectable" environment, chiefly a human or social one. The caretakers who fulfill these vague expectations find in the process that their own developmental needs are met in turn. There is, in other words, a "cogwheeling" of the stages of childhood and adulthood, a mutually beneficial "system of *generation* and *regeneration*" (Erikson, 1964, p. 152). Also part of the expectable environment are certain institutions and traditions that have evolved to safeguard and reinforce the ego strengths that are to be achieved in the sequence of developmental stages. Although the epigenetic phases are presumed to be universal, the typical solutions and institutional safeguards naturally vary from one society to the next.

The Stages of Psychosocial Development

Each of Erikson's eight epigenetic stages is summed up in terms of a bipolar formula. At the one pole is the ego quality that successful resolution of that stage's challenge will establish. At the other pole is that quality's counterpart, the outcome of consistently unfavorable circumstances. No one will fall at one extreme or the other; it is always a matter of the ratio between the two opposing trends. Whether favorable or not, this ratio implies not only certain modes of conscious experience and observable behavior but also unconscious inner states.

In briefly summing up each of these stages here, we first define the ego quality to be attained and the circumstances that favor its development. Next, we identify the human strength or "virtue" that emerges in that stage and, with the others, expresses the integration of these developmental trends. Then we specify the basic element of society—some institution or tradition—that, having evolved in intimate relation with the human life cycle, converges with the individual's unfolding capacities and brings forth the essential virtue. Finally, we note the "potential core pathology" or "basic antipathy" that, as the virtue's counterpart, overshadows it when unfavorable trends prevail (Erikson, 1950, 1982).

Infancy: Basic Trust versus Basic Mistrust: Like each of the other childhood stages, infancy is grounded in particular bodily experience. In terms of erotogenic zones and developing organ systems, this is the oral-respiratory and sensory stage. The primary zone of interaction is the mouth, and the dominant mode of approach—generalized to the entire body surface—is incorporation. Through the repeated pleasure of nursing and the lovingly sensitive ritual of daily caretaking, the infant gradually develops a sense that the surrounding world is a benign, predictable, and thus trustworthy place to be. In this early experience of "mutual regulation" the infant also discovers trust in the self (Erikson, 1950, p. 68).

With the eruption of teeth, however, the main locus of pleasure becomes the source of gnawing pain. Furthermore, the urge to alleviate that pain through biting may provoke the mother to withdraw—abruptly and perhaps in anger—from the nursing child. The traumatic character of these events and the changes they bring about are intensified by their closeness to the time of weaning and the mother's return to work or preoccupation with another pregnancy. The outcome, says Erikson, may be an abiding impression that "Once upon a time one destroyed one's unity with a maternal matrix." This "earliest catastrophe" in the person's relation to self and the world "is probably the ontogenetic contribution to the biblical saga of paradise, where the first people on earth forfeited forever the right to pluck without effort what had been put at their disposal; they bit into the forbidden apple, and made God angry" (p. 79). The lasting sense of mistrust introduced by this universal experience of "evil," of being deprived and abandoned, will be minimized and outweighed, says Erikson, if the early unity is deeply satisfying and the inevitable changes are gently introduced.

The successful resolution of the stage of infancy gives rise to the essential virtue of *hope*, which is not only the first of the vital ego strengths to appear but also the most basic and lasting. Hope, writes Erikson (1964), "is the enduring belief in the attainability of fervent wishes, in spite of the dark urges and rages which mark the beginning of existence" (p. 118). Fostered by the parents' faith that what they do has meaning, the child's generalized sense of hopefulness will in time itself be transformed into a mature faith, a confidence requiring neither evidence nor reason that the universe is trustworthy (p. 153).

Institutional confirmation of hope and its mature derivation, faith, has in the course of human history come chiefly from *religion*. It is true, says Erikson, that religion has appropriated power by exploiting humankind's infantile past, "not only by offering eternal guarantees for an omniscient power's benevolence (if properly appeased) but also by magic words and significant gestures, soothing sounds and soporific smells—an infant's world" (p. 153). Yet through its formulations and stylized gestures, religion has at the same time universalized the personal heritage of trust and mistrust, creating a common faith and a common perception of evil. The private longing for restoration, for renewed hope to counter the residual of threatening separation, finds its fulfillment in the shared ritual of a trusted community. The challenge to the nurturing adult, Erikson suggests, is not simply to convey a coherent and hopeful world-image to the child but also to preserve or transform the institutions that sustain a tradition of faith (Erikson, 1968, p. 106; 1964, p. 153).

Rather than determining how religion should be practiced, the psychologist must decide, says Erikson (1959), whether religious tradition is a living force in the parent's life, creating a faith that undergirds the child's sense of trust. "The psychopathologist cannot avoid observing," he writes, "that there are millions of people who cannot really afford to be without religion, and whose pride in not having it is that much whistling in the dark." Many, however, have found a viable source of faith apart from traditional religious doctrines—in fellowship, social action, productive work, or artistic creation. Many, too, profess faith while yet mistrusting their fellow humans and even life itself (p. 64). In them we may see hope's counterpart, the basic antipathy of *withdrawal*.

Early Childhood: Autonomy versus Shame and Doubt: In the second, anal-urethral and muscular stage, the anal zone becomes the locus for two conflicting modes, retention and elimination. The same modes are expressed more generally by the developing muscle system as a whole, in such actions as holding on to things or throwing them away. In this stage, says Erikson (1950), and especially in societies that take toilet training seriously, the mutual regulation between caretaker and child is put to its severest test. When the child's faltering and often violently contradictory efforts to gain self-control and act independently are supported by tolerant and firmly reassuring control from others, the still highly dependent child may strive for autonomy without fear of jeopardizing the basic trust achieved in the first stage. If, however, the child is unprotected from repeated loss of self-control or is subject to excessive parental restraint, the outcome may well be a lasting sense of doubt—both in the self and in the wisdom of the parents—as well as a feeling of shame.

No less vital than hope is the virtue of *will*, the distillate of a satisfactory resolution of the early childhood stage. According to Erikson's (1964) formulation, will "is the unbroken determination to exercise free choice as well as self-restraint, in spite of the unavoidable experience of shame and doubt in infancy" (p. 119). Individually, will provides a basis for accepting, even "choosing," the inevitable. Socially, the mutual limitation of will among those who have learned willingness allows the exchange of "good will." The lasting need to have the person's will affirmed in a social context of mutually agreed-upon privileges and obligations is safeguarded by the *principle of law and order,* whether embodied in courts of law or in the political and economic regulation of daily life. More immediately, the child's confidence in the lasting worth of the autonomy achieved in childhood will be sustained by the "sense of rightful dignity and lawful independence" of nurturing adults. Where the will remains rudimentary, however, slavish *compulsion* and willful *impulsivity* may rule instead (Erikson, 1950, p. 254; 1982, p. 78).

Play Age: Initiative versus Guilt: What Freud called the phallic stage Erikson labels the infantile-genital and locomotor stage. Erikson, too, imputes to this developmental era the complex of sensations, wishes, and fears that compose the Oedipus complex. But he frames this crisis in the broader context of the child's new capacities: for independent and vigorous movement; for understanding—and misunderstanding—language; and for imagining wild and sometimes terrifying possibilities. The intrusive mode that has its ground plan in early though vague genital awareness becomes generalized as aggressive activity and exuberant discovery.[1] The danger of this stage, says Erikson, is a deep and abiding sense of guilt over forbidden wishes and jealous rivalry, perhaps expressed in aggressive acts that seem frighteningly out of control. Once these fantasies are repressed and the rage denied, restrictive inhibition and intolerant self-righteousness may result. Yet the secret guilt may also serve to redirect the individual's curiosity and energy away from the family and toward the world of facts, worthy ideals, and practical goals (Erikson, 1950, p. 257; 1959, p. 75).

The new temporal perspective required for the development of *purpose*, the vital virtue that belongs to this stage, emerges in the context of the "intermediate reality" of infantile play. In the simplified world of make-believe, the child gradually works through the failures of the past and appropriates a future of realizable goals. In time, the family must convey by example the bounds of fantasy and play, the demands of an unchangeable reality, and the ideals of purposeful action. Purpose, says Erikson (1964), "is the courage to envisage and pursue valued goals uninhibited by the defeat of infantile fantasies, by guilt and by the foiling fear of punishment" (p. 122). In society at large, Erikson notes, initiative and purpose find fullest support in an *economic order* that fosters a "truly free sense of enterprise" (Erikson, 1950, p. 258; 1959, p. 82). In the absence of such freedom we find the core pathology of *inhibition*.

---

[1] Phallic intrusiveness is, of course, chiefly the prerogative of the boy. To the girl in this stage Erikson ascribes the modes of feminine inception and maternal inclusion, both of which resemble the incorporative mode of the first stage. Thus the stage of initiative has a distinctly masculine cast to it. Although critics have challenged Erikson's (1968) claim that these modal sex differences are consistently reflected in the ways boys and girls play with toys, other research has confirmed it (Robert May, 1980).

School Age: Industry versus Inferiority: According to the orthodox psycho-analytic view, the resolution of the Oedipus complex and the formation of the superego bring the psychosexual stages to a climax and inaugurate the period of latency, that "halt and retrogression in sexual development" (Freud, 1916–1917, p. 326). Although Erikson agrees that the first three stages have greater importance than any of those that follow, and asserts that the fourth stage is the first to entail no "swing from an inner upheaval to a new mastery," he finds "latency" a signif-icant stage nonetheless. It is the time of systematic instruction, whether in class-rooms under the tutelage of certified teachers or, in nonliterate societies, in the field or jungle under the guidance of gifted adults or knowledgeable older children. Moving beyond the immediate family circle and playful exploration of bodily modes and emergent capacities, the child in this stage learns to use the practical tools and utensils of the adult world, thus developing a sense of industry. When success in this endeavor eludes the child, or the goals themselves are indistinct, a sense of inadequacy or inferiority will likely follow.

When industry is rewarded, the foundations are laid for the virtue of *competence* and for the more specific adult form, workmanship, the vital source of lasting self-verification and ego strength. Allowed to postpone the challenges of further psy-chosexual development, the child must now learn the skillful use of body, mind, and material objects for practical and lasting achievements. Competence—"the free exercise of dexterity and intelligence in the completion of tasks, unimpaired by infantile inferiority"—finds its institutional underpinnings in the *technological order* and the ethos of production. Through the guidance and example of teachers and peers, the developing child gradually becomes a competent participant in the technologies of the surrounding culture (Erikson, 1964, pp. 123–124). When the sense of competence remains elusive, however, we may observe the antipathic quality of *inertia,* which remains a continuing threat to a person's productivity (Erikson, 1982, p. 76).

Adolescence: Identity versus Identity Confusion: Silently at work through-out all the preceding stages, beginning with the earliest exchange of smiles between baby and parent, is a lifelong development that reaches its critical time with the advent of puberty. This process is the formation of IDENTITY, an expression enor-mously enriched by Erickson's famous if elusive elaborations of it. In his writings, Erikson (1959) suggests, the term identity has at least four connotations: (1) a conscious sense of being a separate and unique individual; (2) a feeling of "inner sameness and continuity" over time, the relative attainment of unconscious striving; (3) the wholeness achieved through the silent, synthesizing functions of the ego; and (4) a sense of deep accord ("inner solidarity") with the self-definition and ideals of some group that affirms in turn a person's own identity (pp. 89, 102).

At the time that rapid body growth and genital maturation call into question the "sameness and continuity" achieved in the preceding years, the pubescent youth is confronted with the problem of connecting the ego qualities and know-how learned in childhood with the adult roles that loom on the horizon. The "evolving configuration" that is gradually established in the process of identity formation encompasses not only a consistent set of satisfying roles, recognized by others, but also one's particular constitutional endowment and libidinal needs, successful defenses and valued sublimations, preferred capacities and meaningful identifications. In societies in which technological innovation has expanded the years of preparation required for access to the adult world of specialized work, the adolescent requires a psychosocial MORATORIUM, a stage of suspension, as it were, between the ways of childhood and the responsibilities of the adult years. The adolescent moratorium provides an opportunity for role playing and experimentation as a means of achieving a durable sense of inner unity and of settling on some occupational role.

Adolescents in the throes of an IDENTITY CRISIS may seek a temporary solution in overidentifying with some popular hero, to the point of total identity loss. They may also join some clique that cruelly separates insiders and outsiders in terms of superficial and stereotyped features. The forming of such groups, while warding off the sense of identity confusion, also serves to test the members' capacity to pledge fidelity, the virtue that emerges in the adolescent stage (Erikson, 1950, p. 262). When the dominant images of a society do not inspire commitment—as in recent times the American culture has not—the values of conventional adulthood may be indefinitely refused. Among certain detached youth, the outcome is a fragmentation of identity, a present-centered cult of experience, and fantasies of a selfless mystical fusion (Keniston, 1965).

The cornerstone of identity, says Erikson (1964), is the virtue of *fidelity,* "the ability to sustain loyalties freely pledged in spite of the inevitable contradictions of value systems" (p. 125). Fidelity, we have noted, may be inspired by the acceptance and affirmation of one's peers. It is also sustained by IDEOLOGY or at least a world-view, the societal element that Erikson associates with the fifth, adolescent stage. The mind of the adolescent is an ideological mind, he observes, for in devotion to some creed or doctrine youth finds both inner coherence and a definition of evil. Ritually confirmed as a member of some tribe or tradition, the adolescent pledges fidelity to a new, larger family. Tragically, such group identity simultaneously fosters the conviction that otherness is harmful; outsiders may be defined and attacked as a dangerous enemy. The challenge to the adult world, Erikson suggests, is twofold: to provide values that attract the loyalty and energies of youth, on the one hand, and to identify objects worthy of its repudiation on the other (p. 126). Both were missing from the lives of Kenneth Keniston's (1965) uncommitted youth, whose alienation took the form of an ideological distrust of all ideology (p. 192). Such lives as these illustrate fidelity's antipathic counterpart, *role repudiation.*

Young Adulthood: Intimacy versus Isolation: With the attainment of identity, the individual is at last ready—indeed, eager—to fuse that identity with the identity of others, in intimate relation. Erikson chiefly elaborates on heterosexual relationships of orgasmic mutuality, which he says can develop fully only with the capacity for abiding commitment. Yet intimacy also enters into other situations of self-abandon, including close friendships, inspiration from teachers, and intuitive insights. When fear of ego loss compels a person to avoid such experiences, however, a profound sense of self-absorbed isolation may result.

With intimacy comes the virtue of *love.* Anticipated by the forms of love known in the earlier stages, love in young adulthood represents the transformation of these earlier forms into the selfless care given to others, actively and by choice, throughout the rest of the life cycle. In the lives of young adults, Erikson (1964, p. 129) maintains, the decisive biological differences between the sexes finally reach their own crisis and resolution, yielding a lasting polarization of the two sexes in terms of their typical patterns of love and care. These mutually enhancing patterns are reflected most obviously in the differing roles played in procreation, but they appear elsewhere as well, even in the forms that religion takes. Whereas men seek verification of faith in a logic that permits action free of guilt, women find it in what they are able to do with faith itself—establish trust and foster hope in the new generation (p. 152). Love, writes Erikson, "is mutuality of devotion forever sub-duing the antagonisms inherent in divided function." It is, he adds, "the basis of ethical concern," though it may also be a "joint selfishness" in the service of some narrowly circumscribed loyalty (pp. 129–130). Intimacy and love find their institutional support in the *patterns of relationship* a society defines and facilitates. They require, too, a measure of *exclusivity,* which, as their antipathic counterforce, may also become destructive (Erikson, 1982, p. 71).

Adulthood: Generativity versus Stagnation: Given the enormous role that learning and cultural transmission play in human lives, notes Erickson (1950), the theme of *generativity* might well be considered the most important of all. The heart of generativity lies, he says, in "establishing and guiding the next generation," whether it be directly, in rearing one's own offspring, or through a more generalized productivity and creativity. Adults need to be needed, and they rely on receiving encouragement, guidance, and self-verification from those who are the objects of their productivity and care (p. 267). Self-absorbed individuals for whom such an expansion of interests and investment of energy is foreign are likely to be personally impoverished and experience a deep-felt sense of stagnation.

The virtue of the adulthood stage is *care,* "the widening concern for what has been generated by love, necessity, or accident; it overcomes the ambivalence adhering to irreversible obligation" (Erikson, 1964, p. 131). It is a quality, he says, that is essential for psychosocial evolution and the successful attainment of the various ego qualities. No one institution safeguards generativity, Erikson (1950) observes; "one can only say that all institutions codify the ethics of generative succession" (p. 267). Even the impulse of monastic religious traditions to renounce biological procreation reveals a striving for a deeper understanding of care as it has been projected onto a superhuman agency. This agency must "be strong enough to guide (or at least forgive) man's propensity for freely propagating offspring, causing events and creating conditions which, ever again, prove to be beyond him" (Erikson, 1964, p. 131).

Like exclusivity, which in some measure is essential to intimacy and love, *rejectivity* is the necessary countertrend to sympathy and care. As Erikson (1982) observes, "One cannot ever be generative and care-ful without being selective to the point of *some* distinct rejectivity" (p. 68). Yet rejectivity may expand ruthlessly, a concern not only of law and ethics but also of the religious and ideological traditions that advocate an ideal of universal care.

Old Age: Integrity versus Despair: When the fruits of each of the preceding seven stages successfully form and ripen in turn, the harvest in old age is a sense of integrity, the last and most encompassing of the ego qualities to emerge. Suggesting both coherence and wholeness, the term *integrity* implies an emotional synthesis of the other ego qualities in their most mature forms. There is a quality of closure to a life of integrity, a sense of world order and spiritual meaning. A new, timeless, and accepting love is felt toward one's parents and the other significant persons in one's life. A person also feels a comradeship with peoples of distant times and other callings, with those who have left a heritage expressing human dignity and love. Integrity's touchstone can be found in "the acceptance of one's one and only life cycle as something that had to be and that, by necessity, permitted of no substitutions," an acceptance most tangibly evident in a courageous facing of death. The lack of ego integrity, on the other hand, is signaled by despair—over the fleeting passage of time and the impossibility of starting over. Unable to accept as ultimate the life cycle drawing to a close, the despairing individual approaches death with fear and disgust (Erikson, 1950, pp. 268–269; 1959, p. 98; 1964, p. 134; 1982, p. 65).

When despair is outweighed by ego integrity, we find the virtue of *wisdom*, "detached concern with life itself, in the face of death itself" (Erikson, 1964, p. 133). An amalgam of such elements as refined discernment, mature judgment, and accumulated knowledge, wisdom preserves the integrity and meaning of experience in the face of declining physical and mental abilities. At the same time, it provides for the next generations a heritage upon which they in turn can build. For most persons, wisdom's essence is not an individual achievement but is provided, rather, by a living *religious or philosophical tradition* (Erikson, 1968, p. 140). Even the wise, however, are naturally inclined to react to weakness and helplessness—including their own—with *disdain*, the antipathic counterpart to wisdom (Erikson, 1982, pp. 61, 64).

Reflecting on the final stage as an old man himself, Erikson (1982) indicates that the role of old age may have to be reevaluated in the light of its changing image. Overshadowing the few, long-surviving "elders" who quietly lived up to their assignment of wisdom and dignity are the increasingly numerous "elderlies" who are distinguished by little more than advanced age. As Erikson's schema stands today, however, successful completion of the life cycle takes us full circle, bringing not despair but the fulfillment of hope, the virtue that in its final, most mature form has become faith (p. 62).

Ritualization and Its Elements

The ego qualities and vital virtues of the first and last stages, Erikson says, have in the course of history been safeguarded primarily by the religious traditions. Most of the virtues of the intermediate stages—will, purpose, competence, fidelity, love, and care—also bear religious connotations, especially in the Christian context. So, too, does Erikson's notion of *ritualization*, which not only is linked to religious ritual but also casts new light on it.

As Erikson (1966) uses the term, ritualization consists of "an agreed-upon interplay between at least two persons who repeat it at meaningful intervals and in recurring contexts" (p. 337). It is also characterized by careful attentiveness to the ceremony's form and details; a sense of higher symbolic meaning; active engagement of all participants; and a feeling of absolute necessity (p. 343). A regular feature of everyday life, such ritualized interplay is adaptive for each of its participants. It fosters the growth of the individual ego, helping the person to avoid both uncontrolled impulsivity and excessive self-restriction, and it makes familiar a particular understanding of human existence.

In addition to these positive functions, ritualization regrettably promotes humankind's proclivity for PSEUDOSPECIATION, the conviction that a person's own group and its ways define what is essentially human, and that other pseudospecies, lacking such divine election, are a threat to the group members' identity and fate. Pseudospeciation presents us with a fundamental antinomy. On the one hand, it undergirds cooperation and loyalty and inspires invention and heroism. On the other hand, its prejudicial attitude is expressed in clannishness and fearful avoidance if not also moral hatred and mutual destruction (Erikson, 1977, p. 77; 1982, p. 69).

Among ritualization's positive functions, says Erikson (1977), is the successive development of the essential elements composing adult rituals. Occurring in a variety of contexts, these rituals are marked by "a deepened communality, a proven ceremonial form, and a timeless quality from which all participants emerge with a sense of awe and purification" (p. 78). Just as each of the eight developmental stages is defined in terms of an ego quality and its negative counterpart, a vital virtue and an antipathic trend, so each of them is associated with a positive ritual element as well as a RITUALISM, a pathological equivalent that is a mere shadow of playful ritualization. Like the ego qualities and virtues, each element of ritualization, once it has emerged, is taken up and renewed in all subsequent stages, forming with the others the whole that is true ritual (p. 98). A summary of all these thematic elements can be found in Table 9.2.

The Numinous: The first of these ritual elements is the numinous, a pervasive quality signifying the presence of the holy. Although the numinous is naturally more often associated with religious settings and rituals, Erikson considers it indispensable to any ritual observance incorporating the devotional element. The "ontogenetic source" of the numinous, he says, lies in the mutual recognition and affirmation that constitute the "greeting ceremonial" that occurs each morning between mother and infant.[2] Addressing the child by name and referring to herself, too, by some special term, the mother attends in a highly ritualized way to the physical needs of her increasingly responsive offspring. At the same time, this exchange between two obviously unequal participants serves the emotional needs of both. The familiarity of such periodic caretaking and the recurring "sense of a *hallowed presence*" lend coherence to infantile experience and forestall a feeling of separation by abandonment. For the mother, this ritualization helps to overcome her ambivalence toward the demanding child and to affirm her as the kind of benevolent mother she is trying to be (Erikson, 1966, pp. 338–340; 1977, pp. 85–90).

Later in life, this seemingly inborn need for periodic recognition and affirmation is met by the numinous element in religious ritual. The numinous "assures us of *separateness transcended* and yet a *distinctiveness confirmed,* and thus of the very basis of a sense of 'I,' renewed (as it feels) by the mutual recognition of all 'I's joined in a shared faith in one all-embracing 'I Am.' " That the numinous has its ontogenetic origin in infancy is suggested not only by the special appeal of Madonna-and-Child images but also by the attitudes and gestures of childlike dependence that are directed toward securing "the privilege of being lifted up to the very bosom of the divine which, indeed, may be seen to graciously respond, with the faint smile of an inclined face" (Erickson, 1977, pp. 89–90). Rejecting the perspective of what he calls ORIGINOLOGY, which would simply reduce religion to these infantile origins, Erikson maintains that a "true sense of veneration or even adoration" is inherently integrative, both psychosocially and generationally. Yet reverence for the numinous can be distorted through the perversion of *idolism,* a nonintegrative attitude of adulation that Erikson says implies an illusory and narcissistic image of perfection.

The Judicious: The second basic element in ritual is the judicious, a term chosen to suggest discrimination between right and wrong. Most fully elaborated

---

[2] In his more recent writings on ritualization, Erikson (1977) initially substitutes "maternal person" for mother, allowing us to infer that fathers who participate in this ceremonial may contribute and gain to the same effect. Yet Erikson quickly shifts to "she" and "mother," and he suggests that the interplay with the infant is enhanced by the mother's "postpartum condition" and perhaps also by an "instinctive sense of mothering" (pp. 86–87). As we noted earlier, Erikson posits enduring sex differences in typical patterns of love and care. Thus Erikson, too, seems to underscore the maternal component that human ontogeny contributes to religious tradition.

Table 9.2 SUMMARY OF THE THEMES CONSTITUTING ERIKSON'S STAGES OF DEVELOPMENT

Psychosocial Stage	Psychosexual Stage	Psychosocial Crisis: Ego Quality	Psychosocial Crisis: Counterpart	Virtue	Basic Antipathy	Societal Element	Ritual Element	Ritualism
Old Age		Integrity	Despair, disgust	Wisdom	Disdain	Religious or philosophic tradition	Integral (philo-sophical)	Dogmatism
Adulthood		Generativity	Stagnation	Care	Rejectivity	(various)	Generational	Authoritism
Young Adulthood	Genitality	Intimacy	Isolation	Love	Exclusivity	Patterns of relationship	Affiliative	Elitism
Adolescence	(Puberty)	Identity	Identity confusion	Fidelity	Repudiation	Ideology	Ideological	Totalism
School Age	Latency	Industry	Inferiority	Competence	Inertia	Technological order	Formal	Formalism
Play Age	Infantile-genital and locomotor	Initiative	Guilt	Purpose	Inhibition	Economic order	Dramatic	Impersonation
Early Childhood	Anal-urethral and muscular	Autonomy	Shame, doubt	Will	Compulsion, impulsivity	Law and order	Judicious	Legalism
Infancy	Oral-respiratory and sensory	Basic trust	Mistrust	Hope	Withdrawal	Religion	Numinous	Idolism

Source: Modified from pages 32–33 in Erikson, 1982.

in a court trial, the judicious is an essential feature of every ritual, "for there is no ritual—up to the Last Judgment—which does not imply a severe discrimination between the sanctioned and the out-of-bounds" (Erikson, 1977, p. 92). The judicious has its ontogenetic source in early childhood, the stage of autonomy and will and the testing of limits under the watchful eyes of superior persons. Because at this age we are taught not only what we can be by "watching out" but also what we might become if our vigilance fails, the foundations are also laid for the NEGATIVE IDENTITY. An image of all that a person is not supposed to be, the negative identity plays an essential part in pseudospeciation. When the forms of the judicious are learned rather than the spirit, we see the pathological ritualism of *legalism,* expressed in shameless self-righteousness or moralistic adherence to the letter of the law (pp. 94–97).

The Dramatic: The third ritual element, dramatic elaboration, finds its fullest expression on the stage. There, by means of artful condensation of space and time, human conflicts are played out in representative forms that are intensely cathartic for players and audience alike. The dramatic element is indispensable to every rite or ceremony, according to Erikson, and in all ritual performance, he claims, fateful guilt is among the prominent themes. Erikson finds the source of the dramatic element in the play age, when the child employs newly emergent capabilities to play-act and perhaps revise past events as well as to anticipate a future of purposeful striving. At this age, play is often dominated by "the impersonation of victorious self-images and the killing off of weak and evil 'others,' " often with a sense of guilt (p. 100). In adulthood, *impersonation* is the ritualism that corresponds to the dramatic. In the place of an authentic integration of initiative and guilt, a person role-plays the stance of idealized others.

The Formal: Binding together the preceding elements is a fourth one, the formal aspect, which ensures that the ritual is carried out with an eye to perfection. The capacity for such serious attentiveness to orderly detail arises in the school age and under the influence of systematic instruction in basic techniques. In the interplay among pupils and teacher, ritualization becomes genuinely cooperative. If, however, the formal element later becomes an end in itself, rather than a means of participating in a higher order, it becomes transmuted into *formalism,* the empty, compulsively perfectionistic ritualism that other psychoanalysts have mistaken as the model of religious ritual.

The Ideological: The four elements of ritualization that originate in childhood find in the fifth, adolescent element a coherence of a different kind, that of ideology. Ritualization formally appears in adolescence in the traditional rites of induction, confirmation, or graduation. By these means adolescents are at last enjoined to become full and responsible members of their pseudospecies and to affirm a shared world image. Yet adolescents also improvise their own rites, both to set their generation apart and to regulate their relations with each other. This age is likewise prone to the ritualistic element of *totalism,* "a fanatic and exclusive preoccupation with what seems unquestionably ideal within a tight system of ideas" (p. 110). In the twentieth century, totalitarian regimes have exploited this tendency by providing young people with an ideological commitment that assigns traditional values to a decidedly negative identity. By the Nazis in particular, these disastrous commitments were impressively staged in rituals of massive scale (Erikson, 1966, p. 347).

The Affiliative: When Erikson (1966) first published his reflections on ritualization, he identified a total of six elements: the five we have so far reviewed and a sixth, generational element of the adulthood years. In his later writings, he briefly notes two additional elements—the affiliative and the integral—apparently to complete the charts that Erikson (1977, p. 116) confesses may be his own ceremonial reassurances.[3] The affiliative element, with origins in the stage of young adulthood, corresponds to the ego quality of intimacy and is expressed in friendship, love, and work. When such mutuality is little more than shared narcissism, we find an *elitism* of exclusive association.

The Generational: To understand the seventh of the eight ritual elements, the generational, we must shift our focus from the experience of the maturing individual to the perspective of the adult ritualizer. In such authoritative roles as parent, teacher, or healer, adults require confirmation that they have successfully become "a numinous model in the next generation's eyes" as well as a "judge of evil and the transmitter of ideal values." Ritual participation itself provides a measure of reassurance. In addition, the notion of an omniscient Father–God in whose image we have been created, or the convincing pronouncements of a revered founder or prophet, reinforce our sense that we know what we are doing. Corresponding to the generational ritualization is the danger of a "self-convinced and yet spurious usurpation of authority," a form of ritualism that Erikson calls *authoritism*. This perversion, he intimates, underlies much of traditional male dominance (p. 111).

The Integral: Traditionally, a society's elders affirm the meaning of the human cycle of life by personifying ritual wisdom. Thus their contribution to ritualization is the *integral*, or what a few years later Erikson called the "*philosophical*," for in maintaining a sense of integrity in the face of physical and mental decline, the elderly "advocate a durable hope in wisdom." The corresponding ritualistic danger, the mere pretense of having attained integrity and wisdom, Erikson first called *sapientism*. Later he labeled it *dogmatism*, which in conjunction with power can become coercive orthodoxy (Erikson, 1977, p. 112; 1982, p. 64).

In combination, these diverse elements of ritual help to preserve certain basic features of society: "faith in a cosmic order, a sense of law and justice, a hierarchy of ideal and evil roles, the fundamentals of technology, and ideological perspectives" (Erikson, 1977, p. 113). What is to happen, then, in a technological age when traditional forms of ritual are widely neglected? According to the "slow laws of ontogeny," when old ritualizations are abandoned, new ones will take their place. There is abundant evidence today, Erikson reports, of a vital and playful "re-ritualization of everyday life." Optimistically anticipating the decline of pseudo-speciation, Erikson maintains that "new sources of numinous and judicial affirmation as well as of dramatic and aesthetic representations can obviously come only from a new spirit embodying an eventual identification of the whole human species with itself" (pp. 116, 118).

The Vitality of Religion

By now it is apparent how radically Erikson differs from Freud on the matter of religion. Erikson grants that individual religious faith is vulnerable to pathological distortion, that religious traditions have correspondingly exploited human weak-

---

[3] Only the master chart in Erikson's (1982) most recent summary actually incorporates these two additional elements. In his book-length study of ritualization, Erikson (1977) reprints without change the original chart of 1966.

ness and fostered malevolent intolerance. Yet he also maintains that faith and tradition, in their positive and mutually activating forms, are vital for the attainment of human maturity. Although human development requires a variety of societal supports, it is chiefly religion that deals with the first and last things: basic trust and a sense of cosmic order.

Religion's role in these consequential matters was explored in an interview study carried out by Erikson in collaboration with his wife, Joan—an often invisible yet frequently acknowledged collaborator in virtually all of Erikson's work—and clinical psychologist Helen Kivnick (Erikson, Erikson, and Kivnick, 1987). The subjects of their study were 29 octogenarians who were the parents of children whose lives had been followed for more than five decades at the Institute of Human Development of the University of California at Berkeley. Like their children, they had been repeatedly interviewed over the years.

These contemporaries of the Eriksons were struggling in various ways to shift the balance from despair over the prospects of debilitation and death to the sense of integrity, which for them found its primary nourishment in concern for the well-being of their grandchildren, if not also for the world as a whole. For many, an important source of continuity and hope was their religious faith, which had long informed their life's decisions. Assailed by "the kind of newly serious questioning that emerges as part of later life" (p. 227), these elders troubled themselves little with theological subtleties. Critical of religious organizations in a way that denied any of them ultimate authority while yet frequently still active participants, they found it challenging enough to affirm a basic faith. Articulated in widely varying ways and sometimes directed toward nature, this faith reflected their struggle "to trust in the face of mistrust, to accept in the face of the incomprehensible" (p. 224).

Whatever the outcome of this struggle, most of them felt it important that their children and grandchildren should attend religious services, even when they themselves did not. Struck by their subjects' inability to explain this discrepancy, Erikson and his co-authors speculate that these elders may have felt that "going to church," along with the faith, values, and commitments associated with it, would somehow shield their families from the dangers in today's world. Those elders who themselves no longer attended services may have believed that the abandonment of this ideal is justified only later in life, as the principled expression of a lifelong search (pp. 226–227).

HOMO RELIGIOSUS

Erikson's interest in religion extended beyond its role in ordinary lives to encompass the true HOMO RELIGIOSUS, that rare individual for whom the final challenge of integrity, he says, is a lifelong crisis. Such a person "is always older, or in early years suddenly beomes older, than his playmates or even his parents and teachers, and focuses in a precocious way on what it takes others a lifetime to gain a mere inkling of" (p. 261). Unsatisfied by traditional answers to the final, difficult question of life's meaning, such influential religious figures as Martin Luther, Søren Kierkegaard, and Mohandas Gandhi are burdened by the "melancholy world mood" that Erikson (1958), in the spirit of William James, says is "the truest adaptation to the human condition" (p. 40).

For persons of the melancholic type—the sick souls in James's typology—the identity crisis of adolescence is peculiarly severe, for not only does the search for perspective and direction anticipate the final, existential crisis but it also recalls the first one, the crisis of trust in the world as a whole. "This concentration in the cataclysm of the adolescent identity crisis of both first and last crises in the human life may well explain why religiously and artistically creative men often seem to be suffering from a barely compensated psychosis, and yet later prove superhumanly gifted in conveying a total meaning for man's life" (p. 261). Estranged from the ideology of their time, they eventually find a new truth and thus a new beginning in the totality of their own experience, intended for humankind as well as for themselves.

In his book-length studies of two contrasting *homines religiosi,* Luther and Gandhi, Erikson underscores the dynamic relation that exists between the lives of such gifted but troubled innovators and the society whose own crisis is providentially resolved—albeit perhaps at a cost—by the innovator's own cure, in the form of an ideological breakthrough. Without a larger stage and essential counterplayers to enact the extended drama of an identity crisis become existential, these lives might have remained obscure and neurotic at best. On the other hand, without precocious and conflicted youth desperate for a cause, a society whose world-images are no longer convincing would find itself bereft of vital resources for its own renewal.

Martin Luther

Born into a time of great religious and political turmoil, Luther was to become famous for battling the corrupt doctrine and hierarchy of the medieval church. In this momentous struggle, he found a solution to his own neurotic conflict. At the same time, his new vision initiated the momentous Protestant Reformation and thus contributed to widespread social and political revolution.

Luther, we may recall, was chosen by Schjelderup and Schjelderup (1932) as their historical example of father-centered piety. This type of religious attitude is said to be formed largely in accord with unconscious infantile impressions of a demanding father who is both loved and feared. Such origins are said to yield a type of religious experience dominated by guilt, anxiety, and longing for atonement. In Luther's breakthrough, observe the Schjelderups, it is these very elements, centered upon a fear of God and of Christ, that stand out.

In his own study of Luther, Erikson (1958) reaches much the same conclusion: "In this book," he writes, "we are dealing with a Western religious movement which grew out of and subsequently perpetuated an extreme emphasis on the interplay of initiative and guilt, and an exclusive emphasis on the divine Father–Son" (p. 263). The story he recounts, says Erikson, has an overwhelmingly masculine tenor. On the one hand, Luther provides new elements of identity and a new inventory of roles that are appropriate chiefly for the Western male. On the other hand, Luther was instrumental in dethroning the Mother of God, "that focus of women's natural religion-by-being-and-letting-be" (p. 71). As Erikson sees it, the story of Luther and his theological innovations testifies not only to an age in crisis over the moral authority of its religious and political leaders, but also to a crisis of relation between a particular father and son.

Luther's World: Martin Luther was born on November 10, 1483, at Eisleben in Thuringian Saxony. His father, Hans Luther, was a simple farmer-turned-miner who, thrifty and hard working, became a shareholder in the mining operation and thus found a place in the managerial class. Hans was no less ambitious for his eldest son. He sent Martin to a Latin school and to the University of Erfurt, expecting

Hans Luther, the father of Martin Luther (after a painting by Lucas Cranach).

Margareta Luther, Luther's mother (after Cranach).

him to become a lawyer. As Martin began his legal studies, his father set about to find him a bride from an honorable and well-to-do family.

According to Erikson's reconstruction of the evidence, Hans Luther was as excessively harsh as he was unrelentingly ambitious. He "apparently had a towering temper," which Erikson says was most evident when Hans tried to curtail his children's own anger (pp. 57–58). Luther himself recalls an occasion when he fled from his father after a whipping. He was also caned at school, one stroke on the buttocks for each occurrence of bad behavior recorded by a secretly appointed informant (pp. 64, 78). Luther's relation to his father was pathological, Erikson concludes, and the overall climate of that time oppressive.

Of Luther's mother we know very little. She also was said by her son to have beat him, and Luther implies, says Erikson, that her strict discipline was responsible for the neurotic quality of the piety of his monastic years. Otherwise he hardly mentions her at all. Erikson (1958) himself discerns her influence in Luther's fondness of children and of music and in his evident capacity for love. Yet from uncited remarks about women and marriage Erikson also infers a deep disappointment in his early maternal experience (pp. 65–73, 237, 250).

The late medieval world into which Luther was born was rife with superstition and fear. Although living on the threshold of widespread intellectual revolution, Luther and his contemporaries felt themselves surrounded by spiritual and physical dangers. The unpredictable course of adversity was understood as the workings of evil spirits if not the Devil himself, whose presence was suspected in the howling of the wind or the ominous shadows of twilight. The Thuringian miners were among the most superstitious of their time, Erikson reports, reflecting not only a regional tendency, apparently, but also the peculiarities of their work, subject as it was to mistaken leads, lucky finds, and sudden disasters. The fear of catastrophe that is the miner's constant companion, suggests Erikson, "gave Luther's work an orientation toward sudden death, and thus a constant alertness toward the judgment which might have to be faced at any moment" (p. 59).

In the populous spiritual world, there were also numerous mediators and protectors, a saint for every misfortune and disease. Safeguarding the well-being of the miners was Saint Anne, the mother of the Virgin Mary. It was to her that Luther one fateful day addressed an appeal that changed the course of his life and thus also of Western culture. Luther had received with distinction an M.A. degree and, at the age of 21, was in the first semester of his study of law. Unexpectedly, he requested a short leave of absence and went home. There, some speculate, he may have expressed dissatisfaction with law and perhaps also an interest in the monastic life. Choosing this would naturally abort his father's efforts to arrange a prosperous marriage. On his way back to school, Luther reports, he was overtaken by a severe thunderstorm. When a bolt of lightning suddenly struck near him, rousing in him a deep fear of imminent death, Luther cried out, "Help me, St. Anne . . . I want to become a monk" (p. 92).

At some level, he immediately realized, he wanted no part in the monastic life. He knew, moreover, that his desperate appeal to Saint Anne was not really a vow. Yet the whole experience seemed to him a terrifying call from heaven, and he took his response to be an imposed and binding promise. Accordingly, two weeks later he presented himself at the door of the Augustinian monastery in Erfurt, where he was admitted for the standard year of probation. Only then did he tell his father.

A Prolonged Crisis of Identity: Hans Luther was furious, and he initially withheld his permission even for the provisional year. When two other sons subsequently died, however, friends of Martin managed to convince the grieving Hans to hand over to God his eldest son as well. Two years later, during the banquet following Luther's first mass, Hans again expressed his displeasure, this time suggesting that the calling by thunderstorm might have been the Devil's work. The Mass itself had been an occasion of great anxiety, for the moment had come, it seemed, when the scrupulous and ambivalent Luther would for the first time speak to The Father directly—and that in the presence of his earthly father, whom he had not seen since the fateful thunderstorm. Still torn in his obedience to the two fathers and longing for recognition from both, Luther heard his father's angry words as if spoken by God Himself.

Denied the sense of justification by both fathers, Luther became subject, says Erikson, to reawakened infantile conflicts and a prolonged identity crsis. He manifested symptoms of "a borderline psychotic state," including highly ambivalent obsessive–compulsive preoccupations as well as rapidly shifting and seemingly hysterical anxiety attacks and hallucinations. Terrified of the Devil, he came also "to fear and even hate Christ . . . as one who came only to punish" (pp. 147–148). Even toward God he expressed an "obsessive-blasphemous ambivalence," a consequence in part of a totalism that established God "in the role of the dreaded and untrustworthy father" (pp. 29, 164).

In becoming a monk, according to Erikson, Luther temporarily chose a negative identity, and the years of anonymity and regimentation in the monastery constituted a badly needed psychosocial moratorium. In due time, after he was transferred to the monastery in Wittenberg, where a new university had been established, Luther found in John Staupitz, the vicar-general of the province, a valuable and benevolent sponsor for a new, more positive identity. Having suffered the aggravations of identity diffusion that Erikson says are part and parcel of any system of indoctrination, Luther was taken in hand by Staupitz. As Luther's confessor, Staupitz awakened in him a sense of trust and evoked a largely positive father transference. Staupitz undertook to groom Luther for his own chair in theology at Wittenberg, which Luther was to occupy for 30 years. Luther later credited Staupitz with having saved him from the doubts and temptations that assailed him during these critical years. He considered Staupitz the father of the ideas that faith is primary and that one may face, without terror, God's son as a real person. Staupitz was not only a wise therapist, says Erikson, but also the best father figure that Luther ever knew (pp. 134, 167, 169, 37).

The solution to Luther's protracted identity crisis emerged around the age of 30, when the coalescence of new insights at last won him a sense of justification. Although evidence indicates that Luther had been formulating these insights over some period of time, he reports that they came to him as a revelation while in the monastery tower. "As Luther was reviewing in his mind Romans 1:17, the last sentence suddenly assumed a clarity which pervaded his whole being and 'opened the door of paradise' to him: 'For therein is the righteousness of God revealed from faith to faith: as it is written, *the just shall live by faith*' " (p. 201). Through these words Luther came to see that God is not a wrathful judge assessing the collective worth of one's meritorious acts—a view reflecting both Luther's personal conflicts and the theology of his day—but the merciful source of justice in the here and now, available through faith in the grace and love of Christ. Taking recourse to the "massive totalisms" that Erikson says typify persons recovering from mental oppression, Luther declared human beings to be at the same time totally sinners and—through God's grace—totally just. According to Erikson, in this seemingly illogical formulation Luther has pointed to a fundamental psychological truth. That is, the ego recovers its initiative to the degree that it accepts the power both of the drives and of conscience, as long as it also sustains the combination of love and work that alone confirms human identity. Luther's regaining of ego initiative, declares Erikson, is signified by his own recovery of faith (pp. 216–217, 206).

Defiant Son and Anxious Father: Luther's new identity as Reformation leader, which he acquired after his adamant attack on the selling of indulgences led to his excommunication by Rome, did not spell the end of his massive inner conflict. Replacing his fixation on his father, says Erikson, was a fixation on the Devil and on the Pope, whom Luther came to see as the Antichrist. A prominent theme in this transference was an anal defiance that exceeded the bounds even of medieval uncouthness. When the buttocks are assaulted as they often were in Luther's day, Erikson writes, the anal zone can become the locus of stubborn and defiant associations. "The devil according to Luther, expresses his scorn by exposing his rear parts; man can beat him to it by employing anal weapons, and by telling him where his kiss is welcome" (p. 79). "No doubt," Erikson adds, "when Martin learned to speak up, much that he had to say to the devil was fueled by a highly-compressed store of defiance consisting of what he had been unable to say to his father and to his teachers; in due time he said it all, with a vengeance, to the Pope" (p. 122). Erikson concludes that Luther's explosive and repudiative profanity served as a safety valve whenever "he was again about to repudiate God in supreme rebellion, and himself in malignant melancholy" (p. 247).

With the crisis of identity behind him, Luther was at last free to grapple with the further challenges of intimacy and generativity. Luther's crisis of intimacy, forestalled for some years by the monastic rules of intentional isolation, eventually

ADORATVR PAPA DEVS TERRENVS.

Bapſt hat dem reich Chriſti gethon
Wie man hie handelt ſeine Cron.
Machts jr zweifeltig: ſpricht der geiſt Apoc.18.
Schenckt getroſt ein: Gott iſts ders heiſt.
Mart: Luth: D.

The Pope, God of the World, Is Worshiped—one of eight cartoons by Cranach, commissioned by Luther to express his contempt for the papacy.

HIC OSCVLA PEDIBVS PAPAE FI-
GVNTVR.

Nicht Bapſt: nicht ſchreck vns mit deim ban
Vnd ſey nicht ſo zorniger man
Wir thun ſonſt ein gegen wehre
Vnd zeigen dirs Bel vedere.
Mart. Luth. D.

Kissing the Pope's Feet—another of the cartoons of ridicule commissioned by Luther and rendered by Cranach.

found its time and resolution. Long conflicted over his sexual urges, Luther at the age of 42 married Catherine von Bora, a nun who had renounced her vows under the influence of Luther's teachings. His capacity and need for intimacy were also reflected in the frankness with which he wrote of his emotional life to male friends; in the effectiveness of his preaching and table talks; and even in his extraordinarily inspired translation of the Bible, which touched the very heart of the German people (p. 259).

Luther's crisis of generativity, says Erikson, was fused with the crisis of intimacy, the outcome of his prolonged identity crisis and the delay in sexual intimacy. The father of six children, Luther was at the same time progenitor to a major historical movement. Yet some of his followers proved to be righteously rebellious, too, and they so thoroughly expunged basic elements of sacred ritual that Luther, who in certain respects was deeply conservative, "could hardly recognize what he had generated" (p. 234). More disturbing still was the revolt of the peasants, who, over Luther's objections, extended his defense of spiritual freedom to the political and economic realms as well. When the peasants ignored his recommendation of compromise, the once-sympathetic Luther issued a tract urging the violent suppression of what he came to see as a demonic manifestation. By the end of the infamous Peasants' War of 1524–1525, 130,000 peasants had been massacred, and Luther lost much of his support among the increasingly mystical and revolutionary lower classes. Luther continued to foster the Reformation movement, however, both through personal attention to its schools and churches and through the composition of catechisms, hymns, model sermons, and new liturgical forms. Yet to the end, Luther remained subject to episodes of anxiety and melancholy over what his rebellion had inadvertently created at all levels of society (p. 242).

Mohandas Gandhi

"The danger of a reformer of the first order," writes Erikson (1958), "lies in the nature of his influence on the masses." Drawn to the reformer by their own intense need for periodic renewal of trust and of day-to-day meaning, the common people inevitably respond to the new truth in terms of their own limitations: "The best of them will fall asleep at Gethsemane; and the worst will accept the new faith only as a sanction for anarchic destructiveness or political guile" (p. 262). In the second of his book-length studies of the *homo religiosus,* Erikson (1969) provides a more recent illustration of this regrettable principle. The subject of this work is Mohandas Karamchand Gandhi (1869–1948), the enormously influential political and spiritual leader of India who through his campaigns of SATYAGRAHA—"truth force," literally, but often less satisfactorily rendered as "passive resistance"—helped to bring more than a century of British rule to an end. Like Luther, Gandhi saw his inspired vision undermined by large-scale violence. Revered throughout India as a saint and addressed as Mahatma, "great-souled," Gandhi was even to die from an assassin's bullets.

Erikson's study of Gandhi, however, is not intended to convince us of the hopelessness of the Mahatma's vision. To the contrary, Erikson came to see Gandhi's truth, and the ritualization—*satyagraha*—that he created, as a heritage essential to humankind's survival, a vital antidote to the pervasively destructive trend of pseudospeciation. Impressed, too, by the apparent kinship of Gandhi's and Freud's methods, Erikson proposes that psychoanalysis be considered a counterpart to *satyagraha,* a means by which to confront the enemy *within oneself* nonviolently. That, Erikson respectfully suggests, the dogmatically moralistic Gandhi had not always succeeded in doing. In *Gandhi's Truth,* then, Erikson explores not only the origins and deep ambivalences of the Mahatma's embodiment of *satyagraha* but also the means by which nonviolence, within and without, can become a true force for the survival of humankind.

A Childhood in India: Mohandas Gandhi was the last of four children born to the prime minister of a small city–state in western India and his fourth and much younger wife. Although the Gandhis were well off, their capacious home was crowded by the presence of a large extended family. In accord with Indian tradition, both of Gandhi's parents served as caretakers to all members of the clan, and thus Gandhi and his siblings, Erikson infers, were subject in some measure to the diffuse mothering and familial intimacy that foster a "deep nostalgia for fusion" as well as potential patterns of guilt and resentment that are common in India but largely unknown in the West (pp. 42–43).

Gandhi's illiterate mother was a deeply religious Hindu who worshiped at the temple daily and fasted periodically. Her piety, Erikson observes, was utterly undogmatic, a pervasive and personalized "sense of being carried along by a demanding and yet trustworthy universe" (p. 111). Young Gandhi was surrounded, too, by the practices and values of the Vaishnava and Jain traditions, including vegetarianism and especially *ahimsa,* the principle of noninjury to any other living being. Erikson discerns a degree of ambivalence in the later reforms in diet and daily living that Gandhi credited to his mother's influence. Yet through his relation to her he often did succeed, Erikson says, in uniting the feminine and masculine aspects of piety, for himself and for the masses (p. 112). One must further assume, Erikson adds, that Gandhi's inclination to enter into "one intense relationship at a time and this a relationship of service, nay, salvation of the other" also derives from his loving relation with his mother (p. 114).

Mohandas Gandhi.

Gandhi's later identification with his father, according to Erikson, was more complex and competitive than that with his mother. Indeed, Erikson discerns in Gandhi's life "a son-father and father-son theme of biblical dimensions" (p. 128). Gandhi's loving attachment is evident in the great joy he said he experienced in diligently nursing his long-ailing father. At the same time, he was never able to forgive his father for prematurely provoking his sexual appetite by forcing him into an early marriage, at the age of 13. Moreover, that passion was to underlie an "existential debt" to his father that Gandhi would never be able to repay. On the very evening that his father was to die, the 16-year-old Gandhi left the nursing care to an uncle, in order to join his then pregnant wife in their bedroom. Summoned a short while later, he was devastated to find that his father had died in his absence— " 'a blot,' Gandhi writes, 'which I have never been able to efface or to forget' " (p. 128).

An Existential Curse: Erikson identifies this experience as Gandhi's version of "the curse" that marks the lives of other morally precocious spiritual innovators and that in Luther's case was paternal brutality (Erikson, 1964, p. 202). A single such episode is not itself the cause of the curse, the psychoanalyst quickly adds. It is, rather, a COVER MEMORY, "a condensation and projection of a pervasive child-hood conflict on one dramatized scene." That conflict is the Oedipus complex, which Erikson also calls the generational complex, for it has its roots in the child's dawning awareness of aging, death, and the inevitable succession of generations. This realization appears at a time when the child is given to intense, irrational guilt, and it is intensified in rare persons who early sense an originality that points beyond competition with their own fathers. "To better the parent thus means to replace him; to survive him means to kill him; to usurp his domain means to appropriate the mother, the 'house,' the 'throne.' " Young Gandhi's " 'feminine' service" to his father, Erikson suggests, was a means of denying his wish to take his aging father's place in relation to his mother as well as to outdo him in the public realm. "Thus the pattern would be set for a style of leadership which can defeat a superior adversary only nonviolently and with the express intent of saving him as well as those whom he oppressed." This interpretation, Erikson adds, is consistent with the Mahatma's expressed intention (Erikson, 1969, pp. 128–129, 132).

Another memorable incident involving his father seems to have been a "youthful antecedent" of *satyagraha* (p. 320) in Gandhi's life history. At the age of 15, Gandhi wrote a letter of confession to his convalescing father, asking his forgiveness for having sold a bit of gold to settle a debt of his brother's. He requested appropriate punishment and promised never to steal again. His father read the note in apparent agony, with tears running down his cheeks, and then merely tore it up and lay down once again on his bed. Receiving "sublime forgiveness" from his "wonderfully peaceful" father rather than the expected angry words and gestures, Gandhi attributed his short-tempered father's transformation to his own "clean confession," and thus found in this occurrence "an object-lesson in Ahimsa." Beyond its importance in the evolution of Gandhi's "sense of superior destiny," this story reveals, says Erikson, "an early assumption of moral responsibility for a parent" that is typical of other world leaders who have subsequently extended that responsibility to humankind itself (pp. 124–125).

Ambivalence and Conflict: Gandhi's favorable relation with his parents, we are told, not only allowed him to acquire their strengths but also fostered his sense of having a special calling. His positive (if inevitably ambivalent) identification with both of them, including a father known for his unusual willingness to help with household chores, apparently contributed to the "bisexuality"—today we might say androgyny—in which Gandhi seemed almost to pride himself. There are, to be sure, cultural antecedents: India's persisting mother–goddesses, Erikson supposes, are responsible for her basic bisexuality. Yet this national trend, he says, combined in Gandhi with a profoundly personal need, which was reflected not only in his famous love for home spinning but also in the marked maternalism that governed his various relationships. The autocratic Gandhi finally resolved his deeply rooted "conflict between phallicism and saintliness" by resolutely (and unilaterally) renouncing sexual relations. Like other innovators, he then absorbed his "phallic maleness . . . in the decisive wielding of influence—and in a certain locomotor drivenness" (p. 402). That the elderly Gandhi occasionally asked some of his women helpers to cradle him for warmth at night, whenever he suffered severe attacks of shivering; and that he publicly declared the presence of these sometimes naked women as a test of the thoroughness of his renunciation, points, says Erikson, "to a persistent importance in Gandhi's life of the theme of motherhood, both in the sense of a need to be a perfect and pure mother, and in the sense of a much less acknowledged need to be held and reassured," especially at a time when widespread communal riots seemed to dash all hopes for a unified India (pp. 404–405).

Gandhi's exceptional openness about such matters, along with his proclivity, in his autobiography, to present himself as a case study, has tempted others to emphasize the seemingly pathological trends in Gandhi's life, especially his renunciation of sex, his negatively obsessive concern with food and eating, and his insensitivity to his wife and four sons. Erikson, of course, considers these matters too, chiefly in a long personal aside appearing at the book's midpoint and addressed directly to the Mahatma. Quoting Gandhi back to himself, Erikson tactfully points to elements of vindictiveness and even violence in Gandhi's own conduct—evidence, Erikson says, of an unrecognized ambivalence that threatens the future of *satyagraha*. He declares that *satyagraha* will attain universal relevance only when it is directed inwardly as well, at the instinctual tendencies that Gandhi so resolutely attacked with moral absolutism. Genuine peace can only be achieved, Erikson maintains, in moments when a person's sensual, logical, and ethical experiences are brought into harmonious balance (p. 251).

If Gandhi's own conduct, then, and the tragic suffering of his renegade eldest son, Harilal, testify to a current of untruth in the Mahatma's life, Erikson yet saw him as "one of the wholest of men and one of the most miraculously energetic" (p. 378). The real challenge to the psychohistorian, Erikson suggests, lies not in demonstrating the presence of universal human conflicts and even pathological disturbances in such figures as Gandhi, but in accounting for the emergence of the identity of a reformer, the discovery of a new truth, and the effective transmission of this truth to the masses.

Becoming a Reformer: As was true of Luther, the establishment of Gandhi's sense of identity was long in coming. Gandhi was not only gifted in specific ways, according to Erikson, but was also probably conscious—"early and painfully"—of a "special mission," undoubtedly in part because of his favored position as the last born of a young mother and an "aging patriarch." Alleviating his evident moral precocity was the lifelong pleasure he took in laughing and making others laugh, even while subtly admonishing them. This "seasoned playfulness," Erikson thinks, may be an essential element in all nonviolence (pp. 100, 106, 133).

That so conscientious a boy should at the same time have "experimented" with delinquency presents any interpreter with a difficult challenge. Erikson finds in Gandhi's puzzling relationship with Sheik Mehtab, a Muslim youth who not only served as Gandhi's mesomorphic protector but also successfully tempted him to eat meat and to visit prostitutes, the dynamics of a negative identity. Gandhi had projected onto Mehtab his own "personal devil," the unacceptable elements within himself that he vigorously sought to subdue. At risk of becoming enslaved to an overweening sense of moral superiority, Gandhi could not have attained his mature ethical stature, Erikson maintains, without first facing his negative identity. "By choosing Mehtab as a friend, he unconsciously tested himself in order to prove to himself that he *could* sin—and test the limits of that experience, too." Only years later, when he at last resolved his identity struggle, could Gandhi finally break with his Muslim alter ego (pp. 136, 174).

Gandhi was doubtless also tempted by a multitude of sins in London, where at the age of 19 he undertook the study of law. At his mother's instigation, however, he had taken an oath before a Jain monk, vowing never to touch wine, women, or meat. Only that vow, says Erikson, could safeguard Gandhi's solitary years in England and make of them a genuine moratorium, "a period of apprenticeship between the childhood that was over and a future leadership of unforeseeable dimensions" (p. 139). At the same time that learning to cook his own vegetarian meals helped him "to develop the householder's habits with which he would later take care of ever bigger things" (p. 146), his success in keeping to his vow secured his tie to his mother and to her religious faith. That victory, adds Erikson, though later enormously important for Gandhi's ethical stature in India, reinforced his "obsessional trends, set him against women and even against milk, and in no way furthered his capacity to appreciate or even tolerate sexual intimacy" (p. 152).

Gandhi sailed back to India three years later, still without a sense of vocation. Arriving home, he was stunned by the belated news that his beloved mother had died. Feeling lost as never before, Gandhi made the acquaintance of a saintly philosopher–poet named Rajchandra, who came to serve as "the anchor of young Gandhi's religious imagination." The first to affirm Gandhi's still inarticulate ethical direction, the 25-year-old Rajchandra "succeeded in translating for him the highly personal commitment of his vow into the ideological terms of the Jain community." Along with the writings of Tolstoy, Ruskin, and Thoreau, to which Gandhi had been introduced by the British vegetarian community, Rajchandra helped Gandhi to shape the ideology that was integral to his identity and for which he would later be famous (pp. 162–163).

Householder in South Africa: Gandhi had at last come to see himself as a reformer. But not until his fateful ejection from a first-class train compartment in South Africa, where, following a brief and unsuccessful stint as a lawyer in India, he had come to represent a Muslim law firm for a year, did Gandhi find himself committed to a cause outside the boundaries of his own home. Becoming himself a victim of the prejudices that his fellow Indians had long faced in South Africa, Gandhi resolved then and there "to root out the disease and suffer hardships in the process." "The central identity which here found its historical time and place," writes Erikson, "was the conviction that among the Indians in South Africa he was *the only person equipped by fate* to reform a situation which under no conditions could be tolerated" (p. 166).

Gandhi brought his family to South Africa and stayed on for another 20 years, during which time he finally came to realize his vocation in life. A series of governmental maneuvers, designed to disenfranchise and curtail the free movement of the nonwhites, prompted the evolution of Gandhi's new instrument of peace, the principles of which gradually took shape through successive improvisations. During these years he finally broke altogether with "the identity remnant of the well-dressed, highly educated, and fair skinned 'coloured' citizen of the British Empire" and, indeed, with every other identity element that precluded a truly universal identity. These were Gandhi's householding years, constituting the second of the four traditional Hindu stages of life and coinciding with Erikson's stages of intimacy and generativity. For Gandhi, however, householding came to take on universal connotations, for it was during these years of increasing emphasis on renunciation and self-control that he foreswore sexual intimacy for a "wider communal intimacy," embraced poverty as integral to celibacy, and extended his generative concerns beyond his own, sometimes neglected family to the whole of the living world (pp. 191–192, 177).

A Religious Actualist and His Followers: Of the increasingly momentous events that followed the middle-aged Gandhi's return to India in 1914, after governmental concessions convinced him that his work in South Africa was finished, Erikson chose to make the 1918 strike of millworkers in Ahmedabad "the Event" in his study of Gandhi's life. Although neither Gandhi himself nor his other biographers have accorded so central a position to this "first full application of the instrument of Satyagraha" (p. 257), Erikson sensed there was "more to the story than the books allowed" (p. 10). In 1962, when Erikson went to India to conduct a seminar on the human life cycle, he found himself the guest of the very mill owner who in 1918 had been Gandhi's main opponent. Living next door was the elderly mill owner's saintly sister, who paradoxically was Gandhi's chief supporter during the lockout and strike. Introduced to still other opponents or followers from that time, Erikson came to suspect that the obscure three-week campaign was of major significance in Gandhi's rise to national leadership.

Justifiable or not, Erikson's featuring of the Ahmedabad strike allowed him—as his study of Luther of course did not—to incorporate evidence from interviews of contemporary witnesses. In becoming personally acquainted with some of Gandhi's disciples, Erikson frequently found himself the recipient of recollections that offered his "third ear" clues to his informants' youthful motives. Chary of exploiting these confidences, Erikson reports the growing conviction that

> all these informants harbor a sense (maybe unconscious, maybe unverbalized) of having vastly outdistanced their childhood loyalties, and with these, their personal DHARMA [moral duty], by serving a man who had the power to impose his *dharma* on his contemporaries—a very special kind of guru who would make radical and total use of an age-old emotional (and once well institutionalized) necessity for finding a second, spiritual father (p. 407).

Gandhi was in some degree responsible for the curse that his followers seemed to bear: the memory of having deeply hurt a perhaps already estranged parent or other relative when they acceded to Gandhi's increasingly stringent demands for total devotion. Yet his highly gifted disciples seemed to have come to him already in possession of "an early and anxious concern for the abandoned and persecuted," with whom they strongly identified. If they thus came to him with "the 'right conflicts' and the right interests and talents," at the same time crucial in their own lives and in history, they undoubtedly also harbored a deep ambivalence toward the man whose miraculous confidence inspired a virtual conversion (pp. 308, 85).

The Ahmedabad campaign also illustrates Gandhi's readiness to improvise new rituals as a situation might require them. Each day of the strike he issued a printed leaflet to inform and educate the striking workers and to strengthen their resolve. In the late afternoon thousands of illiterate men and women would gather outside the main city gate to hear a reading of the leaflet and Gandhi's discourse on it. The meeting culminated with a mass reaffirmation of the workers' pledge to strike peacefully until they secured their targeted wage increase, and it concluded with the singing of songs newly composed for the occasion. Two weeks later, when widespread disillusionment threatened the movement and its increasingly religious spirit, Gandhi undertook the first of his famous fasts "to the death" for a public cause. When he publicly broke his fast several days later, after the strike had finally been settled in accord with Gandhi's principle that neither party to the dispute be harmed, the mill hands placed him and the leading mill owner and his sister in a carriage and pulled them through the streets.

Within a year of the Ahmedabad campaign, Gandhi had introduced *satyagraha* to the whole of the Indian nation, and by 1920 he was indisputably India's political and spiritual leader. He was, in Erikson's terminology, a *religious actualist*. He had effectively actualized, through a process of mutual activation, the wisdom he had absorbed from Indian culture. Like other gifted leaders, Gandhi creatively reenacted an inescapable existential curse through deeds that spoke to and liberated countless others of this time. And like other religious actualists, Gandhi courageously faced "the central truth of our nothingness," which the mass of humanity denies but cannot quite forget. From it he miraculously derived strength that drew others to him—including, in our day, Erikson himself. Gandhi's truth, Erikson suggests, may fairly be interpreted to mean that, ethically speaking, "A man should act in such a way that he actualizes both in himself and in the other such forces as are ready for a heightened mutuality." Truth in action, he emphasizes, requires an encounter that leads to change in both partners, a transformation that is possible only when one has learned nonviolence, toward oneself as well as toward others (pp. 396–397, 133, 413, 439). The ritualization that Gandhi created "in his immense intuition for historical actuality and his capacity to assume leadership in 'truth in action' " may finally allow human beings to transcend pseudospeciation and, like other species engaged in instinctive rituals of pacification, to face one another in mutual confidence (p. 433).

Jesus of Galilee

When writer Louis Fischer visited Gandhi in 1942, the sole decoration on the walls of the Mahatma's hut was a picture of Jesus. Under it was written "He is Our Peace." Gandhi was a Hindu, yet he also professed to be a Christian—as well as a Muslim and a Jew. For him, the heart of the Christian message lies in Jesus' Sermon on the Mount, which Gandhi felt was negated by much that passes as Christianity. This message so influenced Gandhi that Christian missionary friends considered him to be among the most Christlike persons they knew (Fischer, 1954, pp. 130–131).

From his youth, Erikson had also seen an affinity between Gandhi and Jesus. What they have in common, he says, is a "pervasive presence," though they would seem also to share the role of *homo religiosus* (Erikson, 1969, p. 20; 1958, p. 261). In his essay on Jesus, however, Erikson (1981) does not provide yet another psychohistorical study, probably because, as he remarks, the creative mythologizing of Christ's life has distorted its meaning, even encouraging a destructive new pseudospeciation.

Like Gandhi, Erikson (1981) finds the authentic Jesus to be most conspicuous in the sayings attributed to Jesus during the Galilean period of his ministry. In his study of these sayings, Erikson proposes a new, psychological criterion for establishing their authenticity: the presence of a "pervasive healing quality" directed not merely to some particular disease or misfortune but to the vital core of the individual, the sense of "I" (p. 328). This message, referring to the immediate present rather than some future state of reward or punishment, was addressed to a people whose sense of *I* of identity, had been virtually lost. Like other *homines religiosi*, then, Jesus offered to his contemporaries a new set of images that promised them renewal.

Ancient Israel, Erikson points out, wholly lacked the reassuring "space–time qualities" required for the sense of *I* and the corresponding sense of *We*. These vital qualities include a position of centrality, continuity through time, and the possibility of action—all reliably secured by strong boundaries (p. 333). The geographical location of Palestine made it lastingly vulnerable, for it was both corridor and buffer zone for the contending nations lying nearby. The Jewish people had suffered a succession of exiles, captivities, and occupations, and their temple, "the one symbol of central focus and inner autonomy," was subject to foreign intrusion and control. Such conditions, says Erikson, "obviously violate every dimension of that sense of *I* which any collective must provide; and one could conclude that such a nation had no identity with a chance of survival in centuries to come" (p. 335).

The Jewish people were not utterly bereft, however, for their monotheistic tradition and the active and everlasting God that had chosen them provided an enduring sense of identity and a framework for accepting disaster. Yet there was a negative side to their belief in so overwhelming a deity as Jehovah. Especially with the threat of political and cultural dissolution, their once-rejuvenating periodic ritualizations became merely repetitive, transforming them into deadening and compulsively scrupulous ritualisms. Idolism, legalism, and dogmatism were the unfortunate outcomes.

Compensating for these regrettable trends in the patriarchal tradition were the

The Prodigal Son, by Rembrandt.

ritualizations of everyday life overseen by the Jewish mother. Daily playing the role of "a most down-to-earth goddess of the hearth," the Jewish mother continued to nourish the sense of *I* that is born of the early interplay between infant and maternal *Other,* the first of the *I*'s vital counterplayers. The ritualization of family life, Erikson maintains, must have contributed enormously to the survival of the Jewish tradition (pp. 340–341).

These trends, then, were the heritage of Jesus. Through the circumstances he addressed in the simple stories he told, and through vivid encounters with those who came to him in an attitude of active faith, Jesus communicated his deep caring about the conditions that foster the sense of *I.* In rebuking his disciples for turning away children—"for to such belongs the kingdom of God"—Jesus affirms, says Erikson, "the radiant potentials of childhood" and the value of childlike trust for maintaining continuity through the stages of development. By means of his parable of the Prodigal Son, in which a father celebrates the return of his once-profligate but now-repentant younger child in the joyful ritualization of a shared meal, Jesus extols the mutual recovery of generational continuity.

In such stories as these, and in addressing God as "Abba," the Aramaic equivalent of daddy, Jesus rejects the threatening and vengeful patriarchal image of God, replacing it with one far more forgiving, loving, and caring. Erikson sees here "an unobtrusive integration of maternal and paternal tenderness" (p. 349). The suggestion that *the* Father is more intimately *my* father underscores the sense of continuity between generations.

Is the kingdom of God, then, also closer at hand? When Jesus speaks of the Kingdom, Erikson says, he clearly conceives of it as "an experience of inner as well as interpersonal actualization open to every individual who accepts his mediation."

It is not located in some far-off unchanging place or specifiable time, but is dynamically in motion in the here and now. It is a coming or a way, a fulfillment of potential in the immediate present that anticipates the future. It bears the temporal and spatial marks of the sense of *I*, which is characterized by activity, wholeness, and presence at the center of events (p. 347).

If Jesus' therapeutic sayings and his attitude of nonviolence offered healing for the malaise of his time, they may have something to teach us, says Erikson, about the evolution of human self-awareness. They represent, like the great sayings attributed to Lao Tse and others of the same millennium, a step forward in human consciousness: "a more aware *I* related to a more universal *We*, approaching the idea of one mankind" (p. 358). Living as we do in an age of perfected technological destruction, concludes Erickson, we can hardly afford to overlook such insights as these sayings have to offer us.

ERIKSON'S CONTINUING INFLUENCE

In the conclusion to his best-known work, *Childhood and Society*, Erikson modestly remarks that he has nothing to offer his readers but "a way of looking at things," a phrase that became the title of Stephen Schlein's (1987) voluminous selection of Erikson's (1987) papers. That configurational and contextual perspective, as Schlein describes it, along with the principles and concepts Erikson used to develop it, proved to be enormously influential. Psychologists appropriated such notions as *basic trust* and *identity crisis* as essential elements in any account of human development. Erikson's expansion of Freud's psychosexual stages to encompass the entire life cycle, his corresponding emphasis on adaptive ego functions, and his application of his approach cross-culturally gave vital impetus to life-span developmental psychology, just as his vision of the "complex metabolism of individuals, generations, and larger historical trends" (Pomper, 1985, p. 82) added new dimensions to the study of psychohistory. Similarly, Erikson's subtle and humane approach to psychotherapy, within the broader framework of ego psychology, enriched the work of psychotherapists and counselors in a variety of contexts.

For the psychology of religion in particular, Erikson's influence has been most apparent in two rather different undertakings. On the one hand are further studies of famous religious personalities, such as John Wesley and Jonathan Edwards, as well as of particular religious movements or times (Capps, Capps, and Bradford, 1977; Moore, 1979). Although not written on the magisterial scale of Erikson's, these psychohistorical studies illustrate the deepened understanding of the interplay of personal and historical factors that Erikson's work has fostered.

On the other hand are works concerned with religious development in ordinary lives. Some of these books are essentially manuals for applying Erikson's life-cycle theory in religious contexts. For example, Donald Capps (1983), a professor of pastoral theology, uses Erikson's framework for developing a new pastoral-care model that assigns three major roles to the clergy: moral counselor, ritual coordinator, and personal comforter. Along the way, Capps neatly parallels Erikson's eight virtues with the seven deadly sins, or vices, which he expands into a corresponding eight by separating sloth into its original components: indifference and melancholy (see Table 9.3). Similarly finding parallels to the eight stages in the Book of Proverbs, Capps underscores the close fit between Erikson's life-cycle theory and the wisdom literature of the Hebrew Bible.

Other works are intended both for religious educators and for laypersons

Table 9.3 **THE EIGHT DEADLY SINS, OR VICES, AND ERIKSON'S STAGES**

Stage	Psychosocial Crisis	Virtue	Vice
Old Age	Integrity versus Despair	Wisdom	Melancholy
Adulthood	Generativity versus Stagnation	Care	Indifference
Young Adult	Intimacy versus Isolation	Love	Lust
Adolescence	Identity versus Identity Confusion	Fidelity	Pride
School Age	Industry versus Inferiority	Competence	Envy
Play Age	Initiative versus Guilt	Purpose	Greed
Early Childhood	Autonomy versus Shame and Doubt	Will	Anger
Infancy	Basic Trust versus Mistrust	Hope	Gluttony

seeking spiritual direction. Evelyn and James Whitehead (1979), a developmental psychologist and pastoral theologian, respectively, undertake to deepen religious self-understanding by synthesizing Erikson's model of adult development and certain Christian theological concepts. Some less technical works discuss spirituality in relation to all eight of Erikson's stages (e.g., Gleason, 1975; Linn, Fabricant, and Linn, 1988; J. E. Wright, 1982).

Fowler's Stages of Faith

Less apparent but no less profound is Erikson's contribution to the faith development theory of James Fowler, a professor of theology and human development. Building on the work of Piaget and Kohlberg as well, Fowler (1981) describes Erikson's influence on him as more subtle and pervasive. It has touched him, he writes, "at convictional depths that the structural developmentalists have not addressed" (p. 110). Erikson's work, especially his account of stages centered upon emergent crises, became for Fowler an important interpretive framework for his research on faith development. Much like Erikson, as we will see, Fowler offers a stage-centered perspective that attributes to each step an enduring "emergent strength" as well as a potential danger or deficiency.

Fowler and his associates interviewed 359 persons ranging in age from 4 to 84 and representing Protestant (45 percent), Catholic (36.5 percent), and Jewish (11.2 percent) traditions, along with a few others (7.2 percent). The respondents were equally divided by sex and were overwhelmingly white (97.8 percent). On the basis of the audio-recorded and transcribed interview protocols, Fowler and his colleagues identified the following six stages of faith, a term he uses, in the spirit of Wilfred Smith, to refer to "our way of discerning and committing ourselves to centers of value and power that exert ordering force in our lives" (pp. 24–25).

1. Intuitive-Projective Faith: The first formal stage of faith emerges out of the "undifferentiated" or "primal" faith of infancy, which rests on a foundation of basic trust and mutuality. It is a joint product of the teachings and examples of significant adults, on the one hand, and the young child's reigning cognitive egocentrism and developing imaginative capacity on the other. Although in many respects imitative and marked by fluid and fantasy-filled thought patterns unrestrained by logic, this first stage possesses the emergent strength of *imagination,* the capacity to represent the world of experience in powerful and unifying images that also serve to orient the child toward ultimate reality. The danger here is of becoming overwhelmed by terrifying or destructive images, or of being exploited by images used to compel moral or doctrinal conformity.

2. Mythic-Literal Faith: With the resolution of the Oedipal conflict and the development of CONCRETE OPERATIONAL THINKING—that is, the capacity to think logically about processes or objects physically present, which usually appears at about the age of seven—children begin to appropriate systematically the content of their community's tradition. The fluid, image-centered faith of the first stage gives way to a more literalistic and linear way of finding coherence and meaning, particularly in the form of narrative. Story, drama, and myth, which together form the emergent capacity of this stage, become the way of conserving and communicating such experienced meaning. This stage is limited by its anthropomorphic literalism and a morality narrowly conceived as concrete reciprocity. Together, they may lead to self-righteous perfectionism or—if significant others mistreat or reject the child—a feeling of badness and unworthiness, much as we saw in Rizzuto's case of Bernadine Fisher.

3. Synthetic-Conventional Faith: The transition around the age of 12 to FORMAL OPERATIONAL THINKING, which by means of abstract concepts is able to reflect back on itself, marks the beginning of the third stage of faith. The world of experience for the adolescent is much broader and more complex, placing new demands on the orienting function of faith. Whereas Stage 2 typically employs prepersonal anthropomorphisms that lack the nuances required for deep personal relation, Stage 3 marks a recasting of the ultimate environment in more genuinely interpersonal terms. It is a conformist stage, Fowler observes, for the opinions and authority of significant others play a powerful role. The growing capacity for reflection is not yet directed to the cluster of beliefs and values that form the adolescent's ideology; the youth simply takes them and the world they mediate for granted. More evident in this stage is the emergent capacity for a higher level of storytelling, for the shaping of *personal myth* that discerns new meaning in the stories from the young person's past while also projecting him or her into possible roles and relationships in the future. Potentially at risk in this stage is the later development of autonomy, if others' expectations and judgments are too thoroughly internalized and sacralized. A second danger lies in the adolescent's vulnerability to interpersonal betrayal, which may result either in despair about an ultimate personal reality or in a compensatory intimacy with it that is disconnected from other spheres of relationship (p. 173).

4. Individuative-Reflective Faith: Whereas Stage 3 becomes for many adults a permanent resting place, for others it is undermined by contradictions among respected authorities or by experiences that compel reflection on the origins and relativity of their beliefs and values. As William Perry (1970) points out in his study of the course of intellectual and ethical development among college students, the full realization of RELATIVISM represents a drastic revolution that is emancipating for many, yet deeply disturbing for others. Infrequently, when relativism proves to be intolerable, the person will retreat into an authority-oriented dualistic structure of right and wrong.

In Fowler's scheme, Stage 4 is marked by two essential aspects: realizing the relativity of a person's inherited world-view and abandoning reliance on external authority. The "executive ego" emerges and takes on the burden of choosing among the priorities and commitments that will help shape identity. The critical questioning of Stage 4 disrupts the intimate relation between the religious symbol or ritual and its felt meaning, bringing a sense of loss if not also guilt. Yet Fowler finds that such DEMYTHOLOGIZING offers gains as well, among them the clarifying and communicating of meaning. The emerging strength of the person in Stage 4 is the capacity to reflect critically on personal identity and ideology. The dangers consist of overconfidence in the powers of conscious reflection and the temptation to assimilate others' perspectives, and even reality itself, to one's own limited worldview.

5. Conjunctive Faith: The transition to Stage 5 comes with the realization that life is not adequately comprehended by the clarifications and abstractions of individuative–reflective faith. There may be a sense of deeper possibilities within the self, and the symbols and paradoxes of one or another religious tradition may insistently challenge the two-dimensional neatness of Stage 4 faith. Conjunctive faith is so named in recognition of the fact that a person faces the paradoxes and contradictions within the self and experience and attains some measure of integration. In this form of faith, the individual moves beyond Stage 4's reductive conceptualizing of symbol and myth, attaining instead to Ricoeur's SECOND NAÏVETÉ, a postcritical attitude that allows reengagement with the reality expressed by means of these traditional elements: "symbolic power is reunited with conceptual meanings" (p. 197).

Retaining the realization that ours is a relativistic world, the individual in this stage of faith is genuinely open to the truths of other communities and traditions and at the same time humbly recognizes that ultimate truth extends far beyond the reach of every tradition, including his or her own. As Fowler (1984, p. 67) puts it, conjunctive faith "combines loyalty to one's own primary communities of value and belief with loyalty to the reality of a community of communities." The emergent strength of this stage is the *ironic imagination,* the capacity to become powerfully engaged by symbolic expressions, even while recognizing their relativity and ultimate inadequacy for representing transcendent reality. The danger here is becoming paralyzed by the irresolvable paradoxes and polarities, a state of disunity that can lead to a sense of "cosmic homelessness and loneliness" (p. 68).

6. Universalizing Faith: For certain rare individuals, such discomfort serves to call them into a new, transformed relation to the ultimate environment, an attitude that Fowler designates universalizing faith. Two tendencies already developing in the earlier stages become fully realized in the lives of universalizers: the *decentration from self,* through a gradually expanded knowing and valuing of the world as it is experienced by diverse others, and the *emptying of self,* through the detachment that follows from radical DECENTRATION. Represented by Gandhi and Mother Teresa in India and by Martin Luther King, Jr., in America, persons who attain Stage 6 embrace the world as their community and demonstrate an all-consuming commitment to justice and love. Though often still blind and limited in certain respects, these exceptional individuals through their struggle with various difficulties have become selfless proponents for a redeemed world. The chief danger of this stage, we may infer, is martyrdom at the hands of those most threatened by the universalizer's subversive vision and leadership.

Although the stages of faith are naturally related to chronological age, especially in the first two decades when cognitive development is predictable and revolutionary, the correlation is in general not high, as the selected data in Figure 9.1 demonstrate. Of the subjects in the youngest group, 88 percent fall in Stage 1; the rest are in transition to Stage 2. Children between the ages of 7 and 12 also show a strong tendency to share the same level of faith development: 72.4 percent of them are assigned to Stage 2. The remaining age groups, however, span at least three if not four stages of faith. Normal adults may assume enduring faith positions at any stage from the second one onward, though both Stages 2 and 6 are for them exceedingly rare.

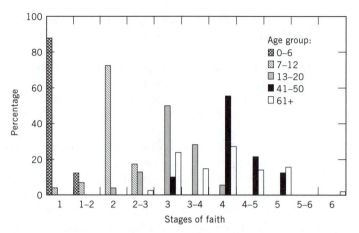

Figure 9.1. The percentage of persons from five age groups in each stage of faith. The age groups 21 to 30, 31 to 40, and 51 to 60 have been omitted from this figure for the sake of clarity. Source: Based on Table B.3 in Fowler, 1981, page 318.

The relation of the faith stages to Erikson's psychosocial eras is less easily assessed. Research suggests, however, that how a person construes and responds to each developmental crisis as it comes along is intimately related to the structural features of that person's stage of faith. These features are so dissimilar that each crisis will in certain respects be a different one for persons at successive stages of faith development. Research by Richard Shulik, for instance, demonstrates that elderly persons in faith Stage 3 construe the process of aging in terms that differ from those in Stages 4 or 5. Similarly, the crisis of intimacy will be experienced differently by someone in Stage 2, who has not yet developed the capacity for mutual perspective taking, in comparison to persons in Stages 3 or 4 (Fowler, 1981, p. 107).

Thoughtfully derived from in-depth research as well as the current thinking of developmental psychologists and scholars of religion, Fowler's faith development theory has won considerable attention in both academic and applied circles. Efforts are now under way to operationalize Fowler's stages with objectively scorable questionnaires that will allow researchers to test hypotheses issuing out of his work. Charles Green and Cindy Hoffman (1989), for example, found that college students who consistently responded to their questionnaire at either Stage 4 or Stage 5 did not discriminate in terms of religious outlook among five hypothetical college applicants whereas those in earlier stages preferred the applicants with religious views more like their own. Using their own nine-item "faith-style" questionnaire, Michael Barnes, Dennis Doyle, and Byron Johnson (1989) found that persons endorsing the literal alternatives on a survey of Catholic beliefs were most likely to be at Stages 3 or 4, whereas those choosing symbolic alternatives were typically at Stage 5.[4] Gary Leak and Brandy Randall (1995), finally, found that their measures of Fowler's Stages 2 and 3 were positively correlated with Altemeyer's (1988) Right-Wing Authoritarianism (RWA) Scale whereas measures of Stages 4 and 5 were

---

[4] None of these research teams has included Stages 1 or 6 in their questionnaire because of the rarity of these stage levels in adult samples. Green and Hoffman had so few respondents in Stage 2 that they omitted these subjects from their analysis.

negatively correlated with it. A "faith stage composite," calculated by summing scores on Stages 4 and 5 and subtracting scores on Stages 2 and 3, yielded a still larger (− .57) negative correlation with RWA scores.

Meanwhile, commentators continue to discuss the strengths and seeming limitations of Fowler's faith development theory (Dykstra and Parks, 1986; Fowler, Nipkow, and Schweitzer, 1991; Streib, 1991). Its conceptual subtleties and broadly conceived empiricism have troubled some objective psychologists, and the themes of relativism and universalism are naturally disquieting to adherents of orthodoxy. Walter Conn (1986) and William Meissner (1987) both express reservations about the heavily cognitive emphasis in Fowler's theory and the corresponding neglect of faith's affective dynamic. Meissner, a Jesuit psychoanalyst, also maintains that Fowler's system is contaminated by liberal attitudes. Nevertheless, he concludes that "Fowler's work represents a fundamental contribution to our understanding of the human experience of faith" (p. 136). Meissner's (1984) own schema of religious development is organized according to five modes of religious experience that are distinguished chiefly in terms of Kohut's theory of an evolving narcissism. Both Conn and Meissner, we should note, also draw on Erikson.

EVALUATION OF ERIKSON'S PERSPECTIVE

Writing at a time when Erikson's fame was at its peak and his standing seemed well secured, Daniel Yankelovich and William Barrett (1970, p. 120) declared that "Not only is Erikson one of the most gifted minds in the analytic pantheon, he probably stands among the very gifted men of the age." Even among psychoanalysts, who are not ordinarily hospitable to practitioners without medical training, Erikson was widely respected for his remarkable clinical insights. The diffusion of his basic concepts and principles throughout the technical literatures in clinical psychology and psychiatry, as well as his pervading presence in more popular psychological works,[5] testified to the high regard in which he was then generally held.

By 1993, when *The Psychohistory Review* brought out a second special issue on Erikson, 17 years after the first one, it was less clear what the fate of his ideas would be. Prevented by age and declining health from inspiring students through his remarkable presence, as he once famously did, he also lacked a school of disciples committed to promoting his views. While urging other innovators to watch carefully over what they had generated, he made no provisions for the institutionalization of his own contributions (Roazen, 1993, p. 103).

GENERAL CRITICISMS OF ERIKSON'S WORK

There are other reasons for why it is hard to predict what Erikson's enduring legacy will be. Even the friendliest of his readers acknowledge the elusive qualities of his richly textured prose and his tendency as a clinician to hint at complexities that are never pinned down. David Andersen (1993), for example, notes that Erikson is "frequently unclear, inconsistent, and vague" (p. 40); his style "tends to be a complex mixture of evocative imagery, psychological jargon, layered meanings, and uneven structure" (p. 36), elements that together make it impossible to know for

---

[5] In a survey of the indexes of 24 introductory psychology textbooks, Terry Knapp (1985) found that Erikson was the fifth most frequently cited authority, following Freud, Piaget, Skinner, and Bandura.

certain what he means to say. Thus it is a difficult and hazardous undertaking to sum up his work in concise principles.

The crucial concept of identity has in particular been singled out for criticism. Joel Kovel (1974) characterizes Erikson's writings on this subject as an "identity salad," a collection of ideas more confusing than clarifying. The notion of the identity crisis, says Howard Kushner (1993), lies at the heart of Erikson's theory and is his main contribution to ego psychology. Yet what stands out about it, he adds, is its shifting definition and lack of theoretical specificity. Erikson's initial, highly tentative constructions of identity, which were framed in terms of the immediate culture, were later expanded to include not just international but also universalist and theological meanings (p. 17). Kushner suggests that the fuzziness of the identity concept may in part reflect Erikson's struggle with his own identity crisis, "the central probem of his life" (p. 21).

In his various writings, Erikson drew on the language and images of a wide range of intellectual perspectives, without adopting any one of them in a systematic way. The outcome of Erikson's "pillaging ways," Andersen (1993) remarks, was "a certain rhetorical wealth and consequent freedom from the clinical-medical imagery of his own discipline" (p. 62–63). These borrowings also add to the difficulties in precisely specifying Erikson's views. In an outstanding review of Erikson's work, for example, Hetty Zock (1990) lays out evidence that, beginning in *Young Man Luther,* Erikson distinguished two developmental trajectories, one psychosocial and the other existential. By the time Erikson wrote *Gandhi's Truth* and the essay on Jesus, Zock suggests, the existential themes—self, encounter, actuality, and so on— had coalesced into a "psychology of ultimate concern." Yet as Andersen (1993) notes, Erikson's borrowings do not reflect a sustained and systematic interest in existential philosophy and theology. Zock's reading of Erikson is surely an interesting one, but it is not the only way to resolve the ambiguities in Erikson's writings.

Critics likewise point to reductionistic trends in Erikson's work, in spite of his explicit rejection of originology (Fitzpatrick, 1976). Kushner (1993) notes in particular the emphasis on individual pathology that is evident in *Young Man Luther.* Aware of the problem, Erikson tried to avoid the same trend in *Gandhi's Truth.* Yet even there, Kushner remarks, Erikson's model tends to direct analysis away from the social conflicts to which Gandhi was responding to the ego conflicts that originated early in Gandhi's life. Cultures, on the other hand, are rarely portrayed by Erikson as pathological. "Even the most careful and creative of his followers cannot avoid pathological assumptions and conclusions when they adopt Erikson's [eight-stage] typology" (p. 12), Kushner concludes.

Another criticism centers on Erikson's assumption that his epigenetic model, the distillate of clinical experience in the modern West, is universally applicable. The recognition of adolescence as a developmental stage is historically a recent phenomenon, John Fitzpatrick (1976) points out, and child-rearing practices vary markedly from one time and culture to another. Illustrating this point, Alan Roland (1988, p. 314) notes that Erikson's tightly organized developmental schema does not fully work in India and Japan, for not only does it emphasize issues—for example, autonomy, initiative, and identity—that are not central in these cultures, but it also leaves out such crucial factors as the early encouragement of dependency needs and the later severe and sustained imposition of hierarchical relations within the family. John Kotre (1984) even doubts that development in the West today, when people are living longer and having fewer children, can be adequately understood in terms of fixed stages. The life cycle, he suggests, is far more flexible than Erikson allows.

The individual stages themselves have been subjected to critical analysis. Kotre points out several problems in Erikson's characterization of the adulthood stage of generativity. Whereas childbearing, a prime component of generativity, begins in very early adulthood for most women, Erikson assigns it to the middle years. Moreover, there is apparently no evidence that generativity dominates more than a few people's lives for the several decades that Erikson allots to it. Rather, it is only intermittently ascendant, and for this reason Kotre prefers conceiving of it as an impulse or *moment* rather than as a stage. Kotre distinguishes four types of generativity—biological, parental, technical (the teaching of skills), and cultural (conserving a symbol system)—each of which may find its own moment and duration, depending in part on chance encounters and accidental circumstances. Whereas Erikson limits the negative side of the stage of generativity to absence of the virtue of care, Kotre points out that generativity can in some lives lead to genuine destructiveness, a potential for evil that is evident even in Erikson's studies of Luther and Gandhi. Thus generativity is more accurately conceived, Kotre says, as an impulse that can manifest itself in vice as well as in virtue.

Others, it must be said, find the potential for active destructiveness fully implicit in Erikson's formulations. Don Browning (1973) takes as Erikson's essential insight the possibility of "irresponsible creativity devoid of a quality of enduring care." For humankind today, says Browning, generativity "has degenerated into mere creativeness, experimentation, and inventiveness; it has become torn apart from that deeper capacity for care which completes and limits the truly generative impulse" (p. 164). From Erikson's writings, Browning deduces three sources of the current nongenerative mentality in America: (1) the Protestant work ethic; (2) the experience of a seemingly limitless frontier; and (3) the extreme differentiation of advanced industrial society.

Doubts regarding Erikson's stages have also been directed toward the first, foundational one, that of basic trust, along with any other formulation that attributes to maternal care a crucial role in the child's later psychological well-being. Some developmental psychologists today argue that these "sentimental views" underestimate the contribution of the child's developing cognitive and motor capacities as well as the major role that even the young infant plays in regulating social contact, through variations in gazing, facial expression, and vocalizing. Thus today there is a growing emphasis on the inherent capabilities that emerge with biological maturation, and on genetically determined individual differences in temperamental disposition, to which most parents learn to accommodate themselves. It is these emerging abilities, Daniel Stern (1985, pp. 22–23) argues, not such clinical issues as trust or autonomy, that mark the progression of a child's development. Rather than being specific to certain phases, these clinical issues remain salient throughout the life-span. Stern suggests that their prominence in recent decades reflects theoretical biases or clinical needs, as well as certain cultural pressures.

Jerome Kagan (1984, pp. 55–56) traces the particular emphasis on the issue of trust to the twentieth-century loss of faith in the inevitability of familial love, as well as anxieties about the future triggered by the world wars, the economic depression, and the threat of nuclear annihilation. The parent–infant bond, Kagan states, remains one of the few sacred themes to which modern Americans are still able to remain loyal. Neither Kagan nor Stern denies that parents play vital roles in their children's lives. Rather, what such researchers are questioning is the prominence given these roles, the special status assigned to certain experiences or modalities (e.g., orality), and the assumption that adult personality is deeply shaped by these factors.

These complex issues are notoriously difficult to test empirically, and much in Erikson can be approached only from a hermeneutical perspective. Yankelovich and Barrett underscore the difficulty of doing justice to the subtleties of Erikson's thought, especially given his disinclination to think through the formal underpinnings of his work. The cost, they say, is systematic misunderstanding. Even analysts highly sympathetic to his ideas have difficulty applying them in their own clinical practice. Furthermore, in blurring his differences from Freud, he has made it more difficult to discern the distinctiveness of his own contributions.

Yankelovich and Barrett grant that Erikson's writings on the concept of identity are confusing, but rather than lamenting over his "identity salad," they set about to clarify its rather large family of meanings, including the least explicit but most fundamental of all: the sheer *is*-ness, or sense of existence, of the individual person. If Erikson's definition seems too subtle, rich, and ambiguous, too all-encompassing, "the phenomena themselves are partly to blame. Ego identity is the outcome of a complex interplay among biological heritage, the unfolding of individual potentialities, the responses of family and other significant persons, and the accumulated values of the culture. None can be ignored if we are to capture the essential way in which a human being manages to become a whole and single person." From Yankelovich and Barrett's perspective, Erikson's emphasis on identity represents an entirely appropriate responsiveness to one of the great themes of today, "the disharmony between ourselves and the quality of modern life" (p. 134). They do not look to him for an objective science valid for all times and all places.

THE HAZARDS OF BRIDGING TIMES AND CULTURES

Erikson intended his theory to be universally applicable, even to figures as remote from the modern West as Luther and Gandhi. His widely acclaimed studies of these two highly influential personalities have stirred considerable controversy, especially among historians accustomed to explaining the past in its own terms. Here we will examine some of the criticisms inspired by these works in particular.

Luther and His Parents

"A besetting difficulty of all Luther biography," writes Ian Siggins (1981, p. 41), "is that the earliest sources, whether friendly or hostile, are anything but dispassionate. Not only are they fiercely partisan and mutually pejorative, written in an age which had perfected the art of vituperation, but they often had specific ideological axes to grind." The more specific, insurmountable problem facing the psychoanalyst, for whom the early years are of greatest importance, is that very little is known of Luther as a child, and even less about his parents. What testimony we have comes—often indirectly—from Luther as an older man, evidence that "wants skeptical, loving evaluation" (Haile, 1980, p. 2).

Erikson, it may be recalled, infers from certain of Luther's comments that his father was ill-tempered and unrelentingly harsh, and that his mother, though the apparent source of certain positive qualities in Luther, was in her own way deeply disappointing. These early parental relations and the unhappy childhood they created, Erikson suggests, were enormously consequential for Luther's later religious and theological views, and thus also for the history of the Christian tradition.[6]

A number of Reformation historians—themselves often Lutheran—find this interpretation thoroughly unconvincing. Some of them quote documents showing that Hans Luther was a loving, if at times stern, father, and that throughout his life Luther felt tender affection toward both his parents. After painstakingly piecing together fragments of information about Luther's mother, Siggins argues that her influence must have been far more positive and fundamental than Erikson (1958, p. 71) concludes when he declares Luther's story to be "an almost exclusively masculine" one. Like Roland Bainton (in Johnson, 1977), Siggins maintains that Luther's attitudes toward women in general and the Virgin Mary in particular were much more favorable than Erikson makes out.

If Erikson's portrait of Luther's father is "demonstrably fabricated," as Steven Ozment (1980, p. 227) puts it, and his reconstruction of Luther's childhood is unverifiable, how then do we account for Luther's anxieties, rages, and strange preoccupations? Though perhaps acknowledging the role of constitutional and temperamental factors such as we examined in Chapter 3, traditional historians are far more inclined to view Luther's difficulties as culturally induced, the product of the intense, fear-motivated piety of the late medieval period. Driven into the monastery by fear of death and God's wrath (not a subconscious wish to defy a tyrannical father), Luther found himself subject to a regimen that, as a distillate of medieval religious culture, served as "a kind of training in mental illness" (p. 229). He remained as long as he did, not because he needed time to resolve an identity crisis, but because he took seriously the acute religious problems confronting him and his contemporaries. His eventual break with the papacy was the end result of careful biblical exegesis, not rejection of a father figure. Lewis Spitz (1977, p. 82) admits in passing that Luther's scatology "poses problems," but others dismiss it as a combination of medieval earthiness and Luther's jovial wit. Luther's contributions to humanity, writes Ozment in summary, are "far better understood and more plausibly explained by a grasp of the religious culture and theology of the Middle Ages than by the importation of the findings of clinical psychology into the sixteenth century" (p. 231).

These historians, in turn, have their critics too. According to Robert Bellah (1977, p. 29), their chief sin is "idolatry of the letter," manifest in their effort to torpedo this reported fact or that one. The only effective critique of Erikson's _Luther,_ he says, would be a portrait of Luther's personal and social development that is more convincing than Erikson's. There will never be a final story of Luther, Bellah points out, but only a succession of interpretations. "What Erikson has given us is _an_ interpretation of Luther, an interpretation which has been compelling for many students of religion in general and of the Reformation in particular, because of the coherence of the pattern he has discerned." This coherence does not depend

---

[6] Pfister (1944) also concluded that Luther had had a severe upbringing, but he remains silent about the specific contributions of Luther's parents. Schjelderup and Schjelderup (1932) are more conservative in reading the evidence. After quoting the same critical passage from Luther that Erikson uses to support his case for Hans Luther's harshness, they remark that too little is known of Luther's childhood to allow reliable inferences (p. 74n).

on the accuracy of every detail, he remarks, nor can these details—the putative harshness and superstitiousness of Luther's father, for example—be simply assessed by some objective criterion. A more sophisticated understanding of the complex web of causal relations is required, Bellah adds, than seems to underlie some of these criticisms.

Cushing Strout (1968a) urges his fellow historians to take ego psychology's potential contribution to their work more seriously. "History without psychological insight drowns the individual in a sea of social forces or elevates him to mythical heights" (p. 295). As Strout demonstrates in his own psychohistorical study of William James, Erikson's theory suggests specific evidence to look for in a subject's life history and provides a conceptual framework by which to make more intelligible the sequence and configurations of this life. But wary of reducing any person to a mere case study, Strout emphasizes that psychology needs in like measure to be enriched by historical insight.

Gandhi and the Hindu Cultural Universe

Erikson's prize-winning book on Gandhi presents a rather different configuration of issues. Outstanding among them is the problem of applying to Gandhi an interpretive schema that has arisen out of the values and outlook of the Judeo-Christian West. The risk here is considerable, given the difference in the Indian family structure and, more importantly, the Hindu cultural universe that Gandhi shared with his multitude of followers.

In sketching out the dimensions of that universe, Arjun Appadurai (1978) delineates the particular emphases and innovative reinterpretations for which Gandhi became widely famous. He was convinced that the end of the British rule would come only with the achievement of individual self-control, attainable through the practice of *ahimsa,* a nonviolence that combines selfless love for one's enemy and a willingness to suffer injury in the service of truth. He also believed that detached moral action (*dharma*), especially in the form of vows, binds a person to ultimate truth. Such vows as celibacy (BRAHMACHARYA), fasting, and nonpossession not only further self-control and detached action, by stilling the passions, but also conserve certain bodily (particularly reproductive) substances or powers and transform them into "soul-force," thus increasing a person's control over the powers governing the universe and the capacity to know and convert others to the truth (pp. 116–121). Much of Gandhi's energy, Appadurai says, went into enacting and comunicating his version of the cultural heritage that governed the lives of most of those in his audiences. "Because he described these essential and enduring elements of Hindu culture with enormous simplicity and clarity, and because his own adherence to these models and meanings was tireless and imaginative, Gandhi had direct access to the Indian popular imagination" (p. 122).

It is seriously misleading, Appadurai says, to interpret elements of Gandhi's life apart from this cultural framework and in accord with a lexicon that associates sexuality with primal sin and rebellion rather than wastefulness; that conceives of ultimate reality as a Father–God instead of an impersonal Godhead and a pantheon of both male and female deities; and that takes guilt, not ignorance, as humankind's chief psychoreligious problem (p. 132). Appadurai illustrates this point by recalling young Gandhi's devastation upon learning that, while he was sexually engaged with his wife, his ailing father had died. Erikson, we may remember, considers this recollection a cover memory for guilty Oedipal wishes that Gandhi had denied through assiduous caretaking of his father. Viewed, however, from the perspective

Gandhi with his "walking sticks," young women whose intimate presence appeared to others to contradict Gandhi's vows of ascetic self-denial.

of one who has grown up in the Hindu cultural world, Appadurai points out, a rather different interpretation suggests itself. What Gandhi experienced on that traumatic occasion was a primordial dramatization of the ancient Hindu principle that sexual indulgence, through its wasting of potent bodily fluid, contravenes fulfillment of *dharma,* the moral law. This event and the earlier memorable confession of theft to his father may well constitute cover memories of certain broadly conceived childhood conflicts, Appadurai allows, but he insists that they be considered "cultural condensations and projections as well—that is, concentrated displays of powerful cultural models in single, dramatic scenes" (p. 133). If these dramatic events were of later significance, "it is because their original social context and their later deliberate formulation draw mutual sustenance from a common cultural universe" (p. 134). Erikson's neglect of this universe, Appadurai declares, is his single major shortcoming.

The Hindu world-view is likewise the necessary framework for understanding Gandhi's treatment of those closely associated with him, especially the members of his own family. Whereas Aijaz Ahmad (1970, p. 8) castigates Erikson for giving insufficient prominence to Gandhi's "monstrous callousness toward others, his refusal to forgive or have mercy, his insistence on making a virtue of not having personal loyalties to anybody," Appadurai argues that Erikson has failed to understand how Gandhi's unmistakable authoritarian and vindictive attitudes, and especially his commitment to celibacy (*brahmacharya*) as a prerequisite for nonviolent resistance (*satyagraha*), emerged out of the Hindu cultural tradition.

Gandhi's sadism toward his family, Appadurai argues, expresses the tension Gandhi felt between his vow of *brahmacharya* and the constant reminder of earlier sexual involvement represented by the presence of wife and children. Moreover, the democratizing tendencies inherent in familial relations complicated or even contradicted the clear-cut relations of authority, the open and unambiguous use of conflict, and the "selfless" love of *ahimsa* that were integral to Gandhi's reformist tactics (pp. 140–141). Susanne Rudolph (1970) notes in addition that, in India, lack of control over one's own family would raise questions about one's capacity or right to lead others, and that Gandhi naturally expected his family to be exemplary in meeting his new standards of virtue. Above all else, she says, it was Gandhi's remorseless practice of asceticism, so characteristic of the saintly person in the Indian context, that lent him his great appeal among villagers and city dwellers alike.

Erikson recommends a rather different vision—a balance of the "sensual, logical and ethical faculties" that "a world-wide technological culture must help make universal at least as an ideal" (1969, pp. 251–252). But in Erikson's enlightened program Appadurai discerns a twofold bias.

> This recommendation of planned parenthood, sexual mutuality, and universal technology, I submit, is part of Erikson's *ideological* quarrel with Gandhi. However, it supports and is interwoven with his strictly psychoanalytic criticism, and is equally in conflict with Gandhi's explicit ideological preferences on these matters. Taken together, these biases show that Erikson's criticism of Gandhi is not simply a disinterested psychoanalytic corrective to *satyagraha*. Rather, they show the degree to which Erikson's cultural presuppositions, expressed in either clinical or ideological terms, render crucial parts of Gandhi's beliefs and activities, from his point of view, either incomprehensible or unappealing or both (p. 139).

Yet even the traditional Hindu is disturbed by certain elements in Gandhi's conduct, notably his long baths and daily massages at the hands of his woman devotees; his routine practice of walking with his hands on the shoulders of young women (his "walking sticks," he would say); and, in a gesture that scandalized even some of his closest disciples, his taking one or another of these young women into bed with him, both of them naked, putatively as a means of testing the perfection of his renunciation—all highly unorthodox practices for a *brahmachari* (Mehta, 1977, p. 195). As full of contempt for Hindu culture as he is for Gandhi, Ahmad finds at the heart of Erikson's book a fundamental contradiction: on the one hand, a commitment to presenting Gandhi and his principle of *satyagraha* as a key to humankind's salvation; on the other hand, a subject who has "totally internalized the oppression, the authoritarianism, the conformism, the reactionary ethics and ideology, and the horror of the human flesh characteristic of the traditional ruling class of India, the Brahmins" (p. 5).

ERIKSON'S RELIGIOUS NARRATIVE

Writing from a much more sympathetic standpoint, Philip Pomper (1970) wonders whether Erikson has not overrated Gandhi. Erikson's "theory of the great *homo religiosus* as savior *pro tempore*" (p. 205) places an enormous burden on such figures as Luther and Gandhi, says Pomper, who doubts that they are always up to the task. The "gifts" they leave behind "are consistently squandered," he notes, and one often suspects that "they create more harm than good" (p. 209). Had Erikson not limited himself to the Ahmedabad textile strike—the importance of which some critics say he overestimates—and to the handful of wealthy, powerful, and well-educated participants who were his chief informants, but like Ved Mehta (1977) had sought out instead a larger number of more intimate and humble associates, he might well have felt impelled to write at greater length about the personal costs of devotion to Gandhi and his cause.

That approach, it seems, would not have served Erikson's larger purposes. For Gandhi is assigned a crucial role in the story Erikson tells of humankind's evolutionary struggle with its wayward instinctual endowment, including a propensity toward violence that technology has made increasingly dangerous to the human race. What we find in Erikson's writings, Roger Johnson (1977) cogently argues, is not merely psychohistory but genuine religious narrative. Featured in Erikson's cast of characters are Hans Luther, an unambiguously demonic figure who appears as a brutally aggressive precursor of economic man today; Martin Luther, the rebellious and neurotic son whose positive legacy is shadowed by his father's excessive ambition; Kaba, Gandhi's father, short-tempered and prone to violence like Hans but restrained toward his son as Hans was not; Gandhi, who through his invention of *satyagraha* corrects and completes the religious movement initiated by Hans's son; Sigmund Freud, who succeeds Luther as champion of an ego emancipated from tyranny and joins Gandhi in promoting a method of truth seeking that is based on noncoercive mutuality; and animal species such as the wolf, whose instinctive, pacifying rituals find their desperately needed human parallel in Gandhi's *satyagraha*. Writes Johnson,

> Gandhi is the prophet who enacts a genuine alternative to a future of mass destruction, the prophet who extends into sociopolitical arenas the strengths of the therapeutic tradition from Luther through Freud while healing the liabilities of that same tradition, and finally, the prophet who recapitulates in himself the prehistory of humanity, manifesting both adaptive instinctive patterns and the healing of instinctual aberrations (p. 153).

Johnson concludes that Erikson is more than a psychologist and psychohistorian. "He is also an ethicist, a religionist, or—in a modified use of the term—an ideologist" (p. 141). Erikson "smuggles the concept of the human spirit through the back door of psychoanalytic theory," concur Yankelovich and Barrett (1970). "He is responding to the human need for meaning and for self-understanding, to the need for a sense of relatedness to a cosmic order, and above all, to the universal search for a bedrock basis for ethical reality in a secular age" (p. 152). Colleagues and commentators agree with Yankelovich and Barrett that Erikson himself possessed wisdom, which in his epigenetic schema is the reward of old age. Some even claim that Erikson was himself a *homo religiosus*. Whether or not his life was marked by the personal dynamics he attributes to this rare type, certainly no one today has been more profoundly disturbed by the human side of the contemporary crisis, and we would have to look far to find more helpful clues to a possible solution.

Such epithets underscore the extent to which Erikson's remarkable achievements are an expression of his particular sensitivities and outlook. As Pomper (1970, p. 203) observes in his review of *Gandhi's Truth*, Erikson is "the creator of a genre of psychohistorical literature so uniquely a product of his peculiar style as a writer and thinker that one fears it will not survive him. There is not, nor is there likely to appear soon, another writer capable of carrying off Erikson's asides, his word games, his apostrophizing, his pleasant side trips, and, above all, his organic, multilevel approach to psychohistorical biography." Whatever shortcomings his work may have or whatever correcting and supplementing it may require, it will long remain essential reading for the psychologist of religion.

10

C. G. JUNG AND THE ANALYTICAL TRADITION

*N*o psychologist has received more attention from contemporary scholars of comparative religion than Carl Gustav Jung. More than any other psychologist, Jung has drawn widely from both Western and Eastern religious traditions for evidence in support of his concepts and theories. He has also demonstrated an unusually sympathetic attitude toward the religious life. Religion, Jung emphasizes repeatedly, is a necessary psychological function, the neglect of which is costly to both individual and society. In this chapter we become acquainted with Jung's life and work, as well as the considerable literature of further studies—and of criticism—that demonstrates the vitality of his continuing influence.

THE LIFE OF C. G. JUNG

Although by now we have an abundance of biographical material on Jung, a definitive work comparable in compass and detail to the best of the available studies on Freud is still on the horizon. The sources currently available are of several types. First there is Jung's posthumously published autobiography, *Memories, Dreams, Reflections* (1962), a deeply revealing yet highly selective reconstruction that Peter Homans (1979) characterizes as automythology. Invited by the publisher Kurt Wolff, this book was originally to have been written by Aniela Jaffé, Jung's personal assistant, on the basis of conversations they held weekly for this purpose. The voice was to be Jung's but Jaffé would organize and edit the material. At a certain point, however, Jung felt impelled to take over the writing of his early recollections, which came to form the first three chapters of the book. Other, briefer portions are also largely of his authorship. Yet because of the selecting and editing process carried out by others, Richard Noll (1994) considers the work an historically unilluminating "product of discipleship" (p. 13). John Kerr (1995), in contrast, sees no reason for disbelieving the statements in Jung's memoirs, especially the first three chapters. Kerr considers the work to be "one of the great publishing coups of the century"

C. G. Jung

(p. 3). Given our interest in the origins of Jung's psychology of religion in his own experience, we, too, rely on this autobiography.

The controversy over Jung's *Memories* reflects two quite distinct literatures on Jung's life and work. On the one hand are the various "biographical memoirs," as Barbara Hannah (1976) labels her own contribution. These works are authored by persons who were intimately associated with Jung, profoundly influenced by him, and convinced that his *Memories* "will always remain the deepest and most authentic source" concerning his life (p. 8). On the other hand are two relentlessly unsympathetic though often plausible works, one of them Noll's (1994) and the other by Paul Stern (1976). Stern, a German-born psychotherapist of Freudian and existential leanings, curiously cites no sources for his surprisingly intimate study. In contrast, Noll, a clinical psychologist who did postdoctoral work in the history of science at Harvard, uses elaborate documentation to press forward his claim that Jung abandoned science and established himself at the center of an irrational mystery cult with roots in the same turn-of-the-century occultism and neo-paganism that gave rise to National Socialism. Designated the best book of the year in psychology by the Association of American Publishers, Noll's work has been criticized by reviewers as "a kind of entrenched literalism" (Gardner, 1995, p. 62) and an "extended hatchet job" with nothing new that is true (McHugh, 1995, p. 620). Kerr (1994) considers the book flawed but nevertheless illuminating.

Ranging in between these extremes of devotion and derogation are a number of more moderate works. The most recent of these is Kerr's (1993) remarkable reconstruction of the early years of psychoanalysis and the dynamics of the complex relationship between Freud and Jung. Other valuable resources include Henri Ellenberger's (1970) lengthy chapter on Jung, portions of which Jung had read and commented on; J. J. Clark's (1992) delineation of Jung's role in the history of modern thought; Renos Papadopoulos's (1992) four-volume collection of key papers on Jung; and a number of other works given over to Jung's life and thought (Bennet, 1961; Brome, 1978; Jaffé, 1979; Staude, 1981; Tenzler, 1975; van der Post, 1975; Wehr, 1985).

A Visionary's Lonely Childhood

C. G. Jung was born in Switzerland on July 26, 1875, into a parsonage in Kesswil, a small village on Lake Constance. His father was a country parson in the Swiss Reformed Church and, before that, a student of philology and linguistics, in which he had earned a Ph.D. Jung's paternal grandfather, also C. G. Jung, was of German origin and, according to an unsubstantiated legend to which our subject occasionally alluded, an illegitimate son of Goethe. He came to Switzerland in 1822 to become professor of surgery at the University of Basel. The legitimate line of descent was traced from the learned Catholic doctor and jurist Carl Jung, who died in 1654. This ancestor lived at a time when pharmacology was still heavily influenced by ALCHEMY, and thus he was probably well acquainted with the writings that were to spring up again into Jungian consciousness 200 years later.

Paul Jung, our subject's father, apparently had been forced by financial circumstances to abandon his philological studies and to take up theology instead. Although he took his profession seriously and was respected and even loved by the villagers he served, he became increasingly subject to despair, according to his son, as he realized the hollowness of his own religious faith. Jung felt much closer to his mother, Emilie Preiswerk Jung, a voluble, warmhearted, and humorous woman. He also saw an uncanny side to her, unpredictable and frightening, and he came to think of her as having two personalities. Early on, his parents' marriage was filled with disappointment and tension, which Jung thought contributed to his father's decline in spirits and health.

When Jung was six months of age, his parents moved from Kesswil to Laufen, where the vicarage stood alone near the castle above the falls of the Rhine. From the years at Laufen, Jung recalls glorious impressions of nature: of sunlight through green leaves, of the Alps at sunset, of waves washing up on shore. The dangerous nearby falls showed Jung another face of the natural world. Its victims' funerals, attended by "black, solemn men in long frock coats," and the sudden disappearance of familiar persons whom Lord Jesus, it was said, had taken to himself, left powerful, even overwhelming, images. Jung's vague fears at night were partially dispelled by a prayer his mother had taught him, in which he asked a winged Jesus to take him, as a chick, in order to prevent Satan from devouring him instead. The sinister parallel of the taking in the prayer and the taking associated with the hole in the ground made the child Jung afraid of Lord Jesus and led, when he was three or four years old, to his first conscious trauma: the terrifying appearance of a black-robed Jesuit emerging from the wooded hilltop near the vicarage, the experience of which kept the horribly frightened Jung in the house for days afterward.

When Jung was three, his mother was hospitalized in Basel for a period of several months. In his autobiography he associates her illness with difficulties in the marriage and a temporary separation of his parents. Her absence deeply troubled the young boy, whose feeling of abandonment was apparently unrelieved by the presence of a visiting aunt and the dark-complected maid who left long-enduring impressions of strangeness yet inexplicable familiarity. Jung attributed his temporary suffering at that time from a generalized dermatitis to the distress he felt over his mother's seeming unreliability.

At about this same time, Jung had a dream—the earliest he could remember—that was to preoccupy him all his life. In this dream, Jung discovered a dark, rectangular, stone-lined hole located in the big meadow behind the sexton's farm. Descending into it with hesitation and fear, he saw behind a heavy green curtain a dimly lit chamber made of stone. A red carpet led across the flagstone floor to a magnificent golden throne. Standing on the throne was what appeared to be a giant tree trunk, but it was made of flesh and possessed a rounded head with a single, upward-gazing eye. The terror that paralyzed Jung grew even more intense when he heard his mother call out, "Yes, just look at him. That is the maneater!" And then he awoke, sweating and terrified. For nights afterward he was fearful that the dream might recur. "The phallus of this dream"—he did not realize until much later that this was what it was—"seems to be a subterranean God 'not to be named,' and such it remained throughout my youth, reappearing whenever people spoke too emphatically about Lord Jesus" (Jung, 1962, p. 13).[1]

When he was four, Jung's parents moved into the eighteenth-century parsonage at Klein-Hüningen, near Basel, where Jung's father also served as Protestant chaplain of the Friedmatt Mental Hospital. The years that followed left in Jung's memory a variety of impressions: the old paintings that hung in the dark room full of fine furniture; a gashed chin suffered on the steps of a Catholic church, an incident that intensified his fear of Catholic churches and priests; and an old, richly illustrated children's book with fascinating pictures of Brahma, Vishnu, and Shiva, the three chief deities of the Hindu tradition. There were also his hatred of going to church, although he celebrated Christmas day with fervor; a living and sacred fire that he built and for a time constantly maintained in an interstice of an old stone wall, and a nearby stone that stood in some secret relationship to Jung; and anxiety dreams and alarming visions that reflected the tense atmosphere of his parent's troubled relationship.

Above all, there was the little manikin, dressed in frock coat, top hat, and shiny black boots, that the nine-year-old Jung carved out of the end of a ruler. He kept it wrapped in a cloak of wool and bedded down in a pencil case, along with a smooth, oblong, blackish stone divided into two halves by means of water colors. The yellow varnished case was hidden on a beam in the attic, where Jung stole from time to time to add little scrolls of paper inscribed in a secret language. This practice, which lasted about a year, was a great, inviolable secret that brought Jung satisfaction and security. It was, he writes, the climax and conclusion of his childhood.

Beginning in his eleventh year, Jung was sent to study at the *Gymnasium* in Basel, leaving behind his rustic playmates and joining the refined sons of the personages who inhabited the "great world." For the first time he became aware of how poor his family was, and he began to understand the cares and worries of his parents. School itself came to bore him; nonetheless, and in spite of his fear of mathematics and his hatred of gymnastics, he managed to reach the top of his class.

---

[1] A strikingly similar series of images, which would have confirmed Jung in his conviction that this dream is archetypal in character, comes from a story associated with Hindu saint Allama Prabhu of the twelfth century C.E. According to tradition, Allama began wandering the countryside, griefstricken and benumbed, in search of his beloved wife after her sudden death from fever. One day, while sitting downcast in a grove of trees, he saw the golden cupola of a temple protruding from the ground. Excavation revealed the closed door of a shrine. He kicked the door open, entered, and found an entranced yogi meditating on the linga (phallus). "Like the All-giving Tree, he sat there in the heart of the temple. The yōgi's name was Animiṣayya (the One without eyelids, the open-eyed one)." Handing over the linga to Allama, Animiṣayya expired and Allama became enlightened. Appearing in virtually all of Allama's religious lyrics, as the traditional signature line, is the name Guhēśvara, or Lord of Caves, which is one of Shiva's names (Ramanujan, 1973, p. 144; I am indebted to Professor Ramanujan for bringing this material to my attention). For Allama, the linga was a long-familiar image representing Shiva; for Jung it was terrifyingly foreign.

Around his twelfth birthday, Jung became obsessed with a terrifying fantasy that he struggled for days to avoid completing, for fear of committing the sin against the Holy Ghost and thus being condemned to hell. Only when he concluded that God Himself had placed him in this desperate situation as a decisive test could Jung finally let the thought unfold itself. He saw before him, as he had earlier, the cathedral of Basel, the sky around it a glorious blue and the sun reflected off of the new, brightly glazed tiles. High above this beautiful sight sits its creator on His golden throne—and then "from under the throne an enormous turd falls upon the sparkling new roof, shatters it, and breaks the walls of the cathedral asunder" (p. 39). At the completion of this vision, Jung experienced an enormous, indescribable relief and an unutterable bliss. He wept with happiness and gratitude for the grace and illumination that had come to him. But God's befouling of His own cathedral was a dreadful thought, and Jung's whole life was overshadowed by the dark and horrible secret that God could be something terrible. Because those around him showed no traces of having had similar experiences, Jung had the feeling that he had been either cursed or blessed by this sinister vision.

His entire youth, Jung says, can be understood in terms of this secret experience, along with his dream of the underground phallus, the encounter with the Jesuit, and the wooden figure that was his first attempt to give shape to his secret. The secret "induced in me an almost unendurable loneliness. My one great achievement during those years was that I resisted the temptation to talk about it with anyone. Thus the pattern of my relationship to the world was already prefigured: today as then I am a solitary, because I know things and must hint at things which other people do not know, and usually do not even want to know" (pp. 41–42).

Jung's Two Personalities

Somewhere in the fringes of his awareness, Jung writes, he always knew that he was two persons. One was the parson's son, with all his weaknesses, insecurities, and ambitions. The other was an old man from another century, "skeptical, mistrustful, remote from the world of men, but close to nature, the earth, the sun, the moon, the weather, all living creatures, and above all close to the night, to dreams, and to whatever 'God' worked directly in him" (pp. 44–45). The first lived an ordinary, everyday existence; the second dwelled in the boundlessness of "God's World," a world of dazzling light and abysmal darkness, of coldly impassive infinite space and time, of chance and uncertainty, of meaning and historical continuity. The play and counterplay between these two personalities, Jung says, occurs in the life of every individual, although the second figure is rarely perceived. In his own life, the second was of prime importance, a fact reflected in the dominance of inner realities over outer events in his autobiography. From the second personality came the dreams and visions, the sense of destiny and inner security, the peace and solitude that characterized Jung's life.

Having directly experienced God's grace and increasingly sensing the reality of "God's World," the 14-year-old Jung expected to participate in the mystery that he was sure must lie behind the sacrament of Holy Communion. His father's instruction for confirmation was boring beyond measure, and Jung was profoundly disappointed when they skipped over the one question that interested him, the problem of the Trinity. Jung nevertheless tried hard to believe without understanding—which was seemingly his father's attitude—and set his last hopes on the rite of Communion, the pinnacle of religious initiation. At the critical moment, when he finally received the bread and wine, nothing happened; nor, apparently, did anything happen for the people around him. As in the theological conversations Jung so often overhead (for eight of his uncles were parsons), the words and acts of this ritual seemed to have no experience behind them. God, who for Jung was one of the most certain and immediate of realities, had been absent. It was, he says, a fatal experience for him. The ceremony proved to be a total loss, and he knew that he would never again be able to participate in it. "For God's sake I now found myself cut off from the Church and from my father's and everybody else's faith" (p. 56).

Jung continued his search for understanding in the books of his father's library, but only with the discovery of Goethe's *Faust* did he find something that spoke to his own experience. *Faust,* which "poured into my soul like a miraculous balm" (p. 60), was the living equivalent of Jung's second personality and finally gave him the reassurance that he was not alone in this world. "My godfather and authority was the great Goethe himself" (p. 87). A few years later, Jung found a second equivalent to his "No. 2," in Nietzsche's *Thus Spake Zarathustra;* but the morbidity of *Zarathustra* and its author's tragic end in madness slammed shut for a long time to come the door that *Faust* had opened.

Between his sixteenth and nineteenth years, Jung slowly emerged from the confusion and depressions of the preceding period, and his first personality grew more and more distinctive. He began a systematic reading of philosophy, in which he found historical analogues for many of his intuitions. The works of Pythagoras, Heraclitus, Empedocles, and Plato were especially attractive to him, but his great find was Schopenhauer and his somber picture of the world. An even greater illumination came with his subsequent reading of Kant, above all his *Critique of Pure Reason.* Beyond laying the idealistic foundations for his later psychology (Nagy, 1991), Jung's study of philosophy radically altered his attitude toward the world and life, and he found himself much more confident and communicative. The effort to overcome the split within himself, however, remained a painful frustration; he repeatedly found himself forced back into "God's World."

The Study of Psychiatry

The division in Jung's personality was reflected in a corresponding dichotomy of interests. He was attracted by the concrete facts of the empirical sciences, especially zoology, paleontology, and geology, but only the humane or historical studies provided the factor of meaning. When people asked him what he wanted to study, he would reply philology, by which he secretly meant Assyrian and Egyptian archaeology. In reality, both the sciences and the humanities attracted him, and he postponed his decision until shortly before he matriculated at the University of Basel. Archaeology was out of the question, for the University had no instructor in that subject, and Jung could not afford to go elsewhere. Two dreams about fascinating natural discoveries, Jung claims, decided him in favor of science. Without money to finance advanced training abroad, however, Jung saw no hopes for a scientific career, and he opted instead for medicine and its wide range of possibilities for later specialization. Finally, when he was preparing for the state examination in medicine, he fell in great excitement upon a vocation that would allow the two currents of his interest to flow together. In psychiatry he found an empirical field that embraced both biological and spiritual facts.

In 1900, after completing his studies and examinations at the University of Basel, Jung took a position as assistant under Eugen Bleuler at the Burghölzli, the prestigious psychiatric hospital and clinic of the University of Zurich. For six months he cloistered himself within the walls of the asylum. He also read through the entire fifty volumes of the *Allgemeine Zeitschrift für Psychiatrie*. He wished to understand the disturbed personality, but he was equally puzzled by the attitudes of his colleagues, which seemed to him strange and reductionistic. He did not share their apparent conviction that delusions and hallucinations are devoid of human meaning or that the individuality of the patient may be ignored.

In 1902 Jung studied for a term with Pierre Janet at the Salpêtrière in Paris. The following year he married Emma Rauschenbach, the daughter of a wealthy industrialist. After bearing one son and four daughters, she herself became an analyst and a specialist on the legend of the Holy Grail (E. Jung and von Franz, 1960). During 1904 and 1905, Jung set up a laboratory for experimental psychopathology at the Psychiatric Clinic, where research on word association and the psychogalvanic response was to bring him an international reputation. In 1905 Jung was appointed lecturer in psychiatry at the University of Zurich and became a senior physician at the Psychiatric Clinic. He resigned the senior physician post four years later, in 1909, when he found himself overwhelmed by a burgeoning private practice.

A Temporary Association with Freud

Jung first met Freud in 1907, in Vienna. From the beginning of Jung's psychiatric career, the writings of Freud, along with those of Breuer and Janet, had been an important stimulus for his own thinking. Jung's experiments with word association corroborated Freud's concept of the repression mechanism, at a time when Freud was still unwelcome in psychiatric and academic circles. Jung championed Freud's cause, at the risk of his own academic career, and soon became a member of Freud's inner circle. They began an eight-year association with a correspondence initiated by a copy of the *Studies in Word Association*, which Jung sent to Freud in 1906. In 1909, in response to independently issued invitations from Stanley Hall, they sailed together for the United States to deliver lectures at Clark University, where they also received honorary degrees.

In spite of his great admiration of Freud, Jung had earlier experienced a growing frustration over the differences between their attitudes. Freud's positivistic and dogmatic attitude, especially in regard to his theory of sexuality, became increasingly disturbing to Jung. Whenever confronted by an expression of the higher reaches of the human spirit, whether in a person or in a work of art, Freud seemed immediately to suspect repressed sexuality. "One thing was clear: Freud, who had always made much of his irreligiosity, had now constructed a dogma; or rather, in the place of a jealous God whom he had lost, he had substituted another compelling image, that of sexuality" (Jung, 1962, p. 151).

The turning point in their relationship came for Jung on the 1909 voyage, during which they daily analyzed each other's dreams. One day, Jung writes, he was attempting to analyze one of Freud's dreams and suggested that much more could be made of it if Freud would provide additional details from his private life. Freud, according to Jung, gave him a look of utmost suspicion and said that he could not risk his authority. At that moment Freud lost it altogether in Jung's eyes, for he seemed to place personal authority above loyalty to truth. The correspondence between Freud and Jung ceased in 1913. The following year Jung resigned the presidency of the International Psychoanalytic Society, which he had held since its founding in 1910, and shortly thereafter he withdrew as a member.

Jung's carved stone in its Tower setting at Bollingen.

Inner Quest and Outer Achievement

The period from 1912 to 1917 was profoundly disturbing and momentous for Jung. Overwhelmed with fantasies and dreams, he found it difficult to lecture, write, or even read. He was, he says, almost literally struck dumb, and he felt that he could no longer offer courses while he was so filled with doubts and confusion. Giving himself over entirely to the task of confronting the chaos of his unconscious, he decided to withdraw from all public appearances. Accordingly, he resigned his lectureship and gave up his academic career.

Much like Freud, according to Ellenberger (1970, p. 672), Jung was suffering a creative illness. And just as Freud had Wilhelm Fliess as a vital link to reality, so Jung was sustained during this period of darkness and extreme loneliness by certain vital relationships. In his autobiography he credits his family and his work as psychotherapist, but to Barbara Hannah (1976, p. 120) he intimated that it was the unfailingly sympathetic and understanding companionship of Toni Wolff—a former patient, collaborator, and longtime lover—that truly saved him. These years seemed to him to have been the most important in his life: "In them everything essential was decided" (Jung, 1962, p. 199). It was during this period that Jung began drawing MANDALAS—circular patterns he came to see as symbolic representations of the SELF, which he soon recognized as the goal of psychic development. In 1918 he began seriously to study the GNOSTIC writers, who were to provide him with rich analogies for the basic processes of the psyche.

The 1920s were outwardly uneventful years for Jung, though not without significance for his inner quest. In 1920 he traveled to North Africa, in an effort, he writes, to find the part of himself that had been covered over by European influences. About this time, too, he began experimenting with the *I Ching,* the ancient Chinese book of wisdom and oracles. In 1923 his mother died (27 years after his father), and two months later construction of the "Tower" was begun on the land he had bought the year before in Bollingen, on Lake Zurich. The Tower was a silent and timeless stone retreat, built in stages, where Jung spent many of his free days. It was, he says, "a confession of faith in stone" (p. 223), "a place of maturation," "a concretization of the individuation process" (p. 225). At Bollingen, he felt that he was most deeply himself.

A triptych on the theme of the anima, carved by Jung on a wall at Bollingen. The bear symbolizes the strength and energy of Artemis and also alludes to Russia. The image of the woman milking the mare anticipates the coming of the Age of Aquarius, when the feminine element will play a special role (Jaffé, 1979, p. 194; Kerr, 1993, p. 507).

In the middle 1920s Jung visited the Pueblo Indians of New Mexico, and shortly thereafter he made a second trip to Africa, this time to its central regions, where he lived for a while with the Elgonyi on the slopes of Mount Elgon in Kenya. In 1928 Richard Wilhelm, then director of the China Institute in Frankfurt, sent him the text of *The Secret of the Golden Flower,* a Taoist alchemical treatise that they were eventually to publish together. This text was a breakthrough for Jung, confirming his ideas about the mandala and shedding light for the first time on the nature of alchemy. He commissioned a Munich bookseller to find other alchemical texts for him, gradually building a library much like the one he claims he had seen before—in a dream prior to his discovery of alchemy.

It took Jung years to penetrate the meaning of alchemy, and it was not until the late 1930s and early 1940s that his alchemical writings began to appear. Alchemy proved to be the missing link between Jung's psychology and the Gnostic writers. As Jung pored over the old texts, he writes, everything seemed to fall into place: his own fantasy images, the empirical material he had gathered from his patients, and the conclusions he had drawn. He finally understood that the unconscious is a *process* and that the psyche undergoes transformation or development in a manner symbolized by the alchemist's abstruse ideas and images. Out of his study of this symbolism and the process of transformation emerged the central concept of his psychology, individuation.

In the 1930s Jung received a number of honors, including membership or honorary presidencies in several major medical societies and honorary doctorates from universities around the world, including Harvard, Oxford, three universities in India, and two in his native Switzerland. During this decade he resumed lecturing, at the Swiss Federal Polytechnic Institute in Zurich, and offered numerous seminars in English. In 1944 he accepted a chair in medical psychology established for him at the University of Basel, but a heart attack forced him to resign within a year.

The period of serious illness that followed was filled with visions, "the most tremendous things I have ever experienced" (Jung, 1962, p. 295). Out of the insight he felt he had gained from these visions, Jung found "the courage to undertake new formulations." "Thus one problem after another revealed itself to me and took shape" (p. 297). A productive period of work followed, culminating in the

Mysterium Coniunctionis, published in two volumes in 1955—the year his wife Emma died—and 1956. "In *Mysterium Coniunctionis* my psychology was at last given its place in reality and established upon its historical foundations. Thus my task was finished, my work done, and now it can stand." Jung had finally "touched bottom" (p. 221). After a brief illness, he died on June 6, 1961, shortly before his eighty-sixth birthday.

The intimate relation of the life and work of an individual is perhaps nowhere more clearly illustrated than in the instance of Jung and his psychology. Jung himself said that his work is a vital and inseparable expression of his own inner development, that each of his writings constitutes a station along his life's way. He wrote because he was compelled to, from within. He was, he said, in the grip of a daimon. His life was filled with vivid dreams and visions, and he was no stranger to remarkable parapsychological phenomena. He lived in a world filled with mystery, a world that cannot be grasped apart from myth and symbol. Yet he knew that he could speak to this age only through empirical facts, and so he gathered them in extraordinary number. To those who find these facts comprehensible and interesting, Jung's achievement can only appear remarkable, whatever its limitations may be. If we evaluate his system by the degree to which it increases self-awareness and promotes psychic growth, Jung's own life would seem to testify to its adequacy. According to those who knew him, Jung died a whole and happy man.

JUNG'S ANALYTICAL PSYCHOLOGY

When we examine Jung's psychology and especially his writings on religion in the light of his autobiography, we find many of the themes prefigured in his own early experience: the division of the personality into two opposing halves; the contrasting forces of darkness and light; a view of God as both good and terrible; the emptiness of contemporary Protestant ritual and dogma; the contrasting power of the Catholic tradition; and the fundamental significance of the doctrine of the Trinity and the rite of the Holy Eucharist. We witness as well his early familiarity with the power of natural symbols—animals, trees, stones, fire. Jung's inclusion of these themes in his autobiography was most certainly influenced by his mature views, including his conviction that any psychologist's writings and personal experience are intimately related. But there is no reason to doubt that the events and experiences he features in this book occurred more or less as he describes them.

Jung declares the subjective factor in psychological work, familiar to us from earlier chapters, to be an unavoidable reality.

> The psychology we at present possess is the testimony of a few individuals here and there regarding what they have found within themselves. The form in which they have cast it is sometimes adequate and sometimes not. . . . Our way of looking at things is conditioned by what we are. And since other people are differently constituted, they see things differently and express themselves differently. . . . Philosophical criticism has helped me to see that every psychology—my own included—has the character of a subjective confession (Jung, 1933, pp. 116–118).

In all fields of knowledge, Jung (1954e) says, we have come to recognize the importance of the "personal equation," of the decisive influence of individual psychological factors. Given that we understand only what we have experienced, the important question becomes, "*Who* saw, heard, or thought what has been reported?" (p. 77). Within the equation, too, we must include the spirit of the age, a time's unexamined and typically dogmatic view of what is true, an emotional tendency to which weaker and more suggestive minds are particularly vulnerable (Jung, 1931a).

A Quest for True Expression

Limited by the confessed boundaries of his own experience, Jung strove to free himself from all uncriticized presuppositions, although he asserted that fundamental assumptions are finally unavoidable and that an overall hypothesis is indispensable. The explanatory speculations of his contemporaries, Jung (1951b) writes, are "based far more on unconscious philosophical premises than on the nature of the phenomena themselves." Because of "the enormous complexity of psychic phenomena, a purely phenomenological point of view is, and will be for a long time, the only possible one and the only one with with any prospect of success" (p. 182).

Reflecting his deep respect for human experience, Jung (1929) set as his goal "true expression," "an open avowal and detailed presentation of everything that is subjectively observed. . . . True expression consists in giving form to what is observed" (p. 334). The psychologist brings together materials for comparison, offers a terminology for discussion, and, where possible, discerns types by which the phenomena might be classified. The concepts of analytical psychology were thus viewed by Jung not as explanatory constructs but as names of recurring forms of experience. Whenever possible, he used the names by which these experiences have always been known.

Although Jung did not wholly repudiate the modern trends toward quantification and causal explanation, he found these approaches inadequate to the task before him. Statistical knowledge allows us to make general statements about human beings as a species, but real facts, Jung writes, are distinguished by their individuality. "The more a theory lays claim to universal validity, the less capable it is of doing justice to the individual facts." For self-knowledge a person must understand these unique individual facts, whose regularity is illuminated very little by theoretical assumptions or general knowledge. "In principle, the positive advantages of *knowledge* work specifically to the disadvantage of *understanding*." To understand, a person must lay aside all general scientific knowledge and adopt a new and unprejudiced attitude (Jung, 1957, pp. 250–251). Even a presupposition as widely accepted as the materialistic hypothesis, which views the psyche as a secondary manifestion or an EPIPHENOMENON, is too bold in the face of experience. It is better to regard the psyche as something unique, as an irreducible phenomenon to be understood in and for itself (Jung, 1954b).

As a psychotherapist Jung pursued the goal of individual understanding, but as a writer of books on psychology he had to generalize. It is almost impossible, he writes, to demonstrate anything with a few words. Individual images require a context that includes both the individual case history and illuminating mythical materials. Such contextual material would be voluminous, requiring an entire book in itself. Realizing as well that it is impossible to convey the power of an image's subjective impression on the patient's psyche, Jung (1951b) says that he used case material most hesitantly and then only in brief.

Beyond Causal Explanation and Critical Reason

In order to do justice to individual empirical facts, Jung added several controversial principles to his generalized conceptual system. Looking beyond the causal question of origins and influences of the past, Jung (1954d) emphasizes the TELEOLOG-

ICAL question of purpose and meaning. Psychic processes are not just the result of past forces still living in the present. They also show spontaneous movement toward goals in the future. Only by answering the question of purpose do we obtain the meaning of a phenomenon. And just as we speak of causality when one event follows an earlier event with apparent dependence, so Jung (1952d) proposes the principle of SYNCHRONICITY to refer to events that occur simultaneously and are meaningfully but not causally connected, as in the case of many parapsychological phenomena. In addition to the principles of causality, teleology, and synchronicity, Jung says, we must recognize the factors of *chance* and *mystery*. "In practice, . . . chance reigns everywhere, and so obtrusively that we might as well put our causal philosophy in our pocket" (Jung, 1943, p. 49). We all must sense, he says, that we live "in a world which in some respects is mysterious; that things happen and can be experienced which remain inexplicable; that not everything which happens can be anticipated. The unexpected and the incredible belong in the world. Only then is life whole" (Jung, 1962, p. 356).

We must content ourselves, says Jung (1935), with the knowledge that "to the critical intelligence, nothing is left of *absolute* reality. Of the essence of things, of absolute being, we know nothing" (p. 218). All we can know are effects, as they present themselves to us through our senses and by way of fantasy. Out of these psychic realities humankind creates myth, which gives meaning to human existence and aids the individual in coming to terms with the world that lies both without and within the self. Unfortunately, increasing emphasis on reason has made it more difficult for the individual to participate in the mythical process. "The more the critical reason dominates, the more impoverished life becomes; but the more of the unconscious, and the more of myth we are capable of making conscious, the more of life we integrate" (Jung, 1962, p. 302). With the regrettable decline of the religious traditions, it has become the task of psychology to understand and foster this process of integration, and psychology must be correspondingly broad and deep, not simply an abstract schema constructed by reason toward limited ends.

As we review the outlines of Jung's psychology, we must keep in mind that Jung, like James, counts experience as far more important than any conceptual system. The highest achievements of human effort—faith, hope, love, and insight—can neither be taught nor learned, he claims, but come only through experience. The way to experience is "a venture which requires us to commit ourselves with our whole being" (Jung, 1932, p. 332). Jung was ever reluctant to refer to his work as a theory or a method; he called it instead "a circumambulation of unknown factors" (Fordham, 1966, p. 11) that constantly requires new definitions and perspectives. If anything, his opus constitutes a new mythical statement, a new embodiment of timeless factors.

THE STRUCTURE OF THE HUMAN PSYCHE

Out of the darkness of prehistory, says Jung, a remarkable phenomenon has struggled into a precarious existence that even today is not fully assured. This phenomenon is human *consciousness*, an achievement of extraordinary moment. It is nature's becoming aware of itself, the capacity to *know* that we live and experience. With it arises the *ego*, the center of the conscious personality, and with it the individual is born. The precariousness of consciousness is perhaps more noticeable among members of nonliterate tribes, for whom the area of consciousness and the capacity for concentrated reflection are said by Jung to be somewhat smaller. Contemporary individuals are only slightly less vulnerable to the twilight and darkness that come with the fading of consciousness—in sleep, mental illness, mass movements, or war. We in the modern world are only relatively less dependent on the dogmas and rituals that nonliterate tribes use to maintain the flickering light of conscious awareness.

The Personal Unconscious

Underlying the vulnerable layer of immediate consciousness is the unconscious, the timeless matrix out of which consciousness arises anew in each succeeding generation. Immediately below conscious awareness is found the *personal uncon-scious,* whose character is determined by the personal past. The contents of this layer of the psyche, which essentially corresponds to Freud's notion of the unconscious, consist of acquisitions of the individual's own lifetime, some of which have been repressed and others of which have simply fallen below the threshold like indifferent memories or passing sense impressions. Within the personal unconscious lie the COMPLEXES, emotionally colored ideas that become split off as a result of traumatic influences or incompatible tendencies and that may help or hinder conscious activity. A complex—for example, one centering on the idea of the mother—can become an autonomous and fragmentary personality that seems to live a life of its own, dominating the individual's feelings, thoughts, and actions. Though usually disturbing and harmful, complexes can act positively by challenging the individual to seek new possibilities. Such unsolved problems, as focal points of psychic life, are in fact essential for psychic activity. It was Jung's exploration of these complexes through the use of the word association test that first brought him widespread recognition (Jung, 1934).

The Collective Unconscious and the Archetypes

Deeper within the dark interior of the psyche are layers that have been formed, not in the personal lifetime of the individual, but during the millennia that the human species has existed. Beneath these layers, says Jung, lie deposits of the experience of prehuman evolutionary forms. All these layers constitute the COL-LECTIVE UNCONSCIOUS, the most important and controversial of Jung's concepts. In the dreams and fantasies of his and other therapists' patients, Jung encountered remarkable ideas and images whose origins could not be traced to the individuals' own past experiences. The resemblance of these contents to mythical and religious themes that have appeared throughout the centuries in widely scattered geographical areas led Jung to refer to them as primordial images and to postulate the existence of underlying ARCHETYPES.

The archetypes are not, Jung (1936) emphasizes, memories of past experiences, but *"forms without content,* representing merely the possibility of a certain type of perception and action" (p. 48). The archetypes are "a kind of readiness to produce over and over again the same or similar mythical ideas" (Jung, 1943, p. 69). "They are the ruling powers, the gods, images of the dominant laws and principles, and of typical, regularly occurring events in the soul's cycle of experience" (p. 95). These "dominants," which are responsible for the human quality of human beings, are not only the effects and deposits of experience but also active agents that cause the repetition of these same experiences (p. 70).

Because we can know only the manifestations of the archetypes—the historical formulations that have evolved through conscious elaboration, the individual images that are colored by the personal consciousness in which they appear—we can say very little about the archetypes themselves. Jung (1936, p. 48) speculates that there are as many archetypes as there are typical persons and situations in human experience. Because a "fluid interpenetration" is part of their nature, however, they cannot be clearly circumscribed or reduced to a formula. The units of meaning that the archetypes form can be intuitively apprehended through a phenomenology of their manifestations and a circumscription of the unconscious cores of meaning (Jung, 1951c, p. 179). Reductive explanation is neither desirable nor possible.

> Not for a moment dare we succumb to the illusion that an archetype can be finally explained and disposed of. Even the best attempts at explanation are only more or less successful translations into another metaphorical language. (Indeed, language itself is only an image.) The most we can do is to *dream the myth onwards* and give it a modern dress. And whatever explanation or interpretation does to it, we do to our own souls as well, with corresponding results for our own well-being. . . . Hence the "explanation" should always be such that the functional significance of the archetype remains unimpaired, so that an adequate and meaningful connection between the conscious mind and the archetypes is assured. For the archetype is an element of our psychic structure and thus a vital and necessary component in our psychic economy (p. 160).

From years of observing and investigating dreams, fantasies, visions, and psychotic delusions, and from his study of parallel images in religious and mythical materials, Jung identified certain frequently recurring situations and figures that appear to exhibit regular patterns of meaning. Among the typical motifs known in human experience, a few stood out for Jung as particularly important, including the PERSONA, the SHADOW, the ANIMA and ANIMUS, the mother, the child, the wise old man, and the self. These archetypes are often reflected in personified forms. Objects, abstract figures, situations, places, and processes can also give expression to them.

The Persona: As the mask that we wear to make a particular impression on others, the persona may at the same time conceal our true nature. This artificial personality is a compromise between a person's real individuality and society's expectations; not infrequently society's demands prove to be the more significant factor. Constructed of professional titles, characteristic roles, habits of politeness, and other such impersonal or collective elements that together simulate individuality, the persona serves both to guarantee social order and to protect the individual's "private life." Unfortunately, many people believe that they are what they pretend to be. That is, the ego identifies itself with the persona. With such an identification, the individual becomes especially vulnerable to influences from the unconscious. People must distinguish between who they are and who they appear to be before the process of self-realization can begin (Jung, 1935).

The Shadow: The first step toward self-realization, or individuation, consists in recognizing and integrating the shadow, the negative or inferior (that is, undeveloped or undifferentiated) side of the personality. The shadow is made up in part of the reprehensible qualities that the individual wishes to deny, including animal tendencies that we have inherited from our infrahuman ancestors. It also contains the modes and qualities that the individual has simply not developed, some of which may be highly desirable. The shadow coincides with the personal unconscious. Because all persons inevitably share in this phenomenon, it is also in some sense a collective manifestation.

The more unaware a person is of the shadow, says Jung, the blacker and denser it will be. The more it is dissociated from conscious life, the more it will display a compensatory demonic dynamism. The unrecognized shadow is projected upon persons or groups who are then thought to embody all the immature, evil, and other repressed tendencies that are actually resident in the individual's own psyche. The image of the devil and the serpent, as well as the doctrine of original sin, represent variants of the shadow archetype. It occasionally happens that the ego identifies with the shadow, producing "the moment of Dionysian frenzy," in which the victim of the archetype feels like a godlike being who is beyond good and evil (Jung, 1943, 1951a, 1954a).

Anima and Animus: When a person has come to terms with the shadow—that is, with the personal unconscious—he or she is then confronted with the problem of the anima or animus, the archetype that personifies the soul, or inner attitude. Because this archetype is complementary to the persona, it takes on the characteristics of the opposite sex (Jung, 1921). The *anima,* the archetypal image of woman present in the unconscious of every man, grows out of three important sources: the individual man's experience of woman as companion; a man's own femininity, which is presumably grounded in the female sex hormones present to some degree in every male body; and the inherited collective image that has been formed from man's experience of woman throughout the centuries (Jung, 1935). The anima often appears in dreams, and as long as she remains unconscious, she is also projected outward onto various women, including, at first, the mother, and then later, the lover or wife. This projection is responsible for passionate attraction or aversion and, more generally, for man's apprehension of the nature of woman. Should a man mistakenly identify with the anima, says Jung, she can produce effeminacy or homosexuality. The anima exists in a compensatory relationship with the outer, conscious attitude. The more a man identifies with a highly masculine persona, the more he will become the victim of an undifferentiated and projected anima. In all men the anima is responsible for moods and is a complication in all emotional relationships. After the middle of life, according to Jung, the anima is essential for vitality, flexibility, and human kindness (Jung, 1935, 1954b).

The anima, the archetype of life itself, is encountered in a wide range of images that reflect her bipolarity. She can "appear positive one moment and negative the next; now young, now old; now mother, now maiden; now a good fairy, now a witch; now a saint, now a whore. Besides this ambivalence, the anima also has 'occult' connections with 'mysteries,' with the world of darkness in general, and for that reason she often has a religious tinge" (Jung, 1951b, p. 199). Historically, the anima is encountered above all in the divine SYZYGIES, the male–female pairs of deities (Jung, 1954b). The anima can also appear as a snake, tiger, bird, or another such animal that symbolizes her characteristics.

The comparable archetype in the female psyche is the *animus,* the woman's image of man. Unlike the anima, which appears as a single feminine figure, albeit one with ambivalent or contradictory qualities, the animus often manifests itself in a plurality of figures, in an indefinite variety. This fact, says Jung, reflects differences in the conscious attitudes of men and women. Whereas a woman's consciousness tends to be exclusively personal and centered upon her own family, the man's is made up of various worlds, of which his family is only one. Thus, the animus and anima, as the opposites of these conscious attitudes, are plural and singular, respectively.

Just as feminine Eros remains undifferentiated in the man's unconscious anima, thus causing disturbing emotions and immature relationships, so the undifferentiated masculine Logos in the woman's unconscious animus is responsible for

A Hindu deity with his consort, or *Śakti,* considered to be the source of his divine energy; from the ornately carved outer wall of the twelfth-century Hoyśaleśvara Temple in Halebīd, India.

unreasoned opinion and critical disputatiousness. According to Emma Jung (1934, p. 20), the animus manifests itself most characteristically in words rather than in images, typically a voice that comments on a person's situation or imparts general rules. When the animus does take on form, as in dreams or fantasies, it appears "either as a plurality of men, as a group of fathers, a council, a court, or some other gathering of wise men, or else as a lightning-change artist who can assume any form and makes extensive use of this ability" (p. 27). The animus may also manifest itself in the single figure of a real man: "as father, lover, brother, teacher, judge, sage; as sorcerer, artist, philosopher, scholar, builder, monk (especially as a Jesuit); or as a trader, aviator, chauffeur, and so forth; in short, as a man distinguished in some way by mental capacities or other masculine qualities." In its positive forms, the animus is characteristically benevolent, fascinating, knowledgeable, or understanding. It may also be cruelly demanding, violently tyrannical, seductive, or moralistic and censorious (p. 29). Distinguished from oneself and brought into consciousness, the animus, like the anima, can be changed from a personified complex into a function that serves as a bridge into the collective unconscious, much as the persona mediates between ego consciousness and the outer world (Jung, 1935).

The Mother Archetype: As for the other archetypes, the variety of aspects under which the mother archetype appears is almost infinite.

The qualities associated with it are maternal solicitude and sympathy; the magic authority of the female; the wisdom and spiritual exaltation that transcend reason; any helpful instinct or impulse; all that is benign, all that cherishes and sustains, that fosters growth and fertility. The place of magic transformation and rebirth, together with the underworld and its inhabitants, are presided over by the mother. On the negative side the mother archetype may connote anything secret, hidden, dark; the abyss, the world of the dead, anything that devours, seduces, and poisons, that is terrifying and inescapable like fate (Jung, 1954e, p. 82).

The range of images that express the mother archetype is thus virtually inexhaustible. Most important are mothers in the literal sense—the personal mother, grandmother, stepmother, and mother-in-law—and then the figurative but personified mothers, including the mother–goddess or Great Mother, especially the Mother of God, the Virgin, and Sophia (the personified "Wisdom" of God in the Gnostic tradition). The mother archetype may also be symbolized in many impersonal forms. Paradise, the Kingdom of God, the church, the university, the city or country, earth, the woods, the sea, the moon, the cornucopia, a garden, a cave, a tree, or deep well, the baptismal font, cooking vessels, and such animals as the cow or the hare are among the images that have a favorable meaning. Evil symbols include the witch, the dragon, the grave, deep water, and death (Jung, 1954e).

The Child Archetype: The archetype of the child can take many forms. It may appear unmistakably as a child, perhaps a child god or a child hero. It may be a dwarf or an elf, or it may seem to be of exotic origin with a dark skin. Finally, it may take the form of an animal, such as the monkey, or of an object, such as the jewel, the chalice, or the golden ball. The child archetype, through one or another of its images, represents original or childhood conditions in the life of the individual and of humankind, in order to remind the conscious mind of its origins and thus to maintain continuity with them. Such a reminder is necessary when consciousness becomes too one-sided, too willfully progressive in a manner that threatens to sever the individual from the laws and roots of his or her being. At the same time, the child points to the future. It signifies the potentiality of future development of the personality, and it anticipates the synthesis of opposites in the achievement of wholeness. In other words, it represents the urge and compulsion toward self-realization. Thus it is that so many of the mythological saviors are child gods. The threats and obstacles that appear before the child god or hero are reminders of the difficulties of the way to psychic wholeness and of the dangers that threaten the newly acquired consciousness. As an expression of psychic wholeness, the child points even beyond death, as exemplified by the cupids on antique gravestones (Jung, 1951c).

The Wise Old Man: The archetype of the wise old man is also known as the archetype of meaning or spirit. Appearing as grandfather, sage, magician, king, doctor, priest, professor, or some other authoritative figure, or as dwarf, hobgoblin, or animal, the wise old man represents insight, understanding, knowledge, wisdom, cleverness, and intuition on the one hand, and moral qualities, such as goodwill and readiness to help, on the other. His appearance serves to induce self-reflection, to warn of dangers, and to provide protective gifts to those who demonstrate the requisite moral qualities. Just as the other archetypes have positive and negative aspects, so also the wise old man sometimes manifests an ambiguous elfin character possessing both beneficent and malevolent features. As our scientific and technological age has made unmistakably clear, the human spirit is capable of working for evil as well as for good (Jung, 1948a).

The Self: The most important archetype, and also the most difficult to comprehend, is the *self*. It is the "midpoint of the personality," a center midway between consciousness and the unconscious that signifies the harmony and balance of the various opposing qualities that constitute the psyche. The self remains essentially incomprehensible, for ego consciousness cannot grasp this superordinate person-

The Kalachakra, or "Wheel of Time," a rare, symbol-filled Tibetan mandala that is painstakingly created over a period of weeks out of colored sand and then destroyed, the sand released into a body of water.

ality of which it is only one element, just as the young child cannot wholly comprehend the adult, or as a part cannot contain the whole.

The symbols of the self can include anything that the ego takes as a greater totality than itself. Thus many of the symbols fall short of expressing the self in its fullest development. Because the self is so far from the conscious mind, and because it is virtually impossible for any person to embody the self fully, this archetype is often expressed by abstract or geometrical forms, above all, by the *mandala* ("circle" in Sanskrit, but applied to a wide variety of concentrically arranged figures) or by the QUATERNITY (any figure with four parts). Prominent among the human figures that express the self are the Buddha, Christ, and Khidr (a legendary Muslim saint). It is also symbolized by the divine child, by various pairs, such as father and son, king and queen, and god and goddess, or by a HERMAPHRODITE. Theriomorphic symbols include powerful animals, such as the dragon, snake, elephant, lion, and bear, and insects, such as the spider, butterfly, and beetle as well as the insectlike crab. The self is also expressed by plants, above all by the lotus and the rose, and by various mythical objects, including the Hiranyagarbha (the "golden germ" that Vedic tradition says arose and created the universe), the Holy Grail, and the philosopher's stone of the medieval alchemist. The self archetype, says Jung, produces the same symbolism that has always expressed the deity; it is impossible, in fact, to distinguish between a symbol of the self and a God image. The self, Jung concludes, is the "God within us" (Jung, 1935, 1948b, 1951a, 1951b, 1952a).

THE DYNAMICS OF SELF-REALIZATION

The process by which a person moves toward the achievement of the self is called *individuation.*

> Individuation means becoming an "in-dividual," and, in so far as "individuality" embraces our innermost, last, and incomparable uniqueness, it also implies becoming one's own self. We could therefore translate individuation as "coming to selfhood" or "self-realization." . . . The aim of individuation is nothing less than to divest the self of the false wrappings of the persona on the one hand, and of the suggestive power of primordial images on the other (Jung, 1935, pp. 173, 174).

Individuation must not be confused with individualism, which overlooks collective factors and seeks only to stress some supposed peculiarity valued by the ego.

Although Jung (1935) refers to individuation as an "ineluctable psychological necessity" (p. 155), he also says that "nature is aristocratic," and that "only those individuals can attain to a higher degree of consciousness who are destined to it and called to it from the beginning, i.e., who have a capacity and an urge for higher differentiation." In these respects, individual differences are enormous (Jung, 1943a, p. 116). The requirements are not superior intelligence or other special gifts, for moral qualities can compensate for intellectual shortcomings (p. 117). The great majority of human beings are still in a state of childhood and are notoriously unconscious. Still struggling with outer necessity and problems of the personal unconscious, the average person remains content within limited horizons that do not include knowledge of the collective unconscious. Nevertheless, wider consciousness may be presumed to be a universal capacity (Jung, 1935).

Psychological Types

The process of individuation occurs in two stages, which Jung calls the morning and the afternoon of life. The tasks of the morning of life require an extraverted attitude, that is, an orientation toward the external world. During these years a person's psychic energy or libido is usually directed into social relations, education, marriage, and family, into becoming both professionally and socially established. During this stage the individual is concerned, in more general terms, with finding a place in the external world of objects and fellow human beings.

The transition from morning to afternoon typically comes between 35 and 40 years of age, according to Jung, and brings with it the urgent need to reexamine accepted values and to appreciate the opposites of earlier ideals. The afternoon of life is properly introverted, for then a person's concerns should become increasingly those of the internal world, of the fuller development of the psyche. The second half of life is the time for culture and wisdom, for the true flowering of the art of life. It is a period governed by its own principles, which are directed toward the end of self-realization through the union of opposites (Jung, 1931c).

The attitudes of extraversion and introversion are only one of a number of pairs of opposites that embody the principle of ENANTIODROMIA: the changing of a phenomenon into its opposite (Jung, 1943a). Equally important are the two pairs of functions, known also as the modes of apprehension. These are sensation and intuition, which are the modes of perception, and thinking and feeling, which are the modes of judgment. *Sensation* refers to the process of perceiving physical stimuli, not only from outward events but also from inner organic changes. It is concerned with what is immediately present to the senses. The opposite of sensation is *intuition,* "the function that mediates perceptions in an *unconscious way*" (Jung, 1921, p. 453). Intuition yields a content that is whole and complete, a knowledge that possesses immediate certainty and conviction. Intuition, when not merely reacting to a concrete situation, can discern the hidden meaning of unconscious images and the new possibilities that lie in the future. Both sensation and intuition are "irrational" functions in the sense that they deliver perceptions that are not grounded in reason. Their fulfillment lies simply in the undirected perception of events, inner or outer (Jung, 1921).

Thinking is concerned with the conceptual relationship of psychic contents, toward the end of making them comprehensible. Active or directed thinking is undertaken intentionally toward the end of some judgment. In passive or intuitive thinking, on the other hand, the conceptual connections seem to establish themselves of their own accord and may lead to judgments that are contrary to the person's intention. Both of these forms of thinking should be distinguished from associative thinking, which produces ideas that form no connections and yield no judgments. Jung considers only directed thinking to be a rational function, for undirected thinking relies on unconscious or irrational processes, and the ideation of associative thinking is really not thinking at all.

The opposite of thinking is *feeling*, a process that responds to psychic content with a subjective judgment of value—of acceptance, rejection, or indifference. Feeling, like thinking, is considered a rational function insofar as it is decisively influenced by reflection and is in accord with the laws of reason. When feeling becomes relatively independent of the momentary contents of consciousness, it appears in the form of a mood; when the intensity of a feeling increases enough to produce physical innervations, it turns into an affect (Jung, 1921).

Ideally, we should develop equally the two attitudes of extraversion and introversion, as well as the four functions of sensation and intuition, thinking and feeling, and thus also the two modes of apprehension, perceiving and judging. Everyone, however, prefers one or the other of the opposites that form these pairs. One function is singled out, perhaps on the basis of constitutional preference, for the fullest development and use; it thereby becomes the dominant or SUPERIOR FUNCTION. Of the four this function is by far the most reliable and the most amenable to intention, and in combination with either extraversion or introversion it forms the conscious attitude of the individual (Jung, 1948a). The opposite of the superior function falls into the unconscious, where it remains, inaccessible, undifferentiated, and autonomous; Jung calls it the INFERIOR FUNCTION.

The remaining two functions become only partially differentiated, one more than the other. This secondary or *auxiliary function* operates in the service of the dominant function, and it becomes an important ally in dealing with the unconscious because it is not antagonistic to the inferior function. Should it become as differentiated as the dominant function, it will interfere with the reigning mode—perception or judgment—and perhaps change that mode into its opposite. The two functions that are relatively or fully unconscious remain in a primitive, undeveloped state. They are not, however, merely dormant. Like all unconscious contents, they can be the source of considerable psychic disturbance, appearing in dreams and fantasies as animals or monsters (Jung, 1921).

Differentiation and Integration

This brief review of Jung's theory of types gives us a clearer perception of what the process of individuation entails. The undifferentiated attitudinal and functional modes are also part of the contents of the unconscious with which a person must finally come to terms in order to realize the self. Because, however, the attitudes and functions consist of opposites that cannot, with their contradictory nature, be realized simultaneously, their development must occur in harmonious alternation, giving to life a certain rhythm. Unfortunately, ordinary conscious acts can disturb the natural law that governs this process. What is required, therefore, is a much higher level of consciousness that will permit the art of these antithetical movements to be developed (Jung, 1943a).

These opposites, and the many others that compose the psyche, provide the polar tension that is the source of psychic energy. Accordingly, they are necessary for self-regulation and renewal.

> However different, to all intents and purposes, these opposing forces may be, their fundamental meaning and desire is the life of the individual: they always fluctuate round this centre of balance. Just because they are inseparably related through opposition, they also unite in a mediatory meaning, which, willingly or unwillingly, is

born out of the individual and is therefore divined by him. He has a strong feeling of what should be and what could be. To depart from this divination means error, aberration, illness (Jung, 1935, p. 196).

The theme of opposites is one of the most pervasive in Jung's writings. It is also one of the most difficult. To the conscious, rational mind, the ubiquitous opposites that preoccupied Jung—including the fundamental antinomies of masculine and feminine, matter and spirit, good and evil—are distinct and irreconcilable. To the unconscious, however, whose own contents "are without exception paradoxical or antinomial by nature" (Jung, 1948a, p. 230), the unification of opposites is an ever-present possibility. For Jung, individuation is an unending process of differentiation and integration that repeats itself on ever-higher planes. The analytical capacities of the conscious mind allow us to distinguish, develop, and contrast the individual components of the psyche. The creative forces of the unconscious, on the other hand, provide symbols that bring these one-sided, opposing elements together again, on a higher level. These symbols direct the energy created by the temporarily incapacitating dividedness of thesis and antithesis into a common channel, and life flows on again, renewed and transformed (Jung, 1921, p. 480). Jung calls this process the TRANSCENDENT FUNCTION. This complex function brings conscious and unconscious together and allows for an organic transition from a lower attitude to a higher one—thus the name "transcendent" (Jung, 1958).

The countless archetypal symbols that express and bring about the union of opposites—in other words, that mediate the process of individuation—are none other than the images, dogmas, and rites that make up the religious traditions. General psychological education toward psychic wholeness, says Jung (1952b), belongs to the very nature of these traditions, "for religion excels all rationalistic systems in that it alone relates to the outer and inner man in equal degree" (p. 7). Only by living in harmony with the primordial images of the unconscious, by bringing our thinking in agreement with them, can we live life fully (Jung, 1931b). Unfortunately, many people today have either mistaken or wholly rejected these images, and thus they have estranged themselves from their own deepest resources. They have also made themselves vulnerable to the powerful and destructive forces that lie in the depths of the undifferentiated psyche.

JUNG'S PSYCHOLOGY OF RELIGION

Religion was always a matter of personal interest to Jung, but only gradually did it find a preeminent place in his theory and practice. This evolution was undoubtedly stimulated by his personal struggles in the years 1912 to 1917. It also reflected his commitment to a comprehensive view of human experience.

> Since religion is incontestably one of the earliest and most universal expressions of the human mind, it is obvious that any psychology which touches upon the psychological structure of human personality cannot avoid taking note of the fact that religion is not only a sociological and historical phenomenon, but also something of considerable personal concern to a great number of individuals (Jung, 1938, p. 5).

Among these individuals were Jung's patients, whose dreams, fantasies, and drawings were to provide him with powerful living symbols that bore remarkable resemblance to historical religious materials wholly unknown to many who consulted with him.

The Development of Jung's Thought on Religion

Jung's earliest discussions of religion are couched in terms that Raymond Hostie (1955) describes as "out-and-out Freudianism" (p. 112). In the first edition of his "The Significance of the Father in the Destiny of the Individual," published in 1909, Jung wrote

> The child is guided by the power of the parents as by a higher destiny. But as he grows up, the struggle between his infantile attitude and his increasing consciousness begins. The parental influence, dating from the earliest infantile period, is repressed and sinks into the unconscious, but is not eliminated; by invisible threads it directs the apparently individual workings of the maturing mind. Like everything that has fallen into the unconscious, the infantile situation still sends up dim, premonitory feelings, feelings of being secretly guided by other worldly influences. These are the roots of the first religious sublimations. In the place of the father with his constellating virtues and faults there appears on the one hand an altogether sublime deity, and on the other hand the devil (Jung, 1949, pp. 320–321).

In the much revised and expanded third edition of this essay, Jung omitted the last two sentences quoted here and added a passage on the preexistent archetype of the father, which constellates both the father image and the divine or demonic figure that is put in the place of the father.

In 1911, in the first edition of his *Symbols of Transformation* (1952c), Jung depicts religion as a positive factor of psychological value. It is also, he wrote, a delusion that keeps human beings in an infantile mental state. The ideal religion would lead a person from submissive belief to understanding: "This would be the course of moral autonomy, of perfect freedom, when man could without compulsion wish that which he must do, and this from knowledge, without delusion through belief in the religious symbols. It is a positive creed which keeps us infantile and, therefore, ethically inferior." Thus Jung saw religion as an error, but a positive one. It "gives man assurance and strength, so that he may not be overwhelmed by the monsters of the universe." The religious symbol is *psychologically true,* for it has allowed humankind to transcend the instinctive stage of the unconscious into the heights of the greatest moral and cultural achievements. For the masses who are unable to pursue moral autonomy, religion may continue to fulfill "its great biological purpose" (quoted in Hostie, 1955, pp. 114, 116).

At first Jung perceived the idea of God as a projection of psychic energy. He viewed the myth of the sun god in particular as a projected description of the rhythmic progression and regression of this energy throughout the life of the individual. With the development around 1918 of the notion of the self and its place in the developing psyche, Jung came to view the idea of God and the whole complex world of religious phenomena not only as projections of psychic processes but also as indispensable symbols that express and draw human beings toward psychic wholeness.

Jung also became increasingly aware of "the spiritual problem of modern man," the profoundly convulsive changes in spiritual life brought about by the horrors of World War I, which tore from humankind the certainties of centuries-old religious, social, and political systems. Genuinely modern individuals are the rare solitary persons who have been born into consciousness, and thus into awareness of the chaotic and dark recesses of their own minds. They know the guilt and burden that are theirs in breaking with tradition and in falling back upon their own unknown resources. Most persons are not truly modern, according to Jung's

(1931b) definition, for to be "the man who stands upon a peak, or at the very edge of the world, the abyss of the future before him, above him the heavens, and below him the whole of mankind with a history that disappears in primeval mists" requires "the most intensive and extensive consciousness, with a minimum of unconsciousness" (pp. 74–75). Whatever their individual achievements, such persons share with the rest of us the profound uncertainty and disillusionment that recent catastrophic events have left in their wake. They, too, live in the midst of a civilization dominated by materialism and the demonic achievements of science and technology, a civilization in which the masses, bereft of adequate symbols, inexorably project the neglected archetypes onto persons and nations, thus transforming them into dangerous enemies.

This spiritual revolution underlies the worldwide preoccupation with psychology and the widespread interest in astrology, THEOSOPHY, spiritualism, and the like. Those in the afternoon of life are especially in need of a comprehensive, essentially religious system that will allow the psyche to develop as it must if it is to avoid psychoneurosis. Only a spiritual standpoint can give the meaning and form that are essential for human life. In a widely quoted passage Jung (1932) reports that

> Among all my patients in the second half of life—that is to say, over thirty-five—there has not been one whose problem in the last resort was not that of finding a religious outlook on life. It is safe to say that every one of them fell ill because he had lost what the living religions of every age have given to their followers, and none of them has been really healed who did not regain his religious outlook (p. 334).

Religion Defined

To have a religious outlook, Jung emphasizes, is not merely to subscribe to a particular creed or to belong to a religious organization. *Creeds,* he (1938) says, are "codified and dogmatized forms of original religious experience." They are substitutes for immediate experience, composed of suitable symbols that are elaborated and framed within organized dogma and ritual. Creeds and dogmas are not as inflexible as some critics maintain, "yet all changes and developments are determined within the framework of the facts as originally experienced, and this sets up a special kind of dogmatic content and emotional value" (p. 9). At the same time that the creed helps to shape over and over again certain limited but valid forms of religious experience, it protects the adherent from the potentially terrifying and disruptive forces that are unleashed in an original religious experience. Unfortunately, like all metaphysical systems, creeds are vulnerable to the probing light of disinterested reason (Jung, 1854f).

Religion, according to Jung (1938), is an attitude that involves

> a careful consideration and observation of certain dynamic factors that are conceived as "powers": spirits, daemons, gods, laws, ideas, ideals, or whatever name man has given to such factors in his world as he has found powerful, dangerous, or helpful enough to be taken into careful consideration, or grand, beautiful, and meaningful enough to be devoutly worshipped and loved (p. 8).

This attitude comes about when persons consciously experience what Rudolf Otto termed the "numinous," "a dynamic agency" that "seizes and controls the human subject, who is always rather its victim than its creator" (p. 7). Individuals often assume that these dynamic factors or powers exist apart from themselves. Jung argues to the contrary, holding that the archetypes in the collective unconscious are their immediate source. An indirect encounter with the archetypes, especially the archetype of the self, in one or another of their manifestations is always a numinous and therefore an awesome and fascinating experience, the intensity of which varies with the clarity of the representation. The apparent independence of these forces from willful activity and conscious understanding naturally leads persons who experience them to assume that these powers have invaded them from outside.

Jung's location of the source of religious experiences and ideas in the human psyche brought down on him charges of psychologism, agnosticism, and even atheism (Hostie, 1955). He responded by emphasizing that he *as psychologist* can say nothing more about God than is given in the psyche; psychology can know only the "typos" or "imprint," not the imprinter. The facts prove, says Jung (1952b), that the psyche possesses a religious function. The psychologist's task lies in helping people to recover the inner vision that depends on establishing a connection between the psyche and the sacred images. Rather than attacking or undermining religion, psychology "provides possible approaches to a better understanding of these things, it opens people's eyes to the real meaning of dogmas, and, far from destroying, it throws open an empty house to new inhabitants" (p. 15). Psychology, unbounded by creed, can help the undeveloped mind to appreciate the value and scope of the paradoxes of faith. Indeed, only through the logical contradictions and impossible assertions of paradox can we hope, according to Jung, to come near a comprehension of the totality of life.

The Difference Between Western and Eastern Traditions

As even a casual reading of his works reveals, Jung was interested in and well acquainted with both Western and Eastern religious traditions. Notably, some of his earliest explorations were of Chinese materials: the *I Ching* and the Taoist *Secret of the Golden Flower*. He eventually wrote essays on these abstruse works as well as on two Tibetan texts, Zen, Eastern meditation, yoga, and India (see Jung, 1969). Yet his chief interest lay in Western spirituality, above all the Christian varieties. Although he was deeply influenced by Eastern religious ideas, especially during the 1920s and 1930s (Coward, 1985), and even practiced "certain yogic exercises" to calm himself during the difficult and momentous period of his self-analysis, most of his writings about Eastern materials were occasioned by requests from other scholars. Underlying his own emphasis on Western symbols and practices was the conviction that Eastern and Western minds are divided by a fundamental and virtually insuperable difference in orientation. The Eastern mind is introverted, one that seeks a deepening or sinking into the source of all existence, into the psyche itself. By contrast, the extraverted Western mind is one of religious exaltation and uplift toward a compelling outer reality, the Wholly Other. To the Western mind, the "style" of the East seems impractical, if not also antisocial and irresponsible; it is abnormal, morbid, or narcissistic. The traditional East, on the other hand, views the West's cherished extraversion as a commitment to the illusory perceptions and desires that chain the ignorant to the world of suffering and from which the Eastern mind struggles to escape (Jung, 1943b, 1954f).

Neither mind, according to Jung, is ordinarily capable of fully comprehending the other. Jung himself was always apologetic for presuming to write about Eastern ideas and practices. To the Westerner who would imitate Indian practices and sentiments, Jung (1943b) addresses a warning.

> As a rule nothing comes of it except an artificial stultification of our Western intelligence. Of course, if anyone should succeed in giving up Europe from every point of view, and could actually *be* nothing but a yogi and sit in the lotus position with all the practical and ethical consequences that this entails, evaporating on a gazelle-skin under a dusty banyan tree and ending his days in nameless non-being, then I should have to admit that such a person understood yoga in the Indian manner. But anyone who cannot do this should not behave as if he did. He cannot and should not give up his Western understanding; on the contrary, he should apply it honestly, without imitation or sentimentality, to understanding as much of yoga as is possible for the Western mind (p. 568).

Jung said that he was "in principle against the uncritical appropriation of yoga practices by Europeans" (p. 571), for not only does the rationalistic Western mind too easily undervalue what it does not know and does not understand, but it also is unwilling and unprepared to have light thrown into the dark corners of its unconscious.

Rather than taking up the spiritual techniques of the East in a forced imitation that is thoroughly Christian, Western seekers would be well advised, says Jung (1954f), to look within their own traditions for an introverted tendency similar to the East's. "If we snatch these things directly from the East, we have merely indulged our Western acquisitiveness, confirming yet again that 'everything good is outside,' whence it has to be fetched and pumped into our barren souls" (p. 483). Individuals who would truly learn from the East will look for the Eastern values within the riches of their own psyches, rather than seeking them outside of themselves. Only by coming to terms with Western "spiritual pride and blasphemous self-assertiveness," and by overcoming their fear of the unconscous, can Western individuals discover the "self-liberating power of the introverted mind" (p. 484).

The way inward is especially difficult for persons in the West, even for those as naturally disposed toward introversion as Jung seemed to be. The reason, he says, is that the West has developed nothing comparable to the Eastern techniques of meditation—nothing, that is, except the psychology of the unconscious. In the course of psychotherapy, Jung's patients brought to him dream and fantasy images with a concentric, radial, or quadratic order. These reminded him of the ancient meditative symbols of the East. Finding remarkable agreement between the insights of the East and the results of his own research, Jung chose the Sanskrit word *mandala* and the Latin-derived term *quaternity* for these central symbols of wholeness and completion (Jung, 1943b). At the same time, he searched into the Western past for further evidence of the dynamics of these and related symbols that he seemed to find everywhere.

Gnosticism

Among the first of the religious traditions to gain Jung's interest was Gnosticism (Hoeller, 1982; Segal, 1992; Segal, Singer, and Stein, 1995). The Gnostic movement came into being during the Hellenistic period of transition and profound spiritual turmoil brought about by the convergence of Greek culture and the Oriental civilizations of the areas conquered by Alexander the Great during the fourth century B.C.E., including Egypt, Palestine, Syria, Babylonia, and Persia. At the beginning of the Christian era, after several centuries of Greek dominance, the already-syncretic East rose up in "spiritual counterattack" and flooded the Hellenic culture with its own content. The outcome was a new and pervasive SYNCRETISM, an intermingling of Babylonian astrology, Hellenistic Judaism, Platonic and Stoic ideas, and various Eastern mystery cults, to name only some of the chief elements. Standing out among the spiritual movements of this time is the group known to us under the name "Gnostic" (Jonas, 1963; Pagels, 1979).

The Gnostic Drama: The reader who knows little or nothing about the Gnostic movement will be astonished to discover the dimensions of the super-cosmic drama about which it was centered. "Out of the mist of the beginning of our era," writes Hans Jonas (1963)

> there looms a pageant of mythical figures whose vast, superhuman contours might people the walls and ceiling of another Sistine Chapel. Their countenances and gestures, the roles in which they are cast, the drama which they enact, would yield images different from the biblical ones on which the imagination of the beholder was reared, yet strangely familiar to him and disturbingly moving. The stage would be the same, the theme as transcending: the creation of the world, the destiny of man, fall and redemption, the first and the last things. But how much more numerous would be the cast, how much more bizarre the symbolism, how much more extravagant the emotions (p. xiii).

At the center of the Gnostic drama is a radical dualism—between good and evil, God and humankind, the divine and the material worlds. The PLEROMA, or the divine realm of light, and its deity, the true God, stand as the remote antithesis to the universe, the realm of darkness. Through a series of increasingly inferior emanations from the pleroma, initiated by the fall of the erring Sophia, our world of darkness and evil was brought into existence. The universe, according to the Gnostics, was created and ruled by seven archons or, alternatively, by the prince of the archons, the DEMIURGE. Ignorant themselves of the true God, the tyrannical archons rule the cosmos like a vast prison, enslaving humankind and preventing at death the return to God of the "pneuma" or "spark" in the human soul, the slumbering portion of the divine substance that lies ensnared in the cosmic creation. The pneumatic spirit in the individual is as alien to the appetites and passions of the body and psyche as God is to the whole of this world. Without redemption, this spirit remains in ignorant and intoxicated captivity.

The saving mystical knowledge, the *gnosis,* comes only through revelation, for the transcendent God is otherwise wholly unknown to this world. The Gnostic drama is basically a plan of salvation, detailing the story of the world's creation, its redemption, and its final dissolution when the deity will regain all its divine substance. The mystical knowledge of salvation is brought from the realm of light by a savior (Primal Man), who awakens the spirit and teaches it the rites and knowledge (often expressible only in negations) necessary for it to find its way through the encircling spheres guarded by the archons.

This extraordinarily elaborate system of teachings, which was championed by some of the greatest minds of the Hellenistic age, represented a serious threat to the early Christian movement, especially from within. Many of the early Christians were themselves Christian Gnostics. They identified the Old Testament god as the evil demiurge and distinguished him from the true God, who sent Primal Man in the form of Jesus to redeem the world through mystical knowledge. The perilous struggle with Gnosticism transformed the slightly organized and doctrinally undefined early Christian church into an institution with a hierarchy of authority, a closed canon, and a notion of orthodoxy. Gnosticism itself lost its initial impetus by the fourth century C.E. and underwent a gradual transformation into new forms that no longer carried its name.

Symbols of the Individuation Process: Among the new manifestations were varieties of mysticism. The Gnostic doctrines depicting the ascent of the soul through the celestial spheres became translated into a technique of subjective inner transformation that culminated—still in this life—in ecstatic union with the Absolute. Such a reinterpretation accords closely with Jung's own views of Gnosticism, views that led some of his critics to charge him with being himself a Gnostic. Jung emphasizes that he writes as a doctor and a scientist proceeding from verifiable facts, not as a Gnostic claiming supernatural knowledge. His chief interest was not in the Gnostic doctrines per se, but in the unconscious processes expressed in these "old religions with their sublime and ridiculous, their friendly and fiendish symbols" (Jung, 1935, p. 204). He found it interesting, too, that "millions of cultivated persons should be taken in by theosophy and anthroposophy," both of which he describes as "pure Gnosticism in Hindu dress" (Jung, 1943, p. 77; 1931b, p. 83).

Gnosticism, ancient and modern, is for Jung a symbolic representation of the differentiation and integration of the psyche. In language that, like the outpourings of the unconscious, is analogical, paradoxical, or circular, the Gnostic described and explored the process of individuation. "It is clear beyond a doubt," concluded Jung (1951a), "that many of the Gnostics were nothing other than psychologists" (p. 222). Much like the individual psyche, the Gnostic's universe begins as an undifferentiated world of chaotic darkness. Sophia, in an act that is reflective and yet driven by necessity, leaves the pleroma and creates the entire world out of her sufferings in the outer darkness, just as the unconscious feminine anima must become separated from the dawning masculine consciousness. The world she creates is ruled by the tyrannical demiurge—the ego—who, thinking that he himself is God, fails to comprehend that he must someday be dethroned by a superordinate authority—the self. Into the world dominated by the archons—representing the relatively autonomous archetypes—comes Primal Man, "the greater, more comprehensive Man, that indescribable whole consisting of the sum of conscious and unconscious processes" (Jung, 1951a, p. 189).

The various accounts of the dramatic progression of the Gnostic cosmos are filled with Jungian archetypal symbols representing the elements of the psyche and their integration. Most obvious is the pervasive principle of opposition, without which there would be no cosmos, no need for salvation, but also no growth or change, just as the psyche would not exist and grow without the energy and challenge from the tension of opposites. Equally clear is the possibility of gradually overcoming the opposites. Primal Man, for example, is composed of four parts (the quaternity) and is hermaphroditic (a union of opposites), both of which are symbols of differentiated wholeness. Such images as the four rivers of Paradise, the incestuous marriage *quaternio*, and the elaborate lists of syzygies also give expression to the process of differentiation and integration that Jung saw as the goal of the life of the human psyche.

Although Gnosticism provided Jung with a rich source of illustrations for his basic principles and insights, his collected works do not contain a comprehensive and systematic analysis of this material (see Segal, 1992). At the time that Jung was first interested in Gnosticism, very few Gnostic texts had been found. Most of what was known about Gnostic teachings came instead from the writings of its Christian opponents. Furthermore, according to Jung, Gnostic speculation and systematization had largely covered over the evidence of the immediate psychic experience. With such inadequate knowledge of the "strange and confused literature" of a movement separated from us by seventeen to eighteen hundred years, Jung turned

The two faces of alchemy: on the right, a man tends the fire under a round flask containing a winged dragon that symbolizes the alchemist's visionary experience; on the left, three men—an abbot, a monk, and a layman—confer in a library (Jung, 1952b, pp. 290–291; from Maier, *Tripus aureus,* 1618).

instead to alchemy, which he saw as the more accessible link between the Gnosticism of the first two centuries of our era and the contemporary psyche, especially the Christian one (Jung, 1938, p. 3).

Alchemy

Known popularly as a medieval precursor of modern chemistry that sought to transmute base metals into gold, alchemy is in actuality a remarkably complicated synthesis of protoscientific, philosophical, and religious ideas at least as old as Gnosticism. Most likely originating in Hellenistic Egypt, with roots in ancient metallurgy and astrology, the alchemical tradition was also known in India, China, Arabia, and—beginning in the twelfth century—western Europe. The word itself is Arabic, reflecting the importance of the Islamic contribution to Western alchemy during the early Middle Ages.

The Alchemical Doctrine: The goal of exoteric or practical alchemy—the transformation of base metals into precious ones—was wholly reasonable, given the reigning theory of matter, which was based on Aristotle's four elements. Aristotle argued that every substance is composed of fire, air, water, and earth, but in proportions that are found in it alone. Any substance can be transformed, it seemed to follow, by changing the proportions of its elements. Such a transformation might be achieved by finding another substance, the proportions of which are complementary to the first substance in a manner that yields the final elemental composition desired. Thus there was sufficient reason to believe that, once the right conditions were found for adjusting the four elements, a metal as dull, heavy, and commonplace as lead could be changed into shining, precious gold (Holmyard, 1957).

Only by the "charcoal burners," however, was alchemy so simply conceived. Esoteric or mystical alchemy involved an elaborate COSMOLOGY in which the microcosm of the human being and the macrocosm of the universe were conceived as intimately interrelated. Like human beings, metals were thought to be born, to change, and to be perfectible, through death and resurrection. To the alchemists, the transformations they sought to carry out in their laboratories were means for the redemption, the recovery of the original perfection, of the divine world-soul, which is mirrored simultaneously in matter and in spirit. Because macrocosm and microcosm correspond to one another, the alchemists' transformation and perfection of metal effected at the same time a transformation and perfection of their own souls (Burckhardt, 1960).

Although it is impossible to spell out precisely how the work was done or what final results were achieved, three distinct stages in the process of tranformation can be characterized. The first of these is the NIGREDO, or blackness stage, which signifies a state of dissolution and decomposition, a return to the original dark chaos of primal matter. Alternatively, if it is assumed that the alchemist is working with a substance already separated into its component parts, the *nigredo* refers to the outcome of the union of opposites and the death of what results from this union. The ALBEDO, or whiteness stage, corresponds on the laboratory level to coagulation, represented by salt or the purified white ash, and on the spiritual plane, to resurrection. The *albedo* denotes the achievement of the first principal goal, the outcome of a series of processes that requires furnaces of varying temperatures and an elaborate array of stills, flasks, and other apparatus, including the alchemist's miraculous spherical vessel. Finally, by raising the heat of the fire to the highest possible intensity, the RUBEDO, or redness stage, follows and the final goal of the alchemist is reached (Eliade, 1956; Jung, 1952b, 1955–1956).

The symbolic character of this process becomes more apparent when we consider the various ways in which the final goal, the *rubedo* stage, is conceptualized. Best known perhaps is the philosopher's stone, which paradoxically is—in words attributed to the Greek alchemist Zosimos—"this Stone which is not a stone, a precious thing which has no value, a thing of many shapes which has no shapes, this unknown which is known of all" (quoted in Eliade, 1956, p. 164). The goal may also be a red or white tincture; the panacea or *elixir vitae* that brings prolongation of life or immortality; philosophical gold or golden glass; a carbuncle or rose; or a winged hermaphroditic creature representing the unity of body, soul, and spirit. It is most unlikely, of course, that any of these or similar substances and forms was actually materialized by the alchemists, who included some of the wisest men of the day. Yet their self-sacrificing persistence would suggest that the inner transformation they simultaneously sought did not wholly elude them.

Symbols of Psychic Transformation: Jung's cautious and painstaking exploration of the vast literature of alchemy convinced him that its authors were dealing primarily with "psychic processes expressed in pseudochemical language" (Jung, 1952b, p. 242). In the alchemist's day, says Jung, matter was essentially an unknown, and into this darkness the alchemists projected their own psychic processes. Some alchemists surely were aware of the deeper symbolic meaning of their art, suggested by the moral and philosophical interpretations they gave it. But the majority, Jung thought, did not realize that the most fundamental and significant transformations were occurring within their own unconscious psyches. With the discovery that many of the fantasy and dream symbols of his patients resembled the images of the alchemists, Jung undertook a study of alchemy that preoccupied him for the last 30 years of his life.

Jung came to believe that alchemy is a highly sophisticated symbol system, boundlessly amplified, representing the archetypes of the collective unconscious and the process of individuation. The alchemist's formula of "dissolve and coagulate" sums up the same process that the analytical psychologist describes as differentiation and integration. The spirit Mercurius, identified by the alchemists with quicksilver, as well as with earth and water, air and fire, spirit and soul, is considered to be both young and old, good and evil, masculine and feminine, and the very

The hermaphroditic Mercurius, standing on sun and moon as befits his dual nature, ripens under the sun's rays in the alchemical vessel (Jung, 1952b, p. 66; from *Mutus liber,* 1702).

transformative substance itself. According to Jung, Mercurius represents the collective unconscious, as well as the individuation process and its goal, the self (Jung, 1952b).

The various stages of the alchemical process symbolize the stages of the process of individuation. The *nigredo* stage, which was experienced as melancholy in alchemy, marks the encounter with the dark shadow. It signals the dawning awareness of the chaos of opposite and conflicting tendencies within the psyche. With confrontation of the archetypes and progressive unification of opposites, achieved only by suffering through the "purgatorial fire" of self-discovery, the unconscious gradually becomes illuminated and the *albedo* state is reached. The final, *rubedo* stage, so variously and remarkably symbolized, represents the fully balanced unification of the differentiated psyche, the ideal of wholeness that Jung calls the self.

The possibility that preoccupation with chemical substances and arcane symbols might bring about constructive and systematic changes within the psyche becomes more comprehensible when we consider the prerequisites for engaging in alchemical work. Success in this endeavor was thought to depend on the alchemist's ethical and religious attitudes. Many alchemists were devout Christians, and, according to Jung (1952b), alchemy in the West was a continuation of or an undercurrent to the reigning Christian tradition. In their desire for a total union of opposites, however, the alchemists also strove to overcome the conflict of good and evil, looking not only for their own salvation but also for the redemption of the entire cosmos. In order to comprehend and carry out this divinely inspired work, the aspirants were forced by the host of paradoxes, obscure symbols, and incomprehensible leaps to recognize the limits of human reason and to turn inward in prayer and meditation. If they were to join the few sages truly endowed with understanding, they also had to renounce all covetousness, all attachment to their own egos, turning instead toward others—or nature itself—in an attitude of compassion. Only then could they hope for permission from a master to undertake the work (Burckhardt, 1960).

Alchemy began to decline with the publication in 1661 of Robert Boyle's revolutionary book, *The Sceptical Chymist,* which undercut the four-element theory that was the apparent foundation of alchemy (Holmyard, 1957). Its spiritual and intuitive outlook was already being challenged in the fifteenth century by the humanistic and rationalistic thought developing at the time, although alchemical writings continued to appear in the sixteenth and seventeenth centuries (Burckhardt, 1960). The passing of alchemy as a living tradition did not, however, leave the Western psyche without a symbol system expressing the process of individuation. The trail along which Jung leads us, from Gnosticism through alchemy, brings us finally to Christian symbols and rites that, though rooted in this remarkable past, remain alive today for large numbers of people.

The Christ Figure

As we have already observed, many of those within the Gnostic and alchemical traditions were Christians. According to the Christian Gnostics, Christ was the Anthropos, Primal Man, who comes from the pleroma with the redeeming mystical knowledge. The alchemists paralleled Christ with the philosopher's stone, the goal of their obscure art (Jung, 1952b). Wherever he appears, Christ is interpreted by Jung as a representative of the most central archetype, the self.

Various of Christ's attributes mark him as a symbol of the self: his CONSUBSTAN-TIALITY with the Father and his birth from a virgin mother; his crucifixion and resurrection; his role as a savior and bringer of healing; his androgynous character, expressed most clearly in noncanonical writings; his assimilation to the image of the fish, which, like the serpent, appears suddenly from out of the depths; or, more generally, his continuity with a variety of other archetypal figures, including Adam and Job, as well as Mithras and a number of other Near Eastern gods who die young and are born again. On the other hand, the sublimity of Christ's perfect goodness indicates that, from a psychological perspective, he lacks archetypal wholeness or totality. Missing is the dark side of the psyche, the element of evil, which in fulfill-ment of the law of enantiodromia appears inexorably as the Antichrist.

The paradox contained in the conflict between perfection and wholeness (see Jung, 1952a) reflects the paradoxicality of all opposites and their conjunction. Christ's crucifixion on the cross (a quaternity symbol) between the two thieves (the

An early nineteenth-century French woodcut of the crucifixion on the Tree of Life. The theme of dis-memberment also suggests psychic metamorpho-sis, through differentiation.

opposites) vividly symbolizes the intense suffering and the apparent annihilation that is part of the conjunction of opposites, especially when emphasis on one of them accentuates their seeming irreconcilability. As with Christ, so for the individual who takes seriously the mandate of individuation, the "acute state of unredeemedness"—including the painful awareness of the world's suffering that sets off delight in life's splendor—comes to an end only with the words, "It is finished" (Jung, 1951a, p. 70). Individuals who would genuinely undertake the "imitation of Christ," Jung (1932) suggests, are required not simply to copy his life and virtues, though that in itself would be far from easy. Rather, they must try to live their own lives as truly as Christ lived his (p. 340), risking the misjudgment, torture, and crucifixion that are the lot of those who run counter to their own times. To follow Christ, in other words, is to tread the lonely and difficult road of individuation, allowing the ego—the ordinary person that one thinks one is—to be put to death in order that the self—the Son of God—may become incarnate within.

The Idea of the Trinity

The psychological meaning of the Christ figure is examined from a somewhat different perspective in Jung's (1948b) analysis of the Christian doctrine of the Trinity—the Father, Son, and Holy Ghost who are three persons and yet one. Jung suggests that the gradually evolved idea of the Trinity symbolically represents a three-part process of maturation that occurs within the individual and expresses itself in various myths and rituals, especially those centering on the events of birth, puberty, marriage, and death. The Person of the Father symbolizes the psyche in its original state of undifferentiated wholeness, the unreflective consciousness of children who accept without question the pattern of life given them by their parents and their society. From the Father is born the Son, who, being of the same substance as the Father, represents the progressive transformation of this substance, the human psyche. The differentiation of the Son from the Father corresponds to the growth of reflection and discrimination, which provides the basis for the conscious effort of young people to separate from, and perhaps even oppose, their parents and habitually learned modes of life. It is a conflictual and relatively brief stage of transition, reflected in the early death of the Son.

The Holy Ghost represents a return to the initial stage of the Father, but with the reason and reflection gained in the second stage remaining intact. Psychologically, the third stage consists of a new level of consciousness that recognizes the authority of the unconscious, perhaps projected—and here lie spiritual dangers—into some external authority. It is the passing beyond childish dependence and adamant independence, through a series of fateful transformations that often have a numinous character, to a state of self-critical and humble submission to a higher reality.

An Incomplete Quaternity: As Jung demonstrates, similar trinitarian ideas can be found in Babylonian, Egyptian, and Greek mystic and philosophical traditions, as well as in contemporary dreams. He suggests, however, that the Trinity is actually a quaternity, a symbol of wholeness, the fourth element of which has been rejected and thereby cast into the role of adversary. If the Trinity is correctly understood as a process, a fourth would be necessary to bring it to wholeness or totality, for a fourth element would provide the energizing opposition essential for the process of actualization. What is missing from the Trinity, like the fourth or inferior function that remains wholly unknown to individual consciousness, is the principle of evil. Without the counterwill of Satan, who is one of God's sons, the

The Trinity—consisting of Father, Son, and Holy Ghost (the dove)—becomes a quaternity in this painting by Valásquez, *Coronation of the Virgin.*

Trinity would have remained a unity. In Jungian terms, without the opposition of the shadow, there would be no psychic development and no actualization of the self.

The Trinity is one-sided not only because it is perfectly good, but also because it is exclusively masculine. Thus, in another context, Jung (1938) suggests that the feminine element would be required to complete the Trinity. In 1950 Pope Pius XII proclaimed the dogma of the Assumption of the Blessed Virgin, whereby "Mary as the bride is united with the son in the heavenly bridal-chamber, and, as Sophia, with the Godhead" (p. 458). Jung (1952a) greeted this restoration of the quaternity, foreshadowed long before in medieval art and literature, as "the most important religious event since the Reformation" (p. 464). Yet, because Mary's immaculate conception left her free of sin, her assumption into heaven introduced no evil into the realm of the Trinity. The Catholic Church's attempt to create a "quaternity without shadow" therefore did not quite succeed, says Jung, because the devil was still excluded (Philp, 1958, p. 219).

Although Jung's answer to H. L. Philp's (1958, p. 216) question "Who compose the quaternity?" provides little real clarification, Jung obviously does not intend both Satan and the Virgin Mary to be included, forming a quinary. The quaternity is an empirical fact, he says, not a logical concept. Yet his brief allusion to the elements of woman and evil in his Terry Lectures (1938), as well as his comments about the Catholic quaternity, would suggest that evil is the essential fourth element and that the feminine is the "matrix of the quaternity," the anima that often personifies the unconscious (p. 63). Jung is vague enough that the puzzlement of various critics (e.g., Dry, 1961; Moreno, 1970; Philp, 1958) is understandable.

Catholic Advantage and Protestant Opportunity: If Mary's assumption into heaven did not truly succeed in creating a quaternity, it is still a dogma that gives the Catholic a distinct edge over the Protestant. Protestantism's neglect of the feminine leaves it, remarks Jung (1952a), with "the odium of being nothing but a *man's religion.* . . . Protestantism has obviously not given sufficient attention to the signs of the times which point to the equality of women" (p. 465).

The neglect of the feminine is but one aspect of the Protestant's abandonment of the dogmatic symbols, codified ritual, and ecclesiastical authority that serve Catholics as "spiritual safeguards" against the powerful forces of the unconscious. Left alone with God, Protestants must accept the grave risk of facing unaided the terrifying power of the images that have sunk back into the unconscious. In accepting the responsibility for their souls, however, they gain the great opportunity for immediate religious experience (Jung, 1938).

Jung was himself a Protestant, belonging to "the extreme left wing," and we sense throughout his works the spirit of a solitary man diligently working out his own salvation. He was nonetheless deeply interested in the doctrines and rites of the Catholic Church. His admiring fascination with the Catholic tradition is further illustrated in his analysis of the Mass.

Transformation Symbolism in the Mass

Jung's essay on the Roman Mass is continuous with his reflections on Gnosticism, alchemy, and the Trinity. He prefaces his study of the rites of the Eucharist with an examination of some of its New Testament sources; a review of the sequences of events in the ritual as represented by the church; and an extended consideration of parallel sacrificial and transformational symbols in "pagan" antiquity, especially in the visions of Zosimos, a non-Christian Gnostic and alchemist of the third century C.E. (Jung, 1954g). "So far as the dramatic course of the Mass represents the death, sacrifice and resurrection of a god and the inclusion and active participation of the priest and congregation," writes Jung (1954f), "its phenomenology may legitimately be brought into line with other fundamentally similar, though more primitive, religious customs" (p. 246). Among the themes that he finds in these comparative materials are the fiery sacrificial sword; bloody rites of flaying, decapitation, and dismemberment; immersion, soaking, and boiling of sacrifical elements; and ritual anthropophagy, the eating of human flesh. However unpleasant these references to gross and undifferentiated images and rites may be—and here Jung reminds us that the story of Christ's crucifixion contains elements hardly less horrifying—Jung believes that these parallels serve to demonstrate that "the most important mystery of the Catholic Church rests, among other things, on psychic conditions which are deeply rooted in the human soul" (p. 267).

In the Mass, says Jung, the participant celebrates a father's deliberate sending of his son into a gravely dangerous situation that inexorably culminates in the son's execution by a method both humiliating and extraordinarily painful. Because the Father and the Son are of the same substance, however, the punishment is in effect inflicted upon God Himself—in the same pattern as the ritual slaying of the king, which was carried out as a rite of fertility and prosperity. Like the king who dies to save his people from famine, God is sacrificed for the salvation of humankind. The Christian tradition asserts, of course, that Christ's death was necessary in order to save human beings from their own sin and guilt. This view, Jung argues, is a misleading rationalization for an otherwise inexplicable cruelty. Yahweh's fits of rage in the Old Testament, and his woefully inadequate efforts as the Gnostic demiurge to create a perfect world, suggest that the guilt is God's, and not that of his faulty creatures. Thus it is He who must be sacrificed.

The Meaning of Sacrifice: Jung attempts to uncover the psychological meaning of the extraordinary events celebrated in the Mass by examining the nature of

Human sacrifice among the Aztecs (from the Codex Magliabecchiano). Thousands of victims were annually offered to the gods to ensure the continued rising and setting of the sun. A Spanish observer was struck by "how cleverly this devilish rite imitates that of our Holy Church, which orders us to receive the True Body and Blood of our Lord Jesus Christ" (Diego Duran, quoted in Fagan, 1984, p. 228).

sacrifice. True sacrifice, he says, requires a conscious giving up of something with which a person has identified, without expecting something in return. That is, a person parts with the gift as though it were to be destroyed (as indeed it is in a burnt offering). If I have truly identified myself with the gift, then I am in effect destroying myself. Such is merely an apparent loss, however, for only those who possess themselves can give themselves away. Thus, to sacrifice myself, forgoing any further claim, is to demonstrate a considerable degree of self-knowledge. It also signals self-control, the capacity to surrender the ego for some higher purpose.

The sacrificial gifts that are presented at the altar during the Mass are the bread and wine, multilayered symbols that are inexhaustibly complex and ambiguous. From one perspective, they are symbols for the physical and spiritual fruits of human civilization, and, as substances derived from plants, for the life that undergoes a seasonal dying and resurrection. From another perspective they are unitary substances made up of countless grains of wheat and many grapes, just as the mystical body of the church is composed of a multitude of believers. From yet another perspective, the masculine wine and the feminine bread represent the androgynous nature of Christ, which signifies the union of opposites within him. What is sacrificed, concludes Jung, is "nature, man, and God, all combined in the unity of the symbolic gift" (p. 255).

The Mystery of Transformation: The sacrificial meal and the ritual that surrounds it constitute, according to Jung, the "rite of the individuation process."

> The psychology of this process makes it easier to understand why, in the Mass, man appears as both the sacrificer and the sacrificed gift, and why it is not man who is these things, but God who is both; why God becomes the suffering and dying man, and why man, through partaking of the Glorified Body, gains the assurance of resurrection and becomes aware of his participation in Godhead (p. 263).

As God sent his Son as a living sacrifice, so the self compels the sacrifice of the ego, which, as the self's exponent in consciousness, is like a son to the self. As Christ is crucified and dies, or the priest–victim in the vision of Zosimos is slain through dismemberment, so the ego must die through the difficult and torturous act of self-recollection. By this means individuals become aware of their selfish aims and fragmented, scattered elements. And as Christ rises up again and returns to the

Father, so the human soul is transformed by the mystery of the Eucharist into a totality, the self that is symbolized by the resurrected Christ.

The Mass, Jung concludes, is the outcome of a process that began many thousands of years ago in the individual psyches of gifted shamans, whose isolated experiences gradually became universalized with the progressive development of consciousness. Under the dramatic cover of "mysteries" and "sacraments," and through a complex of religious teachings and rituals, the individuation process became the collective experience of countless numbers of people. To describe the Mass in psychological terms is not to explain away the mystery, however, for the real nature of the psychic process is itself an unfathomable mystery. Jung sought only to bring this mystery "a little nearer to individual consciousness, using the empirical material to set forth the individuation process and show it as an actual and experienceable fact" (p. 296).

Answer to Job

Published in the last decade in Jung's life and ten years after the first versions of the essays on the Trinity and the Mass, his *Answer to Job* (1952a) returns to some of the themes we have already discussed. With this work Jung decided to "deal with the whole problem," as completely and explicitly as possible and without regard for the storm it would raise. His conclusion that humankind plays a central role in the redemption of God made this book perhaps the most controversial of his writings. It is a complex and occasionally obscure work, and we content ourselves here with a review of the main argument.

A Study of Psychic Facts: At the outset it will be well for us to distinguish among three possible referents for the word "God": God as a metaphysical entity, God as an archetype, and God as an image. As an empirical scientist, Jung consid-

A contemporary concelebration of the Roman Catholic Mass. The broken wafers of bread held by the priests symbolize the broken body of Christ and thus his sacrificial death. A small piece is dropped into the chalice of wine, thereby mingling the body and blood of Christ.

ered himself wholly unqualified to discuss the first of these, which theologians and metaphysicians consider to be largely beyond human experience. The second is an unknown and unknowable psychic force posited by Jung to account for recurrent mythic ideas and images. Only the third referent, the God image, is present in experience, and that, of course, in some considerable variety. The reader of Jung must remember that whenever Jung uses the word "God," as well as words such as "Christ," "Trinity," "Satan," and "pleroma," he is referring to *images,* not to metaphysical entities that exist independent of the human psyche. Although Jung carefully makes this distinction at various places in his works, he often writes, perhaps of necessity, from a subjective view, that is, from within the mythic structure, as though he were taking the images at face value. We must continually remind ourselves that Jung is always writing about *psychic* facts, however he may happen to refer to them.

The Biblical Drama Reconstructed: In his essay on Job, Jung re-creates the divine drama that runs thoughout the Old and New Testaments. Drawing on both biblical and extrabiblical sources, Jung acknowledges that he writes from the personal and emotional perspective of a modern layperson and physician brought up in the Christian tradition and deeply concerned about the contemporary situation.

From out of the eternal perfection of the pleroma, Jung begins, God creates the heavens and the earth. But already on the second day, when God separates the waters and creates the firmament, there is an ominous note. Unlike the work of the other days of creation, the great division of the second day is not greeted by the Creator as good. Into the world below the firmament God places a copy of Himself, Adam, as well as copies of His sons Satan and Christ, in the persons of Cain and Abel. Like Yahweh (the name by which the Hebrews referred to God), who is married to Israel but eternally associated with Sophia, Adam has two wives: Lilith, the daughter of Satan, who is his first wife, and Eve, the wife known to us in the Bible. Life for Adam and Eve is soon disturbed by the appearance of a serpent who, more conscious than they, is an early indication of Satan's penchant for mischief. It is not long before tragedy strikes again, when Cain kills Abel.

The Creator's plan continues to go afoul as Satan takes the human species under his wing, experimenting with it and giving it knowledge that was reserved for the pleroma. Yet even a measure so drastic as drowning all but a chosen few fails to purge Yahweh's creatures of their disobedience. Satan, meanwhile, remains hidden and blameless under the hem of his father's garment. Forgetful of his coexistence with Sophia in the pleroma, Yahweh takes Israel as his wife. His masculine perfectionism, however, closes out Eros and thus genuine relationship, and he thereby becomes a jealous and mistrustful husband who sees no purposes apart from his own. The more completely he forgets Sophia, the embodiment of Wisdom, the more obsessed he becomes with the faithfulness of his people.

One fateful day Satan insinuates that Job, a good man who had heretofore escaped Yahweh's suspicion, is faithful to Yahweh only because life for him has been abundant and happy. Forthwith and in violation of His own commandments, Yahweh unleashes the destructive forces that rob Job of his possessions, his servants, his children, and his health. All that remain are his wife and a few friends, who bring him no consolation. When the pious and obedient Job prostrates himself before Yahweh and asks *why,* Yahweh thunders at him for 71 verses about His own omnipotence. Although Job finally gives way to Yahweh's brute force, he secretly gains a knowledge of God that God Himself does not have. By insisting that Yahweh show him the justice in his terrible fate, Job forces God to reveal the unconscious antinomy in His own nature, the source of His tremendous power. On the one hand Yahweh wants the love and worship of humankind and wants to be praised as wise and just. On the other hand he behaves like an irritable, power-drunk tyrant, wholly indifferent to human life and happiness. Yahweh proves himself to be in some respects less than human, to be an unconscious being who is thoughtless rather than omniscient and who projects his own unconscious side onto Job.

Job's new knowledge of God does not leave Yahweh untouched. "Could a suspicion have grown up in God," Jung asks, "that man possesses an infinitely small yet more concentrated light than he, Yahweh, possesses?" (pp. 375–376). In the few centuries between the writing of the Book of Job and the coming of Christ, the wisdom of Sophia comes gently to the fore, evidenced in the Book of Proverbs and the apocryphal Wisdom of Solomon. Sophia reinforces the growing reflection in Yahweh and compensates for Yahweh's attitude by showing human beings the kind and just side of their God. Her reappearance, like the archetypal visions of Ezekiel and Daniel, signals the imminence of a momentous change: God desires to transform Himself by becoming human. Yahweh had wronged the creature who had surpassed Him, and only by becoming a human being could He expiate this injustice and catch up with the more reflective and morally superior Job. Mary, as an incarnation of Sophia, is prepared with utmost care to become the Mother of God, for Yahweh finally sees the perverse intentions of His dark son, soon to be banished from heaven, and protects Mary by freeing her from original sin. Yahweh's purpose in becoming human at last reaches apparent fulfillment when His son Christ cries out from the cross, "My God, my God, why hast thou forsaken me?" At this moment God experiences what He had made Job suffer, and thus Job is given an answer.

The drama remains unfinished, however, for the incarnation itself is incomplete. Because of his virgin birth and his sinless nature, Christ was not truly an empirical human being. God therefore did not truly become a man and make reparation for the wrong He did to humankind. Reconciliation through the incarnation in Christ was only the beginning. Christ promised that a Counselor, the Holy Ghost, would come after him to indwell in Christ's "fellow heirs." Thus the process of incarnation becomes continuous and broadened, through persons who, without being conceived by the Holy Ghost or born of a virgin, will nevertheless become the children of God and the brothers and sisters of Christ.

In an even more ominous way the drama remains incomplete. Because God, with every good intention, incarnated Himself in a wholly good son and strove in other ways as well to demonstrate that He is Love itself, He failed to recognize and take into account His own dark side. Even His son Christ was suspicious of the radical transformation, and cautiously added the otherwise mysterious phrase "and lead us not into temptation" in his prayer to the Father who might well need reminding of His former inclinations toward humankind. God's benevolent one-sidedness leads to a dangerous accumulation of evil that finally breaks out of the collective unconscious in the visions of John of the Apocalypse, who, if he is also the author of the Epistles, had naively declared that in God there is "no darkness at all," but only love. The terrifying apocalyptic visions of the Revelation to John describe a fearful outpouring of unholy anger and horrible cosmic devastation. "A veritable orgy of hatred, wrath, vindictiveness, and blind destructive fury that revels in fantastic images of terror breaks out and with blood and fire overwhelms a world which Christ had just endeavoured to restore to the original state of innocence and loving communion with God" (p. 438). In incarnating only His light aspect, God paved the way for a tremendous enantiodromia: the Apocalypse and—following

Dürer's *The Apocalyptic Woman.* In the Book of Revelation she gives birth to a child who is snatched away from the dragon waiting to devour him and is borne up to God.

Christ's thousand-year reign—the temporary rule of the Antichrist, the mighty manifestation of the jealous Satan.

In the midst of Saint John's terrible drama there suddenly appears an omen of great moment: the vision of the sun woman, the feminine Anthropos, who is about to give birth. The newborn man-child, a symbol of the unity of opposites and the coming to consciousness of the self, is snatched up to God from the seven-headed dragon waiting to devour it, and disappears. Following further waves of bloody retribution and the brief reign of the Antichrist comes the final vision, the New Jerusalem that is Sophia, who is reunited with God at the end of time and thereby restores the original pleromatic state.

A New Responsibility: Within the more than epic dimensions of this drama, Jung sees the fate both of the individual and of the human race as a whole. The terrible antinomy of God, who must be feared at the same time that He is loved, reflects a dividedness in humankind's own soul. God cannot truly become human— human beings cannot truly become themselves—until the one-sided God image that identifies God with good and humankind with evil is brought more fully into human consciousness. Human beings can no longer remain blind and unconscious, Jung says, but must accept the new responsibility of carrying forward the process of individuation, of uniting within themselves the antinomy of God. Only when God is genuinely incarnated in human beings will Job have his answer.

Whether or not the human species will find itself equal to the remarkable powers that myth says the fallen angels gave to us depends on whether or not human beings can attain to a higher level of consciousness, a higher moral plane.

The four sinister horsemen, the threatening tumult of trumpets, and the brimming vials of wrath are still waiting; already the atom bomb hangs over us like the sword of Damocles, and behind that lurk the incomparably more terrible possibilities of chem-

Dürer's *The Four Horsemen of the Apocalypse,* whose bringing of massive destruction to the earth serves still today as a potent image of impending doom.

ical warfare, which would eclipse even the horrors described in the Apocalypse (p. 451).

Is there any sign of a resurgent longing for wholeness, for a healing of the split in God's, and therefore our, nature? Jung speculates that there is—in the dogma of the Assumption of the Virgin Mary, which suggests the divine marriage in the pleroma and the future birth of the divine child who will be incarnated in living human beings. Only with the conscious realization of wholeness, of the self, can humankind hope to escape the apocalyptic return of God's wrath, of the unconscious destructiveness that lies deep within us. In the apocryphal words of Christ that Jung repeatedly quotes, " 'Man, if indeed thou knowest what thou doest, thou art blessed: but if thou knowest not, thou art cursed, and a transgressor of the law' " (p. 459).

THE CONTINUING INFLUENCE OF JUNG'S PSYCHOLOGY

Although Jung strove to ground his work in a thoroughgoing empiricism, he repeatedly admitted that his writings were a subjective confession. He was writing, as it were, his own personal myth. This private myth, says Philip Rieff (1966), came to Jung as a revelation, and only through it and the prophetic role in which it cast him was he able to escape madness. His psychology is a continuing development of this revelation. It is "a vast collection of illustrations, not data; modes of support rather than actual testing" (p. 126). No clearly defined science, concurs James Olney (1972), could "ever hope to take its bearings in Jung's work," for Jung was more than a scientist. His works constitute "a large and complex metaphor for all that he and he alone knew about the process of becoming a self" (p. 149).

Whether or not these characterizations are fair—and to some degree they are—

Jung's personal myth obviously struck a chord in many others. His influence on certain prominent scholars was undoubtedly facilitated by his regular presence from 1933 to 1951 at the annual Eranos Conferences on the estate of the now deceased Olga Fröbe-Kapteyn near Ascona, Switzerland. Each year Mrs. Fröbe would call together nine or ten of the greatest scholars of the world—including historians of religion, ethnologists, depth psychologists, orientalists, physical and biological scientists, art historians, and theologians—for a "shared feast" (*eranos,* a name suggested by Rudolf Otto) of lectures and discussion dealing with human-kind's deepest experiences and their expression. Attending these conferences at one time or another were Heinrich Zimmer, Friedrich Heiler, Martin Buber, Carl Kerényi, Erich Neumann, Adolf Portmann, Gerardus van der Leeuw, Paul Radin, Mircea Eliade, Gershom Scholem, D. T. Suzuki, R. C. Zaehner, Henry Corbin, Herbert Read, and Joseph Campbell, to mention only some of the more notable contributors. Among the "many historians of religion" that Eliade (1969, p. 22) says were influenced by Jung were Eranos participants Zimmer, Kerényi, Corbin, and Campbell, and, we should add, Eliade himself (Ricketts, 1970; Ulanov, 1992).

Although Eranos was not strictly a Jungian gathering, Jung's presence during the first 20 years of the conferences and the evolving ideas that he presented there provided both focus and continuity. In recognition of his special presence, two of the Eranos Yearbooks, which still appear annually, were published as *Festschriften* to him, on his seventieth and seventy-fifth birthdays, respectively. The meetings held at Ascona in recent years, now sponsored by the Eranos Foundation established by Olga Fröbe, continue to reflect the influence of analytical psychology. A number of the lectures given at Eranos have been translated and brought together for the English reader in six volumes edited by Joseph Campbell (1954–1968), which testify to Ira Progoff's (1966) judgment that "The collected Eranos publications have become a major library of the humanities, an evolving encyclopedia of symbolism as an expression of the human spirit" (p. 311).

Jung's influence today is unmistakable and direct. Indeed, there is a large and still growing secondary literature, most of it with an explicitly religious focus. Some of these works explore and evaluate Jung's own thinking on religion (e.g., Aziz, 1990; Chapman, 1988; Charet, 1993; Edinger, 1992; Jaffe, 1990; Keintzel, 1991; C. D. Smith, 1990; Spies, 1984); others extend it, in a variety of directions. To give the reader a clear sense of this continuing influence, we will briefly review some representative works in six related though separate areas.

The Critique and Renewal of Christianity

Much of the secondary literature mirrors Jung's convictions that (1) we live in an age of crisis, inner and outer; (2) many people today are finding it difficult if not impossible to relate to traditional religious forms; and (3) analytical psychology can help foster a renewal of contemporary piety on both individual and institutional levels. As in Jung's case, the framework for this criticism and analysis is most often Christian.

John Dourley (1984, 1992), for example, who is a professor of religious studies, a Roman Catholic priest, and a Jungian analyst, elaborates on Jung's critique of Christianity as one-sided and cut off from its origins. To counter the trivializing and destructive tendency to reduce religious myth to literal and historical fact—and thus to set one system of revelation against another—Dourley recommends a return to the Gnostic conviction that the truth of the Christian mysteries lies in the human soul. Also seeking to restore the bridge between the external and historically conditioned expressions of story, dogma, and ritual, on the one hand, and the inner experience of contemporary individuals on the other, religious studies professor Wallace Clift (1982) draws on his years as an Episcopal priest to point to evidence of renewal already underway in the Christian community, albeit sometimes in the regrettable framework of an outdated world-view. Pressing like Dourley for a new appreciation of the symbolic meaning of the resurrection of Christ, Clift anticipates a new age of consciousness arising out of a contemporary reinterpretation of the doctrine of the Holy Spirit. The author of a book on Jung's "treatment" of Christianity, Jungian analyst Murray Stein (1985) has also coedited a volume with psychologist of religion and Jungian analyst Robert Moore that brings the Jungian perspective to bear on a variety of contemporary religious issues (Stein and Moore, 1987). Comparable works in the German literature include Gerhard Wehr's (1975) study of Jung and Christianity as well as Gerhard Zacharias's (1954) application of Jungian psychology to the task of theological and liturgical renewal.

The Feminine and Feminist Theology

Among contemporary psychological perspectives, Jung's seems to be exceptionally appealing to women. This is so, Demaris Wehr (1987, p. 6) suggests, because it is "a 'meaning-making' psychology" that takes seriously both inner subjectivity and its outer expression in myth and the creative arts. Jung seems to valorize certain "feminine" preferences and modes from the perspective of depth psychology, much as Carol Gilligan (1982) has done it on the basis of more traditional forms of psychological research. Thus when scholars turn to issues regarding women and the feminine in general, especially in the context of religion, they seem inevitably to draw on Jung's concepts and principles (e.g., Bitter, 1962).

The implications of Jung's perspective on the feminine for Christian theology have been investigated by Jungian analyst Ann Ulanov (1971, 1981), who attributes a number of individual and collective ills to the exclusion of feminine elements from religious symbolism, especially in the Protestant Christian tradition. Edward Whitmont (1982), also a Jungian analyst, celebrates the return of the goddess, the archetypal feminine, in the face of the naturally aggressive and even violent patriarchal trends that, though considered part of the natural evolution of human consciousness, are today threatening us with massive self-destruction. Whitmont finds in the myth of the quest of the Holy Grail a model for reconceiving our relationship to the world and controlling destructive aggression. The complex symbolism of the Grail, it may be recalled, was a long-standing interest of Emma Jung.

Jung's perspective on the feminine is also the subject of considerable criticism. Such feminist theologians as Rosemary Ruether and Mary Daly have rejected Jung's views as fundamentally androcentric (Wehr, 1987, p. 3). They maintain that, although Jung appears to appreciate the feminine, he is actually reducing it to the secondary role of complementing the masculine ego. Naomi Goldenberg (1990), who for years associated herself with the Jungian universe, including a stint at the Jung Institute in Zürich, eventually rejected Jung in favor of psychoanalysis. In positing the existence of disembodied, transcendent forces that shape human experience, she says, Jung's theory of archetypes "tends to be both anti-woman and anti-life" (p. 71). Wehr (1987), who writes as a proponent of both feminism and Jungian psychology, also considers Jung's views to be in certain respects androcentric and misogynistic—attitudes, she says, that are regrettably "ontologized," or made sacred, by the religious character of analytical psychology. While affirming

Jung's emphasis on the spiritual dimension of human experience, she will accept such terms as anima and animus only after they have been "de-ontologized" and liberated from their patriarchal context. A combination of feminism and Jungian psychology, she suggests, will allow a deeper understanding of the feminine as it emerges from women's experience than can be achieved by either approach alone.

Biblical Interpretation

A renewed sensitivity to experience, past and present, is also the goal of the biblical scholars who are turning to Jung's psychology, among others, to revive a field whose traditional methods of textual analysis are thought by some to be yielding diminishing returns (Scroggs, 1982). The general principles that would be featured in a Jungian approach to the Bible are laid out in a work by religious studies professor Wayne Rollins (1983), who has also contributed papers on this topic to several anthologies on Jung and religion (e.g., Martin and Goss, 1985; D. L. Miller, 1995). In addition to providing a glossary of archetypal symbols that appear in the Bible (e.g., numbers, colors, animals, and divine names), Rollins describes how the Jungian methods of amplification and active imagination can be fruitfully applied to scriptural texts. The chief gain of such an approach, Rollins says, would be a deeper appreciation of the role played by the psyche and its unconscious elements in the writing of the biblical texts as well as in reading them, by the authors' contemporaries and by us today.

A brief look at Genesis, chapters 1 through 3, will show how this approach differs from the orthodox psychoanalytic perspective. Jungians interpret these three chapters as a dramatization of the individuation process, of the emergence of the ego out of undivided wholeness—the dark and empty earth before creation—and its gradual differentiation and integration. The first serious threat to the increasingly complex wholeness of the self symbolized by the mandala–garden is the appearance from out of Adam of his feminine side, Sophia or wisdom, through an act of sacrifice (the giving up of a rib). But it is only through encounter with the serpent (symbolizing knowledge or dawning consciousness) and through succumbing to the temptation to eat the apple (seeking wholeness or self-realization) that Adam finally becomes aware of his human individuality and the tension between the conscious and the unconscious. Thus the "sin" of Adam and Eve, rather than being blameworthy, represents growth into consciousness, which inevitably separates the ego from the self. From then onward, Paradise—the self—becomes the background and final horizon of historical existence, an elusive goal symbolizing a new wholeness (Edinger, 1972; Kretschmer, 1955; Sanford, 1981b).

Whereas most efforts at Jungian biblical interpretation have been directed to figures in the Hebrew Bible, or Old Testament (Corey, 1995; Edinger, 1986; Kassal, 1980), Gerald Slusser (1986) provides a detailed Jungian analysis of the life of Jesus. Employing as his framework Joseph Campbell's (1968) monomyth of the hero, the archetype of development and renewal, Slusser argues that the cycle of life, death, and resurrection of Jesus provides a prototype of the true unfolding of human consciousness. Most of us, he thinks, are profoundly alienated from this destiny by our commitment to the rationalistic myth we have inherited from the Enlightenment. Observing a decline today in the myth of rationalism and a resurgence of interest in Eastern traditions and meditative practice, Slusser looks to the myth of Jesus as Hero as a means of illuminating the way toward wholeness.

Archetypal Phenomenology of Religion

An analysis of Jesus' life in terms of the hero myth, Slusser observes, brings home to us the kinship of Christianity with other religious traditions as well as with the PERENNIAL PHILOSOPHY that is said to underlie them all. Some other works inspired by Jung are also centered on some archetypal figure or process that recurs in various religious traditions. Particularly noteworthy is the massive and broad-ranging phenomenology of the idea of salvation carried out by Protestant theologian Hans Schär (1950) somewhat on the model of Friedrich Heiler's *Prayer* (1918). After a preliminary clarification of the contemporary yearning for salvation and an historical overview of the ideas of salvation in the world's religious traditions, Schär lays out a typology of nine forms of the experience, identified not according to content but in terms of their functions in human personality. Included among these types, for example, are *salvation through the experience of community,* which, in religious form, has been most fully elaborated in the Christian tradition; *salvation through boundedness,* a dogmatic acceptance of religious authority that disrupts the dialogue of self and life experiences; *salvation through constriction of the personality,* entailing sacrifice of some portion of a person's potentialities for a higher purpose, a type found in its most extreme varieties in India; and *salvation as the way to psychic wholeness (individuation),* when the ego is displaced by the self as the center of personality. Other notable archetypal studies of this sort include, in addition to Campbell's work on the hero, Erich Neumann's (1955) analysis of the structure and dynamic of the archetype of the Great Mother, Joseph Henderson's (1967) exploration of the archetype of initiation, and studies by various authors of the nature of evil (Beck, 1976; Curatorium, 1961; Sanford, 1981a).

Dialogue with the Religious Traditions

An increasing number of publications on Jungian psychology and religion bill themselves as "dialogues" between the two content areas. Rather than simply using analytical psychology as a framework for interpreting religious phenomena, these works also explore parallels between Jung's thought and the teachings of particular traditions, critically analyze his writings on these traditions, and explore the implications of analytical psychology for religious thinking and practice within specific traditions.

Eastern Religious Traditions: Few psychologists of religion have shown as deep an interest in Eastern thought as Jung, and fewer still have been as profoundly influenced by it. Yet we know that this interest was secondary to his fascination with alchemical and Christian themes, and that he had clear misgivings about any effort to transplant Eastern insights into the Western context. Canadian religious studies professor Harold Coward (1985) provides an invaluable discussion and analysis of Jung's relation to Eastern spirituality, which Jung designates by one of its basic motifs, yoga. Although Jung does give occasional attention to the particular *contents* of yoga, he was far more interested in its *form,* which he felt confirmed his own experiences, including his sense that consciousness extends far beyond the boundaries circumscribed by the Western scientific intellect. Although the influence of Eastern symbols and concepts, including the mandala, is explicit in Jung's formulations of the process of individuation and its goal, the self, his interpretations of them, Coward says, are distinctly his own. Jung was struck in particular by the Eastern notion of the union of opposites—in the divine itself and as the outcome of spiritual practice. Yet he rejected the orthodox Hindu conviction that it is possible to transcend the pairs of opposites in the course of one's life. Coward, assisted by J. F. T. Jordens and John Borelli, who also prepared an annotated bibliography on Jung and Eastern traditions for inclusion in the book, explores the limits of Jung's dialogue with the East and clarifies Jung's understanding of such concepts as KARMA, KUNDALINĪ, PRAKRTI, and PRĀNA.

In a more recent work, philosopher J. J. Clark (1994) places Jung's writings on Eastern thought in the wider context of the East-West dialogue. While noting Jung's considerable ambivalence regarding his Eastern "discoveries," Clark emphasizes the seriousness of these excursions into Eastern thought and their substantial role in shaping Jung's overall point of view. If Jung's accounts of Taoism, Yoga, and Buddhism are frequently flawed, Clark says after reviewing them, they nevertheless represent an admirably courageous effort to transcend the conventional wisdom of the West. Jung's dialogical mode of discourse and his postmodern, pluralistic outlook, which declines to privilege the Western point of view, is offered by Clark as a still-viable way to approach Eastern philosophical and religious materials. Genuine dialogue, he says, will remain forever elusive, but it must be pursued "if the human race is to live at peace with itself" (p. 191). The Jung-Buddhism dialogue in particular is advanced by a work edited by Daniel Meckel and Robert Moore (1992).

More personal accounts of the meeting of Jungian psychology and Eastern thought can be found in three other books. Two of them are coauthored by Marvin Spiegelman, a Jewish Jungian analyst who had early associations with Japanese and Hindu culture. In the first of these works, Spiegelman and Mokusen Miyuki (1985), a Jungian analyst who is also a Buddhist priest, reflect on the conjunction of East and West in their own lives and then undertake an analysis of the Zen tradition's oxherding pictures—believed to express the experience of *satori,* or enlightenment—in terms of the process of individuation. Miyuki also provides a Jungian perspective on various Japanese attitudes and Buddhist principles. In a subsequent work, Spiegelman and Arwind Vasavada (1987), a Hindu Brahmin who became a Jungian analyst, bring analytic psychology and aspects of the Hindu tradition into mutually illuminating dialogue. Vasavada, who spontaneously prostrated himself before Jung when he first met him, considers Jung a "consummate guru" who took on the identity of psychologist and doctor in order to be understood by the Western intellectual mind. In a third work, Radmila Moacanin (1986), a psychotherapist deeply influenced by Jungian psychology and Tibetan Buddhism, especially in its tantric form, provides an introduction to both traditions and then systematically explores their similarities and differences. Suggesting that Tibetan Buddhism serves in the West as a valuable counterbalance to deteriorating Western spiritual values, Moacanin interprets Jungian psychology as pointing to the same universal wisdom.

Western Religious Traditions: The dialogue that Jung initiated between analytical psychology and the Christian tradition was taken up by others well within his lifetime. Particularly notable is the work of Victor White (1952, 1960), an English Dominican priest and Thomistic theologian who, late in Jung's life, became one of his friends and collaborators. Ann Lammers (1994), in a volume in the Jung and Spirituality Series of Paulist Press, traces out this ten-year collaboration, which tragically ended in White's angry break with Jung when it seemed that their association had led to White's rejection by his religious order. The dialogue with Catholicism that White initiated continues today, most comprehensively in a collection of essays edited by Marvin Spiegelman (1988) in his series of books on the

various religious traditions and Jungian psychology. James Arraj (1991), who identifies himself as both Catholic and Jungian, directs his inquiry to the problems,
resources, and requirements for a genuine Jungian-Christian dialogue.

To assemble a volume of Protestantism and Jungian psychology, Spiegelman
(1994) invited the participation of some 50 members of the International Association of Analytical Psychology who were also Protestant clergy. The fact that relatively few responded, resulting in a volume that is noticeably slimmer than its
Catholic equivalent, may reflect, Spiegelman suggests, Jung's own ambivalence
toward Protestantism. Inevitably, given the range of Protestant views, the book
contains a rather diverse set of essays. The possibility of addressing a single Protestant tradition is illustrated by Jack Wallis (1988), who invites his fellow Quakers
to examine their faith and practice in the light of Jungian principles. Noting
fundamental points of harmony between the two traditions—the accent on first-
hand experience, the valorizing of the inner and the spiritual, the goal of harmonizing differences and opposites, the valuing of an inner voice and an inner light
for finding one's vocation, the presence of God in all human nature—Wallis challenges his readers to risk discomfort in facing the shadow side of personality and
considering whether Quaker teachings and practice always promote growth toward
wholeness.

Three other collections of essays take us beyond the Christian tradition. In a
gathering, now, of his own essays that include reflections on his experience of being
"a modern Jew in search of a soul," Spiegelman (1993) carries his series forward
with a volume dedicated to Judaism and Jungian psychology. In the Introduction,
Spiegelman gives his own views on the charge that Jung harbored anti-Semitic
sentiments (see Maidenbaum and Martin [1991] for a definitive review of this
question). Spiegelman's series also contains a book on Sufism and Islam (Spiegelman, Khan, and Fernandez, 1991). With two exceptions, the contributors to this
work are members of one or the other of two Sufi organizations, one centered in
England and the other in Seattle, Washington. The authors explore parallels between Jungian and Sufi principles and consider how Sufi training and practice
promote the individuation process. Joel Ryce-Menuhin's (1994) edited volume,
finally, combines Jungian essays on "the three monotheisms"—Judaism, Christianity, and Islam—with the goal of bringing the three traditions more fully into
dialogue. The essays on Sufism and Islam are almost all written by outsiders or by
Western converts. As Spiegelman points out in the introduction to his own volume,
Islamic scholars have not themselves pursued Jungian psychology the way those of
other faiths have.

Christian Spirituality

Although Coward's book and Martin and Goss's (1985) collection of essays, along
with a number of earlier studies (see Heisig, 1973), demonstrate that Jung's psychology is widely employed in scholarly research, obviously many also view it as a
major resource for personal spiritual growth. In the recent literature on analytical
psychology and religion, works on spirituality—nearly all written from a Christian
perspective—form the largest category. Two particularly prolific writers are Morton
Kelsey and John Sanford, both Episcopal priests trained in Jungian psychology.
Addressing both laypersons and ministers, these authors urge their readers to take
their dreams seriously as important sources of religious insight, and—in the spirit

of Batson's quest orientation—to construe their religious practice as a healing, inner journey toward wholeness and meaning (Kelsey, 1974, 1982; Sanford, 1968, 1981b). In England, the implications of Jung's psychology for the Christian life have been similarly explored by Christopher Bryant (1983), who is a member of an Anglican religious community.

The quite practical turn that this literature can take is represented in Betsy Caprio and Thomas Hedberg's (1986) *Coming Home; A Handbook for Exploring the Sanctuary Within*. The inner home they encourage their readers to seek is none other than the Jungian self. Punctuated with striking personal stories from anonymous contributors, engaging illustrations, and periodic worksheets for appropriating each chapter's ideas, this guide for spiritual growth is at the same time a nontechnical introduction to the principles of Jungian psychology. Another work of a distinctly practical bent is Chester Michael and Marie Norrisey's (1984) study of the relation between personality type and style of prayer. The personality type for each of their 457 participants, 75 percent of whom were women, was determined by means of the Myers–Briggs Type Indicator (MBTI), a highly popular personality test designed to assess individuals in terms of Jung's typology. These persons were then asked to report their experience with different forms of prayer suggested to them over a period of a year on the basis of the authors' theory. Virtually all reported that they found it helpful to use a form of prayer selected to be compatible with their personal disposition. Beyond analyzing a number of traditional forms of Catholic prayer and spirituality in typological terms, this book offers prayer suggestions for each of the 16 types derived from the MBTI.

The Alban Institute, a nondenominational membership organization that conducts research and provides educational, consulting, and publishing services to congregations around the world, has published two guides based on the MBTI. The first of these, which draws on Institute research, is directed to clergy differences in personality type and their implications for religious leadership (Oswald and Kroeger, 1988). The second, much briefer work considers congregational dynamics in the light of MBTI typological differences (L. Edwards, 1993). Otto Kroeger, a partner in a consulting firm that uses the MBTI exclusively, has also co-authored a more general book on the MBTI and its 16 types (Kroeger and Thuesen, 1988).

A dozen outstanding essays on Jung and Christian spirituality, including articles by Sanford and Kelsey, were assembled by Robert Moore (1988) as the inaugural volume in a series of Paulist Press publications on contemporary spirituality—Christian and non-Christian—and spiritual direction. Moore maintains that Jungian psychology is one of the most important resources now available for addressing today's spiritual crisis and the multitude of political, ecological, and social ills that threaten the very survival of our planet. Through its notion of a *collective* unconscious, Moore says, Jungian thought promises a way of transcending the narrow loyalties that Erikson has called pseudospeciation, thus providing a bridge for understanding among diverse cultural and religious communities. Through its recognition of the shadow side of human nature, it possesses vital means for confronting the demonic forces that profoundly disturb our political and social lives. But most important of all, says Moore, through its emphasis on the self as an ego-transcending source of inner wisdom and guidance, Jungian psychology offers an unparalleled resource for "the individual on pilgrimage." The volumes by Moore and Meckel (1990) and Meckel and Moore (1992) are also in this series.

EVALUATION OF THE JUNGIAN APPROACH TO RELIGION

The voluminous secondary literature that we have sampled here testifies to Jung's still-growing popularity among religious studies scholars, philosophers, members of the clergy, psychotherapists, literary critics, artists, and still others from various walks of life (Ulanov, 1992). So also does the increasing number of institutes dedicated to promoting the practice and application of Jungian psychology. Enthusiasm for Jung's work is particularly evident among scholars of religion. Fokke Sierksma (1950), for example, believes that Jung's is the only psychology that makes religious phenomena comprehensible without reducing them. Coward (1985, p. 79) writes that "No other individual in recent times has contributed more towards an understanding of the psychology of religious experience than Jung." Honored in his lifetime by major universities around the world, Jung possesses for many today an unequaled stature.

Others are less enthusiastic about Jung, some decidedly so. Many psychologists, especially those in American academic circles, have largely ignored him, not only because he deals with materials—such as religious symbols and myths—that mystify or repel them, but also because he relies primarily on clinical and armchair techniques of research rather than on experimentation and quantification (Hall and Lindzey, 1978). Jung's refusal to make the paradoxes, antinomies, and complex symbols of religious language conform to the logic and conceptual terms of contemporary science, as well as his tendency to be unsystematic and obscure, have made him relatively inaccessible. Richard Peters (1962), who edited and updated George Brett's classic history of psychology, declares many of Jung's later writings to be "so mysterious as to be almost undiscussable" (p. 730).

Although theologians and scholars of religion praise Jung for his attentiveness to the complex world of human piety, they are frequently critical of his particular interpretations of it. He fails to observe the limits of psychology, some argue, and he also misrepresents or distorts the doctrines, rituals, and images that compose the religious traditions he analyzed. We will examine some of the specific issues raised by these critics after first considering the scientific status of Jung's psychology in general.

A QUESTION OF SCIENCE

Much like psychoanalysis, analytical psychology is summarily dismissed by many psychologists as patently unscientific (Noll, 1994). Freud's advocates, in seeking to regain a proper hearing for his views, have tended to respond in one of two ways. Some have derived testable hypotheses from Freud's writings and then sought supporting evidence gathered by standard empirical procedures. Others have removed his theories from the realm of scientific discourse altogether, by reconceiving psychoanalysis as hermeneutics. The debate over Jung's views has taken a rather different turn. Although his theories, too, have been subjected to friendly reconstruction to ensure compatibility with current scientific thinking (Shelburne, 1988), or have been construed as a psychologial hermeneutic (C. A. Brown, 1981), Jung is often said to be an exemplar of a new, more adequate science that transcends the limited perspective of his critics. According to Fritjof Capra (1982), Jung's basic principles go well beyond the mechanistic view of traditional psychology, bringing his psychology "much closer to the conceptual framework of modern physics than any other psychological school" (pp. 186–187). In particular, the concepts employed by Jung to discuss the collective unconscious are "surprisingly similar to the ones contemporary physicists use in their description of subatomic phenomena" (pp. 361–362).

Traditional research methods have yielded some evidence bearing on Jung's theories, as in Richard Coan's (1974) finding of a pattern of pervasive sex differences that "corresponds well" to Jung's Eros and Logos principles (p. 174). The largest claims for empirical support, however, derive from less conventional research strategies. The outstanding case in point is the psychedelic research of psychiatrist Stanislav Grof (1985). Though acknowledging that even Jung's psychology falls short of encompassing the full range of phenomena observed during hundreds of sessions of LSD psychotherapy, Grof regards it as more adequate than any other. These drug-based observations, he declares, "have repeatedly confirmed most of Jung's brilliant insights." Together with the material that Grof (1988) later gathered during nondrug "holotropic therapy," these findings lend "strong support for the existence of the collective unconscious and for the dynamics of archetypal structures, Jung's understanding of the nature of libido, his distinction between the ego and the Self, recognition of the creative and prospective function of the unconscious, and the concept of the individuation process" (1985, pp. 190–191). In his own psychotherapeutic work with harmaline, a psychotropic plant extract used by shamans, Chilean psychiatrist Claudio Naranjo (1973) found that this substance evokes a remarkable array of Jungian archetypal images. Equally striking was the high rate of therapeutic benefit from a single exposure to the effects of this drug. In accord with Jungian views, encounter with dramatic archetypal material seemed to promote enduring personality integration.

Research on Jung's Typology in Relation to Religion

Such sweeping enthusiasm and exceptional methods themselves raise doubts of various kinds. Thus for now the best avenue of support will likely be more conventional forms of research. Applied to Jung's psychology, these have been largely limited to studies of his personality typology. Leon Gorlow, Norman Simonson, and Herbert Krauss (1966), for example, derived a set of 100 statements from Jung's writings on typology and then asked a group of introductory psychology students to indicate how each of the statements applied to them, by placing the statement along an 11-point scale. Factor analysis of these Q-sort data yielded eight factors, including five that clearly corresponded to Jungian types (e.g., the extraverted-feeling type, which accounted for the largest amount of common variance). After suggesting various explanations for the failure of the three remaining types to appear in their data, these investigators concluded that, on the whole, their results supported Jung's typology.

The most common instrument for researching Jung's typology is the Myers–Briggs Type Indicator. Correlations of the MBTI with standardized tests that have a scale measuring religious orientation in some form, along with data gathered from 2010 religious workers of various denominations, show *feeling* to be the typical superior function among religious individuals (Myers and McCaulley, 1985). A marked preference for feeling is likewise the dominant trend in the MBTI data that Oswald and Kroeger (1988, p. 22) gathered from 1319 ordained clergy representing a wide array of denominations.

Jung's (1921, p. 249) reference to "the intuitive teachings of religion" would also lead us to predict a predominance of intuition over sensing. This preference does in fact appear in conjunction with the Minister scale on the Kuder Occupational Interest Survey (Myers and McCaulley, p. 193), and Oswald and Kroeger's clergy show a much stronger preference for intuition than the general population (57 versus 24 percent). Still, half of Myers and McCaulley's religious workers are sensing types, and the proportion is even higher among the orthodoxly religious. This trend is particularly evident in a study by Tommy Poling and Frank Kenney (1986), who report that 82 percent of their sample of 93 Krishna Consciousness devotees were sensing types. By contrast, a comparison group of 52 Unitarian Universalists, whose tradition is well known for its liberal, nonritualistic views of religion, showed an equally extreme preference for the intuitive function. Christopher Ross's (1993) findings with Canadian subjects are equally striking: whereas 64 percent of the Anglicans indicated an intuitive preference, only 28 percent of the Catholics and 12 percent of the evangelical Protestants showed the same trend.

Warning against too simple a formula relating religiosity to psychological types, Ross (1992) speculates that the intuitive preference is related to a variety of liberal trends in religious thinking and spiritual practice. Among these trends are a less clear separation of religious and secular domains; less emphasis on membership in a religious community and the observation of specific rules of faith; greater openness to other religious traditions and to religious complexity, doubt, and change; and a preference for symbolic and metaphoric interpretations of religious texts. Using questionnaire items that he developed to assess such trends in religious orientation, Ross is now gathering empirical data to test their relation to the MBTI types (Ross, Wiess, and Jackson, 1996).

Although highly interesting in themselves, findings with the MBTI are at best ambiguously related to Jung's psychology of religion. On the one hand, the indicators of religiosity bear no obvious relation to the numinous experience that Jung considered the mark of religion proper. On the other hand, in spite of the MBTI's enormous popularity among proponents of analytical psychology, research indicates that what it measures may not be Jung's types but basic dimensions of personality that also appear—more clearly identified—on other inventories. On the basis of their own findings, Robert McCrae and Paul Costa (1989) propose reinterpreting the MBTI sensing–intuition index as a measure of *openness to experience,* which does seem to be a clearer way of understanding the association of the index's intuition pole with liberal religiosity. Reinterpreting the thinking–feeling scale as a measure of some aspects of *agreeableness,* these researchers note its positive relation to needs for affiliation, nurturance, and succorance, and its negative relation to needs for aggression, counteraction, and dominance. Thus the tendency for religious persons to score in the direction of feeling (i.e., agreeableness) would seem to provide support for object-relations theory rather than for Jung's. McCrae and Costa recommend that the Jungian framework and the MBTI be utterly disengaged from each other.

For the immediate future, those wishing to establish Jung's theories on a traditional scientific foundation will have to rely on indirect support. Toward this end, psychiatrist and researcher Anthony Stevens (1982) has integrated evidence from diverse quarters: the work on mother–infant attachment by John Bowlby, the cross-species ethological studies of Konrad Lorenz, and in particular the recent research on brain lateralization. In light of research over the past several decades, says Stevens, Jung's

> overriding conviction that the life-experience of individual men and women is profoundly influenced by phylogenetically acquired "dominants" is more difficult to refute now than ever before, as is his view of the psyche as a homeostatic system which strives perpetually to achieve a balance between opposing propensities, while at the same time actively seeking its own individuation. As a result, the hypotheses relating to the archetype, collective unconscious, symbol and transcendent function are beginning to receive more sympathetic consideration than Jung could ever have anticipated. Moreover, there is now good reason to suppose that the "command neurons" subserving archetypal systems may be situated in the phylogenetically ancient cerebral regions of the midbrain and brain stem, and that dreams do indeed possess the crucial function that Jung ascribed to them of linking the inherent biogrammar of the species with the conscious awareness of the individual (p. 274).

Those who reject Jung's psychology as unscientific will need to take a new look.

CRITIQUE OF JUNG'S INTERPRETATION OF RELIGION

Traditionally, Freud is viewed as a foe of religion and Jung as a good friend. Various critics have said otherwise, suggesting that, in both obvious and subtle ways, Jung misrepresents the essential spirit and truth of the traditions about which he writes. Jung insisted that he worked strictly as an empirical scientist and as a phenomenologist. He used the term *phenomenologist* to underscore his commitment to the facts of experience apart from any metaphysical or philosophical judgments about them (Jung, 1938, p. 6). Psychology, he argued, is not in a position to take a stand regarding the validity of any particular idea it studies. In truth, however, Jung went far beyond a strictly empirical standpoint, as a number of his critics point out (e.g., Heisig, 1979). Here we will review some of their chief criticisms.

Psychology as Theology

According to his critics, Jung undercuts religion in two ways. On the one hand, he is seemingly indifferent to the striving for truth that lies at the heart of religious aspiration (Fromm, 1950, p. 16); on the other, he denies to metaphysics and theology their self-definitions. Raymond Hostie (1955) accurately notes that Jung considers metaphysical and theological views to be essentially matters of personal faith rather than modes of thought that can hope to approximate truth. "Nothing," says Jung (1955–1956, p. 548), "provides a better demonstration of the extreme uncertainty of metaphysical assertions than their diversity." They are not worthless, however, for they are in part a product of numinous experiences and are therefore valuable to the psychologist who would understand such experiences. Jung's "incorrigible" empiricism would be acceptable, Hostie remarks, if, in his ignorance of these other branches of knowledge, he had not gone beyond the boundaries of psychology in his studies of religious symbolism (pp. 157–158).

Jung may have succeeded in limiting himself to psychological issues while doing research and advancing hypotheses, but he violated these limits, say some of his critics, when as a psychotherapist he dealt with human life as a whole. As Philip Rieff (1966) points out, "Symbols of psychological analysis, if they are intellectually compelling, become what they must be wherever analysis develops fully into therapy: a language of faith" (p. 140). Victor White (1952) similarly emphasizes the religious aura that surrounds Jungian therapy. A patient's dream sequence, he says, has often proved to be "a kind of interior religious pilgrimage which leads progressively to something very like a religious conversion" (p. 49). Not infrequently Jungian analysis appears to be like a religious retreat, and the analyst like a spiritual director or priest. Luis Gómez (1995), on the other hand, is struck by Jung's effort to appropriate the authority of competing spiritual powers by transforming what was originally sacred and communal into a form that is both secular and individual.

Rudolf Affemann (1957) points out that, for Jung, psychology and religion are not sharply differentiated, for they share the same object, the soul; the same purpose, to protect individuals against the dangers that threaten the soul, and to lead them toward self-fulfillment; and the same methods. Jung is therefore mistaken when he claims that he does not deal with metaphysical matters. On the contrary, Affemann concludes, Jung espouses a pantheistic–mystical world-view that goes far beyond empirical observations. Warning theologians of the danger of grounding their work in Jung's (or any other) psychological theory rather than in biblical anthropology, Affemann nevertheless concludes that dialogue between theology and Jungian psychology will for some time to come be of great value for achieving the best in human beings.

Most critical of Jung's empiricism, to the point of dismissal, is Robert Jelke (1948), who laments that Jung's conclusions are not "the outcome of psychology carried out in a genuinely empirical fashion. This "psychology" stands not in the service of genuine research, but in the service of a one-sided and dogmatic fundamental thesis" (p. 43). The result, Jelke intimates, is the substitution of psychological for ecclesiastical dogmas.

To whatever degree these charges are justified, it is true that Jung often fails to make clear that he is referring only to psychological processes. We cannot blame readers who conclude that at times Jung is writing theology instead of psychology. This is especially true of *Answer to Job* (see Corey, 1990). To the charge that, as a therapist, he sometimes took on the role of the priest, Jung (1952b) wrote that he would have been delighted to have left this "anything but easy task" to the church, were it not for the fact that many of his patients were shed from the church "like dry leaves from the great tree and now find themselves 'hanging on' to the treatment" (p. 28).

Questionable Presuppositions and Personal Psychology

On the face of it, Jung is not a phenomenologist. Some of his central concepts, such as the collective unconscious or the self, go far beyond what is given phenomenologically. In contradiction to Jung's claim that his psychology is strictly based on empirical facts and entails no philosophical system, Marilyn Nagy (1992) demonstrates that Jung's work is founded on philosophical postulates that express "an idealist and a metaphysical view of reality." More specifically, his work shows a fundamental similarity to "a certain type of radically subjectivistic neo-Kantianism" that was in vogue at the turn of the century, especially among those hoping to defend religious truths against science (p. 265).

On the other hand, as Roger Brooke (1991) persuasively argues, if we can successfully bypass Jung's metatheoretical assumptions and reread him hermeneutically, we may discover in his insights an existential depth and significance that is otherwise not apparent. Brooke thinks that Jung was close to the truth when he claimed to be a phenomenologist. What Jung lacked was not phenomenological insight but the conceptual tools for expressing his insights in phenomenologically rigorous ways (p. 2). Whereas Jung was at times fully explicit about the value of setting aside preconceived notions, certain presuppositions nevertheless shaped his psychology, including his psychology of religion. Here we examine several of these formative assumptions.

Dreams and Myths as Collective Phenomena: The assumption of the existence of a collective unconscious is justified by Jung and his followers by two claims: (1) highly similar mythic images and themes frequently recur at widely separated places and times around the world, with no evidence that these elements were transmitted culturally; and (2) individuals sometimes experience dreams and fantasies containing ancient mythic themes that cannot be accounted for in terms of the life histories of those experiencing them. The positing of a collective unconscious not only accounts for these reported phenomena but also intimately links them to each other: myth becomes a collective dream, and the dream, potentially, a personal re-experiencing of myth.

Professor of Classics G. S. Kirk (1970) is frankly unconvinced. "Jung," he says, "has somehow succeeded in persuading many people that his general symbols are of universal occurrence; but the probability is that they are nothing of the sort. . . . The earth-mother, the divine child, the anima, and so on, simply do not occur often (or specifically) enough to make a general theory necessary or acceptable; and neither do the typical myth-sequences (swallowing by a sea-monster, betrayal of the hero, and so on) that are implied, rather puzzlingly, to enshrine these symbols" (pp. 275–276).

Oriental archaeologist Henri Frankfort (1958) is of like opinion. Pointing to noticeable differences in the mother imagery of Ancient Egypt and Ancient Mesopotamia, Frankfort denies the existence of universal archetypes. Myths, he says, are always the concern of the community and are occasioned by the course of objective natural events, for example, the sometimes catastrophic change of seasons or the crisis of death. Kirk, following Piaget, suggests that whatever recurring images there are have probably arisen out of universal experiences of the early years of childhood. Kirk does say, however, that it is "important to concede" that there are no compelling arguments against the possibility that modes of thought are inherited, much as modes of behaving are passed on genetically in other species (p. 277).

When seemingly mythic images appear in individual dreams and fantasies, it is naturally impossible to establish with absolute certainty that the images were not earlier encountered, say, in books, art museums, or conversation. Critics say that Jung and his followers have been too quick to rule out such mundane sources. Noll (1994) examines at some length the case of a patient at the Burghölzli who reportedly hallucinated a sun with an erect phallus, the movement of which created the wind. Jung traces this imagery to Mithraic liturgy, which he says the patient could not have known about at that time. Jung frequently cites this case in support of the collective unconscious. Noll in turn reports evidence suggesting not only that the patient could easily have come across such imagery but also that Jung either inadvertently or deliberately distorted the record. Both Jung and Noll undoubtedly make too much of this case, but the question it addresses remains an important one.

Religion as Therapy: Contradicting the phenomenological spirit as well is Jung's occasional tendency to take "from religion only what confirms and illustrates his psychology" (Zaehner, 1957, p. 120). Jung's selectivity, broad though it is, demonstrates that he was interested in religion primarily for its therapeutic value. "The history of religion," Jung (1952b) writes, ". . . is a treasure-house of archetypal forms from which the doctor can draw helpful parallels and enlightening comparisons for the purpose of calming and clarifying a consciousness that is all at sea" (p. 33). If Jung did not force phenomena to conform to the dimensions of his theory, he surely ignored religious phenomena that are not easily interpreted in terms of his system.

A case in point is Jung's insistence on the preeminence of the quaternity. Philp (1958) marshalls evidence against the position that four is the most significant number in alchemy, evidence supported by John Holmyard's (1957) thorough study of this remarkable tradition. Victor White (1960) recognizes the pervasiveness of the quaternity and the vital necessity of living in accordance with adequate models of wholeness, but he wonders why ternary images, such as the Trinity, need be considered incomplete quaternities. Might they not be "archetypal images in their own right, which present a content distinct from that of the quaternity?" (p. 106). Divine beings, White points out, are rarely found in groups of four; far more often they appear in triads or present themselves with three aspects. The Trinity requires three elements, according to Rudolf Arnheim (1969, p. 211), to represent their inherent intertwining; four, he says, would break up the whole into a system of contrasts.

The Solitary Individual: That Jung reconstructed the world in terms of his theory, which in turn was derived from his own personality type,[2] is further evidenced by the discrepancies between his characterization of the alchemists and what others say of them. In contrast to Titus Burckhardt (1960) and Ralph Metzner (1971), who depict alchemy as a tradition passed on through apprenticeships and esoteric societies, Jung (1952b) represents the ancient art as a solitary endeavor: "They rarely have pupils, and of direct tradition there seems to have been very little, nor is there much evidence of any secret societies or the like. Each worked in the laboratory for himself and suffered from loneliness" (p. 314). Jung's account sounds suspiciously descriptive of his own style of scholarly research, as well as of his expectations of what his patients must experience: "The patient must be alone if he is to find out what it is that supports him when he can no longer support himself." Only this experience of being "alone with his own self," which is "the highest and most decisive experience of all, . . . can give him an indestructible foundation" (p. 28). Both Burckhardt and Metzner also contradict Jung's projection theory of alchemy in arguing that the alchemists were for the most part aware of the deeper symbolic meaning of their work.

Jung's depiction of alchemy as a solitary undertaking is paralleled by his stress on the individual and experiential component of religion. This emphasis, Hostie

---

[2] A good number of the characteristics that Jung (1921) assigns to the introverted-thinking type, the type he later said was his own, seem peculiarly descriptive of Jung's work. For example, "External facts are not the aim and origin of this thinking, though the introvert would often like to make his thinking appear so. It begins with the subject and leads back to the subject, far though it may range into the realm of actual reality. . . . Facts are collected as evidence for a theory, never for their own sake. . . . Facts are of secondary importance for this kind of thinking; what seems to it of paramount importance is the development and presentation of the subjective idea, of the initial symbolic image hovering darkly before the mind's eye. Its aim is never an intellectual reconstruction of the concrete fact, but a shaping of that dark image into a luminous idea. . . . Its task is completed when the idea it has fashioned seems to emerge so inevitably from the external facts that they actually prove its validity" (pp. 380–381). Jung also anticipates the reactions his psychology was to inspire: "In his own special field of work [the introverted thinking type] provokes the most violent opposition" (p. 385).

(1955) concludes, is a reaction to the rationalistic spirit dominant at the end of the nineteenth century. White (1960) takes exception to Jung's identification of religion with the numinous experience by pointing to the considerable body of evidence demonstrating that "the experience of 'numinosity' is by no means always religious, nor issues in religion." Jung's own work, White adds, shows that the experience is also the root of magic, art, poetry, as well as of neurosis and psychosis (p. 57). Conversely, phenomena ordinarily called religious may have no connection at all with the numinous experience.

Both White (1952, 1960) and Hans Schaer (1946) urge the adoption of a broader and more balanced definition of religion than we find in Jung. Josef Goldbrunner (1949) especially notes the omission of the I–Thou relationship. For Jung, he says, "the absolutized Self revolves around itself in self-satisfied isolation" (p. 200). Similarly, Rieff (1966, p. 134) states that "Jung is recommending an essentially private religiosity without institutional reference or communal membership." "The narcissistic goal of individuation," cautions Harry Guntrip (1961, p. 191), overlooks the essential role of personal relations in the attainment of integration.

The aristocratic element in Jung's individualism is also noteworthy. To the degree that Jung emphasizes a "higher way" for the privileged few, remarks David Cox (1959), he is guilty of the otherwise debatable charge of Gnosticism. Only uncommon individuals with exceptional personal qualities, years of otherwise uncommitted time, and considerable financial reserves can hope to understand what Gerald Sykes (1962) describes as a "leisurely Goethean search for metaphysical values" (p. 67). To the masses set upon worldly success, Jung has nothing to say. What Jung advocates, agrees R. C. Zaehner (1959), is wholly unsuited to the average person of our day.

Evil as Imbalance: Among the specific elements examined in Jung's psychology of religion, his treatment of evil has probably inspired the most extensive debate. Jung took issue with the widely accepted definition of evil as a *privatio boni,* the privation or absence of good. He argued that good is meaningful only if we can contrast it with an equally palpable opposite, and not merely with its absence. From his experience as a psychotherapist Jung concludes that the *privatio boni* theory constitutes a one-sided emphasis on the good and the dismissal of the indisputably real opposing forces, which as a result become destructive. Because evil is a matter of imbalance, a matter of a distortion of the individuation process, it is a relative thing, though no less real for all that.

Hostie (1955) observes that Jung bases his understanding of the conception of the *privatio boni* on the opinions of misinformed patients and oversimplified texts that do not do justice to this doctrine. Correctly understood, it need not conflict with Jung's views on the problem of evil. Both accept the fact and activity of evil, and both recognize its relativity. Hostie takes issue with Jung only when he projects his empirical discoveries about the nature of psychic evil onto God. Philp (1958) and White (1960) also challenge Jung's expositions on evil. "I must confess," says White, "that for my part I have great difficulty in understanding just what Jung *does* understand by evil, and how, intellectually, he would have us differentiate it from good. And it is not indeed altogether clear what he would have us understand by 'integrating,' 'accepting' and even 'becoming conscious' of it" (pp. 156–157).

The Unity of Personality: Jung shares with other humanistic psychologists the assumption that human personality possesses a natural tendency toward unification and wholeness. Yet according to James Hillman (1975), formerly the Director of

Studies at the C. G. Jung Institute in Zurich and now a proponent of a radical archetypal psychology that deviates in significant ways from analytical psychology, Jung has erroneously literalized the individuation process. By affirming "the comforting teleological fallacy," he has substituted a monotheistic theology for a true archetypal psychology (p. 147). From Hillman's perspective, individuation is only one archetypal fantasy among many, corresponding to just one of the possible perspectives that lie deep within our nature. This process can be taken into account, he says, without elevating it to the fundamental law of the psyche. In his own "revisioning" of psychology, Hillman undertakes to free the individual soul from all partial identifications, especially with the ego and the life in which it is centered, and to engage in "soul-making" through a noninterpretive understanding of the imaginal process. Because the soul expresses itself in images of Gods, Hillman says, a genuine depth psychology must be religious and theistic—even polytheistic given the soul's "native polycentricity" (p. 167)—though not, of course, in any literal sense. Hillman's recasting of Jungian psychology has been helpfully reviewed by Thomas Moore (1980), who also considers its implications for religious studies. Moore's best-selling book, *Care of the Soul* (1992), owes much to Hillman's thinking.

From Rejection to Reverence

The critics we have encountered so far represent a range of moderate positions that combine fundamental appreciation for Jung's approach with thoughtful criticism of it. At the negative extreme are the psychoanalysts Hans Jacobs (1961) and Edward Glover (1950), who draw their conclusions with a confidence and—especially in Glover's case—an animosity that some readers may rightly suspect. Few will agree with Jacobs that Jung does not "possess sufficient religious sensitivity to be a leader in the field of religion" (pp. 142–143), but Jacobs's rejection of Jung's distinction between Eastern and Western minds—earlier repudiated by Swami Akhilananda (1946)—may well be justified. We should balance Jacobs's thorough rejection of Jung's psychology of religion with the contrasting evaluation of the well-known scholar of Eastern religious traditions, R. C. Zaehner (1959), who, though not uncritical of Jung, says that Jung has "done more to interpret Eastern religion to the West than any other man" (p. 403). Elsewhere Zaehner (1957) says that Jung's ideas "seem to illumine much in Oriental religion that has previously been obscure" (p. xvii).

Glover's hostile description of later Jungian psychology as a "mishmash of Oriental philosophy with a bowdlerised psychobiology" (p. 134) suggests an important observation that has been made more thoughtfully by others. Zaehner (1959) judges that, among his followers, Jung's psychology is rapidly becoming a religion itself, an esoteric cult that is individualistic to an extreme. It represents "a re-emergence of some aspects of Buddhism and Taoism in modern dress; it is nature mysticism made respectable for the modern mind by the jargon of psychology" (p. 403). Noll (1994) develops this theme at considerable length.

Among those who have fallen victim to the temptation to treat Jung's psychology as a doctrinal system are associates of the famous C. G. Jung Institute in Zurich, the Mecca of analytical psychology. Edmund Cohen (1975), who studied at the modest Institute in the winter of 1970–1971, found there a worshipful fixation on the person of Jung, whose *Collected Works* were viewed as an encyclopedia of universal knowledge, the revered record of a closed system of thought. Ignorance of other psychologists' work was rife, and critical thinking discouraged. Analysis too often became a matter of giving names to dream images and other psychological phe-

nomena, rather than understanding them as expressions of an individual life situation. Profoundly disappointed by a program whose best students came to it as a
way of entering psychology subsequent to another career, Cohen quickly abandoned his own plans for earning the Institute's three-year diploma. The situation
at the Institute may be different today, of course, but there is no question that, for
analytical psychology, these trends remain a continuing danger.

Being aware of these possibilities, Jung only reluctantly agreed to the founding
of the Zurich Institute, which never realized his vision for it—a center for research,
especially on dreams, mythology, and the psychology of religion (Stern, 1976, p.
249). "I can only hope and wish that no one becomes 'Jungian,' " he wrote to an
associate in 1946, two years before the Institute was finally opened; "I stand for no
doctrine, but describe facts and put forth certain views which I hold worthy of
discussion" (quoted in Cohen, p. 138).

JUNG'S CHALLENGE TO THE PRESENT AGE

Jung's theoretical concepts were not what was most important to him; he was not
offering analytical psychology as a new orthodoxy. Rather, more than anything else
he wished to communicate an attitude and a challenge. The attitude is one of
openness, especially to the nonrational and the mysterious, to what lies beyond the
logic of the philosopher and the instruments of the scientist. It is a recognition of
the infinity that stretches far beyond our understanding, of the powers that lie
outside our comprehension and control. It is, then, also an attitude of humility and
of awe.

The challenge Jung throws out to us is ultimately an impossible one to fulfill:
the challenge of becoming whole. Yet only through growth into conscious integration, many psychologists agree, will the individual truly find meaning and fulfillment. Failure to meet this challenge will bring, on the individual level, neurosis or
psychosis; if unconsciousness is widespread within a society—and Jung says that it
is in ours—the outcome will be discord and destruction. "If ever there was a time
when self-reflection was the absolutely necessary and only right thing, it is now, in
our present catastrophic epoch" (1943, p. 4), wrote Jung in 1916 in words that are
even more applicable today.

The task of psychology is therefore an urgent one. Man, writes Jung (1952a),
"can make no progress with himself unless he becomes very much better acquainted with his own nature. Unfortunately, a terrifying ignorance prevails in this
respect, and an equally great aversion to increasing the knowledge of his intrinsic
character" (p. 460). According to Jung, that knowledge will grow only when psychologists and other students of human nature take into account the full range of
human experience, including the experience of God. God, Jung emphasized repeatedly, is not a matter of belief, but of indisputable and valuable experience.

> No matter what the world thinks about religious experience, the one who has it
> possesses a great treasure, a thing that has become for him a source of life, meaning,
> and beauty, and that has given a new splendour to the world and to mankind. He has
> PISTIS and peace. Where is the criterion by which you could say that such a life is not
> legitimate, that such an experience is not valid, and that such *pistis* is mere illusion? Is
> there, as a matter of fact, any better truth about the ultimate things than the one that
> helps you to live? . . . No one can know what the ultimate things are. We must therefore
> take them as we experience them. And if such experience helps to make life healthier,

more beautiful, more complete and more satisfactory to yourself and to those you love, you may safely say: "This was the Grace of God" (Jung, 1938, p. 105).

Engraved in the stone lintel above the entrance to Jung's house in Küsnacht is a Latin inscription from the Oracle of Delphi: *vocatus atque non vocatus deus aderit*—Summoned or not summoned, God will be present. We could find no better words to epitomize Jung's psychology of religion.

11

WILLIAM JAMES AND
HIS LEGACY

*A*lthough C. G. Jung is ordinarily classified as a depth psychologist, in some respects his views belong among the humanistic perspectives that make up the next three chapters. Like other humanistic psychologists, Jung opposes the reductionistic trends that are evident in objective psychology and psychoanalysis alike. Moreover, he joins the humanists in postulating a complex array of positive, inborn dispositions and capacities that form the matrix out of which human individuality emerges. With other humanists, he emphasizes the positive side of human culture, especially as it promotes self-actualization. In this light he also distinguishes contemporary society's positive and destructive tendencies, including those in the religious sphere.

In contrast to other humanistic psychologists, however, Jung gives little attention to the structure and dynamics of *individual* human experience. He recognizes that "the psychological individual is characterized by a peculiar and in some respects unique psychology" (Jung, 1921, p. 447). Yet he traces this uniqueness to the ways in which the hypothetical psychic elements combine, not to the elements themselves, which he takes to be age-old and universal possessions. It is these collective elements that preoccupied Jung. Whenever he alludes in his writings to the dreams and fantasies of individual patients, it is almost always to illustrate universal archetypal themes and processes.

Far more representative of the humanistic emphasis on individual experience and the corresponding reluctance to employ explanatory concepts or theories is the work of William James. Although James did not altogether abandon the quest for general laws regarding religion's psychic origins, the accent of his classic work *The Varieties of Religious Experience* falls heavily on the solitary experience of individuals. In accord with his conviction that "the stronghold of religion lies in individuality" and that "real fact in the making" can be caught only in the inner recesses of private feeling, James filled the *Varieties* with lengthy quotations from personal documents, most of them brimming with deep, singular emotion (James, 1902, pp. 396n, 395).

The immediate occasion for the writing of the *Varieties* was provided by an invitation to give the Gifford Lectures at the University of Edinburgh.[1] The task James set for himself in these lectures, and the principles he put forward in fulfilling it, reflect lifelong concerns rooted deep in his own character. Like Jung, who acknowledges a profound indebtedness to him, James maintains that to understand another's perspective we must first become familiar with the individual's personal life. This rule applies especially well to James, for the key to his influence is said to lie in his remarkable personality rather than in the principles he expounded, the distinctions he drew, or the few, widely disputed hypotheses he proposed. Readers from his day to ours have been struck by his brilliant and richly furnished mind, his great sympathy for his subjects and their experience, his moral sensibility, and his vivacious spontaneity, evident in a striking literary style. It is most appropriate, therefore, that the last of our biographical studies in the origins of the psychology of religion should focus on James, the author of a work recognized not only as the field's greatest classic but also as one of the most important writings on religion in the twentieth century.

THE LIFE OF WILLIAM JAMES

William James was born in New York City on January 11, 1842, the eldest in a family of four sons and one daughter. His grandfather by the same name was an Irish immigrant who was religiously orthodox and aggressively acquisitive. During a 40-year career in commerce, he became one of the leading citizens of Albany and of New York State, a pillar of the Presbyterian Church, and a financier of enormous wealth. James's father Henry, on the other hand, inherited neither the somber, churchgoing Calvinism nor the preoccupation with money, much to his father's great disappointment. Prone during his college years to drunkenness and profligacy, Henry was also profoundly religious and introspective, traits that were undoubtedly accentuated by the almost four years of acute suffering he endured as an adolescent, when his right leg, severely burned in an accident, refused to heal and twice had to be amputated (Habegger, 1994). After abortive efforts to find a vocation in law—his father's wish—as well as in theology, he settled into the career of a professional student, dedicated to articulating and promoting his own radical conception of God. The "bundle of truth" that served him throughout his life he derived from the writings of Emanuel Swedenborg, following a sudden and terrifying experience of "doubt, anxiety, and despair" in his early thirties and a nearly two-year search for relief (G. W. Allen, 1967, pp. 17–18; see also Habegger, 1994, pp. 211 ff.).

At first his resources for such a career were sharply limited, for according to the punishing terms of his father's will, Henry was to receive but a small annuity until he entered a respectable profession. Four years after his father's death in 1832, however, the will was declared invalid, clearing the way for Henry to inherit a full portion of his father's wealth. With a leisurely life of study and writing now well secured, he also had the means to experiment to an extraordinary degree with his children's education. Driven by an unrealizable educational ideal, Henry James frequently changed his children's schools or tutors as he swept his family from one

---

[1] The Gifford Lectures on Natural Religion were inaugurated in 1888 under an endowment from Lord Adam Gifford, a jurist, to four universities in Scotland—Edinburgh, Glasgow, Aberdeen, and St. Andrew's—among which the lectureship rotates. A list of the lectures published to 1964 can be found in Vande Kemp (1984), pp. 273–280.

William James, in a photograph taken while in Edinburgh, Scotland, to deliver the Gifford Lectures in 1901–1902.

city to another: Albany, New York, Newport, Boston, and Cambridge, as well as London, Paris, Bologna, and Bonn. In the kaleidoscope of new experiences that these travels provided his children, Henry remained a crucial element in their erratic education. Always ready for a spirited exchange of ideas, he entertained interesting people wherever he settled his household, stirred up lively debates at the dinner table, and challenged his gifted and cosmopolitan offspring—including his second son, Henry, later the famous novelist—to outdo him in the witty use of language. Opposed to any merely literal understanding of things, tolerant to a fault of inconsistency and contradiction, and dedicated to an educational philosophy of exceptional openness and freedom, Henry James, Sr., headed a family as remarkable for its breadth of acquaintance with Western culture and public affairs as it was for the bonds of attachment among its members. William's emotional dependence on his father, in spite of enduring differences in outlook and religious conviction, is particularly noteworthy. It not only played a role in seriously prolonging his childhood but also had fateful consequences for the direction of his scholarly work (Allen, 1967; Croce, 1995; Habegger, 1994; Perry, 1935).

An Artist's Education in Science

William, who would someday become America's foremost psychologist as well as one of its leading philosophers, began his vocational preparation as tentatively as his father. Some scholars maintain that the young James's difficulty in choosing a career was an inevitable corollary of his rare combination of artistic and scientific abilities, both of which were evident before his second decade. A person of James's creative genius and unity of vision, Daniel Bjork (1988) says, could not be satisfied by any ordinary career. Others, however, regard James's equivocation as the unfortunate outcome of his father's influence. The "career vacuum" created by Henry James, Sr., says Gerald Myers (1986, p. 21), may have disposed William to worry unduly about choosing a direction of his own. Marian and Edward Madden (1979) blame the elder James's chronic educational experimentation. "The most damaging, pervasive lesson" of James's "rootless and accidental childhood," they write, was one of never making commitments; problems were to be met, rather, by changing the context (p. 382). The result was "a constitutional inability to make decisions, to commit himself," and this incapacity in turn is said to underlie his subsequent

THE LIFE OF WILLIAM JAMES **475**

ill health, which he was already predisposed to view as an obstacle to action. Cushing Strout's (1968a, 1968b) more dynamic interpretation emphasizes James's acute struggle for personal identity, which had been made exceptionally difficult by the excessive and inconsistent influence of his father. Though delaying James's maturity, this influence also enriched it, making the resolution of his struggle a peculiarly fruitful one. Strout notes in particular the resulting dual emphasis on science and religion, of which the *Varieties* is an obvious outcome.

Although for a while it seemed that James would find a direction that harmonized his artistic and scientific talents, at the age of 18 he decided that he was destined to be a painter. He persuaded his father to move the family from Bonn back to Newport, so that he could study painting with William Hunt. Less than a year later, however, in spite of considerable promise as an artist, he suddenly changed his mind. Abandoning a talent that he would never again employ in any serious way, he enrolled the next autumn in the Lawrence Scientific School at Harvard to pursue chemistry and then comparative anatomy, a premedical course of study.

The motives for James's fateful and seemingly abrupt change of mind are the subject of much speculation. Gay Wilson Allen (1967, p. 70) suspects that James's health may have been the chief factor. According to Allen, it was while he was with Hunt in Newport that James first experienced the eye trouble that was to handicap him for the rest of his life. At this time he also developed symptoms of "nervous indigestion," foreshadowing a decade of serious physical and psychic disability. Outer circumstances may have played a role as well. James later said that Hunt had told him that a vocation of painting would go unrewarded in America. Allen suggests that the excitement and indignation stirred up by the outbreak of the Civil War, which coincided with James's decision against painting, may have likewise upset his plans.

Noting the lack of evidence that James was by then experiencing difficulty with his eyes, Howard Feinstein (1984) argues that it was his father, not Hunt, who had successfully opposed a vocation of painting. Henry James, Sr., had long made known his preference for science. Moreover, once they were back in Newport, the elder James suddenly became subject to fainting spells. He predicted he would soon be dead. In a family practiced in the "manipulative politics of invalidism" (p. 196), such a maneuver at last succeeded, according to Feinstein, in propelling William in the direction of science. In a lecture years later, William would equate the rejection of a career underway with the murdering of a self. Yet James the painter lived on—filled with violent anger, according to Feinstein's interpretations of James's sketches, and expressing itself in recurring physical symptoms (p. 145). Feinstein finds a still deeper source for James's illness in the unresolved conflict between Henry James, Sr., and *his* father.

Other scholars think Feinstein has overplayed the father's (and grandfather's) influence in these matters. Gerald Myers (1986) is more inclined to ascribe James's health problems to an inherited predisposition that became combined with an overbearing superego, the product of a "too intense . . . moral and religious upbringing" (p. 21). Bjork (1988) interprets the abandonment of Hunt in Newport as a sign of James's constitutional restlessness and intellectual impatience, as yet another shift of attention in his search for "a suitable medium of creative expression" (p. 32). Rather than disposing James to illness, his painter self eventually effected a brilliant compromise in the form of a "stream of consciousness" psychology (Bjork, 1983).

Cowled Friar, a pencil drawing from a German notebook (ca. 1868) kept by William James. The drawing suggests James's deep sympathy for the "sick soul" and remarkably anticipates his own later appearance.

In any event, that compromise was still far off when James departed for study in Cambridge in 1861, the first time that he had spent more than a few days away from his parents. After three years at Harvard, he was forced by poor health to return home for half a year, during which months he read widely in science, literature, and philosophy. His return to the Scientific School in September 1863 brought a shift from chemistry to comparative anatomy, but the further decision to study medicine was still on the horizon. That choice came only after some months of excruciating indecision, when he felt torn between his fascination for natural science and the more lucrative but self-compromising option of business. If medicine offered James the advantages of both, he nevertheless thought its practice— in which he had no interest—to be filled with humbug and the Harvard program in particular to require disgracefully little of its students. Yet its study was an opportunity for him to pursue his interest in the functioning of the human body, and it undoubtedly saved him for a while from the "unspeakable disgust" over the "dead drifting" of his life that he would later record in his diary (Allen, 1967, p. 149).

James studied medicine between 1863 and 1869, a program from which he twice absented himself. The first interruption came in 1865 when he accompanied one of this teachers, Louis Agassiz, on a collecting expedition to Brazil. Tired of the generalizations and abstractions of his medical courses, James turned with relief to the prospects of an adventure on the Amazon, when he would learn to observe the inexhaustibly complex natural world. During this period he was deeply discouraged by violent illnesses and other hardships. Moreover, the monotonous routine of collecting fish specimens rapidly convinced him that he was not cut out to be a field naturalist. But the nine months he spent with Agassiz did serve to bring home the difference between a life of abstractions and a life lived "in the light of the world's concrete fullness" (James, 1896, p. 50). "No one sees farther into a generalization," James wrote at the time, "than his own knowledge of detail extends" (H. James, 1920, 1, p. 65).

Despair and Deliverance

The second interruption, in 1865, followed a winter of intense suffering from eye trouble, digestive disorders, insomnia, painful back weakness, and profound depression. Later reporting himself to have been "on the continual verge of suicide" (quoted in Allen, 1967, p. 124), James at last decided that he might find relief in the mineral baths at a spa in Germany. The visit there would also give him an opportunity to improve his command of German and to study physiology at one of the famous universities.

The baths did him no good, but his 18 months in Europe were hardly wasted, in spite of his own conviction to the contrary. Although physically incapable of doing laboratory work, he attended lectures in physiology and psychology at the University of Berlin. At the same time, he undertook a heroic course of reading in the massive German literature on the nervous system and psychology as well as in philosophy and literature. The outcome, says Allen (1967, p. 151), was a liberal education such as James could not have obtained even at Harvard College.

James did not see it that way, however, for he returned to Cambridge weary and discouraged. Preparation for his medical school examination, which he passed without difficulty in June 1869, preoccupied him for a time, yet what for others would have marked the beginning of a promising professional career was for James a seeming dead end. He remained wholly uninterested in the practice of medicine, and he lacked the stamina to do laboratory work in physiology. Sustained reading of any kind was difficult, too, for sometimes he could use his eyes no more than two hours a day.

During three lonely and deeply troubled years of invalidism in his parents' home, James managed to read and take notes on a remarkable number of books— on physiology, neurology, psychology, and philosophy. When his mind demanded rest, he turned to German, French, and English literature. Underneath a surface of quiet preoccupation, James struggled in desperation with the profound melancholy and helplessness that, when they did not sweep him to the edge of suicide, convinced him that he was unfit for any affectionate relation. He felt condemned, according to a diary entry, to the life of a joyless spectator.

James describes the extreme of his suffering, which Allen dates from early 1870, in a powerful passage he included in the *Varieties* to illustrate the panic fear that characterizes the "sick soul's" melancholy at its worst. Attributing the experience to an anonymous correspondent, James recounts that, one day at twilight, while in a "state of philosophic pessimism and general depression of spirits about my prospects," he was suddenly overwhelmed by "a horrible fear of my own existence." This feeling of terror was accompanied by the mummylike image of an idiotic and withdrawn epileptic youth whom James had seen in a mental asylum. So horrifying a fate, he felt with a shudder, could in an instant be his own.

> It was as if something hitherto solid within my breast gave way entirely, and I became a mass of quivering fear. After this the universe was changed for me altogether. I awoke morning after morning with a horrible dread at the pit of my stomach, and with a sense of the insecurity of life that I never knew before, and that I have never felt since. . . . [The experience] gradually faded, but for months I was unable to go out into the dark alone.

He escaped insanity, he says, only by clinging "to scripture-texts like 'The eternal God is my refuge,' etc., 'Come unto me, all ye that labor and are heavy-laden,' etc., 'I am the resurrection and the life,' etc." (James, 1902, pp. 134–135).

At the end of his account of this terrifying experience, James cites in a footnote another, extraordinarily similar one—his father's from 1844, at nearly the same age. Like his father, too, James at last found relief in a new intellectual understanding. Whereas the elder James obtained deliverance through the writings of Swedenborg, the younger one found his salvation in the works of the French philosopher Charles Renouvier and the British psychologist Alexander Bain. From Renouvier he obtained a definition of free will to which, at least temporarily, he felt he could subscribe: "the sustaining of a thought *because I choose to* when I might have other thoughts." Fortified by this vindication of free will, James resolved to stop obsessing over philosophical subtleties and to cultivate instead, through carefully selected reading and resolute acts, "the feeling of moral freedom." Bain's analysis of "habit" provided the principles by which to construct such a renewed sense of "individual reality and creative power" (quoted in Allen, 1967, pp. 168–169).

A Great Psychologist Emerges

James's "spiritual crisis" has prompted much theorizing about its causes, ranging from physical and psychological factors—especially the anguishing conflict with his father—to cultural and philosophical ones (see Bjork, 1988, pp. 285–286). Much has also been written about the effects of his depression, once he emerged from it, on the character of his psychology and philosophy. His years as an invalid, brought to a close by his appointment in 1872 as instructor in physiology at Harvard, had provided him with the leisure to read and think about matters that would engage him for the rest of his life. More than this, however, they "gave a personal intimacy and intensity to the deepest problems that philosophy and religion can present to man's understanding." His illness, from which he was never wholly to recover, "developed and deepened the bed in which the stream of his philosophic life was to flow" (H. James, 1920, 1, p. 85). As he wrote in his anonymous confession, it also made him sympathetic to the plight of his fellow sufferers, whose compelling sense of "something wrong" struck him as more than a private perception.

James viewed his appointment in physiology as a helpful diversion from his introspective studies, which he said had bred in him "a sort of philosophical hypochondria" (Allen, 1967, p. 175). At the same time he had growing doubts about scientific methods, and he no longer believed that physiology provides the key to psychic states. To the contrary, his own experience had taught him that the mind could be approached directly, through self-observation. Though welcoming for the time being the "stable reality" of biology's "concrete facts" (p. 182), his interests soon led him in the direction of psychology and then philosophy, the two fields in which he was to make his chief contributions.

In 1878, shortly before his marriage and at the beginning of a period of exceptional productivity, James contracted to write *The Principles of Psychology,* a monumental, two-volume work that has been described from the perspective of 80 years as "without question the most literate, the most provocative, and at the same time the most intelligible book on psychology that has ever appeared in English or in any other language" (MacLeod, 1969, p. iii). Ironically, the publication of this 1400-page work—12 years in the making and destined to become one of the great classics of the Western intellectual tradition—marked the end of psychology's domination in James's life. Transferred to the philosophy faculty in 1880, he increasingly gave his attention to philosophical questions, to the PRAGMATISM and RADICAL EMPIRICISM that were to be his contribution to American philosophy.

A Mystical Germ

Behind the shifting surface of academic titles and scholarly publications lay one of James's perennial concerns, that of religion. If it was not actually the great interest of his life, as he casually declared it to be in a letter to Henry W. Rankin in 1897, it was indisputably a major preoccupation. After reading James's book *Pragmatism,* published in 1907, Oliver Wendell Holmes, Jr., observed, "I now see, as I have seen in his other books that I have read, that the aim and end of the whole business is religious." In like vein, John Jay Chapman remarked on "the great religious impulse at the back of all his work . . . which controlled his whole life and mind, and accomplished a great work in the world" (McDermott, 1967, pp. xx–xxi).

James's religious impulse, however pervasively it may have influenced his work, was by most standards unusually muted. "Personal religious experience," he writes in the *Varieties,* "has its root and centre in mystical states of consciousness"; yet his own constitution, he adds, "shuts me out from their enjoyment almost entirely" (p. 301). The contempt of the elder Henry James for institutions of all kinds virtually guaranteed that, during their childhood at least, William and his siblings would have no official church association, a fact that was for them a source of occasional embarrassment. Although they did exercise their freedom to visit churches from time to time, and James would, as a Harvard professor, regularly attend morning chapel, he otherwise found himself incapable of participating in ordinary expressions of piety.[2] In response to the questionnaire that James Pratt circulated in 1904 as part of his dissertation research, James wrote that "I can't possibly pray—I feel foolish and artificial." Yet prayer, he had written in the *Varieties,* "is the very soul and essence of religion" (p. 365). Far more an abstract ideal than a felt personal presence, God was for him only "dimly" real. Moreover, the Bible offered him no religious authority, for "it is so human a book that I don't see how belief in its divine authorship can survive the reading of it." He was open to the possibility of personal immortality, but he "never keenly" believed in it (H. James, 1920, 2, pp. 213–215).

Of what then did James's religious impulse consist? Although he lacked consciousness of God "in the directer and stronger sense," as he wrote to James Leuba in 1902, he found himself responding sympathetically to the cumulative testimony of others, including especially his father's. His own "mystical germ," undeterred by rational criticism, compelled him to recognize "thither lies truth" (H. James, 1920, 2, p. 211). James had become famous—as well as disliked and criticized—for his apparent openness to every phenomenon that came his way, however much it clashed with medical or scientific orthodoxy. Yet his resonance to religious testimony was more than evidence of a brave and generous spirit. Acutely aware for a time of "that pit of insecurity beneath the surface of life" (James, 1902, p. 135), and recognizing the assurance and new zest for living that religious convictions can provide, James longed for faith in a spiritual world. As a scientist he felt compelled to withhold judgment on so unproved a matter, but as a humanitarian and "popular" philosopher bent on easing life's difficulties and building a better and more enjoyable world, he defended the right of others to affirm what he himself could not.

---

[2] Höffding (1918, p. 193n) writes that "William James told me that he belonged to no denomination [*Konfession*] but loved to hear the singing of Psalms; sermons he could not bear to hear." Whereas Roback (1942, pp. 32–33) infers from the paucity and spirit of musical allusions in the *Principles* that James was in fact little moved by music, James suggests otherwise when, in a letter to Flournoy, he cites as his single example of the "essentials" provided at Stanford University the "fine music" that was offered daily at the school's Memorial Church. Allusions in the *Varieties* likewise suggest an appreciation for music. In his discussion of the sick soul, for example, James compares the effects of illness or disaster on a happy life to the action of a damper on a piano string (p. 116). More significantly, James argues that the mystics' paradoxical expressions "prove that not conceptual speech, but music rather, is the element through which we are best spoken to by mystical truth. Many mystical scriptures are indeed little more than musical compositions" (p. 333). Given that music tends to be localized in the right cerebral hemisphere, James's observation is consistent with the thesis, discussed in Chapter 3, that religious experience also issues out of the right hemisphere.

The type of experience that, in less critical minds, inspires such an affirmation was not entirely foreign to James. Late one July evening in 1898, at the end of a day of hiking with friends through his beloved Adirondack Mountains, he found himself in "a state of spiritual alertness of the most vital description." Leaving his sleeping companions behind in the cabin, he wandered much of the night through the still, moonlit woods. Fermenting within him was a tumultuous mixture of impressions and memories: of magically illuminated nature, of his wholesome companions and beloved family, of the challenging Gifford Lectures that lay ahead. It seemed to him "a regular Walpurgis [Night]," a discordant meeting within himself of the "Gods of all the nature-mythologies" and "the moral Gods of the inner life." Inhumanly remote yet enormously appealing, eternally fresh yet hoary with age and decay, the unearthly scene before him was above all intensely significant. *What* it signified, however, James did not know, nor could he find a single word to express it. "So there it remained, a mere boulder of *impression.*" Experiencing it as "one of the happiest lonesome nights of my existence," James was sure it would leave traces in his Edinburgh lectures (H. James, 1920, 2, pp. 75–77).

Illuminating traces there were, but that long, momentous evening and its aftermath were to be consequential for his lectures in a far more ominous way. Heedless of the fact that he had been up all night, after having slept badly for weeks, James plunged with his rested and youthful companions into a strenuous day of hiking up and down the nearby mountains. The exertion damaged his heart irreparably, though he tried for some months to ignore the painful symptoms. Nearly a year later, three weeks before he was to sail with his wife and daughter for Europe, he took once again to the Adirondacks, convinced that solitary and leisurely walks on the mountainsides would do him no harm. One afternoon, however, he lost his way. Lacking all provisions for an extended hike and fainting twice in the downward scramble, James stumbled, close to midnight, upon a house where he at last obtained help. He made light of his experience through the days of busy preparation for the family's departure to the Continent, but once there he suffered total collapse.

The Gifford Lectures

The summer of rest and the mineral baths at Nauheim offered him only temporary relief. Although James continued reading in the religious biographies he had been collecting since the invitation to give the Gifford Lectures was first extended more than two years before, the discouragement, depression, and homesickness that assailed him in the fall and winter months, as he and Mrs. James moved about England and Europe in quest of comfort and healing, made writing the lectures impossible. It was not until early 1900, after two postponements of the lectures and an extension of his leave from Harvard for a second year, that James, slowly on the mend, finally got them underway. Even then he continued to be easily exhausted, and the progress of his writing was agonizingly slow.

The task James had taken on would not have been easy under the best of circumstances. As he wrote to an old friend in Boston on April 12, 1900,

> The problem I have set myself is a hard one: *first,* to defend . . . "experience" against "philosophy" as being the real backbone of the world's religious life . . . and *second,* to make the hearer or reader believe, what I myself invincibly do believe, that, although all the special manifestations of religion may have been absurd (I mean its creeds and theories), yet the life of it as a whole is mankind's most important function (H. James, 1920, 2, p. 127).

He expected failure in so "well-nigh impossible" a task, "but to attempt it," he added, "is *my* religious act."

It was even more an act of filial piety. So concludes Ralph Barton Perry, James's successor at Harvard, whose two-volume study of James won the Pulitzer prize in biography in 1936. In a letter of farewell to his dying father, which he wrote in England on December 14, 1882, James declared that

> In the mysterious gulf of the past into which the present soon will fall and go back and back, yours is still for me the central figure. All my intellectual life I derive from you; and though we have often seemed at odds in the expression thereof, I'm sure there's a harmony somewhere, and that our strivings will combine. What my debt to you is goes beyond all my power of estimating,—so early, so penetrating and so constant has been the influence (H. James, 1920, 1, p. 219).

Learning of his father's death only a few days later, James made the following request in a letter to his wife, who was to play a vital role in supporting and encouraging him in his work.

> You have one new function hereafter, or rather not so much a new function as a new intellectualization of an old one: you must not leave me till I understand a little more the value and meaning of religion in Father's sense, in the mental life and destiny of man. It is not the *one* thing needful, as he said. But it is needful with the rest. My friends leave it altogether out. I as his son (if for no other reason) must help it to its rights in their eyes. And for that reason I must learn to interpret it aright as I have never done, and you must help me.

"The *Varieties*," concludes Perry (1935, 2, p. 323), "is the fulfillment of this pledge after the lapse of almost twenty years."

In spite of his self-deprecating complaints while preparing them, of "wishy-washy generalities" and slackness in the writing, James's Gifford Lectures proved to be an unmistakable success. The record audience of some 300 persons who were present for the first series of ten, given twice weekly in May and June of 1901, struck the surprised lecturer as extraordinarily attentive and sympathetic. At the next year's series, which James wrote in the fall and winter of 1901 while teaching a course at Harvard on "The Psychological Elements of Religious Life," the audience swelled to 400. The book itself, dedicated to his mother-in-law and appearing within weeks after the final lecture, was immediately so popular that half a dozen reprintings were required in the first year alone. While translators set about to make the *Varieties* available to a wider audience, reviewers hailed it in both scholarly and sectarian journals as a masterful work of deep understanding and penetrating insights (see Wulff, 1995).

The *Varieties* is quintessentially James in many respects—in its emphasis on individuality and feeling, its sympathetic understanding of human suffering and eccentricity, the predominance of vivid fact over abstract formulation. Yet it contains relatively little of his own philosophy, to which he was to give the last decade of his life. In a period of eight years that was punctuated with honorary degrees, visiting lectureships, and still more trips to Europe, for intellectual exchange and medical treatment, James eagerly set about to articulate his philosophy of pure experience. In one series of essays he sought to work out more fully the pragmatic rule of truth, according to which the meaning of any idea whatsoever lies in its experiential consequences. In another series he championed what he considered his most important contribution to philosophy, his pluralistic doctrine of radical empiricism.

Yet the comprehensive work on philosophy that he long dreamed of writing was destined to remain but a fragment. Precarious health and seemingly constant interruptions—to accommodate an international stream of correspondents and callers, to support worthy causes, and to fulfill his duties at Harvard—greatly reduced his opportunities for sustained work. Long-anticipated retirement in 1907 promised more leisure, but the fact was that his time had nearly run out. After a final, hopeful trip to Europe in the spring of 1910, which ended several months later in exhaustion and despair, James returned for the last time to his beloved summer house near Chocorua, New Hampshire, on the southern edge of the White Mountains. There, on August 26, he died, surrounded by the natural beauty that was his most direct access to the spiritual life.

JAMES'S PSYCHOLOGY OF RELIGION

The incomplete work that James left behind contains neither an original principle nor a comprehensive theory around which a school might have formed itself. It is also said that his corpus is shot through with inconsistencies and thus does not form a coherent whole. It may seem remarkable, therefore, that an unbroken succession of scholars has been inspired by his writings (see Capps and Jacobs, 1995; Pettersson and Åkerberg, 1980; Skrupskelis, 1977), and even more so that the interest of the present generation, which has at last produced critical editions of his works and of his voluminous correspondence,[3] is great enough to be considered a revival. The contemporary rediscovery of James is evident especially among some proponents of the phenomenological perspective, who claim him as one of their own (see Edie, 1987; MacLeod, 1969; Spiegelberg, 1972).

As undisturbed by inconsistency as his father was, and convinced that the universe's indeterminate nature requires a pluralistic perspective, James argued that a mere textual analysis of his writings would lead nowhere, especially if it overlooks the character of the audience to which each contribution was addressed. Essential first of all, he insisted, is an imaginative grasping of his center of vision (H. James, 1920, 2, p. 355). "When one attempts to put the very varied contents of his essays and lectures into precise and well-arranged formulae," agrees James's good friend Theodore Flournoy (1911a, p. 40), "one runs the risk of gravely misrepresenting him." To this danger we must remain alert as we consider the contents of his Gifford Lectures.

The Right to Believe

The *Varieties*, we have learned, was intended primarily as a defense of the religious outlook. In an earlier essay, misleadingly entitled "The Will to Believe" (1897), James defended the right to affirm religious propositions solely on the basis of emotional predilection—but only when three conditions hold. The choice confronting a person must be *forced* or inescapable, so that not choosing becomes itself a choice. The alternatives must be *living*, that is, they must be appealing options that can be genuinely embraced. Finally, the decision must be *momentous*, providing

---

[3] *The Works of William James*, edited by F. H. Burkhardt, F. Bowers, and I. K. Skrupskelis and published by Harvard University Press, consists of 19 volumes. *The Correspondence of William James*, edited by I. K. Skrupskelis and E. M. Berkeley and published by the University Press of Virginia, is expected to fill 12 volumes, of which the first three, published between 1992 and 1994, are devoted to James's correspondence with his brother Henry.

a unique opportunity that will make a significant difference in a person's life. It is assumed that the evidence is insufficient for making the choice on intellectual grounds.

Doubtful that any particular religious doctrine is true, and certain that most people need to have their faiths "broken up and ventilated," ridding them of their "sickliness and barbarism," James was explicitly not addressing this essay to a "miscellaneous popular crowd" (p. 7). He intended it, rather, for academics instilled with false and inhibitory notions of science and scientific evidence. It was for this tiny minority—as well as for himself, according to Perry (1935, 2, p. 211)—that James sought to legitimate religious faith.

We spontaneously believe whatever presents itself to our consciousness, James had said in the *Principles* (1890, 2, p. 919), unless it is contradicted by an opposing belief already held. Thus belief may be attained, not by "willing" it, as this essay's title may falsely imply, but by discrediting every contradictory belief. It is to this indirect task that "The Will to Believe" is addressed.

The *Varieties'* Threefold Agenda

The *Varieties*, in turn, represents a direct approach to justifying religious faith, now in terms of empirical evidence. According to the volume's preface, James originally expected to devote the first series of ten lectures to the psychological task of describing humanity's "religious constitution" and the second series to discussing the philosophical implications of his findings. The descriptive component grew, he says, to fill both series, allowing only the briefest summary of his philosophical conclusions in the final lecture. His interest in judging the significance of what he found is nonetheless evident throughout the series.

James identifies two types of judgment, each independent of the other. An *existential judgment,* on the one hand, is directed to a phenomenon's constitution as well as to its origin and history. It begins by means of description and classification, followed by analysis of the causal forces that brought the phenomenon into being. A *spiritual judgment,* on the other hand, is addressed to a thing's value—its significance, importance, or meaning. Applied to religion, such a judgment employs three criteria: immediate luminousness (a feeling that is authoritative, James would eventually conclude, only for those who have it); congruence with facts or principles already held to be true; and helpfulness in the moral sphere—that is, in the attainment of human ideals (James, 1902, pp. 13, 23).

At the heart of the *Varieties* is a judgment of the spiritual type. What, James wanted to know, are religion's fruits for life? Yet as a physician–psychologist, he was naturally interested in the "existential" side of religion as well. Anxious that he not be misunderstood, he issued a sharp warning against "medical materialism," the tendency, evident especially among certain French psychopathologists, to consider religion discredited by tracing various of its manifestations to organic disturbances. Knowledge of the origin or conditions of a phenomenon, he emphasized, does not provide a sufficient basis for judging its value. So why, then, did he pursue his "pathological programme"? Admitting that he was led forward by "irrepressible curiosity," James also maintained that close examination of religion's "exaggerations and perversions, its equivalents and substitutes and nearest relatives elsewhere" would, by revealing its potentialities for corruption, make clearer its peculiar merits (p. 26).

If, then, the two forms of judgment prove not to be entirely independent after all, they nevertheless remain distinct items on James's complex agenda. Joining them is a third discrete theme, which emerges from the abundance of descriptive material that James says he gathered to carry out the task of judgment. In spite of this avowed motive, the material is allowed again and again to stand on its own merits. Its richness, James declares, far exceeds the paltry generalizations that can be made about it.

James, in sum, is speaking to us in a plurality of voices. First there is James the sensitive artist and pioneering phenomenologist, who seeks to understand from within and to appreciate the uniqueness of every individual experience. Second, there is James the empirical scientist and explanatory psychologist, curious about origins, impressed by the lawful regularities of nature, and yet, in the end, doubtful about psychology's ability to discern causal relations. Finally, there is James the liberal Protestant and pragmatic philosopher, who, impatient with every form of dogmatism and yet guided without apology by "common sense" and confessed philosophic prejudices, is set upon judging the overall value of religion for human life. We will listen to each of these voices in turn.

THE *VARIETIES* AS A DESCRIPTIVE WORK

Among psychologists of religion, James's Gifford Lectures have been most highly regarded for the wealth of descriptive material they contain. Although he embodied the spirit of scientific exactness, James was "above all . . . an artist in his extraordinarily vivid and delicate feeling for concrete realities, his penetrating vision in the realm of the particular and his aptitude for seizing on that which was characteristic and unique in everything that he met." The "most typical and masterly example" of this artistic capacity "to penetrate the recesses of other persons' consciousness," continues Theodore Flournoy (1902) in an early review of James's lectures, "is undoubtedly his celebrated book, *The Varieties of Religious Experience*." In a realm in which persons are shut off from one another to a most exceptional degree, James was the first, says the Geneva psychologist, to succeed in pulling down the barriers.

The *Varieties'* great theme, reflected in its title and throughout its pages, is that of religious diversity. Years before, in his *Principles of Psychology,* James had laid the foundations for a radical psychology of individual differences. According to the famous chapter on the stream of thought, the largely vague and ever-changing character of personal consciousness guarantees that even within a single individual every thought or feeling is unique. The differences between individuals may be expected to be even greater, according to the *Varieties,* given the further variability in human needs, capacities, and emotional susceptibilities. "The whole outcome" of his Gifford Lectures, James suspected, would be "the emphasizing to [his listeners' minds] of the enormous diversities which the spiritual lives of different men exhibit" (p. 94).

In sharp contrast to the experimental psychologist striving to characterize the human mind in general, James viewed individual differences not only as a phenomenon worthy of systematic study but also as a matrix of fundamental events. In his essay "The Importance of Individuals," James (1897, p. 193) declares that "the zone of the individual differences, and of the social 'twists' which by common confession they initiate, is the zone of formative processes, the dynamic belt of quivering uncertainty, the line where past and future meet." James makes much

[handwritten: personal vs institutional yet there is a symbiotic relation.]

the same point in the *Varieties*. "Individuality," he writes, "is founded in feeling; and the recesses of feeling, the darker, blinder strata of character, are the only places in the world in which we catch real fact in the making, and directly perceive how events happen, and how work is actually done" (p. 395).

In accord with this principle, James sought the essence of religion—that vital element or quality, found nowhere else, by which religion as a whole can be judged—in the privacy of inner religious experience. Accordingly, James was exclusively concerned with "personal religion," the primordial and solitary experience of direct communion with the divine, an uncommon, spontaneous, and predictably unorthodox occurrence, he says, that prompts a person to individual rather than corporate acts. Little would be gained, James was certain, from studying the contrasting institutional variety, "the chronic religion of the many" (p. 98), which originally evolved out of but now opposes genuine religious inspiration. Contaminated by the spirits of corporate and dogmatic domination and reduced to external ritual practices aimed at placating a childishly conceived god, institutional religion is, according to James, entirely a second-hand affair, a system of secondary accretions that is passed on and maintained by means of imitation and dull habit.

Some Principles of Method

Committed to studying "the acute religion of the few" (p. 98), James was faced by a serious dilemma. Like other psychologists of his day, he took introspection to be his chief and most reliable instrument of research. Moreover, his use of it was said to be unrivaled in terms of accuracy, refinement, and breadth. "With William James," writes John Dewey (1929, p. 114), "introspection meant genuine observation of genuine events, events that most persons are too conventional or too literal to note at all." Yet it was precisely from the religious sphere of events, a realm of exceptionally subtle emotions, that James felt himself most fully closed out.

One can never fathom an emotion or divine its dictates by standing outside of it," he writes in the *Varieties*. "In all these matters of sentiment one must have 'been there' one's self in order to understand them." What, then, was he to do, finding himself "outside the pale of such emotions"? In such a circumstance, he says, "The only sound plan . . . is to observe as well as we are able those who feel them, and to record faithfully what we observe" (pp. 260–261).

Choosing Personal Documents: To make his observations, James assembled a diverse collection of personal documents, most of them from published sources. James was not the first to use personal documents in the psychology of religion: Members of the Clark School, notably Edwin Starbuck, had already employed them, in the form of lengthy, open-ended questionnaires. James was even to borrow some of Starbuck's documents for his own study. Yet James selected and analyzed personal documents in a manner that was fundamentally different from that of the Clark school's.

For his study of conversion, Starbuck (1899) sought questionnaire replies from as broadly representative a sample as he could easily find—mainly women attending conventions of the Woman's Christian Temperance Union and soldiers in Iowa and Tennessee regiments that were stationed in San Francisco. James, in contrast, looked for documents written by those far less common persons who live at the extremes. Only in instances that are "one-sided, exaggerated, and intense," he declared, are we likely to find the religious life lived at first hand. From a study of these "violenter examples," primarily, James hoped to uncover the essential character of religious experience, to "know its secrets as authentically as anyone can know them who learns them from another" (pp. 44, 48, 383).

Persons who experience exceptional religious states, James forewarns his readers, frequently also show symptoms of mental pathology, a realm of phenomena that had interested James for some years (Taylor, 1983). This association should not surprise us, he says, for "In the PSYCHOPATHIC temperament we have the emotionality which is the *sine qua non* of moral perception; . . . the intensity and tendency to emphasis which are the essence of practical moral vigor; and . . . the love of metaphysics and mysticism which carry one's interests beyond the surface of the sensible world" (James, 1902, p. 28). The "psychopathic" temperament does not in itself, of course, guarantee religious genius. Whereas such a temperament may introduce an individual to "regions of religious truth" or perhaps even be an essential condition for such receptivity, a superior intellect is also required if the individual is to avoid "holy excesses," puerile conceptions, or paltry ideals and become an effective force in the world.

For the task before him, James declares in the first lecture of the *Varieties,* he will be most concerned with the works of piety and autobiography of "articulate and fully self-conscious" persons, those who are among the "most accomplished in the religious life and best able to give an intelligible account of their ideas and motives" (p. 12). Among the luminaries whose testimony he assembled are Leo Tolstoy, John Bunyan, Martin Luther, Ignatius Loyola, George Fox, and Walt Whitman. Yet James also draws on the reports of many persons whose piety is of the humblest order. There is Billy Bray, for example, the illiterate English evangelist who tells of twice whipping his quid of chewing tobacco under the church bench, before abandoning the habit altogether, when the Lord asked him to worship Him with "clean lips" (p. 234). Or George Müller, a man of energetic but narrowly literalistic piety for whom God was little more than an obliging assistant and business partner (p. 370). There are even documents reporting experiences that seem to have no religious character at all, or that express attitudes of religious indifference or hostility, as in the case of one of Starbuck's anonymous respondents who thought religion to be "so much mythic bosh" (p. 82).

Whereas all of Starbuck's documents were solicited by means of questionnaires, the great majority of the nearly 200 excerpts that James incorporated into his text were of the "spontaneous" variety, published in confessions, biographies, or inspirational works. Of the roughly 20 percent that were not derived from such sources, about half were taken from Starbuck's collection. Most of the rest were written by James's acquaintances or intimate friends, apparently at his request. Whatever their origin, the documents of the *Varieties* were overwhelmingly composed by persons of Christian faith. It is regrettable, James remarks, that personal confessions are so rare in other traditions, for without them, a literary approach to the "inwardness" of these traditions is virtually impossible (p. 319).

A Vicarious Phenomenology: Starbuck chose a statistical approach to analyze his collection of personal documents. He coded the responses of his subjects into various categories, counted up the number of occurrences, and then summed up the trends through a series of charts and graphs. While James does cite Starbuck's statistics regarding ordinary adolescent conversion, he concludes that the strikingly uniform phenomenon they reveal is the outcome of suggestion and imitation. The more genuine and idiosyncratic forms of piety, James implies, cannot be comprehended by means of representative samples and statistical procedures.

For the analysis of his own collection of documents, James chose a qualitative method that may be described as phenomenological.[4] Indeed, according to James Edie (1987, p. 52), James was the first to undertake a phenomenology of religious experience as such, based on a descriptive study of naive, unreflective experience undistorted by any theory or doctrine. Yet hardly anyone has followed James's lead, says Edie, and his method has been "unaccountably neglected by his successors and disciples."

According to the classic European model, phenomenological description is accomplished in a series of three distinguishable but closely related steps. The first is phenomenological *intuiting*, the act of becoming absorbed in the phenomena to be understood but without becoming totally lost in them. Maintaining some critical distance allows the phenomenologist to compare the phenomena to related ones in terms of similarities and differences and to be alert for factors that might distort or limit one's seeing. The second step is phenomenological *analyzing*. Intended here is not ruthless dissection of the phenomenon into its component parts but a careful discerning of its elements and structural organization. In the third step, phenomenological *describing*, the investigator at last reports what has been "seen," usually by means of some system of classification or through the use of metaphor or analogy. Description proper is necessarily selective, for the phenomenal world is virtually inexhaustible (Spiegelberg, 1965, pp. 659–676).

As a confessed outsider, James was prevented from approaching the world of religious experience directly. Thus he was forced to carry out his analysis vicariously, through a process that Spiegelberg (1975, p. 47) terms "imaginative self-transposal" or that we may simply call empathic understanding. How he carried out the equivalent of the first two steps described above we cannot know, for as Spiegelberg emphasizes, they are performed in patient silence. All we can say is that it must have been difficult, not only because James was an outsider but also because of ill health. Of the third step, on the other hand, much can be said, in spite of James's reticence about his own procedures.

The Method of Serial Study: James's treatment of mystical experiences provides a clear example of his descriptive method. James begins by delineating four characteristics that, for his purposes, identify an experience as mystical. The first two are the most important, sufficient in themselves for defining the mystical.

(1) *Ineffability:* Like states of feeling, mystical experiences cannot be adequately expressed in words and thus can only be known by those who have them.
(2) *Noetic quality:* Mystical states are experienced as states of knowledge, as sources of deeply significant illuminations. Moreover, the truths revealed in them, unknown in ordinary states, typically possess an enduring sense of authority.

The other two characteristics are nearly as common if not so strikingly evident.

(3) *Transiency:* Mystical experiences are fleeting, lasting at most an hour or two. While tending to elude full recollection in normal states of mind, they leave a

---

[4] James himself used the word phenomenology to describe his efforts in the *Varieties*. "We began all this empirical inquiry," he remarked at the outset of his second set of lectures, "not merely to open a curious chapter in the phenomenology of human consciousness, but rather to attain a spiritual judgment as to the total value and positive meaning of all the religious trouble and happiness which we have seen" (p. 259 in the first printing of the *Varieties*). But from the eighth printing (November 1903) onward, "natural history" appears in the place of phenomenology. The significance of this change remains obscure, for the phenomenological movement was only then beginning and James apparently took little notice of it (Spiegelberg, 1965, 1, p. 111).

lasting impression on the inner life and are immediately recognized when they recur.

(4) *Passivity:* Although mystical states can be actively facilitated, through meditation and other spiritual disciplines, once they set in, the individual no longer feels a sense of personal control. The mystic may even feel grasped and held by the Other who is encountered in these states. (pp. 302–303)

Having circumscribed his subject matter, James sets about to acquaint his readers with some typical examples. Essential to their interpretation, he says, is the METHOD OF SERIAL STUDY, which is the *Varieties*'s one explicit methodological device. "Phenomena are best understood," he writes, "when placed within their series, studied in their germ and in their over-ripe decay, and compared with their exaggerated and degenerated kindred" (p. 303). To illuminate mystical experience, James begins by considering the phenomenon of suddenly sensing a deeper significance of some maxim, formula, or single word, or of a particular odor, some musical pattern, or a play of light. Ascending step by step, then, from this ordinary phenomenon that claims hardly any religious significance at all, James examines a variety of other manifestations: DÉJÀ VU, the experience of having "been here before" under precisely the same circumstances; other "dreamy states" in which a person feels surrounded by incomprehensible truths; experiences of intensified awareness of an abstracted self beyond the realities of space and time; and states of consciousness produced by intoxicants and anaesthetics, or awakened by certain aspects of nature, in which a person feels at one with the deepest truth (see Figure 11.1). Having reached the upper end of this series, James explores mysticism more fully through the testimony of recognized authorities, including Sufi philosopher and mystic Al-Ghazzali, "one of the best" of the mystical teachers; Saint Teresa, "the expert of experts" in describing the sensed revelation of new depths of truth; Saint Ignatius Loyola, "one of the most powerfully practical human engines that ever lived"; and Dionysius the Areopagite, "the fountain-head of Christian mysticism" (pp. 303–330 *passim*).

James places other religious phenomena in their respective series, too, including the sense of divine presence, religious melancholy, asceticism, and prayer. Less systematic applications of the principle are represented in occasional comparisons between particular religious occurrences and analogous but nonreligious ones. The place of self-surrender in certain cases of conversion, for example, is made more obvious by reminding the reader that recollection of a frustratingly elusive name

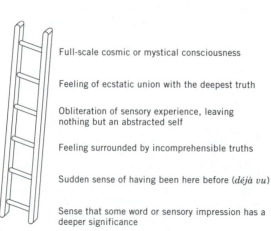

Full-scale cosmic or mystical consciousness

Feeling of ecstatic union with the deepest truth

Obliteration of sensory experience, leaving nothing but an abstracted self

Feeling surrounded by incomprehensible truths

Sudden sense of having been here before (*déjà vu*)

Sense that some word or sensory impression has a deeper significance

Figure 11.1. James's "mystical ladder," illustrating the method of serial study.

sometimes comes only after we stop trying to recall it. The transformative power of religious emotion is said to be analogous to the dramatic effects of maternity on a self-indulgent woman. The altruistic self-forgetfulness of spiritual excitement is observed to occur just as predictably in the joyous phase of a case of manic–depressive psychosis. And the automatisms—visions, voices, or speaking in tongues, for example—of certain religious states show apparent kinship to the effects of posthypnotic suggestion.

It is precisely in "the mass of collateral phenomena" to which he compares diverse religious manifestations that James locates the novelty of his *Varieties* (p. 29). By this method, above all, he provides an avenue of approach to phenomena that may otherwise lie beyond the reader's capacity for empathy. Recall, he says, the temporary "melting moods," especially the tearful states, into which we are occasionally thrown by a novel, play, or real-life experience; observe, then, the softening of the heart and the openness to loftier intentions. So it is with the saints, James says, except that their melting moods come to stay (p. 216). Or consider how the emotion of love transforms both the beloved and the face of nature, endowing them with new significance and value. In like manner does the world appear to change in the "state of assurance" of the religious convert, for whom everything looks vibrantly transfigured (pp. 127, 201). "We all have moments when the universal life seems to wrap us round with friendliness," writes James (p. 221) as he throws up yet another bridge to understanding the religious life from within.

The comparison of religious phenomena to collateral occurrences, both normal and pathological, can also help in making existential and spiritual judgments. On the one hand, by finding parallels between certain manifestations of piety and phenomena that are already to some degree explained—known to reflect, say, a particular temperamental disposition or an exceptional physiological state—we make inferences about some of piety's causes. On the other hand, such parallels may help us to judge the distinctive significance of a religious phenomenon by making evident the qualities that differentiate it from its next of kin.

This, then, is how James proceeds with a typical document. He prefaces the excerpt with a brief characterization of the phenomenon it illustrates, emphasizing the crucial distinction or point he wishes to make. He also introduces the writer of the excerpt and describes any essential historical or contextual factors. Following the lengthy quotation itself—perhaps after he has supplemented it with additional, briefer extracts that either drive home the point or merely demonstrate that so odd a phenomenon is after all not so rare—James adds his own incisive and often sympathetic comments. In these remarks he reiterates the object to be learned, often by means of an analogy. He sometimes also suggests in which series the example lies or in which respects and to what degree it is typical of its class. Interspersed among these documents and their commentary is a variety of other material, including introspective discourses on aspects of human experience, fragments of religious history and sociological analysis, and philosophical reflections on EPISTEMOLOGY and human nature. There are also the existential and spiritual judgments, to which we will shortly turn.

Two Fundamental Types

The generous sampling of personal documents that James submits to us for intuitive comprehension is more broadly framed by several typological distinctions. At their extremes, these types are "somewhat ideal abstractions." Most of our acquaintances, James admits, will appear as "intermediate varieties and mixtures" (p. 140).

Yet he is convinced that only by pushing these types to their limits will we clearly see their distinctive features.

At the heart of the first series of ten lectures—and for many the most memorable theme of the *Varieties*—is James's differentiation of the HEALTHY-MINDED and the SICK SOUL. Strictly speaking, these two types represent, not religious varieties per se, but temperamental predispositions to perceive the world in different ways. Persons of a healthy-minded bent tend to see everything in this life as good; the outcome is a congenital happiness, and in the religious sphere the response is one of grateful admiration and desire for union with the divine. In contrast, the sick soul is peculiarly sensitive to life's discordances. Struck by the precariousness of existence, the ubiquity of suffering, and the inevitability of death, an individual of this inclination finds evil to be an essential clue to the world's dimly perceived meaning. When the outlook of such a person is purely naturalistic, says James, life is bound to end in sadness if not also anxious trembling; but when suffering is seen to have immortal significance, the soul breaks through its melancholy with new-found zest or even ecstatic rapture.

The seeming incapacity for suffering that is inborn in persons at the extreme of healthy-mindedness can be voluntarily and systematically cultivated by others. That is, good may be consciously regarded as the essence of things at the same time that evil is deliberately ignored. The fact is, says James, that each of us cultivates the healthy-minded attitude to some degree, as when we avert our eyes from disease and death or fastidiously avoid thinking about "the slaughterhouses and indecencies without end on which our life is founded" (p. 80). For some, the resolute turning away from such threats to personal happiness eventually establishes an optimistic outlook that embraces the whole of reality.

As the "supreme contemporary example" (p. 75) of healthy-mindedness James chose poet Walt Whitman, whom Canadian psychiatrist Richard Bucke (1901, p. 225) describes, similarly in superlatives, as "the best, most perfect, example the world has so far had of the Cosmic Sense." Others fitting the "infinite varieties" of the healthy-minded type include the leaders and shapers of liberal Protestantism, notably Ralph Waldo Emerson and Theodore Parker. Of greater interest to James, however, was the movement he designates "mind-cure," which derived in part from New England transcendentalism. Teaching that our individual lives are at all times one with God's, the mind-curers systematically inculcated optimistic attitudes of hope, courage, and trust while simultaneously eradicating every negative attitude or emotion. Achieving success often enough to appeal to American practicality, mind-cure found its most radical expression in Christian Science, which denies reality not simply to evil but to the whole of the material world.

From the sick soul's perspective, on the other hand, evil is no easily dismissed chimera born of our ignorance. Nor is it simply a matter of the external world gone awry. Rather, this type experiences a painful discordancy deep within, a heterogeneity of personality that in extreme forms may be the cause of "desperation absolute and complete" (p. 135). However neurotic in constitution it may be, the sick soul is said by James to encompass the broader range of experience, incorporating the genuinely evil aspects of reality—within and without—and thereby opening itself, perhaps, to the deepest levels of truth. Tolstoy and John Bunyan serve as James's most famous cases of religious melancholy (see Excerpts 11.1). For James, Tolstoy represented a profoundly momentous loss of meaning in the outer world, in spite of seemingly fortunate circumstances, and Bunyan, a fearful contempt and despair for his own human self. James finds the sick soul's

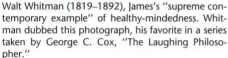

Walt Whitman (1819–1892), James's "supreme contemporary example" of healthy-mindedness. Whitman dubbed this photograph, his favorite in a series taken by George C. Cox, "The Laughing Philosopher."

Leo Tolstoy (1828–1910), who exemplified religious melancholy, in an engraving by T. Johnson.

discordant personality or DIVIDED SELF and its preoccupation with its own sinfulness described with unsurpassed genius in Saint Augustine's *Confessions.*

The healthy-minded and the sick soul live, says James, on the opposite sides of the pain threshold, the one habitually dwelling "on the sunny side of their misery-line," and the other living beyond it, "in darkness and apprehension" (p. 115). They correspondingly require different types of religion. For the ONCE-BORN, a term that James freely adapted from Francis Newman to describe the healthy-minded,[5] the world has one story only, possessing precisely those values it seems to have. For those who must be TWICE-BORN to achieve happiness, however, the world is a "double-storied mystery." The life that appears before us is a deception and a cheat, and only by renouncing it can we hope to discover truth (p. 139).

If asceticism represents "the essence of the twice-born philosophy" (p. 289), conversion constitutes its fulfillment and resolution. Although escape from the sick soul's agonies through transformation and unification is sometimes gradual, James (p. 186) says it is likely to be psychologically more complete when there is a definite crisis. The momentous outcome of this second birth is the state of assurance, an experience of tremendous intensity. At the heart of this state, beyond the conviction of perceiving new truths and the sense of glorious newness in the world and within

---

[5] Francis Newman (1852), who should not be confused with Cardinal Newman, his elder brother, indeed attributes to the once-born individual a "benevolent and healthy mind," but the other qualities he identifies—rigid and conservative formality, preoccupation with law and conscience, joyless lack of passion, and interest in God only in times of trial—sound not at all like those of James's once-born type. The description that James quotes is intended by Newman (p. 81) to describe, not the once-born, but the "feminine character," who by Newman's account tends to be twice-born, that is, governed by feelings and affection and acting on a more positive, creative, and instinctive basis than the once-born.

oneself, is a profound feeling of peace and harmony, a willing acquiescence to life's circumstances.

EXCERPTS 11.1

Illustrative of the documents that James incorporated into the *Varieties* are the following excerpts from two quotations that James abridged from Tolstoy's *My Confession.* Around the age of 50, Tolstoy became increasingly subject to intervals of perplexity, during which life's usual enchantment faded into meaninglessness, leaving him with the unanswered questions "Why?" and "What for?"

I felt that something had broken within me on which my life had always rested, that I had nothing left to hold on to, and that morally my life had stopped. An invincible force impelled me to get rid of my existence, in one way or another. It cannot be said exactly that I wished to kill myself, for the force which drew me away from life was fuller, more powerful, more general than any mere desire. It was a force like my old aspiration to live, only it impelled me in the opposite direction. It was an aspiration of my whole being to get out of life.

Behold me then, a man happy and in good health, hiding the rope in order not to hang myself to the rafters of the room where every night I went to sleep alone; behold me no longer going shooting, lest I should yield to the too easy temptation of putting an end to myself with my gun (quoted in James, 1902, pp. 128–129).

Over a period of two years, it gradually dawned on Tolstoy that the problem was not with life in general but with the conventional, upper-class life of intellectuality and ambition that he had been living. Happiness, he finally concluded, lies in simple living, in tending to elemental needs and believing in God.

I remember one day in early spring, I was alone in the forest, lending my ear to its mysterious noises. I listened, and my thought went back to what for these three years it always was busy with–the quest of God. But the idea of him, I said, how did I ever come by the idea?

And again there arose in me, with this thought, glad aspirations towards life. Everything in me awoke and received a meaning. . . . Why do I look farther? a voice within me asked. He is there: he, without whom one cannot live. To acknowledge God and to live are one and the same thing. God is what life is. Well, then! live, seek God, and there will be no life without him.

After this, things cleared up within me and about me better than ever, and the light has never wholly died away. I was saved from suicide. Just how or when the change took place I cannot tell. But as insensibly and gradually as the force of life had been annulled within me, and I had reached my moral death-bed, just as gradually and imperceptibly did the energy of life come back. And what was strange was that this energy that came back was nothing new. It was my ancient juvenile force of faith, the belief that the sole purpose of my life was to be better. I gave up the life of the conventional world, recognizing it to be no life, but a parody on life, which its superfluities simply keep us from comprehending.

Granting that biochemical processes must also have contributed to the interlude of melancholy, as specialists in depression would assume today, James maintains that Tolstoy's suffering was the logical outcome of the conflict between his inner character and outer pursuits. "His crisis was the getting of his soul in order, the discovery of its genuine habitat and vocation, the escape from falsehoods into what for him were ways of truth" (p. 154).

Happiness at last! Yet how much more complex than the innocent gladness of the healthy-minded, for the twice-born's newfound joy springs not from ignorance but from a deeper, even mystical understanding that no longer finds natural evil a stumbling block. Thus even with the experience of redemption, the sick soul retains its distinctive character, which remains incomprehensible to the once-born's sanguine spirit.

The *Varieties* contains additional type distinctions but no others of comparable significance. To the "carnivorous-minded 'strong man,' " for example, James contrasts the gentle herbivorous saint, both of whom are said to have legitimate roles to play in this world (p. 297). Those who "aim most at intellectual purity and simplification" are juxtaposed with others for whom "*richness* is the supreme imaginative requirement" (p. 362)—the liberal Protestant in contrast to the high church Catholic. And persons whose lives are based on mere *having* are paired off with their opposites, who renounce possessions in the interest of *being* and *doing,* according to some ideal (p. 255).

THE *VARIETIES* AS A WORK OF EXISTENTIAL JUDGMENT

James's penetrating sympathetic study of piety's variations, says Gordon Allport (1942, p. 6), is "a masterpiece of descriptive science." As we know, however, James had more in mind than sheer description and classification of religious experiences. "Forever harping on the need of an explanatory psychology . . . , he rushed impatiently on to what was to him the *real* question, 'What shall we say or do about [these varieties]?' " Explanation and action, not contemplation and imagination, were his preferences in the long run (Perry, 1935, 1, pp. 176, 201).

James thought it peculiarly difficult to form existential judgments about religious experience, to trace out its causal origins. Introspection, he points out, reveals little about causal connections; and of the cerebral correlates of subconscious activity, which serves as James's most notable theoretical construct, science had yet learned nothing. Moreover, he was confronted by events of extraordinary individuality, allowing but the vaguest of general explanations. Within these sharp limits James still thought it possible to infer some of the causal factors responsible for the diversity of human piety.

In accord with his chapter on instincts in the *Principles of Psychology*, James postulates in the *Varieties* an indefinite number of inborn impulses that are apparently common to all human beings. These impulses occupy two spheres, a lower one of "fleshly sensations, instincts, and desires, of egotism, doubt, and the lower personal interests" and a higher, more profound sphere, wherein may be found, for example, the self-forgetful expansive affections and the tendency to subject oneself to strenuous challenge and sacrifice. This duality in human nature, says James, provides "the general basis of all religious experience" (p. 86). The shifting balance of our propensities, whether through gradual mutation or sudden explosion, accounts in large part for the dynamics of the religious life.

To discuss such changes, James finds us forced by our ignorance to resort to the use—illusory though it be—of mechanical or spatial analogies. We might imagine, for example, the emotionally excited human mind as a *polyhedron*. Sufficiently pried up from its habitual position, it may settle onto another of its faces, assuming a new attitude. Similarly, ideas are said to shift from the *periphery* to the *center* of a person's energy; conversion is supposed to show the *high-water mark* of a person's spiritual capacity; and the soul is compared to a *machine* with its own best conditions of efficiency. Earlier we noted that James spoke of the healthy-minded and the sick soul as living on the *opposite sides* of the pain *threshold*. (On James's use of metaphor, see Bozzo, 1977, and Leary, 1990.)

The Subconscious Self

Of James's spatial metaphors, the subconscious is by far the most important. What James refers to with this expression is not some *un*conscious mental state; earlier, in the *Principles,* he had systematically refuted ten proofs for the existence of such states. Rather, he had in mind another level or form of consciousness such as he himself had experienced years before while experimenting with nitrous oxide (James, 1882). The investigations of hypnosis and hysteria by Alfred Binet, Pierre Janet, Sigmund Freud, and Morton Prince, among others, and especially the work of Frederick Myers, a founder of the British Society for Psychical Research and James's intimate friend, contributed compelling evidence of "a consciousness existing beyond the field" of ordinary consciousness. James considered the discovery of this extramarginal consciousness to be "the most important step forward . . . in psychology" since his student days (1902, p. 190). Although others were using the adjective "unconscious," James preferred the vaguer and more obviously metaphorical terms *subconscious* or Meyers's SUBLIMINAL (James, 1901, p. 196). By whatever name, its discovery seemed to James to illumine many of the episodes that punctuate the *Varieties'* pages.

Religion is said by James to have "unusually close relations" to the subliminal region, demonstrated by the near-universality of automatisms among religious leaders. Events in this region may account for the converted individual's abrupt change of heart, after a long period of subconscious incubation, as well as for the revelations of mystical experience, the diabolical no less than the divine. We may also comprehend the saint's extravagant obsessions in terms of these extramarginal occurrences. James observes that the subliminal region is "the abode of everything that is latent and the reservoir of everything that passes unrecorded or unobserved. . . . Our intuitions, hypotheses, fancies, superstitions, persuasions, convictions, and in general all our non-rational operations, come from it." It is, he says, "the fountainhead of much that feeds our religion" (p. 381).

Differences in religious experience reflect differences in the character and accessibility of the subliminal field. The content of this region varies in part with diversity in life experiences, the deposits of which incubate and ripen outside the field of consciousness. The subliminal self, James suggests, is larger in some persons than in others; it may also be more or less active or developed. Furthermore, the margin of a person's conscious field, the dimensions of which are said to reflect constitutional differences, may be relatively "leaky" or "pervious," or—to employ yet another of James's metaphors—may have a door that stands ajar or even wide open, as he says would be true of persons "deep in the religious life" (pp. 197, 381). The conscious person, in sum, "is continuous with a wider self through which saving experiences come" (p. 405). What may lie on the farther side of the little-understood subliminal region is of course a matter of sheer speculation, but James leaves open the possibility that the subconscious self is the doorway through which the divine enters human lives.

Overlapping with variations in the subconscious self are other individual differences that James says are important in shaping religious lives. Beyond the fundamental differences of constitution and temperament, of emotional susceptibility, are variations in needs and wants, in imagination, intellect, and sensibility, in life difficulties and angle of observation. Writing at a time when psychologists were only beginning to recognize the significance of individual differences, James placed their reality at the heart of his analysis. Are we to wonder, he asks, that human piety ranges so enormously? Is it not likely that different persons may be helped best by different religious traditions? Are not all critics or judges most likely to be drawn to traditions that best meet their own needs, making impartial judgments about religious matters effectively impossible?

THE *VARIETIES* AS A WORK OF SPIRITUAL JUDGMENT

Just as he hoped that the *Varieties* might serve as a "crumb-like contribution" to a "psychology of individual types of character" (p. 95), so James wished that his lectures would help to promote a critical "Science of Religions" grounded in the facts of personal experience. Such a science, he thought, could help to remove from both dogma and worship their "historic incrustations," and it could sift out doctrines incongruent with the findings of natural science. What remained could be dealt with as hypotheses for careful testing. Through this process, James hoped that consensus on religious matters might at last be obtained (pp. 342, 359).

To make the spiritual judgments that were his ultimate goal, James had to decide for himself what the abiding, essential core of religion might be. Underneath the great diversity in religious thought, he concludes, is a uniformity in feeling and conduct, elements that best serve to identify religion's essence. Ideas, symbols, and other teachings are only secondary; they are helpful embellishments, perhaps, but not indispensable for the continuance of the religious life. The feelings characteristic of such a life are cheerful and expansive; there may be a sense that "great and wondrous things are in the air" (p. 398). This state of assurance or "faith-state," in Leuba's phrase, imparts courage, meaning, and zest to ordinary life.

Amidst the cacophony of conflicting doctrines, James also finds a common intellectual nucleus, consisting of two impressions. The first is an uneasiness, "a sense that there is *something wrong about us* as we naturally stand," the second "a sense that *we are saved from the wrongness* by making proper connexion with the higher powers." In both impressions the higher self plays a crucial role. It allows us, first of all, to perceive the wrongness within, and second, it is what we identify with our real being. We become aware, says James, that this higher part borders on and is continuous with "a *more* of the same quality." This "more" is active in the universe outside of ourselves and by contact with it we may find salvation (p. 400).

Regarding the objective reality of the "more," James proposes a single, modest hypothesis, which we have already anticipated. "Whatever it may be on its *farther* side, the 'more' with which in religious experience we feel ourselves connected is on its *hither* side the subconscious continuation of our conscious life." According to this hypothesis, the reports of religious individuals claiming to be under the control of something higher are literally true, for it is from "the higher faculties of our own hidden mind" that the objective-appearing invasions come (p. 403).

James recognizes that so meager and abstract a distillate as he has to offer is not likely to rouse the spiritual excitement that he documents and admires in the pages of the *Varieties*. For many individuals, "over-beliefs" of one kind or another are "absolutely indispensable" for lively personal faith (p. 405). These ideas or doctrines, he adds, are generally the most interesting and valuable aspects of a person. Without them, many of the fruits of the religious life would undoubtedly be lost.

It would be a loss indeed, for these fruits, taken as a whole, convinced James that religion is "an essential organ of our life, performing a function which no other portion of our nature can so successfully fulfill" (p. 49). Employing "general philosophical prejudices," an intuitive "standard of theological probability," and a measure of common sense, James argues that saintliness—the collective name for the ripe fruits of religion, said to be much the same in all traditions—must, by today's lights and thus provisionally, be evaluated in terms of "helpfulness in general human affairs" (pp. 263, 265, 283). To what degree, we must ask, do the saintly virtues help us to meet the difficulties of worldly existence? How fully do they satisfy

Mother Teresa, the saintly Catholic nun from Yugoslavia who was awarded the 1979 Nobel Peace Prize, among numerous other honors, for her work with abandoned children and destitute sick and dying adults in Calcutta.

diverse human needs? How lofty—and how probable of attainment—are the ideals toward which they direct us?

For James, institutional religion seems to have little to recommend it, beyond its ability to satisfy certain aesthetic needs for majestic authority and splendor. Yet personal religion, too, could excite his frank disapproval, especially when it combined with concepts of cruel and petty deities who delight in self-inflicted suffering, bask in their devotees' unending adulation, and smile with benign partiality on a select group of favorites. James's pity borders on amused contempt when he describes the swoons and sufferings of the blessed Marguerite Marie Alacoque, the extraordinary precautions against sin of Saint Louis of Gonzaga, and the stereotyped humility and voluble egotism of Saint Teresa. A "feeble . . . intellectual outlook," an intellect "no larger than a pin's head," a genius with "a curious flavor of superficiality"—in each of these cases of holy excess, as in most others, the spirtual excitement is said to be unmet by an intellect even approximately its equal (pp. 276, 283, 277, 298). Lacking balance, the saintly mind is prone to fanaticism, intolerance, and persecution.

At their best, however, nothing can match the saint's extravagances. "The highest flights of charity, devotion, trust, patience, bravery to which the wings of human nature have spread themselves have been flown for religious ideals" (p. 210). By renouncing every demand of the lower self and surrendering absolutely to a higher power, the saint secures a new center of energy and a level of human excellence otherwise unobtainable. In the discipline of ascetic practice, the saint spurns the accident of happy life circumstances and voluntarily takes "the great initiation," confronting the wrongness of the world with the soul's best resources. Here if anywhere may one find the heroic, the "genuinely strenuous life," which James says is required in some proportion "to produce the sense of an existence with character and texture and power" (pp. 290, 210, 240).

The out-and-out saint, according to James, would live at peril in today's world, where the saintly virtues of sympathy, trustfulness, and nonresistance would inevitably invite contempt as well as defeat. Yet without the saint's tender extravagances, he adds, the world would be far worse a place in which to live. Naively confident in the virtue and worth of others, the saint calls into existence potentialities of goodness that the subjects themselves never suspected. Enrichers of our imagination, sources of creative energy, and transmuters of the earthly order, the great saints present to us qualities "indispensable to the world's welfare." Religion, "in a general way" and "on the whole," retains "its towering place in history" (p. 299).

THE *VARIETIES* AS A PERSONAL DOCUMENT

James's Gifford Lectures, we have seen, are far more than a disinterested descriptive work. Inevitably, they reflect their author's philosophic standpoint. Before the tribunal of the pragmatic view of truth, religion is to be judged in terms of its usefulness, the difference it makes in the individual's day-to-day existence. The evidence, in accord with James's radical empiricism, is to come from the realm of human experience, the personal arena in which individual destinies work themselves out. That religion itself is occupied with these private destinies nearly guarantees at the outset a favorable judgment. But the idiosyncratic character of personal experience requires James to reserve his fullest approval for the pluralistic view, which gives place to a diversity of religious types.

James observes that philosophic postures no less than religious ones have their roots in our feelings and intuitions as well as in our experience. Therefore we come round once again to the matter of the personal equation. Elements of James's own inner experience unquestionably crept into the *Varieties*, sometimes as just one more vivid example, other times as a major theme. Knowing as we do that the sufferings of James's anonymous correspondent (p. 134) were in reality his own, we might suspect that other examples are his as well. One candidate is the first case in the appendix following the lectures on healthy-mindedness. Written in the first person, this case describes and then analyzes in terms of subconscious influences the startling effectiveness of the writer's visits to a psychic healer. When the congruency of this case with James's medical history as well as with his attitudes and speculations raised his earliest readers' suspicions, an alarmed James considered deleting the case entirely (Perry, 1935, 2, p. 340).[6]

Even if James had included no documents of his own in the *Varieties*, we might still recognize the testimony of the author's personal experience. Certainly he knew at first hand the "organic thrill . . . we feel in a forest at twilight, or in a mountain gorge" (p. 31). "The fact of the prevalence of tragic death" (p. 289) was also no stranger to him. Indeed, the sudden death from tuberculosis of his devoted cousin Minnie Temple, in March of 1870, may have precipitated his profound crisis of dread (Allen, 1967). And who can doubt that he writes from immediate experience when he describes the absolute loss of pleasure during prolonged seasickness; the proneness to becoming "melancholy metaphysicians" during periods of weakness and pain; or the virtue of obeying a doctor or wife at times of indecision? We might recall, too, James's (1882) earlier experiment with nitrous oxide intoxication, which left him with an unshakable conviction that our ordinary form of consciousness is

---

[6] These suspicions were understandably fueled by the words introducing this case: "My own experience is this: I had long been ill [etc.]" (p. 123 in the original edition). In the first printing of the *Varieties*, James had a slip inserted immediately before the Contents, which reads "*Remark on pages 123–126.—* The two cases printed here are selected from a larger number, kindly furnished me by friends." For subsequent printings, the footnote on page 121 referring to these cases was correspondingly modified and quotation marks were added to both documents.

surrounded by potential forms that are entirely different. This is one of the out-standing conclusions of the *Varieties* (p. 308).

As noted earlier, many scholars contend that James's experience was pro-foundly shaped by his relation to his father. Perry, we may recall, concluded that the *Varieties* was James's way of championing his father's cause, of helping religion "to its rights" in his contemporary's eyes. Inevitably, it seems, his father's views themselves were taken up into the lectures. Flournoy (1911a) points out the per-vasive quality of *seriousness* in the work of both father and son, beneath a surface of charm, wit, and vivacity. "There must be something solemn, serious, and tender about any attitude which we denominate religious," writes the author of the *Varieties* (p. 39), who proceeds, then, to enthrone melancholy and helplessness, risk and heroic struggle, as singularly vital elements in the genuine religious life.

In making his father's "twice-born" outlook the paradigm of religious experi-ence, says Strout (1971), James strikingly narrowed the varieties that he considered in this work.

> The peculiar typology and divided sympathies of *The Varieties of Religious Experience* reflect . . . the long shadow of William James's troubled over-identification with and gradual emancipation from the baffling and inspiring example of his neglected and brilliant father. This explanation cannot validate or undermine the argument of his book, but it can enable us to understand the point of its odd vocabulary, the urgency of its themes, the distribution of its sympathies, and its strategic place in the developing identity of one of America's most original philosophers (p. 151).

Judging the argument of the *Varieties* to have failed in the end, Strout considers psychobiography to be the best means for understanding this enormously popular work.

Drawing on Erikson's concept of an identity crisis, Strout maintains that the *Varieties* was James's way of working through an over-identification with his troubled father. The perspective that James developed in this work, says Strout, was an "ingenious compromise" between his father's dogmatic and mystical theology, which James had edited and published in 1885, and his own scientific and psycho-logical outlook. He vindicated his father's twice-bornness by making it the model of religious experience, and he incorporated his father's socialist-communal em-phasis by advocating the strenuous life for the good of the larger world. Yet by siding with philosophical pluralism, he finally posed a fundamental challenge to his father's monistic view of God. Born too late to find relief in religious conversion and too early for psychoanalytic therapy, James was compelled as he wrote the *Varieties* to be "his own therapist, his own pastor, his own philosopher" (p. 148).

One notable outcome of James's therapeutic approach to religious experience, Strout observes, was his minimizing of the significance of religious symbols. He saw them as inadequate expressions or by-products of original religious experience and the accompanying sense of having perceived truth. Faithful to his liberal Protestant upbringing, he largely disdained the elaborations of story and ritual that are the collective possession of the mass of ordinary devotees. The legends surrounding the lives of the Buddha, Muhammad, and the Catholic saints, for example, he judged to be simply tasteless and silly (James, 1902, p. 274). Yet he grants that the indulgence of human nature by the Catholic tradition, in offering "so much richer pasturage and shade to the fancy," gives the tradition an undeniable advantage. At the same time, however, he reiterates his conviction that Protestant theology, be-cause of its alleged congruity with the structure of the human mind, is spiritually the more profound (pp. 363, 198).

The undeniable Protestant Christian bias of the *Varieties* is most clearly evident in the preponderance of Protestant categories and examples as well as in such collective references as "We English-speaking Protestants" (p. 365). Similarly, his definition of religion—"the feelings, acts, and experiences of individual men in their solitude, so far as they apprehend themselves to stand in relation to whatever they may consider the divine" (p. 34)—projects before us an image of an anti-ecclesiastical Protestant privately communing with God. Yet James also draws heavily on the testimony and example of the Catholic saints, and—more frequently than the original index of the *Varieties* would suggest—he refers to non-Christian materials as well, most often from the Hindu, Buddhist, and Islamic traditions. To fill out his characterization of mystical experience, for example, he considers the Hindu notion of *samādhi*, the Buddhist concept of *dhyāna*, and Al-Ghazzali's autobiographic reflections of the Sufi life. And just as Michael Malone (1983) finds James's distinction of the healthy-minded and the sick soul helpful in bridging the gap between traditionalist and renewalist Episcopalians, so Conrad Hyer (1983) uses it to account for the differences between the Rinzai and Soto schools of Zen Buddhism. Historian of religion Erwin Goodenough (1965, p. xii) must nevertheless be correct when he declares that "No Catholic, Jew, Hindu, or Moslem would have used [James's Protestant categories to outline] the subject or would feel much personal relevancy in James's brilliant description."

THE RESPONSE OF THE CRITICS

To the Protestant Christians who dominated the American psychology of religion James's categories seemed perfectly natural. Moreover, the *Varieties* had the virtue of expanding the narrow focus on conversion characteristic of earlier contributors such as Leuba, Starbuck, and Coe. Yet reviewers of every persuasion, including those whose admiration was otherwise unbounded, pointed to certain apparent shortcomings of James's study. Six overlapping criticisms stand out.

Neglect of Normal Experience

From James's day to ours, the most frequent objection to the *Varieties* is to its overwhelming emphasis on exceptional experience. Anton Boisen (1953, p. 156) maintains that James's interest in the pathological "provides the basis for some of [the *Varieties*] most brilliant insights," but the majority of the book's critics argue that James's extreme cases, because they accent the morbid and the mystical, do not provide an adequate basis for generalizing about religion as a whole. Ezra Crooks (1913, p. 125), for example, after admiring James's "genius for noting the unusual in human experience," warns against "neglecting the vastly more significant central experiences of our lives."

In like vein John Hibben (1903) argues that such normal experiences give rise to impulses that readily adapt themselves to diverse personal needs and changing times.

> These experiences are commonplace; they possess no content of mystic truth; they are accompanied by no dream or trance states, they show neither the heat nor the light of emotional enthusiasm—but they do form a steady stream of influence in every community which makes for the conservation and progress of all forms of social good. . . . In religion the superior court of appeal resides in the common experiences . . . of simple conviction and quiet devotion (p. 184).

Casting his lot in the same direction, Starbuck (1904, p. 104) wonders whether the mass of ordinary persons have not done more in discovering, shaping, and refining the diverse modes of religious life than all the mystics combined. "If the psychology of religion is to have the future it deserves," he warns, "there is an indefinite amount of plodding ahead of it with the prosaic facts of ordinary experience." It is to the "compact mass of humanity" that we must go, he says, "if we are to get the truest picture at last of what religion really is."

In the *Varieties,* James deliberately passes over the ordinary individual's piety as nothing more than dull habit. It is worth recalling, however, that at the time of his spiritual crisis, salvation came to James not in the form of dramatic experience but through the deliberate cultivating of certain habitual practices. In some of his other writings, he argues that habit—the enormous fly-wheel of society, its most precious conservative agent" (James, 1890, 1, p. 125)—is the essential practical means by which even the highest ideals are kept alive. "Every good that is worth possessing must be paid for in strokes of daily effort," he writes, and accordingly, to maintain the "higher spiritual side," he recommends a daily regime of spiritual reading or meditation. Such a discipline, he says, "would infallibly give us in due time the fulness of all we desire," including the "grace of character" that he observed with admiration in a number of Hindu visitors (James, 1899, pp. 51–52). Habit, we may conclude, may be a positive factor in the religious life when consciously placed in the service of some higher goal.

Exclusion of Institutional and Historical Factors

Habitual practices, including not only the individual forms that James had in mind but also various corporate observances, have long been valued by ecclesiastical authorities as a means of fostering the piety of ordinary people. Such traditional practices undoubtedly also played a role in the lives of many of James's experts, whose remarkable experiences were surely exceptional for them as well. Echoing a number of other critics, Friedrich Heiler (1914) faults James for treating his subjects' religious experiences apart from the traditional and historical factors that condition even the lives of religious innovators. Wilhelm Wundt (1911, p. 119) argues that religion, like language and ethics, is a creation of human society. Individual experiences and confessions are therefore meaningful, he claims, only if they are considered in the context out of which they arise. Priest–ethnologist Wilhelm Schmidt (1908, pp. 141–142) emphasizes the interrelatedness of personal and institutional religion. Although they can be distinguished, he says, they cannot be separated, as James sought to do, for each presupposes and conditions the other. In giving no place in his study to institutional religion, James also neglects the role that ecclesiastical organizations play—for better or worse—in making certain fundamental values manifest in the public realm (Adams, 1980).

Overestimation of the Role of Feeling

Integral to James's theory that the origin of religion lies in exceptional individual experience—a theory that many since have taken to be a self-evident fact—is the conviction that feeling is religion's fundamental element, the matrix out of which faith and its expressions arise. A number of his critics have challenged this point, arguing that James exaggerates the extent and significance of immediate feeling in the religious life, and that he correspondingly undervalues the role of the intellectual, the volitional, and the ethical (e.g., Moore, 1938; Schmidt, 1908; Troeltsch,

THE RESPONSE OF THE CRITICS *501*

1904; Uren, 1928). To be sure, James uses the term *feeling* is so broad a sense that it includes both perceptual and cognitive aspects. Yet feeling is "private and dumb," he says, "and unable to give an account of itself"—thus the necessity of interpretations by which we "construe our feelings intellectually" (pp. 341, 342). Friedrich von Hügel, for one, criticizes James's casting of "the analytic and speculative activity of the mind" into nothing more than a secondary role, denying thereby that it may just as well precede and influence the "intuitive-emotional-volitional element." This unjustifed assumption, he says, conflicts with the *Varieties'* empirical method (Adams, 1980, p. 230).

James's similar subordination of activity or will to feeling is challenged by Starbuck (1904), who finds such a position strangely inconsistent with James's own famous theory of emotion, which is never mentioned in the *Varieties*. According to this theory, emotion is a reaction secondary to organic change and bodily movement: I see the bear, I run, and *then* I feel afraid. Starbuck proposes that *both* the rational processes *and* feelings are derivative, from deeper-lying "life-movements." "Religion," he says, "is to be found essentially in the active response the individual makes to the things of life." The cognitive and the affective, according to his view, serve the vital function of giving to consciousness "an account of its own inner life, a report of the facts of the outer world, and an estimation of one's adjustment or lack of adjustment to the sum of outside relations" (pp. 107–108). Thus Starbuck supports James's dethroning of theology and philosophy, but without giving feeling priority.

Inclusion of Pathology

Almost inevitably, James's focus on marked religious feeling brought cases of pathological intensity into the center of his discussion. The thesis that the presence of pathological elements may in fact be a prerequisite for genuine religious experience, as James suggests, was found unacceptable by a number of his critics. Hall (1904, 2, p. 293), for example, was appalled by the bulk of "abnormal" and even "teratological" cases—"the yellow literature of religious psychology"—that James included in the *Varieties*. Not only do they not explain piety, he says, but they also constitute what "true religion" preserves the faithful from. The "psychopathic temperament," he declares, has no advantage beyond the literary. Pratt (1920, p. 66) allows that the dissociated states characteristic of certain abnormal personalities sometimes "do seem to be of real use," lending a peculiar forcefulness to the lives of certain religious leaders. On the whole, however, he concludes that the fruits of such dispositions are negative. Also rejecting the comparison of religious expressions to pathological phenomena, Schmidt (1908) argues in his nearly book-length summary–critique of the *Varieties* that religion exists entirely independent of other factors. The testimony of a person's own inner being, he adds, unequivocally certifies religion as a phenomenon of health, not illness.

Appeal to Unknowable Subconscious Processes

In accord with this view, Schmidt places normal, healthy piety squarely in the realm of consciousness. Hence true religious conversion entails a fully conscious break with a person's former ways, achieved through self-determination and passionate inner struggle. Only then is it a conversion "in spirit and truth" (p. 69). The change of heart and mind, Schmidt emphasizes, is a fact—but the only one that is unequivocal and incontestable. Schmidt is not willing to accept James's speculations regarding causal factors in a subconscious realm. The "subconscious life," he says, is a "refuge of ignorance" (p. 47); we can know nothing of the "incubation and maturing of motives" in the subconscious that James postulates as a means of explanation.

John Moore (1938) also takes issue with James's "metaphors and fictitious entities," especially the subconscious. Employing the subconscious to account for mystical experience, he declares, "represents an attempt to explain the obscure by the almost totally dark" (pp. 199, 201). From among alternative explanations of mystical phenomena, Moore selects Henry Wieman's (1926) as the most satisfactory. According to Wieman's theory, in times of crisis when the usual system of responding is no longer sufficient, "The ordinary narrow and routinized selectiveness of attention is broken down, and instead of attending only to a few familiar data to the exclusion of all else, one becomes aware of a far larger portion of that totality of immediate experience which constantly flows over one" (p. 38). The outcome, he says, is what we call religious experience. The "state of diffusive awareness" may occur under other circumstances as well—such as falling in love, experiencing the grandeur of nature, or joining an excited crowd—as long as they serve to break down a person's habitual pattern of response. Forty years later Arthur Deikman (1966) independently and more elaborately restated this theory. In a widely cited paper on mystical experience, Deikman terms the putative suspension of automatic perceptual and cognitive processes as "deautomatization," a concept developed earlier by Merton Gill and Margaret Brenman (1959) in conjunction with their studies of hypnosis.

Imposition of Philosophic Biases

If both James the phenomenologist and James the explanatory psychologist have been found wanting, so also has James the pragmatic philosopher. It is his preoccupation with defending religion in terms of the pragmatic view of truth that is said to be the origin of the limitations we have thus far reviewed. Hermann Faber (1913), Karl Girgensohn (1921), Leuba (1904), and others have faulted James for being insufficiently empirical. His selection of documents and phenomena, they say, is seriously biased by his philosophical agenda. To James, declares Wundt (1911, p. 109), "the reports of the awakened and converted were not psychology, but merely a foundation for his own pragmatic philosophy." If we set aside James's pragmatic goal, Wundt continues, we are faced with but two possibilities. Either we accept the reports of religious ecstatics—whether they speak out of history or out of mental institutions—as genuine revelations of divinity; or we view them as material for a psychopathology of religious consciousness. Wundt maintains that the effort, notable in Protestant theological circles, to lift James's collection of examples out of their pragmatic framework and to use them for founding an independent psychology of religion is doomed to failure. A psychology that takes into account so limited a group of phenomena, he says, will be incomplete to the highest degree (p. 112).

According to Leuba (1904), James's tendentious selection of documents more evidently serves the end of his emerging philosophy of pluralistic idealism. James sought evidence, says Leuba, in support of the notion that the universe is "a multiverse of spiritual agents" (p. 324) with whom we may come in contact and from whom we may derive higher energies. James speculates that the point of contact lies in the subliminal region. Thus it is, Leuba concludes, that James passes over the more common and less striking forms of piety in which relation to God is more distant and objective. It was for the same reasons, Leuba says, that James assigned to the science of religion so limited an agenda and failed to articulate, in his vigorous and influential way, the task and promise of the still-neglected psychology of religion. "No one," laments James's critic, "could have done as much as he for its advancement" (p. 325).

THE ENDURING INFLUENCE OF THE *VARIETIES*

Others, too, were disquieted by James's "very doubtful pluralistic metaphysics," reminiscent of spiritualism (Girgensohn, 1921, p. 17), and some, like Catholic scholar Jakob Margreth (1909), considered the *Varieties* so fundamentally flawed that they categorically rejected its entire contents. Most of the *Varieties'* readers, however, including Girgensohn himself, found much in these lectures that was stimulating and insightful. Leuba's lament would seem to have been distinctly premature. Speaking for countless others, Lawrence Grensted (1952, p. 51) remarks that the *Varieties* has "deservedly become a classic. Few scientific books have been as brilliantly written or as widely read, and [its] influence was immediate and lasting. Still, fifty years later, [these lectures] form the necessary starting-point for any serious study of the subject."

Villiam Grønbaek's (1970) analysis of 24 books published in this field between 1950 and 1967 attests to James's continuing preeminence in the psychology of religion. Among the authors indexed in these works, James is the most frequently cited.[7] Similarly, Hendrika Vande Kemp (1976), in her survey of American college courses on or related to the psychology of religion, found that the *Varieties* was the book most commonly assigned by the respondents.

These statistics are somewhat misleading, however. In fact, only 17 of Vande Kemp's 49 respondents assigned the *Varieties* to their students, and Grønbaek's sheer counting of citations veils widespread disagreement with James's findings or approach. In our day as well as in his own, James has often served as little more than a prestigious source of striking examples and mellifluous prose. His commonly misunderstood methods, if not simply criticized, have been largely ignored. What the *Varieties* has most often been thought to offer, then, is the *possibility* of a viable psychology of religion rather than its prototype. Karl Busch (1911, p. 81), for example, declares James's "analytical and descriptive psychology of religion" to be a "great step forward" that "merits unreserved appreciation," but he rests his hope for clarification of the field's methodology somewhere in the distant future.

Although often qualified, interest in the *Varieties* was so exceptional that within a decade of its publication it was translated into more than a half dozen European languages (Wulff, 1995). This interest was particularly conspicuous in Germany where James's Gifford Lectures may have been more widely read and discussed than in America (Busch, p. 4). A century earlier, German theologian Friedrich Schleiermacher had argued, like James, that religious experience is more funda-

---

[7] The remaining writers among the ten most frequently cited are, in order, (2) Freud, (3) Allport, (4) Gruehn, (5) Starbuck, (6) Jung, (7) Girgensohn, (8) Lersch, (9) Godin, and (10) Otto. Although Philipp Lersch, a major figure in the German psychology of personality, made few direct contributions to the psychology of religion, European scholars in this field frequently find his work germane to their own.

mental than the interpretations that are made of it. The theme of religious consciousness—and thus the possibility of a psychology of religion—subsequently faded with the resurgence of rational metaphysics. Even those, like Albrecht Ritschl, who sought to reclaim for theology some of Schleiermacher's insights were chiefly influenced by his historical orientation, not the emphasis on experience. So it was that James's *Varieties,* reminiscent in important ways of Schleiermacher's views on religious experience, was hailed as a major contribution (Schär, 1943; Wobbermin, 1907).

The foremost spokesman for this judgment was Protestant theologian Georg Wobbermin (1869–1943). Hopeful that the *Varieties* would stimulate interest among his fellow theologians in a psychological approach to religion, Wobbermin undertook a slightly abbreviated translation into German of this "standard work of the Anglo-American psychology of religion" (Wobbermin, 1907, p. v). In the years that followed, he also wrote a three-volume systematic theology founded upon "the religio-psychological" or "James–Schleiermacher" method. What Wobbermin had in mind was an interpretative understanding of religious experience that begins with one's own experience but alternates, then, with an empathic comprehension of the experience of others. By reciprocally illuminating each other, said Wobbermin, these inner and outer sources of experience will gradually reveal the fundamental motive of all religious life (Wobbermin, 1921, pp. 44–45; 1933, p. 34). In basing his own work on this method, Wobbermin hoped to revolutionize Protestant theology.

Wobbermin was ultimately interested in the nature and truth of Christian doctrine and wished to dissociate himself from pragmatic philosophy. Inevitably, then, he drew far more on Schleiermacher than on James. Furthermore, what he did take from James was not his method, but his valorization of religious experience. As a result, Wobbermin's theology proved to be chiefly a work of textual and historical analysis rather than a phenomenology of religious consciousness. In any event, his efforts met with only slight success. His colleagues regarded his unusual principles largely as a curiosity, and the relation between theology and psychology remained disappointingly cool (Schär, 1943, p. 177; see also Klünker, 1985).

Although the *Varieties* failed, then, to influence the direction of theological discourse, it did inspire in other quarters the study of individual religious lives. According to the eminent Japanese historian of religions, Masaharu Anesaki,

> Since the appearance of Professor James' "Varieties of Religious Experience," the attention of scholars has been strongly drawn toward men of original religious experience, with emphasis on the psychological point of view, disregarding doctrinal considerations. A conspicuous result of the change brought about by this book is that religious psychology has been extended from a study of material taken from the average masses, to the study of strong personalities and their characteristic faith (Anesaki, 1916, p. v).

Anesaki's study of the thirteenth-century Buddhist prophet Nichiren was intended as a contribution to this "newer branch of religious psychology." So, too, in its own tendentiously dramatic way, was Harold Begbie's (1909) study of a dozen or so "twice-born men" living in the same section of London, all of them converted from lives of misery and crime by the Salvation Army. Begbie subtitled his book "A Footnote in Narrative" to James's *Varieties,* and to James he also dedicated this inspirational work, the first in a series written to convince its readers of the unique, saving function of religion.[8]

Influenced by James they certainly were, but writers such as Wobbermin, Anesaki, and Begbie finally went their own ways, leaving James's ill-specified model well behind them. Given the *Varieties'* multiplicity of purpose, its studied indefiniteness (Bruns, 1984), and its disorienting style (Ruf, 1991), on the one hand, and today's continuing obedience to empiricism, objectivity, and generalizability (Dittes, 1973a) on the other, it is understandable that James has not been systematically influential enough to form a school. Nonetheless, a succession of psychologists of religion, extending into the present, explicitly credit James for major elements in their own work. In America we would include James Pratt, Gordon Allport, Walter Clark, and Orlo Strunk. Paul Pruyser also draws heavily on James, although far more critically. In Europe, both Girgensohn and Jung, whose early thinking was shaped by the *Varieties,* are classic contributors, and today aspects of James's approach are evident in other European writers as well (e.g., Åkerberg, 1972, 1975; Milanesi and Aletti, 1973; Pettersson and Åkerberg, 1980).

Paradoxically, the most systematic contemporary effort to appropriate the insight of James's *Varieties* is to be found outside the psychology of religion, in a notable work on American literature by Victor Strandberg (1981). Using the typology of the healthy-minded versus the sick soul as well as James's generalizations regarding conversion, mysticism, and saintliness, Strandberg examines the works of 30 major authors, including Emily Dickinson, Herman Melville, Edgar Allan Poe, William Faulkner, and Henry James. Much as James felt that his analysis of religion left undisturbed "its towering place in history," so Strandberg concludes that his study leaves James "more securely in possession of *his* towering place in American literary history" (p. 234).

JAMES PRATT AND THE RELIGIOUS CONSCIOUSNESS

James's most immediate and influential successor was James Bissett Pratt (1875–1944), long a professor of philosophy at Williams College and author of *The Religious Consciousness* (1920), a book second only to the *Varieties* in longevity and importance. Pratt was a graduate student who studied under James at Harvard, where in 1905 he completed a doctoral dissertation on the psychology of religious belief under his famous mentor's guidance (see Pratt, 1907). That the psychology of religion remained one of Pratt's active, lifelong concerns is a fact of considerable

---

[8] James's *Varieties* was also influential in the creation of Alcoholics Anonymous, the oldest of contemporary support groups and—with a membership exceeding two million worldwide—by far the largest. Shortly after Bill Wilson, a New York stockbroker, experienced relief from his own alcohol obsession and severe depression as a result of a sudden religious illumination, a friend brought him a copy of the *Varieties.* His laborious reading of this book, in conjunction with C. G. Jung's immensely influential remark to an alcoholic acquaintance of Wilson's that his situation was hopeless unless he could become the subject of religious experience, convinced Wilson that the feeling of hopelessness is essential for the experience of spiritual transformation. Observing the important role that other alcoholics played in his coming to acknowledge his own hopelessness, Wilson conceived Alcoholics Anonymous, which he co-founded in 1935 (B. Wilson, 1957; Wilson and Jung, 1963). Directed as Wilson's model is to sick-souled individuals and the fostering of self-surrender, Walle (1992) suggests that it may be too narrowly conceived to be effective with all the varieties of alcoholism.

James Pratt

moment, for Pratt was not only a first-rate scholar with training in philosophy and psychology but also a man of deep piety who is renowned even today for his sympathetic and penetrating understanding of Eastern religious traditions. His book *The Pilgrimage of Buddhism* (1928) is still considered one of the best introductions to Buddhist thought and practice (Adams, 1977; H. Smith, 1991). This book, along with his *India and Its Faiths* (1915), "did much to make these [religious traditions] come alive for the first time for many Western readers; for Pratt had a gift not only of brilliance but of extraordinary human sympathy" (W. C. Smith, 1959, p. 36).

Pratt's rare sympathy, said to be the outstanding feature of all his writings in the psychology of religion (Uren, 1928, p. 96), is only one of several characteristics revealing the continuity of his work with James's. Both were liberal Protestants, not merely in the limited sense of rejecting orthodox views, but in the broader one of commitment to genuine thinking about religious matters, constrained only by loyalty to truth and respect for the facts of human experience (Pratt, 1936; Procter, 1945). Both were defenders of the religious outlook, James primarily against its philosophic critics and Pratt against the widespread erosion of traditional forms of religious expression and cultivation. Both found in private feelings and the fringes of consciousness a major source of religious experience, and to study so subtle and individual a matter, both employed personal documents and questionnaire replies as their chief sources of evidence. Finally, both saw religion as a serious, even heroic, means by which individual lives and the world might be transformed.

IN PRAISE OF ORDINARY RELIGIOUS EXPERIENCE

In other respects, however, James and Pratt stood far apart. Whereas James wrote essentially as an outsider who was disdainful of ordinary piety, Pratt knew at first hand the fruits of deep, though undramatic, religious faith.

> Piety was the centre of his being. His happiness was religious happiness. His great zest for life, his delight in nature, his unfailing love for mankind, his strong sense of value, the simplicity of his character, his quiet strength, the triumph of his spirit over pain and disability, his intense moral energy—all these were manifestations of a soul at almost every moment conscious of God (Procter, 1945, p. 137).

Reared by the deeply religious daughter of a Presbyterian minister, acquainted by marriage with the Catholic faith at its best, and immersed through reading and travel in the spirit of the Eastern traditions, Pratt was qualified as no one before him to write a systematic treatise on the psychology of religion. He was also singularly dedicated to the field. His voyage to India was undertaken for no other purpose than "to gain fresh light on the psychology of religion" (Pratt, 1915, p. ix), and he gave more thought and time—12 years, start to finish—to *The Religious Consciousness* than to any of the dozen other books he wrote (Myers, 1961, p. 223).

Two Types of Conversion

The Religious Consciousness was far more inclusive—both of religious phenomena and of the international literature on the psychology of religion—than any earlier work in the field. What most distinguishes it from James's *Varieties*, however, is its insistence that an exclusive focus on the dramatic experiences of religious experts is bound to be misleading. This point is first brought home in the chapters on conversion. The violent form that James features is neither as common nor as normal as is often suggested, says Pratt. Its stereotypic course, he argues, largely reflects the suggestive influence on susceptible persons of evangelical theology. By taking this form of conversion as the norm, Pratt (1920, p. 151) points out, James and others have unwittingly authenticated the conventions of this theology, including the conviction of sin and the necessity of surrendering effort. The feeling of sinfulness is rare in truly significant cases of conversion, says Pratt, and the doctrine of surrendering effort, he adds, is a dangerous and deplorable fallacy. To this "merely emotional" and essentially spurious type of conversion Pratt contrasts the more ordinary, imperceptible, and lasting "moral" type, for which effort toward new insight or overcoming old habits is, he says, of real importance.

In a questionnaire study designed in part to test Pratt's conclusions, Elmer Clark (1929) found that of his diverse sample of 2174 persons, only 6.7 percent claimed to have undergone a "definite crisis" conversion, equivalent to James's dramatic type. Another 27.2 percent reported an "emotional stimulus awakening." That is, some event, such as undergoing confirmation, stood out for these subjects as an occasion of "definite religious acceptance," yet it was not a time of notable change. The remaining 66.1 percent could point to no particular event that stimulated, even to a mild degree, their religious consciousness. Moreover, Clark found that when stern theological teachings were part of the individual's experience, as only 9.8 percent of those answering the relevant question said they were, the occurrence of definite crisis conversion jumped to 34.6 percent—eight times the rate of those not reporting exposure to such theology.[9] Beyond providing unequivocal support for Pratt's claims, Clark's data suggested that both stern theology and dramatic conversion were on the decline.

Two Types of Mystic Experience

More far reaching than his typology of conversion is the parallel distinction that Pratt (1920) draws between two forms of mystic experience, the mild and the extreme. The mild type, though commonplace, is often overlooked, for those acquainted with it are frequently hesitant or ill prepared to describe what it was like. Such expressions as there are seem to be little more than statements of faith. In contrast, the extreme type has attracted a good deal of attention, from those convinced that it provides evidence of divine grace as well as those who regard it as a form of pathology.

---

[9] This comparative rate is derived from the data summarized in Clark (1929) on page 87. The 340 persons who did not answer the question pertaining to type of theology are presumed not to have been exposed to the stern type.

The importance of distinguishing these two types of mystic experience, says Pratt, cannot be overemphasized. "No just idea can be formed upon the subject and no sound conclusion as to the nature and place and value of mysticism can be reached unless one consistently keeps [this distinction] in mind" (p. 339). Granting that in reality the two types may "blend into each other," Pratt nonetheless maintains that the extreme type involves factors that set it apart from the mild form and make it risky to generalize from one to the other.

The Essence of the Mystic Experience: Both types of mystic report experiencing "the sense of the presence of a being or reality through other means than the ordinary perceptive process or the reason" (p. 337). This immediate and intuitive feeling of presence, of making contact with a life greater than one's own, has a compelling sense of objectivity, much like what a person feels in the presence of another human being but without the sensory elements that are ordinarily its source. Given that the encounter is with the divine, the sense of presence is universally accompanied by intense emotions of happiness. The mystic experience consists minimally, then, of two indissolubly united aspects: its cognitive content of a great truth more or less vividly realized (yet commonly irreducible to discursive language) and its emotional character of joy and sweetness.

The Extreme Type: To the basic portrait the extreme type of mystic adds a number of other elements. Alternating with this unworldly happiness are periods of pain and suffering. A milder, negative kind of pain occurs in periods of "dryness," when the longed-for religious joy remains mysteriously out of reach. A more positive form of pain accompanies a felt sense of separation from a being that is at the same time experienced as present. Usually associated with feelings of unworthiness, this anguished longing for an elusive presence is a quality that mystic experience shares with the dramatic forms of conversion.

Corresponding to the extreme mystic's greater suffering is the prospect of an incomparably greater joy. To attain the stage of ecstasy, the extreme mystic combines ascetic practices designed to root out all interest in worldly pleasures and concern for the personal self with more positive techniques of concentration and meditation. Ecstasy is a passive state of relative unity in which all other content is displaced by awareness of God and the accompanying emotions of love and bliss. It sometimes occurs in conjunction with a variety of other phenomena that are widely associated with mysticism, including visions and inner voices; sudden "ravishment," often accompanied by a sense of levitation; and "ligature," a peculiar loss of will making even inward prayer impossible and accompanied by diminished sense perception and a slowing of involuntary bodily functions. Extreme in its passivity, this blissful stage typically inaugurates an active life of inspired service.

The Types Evaluated: The unusual character of these experiences, the extremity of some of the ascetic practices used to achieve them, and the fact that the mystics themselves frequently employ erotic language and images to describe their ecstasies have convinced some psychologists that mystical experience is essentially pathological. Pratt agrees that some of the lesser mystics of the extreme type are no more than cases of mental disorder, and he grants that pathology may color the experience of the great ecstatics as well. He also emphasizes, however, that the mystics themselves are aware of these tendencies and discount their importance or see them as temptations to be overcome. Close examination reveals important differences between these phenomena and ordinary pathological symptoms, between the lives of the mystics and those of the mentally disturbed. Outstanding among these differences is the mystics' strength of will, their "determination to unify their lives and direct their activities according to the divine purpose'' (p. 463). Following in James's footsteps, Pratt suggests that systematic practice in ascetic self-denial would benefit us all.

At the same time, Pratt acknowledges that the originality and practical service of the ecstatics have been greatly overrated. Their real contribution, he says, has been to the poetic literature of religious inspiration. Most of mysticism's positive fruits, he continues, have come from those of the milder type, whom Pratt, by distinguishing them as a class, sought to preserve from the sweeping criticisms of mysticism at the extreme. Whereas ''even at its best the ecstasy is dangerous and at its worst is altogether evil'' (p. 469), the humbler intimations enjoyed by the mystics of the mild type are, at least for them, of supreme and life-sustaining value. ''Mysticism is by no means *essential* to religion,'' says Pratt, yet ''all intensely religious people have at least a touch'' of it (pp. 18, 477). Especially in an age that so values activity, efficiency, and economic productivity, the soul needs a horizon wider than social and political ideals can afford: ''It needs a chance for spreading its wings, for looking beyond itself, beyond the immediate environment, and for quiet inner growth, which is best to be found in that group of somewhat indefinite, but very real experiences—aspiration, insight, contemplation—which may well be called the mystic life'' (p. 479).

Two Nations of Mystics: Two national surveys, one in the United States and the other in Great Britain, carried out a half century after *The Religious Consciousness* was first published, provide clear and consistent support for Pratt's brief on mysticism. In 1973, Andrew Greeley (1975), William McCready, and their associates asked a carefully selected national sample of about 1460 Americans to indicate the frequency with which they had experienced a variety of paranormal phenomena; personal, social, and demographic information was gathered as well. A surprising 35 percent of their respondents reported that, at least once or twice in their lives, they had felt as though they were ''very close to a powerful, spiritual force that seemed to lift [them] out of [themselves].'' Of the total sample, 12 percent said such an experience had happened several times; 5 percent claimed it happened often. More than 87 million Americans, it may be inferred, have experienced a spiritual sense of presence; 12 million do so frequently.[10]

Is Pratt also correct that this army of heretofore unsuspected ''mild mystics'' is likely not only to be free of the pathology long imputed to persons of a mystic bent but also to be happier than those without such experiences? Evidence suggests that he is indeed. Greeley reports that the occurrence of mystical experience was positively related ($r = .34$) to the Positive Affect Scale devised by Norman Bradburn (1969) as a measure of psychological well-being and negatively related ($r = -.34$) to the Negative Affect Scale, which is consistently related to traditional indicators of poor mental health. When mystical experience was more strictly defined in classical terms—passivity, ineffability, a sense of new life, and the experience of

---

[10] Concerned that some subjects might interpret Greeley's question metaphorically rather than literally, David Hufford (1985, pp. 96–98) asked 30 randomly chosen nonpsychiatric hospital patients to respond to this question and, when their answers were positive, to describe the experience in detail. Fourteen subjects responded affirmatively, of which eight subsequently proved to be false positives—for example, interpreting ''lift you out of yourself'' merely as feeling ''uplifted,'' and without any reference to a spiritual force. Although this small sample cannot be considered representative of Greeley's, the reduction of positive responses from 47 to 20 percent through follow-up questioning suggests that Greeley's results may also be inflated. Yet 20 percent would still be a large number of people. Greeley's percentage was more recently confirmed in a poll conducted for *Newsweek* magazine in November, 1994: Of the adults interviewed, 33 percent reported having had a religious or mystical experience (Kantrowitz, 1994).

being bathed in light—the correlation with positive affect rose to a relatively impressive .52. Compared with the nonmystics, then, the mystics are a notably happier lot, and they are freer from symptoms of mental disorder.

The individuals comprising the British national sample of 1865 persons, also carefully chosen to represent the nation as a whole, were asked whether they had ever "been aware of or influenced by a presence or power, whether referred to as God or not, which was different from their everyday selves" (Hay and Morisy, 1978, p. 257). Greeley and McCready's question was also posed, along with the Bradburn scales, in order to make direct comparisons possible. The results were remarkably close to Greeley and McCready's, with 36.4 percent responding affirmatively to the British version of the "presence" question and 30.4 percent affirmatively to the American one. Well-being once again proved to be positively related to mystical experience, though much less strongly so.

The Feeling Background

Pratt believes that the vague and usually inarticulate intimations of mild mystic experience originate from a region of consciousness that he refers to as the feeling background. In contrast to the cognitive division of consciousness, which is composed of ideation and sensory experience, the feeling background is relatively amorphous and indistinct. It can nonetheless be analyzed, says Pratt (1907, p. 9), into "two kinds of psychic material": feeling and the vague, unfocused "fringe" or halo of relations that James (1890) discusses so brilliantly in his chapter on the stream of consciousness. This nonrational and noncognitive feeling background— described by Pratt as surrounding the small islands of ideation and sensation like a great boiling sea—links us, he claims, not only to our own personal pasts but also "to our ancestors, and to the race,—in fact in a sense to all living things." Anticipating Jung's notion of a collective psyche, Pratt is less willing than Jung to speculate about the nature of this putative storehouse of inherited past experience, and he is reluctant, too, to accept James's account of the subliminal self. Still, he claims that the feeling background possesses "what might be called a *racial* or *instinctive* wisdom which seems to put it in touch, in a perfectly natural manner, with forces hidden from the clearly conscious personality and which makes it in many ways wiser than the individual" (Pratt, 1907, pp. 22–23).

Containing instinctive responses and well-attuned adaptations to the universe, the feeling background not only serves as the origin of life's values but also frequently constitutes that part of the individual that *has* value for others.

> The ideals which have animated and guided the race, the sentiments and passions which do us the most honor, the impulses which raise us above the brutes and which have been the motive forces of history, the intuitions which have marked out the saviors and the saints and the heroes of our earth, have not come from the brightly illuminated center of consciousness, have not been the result of reason and of logic, but have sprung from the deeper instinctive regions of our nature (p. 27).

The vital importance of the instinctive life as it expresses itself in the feeling background and, more particularly, in the religious consciousness is "the one contention" for which Pratt wished his first book to stand.

Three Types of Belief: In his psychological and historical study of religious belief, in which belief is understood as a "mental attitude of assent" (p. 32), articulate or not, Pratt identifies three types: (1) PRIMITIVE CREDULITY, the tendency to believe what one is told until some cause for doubt arises; (2) intellectual belief, which counters doubt with reasons for assent, commonly derived from the authority of experts; and (3) emotional belief, which draws its enormous strength from the feeling background, out of which comes the conviction that satisfaction must be possible for all its instinctive desires.

Primitive credulity, says Pratt, belongs to the childhood of the race and of the individual but lingers on in the lives of a great many adults, out of habit and inertia. "They believe because when children they were taught so to do, and having formed the mental habit, they would find it difficult and unpleasant to make a change" (p. 235). Observing at the same time a general reaction against any belief based on uncritical acceptance of authority, Pratt noted a decline in credulity even among the most religiously orthodox, who were increasingly forced to acknowledge that many of their once-hallowed dogmas were no longer supportable.

The more reflective appeal of *intellectual belief* to a respected authority, which in the Christian context usually means either the Bible or ecclesiastical tradition, was also perceived to be on the decline. To Pratt the growth of scholarly criticism of the Bible and of church teachings seemed the final blow to absolute and un-questionable authority, though he gladly counted the Bible among the profoundly luminous and perennially influential sources of religious inspiration. If no longer able to assure positive belief, critical thought can still serve religious faith, says Pratt, by protecting it from attacks by various antireligious conceptions. More directly, it may reformulate the conceptual expressions of faith to accord with advances in human knowledge and reflection, yet without abandoning what is essential.

Religion is thus forced to take its stand, Pratt concludes, in the realm of instinc-tive demands, intuitions, and feeling. Grounded not merely in the intellectual but in the whole psychophysical organism, *emotional belief* is for Pratt the quintessence of religious faith, an attitude of assent rising up in individual form out of the race itself. As inexplicable and compelling as the bird's urge to build a nest or migrate, the immediate experience of assurance and insight is neither attainable nor refut-able by reason. Personal inner experience, he says, is the only source from which contemporary religion can draw sustenance without fear of historical criticism or scientific advance. Although it clothes itself in diverse forms and symbols that often contradict or displace one another, the inner religious experience is yet said to be unitary: "All the mystics speak one language and profess one faith." In place of the countless dogmas of the "Religion of Thought," the "Religion of Feeling" offers but one. Lying beyond us is a vast reservoir of life, similar in nature to our own and one with which we can make connection. Here, says Pratt, we have "the one doctrine of the real Religion of Humanity" (p. 304).

In his later, more famous work, Pratt (1920, p. 214) carefully emphasizes that his expression "emotional belief" should not be too narrowly interpreted. The affective dimension of human life, he observes, is itself elaborately structured. To denote its enduring complexes of emotional tendencies, which are chiefly disposi-tional and contain a large measure of ideational content, Pratt borrowed the term SENTIMENT. As a sentiment, then, religious belief of the emotional type is said not to depend on the actual arousal of its constituent emotions and, more than merely a "feeling," it crystallizes around a core of meaning. The complexity of this third type of belief, says Pratt, would have been more clearly suggested had he called it *affective* rather than emotional.

A Fourth Type of Belief: Not everyone, of course, is equally prone to the intimations that well up out of the feeling background. "One of the chief ways in which individual minds differ," Pratt writes (p. 362), "is in the relative amount and importance of the fringe region." A relatively narrow and uninfluential margin is typical of the clear, rationalistic thinker, who is most unlikely to experience the sense of divine presence, especially in the midst of daily activities. In contrast, the mystic's wider margin, although making concentration more difficult, permits the individual to combine the mystic sense with practical action.

If a narrow margin largely rules out assent of the "emotional" type, Pratt offers another possibility, designated *volitional belief,* to persons so endowed who yet strongly desire faith. Added in the 1920 volume to the other, more common forms, this fourth type of belief may be systematically cultivated by inhibiting all contrary ideas and consciously focusing and acting upon the content of the desired belief. Pratt cites the case of a woman who, long after having lost the comforting faith of her youth, set about to recover it at a time of crisis.

> I deliberately set to work to recognize the sense of God's presence which I had not had for nearly twenty years. I reinforced my reason by reiterating my reasons for assuming such a personality, and I prayed constantly after the fashion of the old skeptic: 'O God, if there is a God, save my soul if I have a soul." Then one night after a week of this sort of thing, the old sense of God's presence came upon me with overpowering fullness. . . . I felt the thing—whatever it was—so close to me, so a part of me, that words and even thoughts were unnecessary, that my part was only to sink back into this personality—if such it were—and drop all worries and temptations, all the straining and striving that had been so prominent in my life for years and years.

The subject felt "a great upwelling of love and gratitude" toward this source of consolation and strength, and for months afterward thoughts of it calmed her at moments of perplexity or stress (p. 221).

To be sure, Pratt adds, volitional belief rarely yields such a dramatic result. Far more typical is a credulity of an habitual sort, which may nevertheless be vital and sustaining. Wary of the possibility of its degenerating into a "veritable malpractice upon one's own mind," Pratt was convinced of the potential efficacy and value of the proper use of the "will to believe." He was also certain that its role is frequently unrecognized. Whereas only 8 percent of the respondents to his questionnaire gave evidence of volitional belief, he suspected that many others, also indebted to it, were mistaken in crediting mystic feeling or philosophical argument instead.

The Spiritual Power of Symbols

The inclusion of volitional belief in his expanded typology reflects Pratt's appreciation for religion's multiplicity of roots as well as for the diversity of its manifestations. He was especially sensitive to the role of religious symbols in the lives of ordinary people, a theme altogether absent from the *Varieties*. We might even wonder whether Pratt had James in mind when he wrote that "we of the more ultra-Protestant branch of the Christian Church . . . seem extraordinarily, almost perversely blind to the value of visible and tangible symbols." Any thoughtful study of the psychology of religion, he said, will demonstrate the "immense power of spiritual reinforcement" provided by the mental images, tangible objects, and ritual actions that are the heart of a religious tradition for most of its participants (Pratt, 1950, pp. 6–7).

The Role of Imagination: Countering the tendency to overemphasize the well-defined and rational aspects of religious belief, Pratt (1920) draws our attention to the contributions that imagination and the sensory processes make, especially during the early years and in less sophisticated persons. Unless we are strongly disposed to conceptual thinking, Pratt observes, it is exceedingly difficult to believe in objects or events that we cannot imagine. Individuals, for example, who are unable to form

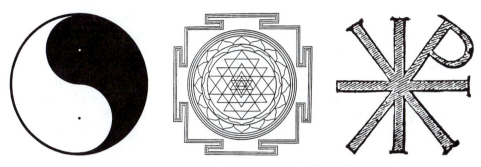

Three abstract religious symbols: the Yin and Yang diagram, the Shrī Yantra meditation symbol, and a stylized Christian cross found in the Catacombs.

persuasive images of a future life are unlikely to affirm the idea of immortality—unless imagining cessation of their own conscious existence is more difficult still. An abstract idea that can be conceived but has no evident imaginal content will ordinarily lack the vividness that is "the primitive touch-stone of reality" (p. 245). But if it is possible to surround such an idea with a wealth of concrete details, the abstraction may borrow their reality–feeling and finally win a measure of assent.

Imagination's contribution may be even more fundamental. In his last, post-humously published book, Pratt (1950, p. 135) argues that the very process of transforming thought into a clear and genuinely usable concept requires that it first be clothed in some form of symbol. What this symbol or image will be in any particular instance is unpredictable, he says, and its relation to the meaning it bears is both complex and obscure; "yet that some symbol there must be if we are to carry on a process of thinking is altogether certain."

If images lend our ideas persuasiveness and clarity, as Pratt argues, they do so, according to psychologist Rudolf Arnheim (1969), because they are the very medium of thought. Psychologists who early in this century concluded that certain forms of thought are imageless were misled, says Arnheim, by their assumption that the images they were looking for would in every case be more or less faint replicas of perceptual experience. Furthermore, they presumed that the existence of such mimetic images would always be apparent to reflective consciousness. Arguing to the contrary, Arnheim maintains that these observers overlooked the simple, often vague, generic images that best serve productive thinking. These fleeting, essentially NONMIMETIC images are formed by abstracting from the object of thought the qualities that are essential to it. For theoretical problems, such images typically take on a topological or geometric shape located only faintly in mental space. The ancient Yin–Yang symbol of Chinese religion, the stylized crosses familiar to Christians, and the elaborate diagrams employed in Buddhist meditation would all seem to be derived from this kind of imagery.

What Pratt has chiefly in mind, however, is the mimetic type of image, which undoubtedly plays by far the largest role in everyday piety. Ordinary Christian worshipers take much greater delight in picturing to themselves the details of the story of Jesus' birth than in contemplating a highly abstract image—if indeed they can produce one—of the triune God. The feeling of reality may be heightened even more when these details are vividly presented to the senses, especially through pictures, sculpture, and song. What observer of folk piety has not seen, for example, the rapture of a devotee lovingly caressing an image of the divine? Opponents of "idolatry" are doubly mistaken, according to Pratt (1950, p. 5), for they overlook the powerful psychological advantage of tangible symbols sanctified by the ages, and they fail to realize that the palpable image is viewed at most as a temporary dwelling place for divinity, not as divinity itself.

It is the relatively nonmimetic image, Pratt would likely agree, that most powerfully demonstrates the symbol's important capacity to suggest "the indefinable, the illimitable, the ineffable." Half magically, the religious symbol suffuses the mind with a "dim religious light," rousing within one a strong emotional response (Pratt, 1920, p. 205). As Arnheim points out, language may serve this process by stabilizing, preserving, and then evoking the image anew, specifying at the same time the appropriate level of abstractness. Pratt would add that the verbal expression may itself become a symbol, taking on a meaning far deeper than that discerned by the intellect. The creedal statement or theological dogma that has traditionally been accepted as a literal account of historical events may be taken by another type of mind as a symbol of reality irreducible to propositional statements. The very syllables themselves become sacred. Whether or not the language is even understood, these hallowed formulas serve, especially when recited with persons who share one's faith, to induce the "emotion of belief" and establish a certain enduring mental set (pp. 284–285).

The religious symbol's capacity to bring about such changes depends largely, of course, on the individual's attitude. If we misunderstand the dynamic of symbolism, says Pratt (1950, pp. 140–143), we may make one of two "great and costly mistakes." The first is a scrupulous intellectual sincerity that abstains from sharing in any symbolic expression that appears inadequate or unreasonable to the intellect. Persons who so limit themselves to a set of "coldly inadequate symbols" or even force themselves into silence regarding religion's great themes will find their worship impoverished and their deeper emotions paralyzed. For naught, says Pratt, will we be left with abstract philosophy and social morality.

Far more common is the second mistake, which consists in taking symbols too literally, "identifying the little thing that they *say* with the great thing that they *mean*." Pratt considered the fundamentalist tendency to think too literally to be particularly a Western error. The East seemed to him far more appreciative of the possibility of believing in something without requiring it to be literally true. Whereas many highly educated Japanese Buddhists consider Amida, the enormously popular Buddha of Infinite Light, to be nothing more than a name of the Absolute, they still find the beloved image of this compassionate deity to be an invaluable aid in their spiritual lives. Similarly, Indian Vedantists affirm the sole reality of Brahman, the impersonal Absolute, yet turn to Shiva in meditation and worship. The finite Shiva's far greater appeal to the imagination paradoxically allows the cultivation of an attitude that finally transcends the finite.

A Childhood Prerequisite: An understanding of the nature and function of religious symbols that avoids such errors is yet no guarantee that these sacred images will resonate deep in the feeling background. More important still is the factor of immersion in a living system of religious images, words, and acts during the early, impressionable years of life. "Nearly all the religious symbolism that ever becomes really potent in an individual's experience," writes Pratt (1920, p. 286), "comes into his life in childhood." The Bible, for example, in spite of its inherent nobility, gains the power it has only if its passages are "learned and loved *in early childhood and as sacred words*" (Pratt, 1923, p. 602). An adult convert to a religious tradition may achieve a meaningful intellectual relation to its initially unfamiliar symbols,

Amida, the Buddha of Infinite Light, in an open setting in Japan.

but their emotional and volitional significance will most likely remain slight at best. "It is seldom after those formative years," Pratt (1920, p. 286) maintains, "that the close association between object and emotion can be wrought which is essential to religious symbolism."

The obverse is true as well. That is, even adults who actively reject the religious teachings and sentiments of their early years are destined by the conservative nature of the nervous system to remain to some degree under their influence, often in subtle and unrecognized ways. The preservation of early habits of piety is especially true of religious customs, including bodily gestures and ritual acts, which are learned and associated with the religious sentiment earlier than doctrine and are less subject to rational discussion and refutation. We may resolutely found our adult faith in some reasoned argument, but in moments of weariness the tradition and habits of childhood will likely reemerge from the background to become the decisive factor (pp. 62, 85–86, 226, 281–291).

For the traditional objects, sacred texts, and hallowed rites to become suffused over time with the religious feeling that makes them genuinely symbolic, Pratt says that, as a rule, the child's whole social environment must act as a single, unanimous force. Pratt advises that parents who wish to bequeath to their child a vital, deeply rooted faith should make the outward expressions of their own piety exceptionally obvious to the child. In accord with the law of imitation, the child will spontaneously mimic these gestures and thereby begin to share in the attitudes and feelings they express. This indirect influence may be followed by direct instruction, but preferably not until the child voices curiosity about what the parents are doing.

Although Pratt maintains that religion must become articulate if it is to be a genuine force in life, he cautions against teaching doctrine to children before they are capable of conceptual thought. Otherwise, they are likely to be subjected to unnecessary doubts raised by conflict with their own experience, by their growing sense of justice and morality, and by their loyalty to truth. Instead—and here Pratt writes as a Christian addressing other Christians—he would have children learn the significance of the tradition's worship and experience from persons of exceptional spirituality. They would be taught to sing the great hymns of the church, to pray some of its great prayers; they would come to know the origins of the Communion service and witness its remarkable emotional force. Only by such means, Pratt was convinced, would children be reliably won to a lifelong association with the church (1950, pp. 58–59).

If childhood immersion in a religious community is a virtual prerequisite for a vital adult faith, what hope is there then for the missionary enterprise? From a purely psychological standpoint, Pratt agrees that there are real grounds for discouragement.

> The religion native to a land has enormous advantages over every newcomer, advantages of an emotional and authoritative character so great that one should certainly think many times before seeking to replace it with a foreign religion, which might be a little but only a little better. For to destroy an old religion is a very difficult process; and, moreover, if one succeeds in so doing there is the great danger that in destroying one religion he may have undermined the foundations of religion as such, and opened the way only to a godless and reckless skepticism or naturalism (Pratt, 1915, p. 432).

Pratt notes, too, that the vast majority of Christian converts in India are drawn from the lowest ranks of society, for whom conversion has certain practical and social advantages. Superficial as it often is under such circumstances, conversion may lead to little more than the incorporation of Christian elements into the old rites and ceremonies, and in some instances morality may actually decline.

History demonstrates that, in spite of such difficulties, the religious traditions have been able over the centuries to sink deep and lasting roots into foreign soil. Indeed, some survive more successfully in their adopted lands. Reflecting on Christian evangelism, Pratt thought the positive results more than sufficient to justify the costs of the missionary effort, especially given his conviction that, all told, Christianity is unmistakably superior to the other traditions. Although unusually sympathetic to Eastern piety, Pratt perceived in liberal Christianity psychological and moral advantages over the other traditions, even when taken at their best. Chief among these advantages is the "partly historical and partly metaphysical" image of Jesus, which seemed to Pratt unequaled in its power over the imagination and the moral life. Admirable though other historical personalities may be, says Pratt, none of them has so fully embodied the ideals of sacrifice and service or so inspired effort toward "the highest form of self-forgetful usefulness and active love" (p. 452).

Among the other qualities that Pratt counts in the Christian tradition's favor are the simplicity of its message, so that the humblest of souls can grasp it and be transformed by it; its accent on the importance of the individual and of personal responsibility; and its practical organization for communicating ideas and ideals, including its unusually accessible scriptures, its well-trained and sincerely devoted clergy, and its elaborate system of religious education.[11] Liberal that he was, how-

---

[11] A comprehensive survey of the history, principles, methods, and agencies of Christian religious education is offered in a book edited by Marvin Taylor (1960). The new foundations for religious education offered by contemporary moral and faith development theory are laid out in the report of an international conference convened by Christiane Brusselmans (1980). Only recently has systematic attention been given to non-Western approaches to religious education. Conceiving such education in existential terms, as the establishing of a horizon of cosmic meaning that enables individuals to find a place in the world as a whole and to live a fully human life, German theologian Fritz Köster (1986) examines Hindu, Buddhist, and Islamic approaches in the light of current developments. A still-wider range of the world's religious traditions are considered in a work edited by Norma Thompson (1988).

ever, he envisaged a purified adaptation of Christianity, free of indefensible dogmas and incorporating the noble and genuinely spiritual aspects of other traditions. What it would be called and how it would clothe itself seemed to him unimportant, as long as it retained Christ's spirit of loving service.

Understanding Another's Symbols: Whereas work in the mission field continues apace, contemporary scholars of "comparative religion" are far less inclined than Pratt to compare traditions in order to judge their relative merits. More germane to their task are Pratt's reflections on the difficulties of understanding another's faith. If it is true that we must grow up with a symbol to comprehend its significance, says Pratt, "it follows that one can never completely understand the full force and the emotional meaning and value of a symbol belonging to a strange people and a strange culture." We in the West cannot understand, for example, "how any one can find strength or comfort in Kali, the great Hindu Mother, with her string of skulls and her bloody mouth" (p. 13).

Even so, Pratt thought it possible to cultivate an attitude toward such symbols that is sufficiently sympathetic to yield a measure of insight into their spiritual value. In support of this claim, he recounts the story of how the Irish woman Margaret Noble first learned the meaning of Kali to the Hindu.

> One evening shortly after her arrival in Calcutta, she heard a cry in a quiet lane, and following her ears, found it came from a little Hindu girl who lay in her mother's arms, dying. The end came soon, and the poor mother for a time wept inconsolably. Then at last, wearied with her sobbing, she fell back into [the Irish woman's] arms, and turning to her, said: "Oh, what shall I do? Where is my child now?"

At that moment, says Margaret Noble, she found the key.

> "Filled with a sudden pity, not so much for the bereaved woman as for those to whom the use of some particular language of the Infinite is a question of morality, I leaned forward. 'Hush, mother!' I said, 'Your child is with the Great Mother. She is with Kali!' And for a moment, with memory stilled, we were enfolded together, Eastern and Western, in the unfathomable depth of consolation of the World-Heart" (p. 14).

Drawn to India by an encounter in London with Swami Vivekananda, Margaret Noble stayed on to become, under the name Sister Nivedita, one of his devoted disciples and herself a child of the Great Mother.

First we must recognize, Pratt says, that the same truth or emotional attitude may be symbolized in a great variety of forms. Thus underneath alien symbols may lie familiar and comprehensible insights or sentiments. Furthermore, as Sister Nivedita discovered, our most valuable clues to the inner meaning of others' images and rites come not from gazing at these outward manifestations but from observing their effects on the devotees, revealed chiefly in their faces. "For though the human face also is a symbol, it is a symbol which we all can understand." Himself intently watching a worshiper leaving a Shiva temple in Banaras, Pratt concludes that "If one may trust the expression on her face, she is taking with her something that she did not bring. She has found something in that shrine, something like comfort or hope, or at least a sense of duty done and God pleased. In some sense or other she has met God in the Hindu temple" (pp. 25–26).

OBJECTIVE AND SUBJECTIVE WORSHIP

The comfort that Pratt's worshiper derived from ancient ritual was undoubtedly dependent on her conviction that something objectively occurred within the dark and noisy interior of the temple. Had someone convinced her, however, that the

A Buddhist worshiper making an offering of flowers at the Temple of the Tooth. Kandy, Ceylon. Facial expressions, Pratt argues, give us valuable clues to the meaning of others' rituals.

Ganges water, rice, and flower petals with which she honored the divine images were nothing but superstitious remnants of ignorant, magical rites, the subjective effects reflected in her face would most likely disappear. But what if, instead, she had been persuaded that the chief value of such ritual observance lay precisely in the joy and renewed strength that issued out of it? Paradoxically, the outcome would be much the same, for worship that is carried out for its subjective effects is likely no longer to provide them.

Pratt (1920, 1926, 1950) proposes a simple typology to aid our thinking about the relation of objective and subjective factors in religious practice. OBJECTIVE WORSHIP, on the one hand, aims to communicate with and perhaps please or influence some supernatural being. SUBJECTIVE WORSHIP, on the other, seeks primarily to induce some desired mental state in the worshiper. The same distinction can be equally well applied to other elements of religious observance, especially prayer. We recall, for example, that Francis Galton found sufficient evidence to convince himself that prayer has no objective efficacy, yet he continued to employ it for its subjective effects.

Religious observance in the distant past was without a doubt naively objective, Pratt says. According to his reconstruction, over time it gradually became apparent that cultic practices influence the worshiper as well and that they can be modified to increase this effect. "The entire history of religion might be written from the point of view of this process," says Pratt (1926, p. 43; 1950, p. 27). By illustration he contrasts the naively objective worship of Shiva with one of the ceremonies of the Arya Samaj, an aggressive and highly self-conscious Hindu reform movement founded in 1875. In place of the image-centered polytheism of popular temple worship, which they passionately opposed, the highly rationalistic Aryas substituted a daily ritual of chanting ancient Sanskrit verses around a fire into which liquified butter was periodically ladled, a rite said to underscore their connection with the great Vedic period of Indian religion. Although the ritual's only acknowledged objective purpose was to purify the air, "The earnest religious feeling which it arouses among them is patent to every visitor" (Pratt, 1920, p. 292). Pratt finds the

A praying barrel in Tibet. The prayer formulas placed inside the turning barrel are continuously "prayed" in the absence of any human participants, illustrating an extreme form of objective prayer.

extreme of subjective worship in the practice of certain learned Buddhist monks who offer flowers and recite ancient praises to a Buddha they consider beyond all prayers and offerings. "The enlightened Buddhist is to act *just as if* he believed various things which he does not believe, because the performance of these acts has been found to be helpful in the production of a desirable inner state of mind" (p. 294).

Catholic and Protestant: Two Contrasting Types

Within the Christian context, traditional Roman Catholic observance most clearly exemplifies the objective type of worship. Believing that the glorifying of God, whether or not a congregation is present, is among its chief duties, the Catholic Church instituted a variety of practices in which the objective element is plainly evident. The constant presence of the Blessed Sacrament in every Catholic church makes the ornately furnished building a sacred dwelling place that a person enters, whatever the day or hour, with the attitude and gestures of reverence. Perpetual adoration of the Sacrament was the founding purpose of several Catholic orders whose members maintained in turn an unbroken vigil night and day. Extended if not strictly continuous periods of adoration may be undertaken once a year by other religious communities as well. Priests and others called to the religious life are under obligation to spend a portion of each day reading the Liturgy of the Hours (the Divine Office) not because of its subjective effects on them but to sanctify the day through the praise of God. Before the sweeping changes that issued out of the Second Vatican Council in the 1960s, the impressive and deeply stirring Mass itself was said in Latin, a language unknown to many worshipers, and much that occurred around the altar could be neither seen nor heard.

Minimizing or even renouncing the elaborations of Catholic liturgical practice, the Protestant traditions have evolved a form of worship that is clearly subjective in its intent. The minister's words, even when they are addressed to God, are meant for the hearing of the congregation, the presence of which is a prerequisite for services to be held. Often plainly appointed, the Protestant chancel may double on weekdays as a concert stage or a lecture platform, evoking applause or laughter instead of reverence and awe. For the most liberal Protestants, Sunday worship is little more than a music recital combined with an edifying talk.

The Protestant's loss is profound, according to Pratt. No combination of candles, music, and intonation, he says, can fill the void left by the loss of the peculiar sense of divine presence that is at the heart of the Catholic Mass. It matters little that the Catholic worshiper may not hear or understand what is going on,

> for he finds—and this sums up the subjective value of the mass—that a church in which mass is being said is an excellent place to pray, that the service gives him an intense realization of the closeness of God to human life, and that he goes away from it with a sense of spiritual refreshment (Pratt, 1920, p. 299).

Or at least that is how it used to be, for the Mass has undergone radical changes since the Second Vatican Council. Today Catholics hear the Mass said in their own language by a priest facing them from behind a relocated altar. After listening to a Protestant-style sermon, they may rise to sing a Protestant-authored song. Modified to engage the understanding and participation of its witnesses, today's mass is more didactic and less mysterious; it doubtless inspires less awe. The Divine Office has also been modified, along with many other aspects of Catholic practice, to make room for genuine personal response. With the decline of the regimented cloistered life, perpetual adoration of the Sacrament has largely ceased (O'Brien, 1979). Whether these changes ultimately signify gain or loss, the Catholic retains one fundamental and irreplaceable advantage: a service of worship still centered on a dramatic objective event—the transformation of bread and wine into the body and blood of Christ.

Corresponding to this undeniable strength is a serious weakness. That is, subjective gains are possible only for those who implicitly believe in the objective occurrence. Yet as Pratt (1950) declares, this is increasingly difficult in our present age. "Objective worship of the old and naive sort, for better or for worse, is hopelessly behind us" (p. 59). Problematical, too, is the Mass's requirement of at least a touch of the mystical temperament.

Old Symbols and a New Faith

Protestant that he was, Pratt did not entirely despair. On the one hand, he recognized the peculiar strengths of the cognitive emphasis in Protestant worship, especially its capacity to reconcile reason with belief and to enlarge the sympathies and moral outlook of its participants. On the other hand, he thought it possible to

St. Peter's Basilica. Pope Paul VI and 24 prelates concelebrate a Latin Rite Mass attended by 2500 bishops who gathered in 1964 from around the world for the Second Vatican Council's third session.

First Baptist Meeting House, Providence, Rhode Island. Brown University students stop here on commencement day to be addressed by fellow graduating seniors. A strictly secular event of this type would be unthinkable in a traditional Roman Catholic church.

retain enough of the sense of objectivity to allow a form of worship that nourishes the religious sentiment without offending the intellect. He conceived that worship as "an active search," "an ontological venture or achievement of the soul" founded in the sense of kinship between the human spirit and the cosmic spiritual realm (pp. 59–60). In place of petitionary prayer that seeks material help from a personal god, Pratt would foster the "prayer of aspiration and realization," a meditative mood characterized by an "intense longing for the attainment of all that is highest in our own potentialities," including the realization of the immensities of the cosmos and of our own finitude and littleness by comparison—the sense, in short, of the numinous (pp. 78–79).

Where will we find the symbols to help us cultivate this new form of worship? Faithful to his notion that symbols are derived historically from naive belief in objectively conceived entities, Pratt concludes that the forging of new symbols is no longer possible in the modern world. The great religious symbols, he says, "have their roots not only in a remote past but in a religious past." They derive their vitality and authority from "the symbol-making Ages of Faith," which he says are gone forever. It follows, then, that we will have to get along with the existing store of symbols, "an irreplaceable part of our spiritual heritage" that he urges us to conserve as one of our most valuable natural resources (pp. 138–139).

The symbols themselves are useless, of course, if we lose the capacity to understand their deeper meaning. According to Pratt, we have been living off of the reserve of "ontological realization" that we have inherited from our predecessors, an endowment we are rapidly using up. The blatantly subjective use of symbols and rites is possible for us only because we are still able to draw against the reserve of meaning left by those for whom these symbols pointed to a felt objective reality. "We need to see the Unseen for ourselves," says Pratt; "or, if that may not be, we need at least to feel a deeper reverence for it" (p. 50).

According to Pratt, the finding of new forms of faith and the appropriation of new methods of spiritual cultivation is a task for the social group and its leaders, not for the rare religious genius of former days. Although as a result Pratt expects far less unanimity in belief, he still hopes for an underlying religious accord. Seeking to impress upon the younger generation and its successors the enormity of the issues at stake, Pratt declares "that religion is a pearl of great price; that the spiritual life, though it can never be killed out of the race, is a tender plant which gives its fairest flowers only after careful culture; that liberty is not the only thing whose price is eternal vigilance'' (Pratt, 1923, p. 613).

A Monument for Succeeding Generations

Much like the *Varieties'* author, Pratt advanced neither a fundamental thesis nor a comprehensive explanatory principle. His aim, he said, was "purely descriptive" and his method, a "purely empirical" record of human experience (1920, p. vii). Whereas he does identify certain "laws" that function in the religious realm—the laws of habit and of rhythm, for example—we would not formulate them, he says, without a wink (p. 456). In any event, these laws play only a minor role in his work as a whole. Unorthodox in his scientific views like other humanistic psychologists, Pratt rejected all attempts to assimilate psychology to the physical sciences. Its explanations, he writes, "will be only the most general sort of description," made possible largely by the fact that human personalities are grounded in essentially the same physiological processes. "And this generalized description—which is psychology—would still hold even if these selves were surrounded by a non-human spiritual world with which they had actual commerce," though this world could not itself become an object of scientific study (p. 459).

Pratt's *Religious Consciousness* was quickly recognized as one of the field's best introductions, if not the finest of them all. Rudolph Uren (1928), who places it even before James's *Varieties,* judged it to be "the most thorough and comprehensive" of the works then available. He praises Pratt's lucid discussion of psychological method; his judicious balance between individual and social factors; his inclusion of neglected phenomena, especially from India, China, and Japan; his unsurpassed sympathy for every aspect of the religious life; and his balanced treatment of the varieties of conversion and mystical experience.

Edward Schaub (1921) points out that, in taking a descriptive approach free of the constraints of a guiding principle or law, Pratt was able to introduce the reader to an exceptional range of religious phenomena and to allow them to speak for themselves. Having no fundamental thesis to defend—for example, that desire plays a larger role in religion than intellect—Pratt drew conclusions that Schaub thought were unusually fair. Yet such an approach has its costs: "The facts are knit less closely together, and the relationship between the major topics, and that between religious experience as a whole and other types of experience, are less clear" (p. 211). Like other critics, Schaub regrets that Pratt did not take the challenge of explanation more to heart, especially the question of how belief in God originated. "No one, however, can give careful study to the volume without realizing that, within the limits it sets itself, it offers a rarely judicious treatment of the more fundamental aspects of the religious life and that, in addition, it presents not a few contributions of permanent value" (p. 217).

In the psychology of religion as a whole, Pratt's book rapidly took its place alongside the *Varieties* as a pervasively influential work, though the range of its influence has largely been limited to the English language literature. His famous and much misunderstood distinction of objective and subjective worship was widely regarded as too sharply drawn, but many of his other findings were eventually assimilated as virtual articles of truth.

Coming as it did near the end of the inaugural period of the American psychology of religion, Pratt's 1920 classic stood as a monument to the research and reflection of that period rather than as a beacon to a new generation of similarly competent and dedicated scholars. With few exceptions, the work in England and

America that followed was merely imitative and apologetic. Reprinted with a frequency second only to the *Varieties,* Pratt's never-revised book remained for decades the field's most comprehensive and authoritative source.

On the Continent, by contrast, the interval between the wars was especially productive for the psychology of religion. Most of Freud's contributions fall in this period, along with many of those of his followers. So, too, do some of the classics of the German descriptive tradition, which constitutes an important but, in America, largely neglected current in the humanistic stream. As we will see in the next chapter, the work of the German-speaking psychologists of religion—past and present—has been substantial, constituting a literature of much larger proportions than that authored by their humanistic counterparts on the other side of the ocean.

12

THE GERMAN
DESCRIPTIVE TRADITION

*H*umanistic psychologists are a diverse group of scholars who are united not by a common theoretical framework but by a shared understanding of the human condition. Because the inner world of subjective experience is the starting and end point in their thinking, they reject in one voice the ideal of an objective science of observable behavior. They likewise decline the psychoanalytic assumption that unconscious forces are a controlling factor in every human life. Most agree that the human experiential world is both subtle and elusive, requiring great care if investigators are to avoid misapprehending or distorting it. In other respects, however, humanistic psychologists vary widely, notably in the degree to which they incorporate elements of humanistic philosophy, including its rejection of supernaturalism, and in the effort they give to developing research methods appropriate to the study of human subjectivity.

It is in these two respects that the German descriptive tradition most strikingly differs from American humanistic psychology. German psychologists of religion, usually educated as philosophers or theologians, are far more inclined explicitly to define the limits of the field and to locate philosophical or theological questions outside its domain. The psychology of religion is nevertheless viewed as an essential element in theological discourse. Although committed to a position of neutrality, the German tradition reveals a fundamental kinship with German idealist philosophy and liberal Christian thought. In contrast, the American humanists are likely to be psychologists working entirely outside of any theological context. Relatively unconcerned with traditional philosophical and theological issues, including the question of boundaries, they have not hesitated to incorporate humanistic philosophical elements into their psychology. In their hands psychology sometimes takes on a distinctly religious character, although references to a transcendent dimension typically remain oblique.

Although the German scholars tend to employ a Christian idealist conceptual framework, they are highly self-conscious about method and rigorously systematic in its application. Carefully attentive to the diverse manifestations of a phenomenon, they have produced impressive tomes both subtle in analysis and rich in illustration. The American humanists, on the other hand, have shown little interest in exploring the intricacies of religious experience. They have mainly limited themselves instead to the enunciation of general principles and broad conclusions. Where evidence is not merely impressionistic or drawn from generalized human experience, it may well be gathered by means of the objective psychologist's correlational techniques. Thus, whereas most of the Germans consider inductive and intuitive methods to be essential for an understanding of the world of human subjectivity, the Americans willingly adopt some of the hypothetico–deductive techniques developed by the explanatory sciences when they wish to test their humanistic propositions. For them psychology may remain an explanatory science that happens to have chosen an unusually complex and elusive object.

In this chapter we review the most prominent contributions to the German descriptive literature. We begin by examining "the RELIGIOUS ACT," which serves to introduce the phenomenological approach. Then, in the context of a more encompassing methodological framework, we review Rudolf Otto's analysis of the experience of the holy and Friedrich Heiler's psychological and historical study of prayer. The existential–interpretive approach as exemplified by Eduard Spranger is featured next, followed by the work of Karl Girgensohn and other members of the Dorpat school of religious psychology. After a brief look at more recent contributions to this literature, we undertake an overall assessment of the phenomenological–interpretive perspectives.

PHENOMENOLOGICAL AND INTERPRETIVE PSYCHOLOGIES

German contributions to the psychology of religion are typically phenomenological. Here this term designates any approach that systematically describes phenomena occurring in human experience without imposing a theoretical framework and with no other goal than the faithful illumination of the phenomena. Thus defined, the phenomenological attitude may be found in some measure in a variety of related psychologies, each identified by the methodological or thematic principle to which it gives particular emphasis. Most notable among these are *verstehende* ("understanding") psychology, which we will call INTERPRETIVE PSYCHOLOGY, and existential psychology, which, though self-consciously phenomenological, is known chiefly for its concern with the fundamental structure of human existence.

THE RELIGIOUS ACT

At the heart of the phenomenological approach to religion is the notion of "the religious act." The term *act,* once widely regarded as the fundamental concept of psychology, designates a psychological unit that combines cognitive, affective, and CONATIVE aspects of a person's relation with the outer world (English and English, 1958). It is thus more inclusive—and correspondingly more adequate—than such contemporary terms as "behavior" or "response." Although it is sometimes used interchangeably with *experience,* the word *act* more clearly denotes the aspect of purposeful striving.

An act is by definition always "intentional." That is, in every instance it implies some object or refers to some content. The *religious act* in particular is defined not in terms of a specifically religious feeling, function, or sense, but in relation to that "something" we are conscious of, the act's so-called INTENTIONAL OBJECT or correlate (Stavenhagen, 1925, p. 6; Potempa, 1958; James, 1902, p. 31, makes the same point). "One cannot describe the religious act," says Wolfgang Trillhaas (1953, p. 29), "without reference to its intentional correlate, without indicating the object-sphere to which it refers. Religious acts . . . are those that refer to the 'divine,' a term that one must naturally apprehend in a sufficiently broad sense." At the same time psychology can say nothing about the existence and nature of the intentional object, and correspondingly, it cannot judge whether the experiences and perceptions of the divine are "true" or "false."

According to the phenomenologists, every psychic act has the quality of "transcendence," the "climbing beyond" the self's immediate standpoint. This capacity to transcend the momentary situation is engaged when we reflect on the past and anticipate the future, when we think and talk in symbols, and when we participate in responsible social relations (May et al., 1958, pp. 71–76). Peculiar to the religious act, however, is transcendence of *the world as a whole*. All aspects of a person's experience, including all objects of a finite and contingent character, are first gathered together under the rubric "the world." This whole is then transcended in the religious act, for absolutely no finite object or good can fulfill its intention. Viewed from a worldly standpoint, the religious act will thus appear groundless and aimless. From a religious perspective, however, the inability of any imaginary finite good or human perfection to satisfy the intention of the act demonstrates its genuinely religious character (Scheler, 1921, pp. 250–251).

The Structure of the Religious Act

The religious act is more complex than it may at first seem. As Otto Gründler (1922) points out, it is not a simple act comparable to an act of sensory perception, but a layered arrangement of partial acts. He divides the partial acts into two groups: (1) theoretical acts of noticing or of taking cognizance (*die Kenntnisnahmen*) and (2) the subsequent emotional and practical acts of taking a position or stand (*die Stellungnahmen*).

Acts of Taking Cognizance: According to Gründler, "The theoretical act consists here not in the mere perception of a thing but in the grasping of a value. From this value knowledge is derived, its presence and specific quality grasped in an originally intuitive act; that is the fundamental experience" (p. 44). At first, he says, there is no clear idea of the object that possesses the value; this comes only gradually, through clarification and inference. Once such objects emerge, however, there is a common but erroneous tendency to treat them as essential aspects of divinity itself rather than as elements in a person's experience of the divine. They should be conceived, Gründler says, as pointers or signposts that make it possible to perceive what would otherwise be imperceptible.

Gründler identifies two contrasting attitudes that can lead to the grasping of religious values. On the one hand is the *world-rejecting attitude,* which opposes all finite values and thus finds no pleasure or positive meaning in the things of this world. Individuality itself is rejected as a delusion. Citing as examples the writings of Meister Eckhart and various ancient Hindu scriptures, Gründler suggests that the nothingness remaining for this attitude at its extreme may be said to have taken on the mediating role of the value-bearing object, unless one prefers to regard the "pure" ego emptied of all individuality and objective orientation as itself the mediator (p. 48).

For the *world-affirming attitude,* on the other hand, any object can serve as the religious act's intentional correlate, as long as it possesses an absolute value rather than a finite one, and its existence is experienced as a miracle and a gift. Gründler discusses four groups of objects that bear religious values: the world of nature in its vital, aesthetic, and lawful aspects; inspired works of art that have a certain loftiness and grandeur, whether or not the content is obviously religious; historical and personal events that suggest, in conjunction with other religious experiences, an insight and will that is more than human; and, finally, the testimony of finite human beings, including one's own conscience ("the voice of God") but especially saintly persons, who, unlike natural objects, may themselves be thought to be essentially divine or holy.

Acts of Taking a Stand: Dependent on the theoretical acts, yet frequently influencing them in turn, are the acts of taking a stand. The value grasped in the theoretical act demands by its very nature a response that accords with the value's character. The form of this response may be either emotional or practical. *Emotional attitudes* include faith, confidence, trust, hope, fear, awe, humility, devotion, and love. Paradoxically, faith and love are not only responses to values observed in the theoretical acts but are also the conditions necessary for a genuinely insightful comprehension of the divine. As this knowledge grows, so also do they, in depth and intensity, allowing a more profound understanding in turn.

A person's response may also appear outwardly in word, gesture, or deed. These *practical attitudes* encompass the whole sphere of ethical and moral action, on the one hand, and the various kinds of worship and cultic practice on the other. Scheler (1921) maintains that both of these manifestations—purposeful conduct no less than expressive action—bear a reciprocal relation to the act of taking cognizance akin to that ascribed by Gründler to faith and love. "Good will and conduct do more than reflect religious awareness," writes Scheler. "At every step they widen and *deepen* one's concrete knowledge of God." Similarly, in a manner analogous to the artist's penetrating the world in the very process of representing it, "Religious knowledge is not wholly present *before* liturgical expression; ritual is an essential *vehicle* of its growth" (p. 265). The apparent interdependence of the idea of the religious object and the form of ritual response, of theory and practice, leads Scheler to conclude that "They who pray kneeling have not seen God in the same light as they who pray standing" (p. 266). Thus he advises those who wish to enter into the faith of another tradition to follow its rules of conduct as well as its moral precepts.

The Object of the Religious Act

Analysis of the religious act, Gründler emphasizes, must not be allowed to obscure its essential and indissoluble unity, which both derives from and includes its object. Thus the act of worship, says Scheler, forms a unity with the Highest Good, the object that is its fulfillment. Yet unlike all other types of cognitive acts, he adds, the religious one finds its fulfillment only in an act of reciprocity. That is, the religious act demands from its intentional object an answer corresponding to its primary intention. Thus "One may only speak of 'religion' where the object bears a *divine personal form* and where revelation (in the widest sense) on the part of this personal object is what fulfils the religious act and its intention" (p. 253). In short, the truth "intended" or the salvation sought must be experienced as somehow *received*.

No one can avoid performing the religious act, according to Scheler, who considers it "an essential endowment of the human mind." All that remains in question is the adequacy of its object. A person has but two choices, he says: the absolute good that is God or some finite and contingent object, which, elevated to the absolute sphere that corresponds to the religious act, becomes an idol.

Everybody *has* a particular something, an object bearing (for him) the hallmarks of the supremely valuable, to which he knowingly, or by the unconscious test of practical conduct, accords precedence over all else. This object is for the leading minority in this capitalist age, to give an example, the maximal acquisition of economic goods, or of their measure—money (mammonism). For the nationalist it is his nation, for the Faustian limitless knowledge, for the Don Juan repeated conquests of woman. In principle any finite good may enter the absolute sphere of being and values in any concrete mind, and thereafter be striven for with "unending endeavour." In such a case the good invariably becomes a false god (p. 269).

To guide the religious act to its proper object, Scheler advocates what he calls the "shattering of idols," demonstrating to the individual that a finite good has been installed in the place of God. "In thus bringing a man to *disillusion* with his idol, once we have exposed it in analysing his life, we bring him *of his own accord* to the idea and reality of God." At the same time the individual is thereby brought back into the human community, says Scheler. For not only do we tend to think of God as bearing the same relation to all persons, but also "Precisely because the religious is man's most personal and individual act, it is necessarily one which can *fully* attain its object only in the form of the general concert of men" (p. 267). Hence every religious act is simultaneously individual and social.

Types of Religious Acts

Much as religious experience has been distinguished according to its varieties, so too the religious act has been differentiated according to type. Albert Lang (1957, p. 34), for example, identifies the act in the form we have thus far encountered it here as the *primary religious act,* that is, one that "arises out of religious motives and refers to religious objects." *Secondary religious acts* constitute, then, the effects of religious motives in the ethical, political, and social arenas. Within the primary religious act Lang further distinguishes the core religious experience or the central religious act—that is, personal encounter of the holy—from acts that are preparatory and those that follow as aftereffects.

Helpful though they may be, these distinctions are not universally accepted. Although Wilhelm Pöll (1965) grants the legitimacy of identifying a dramatic encounter with the divine as the "core experience" or the "central act," he objects to reducing other religious experiences to "peripheral acts." Religious longing or repentance may equally well fall in the center of the sphere of personal experience, he says, and contrariwise, the numinous experience may first arise in the periphery. Pöll proposes that we retain the labels "basic religious experience" or "fundamental religious act" for the numinous experience, but that we denominate the rest as "consequential religious experiences" or "consecutive religious acts." Even these distinctions, he warns us, should not mislead us into thinking that experience orders itself according to our categories, or that "partial acts" form less of a whole than "total" ones (pp. 113–114).

FOUNDATIONS FOR AN INTERPRETIVE PSYCHOLOGY OF RELIGION

Although phenomenology is sometimes represented as a method, it is difficult to say precisely what its practitioners *do* to arrive at their distinctions and insights. It would be more accurate to think of phenomenology as an attitude that is informed by certain basic principles. Among these is the proposition that no preestablished set of procedures shall govern the research process. Moreover, in contrast to objective scientists, who proceed on the basis of impersonal and precisely formulated hypotheses, phenomenologists start with what deeply interests them in their own experience and then explore the phenomena in an open, questioning mood. Readers of their subsequent descriptions and interpretations will ideally find themselves wondering about the phenomena with a similar attitude (van Manen, 1990).

Methodological principles, and even specific procedures and techniques, may nevertheless be helpful in carrying out phenomenological research. In the literature on the psychology of religion, the fullest discussion of such principles is contained in a small volume by German theologian Wilhelm Koepp (1920). The method he presents, says Koepp, is "purely empirical," meaning that it is strictly grounded in human experience. To employ the method, then, the investigator must personally gain access to the realm of religious experience. To be a psychologist of religion, Koepp declares, one must possess the rare combination of a deep piety of one's own, the gift of the purest self-observation, and an extraordinarily broad acquaintance with the religious expressions of others, from diverse traditions and times. Vital as well to the phenomenological work is a measure of artistic sensitivity.

Understanding

Wilhelm Dilthey, the great nineteenth-century pioneer of the human sciences (the GEISTESWISSENSCHAFTEN), argued that the world of human experience and creativity requires an approach markedly different from the methods of the natural sciences. Unlike the world of physical objects, the human realm is shot through with experienced meaning, which is expressed outwardly in a myriad of forms, from posture and simple gestures to literature, art, and religion. The process by which we comprehend the underlying meaning of these expressions is called "understanding" (VERSTEHEN), an everyday term that Dilthey and those who followed him used in a highly technical way.

According to Dilthey, understanding is not simply an intellectual operation but employs all of the mind's capacities operating in concert. It is correspondingly resistant to precise definition and logical analysis. This fundamental, irreducible disposition is known to all of us in the primal form we automatically use to make sense of everyday human expressions and situations. The higher, more self-critical, and more encompassing forms of understanding offer access to more complex and elusive expressions and place them in much broader contexts of meanings. In all of its forms, understanding underlies *interpretation,* the process by which we make sense of what is present to us. Like understanding, interpretation occurs on varying levels of sophistication and adequacy. *Hermeneutics* is the enterprise that reflects on the possibilities of interpretation and establishes principles by which to carry it out (Ermarth, 1978; Hodges, 1952; Palmer, 1969; Rickman, 1979).

Understanding at any level is grounded in a person's own lived experience. I understand another's experience to the degree that I am able to relive it or to reconstruct it imaginatively, by drawing on similar experiences of my own. Furthermore, to comprehend the elements of another's experience—say, momentary thoughts or passing desires—they must be placed in the context of the whole of which they are a part: the coherent structure of the other person's mental life. To see such connections, however, I must first be familiar with them in my own experience.

There are still other requirements. Understanding, says Dilthey, is "an intellectual process involving the highest concentration" (Hodges, 1952, p. 124). In every instance, adds Eduard Spranger (1929, p. 165), understanding depends on the researcher's "spiritual" or intellectual breadth and maturity, qualities that imply not simply a high level of educational and cultural attainment but also the capacity for "originality of seeing." However much experience and vision a person may have, understanding is always a relative achievement, a process that is never complete.

Koepp's Schema for Interpretive Understanding

In his account of the process of understanding religious phenomena, Koepp distinguishes two major stages: the gathering of materials and the systematic treatment of them. He calls the first stage phenomenology, which he defines as observation and description of the facts of human experience exactly as they are given, without distorting them through preconceptions, theoretical interpretations, or judgments about their truth or value. If it is impossible wholly to set aside our presuppositions, says Koepp, much can be gained in making the effort. A person's attitude, he emphasizes, must embody a strictly inductive empiricism that desires nothing more than contact with reality as it is given in human experience.

Phenomenology: For the psychology of religion, Koepp maintains, the gathering of materials presents peculiar difficulties. The most direct avenues of investigation—self-observation and experimentation—are largely closed to it, for it is impossible, he says, to observe a religious phenomenon introspectively or experimentally without changing its fundamental character. So sensitive a process as religion cannot be made to serve a scientific or any other foreign aim; it can only be called forth for its own sake. The psychology of religion must therefore rely above all on "indirect observation," carried out chiefly by means of personal documents that were written not for scientific study but for such purposes as self-examination, the edification of other members of the religious community, or the solicitation of those outside of it. The collection of such materials, especially from great or influential religious persons, must be undertaken in close cooperation with the historian of religion. History, says Koepp, provides the psychology of religion with a natural laboratory.

Comprehension of personal documents and other such historical materials is dependent, Koepp says, on our own self-understanding, limited though it is by the difficulties of self-observation and other factors. The relation between these two fundamental sources—the historical and the personal—is in fact intimately reciprocal, forming a HERMENEUTICAL CIRCLE. The familiarity with historical materials that is facilitated by self-understanding is in turn a vital basis for more deeply comprehending our own lives. Broad acquaintance with the piety of our contemporaries, even when it is largely imitative or shallow, is also an essential ingredient for the psychology of religion, although here again the methodological difficulties are considerable. Maintaining that personal documents are always the surest source of material, Koepp asserts nonetheless that even the more problematic modes of observation must be occasionally used if the psychology of religion is to be truly universal, encompassing both past and present, both historical tradition and individual faith.

Interpretation: The second stage in Koepp's methodological schema consists of two complementary ways of processing the phenomena gathered and described in the phenomenological stage. We may seek, on the one hand, to penetrate to the heart of a single phenomenon, perhaps one that is especially prominent or characteristic; this is the way of *analysis*. On the other hand, we may begin with a diversity of phenomena, ordering them according to their similarities, differences, and relations; this is the way of synthesis or the *formation of types.* Equally valid and neither more essential than the other, these two ways, says Koepp, must ultimately be carried out in intimate relation to each other. Often, however, investigators will justifiably emphasize one over the other.

Analysis: Koepp identifies four steps in the conduct of analysis. The object chosen for study, whether it be as exceptional as some famous religious personality or as nearly universal as priesthood or prayer, must first be clearly identified. By carefully isolating and delimiting the object, we can make apparent its unique features and coloring. Perhaps more than any of the other steps, says Koepp, this first one requires unusual artistic receptivity and empathy.

The second step of analysis takes into account the human capacity for conscious awareness, for reflecting on the past and pursuing goals imaginatively projected into the future. Unlike the essentially blind and automatic behavior of many animals, for which mechanistic explanatory principles seem adequate, human conduct is conspicuously purposive, a quality that Koepp says only a teleological perspective can comprehend. Even on levels where active striving is not apparent, where it may seem that the behavioristic assumption of passive reactivity holds true, the psyche is best characterized by *receptivity.* The human mind participates in the taking in of external stimuli, seizing them and actively shaping and adapting them according to its own purposes. The higher the level of psychic life, Koepp maintains, the clearer the teleological, purposive structure will appear in analysis. Because the psychology of religion strives to comprehend one of the highest of the psychic provinces, it must rely to an exceptional degree on the teleological principle. The second step of analysis, then, is the crucial one, for in it we attempt to discern the *telos,* the goal or purpose of the phenomenon we seek to understand. With its discovery, we have in hand the unifying element that gives meaning to the whole.[1]

The third step consists of the "teleological illumination of structure." Whether the phenomenon be an individual, a particular religious experience, a dogmatic proposition, a cultic act, or an artistic expression, we trace the *telos* or goal back through the structure of the phenomenon as a whole, thereby illuminating it in its totality. What may at first have appeared to be incomprehensible or "superstitious" proves in the end to be meaningful—illustrating, in Koepp's words, the "life-functions" or "teleological laws" of religion.

In the fourth step, we place the phenomenon being studied into the larger context of related and contrasting religious manifestations, where comparison may shed new light on the phenomena themselves as well as their interrelations. With this final step, analysis passes over to the other of Koepp's two complementary ways of handling phenomena, the identification of types.

Formation of Types: According to interpretive psychologists, the goal of typology is the construction of a fundamental set of IDEAL TYPES that can serve as an orienting schema for comprehending the nature and dynamics of individual forms. These types are ideal in the sense that they are purified, imaginative constructions that are most unlikely to correspond exactly to any existing form. Somewhat the same process is involved when the psychopathologist creates a portrait of the "typical" paranoid schizophrenic, who, combining in full blossom each of the defining

---

[1] Berguer (1920) makes the same point. "Religion is not merely an assemblage of states of consciousness of a special kind; it is also a struggle with destiny; it is directed towards an end, towards an aim; the devotee is in search of something, he follows a plan" (p. 11).

characteristics of this variety of mental disorder, is in fact rarely if ever encountered. Familiarity with such types is valuable, however, for it provides a basis for diagnosing and treating individual patients.

According to Koepp's schema, the formation of types begins with the sensitive and self-critical comparison of phenomena. Both their similarities and their differences are considered, especially with regard to the fundamental tendencies discerned in the process of analysis. This first, comparative step, he says, requires intuitive and artistic capabilities combined with extraordinary diligence and patience. A multitude of alternative ways for ordering, arranging, and typifying the phenomena must be tested and rejected in turn until one is found that closely corresponds to empirical reality.

The results of such painstaking comparison are given final form in two parallel steps. To the degree that the phenomena possess an unchanging identity, they may be characterized through the formation of static types, which is typology in the narrower sense. Because the enduring type is inconceivable apart from a certain inner dynamic, religious phenomena may also be typified in terms of the laws or functions that govern their change or alteration (NOMOLOGY). Useful though such distinctions are, Koepp adds, we must always keep in mind that they are invented human constructs.

The final step of typology in the broader sense consists of psychological clarification and interpretation of the similarities, types, and lawful developments that have been discovered. Merely accidental and superficial similarities must be distinguished from genuine and deeply rooted ones. We must separate out as well, Koepp says, all the elements that are geographically or historically conditioned. We seek to retain only what is essential and intrinsic to the phenomena, in order to make their deeper meaning as clear as possible. With this step we again draw on the way of analysis, but this time in relation to a variety of phenomena.

Koepp's schema for an interpretive psychology of religion is summarized in Table 12.1. According to his view, a full account of the religious life in all its varieties and manifestations will be based on comprehensive phenomenology, penetrating analysis, and astute typology—all carried out in intimate relation to one another and with the fullest possible attention to the reality of human experience. This approach is purely empirical, Koepp repeatedly emphasizes, and thus it excludes theoretical interpretations of every kind. Its goal is explicitly not to solve the religious *mysterium*, Koepp says, but only to bring enough of this mystery into comprehensible order to allow its facts to speak to our understanding.

TWO CLASSIC EXAMPLES: RUDOLF OTTO AND FRIEDRICH HEILER

As examples of the interpretive approach, Koepp cites two German works, contemporary to his own, that have become world-famous classics: Rudolf Otto's *The Idea of the Holy* (1917), which Koepp identifies as exemplary of the way of analysis, and Friedrich Heiler's *Prayer* (1918), which illustrates the use of typology. Otto (1869–1937) was a liberal Lutheran philosopher–theologian whose broad and penetrating knowledge of the great religious traditions was founded not only in close study of original texts, chiefly Hindu, but also in extensive travel, most notably to North Africa, India, China, and Japan (Wach, 1951). Heiler (1892–1967), who was recruited by Otto to the University of Marburg, was a distinguished historian of religion whose deep longing for the unity of the religious traditions was reflected in his own shift, in 1918, from Roman Catholic affiliation to a lifelong intermediate

Table 12.1 **KOEPP'S SCHEMA FOR AN INTERPRETIVE PSYCHOLOGY OF RELIGION**

A. Phenomenology

1. Gathering of personal documents and other expressions of religious experience, past and present.
2. Pure description of the religious phenomena.

B. Interpretation

I. Analysis	**II. Typology and Nomology**
1. Isolation, delimitation, and concentration of a religious phenomenon.	1. Comparison of religious phenomena according to similarities and contrasts.
2. Identification of the *telos,* the goal or fundamental motive of the phenomenon.	2. Formation of types: religious phenomena viewed in terms of their enduring identity.
3. Illumination of the inner structure of the phenomenon in the light of the *telos.*	3. Discovery of laws: religious phenomena viewed in terms of their systematic alterations.
4. Comparison with related religious phenomena.	4. Clarification and interpretation.
Exemplar: Rudolf Otto's *The Idea of the Holy* (1917).	Exemplar: Friedrich Heiler's *Prayer* (1918).

Source: Based on Koepp, 1920, page 95.

posture of "evangelical [i.e., Lutheran or Protestant] catholicity." A well-traveled historian knowledgeable in several Oriental languages, a major contributor to the phenomenology of religion, and a feminist in both religious and secular circles, Heiler shared with Otto a profound personal apprehension of religion's great mysteries as well as an exceptionally empathic understanding of the diversity of human response (Schimmel, 1968). It is to such psychologically trained scholars as Otto and Heiler, says the eminent Dutch scholar Gerardus van der Leeuw (1926, p. 2), that we owe the realization that no single principle or method is sufficient to explain reality's rich and manifold character.

The Experience of the Holy

Otto's famous and extraordinarily influential study takes as its object "the nonrational factor in the idea of the divine," the experiential substratum, often overlooked, that constitutes the essential, living core of every religion. The nonrational or feeling element is neglected, according to Otto, because of the dominant role that language plays in religious traditions. Sacred texts, edifying discourses, and theological instruction almost inevitably accent the conceptual. Although Otto clearly appreciates the ethical and other "rational" aspects of religious tradition, he emphasizes that conceptualization invariably diminishes the experience of the holy, if it does not exclude it altogether. The experience is therefore most directly expressed by negative means: in darkness, emptiness, and silence.

The tendency for the rational to distort and displace the nonrational is demonstrated in the fate of the word "holy" itself. Originally used in reference to a unique and profoundly moving feeling response, "holy" now chiefly denotes the ethical quality of absolute goodness, a meaning that is derivative at best. To recover the original sense of this word, apart from any "rational" aspects, Otto adopted the word "numinous," derived from the Latin *numen,* meaning divine will or power.

Rudolf Otto   Friedrich Heiler

The focus of Otto's study, then, is the *numinous consciousness,* a complex feeling state that, given the accompanying intimations of its object, is also in some sense cognitive, even before it is schematized by rational concepts. Emphasizing the insufficiency of any attempt to articulate this nonrational experience, Otto maintains that his own analysis will be comprehensible only to those who have themselves had the experience and in whom, therefore, it can be evoked anew. All he can offer us, he says, are pointers or "ideograms," analogical notions derived from events in the natural sphere. The numinous experience itself is irreducible to these or any other analogous terms, for this experience, claims Otto, is in every respect unique. More than that, it is strictly beyond utterance.

Otto describes the numinous consciousness in terms of a dual structure corresponding to the twofold character of its object, the *mysterium* (which presumably constitutes the *telos* in Koepp's system of analysis). On the one hand, it is the *mysterium tremendum,* an object that is awesome and daunting. On the other, it is the *mysterium fascinans,* which is attractive and fascinating as nothing else can be (Figure 12.1). The "strange harmony of contrasts" formed by these opposing qualities yields a dual structure that "is at once the strangest and most noteworthy phenomenon in the whole history of religion" (Otto, 1917, p. 31).

Mysterium Tremendum: In analyzing the first of these aspects, the *tremendum,* Otto distinguishes three related elements.

1. The element of *awfulness,* emerging first as uncanniness, shuddering, or demonic dread, becomes in higher forms of experience a religious or mystical awe. The numen is correspondingly characterized by "absolute unapproachability."
2. The element of *majesty* or "absolute overpoweringness" is chiefly responsible for the sharply contrasting subjective feeling of "creature-consciousness," the sense of personal nothingness, out of which may come the feeling of religious humility.
3. The element of *energy* or urgency underscores the living character of the numinous object and is symbolically represented in such expressions as passion, will, force, and activity.

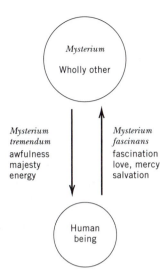

Figure 12.1. The experience of the holy as conceptualized by Rudolf Otto. The arrows indicate the direction of the human response, either away from or toward the *mysterium,* depending on which aspect predominates.

Whereas the adjective *tremendum* allows some positive if only analogical definition, the noun *mysterium* is essentially negative in meaning. What is mysterious is "wholly other," lying beyond our ordinary experience and categories and filling us with absolute, dumb amazement. Progressively contrasted with familiar objects and then with nature in its entirety, the Wholly Other becomes in time the "supernatural" and finally the "supramundane," when it is at last exalted above the world order as a whole. Thus conceptual thought is left with only negation and paradox as the means by which to apprehend the *mysterium* (p. 29).

Mysterium Fascinans: Contrasting with the holy's awesomeness is the element of fascination. The object that inspires dread is at the same time uniquely alluring and captivating, potentially to the level of frenzied intoxication. The moment of fascination is present, too, on occasions of solemnity, whether public or private. Just as "wrath" serves as an ideogram for the element of awfulness, without exhausting it, so the element of fascination is schematized by the ideas of perfect love, mercy, pity, and comfort as well as by doctrines of salvation. With the addition of this element, what would otherwise prompt worship only in the form of expiation and propitiation now becomes the object of desire and yearning, inspiring a search carried out for its own sake, not merely for help in the natural sphere.

Possession of or by the numinous object, first sought in order to appropriate its powers for practical purposes, becomes an end in itself, even a way of salvation. The diverse magical and shamanistic procedures give way to ascetic practices, and with further maturation and purification, the highest reaches of the spiritual life are attained. At these sublime levels, "The *mysterium* is experienced in its essential, positive, and specific character, as something that bestows upon man a beatitude beyond compare, but one whose real nature he can neither proclaim in speech nor conceive in thought, but may know only by a direct and living experience" (p. 33).

Expressions of the Holy: Just as the numinous consciousness cannot be contained in words, so it cannot be taught to another. Yet because, as Otto claims, it exists as an inborn capacity, it can be induced or awakened. Words and images, though they serve as an often dramatic means of interpreting and preserving an apprehension of the holy, are least likely to incite it in another. What are needed, rather, are the dynamic expressions of living persons, whose voices and gestures and reverent attitudes embody the experience far more than words can. No other element in religion, says Otto, so requires "transmission by living fellowship and the inspiration of personal contact" (p. 61).

Art, too, may represent the numinous, most effectively in the form of the sublime, and that especially in architecture. Whatever the medium, however, art's representation of the numinous is indirect at best. At some point art must retreat, giving way to darkness and silence. It is in semidarkness that the "mystical" effect begins, says Otto, who recalls for us the quickening of the soul in dimly lit cathedrals, temples, and mosques or in the play of light and shadow on the forest path (the circumstances, we remember, of William James's mystical experience). Music, too, must be restrained, even to the point of silence, if it is to achieve the fullest expression of the *mysterium*. The most mystical moments of Bach's Mass in B Minor, Otto observes by way of illustration, are not the gloriously stirring "Sanctus" but the hushed and lingering "Et incarnatus est" of the "Credo."[2]

To the darkness and silence that are well known in Western art, the Eastern traditions add a third indirect means of expressing the numinous: emptiness and empty distance. Otto calls to mind the meticulously laid out though nearly empty courtyards of Chinese and Japanese temple architecture and especially the numinous simplicity of Oriental paintings, whose power far exceeds the economy of strokes. The void itself seems to become the subject of many of these paintings, says Otto, especially those associated with contemplation. A far cry from the Gothic works of art that are most strikingly numinous to the Westerner, these Oriental expressions are nonetheless accessible to us by means of a "penetrating imaginative sympathy" (p. 60).

The Varieties of Prayer

Given the centrality of expression in any genuine interpretive psychology (Rickman, 1979), we will not be surprised to discover that it is thematic in Heiler's work as well. Heiler's widely admired book on prayer, which is considerably abridged in the English translation, is chiefly a study in typology. As we will see, however, it is also a work of analysis, in Koepp's sense of teleological illumination. It accords more clearly with Koepp's schema than does Otto's work, in fact, and may be regarded as a model of Koepp's twofold approach.

Prayer, according to Heiler, is the central and most revealing expression of religious faith.

> Not in dogmas and institutions, not in rites and ethical ideals, but in prayer do we grasp the peculiar quality of the religious life. In the words of a prayer we can penetrate

---

[2] For one of Hardy's (1979) respondents, the "Sanctus" elicited a full-blown experience of the *mysterium tremendum*. The seventy-year-old man writes: "A friend persuaded me to go to Ely Cathedral to hear a performance of Bach's B Minor Mass. I had heard the work [before], indeed I knew Bach's choral works pretty well. I was sitting towards the back of the nave. The Cathedral seemed to be very cold. The music thrilled me . . . until we got to the great SANCTUS. I find this experience difficult to define. It was primarily a warning. I was frightened. I was trembling from head to foot, and wanted to cry. Actually I think I did. I heard no 'voice' except the music; I saw nothing; but the warning was very definite. I was not able to interpret this experience satisfactorily until I read—some months later—Rudolf Otto's 'Das Heilige.' Here I found it—the 'Numinous.' I was before the Judgement Seat. I was being 'weighed in the balance and found wanting.' This is an experience I have never forgotten" (p. 85). Hardy reports that of the more than 4000 first-hand accounts of religious experience that he and his colleagues had collected, 607 offered "splendid examples" of Otto's numinous consciousness (p. 66).

The timeless Ryoanji Zen garden at Kyoto, created around 1500 C.E., consists of five clusters of rocks surrounded by meticulously raked white sand and gravel.

into the deepest and the most intimate movements of the religious soul (Heiler, 1932, p. xv).

Differences not only among individuals but also among cultures and traditions mean that prayer will manifest itself in a great diversity of forms. Indeed, it appears

as the calm collectedness of a devout individual soul, and as the ceremonial liturgy of a great congregation; as an original creation of a religious genius, and as an imitation on the part of a simple, average religious person; as the spontaneous expression of upspringing religious experiences, and as the mechanical recitation of an incomprehensible formula; as bliss and ecstasy of heart, and as painful fulfilment of the law; as the involuntary discharge of an overwhelming emotion, and as the voluntary concentration on a religious object; as loud shouting and crying, and as still, silent absorption; as artistic poetry, and as stammering speech; as the flight of the spirit to the supreme Light, and as a cry out of the deep distress of the heart; as joyous thanksgiving and ecstatic praise, and as humble supplication for forgiveness and compassion; as a childlike entreaty for life, health, and happiness, and as an earnest desire for power in the moral struggle of existence; as a simple petition for daily bread, and as an all-consuming yearning for God Himself; as a selfish wish, and as an unselfish solicitude for a brother; as wild cursing and vengeful thirst, and as heroic intercession for personal enemies and persecutors; as a stormy clamour and demand, and as joyful renunciation and holy serenity; as a desire to change God's will and make it chime with our petty wishes, and as a self-forgetting vision of and surrender to the Highest Good; as the timid entreaty of the sinner before a stern judge, and as the trustful talk of a child with a kind father; as swelling phrases of politeness and flattery before an unapproachable

> King, and as a free outpouring in the presence of a friend who cares; as the humble petition of a servant to a powerful master, and as the ecstatic converse of the bride with the heavenly Bridegroom (p. 353).

Heiler took as his main task the construction of a typology of prayer that would serve to characterize this astonishing richness of individual forms. He identified nine general types.

Naive Prayer of Primitive Man: Heiler considers the first of his nine types, the impulsive petitionary prayer of the nonliterate individual, to be the "prototype of all prayer" (p. 1). Accordingly, he dwells on it far longer than on any other type, excepting prayer of great religious personalities. These two featured types, in fact, share certain essential features. Both are spontaneous expressions, free equally of reflective criticism and traditional form. Both are directed to a living, present, and personalized god, with whom a person may enter into relation and from whom a response may be expected. Finally, in both types this encounter takes the form of a social relation, most often of kinship but also of subjection or of friendship, involving thereby some combination of familiarity, awe, humility, warmth of feeling, trust, and confidence (Heiler, 1918, pp. 139–147; 220–221; 1932, pp. 58–64; 104–105). Yet fundamental differences remain between these two types, as we will see.

Naive prayer, which may be no less spontaneous and heartfelt for its occasional use of a formula, is typically incited by a sudden threat to the well-being of the individual or the group. It may also be prompted by a felt practical need or by feelings of gratitude. The powerful supernatural being to whom the prayer is addressed is assumed to share many of the qualities of human beings, including not only a body of some, often considerable, age and of a specific sex, but also various impulses and needs. In order to appeal to divinity's putative egoism, the individual's petition is almost always accompanied by sacrifice and sacrificial formulas or—in accord with a later development—by a vow, which boldly and irreverently makes the gift contingent on the granting of the petitioner's request. Praise, flattery, and appeals to sympathy, or even threats and insults, may also be employed, much as they are with other human beings, especially rulers. In many traditions today, the function of sacrifice has been taken over by attendance at religious services, monetary offerings, fasting, and pilgrimages to holy sites (Heiler, 1932, pp. 2–35).

Invariably accompanying the spoken elements of prayer—and sometimes taking their place—are certain gestures and bodily attitudes. The wishes and feelings that impelled the petitioner into prayerful action are most clearly and directly reflected, according to Heiler, in the free play of facial expression. Yet bodily movements so spontaneous, individual, and ephemeral as these, says Heiler, elude systematic comprehension. He turns instead to the larger, more accessible bodily gestures that, even more rapidly than the words of prayer, become conventionalized in ritual forms.[3] Only in moments of extreme need, he reports, are word and gesture likely to break entirely free of these traditional patterns (Heiler, 1918, pp. 98–99).

Roughly half of Heiler's (1918) extended section on posture and gesture in

---

[3] When discursive thought is forced into silence, the photographic image can often speak eloquently. For a striking exploration of the facial expressions and other gestures of prayer, see Abraham Menashe's *The Face of Prayer* (1983). The symbolic value of facial expression for representing the depths of emotion and individual character is reflected in Denis Thomas's *The Face of Christ* (1979), a work depicting the search of artists and popular piety over the past 18 centuries for the visage of "the most famous man who ever lived" (p. 12).

Pilgrims circumambulate a shrine on the outskirts of Banaras, India, as part of their larger circumambulation of the great sacred city as a whole.

prayer describes the various movements themselves and documents their occurrence in a great variety of religious traditions. Standing is the most frequently observed posture in prayer, followed by kneeling. Both positions are typically preceded by prostration or by inclination downward of a portion of the upper body. Also common as a preface to prayer is bodily rotation, which Heiler identifies as an abbreviated form of sacred CIRCUMAMBULATION. The ritual of walking around a sacred object, usually with the right side of the body nearest the object and the hand touching it, can be found in various parts of the world.[4]

The positioning of the arms and hands during prayer can follow any of a number of patterns. Most frequently, the arms are raised or spread out, the palms opened toward the deity; Heiler identifies this as the earliest pattern. Alternatively, a single arm may be held aloft, the other remaining at the side or holding a ritual object. Sometimes the hands are pressed together over the head, occasionally in conjuction with prostration, or a hand may simply be placed on the head. Prayer is very often punctuated with a clapping of the hands, and in extreme circumstances the hands may strike the breast or tear the hair. When the deity or power is associated with the earth, the prayer gestures are extended downward and may include touching or tapping the ground. Clasping of the hands, the typical Christian gesture of prayer, has early roots in Hindu and Buddhist practice, and the familiar interlacing of the fingers was employed by the ancient Sumerians. The hands may also be crossed on the breast or even behind the back, as though the petitioner were fettered.

In contrast to the foregoing gestures, which acknowledge and preserve the petitioner's distance from the deity, others are intended to establish and intensify intimate contact. Ritual acts of touching, stroking, embracing, or kissing the sacred image or object are common in many traditions. When such contact occurs with a personified image, it is usually limited to the extremities—the hands, knees, or feet.

The final grouping of prayer gestures that Heiler describes and documents

---

[4] This expression is not unknown even in America. Since 1976, when the Liberty Bell was made publicly accessible, countless visitors to Philadelphia have reverently touched and circumambulated this traditional symbol of freedom, which is inscribed with a verse from the Hebrew book of Leviticus. Here we have a concrete manifestation of what Bellah (1970a) calls "civil religion."

Camped in the open air with their belongings, a Muslim family prays to Allah for protection following a 1957 series of savage earthquakes in Iran.

consists of some modification in dress, most often the removal of shoes. The uncovering of the head is also common, and in some traditions the upper part of the body—or the whole of it, especially in the mystery cults—may be exposed. Curiously, we also find the opposite practice, the ritual covering of the body, most often the head, but sometimes the mouth or hands (Heiler, 1918, pp. 100–105).

Discerning the origins and meaning of these diverse and ancient gestures is not easy, according to Heiler, given that they are forms long fixed by traditional practice rather than spontaneous expressions of individual religious experience. The earliest commentators thought prayer's gestures testified to feelings of powerlessness, dependency, and longing, akin to the small child's reaching up to the beloved parent for protection and consolation. In contrast, historians of religion of the nineteenth and early twentieth centuries interpreted the gestures of prayer as magical practices performed either to secure the power of divinity or to protect the person from it. Weighting the first interpretation over the second, Heiler observes that both have overlooked the fundamental key to understanding. All the gestures and bodily attitudes employed in prayer, he claims, served earlier as secular forms of greeting or paying respect.

Historically, Heiler suggests, greeting gestures first expressed social feelings; later they also came to constitute a means by which to share in the power of the other or to ward it off. Once transferred to the religious sphere, these modes of greeting tended to disappear from secular life. Heiler grants that the acts of stretching out or folding the hands were probably gestures of supplication from the beginning. He argues that the rest of the prayer's bodily accompaniments should be interpreted not as petitionary movements but as gestures of greeting.

The Ritual Prayer Formula: The second of Heiler's types of prayer contrasts sharply with the first. Although the content is more or less the same, the form is no longer spontaneous. In place of the impulsive cry for help stands the ritual formula, its solemn wording sacrosanct and inviolable, the form of its utterance—whether recitation, singing, or murmuring—strictly prescribed. The mastery of prayer formulas and the complicated ritual acts with which they are associated become in many traditions the specialized concern of a priestly class. Those who look on may find themselves awed by the scrupulously intoned words, perhaps unintelligible even to the priest, but often they irreverently ignore the mysterious proceedings entirely. Exactly recited, the formula is thought to be valuable and efficacious in itself, requiring no inner sympathy with its content.

How did such "coldness and estrangement" come to enter in? Heiler suggests that between the stage of prayer that is a free outpouring of the heart and the point at which it becomes a fixed, even magical formula passed from one generation to the next and recited without feeling is an intermediate stage. Here prayer is a "flexible, elastic outline," derived from inspired spontaneous expressions and freely adaptable to momentary needs. The progressive "process of petrification and mechanization" is favored, says Heiler, by the frequency with which the occasions for prayer recur and by their close association with established ritual forms. "Acts of worship harden with amazing swiftness into sacred rites." Fixed formulas also allay the uncertainties that grow as the sense of divine presence diminishes, and they give a voice to those individuals incapable of framing their own expressions (Heiler, 1932, p. 66).

The Hymn: Heiler's third type of prayer, the hymn,[5] is marked by such formal aesthetic elements as rhythm, rhyme, and metrical structure. Gradually emerging out of "primitive" prayer, the hymn came into its own when the great religious traditions of the ancient world became established. Deliberately crafted for practical ritual purposes, hymns were the possession of the priests, who composed, recited, and preserved them. In certain respects the *cultic hymn* resembles naive prayer. It, too, is directed to an anthropomorphic deity, though one of a more complex, syncretic character, and it seeks much the same objects. It is distinguished, however, not only by its formal structure but in particular by an overlay of extravagant and ingratiating praise.

The elaborate celebration of divine power and goodness, says Heiler, springs from a refined egoism. By glorifying the deity's qualities and surrounding the divine nature with deep secrecy, the priests sought to indulge the vanity of God and to win rich favors in return. Hoping to disguise the true intent of their hymns, the priests conceived their requests in the most general terms and then appended them, almost as an afterthought, to this flood of divine flattery. Observing the loss of the freshness and naïveté of spontaneous prayer, Heiler concludes that the cultic hymn, reduced finally to a magical formula, is the product of a degenerative process.

In certain gifted individuals, the cultic hymn may arouse a genuine love of God and inspire the composition of hymns of a rather different character. Overlapping in time with the cultic hymn is another type, which Heiler calls the *literary hymn*. Unlike the variety composed for cultic functions, the literary hymn is the spontaneous expression of the feelings of a layperson, who employs not the ponderous, sacred language of the priest but the light and fluent expressions of everyday speech. The deities extolled in literary hymns are chiefly gods of nature, most notably the sun; given the pantheistic tendency underlying these hymns, anthropomorphism is minimal. Heiler notes the ethical trend of the individual literary hymn as well as the mystical intimations of an aesthetic type. Although petition is not entirely absent from these hymns, the predominance of praise is judged to be sincere, an end rather than a means. In the literary hymn, concludes Heiler, we have the beginnings of interior religion (Heiler, 1918, pp. 157–190).

Prayer in the Religion of Greek Civilization: Heiler's fourth type of prayer, that of Greek religion as it existed in the fifth century B.C.E., shares certain essential

---

[5] This type and Heiler's discussion of it are entirely omitted from the English translation.

qualities of primitive prayer: its simple, spontaneous character; its focus on personal well-being or happiness; its appeal to an unnumbered variety of higher beings; and its ascription of human qualities to the gods, with whom the individual can therefore enter into personal relation. Yet Greek prayer, says Heiler (1932, p. 85), "stands incalculably higher," for it is pervasively influenced by high ethical ideals. Indeed, Hellenic religion incorporates with exceptional clarity and harmony all cultural ideals—intellectual, social, aesthetic, and material. Every activity, however insignificant, was consecrated by prayer and sacrifice. Although a measure of naïveté remained, most evidently in prayers of cursing and vengeance, prayer at the height of Greek civilization centered on the petitioning for moral values (Heiler, 1932, pp. 74–86).

Prayer in Philosophical Thought: To the reflective thinker unable to affirm the real presence of the changeable, anthropomorphic god presupposed by the various forms of spontaneous prayer, praying itself becomes seriously problematical. Contrary to what we might logically expect, however, prayer is seldom utterly rejected. Instead, it is reconceptualized to accord with philosophy's ethical and rational ideals. Looking with critical disdain on simple piety's too-human god, its self-seeking motives, and its prescribed rituals, philosophical thought champions an ideal, purified form of prayer, the fifth of Heiler's types.

Philosophical prayer has a threefold content. First, rejecting prayers for health and food, for children and possessions, for victory and honor as unworthy and immoral, the philosopher asks only for the realization of the highest ethical ideals, not only in the life of the individual who prays but in the lives of all others as well. Second, for some, the element of petition vanishes altogether; in its place stand renunciation of every desire and absolute surrender to the course of destiny. A third element of philosophical prayer is solemn contemplation—of the divine greatness revealed in all things, of the riddle of existence, and of the aims of life. More orthodox forms of prayer may also be retained, out of respect for tradition or as a means of training. In any event, prayer's acknowledged significance is merely subjective and psychological.

The prayer of the philosopher is thus no longer a necessity; it has ceased to reside at the heart of religion. In truth, says Heiler, it is but "a halting-place on the road to the dissolution of prayer" (p. 102). Such is the fate of prayer for those who are committed foremost to a life of reason. For those ordinary men and women whose lives remain untouched by philosophical criticism and ideals, spontaneous prayer will live on indestructibly, as an inner necessity and a vital source of constructive energy (Heiler, 1932, pp. 87–103).

The Prayer of Great Religious Personalities: Nowhere is the potential "psychic depth and native energy" of natural prayer as evident, according to Heiler, as in the devotional lives of great religious persons. "The prayer of men of religious genius," Heiler's sixth type, "is the most living, the most powerful, the most profound, and the most fervent species of prayer; it towers as the loftiest peak among the various types" (Heiler, 1932, p. 286). Although sharing essential features of primitive prayer—its spontaneity, its felt relation to a present and personal god, and its conception of this relation in social terms—the prayer of the great masters possesses other qualities that identify it as something entirely new.

In contrast to the other types we have examined, the prayer of the religious genius is not limited to certain ritual occasions or to situations of need but becomes instead a means of continuous intercourse with God. This veritable life of prayer finds its moments of intensification not in some particular sacred place but in "the still silence of the heart.'' This realm of inner perception is best attained in solitude, whether of the forest retreat or of one's own room. The outcome of a recognizable historical development, which Heiler traces in some detail, the personal prayer of genius is experienced as a revelation of God at work in the soul, as a divine gift rather than as a human achievement. It is something to be intentionally and methodically cultivated, by various arts and techniques. The end sought in such prayer is not the earthly aims that we have earlier encountered but nothing less than God and spiritual salvation. Accordingly, petition is displaced from the primary place, and instead, prayer comes to express everything that stirs the soul.

Heiler's discussion of the prayer of great religious souls centers upon two fundamental types of piety: the mystical and the prophetic. The *mystical type* wearily turns away from the world and its objects, including the ego, and orients itself instead to the Infinite and the delight of ecstatic union. This intentional, extremely individualistic, and ''feminine'' outlook is notable for its subtle speculations, meticulous self-analysis, and broad tolerance for those not called to ''perfection.'' It is best known for the extraordinary experiences in which it culminates. The *prophetic type*, in contrast, is firmly anchored in the social world, passionately affirming life and vigorously seeking to realize its ideals in the spheres of faith and moral action. Spontaneous, unreflective, and ''masculine,'' prophetic piety is scornful of any form of systematic training or psychological technique. Yielding an inner religious life that is correspondingly richer and more diverse than that of the mystical type, it is also strikingly less tolerant, opposed as it is to every expression that falls below the prophetic ideal.

For the religious genius of the mystical type, prayer has only one theme: the Highest Good and the soul that seeks to attain a vision of it and union with it. Beginning in meditation centered on some religious ideal, perhaps derived from an edifying text or a devotional formula, mystical prayer always tends to pass beyond discursive thought into silent contemplation of God. Such wordless prayer may itself pass away, when the felt separation of ''I'' and ''Thou'' finally dissolves in ecstatic union. Without consciousness of the presence of God there can be no prayer, says Heiler. Short of this supreme moment, however, prayer serves the mystic as a means of achieving detachment from the world and the desires of the self— hence the unequivocal rejection of praying for earthly things—as well as a vehicle for unifying and intensifying the inner life and for drawing ever closer to God. Mystical prayer overflows with expressions of repentant sorrow and ardent longing, of surrender and resignation, of praise and thanksgiving, of exalting adoration and a feeling of unworthiness. Although the mystics often address God in the anthropomorphic language of naive prayer, the human contours of the Highest Good gradually fade as the purely contemplative level is attained.

For prophetic piety, in contrast, God is no static and impersonal final Good but a being who thinks, feels, and wills, and who is therefore subject to persuasive appeals to His own interests, to the kindness and pity recalled for Him in His earlier deeds, to His divine sense of righteousness. Gone are the gross features of the capricious, localized gods whose material needs and desires may be gratified through offerings and sacrifice. Prophetic prayer, like the primitive variety, is a free outpouring impelled by intense, usually painful emotions, and in it, too, a person may petition fervently for health or daily bread. Playing far greater a role, however, are emotions welling up out of experiences of spiritual value. Recovery of self-respect, forgiveness of sins, freedom from perplexity, security of life—these are the most frequent objects of prophetic petition. So, too, is the salvation of others, even those remote from a person's own community of faith, and of supreme importance is the petition for final fulfillment of an ideal reality, the Kingdom of God. Although the declaration of need, through complaint and supplication, forms the chief content of prophetic prayer, often it is suddenly and involuntarily displaced by a mood of assurance and peace. Such prayer, then, comes also to express confidence and trust, resignation and surrender, thanksgiving and praise, yearning and vision. Although prophetic prayer, like mystical consciousness, is directed to an ultimate highest good, it never becomes extinguished in the ecstasy of union. Throughout the prayer the relation between devotee and divinity remains a dynamic, social one (Heiler, 1932, pp. 104–285).

The Individual Prayer of Great Artists and Poets: In the prayers of great persons, most notably artists and poets, Heiler finds his seventh type, which in many respects is akin to the prayer of religious genius. Heiler has in mind forms of prayer that issue out of lives belonging to a higher sphere but in which religion does not reside at the center. Although prayer therefore does not have a controlling place, it is no less spontaneous, vigorous, and original, and it serves in its vitality as a major source of artistic inspiration.

Much like the prayer of great religious persons, that of artists and poets can be distinguished according to two types: the aesthetic–contemplative and the emotional–ethical. These types parallel the mystical and prophetic types of religious genius, but they are discernibly different. Although the aesthetic–contemplative type shares mystical prayer's content of contemplative longing, surrender, adoration, and union, it differs from it in retaining the value of human personality and in finding its pantheistic god in the beautiful and noble things of this world. The simple petition and complaint of the emotional–ethical type, though reminiscent of prophetic piety, is centered not on the fulfillment of moral values and the Kingdom of God but on an ideal of artistic creation and embodiment. As is true of the mystical and prophetic varieties, these types are not mutually exclusive but may combine in the same personality (Heiler, 1932, pp. 286–295).

Prayer in Public Worship: The strongly social character of prophetic prayer, manifested in its concern for the salvation of all humanity, presses on to the *united* prayer of congregational worship, Heiler's eighth type. Expressing the shared experiences of religious communities closely bound together, congregational prayer serves not only to awaken and intensify the religious spirit but also to lift individual members to higher stages of devotion. Initially the central feature and culmination of collective worship and a free expression of the consciousness of a present, living god, common prayer tends inexorably to harden into a subordinate element of fixed, complex, and obligatory ritual. Religious reform regularly seeks to restore to public prayer its original character.

Once the spontaneous outpouring of any member of the congregation, common prayer usually becomes the possession of a liturgist who intones its dignified and ornate phrases with solemnity and measured rhythm. The congregation participates through silent gestures and brief verbal responses. When entirely fixed in form, public prayers may also be spoken antiphonally, between prayer leader and congregation, or rhythmically in chorus by the assembled people. Such prayer may also be sung or shared silently. The content of liturgical prayer is for the most part praise and thanksgiving, in contemplation of God's redemptive power and holiness, though petition and intercession, primarily for spiritual benefits, are also common (Heiler, 1932, pp. 296–346).

Individual Prayer as a Law of Duty and Good Works: The last of Heiler's types, prescribed and meritorious prayer, derives its content from the experiences of prophetic geniuses, but its motives are radically different. In the place of deep anguish or inner longing is fear of punishment and hope of reward. Prayer in this sense has become an authority-imposed duty, an offering presented to God, perhaps in combination with other "good works" such as fasting and almsgiving, in order to accumulate merit and receive divine blessings. To omit it entirely is to risk divine judgment. Recited mechanically and unthinkingly, the lofty phrases of obligatory prayer may become emptied of all genuine religious value. Often, however, they help to sustain a spiritual mood, and when prayed with thought and concentration, they may strengthen and purify the religious life. For the great mass of persons for whom the ideal of prophetic prayer is impossible, says Heiler, prescribed prayer has served invaluably to impel and elevate the spiritual life (Heiler, 1932, pp. 347–352).

The Essence of Prayer

In the final chapter of his long and richly illustrated book, Heiler turns from the task of typology to that of analysis. Given prayer's astonishing multiplicity, he asks, is it possible to discern something that all the forms share, some essential core? To aid in this task, Heiler sorts the nine types into two broad classes. The *primary* types include naive prayer of primitive man, the prayers of great religious personalities, the prayers of great artists and poets, and prayer in public worship as long as it retains its original character. Each of these types expresses an original and profound experience, and it is in these forms that we will find the essence of prayer. The remaining, *secondary* types are imitative, a petrifaction of living personal experience, or a cold abstraction.

In its essence, says Heiler (1932, p. 358), prayer is "a living communion of the religious man with God, conceived as personal and present in experience, a communion which reflects the forms of the social relations of humanity." The common psychological root of all prayer, whether it be self-seeking, ethical, or purely religious, is the effort to enhance life. "Prayer is the expression of a primitive impulse to a higher, richer, intenser life" (p. 355). It is the center of religion, "the soul of all piety" (p. 362).

The "severely non-rational character of religion," according to Heiler, is nowhere else so evident as in prayer. A person has but two choices, he says: either to affirm genuine prayer decisively, with all its difficulties, or to substitute for it reverent contemplation of a supreme good or solemn and exalted absorption. Contemplation and absorption, which belong to the secular and religious realms alike, often accompany prayer, says Heiler, but they must not be mistaken for it.

SPRANGER'S EXISTENTIAL–INTERPRETIVE PSYCHOLOGY OF RELIGION

As the work of Otto and Heiler illustrates, phenomenological studies almost always proceed in general, impersonal terms. If the experiences of specific individuals should come into discussion (as they do occasionally in Heiler's work), they serve only as examples (Oesterreich, 1917). Even when the singularity of individual experience is underscored, individual differences rarely figure in the results. James, as we have seen, is an exception, if we are willing to classify the *Varieties* as a work in phenomenology. So also is the German philosopher, psychologist, and educator Eduard Spranger (1882–1963), though for him, too, we may hesitate to apply a label that the writer himself did not employ. Defined in his own terms, Spranger

Eduard Spranger

is a *verstehende* psychologist. As Dilthey's most famous disciple, he is the leading advocate of the human-scientific (*geisteswissenschaftliche*) psychology that Dilthey outlined at the end of the nineteenth century. In this role, Spranger made significant contributions to the psychology of religion, particularly in regard to individual differences.

Spranger, the son of a Berlin storekeeper, aspired in his adolescent years to becoming a professional musician. Though already an accomplished pianist, he was persuaded instead to study philosophy at the University of Berlin. His interest in pedagogy became firmly established when, to support his graduate studies, he successfully undertook part-time teaching at a private school for girls. Called first to the University of Leipzig as professor of philosophy and pedagogy and then, in 1920, back to Berlin, he became widely influential in the *Geisteswissenschaften,* the human sciences or studies, as well as throughout the German educational system.

In 1933, when the new National Socialist regime intruded into university politics, Spranger submitted his resignation in protest, and in 1936 he became the first German exchange professor to Japan, where he formed many enduring friendships. Soon after his return a year later, he was drafted as a military psychologist, and in 1944 he was arrested and imprisoned, chiefly for his association with a group of anti-Hitler conspirators. The Japanese ambassador to Germany effected his release ten weeks later. After the war, the Allied military government appointed Spranger rector to the University of Berlin. When his efforts to restore the famous university to its former greatness were frustrated by the Soviet and East German authorities, he accepted a professorship in philosophy at Tübingen, a post he held until his retirement in 1954 (Spranger, 1964).

Spranger lived in the tradition of Goethe, the world of German classicism and idealism. He was a dedicated champion of humanism, which he defined as investigation of human nature in the light of what human beings have achieved in the past and the powers they may yet realize in the future (p. 47). An eloquent man of profound moral sensibilities and striking personal presence, Spranger was admired the world over. Albert Schweitzer, for example, credited him with having made the idea of reverence for life visible to the world, and Zakir Husain, who some years after studying with Spranger became president of India, saw in Spranger's wisdom and intuitive powers the signs of a mystic. On his eightieth birthday, his own government bestowed on him its gold medal, the highest distinction in the land (Bähr and Wenke, 1964). Spranger's thought is seldom encountered today outside of the German literature, except for fleeting references to his schema of personality types. Even less well known are his reflections on the nature of human existence and on religious faith. In his later writings especially, these reflections take on the contours of contemporary existential philosophy and psychology. Thus a review of Spranger's psychology of religion will serve not only to exemplify the *verstehende* approach to individuality, but also to introduce the existential perspective on the human condition.

An Existential Prolegomenon

All of us, Spranger says, live our lives on the basis of silent presuppositions—seldom thought out, largely unrecognized, yet absolutely essential. Psychology, too, is founded on such presuppositions. Today, both in our personal lives and in our conduct of psychology, we in the West have so narrowed our thinking that many of us assume that truth consists only of external facts, logically consistent proposi- tions, and causal explanations. The inevitable result, in Spranger's judgment, is a society of alienated individuals seeking escape from their impoverishment through intoxication and other forms of diversion. The narrow conviction that truth lies only in outer facts is evident as well, Spranger (1947) observes, in contemporary forms of Christianity, the tradition that provides the context but not the boundaries for his reflections on religion. The Christian tradition's profound symbols, he says, are seriously misunderstood if taken to describe historical events occurring in the external world. Instead, he maintains, they refer to the inner kingdom of the soul and the possibilities therein for magical transformation. Psychology, too, with its emphasis on observable behavior, has fallen victim to the externalization of truth; in its meagerness, he says, it knows nothing of the "magic of the soul." It was with a sense of mission, therefore, that Spranger (1964, p. 13) sought not only to give ear to "the powers and destinies that rise up out of the human soul," but also to preserve and cultivate them. Like James, then, he was not only a descriptive psy- chologist but also a fervent advocate of a particular point of view.

"As human beings bound to nature," wrote Spranger (1954, p. 75) late in his life, "we all live in profound darkness regarding our being and our fate." Only one fact seems indisputably apparent: this world is not sufficient for our longings. We yearn in myriad ways for happiness, but the more deeply involved in life we become, the more happiness seems to elude us. When hope and consolation take the place of happiness, they, too, are called into question, by the inevitability of death.

Chief among the mysteries of this world, Spranger (1954, p. 85) continues, is time, which tantalizingly points us beyond the very limits it sets. Time, he reminds us, is not only a succession of fleeting moments, each vanishing in turn into noth- ingness; it is also duration, albeit always a limited one. It is humankind's most tragic fate, Spranger says, to be subject to time's ruthless limitations and simultaneously to be driven by an incessant longing to conquer them, to win a place in eternity. Filled with the sadness, doubt, guilt, anxiety, desperation, and dread by which we respond to the felt narrowness of this world, we flee from it as a place where we cannot feel at home (Spranger, 1941).

Yet from this very experience of insufficiency, Spranger (1942, p. 253) claims, comes faith in its purest form. Driven forward by unfulfilled longings, the individual soul is startled to see opening before it a new and higher world. Breaking through the horizontal dimension in which life in this world is lived is another, vertical one,

the metaphysical dimension. With this revolution of the inner world, the outer world appears in a new light. Suffering and death, which once were only sources of dread and despair, become the way of the highest transformation, the way to salvation. In the "outer world," at last, we find our fulfillment, our home.[6]

Already, then, we may see elements of the existential perspective in Spranger's thought, even though he does not consistently employ its vocabulary. Restated in terms used by the existentialists, this prolegomenon might be summarized as follows. We human beings are "thrown" into this world at a particular place and time but without any apparent purpose. Endowed with awareness and the capacity to transcend experience in thought and imagination, we recognize the contingency of our existence and respond with anxiety and dread. At the same time, this capacity of transcendence allows us to pass beyond the limits of the objective world of time and space into a new modality, denominated "being-beyond-the-world" by Ludwig Binswanger, in which TEMPORALITY takes the form of "eternity," and SPATIALITY the form of "at-home-ness" (in German, *Heimat*).

The Structure of the Personal World

The existentialists have coined or redefined such terms as *thrownness, transcendence, temporality,* and *spatiality* so that they can speak with relative precision about the subtleties of human experience. Another such expression is *world,* which here refers not to the objective, external world (the environment) but to the structured, experiential whole that is formed by the individual's meaningful relationships. Three aspects of this personal world are commonly distinguished: the *Umwelt* ("world-around"), the experienced natural world, including one's own body; the *Mitwelt* ("world-with"), the world of interpersonal relationship; and the *Eigenwelt* ("own-world"), the world of relation with oneself (May et al., 1958, p. 61).

How we experience *the* world depends in part on the particular biological organization of the human body, most notably our organs of perception and the bodily structures that enable us to act on the world (Spranger, 1942, p. 260). Yet sharing a common biological endowment does not mean that individuals perceive events in the same way. The meaning that the world has for each of us, says Spranger, is bestowed on it from within, by the attitude of *faith*.

Like Wilfred Smith, Spranger uses the word faith in a broadly religious sense, to designate one's fundamental orientation toward the world. Like Smith, too, he warns against equating the inner disposition of faith with outward confessions of belief; in most persons, he says, the two do not correspond. Anticipating Erikson, Spranger says that faith is a sense of trust in the world, a trust that is built into the very foundations of the personal life-structure and that decisively determines the course of one's life (p. 252). Possessing the inner security of faith, we find life bearable, if not also meaningful and valuable; without it, we are subject to lasting desperation and a manifold of psychic disorders.

At first, according to Spranger, faith is nothing more than an inner disposition

---

[6] A vivid example of the sudden emergence of the metaphysical dimension is offered by Rufus Jones (1947). An English friend of his, he reports, was on the threshold of young manhood and "beginning to feel the dawning sense of a great mission" when he realized that "he was slowly losing his sight and hearing. His London doctor told him that before middle life he would become totally blind and deaf, as the result of an insidious disease. Dazed . . . , he staggered from the doctor's office to the street and stood there quite overwhelmed with the report of his condition. Suddenly he felt the love of God wrap him about as though a visible presence enfolded him, and a joy filled him such as he had never known." Until his death in his mid-thirties, "he was a gloriously joyous and happy man" (p. 77).

or a nucleus of energy. With time, it gives birth to the outward expressions of *mythos* and *magic.* Mythos, consisting of poetic ideas that clarify the meaning of the world, represents the cognitive side of faith. Magic, consisting of ethically attuned actions, represents its practical side. Although at first glance both seem to refer largely or wholly to the outer world, Spranger maintains that they are concerned chiefly with powers acting within the human soul. The intimate relation of inner and outer, expressed in the concept of the personal world, will become clearer when we examine the three modes of this world.

Relation to the Natural World: According to Spranger (1947), the *Umwelt* takes one or the other of two radically different forms. The "external world" may be viewed as a realm of merely physical, lawful reality, filled with lifeless objects that bear no essential relation to the observer. Or it may be viewed as a living reality with which it is possible to establish an I–Thou relation. A deep empathy springs up between subject and object, perhaps even a feeling of oneness, and the fate of the one is perceived as inextricably bound up with the fate of the other. This "magical view of the world" is natural for the child, who typically suffers disappointment when taught that the material world cannot be "understood," empathically, but can only be explained. Preliterate societies likewise hold this magical view. That we moderns have so thoroughly renounced it, often with a measure of self-satisfaction, is viewed by Spranger as a fact of serious consequence for the life of the soul.

The human soul, Spranger argues, cannot be at home in the midst of a lawful, dead reality. To reduce the outer world to neutralized objectivity is to sever the vital connections between the inner and outer realms. The outer world is meaningful, he says, only to the degree that it is bound up with the inner one. At the same time, the inner world depends on the outer one as a source of *symbols,* which, though necessarily inadequate, are essential for the ordering, unfolding, and expression of the inner life. Yet if the external world is to speak for us in the language of symbol and thereby to take on meaning itself, we must retain the capacities for identification and participation that are integral to the magical mode of experience.

We have not entirely lost the capacity to participate in the magical world-view, Spranger points out, for we can still be irresistibly seized by some rhythm or be captivated by an intense color. In poetry, too, we may momentarily restore to the outer world its friendly or hostile PHYSIOGNOMY, perceiving objects as animated beings with emotions and intentions much like our own. But if we truly perceived the world physiognomically, if we experienced life as a continuous struggle in a demon-filled realm where possession or dramatic self-transformation were ever possible, our contemporaries would likely think us mad.

Relation to Other Persons: In the *Mitwelt,* the possibility of the I–Thou encounter remains open to us. In the realm of interpersonal relations, says Spranger, we may still find aspects of the magical world. Each of us represents, as it were, a "field of power" or an "atmosphere," sensible even in a momentary encounter. The magical principle that possession of a part—say, a lock of hair—gives one access to the whole—the person whose hair it is—is a principle we find untenable in the physical world. It finds new meaning, according to Spranger, in the psychic realm. Through the contagion of energy, temperament, or mood, even fleeting contact with another can transform a person's psychological condition as a whole, creating a new totality. In such a light, Spranger would doubtless agree, can we understand the meaning of a Hindu's taking DARSHAN of a guru or a Catholic's seeking an audience with the Pope. The same principle applies to the enshrining

Widely revered as a saint and even the Divine Mother, Anandamayi Ma (1896–1982) was famous for the extraordinary effect she had on those who came to her for *darshan*. Among her devotees was India's Prime Minister Indira Gandhi (right), who wrote that "Just with a glimpse of Her, countless problems are solved." After his first meeting with Anandamayi Ma ("Bliss-Permeated Mother"), a prominent French physician said, "I was in a strange state—my heart swelled with jubilation, with joyful exultation—the state of one who has found what he has always yearned for in the innermost recesses of his heart." According to yet another follower, "It is difficult to describe how [her devotees'] souls became steeped in tranquil bliss in Her presence" (Hallstrom, 1987).

of some bodily part of a beloved founder or saint, for even so tenuous a link to the revered personality as a hair or a tooth can be sufficient to effect inner transformation.[7]

The significance of the *Mitwelt* for Spranger's analysis is not exhausted in such mysterious interactions, including the earliest of them—the intimate mother–child relation that forms a vital part of the preverbal life unity on which every later I–Thou encounter is said to depend. The *Mitwelt* is also a source of experienced demands. Every human group orders itself in terms of a moral code, the sanctity and authority of which each member must accept if it is to be effective. Morally ordered relations limit and obligate us, says Spranger (1942, p. 263); they make us SCHULDIG to each other in many ways. The German word *schuldig* means both "guilty" and "indebted": Martin Heidegger and other existentialists use it not simply to describe the vagaries of individual conscience, but to point to a fundamental characteristic of human existence. To exist in the society of our fellow human beings is to be indebted to them in countless ways. To deny this "guilt," or to assume it can be discharged in a measured number of charitable acts, is to blind

---

[7] Scientific evidence for the power of indirect contact with revered persons is reported by David McClelland in an interview with Joan Borysenko (1985). In a group of Harvard undergraduates who had just viewed a film of Mother Teresa in Calcutta, McClelland discovered an increase in salivary immunoglobulin A, a chemical change that marks the body's first defensive response to a cold virus. This improvement in the immune system proved to be unrelated to whether or not the student liked or approved of Mother Teresa and her work. Skeptics will undoubtedly prefer an alternate explanation of this finding: viewing pictures of ill or dying persons may be the factor responsible for the observed change.

ourselves, it is said, to the nature of our existence. We also thereby set limits on personal self-realization (see May et al., 1958, p. 54).

Relation to Oneself: A person may also be "guilty" in the other relational modes, including the *Eigenwelt*. The mode of relation to oneself, largely neglected by other contemporary Western psychologists, is particularly emphasized by the existentialists. Although Spranger does not himself use the term *Eigenwelt*, the complex aspect of world to which it refers is crucial in his thinking nonetheless. The I–Thou relation, "the fundamental category of the life of the soul," is also possible within: "I can speak Thou to its own self." By its very nature, says Spranger (1947, p. 50), the soul is divided into a lower self, which lives life spontaneously and unreflectively, and a higher self, which acts as an onlooking observer. The higher self is the source of the "solitary voice," a fundamental phenomenon, Spranger (1942, p. 265) says, to which we give a variety of mythic interpretations. We call it in turn conscience, the better self, or the voice of God. From this experience emerges the idea of a higher principle, identifed with the soul, and ultimately, the idea of a spiritual being—"the unknown God"—that lives within us and that the "lower level" of the soul addresses as Thou. Spranger (1947) maintains that these "fundamental facts," which lie outside any kind of rational explanation, form the basis for all higher life of the spirit, above all, for the emergence of religiosity, which Spranger defines as "the bond of the I to higher powers" (p. 51).

Toward a New Psychology of the Soul

When Spranger speaks of the "universe" within or the "magic of the soul," in an effort to articulate the dynamics of the inner life, he is employing symbols and metaphors derived inevitably from the outer world. It is important, he says, that their limits be recognized. A new, higher logic is required, says Spranger (1947, p. 29), if we are to comprehend life's struggles and contradictions. This dialectical mode of reasoning is foreshadowed in the ancient, religiously conditioned logic of a higher unity of opposites. How else, he asks, are we to comprehend the mysterious power within that transforms the negations of insufficiency, meaninglessness, and guilt into a positive posture of faith? Or the paradox that we must already possess the power of faith—a gift from God, it is said—in order to win it?

Anticipating his critics, Spranger denies that his is a call for a new romanticism or a return to esoteric doctrine or a mysticism of inner experience. Rather, he seeks to develop a deeper psychology, one that draws on the religious life as well. He would restore to contemporary persons the transformative powers within that are denied or repressed by every one-sided commitment to the outer world. The inner realm, he says, is a source of illuminations underivable from the purely external course of the world and possessing unique motivational potential for the living of life in the highest sense. Our difficult task is learning to dwell on the boundary between the two worlds—the outer and the inner, "this world" of apparent insufficiency and discord, and "the world beyond" of fulfillment and eternal love.

In speaking of "a magic of the soul that arises out of the deepest ethical and religious earnestness," Spranger sought, much like Jung, to restore to us the original language used to express an eternally valid content. Both sought to provide a new grammar and a system of interpretation appropriate to our time (Spranger, 1947, pp. 62, 71). Yet whereas Jung also writes of inner "powers" that are expressed in outer symbols, his discussion of these expressions is far more explicit and systematic than the treatment offered by Spranger, who of the two was far less the historian of religion. On the other hand, although both of these psychologists emphasize the positive value of the religious attitude, Spranger is the more attentive to the diversity of individual forms.

The Religious Type and Its Varieties

In the English-speaking world, Spranger is best known for his system of personality types. Not only does it structure his only work translated into English (Spranger, 1925), but it is also the inspiration for the once widely popular test called the Study of Values (Allport, Vernon, and Lindzey, 1970). Interpretive psychology, we may recall, finds its fullest expression in the discernment of ideal types—schematic, timeless, and purified portraits of fundamental tendencies. As Spranger's system demonstrates, behind these abstractions may lie an enduring appreciation for individual, existing forms.

To understand other persons, Spranger says, we must discern the fundamental values that underlie their mental acts, which are manifest in a multitude of outward and subtle expressions. There are, he suggests, six basic personality types, corresponding to the six value orientations that may dominate an individual's life. These six types are theoretic, economic, aesthetic, social, political, and religious. Although our interest in the psychology of religion naturally leads us to focus here on the religious type, it stands out of its own accord as the most comprehensive and thus the most adequate of the six value orientations.

Spranger maintains that every person is religious to some degree, for each of us has faith, however dimly felt and inarticulate, that life as a whole has meaning. For many, this faith remains largely in the background, subordinated to other, more limited commitments, including the practical demands of day-to-day existence. In contrast, a person of the religious type is one "whose whole mental structure is permanently directed to the creation of the highest and absolutely satisfying value experience" (Spranger, 1925, p. 213).

To speak of "the religious type" is misleading in at least two respects. On the one hand, the five other types may also be religious, albeit each in its own one-sided way. On the other hand, the religious type itself proves to be divisible into an indefinite number of alternate subtypes. Everyone, he says, experiences the meaning of the world in a personal way. "Everyone has his own God" (p. 240). Having affirmed the radically individual character of the religious attitude, Spranger proceeds to isolate and idealize its fundamental directions.

Spranger identifies the religious type with the mystic, who, from one or another perspective, "searches for the absolute unity of the highest values" (p. 213n). There are two fundamental types of mystics. The *immanent mystic* is life-affirming, for such a person finds evidence of God in every sphere of human activity—indeed, in every aspect of life. Yet the heroic desire to embrace the whole, to find and sympathize with that "something more" in everything, is doomed to frustration. Foundering in human finitude, the immanent mystic may finally look to death as an opportunity for the transformation and purification that is otherwise so elusive. The *transcendent mystic*, on the other hand, finds the highest goal by negating the world of immanent values. From the start, attention is given to a world beyond. Here is the ascetic who sees the values of this world as meaningless hindrances to the true comprehension of God. In their place is cultivated the capacity for ecstasy, "the mysterious gift of perceiving the imperceptible and communicating with God, the final meaning of the world" (p. 216).

Even in the idealized realm of typology sharp distinctions are not always possible. There is a third fundamental religious type, or rather a range of types, lying between the relatively rare immanent and transcendent extremes. According to Spranger, religiosity usually combines elements of both, thus affirming some aspects of life and rejecting others.

The Dialectic of the Religious Sphere: The religious type is further differentiated by the part played by each of the other five idealized attitudes. The *theoretic* attitude seeks to know what is objectively true or valid by means of the intellect. The person of a theoretical bent who knows no passion apart from cognitive knowledge may, like the positivist, reject religion as a mistaken and untenable means of cognition. On the other hand, the theoretically oriented individual who affirms the fundamental tendency of religion is likely to maintain that the highest value or the transcendent is accessible to us chiefly through reason. Thus we have the metaphysician.

The utilitarian interests of the *economic* type, who views everything in terms of its usefulness for self-preservation, may similarly either preempt or combine with a genuine religious attitude. A passion for wealth without regard for the means used to acquire it may lead to the worship of the mundane power imagined to be in control of "the great world-lottery" (p. 138). Worship of a deity, when it occurs, may have its chief origin in economic interests. An analysis of a diversity of religious traditions, especially "primitive" ones, would undoubtedly "lead to a wealth of such symbols," says Spranger, symbols that "originated in fear or hope, in the desire and will to live, and in the psychology of work and enjoyment" (p. 139). In contrast, the perception of economic prosperity as a sign of God's grace suggests a concern that is primarily religious, not economic.

We need not look far to observe that the *aesthetic* attitude, which seeks to give expression or form to emotionally significant psychic content, has often combined with the religious attitude. A person with an aesthetically conditioned faith views God as "the highest ordering and form-giving Power" (p. 161); the aesthetic type may affirm a religion of beauty. For the fundamentally religious type, however, the aesthetic may be simply a means of expressing a person's experience of value, whether in painting, ritual, music, or dance. According to Spranger, aesthetic expression is able neither to represent the whole of lived experience nor to give direct access to the world's ultimate structure of meaning. One-sided, incomplete, and living only at second hand, it is finally rejected by a wholly spiritualized religious faith.

The *social* attitude, which seeks to give of itself to another in love, comes closest of all to the religious type. Love's selfless affirmation of another person as the locus of value is itself a religious act, although it is not obviously so until it embraces everyone—perhaps everything—with such an attitude. In the perception that all life is sacred do we find the defining characteristic of religion, that is, a total evaluation of existence. The religious character of love is made explicit in the use of the figure of love to describe the relation between God and humankind. Although love between persons serves to create religious community, it never wholly succeeds in breaking down the barriers of individuality. Thus it, too, may be renounced as insufficient or incomplete. In any event, says Spranger, periods of solitary recollection are necessary to restore love's dynamic (p. 231).

The concern with power and competition that defines the *political* attitude may combine with religion in several ways. The purely political type sees religion, like all other areas of value, simply as a means of gaining personal power. If a person is literally a politician, he or she may pragmatically advocate the inculcation of religious teachings in order to control the masses. Where the religious attitude is more genuine, a ruler may feel cast in the role of servant–agent to God, who is regarded above all in terms of power and deeds. The very relation to God may be construed in terms of political and legal categories. A host of religious phenomena, from certain forms of prayer and a sense of religious power to the hierarchies of religious organizations and the undertaking of religious wars, reflect the combination of political and religious strivings. Like the other attitudes, the political is one-sided and thus a threat to religion's encompassing vision. However, the religious sphere cannot be wholly separated from these partial attitudes, even in the instance of the transcendent mystic, who is bound to show the coloration of one or another of the other five value types. Thus we have "the unique DIALECTIC of the religious sphere" (p. 235).

In the light of his analysis, Spranger suggests that we may classify religious persons in terms of the value type that served as the starting point, chief impetus, or context for a more comprehensive view. Thus we may observe whether an individual's religiosity, or even a religious tradition as a whole, is predominantly theoretic, economic, aesthetic, social, or political in character. It is also possible, of course, for two or more of these attitudes to work in combination.

Spranger offers several other typological distinctions for depicting the religious attitude. First, there is the contrast between the religiously creative prophet or savior who experiences a new revelation of the highest value, and the receptive followers of orthodox tradition, for whom something is sacred because others before them believed it to be so. Similar to this distinction is another, that between the individualist who "forges his own way to God" (p. 241) by means of moral or rational considerations and the follower of a historical religious tradition who requires an external revelation or spiritual authority. We may also classify religious experience in terms of its rhythm or method. For some persons religion is steady and unobtrusive, like constant background music, whereas others, like the ecstatic mystics, swing back and forth between religious exaltation and exhaustion. Some are suddenly and unexpectedly seized by the divine, whereas others systematically set about to cultivate the experience. Some see everything, even the most mundane objects, in a religious light; for others only certain objects, places, and times have a religious character. Finally, we may distinguish those who symbolize the ultimate world principles in the personality of God and those who eschew all anthropomorphism but continue to love and honor their fate as a meaningful destiny.

Is there also an irreligious type? Traditional religious concepts and institutions may be rejected, Spranger says, in the name of a higher religiosity or value. Only if a person is profoundly convinced that there are no values, that life therefore has no meaning, may he or she be truly designated irreligious. Such a person, Spranger thinks, is scarcely to be found.

The Course of Religious Development

Whatever the strengths of Spranger's famous study of types, it is doubly removed from the ordinary personalities that we might wish to understand. It presents idealized portraits, not case studies of living persons. When it does illustrate its fundamental types, it draws on well-known historical figures—Plato, Goethe, Schleiermacher, Tolstoy, to name just a few. We may rightly wonder to what degree a typology based on so rarified a company of personages illuminates the rest of humanity.

We may also wish to know more about the developmental course of each of the types, the task of nomology in Koepp's schema. Spranger's typology represents enduring structures of personal disposition at the stage of maturity. It was not intended to represent the years of immaturity, when the personality structure is still undergoing growth and transformation.

Spranger himself recognized these limitations. In the second of his two major works, a frequently reprinted book on the psychology of youth, Spranger (1924) not only introduces a developmental perspective but also tests his methods and conclusions by applying them to ordinary, living persons. His subjects were contemporary German youth, primarily Protestant, middle-class, and educated. Here we will limit ourselves to the chief findings reported in "The Religious Development of Young People," the longest chapter of this finely nuanced book.

The Notion of Religious Development: When we speak of "religious development," Spranger points out, we make certain assumptions that in reality may not hold. Development, Spranger (1974) writes in a posthumously published paper, is a category for comprehending changes over time in a living organism or life structure. These changes meet the following conditions:

1. The process is set in motion from within; outer influences only support it.
2. It is directed toward a goal; that is, the end state is already foreshadowed in the initial stage.
3. It proceeds, therefore, from inner predispositions (ANLAGEN) to mature characteristics and activities.
4. Through differentiation and integration, it achieves a unified wholeness.
5. It can thus be conceived as a growing self-realization.

Do changes in religious faith meet these criteria? According to Spranger, there is indeed a religious predisposition, consisting of the impulse to search for a meaningful interpretation of the world we experience. Furthermore, the unfolding of this predisposition is indisputably dependent on general intellectual and ethical maturation. Yet unlike biological growth, the process of religious development is highly dependent on and influenced by the social and historical contexts in which it occurs. In particular, it requires religious language, although such language can be effective only if it is met with a religious attitude. Similarly, the notion of an orderly or progressive religious development is called into question by the decisive factor of encounter with the Wholly Other, which manifests itself in unpredictable ways. Revelation, illumination, conversion, the experience of grace—none of these, Spranger declares, may be considered the outcome of orderly development (p. 12).

Spranger concludes that religious maturation cannot be wholly comprehended by the principles of development. Development is, after all, a human category of thought based on the model of the physical growth of organisms. Applied to psychological or historical phenomena, he says, it requires certain modifications. Religious events, especially encounters with the numinous, may elude it altogether. Without psychic development, he says, there will be no encounter with God, but religious growth cannot be wholly comprehended in terms of individual and societal factors.

Spranger declares the conceptual apparatus of the psychology of religion to be inadequate—and inevitably so—for approaching the heart of religious experience, especially of persons distant from us in time or personal disposition. Yet he did think it possible to trace certain lawful regularities in the growth of religious faith. A crucial factor in such development, he reports, is the character of the religious milieu, of which three types are distinguished: the moderate, the intense, and the indifferent or hostile. Each type of atmosphere predictably yields a different course of development.

Development in the Moderate Religious Milieu: In a moderate religious atmosphere, the child's faith is marked by four familiar qualities. Like the child's thinking generally, religious ideas at this age are thoroughly *egocentric* and *anthropomorphic.* The powers of the world, good and bad, are personified as adult human beings who are peculiarly interested in the child's personal circumstances and happiness. The child relates to these powers as I to Thou and attributes to the world in general a shifting physiognomic character—both aspects of the *magical* world-view on which, in more mature form, the life of inwardness and relationship depends. A *primitive morality* likewise testifies to the child's limited capacities and unreflectiveness. Edwin Starbuck was correct, says Spranger, in declaring credulity to be the most obvious feature of the child's faith. Religious content does not yet lie at the center of personality, for such a center remains unformed.

The period of youth, which encompasses roughly the second decade of life and is inaugurated by the emergence of an inner life, is said by Spranger to contain three stages of religious development. The distinctive mark of the first stage is the character of newness: long-familiar objects and ideas seem suddenly to take on a depth of meaning and significance. Such a discovery normally requires exposure to a truly living religious tradition. Regardless of the nature of the milieu, however, the first stage is regularly followed by a period of doubt and denial. Active dissociation from the family's tradition may represent the youth's positive effort to be faithful to personal religious experience or to employ the language of his or her own generation. It may also be a negative act, usually prompted by one of three factors. First, the youth's expectations of deeply moving and transformative experience may meet with profound disappointment, as happened to the 14-year-old Jung (1962, p. 54). Alternatively, when the cognitive need is strong and the *Zeitgeist* is dominated by scientific and positivistic values, religion's enigmas, contradictions, and miraculous events may form an insuperable barrier. Finally, the experience of evil and the difficulties of justifying God's ways in the face of it—the problem of THEODICY—may lead to dissociation on ethical grounds.

Spranger considers the negativity of the second stage to be essential preparation for the third one, the establishment of a personal and relatively enduring perspective. The Christian youth who were Spranger's subjects exemplified three general outcomes: a state of apparent religious indifference and emptiness, underlying which Spranger suspected there was a faith of some kind; a decisive break from historical Christianity into a personal religiosity of strikingly different character; and a reconstruction of Christian conviction, either by returning to the earlier faith or by combining selections from it with personal appropriations and reinterpretations. In spite of its exceptional diversity, Spranger finds the third stage typified by a single tendency: the happy conviction that one at last possesses truth. An underlying uncertainty often remains, however, which manifests itself as an intolerant and exclusive defense of the perceived truth against the claims of others.

Beyond the three stages of religious development in youth is a final one, that of maturity, which Spranger considers only briefly. Passion and feverishness are in general left behind, although new waves of the old storm and stress are not unknown. If new themes are rare, there may yet be a discovery of new, unsuspected depths. In any event, "in the religious realm, a final state of equilibrium is almost never reached" (p. 307).

Development in Exceptional Milieus: To this point we have been tracing the changes that occur in the moderate religious environment. When surrounding religious attitudes are extreme, we may naturally expect somewhat different patterns of development. In an intensely religious milieu, youth are strongly encouraged to share the ardor of their elders' piety at the same time that alternatives are actively opposed. Spranger identifies three varieties of such a milieu, corresponding, respectively, to emphasis on thought, action, or feeling. The first two, in which the accent is on fixed religious doctrine or particular ethical demands, are likely to meet with resistance from adolescents, for although both promise certainty, they allow no room for personal growth or the youthful sense of vitality and self-sufficiency. The third, emotional variety of milieu, given its emphasis on self-analysis and individual experience, is far more likely to gain youth's sympathy than dogmatic or ethical orthodoxy.

For insights into development in "irreligious" environments, Spranger draws heavily on Günther Dehn's (1923) study of working-class youth. Dehn's subjects tend to view religion as of a piece with middle-class and establishment values and thus to see it as a politically motivated institution of the rich. At the same time that traditional religious expressions are therefore alien to them, opportunities for inner religious development are essentially absent. Thrust prematurely into the struggle for existence, youth of this culture lack the quiet and solitude that Spranger thinks are necessary for developing the inner life, including the powers of imagination that are the bridge to all that is higher in humankind—above all, its ideals. Moreover, there is usually no one who embodies the religious life and can awaken working-class youth to the possibilities that lie within and guide their development with deep and loving care. Spranger contends that only such uncommon persons, not books or instruction, can truly provide access to the soul's deepest possibilities. Working-class youth may nevertheless evince a sense of religion's traditional powers. The women in particular are likely to turn to the church to mark life's great transitions, through baptisms, weddings, and funerals. Spranger suggests that beneath the abundant resentment and opposition that are otherwise typical of these youth, the psychologist of religion may discern traces of disappointed religious longing, however literalistic or primitive its expression. Even an inhospitable milieu cannot utterly suppress the religious predisposition.

THE DORPAT SCHOOL: SYSTEMATIC EXPERIMENTAL INTROSPECTION

Although Spranger's interpretive psychology proved to be widely influential, some researchers had doubts about methods that were so heavily dependent on vaguely specified intuitive processes. No less descriptive in its intent but lying at the other extreme of methodological explicitness is the approach of the Dorpat school of religious psychology, an international group of scholars whose harmoniously orchestrated program deserves more than any other in the psychology of religion the designation of "school." Named after the Baltic city and university where it was founded early in the twentieth century, the Dorpat school is distinguished for applying the method of systematic experimental introspection to religious experience. This method was developed by the famous Würzburg school of psychology and its leader, Oswald Külpe (Wulff, 1985a).

THE METHOD OF EXPERIMENTAL INTROSPECTION

The method employed by Külpe and his associates was elegantly simple. Well-trained subjects were presented with a problem to be solved or a passage to be interpreted. Once they found and reported the solution, they were asked to describe as fully and precisely as possible the contents of their conscious experience. The interval of time required to find a solution was carefully noted, and the reports that followed were transcribed verbatim. Word association experiments were carried out in a similar manner, but the observers were instructed to provide responses of a particular class, for example, the whole of which the presented concept is a part. Again they were asked to report what occurred in consciousness between the presentation of the stimulus word and the report of their responses.

Strictly speaking, the Würzburg researchers employed what William Stern (1935) calls "primary self-remembrance," for the subjects made their observations retrospectively, immediately following the experience. This procedure was thought to be superior to ordinary self-observation in several ways. First, the phenomena to be observed were limited to those that occurred in the interval immediately preceding the observational effort. By limiting the events to be observed to the immediate past—and by carefully separating experience from observation and report—the Würzburg researchers minimized the inevitable distortions of memory and the disrupting effects of observational effort. Second, the introspective task concerned a single, carefully selected stimulus event, which was presented under the same conditions to other, similarly trained observers. This arrangement provided a more adequate basis for ensuring reliability and carrying out intersubjective validation and comparison. Third, by assigning the work of introspection to someone other than themselves, the researchers were able to minimize the systematic influence of their own expectations and bias. Finally, laboratory conditions permitted precise measurement of the reaction times, which served as a basis for judging how promptly and therefore how reliably the observations were made.

Piety in the Laboratory

Wilhelm Stählin (1914) first applied the Würzburg school's method to religious experience, but it fell to Lutheran theologian Karl Girgensohn (1875–1925) to found a school upon it. As a pious Latvian youth, Girgensohn had become a convert

Karl Girgensohn

to the "spirit of positivistic enlightenment." However, the writings of Friedrich Schleiermacher, Hermann Lotze, and Auguste Sabatier eventually led him to a mystical–pantheistic way of thinking. Their emphasis on the subjective side of religion may also have prompted him, while studying theology in Berlin, to attend lectures in psychology as well. The most influential of his teachers from this time was Karl Stumpf, an outstanding student of Franz Brentano, a close friend of William James, and the founder of experimental phenomenology. A few years later, a colleague at Dorpat University introduced Girgensohn to the revolutionary work of the Würzburg school. Accepting Külpe's invitation in 1910 to spend a term with him at Bonn, Girgensohn soon became a convinced adherent of the school's procedures (Girgensohn, 1926).

Girgensohn and his associates embraced experimental introspection as the best method that psychology then had to offer. Yet they also recognized that its application to personal religious experience could present special problems. In order to ensure a trusting and open relation with each observer, the Dorpat researchers took four precautions.

1. Observers were chosen from among persons who already knew and trusted the investigator.
2. Little-known stimulus texts were selected, not simply to reduce the likelihood of habitual responses to familiar material, but also to avoid passages that might trigger profoundly personal meanings.
3. Observers were assured that they were free to remain silent about painfully intimate matters, though they were requested to indicate the occurrence of each such omission.
4. Observers were given sufficient practice with nonreligious materials to accustom them to the procedures.

Seldom mentioned, but apparently frequently employed, was a fifth measure. Some investigators began and ended the experimental sessions with prayer. These five precautions seem to have succeeded in their purpose. That is, deeply emotional responses were not unknown, yet omissions were reportedly rare. Testifying to the degree of trust that Girgensohn established, the mother of an observer who later died said of her son's protocols: "It was for me as if my dead son had once again sat down with me, and, in his own words and turns of phrase, began to speak about God and man, just as he did in our closest times together" (Girgensohn, 1923b, p. 10). Georg Siegmund (1942), a Roman Catholic priest and psychologist who adopted Girgensohn's methods for the study of faith, reports that one of his observers volunteered afterward that he had never before confided so openly about his own inner life.

The members of the Dorpat school emphasized that they did not aim to elicit full-blown religious experiences in the experimental laboratory. They doubted that anyone could experiment with religion without altering it fundamentally. Girgensohn (1921, pp. 12–13) proposed instead to discern the traces left by religious experience in the psychic structure as a whole, to explore the role played in this matter by the individual's general type, and to experiment with *thoughts about* religion. Religious thinking, however, especially when it expresses an attitude of yearning or devotion, cannot in living persons be separated from religious affect. As a result of presenting such texts to their observers, who were instructed to read them as freely and naturally as possible, the Dorpat researchers found themselves witnesses to a range of religious emotions. Although the observers' experiences were on the whole not as deep or compelling as the "naturally occurring" variety, they were thought to be genuine and psychologically valuable.

GIRGENSOHN ON THE NATURE OF RELIGIOUS EXPERIENCE

The Dorpat school came into full prominence with the publication in 1921 of Girgensohn's classic book, *Der seelische Aufbau des religiösen Erlebens* (The Psychic Structure of Religious Experience). In this ambitious work, Girgensohn sought to mediate the dispute over the psychic nature of religion, a controversy that had grown acute since the time of Feuerbach. In particular, Girgensohn wished to test Schleiermacher's theory, which found the essence of religion in the feeling of absolute dependence. Hegel disputed Schleiermacher's notion, arguing that the heart of religion consists of a complex of representations and ideas. In contrast to both Schleiermacher and Hegel, Kant found the decisive factor to lie in the human will; religion fulfills its meaning, he thought, in its service to morality. Still others have sought to synthesize these three points of view, proposing that religion is a complex structure incorporating, in more or less equal measure, all three of the classically conceived functions of the human psyche (Girgensohn, 1921, pp. 1–2).

The Experimental Procedures

Rejecting historical sources as inadequate for any final solution to the question of religion's nature, Girgensohn turned instead to experimental psychology. Between 1911 and 1913, he laboriously recorded the observations of 14 individuals, including himself (to the degree that it was possible). Divided equally between the two sexes, his observers ranged in age from 20 to 37; all were highly educated. As stimulus texts, Girgensohn used 26 little-known religious poems and hymns, such as Theodor Fontane's "Bekenntnis" ("Confession") and Saint Francis of Assisi's "Canticle of Brother Sun" (see Excerpt 12.1). All these texts were chosen for their apparent usefulness in uncovering the formal characteristics that distinguish the life of faith.

EXCERPT 12.1

The Canticle of Brother Sun

Most high, all-powerful, all good, Lord!
  All praise is yours, all glory, all honour
  And all blessing.
To you, alone, Most High, do they belong.
  No mortal lips are worthy
  To pronounce your name.
All praise be yours, my Lord, through all that you have made.
  And first my lord Brother Sun,
  Who brings the day; and light you give to us through him.
How beautiful is he, how radiant in all his splendour!
  Of you, Most High, he bears the likeness.
All praise be yours, my Lord, through Sister Moon and Stars;
  In the heavens you have made them, bright
  And precious and fair.
All praise be yours, my Lord, through Brothers Wind and Air,
  And fair and stormy, all the weather's moods,
  By which you cherish all that you have made.

All praise be yours, my Lord, through Sister Water,
  So useful, lowly, precious and pure.
All praise be yours, my Lord, through Brother Fire,
  Through whom you brighten up the night.
  How beautiful is he, how gay! Full of power and strength.
All praise be yours, my Lord, through Sister Earth, our mother,
  Who feeds us in her sovereignty and produces
  Various fruits with coloured flowers and herbs.
All praise be yours, my Lord, through those who grant pardon
  For love of you; through those who endure
  Sickness and trial.
Happy those who endure in peace,
  By you, Most High, they will be crowned.
All praise be yours, my Lord, through Sister Death,
  From whose embrace no mortal can escape.
Woe to those who die in mortal sin!
  Happy those She finds doing your will!
  The second death can do no harm to them.
Praise and bless my Lord, and give him thanks,
  And serve him with great humility.

Source: From *The Writings of St. Francis of Assisi,* translated by B. Fahy. Chicago: Franciscan Herald Press, 1964, pages 130–131.

The work with each observer, which required an average of 30 sessions, began with approximately three hours of preliminary experiments, during which the observer was carefully schooled in the complexities of the observational task and accustomed to the experimental methods. Proceeding, then, with the first of the 26 poems, Girgensohn asked the observer to read the presented text through once, in as natural a manner as possible. Next, he asked the observer to describe the accompanying experience. When Girgensohn thought that additional readings and observations might yield further clarification, they followed without interruption. Taking a clue from Freud, Girgensohn also asked his observers to free-associate to the poem, a technique that proved of particular value when the earlier protocols hinted at factors only dimly perceived by the observer.

At preestablished intervals punctuating this series of 26 observations were several supplementary procedures. First, Girgensohn inquired about the ultimate grounds for the observer's faith, initially by direct inquiry and then by challenging the observer's position. At another point, he initiated a conversation on the subject of trust, using persons in the observer's own experience as the focus. Finally, an alternate experimental task was interpolated, using catechetical terms (e.g., the love of God) as stimuli and limiting the observer to conceptual thinking. Work with each observer was at last brought to a close by "control and supplementary trials" that repeated a few of the standard poems as well as several hymns that the observer had particularly liked or disliked in the first conversation.

Girgensohn's Findings

Much like James, Girgensohn considered it essential to anchor his conclusions from this mass of introspective reports in a generous sampling of his subjects' prose. Filling half of his book's 700 pages, the protocol excerpts are organized around the structural elements that are blended together in religious experience:

1. "Feelings," a broadly used term that refers variously to pleasant and unpleasant states, organic sensations, intuitions, and EGO FUNCTIONS.
2. Representations or images, defined by Girgensohn simply as "reproductions of physical sensations experienceable as tangibly evident" (p. 512).
3. Processes of willing, "ego functions combined with the consciousness of freedom and self-determination that are directed toward a specific behavior" (p. 575).

After clarifying the usage of these terms, Girgensohn sought to determine what role each element of the inner life had in religious experience.

Religion's Two Essential Components: Among the conclusions that Girgensohn draws from his voluminous data, several stand out. The leading structural element in religious experience, he says, is *intuitive thinking*. In contrast to the DISCURSIVE variety, intuitive thought tends to be vague and unformulated, uncontrollable and unrepeatable, and associated less with logic than with feelings of pleasure and displeasure as well as with symbols derived from organic sensations (p. 339). Schleiermacher's "feeling of absolute dependence" is said to be just such an intuition, and, indeed, Girgensohn happily notes the essential harmony of his own conclusions with Schleiermacher's. Both assign to religious thought of the discursive or reflective type a secondary role only, interpreting it as a symbolic expression of original experience and not the experience itself. In comparison to Schleiermacher, however, Girgensohn ascribes to systematic thinking a much greater significance for the practical religious life (p. 495).

Fused with intuitive thoughts in the course of religious experience is a second essential component, the so-called *ego functions*. Presented with a new set of ideas, the ego first responds intellectually, evaluating the ideas in terms of its existing store of cognitive principles. With time, however, may come not only cognitive assent but also genuine appropriation, so that the thoughts in effect become the person's own. Yet the objects of religious thinking are such that, if they are in some sense taken to be real, a merely cognitive attitude toward them will not suffice. Accordingly, the ego is called upon to take a position or stand in relation to these realities. Such a stand, says Girgensohn, may proceed along either of two lines: defiant resistance to the divine or self-surrender to it, the act of faith or trust.

Emphasizing the inseparable relation of intuitive thought and ego function in religious experience, and simultaneously countering those who minimize the intellectual element, Girgensohn maintains that, as a rule, faith and other postures of the ego do not exist without some object in mind. Thus, he says, an attitude of trust cannot occur without some object toward which it is directed. "To trust is first of all to open and disclose oneself to the object of one's trust; secondly, it is steadfastly to entrust oneself to that object, supported by the confidence that it can and will act rightly" (p. 465).

As the dynamic relation of ego and religious object evolves, the ego is said to undergo transformation. The more fully and unreservedly the ego enters into relation with a religious object, so that the ego is increasingly dominated and guided by it, the deeper, more powerful, and more expansive the ego will feel (p. 485). Paradoxically, a point may finally be reached when in a moment of ecstasy the ego experiences itself to be entirely extinguished.

Thus, for Girgensohn the religious experience possesses a dual structure. On the one hand is the peculiar activity of the ego, which is a basic prerequisite of all religious experience. On the other is the equally indispensable intuited object, which lies beyond the mundane world. In genuine religious experience the two components form a living unity; only in theoretical discourse can they be separated and analyzed.

Images and Willing as Secondary Expressions: This dynamic whole manifests itself secondarily in images and acts of willing that express its essential nature. Viewed in isolation, religious images frequently seem contradictory or nonsensical, but if interpreted in the light of the whole they express, says Girgensohn, their meaning will become clear. Even when images appear to be immediately meaningful, as they do when depicting objects or events that could occur in real life, they carry a surplus of intuitive content that cannot be visualized with the image and would be lost if the image were analyzed in isolation. Ways must be found, says Girgensohn, to interpret images aright, carefully determining the thought processes to which they give palpable form (p. 559).

Girgensohn likewise considers the complexly constituted processes of willing to be secondary to the dynamic whole formed by religious thought and the religious attitude of the ego. They are a by-product of inner change, he says, an ineluctable expression of the new life. The fundamental mystery of religion lies not in acts of willing but in the new attitude of the ego, which expresses itself without consciousness of freedom (p. 582). Although such an attitude may be responsible for a radical redirection of willing, he adds, it is not in itself a volitional act.

Even though religious experience lends itself to analysis in terms of structural elements, Girgensohn emphasizes that the larger whole cannot be reconstituted simply by adding up the qualities of its parts. Religion, says Girgensohn, synthesizes to the highest possible degree all of the fundamental human capacities. Out of an abundance of experiences and relations it forms a unity that is different from any of its constitutive elements (p. 436). Thus we see that religion, too, follows the fundamental principle of Gestalt psychology, perhaps the best-known successor of the Würzburg school.

CONTRIBUTIONS TO A DIFFERENTIAL PSYCHOLOGY OF RELIGION

Although Girgensohn was interested primarily in the general nature of religious experience, he soon also recognized the value of experimental introspection for the study of individual differences. In a major theological work, Girgensohn (1924) identifies "differential psychology of religion" as one of the three topic areas of the field as a whole, alongside "analytic psychology of religion," which deals with the structural character of religious experience (the subject of *Der seelische Aufbau*), and "social psychology of religion," which considers the functions of religion in human society. In 1913 Girgensohn published a paper, "On the Differential Psychology of Religious Thought," in which he deals chiefly with the diverse objects of religious thought, though he also considers individual variation in the capacities for abstraction and for making religious interpretations. Some years later, in the lecture containing his responses to the critics of his *Der seelische Aufbau*, Girgensohn (1923b) noted the relative neglect of individual differences in his massive work and called for the earliest possible remedy. His own efforts toward this end, in a study concerned with intuitive thinking, were published in preliminary form the same year (Girgensohn, 1923a).

With Girgensohn's premature death in 1925, the task of developing the differential psychology of religion was left to other members of the school. The challenge was most systematically taken up by Carl Schneider, who worked with Girgensohn at the University of Leipzig where he was studying theology while completing a Ph.D. in psychology with the influential holistic psychologist Felix Krueger. Schneider assembled an educated but religiously diverse group of 20 observers, including a Jewish mathematics student and an advanced student of modern languages who proclaimed himself to be wholly irreligious. In a series of experimental sessions, 100 stimulus texts were presented to each observer in a manner identical to Girgensohn's. Regrettably, Schneider published only fragments of his results; his reports are nonetheless valuable for their careful attention to the central and complex factor of individuality, which today is still too often overlooked.

Four Responses to a Solitary Wanderer

Let us consider one of Schneider's (1926) examples. Each of the observers was asked "to appropriate" to the greatest degree possible the content of the following verse:

> I am a wanderer with no one at my side;
> That I not lose my way to heaven, dear God with me abide.[8]

Of the protocols recorded for this text, Schneider selected for analysis those provided by four markedly different observers. The first of these subjects, a Protestant student of theology, reported an image of a solitary figure resolutely striding down a long road at night, undisturbed by the howling wind and flashes of lightning yet inwardly full of yearning. "So it often is with me," said this student. In the company of most other people, he added, he would dread losing the way. A strong conviction then came to him that even under these circumstances it is possible to talk with God. Further images—including Jacob's struggle with God—finally culminated in a feeling of great power.

The second observer, a South African teacher studying psychology at Leipzig who "at least was not irreligious," stated that the verse's first line reminded him of John Bunyan's book *A Pilgrim's Progress*. With the second line he turned to thoughts of prayer and the indescribable complex of mystical feelings that accompanied it for him. This complex combined very pleasant feelings of power and confidence with unpleasant feelings of vagueness and tension.

The third observer, the irreligious language student, responded to the first line with the cynical thought, "Well, why not, are you so disgusting a fellow that no one will go with you?" This must have been written long ago, he reflected, and then the thought of losing the way suggested to him that the wanderer ought to purchase a good map. "As for the rest, no, that doesn't concern me."

The fourth observer, the Jewish student, responded to the verse with a succession of images: an apprentice, an evangelist, Jesus leading a person by the arm, a prodigal son, a monklike man on a pilgrimage to Jerusalem, Saint Augustine. "It is always the same," he remarked, "and I rejected that today—I can't, I couldn't say it that way, but I felt, I must yet also say, in the background I sensed a measure of repentance that I am unable to say it." It was, he added, a most glorious feeling.

As Schneider demonstrates in his analysis, we may first approach these protocols individually, noting the distortions in meaning introduced by the observer's

---

[8] The original German text reads as follows:
> *Ich bin ein Wandersmann und keiner geht mit mir.*
> *Ich bitte Gott, dass ich den Weg zum Himmel nicht verlier.*
The English translation is mine.

personal disposition. We may note, for example, the first observer's strongly individualistic tendency. He illustrates, says Schneider, a religious type characterized by a polarity of religious experience—a feeling of anxiety among other persons and a feeling of power, courage, and defiance in relation to the divine. The third observer, on the other hand, shows no evidence of religious experience whatsoever. Other protocols confirm the impression we get of him here; skeptical, sarcastic, and blasé, he greets everything with critical and satiric derision (Schneider, 1929).

Alternatively, some of the protocols lend themselves to detailed comparative analysis, as Schneider illustrates with the first two observers we are considering. The experience of the first one is predominantly oriented toward the outer world and consists of a well-defined set of opposites. The experience of the second, in contrast, is rooted deep within and reveals itself only reluctantly and vaguely, employing far fewer concepts and images. For both observers, concludes Schneider, their experiences reflect their unique individualities. Religious experience, he maintains, is individually structured even in its subtlest aspects, and it always bears a peculiarly personal stamp.

A Schizothyme's Apocalyptic Vision

That a knowledge of these subtle differences can be of value to the historian of religion is demonstrated by Schneider (1930) in a study of the APOCALYPTIC experience recounted in the New Testament book The Revelation to John (see Excerpt 12.2). Drawing on contemporary research on dreams, hallucinations, and a variety of other forms of imagery, Schneider concludes that the diverse elements of John's extraordinary account were not pieced together from the experience of others; rather, they form a unique and authentic whole. More specifically, the sharply contrasting feelings of horrible destruction and ecstatic rapture, along with the primarily auditory character of the exceptionally intense hallucinations, suggested to Schneider that its author possessed a schizothymic temperament. This disposition, we learned in Chapter 3, is marked by outer reserve and formality juxtaposed with passionate hidden feelings and antipathies. Close analysis of the peculiarities of the experience recorded in the book of Revelation, Schneider observed, might also cast light on the relation of the Apocalypse to the other Johannine writings. Whereas comparison in terms of content, vocabulary, and style seems to set the book of Revelation and the Gospel of John apart, Schneider found striking similarities in the kinds of feelings expressed, the inner tension of opposites, the predominance of auditory elements, and the manner of thinking—evidence for a common authorship.

EXCERPT 12.2

From The Revelation to John, Chapter 9

9 . . . Then the sixth angel blew his trumpet, and I heard a voice from the four horns of the golden altar before God, saying to the sixth angel who had the trumpet, "Release the four angels who are bound at the great river Euphrates." So the four angels were released, who had been held ready for the hour, the day, the month, and the year, to kill a third of mankind. The number of the troops of cavalry was twice ten thousand times ten thousand; I heard their number. And this was how I saw the horses in my vision: the riders wore breastplates the color of fire and of sapphire and of sulphur, and the heads of the horses were like lions' heads, and fire and smoke and sulphur issued from their mouths. By these three plagues a third of mankind was killed, by the fire and smoke and sulphur issuing from their mouths. For the power of the horses is in their mouths and in their tails; their tails are like serpents, with heads, and by means of them they wound.

Schneider offers yet another application for his findings. He proposes that they may explain the diversity of responses to the book of Revelation. To Luther, who was more the outgoing and variable cyclothymic type, the Apocalypse was at first too mysterious in its content, too rich and ambiguous in its language, to allow him to make any sense of it. Later in his life, however, he came to see in it a representation of his struggle with the papacy. Thus, "out of the ambivalent, schizothymic book of longing emerged a practical, cyclothymic manual of war" (p. 144). In contrast, Albrecht Dürer demonstrated in his woodcuts of the Apocalypse a profound understanding and affinity for the work's underlying schizothymic yearning.

DEMISE AND ITS SURVIVORS

The full sweep of the program of the Dorpat school, including its concern with individual differences and the practical matters of religious education and pastoral care, is represented in the large handbook written by Girgensohn's successor, Werner Gruehn (1887–1961). This book, *Die Frömmigkeit der Gegenwart* (Contemporary Piety), was published in 1956. By that time, however, the Dorpat school was largely a thing of the past. The decade or so of research that followed Girgensohn's ground-breaking study and a parallel one by Gruehn (1924) on religious valuation (see Wulff, 1985a) was brought to a virtual halt by the rise of National Socialism and the tragic events of World War II. Some of the earlier work had also suffered severely under existing political circumstance—Gruehn (1924) relates that one of his observers at Dorpat was arrested by the Russian secret police in the middle of an experiment (p. viii)—but this time the devastation was nearly complete. Gruehn and Schneider, for example, lost virtually everything, including their large personal

Dürer's *The Four Avenging Angels of Euphrates.*

libraries. The Russians dismantled the Dorpat school of theology and its Institute for Religious Psychology after they annexed Estonia in 1940.[9]

Villiam Grønbaek: The spirit of the Dorpat school lived on in the work of several of Gruehn's students. Outstanding among them is the Danish pastor and scholar Villiam Grønbaek (1897–1970), whom Gruehn identifies in the foreword to Grønbaek's (1958) untranslated survey of the field as, at that time, "indisputably the most important Protestant psychologist of religion . . . in the world" (p. 6). An admirer in particular of Starbuck and James, Grønbaek was more open than Gruehn to other research approaches. Indeed, he looked forward to the day when there would be but one psychology of religion. His chief loyalty, however, remained with the "experimental" approach, albeit transmuted into a more productive "conversational method" carried out in the service of pastoral care (Grønbaek, 1967, pp. 93–95). Like others in the Dorpat traditon, Grønbaek brought to his study of religious experience a practical interest in developmental processes, not only in children and adolescents but also, notably, in the elderly (Åkerberg, 1973). Of particular interest are his studies of the complex dynamics of the child's experience of religious art (Grønbaek, 1964) and of the spontaneous visual representations experienced by the aging during prayer (Grønbaek, 1969). In his 1969 study, Grønbaek reports that clear visual images were surprisingly common among his elderly subjects, especially the women. Whereas about one-fifth of his male subjects reported such occurrences, virtually half of the females did.

Alfons Bolley: Among the few Catholics in Gruehn's circle of students and the only university teacher, Alfons Bolley (1898–1989) followed his own early work on adolescent prayer (Bolley, 1930) with a series of studies on meditation (see Thomas, 1973, p. 118). Of particular moment for us is his finding of two basic forms between which the consciousness of God fluctuates: the experience of *distance*, typically mediated by images of spatial remove and accompanied by feelings of fear, awe, and unworthiness; and the experience of *contact*, expressed in the sense of being touched or embraced and associated with such feelings as purification, tranquillity, and joy. Here is empirical evidence, says Bolley (1949, 1965, 1976), for Otto's "strange harmony of contrasts." Notable, too, is Bolley's highly suggestive analysis of meditation as a progression of various forms of empathy (*Einfühlung*) culimating in experiences of feeling-at-one (*Einsfühlung*). Like Scheler, upon whose phenomenology of sympathy this work is based, Bolley takes for granted that the religious object possesses a personal form (Bolley, 1964; Thomas, 1973).

Kurt Gins: The investigations of Lutheran pastor Kurt Gins have centered on mystical experience. Following in the footsteps of Girgensohn and Gruehn, Gins (1961, 1967, 1982) set about to identify, describe, and order the mystical elements in both contemporary and classic piety. From the reports of his laboratory subjects, Gins (1992) identified three forms of pre-mystic experience, which differ according to whether the self or the object dominates the experience and the degree to which the self and the object merge. In the *object-oriented pre-mystic form*, the self joins in pre-mystic union with the dominating religious image but without losing its separate identity (hence it is mystical rather than ecstatic); in the *self-oriented pre-ecstatic form*, the object is created by the self, perhaps in its own image, and is subsequently absorbed by the self in a state of oneness; and in the *object-oriented pre-ecstatic form*,

---

[9] Following the collapse of the Soviet Union in 1991, the University of Tartu—the former Dorpat University—reestablished a program in theology, which now includes a position in the psychology of religion.

the self is absorbed into the strongly dominant image, to the point of virtual disappearance. Gins found that parallel distinctions can be made in the experiences of the classical mystics. Grønbaek (1970) cites Gins's work, together with that of Bolley, as evidence of the continuing serviceability of the experimental method.

DESCRIPTIVE RESEARCH IN THE POSTWAR LITERATURE

In spite of the growing prominence today of the objective and depth psychologies among German-speaking scholars, the postwar literature contains a variety of notable works in the descriptive tradition. Several of these works are integrative, summing up and building on the earlier literature (e.g., Pöll, 1965, 1974; Potempa, 1958; Trillhaas, 1953; Wyss, 1991). Others report original research on particular phenomena or themes. To illustrate the continuing vitality of this approach, we will conclude our survey by reviewing the work of three researchers whose findings significantly complement the classic studies we have surveyed. Focusing as they do on topics that are usually approached by other methods, they will also remind us of what more is to be gained by phenomenological and interpretive means.

THE PHENOMENOLOGY OF MYSTICAL CONSCIOUSNESS

Most of the contributors to the German descriptive tradition wrote as teachers of theology, philosophy, or religion, or, especially in the case of the Dorpat school, as ministers and pastoral counselors. A striking exception is Carl Albrecht (1902–1965), a physician who practiced internal medicine but who, with systematic training in psychology, philosophy, and theology, was also a psychotherapist and a researcher of mystical experience. While investigating the therapeutic value of various meditative practices, especially yoga, Albrecht was astonished to observe the healing and integrative power of the state of consciousness attainable through meditation. When he sought to clarify and interpret the occurrences in this state, he discovered a remarkable technique by which he was able to elicit a verbal report from a handful of his patients while they were in the state of absorption. Albrecht himself learned to employ it, and from his patients' experiences and his own, he constructed a phenomenology of mystical consciousness (Fischer-Barnicol, in Albrecht, 1974).

Albrecht's (1951) finely wrought analysis is divided into two parts, one devoted to the process of "centering down" (*die Versenkung*) and the other to absorption (*die Versunkenheit*), the end state of this process. Centering down, says Albrecht, is initiated through a conscious act of resolve that includes an idea of its goal and a "determining tendency." Progression is marked by a slowing down of the life current, a loosening of the ties to the surrounding world, and an emptying of the mind. The entire experience is marked by a special mood of peacefulness, and an "enormous clarity" progressively fills the entire sphere of consciousness.

Absorption, the end result of centering down—though it may also occur spontaneously—is an undivided and fully integrated state of consciousness. Empty of all content not uniquely its own and possessing an extraordinary clarity, the structure of this state is the most orderly known in human experience. For its duration, the stream of consciousness flows slowly onward and the dominant mood is one of peace. Located within it as its only function is a purely receptive ego, *die Innenschau* (literally, "view within"), which Albrecht carefully distinguishes from all ordinary modes of perception, including illusions and hallucinations.

Albrecht identifies two groups of experiences that make up this state of absorption. The first, reflecting its orderliness and clarity, is an objectively observable improvement in the performance of various tasks, such as thinking or remembering. More remarkable is the second one, a phenomenon that Albrecht calls "the arriving" (*das Ankommende*), a term designating the complex whole that gradually emerges into consciousness in a series of experiences. This emergent whole, because it stands in a complementary relation to the purely receptive ego, is not comparable to objects known to the ego in other states of consciousness. The forms in which it may appear are manifold, including movielike images, feelings, symbols, and metaphors as well as bodily paroxysms, vivid self-understandings, intuitions, and unexpected and often incomprehensible words or phrases.

This phenomenon may also take the form of an absolutely ungraspable essence that has come from an unknown realm and mysteriously contains within its comprehensive unity all experience—past, present, and future. Possessing a numinous character, this form of "the arriving" is called "the encompassing" (*das Umfassende*), to express the feeling of being grasped and enveloped. Its specific forms may range from impersonal ones, such as all-encompassing peace (to which Otto's schema can be applied only conditionally, says Albrecht), to a personal Thou experienced as an invisible presence, as internal harmonies or an inner voice, or as the cause of bodily sensations such as being grasped or branded. The coming of "the encompassing," whatever its form, in the state of absorption constitutes mystical experience, according to Albrecht. In a second book published a few years later, Albrecht explores the phenomenological structure of the mystical relation as well as important philosophical and hermeneutical questions (Albrecht, 1958).

Clues to Albrecht's technique can be found in a posthumously published selection of his literary remains, including letters to the volume's editor and mystical declarations made in the state of absorption (Albrecht, 1974). Long undecided about publishing the particulars of his technique as well as the minutely detailed protocols of his patients, for fear of their misuse, he destroyed the voluminous material in its entirety shortly before his death in 1965. He died less than three months after his 24 years of speaking out of the mystical state had found its fulfillment in "a repose in a silent luminosity" (p. 18).

STUDIES OF RELIGIOUS DEVELOPMENT

Worldwide, the interest in religious development has continued unabated since the beginnings of the psychology of religion (Helve, 1993; Hyde, 1990; Reich, 1992; Tamminen, 1991). Within the German literature we will examine the well-conceived work of two investigators, Theophil Thun and Maria Bindl, both of whom have grounded their efforts in an intimate acquaintance with earlier research and reflection. Particularly influential in their thinking is the work of Otto and Spranger, as may be apparent. These researchers illustrate rather different means by which psychologists can elicit expressions of religious experience.

Religion Through the Life Cycle

In a series of related studies employing subjects of three distinct age groups, professor of education Theophil Thun has provided an overview of religiosity through the course of the human life cycle. In each study he used methods designed to encourage his participants to report their religious thoughts and experiences as freely and openly as possible. Thun's skill in establishing rapport with his subjects, a prerequisite for the success of these methods, is evident in each study.

Childhood and Metamorphosis: The subjects in the first of Thun's (1959) investigations were four groups of children, both Protestant and Catholic, who were enrolled in one of the first four grades of either a village or a city school. In a series of weekly "reflection hours," Thun posed to these children a sequence of 26 questions on such themes as the form of Christ, heaven and hell, prayer, and the experience of death. The children were asked to listen quietly to each question, with eyes closed, and to formulate their own answers silently. The class would then discuss the question in a free conversation. Given the enthusiastic outpouring of answers, only one or two questions were discussed each week.

From the rich material he gathered by this means, Thun identified five characteristics of the child's religion.

1. Evident, first of all, is the child's *readiness* for religion. The eager response of the children to Thun's questions demonstrated not only an uncritical predisposition to believe in these religious doctrines but also a spontaneous tendency to think about them without special prompting. The first glimmerings of skepticism appeared in the third grade, when classmates' statements were occasionally criticized.

2. Obvious, too, from the second grade on, was the *capacity for experience,* notably of the *mysterium tremendum*—though not its components of horror, astonishment, and creature consciousness—and also of the *mysterium fascinans,* especially in church.

3. Though *dependence* on environmental factors is also a characteristic of childhood piety, says Thun, it does not sharply distinguish the child from the adult, in whom the ideal of an autonomous faith is seldom realized. The impress of the environment was evident in the differences that Thun found between Protestant and Catholic, villager and city dweller, the store owner's child and the child of the industrial worker. Family, neighborhood, school, and church are all influential factors, he concludes, and so too are picture books, magazines, and television.

4. The factor of *limitation* in the child's religion is reflected in four characteristics that Thun observed: (a) *magical thinking,* both in interpreting divine action and in conduct, for example, of prayer; (b) *anthropomorphism,* which is fostered by aspects of Christian theology and solidified by the religious picture books that well-meaning adults provided for children; (c) *egocentrism*—but again, a quality common in adults and counterbalanced to some degree by the religiously educated child's theocentric world-view and by empathic concern for other living things; and (d) *realism,* applied to every level of the homogeneously conceived world, even to the most abstract and speculative matters.

5. The quality of *changeableness* means that the metamorphosis of this childhood faith is inevitable, but whether change will lead to religious maturity or to infantile self-defense or indifference depends on the factor of spiritual cultivation.

Adolescence in a Culture in Crisis: To explore the changes that occur in the adolescent years, Thun (1963) carried out a second study, employing 375 students enrolled in the eighth grade, in high school, or in a trade school in one of three different cities. Over the course of four to six months he distributed a series of

Pictures such as Rudolf Schäfer's *Our Father* embody and perpetuate anthropomorphic thinking about God.

printed questions on 16 themes, progressing from peripheral though important matters (e.g., use of leisure time or the problems of sexuality) to specifically religious issues, akin to those addressed to the children in the previous study. Free group conversation followed collection of these anonymously completed pages.

Among his subjects, some chacteristics of childhood religion occasionally carried over into adolescence, for example, magical understanding of prayer or an outlook of pervasive realism. Most of his subjects, however, had by this age left behind the naive and harmoniously coherent world of the child as well as its simple piety. Some, whom Thun identifies as a "religious elite," had undergone an intensification and deepening of their faith, reflected both in reports of profound inner experience and in concordant expressions of insight. But for the majority, who in their struggle or indifference embodied the contemporary religious crisis, genuine religious experience remained entirely foreign. Some self-confidently assumed the arrogant posture of the enlightened positivist. Others, deeply troubled by the ancient problem of theodicy, vacillated on the boundaries of disbelief. Still others, disillusioned especially by religious hypocrisy, actively opposed all religious faith. Among the trade school students, whose thinking was marked by contradictions and incoherence, religious indifference reigned supreme.

How is one to understand the decline of religious experience? According to Thun, it is a symptom of "the spiritual destruction of modern, uprooted man," one component of which is the rapid decline in the capacity for experience (p. 310). When abstract conceptual thinking becomes as dominant as it has in our day, says Thun, the language of images becomes alien and the inner world of wholeness is lost. The disappearance of inner images is reflected, he suggests, in an intensified visual need, which a vast system of commercial enterprises today seeks to exploit. Symptomatic, too, is the craving for experience, which in adolescence may become insatiable. Nonetheless, at the end of this study, Thun observes hopeful signs of positive development, including the rise of a religious elite.

Old Age and Its Destiny: To complete his studies of the course of piety through the life-span, Thun (1969) moved from the first two decades of life to the last several, when the "boundary situation" of growing old commonly leads to earnest reflections on one's life as a whole and on one's personal fate. In leisurely conversations that lasted three to four hours each, Thun interviewed 65 men and women who were between the ages of 60 and 87 and represented a broad variety of occupations and world-views. Following an initial inquiry into their personal history, general interests, and their image of an ideal person, these subjects were asked to talk about many of the religious themes addressed in Thun's earlier studies.

As in those previous works, Thun analyzes the pattern of responses to certain of these themes, but the heart of this book consists of 36 of his subjects' protocols, along with a summary of Thun's impressions of each. These brief case studies are organized according to six typical trajectories taken by the "religious destiny": (1) personalities with a religious development unbroken by crisis since childhood; (2) individualists with an independent religious development within the denomination they inherited from their parents and grandparents; (3) converts to another denomination; (4) seekers who, estranged from their inherited denomination, have come to feel at home in another religious community; (5) personalities whose religious destinies were influenced by contact with socialism; and (6) personalities whose religious destinies were shaped by estrangement from their inherited denominations and by continued dissociation from a community of faith.

In reflecting on their own lives, Thun's older subjects provided additional testimony regarding the piety of childhood and adolescence. Once again the paramount significance of the early influences in a person's life becomes evident. Most important is the influence of the mother, although the father may also play a major role. School and church, especially relations with teachers and religious personnel, frequently have notable effects, for better or worse, and decisive life experiences of diverse kinds, in the broader context of historical events, constitute still another set of influences. Yet in the end, says Thun, the religious fate of the individual—ultimately mysterious and impenetrable—remains inaccessible to rational analysis (p. 217).

Drawings as a Mirror of Religious Development

Like virtually all other researchers in this field, Thun relied for the most part on the vehicle of words to gain insight into the piety of his subjects. The apparent superiority of language for the transmission of ideas and principles is recognized by the religious traditions themselves. Indeed, most historians of religion rightly agree that a mastery of the languages in which a tradition expresses itself is a prerequisite for any genuine understanding of it.

Projective Techniques: There are doubts abroad, however, regarding the capacity of words to give free and adequate expression to the subtleties of individual experience. Certainly at times we are all convinced that it is hopeless to try to put our feelings into words. Yet even if, in principle, we grant language the capacity to represent our inner lives, we are often only vaguely aware of events transpiring therein, and we rarely have sufficient perspective to represent this complex inner world as a whole. Furthermore, even though we have some understanding of ourselves, various factors may prompt us to conceal it from others. In sum, much remains to be learned about the private world of another that the individual cannot or will not articulate. Religious faith in particular, according to Wilfred Smith (1959, p. 39), "cannot adequately be expressed in words, not even by a man who holds it devoutly." We may also recall Otto's claim that, within the religious process itself, language tends to foreclose the depths of nonrational experience.

In an effort to bypass these difficulties, psychologists have developed a wide variety of projective techniques. Subjects are presented with a set of objects that are relatively unstructured—inkblots, ambiguous pictures, materials for constructing a scene or picture. The way in which individuals interpret or organize these objects is assumed to reflect the structure and organization of their private worlds. Projective techniques are thought to have various advantages over standardized assessment procedures, including the capacity to represent the personality as an organized whole and sensitivity to private, idiosyncratic meanings. They are also thought to be particularly effective in revealing latent or unconscious trends. These very strengths, however, make it difficult to standardize these procedures and to establish adequate reliability, validity, and norms (Anastasi, 1988; Frank, 1939).

Standard projective techniques, such as the Rorschach inkblot test and the Thematic Apperception Test, have on occasion been used to evaluate the general psychological status of persons of a particular religious outlook. To elicit expressions of the religious outlook itself, however, these procedures have had to be modified, making the task more explicitly religious (see Wulff, 1985b, pp. 64–66). When Ana-Maria Rizzuto (1979) asked her subjects to draw pictures of God, she was employing just such a technique.

Changing Views of the Wholly Other: A similar method was used by Maria Bindl (1965), who gathered drawings on religious themes from 8205 Roman Catholic students between the ages of 3 and 18. These drawings, which were merely scribblings for the youngest children, were made in response to a retelling of one or another of six relatively unfamiliar stories, for example, episodes selected from the Revelation of John. They served as the basis for judging the character of each child's experience and for describing the course of religious development.

Bindl argues that the expressive technique of drawing is peculiarly appropriate for studying the inner lives of both children and adolescents. For the young, still-inarticulate child, she says, there is no other method that is equally serviceable. More primitive and motoric than conceptual formulation, graphic expression can be intensely engaging, yielding a product of subtle yet evident affectivity. For the older child or adolescent, who is both more verbal and self-conscious, there are additional advantages. On the one hand, because the drawing seems less revealing than the spoken word, it is less threatening for the sensitive individual. On the other, because it reflects more directly the depths of inner experience, it lends itself less readily to dissimulation. In any event, the presence of artificiality will likely be evident. In contrast to verbal testimony, moreover, the drawing is less easily rendered in a form that is impersonal and stereotyped or that is intended to be "right." All external standards such as accuracy or artistic merit are irrelevant, Bindl contends, when drawings are examined for their psychic content (pp. 101–102).

To interpret these drawings, Bindl used principles that the prominent German graphologist Ludwig Klages and his successors developed for handwriting analysis (see Roman, 1952).[10] In both types of expression the complementary factors of *movement* and *form* prevail, though in the drawing, form and therefore space are predominant, whereas in handwriting, movement and hence time take the lead. Thus, in the interpretation of drawings, the accent lies more heavily on the overall impression of the content than on the process by which it was created. Bindl gave her attention to five aspects in particular: (1) spatial arrangements of symbolic significance (e.g., high versus low, right versus left); (2) symbolism of the drawing's elementary components (e.g., point and line, vertical and horizontal, circle and cross); (3) symbolism of imagery in the form of the human body; (4) symbolism of color; and (5) the feeling content of the whole (e.g., as revealed in a figure's facial expression). Bindl illustrates her interpretive approach by commenting in detail on 49 of her subjects' scribblings and drawings.

In seeking for the most meaningful way to conceptualize the developmental changes that she saw reflected in these graphic expressions, Bindl turned to Otto's description of the numinous consciousness. Revealing itself in the course of development, she says, is the intensely dynamic and ever-shifting relation of *tremendum* and *fascinans*. This relation knows no perfect form and reaches no ultimate developmental stage or stable balance. Even so there is a predictable pattern of change over the course of the first decades of life.

Bindle discerns four major phases in the course of development. In the first phase, of *naive relatedness to the Wholly Other,* which extends approximately to age seven, divinity is experienced in an emotional and personified I–Thou relation free of any signs of incredulity. In the earliest expressions of religious experience, Bindl says, the *tremendum* emerges first and without form. In due time it is joined by and then gives way to the *fascinans,* which imagination seeks to fathom in a delightful profusion of magical imagery.

In the second phase, of *decline in spontaneous experience of the numinous,* which may announce itself as early as the sixth year, the compelling reality of the Wholly Other gradually fades for the child. As reason progressively displaces fantasy, unreserved surrender to the *mysterium* in an extravagance of feeling gives way to a more rational and selfish interestedness.

The changes of puberty inaugurate the third phase, of *narcissistic reversion toward one's own self,* a time not only of crisis but also of religious need. With the naive and unselfconscious unity of the child's world shattered, this stage is marked by a critical and objectifying stance. What was once taken as natural and a matter of course now becomes problematical. The great danger of this phase, says Bindl, is an inward

---

[10] Handwriting itself has been thought to provide clues to piety. Klages (1927) suggests that an upward prolongation of the final stroke of a word is common in the handwriting of persons who are in some sense religious. This "religious curve" is found most frequently, he claims, in the script of ministers. Unfortunately for Klages's hypothesis, this distinctive upward curve is hardly to be found at all in the handwriting samples of 32 Roman Catholic saints that Girolamo Moretti (1952) analyzed blind for traits of intelligence and character. Nor does it appear in more than one of the seven cases, drawn from a much larger number, that Hans Jacoby (1939) cites in his graphological study of the changes of character that result from religious conversion. Jacoby features handwriting samples that illustrate how variable, dramatic, and prolonged the dynamic course of religious change can be, initiating in turn both disturbing and healing processes. The most specifically religious graphological indicator for Jacoby is also a spatial one, in this instance the relative proportion of "uncovered writing space," the amount of room left between words and lines. In these "creative pauses and intervals," he says, "the super-personal can make itself heard." We should note that the prominent graphologist employed by Cantril, Rand, and Allport (1933) to test whether personal interests can be judged from handwriting was entirely unsuccessful in estimating college students' religious scores on the Allport–Vernon–Lindzey Study of Values.

reversion that transforms dialogue into monologue, the I into its own Thou. Others, including the Wholly Other, exist only as aspects of one's own experience. On balance, however, it is only by becoming uprooted and exiled from the paradise of naive faith, says Bindl, that the adolescent will become an individual "who once and for all stands solitary and free before his God" (p. 279).

In the final phase, of a *consciously-striven-for relation to transcendence*, the distant yet accessible Wholly Other that appears spontaneously in the child's experience becomes the transcendent Thou, to which relation, consciously desired out of the depths of existence, is actively sought. Freed from the bonds of narcissistic demands, the imagination strives once more to make of the transcendent Thou a living presence, felt predominantly in the form of religious longing.

Much like Ernst Rolffs (1938), who in a work dedicated to Otto compares the role of imagination in religion to that of an induction coil,[11] Bindl concludes that the formation of religious images is an essential means by which religious experience is clarified and deepened, promoting and intensifying thereby the process of becoming. In the freedom of mind that is uniquely attained by the act of imagining, says American phenomenologist Edward Casey (1976), we come to know what is *possible* in human experience. Imagining, he says, is mind in the process of completing itself. Rolffs ventures further: "What the imagination creates is no phantom: its creation is the mirror image of the Creator, the expression and symbol of eternal truth" (p. 190).

EVALUATION OF THE GERMAN DESCRIPTIVE APPROACH

Whereas the phenomenological–interpretive perspective has long been at home in the German psychological literature, it is either ignored or viewed with suspicion by most American psychologists. Judging from how it is represented in standard textbooks, it is also widely misunderstood. It may therefore be helpful to address the most common misgivings regarding phenomenology and typology before we evaluate their application to the study of religion. To the degree that James and Pratt approach religion descriptively, this evaluation may be applied to their work as well.

MISGIVINGS REGARDING THE METHODS THEMSELVES

Some Questions about Phenomenology

Phenomenology's critics frequently raise the following questions. The answers summarize the responses that phenomenologists have made to them in one context or another.

Is not phenomenology a return to naive introspection, whose claims to self-knowledge have been refuted by modern COGNITIVE PSYCHOLOGY? Phenomenology, it is true, begins whenever possible with the investigator's own experience. Unlike traditional introspection, however, it does not limit itself to what is given "in the mind." Rejecting the split between subject and object that has haunted Western thought since Descartes, phenomenologists underscore the *intentional* character of all experience.

---

[11] An induction coil is a device for increasing the voltage of an electric current.

The focus is not on "the contents of one's mind" but on the *objects of experience*, whether they be "subjective" images or feeling states or "objective" events in the outer world.

But what of the evidence from cognitive psychology that research subjects cannot accurately represent how they deal with the objects of their experience (Flanagan, 1984, pp. 192–198)? From the phenomenological perspective, these experiments are flawed in at least two respects. First, the subjects are naive observers untrained in phenomenological description; and second, the experimenters evaluate their introspective reports in terms borrowed uncritically from other domains. Neither the experimenters nor the subjects, it appears, were alert to the presuppositions that shaped their judgments. A proper examination of the implicit assumptions of today's cognitive psychologists, says Carl Graumann (1988, p. 42), would yield a list both colorful and depressing.

By taking experience as its object, does not phenomenology limit itself to merely subjective or private phenomena? The term *subjective* is used here in a pejorative sense, suggesting uncritical, unverifiable, and thus unscientific observation of idiosyncratic inner events. Phenomenologists object to such a usage on several grounds. The objects of our experience, they would remind their critics, frequently come to us, as it were, from the outside. Thus phenomenology is hardly limited to inner events. Moreover, although phenomenology is directed to experience as it is naively apprehended, phenomenological description does not consist of "merely subjective" reports of naive observers. To the contrary, it requires "a considerable degree of aptitude, training, and conscientious self-criticism" (Spiegelberg, 1965, p. 666). Furthermore, the dogmatic assumption that experience is "private" and cannot be shared is belied by considerable evidence. It would be "preposterous and self-defeating," says Spiegelberg, to assume that any particular phenomenon is utterly private before we have checked to see whether it is shared by others. "Even merely private phenomena," he adds, "are facts which we have no business to ignore. A science which refuses to take account of them as such is guilty of suppressing evidence and will end with a truncated universe" (p. 668).

The phenomenologists acknowledge that their approach is particularly demanding, and that it is seductively attractive to certain unprepared minds. The temptation to use its method "purely subjectively or capriciously," says Albert Wellek (1957, p. 284), "seems to be greater and more acute in phenomenology than in most other fields." Yet, he adds, objective methods can also be misused, as frequently happens when a scale is assumed to be valid without sufficient evidence.

Is not phenomenology limited in any case to conscious experience, thus foreclosing to it the layers explored by the depth psychologies? "To be conscious and to be unconscious are two complementary modes of the ontological structure . . . of every human being," writes psychiatrist Henri Ey (1968, p. xix), who employs phenomenology to illuminate the relation between these two conflicting modes. Although the unconscious content postulated by the psychoanalysts is naturally unavailable for direct phenomenological study, Ey, Ricoeur, and others demonstrate that phenomenology can contribute vitally to a discussion of consciousness itself and also provide new perspectives on theories of the unconscious and its potential for disclosure. Some phenomenologists, it is true, consider "the unconscious" to be a regrettable reification, but all would surely agree with Ricoeur (1965, p. 393) that "the lived meaning of a behavior extends beyond its representation in conscious awareness," and that this meaning is a proper object for phenomenological study.

By what means do the phenomenologists validate their conclusions? Is not one interpretation as good as another? Like every other area of research, phenomenology has a community of scholars who continually read and evaluate each other's work. More fundamental than this public mode of verification, however, is a strikingly immediate and personal one. When the phenomenologist attains a new insight, the "shock" of understanding—the sense of immediate illumination—is itself a form of validation, though hardly an infallible one. If the resulting description is adequate, its readers should experience this illumination in turn. Wilfred Smith (1971, p. 17) suggests yet another validating criterion: the capacity of an individual's interpretation to be "existentially appropriated" by those to whom it applies.

The immediate goal of phenomenology, it is said, is not the accumulation of an inventory of verified facts but an enlarging and deepening of the realm of immediate experience—of the world, of ourselves, and of meanings and values (Spiegelberg, 1975, pp. 60–61). Thus "verification" would consist in the felt or observed expansion of the experiential horizon, in oneself or in others. Just as that awareness is always relative and partial, so any interpretation of experience is only approximate. The quest for understanding is a never-ending one, requiring a continual interplay between observation and reflection (Graumann, 1988).

On the Value of Typology

According to the interpretive psychologists, understanding the experience of others can be advanced by the formation of types. The disposition to think of people in terms of a simple typology goes back at least to Hippocrates. In this book we have encountered a variety of such schemata, including the types empirically derived from the Intrinsic, Extrinsic, and Quest scales as well as the typologies of Jung, James, Heiler, and Spranger. Despite its long history, many contemporary psychologists have doubts about the typological approach. Two major criticisms have been made. First, to some critics the lack of convergence among these typological systems suggests that they tell us more about the interests and values of their authors than about people in general. Second, most people cannot be sorted into the discontinuous categories of a typology; the facts of personality are said to require instead a system of continuous trait dimensions (Allport, 1961).

These criticisms are in certain respects well taken, especially when typologies are used for classifying individuals. It should be remembered, however, that some typologies—notably Spranger's—are not intended for such purposes. Rather, these "ideal" types were developed as schemata for discerning fundamental patterns that recur in individual lives. Unlike a system of traits, they allow us to represent the holistic and dynamic character of human personality. As Rudolf Arnheim (1969, p. 174) reminds us, types are abstractions designed to aid thinking about structural properties, not containers intended for identifying and sorting individuals. Just as different systems of thought can be equally interesting and helpful, so too can different typologies.

THE DESCRIPTIVE APPROACH TO RELIGION

Given the sympathy and even reverence with which the phenomenological–interpretive view has been applied to religion by such "insiders" as Otto, Heiler, and Spranger, it is not surprising that it has been well received in the religious community. Its exponents are highly regarded not simply for the depth of their piety but for the essential new insights they give into the nature of religion. Otto, for example, is to Gifford lecturer Charles Campbell (1957, p. 327) "by a wide margin the most illuminating religious thinker of modern times." "No one," writes John Moore (1938, p. 84), "has been more successful than [Otto] in describing and analyzing certain of the subtle and manifold kinds of feelings which characterize the religious life." Edmund Husserl, who was deeply moved by Otto's *The Idea of the Holy*, considered the descriptive and analytic portions of the book to be a true beginning for a phenomenology of the religious. For the psychology of religion in particular, says German theologian Ulrich Mann (1973, p. 37), it would be impossible to overestimate the value of this work. The continuing influence of Otto's schema is clearly evident in the writings of Bolley, Pöll, Thun, and Bindl, all of whom are cited in this chapter, but earlier we saw it in the psychoanalytic work of Weston La Barre and especially in the analytical psychology of C. G. Jung. Whether or not Otto overgeneralized his analysis and thus overlooked other important forms of religion, as some of his critics say, he has clearly and profoundly affected generations of scholars.

Spranger's contributions, too, were in their own way revolutionary. According to Erich Eichele (1928, p. 22), Spranger more than anyone else helped to bring about a radical change in psychology. Until the appearance in 1924 of Spranger's book on adolescence, this momentous stage of development was largely ignored in German circles. Moreover, says Eichele, Spranger's emphasis on understanding the structural totality formed by the individual provided a new direction in psychological science as well as new methods for studying the inner life. Eichele's own classic investigation of adolescent piety is explicitly grounded in Spranger's methodological approach.

Various aspects of Spranger's work have guided the research of other scholars. Heinrich Vorwahl (1933), for example, found in Spranger's three stages of adolescent piety a valuable schema for organizing the spontaneous remarks about religious attitudes and background appearing in a collection of adolescent self-histories. Gottfried Ewald (1932) was challenged to search for the physiological underpinnings of Spranger's six types. The eminent Dutch phenomenologist of religion, Gerardus van der Leeuw (1926, 1928, 1933), found in Spranger's thought important foundational elements for his own typological efforts. In America and Great Britain, where his influence is less apparent, Spranger is best known for inspiring the Allport–Vernon–Lindzey Study of Values, which we will encounter again in the next chapter. There we will review findings that provide unanticipated support for Spranger's "dialectic of the religious sphere." In the German literature, Spranger's importance remains evident to this day, most obviously in the publishing of his collected works but in secondary sources as well (e.g., Müller-Pozzi, 1979; Reich, 1990).

Psychologists of religion outside of the phenomenological–interpretive tradition, on the other hand, seem ambivalent at best about its intuitive approach. Although Otto in particular is still frequently cited in passing, the perspective is otherwise largely ignored. Occasional allusions suggest why. Its mode of thought is considered too speculative, and its methods, too subjective or ill defined. Moreover, its appreciative, nonreductionistic attitude seems to foreclose any critical judgment or any program for change. Some undoubtedly wonder whether this "merely descriptive" approach is psychology at all.

Psychology of religion it is, however, at least in the eyes of those sympathetic to its objectives. Even its proponents, however, have unsettled questions, especially regarding method. The debate was at its liveliest during the heyday of the Dorpat school, which was both source and object of much criticism. A brief review of this debate will clarify some of the basic issues.

Which Method Is Best?

Contrasting their approach with Spranger's system of abstract types, members of the Dorpat school argued that experimental introspection made possible a faithful and complete "photography of the soul." The use of this "microscopic" technique, Girgensohn (1923b, p. 9) maintained, allows us to make the subtlest of distinctions in the highest and deepest aspects of human existence without losing sight of their living quality. "Macroscopic" approaches such as Spranger's, though acknowledged as sources of insight, seemed to the Dorpat school's proponents to incorporate facts with far less exactness and thus to be much less strictly empirical. Spontaneous expressions of piety, on which macroscopic efforts usually rely, were thought to allow only in the most exceptional instances a direct and undistorted view of the original experience in all its complexity (Raitz von Frentz, 1925).

The response to Girgensohn's work was distinctly mixed. Some scholars viewed it as a masterful achievement of unparalleled significance, the starting point and foundation for all future work in the psychology of religion. Others were decidedly less enthusiastic. Perhaps the most negative of all was Oskar Pfister (1922), who declared Girgensohn's now-classic book to be a work of "truly amazing superficiality"—tedious in the laying of the psychological foundations, narrowly bounded in the range of phenomena investigated, and impoverished in its conclusions and implications. It confirmed his conviction, he says, that the greatest enemy of the psychology of religion is the "straining of gnats and swallowing of camels."[12] In Pfister's view, Girgensohn should instead have undertaken a genetic study of religious experience, tracing its development in the context of individual life histories, especially of persons suffering from religious and sexual abnormalities. Only by this means, he says, can the psychology of religion meet "the burning need to help human beings with psychic inhibitions" (pp. 374, 396).

Among those who accepted Girgensohn's rather different agenda—the essentially descriptive task of discerning the structural elements of religious experience in normal, educated, and articulate adults—criticisms were more moderate. The principal objections were these.

1. Religious experience cannot be studied in the laboratory; what Girgensohn's observers reported were secondary or artificially created fragments of minor significance at best.
2. Girgensohn's studies were neither "experimental" nor "exact," according to ordinary scientific usage of these terms.
3. In any event, his techniques were unnecessarily elaborate and certainly not essential.
4. Girgensohn's "experimental" approach is limited in application to ordinary persons; it cannot be used to study the more informative great personalities in the history of the religious traditions.
5. Girgensohn employed too few observers, or observers of too limited a range of personal characteristics (Wulff, 1985a).

---

[12] Pfister is referring here to the words of Jesus in Matthew 23:24. Jesus chastises the hypocritical scribes and Pharisees for being "blind guides, straining out the gnat and swallowing the camel!" While attending to such trivial matters as the tithing of spices, they neglected the weightier ones of "the law, justice and mercy and faith."

Although Girgensohn eventually did acknowledge that his quest for exactness may have excluded essential matters from his research, he and his associates unequivocally reaffirmed the value of "microscopic observations" for discerning the nuances supposedly overlooked by macroscopic methods. They argued that their procedures had revealed deep and essential aspects of their subjects' religious lives. Though certainly not as dramatic as full-scale encounters with divinity, the experiences they evoked seemed to them genuine and valuable. In contrast, the work of Heiler (1918)—who rejected the experimental approach as "a feelingless anatomy of the religious psyche" (p. vi)—was criticized for relying on material once or even twice removed from the original experience (Gruehn, 1924, p. 67).

In defending his use of the term *experimental,* Girgensohn (1921, p. 675) defines experiment as "an artificial intervention in the natural course of events for the purpose of more exact observation and better command of the phenomenon." As we noted in Chapter 5, such a usage is historically permissible but today confusing. Although its proponents may not have thought so, the Dorpat approach is much more akin to the phenomenological method than to the techniques of contemporary experimental psychology.

The Dorpat tradition shows other similarities to phenomenology. Girgensohn had pointed out that every attitude of the ego requires an object—the phenomenological principle of intentionality. The reliance of these researchers on a few well-trained subjects, studied in depth, is also consonant with the phenomenological method. Most striking of all is the convergence of Girgensohn's conclusions with those of Scheler and Gründler in their studies of the religious act, which were published at virtually the same time as Girgensohn's much larger work. Should we conclude that the elaborate "experimental" procedures of the Dorpat school are unnecessary? Gruehn (1930, p. 726) acknowledges the value of Scheler's exceptionally well-developed gift of intuitive observation but argues that so individual a capacity can never attain the rank of a scientific method. Pointedly observing the lack of agreement in the findings of those employing intuitive methods, Gruehn maintains that the experimental psychology of religion alone offers a basis for decisively establishing the validity of phenomenologically derived results.

Although Gruehn seems unnecessarily dogmatic in this instance, he makes a point that others have also emphasized. Interpretive understanding, he says, is dependent on intellectual and personal qualities that are relatively rare. Many of these prerequisites can be patiently acquired, through years of study and wide experience. It is also said that certain essential qualities of personality simply cannot be learned. Moreover, for those who are drawn to the "openness" of this approach and its "fidelity to experience," there is the danger of getting lost in a "wayward impressionism" or "formless wonder" (Ermarth, 1978, p. 348). Hence it is perhaps not surprising that many observers dismiss interpretive psychology as "fuzzy-minded."

The Continuing Challenge of More Adequate Description

Judging from the content of recent issues of the *Archiv für Religionspsychologie,* the phenomenological–interpretive approach has now been eclipsed in the German literature by other perspectives, especially those of Freud and Jung. The depth—and objective—psychologies seem to be in ascendance elsewhere as well, though occasional works appear that are explicitly phenomenological (e.g., Bradford, 1984; Sneck, 1981; see Wulff, 1995b). These trends reflect the widely felt sentiment that what the psychology of religion needs most is not renewed emphasis on description but a more adequate theoretical base.

Swiss psychologist Willy Canziani (1959, p. 415) states that to limit the psychology of religion to a descriptive science, as Gruehn would have us do, would be to leave its work half done. Every psychology of religion begins with "empirical" description, he says, but it must eventually proceed to the task of theoretical interpretation. Only then will the science be complete. It is with the addition of the theoretical-interpretive aspect, he says, that the psychology of religion at last becomes genuinely useful, especially for pastoral counseling.

Most contemporary psychologists of religion would undoubtedly agree with Canziani's position. The phenomenologist, however, would want to emphasize that the critically important work of description must first be properly carried out. Those laudable few who propose to integrate phenomenological description into a more conventional psychology should be certain they understand the radical critique demanded by any genuine phenomenology, which will brook no assimilation to a narrowly or dogmatically conceived science. In particular, the exceptional openness to a phenomenon that is necessary for adequate description requires setting aside— at least temporarily and as completely as possible—all theoretical or interpretive presuppositions. As Erwin Goodenough (1965, p. xi) has put it, "The business of the 'psychology of religion' is not to fit religious experiences into the pigeonholes of Freud or Jung or into the categories of *Gestalt* or stimulus–response or any other, but rather to see what the data of religious experience themselves suggest." No theory will suffice, the phenomenologists insist, until that demanding task is adequately carried out.

13

THE AMERICAN HUMANISTIC SYNTHESIS

*T*he humanistic tradition, it should now be apparent, has a much longer past than many have suspected. Humanistic trends have been evident in the psychology of religion virtually from its beginnings. In a work of the eminent Danish psychologist and philosopher Harald Höffding (1901), which antedates James's *Varieties* by a year, we find, for example, an unusually sensitive analysis of the subtleties of the religious life. Famous for his "axiom of the conservation of value," said to express the fundamental tendency of all religious traditions, Höffding maintains that when religion is genuine and original, "All the elements of psychical life work together with an energy and harmony which is hardly to be found within any other sphere" (pp. 95–96). According to his "principle of personality," which emphasizes that individual personalities are centers of both experience and evaluation, individual differences are to be revered and fostered as realizations of the richness of existence. Höffding's insightful analysis of religious experience includes a typology of personal differences that anticipates James's more famous classification. A methodological pluralist who counted autobiographies among the psychology of religion's most instructive materials, Höffding demonstrates in this and other works what long experience and a well-furnished mind can yield from the liberal humanist's armchair.

HUMANISTIC ELEMENTS IN THE EARLY AMERICAN EMPIRICISTS

American psychologists of religion more or less contemporary to James also give expression to certain elements of the humanistic outlook in psychology. Edwin Starbuck is a case in point. The source of some of James's documents, Starbuck (1899) carried out his own research with the hope that it would ultimately help to foster growth toward maturity in the moral and religious spheres. Toward that end, he emphasizes the factor of individual differences as well as the differing capabilities and needs of each stage along the way. Although his data suggested an association between religious awakening and the changes of puberty, he insisted that "Religion has not been nourished from a single root, but that, on the contrary, it has many sources" (p. 403). A "birthright" member of the Religious Society of Friends who retained for life the Quaker spirit though not the practice (Booth, 1981), Starbuck (1937) wrote as one who knew at first hand the mystical "sense of an interfusing Presence" (p. 205).

We may add other candidates for the roster of early American humanists headed by James and Pratt. Unlike Starbuck, George Coe was doubtful about the value of mystical experience; certainly it was not an element in his own life. But religion itself—which he defines, in the spirit of Höffding, as the completing, unifying, and conserving of values—he considered life's most important undertaking. Coe's view was both personal and social. Persons, he said, are the supreme reality, and life's meaning adheres in social relations. The functional and genetic psychology he advocated was above all "a psychology of self-realizations" that characteristically concerned itself with the experience of values (Coe, 1916, pp. 30–31). Perceiving the ethical will as the center of religion, Coe became increasingly concerned in his later years with religion's ambiguous relation to the social, economic, and political factors that either distort or suppress personality in Western culture (Coe, 1937, 1943).

Whereas Coe was most critical of the practices of a capitalistic society, James Leuba concentrated on the churches themselves. Famous for the unseemly enthusiasm with which he documented the "momentous evils" of the religious traditions as well as the decline of belief among eminent scientists, Leuba was a highly competent scholar whose writings on the psychology of religion commanded worldwide attention. He was a humanist in the philosophic sense principally, for he denied the existence of a mysterious realm of supernatural beings and events, whereas he affirmed, as the deepest and most significant factor of human nature, the presence of an urge toward perfection, "to make all things better and to realize moral ideals" (1950, p. 146). Leuba's (1950) last, posthumously published book is a program for transforming the churches into more effective instruments for fostering human ideals and preserving the integrity of the individual.

Viewed from the perspective of twentieth-century behaviorism, Starbuck, Coe, and Leuba are unequivocally humanists, for they postulate positive inborn potentialities, emphasize the importance and uniqueness of the individual, and recognize and seek to promote spiritual needs and values. From a European perspective, however, what is striking about these American scholars is their commitment to the new empirical methods of increasingly objective scientific research. Coe (1916, p. 55) may seem to be an exception, for he warns his readers against taking the notion of method too seriously. Höffding's noteworthy analysis of religious experience, he observes, was the result of no clearly defined techniques. Yet Coe was hopeful with the others that the new science of psychology and its methods would deepen our understanding of the religious life. On the Continent, it was widely thought that the scientific principles and methods embraced by the Americans were not only inadequate for comprehending religion but also a potential threat to its very life. A phenomenon conceived in humanistic terms, they argued, requires methods that are humanistic in turn (Faber, 1913; Jelke, 1948; Koepp, 1920; Wobbermin, 1928).

In this final chapter on the humanistic movement, we will examine the work of three major American contributors: Gordon Allport, Erich Fromm, and Abraham Maslow. We will also consider two existential thinkers—Rollo May and Viktor Frankl—who, though less influential, have attained a measure of prominence in the American literature. Along the way, transpersonal psychology is also discussed.

As will become apparent when we examine the empirical research that these think-ers have inspired, some American humanists still regard objective research methods as the ideal means for establishing the validity of their generalizations about human experience.

GORDON ALLPORT AND THE RELIGIOUS SENTIMENT

The tension between humanistic conception and rigorous science is evident in the work of Gordon Allport (1897–1967), the most broadly influential contributor since James and Pratt to the American humanistic psychology of religion. Reared in a Midwestern home "marked by plain Protestant piety and hard work" and by a mother who "brought to her [four] sons an eager sense of philosophical questing and the importance of searching for ultimate religious answers," Allport became, as a Harvard professor, a world figure in personality and social psychology (Allport, 1967, p. 379). As a leading authority in these fields and as an occasional writer on human piety and its role in the economy of the personality, Allport lent to the American psychology of religion not only a fund of distinctive principles but also a new measure of visibility and prestige. It is doubtless appropriate that Grønbaek (1974) dates the postwar revival of the field worldwide with the publication of Allport's modest but influential book, *The Individual and His Religion* (1950).

Full-Bodied Persons and Rigorous Science

Evident in this work no less than in Allport's other writings is a dual commitment: to a faithful understanding of the complexities of personal and social existence, on the one hand, and to orthodox principles of scientific research, on the other. A devout Episcopalian and a periodic contributor over many years to the daily worship service at Harvard's Appleton Chapel, Allport (1978) knew at first hand the fruits of a life permeated with a sense of value and mystery. Although a lifelong acade-mician, he focused much of his scholarly effort on urgent, real-world problems such as wartime rumor and intergroup prejudice. Ever the critic of any one-sided or dogmatic outlook and himself a gently persuasive advocate of an open-minded and ECLECTIC psychology, Allport also demonstrated a surprising allegiance to the causal and quantitative model of science that measures success in terms of predic-tion and control. Although he was America's most vocal proponent of IDIOGRAPHIC

Gordon Allport

or individual-centered research techniques, when Allport undertook studies of his own, paradoxically, he most often chose NOMOTHETIC methods aimed at establishing general laws.

Themes from Stern and Spranger: Allport's famous distinction between idiographic and nomothetic methods, which he adopted from the German philosopher Wilhelm Windelband (1848–1915), was one of the fruits of his profoundly stimulating postdoctoral year in Germany. Indeed, most of the themes that set Allport apart from the mainstream of American psychology—the holistic emphases on the self, personal values, and a philosophy of life, for example, or the principle of intentionality and the accent on conscious forces—were derived from this year of study abroad. Allport was particularly influenced by his teachers William Stern and Eduard Spranger, but he rejected the implications of their radical critique of explanatory psychology, advocating instead the ideal of an inclusive and systematic eclecticism (Allport, 1937, 1964, 1967; Evans, 1971). Although he did not himself approximate that ideal and even wondered if its achievement was possible, more than anyone else he represents the effort to synthesize European and American views.

The Influence of James: Among his American sources, the pervasive influence of William James is unmistakable, not only in Allport's tentative and pluralistic outlook but especially in his work on religion. Much like his predecessor, Allport chose as his central theme the endless diversity of individual forms in which human piety appears. This variegation, as both Allport and James maintained, disallows any simple accounting of piety's origins, and for both it underscores the solitariness of religious faith. James and Allport also agreed that to become acquainted with this diversity, personal documents are of supreme value. The religious life, concluded Allport (1942, p. 38) after praising the *Varieties,* "has never been studied with even partial adequacy by any [other] means." Finally, both were convinced that in the life economy of many individuals, religion plays a positive, central role.

In other respects, Allport's work diverges fundamentally from James. In spite of his enthusiasm for personal documents, Allport used them infrequently and only with great caution. Like the great majority of American psychologists today, he apparently preferred to ground his reflections in representative samples, standardized questionnaires, and statistical analysis. Allport departed from James, too, in emphasizing the cognitive side of religion. Whereas James thought that the heart of the matter lies in the hidden recesses of feeling, Allport accented the more accessible "conceptual objects and principles" that provide the individual with orientation and meaning. James's effort to assess religion's potential helpfulness in meeting the difficulties of life is displaced in Allport's work by an interest in the dynamic qualities of the "religious sentiment" itself, as they are illuminated by principles of personality functioning and development. In contrast, then, to James's uncommon "experts," individually summoned to testify on behalf of religion at its deepest and best, stands Allport's mass of anonymous students and ordinary church members, who give voice to religious faith in its everyday forms (Allport, Gillespie, and Young, 1948; Gillespie and Allport, 1955; Allport and Ross, 1967).

Yet, in his own way, Allport, too, was a defender of religious faith. On the one hand, he criticized his fellow psychologists for the shallowness and youthful arrogance that he said was evident in their neglect of religion and such related matters as will, conscience, subjective values, and the self (Allport, 1948). On the other hand, he tried to make plain in his own writings "the autonomous and unifying character of the religious sentiment in personality and the essential dependence of all human life upon faith'' (p. 112). Recognizing no less than James that piety takes higher and lower forms, Allport made a lasting contribution to their differentiation by setting forth a model of the mature religious sentiment. This model, derived from his theory of personality, forms the core of his contribution to the humanistic psychology of religion.

The Religious Sentiment in the Developing Individual

Allport (1950) uses the term *sentiment* to designate a relatively stable component of personality that combines affective and cognitive factors and is directed toward some definable object of value (p. 55). A sentiment is ordinarily distinguished in terms of an easily specified object, but for the more abstract religious sentiment, the matter of definition is not so simple. True to his emphasis on individuality, Allport rejects any single formula—say, of Schleiermacher, Otto, or Freud—as insufficient. Rather, he defines the religious sentiment as ''a comprehensive attitude whose function it is to relate the individual meaningfully to the whole of Being'' (Allport, 1955, p. 94). Although experience disposes the religious sentiment to respond to widely varying conceptual objects, these objects will by definition be of ultimate importance to the individual, who regards them as related to enduring or central aspects of reality (1950, p. 56).

A Classic Study of Student Piety: Allport retraces the now-familiar course of development of the religious sentiment through the years of childhood and adolescence. He dwells on his own findings with Harvard and Radcliffe students, whose questionnaire replies again reveal the importance of religious upbringing for a lasting religious orientation. Personal influences, chiefly those of the parents, were most often cited as underlying their sense of religious need, though a variety of other factors were reported to play a role as well. Among the 70 percent who claimed to have such a need, dissatisfaction with institutional religion was widespread and most of them deviated from theological orthodoxy. Despite this discontent, a majority still maintained some kind of traditional religious practice, including some form of prayer (Allport, Gillespie, and Young, 1948).

Allport's famous study was soon replicated at a variety of educational institutions in the United States and abroad, yielding largely similar results (e.g., see Vinacke, Eindhoven, and Engle, 1949; Wells, 1962; Zunini, 1954). Twenty years after the initial study, Allport himself repeated it at Harvard, in cooperation with doctoral student Dean Hoge. By 1966, their data clearly showed that religious beliefs among Harvard and Radcliffe students had become more liberal, traditional religious practices had declined, and religious commitment was less common. Surprisingly, these changes were more marked among the Radcliffe women, who this time proved to be less conservative and committed than the Harvard men (Eddy, 1968). Comparable data gathered at about the same time at Clark University showed similar trends overall, though the women at Clark were somewhat more favorable toward religion than those at Radcliffe. Once again, religious upbringing was found to be the factor most strongly associated with positive religious attitudes (Jones, 1970).

Attributes of the Mature Religious Sentiment

As persons on the threshold of the ''irreligious twenties,'' college students are unlikely, of course, to embody the mature religious sentiment. Yet because a person's religious views are ordinarily regarded as a private matter and are therefore less subject to the environmental pressures that force maturity in other respects, we cannot be confident of finding religious maturity in adults of any age. Indeed, Allport (1950) concludes that "In probably no [other] region of personality do we find so many residues of childhood as in the religious attitudes of adults" (p. 52). Moreover, because it is assigned the task of synthesizing all that is "central in the nature of things," the religious sentiment, more than any other, is destined in all lives falling short of religious genius to remain less than perfectly consistent and complete. Thus to delineate the qualities of the mature religious sentiment, Allport (1950, 1978) relies on armchair reflection rather than replies to questionnaires. According to his analysis, the mature sentiment is (1) well differentiated, (2) dynamic though derivative, (3) consistently directive, (4) comprehensive, (5) integral, and (6) fundamentally heuristic.

Well Differentiated: With increasing differentiation, a religious sentiment becomes richer and more complex, encompassing a multiplicity of elements that together form a pattern of intricate design. Articulation of the sentiment's parts begins in late childhood and adolescence, when the capacity for critical reflection gives the individual perspective on the oversimplified and secondhand faith of the earliest years. Over time, the gradually amended and reorganized sentiment embraces and orders an ever-larger number of objects, issues, and interests. Allport acknowledges the possibility that, as some traditions claim, this process may culminate in the overwhelming sense of wholeness that constitutes mystical experience. Yet these transient moments of union, he adds, are not themselves a token of maturity.

Dynamic Though Derivative: According to Allport's second criterion, a religious sentiment is mature in proportion to the autonomy of its motives. Granting that organic desires, especially when heightened by deprivation or threat, play a significant role in the course of religious development, Allport maintains nonetheless that the mature sentiment is distinguished by having largely broken free of these desires, establishing itself as a force in its own right.

Allport was not the first to point out the possibility for such transformation of motives. Among psychologists of religion, for example, Coe (1916, p. 217) suggests that the evolution of mental functions leads to genuinely new wants in the species as a whole, and Edward Schaub (1926) writes that

> even though conscious processes may in their beginnings be . . . subservient to the demands of life, they in time win their emancipation and become ends in themselves, masters no less truly than servants. They develop along autonomous lines, under the guidance of self-critical reason and consciously evaluated norms. They initiate novel insights and values, besides conserving those attested in the past (pp. 128–129).

Governing this process of emancipation, says Allport, is the principle of FUNCTIONAL AUTONOMY, which, once he had named it, he elaborated as a foundation stone in his theory of personality.

The capacity of mature religious faith to lift persons above the realm of petty self-interest and even to transform their lives is a consequence, says Allport, of its functional autonomy. The "push" of childhood needs gives way to the "pull" of adult intentions, the future-oriented seeking of some value or goal. The diverse forms of religious intention may best be summed up, Allport suggests, in Spranger's notion of a longing for total harmony, the mystical goal of oneness. Yet Allport himself preferred to keep the individual differences that characterize the religious sentiment well in sight. Dynamically independent, the mature sentiment is neither fanatic nor compulsive. Thus free of the unconscious, defensive qualities of the unreflective and undifferentiated sentiment, it may retain its fervor, he says, as long as it preserves its central position among the systems composing the personality.

Consistently Directive: The mature sentiment is consistent in its moral consequences. It may even be a prerequisite, Allport (1950) thinks, for the formation of a conscience with high ethical standards. When such standards survive independently of a religious outlook, as often seems to be true among college students, Allport suspects that they are drawing on the momentum of the previous generation's faith. How long, he asks, can that momentum last? "Ethical standards are difficult to sustain without idealism; and idealism is difficult to sustain without a myth of Being" (p. 66). Allport optimistically observes that the religious sentiment comes forth anew in each generation, yielding a fresh reserve of moral power.

Comprehensive: The mature personality, Allport (1937) had earlier argued, requires a unifying philosophy of life, a frame of reference that brings the diverse elements of human experience into some kind of order and provides a sense of purpose. Secular philosophies of various sorts have often served these needs, but none of them is as comprehensive and thus as adequate as a religious outlook, he says. Only religion seeks to encompass the whole of existence. Meditation, Allport (1978, p. 72) observes, begins with a focus on a person's own circumstances, but it often proceeds by placing these particulars in the framework of the whole. "When one is genuinely thinking of the whole, the embracing context of his life, one is being purely religious." The individual who seeks the most comprehensive possible outlook, he adds, is also likely to be tolerant, for such a person recognizes that no single life embraces the whole of truth. Tolerance is presumably also a by-product of another trend in the mature sentiment, the joining of deeply solitary personal faith to social living (1950, p. 69; 1978, p. 60).

Integral: For the mature individual, the religious sentiment is not only differentiated and comprehensive but also integral; its pattern forms a harmonious whole. Although any consistently followed system of values may serve the process of integration, Allport (1937) observes, the religious motive has a twofold advantage. As the most comprehensive of all the sentiments, it "holds everything in place at once, and gives equal meaning to suffering and to joy, to death and to life" (Allport, 1978, p. 21); and, being ever incomplete, it best sustains the constant striving that unifies the personality.

Today, the task of integration is especially difficult, for along with the eternal problem of evil, including the suffering of innocent people, we must now also accommodate the findings of modern science, especially of psychology and psychiatry. In particular, the troubling fact that much of what we do is determined by factors beyond our choosing must be admitted into the religious sentiment. At the same time it must be recognized that what we believe about this matter is itself a factor in establishing the regions in which aspiration and effort may truly make a difference.

Heuristic: Allport's final attribute of the mature religious sentiment is its "essentially HEURISTIC character." In psychology, a heuristic theory is one that, though lacking sufficient empirical support, is still valuable for the vital impetus it gives to therapy or research. For the mature individual, says Allport (1950), religious faith has a similar function, serving as a working hypothesis that generates energy and conserves values. "Religion," he writes, "is chiefly a matter of reaching for more than we can grasp. It is a matter of stretching . . . beyond the knowledge now available to us" (1978, p. 41). Fully aware that the grounds of faith are necessarily uncertain, the mature person optimistically risks the probability of error in order to discover some measure of truth. Tentative at first and assailed by doubt, mature faith gradually finds strength in the successive acts and helpful consequences of a growing commitment. Even if doubt should remain, the mature mind finds enough validation to act wholeheartedly.

Factors Favoring the Mature Religious Sentiment

Are there identifiable conditions that favor the development of a mature religious sentiment? In completing a doctoral dissertation under Allport's guidance at Harvard, Vera French (1947) found some suggestive clues. On the basis of an intensive personality evaluation of 20 Swarthmore College undergraduates and 15 faculty members, French distinguished two groups: one with highly organized "philosophicoreligious sentiments" and a second with less highly organized sentiments. The subjects in both groups were predominantly women.

The highly organized sentiments of the one group were by comparison (1) more elaborately differentiated; (2) less clear-cut and emotionally intense; (3) more ambivalent, recognizing both positive and negative aspects of religion and responding to it with mixed feelings; (4) more hierarchically integrated; and (5) more largely conscious. Because the subject group with highly organized sentiments was made up for the most part of faculty members, it is not surprising that the group showed evidence of a higher level of intelligence, reported more serious interests (including more challenging reading material), took more courses in philosophy and religion, and more often included teachers among the influences on their outlook. They also demonstrated a higher level of organization in their other sentiments, including those for parents and other persons, for institutions and activities, and for sociopolitical issues.

French found evidence, too, of a differential pattern of parental influence. The "highs" tended to feel closer to their mothers than to their fathers during childhood and then to shift to the father as the closer parent in adulthood. The "less highs" more often felt equally close to both parents in childhood. These relational patterns changed very little during the ensuing years. When the "highs" acknowledged a similarity between their own philosophicoreligious sentiments and those of their parents—which they did far less frequently than the "less highs"— it was without exception the father's that theirs were said to resemble. Their fathers, half of whom held degrees beyond the B.A., tended far more than any of the other parents to be thoughtfully critical of religion and thus, like their children, to have more highly organized sentiments.

French could not anticipate, of course, that the exceptional relation of the "highs"—mostly women—to their fathers, as well as the tendency for these fathers to be professionals and more highly educated than their wives, would reappear in later studies of creative women. Revenna Helson (1971, p. 218) describes other aspects of the recurring constellation: "ambivalence toward the mother, the need for autonomy, and the development of strong symbolic interests, a father who seems to have modeled the use of intellectual activity for self-expression and for purpose in life" and with whom the subject had identified. This constellation of factors, perhaps specific to women, does not exhaust the characteristics of personality and background that may play a role in fostering religious maturity, as Allport and French define it. It does serve to remind us, though, that religious maturity does not automatically come with age.

A Study of Values

Though apparently convinced that the religious sentiment, however mature, is best studied by means of personal documents, Allport has exercised far more influence in the psychology of religion through the scales he developed to quantify the religious trends of personality. The first of these scales is a component of his long-lived Study of Values, an assessment device first published in 1931 in collaboration with Philip Vernon and revised in 1951 with the additional help of Gardner Lindzey. The manual appeared in further revisions in 1960 and 1970. *The Eighth Mental Measurements Yearbook* (Buros, 1978) lists more than one thousand references for the Study of Values, placing it among the half-dozen standardized personality tests that, at that time, had been most frequently used for conducting research.

The Test Format: The Study of Values (SV) represents Allport's effort to translate Spranger's six personality types into the format of a standardized questionnaire on values. Unlike the great majority of personality tests, the SV employs IPSATIVE scoring. That is, rather than allowing the subjects to score high or low on all the scales, the item format forces them to rank the six values in the order of their importance. In other words, to score high on one scale, the subject must score lower on another. Thus a person who assigns more points than someone else to the Religious scale is not necessarily more religious in an absolute sense but merely considers this area of value to be of greater relative importance. The individual, not some normative sample, serves as the frame of reference. But because certain well-defined groups tend to agree on the order of their rankings, it is possible to accumulate normative data of a limited kind. Such group differences are featured in the test's manual as evidence of the instrument's validity. As we might predict, engineering students have relatively high Theoretical, Economic, and Political values, ministers score highest on Religious and Social values, and art and design students give first rank to the Aesthetic value. The cumulative evidence for validity was apparently sufficient, in spite of certain psychometric and other shortcomings, to maintain the test's popularity for several decades (see Hogan, 1972).

A relatively valid measure of Spranger's personality types could, of course, serve as a valuable tool for checking the accuracy and generality of his various interpretations. Most users of the SV, however, have employed it for their own purposes, tacitly assuming that it is an essentially valid test representing Spranger's personality types reasonably well. The few investigators who have sought to assess the validity of Spranger's typology itself, by factor-analyzing items from the SV or items similar to them, are less content. From their quite similar results they conclude that the structure of the domain of human values is not well represented by Spranger's typology and that the Study of Values should be revised (Brogden, 1952; Gordon, 1972; Lurie, 1937). They do not consider that the Study of Values may misrepresent Spranger's thought in fundamental ways.

The Character of the SV Religious Scale: The Religious (R) scale in particular has been found to be problematic. Leonard Gordon (1972) points out that it is not Spranger's mystic that we find represented in the scale but rather the Christian conservative. A factor analysis of the scale in conjunction with a slightly modified form of the Aspects of Religious Belief Questionnaire (Allport, Gillespie, and Young, 1948) led Richard Hunt (1968, p. 70) to conclude that "The R scale is primarily measuring an individual's involvement in traditional religious institutions as a means of making life meaningful." Those who score high on it, he allows, may to some degree resemble Spranger's "immanent mystic," but he thinks it would be more accurate to describe them as "activists who approach religion intellectually and rationally and seek to apply it to daily living." Spranger's "transcendental mystic," on the other hand, is almost entirely overlooked.

Douglas Heath (1969) identified two different clusters of items on the R scale, the larger one forming a Traditional Belief Index, which is defined by conventional religious beliefs and values, and the other constituting a Religio-Philosophical Index, which is unrelated to particularistic views. This division of the R scale, which could equally well be inferred from the SV's pattern of factor loadings found by A. J. Wearing and L. B. Brown (1972), allowed Heath to demonstrate that underlying the widely observed decline in religious orthodoxy is a sustained interest in finding some meaning and orientation in life.

Correlates of the Religious Scale: Often we get a clear sense of what a scale is measuring by examining its pattern of correlations with other measures. With the R scale, however, this pattern is inconsistent. Some researchers have found it to be either unrelated or negatively related to authoritarianism as measured by the California F scale and to be positively related to the Lovibond Humanitarian Scale (Nolan, Bram, and Tillman, 1963; Fehr and Heintzelman, 1977). In another study, National Merit Scholarship holders and finalists tended to have higher Religious scores than any comparison group at the same time that they showed—on a preliminary version of the Omnibus Personality Inventory—not only higher intellectual disposition but also lower levels of maladjustment and authoritarianism (Warren and Heist, 1960).

In contrast, other investigators report that R scores are *positively* related to various aspects of the authoritarian personality. It has been found, for example, that high R scores are predictive of social acquiescence (Fisher, 1964; Vaughan and Mangan, 1963) as well as dogmatism (M. B. Jones, 1958; Juan et al., 1974). In a factor-analytic study, items from the R scale loaded on a second-order Punitiveness factor, in the company of militarism, conservatism, nationalism, and misanthropy (Eckhardt, 1969, p. 50).

Empirical Evidence of the Religious Sphere's Dialectic: As Richard Evans (1952) points out, the inconsistent pattern of relations shown by the Study of Values R scale is evidence that this measure does not distinguish between persons who are religious in a humanitarian sense and those whose piety is relatively narrow and ethnocentric. That these trends might be at least partially disentangled by viewing the other SV scales as factors mediating, in effect, the R scale's relation to external variables is suggested by Evans's own data, especially if we view them in the light of the dialectic that Spranger ascribes to the religious sphere. Evans reports that the SV Economic and Political scores showed significant positive correlations with the Levinson–Sanford Anti-Semitism Scale, whereas the Social and Aesthetic scales correlated negatively with it. He also records a slight, negative trend for the Theoretical and Religious scales. Might we suspect, therefore, that the R scale is predominantly a measure of conservative tendencies when the Economic and Political scores are high, and of more liberal, humanitarian tendencies when the Social, Aesthetic, and Theoretical values take the lead?

Gratton Kemp (1960) found evidence that strongly supports this hypothesis. The rank order of the six value means—Religious, Social, Political, Economic, Theoretical, and Aesthetic—found when he first administered the Study of Values to a group of religiously oriented students at a Presbyterian college, bore no relation to the students' dogmatism scores. Six years later, however, Kemp observed a striking shift in value preferences. The R score remained in the first position for students at all levels of dogmatism, but the other values shifted differentially. For the quarter of the subjects classified as open-minded, the Social value continued to be ranked second, the Theoretical value rose from fifth to third place, and the Political and Economic values dropped to fourth and sixth positions respectively. For those in the closed-minded group, the Social value dropped from second to fifth place, the Political value moved up from third to second, and the Economic value changed from fourth to third (see Table 13.1). Thus for the open-minded group the religious value is embedded in social and theoretical values, and for the close-minded group it is qualified by political and economic values.

Independent confirmation of precisely this pattern, as well as of Spranger's typology of values itself, is unexpectedly provided by an interview study of 80 randomly selected members of the Ninety-Sixth United States Congress carried out in 1980 by the staff of the Search Institute in Minneapolis (Benson and Williams, 1982). A cluster analysis of their 13 multiple-item religion scales, each measuring a different variable or theme and none explicitly derived from either Allport's or Spranger's thought, yielded six religious types. Two of these types do not show any defining thematic accent: the *integrated* religionists, who give moderate to considerable emphasis to all the themes, and the *nominal* religionists, who show enthusiasm for almost none. The remaining four, however, seem to illustrate rather well how Spranger's other value orientations can give a peculiar accent to the religious type.

Benson and Williams's *legalistic* religionists, who think of religion in terms of guidance, discipline, and self-restraint, and of God as a lawgiver, reveal the outlook of Spranger's political type. The *self-concerned* religionists, who are distinguished by their emphasis on their relationship to God and the comfort and solace it provides, show the accent of the economic type on what is useful for self-preservation. The *people-concerned* group stood out for its strong concern for others and its commitment to social action—Spranger's social type. Finally, the *nontraditional* religionists are distinguished by the intellectual energy they give to conceptualizing their distant and highly symbolic God, a focus that calls to mind the theoretical type. The correspondence between these two independently derived typologies is confirmed by the voting pattern of Benson and Williams's types. The legalistic and self-concerned religionists (political and economic types) were the most conservative, whereas the people-concerned and the nontraditional religionists (social and theoretical types) were the most liberal (see Table 13.2). The absence of the aesthetic type from Benson and Williams's study, rather than casting doubt on Spran-

Table 13.1 **VALUE RANKINGS IN COLLEGE AND SIX YEARS LATER IN RELATION TO LEVEL OF DOGMATISM**[a]

Open-Minded (*N* = 25)		Closed-Minded (*N* = 25)	
In College	**Six Years Later**	**In College**	**Six Years Later**
1. Religious	1. Religious	1. Religious	1. Religious
2. Social	2. **Social**[b]	2. Social	2. **Political**
3. Political	3. **Theoretical**	3. Political	3. **Economic**
4. Economic	4. Political	4. Economic	4. Theoretical
5. Theoretical	5. Aesthetic	5. Theoretical	5. Social
6. Aesthetic	6. Economic	6. Aesthetic	6. Aesthetic

[a] The 104 subjects, all recruited from a special training program, completed the Rokeach Dogmatism Scale at the time of the follow-up assessment.
[b] The values in boldface suggest the difference in meaning the Religious value has for open-minded and closed-minded individuals.
Source: Based on Table 18.1 in Kemp, 1960, page 339.

Table 13.2 RELIGIOUS TYPES AMONG 80 MEMBERS OF THE NINETY-SIXTH UNITED STATES CONGRESS

Benson–Williams Religious Type	Equivalent Spranger Type	Liberalism Index[a]	Proportion of Members, percent
Legalistic	Political	24	15
Self-concerned	Economic	27	29
People-concerned	Social	73	10
Nontraditional	Theoretical	72	9
Integrated		57	14
Nominal		48	22

[a] The political liberalism index, developed by Americans for Democratic Action, indicates the proportion of votes on key issues that were cast in the liberal direction.
Source: Based on Table 8-1 and Figure 9-1 in Benson and Williams, 1982, pages 124–125 and 149.

ger's schema, merely reflects the omission of aesthetic elements from the questionnaire they employed.

Within the Study of Values itself, does the R scale show a tendency to combine with one set of values rather than another? Although the SV's ipsative scoring forces the six scales to show an overall negative pattern of intercorrelations and disallows any precise interpretation of them, it is interesting to note that, for both sexes, the R scale correlates positively with the Social scale, as Spranger would have expected, and negatively with all the others, especially the Economic and Political scales for the men and the Theoretical and Aesthetic for the women (Allport, Vernon, and Lindzey, 1970, p. 10). That the men come closer to the pattern of relation we have been seeing is perhaps no coincidence, for 87 percent of Kemp's subjects and 94 percent of Benson and Williams's sample were males. Sex differences aside, the intercorrelations of the scales reflect the R scale's ambiguity. Its positive correlation with the Social scale and its negative relation with the Economic and Political scales suggest a liberal, humanitarian trend, whereas negative correlations with the Theoretical and Aesthetic scales seem to indicate a conservative trend.

The Religious Orientation Scale

The failure of the SV R scale to show an unequivocal relation to positive social attitudes may have been a factor in prompting Allport to develop the Religious Orientation (RO) Scale (Allport, 1966; Allport and Ross, 1967). This 20-item questionnaire, discussed more fully in Chapter 6, was originally designed to assess individuals on a continuum ranging from a consistently extrinsic religious orientation to a consistently intrinsic one. The extrinsic orientation, we may note, is conceptually equivalent to the piety of Spranger's economic type. Religion is valued for its usefulness to the self's other interests. In contrast, the intrinsic orientation suggests Spranger's all-embracing religious type. As Allport would put it, intrinsic religious motivation possesses a PROPRIATE FUNCTION. Operating at the warm center of personality, it "floods the whole life with motivation and meaning," thus serving the process of unification (Allport, 1961; 1966, p. 232). Although the intrinsic scale items include only one or two that refer to mystical experience, the hallmark of Spranger's religious attitude, Hood (1973, 1975) found evidence that an intrinsic orientation is indeed associated with the experience of transcendence.

As the literature reviewed in Chapter 6 makes evident, the Religious Orientation Scale has proved to be more complex psychometrically than Allport anticipated. The curious independence of the Intrinsic and Extrinsic subscales, the somewhat inconsistent results with the Intrinsic scale (including its virtual disappearance in King and Hunt's [1972b] factor-analytic study), and the underlying conceptual confusion have raised serous doubts about the RO Scale's serviceability. That it remains popular is testimony both to its conceptual appeal, especially to those who share Allport's wish to preserve genuine piety from the opprobrium attached to religious bigotry, and to the lack of equally convenient alternatives. Its continuing use may also reflect Allport's enduring reputation.

Allport's Continuing Influence

There is no question that Allport has been broadly influential. On a questionnaire circulated some years ago among practicing clinical psychologists, asking them to name the personality theorist who was most helpful in their clinical work, Allport was second only to Freud (Hall and Lindzey, 1978, p. 468). His influence in the psychology of religion, a field in which he was by no means a specialist, has been similarly pervasive. Indirectly, his criticisms of behavioral and psychoanalytic views gave fresh resolve to those who sought a more positive approach to human piety. More direct contributions are evident both in his own writings on religion and in the work of his students. Walter Clark (1902–1994) is a preeminent example. Allport not only encouraged and directed him in his doctoral study of the Oxford Group (Clark, 1951), but through his writings he also contributed—along with James and Pratt—to the conceptual foundations and content of Clark's (1958) survey of the field, a work that Clark appreciatively dedicated to him. Paul Johnson (1959) and Orlo Strunk (1962, 1965), though not among his students, also found Allport a major stimulus in their writings.

Even in the work of those who are more sympathetic to experimental or correlational methods, Allport has won a place of honor. His research and writings are a major resource, for example, in *Religion and the Individual,* by Daniel Batson, Patricia Schoenrade, and Larry Ventis (1993), whose "religion as quest," a third orientation proposed to complement the intrinsic and extrinsic orientations, is explicitly intended to incorporate the elements of Allport's mature religious sentiment—complexity, doubt, and tentativeness—missing from the questionnaire measures of intrinsic religion. From research evidence cited in Chapter 6, Batson and his associates provisionally conclude that only the *appearance* of humanitarian attitudes is impelled by an intrinsic orientation, whereas genuinely expressed tolerance and compassion are associated with the quest orientation. In Mary Jo Meadow and Richard Kahoe's *Psychology of Religion* (1984), for another example, Allport is cited more frequently than any other source, except James. Their book is dedicated to both of these psychologists.

Grønbaek (1970), we may recall, found that Allport ranked third, behind James and Freud, in frequency of citation in books on the psychology of religion published in America and Europe between 1950 and 1967. Works published abroad since then continue to show Allport's influence. Survey volumes, including Grønbaek's (1974) posthumously published history and the Italian handbook by Giancarlo Milanesi and Mario Aletti (1973), devote entire sections to Allport's thought. His ideas are also apparent in focal studies. Hans Åkerberg (1975, 1978) was guided by Allport's writings in two idiographic studies of Swedish public figures, one of scholar and archbishop Nathan Söderblom and another of social scientist and journalist Herbert Tingsten, whose anxious NIHILISM contrasts sharply with Söderblom's experience of an "overwhelming and saving God." That idiographic and nomothetic procedures can be mutually informative, as Allport maintained, is demonstrated in the startling parallels between Tingsten's life and the trends that George Vetter and Martin Green (1932) report in their questionnaire study of atheists (see Wulff, 1985b, pp. 55–57). Allport's continuing influence on European work in the psychology of religion is most evident, however, in ongoing research using the Allport-Ross Religious Orientation Scale.

ERICH FROMM: THE HOPE OF A HUMANISTIC FAITH

Like other committed Christian psychologists, Allport found in the intrinsic–extrinsic distinction a tentative answer to the age-old problem of distinguishing genuine piety from false or deteriorated forms. Erich Fromm was also challenged by this problem, though as a Jewish psychoanalyst who had given up all religious practice by his late twenties, he approached it from a rather different angle. The distinction he came to draw between authoritarian and humanistic religious traditions provides a unifiying thread in much of his work and offers us yet another perspective on human piety.

Erich Fromm (1900–1980) grew up an only child in an orthodox Jewish home in Frankfurt, Germany. Descended from a long line of rabbis and deeply impressed by the traditional rabbinic values of learning and of just and loving relations, he felt himself a stranger in a world governed by wealth and power. The hatred and nationalism he witnessed during World War I helped to solidify what became for him a lifelong commitment to the quest for peace and international understanding. Although he had abandoned religious observance in early adulthood, he was profoundly and lastingly influenced by the prophetic writings of the Hebrew Bible and especially the humanistic principles and values of his Talmudic teachers, all of whom were strictly observant rabbis (Landis and Tauber, 1971).

Fromm's humanist–socialist view was secondarily shaped by the writings of Karl Marx and Sigmund Freud. The humanistic and revolutionary spirit of Marx (in contrast to the vulgar Soviet misinterpretations of the recent past) seemed to Fromm a contemporary manifestation of the radical HUMANISM expressed in the messianic vision of the Hebrew prophets (Landis and Tauber, 1971, p. xi). Freud he valued, in spite of important limitations, for a number of fundamental discoveries: the discrepancy between what we think and who we are; the intensity of the boy's attachment to his mother; the phenomenon of transference, a powerful factor not only in therapy but also in social, political, and religious life; the self-"love" of narcissism; the dynamic structure of passions that forms a person's character; the significance of early childhood; the art of dream interpretation; and his vision of

Erich Fromm

the life and death impulses (Fromm, 1980). Fromm trained as an orthodox psychoanalyst after completing a Ph.D. in philosophy, and it was only gradually that his own distinctive perspective emerged, after he emigrated to the United States in 1934. The writer of a number of highly readable (if sometimes repetitive) books that contain as much social criticism and moral philosophy as they do psychology, Fromm has much to say on the nature of human piety.

The Human Situation

Usually classified among the neo-Freudians who transmuted psychoanalysis by combining it with the outlook of twentieth-century social psychology, Fromm exhibits elements of the existential–phenomenological view as well, especially when he writes of the human situation. Cast by chance into a particular time and place, we enter this world faced by a fundamental split in our nature. Like other embodied creatures who are part of the natural world, we are subject to immutable natural laws. But the instinctual harmony that characterizes animal existence is disrupted in us by the evolutionary appearance of self-awareness, reason, and imagination. A part of nature, we have at the same time transcended it, exchanging the irretrievable state of original oneness for a sense of anxious homelessness and a realization of the limitations of our own lives. Existence has itself become an inescapable problem that demands of us a solution (Fromm, 1947, 1956).

The split in human nature manifests itself in several "existential dichotomies": living existence and its perpetual defeat by death; the promise of human potential and the insufficiency of time for its realization; the fundamental aloneness in an indifferent universe and a simultaneous relatedness to one's fellow human beings. Unlike the many historical contradictions in individual and social life—the contrast, for example, between the abundant means for material satisfaction and our present inability to limit their use to constructive ends—the existential dichotomies are forever insoluble (Fromm, 1947).

To avert the eventuality of madness—a specifically human danger—which can result from the experience of uprootedness, helplessness, and isolation, the individual requires some *frame of orientation* and an *object of devotion*. These needs are among the most powerful sources of energy in human beings and can be met in various ways. The singlemost common answer to the orientational need is submission to a strong leader, such as a priest, king, or god. Endowed with extraordinary qualities, the leader is presumed to have both the knowledge and the intention to do what is best for the group. To secure an object of devotion that satisfies the deeply felt need for relatedness to the world beyond themselves, human beings have most frequently reaffirmed the "primary ties" of childhood—to mother and father, to soil, ancestors, and race, and, in more complex societies, to religion, nation, and class. In returning to nature or to submissive dependence on an authority figure, in order to feel at home in the world, a person pays a tremendous price: the blockage of the full development of human capacities—to reason, love, and create (Fromm, 1947, 1968).

Two Types of Religion

Fromm (1950, p. 21) defines religion as "any system of thought and action shared by a group" that provides the individual with a frame of orientation and an object of devotion. From his perspective, then, no one is without a religious need, though the means by which it is satisfied may have none of the outward appearances of traditional religious forms. Such traditional forms may also serve as a veneer that disguises and contradicts the more primitive and neurotic religion underneath. "The question is not *religion or not* but *which kind of religion*"—either a religion that contributes to the realization of human potentialities or one that stifles them (p. 26). These two types—the humanistic and the authoritarian—constitute what Fromm considers the most fundamental distinction within the diversity of religious types. They also provide us with another way of thinking about religion's ambiguous relation to humanitarian attitudes.

Authoritarian Religion: The essential element in religion of the authoritarian type, says Fromm, is self-deprecating surrender to a power that transcends humankind. Its principle virtue is obedience; its cardinal sin is disobedience—not because of the deity's moral qualities but simply because it has controlling power. In the authoritarian posture, individuals completely surrender to the higher power, exchanging worth, independence, and integrity for the feelings of belonging and being protected. Calvin's theology provides Fromm with a theistic example, and National Socialism and other authoritarian political systems, with secular illustrations. The controlling ideals of authoritarian religion, whatever its form, are frequently so vague and distant that they rarely touch the everyday lives of real people. Nonetheless, they serve to justify whatever means are necessary for exerting control (Fromm, 1950).

Humanistic Religion: The center of humanistic religion is humankind and its strengths. "Man's aim in humanistic religion," says Fromm, "is to achieve the greatest strength, not the greatest powerlessness; virtue is self-realization, not obedience." A person's own capacities for thinking and feeling, not assent by fiat to someone else's propositions, serve as the foundation for faith, and religious experience is "of oneness with the All, based on one's relatedness to the world as it is grasped with thought and with love." Rather than the sorrow and guilt of the authoritarian type, the prevailing mood is one of joy. In the theistic forms of humanistic religion, God is a symbol of the powers that may be realized in human lives, rather than a symbol of force and domination over humankind. Fromm discerns the humanistic spirit in early Buddhism and Taoism; in the teachings of the Hebrew prophet Isaiah and of Jesus, Socrates, and Spinoza; in certain mystical trends in the Jewish and Christian traditions; and in the religion of Reason of the French Revolution (p. 37).

To help us understand the dynamics of authoritarian religion, Fromm (1950) reiterates a view that Marx borrowed from Feuerbach. Persons of an authoritarian outlook, Fromm says, project their most valuable human qualities onto God, progressively impoverishing themselves as a result. Whereas God has become a being of love, wisdom, and justice, they have become nothing. Alienated in this way from themselves, they can recover their humanity only through the mercy or grace of God. In becoming slavishly dependent on God, they have lost a sense of their own capacities to love and to reason—and with it, their faith in themselves and one another. Feeling empty and sinful, they act without love in their daily affairs.

In humanistic religion, on the other hand, God is a symbol of the higher self, of what a person may or ought to become. Although the aims of humanistic religion—"overcoming the limitations of an egotistical self, achieving love, objectivity, and humility and respecting life so that the aim of life is living itself, and man becomes what he potentially is"—are evident in the great Western and Eastern traditions alike, Fromm (1960, p. 80) considers Taoism and Buddhism, because they are not "burdened with the concept of a transcendent father–saviour," to possess a superior rationality and realism. Fromm's admiration of Zen Buddhism in particular is evident not only in his essay on psychoanalysis and Zen Buddhism (1960), but also in frequent references elsewhere to Zen Buddhist principles.

Faith as Having or Being

Paralleling Fromm's distinction between authoritarian and humanistic religions is the further, more recently elaborated contrast between faith shaped by the having mode of existence and faith in the being mode. The having mode, which has its origins in the impulse for survival, centers on acquiring and owning private property as well as such nonmaterial possessions as one's own ego, other persons, reputation, and knowledge. Because the having mode is grounded in relations of power and aggression and necessarily excludes others, it fosters greed, envy, and violence. It also transforms the possessor, for if I rest my sense of identity on what I have, I become a thing possessed by it in turn. Moreover, because no object is permanent, my possessing of it is merely transitory and thus in reality I have nothing.

The being mode centers not on things but on experience; it is correspondingly less easily described. To enter into the mode of being, a person must become free from the illusions and blinders that are integral to "characterological having," in contrast to the "existential having" required for survival. The fundamental characteristic of being, according to Fromm, is free and purposeful activity that makes use of human powers and animates whatever is touched. The being mode, which owes its strength to the need for union with others, implies self-transcendence, growth, selflessness, interestedness, and love. Because both tendencies—having as well as being—are present in each individual, the values and norms of a society will determine which will become dominant.

Having Faith: In the having mode, faith consists in the confident possession of formulations accepted from a powerful bureaucracy as ultimate and true. The certainty that distinguishes the having mode derives not from independent use of our own reason—for that has been surrendered—but from the seemingly unshakable power of the bureaucracy. Once a symbol for the highest within us, God in the having mode becomes an idol, a thing of our own making to which we surrender certain of our own qualities, such as intelligence, physical strength, power, and fame. Not only are we dependent on the idol, but by identifying with these partial, having-oriented aspects, we also lose our totality and cease to grow (Fromm, 1976, 1966, p. 44). Unmistakable in the having mode, then, are the contours of authoritarian religion.

Being in Faith: In the being mode, faith is not primarily a set of beliefs but an inner orientation or attitude. Rather than a faith that we *have,* it is a faith that we *are in*—toward ourselves and others, as well as toward God. This faith, too, implies certainty, but one derived from our own subjective experience of the other's character, not submission to dogmatic authority. In the being mode, faith in God "is vouched for by inner experience of the divine qualities in oneself; it is a continuous, active process of self-creation—or, as [Meister] Eckhart puts it, of Christ's eternally being born within ourselves" (Fromm, 1976, p. 43). In the mode of being we may recognize the qualities of humanistic religion.

Correlates of the Having Mode of Faith: The predominance of the having mode in Western culture and thus of authoritarian religion makes understandable the persistent finding of a correlation between piety and prejudice. Fromm's distinctions may also provide a basis for rethinking the specific findings obtained with Allport's Religious Orientation Scale. Eugene Tate and Gerald Miller's (1971) indiscriminately antireligious subjects, so classified because they tended to disagree with both intrinsic and extrinsic items on the RO Scale, were distinguished from the three religious groups by giving higher rankings to Freedom, Mature Love, Self-Respect, and Independent, all values of Fromm's humanistic, being-oriented piety. Although their relatively low rankings of A World at Peace and True Friendship, on the other hand, suggest that they do not fully represent the type, the "indiscriminately antireligious," as identified by the RO Scale, do tend to be among the least prejudiced.

A careful reading of the RO Scale (see Table 6.4) reveals that items in both the extrinsic and the intrinsic subscales are expressed in the language of the having mode. The very idea of assessing piety as a quality that we possess *independent of* our way of being appears to be a product of the having orientation. Thus Fromm's distinction seems not only to raise doubts about the RO Scale in particular but also to call into question the whole enterprise of searching for piety's correlates. These "correlates" themselves, Fromm would argue, not the veneer of professed piety, are the truest measure of a person's religious faith.

The Religious scale of the Allport–Vernon–Lindzey Study of Values also partakes of the having mode. Fromm maintains that experience in the mode of being—of creativity, love, joy, or grasping truth—exists only in the "eternity" (i.e., timelessness) of the here and now. The mode of having, on the other hand, exists only *in* time, especially the past, when a person amassed the objects to which he or she is bound, and the future, the zone of concern for preserving what the person has and for adding to it. Although the nature of bodily existence and the physical world forces us to respect time, only in the mode of having do we *submit* to it, allowing it to become our master (Fromm, 1976, pp. 127–129). In an investigation employing the Study of Values in conjunction with a questionnaire designed to assess the dimensions of temporal experience, the SV Religious scale proved to be positively related to concern for past and future, and unrelated to the experience of immersion in a fulfilling timeless present. Interestingly, the SV Aesthetic scale did show a significant positive relation to the experience of a timeless here and now, whereas the Economic scale—and, to a lesser degree, the Political scale—showed a negative relation (Wulff, 1970).

Radical Humanism in the Jewish Tradition

The contrasts between authoritarian and humanistic religion, between the modes of having and being, provide the framework for Fromm's reflections on the history of religion, especially of the Jewish tradition. This perspective, we should note, emerged only after Fromm had practiced for some years as an analyst. Initially, Fromm was a thoroughgoing Freudian, as he demonstrates in his 1927 paper on the Sabbath. In this essay he interprets the rules governing the Sabbath day of rest in Oedipal terms. He views the weekly forbidding of all "work" affecting (mother) nature as penance for the primal crime and as a means of warding off contemporary incestuous longings. It is nonetheless a joyful time, he adds, because it also symbolizes a realization of these longings, through a regressive return to the mother's womb. Eventually, however, Fromm came to regard incestuous wishes as themselves symbolic—of the human longing for the original harmony with nature. The key to Fromm's (1951) later understanding of the Sabbath and the intricacies of its ritual can be found in the concept of work and rest that he says underlies the biblical and later the Talmudic tradition. " 'Work' is any interference by man, be it constructive or destructive, with the physical world. 'Rest' is a state of peace between man and nature" (p. 244). Hence the Sabbath, by disallowing any human interference with the natural process as well as any business transactions, symbolizes a state of perfect harmony with nature and among individuals. More than a mere day of rest, as we tend to think of it today, the Jewish Sabbath stands as a precursor of the salvation and freedom to be attained in messianic time. On the Sabbath, says Fromm (1976, p. 51), "One lives as if one *has* nothing, pursuing no aim except *being,* that is, expressing one's essential powers: praying, studying, eating, drinking, singing, making love." It is a joyful day, for in the timelessness of pure being and harmony, we are at last fully ourselves.

The golden age of messianic time that is anticipated by the observance of the Sabbath stands in a dialectical relation with Paradise before the "fall" (Fromm, 1966). Both represent a state of harmony. The innocent harmony of Paradise reflects humankind's not yet having been born into awareness and independence, whereas the harmony of messianic time is attained only after the loss of innocence and the achievement of full birth into human existence. Between these beginning and end points of Jewish aspiration, Fromm discerns the unfolding of an evolutionary process—from a primitive authoritarian and ethnocentric outlook to a perspective of radical freedom and universal brotherhood. As the record of this evolution, the Hebrew Bible "is a *revolutionary* book; its theme is the liberation of man from the incestuous ties to blood and soil, from the submission to idols, from slavery, from powerful masters, to freedom for the individual, for the nation and for all of mankind" (Fromm, 1966, p. 7). As persons living in a time of increasing emancipation from the bondage of tradition, suggests Fromm, we may today be able to understand the Hebrew Bible and the continuing developments of the postbiblical tradition better than in any earlier age. To this task of reinterpretation Fromm brings the perspective of radical humanism, defined as a global philosophy that emphasizes the oneness of the human race and the capacity of humankind to

Cranach's *Adam and Eve* suggests the state of innocence and utter harmony that Fromm says preceded the birth into human awareness.

develop its own powers and to achieve independence, inner harmony, and a world of peace (p. 13).

The Evolution of God: In the first stage of the evolution recorded in the biblical tradition, God is represented as a ruler with absolute and arbitrary power. His supremacy is soon challenged by the disobedience of the human beings He created. Fearful that they would "become like one of us"—that is, realize the potential divinity within themselves—by eating both of the tree of knowledge and the tree of life, God banished them forever from the Garden of Eden.

From the authoritarian view, Adam and Eve's eviction from Paradise is punishment for the sin of disobedience, which can be overcome only by repentence and renewed submission. Also implied in this story is a radically different meaning, which Fromm says is rooted in the nonauthoritarian mode of being. From this perspective, Adam and Eve's sin is one of unresolved estrangement. In becoming fully human and thus aware of good and evil and of their own separateness from each other, Adam and Eve lost their original oneness and became strangers instead. Facing each other as isolated and selfish human beings who are unable to bridge their separation through love, they are overwhelmed with a deep sense of shame. Their "sin"—it is not called that in the Bible—can be overcome only by "the full unfolding of reason and love, by at-onement" (Fromm, 1976, p. 125).

The first act of disobedience, therefore, marked the beginning of human freedom, of the progressive emancipation from God's supremacy and the gradual realization of the potential Godhood that lies within. In the second stage, beginning with the conclusion of the covenant with Noah and his descendants, in which He promises never again to flood the earth, God is tranformed from an absolute ruler into a "constitutional" monarch who is no longer free to rule arbitrarily but is now bound by the principles of justice and love.

The third stage is reached when God reveals Himself to Moses as the nameless God of history. In response to Moses' repeated pleas to reveal His name, rather than merely saying that He is the God of Abraham, Isaac, and Jacob, God declares that "I AM WHO I AM. . . . Say this to the people of Israel, I AM has sent me to you" (Exodus 3:14). A free translation of the Hebrew text, says Fromm, would read: "My name is *Nameless;* tell them that 'Nameless' has sent you" (p. 31). Having a name is the essence of an idol, according to Fromm; yet only *things*, complete in time and space, can have names. A *living* God cannot be named, nor can it be represented by any other kind of image.

The evolution of divinity from tribal chief to nameless God culminated fifteen hundred years later in the negative theology of Moses Maimonides. According to Maimonides, the foremost Jewish philosopher of the Middle Ages, the unknowability of God's essence necessarily limits us to negative statements, of what God is *not*. Only of His action can we make positive attributions. Thus in the Jewish tradition, "There is only one thing that matters, namely, that God *is*. Little importance is attached to the speculation *about* God's nature and essence; hence, there has been no theological development comparable to that which grew up in Christianity" (p. 42).

Jewish theology is negative in another, perhaps more fundamental sense. The acknowledgment of God is the negation of idolatry. As a shadow of humankind that is recoverable only through submission, the idol, says Fromm, is incompatible with human freedom and independence. In the biblical and later Jewish tradition, he observes, the prohibition of idolatry—and thus of narcissism, for in effect a person is worshiping the self—ranks in importance with the worship of God. Indeed, he argues that the fight against the attitude of idolatry, which can make even God into an idol, might unify persons of every faith.

In *The Art of Loving* (1956), Fromm clarifies what it means for truly religious individuals when God becomes the nameless One about whom no one can speak. Such persons will expect nothing from God, will pray for nothing, and will perhaps not even mention God's name. Yet they will have faith in and strive to fulfill the principles that "God" through time has come to represent: love, truth, and justice. Life is valuable to them only insofar as they have the opportunity to achieve a fuller realization of their human powers, "the only reality that matters." To love God, then, would mean "to long for the attainment of the full capacity to love, for the realization of that which 'God' stands for in oneself" (p. 71).

The Authoritarian Spirit of the Christian West

The humanistic qualities that Fromm discerns in the Jewish tradition are present in the Christian tradition as well, but there, he says, they have encountered more persistent opposition from the authoritarian trend. Judging from the spirit and text of Jesus' teachings, early Christianity was fundamentally humanistic in spirit and demanded total renunciation of the having mode. But once the tradition had passed from the hands of the humble and dispossessed into the grasp of those ruling the Roman Empire and itself became centered in a powerful organization, the authoritarian spirit became dominant, surviving even the emancipation from ecclesiastical authority brought by the Protestant Reformation. The humanistic element nonetheless remained a living force, especially through the teachings of the mystics, most notably those of Meister Eckhart (Fromm, 1941, 1950, 1976, 1994).

The supposed Christian conversion of Europe under Constantine and in the centuries following was for the most part a sham, according to Fromm, for it led to no corresponding changes in social character. The victorious pagan hero who conquers, exploits, and destroys, not the self-sacrificing Christian martyr, remains to this day the prevailing model in both Europe and North America, as evinced, for example, in the popularity of the Olympic Games. Luther's elimination of the motherly element from the church, and thus of unconditional love and cooperation with nature, was among the factors preparing the way for the new paganism that today threatens to destroy humankind. Under a Christian façade but in diametric opposition to it arose the "industrial" and "CYBERNETIC" religions, the industrial centering on the valuing of work, profit, and power, and the cybernetic on the worship of the machine. Industrial religion had its basis in the authoritarian–obsessive–hoarding character that emerged in the 1500s and remained dominant until the end of the nineteenth century. Gradually replacing this social character, and incorporating certain of its elements, is a new one, the *marketing character,* which represents human beings as commodities to be exchanged on the "personality market." Persons of this characterological type are profoundly alienated— from themselves, their work, other human beings, and nature. Although they have little personal interest in philosophical or religious questions and are so emotionally stunted that they cannot distinguish between genuinely religious persons and those who fake religious emotion for politial ends, they are in their own way religious. They worship the machine and, by serving it, imagine themselves to have become godlike. Having in actuality become the impotent slaves of technique, these proponents of cybernetic religion have been transformed into worshipers of the goddess of destruction (Fromm, 1976).

Toward a Social Character of Being

Is there hope for averting catastrophe by fostering a more fitting religious outlook that corresponds to a new and benign social character? Fromm thinks so, however slim its chances of realization from an objective point of view. The founders of such an outlook span the millennia—from the Buddha to Eckhart to Marx and Albert Schweitzer. According to Fromm's interpretation, these seminal thinkers share certain essential elements: "their radical demand for giving up the having orientation; their insistence on complete independence; their metaphysical skepticism; their godless religiosity, and their demand for social activity in the spirit of care and human solidarity" (Fromm, 1976, p. 63).

The realization of a new character structure founded in the mode of being will depend, according to Fromm, on the devotion of the best minds to the development of a new "humanistic science of Man" and an effective governmental system, based in participatory democracy, for promoting the vision of a saner and healthier society. The marketing character must be replaced by the productive, loving character and cybernetic religion by a new radical humanistic spirit—a "religiosity" without dogmas and institutions and permeating the whole of social life. Such a religiosity, he says, would foster a new, more mature sense of relatedness to nature and other human beings as well as the optimal development of the human capacities for reason, courage, compassion, and love. Fromm's view is a new vision, a synthesis of the late medieval City of God and its antithesis, the contemporary Earthly City of Progress. Fromm sees this synthesis as the only alternative to chaos; he calls it the City of Being (p. 202).

Confirmation Through Factor Analysis: Although Fromm's radical humanistic formulations have inspired little empirical research in the psychology of religion, at least one study, carried out independently of his thinking, offers partial support for his basic typology. From interviews of a representative sample of 142 ministers, priests, and rabbis, Jack Shand (1961) obtained 2400 items, later classified into 180 subgroups, defining the term *religious*. A single word or phrase was selected to represent each subgroup, and then a representative sample of Chicago-area clergy was asked to sort these 180 expressions on an 11-point scale according to the degree that each item characterized a "religious" person. Factor analysis of these ratings yielded two basic conceptions of what it means to be religious, one "fundamentalist" and the other "humanisic"; several subtypes of each were also identified.

The essential correspondence between Shand's and Fromm's types is suggested by the characteristics of being religious that were given the highest ratings by each group of clergy identified through factor analysis. A religious person, according to the *humanistic* clergy, is one who "is seeking the truth"; "has a deep human sympathy and understanding"; "has a spirit of brotherhood in all human relations"; "is interested in any cause that advances human welfare"; "has a love of others"; "wants to make the world a better place to live in"; "has a sense of purpose to life"; "has a feeling of . . . at-homeness in the universe"; and "is interested in world peace." In addition, theistic humanistics give similarly high ratings to "is conscious of God's presence in all life" and "has a deep faith in God." The *fundamentalist* clergy, on the other hand, characterized the religious individual as a person who "believes that Jesus Christ is the Son of God"; "believes in . . . the Scriptures"; "has repented his sins"; "has assurance of salvation"; "has a personal relationship to God"; "has hope for the future after life"; "has peace of conscience"; "comes to public worship regularly"; "has a love of God"; and "fears

God." Broen's (1957) Fundamentalism–Humanitarianism factor, which emphasizes human sinfulness and fear of a righteously punitive God at one pole and the human capacity for independent actualization of inherent goodness at the other, also substantiates Fromm's distinction without the investigator's having sought explicitly to test it.

We must be cautious, of course, in attributing the dynamics of Fromm's authoritarian religion to any specific individual of fundamentalist orientation—or, indeed, in assuming their absence among humanists. For *groups* of persons, however, as we saw in Chapter 6, measures of doctrinal orthodoxy consistently show a positive relation to scales of authoritarianism. Furthermore, if James Barr (1980) is correct, this relation is not merely an artifact of biased research instruments. Himself a former conservative evangelical, Barr maintains that the Fundamentalist outlook actually produces authoritarian personality traits: "Young evangelical Christians, open, free and delightful, are often quickly reduced through the life of their society and the pressure of their doctrine to a strained, suspicious and exclusivist frame of mind" (p. 69). This pattern, he adds, should be familiar to anyone who is well acquainted with the movement.

The problems of adjustment that are frequently experienced by former fundamentalists prompted lawyer Richard Yao in 1985 to found Fundamentalists Anonymous (FA), a support group that now has dozens of chapters across the United States. Himself a former Baptist Fundamentalist who later earned a master's degree in divinity at Yale, Yao (1987) delineates a complex of symptoms he calls the "shattered faith syndrome": chronic guilt, anxiety, and depression; low self-esteem; loneliness and isolation; distrust of other people or groups; aversion to any structure or authority; bitterness and anger over lost time; distressing recurrences of the fundamentalist consciousness; lack of basic social skills; and, in some instances, sexual difficulties, including guilt and anxiety about sex if not actual sexual dysfunction. Typically unable to talk about their past, former fundamentalists are encouraged to share their experiences, outside the FA group as well as within it. Noting the similarity between the symptoms described by Yao and the distress syndrome that accompanies other major life transitions and crises, psychologist Gary Hartz (1987) observes that the heart of crisis intervention is empathic support, which is precisely what Fundamentalists Anonymous offers.

ABRAHAM MASLOW AND THE RELIGION OF PEAK EXPERIENCES

Among humanistically oriented psychologists, Fromm's views continue to have considerable appeal. They serve Sidney Jourard (1974), for example, as the foundations of his own discussion of healthy and unhealthy forms of religion, and they are also featured in Meadow and Kahoe's (1984) survey volume. Another psychologist stimulated by Fromm's work was Abraham Maslow (1908–1970), a highly influential humanistic psychologist who placed his own thinking on religion in direct line with James's *Varieties* and Fromm's *Psychoanalysis and Religion*. In contrast to Fromm, Maslow gave little systematic attention to religion in his various writings. Although he possessed, like Fromm, a messianic vision and was himself a Jew, he shared none of Fromm's enthusiasm for the Hebrew Bible and the rabbinical tradition—if indeed he was familiar with them at all. Yet because Maslow has played a far more prominent role in the humanistic movement in American psychology, his views on religion are probably better known. They surely have inspired more research.

Maslow grew up in Brooklyn, New York, the shy, solitary child of uneducated

Abraham Maslow

and struggling Russian immigrants. A proudly militant atheist from his early years, he apparently identified with his respected father, an avowed freethinker; from his "religious" and "superstitious" mother, on the other hand, he was intensely disaffected. He remained throughout his life an opponent of theism, which in the privacy of his journal he disparages as "the childish looking for a big Daddy in the sky." Church attendance, praying, and reading the Bible all seemed to him a waste of positive human impulses. Like James, however, Maslow also harbored a mystic germ. From his youth he was himself capable of being deeply moved by music, art, and nature—and eventually even by reading scientific journals (Lowry, 1973, pp. 12–15; Lowry, 1979, pp. 6, 12; Maslow, 1966, p. 149).

At first an enthusiastic proponent of Watsonian behaviorism and its bold promises of a better world, Maslow grew increasingly impatient with the narrowness of its scientific vision. Traditional science seemed adequate enough in his early research in primate psychology, but the study of human beings, he was finally to conclude, requires a new model. Like Allport, he retained the ideal of public observation and measurement, but for the humanistic science he envisioned, he disavowed the aims of prediction and control. "If humanistic science may be said to have any goals beyond sheer fascination with the human mystery and enjoyment of it, these would be to release the individual from external controls and to make him *less* predictable to the observer . . . even though perhaps more predictable to himself" (Maslow, 1966, p. 40). Ideally, he said, science should encompass both pure receptivity to reality, even loving fusion with it ("experiential knowledge"), on the one hand, and the economical simplifications of good abstract theory ("spectator knowledge"), on the other. Defined in terms of its beginnings, science is merely looking at things for oneself. At the highest level, it is "the organization of, the systematic pursuit of, and the enjoyment of wonder, awe, and mystery." Science, he concluded, can be the religion of the nonreligious, a source of deeply rewarding religious experience (p. 151).

The Study of Self-Actualization: Maslow's new science of psychology required a new object as well. For too long, he argued, psychologists have based their generalizations about human nature on immature, neurotic, or ordinary human beings, or on dubious extrapolations from other species. Convinced from his undergraduate years of the "wonderful possibilities and inscrutable depths" that testify to

Eleanor Roosevelt (1884–1962), the highly influential American humanitarian and reformer who dedicated her last years to promoting the United Nations's Human Rights Declaration, which she had helped to pass.

"the greatness of the human species," he finally decided that the positive side of human potential could be understood only by studying individuals in whom it was unequivocally evident. As he searched for criteria in the literature on saints, great persons, and heroes, Maslow screened students for an in-depth study of "Good Human Beings" ("GHBs"). Disappointed by the rarity of undergraduate GHBs— he found only one immediately usable subject among three thousand students— and by the apparent "need for privacy" of those with some promise, he finally relied on personal acquaintances and friends as well as public and historical figures. His final, overwhelmingly male "sample" consisted of 18 "fairly sure" or "highly probable" figures (e.g., Thomas Jefferson, Eleanor Roosevelt, William James, and Albert Schweitzer), 5 "partial cases" (all anonymous contemporaries), and 37 "potential or possible cases" (e.g., Goethe, Martin Buber, D. T. Suzuki, Benjamin Franklin, and Walt Whitman). The data he was forced to rely on, Maslow notes with a measure of regret, consisted of intuitive global impressions of the ordinary, gradually formed sort (Lowry, 1973, p. 15; Maslow, 1970, p. 152).

A Hierarchy of Needs: According to Maslow's (1970) "holistic–dynamic theory," human beings are universally endowed with certain vaguely delineated fundamental needs. Rejecting any detailed listing of them as seriously misleading, Maslow contents himself with distinguishing five hierarchically ordered types. At the bottom of the hierarchy, as the most PREPOTENT of all, are the *physiological needs*, such as for food, water, and sleep. Persons dominated by these needs will not only be impelled to satisfy them but will view the world and shape their aspirations in terms of them as well. When the physiological needs are more or less satisfactorily met, a new set emerges and becomes dominant: the *safety needs*, for protection, security, predictability, structure, order, and so on. That these needs, too, can dominate the entire organism is evident in the lives of children, the mentally disturbed, and the economically and socially deprived. In healthy and fortunate

Albert Schweitzer (1875–1965), the French doctor, clergyman, musician, ethical philosopher, and Nobel Peace Prize winner who gave much of his life to serving as a medical missionary in Africa.

adults, however, safety needs may be apparent only in an interest in the orienting principles of religion, philosophy, or science. At the third level of the hierarchy we find *belongingness and love needs,* including the needs for roots, for home and family, for neighborhood and friends, for contact and intimacy. *Esteem needs* emerge next and encompass the desire for adequacy, competence, achievement, independence, and freedom as well as for deserved recognition, appreciation, and respect from others. As Hetherington (1975, p. 23) points out, religious teachings have frequently either opposed this set of needs by promoting humility or have intensified them by emphasizing sinfulness. Together these four levels constitute the "lower" or "deficiency" needs, so called because they are actuated by the absence of the needed object. The lower the need in the hierarchy, the more compelling it is, the earlier it arises, and the more serious the state of deprivation.

The "higher" or "growth" needs form the fifth level of the hierarchy, the generic need for *self-actualization.* Ordinarily appearing only after the prior satisfaction of the other four needs, the peculiarly human desire to actualize potentialities, to attain fuller knowledge of one's nature and higher levels of integration, is the least prepotent of the needs and the least debilitating if unmet. In contrast to deficiency needs, which subside when they are satisfied, growth needs are intensified by gratification. Whether a person aspires to be a good doctor or a skilled carpenter, an accomplished musician or a proficient artist, or simply a good human being, growth is in itself rewarding and impels him or her onward to ever-higher levels of attainment (Maslow, 1968, 1970).

A Portrait of the Self-Actualizer: Maslow was particularly interested in the rare, healthy, and inevitably older individuals whose lives are animated by the METANEEDS of self-actualization. Although individual differences are most obvious at this level, he says, these persons resemble one another in significant ways. Briefly summarized, the most important characteristics of self-actualizing persons are said to be the following: more accurate perception and acceptance of reality, including human nature; spontaneity, freshness of appreciation, and creativeness in everyday activities; relative detachment from the immediate physical and social environment and from the culture at large; deeper, more satisfying interpersonal relations, most likely with a small number of other self-actualizing persons; strong feelings of identification and sympathy for all other human beings; democratic (nonauthoritarian) character structure; nonhostile, philosophical humor; centeredness in problems lying outside themselves and reflecting a broad framework of values; clear moral and ethical standards that are consistently applied; and the felt resolution of apparent dichotomies or pairs of opposites (Maslow, 1970).

One other characteristic stands out. Maslow found that it was "fairly common" for his subjects to report mystical experiences. To dissociate such ecstatic states from all traditional religious interpretations and, on the contrary, to emphasize their entirely natural origin, Maslow called them PEAK EXPERIENCES. Associated with a variety of contexts, peak experiences are marked by feelings of wholeness and integration, of relatively egoless fusion with the world, of spontaneity and effortlessness, of fully existing in the here and now. Individuals not only feel more self-activated, more fully functioning, more creative, but objective observers are likely to perceive them that way as well. Profoundly satisfying in themselves, peak experiences may revolutionize the lives in which they occur. They contribute to the feeling that life is truly worth living (Maslow, 1964, 1968).

Cognition of Being: The states of being that are associated with these short-lived but potentially recurrent moments of wonder and awe are marked, says Maslow, by a particular form of cognition, which he calls COGNITION OF BEING or, more conveniently, B-cognition. In contrast to ordinary D-cognition, so called because it is organized in accord with the deficiency needs of the individual, B-cognition is receptive and purposeless, and it seems to encompass, in a holistic way, all that there is. It sees things as they are in themselves, not as they serve human purposes or compare with other objects. Directly apparent to B-cognition is a realm of values that contrasts sharply with such D-values as usefulness or desirability. These B-values, perceived as "out there" and absolute, include wholeness, perfection, truth, jusice, aliveness, richness, simplicity, beauty, goodness, playfulness, and self-sufficiency (Maslow, 1968, p. 83). To attain, if only momentarily, the lofty reaches of B-cognition, says Maslow, is to become godlike in perspective and understanding.

Two Types of Actualizers: Some self-actualizers, Maslow observes, are not disposed to experience peak experiences and B-cognition. Spranger would doubtless see in them a combination of the political and economic types, oriented toward what is effectively practical—both for survival and self-actualization. "Such persons live in the world, coming to fulfillment in it. They master it, lead it, use it for good purposes, as (healthy) politicians or practical people do" (Maslow, 1971, p. 281). Active rather than contemplative, perhaps mesomorphic rather than ectomorphic, these "merely healthy" self-actualizers happily live out their lives in the D-world. The "transcenders," on the other hand, have their center of gravity in the B-realm and its values, giving them a superior perspective on the D-realm and its necessary evils, which may make them prone to "a kind of cosmic-sadness or B-sadness," in spite of their own ecstatic experiences. The more profoundly religious of the two types, the transcenders go beyond even self-actualization.

Somewhat to his surprise, Maslow discovered that peak experiences may also occur in the lives of people who are not self-actualizers, even in the lives of despicable persons. Yet in these instances, his evidence suggested, the experience will be relatively rare and lack cognitive content. Otherwise peak experiences signal at least temporary admission into the ranks of the self-actualizing; they are the moments of a person's greatest fulfillment and maturity.

The High-Plateau Experience: What for ordinary persons are momentary changes in character are for self-actualizers enduring personality dispositions. With time, the peak experiences themselves may become less frequent and less intense, but taking their place, in effect, is something no less valuable, a kind of precipitate of a life of insight and deep experience. Maslow calls this more enduring phenomenon the HIGH-PLATEAU EXPERIENCE. More voluntary than the peak experience and invariably possessing a cognitive element, the high-plateau experience consists of a continuing sense of illumination, of perceiving the miraculous in ordinary things. It is far more serene than the peak experience, though perhaps no less deep or touching. It also contains an element of sadness, Maslow says, for in "witnessing eternity," we become more aware of our own mortality and the transitoriness of all things. Thus there is a certain poignancy in our enjoyment of the precious moment, free of competition or planning for the future (Krippner, 1972; Maslow, 1968, 1971).

Peak and high-plateau experiences, along with the values and insights associated with them, have long been the province of the religious traditions. Yet, says Maslow, traditions of every kind, including both religious and humanistic, have failed us as an effective source of values. Maslow regrets in particular the marked tendency to form dichotomies, a proclivity that has separated religion from science, the sacred from the profane. A "dichotomized religion" is doomed, he maintains, for it claims eternal validity for its founding revelation while vigorously opposing all other sources of truth. Dichotomized science, on the other hand, refuses to deal with anything that is not immediately visible and concrete; it becomes sheer technology, dangerously isolated from human ideals and values. The corresponding split between sacred and profane has removed the "sacred" from the realm of nature and associated it instead with particular times and places, particular ceremonies, and particular language, musical instruments, and food. Rather than infusing all of life with value, such an outlook ruptures the dynamic interplay between the actual and the ideal and fosters a "pie-in-the-sky kind of religion," which not only tolerates but actually supports human exploitation and degradation (Maslow, 1964, p. 15).

Humanistic Psychology and a Naturalistic Faith

In the new humanistic psychology, Maslow saw the possibilities of healing this split. By wresting the "intrinsic core" of religion—the private illumination of some acutely sensitive prophet—from the hands of the organizers or legalists (who, Maslow says, have distorted it in their own efforts to comprehend and communicate it) and then bringing this core into the realm of humanistic science, Maslow hoped both to gain a deeper understanding of it and to foster it. The outcome of reclaiming the intensely personal religious experience—the peak experience—from the religious traditions and making it more widely available, Maslow suggests, will be a recognition that the "paraphernalia of organized religion—buildings and specialized personnel, rituals, dogmas, ceremonials, and the like" are not only distinctly secondary in importance but may actually constitute a danger, either suppressing the core experience or serving as a defense against it.

These "localisms" are also divisive. The peak experience, by contrast, is a "meeting ground" for persons of every persuasion or type. What finally divides humankind in terms of religion, says Maslow, is the presence or absence of the intrinsic core experience:

> The two religions of mankind tend to be the peakers and the non-peakers, that is to say, those who have private, personal, transcendent, core-religious experiences easily

and often and who accept them and make use of them, and, on the other hand, those who have never had them or who repress or suppress them and who, therefore, cannot make use of them for their personal therapy, personal growth, or personal fulfillment (Maslow, 1964, p. 29).

In the history of religion, says Maslow in agreement with James, the same unfortunate pattern repeats itself again and again. That is, the lonely prophet has a mystical experience; an organization springs up to give expression to, communicate, and apply that experience; and then the nonpeakers who receive these symbolic expressions mistake them for the revelation itself and thus treat the verbal formulas, the ritual objects, and even the organization itself as the things to be revered. The original meaning becomes lost in idolatry, and renewed perceptions of it are treated as heresy.

Rescued from this recurring fate by the new humanistic psychology, the peak experience and the ultimate values associated with it will become, Maslow claims, the far goals of all education—and perhaps of every other social institution as well. Answers to the ancient questions will be based increasingly on "natural, empirical fact" and less on religious custom and sacred text. To an age that has suffered a collapse of traditional values, humanistic psychology offers the possibility of a positive, naturalistic faith that may—but need not—be expressed in traditional form. Every aspect and nuance of the experience of the holy described by Rudolf Otto can be accepted as real by theist and atheist alike, and so, too, the empirical spirit and the recognition that our knowledge, though conditioned by historical and cultural factors and relative to human capacities, "can yet come closer and closer to 'The Truth' that is not dependent on man" (Maslow, 1964, p. 55).

Research on Religion Inspired by Maslow's Theories

In spite of the self-acknowledged tentativeness of much that he wrote, Maslow's theories have attracted a great deal of interest. In an article reviewing the research on the need hierarchy in particular, Mahmoud Wahba and Lawrence Bridwell (1976) note that it is one of the leading theories of motivation in the literature on management and organizational behavior. At the same time, they observe that factor-analytic studies designed to test it have found little consistent evidence in its favor, beyond some data suggesting that deficiency and growth needs may form some kind of hierarchy. It does not easily lend itself to traditional empirical testing, and much about it remains conceptually unclear, including the concept of need itself. However, it has served to explain a variety of research findings and to provoke further reflections on human motivation.

Religious Thinking and Dominant Need: In an unusual study relating the need hierarchy to religion, David MacRae (1977) sought to demonstrate that the level of need at which an individual is functioning will be reflected in that person's religious concepts and preferences. MacRae employed the Cantril Self-Anchoring Questionnaire to assess the level of psychological need and a series of questions designed to elicit the respondent's notions of heaven as well as a favorite book, character, and verse in the Bible. Subjects also rated 30 adjectives for God and 50 verses from the Bible, each of which was chosen to represent one of the need categories. Statistical analysis suggested that, indeed, the anticipated satisfactions of heaven correspond to the individual's predominant need level; that the attributes of God and the verses from the Bible considered most meaningful also correspond to this level; and that a person's reasons for choosing a favorite book, verse, or character of the Bible bear the impress of that person's dominant needs. No subjects, it might be observed, appeared to be operating at the lowest, physiological level.

Correlates of Peak Experience: Maslow's efforts to promote the study of peak experiences, which he associated with the highest level of the need hierarchy, have been realized in a small but growing body of empirical research. Overall, the findings thus far lend considerable support to Maslow's more impressionistic claims. For example, of the 1000 persons living in the San Francisco Bay area who were randomly selected for participation in the Berkeley Religious Consciousness Project (Wuthnow, 1978), 50 percent reported that they had had a feeling of contact with "something holy or sacred," 82 percent said that they had felt deeply moved by the beauty of nature, and 39 percent claimed that they had had a feeling of harmony with the universe, thus confirming Maslow's report that these experiences are not unusual. For each kind of peak experience, those who had experienced it in a "deep and lasting way" were more likely than others to report that their lives were more meaningful; that they thought a good deal about the purpose of life; that they spent time meditating about their lives; and that they possessed certain desirable qualities, such as intelligence, organizational skills, and self-confidence, from which a measure of self-assurance might be inferred. Those who had reported experiencing contact with the sacred were also more likely to say that they knew the purpose of life (see Table 13.3). These associations of peak experience

Table 13.3 **PERSONAL CORRELATES OF PEAK EXPERIENCES**

Item	Percentage Response to Each Peak Experience Item				
	Yes, within one year	Yes, not within one year	Yes, but not lasting	No, but would like to	No, and wouldn't care to
Experience: Contact with the Sacred					
Life very meaningful[a]	68	46	46	39	36
Think about purpose a lot[a]	54	41	28	24	19
Meditate[a]	82	78	71	66	55
Know purpose of life[a]	65	44	30	18	21
Self-assured[a]	47	39	39	22	31
Total *N*	127	141	231	252	242
Experience: The Beauty of Nature					
Life very meaningful[a]	55	40	39	41	36
Think about purpose a lot[a]	39	29	26	23	12
Meditate[a]	80	72	62	53	40
Know purpose of life	33	35	31	25	23
Self-assured[a]	45	28	28	24	26
Total *N*	342	147	325	137	46
Experience: Harmony with the Universe					
Life very meaningful[a]	63	54	46	37	40
Think about purpose a lot[a]	49	54	26	24	22
Meditate[a]	86	91	79	66	47
Know purpose of life	39	50	29	25	33
Self-assured[a]	55	38	36	26	26
Total *N*	169	53	168	335	266

[a] Significant at .05 level (chi square).
Source: From Table 2 in Wuthnow, 1978, page 66.

with the tendencies to be more reflective, inner directed, self-aware, and capably self-assured supports Maslow's assertion that such experiences happen more often to self-actualizing persons.

Maslow's further claim that self-actualizers who have peak experiences become centered in the Being-realm and its values is confirmed by this study's findings that, compared with persons who have had no enduringly influential peak experiences, those with deep and lasting experiences gave higher rankings to social concerns and lower rankings to materialistic and status values. The association of peak experiences and B-realm values was also confirmed by Eugene Mathes and his associates (1982), who have developed a highly reliable, 70-item Peak Experience Scale for assessing the tendency to report such experiences.

Piety and Self-Actualization: The largest body of research bearing on Maslow's psychology of religion is that investigating the relation of religious outlook and self-actualization. Like Jung, Maslow attributes to religion both positive and negative functions. Religion as intense, personal experience is to be cherished and fostered as an aspect of self-actualization. Religion as orthodox creed and pious habit, on the other hand, is said to serve a defensive function and thus is associated with lower levels of human well-being. The studies by Greeley (1975) and Hay and Morisy (1978), cited earlier in conjunction with Pratt's reflections on mysticism, indicate that persons who report mystical experience are on the whole both happier and psychologically healthier than those who do not. And according to George Breed and Joe Fagan's (1972) findings, peak experiences are most likely to be reported by persons who do not subscribe to conventional religious beliefs.

Most of the research on the relation of religiousness to self-actualization employs the Personal Orientation Inventory (POI), a standardized personality test purporting to measure self-actualizing tendencies (Shostrom, 1966). Based on the writings not only of Maslow but also of David Riesman, Rollo May, and Fritz Perls, the POI consists of 150 paired statements representing extreme, categorical positions on a number of general or abstract issues. Respondents are asked to indicate their own views by choosing one statement from each pair. According to the POI's 12 scales, self-actualizers are persons who like themselves in spite of recognized weaknesses and hostile feelings; who flexibly follow their own principles; who are sensitive to and freely express their own feelings and needs; who live in the present, unworried about past or future; who have a capacity for intimacy without becoming slaves to others: who believe that human beings are essentially good and that life's opposites have something in common. The POI has in recent years become one of the most frequently used personality tests in the correlational psychology of religion.

Some of the studies using the POI simply correlate its scores—usually of college students—with one or several measures of conventional piety. Leonard Gibb (1968), for example, found that students at a Midwestern state university who received formal religious instruction as children or who attended parochial schools tended to score lower on a majority of the POI scales than those without such formal religious education. The differences were even more marked for current religious participation, with students who reported attending church "seldom or never" scoring significantly higher on a majority of the scales in comparison to those attending "most or part of the time." Robert Lee and Fred Piercy (1974) and Larry Hjelle (1975) also found church attendance and a majority of the POI scores to be negatively related. The more complex measure of religious commitment employed by Robert Graff and Clayton Ladd (1971) showed the same negative pattern for all four of its scales—Belief, Practice, Experience, and Knowledge.

Maslow's claim that peak experiences are more common among self-actualizing persons finds support in the significant positive association ($r = .22$) that Ralph Hood (1977) found when he correlated the encompassing Inner Support (I) scale of the POI with his own Mysticism Scale for a group of psychology students. In accord with Maslow's views, this correlation was accounted for by Factor I, General Mysticism, and not by Factor II, Religious Interpretation, which reflects a more traditional religious orientation. In another group of subjects, selected for their high mysticism scores, those who were also high on the POI I scale more frequently reported having mystical experiences triggered by sex or drugs, whereas those low on this scale more likely had their mystical experiences in religious or natural settings.

The POI has also been used to evaluate self-actualizing trends among members of the clergy as well as among seminarians. The New Zealand Protestant ministers whom Alan Webster and Robert Stewart (1973) assessed proved, in comparison to their standardization group, to be more self-accepting, more integrated, more able to live in the present, and better at interpersonal relations. They scored significantly lower only on awareness of their own feelings. Within the same group, the majority of the POI scales proved to be negatively correlated with general and theological conservatism, ethnocentrism, and dogmatism. In a sample of evangelical seminary students, Donald Lindskoog and Roger Kirk (1975) found that those who scored higher on the POI scales were more ecumenical in their outlook, had more liberal political and social attitudes, came from higher socioeconomic backgrounds, and more frequently had plans for work other than the ministry or Christian education. The two groups showed no differences, on the other hand, in religious background, beliefs, or mystical experience.

In the study of American Catholic priests that was comissioned by the National Council of Catholic Bishops and carried out by a group of psychologists at Loyola University in Chicago (Kennedy and Heckler, 1972; Kennedy, Heckler, Kobler, and Walker, 1977), the POI was one of four psychological tests selected to supplement the in-depth clinical interviews. On the basis of these interviews and independent of the tests, the 271 priests who participated in this study were assigned to one of four groups representing varying levels of sociopsychological development: developed (6 percent), developing (29 percent), underdeveloped (57 percent), and maldeveloped (8 percent). When compared in terms of POI scores, the developed and developing subjects showed a consistent tendency to score higher than the other two groups. Across the four groups these differences reached statistical significance on four of the scales, indicating that the more mature priests showed greater inner-directedness, more flexibility in applying values, greater freedom in expressing feelings, and less tendency to view life's opposites as antagonistic.

Two additional findings are noteworthy here. Contrary to the overall trend, curiously, the developing group scored higher than the developed group on all but one of the POI scales (see Figure 13.1). Striking, too, is the fact that the 271 priests as a group scored consistently lower on all the POI scales than Shostrom's (1966) unspecified adult normative sample. Kennedy and Heckler conclude from this study that the majority of American priests are psychologically underdeveloped, primarily in their relations with other persons but also in their religious faith. This relative immaturity, they add, underscores their kinship with the rest of the American male population.

PROFILE SHEET FOR THE PERSONAL ORIENTATION INVENTORY

		Valuing		Feeling		Self Perception		Synergistic Awareness		Interpersonal Sensitivity	
TIME COMPET-ENT Lives in the present	INNER DIRECTED independent, self supportive	SELF-ACT-UALIZING VALUE Holds values of self-actualizing people	EXISTENTI-ALITY Flexible in application of values	FEELING REACTIVITY Sensitive to own needs and feelings	SPONTA-NEITY Freely expresses feelings behaviorally	SELF REGARD Has high self-worth	SELF-ACCEPTANCE Accepting of self in spite of weaknesses	NATURE OF MAN. CON-STRUCTIVE Sees man as essentially good	SYNERGY Sees oppo-sites of life as meaning-fully related	ACCEPTANCE OF AGGRESSION Accepts feelings of anger or aggression	CAPACITY FOR INTIMATE CONTACT Has warm interpersonal relationships
T_c	I	SAV	Ex	Fr	S	Sr	Sa	Nc	Sy	A	C

ADULT NORMS

Group	Number
Developed	11
Developing	39
Under developed	149
Maldeveloped	19

| TIME INCOMPE-TENT Lives in the past or future | OTHER DIRECTED Dependent, seeks sup-port of others' views | Rejects values of self-actualiz-ing people | Rigid in application of values | Insensitive to own needs and feelings | Fearful of expressing feelings behaviorally | Has low self-worth | Unable to accept self with weaknesses | Sees man as essentially evil | Sees opposites of life as antagonistic | Denies feelings of anger or aggression | Has diffi-culty with warm inter-personal relations |

Figure 13.1. Personal Orientation Inventory Scores for Roman Catholic priests at four levels of development. On each scale, a standard score of 50 is equal to the mean of the normative group, and a deviation of ten points in either direction is equal to one STANDARD DEVIATION. Source: From Figure 2 in Kennedy and Heckler, 1972, page 158. (Profile sheet copyright © 1965 by Educational & Industrial Testing Service, San Diego, California 92107; reproduced with permission.)

Modeled on the Kennedy and Heckler study and thus inviting comparison is another, of one hundred women randomly selected from 211 participants in the 1975 Detroit Ordination Conference who had signed a public statement declaring that they felt personally called to ordination in the Catholic Church (Ferder, 1978). Like the priests, these women were rated on the basis of clinical interviews accord-ing to psychological adjustment: 54 percent were judged developed, 37 percent developing, 8 percent underdeveloped, and 1 percent maldeveloped. Paralleling these strikingly higher ratings in psychological maturity were higher POI scores. The majority of these women scored above the mean of the normative group on all the scales. Although scale–score differences were not large for the subgroups of women, the better adjusted showed a clear tendency to have higher POI scores. As Ferder points out, her subjects were in several ways not comparable to Kennedy and Heckler's priests. Her women were self-selected (through attendance at the conference), devoted to an innovative and unifying cause, and seeking a nontraditional and officially discouraged position in life. Accordingly, it is not surprising that they appear psychologically healthier than the randomly selected priests.

Finally, the POI has served to evaluate the gains of meditation. William Seeman, Sanford Nidich, and Thomas Banta (1972) found that experimental subjects who practiced transcendental meditation (TM) regularly over a period of two months showed significant gains on 6 of the 12 POI scales when compared to a control group of nonmeditators. In a replication of this study, significant differences between experimental and control subjects were found on ten of the scales, all in the predicted direction of increasing self-actualization (Nidich, Seeman, and Dreskin, 1973). Similar results were obtained by Hjelle (1974) when he compared a group of novice meditators with persons who had been practicing TM for an average of nearly 23 months. Experienced meditators scored higher than the beginners on seven of the POI scales. On the other hand, two studies employing less highly motivated subjects, somewhat different techniques of meditation, and shorter time intervals, did not find significant differences in POI scores (Bartels, 1977; Kubose, 1976).

These findings seem to confirm Maslow's conviction that self-actualization is hindered by involvement in traditional religious beliefs and practices, especially if they are conservative. Self-actualization appears to be advanced, on the other hand, by active participation in certain less orthodox practices such as meditation or encounter groups (Knapp, 1990). To draw this conclusion, we must be confident that the POI is a reasonably valid measure of self-actualization. Everett Shostrom's (1966) chief evidence for the POI's validity is the repeated finding that persons nominated as "relatively self-actualized" by clinical psychologists score significantly higher on most or all of the POI scales than persons nominated as not-self-actualized or identified as psychiatric patients. It may be, however, that these studies chiefly confirm that a majority of clinical psychologists, including the developers of the POI, share a common set of presuppositions, among which are certain nonconventional attitudes and a rejection of traditional religion (Watson, Morris, and Hood, 1987).

More objective studies assessing the POI's construct validity raise doubts about the test's adequacy as a measure of self-actualization. The factor analysis of the POI's scales carried out by Donald Tosi and Susan Hoffman (1972) found that 72 percent of the variance on the POI's highly intercorrelated scales can be explained in terms of only three factors: (1) *extraversion,* a basic personality dimension reported to have two main components, impulsivity and sociability (Sparrow and Ross, 1964), and sometimes found to be negatively correlated with religiosity (Francis, Pearson, Carter, and Kay, 1981); (2) *open-mindedness* (though James's healthy-mindedness would seem to be a more accurate label); and (3) *existential nonconformity,* a factor distinguished by uncritical self-acceptance and flexibility in following principles. Apart from challenging the value of the POI's multiplicity of scales, these factors evoke less the image of a mature self-actualizer than that of a young, free-spirited American. Confirming this impression is the finding that POI scores, rather than increasing with age, as Maslow's theory and common sense would predict for a measure of self-actualization, tend to decline in older subjects (Greeley, 1970, in Knapp, 1990, p. 85; Rizzo and Vinacke, 1975). The POI similarly failed to show the predicted relationships when correlated with the Peak Experience Scale by Mathes and his associates (1982).

The POI's correlations with other standardized personality tests also raise doubts about what it is measuring. For example, the correlations with the Study of Values that Shostrom (1966, p. 31) reports without interpretation point not to the altruism, moral consistency, aesthetic sensitivity, and problem-centeredness that Maslow attributes to self-actualizers but rather to a predominance of self-interest and a desire for power. Correlations of the POI with the Sixteen Personality Factor Questionnaire led Shostrom to conclude that "The self-actualizing student might be described as comparatively more assertive, happy-go-lucky, expedient, venturesome, and self-assured" (p. 32)—hardly a satisfactory description of an Eleanor Roosevelt or an Albert Schweitzer but suggestive, perhaps, of qualities that distinguish Ferder's woman aspirants to the priesthood from the typical American priest. Observing the POI's bias in favor of extraversion, individual autonomy, and living in the here and now, and regretting the lack of sophistication in test item formulation, Richard Coan (1972) expresses the hope that more adequate instruments for measuring self-actualization will soon be developed. These instruments will perhaps someday enable more satisfactory testing of Maslow's hypothesis.

TRANSPERSONAL PSYCHOLOGY

Maslow's thinking has inspired yet another research trend, this one much larger in scope and extending even beyond the boundaries of humanistic psychology. In the late 1960s, only a few years after the founding of the *Journal of Humanistic Psychology* and the Association for Humanistic Psychology, Maslow and others became increasingly aware that their research was leading them beyond the strictly "humanistic" to matters of cosmic meaning or ultimate concern. After some debate over what to call the emerging new trend, they christened it "transpersonal psychology," which some viewed as a "fourth force," paralleling behaviorism, classical psychoanalysis, and humanistic psychology. The first public presentation of transpersonal psychology was a lecture Maslow gave in 1967 at the First Unitarian Church in San Francisco. Summing up portions of his own research on self-actualization and peak experiences, this lecture became the lead article in the inaugural issue of *The Journal of Transpersonal Psychology*. Identified in the same issue as transpersonal psychology's "philosophical father," Maslow (1968, pp. iii–iv) came to think of humanistic psychology as a transitional science, preparatory to the still "higher" transpersonal form.

Much like its predecessor, transpersonal psychology seeks to illuminate a large variety of phenomena and concepts that have otherwise been neglected by contemporary psychologists. Following Maslow's emphatically repeated recommendation, the advocates of transpersonal psychology have sought to apply to these matters the most rigorous scientific methods possible. According to the *Journal's* initial Statement of Purpose, transpersonal psychology encompasses the empirical study of

> metaneeds, ultimate values, unitive consciousness, peak experiences, ecstasy, mystical experience, B values, essence, bliss, awe, wonder, self-actualization, ultimate meaning, transcendence of the self, spirit, sacralization of everyday life, oneness, cosmic awareness, cosmic play, individual and species-wide synergy, maximal interpersonal encounter, transcendental phenomena; maximal sensory awareness, responsiveness and expression; and related concepts, experiences, and activities. (Vol. 1, No. 1, p. i)

From more than two decades of subsequent work, Denise Lajoie and S. I. Shapiro (1992) have distilled the following, more succinct definition: "Transpersonal psychology is concerned with the study of humanity's highest potential, and with the recognition, understanding, and realization of unitive, spiritual, and transcendent states of consciousness'' (p. 91). To mark its 25th year, the *Journal* published a history of the field and "state of the art" evaluation by psychiatrist Roger Walsh (1993).

Explicitly concerned with a number of phenomena that have traditionally occupied psychologists of religion, transpersonal psychology represents nonetheless a significant departure from this earlier work. Most obvious is the much larger place given to Eastern religious experience, most notably meditation. Research of this type has been reviewed earlier, chiefly in Chapter 5. More divergent still are transpersonal psychology's efforts to appropriate the psychological insights of the great religious traditions—primarily, again, those of the East—in order to develop a new paradigm of scientific understanding. The severe difficulties of appropriating insights from the East are addressed by the Swiss existential psychotherapist Medard Boss (1959) in a sensitive retelling of his own, first-hand encounter with the traditional wisdom of India.

The quest for a new paradigm has received special impetus from the holistic "systems view" of contemporary physics, which, according to physicist Fritjof Capra (1975), shows striking parallels to ancient mystical teachings, especially Eastern traditions. The revolution in twentieth-century physics, Capra (1982) maintains in a more recent work, signals a wider revolution, a "turning point" in all the sciences and a new vision of reality that promises transformation and healing for individual, society, and environment alike. Ken Wilber's (1977, 1981, 1995) efforts to delineate a multilevel "spectrum of consciousness" and to construct a model of humankind's evolution toward "integral Wholeness and Spirit" (1981, p. 11) illustrate the bold tendency among some advocates of the transpersonal orientation to equate a considerable diversity of psychological and religious concepts (the latter primarily from the East) and to order them according to some syncretic and all-embracing vision of reality. Collections of representative essays can be found in the books edited by Ornstein (1973), Tart (1975, 1990), Walsh and Shapiro (1983), and Walsh and Vaughan (1993).

The "ebullient rhetoric favored by the transpersonal psychologists" (Zaleski, 1987, p. 107) suggests less a psychology *of* religion than a modern-day effort at integration—of Western psychology and Eastern religion. As Michael Washburn (1995) puts it, "Transpersonal psychology is a comprehensive enterprise; it is a *Geisteswissenschaft* that draws upon several humanistic disciplines without itself being strictly subsumable under any of them" (p. ix). Because of its multidisciplinary character and its goal of holistic understanding, he continues, transpersonal psychology might better be called transpersonal *theory*. Whatever we call it, it serves today mainly as an expanded context for a form of psychotherapy that adds authentic spirituality to the usual goals of healthy functioning (Vaughan, Wittine, and Walsh, 1996). The possibilities for cross-fertilization between transpersonal psychology and the scientific study of religion are suggested in a book dedicated to the problem of choosing among the diverse offerings of the new American "psychospiritual "supermarket'" (Anthony, Ecker, and Wilber, 1987, p. 1).

Although the field of transpersonal psychology extends well beyond the boundaries of traditional psychology of religion, we examine here two related subtopics that have interested at least some psychologists of religion: near-death experience and parapsychology. Both are controversial topics about which psychologists and laypersons alike have strong feelings. The challenge to us is to resist prejudging these areas and to examine them with open but critical minds. The experiences they address are compellingly real and sometimes dramatically transforming for the many people who have them. Whether or not we agree that these experiences are evidence of some larger reality, they invite the interest of every serious student of the psychology of religion.

Near-Death Experiences

Anecdotal evidence of what are today called near-death experiences (NDEs) has been available for centuries, but it was not until late in the nineteenth century that any of it was systematically assembled. Albert Heim (1892), a Swiss geology professor and himself the subject of such experiences, collected over a period of decades the reports of survivors of serious accidents, especially persons who had suffered life-threatening falls in the Alps. Heim concluded that for about 95 percent of such accident victims—and presumably also for the great majority of those who do not survive—the experience of impending death is exceedingly pleasant. Free of the pain or anxiety that might paralyze a person in less grave situations, these subjects experienced heightened alertness, greatly accelerated mental activity, and profound feelings of peace and acceptance. Some witnessed a rapid review of their lives and reported visual and auditory experiences of the most transcendent beauty.

The phenomenon of near-death experience became the subject of widespread interest with the publication of Raymond Moody's *Life After Life* (1975), a popular report on the experience of about 50 people the author had interviewed. A philosopher and a physician, Moody combined the frequently recurring elements in these reports to construct the following "ideal" case:

> A man is dying and, as he reaches the point of greatest physical distress, he hears himself pronounced dead by his doctor. He begins to hear an uncomfortable noise, a loud ringing or buzzing, and at the same time feels himself outside of his own physical body, but still in the immediate physical environment, and he sees his own body from a distance, as though he is a spectator. He watches the resuscitation attempt from this unusual vantage point and is in a state of emotional upheaval.
>
> After a while, he collects himself and becomes more accustomed to his odd condition. He notices that he still has a "body," but one of a very different nature and with very different powers from the physical body he has left behind. Soon other things begin to happen. Others come to meet and to help him. He glimpses the spirits of relatives and friends who have already died, and a loving, warm spirit of a kind he has never encountered before—a being of light—appears before him. This being asks him a question, nonverbally, to make him evaluate his life and helps him along by showing him a panoramic, instantaneous playback of the major events of his life. At some point he finds himself approaching some sort of barrier or border, apparently representing the limit between earthly life and the next life. Yet, he finds that he must go back to the earth, that the time for his death has not yet come. At this point he resists, for by now he is taken up with his experiences in the afterlife and does not want to return. He is overwhelmed by intense feelings of joy, love, and peace. Despite his attitude, though, he somehow reunites with his physical body and lives.
>
> Later he tries to tell others, but he has trouble doing so. In the first place, he can find no human words adequate to describe these unearthly episodes. He also finds that others scoff, so he stops telling other people. Still, the experience affects his life profoundly, especially his views about death and its relationship to life. (Moody, 1975, pp. 23-24)

Although none of his informants reported this composite experience in its entirety, many described a majority of the 15 separate elements. The ordering of these elements varied somewhat, too, but marked deviations were unusual. In a sequel

Hieronymus Bosch's *Ascension to the Empyrean,* from the sixteenth century, depicts death as a passage from darkness through a tunnel of brilliant light.

to his first report, Moody (1977) added four other, far less common elements: a transitory vision of complete knowledge or universal insight, forgotten in its particulars when consciousness is regained; an indescribably beautiful city of light; a realm of bewildered spirits still unable to surrender their attachment to the physical world; and supernatural rescue from physical death by some spiritual being or agent.

A variety of other studies, including several that antedate Moody's, have reported similar patterns of experience (see Basford, 1990; Lundahl, 1982; Sabom, 1981; Siegel, 1980). Bruce Greyson (1990), for example, found that at least 40 percent of his sample of 183 people reporting NDEs during close brushes with death checked off the following experiences on Greyson's NDE Scale: time stopped or lost its meaning, or everything seemed to happen at once (74 percent); a feeling of incredible peace or pleasantness (74 percent) or of incredible joy (57 percent); a sense of harmony or unity with the world (55 percent); seeing or feeling surrounded by an unusually bright light or a light of otherworldly origin (72 percent); finding one's senses more vivid than usual (66 percent); leaving the physical body and existing outside of it (55 percent); entering a mystical or unearthly realm (56 percent); and encountering a definite being or voice of otherworldly origin (50 percent). All 16 items on Greyson's scale significantly distinguished the 183 participants reporting NDEs from 63 others who similarly came close to death but denied having NDEs.

With the refinement of standardized questionnaires and the gathering of cross-cultural evidence, researchers in the field of near-death studies are increasingly able to specify to whom and under what conditions the various elements of the near-death experience are likely to occur. It is estimated that upwards to 50 percent of people who come close to dying have NDEs and that 5 percent of Americans have had them to some degree. Researchers concur that the likelihood of NDEs is unrelated to age, sex, level of education, socioeconomic status, occupation, marital status, and religious background (Roberts and Owen, 1988). Age apparently does make a difference, however, in the character of the experience. Whereas the children with NDEs in Nancy Evans Bush's (1983) study described encounters with a spiritual being or presence about as frequently as adults, they reported no life reviews. The experience of light, on the other hand, was described by 65 percent of them, nearly double the rate in a comparison group of adults.

Some researchers think there may be an NDE-prone personality, especially given evidence suggesting that adults who have NDEs are more likely than others to report a childhood marked by abuse, illness, or a troubled home-life and to score higher on a dissociation scale (Ring and Rosing, 1990). Other investigators have found NDEs to be associated with a greater openness to alternate states and a tendency to direct attention inwardly. Because these data are retrospective, however, they may have been influenced by the NDEs (Roberts and Owen, 1988). Susan Blackmore (1993) thinks it is too early to draw conclusions about the contributions of personality.

The role of cultural factors is suggested by Karlis Osis and Erlendur Haraldsson's (1986) report that, in both the United States and India, the hallucinatory beings whom the dying sometimes see and usually take to be guides to another world are predominantly either persons who earlier died, usually relatives, or religious figures, such as angels, Jesus, or Shiva. Americans, however, are five times more likely to see apparitions of the dead than of religious figures, whereas Indians, including Christian patients, more often see religious figures (p. 65). In other respects, however, Osis and Haraldsson find the experiences in these contrasting cultures to be more similar than different. Furthermore, these researchers found that the visionary experiences of the dying often contradicted specific Christian or Hindu teachings about the afterlife.

NDEs occur at about the same overall rate for persons who attempt suicide and survive as for other near-death survivors. Curiously, however, a significant sex difference has appeared in these data. Whereas only 35 percent of the women who attempted suicide reported NDEs, 80 percent of the men did. The men's higher rate, approaching that reported by Heim, may reflect the well-known fact that men tend to employ more lethal means of self-destruction and are thus more likely, if they survive, to have come close to dying. Contrary to what one might expect, suicide-related NDEs are usually very positive and sometimes exceptionally beautiful. Furthermore, the often-profound transformations associated with NDEs occur under these circumstances as well. Those attempting suicide who experience NDEs, the evidence suggests, are unlikely to try again (Greyson, 1981; Ring and Franklin, 1981-82).

Persons who have undergone near-death experiences frequently report one or more elements of a coherent pattern of positive attitude change. Included among these elements are (1) a marked reduction in the fear of death; (2) a feeling of relative invulnerability; (3) a sense of having been chosen for some unique but still unknown mission; (4) a conviction that it was God or some other outside force that was responsible for their new sense of destiny; and (5) a new or intensified belief in some form of life after death. The enduring sense of death's reality that many report frequently brings with it a new appreciation of life's preciousness, a reorganization of priorities along with a new sense of urgency to live life more fully, and a more passive acceptance of life events, now perceived as less controllable than once thought (Noyes, 1980). Using Kenneth Ring's (1980) index for assessing the depth of near-death experience, Steven McLaughlin and Newton Malony (1984) found that depth of experience was significantly associated with increases in rated importance of religion ($r = .46$) and in religious activity ($r = .38$). Retrospective estimates of pre-NDE piety, on the other hand, bore no relation to the depth index, confirming the widely held view that a person's earlier religious outlook influences at most the interpretation of NDEs, not their occurrence or content.

The recurring though still variable pattern of elements making up NDEs has tempted some researchers to agree with their informants that such experiences provide evidence of post-death survival. As psychiatrist and parapsychologist Ian Stevenson (1977b) points out, however, NDEs have so far provided no objective evidence in support of the survival hypothesis. Rather, he says, such experiences may merely reflect adaptive processes triggered by the threat of death, a view that is elaborated by Russell Noyes and Roy Kletti (1976). Any interpretation must also take into account the small minority of NDEs that are unpleasant, frightening, or even hellish (Greyson and Bush, 1992).

Of those who have offered strictly naturalistic explanations for NDEs, Blackmore (1993) provides the fullest and most accessible account. She argues that NDEs are the result of a combination of processes that occur whenever the brain begins to die. The main trigger of NDEs, Blackmore proposes, is cerebral anoxia, or lack of oxygen in the brain. Drawing on research on the loss of consciousness that fighter pilots experience during marked acceleration, she concludes that anoxia is responsible for the elements of euphoria, out-of-body experience, vividly beautiful visions, and the failure to move or communicate. The experience of light at the end of a tunnel, which is more common under extreme medical conditions, is traced by Blackmore to the random neural firing that would result from anoxia's disinhibition of the visual cortex. Endorphins are also thought to play a role. According to Blackmore, these neurotransmitters induce the feelings of peace, happiness, and well-being that are characteristic of NDEs, and by setting off seizures in the limbic system and the temporal lobe of the cortex, they create flashbacks and associated feelings of familiarity and meaningfulness—the life review that 25 percent of Greyson's (1990) NDE subjects reported. The subsequent changes in personal outlook, including the loss of fear of death, are traced by Blackmore to the breakdown, under crisis, of the individual's normal model of reality and the accompanying dissolution of the illusory sense of self.

The sense of self and NDEs may emerge from the same neurocognitive processes, according to Michael Persinger (1994). Persinger has found that a "significant number" of brain-injured people—who very commonly report a change in the sense of self, especially if the temporal lobes are involved—also report NDEs around the time they realized they were different persons. Persinger notes that NDEs are more commonly associated with oxygen insufficiency, to which he too attributes a number of specific NDE phenomena. Among them is the sense of a presence, which he takes to be an intrusion of the right hemisphere's equivalent of the self into the left hemisphere, which is more vulnerable to oxygen deprivation. Persinger speculates that the traumatic events commonly associated with NDEs may lead to a lasting restructuring of the areas of the brain that mediate the sense of self.

Does tracing NDEs to neurophysiological processes invalidate them as evidence of an afterlife? That certainly is the view of Ronald Siegel (1980), who concludes that NDEs are hallucinations based on stored images in the brain and induced by drugs and other conditions affecting the central nervous system. Melvin Morse (1990) represents the opposite view. After concluding from Penfield's brain stimulation research that the NDE originates in the Sylvian fissure in the right temporal lobe, Morse argues that, by locating the "circuit board" for such mystical experiences, researchers have established the NDE as a normal event in the dying. Spirituality and a soul separate from the body should thus be easier for medical professionals to accept, says Morse, who found himself transformed by his near-death research. What impressed him most, it appears, is the phenomenon of the light, which he takes to be the key element of the NDE. It happens also to be, he claims, the one element that brain researchers "can't even come close to explaining" (pp. 170, 117).

As Greyson and Bush (1992, p. 107) remark, "although many of the existing theories might explain some aspects of the near-death experience, few do so with precision, and none adequately describes all aspects of this still idiopathic event." In a masterful study of the NDE literature in the wider historical framework of visionary otherworld journeys, Carol Zaleski (1987) is likewise doubtful that the full range of near-death experiences can be accounted for by neuropsychological theories. She proposes instead that we conceive of the otherworld journey as a product of the religious imagination, serving both as a picture for orienting ourselves in the cosmos and as a system of instruction for moral and spiritual living. Translated into object-relations terms, NDEs may thus be thought of as illusionistic transitional phenomena, which help us to find ourselves at home in this world rather than our way into the next one.[1]

Parapsychology

Whether Stevenson's (1975, 1977a) own research on cases suggestive of reincarnation should also be subsumed under transpersonal psychology is unclear, for some students of the field would prefer to keep it separate from such parapsychological matters (Boucouvalas, 1980). Research on near-death experience might be excluded from transpersonal psychology on the same grounds, for some of its components, including out-of-the-body experience, have long interested parapsychologists. With the notable exceptions of William James, Theodore Flournoy, and Robert Thouless, psychologists of religion also seem to be suspicious of so-called paranormal or psychic phenomena, for references to them are rare indeed in the literature.

Flournoy (1911b) argues that scientific investigators are greatly mistaken in neglecting this realm, for it may cast unexpected light on human nature and its capacities. Although he is convinced that spiritism—the doctrine that spirits of the dead occasionally intervene in human life—is completely erroneous, Flournoy does grant the possibility of such paranormal phenomena as TELEPATHY, CLAIRVOYANCE, and TELEKINESIS, the existence of which he predicts will someday be well established by experimental research. The best of the evidence gathered in the first half of the twentieth century and bearing on these and related phenomena, including survival

---

[1]The World-Wide Web offers a growing array of resources on NDEs, including book reviews and interviews of researchers. Start with http://www.mindspring.com/~scottr/end.html

of death, is reviewed in a book by Gardner Murphy in collaboration with Laura Dale (1961). Murphy, an eminent American social psychologist (Hilgard, 1987), courageously risked his reputation in lending support over many years to so suspect a field. Among his other contributions is an edited volume of James's writings on psychical research (Murphy and Ballou, 1960).

According to Lawrence Grensted (1952, p. 165), the implications of parapsychological research for the psychology of religion "may in the end be considerable." Focusing in particular on telepathy, zoologist Alister Hardy suggests that perhaps the most important issue facing the psychology of religion is

> whether the power that may be called God is entirely within the individual—deep in the subconscious—or [whether it is], at least in part, transcendent. If it could be shown beyond doubt that one mind may communicate with another mind by other than physical means—that in fact elements of our mental life may extend beyond the physico-chemical structure of the brain—then it would at least lend plausibility to the idea that our minds, subconscious or conscious, might be in touch with some larger mental field, possibly like that of the shared subconscious suggested by Jung, beyond our individual selves, or perhaps with something inconceivably greater. It would be an important step towards the scientific recognition of a nonmaterial mental world in which perhaps the numinous—to use Otto's term for the "mysterium tremendum" of religion—might be thought to lie (Hardy, 1975, p. 121).

Our view of religious experience would be profoundly affected, Hardy argues, if the evidence for telepathy could be so improved that it became widely accepted as scientific fact.

The religious implications of parapsychological research have been explored in some detail by Alson Smith (1951), an Episcopal priest well acquainted with the accumulated evidence of anecdotal and experimental research. He maintains that these findings may help to mend "the broken circle of faith," by providing assurance that every human being has a soul and that it *may* survive bodily death; by postulating the existence of a universal spirit and a spiritual homeland; by demonstrating a margin of human freedom and the possibility of intercessory prayer; and by providing the foundations for a more universal social ethic, by underscoring that all persons share in "the treasury of spirituality" (pp. 160–175). The more measured analysis of Robert Thouless (1971), who considers the evidence for some paranormal events to be "overwhelming," emphasizes parapsychology's role in making more plausible a view that "includes a spiritual world and a life after death, and [that] seems to make more understandable such facts of religious narratives as miracles, prophecies, and visions" (p. 88). At the same time he considers "the central elements of religious faith" to be inaccessible to direct experimental study. Alan Angoff (1966) emphasizes the vastness and formlessness of the literature on religion and parapsychology in a special issue of the *International Journal of Parapsychology* dedicated to this subject.

Like others sympathetic to the field of psychic research, both Smith and Thouless point out that the claims of the parapsychologists pose a fundamental challenge to orthodox science. It is therefore understandable that most researchers have steered clear of this controversial area. The fact is, however, that paranormal experiences are far more widespread than many have suspected. In Greeley's (1975) national sample of Americans, 58 percent reported at least one experience of being in touch with someone while they were far away, 24 percent claimed having seen on one or more occasions events occurring at a great distance, and 28 percent said that they had felt, at least once or twice, that they were in touch with someone who had died. In their search for personal or demographic factors associated with paranormal experience, Greeley and his associates found that those who have such experiences tend to report the presence of tension either within their family of origin or in their own marriages, a factor that might well contribute to their seemingly greater sensitivity. These researchers demonstrate the possibility of investigating the conditions associated with the experience of paranormal phenomena—one of the psychology of religion's chief tasks, according to Karl Beth (1926)—without becoming entangled in the exceedingly difficult issue of their VERIDICALITY. If we are actually facing a paradigm shift, as the transpersonal psychologists and others maintain, paranormal phenomena may yet find a place within the subfields of psychology. As Murphy notes, however, "Areas which are taboo do not change rapidly, even under considerable corrosive influence" (in Farberow, 1963, p. 58).

TWO EXISTENTIAL PERSPECTIVES ON RELIGION

Two other prominent contributors to the American humanistic synthesis require our attention: Rollo May and Viktor Frankl. May (1909–1994), a clinical psychologist who was long associated with the William Alanson White Institute in New York, is perhaps the best known American proponent of the European existential perspective as developed by such psychologists and psychiatrists as Ludwig Binswanger and Medard Boss. He was also profoundly influenced by the melancholic Danish theologian Søren Kierkegaard, whose existential writings helped May confront the profound anxiety he endured during a protracted and potentially fatal bout with tuberculosis. Frankl (1905–1997), a psychiatrist who for years was the director of the Neurological Polyclinic of the University of Vienna, has long been known around the world for his psychological reflections on the horrors he witnessed and suffered during three terrifying years in Nazi concentration camps (Frankl, 1962). Initially associated with Alfred Adler, Frankl eventually rejected Adler's organizing principle of the "will to power" as well as Freud's "will to pleasure" in favor of his own, the "will to meaning" (Fabry, 1968).

A Bridge Between Psychology and Religion

Among liberal religious thinkers, the existential outlook represented by May and Frankl is naturally appealing, for the themes they and others have enunciated are also momentous in religious reflection. As we have already seen in the work of Eduard Spranger, the existential perspective has also been taken up into the psychology of religion. Writing at a time when a self-consciously existential psychology was only beginning to emerge, Karl Beth (1933) was convinced that the psychology of religion must reconstitute itself as just such an approach. It must recognize, he says, the unique character of individual human existence as it comes to know itself as goal-oriented and an integral part of a given historical situation.

Years later, after the popular excitement over the existential movement had largely subsided, Joseph Royce (1962) identified existentialism as a means of bridging the regrettable gulf between psychology and religion. Hopeful that the phenomenological approach of the existentialist might gain a more sympathetic hearing from psychologists than "the typically non-empirical approach" of the religionist, Royce discusses four existential themes equally of concern to psychology and religion: (1) the importance of self-realization of authentically living out one's values; (2) the centrality of the nonrational in human life; (3) the significance of

Rollo May

anxiety; and (4) the role of symbolic processes. When existential insights cannot be tested empirically, Royce suggests, it may be possible to subject them to the criterion of existential validity: effectiveness in changing lives.

Rollo May: Religion as Resource or Refuge

The consonance of existential psychology with a religious outlook is reflected in Rollo May's having served as a Congregational minister before he undertook his doctoral studies in clinical psychology at Columbia University. A large proportion of those who later came to consult with him, we might also note, were ministers, students of theology, and other religious persons. An even larger circle of religious professionals came under his influence through his dozen or so books, most of them aimed at a lay readership, as well as the excerpts from his various writings that occasionally appeared in the popular journal *Pastoral Psychology*. Although religion is not an explicit theme in most of May's writings, especially the later works, he nonetheless demonstrates an enduring appreciation for the positive role of the religious outlook.

In the first of his books, published the year after he completed his studies at Union Theological Seminary, May (1939, p. 207–224) declares that "true religion," understood as the finding and affirming of ultimate meaning and individual purpose in the life process as a whole, is essential to a healthy personality. Every genuine atheist with whom he had worked, he says, had shown "unmistakable neurotic tendencies," for each lacked an integrating sense of purpose and direction. Although Freud, Jung, and Adler are the most conspicuous influences in this early work, May's thinking also shows the impress of his teacher and lifelong friend Paul Tillich, who sought in his systematic theology to correlate the questions implicit in the human existential situation with the answers contained in the Christian message (see Tillich, 1952).

The explicitly Christian cast of May's first works (see also May, 1940) is no longer apparent in the later writings, in which the existential perspective is much more fully developed. The one theme that remains constant throughout is that *religion may be either a source of strength or a refuge for weakness*. In accord with the human spirit's capacity for both good and evil, religion may strengthen the individual's sense of personal dignity and worth, promote the affirmation of values in life, and foster the development of ethical awareness and personal responsibility. Or religion may diminish a person's sense of freedom, engender an expectation of being taken care of, and allow the individual to avoid the anxiety that inevitably accompanies any genuine facing of human possibilities. Psychology can help to promote the positive side of religion, May suggests, by making evident the errors of dogmatic faith and clearing the way for genuine inner conviction. Psychology and religion may also cooperate in making possible the awe and wonder felt by the healthy, creative human being, in whom the possibilities of the human spirit are actualized (May, 1953, 1957).

May carefully avoids identifying religion with its traditional forms, any of which, he suggests, may serve as a reassuring though encapsulating "stockade of dogma." Yet he thinks that they are potentially of considerable importance: "We have only ourselves to pauperize if we neglect the wisdom that comes down to us through the historical traditions in ethics and religion" (May, 1957, p. 183). His own appropriation of the insights of the religious traditions as they coalesce in the emerging "new polytheism" (see Miller, 1981) is revealed in the meditative practice with which he began each day of his clinical practice. Starting with reflection on his dreams from the night before, he continued with a Hindu- and Buddhist-inspired phase of meditating on nothingness, which served to free him from everyday pressures and resentments and sometimes eventuated in a still-deeper "experience of Being" marked by ecstasy, pervasive calmness, and a sense of beatitude. There was generally also a third phase, reflecting his Protestant Christian heritage, in which certain vague images came to him and a message formed itself, often taking him by surprise (May, 1973, pp. 94–96). In sum, it would appear that the phenomena of centering down and absorption as they are described by Carl Albrecht (1951) were familiar to May as well.

Viktor Frankl: The Search for Meaning

Frankl is the originator of a therapeutic approach known as LOGOTHERAPY, which is derived from European existential and phenomenological sources. It is phenomenology's role, Frankl (1975) asserts, to render articulate the "pre-reflective ontological self-understanding" possessed by all human beings. This intuitive understanding consists of two aspects: a prelogical understanding of human existence itself, and a premoral understanding of meaning—or, in a word, conscience. Once phenomenology has carried out its work, it is then logotherapy's task to retranslate this "wisdom of the heart" into simpler language, in order to make it available to ordinary people (pp. 130–131).

Normal human existence, says Frankl, is always directed not to the self but toward other persons or things. Through this intentional movement of "self-transcendence," Frankl claims, human beings strive to find meaning and purpose, which are essential for human fulfillment and happiness. The beacon that guides a person in the "search for meaning" is the *conscience,* which Frankl takes to be an irreducible phenomenon of a transcendent origin. Phenomenological–existential analysis, he maintains, points a person beyond the merely psychological dimension to an unconscious *logos,* a "noölogical dimension"[1] of spiritual depth. Here we find an "unconscious religiousness," a "latent relation to transcendence" inherent in all persons. Thus the spiritual unconscious is also the "transcendent unconscious," the intentional referent of which may be called "God."

Frankl says that this "primary" or "intrinsic" religiousness remains uncon-

---

[1] "Noölogical" is derived from "noetic," meant here to refer to "meaning" or "spirit" (*logos*).

Viktor Frankl

scious, if not also repressed, in many people today. The result, he says, is the sense of emptiness, meaninglessness, and futility that is becoming increasingly evident, especially in America. This "existential vacuum" is reflected worldwide in depression and suicide, in drug addiction and alcoholism, and in destructive aggression. Healing for the individual and society will come only with the integration of all three aspects of the human being: the somatic, the psychic, and the religious. Though wary of degrading religion by making it one more tool for promoting mental health, or of making psychotherapy the handmaiden of some religious view, Frankl argues that it is the logotherapist's task to remind the patient of his or her personal spiritual core.

Otherwise, the therapist must wait for religiousness to unfold as it will. Defining religion as the "search for *ultimate* meaning" (p. 13), Frankl argues that, for religiousness to be genuine, it must be spontaneous and personal. It cannot be commanded or willed. Frankl rejects sectarian efforts to promote a particular god that demands to be believed in, or the preaching at others to have faith, hope, or love. Moreover, to attempt to will these intentional acts is to make *them* into objects, and thus to risk losing sight of the objects to which they refer. If you wish others to have faith in God, he says, you must "portray your God believably—and you must act credibly yourself" (pp. 14–15). You cannot give meanings to others, but only an example of your own existential commitment to the search for meaning.

In an age of waning traditions and values, Frankl says, the primary task of education becomes refining the individual conscience, preparing it to meet responsibly and with increasingly comprehensive meaning the countless life situations ahead. Individual survival, Frankl discovered while imprisoned at Auschwitz and Dachau, depends on finding a meaning that points toward the future. The same principle holds for the survival of the human race, he says, but it must be a common meaning, "an awareness of common tasks." Belief in one God, Frankl concludes, is not enough; what is also required is an awareness of the oneness of humankind (p. 140).

Frankl's writings on logotherapy have predictably attracted critical attention in both psychotherapeutic and theological circles, in Europe (e.g., Böschemeyer, 1973), as well as in America (Tweedie, 1961). Perhaps surprisingly, they have also inspired a modest body of correlational research, based on the Purpose-in-Life Test

(PIL) developed by James Crumbaugh and Leonard Maholick (1964) to measure the degree to which life is perceived to have meaning and purpose. Although these authors found this test to be essentially unrelated to any of the six value dimensions assessed by the Allport–Vernon–Lindzey Study of Values, it has shown significant relations to two other scales familiar to us. Frankl's claim that meaning is not to be found in the pursuit of self-centered pleasure is supported by the finding that the higher we rank the hedonistic values of Pleasure, An Exciting Life, and A Comfortable Life on the Rokeach Value Survey, the lower our Purpose-in-Life scores will likely be. A high ranking of Salvation, however, is predictive of a high PIL score (Crandall and Rasmussen, 1975). Allport's (1966, p. 455) claim that an intrinsic religious orientation "floods the whole life with motivation and meaning" is supported by the finding in two studies that the RO Intrinsic scale is positively related to PIL scores (Bolt, 1975; Crandall and Rasmussen, 1975). Though an existentialist in spirit, Frankl (1975) takes obvious satisfaction in empirical findings of this sort.

EVALUATION OF THE AMERICAN HUMANISTIC APPROACH

American humanistic psychology has proved to be widely popular. In place of the mechanistic or darkly deterministic theories of the objective and depth psychologists, the humanists offer a lofty vision of human possibilities that is at once familiar and inspiring. These reflections are sometimes undergirded with a substantial body of empirical research. Even though much of this research is suspect in the eyes of more rigorously scientific psychologists, the humanistic outlook has become an obligatory presence in current psychological textbooks, both introductory and personality.

These humanistic psychologists are also major figures in some textbooks on the psychology of religion (Byrnes, 1984; Crapps, 1986; Meadow and Kahoe, 1984). As we have seen, the humanists ascribe to religion—broadly defined—a major role in the dynamics of the self-actualizing process. Only certain forms of religion are thought to support the realization of human potential, however, and thus a major feature of this literature is the distinguishing of religious types. These simple typologies are by now familiar: intrinsic versus extrinsic (Allport), humanistic versus authoritarian (Fromm), peakers versus nonpeakers (Maslow). Although May and Frankl are apparently less given to typology, they, too, have a vision of genuine religiousness. It must arise anew from within, they say, free of sectarian dogma, if it is to be a source of purpose and meaning.

A RE-VISIONING OF RELIGION

Critics of the humanistic approach find in this spirit of advocacy the markings not of disinterested scholarship but of religion itself. The prophetic spirit or messianic vision that pervades this literature, says its critics, has fostered a highly selective and even distorted view of the religious traditions. Just as humanistic psychologists minimize the dark side of human nature, so, too, do they turn away from the disturbing aspects of religion—including the dread, agony, and violence associated with the *mysterium tremendum*—either by ignoring them altogether or by assigning them to religion's spurious forms.

Maslow's work is particularly vulnerable to this criticism. Whereas his term *peak experience* is intended to encompass mystical experience of every kind, it contains none of the bipolarity featured in Otto's analysis of the experience of the holy. In the joyful afterglow of peak experience, according to Maslow (1964, p. 76), even death loses its dreadful aspect, becoming transformed into "*sweet* death." Such "highly valuable" and "self-validating" experiences are the benchmarks, he suggests, of the progressive maturation implied by self-actualization. According to psychologist William Blanchard (1969), however, the peak experience is in reality an "all-directional" moment of free creativity that is genuinely dangerous to a person's identity. It is at such moments, he says, that the familiar world and even the self are thrown into question, so that the individual has nothing to hold on to. This "element of strangeness and unreality" (p. 107) is simultaneously attractive and disturbing, a source of fear that, if not too strong, can be a catalyst to creativity. In sum, the peak experience "like life itself, is filled with possibilities for both joy and tragedy. It can lead to self-fulfillment or self-destruction" (p. 111).

Blanchard also challenges Maslow's claim that the peak experience is largely the prerogative of self-actualizing persons. This conclusion, Blanchard says, is a modern version of the old idea that, somehow, virtue—that is maturity—will have its reward. He sees no convincing evidence that peak experiences are more common or of a higher quality in more fully actualized persons.

Blanchard doubts that the satisfaction of deficiency needs increases the likelihood of self-actualization; indeed, he argues that the frustration of certain of these needs might produce a state of longing that facilitates the occurrence of a peak experience. As an illustration, Blanchard observes that philosopher Jean-Jacques Rousseau, "one of the greatest of the great thinkers of his time" and the subject of a life-changing peak experience that "unleashed his creativity" (p. 104), suffered acute frustration of his deficiency needs and even psychotic episodes. Maslow's formula also overlooks the principle pointed out by Freud, Adler, and others that *excessive* gratification of basic needs can lead to serious psychological problems (Schneewind, 1984, p. 44).

The absence in Maslow's work of the *mysterium tremendum* as well as certain other aspects of traditional religious experience leads Lucy Bregman (1976) to conclude that Maslow did not really comprehend "the immense multiplicity and sheer 'otherness' of religious phenomena." When in his writings he does make reference to religious figures and ideas of the past, he so thoroughly reinterprets them, she says, that "they sound almost like twentieth-century autonomous individuals in search of . . . their true inner selves" (p. 161).[2] Bregman rejects as unsupportable Maslow's reconstruction of religious history along with his widely shared assumption that mystical experience is the core of religion and in essence is always the same.

Doubts have similarly been raised about Fromm's historical reconstructions and interpretations. Particularly cogent is the critique of philosopher Walter Kaufmann (1958), who considers Fromm's central dichotomy to be untenable. Not only does Fromm overlook the authoritarian elements in his models of humanistic religion—the emphasis of Jesus on obedience, for example, or the authoritarian relation of master and pupil in Zen Buddhism—but, contrary to logic and history, he also conceives the themes of love and justice to be the universal and exclusive

---

[2] This tendency is most strikingly apparent in Maslow's (1964, p. 39) misquotation of one of his sources. "Now is the point in history," he ostensibly quotes from John Macmurray, "at which it becomes possible for man to adopt consciously as his own purpose the purpose which is already inherent in his own nature." Macmurray's statement actually begins "*Jesus marks* the point in history . . ." (emphasis added).

possession of the humanistic trend. Although Kaufmann praises Fromm for focusing attention on the humanistic elements in various religious traditions, he concludes that "There never has been any 'humanistic religion' in Fromm's sense: there have only been humanistic tendencies in most religions." In order to evade erosion, all religious traditions "have cultivated a strong authoritarian undercurrent. Individual religiousness is possible without any touch of authoritarianism; but no historic religion has dispensed with it entirely" (pp. 345, 346). Robert Banks (1975) also questions Fromm's historical perspective, notably his account of the development of the biblical idea of God.

The still widely popular intrinsic–extrinsic typology championed by Allport has likewise come under fire. Comparing it to the troublesome though durable church–sect distinction of the sociologists, James Dittes (1971) argues that both typologies have been inspired primarily by a prophetic concern to identify and preserve a purified essence of religion. As we saw in Chapter 6, various proponents of the intrinsic–extrinsic dichotomy have sought to establish it on a firm foundation of scientific research. The continuing elusiveness of consistent findings is evidence, Dittes states, that the distinction is not truly scientific at its core, but evaluational if not evangelical. The intrinsic–extrinsic typology, he says, is obviously a Western Christian construction, "reminiscent of issues on the conscience of small town Middle America" (p. 381). Allport's apparently unwitting reduction of Spranger's mystical types to conservative Christian piety is understandable in the same light.

A PSYCHOLOGY WITHOUT DEPTH?

None of the humanistic psychologists considered here was committed to developing a truly comprehensive psychology of religion. Rather, each was inspired to promote a particular religious vision or—as Küng (1979, p. 117) suggests of Frankl—even a theology. Had they truly sought to encompass religion in its full breadth and depth, some critics doubt that their psychological principles would have been adequate to the task. James Hillman (1975), for one, finds humanistic psychology disturbingly one-sided and superficial. He faults it for its innocently simplistic and romantic notion of growth and its neglect of human limitation, irrationality, and pathology. Describing its understanding of the psyche as "naïve if not delusional," Hillman asks, "Where is sin, and where are viciousness, failure, and the crippling vicissitudes that fate brings through pathologizing? . . . By insisting on the brighter side of human nature, where even death becomes 'sweet,' humanistic psychology is shadowless, a psychology without depths" (p. 65). We may wonder indeed what positive sense these humanists could make of religion's elaborate rites and symbols, its panoply of divine and demonic beings, and the countless martyrs and saints who have disdained self-actualization for self-abnegation.

At the same time we must avoid oversimplifying the humanistic perspective. Although it may be true, as some critics say, that the writings of Allport, Fromm, Maslow, and May, among others, have served to sanction selfishness and even promote self-worship (Vitz, 1977; Wallach and Wallach, 1983), a close examination of this literature reveals an appreciation that self-centered pursuit of happiness is bound to fail. This theme is most clearly enunciated by Frankl, who developed a number of therapeutic techniques to counter the self-preoccupation of his neurotic patients (Wallach and Wallach, pp. 234–236). "Self-actualization," Frankl (1966, p. 99) writes, "if made an end in itself, contradicts the self-transcendent quality of human existence. . . . Only to the extent to which man fulfills a meaning out there in the world, does he fulfill himself.'' As Frankl notes, this view is in accord with Maslow's findings. His self-actualizing subjects, Maslow (1970, p. 159) reports, are uniformly dedicated to nonpersonal or unselfish tasks lying outside themselves.

What the humanists may not have fully appreciated is how complex and even contradictory the self-actualizing process may be. When Richard Coan (1974) factor-analyzed the responses of 291 university students to a six-hour battery of tests measuring aspects of the optimal personality, he found no general factor he could call self-actualization. Rather, his analysis yielded 19 largely independent factors. Judging from the modest correlations among these factors, some of the elements ascribed to the self-actualizing process may tend to be mutually exclusive. Self-insight and openness to experience, for example, were positively related to anxiety, or proneness to distress, and negatively related to experienced control. Although Maslow argues that self-actualizing people are able to resolve the contradictions that are manifested in ordinary lives, Coan recommends that we abandon the notion of a single pattern of personality characteristics that develop uniformly to an optimal level. We should think instead in terms of ''a variety of patterns that are desirable for a variety of purposes, each pattern being ideal when viewed from an appropriate perspective'' (p. 198).

A return to the distinction between types and traits may cast some light on this issue. Maslow's pattern of characteristics for self-actualizing persons is probably best conceived as constituting an *"ideal" type,* a purified abstraction that in reality is rarely attained. Maslow's critics would therefore be correct in saying that Maslow already had these characteristics in mind when he chose his ''sample'' of self-actualizing persons; they are rare *examples* of the type more or less in full bloom, not sources from which we might derive a replicable set of highly correlated traits. Maslow's error, then, was not in his procedure, as his critics say, but in his insistence on conceptualizing it in narrowly scientific terms. If we translate this type into a pattern of individually varying traits, as Maslow's representation of it tempts us to do, it may well fall apart, especially in an unselected sample of young subjects. As Allport's effort to translate Spranger's typology into measurable dimensions also demonstrates, the humanistic goal of synthesizing the phenomenological–interpretive outlook with contemporary psychological science may itself be an unattainable ideal.

THREE DOUBTFUL ASSUMPTIONS

If self-actualization is in reality a less uniform process than the humanists assume, might peak experiences prove to be similarly diverse? Maslow's concept of peak experience is founded on three generally held assumptions: (1) all religious traditions originate in individual religious experience that is at its heart mystical; (2) the historically conditioned interpretations of these experiences can be stripped away to reveal their original contours; and (3) the experiences thus uncovered will be in essence the same, what Maslow calls ''the core religious experience.'' These assumptions go back at least to James (1902), who, placing mystical consciousness at the center of religious experience, takes it to be ''the primordial thing'' (p. 33), the essential inspiration of every founder of a religious tradition. Moreover, he finds among these mystics ''a unanimous type of experience'' (p. 336), summed up by his four characteristics of mystical experience—ineffability, noetic quality, transiency, and passivity—as well as the qualities of pantheism, optimism, and antinaturalism.

Although some contemporary scholars of religion also subscribe to the notion of a unified "perennial philosophy" or "primordial tradition" underlying religion's diverse historic forms (e.g., H. Smith, 1976), many others reject this assumption unequivocally. At the extreme, proponents of the pluralistic conception of mysticism maintain that there is *no* unmediated or neutral mystical experience that is then subsequently interpreted by the mystic. To the contrary, the very experience itself is said to be shaped in every respect by the traditional concepts that the mystic brings to it. Thus mystical experience is always *particular* and cannot be meaningfully lifted out of its cultural and historical context (Katz, 1978; Scholem, 1960).

Sallie King (1988) recommends a more moderate position. Objecting that the pluralistic conception reduces mystical experience to doctrine and leaves unexplained the affinity and mutual understanding expressed by mystics of various traditions, she argues that mystical experience, like the experience of music, cannot be reduced to the context in which it occurs. Surely it is obvious, she argues by analogy, that some aspects remain free of "the conditioning power of tradition" (p. 269). Just as a composer can invent a new musical style, so can the mystic create a new religious tradition. Yet King remains far from an exponent of the primordial tradition of Maslow and others. Even James, it must be said, finally comes round to a more moderate position, when he confesses that he exaggerated mysticism's unanimity for the sake of exposition (1902, p. 336).

If we deny mysticism a universal core, but instead define it in terms of the tradition in which it arises, we will naturally decline to ascribe to it the origin of the religious traditions. Such is the position of Scholem, who places the rise of mysticism at a later stage in the historical development of religion. Even religious experience as immediate feeling has been denied the essential originative role in the various elements of religious tradition: "Religious experience, the religion of the spirit, is an all-important aspect of religion, but it cannot exist by itself, and it is not the source of religion or even of all that is progressive and highest in it" (Moore, 1938, pp. 73–74). These are not merely historical questions but conceptual queries as well, and even today the vague and ambiguous term *religious experience* is subject to varying interpretations (Proudfoot, 1985).

Whatever their shortcomings, both historical and phenomenological, the humanistic interpretations of religion possess a certain plausibility that will likely sustain the interest of both students and researchers for years to come. Undoubtedly, genuine insights are to be found in these works, and they have clearly facilitated an appreciation of religious values and experience among persons otherwise alienated by traditional religious language. The advancement of a humanistic psychology of religion will be best served, however, by recognizing that the movement has fallen short of its potential. The foundations for a truly humanistic psychology that have been laid by Allport, Maslow, May, and others we have encountered in the last three chapters could support a far more penetrating understanding of religious faith and tradition than these psychologists now offer. If we appropriated their insights into the "upper floor" of the human psyche—using here the metaphor employed by Freud and Binswanger in discussing their differences—and combined them with the understanding of the "ground floor and basement" offered by the depth and objective psychologists, we might at last have a psychology of religion worthy of so sweeping a name.

EPILOGUE

As we step back to reflect on the mass of material we have surveyed in the chapters of this book, one conclusion is inescapable: religion is through and through a *human* preoccupation. This is not to say, of course, that religion's transcendent referents are unreal, for that judgment lies beyond the competence of the psychologist. But what cannot be denied is how comprehensively religion reflects ordinary human experience: of the body and other aspects of the self; of other human beings and a person's relation to them; and of the many facets of the natural world. Religion makes little sense considered apart from this human context, although the word "religion," because it so easily suggests an abstracted essence, tempts us to overlook how pervasively influential this context is. Thus it is that we have preferred the terms *religious faith* and *religious tradition*, in order to remind ourselves that religion cannot be separated from its personal and cultural expressions. Instead of saying that *religion* does this or that, we should remember that *human beings* do what is done, out of perceptions and motives that we have come to call religious.

A corollary of this fundamental insight is religion's *diversity*, which appears limited only by the structure and capacities of the human body and by the outer boundaries of human inventiveness. Various specialists in the study of religion have brought home for us the multiformity of the world's religious traditions. What psychologists of religion are peculiarly competent to demonstrate is the reign of diversity among *individuals*, even within a single tradition. Indeed, we might say that documenting and accounting for these individual differences is the task that has most engaged psychologists of religion.

Diversity is characteristic of these researchers as well, as the dizzying array of psychological perspectives composing this book well testifies. The biographical emphasis of this work is intended to demonstrate how our perspective in psychology emerges from our personal disposition and life experience. These pervasive factors influence the presuppositions we adopt, the questions we ask, the methods we employ. More particularly, they shape what we take religion to be and how we go about studying it. Just as with religious faith, so with psychological perspectives: tracing out their origins does not invalidate them. At the same time, such an exercise should sensitize us to the thoroughgoing relativity of any point of view, religious or psychological, including our own.

Our most immediate response to the diverse perspectives of this book is thus likely to be deeply personal. Greenberg and Mitchell (1983, p. 407) say that a "Theory stands or falls on how compelling it appears to be, on its underlying vision of human life. Does the theory speak to you? Does it seem to account for your deepest needs, longings, fears?" At the very least, Hocking (1912, p. xiii) suggests, any theory claiming to be true ought to be *interesting:* "A proposition that falls on the mind so dully as to excite no enthusiasm has not attained the level of truth." Furthermore, "If a theory has no consequences or bad ones; if it makes no difference to men, or else undesirable differences; if it lowers the capacity of men to meet the stress of existence, or diminishes the worth to them of what existence they have; such a theory is somehow false." The test is not mere agreeableness, Hocking quickly adds, but conservation of the creative power that comes with the deepening of consciousness and the sensing of possibilities and risks in human existence.

Beyond these pragmatic and highly individual criteria are the more general principles of evaluation we have employed at various points throughout this book. Most important is the perspective's phenomenological adequacy. How large a range of religious experience and practice does it take into account? How faithfully does it represent these phenomena as they actually occur in human lives? The range is regrettably narrow in many instances, and in their enthusiasm for reduction, some of our commentators have neglected to reconstruct the complexity of religion as it is lived. Thus their generalizations about religion are often ill founded or too sweeping. Nevertheless, there is something to be learned from each of the approaches, and collectively, they touch on an impressive array of religious manifestations. If no one of these perspectives is adequate in itself, together they illuminate a large portion of the landscape of human piety.

A SUMMARY SCHEMA

In Chapter 2, as a way of orienting ourselves within the psychology of religion, we identified two fundamental trends: the descriptive and the explanatory. Now that we are better acquainted with the various theories or perspectives that constitute this field, as well as with certain fundamental principles, we are prepared to consider a more technical schema for ordering the contents of this book. This schema, it will become apparent, can serve to classify both individuals and psychological approaches. Although our chief interest here is in clarifying the formal perspectives, a framework that links them to personal views will serve once again to underscore the role of the personal equation. This framework will also direct our attention to some perennial problems encountered by this field.

The various approaches can be roughly located in a two-dimensional space defined in terms of two fundamental variables (see Table E.1). The vertical axis specifies the degree to which the objects of religious interest are explicitly granted participation in a transcendent reality or, to the contrary, are limited to processes immanent within the mundane world.[1] The horizontal axis indicates how consis

---

[1] We might be tempted to use Piaget's (1930) typology of religious attitudes—transcendence versus immanence—to define this dimension, but as Wilfred Smith (1988) cogently argues, the two terms are not mutually exclusive. Beauty, for example, transcends any particular instance of it while yet being immanent within the beautiful object (p. 11).

Table E.1 SUMMARY SCHEMA OF VIEWS IN THE PSYCHOLOGY OF RELIGION

	Inclusion of Transcendence

Literal Affirmation	**Restorative Interpretation**
(religious fundamentalism)	(conjunctive faith)
	phenomenology interpretive psychology
correlational psychology	analytical psychology
1	4

Literal ——————————————————————————————— Symbolic

2	3 Erikson's ego psychology
sociobiology	humanistic psychologies
	object-relations theories
medical materialism theoretical behaviorism (rational fundamentalism)	orthodox psychoanalysis
Literal Disaffirmation	**Reductive Interpretation**

Exclusion of
Transcendence

tently the expressions of religion faith—whether beliefs, images, or rituals—are interpreted either literally or symbolically. It is not accidental that the objective approaches in psychology are grouped together at the literal end, for in denying itself direct access to human subjectivity, the objective attitude sharply limits its capacity to comprehend metaphoric or symbolic meaning.

Four Fundamental Attitudes

Literal Affirmation: The two dimensions define four basic attitudes toward religion. The upper left quadrant represents affirmation of the literal existence of the religious objects, a position most clearly embodied by religious fundamentalism. Elements of this posture also appear among those who are not particularly conservative. As James Barr (1978) observes, many mainstream Christians, though not requiring that all the events and sayings in the Bible be literally true, "just want so much to be told that at least this one really happened, that at least this one saying was really uttered by Jesus. . . . They do not want to hear that stories are legends, or that they emerged from the consciousness of the primitive church." This "conservatism of the committed," though not fundamentalist, still shares in "the basic cultural structures upon which fundamentalism also developed" (p. 334). Of the psychological approaches we have studied, only the correlational one might be thought to belong in this first quadrant, both because its questionnaires have tended to define religion in literalistic terms and because much research of this type has been carried out in defense of more or less conservative views. It is nevertheless placed near the other quadrants in recognition of important exceptions to these trends, such as Batson's Quest scale, Hood's Mysticism Scale, and above all, the questionnaire that Hutsebaut (1996a) designed to operationalize the attitudes represented by this schema.

The research and reflections of many contributors to this book form a virtual consensus that, however sincere and high-minded religious fundamentalists may be, their position does not fare well under psychological scrutiny. It is the literal believers who tend to score higher on measures of prejudice, we may recall, and to be rated lower on level of cognitive development. Pratt and Pruyser, among others, consider such literal belief a fundamental error. Although the posture of "naive credulity" may reflect intellectual immaturity, as in the instance of the child, if not enduring personal incapacity, the milieu frequently sets limits beyond which only an exceptionally courageous, independent, and capable mind can see. The personal costs of the fundamentalist outlook may be considerable, judging from the reports of those who have joined Fundamentalists Anonymous. "The harm that has been done to souls," writes Paul Ricoeur (1960), "during the centuries of Christianity, first by the literal interpretation of the story of Adam, and then by the confusion of this myth, treated as history, with later speculations, principally Augustinian, about original sin, will never be adequately told" (p. 239). The interpersonal costs are considerable, too, for as Barr (1978) points out, the fundamentalist ideology can be sustained only by rejecting, as thinkers and as religious persons, all those who doubt the validity of the conservative view (p. 315). What orthodox believers forget, remarks Sabatier (1897), are the historical and psychological factors that condition *all* doctrines. As a field dedicated to the clarification of such factors, the psychology of religion has naturally not been well received among the conservatively religious.

Literal Disaffirmation: Like persons in the first quadrant, those in the second one assume that religious language is to be understood in a literal way. They differ by rejecting rather than affirming what is written or said. Religious fundamentalists may seem themselves to fall into Quadrant 2 in relation to any religious system other than their own. But they do not really belong here, for the permanent residents of this quadrant are distinguished by their resolute rejection of all claims of revealed truth. Speaking as a proponent of this position, which he calls "rational fundamentalism," anthropologist Ernest Gellner (1992) says that it desacralizes everything and excludes the miraculous along with all other privileged facts, individuals, and institutions. If anything is absolutized, he says, it is rational fundamentalism's formal principles of knowledge, or scientific method.

Fundamentalism, Wilfred Smith (1988) suggests, is the religious response to a waning sense of transcendence. "It is the disastrously mistaken supposition that the mundane forms are themselves the transcending reality" (p. 14). Still more calamitous, some would argue, is the position of literal disaffirmation, which in its literalness, utterly cuts itself off from the resources of religious metaphor. Although Stanley Hall (1917), for example, placed belief in a "literal flesh and blood Jesus" low on the pedagogic scale, he nevertheless considered such "objectivizations . . . vastly better than aloofness or negation" (p. viii). "It is better to believe with men who have a childish conception of God," agrees Raymond Cattell (1938) in his book on the religious quest, "than to make the greater error of not believing at all" (p. 185).

Behavioral and social scientists seem particularly prone to this error. As Donald

T. Campbell (1975) observes, they often match the fundamentalist's scriptural literalism with an opposing literalism of their own. "Because such behavioral scientists no longer believe in what they assume to be the literal referents of religious words, they lose sight of the possibility that these words refer to truths for which there is no literal language," truths that "must be metaphorically or figuratively expressed if to be communicated at all." The modern philosopher's humble and relativistic understanding of human knowing, says Campbell, could help these scientists be more open to truths that are expressed through metaphor or other nonscientific language (pp. 196–197).

Most clearly exemplifying literal disaffirmation are such theoretical behaviorists as Vetter and Skinner. Belonging in Quadrant 2 as well are the "medical materialists," who conclude from the findings of neuropsychology that religion is nothing but a matter of disordered physiology. Although sociobiologists such as Edward Wilson show a similar inclination toward literal disaffirmation, Campbell's sociobiologically based argument for the adaptive value of traditional religious teachings wins sociobiology a somewhat higher position in this quadrant.

In Chapters 6 and 7 we reviewed some of the psychological correlates of the position of literal disaffirmation, identified in the literature variously as the indiscriminately antireligious orientation or simply atheism. We saw, for example, that persons who score low on both Intrinsic and Extrinsic Religious Orientation scales tend to be less dogmatic and more intellectual than many of the religious subjects. We also learned that the atheistic position is often motivated by a loss or other deep disappointment early in life. Many of Vetter and Green's (1932) atheists, it may be recalled, reported parental loss or unhappy childhoods. Among the 50 alumnae of a women's college whom Frank Barron (1963) assessed 25 years after they graduated, the seven atheists stood out not only for their devotion to thinking and extremely high scores on intelligence tests, but also for the "sharp disillusionment" and "terrible sense of loss" that marked an adolescent religious crisis recurringly associated with death or desertion by the father. At least for this group of women, says Barron, "Atheism seemed to represent disappointment in the father, anger against him, repudiation of a need for his love, and affirmation of the self alone as sufficiently potent to carry on in life" (p. 155). Indeed, compared to the rest of the sample, a larger proportion of them lived alone—six of the seven— and claimed to like it.

For another phase of his research, Barron used the Inventory of Personal Philosophy, which contains four religious belief scales: Fundamentalist Belief and Fundamentalist Disbelief—equivalent to Quadrants 1 and 2—as well as Enlightened Belief and Enlightened Disbelief. In a group of 100 military officers, high scorers on *either* fundamentalism scale tended to be rated as rigid and low in ability to adapt. In addition, the Fundamentalist Disbelief scale, with items highly reminiscent of the antireligious prose of Watson and Vetter, was negatively correlated with capacity to evaluate ideas, intelligence ratings (based on handwriting), and fairmindedness. The switch in direction of disbelief's relation to intellectual capacity or interests, when disbelief takes the extreme and angry form measured by this scale, suggests the likely possibility of alternative paths to literal disaffirmation.

Reductive Interpretation: The designations of Quadrants 3 and 4 are derived from the work of Paul Ricoeur (1965), who proposes that modern hermeneutics faces two opposing though potentially complementary tasks: on the one hand, *reduction* or demystification, in order to clear away from religious symbols the excrescence of idolatry and illusion; and on the other hand, *restoration* or recollection of meaning, so that the object of suspicion may once again become an object of understanding and faith. This is a "rational faith," to be sure, because it interprets, yet it is a faith nevertheless because "it seeks, through interpretation, a second naïveté" (p. 28). In isolation and in its most resolute form, reductive interpretation stands with literal disaffirmation in denying reality to the transcendent referent of religious language and practice. It then goes beyond this merely negative stance to claim a privileged perspective on what it considers to be the true, hidden, and wholly mundane meaning of religion's myths and rituals. The clearest and most aggressive example of this reductionistic approach is represented by Freud and his orthodox followers (though Ricoeur finds even in Freud the makings of a hermeneutics of restoration, as we noted in Chapter 7).

A less strident and more humble approach to demystification is possible, as demonstrated by Ricoeur as well as many of the psychologists of religion we have encountered in this survey. Although the other psychoanalytic approaches and even the humanistic psychologies, taken as a whole, are assigned to Quadrant 3, they are placed high enough to suggest that their unveiling of religion's neuroticisms and immaturities and their delineation of more mature forms are ultimately aimed at restoring to religion some fundamental, positive meaning. The distinctions favored by the correlationists are in their own way directed toward the same end, and thus they too are located near Quadrant 4.

Restorative Interpretation: The task of the hermeneutics of restoration is to reengage with the objects of religious faith in a way that allows them to speak of the transcendent reality toward which they point. Like literal affirmation, this interpretive posture posits the transcendent realm as real, though not in the same, absolute sense. Furthermore, it scrupulously avoids identifying religious ideas or objects with that realm, as literal affirmation tends to do, but searches instead for the symbolic meaning that resides within and ultimately points beyond these objects. Moreover, this meaning is not reducible to merely cognitive terms, but engages the inner life as a whole. We are concerned here with "non-objective symbols," writes Robert Bellah (1970a), "which express the feelings, values, and hopes of subjects, or which organize and regulate the flow of interaction between subjects and objects, or which attempt to sum up the whole subject–object complex, or even point to the context or ground of that whole" (p. 93). We may consider ourselves to have attained to the meaning of such a symbol, according to Sabatier (1897), only when it "has produced in us the emotions, the transport, the enthusiasm, the faith" that inspired its creator to engender it in the first place (p. 324).

Bellah, who advocates this interpretive approach under the name of "symbolic realism," urges his fellow social scientists to abandon reductionism altogether and to allow religious symbols to speak to them directly. Of those we have studied, the phenomenologists and interpretive psychologists most nearly approximate this position. In many respects, the analytical psychology of C. G. Jung belongs in Quadrant 4 as well, though a somewhat lower position will serve to acknowledge the reductive tendencies pointed out by his critics. As we have already observed, the restorative intention is in some measure present in virtually all the perspectives in Quadrant 3—though in widely varying degrees, as Freud and Pfister illustrate for the psychoanalytic perspective—as well as in the correlational approach, in Quadrant 1.

Characterizing persons who occupy the positions of Quadrants 3 and 4 is somewhat more difficult, for until recently they have been largely neglected in the empirical research literature. The postures themselves, in the forms they might take in individual lives, are represented by James Fowler's stages 4 and 5, indivi-duative reflective faith (Quadrant 3) and conjunctive faith (Quadrant 4). Thus research with scales designed to operationalize Fowler's stages may be thought to cast light on these two positions. More obviously relevant is the ongoing research of Dirk Hutsebaut (1996a, 1996b), who has developed scales specifically designed to measure the attitudes represented by this summary schema.

To fill out our portrait of persons in Quadrant 3, Reductive Interpretation, we need also to draw on findings from several other, closely related scales, including Hunt's Mythological scale, Batson's Quest scale, and Barron's Enlightenment Dis-belief scale. Taken together, the correlates of these various scales suggest that persons in this stage of "disillusion" may be described as complex, socially sensitive and insightful, relatively unprejudiced, original, but also *anxious*. On scales that Hutsebaut (1996b) used to measure Erikson's various dimensions of ego develop-ment, persons scoring high on External Critique—Hutsebaut's equivalent of Quad-rant 3—show a tendency toward identity diffusion and negative ego integrity, or despair. For many individuals, as we noted in Chapter 6, this stage is a temporary one.

The "second naïveté" of Quadrant 4, given its profoundly individual character, is the most difficult of the four attitudes to operationalize with standardized ques-tionnaires. Hutsebaut's initial findings with his Historical Relativism scale do sug-gest, however, that the task is not impossible. Persons scoring high on this scale, he reports, reveal a distinct tendency toward metaphorical thinking and tend to show positive ego integrity. Further qualities are suggested in Barron's summary of interviews with the 27 women in his sample of 50 who possessed a deep and personally evolved religious faith. These women were similar to the atheists and agnostics in their relatively high intellectual orientation and the absence of au-thoritarian or ethnocentric attitudes. They were distinguished from them, however, by high ratings on ego strength, richness of personality, and psychological health; on inner-directedness, genuine autonomy, and growth orientation; and on desire for community status and leadership. This religious orientation, it is interesting to note, is positively correlated with affection toward parents and happiness in child-hood. From his findings, Barron concludes that religious belief

> is not dogma, not a set of forever-prescribed particularities, not static abstraction at all, but a formative process with faith as its foundation and vision as its goal—faith in the intelligibility and order of the universe, leading through necessary difficulties of interpretation and changing meanings to moments of spiritual integration which are themselves transient. (p. 169)

Reflections on the Summary Schema

Research in the psychology of religion, we may infer from this schema, inevitably entails taking some fundamental stance in relation to religious content. With the exception of the correlational approach, the most fully developed perspectives are strongly inclined to interpret religion as a system of symbols whose meanings are multilayered, richly complex, and deeply embedded in human experience. To many scholars today this understanding of symbols is so commonplace that it requires no justification. Others, however, are disposed to interpret religious con-tent more or less literally. Some also affirm this content as the revelations of a supernatural agency. Confronted by research findings that challenge such a view, these religious literalists argue that the measures and developmental frameworks from which such findings are derived are the biased products of naturalism and empiricism. They seem less able to recognize the contingent character of their own position.

A more subtle and difficult issue is presented by the factor of transcendence. According to Flournoy's first principle, the psychology of religion must exclude the transcendent, in the sense that it may neither affirm nor deny the reality of the religious object. It is not the intent of this principle, however, to exclude acknowledgment of the importance of transcendence to faith or to prohibit study of the variations in its conception and observance.

In the abstract, this principle sounds reasonably easy to follow. In practice, however, a person's success would seem to depend on how transcendence is conceived. If we identify a tradition's tangible symbols with the transcendent reality itself, then naturally *any* interpretation of these symbols as human constructs will be viewed as a violation of Flournoy's principle. On the other hand, if we think of religious symbols as historically conditioned expressions of the human imagination that point to an otherwise incomprehensible transcendent realm beyond themselves, only a "nothing-but" interpretation that denies the very existence of this realm will count as a violation. The majority of the subjective psychologies of religion seem to incorporate the second of these two interpretive standpoints, and even those, like Freud's, that include the "nothing-but" clause could be used without it, as Oskar Pfister demonstrates.

Exclusion in the limited sense intended by Flournoy could be said to be represented by the middle third of the vertical axis in Table E.1, where most of the subjective psychologies are found. Those in this middle third that fall in the upper quadrant more explicitly *include* transcendence, yet they do so only in a "neutralized mode." They believe with the believers but "without positing absolutely" the objects of their belief (Ricoeur, 1965, p. 29). Conjunctive faith, unconstrained by the bracketing of absolute reality required of the scientist, is free to affirm it wholeheartedly even while recognizing the relativity and insufficiency of the various symbols that refer to it. Psychoanalysis is positioned at the opposite pole to represent Freud's frank denial of the reality of the transcendent and his reduction of religious myths and rituals to the most mundane reality.

Table E.1 is offered as a heuristic device for thinking about these issues, not as a precise representation of the structure of the field. In truth, the positioning of these perspectives is only approximate, for most entries represent the views of more than one contributor, and few address these issues explicitly and consistently, especially the matter of transcendence. Furthermore, some contributors are not easily located in it. James is a singularly instructive example. His disdain for religious symbols invites placement in Quadrant 2; his theory of the subconscious self and his emphasis on faith's consequences, in Quadrant 3; and his sensitivity to others' transcendent experiences, in Quadrant 4. James is an exception, no doubt, but so important an exception does remind us of the limits of this schema.

This framework will have served its purpose, however, if it alerts the reader to these fundamental issues, especially the daunting problem of including transcendence in a psychology of religion without at the same time implying something about its ultimate nature and the adequacy of its representations. Scholars from the early twentieth century onward have debated the possibility of a genuine psychology of religion, in the light of this dilemma and others as well. Even today there is still no consensus on what the objects and goals of its study should be, or on what methods it can meaningfully employ. Ulrich Mann (1973, p. 39) concludes that this "crisis situation" is in fact a permanent heritage of the field. Rather than despairing over it, he recommends that we incorporate the insights that exist in every psychology of religion but remain cautiously alert to the limitations and prejudices of each. The present work was designed to invite its readers to undertake just such a task.

A SITUATION OF CRISIS

For some contributors to this field, the situation of crisis that looms largest is not the internal one that has troubled the field from its beginnings. Rather, it is the contemporary ecological, political, and social crisis confronting the whole of humanity. From its beginnings the psychology of religion has had an applied orientation, chiefly to religious education and pastoral care. Now these still-vital interests are framed by a much larger concern. Pruyser (1971) identifies the ecological crisis as the single most important challenge to contemporary religion. It has roots, he says, in the theological misconstruction that has given humankind dominion over the rest of nature.

Pruyser's allusion is to Genesis 1:26, which enjoins human beings to have "dominion over . . . every living thing." In a highly influential article published in *Science,* historian Lynn White (1967) argues that today's ecological crisis has its roots in this biblical teaching. In sanctioning an exploitative ethic toward the earth's resources, this outlook has fostered, he says, the fateful growth of science and technology. Thoroughly permeated as they are with "orthodox Christian arrogance toward nature" (p. 1207), science and technology cannot alone provide a solution. Because the crisis of environmental degradation has roots that are mainly religious, White concludes, the remedy must also be essentially religious.

Thomas Merton (1968) likewise traces to the Hebrew Bible a "certain kind of Christian culture" that is actively hostile toward nature and promotes wilderness-destroying values. The Puritans, he points out, regarded the desolate wilderness of America "as though it were filled with conscious malevolence against them. They hated it as a *person,* an extension of the Evil One, the Enemy opposed to the spread of the Kingdom of God." Because nature was conceived of as "fallen" and "corrupt," it became the Christian's duty "to combat, reduce, destroy, and transform the wilderness." The earthly reward for carrying out "God's work" was "prosperity, real estate, money, and ultimately the peaceful 'order' of civil and urban life" (pp. 38–39).

While others, too, have declared that the Christian tradition is to some degree responsible for the ecological crisis, it is mainly White's provocative essay to which religious leaders and social scientists alike have responded. At the time of its publication, there were already stirrings of a Christian environmentalist movement. White's critical judgments proved to be a powerful stimulant to this movement and shaped much of its discussion. By now, every mainline Protestant denomination has taken a stand in support of ecological concerns, and many of the mainline presses have published books proclaiming the new environmental gospel. Conservative Protestant groups have been much slower in addressing environmental issues, but many of them, too, have now joined the cause (R.B. Fowler, 1995).

Social scientists, meanwhile, have set about to test White's thesis, along with related propositions regarding the connection between religiousness and environmentalism. Some data do support White's claims. In one study, for example, professed Christians more often affirmed the human mastery of nature and showed less concern for the environment than agnostics, atheists, and others with no religious preference (Hand and Van Liere, 1984). In other studies, biblical literalism and disbelief in evolution predicted less support for environmental action (Eckberg and Blocker, 1993, 1996; Greeley, 1993). Yet the findings are not entirely consistent. Eric Woodrum and Thomas Hoban (1994), for example, found no relation between their measure of dominion belief and either biblical literalism or environmental attitudes.[2] Moreover, when researchers control for demographic variables—age, education, social class, and so on—the already modest relationships are sometimes reduced to insignificance. There are also studies that report a *positive* relationship between environmental concern and religious participation, though the latter may be more a measure of organizational involvement than of religiosity (Eckberg and Blocker, 1996).

One finding nevertheless remains consistent: the more theologically conservative people are, the less likely they are to be environmentally concerned. Political conservatism is itself a strong predictor of lower levels of environmental concern, but the combined direct and indirect effects of Fundamentalism were even more striking in a study by James Guth and his associates (1993). Among their subjects classified as members of the Christian Left—mainline Protestants and liberal Catholics—47 percent listed the environment as the most important problem facing America; of those associated with the Christian Right—evangelical, charismatic, and Fundamentalist Protestants—only 3 percent gave the environment such priority.

What remains unclear is the source of this "fundamentalism effect" (Eckberg and Blocker, 1996). Altogether, the findings do seem to provide at least partial support for White's argument that biblical teachings dispose people to exploit the natural world. Yet for many Fundamentalists, the more obvious source of their indifference to the fate of the environment is end-times thinking. If the world is soon to reach its apocalyptic conclusion, as many believe, then the important thing is accepting Jesus and encouraging others to embrace him as well. The world itself may be left to the care of God. When Fundamentalists prove to be hostile toward the environmentalist movement, it is often because they associate it with liberal and secular values (R.B. Fowler, 1995). This hostility is reflected in the consistent and substantial negative correlation between environmental concern and Altemeyer's Right-Wing Authoritarianism Scale (Peterson, Doty, and Winter, 1993; Schultz and Stone, 1994).

Of the specific environmental attitudes that have been found to be related to piety, perhaps the most robust and consequential bears on overpopulation. When Carl Hand and Kent Van Liere (1984) controlled for the effects of age, education, and income on their five environmental concern scales, their Population Control Scale proved to have the most variance (11 percent) explained by religious affiliation. The negative correlation between religious attendance and concern for population control was most striking for Catholics ($-.43$) and Mormons ($-.83$), but other religious groups showed the trend as well. Similarly, of the several variables that Mark Harvey and Paul Bell (1995) correlated with their Population Concern

---

[2] It should be noted, however, that subjects who personally reject the attitude of dominion may nevertheless agree with the statement Woodrum and Hoban used to measure it, "[a]ccording to the Bible humans are supposed to use nature to their own advantage." The statements used to assess the other variables more clearly ask for the respondent's own attitudes.

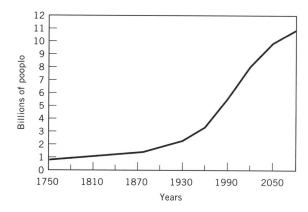

Figure E.1. World population estimates and projections. Source: Data obtained from the Population Reference Bureau, Washington, D.C.

Scale, only the religious one—church attendance—proved to have a significant relationship: as church attendance went up, population concern tended to go down.

The exponential growth in the world's population (see Figure E.1) is arguably the most serious of the problems we face today, for virtually every other problem grows as the number of the earth's inhabitants increases. As Pruyser (1971, p. 88) observes, the biblical injunction to "be fruitful and multiply"

> may have been constructive in an agrarian society with a high infant mortality rate, but it is becoming destructive in today's world. To take this text out of context and to turn it into an everlasting moral injunction is a pernicious form of fundamentalism—pernicious not only because of its disastrous consequences, but also because it fails to come to grips with the moral issue involved in self-reduplication. The issue is no longer whether *I* can survive in *my* offspring, whether *my* family or tribe or nation can survive, but whether mankind can survive.

In a study of a group of ministers in a South Texas town, Christian Buys and his associates (1977) found that the more conservative, or literalistic, the ministers were in their religious beliefs, the less likely they were to be concerned about overpopulation. A conservative outlook also inclined them to attribute the problem of overpopulation to sinful human nature and the work of Satan and to emphasize personal salvation and prayer as solutions, rather than social or political action. Reporting that only 38 percent had moderate to strong feelings that overpopulation was an appropriate topic for a sermon, and that only a small minority of *these* gave more than one sermon per year on the subject, Buys and his colleagues conclude that the ministers' strong otherworld orientation "holds little hope for large social movements aimed at ameliorating the overpopulation problem" (p. 569).

The environmental devastation that overpopulation can bring is already apparent in many parts of the world. For hundreds of millions of people in third-world countries especially, the catastrophe forecast by ecologists is an all-too-present reality. Judging from the silence about this problem in psychology textbooks, most psychologists see it as the concern of other specialists—biologists, sociologists, economists, political theorists, and so on. Yet some recognize that psychology and social psychiatry also have important roles to play, from basic attitude research to the shaping of implementation policies (Back, 1974; Carleton and Stentz, 1976; Cautley and Borgatta, 1973; Howard, 1993).

Religion's contribution to the environmental crisis is noted by Roman Catholic psychologist George Howard (1994), who urges the hierarchy within his own religious tradition to reconsider its position on birth control. Although the Vatican's stance against contraceptives is said to be responsible for incalculable suffering, especially in third-world countries, some of the lowest reproductive rates today are found in Catholic nations. Many Islamic nations, on the other hand, show high growth rates, in spite of the absence of official Muslim policy on contraceptives and a recent declaration, signed by representatives of 24 Muslim states, that acknowledges the threat of overpopulation and calls for accessible family planning, including contraceptives. The declaration also presses for the eradication of illiteracy among women, which would be a major step in increasing their status and giving them greater control over their own fertility (Ehrlich, Ehrlich, and Daily, 1995, pp. 125, 132). Maintaining control over women, including their sexuality and reproductive power, is a prominent item on the fundamentalist agenda, whatever the tradition (Hawley, 1994). Yet equity—between men and women, first of all, but among all the nations as well—is said to be crucial for a solution to our contemporary predicament (Ehrlich, Ehrlich, and Daily, 1995).

The solution will ultimately have to be a political one, as the nations struggle to reach a timely and workable accord. Yet White may be correct when he argues that the heart of the remedy must be in some sense religious, for it requires that we "rethink and refeel our nature and destiny" (White, 1967, p. 1207). It is this very task that many of the psychologists in this book are urging us to undertake. For some, particularly Hall, Jung, Spranger, and Fromm, an essential aspect of this undertaking is the recovery of a sense of intimate relatedness to nature, of the alchemical insight that the inner and outer worlds bear a reciprocal relation to each other. Other psychologists, particularly the psychoanalysts, emphasize the necessity of remediation in the interpersonal sphere, where pseudospeciation, projection, and other destructive processes now threaten the very survival of our planet. And still others, including the transpersonal psychologists (Walsh, 1984; Grof and Valier, 1988), accent the importance of an inner, conscious evolution, a transformation in self-awareness and self-identity that links us to the wisdom of the ages and promises a global spirituality.

The study of religious faith and tradition becomes a way, then, for psychologists to gain new insights into human nature and to seek solutions to the manifold problems we face. For some psychologists, such as Freud and Vetter, the remedy lies in the utter abandonment of religion and reliance instead on the constructions of science. Others, however, regard religion, not as something external to human beings that can be set aside and done without, but as individual faith, the fundamental way in which one perceives and responds to the totality of one's world in the light of a transcendent dimension.

Fundamenalism, it was earlier said, is the religious response to a diminishing sense of transcendence. In his study of what members of the clergy understand religion to be, Jack Shand (1961) found that the ratings for "has a feeling of security, at-homeness in the universe" were exceptionally high for the humanistic clergy but unusually low for the fundamentalists. The more recent research we have reviewed shows that fundamentalists are less concerned than others about the degradation of the biosphere and are sometimes even hostile to the environmental movement.

In those for whom the sense of transcendence is strong we find a rather different attitude. Among the predictable characteristics of mystical experience are a sense of the sacredness of all life and a desire to establish a new, more harmonious relation with nature and with other human beings. There is a corresponding re-nunciation of the various expressions of self-seeking, including the ethos of manip-ulation and control. Mystical experience is manifest in a great many forms, some of which are of rather doubtful value. But only an empathic, self-forgetting mystical outlook, it could be argued, can restore to humankind the attitude toward life that will make possible its long-term survival.

Some psychologists of religion treat mystical experience as an optional element of religion, a potential correlate of one or another way of being religious. For others, however, the mystical attitude is *the* defining feature of religion, whatever traditional or individual forms it may take. Construed broadly enough to encompass James's "something more," Otto's *mysterium*, or Smith's sense of transcendence, mystical experience may be considered essential to any living religious faith or tradition. Some may prefer to call it something else, as Maslow does with his phrase "peak experience." What is crucial is not what we label this dimension of experi-ence but that we take it into account. Perhaps we need today a new principle, the PRINCIPLE OF THE INCLUSION OF THE TRANSCENDENT, to balance Flournoy's classic principle of exclusion. Taken together, these principles might encourage psychol-ogists of religion to give the experience of transcendence the prominence it de-serves, but without reifying it or identifying it with any one tradition's symbols. Consistently applied throughout the literature, these principles might help to cast new light on a number of unsolved problems, perhaps giving the field a new coherence and sense of direction.

One likely outcome would be a new generation of religiosity measures that would serve to clarify the relation of the experience of transcendence to environ-mental and interpersonal attitudes. Another predictable result would be a reinter-pretation and reappropriation of insights scattered throughout the existing litera-ture. If we may expect a deeper sense of the complexities of the problems that confront us, we may also hope for a clearer understanding of effective ways in which to address them. Undertaken with caution and humility, the psychology of religion may well play a significant role in meeting the crisis of our age.

GLOSSARY

Abstraction The cognitive process of extracting from a phenomenon its essential features. According to Arnheim (1969), abstraction is a prerequisite for both meaningful experience and productive thinking.

Acquiescence Marked tendency to agree—or, by extension, to disagree—with questionnaire items, regardless of content.

Advaita vedanta A nondualist Indian philosophy that identifies the embodied soul with the unchanging eternal reality (Brahman).

Adventitious reinforcement Increase in the probability of a particular response as a result of a reinforcing stimulus that happens to follow but is not contingent on this response.

Aetiological myth A story explaining the origin of a particular phenomenon.

Agnosticism The withholding of belief (e.g., in the existence of God) on the grounds that the evidence for it is insufficient. Unlike the atheist, the agnostic remains open to the possibility of the existence of a supreme being.

Ahimsa The Hindu principle of non-injury, expressing the view that all life is sacred.

Albedo In alchemy, an intermediate stage and first goal, represented by the coagulation of a white substance on the material level and resurrection on the spiritual.

Alchemy An ancient system of scientific, religious, and philosophical speculation that, conjoined with laboratory experimentation, centers on the simultaneous transformation of matter and spirit.

Alpha rhythm An EEG brain wave pattern typical of a relaxed, wakeful state. The waves vary from 8 to 13 cycles per second.

Altruism Selfless concern for or devotion to the well-being of others.

Amnesia Partial or total inability to recall past events when such recollection would ordinarily be expected.

Amulet An object thought to secure benefits for the person who wears it.

Anal stage The second of Freud's four psychosexual stages, in which the focus of bodily pleasure is on the retention and expulsion of feces.

Analysand A person who is undergoing psychoanalysis.

Analysis of variance A statistical procedure for determining whether or not the observed variability in scores on some measure (e.g., conservatism) is consistently related to variation on some other measured variables (e.g., age and education).

Analytical psychology The expression chosen by Jung to designate his own approach in psychology in contradistinction to Freud's and Adler's.

Androcentric Centering on the male; favoring male interests and points of view.

Androgynous Possessing both male and female characteristics and thus not clearly belonging to one sex or the other.

Aniconic Without the characteristics of an icon, or literal image, hence nonrepresentational or abstract.

Anima/animus In Jungian psychology, the archetype of the soul, which, because it bears a compensatory relation to consciousness, takes on the characteristics of the opposite sex. Thus for men, the anim*a* personifies femininity, and for women, the anim*us* personifies masculinity.

Animistic Representing objects of the natural world as animated by spirits.

Anlage A natural tendency or disposition that shapes the subsequent development of an organism.

Anorexia nervosa An eating disorder characterized by severe loss of appetite, a dread of becoming fat, and a distorted body image.

Anthropomorphic (1) Described as or thought of as having the attributes of human beings. (2) Ascribing human qualities to nonhuman objects.

Anticathexis As postulated by Freud, a psychic mechanism that opposes the formation of a cathexis, or pleasure-giving object choice, and thus promotes repression.

Antinomy An apparently irresolvable conflict between two ideas, tendencies, or principles.

Anti-Semitism The expression of prejudicial or hostile attitudes toward Jews.

Apocalyptic Foreboding imminent catastrophe if not also ultimate victory over evil.

Apocryphal (1) Scriptural in form or content but excluded from the canon. (2) Lacking a known reliable source.

Apologetics Systematic discourse in defense of particular fundamental doctrines.

Apostasy Falling away from or renunciation of a particular religious faith and tradition.

Archetypes Inherited structural elements in the collective unconscious postulated by Jung to account for recurring themes in myths and fairy tales as well as in contemporary dreams, fantasies, and delusions.

Ascetic Given to practicing systematic self-denial of bodily pleasure, if not also self-imposition of displeasure, as a means of attaining a higher spiritual state.

Ashram The secluded dwelling place of a Hindu ascetic or sage, typically with accommodations for disciples.

Associationism An eighteenth-century doctrine that explains the mind's activity in terms of the association of elementary sensations, images, and ideas.

Assurance In the Protestant Christian context and especially the Methodist tradition, the deep feeling of certainty that personal salvation will be attained.

Atavistic Relating to the recurrence in an organism of a form or characteristic typical of a remote and less evolved ancestor, usually as a result of genetic recombination; hence, primitive.

Athletic One of Kretschmer's three body types, characterized by a muscular, heavily boned physique.

Attribution theory The view that the experience of self, others, and the natural world is shaped to a large degree by the cognitive need to make sense of inner and outer events and to exercise control over them.

Authoritarianism A personal disposition to submit unquestioningly to some authority and to be suspicious of and hostile toward all persons outside one's own circle of associates; said to be marked by rigidity, conventionality, and intolerance of ambiguity.

Autistic Characterized by illogical, self-centered, and utterly private mental activity (e.g., dreaming, reverie, hallucinating) that is untempered by external reality or cultural forms.

Automatisms Actions that are carried out without awareness or at least without the attention that is usually required for their successful performance.

Autosuggestion Deliberate self-induction of certain beliefs, feelings, or courses of action in order to improve physical or psychological well-being.

Axis mundi (Latin, "world axis") Any of a variety of vertically oriented objects, such as a pillar, tree, ladder, or mountain, that is taken to mark the center of the world and to connect it with heaven above if not also the underworld below.

B.C.E. "Before the common era"; a non-Christocentric equivalent to B.C., "Before Christ."

Behavior theory Any approach in psychology that seeks to explain observable behavior in relation to environmental stimuli.

Behavioral Pertaining or limited to observable behavior.

Behaviorism A philosophy and ideology that (1) takes psychology to be a natural science strictly limited to the study of objectively observable behavior, and (2) assumes that such behavior consists of elements that are the invariable and lawful consequences of environmental events. Methodological behaviorism accepts the first proposition but not the second.

Behaviorist (noun) A proponent of behaviorism; (adjective) characteristic of behaviorists or of behaviorism.

Behavioristic Resembling the behaviorist perspective in some but not all respects.

Bicameral mind The "two-chambered" mind postulated by Julian Jaynes to have been characteristic of human beings as recently as 1000 B.C.E. and occasionally to recur even now. In contrast to today's conscious, unitary mind situated primarily in the left hemisphere, the bicameral mind possesses two seats of activity, both lacking reflective consciousness and the right hemisphere dominating as the voice of a god, especially in times of stress or crisis.

Biofeedback A procedure for facilitating certain mental or physical states by providing continuous feedback to the subject regarding one or another physiological variable, such as alpha rhythm or blood pressure.

Blocking The disruption of a particular brain wave pattern by introducing an incompatible stimulus.

Bodhisattva In the Buddhist tradition, a revered or worshiped "being of enlightenment" who is qualified to enter nirvana but compassionately chooses instead to work for the salvation of others.

Borderline A personality disorder characterized by (1) marked changeability in mood and attitude, with anger and self-destructiveness as frequent manifestations; (2) instability of the sense of identity and, consequentially, excessive dependence on others and dread of loss; and (3) recurrent setbacks in interpersonal relations and attainment of goals.

Brahmacharya In the Hindu tradition, the practice of strict sexual continence, along with other forms of ascetic self-denial, in order to concentrate the energies in the direction of spiritual attainment.

Brahman In the Hindu tradition, the impersonal and indescribable ultimate reality, to which all other deities may be assimilated.

Brahmin A Hindu of the highest caste, or hereditary social class.

C.E. "Common Era"; a non-Christocentric equivalent to A.D. (*anno Domini,* "in the year of the Lord").

Cain jealousy Suttie's designation for an older child's hostility toward a younger sibling for usurping the mother's attention and care. It is the dominant recurring theme in mother cults, according to Suttie.

Canonical Officially accepted as part of the canon, the authoritative list of writings constituting a religious tradition's scriptures.

Castration complex In psychoanalytic theory, the intense fear of genital mutilation (in the boy) or the resentful conviction of having already been mutilated (in the girl) that is at the center of the Oedipus complex.

Catalepsy A sustained bodily state of muscular rigidity.

Catatonic Characterized by pathological symptoms of marked reduction in motor activity, even to the point of stupor or catalepsy, or alternatively, of excitement and heightened motor action; a form of schizophrenia.

Catharsis The alleviation of tension and anxiety by reliving, often with the aid of hypnosis, the originating circumstances; a method antecedent to psychoanalysis.

Celibacy Abstention from marriage or sexual intercourse, usually as an expression of some higher principle or religious commitment.

Cerebellum The "little brain" projecting backward from the brain stem and mediating coordinated movements.

Cerebral cortex The highly intricate outer layer of neural cells of the cerebral hemispheres. It is the area of the brain most critically involved in higher mental processes.

Cerebral lateralization The tendency of the two hemispheres of the brain to develop specialized functions.

Cerebrotonia The component of temperament said by Sheldon to correspond to the ectomorphic body type. It is marked by restrained inhibition, overquick reactiveness, love of privacy, and mental overintensity.

Chastity Abstention from sexual intercourse, either categorically or apart from the circumstances under which it is sanctioned by the society.

Choleric Said of a person who is quick-tempered or easily aroused to anger; one of the four basic temperaments identified by Hippocrates and Galen.

Circumambulation The ritual of walking around a revered object or sacred space, usually with the right side oriented toward the object.

Circumcision The excision of the foreskin of the male. The term is sometimes broadly used to designate genital mutilation of either sex.

Clairvoyance The direct perception of objects or events that are not present to the senses.

Clark school The group of American researchers, including James Leuba and Edwin Starbuck, who joined with Stanley Hall, the school's founder and president of Clark University, to study religious development, conversion, and other such phenomena by means of questionnaires and statistical analysis.

Cognition of being Maslow's term for the receptive, purposeless, and holistic form of awareness that accompanies peak, or mystical, experiences.

Cognitive Having to do with the process of becoming aware or gaining knowledge of the objects of experience.

Cognitive dissonance The discomforting awareness of inconsistency between what we know or believe and what we do. It is assumed to motivate efforts to reduce the inconsistency or to avoid information or situations likely to increase the dissonance.

Cognitive psychology A behavioral psychology that emphasizes the role of internal, mental processes, usually conceived in mechanistic terms, in the determination of behavior.

Collective unconscious The deeper-lying portion of the unconscious postulated by Jung to be the repository of universal dispositions toward certain forms of experience, represented by the archetypes.

Comparative psychology Usually, the branch of psychology that studies human and other animal species in relation to each other; used earlier to refer to the study of individual differences among human beings.

Complex According to Jung, a psychic fragment or representation in the personal unconscious that is a disturbing factor in, and yet an essential stimulus for, conscious activity.

Compulsion A persistently recurrent and often irresistible impulse to carry out certain stereotyped actions.

Conative Having to do with purposeful striving or acting.

Concrete operational thinking The mode of thinking ascribed by Piaget to 7- and 12-year-old children. Although capable of transcending immediate visual impressions and carrying out logical manipulations, such children continue to require concrete objects on which to perform these operations. See *Formal operational thinking.*

Constancy principle Freud's principle according to which internal and external stimulation are so adjusted that the level of excitation in the nervous system is held constant.

Constitution An individual's particular configuration of enduring physical characteristics, including height, weight, bodily proportions, sexual differentiation, and facial features.

Consubstantiality The quality or state of being of the same substance, hence intimately related or continuous with.

Contiguity The condition of occurring together in time or space.

Contingencies of reinforcement The pattern of relation existing between a certain behavior and the reinforcing stimuli that follow it.

Control group The subjects in an experiment who are not exposed to the independent variable and to whom, then, the subjects in the experimental group are later compared to assess the effects of that variable.

Conversion A definite and frequently sudden change in essential outlook or allegiances, accompanied by the usually joyful conviction that the new beliefs or attitudes accord with reality.

Coprophilia Abnormal interest in excrement or in sensory experience reminiscent of it.

Correlation The tendency of two or more variables to vary together and thus to serve as predictors of each other. The term is also used to designate the statistical procedure by which this tendency is assessed, as well as the coefficient (r) that is obtained.

Cosmic narcissism In Kohut's theory, a higher and relatively rare form of narcissism in which libido is transferred from the self to self-transcending ideals. The outcome is a timeless cosmic perspective that makes personal mortality acceptable.

Cosmology Speculations or teachings regarding the nature of the universe.

Countercontrol A pattern of responses aimed at counteracting or defeating an agency's aversive efforts at control.

Cover memory In psychoanalysis, an indifferent or unimportant memory, often from childhood, recalled in the place of associated but far more significant impressions that have been repressed; also called screen memory.

Creationism The view that takes the account of creation in the book of Genesis as literal history. It vigorously opposes the evolutionary theory of the origin of animals and plants. See *Evolutionism.*

Critical symbolism French theologian Auguste Sabatier's theory of religious knowledge, according to which religious doctrines are transient symbols, the inadequate secondary expressions of abiding primary religious experience.

Cross tolerance The immediate appearance, after taking an initial dose of some drug, of the diminished responsivity that has developed over time to another substance, which is then presumed to be similar in its action.

Cumulative tradition The totality of the observable aspects of religious life that are transmitted from one person or generation to another.

Curvilinear Represented by a curved line; said of relationships, such as that of prejudice and church attendance, that vary in strength or direction over the range of the two variables.

Cybernetic religion The worship of the machine and hence of destruction, said by Fromm to typify the alienated and technique-enslaved character type common today in the Western world.

Cyclothymic Said of the person who is subject to alternating periods of elation and depression, of uninhibited gregariousness and social withdrawal, but without psychotic proportions.

Darshan (Sanskrit) "Seeing" the divine by being in the presence of and beholding a holy person or a sacred image or place.

Dasein (German, "being there") The term used by existential psychologists and philosophers to designate the uniquely human mode of self-aware existence.

Decentration Piaget's term for the realization that a person's own, egocentric view of the physical and social worlds is but one perspective among a multitude of others. The decentering

of cognitive constructions is a prerequisite for the development of mental operations.

Deicide The killing of a divine being in human or animal form.

Déjà vu (French, "already seen") The sudden experiencing of a situation as intensely familiar while yet knowing that one has not been in that exact situation before; a phenomenon distantly related to mystical experience, according to James.

Delusion A mistaken conviction that is resistant both to reasoning and to compelling contradictory evidence.

Demiurge In the Gnostic tradition, the inferior deity who created and guards over the material world we inhabit.

Demythologizing The interpretive process of divesting some text of its mythical elements in order to reveal the underlying meaning.

Depersonalization A psychological state in which a person loses the ordinary sense of his or her own reality.

Depression An incapacitating state of sadness and despondency usually accompanied by loss of appetite, diminished self-esteem, and indecisiveness.

Dhāraṇā Concentration of thought on a single point or object; one of the last stages of yogic technique.

Dharma In the Hindu tradition, an individual's duty or the totality of actions required according to his or her station and stage in life.

Dhikr (Arabic, "recollection") In the Sufi tradition, the spiritual exercises by which the devotee draws near to God. The *solitary* type of *dhikr* entails breath control and other ascetic practices, whereas the *collective* type proceeds by way of music and ecstatic dance.

Dhyāna Yogic meditation, properly so-called; a lucid state in which the essence of the object of concentration is magically penetrated and assimilated. This stage of yogic technique immediately precedes *samādhi.*

Dialectic Dynamic interaction among opposing ideas, values, or points of view, sometimes resulting in synthesis or resolution.

Dialectical theology The highly influential Christian theology put forward early in the twentieth century by Karl Barth, who maintained that the radically transcendent nature of God requires that every statement regarding

God be balanced by the affirmation of its negation.

Dionysian Possessing the frenzied or orgiastic character of the rites associated with Dionysus, the Roman god of wine.

Discriminative stimulus In operant conditioning, a stimulus that allows an organism to discriminate between when an operant response will be reinforced and when it will not.

Discursive Systematic and rational in character rather than intuitive.

Disinterested Devoid of self-interest or partiality; unbiased.

Displacement In psychoanalytic theory, a defense mechanism whereby an impulse is redirected from its proper object to a less dangerous or threatening one.

Dissociation The splitting off from the rest of the personality of certain processes that then function more or less independently.

Divided self As used by James, the discordancy or heterogeneity of personality that is the psychological origin of the sick soul's suffering.

Doctrine of scriptural inerrancy The conviction of Fundamentalists that the Bible is in every respect free of error and thus may be relied on as the literally true word of God.

Dogmatic (1) Pertaining to the dogma, or authoritative teachings, of a particular tradition. (2) Inclined to dogmatism.

Dogmatism Rigid and unquestioning adherence to a belief system most likely derived from some authority other than reason, with a corresponding unwillingness to consider opposing views.

Dorpat school The international group of researchers who, under the leadership of Karl Girgensohn at Dorpat University, Estonia, and later in Greifswald and Leipzig, applied the Würzburg school's method of experimental introspection to religious experience.

Double-blind Said of an experimental procedure in which neither the experimenters nor the subjects know to which group—the experimental or the control—each subject has been assigned.

Dream work According to Freud, the complex mental operations carried out by the ego to transform the unconscious thoughts and wishes of the id into well-disguised and more coherent dream fantasies.

Driving The occurrence of an electrical brain wave pattern of the same frequency as the rhythmic stimulus that is producing it.

Dustbowl empiricism The opportunistic collecting and analyzing of quantified data, often on a large scale, without a guiding theoretical framework.

Ecclesiastical Pertaining to a church or other formal religious institution.

Eclectic Composed of the best or most serviceable elements drawn from a variety of perhaps conflicting sources, no one of which is considered adequate in itself.

Ecstasy Strictly, a trancelike state of profound emotionality in which awareness is limited to the object of contemplation. Also loosely used to refer to any exalted state of emotion.

Ectomorphy The component in Sheldon's model of body types that reflects the individual's degree of slenderness, delicacy, and fragility.

Ego (1) In psychoanalytic psychology, the largely conscious portion of the psyche that is reality-oriented. (2) In analytical psychology, the center of the field of consciousness.

Ego Functions (1) In psychoanalytic thinking, any of the adaptive activities carried out by the ego. (2) In the writings of the Dorpat school, the totality of possible personal responses to the objects of experience. Girgensohn distinguishes three groups of ego functions in relation to religious thought: (a) appropriation of the thought as one's own; (b) the taking of a stand toward the realities represented in the thought; and (c) transformation of the ego, or self, in proportion to the dominance of the religious objects.

Egocentric Viewing events exclusively from one's own point of view or in terms of one's own interests and needs.

Eidetic image A mental image nearly as vivid and detailed as an actual perception, though the subject—most often a child—usually realizes that the object is not literally present.

Eigenwelt In existential thought, the aspect of the personal world that is constituted by a person's relation to his or her self.

Electroencephalogram (EEG) The linear tracings produced by an electroencephalograph as a graphic representation of the electrical activity in an individual's brain.

Empathy Imaginative participation in the experience of another person; an essential element in the process of understanding. See also *Verstehen*.

Empirical Related to or based on experience rather than speculation. In contemporary psychology, the meaning of this term is commonly narrowed to include only objectively observable and measurable events.

Enantiodromia In analytical psychology, the eventual emergence of the unconscious opposite of some conscious psychic tendency, especially if it is one-sided and extreme.

Endomorphy The component in Sheldon's model of constitutional types reflecting the relative prominence of the digestive viscera and thus the tendency to become fat.

Endorphins A group of opiatelike neurotransmitters occurring naturally in the brain and serving under certain conditions to reduce pain and produce euphoria.

Epicureanism The experience-centered philosophy of Epicurus (341–270 B.C.E.), who viewed the calm and lasting pleasure derived from activities of the intellect and from friendship to be the highest good. The gods, he felt, should serve as perfect examples of tranquillity, not as objects of fear.

Epigenesis The emergence, in the course of an organism's development, of characteristics or properties that were not earlier apparent.

Epilepsy A disorder of the central nervous system characterized by episodic disturbances of consciousness during which convulsions of varying severity may occur.

Epiphenomenon An event derived from an accompanying phenomenon and possessing no causal efficacy of its own.

Epistemology The study of the nature and limits of human knowledge.

Epistemophilia The impulse to gain knowledge, a component of the sexual instinct thought by Freud to be most evident in the phallic-stage interest in the parents' sexual life. Some psychoanalysts regard philosophy and mysticism as sublimations of this drive.

Ergotropic arousal Increased activation of the sympathetic nervous system with attendant emotional excitement; the outcome of various ecstatic practices.

Erotogenic zone Any area of the body that yields distinctly pleasurable sensations when appropriately stimulated.

Error variance The variability in a set of scores that is the result of conditions irrelevant to the purposes of the measuring instrument.

Eschatology Teachings regarding events expected to occur at the end of the world or of human history.

Ethnocentrism The tendency to consider the members, values, or ways of one's own group as superior to those of others.

Ethnology The study of the origins, distribution, and culture of various ethnic, or racial, groups.

Ethology The biological and comparative study of animal behavior as it occurs in the species' natural habitats, with particular attention to the behavior's survival value.

Eucharist A central Christian ritual, also known as Holy Communion or the Lord's Supper, in which bread and wine, conceived as symbolizing or even having become the body and blood of Christ, are partaken in commemoration of the Last Supper and the subsequent sacrificial death of Christ.

Eugenics The application of the science of genetics to improve the hereditary qualities of a species, especially the human one.

Euphoria An intense feeling of well-being or elation.

Evangelical (From the Greek *euangelion*, "good news, gospel") A term designating any of a variety of Protestant views that emphasize the divinity and teachings of Christ. Although applicable to the liberal proponents of the Social Gospel movement early in the twentieth century, this term is understood today to refer chiefly to those more conservative Protestants who stress the sinful nature of humankind and the importance of being "born again."

Evolutionism The view that all forms of life and even the universe itself are products of a continuous, progressive development. The evolutionary hypothesis can be found in the earliest Indian and Greek speculation, but it was not until the nineteenth century that Charles Darwin provided a scientific basis for it. It has been challenged for its assumption that all evolution is progressive and is entirely rejected by creationists. See also *Creationism*.

Exegesis The systematic interpretation of a text through the application of a body of general hermeneutical principles.

Existential psychology A phenomenologically oriented psychology that takes as its object the structure or fundamental character of human existence as it is manifest in individual lives.

Exorcism The expelling of an evil spirit from a possessed person (or an object or place) by means of ritual formulations that address the possessing spirit in the name of a more powerful spirit or deity. As a rule, exorcism must be applied repeatedly, even over a period of months or years.

Experimental introspection The method of controlled self-observation by trained laboratory subjects that was adopted from the Würzburg school by Karl Girgensohn and other members of the Dorpat school to study religious experience.

Expiation Action carried out in reparation for some offense.

Extinction The process by which a conditioned response ceases to occur as the result of removing the reinforcing stimulus event.

Extraversion In the context of Jung's system of personality types, the directing of psychic energy toward the objects of the outer world. In ordinary usage, this term is understood as *social* extraversion, an orientation toward other persons.

Extravertive mystical experience The usually spontaneous and uncontrollable form of mystical experience in which a person vividly perceives an ultimate unity shining through the multiplicity of material objects that are apparent to the physical senses.

Extrinsic religious orientation An instrumental or utilitarian relation to various aspects of religious tradition, which are selected and shaped by an individual as a means of promoting his or her personal and social well-being.

F (fascism) scale The 30-item scale developed by Theodor Adorno and his colleagues (1950) to measure authoritarian, or antidemocratic, personality tendencies. Also called the California F Scale.

Factor analysis A complex statistical procedure for identifying the relatively few underlying factors responsible for the pattern of correlations among a large number of variables.

Faith A person's fundamental orientation or total response to the objects of experience, including oneself, other persons, and the natural world.

False positive In statistical analysis, the relatively rare though theoretically predictable mis-identification of some difference as statistically significant when in fact it is the result of chance variation. According to theory, the probability of such an occurrence is five in a hundred at the .05 level of significance, the usual minimally acceptable level. See also *Significance level.*

Fetishism Reverence for an inanimate object perceived as having magical powers.

Fixation In psychoanalytic theory, an arrest in psychosexual development, usually in a pregenital stage.

Flagellation The infliction of bodily pain, commonly by whipping and often self-administered, as penance for sin.

Folk psychology The historically and ethnographically based psychology that Wundt maintains is essential for understanding the higher mental processes and their expressions, including religion.

Formal operational thinking The thinking that is characteristic of persons who have reached the final stage in Piaget's schema of cognitive development, a level that is normally attained around the age of 12. Such persons are able to perform logical operations on concepts and propositions—that is, to think about thinking. See *Concrete operational thinking.*

Free association The "basic rule" or fundamental technique in orthodox psychoanalysis, according to which the analysand relates whatever comes to mind, perhaps beginning with some dream element or casual remark. From the course of associations, and especially the moments of inevitable resistance to the task, the analyst infers the nature of the analysand's unconscious conflicts.

Functional autonomy Allport's name for the principle that psychological processes may in time become ends in themselves, persisting independently of the needs or motives in which they originated.

Fundamentalism The strict adherence to a set of basic doctrines that are taken to be literally true. When capitalized, the term refers to the twentieth-century Protestant movement from which the expression derives. The "fundamentals" of this movement include the inerrancy of the Bible, the virgin birth of Christ, his bodily resurrection, and his imminent second coming.

Galvanic skin response (GSR) A measured change in the skin's resistance to a weak electrical current, reflecting a change in the organism's level of arousal.

Geisteswissenschaften (German, "sciences of the spirit, or mind") The fields of study, including psychology, that Dilthey sharply distinguished from the natural sciences in terms of both methods and goal. Whereas the natural sciences gather data through sensory observation toward the end of causal explanation, the human sciences are founded in lived experience and aim at empathic understanding.

Generativity In Erikson's epigenetic theory, the productivity and creativity entailed in establishing and guiding the next generation. It is the ego quality that under favorable conditions emerges in the seventh, adulthood stage.

Glossolalia Speaking in an incomprehensible, apparently self-invented "language," usually in religious settings and while in an altered state of consciousness; also known as speaking in tongues.

Gnosticism A group of pre-Christian religious movements synthesizing Greek and Oriental elements and centering on secret knowledge (*gnosis*) regarding salvation.

God representation The frequently complex and highly personalized image of God that is said by the psychoanalysts to be derived from a person's early experiences and fantasies of his or her parents as well as from evolving self-representations and religious instruction. It may contradict the individual's later *concept* of God and be the object of disbelief.

Grandiose self In Kohut's self psychology, an inflated self-image that serves in early childhood as an adaptive replacement for primary narcissism. In normal development, this configuration of perfection gives way to a realistic sense of self-esteem and pleasurable engagement in purposeful activity.

Graves' disease A disturbance in the body regulation system resulting from overactivity of the thyroid gland and frequently accompanied by serious mental disorder.

Guru (Sanskrit, "venerable") In the Hindu tradition, a deeply respected teacher or spiritual guide to whom individuals give their allegiance.

Gynandromorphic Possessing physical characteristics usually associated with the opposite sex.

Habituation The reduced responsiveness to a stimulus that usually results from repeated presentation of the stimulus.

Hallucination Complex false perceptions seen with open eyes and experienced as real.

Hallucinogenic Serving to produce extraordinarily vivid, hallucination-like experiences.

Hasidic Judaism An ecstatic mystical sect established in Poland in the middle of the eighteenth century by Israel the Baal Shem-Tob (1700–1760). Embraced by nearly half of the world's Jewish population in the early nineteenth century, Hasidism remains influential today in Israel and the United States.

Healthy-minded Of James's two temperamental types, the one that is disposed to see everything in this life as good and, accordingly, to respond to the divine with grateful admiration and desire for union. See *Sick soul.*

Heliotropism A reflexive tendency, found in many living organisms, to orient themselves toward the sun.

Hermaphroditic Possessing both male and female reproductive organs.

Hermeneutical circle The interpretive principle that emphasizes the circularity of understanding: every act of understanding begins with something already understood, a "preunderstanding" that is then reciprocally altered through the new act of understanding.

Hermeneutics The science of the methodological principles that underlie interpretation.

Heuristic Said of an idea or method that is justified by its capacity to stimulate further discovery.

High-plateau experience The enduring sense of illumination that Maslow says eventually replaces peak experiences in self-actualizing persons.

Hippocampus The curved, elongated structures within the brain's limbic system that mediate memory processes.

History of religions The equivalent in English of the German *Religionswissenschaft,* the science or scholarly study of the world's religious traditions. It is both historical, in the narrower sense, and systematic.

Homo religiosus (Latin, "religious man") In Erikson's writings, the rare, gifted, and melancholic individual whose public enactment of a cataclysmic identity crisis and subsequent ideological breakthrough serve to resolve the larger society's crisis as well.

Humanism Any system of thought in which the potentialities and fate of human beings are central.

Humanistic psychology Any of a variety of psychologies sensitive to human subjectivity and emphasizing the positive character of human potentialities, the progressive realization of which is considered essential for psychological well-being.

Hyperphrenia Greatly accelerated mental activity.

Hypersuggestibility An exceptional state of heightened suggestibility or openness to external influences.

Hyperventilation Abnormally rapid and deep breathing, resulting in carbon dioxide depletion and such symptoms as reduced blood pressure, constriction of the blood vessels, and sometimes fainting.

Hypnagogic image A peculiarly vivid image occurring as a person is falling asleep.

Hypochondriacal Marked by excessive preoccupation with bodily well-being, with a tendency to exaggerate or imagine symptoms of illness.

Hypomanic In a mild state of mania, thus exhibiting heightened activity, self-confidence, and good spirits, all of which might be taken as normal were it not for the attendant discontinuity in actions or ideas and intolerance of the slightest frustration.

Hypoventilation Abnormal reduction in the amount of air in the lungs, resulting in oxygen depletion and retention of carbon dioxide.

Hysteria An emotional disorder known from antiquity and first systematically studied by French psychopathologists in the nineteenth century, when this puzzling syndrome had become particularly prominent. Conspicuous among the symptoms are blindness, hearing impairment, and bodily paralysis, none of which can be traced to organic disturbances. The study of hysteria contributed to the rise of modern psychiatry.

I–Thou relation A relation of genuine and mutual encounter that engages a person's whole being and opens it to reciprocal influence from the other, whether a person, an aspect of nature, or a spiritual being.

Id (Latin, "it") In Freud's model of the psyche, the unconscious and enduringly influential reservoir of life and death impulses.

Idealized parental imago In Kohut's self psychology, a psychic representation formed in infancy and cathected with narcissistic libido as a means of preserving the original impression of parental perfection. Under favorable circumstances, this configuration is gradually reinternalized as the superego.

Ideal type An abstracted representation of some fundamental trend or disposition, the structural essence of which is thereby made clearer to the understanding. Ideal types are not intended for classifying individuals.

Identification The process of taking on the fundamental character of a deeply respected person and making it one's own. According to the psychoanalysts, it is the means by which the superego is formed at the end of the phallic stage.

Identity In Erikson's usage, the feeling of an enduring and integrated inner sameness that is affirmed by others with whom the person has a sense of solidarity.

Identity crisis The uncertainty or confusion regarding who one is and to what one should commit oneself that Erikson says is characteristic of adolescence.

Ideology An integrated system of ideas and values that serves to define reality and to unite individuals in a common cause.

Idiographic Directed toward an understanding of particular individuals or events. Contrast with *nomothetic*.

Illusion (1) In general, the perceiving of something in a manner that gives a mistaken impression of its true nature. (2) According to Freud's usage, a belief derived from human wishes but not necessarily false.

Illusionistic world Pruyser's term for the realm established between the autistic and realistic worlds by playful and creative imagining. It is the world of transcendent objects and thus of religion.

Imago In psychoanalysis, the unconscious inner representation of a person, usually a parent, that is formed early in childhood.

Immanence The condition of existing within a particular realm, for example, the mundane world.

Inclusive fitness The sociobiological principle according to which traits such as altruism are selected if they contribute to the fitness either of the organism or of relatives who also carry the trait's gene.

Individuation Jung's term for the process of attaining psychic wholeness and balance. It consists in the *differentiation* of the diverse contents of the unconscious and the *integration* of them into consciousness by means of archetypal symbols.

Ineffable Incapable of being described or expressed in words.

Infantile amnesia The ordinary inability to recall the feelings and experiences of early childhood, the result, according to the psychoanalysts, of active repression.

Inferior function In Jung's psychology, the least developed and most nearly unconscious of the four functions, the particular modes a person uses in perceiving and judging inner or outer events.

Innate releasing mechanism The postulated inherited mechanism that is engaged by instinctual display activities of another member of the same species, resulting in a series of repetitive exchanges that serve to coordinate movement, control aggression, or effect pair-bonding.

Instinct An inherited tendency in an organism to carry out certain complex, species-specific patterns of behavior under particular environmental conditions.

Instinctive drift The tendency for behavior artificially shaped in the laboratory to give way to more natural, species-specific behavior, especially when the organism is placed in a situation more closely resembling its natural environment. A term coined by Breland and Breland (1961).

Intentional object The term used by phenomenologists to specify the object or content to which a psychic act refers; also called intentional correlate.

Interpretive psychology Any psychology that seeks to comprehend human experience by means of empathic understanding rather than causal explanation.

Intrinsic religious orientation The consistent harmonizing of all aspects of one's life with some religious ideal or set of precepts.

Introjection In psychoanalysis, the process of incorporating some attribute of another person and making it one's own. Identification constitutes a wholesale introjection of the other's character.

Introspection Observation of one's own experience. Although literally meaning "to look within," in reality one's focus is not on the "contents of one's mind" but on the objects of one's experience, including "subjective" images or feeling states and "objective" events in the outer world.

Introversion In the framework of Jung's personality types, the withdrawal of psychic energy from objects of the outer world and the redirection of it inwardly, toward the subject's own thoughts and feelings.

Introvertive mystical experience The systematically cultivated form of mystical experience in which the usual multiplicity of externally perceived objects vanishes, along with all other mental contents, leaving a void that is experienced as the One, or the Absolute.

Ipsative Pertaining to a scoring procedure that requires the respondent to divide a limited number of points among the various scales, so that scoring high on one will mean scoring lower on another. The resulting scores, because they are relative to the others rather than absolute, must be interpreted and compared with exceptional caution.

Ithyphallic Possessing a perpetually erect penis; an attribute represented in images of such gods as Shiva and Priapus.

Kabbala (Hebrew, "tradition") The sum of medieval and modern Jewish mysticism, the esoteric teachings of which maintain that the historical experience of the Jewish people is symbolic of the cosmic process.

Karma (From Sanskrit *kṛ*, "do" or "act") In the Hindu and Buddhist traditions, the absolutely binding moral law of cause and effect, whereby an individual's present circumstances are the result of his or her past actions, including those in previous lives. It perpetuates the ceaseless round of birth and rebirth.

Kin selection The sociobiological principle according to which a trait such as self-sacrifice will be selected if it increases the reproductive potential of relatives who also carry the gene for the trait.

Kinesthetic Pertaining to the sensory experience produced by bodily movements and tensions.

Koan A seemingly absurd and insoluble problem given by a Zen master to a student as a way of freeing the mind from sheer reason and preparing it through concentration for the moment of sudden illumination. Example: What is the sound of one hand clapping?

Kuṇḍalinī In the Hindu tantric tradition, the "serpent power" that yogic practice seeks to awaken and progressively raise through the seven *chakras*, or bodily centers, the successful completion of which represents the uniting of the opposites of experience as well as the transcending of them.

Laius jealousy Suttie's designation for the father's regressive jealousy of the child's nurtural favors from the mother.

Latency In Freud's account of psychosexual development, the uneventful interval between the phallic and genital stages.

Lateral geniculate A subcortical nucleus of brain cells that transmits visual signals to the cortex.

Law of parsimony The general scientific principle according to which an explanation is to be kept as simple as the phenomenon will allow.

Leptosomic Of Kretschmer's three bodily types, the one characterized by a lean and narrowly built physique.

Levitation The rising into the air of an object or person by means thought to be supernatural.

Liberalism An approach that grounds the quest for truth in reflection on human experience rather than in authority based on divine revelation. Prominent in nineteenth- and twentieth-century theology, liberalism manifested its disposition toward change in the *Social Gospel movement* (which see).

Libido Sexual energy (Freud) or, more generally, psychic energy (Jung).

Limbic system A collection of subcortical structures of the brain that are the chief regulators of emotional states.

Limbo According to Roman Catholic theology, an abode for virtuous souls excluded from heaven by the lack of baptism. While thus forever deprived of the beatific vision of God, souls in this realm are said nevertheless to know God and to enjoy a perfect natural happiness.

Liminal (From the Latin *limen*, "threshold") Used by Victor Turner to refer to the reversals, reconciliations, and imaginings that characterize the transition period in a rite of passage.

Linga (Sanskrit, "phallus," "characteristic") A stylized phallic symbol, usually rendered in stone or metal, representing the Hindu god Shiva and serving as the focus of his worship. See also *Shiva, Yoni*.

Lobectomy Surgical removal of one of the temporal lobes of the brain.

Locus coeruleus A small nucleus in the brain stem widely connected to other brain cells and serving to modulate emotional states.

Locus of control A construct issuing out of social learning theory and assessed by a scale that measures an individual's generalized expectation of *internal* versus *external* control of reinforcement.

Logotherapy The meaning-centered therapeutic approach derived by Frankl from existential and phenomenological sources.

Mādhurya bhāva (Sanskrit, "mood, or emotional state, of sweetness") Of the several traditional ways of relating to divinity in the Hindu tradition, the one in which the devotee relates to God as a woman to her lover.

Mandala (Sanskrit, "circle") A predominantly circular design, often highly elaborated, that Jung took to be a symbol of psychic wholeness or totality.

Mantra A sacred or mystical formula used as an aid to meditation in the Hindu and Buddhist traditions.

Masochistic Taking pleasure in being subjected to pain or in being mistreated or dominated.

Materialism The philosophic theory that takes physical matter to be the only kind of reality.

Matriarchal Under the control of or dominated by women, for example, as pertaining to family organization.

Mechanism The doctrine that the experience and behavior of all living organisms are mechanically determined and can be wholly explained in terms of physical and chemical principles.

Mediating variable A third, perhaps hypothetical variable that serves to explain the observed relation between two other variables.

Medical materialism A term used by James for the assumption that identification of a religious phenomenon's psychophysiological correlates serves to invalidate any claims for its genuineness.

Megalomania A mental disorder marked by delusions of grandeur and feelings of personal omnipotence.

Melancholic Tending toward sadness or depression; one of the four basic temperaments put forward by Hippocrates and Galen.

Mesomorphy The component in Sheldon's model of constitutional types that indicates the degree of muscularity and bone development.

Messianic Possessing inspiration and a crusading spirit to bring about the fulfillment of some foreseen ideal.

Metaneed In Maslow's usage, one of the higher needs motivating the self-actualizing person.

Metaphysics The division of philosophy concerned with the nature of existence.

Method of serial study James's technique of placing a phenomenon in a graduated series of related occurrences, a procedure he considered essential to the process of interpretation.

Methodological behaviorism The perspective in psychology that shares behaviorism's exclusive commitment to quantitative and experimental methods but not its mechanistic and reductionistic emphasis on environmental determinants.

Mezuzah (Hebrew, "doorpost") In the Jewish tradition, a small parchment scroll inscribed with biblical passages and placed in a case attached to the doorpost, where it serves as a reminder of God.

Mimetic Imitative; descriptive of religious images, objects, and practices that represent the natural and social worlds in literal rather than abstract terms. Contrast with *Aniconic* and *Non-mimetic*.

Mind-body problem The philosophical question regarding the ultimate relationship between mental activity and the brain.

Mitwelt In existential thought, the aspect of the personal world that is constituted by a person's relation to his or her fellow human beings.

Mnemonic Aiding the process of remembering.

Moral realism As characterized by Piaget, the conviction common among children that good and bad or right and wrong are inherent and objectively perceptible attributes of certain acts, rather than socially conditioned judgments.

Moratorium A legally or socially sanctioned period of delay before a person must assume some obligation or responsibility.

Mortification Subjecting oneself to bodily discomfort or pain as a form of penance or a means of subduing the passions; considered essential to ascetic practice.

Multiple regression A statistical procedure for combining two or more variables in a way that maximizes the predictability of another, related variable.

Mundane Having to do with the transitory pleasures and practical activities of everyday life, in contrast to what is eternal and transcendent.

Mysterium tremendum et fascinans (Latin, "tremendous and fascinating mystery") Otto's summary formulation for characterizing the bipolar structure of the experience of the holy.

Mystical Related to a spiritual reality not ordinarily present to the senses or comprehended by the intellect.

Myth A class of engaging and tradition-sanctified stories dealing with the origin, nature, and purpose of the world and its inhabitants. Often featuring divine beings, these stories are sometimes taken as true in the narrow historical sense. Psychologists, among other scholars, tend to view them instead as creative imaginings that serve vital personal, social, and religious functions.

Narcissism Egocentric overvaluation and admiration of oneself; preemptive self-love. See also *Primary narcissism.*

Nationalism The conviction that one's own nation is superior to all others and that its culture and interests should thus be favored.

Near-death experience The variable configuration of remarkable perceptions and intensely positive feelings reported by persons who have come close to dying.

Necrophilia A disposition to find corpses sexually exciting.

Negative identity In Erikson's thinking, an identity perversely based on certain personal qualities and social roles that had earlier been presented to the individual as wholly undesirable or even dangerous.

Negative reinforcement Increasing the probability of some response by making the removal of an aversive stimulus event contingent on that response.

Neoteny The preservation into adulthood of certain juvenile characteristics.

Neurotic Pertaining to an often debilitating mental disorder characterized by enduring or recurrent symptoms experienced by the individual as alien and unacceptable. In contrast to psychosis, reality testing remains essentially intact, and the individual's behavior does not conspicuously violate social norms.

Neurotransmitter A chemical substance that serves to transmit an electrical impulse from one neuron to another.

Nigredo An initial stage in the alchemical work, represented by blackness or dark chaos on the material level and by death on the spiritual.

Nihilism The deeply pessimistic view that nothing is knowable or of value, and that existence is therefore meaningless.

Nirvana In the Buddhist tradition, the final state of unspeakable bliss resulting from transcendence of desire, suffering, and the cycle of birth and rebirth.

Nomology In interpretive psychology, the typifying of phenomena in terms of the laws or functions that govern their change or alteration.

Nomothetic Pertaining to laws of general applicability. Contrast with *Idiographic.*

Noncanonical Falling outside a religious tradition's canon, or authoritative body of scriptures, yet similar in form and content.

Nonmimetic Nonimitative, thus nonrepresentational or abstract.

Nonrational Incapable of being grasped by conceptual thought.

Norepinephrine A major neurotransmitter secreted mainly in the locus coeruleus of the brain stem and regulating emotional response.

Novitiate A person admitted to a religious community for the traditional period of probation, or preliminary testing, that precedes full membership.

Null hypothesis In statistical analysis, the precisely testable hypothesis that the differences observed among the assessed varables may be attributed solely to chance variation. If the differences prove to be large enough to allow rejection of the null hypothesis, in effect one's true hypothesis is affirmed, that among the variables there is a statistically significant but otherwise unspecifiable difference.

Numinous The term employed by Otto to designate the category of value and the associated complex of feelings originally implied by "the holy." Otto initially assumed he was the first to coin this term, but he later discovered that the Latin *numinis* was used as early as the sixteenth century, by Calvin.

Objective psychology Any of a variety of approaches in psychology that restrict themselves to data that are publicly observable.

Objective worship According to Pratt's distinction, the form of worship aimed at communicating with and perhaps influencing some supernatural being. Contrast with *Subjective worship.*

Obsessional neurosis A disabling mental disorder in which the person is plagued by persistent irrational or repugnant ideas, thoughts, or images that lie beyond his or her control; referred to more often today as obsessive–compulsive disorder.

Occipital cortex The uppermost layer of the cerebral hemispheres in higher animals, including human beings; commonly called gray matter in accord with its appearance.

Oceanic feeling A term, ultimately derived from Sanskrit sources, used to refer to unbounded mystical experience. Borrowing the term from Romain Rolland, Freud takes its referent to be the limitless narcissism of infancy.

Oedipus complex The crucial pattern of object relations in the phallic stage when the child experiences sexual desire toward the parent of the opposite sex and jealousy and rage toward all rivals, especially the parent of the same sex. In the *inverse* Oedipus complex, which orthodox psychoanalysts take to be almost as common, the roles of the parents are reversed.

Omnipotence The quality or state of having unlimited power or influence.

Omnipotence of thoughts In psychoanalysis, the delusional conviction that the mere thinking of some outcome is sufficient to bring it about.

Omniscience The quality or state of having unlimited awareness, knowledge, or understanding.

Once-born A term freely borrowed by James from Francis Newman to describe the healthy-minded type, whose happiness does not require the agonizing second birth of the twice-born.

Ontogeny The course of development of an individual organism.

Ontological Pertaining to being or existence.

Operant behavior Emitted responses that operate on the environment and produce reinforcing effects.

Operational definition A definition of some characteristic or process in terms of the operations or procedures used to identify and measure it (e.g., defining religiosity in terms of a particular scale purporting to assess it).

Oracle The answer spoken by the representative of some divinity in response to an inquiry. The term is also applied to the representative and to the shrine where the oracles were given.

Oral sadism The taking of pleasure in injuring or destroying by biting; said by psychoanalysts to derive from experience late in the oral stage.

Oral stage The first of Freud's psychosexual stages, during which the mouth serves as the primary source of pleasure.

Originology A term proposed by Erikson to designate a too-facile explanation of a phenomenon in terms of its origins.

Orthodoxy Faithful subscription to a set of beliefs established as correct by some authority.

Orthopraxy Faithful observance of the practices prescribed by some authority.

Overdetermination The principle, emphasized by psychoanalysis, that every behavior or experience has a variety of causes, any one of which may be sufficient to maintain the phenomenon.

Pantheism The doctrine that equates God with the whole of the universe.

Paradigm In general, a particularly clear example of something. More specifically, a model of scientific conduct—including theory, principles, methods, results, and applications—that guides the continuing research of a community of adherents.

Paranoid Subject to irrational suspiciousness and delusions of persecution.

Parapsychology The serious and systematic investigation of such paranormal phenomena as telepathy, clairvoyance, and apparitions of the dying and deceased, with the aim of establishing their nature and laws and ultimately placing them in a broader and generally acceptable scientific framework.

Parricide The murdering of a close relative.

Pathological method The illumination of more or less normal phenomena by studying instances of pathological exaggeration.

Patriarchal Under the control of or dominated by men.

Patricide The killing of one's own father.

Peak experience Maslow's term for mystical experience, chosen in order to study such experience apart from its traditional religious context and to make it more widely available.

Pedagogy The study of educational methods, processes, and goals.

Penance Assigned or self-imposed punishment, ranging from bodily suffering to the performance of good works, that is required for the forgiveness of sins.

Perennial philosophy The unanimous core of truth said by some commentators to underlie the surface variety of religious traditions. Huston Smith (1976) prefers to call this putative underlying unity "the primordial tradition" in order to avoid the suggestion that it operates as an articulate formal philosophy.

Perseveration The persistence of some goal-directed behavior usually to an exceptional degree or beyond a desired point.

Persona In Jung's theory, the social mask or outer attitude a person assumes to meet society's expectations while yet preserving his or her true nature.

Personal document Any record, such as a letter, journal, or autobiography, that through analysis or interpretation yields insight into the experience or personality of the writer.

Personal equation The totality of individual peculiarities in outlook and experience that influence any undertaking, including the conduct and evaluation of psychological research.

Phallic stage The third and most crucial of Freud's psychosexual stages, during which the genitals become the primary erotogenic zone.

Phallus The penis, especially when represented as a symbol.

Phenomenology The descriptive study of the contents of human experience, carried out as free as possible of any presuppositions or theoretical framework.

Phlegmatic Characterized by sluggishness and apathy; one of the four basic temperaments identified by Hippocrates and Galen.

Phobia A persistent and often debilitating irrational fear of some object or situation.

Photism An impression of bright light in the absence of an adequate stimulus.

Photobiology An interdisciplinary field of study that investigates the role of light in the functioning of living organisms.

Phylogeny The evolutionary development of a species.

Physiognomy In traditional usage, the ancient art of judging character from the appearance of the face. The term is now used by phenomenologists to refer to the appearance of the outer world in an individual's experience, for example, as threatening, friendly, or calming.

Pietism A seventeenth-century reform movement in Germany reasserting the importance of heartfelt personal piety as over against the formality and intellectualism of the Lutheran and Calvinist traditions.

Pistis A Greek word meaning "trust" or "trustful loyalty," which for Jung is equally a mark of religious experience and a mark of fidelity to the laws of the individual's own being.

Placebo effect Positive change occurring in response to some factor, not because the factor is efficacious in itself, but because the individual confidently expects it to work.

Pleasure principle In psychoanalysis, the id's blind dedication to maximizing pleasure and minimizing displeasure, without regard to reality. Although eventually displaced by the reality principle, it remains a strong disposition within the psyche throughout life, sometimes even overcoming the reality principle.

Pleroma In the Gnostic tradition, the remote and self-contained realm of divine light.

Pluralism An outlook that respectfully acknowledges today's diversity of intellectual, cultural, and religious views and thoughtfully takes them into account in the process of establishing commitments in a relativistic world. See also *Postmodernism.*

Polymorphous perversity The indifference of the id, and hence of the infant, to who or what the object of gratification is.

Positivistic Characterized by disdain for subjective, intuitive, or speculative approaches to the world of human experience and a corresponding deep admiration for the objective procedures of the natural sciences.

Possession A sometimes voluntarily provoked trance state, usually marked by intense motor activity and emotional excitement, in which the ordinary personality is displaced by another, often alien one that is interpreted as a possessing spirit. Among onlookers, possession evokes all the emotions, including uncanniness and dread, that Otto sums up in the expression *mysterium tremendum.*

Post hoc analysis The choosing of some form of statistical analysis after the data have been collected and examined. Although it makes the obtaining of significant results more likely, it also increases the probability of a *false positive* (which see).

Posthypnotic suggestion A suggestion made during hypnotic trance that the subject will react in a specified way in the subsequent waking state.

Postmodernism The contemporary view that the confident beliefs and values of the modern era are not true in any absolute sense but are human creations that represent alternate ways of making sense of human experience in a universe that will forever remain mysterious. See also *Pluralism, Social constructionism, Relativism.*

Pragmatism The philosophical system championed by James according to which the meaning or truth of an idea is to be found in its practical consequences.

Prakṛti (Sanskrit) Primeval matter or substance; with *purusha* (Sanskrit, "man"), one of the dual bases of all existence, material and spiritual, according to *Sankhya,* one of the oldest major systems of Indian philosophy.

Prāṇa (Sanskrit, "breath") The term for "life energy" or "vital air" in Indian philosophy.

Prāṇāyāma (Sanskrit, "breath-restraint") The disciplining of respiration, which constitutes the fourth of the eight stages of yogic progression.

Pre-Oedipal Pertaining to events or attitudes that characterize the developmental period preceding the Oedipus conflict.

Prepotent Taking precedence over others in power or influence. In Maslow's hierarchy of needs, the lower a need is in the hierarchy, the more prepotent it is.

Presence See *Sense of presence.*

Primary narcissism In psychoanalysis, the infantile psychic disposition to cathect one's own body as an object of sexual pleasure.

Primary process The autistic and illogical laws governing the infantile psyche in its pursuit of the *pleasure principle* (which see).

Primitive credulity The tendency, most evident in children, to believe what one is told until there is some occasion for doubt.

Principle of biological interpretation Proposed by Flournoy in 1903, this principle maintains that an adequate psychology of religion is (1) *physiological* in its attentiveness to organic conditions; (2) *genetic* or *evolutionary* in its concern with development; (3) *comparative* in its sensitivity to individual differences; and (4) *dynamic* in its recognition of the dynamic interplay of many factors in the religious life.

Principle of psychoreligious parallelism Berguer's principle that every religious phenomenon possesses two parallel aspects: a psychological state and an impression of value and objective significance. Because the psychology of religion can address only the first of these factors, he argues, it cannot give a full account of religion.

Principle of the exclusion of the transcendent Flournoy's classic principle according to which the psychologist of religion will neither reject nor affirm the independent existence of the religious object.

Principle of the inclusion of the transcendent The principle, suggested here as a complement to Flournoy's exclusionary principle, maintaining that the psychology of religion must take into account the *experience of* transcendent objects.

Progressivism A term first used by participants and later by historians to refer to the group of reform movements that swept across America from the 1890s to 1917. It was a major factor in the rise of the psychology of religion. See also *Social Gospel movement.*

Projection The unwitting attribution to others of trends within a person's own personality; considered a defense mechanism when the person first represses and denies such trends.

Projective technique Any of a variety of procedures that elicit a projection of the individual's private world of perceptions, thoughts, and feelings by providing a relatively unstructured field that the individual must organize.

Propaedeutic (Greek, "to teach beforehand") Preparatory study or practice needed as a foundation for some subsequent undertaking or achievement.

Propitiate To appease or regain the favor of.

Propriate function Allport's term for any of the activities or functions of the self (pro-

prium), all of which serve to integrate the personality.

Protocol The original record of an interview or of the results of an experiment or other investigation.

Pseudospeciation In Erikson's theory, the conviction that a person's own group and its ways define what is essentially human, and that other groups, viewed as if of a different species, are a threat to the person's own identity and fate.

Psychasthenia A term used by Janet for what today is called an obsessive–compulsive disorder.

Psychedelic "Mind-manifesting," a term coined by Humphry Osmond as a neutral label for drugs that induce ecstatic or mystical experiences. It is also used to describe the experiences themselves.

Psychologism A term of reproach designating the tendency to reduce philosophical and theological reflection to psychological processes, hence making psychology the fundamental discipline.

Psychometrics The quantitative assessment of individual differences in abilities, attitudes, interests, traits, and other such personal qualities.

Psychopathic (1) Most generally, and as used by James, characterized by unspecified mental disorder. (2) More recently and specifically, pertaining to individuals who chronically engage in antisocial activities without guilt or anxiety and are seemingly incapable of lasting, warm, and responsible relationships; also called sociopathic.

Psychotic Pertaining to serious mental disorder in which the person unmistakably loses contact with reality, and thinking, perception, and emotion may be profoundly disturbed.

Punishment In operant conditioning, an aversive stimulus that suppresses the occurrence of the behavior it follows.

Purgatory According to Roman Catholic doctrine, a place or state of punishment where departed souls undergo purificatory suffering for the interval of time required to atone for their sins.

Pyknic One of Kretschmer's three bodily types, characterized by a physique that is soft, heavy, and round.

Quasi-experimental Descriptive of various research designs that, for ethical or practical reasons, depart in one or more ways from the usual rigorous standards for an experiment, for example, relying on naturally occurring differences on an independent variable rather than trying to manipulate them.

Quaternity Any figure or assemblage having four elements or parts; said by Jung to symbolize the archetype of the self.

Quest religious orientation An understanding of religion, not as a shared body of established truths and obligatory practices, but as an active and personal search for deeper understanding of and contact with ultimate reality.

Radical empiricism James's late-developed metaphysics according to which the universe is composed of pure, or unanalyzed, experiences, which are interpreted either as objects in the world or as events in the mind, depending on the person's practical purposes. This philosophy of pure experience, of life as it is actually lived through, is close in spirit to modern-day phenomenology.

Ramadan The ninth month in the Arabian lunar calendar, during which all able-bodied Muslims except soldiers and young children fast from sunrise to sunset to commemorate Muhammad's initial revelation as well as his later flight from Mecca to Medina, the occasion from which Muslims date their calendar.

Rapture According to mystical tradition, an ecstatic state in which the soul is lifted out of itself by divine power, allowing it to see things beyond the reach of ordinary human vision.

Rationalism Reliance on reason, as opposed to sense experience, for establishing what is true.

Reaction formation A defense mechanism whereby a person exhibits a trait or pattern of behavior that is diametrically opposed to the wishes or tendencies he or she has denied and repressed.

Reality principle In psychoanalysis, the realization that there is an independent world of reality that requires considerable compromise if pleasure is ultimately to be obtained. This principle, which is the possession of the ego, ordinarily displaces the pleasure principle.

Recapitulation theory The hypothesis that individual development proceeds through a series of stages paralleling those in the evolutionary development of the species. (In a phrase, ontogeny recapitulates phylogeny.)

Redintegration The postulated process by which a total experience is brought back into consciousness by a single associated stimulus.

Reductionism The explanation of complex phenomena in terms of simpler, underlying processes.

Reflex arc The classic theoretical unit characterizing the function of the nervous system. A receptor nerve, excited by a stimulus, transmits this excitement through an intermediate neuron to an effector nerve, which activates the corresponding muscle or gland.

Regression In psychoanalysis, the retreat to earlier, less mature ways of thinking, feeling, and acting, usually as a mechanism of defense.

Reification The treating of some process or abstract construct as though it were an independently existing thing. The notion that a person "has a religion" is an example of such an error.

Reinforcement In operant conditioning, the process of increasing the probability that some behavior will occur by following it with a stimulus event known to have reinforcing properties. The term also serves to designate the stimulus event.

Relativism The view that all knowledge is relative to the historical and personal context in which it is formulated and interpreted.

Reliability The relative capacity of a measuring instrument to give consistent results, either within itself or from one occasion to another. It is expressed as a correlation coefficient. Distinguish from *Validity* (which see).

Religionswissenschaft (German, "science of religion") The science or scholarly study of the world's religious traditions; usually translated as "history of religions."

Religious act The phenomenological expression referring to the individual's complex relation to the religious object. It includes the partial acts of taking cognizance of the object and of taking a stand in relation to it.

Repression The exclusion of disturbing impulses, images, or thoughts from consciousness by an ongoing process that itself lies outside of awareness; the most elemental defense mechanism.

Respondent behavior Behavior elicited by an unknown stimulus.

Response set A certain disposition—for example, acquiescence—to respond to questionnaire items in terms other than those intended by the test developer.

Reticular activating system (RAS) A fibrous network of neurons in the brain stem that plays a major role in regulating general arousal and excitability.

Ritualism In Erikson's theory, a pathological distortion of one of the elements of ritualization.

Ritualization (1) In ethology, a complex series of repetitive exchanges initiated in many animal species by instinctive display activities and serving to coordinate movement and modulate behavior. (2) In Erikson's theory, periodically recurrent interplay between at least two persons and carried out with attentiveness to form and detail, a sense of higher symbolic meaning, and a feeling of absolute necessity.

Role taking Assuming or appropriating the role of another person by identifying with that person. Also used by Sundén in the more limited sense of imagining oneself in the other's place in order to anticipate how the other will respond.

Rosary A Roman Catholic devotion centering on the mysteries of Christ's life and recited with the aid of a circular string of beads also called a rosary. The most common rosary consists of 150 Hail Marys (the angel's salutation to Mary on telling her she was to give birth to Jesus), arranged in groups of ten, or decades, with each decade preceded by an Our Father and followed by a Gloria.

Rubedo The final stage and goal of the alchemical work, symbolized by the mysterious philosopher's stone and a number of other mythic, sometimes red objects suggesting ultimate transformation and immortality.

Sadistic Taking pleasure in inflicting physical or mental pain on another person.

Sadomasochistic Combining both sadistic and masochistic tendencies.

Salvation The variously conceived ultimate goal of religious devotion, the highest good offered by a tradition to its followers.

Samādhi A state of supreme concentration in which opposites are paradoxically transcended and union is attained; the final stage of yogic progression. Of the grades of *samādhi*, *savichāra samādhi* entails penetration to the "subtle" aspects of matter whereas in *nirvichāra samādhi*, thought becomes one with the essence of the physical world, leaving behind all consciousness of time and space as well as feelings of suffering or pleasure.

Sanguine Typified by warmth, cheerfulness, and optimism; one of the four basic temperaments delineated by Hippocrates and Galen.

Satori The joyful and ineffable experience of sudden illumination that is the immediate aim of Zen Buddhist meditation.

Satyagraha (Sanskrit, "truth force") The ritualized program of friendly passive resistance that Gandhi and his followers used to effect political and social reform.

Scatological Having to do with excrement.

Schizoid A personality disorder in which the person is emotionally aloof, lacks warm feelings for others, and is indifferent to the praise or criticism of others.

Schizophrenic Exhibiting certain symptoms of psychosis, including delusions, hallucinations, and disordered thought processes. The person's sense of self is frequently disturbed, affect is blunted or inappropriate, and the individual tends to withdraw from the world.

Schizothymic In Kretschmer's typology, a class of temperaments consisting of a complex amalgam of divided tendencies that give the outward appearance of coolness, polite sensitivity, adaptability, and refinement while hidden within may be passionate feelings, rebelliousness, vulgarity, and maliciousness. Kretschmer associates this temperamental type with the lean and narrowly built physique of the leptosome.

Schuldig A German word meaning both "guilty" and "indebted"; used by existential psychologists to characterize human relation to the natural world, other persons, and oneself.

Scopophilia (Also scoptophilia) The impulse to look, especially at what is forbidden or unknown. Freud said that this impulse, a component of the sexual instinct, is most conspicuous in the phallic-stage interest in the sexual organs. Psychoanalysts maintain that the interest in looking, as well as its counterpart, showing, is sublimated in various religious practices.

Scrupulosity Anxious overattentiveness to the details of moral or religious requirements.

Second naïveté Ricoeur's term for the postcritical attitude of openness to the objects of religious faith, an attitude said to be fostered by phenomenology through its hermeneutics of restoration.

Secondary process In psychoanalysis, the more or less logical form of thinking characteristic of the conscious ego.

Secularization The progressive substituting of nonreligious and frequently scientific interpretations of events for the traditional religious ones.

Self In Jungian psychology, the archetype of psychic harmony, balance, and wholeness. In its various manifestations it symbolizes the never wholly attained goal of individuation.

Self-actualization The realization to a marked degree of a person's inherent potential.

Self-grandiosity The solipsistic attitude of extravagantly favorable self-evaluation, an attitude denoted by the psychoanalytic principle of primary narcissism.

Self-objects In Kohut's theory, any objects that are felt to be a part or extension of the self and are therefore cathected with narcissistic rather than object libido.

Self-representation In psychoanalysis, the relatively enduring precipitate of past experiences by which the ego represents itself to itself.

Semantic differential A standardized rating device consisting of a series of seven-point bipolar scales for assessing the connotative meaning of some concept or object.

Sensationalism The view that all knowledge is ultimately derived from sensory experience.

Sense of presence A usually vivid and often overwhelming sense of the presence of an invisible spirit or divine being who, although only vaguely represented, is often precisely localized.

Sentiment In relation to some object, a complex personal disposition that is primarily affective and conative in organization while yet possessing considerable cognitive content.

Serotonin A neurotransmitter produced in the raphe nuclei and exerting an excitatory function at some brain synapses and an inhibitory function at others. Its chemical structure is strikingly similar to that of LSD.

Shadow In analytical psychology, the denied and undeveloped side of the personality, which, though individual in form, is archetypal in its universality, dynamics, and symbolism.

Shaman A term of northeast Asian origin now applied to any priest or medicine man whose specialized functions as prophet and spiritual healer are carried out in a state of voluntary possession trance.

Shiva The Destroyer in the Hindu divine Triad, in which Brahma is Creator and Vishnu is Preserver. Variously represented as the Lord of Dancers, as an ithyphallic ascetic, and as a deity who is half male and half female, Shiva is most commonly worshiped in the form of the *linga,* an emblem of the creative energy of the universe. See also *Linga.*

Sick soul In James's typology, the person of melancholic temperament, whose peculiar sensitivity to the evil aspects of reality is founded in an agonizing inner dividedness or discordancy of the self manifested in a conviction of sinfulness.

Significance level In statistical analysis, the probability of wrongly concluding that obtained results are statistically significant. By convention, the largest acceptable probability is usually .05. See also *False positive.*

Social constructionism The view that all human knowledge and understanding is created and shaped through a process of negotiation among persons living within particular cultural contexts. See also *Postmodernism.*

Social Gospel movement A late nineteenth-century reform movement in America dedicated to bringing the Christian gospel to bear on the economic, political, and social problems created by industrialization. See also *Liberalism, Progressivism.*

Social learning theory A cognitively oriented behavior theory that accounts for the learning and enactment of complex patterns of behavior in terms of observation and selective imitation.

Social releaser A ritualized pattern of behavior that serves to trigger an innate releasing mechanism in another member of the same species, thereby instigating a series of repetitive exchanges that serve to modulate and coordinate behavior.

Sociobiology A field of study employing what has been learned about ethology, ecology, and population genetics to predict features of a population's social organization, given its size, density, and age distribution and the behavioral constraints that the population's shared genetic constitution imposes.

Solipsism The conviction that the self is the whole of reality, and thus that other persons and the rest of the world are a person's own creations. Ascribed by some psychologists to the young infant, this view has, in modified form and to varying degrees, been espoused as an epistemological doctrine by nearly every major philospher since Descartes. Jung expresses this doctrine when he says that all we can know is our own experience.

Soma In ancient India, an intoxicating plant juice and the god associated with its use that were the subject of lyric hymns in the *Rig Veda*.

Somatotonia The component of temperament said by Sheldon to correspond to the mesomorphic body type. Among its traits are energetic and noisy assertiveness, love of risk and physical adventure, and psychological callousness.

Somatotype One or another of the basic body builds identified in some typological schema, usually under the assumption that each type is associated with a certain configuration of psychological traits.

Spatiality A fundamental phenomenological category encompassing the totality of an individual's subjective experience of space. See also *Temporality*.

Speaking in tongues See *Glossolalia*.

Spike activity Large and sudden changes in the electrical potential of nerve cells, as superimposed on the slower wave rhythm reflected in an electroencephalogram.

Standard deviation (SD) The descriptive statistic most commonly used to specify the variability of scores in a distribution. It is equal to the square root of the variance. In a normal distribution, 34.13 percent of the scores fall between the mean and one SD. See also *Variance*.

Stigmata In the Christian tradition, marks or actual bleeding sores resembling the traditional wounds of the crucified Christ and welcomed by their recipients as a sign of intimate participation in the renunciatory suffering of their Lord.

Subjective worship In Pratt's typology, the form of worship chiefly intended to induce some desired mental state in the worshipers. Contrast with *Objective worship*.

Sublimation In psychoanalysis, the unconscious diverting of illicit impulses into more highly refined and elaborated interests that, though socially acceptable, also allow partial satisfaction of the instigating needs.

Subliminal Occurring below the threshold of conscious awareness.

Superego In Freud's conception of the psyche, the largely unconscious division formed by the introjection of parental attitudes and experienced as the conscience.

Superior function In analytical psychology, the mode of perceiving or judging inner or outer events that is most developed and most frequently used.

Suppression Conscious renunciation of certain instinctual impulses, a process that Freud says is likely to be only temporarily successful.

Sutras The collection of aphoristic teachings in the late Vedic scriptures of ancient India.

Synapse The juncture where a nervous impulse passes from one neuron to another.

Synchronicity The principle proposed by Jung to account for the temporal concurrence of certain events that are not causally linked.

Syncretism In the history of religions, the gradual and usually spontaneous mingling of two or more traditions, eventually resulting in a new whole.

Synesthesia A concomitant subjective sensation or image in one sensory modality in response to a stimulus that is presented to another (e.g., seeing colors in response to certain sounds).

Syzygy (From Latin, *syzygia*, "conjunction") In analytical psychology, the conjunction of male and female, usually in the form of a divine couple.

Talion punishment Retribution taking a form corresponding to the injury or the crime committed (e.g., an eye for an eye).

Tallith (Hebrew) A prayer shawl, typically white with blue or black stripes and usually made of wool, worn by Jewish males during the morning prayers as well as during all services on the Day of Atonement, if not on other occasions as well. Wearing the *tallith* denotes symbolic subjection to the will of God.

Talmud An authoritative encyclopedia of ancient Jewish thought supplementing the Hebrew Bible and concerned chiefly with law.

Tantric Pertaining to a pan-Indian mystical movement centering on the worship of Shakti, the Divine Woman and Mother. It arose in the fourth century C.E. and has been assimilated into both Hindu and Buddhist traditions.

Tefillin (Hebrew, "phylacteries") Two black leather boxes that are ritually bound by leather straps on the head and the left arm (the right arm of left-handed persons) of Jewish males who have reached religious majority (age 13). Worn on weekdays but not on the Sabbath or festivals, the *tefillin* contain scriptural passages and are said to fortify the wearer against sinning.

Telekinesis The movement of objects without contact or other apparent physical means.

Teleological Pertaining to purposes or goals.

Telepathy The conveying of an impression from one mind to another without the use of the sense organs.

Telesphoros A deity, often represented as a child, who attended Asclepius, the Greek god of healing.

Telic Tending toward some end or goal.

Telos (Greek, "end," "purpose") In Koepp's schema of interpretive understanding, the purpose or goal, and thus the unifying element, of the phenomenon a person seeks to understand.

Temperament An enduring inclination toward a certain quality of emotional response and mood.

Temporality A fundamental phenomenological category encompassing all aspects of the subjective time of the individual's world of experience, including personal tempo, the dynamically interrelated structures of past, present, and future, and the relation to social, historical, and cosmic time. See also *Spatiality.*

Temporal lobe A large lobe of the cerebral hemisphere positioned in front of the occipital lobe and below the lateral fissure, thus located roughly at ear level.

Tetany A nervous disorder characterized by intermittent tonic, usually paroxysmal spasms involving the extremities.

Theocracy Rule of a society or state by immediate divine guidance or by representatives of God, usually priests.

Theodicy The attempt to justify the ways of God in the face of the existence of evil.

Theophagy The sacramental eating of a god in the form of a sacrificed human being or animal, the firstfruits of a harvest, baked bread, or some other substance.

Theophany Some perceptible manifestation of a deity.

Theosophy (1) Any system of thought (e.g., Gnosticism) purporting to offer mystical knowledge of God and of the universe in relation to God. (2) The philosophy derived from Buddhist and Hindu sources by the Russian medium Madam Blavatsky (1831–1891) and promulgated by the Theosophical Society she founded in America in 1875. Annie Besant (1847–1933), a nationalist leader in India, headed the society from 1907 until her death. *Anthroposophy* is a separatist movement initiated in Germany by Rudolf Steiner (1861–1925), who emphasized the *natural* availability of divine wisdom. See also *Gnosticism.*

Theriomorphic Having the form of an animal.

Threshold The point at which an increasingly intense stimulus produces a physiological or psychological effect.

Totemism A social system centered on a shared mystical relation with some animal or plant that is venerated as a symbol of the tribe and the members' common ancestry.

Trance A state of profound absorption frequently accompanied by vocal and motor automatisms that in some contexts are interpreted as signs of spirit possession.

Transcendence The crucial, ultimate dimension toward which all religious expression is directed and in which, to varying degrees, it participates.

Transcendent function Jung's term for the complex process in which opposing elements of the individual psyche are brought together by means of unifying symbols, thus facilitating the transition from a less developed attitude to a more advanced one.

Transference In psychoanalysis, the therapeutically invaluable tendency of the patient to see the therapist as a virtual reincarnation of some important figure in the patient's childhood and thus to reenact this past relationship in the therapist's presence.

Transitional object Some childhood object such as a blanket or teddy bear that symbolizes the mother and helps to ease the young child's transition from hallucinatory omnipotence to recognition and acceptance of objective reality.

Transitional phenomena The broad class of cultural possessions, including especially art and religion, to which Winnicott assigns the function of creating an illusory, intermediate realm of experience that helps throughout life to bridge inner and outer realities. The child's transitional object is the prototype of all later such phenomena.

Transmarginal inhibition A protective reaction of the nervous system to overstimulation.

Transpersonal psychology An offshoot of humanistic psychology that encompasses a wide range of self-transcending phenomena, including ecstatic and mystical experiences. Its proponents seek to appropriate insights from the great religious traditions, especially those of the East, in order to develop a new paradigm of scientific understanding.

Transvestite A person who takes pleasure in adopting the dress and manner of the opposite sex.

Trophotropic arousal Increased activation of the parasympathetic nervous system with attendant relaxation and quietude; the outcome of various meditative practices.

Tropism Automatic orientation by an organism toward or away from a source of stimulation.

Twice-born An alternate term used by James to refer to the sick soul, who must undergo the second birth of conversion in order to attain happiness.

Typology The construction of a fundamental set of "ideal" types as an orienting schema for comprehending individual forms. The term is also applied to the system of types itself.

Umwelt In existential thought, the aspect of the personal world that is constituted by one's relation to the surrounding natural world, including one's own body.

Upanishads A class of sacred texts in the Hindu tradition containing speculations regarding the nature of the world and of ultimate reality and how salvation may be attained.

Vaishnava Pertaining to the major Hindu sect that centers on the worship of Vishnu or one of his incarnations. The other major sect, the Shaivite, centers on Shiva.

Validity The degree to which something is well grounded or supported by appropriate means. In psychometrics, it is the degree to which an assessment device actually measures what it is supposed to measure. Establishing the validity of a test or questionnaire is a complex and cumulative undertaking, the results of which require careful interpretation.

Variance A descriptive statistic for specifying the extent to which individual scores in a distribution deviate from the mean. It is calculated by squaring the deviation of each score from the mean and then averaging these squared deviations.

Vedas The four canonical collections of hymns and prayers that constitute the most ancient of the Hindu scriptures. Of the four, the *Rig Veda* is the most important.

Veridical True or accurate; not illusory.

Verstehen (German, "understanding") The intuitive process, grounded in a person's own lived experience and capacity for empathy, by which the felt meaning that underlies any of a great variety of expressions, from bodily gestures to literature, art, and religion, is discerned. See also *Empathy*.

Viscerotonia The component of temperament said by Sheldon to correspond to the endomorphic body type. Its traits include love of physical comfort and eating, complacency, sociability, and love of ceremony.

Viscous In Kretschmer's typology, the temperament ordinarily characterized by phlegmatic equanimity and stability but capable of explosive anger and massive violence. Kretschmer ascribes this temperamental type to the athletic physique.

Vishnu The Preserver in the Hindu divine Triad, in which Brahma is Creator and Shiva is Destroyer. Among Vishnu's incarnations, Krishna and Rama are the most important.

Volitional Having to do with the processes of choosing or deciding.

Würzburg school The group of psychologists who, under the leadership of Oswald Külpe at Würzburg University, used systematic experimental introspection to study thought processes.

Yoga (Sanskrit, "yoking") An ancient Hindu system of doctrines and physical practices directed toward the attainment of pure Being or liberation. Of the many types of yoga, the best known are *hatha* (yoga by way of bodily purification and discipline), *raja* (concentration), *jnana* (knowledge), *bhakti* (loving devotion), and *karma* (action).

Yoni The pear-shaped base, representing the female genitals, out of which the Shiva *linga* rises.

Zazen The practice of seated meditation that constitutes the heart of Zen Buddhist training.

Zeus jealousy Suttie's designation for a man's jealousy of the woman's capacity to bear and suckle children.

Zizith (Hebrew, "fringes") The tassels attached to the four corners of special garments worn by Jewish males according to biblical command as protection against immoral conduct.

REFERENCES

Aaronson, B. S. (1966). Behavior and the Place Names of Time. *American Journal of Hypnosis: Clinical, Experimental, Theoretical,* 9, 1–17.

Aaronson, B. S. (1967). Mystic and Schizophreniform States and the Experience of Depth. *Journal for the Scientific Study of Religion,* 6, 246–252.

Aaronson, B. S. (1968). Hypnotic Alterations of Space and Time. *International Journal of Parapsychology,* 10, 5–36.

Aaronson, B. S. (1969a). Hypnosis, Depth Perception, and the Psychedelic Experience. In C. T. Tart, *Altered States of Consciousness,* pp. 315–323. (Paper first published 1969)

Aaronson, B. S. (1969b). *The Hypnotic Induction of the Void.* Paper presented at the meeting of the American Society of Clinical Hypnosis, San Francisco.

Aaronson, B. S. (1970). Some Hypnotic Analogues to the Psychedelic State. In B. Aaronson and H. Osmond, *Psychedelics,* pp. 279–295.

Aaronson, B. S., and Osmond, H. (Eds.). (1970). *Psychedelics: The Uses and Implications of Hallucinogenic Drugs.* Garden City, N.Y.: Anchor Books.

Aberle, D. F. (1966). *The Peyote Religion Among the Navaho.* New York: Wenner-Gren Foundation for Anthropological Research.

Abraham, K. (1913). Restrictions and Transformations of Scoptophilia in Psycho-neurotics; With Remarks on Analogous Phenomena in Folk-Psychology. In K. Abraham, *Selected Papers,* pp. 169–234. (Paper first published 1913)

Abraham, K. (1920). The Day of Atonement: Some Observations on Reik's *Problems of the Psychology of Religion.* In K. Abraham, *Clinical Papers and Essays on Psycho-Analysis.* London: Hogarth Press, 1955, pp. 137–147. (Paper first published 1920)

Abraham, K. (1924). The Influence of Oral Erotism on Character Formation. In K. Abraham, *Selected Papers,* pp. 393–406. (Paper first published 1924)

Abraham, K. (1949). *Selected Papers of Karl Abraham.* Translated by D. Bryan and A. Strachey. London: Hogarth Press.

Abramson, H. A. (Ed.). (1967). *The Use of LSD in Psychotherapy and Alcoholism.* Indianapolis: Bobbs-Merrill.

Ackerman, S. H., and Sachar, E. J. (1974). The Lactate Theory of Anxiety: A Review and Reevaluation. *Psychosomatic Medicine,* 36, 69–79.

Acklin, M. W. (1985). An Ego Developmental Study of Religious Cognition (Georgia State University, 1984). *Dissertation Abstracts International,* 45, 3926B. (University Microfilms No. 85–03799)

Adams, C. J. (Ed.). (1977). *A Reader's Guide to the Great Religions* (2nd ed.), New York: Free Press.

Adams, J. L. (1980). Letter from Friedrich von Hügel to William James. *Downside Review,* 98, 214–236.

Adler, A., and Jahn, E. (1933). *Religion und Individualpsychologie: Eine prinzipielle Auseinandersetzung über Menschenführung.* Frankfurt: Fischer, 1975. (First published, with authors reversed, in 1933; Adler's contribution is translated in H. L. Ansbacher and R. R. Ansbacher [Eds.], *Superiority and Social Interest.* Evanston, Ill.: Northwestern University Press, 1964)

Adorno, T. W., Frenkel-Brunswik, E., Levinson, D. J., and Sanford, R. N. (1950). *The Authoritarian Personality.* New York: Harper & Brothers.

Åkerberg, H. (1972). The Significance of William James's Psychology of Religion Today. *Studia Theologica,* 26, 141–158.

Åkerberg, H. (1973). Hauptpunkte der Religionspsychologie William Grønbaeks. *Temenos,* 9, 108–146.

Åkerberg, H. (1975). *Omvändelse och kamp: En empirisk religionspsykologisk undersökning av den unge Nathan Söderblöms religiösa utveckling 1866–1894.* Lund: Studentlitteratur.

Åkerberg, H. (1978). Attempts to Escape: A Psychological Study on the Autobiographical Notes of Herbert Tingsten 1971–1972. In T. Källstad, *Psychological Studies on Religious Man*, pp. 71–92.

Affemann, R. (1957). *Psychologie und Bibel: Eine Auseinandersetzung mit C. G. Jung.* Stuttgart: Ernst Klett.

Aghajanian, G. K. (1980). Mescaline and LSD Facilitate the Activation of Locus Coeruleus Neurons by Peripheral Stimuli. *Brain Research*, 186, 492–498.

Aghajanian, G. K., Sheard, M. H., and Foote, W. E. (1970). LSD and Mescaline: Comparison of Effects on Single Units in the Midbrain Raphe. In D. H. Efron, *Psychotomimetic Drugs*, pp. 165–170.

Ahmad, A. (1970). Erikson's Untruth. *Human Inquiries: Review of Existential Psychology and Psychiatry*, 10, 1–21.

Akhilananda, S. (1946). *Hindu Psychology: Its Meaning for the West.* New York: Harper & Brothers.

Akil, H., Watson, S. J., Young, E., Lewis, M. E., Khachaturian, H., and Walker, J. M. (1984). Endogenous Opioids: Biology and Function. *Annual Review of Neuroscience*, 7, 223–255.

Akishige, Y. (Ed.). (1977). *Psychological Studies on Zen* (2 vols.). Tokyo: Komazawa University. (Vol. 1 was first published in 1968)

Albrecht, C. (1951). *Psychologie des mystischen Bewußtseins.* Bremen: Carl Schünemann.

Albrecht, C. (1958). *Das mystische Erkennen: Gnoseologie und philosophische Relevanz der mystischen Relation.* Bremen: Carl Schünemann.

Albrecht, C. (1974). *Das mystische Wort: Erleben und Sprechen in Versunkenheit.* Presented and edited by H. A. Fischer-Barnicol. Mainz: Matthias-Grünewald.

Aletti, M. (1992). The Psychology of Religion in Italy. *International Journal for the Psychology of Religion*, 2, 171–189.

Alexander, F. (1923). Buddhistic Training as an Artificial Catatonia (The Biological Meaning of Psychic Occurrences). *Psychoanalytic Review*, 1931, 18, 129–145. (Original German edition 1923)

Alexander, F. G., and Selesnick, S. T. (1966). *The History of Psychiatry: An Evaluation of Psychiatric Thought and Practice from Prehistoric Times to the Present.* New York: Harper & Row.

Allen, G. W. (1967). *William James: A Biography.* New York: Viking.

Allen, M. K. (1955). Personality and Cultural Factors Related to Religious Authoritarianism (Stanford University, 1955). *Dissertation Abstracts*, 15, 2324. (University Microfilms No. 13,253)

Allen, R. O., and Spilka, B. (1967). Committed and Consensual Religion: A Specification of Religion-Prejudice Relationships. *Journal for the Scientific Study of Religion*, 6, 191–206.

Alliott, R. (1855). *Psychology and Theology; or, Psychology Applied to the Investigation of Questions Relating to Religion, Natural Theology, and Revelation.* London: Jackson and Walford.

Allison, J. (1968). Adaptive Regression and Intense Religious Experience. *Journal of Nervous and Mental Disease*, 145, 452–463.

Allport, G. W. (1937). *Personality: A Psychological Interpretation.* New York: Henry Holt.

Allport, G. W. (1942). *The Use of Personal Documents in Psychological Science.* New York: Social Science Research Council.

Allport, G. W. (1948). Psychology. In *College Reading and Religion.* New Haven, Conn.: Yale University Press, pp. 80–114.

Allport, G. W. (1950). *The Individual and His Religion: A Psychological Interpretation.* New York: Macmillan.

Allport, G. W. (1954). *The Nature of Prejudice.* Reading, Mass.: Addison-Wesley.

Allport, G. W. (1955). *Becoming: Basic Considerations for a Psychology of Personality.* New Haven, Conn.: Yale University Press.

Allport, G. W. (1959). Religion and Prejudice. *Crane Review*, 2, 1–10. (Reprinted in G. W. Allport, *Personality and Social Encounter: Selected Essays.* Boston: Beacon Press, 1960, pp. 257–267)

Allport, G. W. (1961). *Pattern and Growth in Personality.* New York: Holt, Rinehart and Winston.

Allport, G. W. (1964). The Fruits of Eclecticism: Bitter or Sweet? *Acta Psychologica*, 23, 27–44. (Reprinted in Allport, 1968)

Allport, G. W. (1966). The Religious Context of Prejudice. *Journal for the Scientific Study of Religion*, 5, 447–457.

Allport, G. W. (1967). [Autobiography]. In E. G. Boring and G. Lindzey (Eds.), *A History of Psychology in Autobiography*, Vol. 5. New York: Appleton-Century-Crofts, pp. 1–25. (Reprinted in and cited from Allport, 1968)

Allport, G. W. (1968). *The Person in Psychology: Selected Essays.* Boston: Beacon Press.

Allport, G. W. (1978). *Waiting for the Lord: 33 Meditations on God and Man.* Edited by P. A. Bertocci. New York: Macmillan.

Allport, G. W., Gillespie, J. M., and Young, J. (1948). The Religion of the Post-war College Student. *Journal of Psychology*, 25, 3–33.

Allport, G. W., and Ross, J. M. (1967). Personal Religious Orientation and Prejudice. *Journal of Personality and Social Psychology*, 5, 432–443. (Reprinted in Allport, 1968)

Allport, G. W., Vernon, P. E., and Lindzey, G. (1970). *Manual, Study of Values: A Scale for Measuring the Dominant Interests in Personality* (revision of 3rd ed.). Boston: Houghton Mifflin.

Almquist, A. J., and Cronin, J. E. (1988). Fact, Fancy, and Myth on Human Evolution. *Current Anthropology*, 29, 520–522.

Alston, W. P. (1964). Psychoanalytic Theory and Theistic Belief. In J. Hick (Ed.), *Faith and the Philosophers.* New York: St. Martin's Press, pp. 63–102.

Altemeyer, B. (1988). *Enemies of Freedom: Understanding Right-Wing Authoritarianism.* San Francisco: Jossey-Bass.

Altemeyer, B. (1994). Reducing Prejudice in Right-

Wing Authoritarians. In M. P. Zanna and J. M. Olson (Eds.), *The Psychology of Prejudice: The Ontario Symposium*, Vol. 7. Hillsdale, N.J.: Lawrence Erlbaum Associates, pp. 131–148.

Altemeyer, B., and Hunsberger, B. (1992). Authoritarianism, Religious Fundamentalism, Quest, and Prejudice. *International Journal for the Psychology of Religion*, 2, 113–133.

Ames, E. S. (1910). *The Psychology of Religious Experience*. Boston: Houghton Mifflin.

Amón, J. (1969). *Prejuicio antiprotestante y religiosidad utilitaria*. Madrid: Editorial Aguilar.

Amón, J., and Yela, M. (1968). Dimensiones de la religiosidad. *Revista de Psicologia General y Aplicada*, 23, 989–993.

Anand, B. K., Chhina, G. S., and Singh, B. (1961). Some Aspects of Electroencephalographic Studies in Yogis. *Electroencephalography and Clinical Neurophysiology*, 13, 452–456. (Reprinted in Tart, 1990)

Anand, B. K., Misra, S. S., Narayana, B., and Narayanaswami, V. (1962). *Report of the Committee on Evaluation of Therapeutic Claims of Yogic Practices*. New Delhi: Ministry of Education, Government of India (Publication No. 633).

Anastasi, A. (1988). *Psychological Testing* (6th ed.). New York: Macmillan.

Andersen, D. C. (1993). Beyond Rumor and Reductionism: A Textual Response to Erik H. Erikson. *The Psychohistory Review*, 22, 35–68.

Anderson, S. (1923). The Whirling and Howling Dervishes. *The Moslem World*, 13, 181–191.

Andres, F. (1944). Das religiöse Leben und seine psychologische Erforschung. *Zeitschrift für Aszese und Mystik*, 19, 39–52.

Anesaki, M. (1916). *Nichiren the Buddhist Prophet*. Cambridge, Mass.: Harvard University Press.

Angoff, A. (1966). The Literature of Religion and Parapsychology. *International Journal of Parapsychology*, 8, 321–334.

Annis, L. V. (1976). Emergency Helping and Religious Behavior. *Psychological Reports*, 39, 151–158.

Ansbacher, H. L. (Ed.). (1971). Religion and Individual Psychology. *Journal of Individual Psychology*, 27, 1–48.

Anthony, D., Ecker, B., and Wilber, K. (Eds.). (1987). *Spiritual Choices: The Problem of Recognizing Authentic Paths to Inner Transformation*. New York: Paragon House.

Appadurai, A. (1978). Understanding Gandhi. In P. Homans (Ed.), *Childhood and Selfhood: Essays on Tradition, Religion, and Modernity in the Psychology of Erik H. Erikson*. Lewisburg, Pa.: Bucknell University Press, pp. 113–143.

Arbman, E. (1963–1970). *Ecstasy, or Religious Trance, in the Experience of the Ecstatics and from the Psychological Point of View* (3 vols.). Norstedts: Svenska Bokförlaget.

Argyle, M. (1958). *Religious Behaviour*. London: Routledge & Kegan Paul.

Argyle, M., and Beit-Hallahmi, B. (1975). *The Social Psychology of Religion*. London: Routledge & Kegan Paul. (Revised edition of Argyle, 1958)

Arlow, J. A. (1964). The Madonna's Conception Through the Eyes. *Psychoanalytic Study of Society*, 3, 13–25.

Armstrong, J. R. (1977). Trends in American Eschatology: An Application of Skinnerian Concepts in an Analysis of Changes in Religion and Culture (Boston College, 1976). *Dissertation Abstracts International*, 37, 3575B–3576B. (University Microfilms No. 76–30,375)

Arnheim, R. (1969). *Visual Thinking*. Berkeley: University of California Press.

Arraj, J. (1991). *Jungian and Catholic? The Promises and Problems of the Jungian-Christian Dialogue*. Chiloquin, Ore.: Inner Growth Books.

Aziz, R. (1990). *C. G. Jung's Psychology of Religion and Synchronicity*. Albany: State University of New York Press.

Back, K. W. (1974). Human Nature, Psychological Technology, and the Control of Population Growth. *Journal of Social Issues*, 30, 279–295.

Badcock, C. R. (1980). *The Psychoanalysis of Culture*. Oxford: Basil Blackwell.

Badcock, C. R. (1986). *The Problem of Altruism: Freudian-Darwinian Solutions*. Oxford: Basil Blackwell.

Bähr, H. W., and Wenke, H. (Eds.). (1964). *Eduard Spranger: Sein Werk und sein Leben*. Heidelberg: Quelle & Meyer.

Bagchi, B. K., and Wenger, M. A. (1957). Electrophysiological Correlates of Some Yogi Exercises. *Electroencephalography and Clinical Neurophysiology, Supplement*, 7, 132–149.

Bagley, C., and Boshier, R. (1975). Demographic Predictors of Conservatism and Racial Prejudice. *The Australian and New Zealand Journal of Sociology*, 11, 65–68.

Bagley, C., Boshier, R., and Nias, D. K. B. (1974). The Orthogonality of Religious and Racialist/Punitive Attitudes in Three Societies. *Journal of Social Psychology*, 92, 173–179.

Bakan, D. (1958). *Sigmund Freud and the Jewish Mystical Tradition*. Princeton, N.J.: Van Nostrand.

Bakan, D. (1960). Freud and the Zohar: An Incident. *Commentary*, 29, 65–66.

Bakan, D. (1965). The Mystery-Mastery Complex in Contemporary Psychology. *American Psychologist*, 20, 186–191. (Reprinted in Bakan, 1967)

Bakan, D. (1966a). Behaviorism and American Urbanization. *Journal of the History of the Behavioral Sciences*, 2, 5–28.

Bakan, D. (1966b). *The Duality of Human Existence: An Essay on Psychology and Religion*. Chicago: Rand McNally.

Bakan, D. (1966c). The Test of Significance in Psychological Research. *Psychological Bulletin*, 66, 423–437. (Reprinted in Bakan, 1967)

Bakan, D. (1967). *On Method: Toward a Reconstruction*

of Psychological Investigation. San Francisco: Jossey-Bass.

Bakan, D. (1971). *Slaughter of the Innocents: A Study of the Battered Child Phenomenon.* San Francisco: Jossey-Bass.

Bally, G. (1961). *Einführung in die Psychoanalyse Sigmund Freuds.* Reinbek bei Hamburg: Rowohlt.

Balmary, M. (1979). *Psychoanalyzing Psychoanalysis: Freud and the Hidden Fault of the Father.* Translated by N. Lukacher. Baltimore: Johns Hopkins University Press, 1982. (Original French edition 1979)

Balodhi, J. P., and Mishra, H. (1983). Pātanjala Yoga and Behavior Therapy. *The Behavior Therapist, 6,* 196–197.

Bandura, A. (1977). *Social Learning Theory.* Englewood Cliffs, N.J.: Prentice-Hall.

Banks, R. (1973). Religion as Projection: A Re-Appraisal of Freud's Theory. *Religious Studies, 9,* 401–426.

Banks, R. (1975). A Neo-Freudian Critique of Religion: Erich Fromm on the Judeo-Christian Tradition. *Religion, 5,* 117–135.

Banquet, J. P. (1973). Spectral Analysis of the EEG in Meditation. *Electroencephalography and Clinical Neurophysiology, 35,* 143–151.

Barber, T. X. (1970). *LSD, Marihuana, Yoga, and Hypnosis.* Chicago: Aldine.

Barnard, M. (1963). The God in the Flowerpot. *The American Scholar, 32,* 578–586.

Barnes, M., Doyle, D., and Johnson, B. (1989). The Formulation of a Fowler Scale; An Empirical Assessment Among Catholics. *Review of Religious Research, 30,* 412–420.

Barr, H. L., Langs, R. J., Holt, R. R., Golderberger, L., and Klein, G. S. (1972). *LSD: Personality and Experience.* New York: John Wiley & Sons.

Barr, J. (1978). *Fundamentalism.* Philadelphia: Westminster Press.

Barr, J. (1980). *The Scope and Authority of the Bible.* Philadelphia: Westminster Press.

Barron, F. (1963). *Creativity and Psychological Health: Origins of Personal Vitality and Creative Freedom.* Princeton, N.J.: D. Van Nostrand.

Bartels, W. J. (1977). The Effects of a Western Meditation on a Measure of Self-Actualization (Oklahoma State University, 1976). *Dissertation Abstracts International, 37,* 5596A. (University Microfilms No. 77–5035)

Basford, T. K. (1990). *Near-Death Experiences: An Annotated Bibliography.* New York: Garland.

Bastide, R. (1931). *The Mystical Life.* Translated by H. F. Kynaston-Snell and D. Waring. New York: Charles Scribner's Sons, 1935. (Original French edition, 1931)

Batson, C. D. (1976). Latent Aspects of "From Jerusalem to Jericho." In M. P. Golden (Ed.), *The Research Experience.* Itasca, Ill.: F. E. Peacock, pp. 205–214.

Batson, C. D. (1977). Experimentation in Psychology of Religion: An Impossible Dream. *Journal for the Scientific Study of Religion, 16,* 413–418.

Batson, C. D. (1983). Sociobiology and the Role of Religion in Promoting Prosocial Behavior: An Alternative View. *Journal of Personality and Social Psychology, 45,* 1380–1385.

Batson, C. D. (1990). Good Samaritans—or Priest and Levites? Using William James as a Guide in the Study of Religious Prosocial Motivation. *Personality and Social Psychology Bulletin, 16,* 758–768.

Batson, C. D., Beker, J. C., and Clark, W. M. (1973). *Commitment Without Ideology.* Philadelphia: Pilgrim Press.

Batson, C. D., and Burris, C. T. (1994). Personal Religion: Depressant or Stimulant of Prejudice and Discrimination? In M. P. Zanna and J. M. Olson (Eds.), *The Psychology of Prejudice: The Ontario Symposium,* Vol. 7. Hillsdale, N.J.: Lawrence Erlbaum Associates, pp. 149–169.

Batson, C. D., Flink, C. H., Schoenrade, P. A., Fultz, J., and Pych, V. (1986). Religious Orientation and Overt Versus Covert Racial Prejudice. *Journal of Personality and Social Psychology, 50,* 175–181.

Batson, C. D., and Flory, J. D. (1990). Goal-Relevant Cognitions Associated with Helping by Individuals High on Intrinsic, End Religion. *Journal for the Scientific Study of Religion, 29,* 346–360.

Batson, C. D., and Gray, R. A. (1981). Religious Orientation and Helping Behavior: Responding to One's Own or to the Victim's Needs? *Journal of Personality and Social Psychology, 40,* 511–520.

Batson, C. D., Naifeh, S. J., and Pate, S. (1978). Social Desirability, Religious Orientation, and Racial Prejudice. *Journal for the Scientific Study of Religion, 17,* 31–41.

Batson, C. D., and Raynor-Prince, L. (1983). Religious Orientation and Complexity of Thought about Existential Concerns. *Journal for the Scientific Study of Religion, 22,* 38–50.

Batson, C. D., and Schoenrade, P. (1991a). Measuring Religion as Quest: 1) Validity Concerns. *Journal for the Scientific Study of Religion, 30,* 416–429.

Batson, C. D., and Schoenrade, P. (1991b). Measuring Religion as Quest: 2) Reliability Concerns. *Journal for the Scientific Study of Religion, 30,* 430–447.

Batson, C. D., Schoenrade, P., and Ventis, W. L. (1993). *Religion and the Individual: A Social-Psychological Perspective.* New York: Oxford University Press. (Revised edition of Batson and Ventis, *The Religious Experience,* 1982)

Batson, C. D., and Ventis, W. L. (1985). Misconception of Quest: A Reply to Hood and Morris. *Review of Religious Research, 26,* 398–407.

Beale, L. (1989). Pulling for the Lord—Hallelujah! *The Providence Journal-Bulletin,* February 8, pp. D1–D2.

Bear, D., and Fedio, P. (1977). Quantitative Analysis of Interictal Behavior in Temporal Lobe Epilepsy. *Archives of Neurology, 34,* 454–467.

Beck, C. (1986). Education for Spirituality. *Interchange*, 17, 148–156.

Beck, I. (1976). *Das Problem des Bösen und seiner Bewältigung: Eine Auseinandersetzung mit der Tiefenpsychologie von C. G. Jung vom Standpunkt der Theologie und Religionspädagogik*. Munich: Ernst Reinhardt.

Becker, E. (1973). *The Denial of Death*. New York: Free Press.

Bedell, K. B. (1996). *Yearbook of American & Canadian Churches 1996*. Nashville: Abingdon Press.

Begbie, H. (1909). *Twice-Born Men: A Clinic in Regeneration*. New York: Fleming H. Revell.

Behanan, K. T. (1937). *Yoga: A Scientific Evaluation*. New York: Macmillan.

Beit-Hallahmi, B. (1978). *Psychoanalysis and Religion: A Bibliography*. Norwood, Pa.: Norwood Editions.

Beit-Hallahmi, B. (1996). *Psychoanalytic Studies of Religion: A Critical Assessment and Annotated Bibliography*. Westport, Conn.: Greenwood.

Bell, G. H., Emslie-Smith, D., and Paterson, C. R. (Eds.). (1980). *Textbook of Physiology* (10th ed.). Edinburgh: Churchill Livingstone.

Bell, R. M. (1985). *Holy Anorexia*. Chicago: University of Chicago Press.

Bell, R. R. (1974). Religious Involvement and Marital Sex in Australia and the United States. *Journal of Comparative Family Studies*, 5, 109–116.

Bellah, R. N. (1970a). *Beyond Belief: Essays on Religion in a Post-Traditional World*. New York: Harper & Row.

Bellah, R. N. (1970b). Christianity and Symbolic Realism. *Journal for the Scientific Study of Religion*, 9, 89–96.

Bellah, R. N. (1970c). Confessions of a Former Establishment Fundamentalist. *Bulletin of the Council on the Study of Religion*, 1(3), 3–6.

Bellah, R. [N.] (1977). *Young Man Luther* as Portraiture: A Comment. In Capps, Capps, and Bradford, *Encounter with Erikson*, pp. 29–31.

Belzen, J. A. (1994). Between Feast and Famine: A Sketch of the Development of the Psychology of Religion in The Netherlands. *International Journal for the Psychology of Religion*, 4, 181–197.

Belzen, J. A. van, and Lans, J. M. van der. (Eds.). (1986). *Current Issues in the Psychology of Religion: Proceedings of the Third Symposium on the Psychology of Religion in Europe*. Amsterdam: Rodopi.

Bennet, E. A. (1961). *C. G. Jung*. London: Barrie and Rockliff.

Benson, H. (1975). *The Relaxation Response*. New York: William Morrow.

Benson, H. (1984). *Beyond the Relaxation Response*. New York: Times Books.

Benson, H. (1987). *Your Maximum Mind*. New York: Times Books.

Benson, H. (1996). *Timeless Healing: The Power and Biology of Belief*. New York: Scribner.

Benson, P. L. (1992). Religion and Substance Abuse. In J. F. Schumaker, *Religion and Mental Health*, pp. 211–220.

Benson, P. L., Dehority, J., Garman, L., Hanson, E., Hochschwender, M., Lebold, C., Rohr, R., and Sullivan, J. (1980). Intrapersonal Correlates of Nonspontaneous Helping Behavior. *Journal of Social Psychology*, 110, 87–95.

Benson, P.[L.], and Spilka, B. (1973). God Image as a Function of Self-Esteem and Locus of Control. *Journal for the Scientific Study of Religion*, 12, 297–310.

Benson, P. L., and Williams, D. L. (1982). *Religion on Capitol Hill: Myths and Realities*. San Francisco: Harper & Row.

Benz, E. (1969). *Die Vision: Erfahrungsformen und Bilderwelt*. Stuttgart: Ernest Klett.

Bergin, A. E. (1983). Religiosity and Mental Health: A Critical Reevaluation and Meta-analysis. *Professional Psychology: Research and Practice*, 14, 170–184.

Bergin, A. E., Masters, K. S., and Richards, P. S. (1987). Religiousness and Mental Health Reconsidered: A Study of an Intrinsically Religious Sample. *Journal of Counseling Psychology*, 34, 197–204.

Bergman, R. L. (1971). Navajo Peyote Use: Its Apparent Safety. *American Journal of Psychiatry*, 128, 695–699.

Berguer, G. (1908). *La notion de valeur: Sa nature psychique, son importance en théologie*. Geneva: Romet.

Berguer, G. (1914). Revue et bibliographie générales de psychologie religieuse. *Archives de Psychologie*, 14, 1–91.

Berguer, G. (1920). *Some Aspects of the Life of Jesus from the Psychological and Psycho-Analytic Point of View*. Translated by E. S. Brooks and V. W. Brooks. New York: Harcourt, Brace, 1923. (Original French edition 1920)

Berguer, G. (1946). *Traité de psychologie de la religion*. Lausanne: Payot.

Berman, L. (1927). *The Religion Called Behaviorism*. New York: Boni & Liveright.

Bernard, T. (1944). *Hatha Yoga*. New York: Columbia University Press.

Bernays, A. F. (1940). My Brother, Sigmund Freud. *American Mercury*, 51, 335–342. (Reprinted in Ruitenbeek, 1973)

Bernt, F. M. (1989). Being Religious and Being Altruistic: A Study of College Service Volunteers. *Personality and Individual Differences*, 10, 663–669.

Beth, K. (1926). Die Aufgaben der Religionspsychologie. *Religionspsychologie; Veröffentlichungen des Wiener Religionspsychologischen Forschung-Institutes*, 1, 4–14.

Beth, K. (1933). Religionspsychologie als Existenzialpsychologie. *Zeitschrift für Religionspsychologie*, 6, 1–12.

Bettelheim, B. (1962). *Symbolic Wounds: Puberty Rites and the Envious Male* (rev. ed.). New York, Collier.

Bettelheim, B. (1976). *The Uses of Enchantment: The Meaning and Importance of Fairy Tales*. New York: Alfred A. Knopf.

Bettelheim, B. (1983). *Freud and Man's Soul*. New York: Alfred A. Knopf.

Beyer, P. (1994). *Religion and Globalization.* London: Sage.

Bharati, A. (1965). *The Tantric Tradition.* London: Rider.

Bhushan, L. I. (1970). Religiosity Scale. *Indian Journal of Psychology,* 45, 335–342.

Bhushan, L. I. (1971). *Religiosity Scale (Hindi Version).* Agra: National Psychological Corporation. (English translation provided by the author)

Bibby, R. W. (1995). *Beyond Headlines, Hype, and Hope: Shedding Some Light on Spirituality.* Paper presented at the annual meeting of the Society for the Scientific Study of Religion, St. Louis, October.

Bindl, M. F. (1965). *Das religiöse Erleben im Spiegel der Bildgestaltung: Eine entwicklungs-psychologische Untersuchung.* Freiburg: Herder.

Binswanger, L. (1956). *Sigmund Freud: Reminiscences of a Friendship.* Translated by N. Guterman. New York: Grune & Stratton, 1957. (Original German edition 1956)

Biot, R. (1955). *The Enigma of the Stigmata.* Translated by P. J. Hepburne-Scott. New York: Hawthorn, 1962. (Original French edition 1955)

Biran, M. de (1814–1824). *Journal* (3 vols.). Edited by H. Gouhier. Neuchatel: Éditions de la Baconnière, 1954–1957. (Written 1814–1824)

Bitter, W. (Ed.). (1962). *Krisis und Zukunft der Frau: Psychotherapie—Religion—Gesellschaft.* Stuttgart: Ernst Klett.

Bjork, D. W. (1983). *The Compromised Scientist: William James in the Development of American Psychology.* New York: Columbia University Press.

Bjork, D. W. (1988). *William James: The Center of His Vision.* New York: Columbia University Press.

Blacker, C. P. (1946). Galton's Outlook on Religion. *Eugenics Review,* 38, 69–78.

Blackmore, S. (1993). *Dying to Live: Near-Death Experiences.* Buffalo, N.Y.: Prometheus.

Blanchard, W. H. (1969). Psychodynamic Aspects of the Peak Experience. *Psychoanalytic Review,* 56, 87–112.

Blanton, S. (1971). *Diary of My Analysis with Sigmund Freud.* New York: Hawthorn.

Bloom, A. (1954). Yoga and Christian Spiritual Techniques: Somatopsychic Techniques in Orthodox Christianity. In P. A. Sorokin, *Forms and Techniques of Altruistic and Spiritual Growth,* pp. 93–107.

Bloomfield, H. H., Cain, M. P., Jaffe, D. T., and Kory, R. B. (1975). *TM: Discovering Inner Energy and Overcoming Stress.* New York: Delacorte Press.

Bock, D. C. (1973). Obedience: A Response to Authority and Christian Commitment (Fuller Theological Seminary, Graduate School of Psychology, 1972). *Dissertation Abstracts International,* 33, 3278B-3279B. (University Microfilms No. 72-31,651)

Bock, D. C., and Warren, N. C. (1972). Religious Belief as a Factor in Obedience to Destructive Commands. *Review of Religious Research,* 13, 185–191.

Böschemeyer, U. (1977). *Die Sinnfrage in Psychotherapie und Theologie: Die Existenzanalyse und Logotherapie Viktor E. Frankls aus theologischer Sicht.* Berlin: Walter De Gruyter.

Boisen, A. T. (1936). *The Exploration of the Inner World: A Study of Mental Disorder and Religious Experience.* New York: Harper & Brothers.

Boisen, A. T. (1953). The Present Status of William James' Psychology of Religion. *Journal of Pastoral Care,* 7, 155–157.

Boisen, A. T. (1960). *Out of the Depths: An Autobiographical Study of Mental Disorder and Religious Experience.* New York: Harper & Brothers.

Bolley, A. (1930). *Gebetsstimmung und Gebet: Empirische Untersuchungen zur Psychologie des Gebetes, unter besonderer Berücksichtigung des Betens von Jugendlichen.* Düsseldorf: Pädagogischer Verlag.

Bolley, A. (1949). Das Gotteserleben in der Betrachtung. *Geist und Leben,* 22, 343–356.

Bolley, A. (1964). Die Bedeutung von Einsfühlungs- und Einfühlungserlebnissen in der Meditation. *Archiv für Religionspsychologie,* 8, 145–155.

Bolley, A. (1965). Recent Research into the Psychology of God-Consciousness in Meditation. In A. Godin, *Child and Adult Before God,* pp. 45–54.

Bolley, A. (1976). Das meditative Gotteserlebnis als personal bedingtes seelisches Gefüge. *Archiv für Religionspsychologie,* 12, 85–104.

Bolt, M. (1975). Purpose in Life and Religious Orientation. *Journal of Psychology and Theology,* 3, 116–118.

Bolt, M. (1977). Religious Orientation and Death Fears. *Review of Religious Research,* 19, 73–76.

Boos-Nünning, U. (1972). *Dimensionen der Religiösitat: Zur Operationalisierung und Messung religiöser Einstellungen.* Munich: Chr. Kaiser; Mainz: Matthias-Grünewald.

Booth, H. J. (1981). *Edwin Diller Starbuck: Pioneer in the Psychology of Religion.* Washington, D.C.: University Press of America.

Boring, E. G. (1950). *A History of Experimental Psychology* (2nd ed.). New York: Appleton-Century-Crofts.

Borysenko, J. Z. (1985). Healing Motives: An Interview with David C. McClelland. *Advances,* [Journal of the] *Institute for the Advancement of Health,* 2(2), 29–41.

Boss, M. (1959). *A Psychiatrist Discovers India.* Translated by H. A. Frey. London: Oswald Wolff, 1965. (Original German edition 1959)

Boston, R. (1988). Holy Terrors. *Church & State,* 41, 154–156.

Boucouvalas, M. (1980). Transpersonal Psychology: A Working Outline of the Field. *Journal of Transpersonal Psychology,* 12, 37–46.

Bourguignon, E. (1968). Trance Dance. *Dance Perspectives,* No. 35. (Reprinted in part and without pictures in J. White, 1972)

Bouwsma, W. J. (1988). *John Calvin: A Sixteenth-Century Portrait.* New York: Oxford University Press.

Boven, W. (1919). Religiosité et épilepsie. *Schweizer Archiv für Neurologie und Psychiatrie*, 4, 153–169.

Bovet, P. (1925). *Le sentiment religieux et la psychologie de l'enfant* (2nd ed.). Neuchâtel: Delachaux et Niestlé, 1951. (First edition 1925 [translated as *The Child's Religion*, 1928])

Bower, G. H., and Hilgard, E. R. (1981). *Theories of Learning* (5th ed.). Englewood Cliffs, N.J.: Prentice-Hall.

Bowker, J. (1973). *The Sense of God: Sociological, Anthropological and Psychological Approaches to the Origin of the Sense of God.* London: Oxford University Press.

Bowlby, J. (1969–1980). *Attachment and Loss* (3 vols.). New York: Basic Books.

Bowman, E. S. (1989). Understanding and Responding to Religious Material in the Therapy of Multiple Personality Disorder. *Dissociation*, 2, 231–238.

Boyer, P. (1994). *The Naturalness of Religious Ideas: A Cognitive Theory of Religion.* Berkeley: University of California Press.

Bozzo, E. G. (1977). James and the Valence of Human Action. *Journal of Religion and Health*, 16, 26–43.

Bradburn, N. M. (1969). *The Structure of Psychological Well-Being.* Chicago: Aldine.

Bradford, D. T. (1984). *The Experience of God: Portraits in the Phenomenological Psychopathology of Schizophrenia.* New York: Peter Lang.

Braginsky, B. M., and Braginsky, D. D. (1974). *Mainstream Psychology: A Critique.* New York: Holt, Rinehart and Winston.

Brand, C. (1981). Personality and Political Attitudes. In R. Lynn (Ed.), *Dimensions of Personality: Papers in Honour of H. J. Eysenck.* Oxford: Pergamon Press, pp. 7–38.

Brannon, R. C. (1970). Gimme That Old-Time Racism. *Psychology Today*, 3(11), 42–44.

Breed, G., and Fagan, J. (1972). Religious Dogmatism and Peak Experiences: A Test of Maslow's Hypothesis. *Psychological Reports*, 31, 866.

Bregman, L. (1976). Maslow as Theorist of Religion: Reflections on His Popularity and Plausibility. *Soundings*, 59, 139–163.

Breland, K., and Breland, M. (1961). The Misbehavior of Organisms. *American Psychologist*, 16, 681–684.

Brenner, C. (1973). *An Elementary Textbook of Psychoanalysis* (rev. ed.). New York: International Universities Press.

Breuer, J., and Freud, S. (1895). *Studies on Hysteria.* In S. Freud, *Standard Edition*, Vol. 2, 1955. (Original German edition 1895)

Brody, S. (1980). Transitional Objects: Idealization of a Phenomenon. *Psychoanalytic Quarterly*, 49, 561–605.

Brody, S. (1982). Psychoanalytic Theories of Infant Development and Its Disturbances: A Critical Evaluation. *Psychoanalytic Quarterly*, 51, 526–597.

Broen, W. E., Jr. (1957). A Factor-Analytic Study of Religious Attitudes. *Journal of Abnormal and Social Psychology*, 54, 176–179.

Brogden, H. E. (1952). The Primary Personal Values Measured by the Allport-Vernon Test, "A Study of Values." *Psychological Monographs*, 66 (Whole No. 348), 1–31.

Brome, V. (1978). *Jung.* New York: Atheneum.

Brook, R. (1991). *Jung and Phenomenology.* London: Routledge.

Brosse, T. (1946). A Psycho-Physiological Study [of Yoga]. *Main Currents in Modern Thought*, 4, 77–84.

Brosse, T. (1954). Contribution to the Experimental Study of Altruism: Instrumental Explorations of Yoga Techniques. In P. A. Sorokin, *Forms and Techniques of Altruistic and Spiritual Growth*, pp. 189–282.

Brosse, T. (1963). *Etudes instrumentales des techniques du yoga: expérimentation psychosomatique.* Paris: Ecole française d'Extrême-Orient (Dépositaire: Adrien-Maisonneuve).

Broughton, W. (1975). Theistic Conceptions in American Protestantism. *Journal for the Scientific Study of Religion*, 14, 331–344.

Brown, B. B. (1974). *New Mind, New Body.* New York: Harper & Row.

Brown, C. A. (1981). *Jung's Hermeneutic of Doctrine: Its Theological Significance.* Chico, Calif.: Scholars Press.

Brown, F. C. (1972). *Hallucinogenic Drugs.* Springfield, Ill.: C. C. Thomas.

Brown, J. A. C. (1964). *Freud and the Post-Freudians* (expanded edition). Baltimore: Penguin.

Brown, K. M. (1994). Fundamentalism and the Control of Women. In J. S. Hawley, *Fundamentalism and Gender*, pp. 175–201.

Brown, L. B. (1962). A Study of Religious Belief. *British Journal of Psychology*, 53, 259–272. (Reprinted in Brown, 1973)

Brown, L. B. (1966). The Structure of Religious Belief. *Journal for the Scientific Study of Religion*, 5, 259–272.

Brown, L. B. (Ed.). (1973). *Psychology and Religion: Selected Readings.* Baltimore: Penguin.

Brown, L. B. (1994a). *The Human Side of Prayer: The Psychology of Praying.* Birmingham, Ala.: Religious Education Press.

Brown, L. B. (Ed.). (1994b). *Religion, Personality, and Mental Health.* New York: Springer-Verlag.

Brown, N. O. (1959). *Life Against Death: The Psychoanalytic Meaning of History.* Middletown, Conn.: Wesleyan University Press.

Browning, D. S. (1973). *Generative Man: Psychoanalytic Perspectives.* Philadelphia: Westminster Press.

Browning, D. S. (1987). *Religious Thought and the Modern Psychologies: A Critical Conversation in the Theology of Culture.* Philadelphia: Fortress.

Bruder, E. E. (1947). Some Considerations of the Loss of Faith. *Journal of Clinical and Pastoral Work*, 1, 1–10.

Bruns, G. L. (1984). Loose Talk about Religion from William James. *Critical Inquiry,* 11, 299–316.

Brush, S. G. (1974). The Prayer Test. *American Scientist,* 62, 561–563.

Brusselmans, C. (Ed.). (1980). *Toward Moral and Religious Maturity.* Morristown, N.J.: Silver Burdett.

Bryant, C. (1983). *Jung and the Christian Way.* Minneapolis: Seabury Press.

Bucke, R. M. (1901). *Cosmic Consciousness: A Study in the Evolution of the Human Mind.* New York: E. P. Dutton, 1923. (First published 1901)

Bufford, R. K. (1981). *The Human Reflex: Behavioral Psychology in Biblical Perspective.* San Francisco: Harper & Row.

Bukin, V. R. (1969). *Psikhologiya veruyushchikh i ateisticheskoe vospitanie.* Moscow: Mysl'.

Burckhardt, T. (1960). *Alchemy: Science of the Cosmos, Science of the Soul.* Translated by W. Stoddart. Baltimore: Penguin, 1971. (Original German edition 1960)

Buri, J. R., and Mueller, R. A. (1987). *Conceptions of Parents, Conceptions of Self, and Conceptions of God.* Paper presented at the convention of the American Psychological Association, New York, August.

Burns, J. F. (1996). From Cold War, Afghans Inherit Brutal New Age. *The New York Times,* February 14, A1, A8.

Buros, O. K. (1978). *The Eighth Mental Measurements Yearbook.* Lincoln: University of Nebraska, Buros Institute of Mental Measurements.

Burtchaell, J. T. (1970). A Response to "Christianity and Symbolic Realism." *Journal for the Scientific Study of Religion,* 9, 97–99.

Burton, R. (1621). *The Anatomy of Melancholy.* Edited by F. Dell and P. Jordan-Smith. New York: Tudor, 1927. (First edition 1621)

Burtt, H. E., and Falkenburg, D. R., Jr. (1941). The Influence of Majority and Expert Opinion on Religious Attitudes. *Journal of Social Psychology,* 14, 269–278.

Busch, K. A. (1911). *William James als Religionsphilosoph.* Göttingen: Vandenhoeck & Ruprecht.

Busch, N. E. (1983). The Near-Death Experience in Children: Shades of the Prison-House Reopening. *Anabiosis—The Journal of Near-Death Studies,* 3, 177–193.

Buys, C. J., Word, E. D., Jank, D. R., Ligon, R. W., Mauritz, M. N., Pena, R. H., and Vogt, M. B. (1977). Ministers' Attitudes Toward Overpopulation. *Personality and Social Psychology Bulletin,* 3, 567–570.

Buytendijk, F. J. J. (1951). Zur allgemeinen Psychologie des Tanzes. In G. Ekman et al. (Eds.), *Essays in Psychology Dedicated to David Katz.* Uppsala: Almqvist & Wiksells, pp. 48–64.

Bynum, C. W. (1987). *Holy Feast and Holy Fast: The Religious Significance of Food to Medieval Women.* Berkeley: University of California Press.

Byrd, R. C. (1988). Positive Therapeutic Effects of Intercessory Prayer in a Coronary Care Unit Population. *Southern Medical Journal,* 81, 826–829.

Byrnes, J. F. (1984). *The Psychology of Religion.* New York: Free Press.

Caird, D. (1988). The Structure of Hood's Mysticism Scale: A Factor-Analytic Study. *Journal for the Scientific Study of Religion,* 27, 122–127.

Campbell, C. A. (1957). *On Selfhood and Godhood.* London: Allen & Unwin.

Campbell, D. P. (1971). *Handbook for the Strong Vocational Interest Blank.* Stanford, Calif.: Stanford University Press.

Campbell, D. T. (1975). On the Conflicts Between Biological and Social Evolution and Between Psychology and Moral Tradition. *Zygon,* 1976, 11, 167–208. (First published in *American Psychologist,* 1975, 30, 1103–1126)

Campbell, J. (Ed.). (1954–1968). *Papers from the Eranos Yearbooks* (6 vols.). Princeton, N.J.: Princeton University Press.

Campbell, J. (1959). *The Masks of God: Primitive Mythology.* New York: Viking.

Campbell, J. (1968). *The Hero With a Thousand Faces* (2nd ed.). Princeton, N.J.: Princeton University Press. (First edition 1949)

Cantril, H., Rand, H. A., and Allport, G. W. (1933). The Determination of Personal Interests by Psychological and Graphological Methods. *Character and Personality,* 2, 134–143.

Canziani, W. (1959). Religionspsychologie als empirische Wissenschaft. *Der Psychologe,* 409–420, 472–480.

Caplovitz, D., and Sherrow, F. (1977). *The Religious Drop-Outs: Apostasy Among College Graduates.* Beverly Hills: Sage.

Capps, D. (1983). *Life Cycle Theory and Pastoral Care.* Philadelphia: Fortress Press.

Capps, D., and Jacobs, J. L. (Eds.). (1995). *The Struggle for Life: A Companion to William James's The Varieties of Religious Experience.* [West Layfayette, Ind.]: Society for the Scientific Study of Religion.

Capps, D., Capps, W. H., and Bradford, M. G. (Eds.). (1977). *Encounter with Erikson: Historical Interpretation and Religious Biography.* Missoula, Mont.: Scholars Press.

Capps, D., and Carroll, M. P. (1988). Praying the Rosary. *Journal for the Scientific Study of Religion,* 27, 429–441.

Capps, D., Rambo, L., and Ransohoff, P. (1976). *Psychology of Religion: A Guide to Information Sources.* Detroit: Gale Research Co.

Capps, D., Ransohoff, P., and Rambo, L. (1976). Publication Trends in the Psychology of Religion to 1974. *Journal for the Scientific Study of Religion,* 15, 15–28.

Capra, F. (1975). *The Tao of Physics.* Berkeley: Shambhala.

Capra, F. (1982). *The Turning Point: Science, Society, and the Rising Culture.* New York: Simon and Schuster.

Caprio, B., and Hedberg, T. M. (1986). *Coming Home: A Handbook for Exploring the Sanctuary Within.* Mahwah, N.J.: Paulist Press.

Captain, P. A. (1975). The Effect of Positive Reinforcement on Comprehension, Attitudes, and Rate of Bible Reading in Adolescents. *Journal of Psychology and Theology,* 3, 49–55.

Cardwell, J. D. (1969). The Relationship Between Religious Commitment and Premarital Sexual Permissiveness: A Five Dimensional Analysis. *Sociological Analysis,* 30, 72–81.

Carey, J. W. (1988). Editor's Introduction: Taking Culture Seriously. In J. W. Carey (Ed.), *Media, Myths, and Narratives: Television and the Press.* Newbury Park, Calif.: Sage, pp. 8–18.

Carleton, J. L., and Stentz, K. T. (1976). Socio-Cultural Modalities in Population Control. *Mental Health and Society,* 3, 197–204.

Carrette, J. R. (1993–94). The Psychology of Religion: Re-Examining the Psychological "Subject." *Journal of the Psychology of Religion,* 2/3, 171–199.

Carroll, M. P. (1987). Praying the Rosary; The Anal-Erotic Origins of a Popular Catholic Devotion. *Journal for the Scientific Study of Religion,* 26, 486–498.

Carstairs, G. M. (1957). *The Twice-Born: A Study of a Community of High-Caste Hindus.* London: Hogarth Press.

Carus, P. (1900). *The History of the Devil and the Idea of Evil, from the Earliest Times to the Present Day.* Chicago: Open Court.

Casey, E. S. (1976). *Imagining: A Phenomenological Study.* Bloomington: Indiana University Press.

Casey, R. P. (1938). The Psychoanalytic Study of Religion. *Journal of Abnormal and Social Psychology,* 33, 437–452.

Casey, R. P. (1942). Oedipus Motivation in Religious Thought and Fantasy. *Psychiatry,* 5, 219–228.

Casler, L. (1968). Instrumental Learning. In D. L. Sills (Ed.), *International Encyclopedia of the Social Sciences,* Vol. 9. New York: Macmillan and the Free Press, pp. 130–135.

Cattell, R. B. (1938). *Psychology and the Religious Quest: An Account of the Psychology of Religion and a Defence of Individualism.* London: Thomas Nelson.

Cautley, P. W., and Borgatta, E. F. (1973). Population Growth: A Challenge to Psychologists. *Representative Research in Social Psychology,* 4, 5–21.

Cavander, K. (1974). Voyage of the Psychenauts: A Report on a Journey Inside the Mind. *Harper's Magazine,* 248(1484), 68–72, 74.

Chalmers, R. A., Clements, G., Schenkluhn, H., and Weinless, M. (Eds.). (1989). *Scientific Research on Maharishi's Transcendental Meditation Program and TM-Sidhi Program: Collected Papers,* Vols. 2–4. Vlodrop, The Netherlands: MVU Press.

Chapman, J. H. (1988). *Jung's Three Theories of Religious Experience.* Lewiston, N.Y.: Edwin Mellen.

Charet, F. X. (1993). *Spiritualism and the Foundations of C. G. Jung's Psychology.* Albany: State University of New York Press.

Chau, L. L., Johnson, R. C., Bowers, J. K., Darvill, T. J., et al. (1990). Intrinsic and Extrinsic Religiosity as Related to Conscience, Adjustment, and Altruism. *Personality and Individual Differences,* 11, 397–400.

Chave, E. J. (1939). *Measure Religion: Fifty-two Experimental Forms.* Chicago: University of Chicago Book Store.

Chevreau, G. (1994). *Catch the Fire: The Toronto Blessing: An Experience of Renewal and Revival.* Toronto: HarperCollins.

Cheyne, John. (1843). *Essays on Partial Derangement of the Mind in Supposed Connexion with Religion.* Dublin: William Curry, Jun. and Co.

Christ, C. P. (1995). *Diving Deep and Surfacing: Women Writers on Spiritual Quest* (3rd ed.). Boston: Beacon Press.

Clark, E. T. (1929). *The Psychology of Religious Awakening.* New York: Macmillan.

Clark, J. J. (1992). *In Search of Jung: Historical and Philosophical Enquiries.* London: Routledge.

Clark, J. J. (1994). *Jung and Eastern Thought: A Dialogue with the Orient.* London: Routledge.

Clark, K. E. (1957). *America's Psychologists: A Survey of a Growing Profession.* Washington, D.C.: American Psychological Association.

Clark, W. H. (1951). *The Oxford Group: Its History and Significance.* New York: Bookman Associates.

Clark, W. H. (1958). *The Psychology of Religion: An Introduction to Religious Experience and Behavior.* New York: Macmillan.

Clark, W. H. (1969). *Chemical Ecstasy: Psychedelic Drugs and Religion.* New York: Sheed & Ward.

Clayton, R. R. (1971a). 5–D or 1? *Journal for Scientific Study of Religion,* 10, 37–40.

Clayton, R. R. (1971b). Religiosity and Premarital Sexual Permissiveness. *Sociological Analysis,* 32, 81–96.

Clayton, R. R., and Gladden, J. W. (1974). The Five Dimensions of Religiosity: Toward Demythologizing a Sacred Artifact. *Journal for the Scientific Study of Religion,* 13, 135–143.

Clift, W. B. (1982). *Jung and Christianity: The Challenge of Reconciliation.* New York: Crossroad.

Cline, V. B., and Richards, J. M., Jr. (1965). A Factor-Analytic Study of Religious Belief and Behavior. *Journal of Personality and Social Psychology,* 1, 569–578.

Coan, R. W. (1972). [Review of the Personal Orientation Inventory]. In O. K. Buros (Ed.), *Seventh Mental Measurements Yearbook,* Vol. 1. Highland Park, N. J.: Gryphon Press, pp. 292–294.

Coan, R. W. (1974). *The Optimal Personality: An Empirical and Theoretical Analysis.* New York: Columbia University Press.

Cobb, J. B., Jr. (1990). Response to Relativism: Common Ground, Deconstruction and Reconstruction. *Soundings,* 73, 595–616.

Coe, G. A. (1900). *The Spiritual Life: Studies in the Science of Religion.* New York: Eaton & Mains.

Coe, G. A. (1916). *The Psychology of Religion*. Chicago: University of Chicago Press.

Coe, G. A. (1937). My Own Little Theatre. In V. Ferm, *Religion in Transition*, pp. 90–125.

Coe, G. A. (1943). *What is Religion Doing to our Consciences?* New York: Charles Scribner's Sons.

Cohen, E. D. (1975). *C. G. Jung and the Scientific Attitude*. New York: Philosophical Library.

Cohen, M. (1946). The Dark Side of Religion. In M. Cohen, *The Faith of a Liberal: Selected Essays*. New York: Henry Holt, pp. 337–361.

Cohen, S. (1966). *The Beyond Within: The L.S.D. Story*. New York: Atheneum.

Colaizzi, P. F. (1978). Learning and Existence. In R. S. Valle and M. King (Eds.), *Existential-Phenomenological Alternatives for Psychology*. New York: Oxford University Press, pp. 119–135.

Coles, R. (1970). *Erik H. Erikson: The Growth of His Work*. Boston: Little, Brown.

Conn, J. C. M. (1939). *The Menace of the New Psychology*. London: The Inter-Varsity Press.

Conn, W. (1986). *Christian Conversion: A Developmental Interpretation of Autonomy and Surrender*. Mahwah, N.J.: Paulist Press.

Conze, E. (1956). *Buddhist Meditation*. London: George Allen & Unwin.

Coppens, J. (1948). *La Connaissance du Bien et du Mal et le Péché du Paradis: Contribution à l'interprétation de Gen., II-III*. Louvain: É. Nauwelaerts, [1948].

Corby, J. C., Roth, W. T., Zarcone, V. P., and Kopell, B. S. (1978). Psychophysiological Correlates of the Practice of Tantric Yoga Meditation. *Archives of General Psychiatry*, 35, 571–577.

Corey, L. G. (1990). For the Sake of God: A Reply to Jung. *San Francisco Jung Institute Library Journal*, 9, 27–37.

Corey, M. A. (1995). *Job, Jonah, and the Unconscious: A Psychological Interpretation of Evil and Spiritual Growth in the Old Testament*. Lanham, Md.: University Press of America.

Cortés, J. B., and Gatti, F. M. (1970). Physique and Propensity. *Psychology Today*, 4(5), 42–44, 82–84.

Cortés, J. B., and Gatti, F. M. (1972). *Delinquency and Crime: A Biopsychosocial Approach*. New York: Seminar Press.

Corveleyn, J., and Hutsebaut, D. (Eds.). (1994). *Belief and Unbelief: Psychological Perspectives*. Amsterdam: Rodopi.

Corveleyn, J., and Lietaer, H. (1994). A Critical Review of Current Psychological Research on the Interaction Between Religion and Mental Health. In J. Corveleyn and D. Hutsebaut, *Belief and Unbelief*, pp. 203–218.

Coursey, R. D. (1974). Consulting and the Catholic Crisis. *Journal of Consulting and Clinical Psychology*, 42, 519–528.

Coward, H. (1985). *Jung and Eastern Thought*. Albany: State University of New York Press.

Cox, D. (1959). *Jung and St. Paul: A Study of the Doctrine of Justification by Faith and Its Relation to the Concept of Individuation*. New York: Association Press.

Craddick, R. A., Thumin, F. J., and Barclay, A. G. (1971). A Semantic Differential Study of the Yin-Yang Symbol. *Journal of Personality Assessment*, 35, 338–343.

Crandall, J. E., and Rasmussen, R. D. (1975). Purpose in Life as Related to Specific Values. *Journal of Clinical Psychology*, 31, 483–485.

Crapps, R. W. (1986). *An Introduction to Psychology of Religion*. Macon, Ga.: Mercer University Press.

Creelan, P. G. (1974). Watsonian Behaviorism and the Calvinist Conscience. *Journal of the History of the Behavioral Sciences*, 10, 95–118.

Cremer, K. J. (1934). *De Duitsche Godsdienstpsychologie*. Delft: Naamlooze Vennootschap W. D. Meinema.

Croce, P. J. (1995). *Science and Religion in the Era of William James. Vol. I. Eclipse of Certainty, 1820–1880*. Chapel Hill: University of North Carolina Press.

Cronbach, A. (1926). Religion and Psychoanalysis. *Psychological Bulletin*, 23, 701–713.

Cronbach, A. (1931–1932). The Psychoanalytic Study of Judaism. *Hebrew Union College Annual*, 8–9, 605–740.

Cronbach, A. (1946). New Studies in the Psychology of Judaism. *Hebrew Union College Annual*, 19, 205–273.

Cronbach, L. J. (1957). The Two Disciplines of Scientific Psychology. *American Psychologist*, 12, 671–684.

Crook, J. H. (1980). *The Evolution of Human Consciousness*. London: Oxford University Press.

Crooks, E. B. (1913). Professor James and the Psychology of Religion. *Monist*, 23, 122–130.

Crumbaugh, J. C., and Maholick, L. T. (1964). An Experimental Study in Existentialism: The Psychometric Approach to Frankl's Concept of "Noögenic Neurosis." *Journal of Clinical Psychology*, 20, 200–207.

Cunningham, M. R. (1979). Weather, Mood, and Helping Behavior: Quasi Experiments With the Sunshine Samaritan. *Journal of Personality and Social Psychology*, 37, 1947–1956.

Curatorium of the C. G. Jung Institute, Zurich (Eds.). (1961). *Evil*. Evanston, Ill.: Northwestern University Press, 1967. (Original German edition 1961)

Cutten, G. B. (1908). *The Psychological Phenomena of Christianity*. New York: Charles Scribner's Sons.

Dalal, A. S., and Barber, T. X. (1969). Yoga, "Yogic Feats," and Hypnosis in the Light of Empirical Research. *American Journal of Clinical Hypnosis*, 11, 155–166. (Reprinted with slight revision in Barber, 1970)

Dalbiez, R. (1936). *Psychoanalytic Method and the Doctrine of Freud. Vol. 2. Discussion*. Translated by T. F. Lindsay. London: Longmans, Green, 1941. (Original French edition 1936)

Daly, C. D. (1927). *Hindu-Mythologie und Kastrationskomplex*. Leipzig: Internationaler Psychoanalytischer Verlag.

Daniélou, A. (1961). The Influence of Sound Phenomena on Human Consciousness. Translated by P. Huebner and R. Metzner. *The Psychedelic Review,* 1966, No. 7, 20–26. (Original French version 1961)

Daniels, A. H. (1893). The New Life: A Study of Regeneration. *American Journal of Psychology,* 6, 61–103.

Danziger, K. (1990). *Constructing the Subject: Historical Origins of Psychological Research.* Cambridge: Cambridge University Press.

d'Aquili, E. G., Laughlin, C. D., Jr., and McManus, J. (1979). *The Spectrum of Ritual: A Biogenetic Structural Analysis.* New York: Columbia University Press.

Darley, J. M., and Batson, C. D. (1973). "From Jerusalem to Jericho": A Study of Situational and Dispositional Variables in Helping Behavior. *Journal of Personality and Social Psychology,* 27, 100–108.

Das, N. N., and Gastaut, H. (1957). Variations de l'activité électrique du cerveau, du coeur et des muscles squelettiques au cours de la méditation et de l'extase yogique. *Electroencephalography and Clinical Neurophysiology,* Supplement, 6, 211–219. (With English abstract; longer English abstract in *R. M. Bucke Memorial Society Newsletter-Review,* 1972, 5, 50–54)

Davenport, F. M. (1905). *Primitive Traits in Religious Revivals.* New York: Macmillan.

Davidson, J. M. (1976). The Physiology of Meditation and Mystical States of Consciousness. *Perspectives in Biology and Medicine,* 19, 345–379.

Davis, B. D. (1980). The Importance of Human Individuality for Sociobiology. *Zygon,* 15, 275–293.

Dawson, G. E. (1900). Children's Interest in the Bible. *Pedagogical Seminary,* 7, 151–178.

Day, J. M. (1994). Moral Development, Belief and Unbelief: Young Adult Accounts of Religion in the Process of Moral Growth. In Corveleyn and Hutsebaut, *Belief and Unbelief,* pp. 155–173.

DeBold, R. C., and Leaf, R. C. (Eds.). (1967). *LSD, Man & Society.* Middletown, Conn.: Wesleyan University Press.

Deconchy, J. P. (1971). *L'orthodoxie religieuse: Essai de logique psychosociale.* Paris: Les Éditions ouvrières, 1971.

Deconchy, J. P. (1980). *Orthodoxie religieuse et sciences humaines,* with an English summary: (Religious) Orthodoxy, Rationality and Scientific Knowledge. The Hague: Mouton.

DeFronzo, J. (1972). Religion and Humanitarianism in Eysenck's T Dimension and Left-Right Political Orientation. *Journal of Personality and Social Psychology,* 21, 265–269.

Dehn, G. (1923). *Die religiöse Gedankenwelt der Proletarierjugend.* Berlin: Furche.

Deikman, A. (1966). Implications of Experimentally Produced Contemplative Meditation. *Journal of Nervous and Mental Diseases,* 142, 101–116.

DeJong, G. F., Faulkner, J. E., and Warland, R. H. (1976). Dimensions of Religiosity Reconsidered: Evidence from a Cross-Cultural Study. *Social Forces,* 54, 866–889.

Delacroix, H. (1908). *Études d'histoire et de psychologie du mysticisme. Les grand mystiques chrétiens.* Paris: Félix Alcan.

Denton, R. T., and Denton, M J. (1992). Therapists' Ratings of Fundamentalist and Nonfundamentalist Families in Therapy: An Empirical Comparison. *Family Process,* 31, 175–185.

Derks, F., and Lans, J. M. van der. (1986). Religious Attitudes: A Theoretical Approach. In J. A. van Belzen and J. M. van der Lans, *Current Issues in the Psychology of Religion,* pp. 200–204.

de Ropp, R. S. (1957). *Drugs and the Mind.* New York: St. Martin's Press.

DeSano, C. F., and Persinger, M. A. (1987). Geophysical Variables and Behavior: XXXIX. Alterations in Imaginings and Suggestibility During Brief Magnetic Field Exposures. *Perceptual and Motor Skills,* 64, 968–970.

Deutsch, A. (1975). Observations on a Sidewalk Ashram. *Archives of General Psychiatry,* 32, 166–175.

Dewey, J. (1929). *Characters and Events: Popular Essays in Social and Political Philosophy,* Vol. 1. Edited by J. Ratner. New York: Henry Holt.

Dewhurst, K., and Beard, A. W. (1970). Sudden Religious Conversions in Temporal Lobe Epilepsy. *British Journal of Psychiatry,* 117, 497–507.

Dicker, H. I. (1977). Extrinsic-Intrinsic Religious Orientation and Ethnocentrism in Charitable Volunteering (St. John's University, 1975). *Dissertation Abstracts International,* 37, 4214B. (University Microfilms No. 77–1568)

Diller, J. V. (1991). *Freud's Jewish Identity: A Case Study in the Impact of Ethnicity.* London: Associated University Presses.

Dimond, S. G. (1926). *The Psychology of the Methodist Revival: An Empirical and Descriptive Study.* New York: Oxford University Press.

Dittes, J. E. (1969). Psychology of Religion. In G. Lindzey and E. Aronson (Eds.), *The Handbook of Social Psychology,* Vol. 5 (2nd ed.). Reading, Mass.: Addison-Wesley, pp. 602–659.

Dittes, J. E. (1971). Typing the Typologies: Some Parallels in the Career of Church-Sect and Extrinsic-Intrinsic. *Journal for the Scientific Study of Religion,* 10, 375–383.

Dittes, J. E. (1973a). Beyond William James. In C. Y. Glock and P. E. Hammond, *Beyond the Classics?,* pp. 291–354.

Dittes, J. E. (1973b). *Bias and the Pious: The Relationship Between Prejudice and Religion.* Minneapolis: Augsburg Publishing House.

Doblin, R. (1991). Pahnke's "Good Friday Experiment": A Long-term Follow-up and Methodological Critique. *Journal of Transpersonal Psychology,* 23, 1–28.

Dodrill, C. B. (1976). Brain Functions of Christians

and Non-Christians. *Journal of Psychology and Theology,* 4, 280–285.

Dodrill, C. B., Bean, P., and Bostrom, S. (1973). The Assessment of Religiosity in Evangelical College Students and Its Relationship to Prior Family Religious Involvement. *Journal of Psychology and Theology,* 1, 52–57.

Dörr, A. (1987). *Religiosität und Depression: Eine empirisch-psychologische Untersuchung.* Weinheim: Deutscher Studien Verlag.

Dörr, A. (1992). Religiosität und Depression. In E. Schmitz, *Religionspsychologie,* pp. 159–180.

Donahue, M. J. (1985). Intrinsic and Extrinsic Religiousness: Review and Meta-Analysis. *Journal of Personality and Social Psychology,* 48, 400–419.

Doody, J. A., and Immerwahr, J. (1983). The Persistence of the Four Temperaments. *Soundings,* 66, 348–359.

Douglas, W. (1963). Religion. In N. Farberow, *Taboo Topics,* pp. 80–95.

Dourley, J. P. (1984). *The Illness That We Are: A Jungian Critique of Christianity.* Toronto: Inner City Books.

Dourley, J. P. (1992). *A Strategy for a Loss of Faith: Jung's Proposal.* Toronto: Inner City Books.

Drawbridge, C. L. (1932). *The Religion of Scientists, Being Recent Opinions Expressed by Two Hundred Fellows of the Royal Society on the Subject of Religion and Theology.* New York: Macmillan.

Dry, A. M. (1961). *The Psychology of Jung: A Critical Interpretation.* New York: John Wiley & Sons.

Dulaney, S., and Fiske, A. P. (1994). Cultural Rituals and Obsessive-Compulsive Disorder: Is There a Common Psychological Mechanism? *Ethos,* 22, 243–283.

Dumoulin, H. (1959). *A History of Zen Buddhism.* Translated by P. Peachey. New York: Pantheon, 1963. (Original German edition 1959)

Dunlap, K. (1946). *Religion: Its Functions in Human Life: A Study of Religion from the Point of View of Psychology.* New York: McGraw-Hill.

Dupain, J.-M. (1888). *Étude clinique sur le délire religieux (essai de séméiologie).* Paris: Delahaye et Lecrosnier.

Dwelshauvers, G. (1920). *La psychologie française contemporaine.* Paris: Félix Alcan.

Dykstra, C., and Parks, S. (Eds.). (1986). *Faith Development and Fowler.* Birmingham, Ala.: Religious Education Press.

Earle, J. B. B. (1981). Cerebral Laterality and Meditation: A Review of the Literature. *Journal of Transpersonal Psychology,* 13, 155–173.

Eccles, J. C., and Robinson, D. N. (1984). *The Wonder of Being Human: Our Brain and Our Mind.* New York: The Free Press.

Eck, D. L. (1985). *Darśan, Seeing the Divine Image in India* (2nd ed.). Chambersburg, Pa.: Anima Books.

Eck, D. L. (1993). *Encountering God: A Spiritual Journey from Bozeman to Banaras.* Boston: Beacon Press.

Eckberg, D. L., and Blocker, T. J. (1989). Varieties of Religious Involvement and Environmental Con-

cerns: Testing the Lynn White Thesis. *Journal for the Scientific Study of Religion,* 28, 509–517.

Eckberg, D. L., and Blocker, T. J. (1996). Christianity, Environmentalism, and the Theoretical Problem of Fundamentalism. *Journal for the Scientific Study of Religion,* 35, 343–355.

Eckhardt, W. (1969). Ideology and Personality in Social Attitudes. *Peace Research Reviews,* 3(2), 1–106.

Eddy, J. P. (1968). Report of Religious Activities at Harvard and Radcliffe. *College Student Survey,* 2(2), 31–34, 37.

Edelson, M. (1988). *Psychoanalysis: A Theory in Crisis.* Chicago: University of Chicago Press.

Eder, M. D. (1933). The Jewish Phylacteries and Other Jewish Ritual Observances. *International Journal of Psychoanalysis,* 14, 341–375.

Edie, J. M. (1987). *William James and Phenomenology.* Bloomington: Indiana University Press.

Edinger, E. F. (1972). *Ego and Archetype: Individuation and the Religious Function of the Psyche.* New York: G. P. Putnam's Sons.

Edinger, E. F. (1986). *The Bible and the Psyche: Individuation Symbolism in the Old Testament.* Toronto: Inner City Books.

Edinger, E. F. (1992). *Transformation of the God-Image: An Elucidation of Jung's* Answer to Job. Toronto: Inner City Books.

Edmonds, E. M., and Cahoon, D. D. (1993). Effects of Religious Orientation and Clothing Revealingness on Women's Choice of Clothing. *Journal of Social Behavior and Personality,* 8, 349–353.

Edwards, J. (1746). *A Treatise Concerning Religious Affections.* Edited by J. E. Smith. In *The Works of Jonathan Edwards,* Vol. 2. New Haven, Conn.: Yale University Press, 1959. (First published 1746)

Edwards, L. (1993). *How We Belong, Fight, and Pray: The MBTI as a Key to Congregational Dynamics.* Bethesda, Md.: Alban Institute.

Efron, D. H. (Ed.). (1970). *Psychotomimetic Drugs.* New York: Raven Press.

Efron, D. H., Holmstedt, B., and Kline, N. S. (Eds.). (1967). *Ethnopharmacologic Search for Psychoactive Drugs.* Washington, D. C.: U. S. Department of Health, Education, and Welfare.

Ehrlich, P. R., Ehrlich, A. H., and Daily, G. C. (1995). *The Stork and the Plow: The Equity Answer to the Human Dilemma.* New York: G. P. Putnam's Sons.

Eichele, E. (1928). *Die religiöse Entwicklung im Jugendalter.* Gütersloh: C. Bertelsmann.

Eilberg-Schwartz, H. (1994). Homoeroticism and the Father God: An Unthought in Freud's *Moses and Monotheism. American Imago,* 51, 127–159.

Eisinga, R., Konig, R., and Scheepers, P. (1995). Orthodox Religious Beliefs and Anti-Semitism: A Replication of Glock and Stark in the Netherlands. *Journal for the Scientific Study of Religion,* 34, 214–223.

Elder, G. R. (1987). Phallus. In M. Eliade, *The Encyclopedia of Religion,* Vol. 11, pp. 263–269.

Eliade, M. (1951). *Shamanism: Archaic Techniques of*

Ecstasy. Translated by W. R. Trask. New York: Pantheon, 1964. (Original French edition 1951)

Eliade, M. (1954). *Yoga: Immortality and Freedom* (2nd ed.). Translated by W. R. Trask. Princeton, N.J.: Princeton University Press, 1969. (Original French edition 1954)

Eliade, M. (1956). *The Forge and the Crucible*. Translated by S. Corrin. New York: Harper & Brothers, 1962. (Original French edition 1956)

Eliade, M. (1957). *The Sacred and the Profane: The Nature of Religion*. Translated by W. R. Trask. New York: Harcourt, Brace, 1959. (Translated from the unpublished French original; first published, in German, 1957)

Eliade, M. (1962). *The Two and the One*. Translated by J. M. Cohen. New York: Harper & Row, 1965. (Original French edition 1962)

Eliade, M. (1967). Cultural Fashions and the History of Religions. In J. M. Kitagawa (Ed.), *The History of Religions: Essays on the Problem of Understanding*. Chicago: University of Chicago Press, pp. 21–38.

Eliade, M. (1969). *The Quest: History and Meaning in Religion*. Chicago: University of Chicago Press.

Eliade, M. (Ed.). (1987). *The Encyclopedia of Religion* (16 vols.). New York: Macmillan.

Elkind, D. (1971). The Development of Religious Understanding in Children and Adolescents. In M. P. Strommen, *Research on Religious Development*, pp. 655–685.

Ellenberger, H. F. (1970). *The Discovery of the Unconscious: The History and Evolution of Dynamic Psychiatry*. New York: Basic Books.

Eller, C. (1993). *Living in the Lap of the Goddess: The Feminist Spirituality Movement in America*. Boston: Beacon Press.

Elliott, A. (1994). *Psychoanalytic Theory: An Introduction*. Oxford: Blackwell.

Elliott, D. (1994). The Impact of Christian Faith on the Prevalence and Sequelae of Sexual Abuse. *Journal of Interpersonal Violence, 9*, 95–107.

Ellis, C. C. (1922). *The Religion of Religious Psychology*. Philadelphia: The Sunday School Times Co.

Ellis, H. (1910). The Auto-Erotic Factor in Religion. In *Studies in the Psychology of Sex*, Vol. 1, Part One (3rd ed.). New York: Random House, pp. 310–325.

Ellison, C. G. (1996). Conservative Protestantism and the Corporal Punishment of Children: Clarifying the Issues. *Journal for the Scientific Study of Religion, 35*, 1–16.

Emblen, J. D. (1992). *Religion* and *Spirituality* Defined According to Current Use in Nursing Literature. *Journal of Professional Nursing, 8*, 42–47.

Engelman, E. (1976). *Berggasse 19: Sigmund Freud's Home and Offices, Vienna 1928: The Photographs of Edmund Engelman*. Introduction by P. Gay. New York: Basic Books.

English, H. B., and English, A. C. (1958). *A Comprehensive Dictionary of Psychological and Psychoanalytical Terms*. London: Longmans, Green.

Erikson, E. H. (1950). *Childhood and Society* (2nd ed.). New York: W. W. Norton, 1963. (First edition 1950)

Erikson, E. H. (1958). *Young Man Luther: A Study in Psychoanalysis and History*. New York: W. W. Norton.

Erikson, E. H. (1959). *Identity and the Life Cycle: Selected Papers*. New York: International Universities Press.

Erikson, E. H. (1964). *Insight and Responsibility: Lectures on the Ethical Implications of Psychoanalytic Insight*. New York: W. W. Norton.

Erikson, E. H. (1966). Ontogeny of Ritualization in Man. In J. Huxley, A Discussion of Ritualization of Behaviour in Animals and Man, pp. 337–349. (Reprinted in Erikson, 1987)

Erikson, E. H. (1968). *Identity: Youth and Crisis*. New York: W. W. Norton.

Erikson, E. H. (1969). *Gandhi's Truth: On the Origins of Militant Nonviolence*. New York: W. W. Norton.

Erikson, E. H. (1975). *Life History and the Historical Moment*. New York: W. W. Norton.

Erikson, E. H. (1977). *Toys and Reasons: Stages in the Ritualization of Experience*. New York: W. W. Norton.

Erikson, E. H. (1981). The Galilean Sayings and the Sense of "I." *Yale Review, 70*, 321–362.

Erikson, E. H. (1982). *The Life Cycle Completed: A Review*. New York: W. W. Norton.

Erikson, E. H. (1987). *A Way of Looking at Things: Selected Papers from 1930 to 1980*. Edited by S. Schlein. New York: W. W. Norton.

Erikson, E. H., Erikson, J. M., and Kivnick, H. Q. (1987). *Vital Involvement in Old Age: The Experience of Old Age in Our Time*. New York: W. W. Norton.

Ermarth, M. (1978). *Wilhelm Dilthey: The Critique of Historical Reason*. Chicago: University of Chicago Press.

Ernsberger, D. J., and Manaster, G. J. (1981). Moral Development, Intrinsic/Extrinsic Religious Orientation and Denominational Teachings. *Genetic Psychology Monographs, 104*, 23–41.

Ervin, F. R., Palmour, R. M., Pearson Murphy, B. E., Prince, R., and Simons, R. C. (1988). The Psychobiology of Trance, II: Physiological and Endocrine Correlates. *Transcultural Psychiatric Research, 25*, 267–284.

Evans, R. I. (1952). Personal Values as Factors in Anti-Semitism. *Journal of Abnormal and Social Psychology, 47*, 749–756.

Evans, R. I. (1971). *Gordon Allport: The Man and His Ideas*. New York: E. P. Dutton.

Everett, C. C. (1902). *The Psychological Elements of Religious Faith*. Edited by E. Hale. New York: Macmillan.

Ewald, G. (1932). *Biologische und "reine" Psychologie im Persönlichkeitsaufbau: Prinzipielles und Paralleles*. Darmstadt: Wissenschaftliche Buchgesellschaft, 1969. (First published 1932)

Ey, H. (1968). *Consciousness: A Phenomenological Study of Being Conscious and Becoming Conscious*. Translated by J. H. Flodstrom. Bloomington: Indiana University Press, 1978. (Second French edition 1968)

Faber, H. (1913). *Das Wesen der Religionspsychologie und ihre Bedeutung für die Dogmatik.* Tübingen: J. C. B. Mohr (Paul Siebeck).

Fabry, J. B. (1968). *The Pursuit of Meaning: Logotherapy Applied to Life.* Boston: Beacon Press.

Fagan, B. M. (1984). *The Aztecs.* New York: W. H. Freeman.

Fairbairn, W. R. D. (1927). Notes on the Religious Phantasies of a Female Patient. In *Psychoanalytic Studies of the Personality.* London: Tavistock, 1952, pp. 183–196. (Paper presented in 1927)

Fairbairn, W. R. D. (1943). The Repression and the Return of Bad Objects (With Special Reference to the "War Neuroses"). *British Journal of Medical Psychology,* 19, 327–341.

Fairbairn, W. R. D. (1955). Observations in Defence of the Object-Relations Theory of the Personality. *British Journal of Medical Psychology,* 28, 144–156.

Falk, N. A., and Gross, R. M. (1989). *Unspoken Worlds: Women's Religious Lives* (2nd ed.). Belmont, Calif.: Wadsworth.

Farber, B. (1968). *Mental Retardation: Its Social Context and Social Consequences.* Boston: Houghton Mifflin.

Farberow, N. (Ed.). (1963). *Taboo Topics.* New York: Atherton.

Faulkner, J. E., and DeJong, G. F. (1966). Religiosity in 5–D: An Empirical Analysis. *Social Forces,* 45, 246–254.

Faulkner, J. E., and DeJong, G. F. (1969). On Measuring the Religious Variable: Rejoinder to Weigert and Thomas. *Social Forces,* 48, 263–267.

Feagin, J. R. (1964). Prejudice and Religious Types: A Focused Study of Southern Fundamentalists. *Journal for the Scientific Study of Religion,* 4, 3–13.

Fehr, L. A., and Heintzelman, M. E. (1977). Personality and Attitude Correlates of Religiosity: A Source of Controversy. *Journal of Psychology,* 95, 63–66.

Feinstein, H. M. (1984). *Becoming William James.* Ithaca, N.Y.: Cornell University Press.

Feldman, S. (1941). The Blessing of the Kohenites. *American Imago,* 2, 296–322.

Feldman, S. S. (1959). Notes on Some Religious Rites and Ceremonies. *Journal of the Hillside Hospital,* 8, 36–41.

Félice, P. de. (1936). *Poisons sacrés, ivresses divines. Essai sur quelques formes inférieures de la mystique.* Paris: Albin Michel, 1970. (First published 1936)

Félice, P. de. (1947). *Foules en délire. Extases collectives. Essai sur quelques formes inférieures de la mystique.* Paris: Albin Michel.

Fenichel, O. (1945). *The Psychoanalytic Theory of Neurosis.* New York: W. W. Norton.

Fenwick, P. (1987). Meditation and the EEG. In M. A. West, *The Psychology of Meditation,* pp. 104–117.

Ferder, F. (1978). *Called to Break Bread? A Psychological Investigation of 100 Women Who Feel Called to Priest-hood in the Catholic Church.* Mt. Rainier, Md.: Quixote Center.

Ferguson, L. W. (1939). Primary Social Attitudes. *Journal of Psychology,* 8, 217–223.

Ferguson, L. W. (1944a). A Revision of the Primary Social Attitude Scales. *Journal of Psychology,* 17, 229–241.

Ferguson, L. W. (1944b). Socio-psychological Correlates of the Primary Attitude Scales: I. Religionism; II. Humanitarianism. *Journal of Social Psychology,* 19, 81–98.

Ferm, V. (Ed.). (1937). *Religion in Transition.* New York: Macmillan

Feuerbach, L. (1841). *The Essence of Christianity.* Translated by G. Eliot. New York: Harper & Brothers, 1957. (First English edition 1854; original German edition 1841)

Fine, R. (1979). *A History of Psychoanalysis.* New York: Columbia University Press.

Fingert, H. H. (1954). Psychoanalytic Study of the Minor Prophet, Jonah. *Psychoanalytic Review,* 41, 55–65.

Finn, M., and Gartner, J. (Eds.). (1992). *Object Relations Theory and Religion: Clinical Applications.* Westport, Conn.: Praeger.

Finner, S. L. (1970). Religious Membership and Religious Preference: Equal Indicators of Religiosity? *Journal for the Scientific Study of Religion,* 9, 273–279.

Finner, S. L., and Gamache, J. D. (1969). The Relation Between Religious Commitment and Attitudes Toward Induced Abortion. *Sociological Analysis,* 30, 3–12.

Fischer, L. (1954). *Gandhi: His Life and Message for the World.* New York: New American Library.

Fischer, R. (1969). The Perception-Hallucination Continuum (A Re-Examination). *Diseases of the Nervous System,* 30, 161–171.

Fischer, R. (1971). A Cartography of Ecstatic and Meditative States. *Science,* 174, 897–904.

Fischer, R. (1972). Letter to Raymond Prince. *R. M. Bucke Memorial Society Newsletter-Review,* 5, 42–45.

Fischer, R. (1975). Transformations of Consciousness. A Cartography. I. The Perception-Hallucination Continuum. *Confinia Psychiatrica,* 18, 221–244.

Fischer, R. (1978). Cartography of Conscious States: Integration of East and West. In A. A. Sugerman and R. E. Tarter (Eds.), *Expanding Dimensions of Consciousness.* New York: Springer, pp. 24–57.

Fischer, R. (1986). Toward a Neuroscience of Self-Expression and States of Self-Awareness and Interpreting Interpretations. In B. B. Wolman and M. Ullman, *Handbook of States of Consciousness,* pp. 3–30.

Fisher, S. (1964). Acquiescence and Religiosity. *Psychological Reports,* 15, 784.

Fisher, S. (1973). *The Female Orgasm.* New York: Basic Books.

Fisher, S., and Greenberg, R. P. (1977). *The Scientific*

Credibility of Freud's Theories and Therapy. New York: Basic Books.

Fitchett, G. (Ed.). (1982). Religion and the Self-Psychology of Heinz Kohut: A Memorial Symposium. *Journal of Supervision and Training in Ministry,* 5.

Fitzpatrick, J. J. (1976). Some Problematic Features of Erik H. Erikson's Psychohistory. *The Psychohistory Review,* 5(3), 16–27.

Flakoll, D. (1974). *Self-esteem, Psychological Adjustment, and Images of God.* Paper presented at the annual meeting of the Society for the Scientific Study of Religion, Washington, D.C.

Flanagan, O. J., Jr. (1984). *The Science of the Mind.* Cambridge: MIT Press.

Flattery, D. S., and Schwartz, M. (1989). *Haoma and Harmaline: The Botanical Identity of the Indo-Iranian Sacred Hallucinogen "Soma" and Its Legacy in Religion, Language, and Middle Eastern Folklore.* Berkeley: University of California Press.

Fleck, U. (1935). Über die Religiösitat der Epileptiker. *Archiv für Psychiatrie und Nervenkrankheiten,* 103, 122–135.

Flew, A. G. N. (1973). B. F. Skinner: Human Psychology Dehumanized. *Question 6,* January, 97–107.

Flournoy, T. (1899). *From India to the Planet Mars: A Study of a Case of Somnambulism with Glossolalia.* Translated by D. B. Dermilye. New York: Harper & Brothers, 1900. (Original French edition 1899)

Flournoy, T. (1902). The Varieties of Religious Experience [according to William James]. In *The Philosophy of William James,* pp. 217–244. (First published in French 1902)

Flournoy, T. (1903a). Les principes de la psychologie religieuse. *Archives de Psychologie,* 2, 33–57.

Flournoy, T. (1903b). Observations de psychologie religieuse. *Archives de Psychologie,* 2, 327–366.

Flournoy, T. (1904). *Le génie religieux.* Saint-Blaise: Foyer Solidariste.

Flournoy, T. (1911a). *The Philosophy of William James.* Translated by E. B. Holt and W. James, Jr. New York: H. Holt, 1917. (Original French edition 1911)

Flournoy, T. (1911b). *Spiritism and Psychology.* Abridged and Translated by H. Carrington. New York: Harper & Brothers, 1911. (Original French edition 1911)

Flournoy, T. (1915). Une mystique moderne. (Documents pour la psychologie religieuse). *Archives de Psychologie,* 15, 1–224.

Fodor, A. (1954). The Fall of Man in the Book of Genesis. *American Imago,* 11, 203–231.

Fordham, F. (1966). *An Introduction to Jung's Psychology* (3rd ed.). Baltimore: Penguin.

Forem, J. (1974). *Transcendental Meditation: Maharishi Mahesh Yogi and the Science of Creative Intelligence.* New York: E. P. Dutton.

Forrest, D. W. (1974). *Francis Galton: The Life and Work of a Victorian Genius.* New York: Taplinger Publishing Co.

Fortune, M. M. (1989). *Is Nothing Sacred?* San Francisco: Harper & Row.

Fortune, R. F. (1926). The Symbolism of the Serpent. *International Journal of Psychoanalysis,* 7, 237–243.

Foster, G. W. (1985). *The World Was Flooded with Light: A Mystical Experience Remembered.* Pittsburgh: University of Pittsburgh Press.

Fowler, J. W. (1981). *Stages of Faith: The Psychology of Human Development and the Quest for Meaning.* San Francisco: Harper & Row.

Fowler, J. W. (1984). *Becoming Adult, Becoming Christian: Adult Development and Christian Faith.* San Francisco: Harper & Row.

Fowler, J. W., Nipkow, K. E., and Schweitzer, F. (Eds.). (1991). *Stages of Faith and Religious Development.* New York: Crossroad.

Fowler, R. B. (1995). *The Greening of Protestant Thought.* Chapel Hill: University of North Carolina Press.

Fraas, H.-J., and Heimbrock, H.-G. (Eds.). (1986). *Religiöse Erziehung und Glaubens-Entwicklung: Zur Auseinandersetzung mit der kognitiven Psychologie.* Göttingen: Vandenhoeck & Ruprecht.

Fraenkel, E. (1959). La doctrine de Sigmund Freud et le Judaisme. *Revue d'Histoire de la Médecine Hébraïque,* 12, 79–97.

Francis, L. J., and Evan, T. E. (1995). The Psychology of Christian Prayer: A Review of Empirical Research. *Religion,* 25, 371–388.

Francis, L., Pearson, P. R., Carter, M., and Kay, W. K. (1981). Are Introverts More Religious? *British Journal of Social Psychology,* 20, 101–104.

Frank, L. K. (1939). Projective Methods for the Study of Personality. *Journal of Psychology,* 8, 389–413.

Frankfort, H. (1958). The Archetype in Analytical Psychology and the History of Religion. *Journal of The Warburg and Courtauld Institutes,* 21, 166–178.

Frankl, V. (1962). *Man's Search for Meaning: An Introduction to Logotherapy* (rev. ed. of *From Death Camp to Existentialism*). Translated by I. Lasch. Boston: Beacon Press. (Original German edition 1946)

Frankl, V. (1966). Self-Transcendence as a Human Phenomenon. *Journal of Humanistic Psychology,* 6, 97–106.

Frankl, V. (1975). *The Unconscious God: Psychotherapy and Theology.* New York: Simon and Schuster. (Expanded translation of *Der unbewußte Gott,* 1948.)

Franzblau, A. N. (1934). Religious Belief and Character Among Jewish Adolescents. *Teachers College Contributions to Education,* No. 634.

Freemon, F. R. (1976). A Differential Diagnosis of the Inspirational Spells of Muhammad the Prophet of Islam. *Epilepsia,* 17, 423–427.

French, V. V. (1947). The Structure of Sentiments. *Journal of Personality,* 15, 247–282; 16, 78–108, 209–244.

Freud, E. L. (Ed.). (1970). *The Letters of Sigmund Freud and Arnold Zweig.* New York: Harcourt, Brace and World.

Freud, M. (1957). *Sigmund Freud: Man and Father.* New

York: Vanguard Press, 1958. (British edition 1957)

Freud, S. (1953–1974). *The Standard Edition of the Complete Psychological Works of Sigmund Freud* (24 vols.). Translated from the German under the general editorship of J. Strachey. London: Hogarth Press and the Institute of Psycho-Analysis.

Freud, S. (1900). *The Interpretation of Dreams.* In *Standard Edition*, Vols. 4 and 5. (First German edition 1900)

Freud, S. (1901). *The Psychopathology of Everyday Life.* In *Standard Edition*, Vol. 6, 1960. (First German edition 1901)

Freud, S. (1905). Three Essays on the Theory of Sexuality. In *Standard Edition*, Vol. 7, 1953, pp. 123–243. (First German edition 1905)

Freud, S. (1907). Obsessive Actions and Religious Practices. In *Standard Edition*, Vol. 9, 1959, pp. 115–127. (Original German edition 1907)

Freud, S. (1908). Character and Anal Erotism. In *Standard Edition*, Vol. 9, 1959, pp. 167–175. (Original German edition 1908)

Freud, S. (1910). Leonardo da Vinci and a Memory of His Childhood. In *Standard Edition*, Vol. 11, 1957, pp. 57–137. (First German edition 1910)

Freud, S. (1911a). "Great is Diana of the Ephesians." In *Standard Edition*, Vol. 12, 1958, pp. 342–344. (Original German edition 1911)

Freud, S. (1911b). Psycho-Analytic Notes on an Autobiographical Account of a Case of Paranoia (Dementia Paranoides.). In *Standard Edition*, Vol. 12, 1958, pp. 1–82. (First German edition 1911)

Freud, S. (1913). Totem and Taboo: Some Points of Agreement Between the Mental Lives of Savages and Neurotics. In *Standard Edition*, Vol. 13, 1953, pp. 1–161. (First German edition in one volume 1913)

Freud, S. (1914). On Narcissism: An Introduction. In *Standard Edition*, Vol. 14, pp. 67–102. (Original German edition 1914)

Freud, S. (1916–17). *Introductory Lectures on Psycho-Analysis.* In *Standard Edition*, Vols. 15 and 16, 1961, 1963. (First German edition 1916–1917)

Freud, S. (1918). From the History of an Infantile Neurosis. In *Standard Edition*, Vol. 17, 1955, pp. 1–123. (Original German edition 1918)

Freud, S. (1921). Group Psychology and the Analysis of the Ego. In *Standard Edition*, Vol. 18, 1955, pp. 67–143. (Original German edition 1921)

Freud, S. (1923a). The Ego and the Id. In *Standard Edition*, Vol. 19, 1961, pp. 1–66. (Original German edition 1923)

Freud, S. (1923b). A Seventeenth-Century Demonological Neurosis. In *Standard Edition*, Vol. 19, 1961, pp. 67–105. (Original German edition 1923)

Freud, S. (1924). The Dissolution of the Oedipus Complex. In *Standard Edition*, Vol. 19, 1961, pp. 171–179. (Original German edition 1924)

Freud, S. (1925a). An Autobiographical Study. In *Standard Edition*, Vol. 20, 1959, pp. 1–74. (First German edition 1925)

Freud, S. (1925b). Some Psychical Consequences of the Anatomical Distinction Between the Sexes. *Standard Edition*, Vol. 19, 1961, pp. 241–258. (Original German edition 1925)

Freud, S. (1926a). Address to the Society of B'nai B'rith. In *Standard Edition*, Vol. 20, 1959, pp. 271–274. (Original German edition 1941; read in 1926)

Freud, S. (1926b). The Question of Lay Analysis: Conversations with an Impartial Person. In *Standard Edition*, Vol. 20 1959, pp. 177–258. (Original German edition 1926)

Freud, S. (1927). The Future of an Illusion. In *Standard Edition*, Vol. 21, 1961, pp. 1–56. (First German edition 1927)

Freud, S. (1928). A Religious Experience. In *Standard Edition*, Vol. 21, 1961, pp. 167–172. (First German edition 1928)

Freud, S. (1930). Civilization and Its Discontents. In *Standard Edition*, Vol. 21, 1961, pp. 57–145. (Original German edition 1930)

Freud, S. (1933). New Introductory Lectures on Psycho-Analysis. In *Standard Edition*, Vol. 22, 1964, pp. 1–182. (Original German edition 1933)

Freud, S. (1939). Moses and Monotheism: Three Essays. In *Standard Edition*, Vol. 23, 1964, pp. 7–137. (Original German edition 1939)

Freud, S. (1940). An Outline of Psycho-Analysis. In *Standard Edition*, Vol. 23, 1964, pp. 139–207. (Original German edition 1940)

Freud, S. (1960). *Letters of Sigmund Freud.* Edited by E. L. Freud; translated by T. and J. Stern. New York: Basic Books.

Freud, S. (1985). *The Complete Letters of Sigmund Freud to Wilhelm Fliess, 1887–1904.* Edited and translated by J. M. Masson. Cambridge: Belknap/Harvard University Press.

Friedlander, I. (1975). *The Whirling Dervishes.* New York: Macmillan.

Friedrichs, R. W. (1959). Christians and Residential Exclusion: An Empirical Study of a Northern Dilemma. *Journal of Social Issues,* 15, 14–23.

Friedrichs, R. W. (1960). Alter versus Ego: An Exploratory Assessment of Altruism. *American Sociological Review,* 25, 496–508.

Fromm, E. (1927). Der Sabbath. *Imago,* 13, 223–234.

Fromm, E. (1930). The Dogma of Christ. Translated by J. L. Adams. In *The Dogma of Christ and Other Essays on Religion, Psychology and Culture.* New York: Holt, Rinehart and Winston, 1963. (Original German edition of the title essay 1930)

Fromm, E. (1941). *Escape from Freedom.* New York: Rinehart.

Fromm, E. (1947). *Man for Himself: An Inquiry into the Psychology of Ethics.* New York: Rinehart.

Fromm, E. (1950). *Psychoanalysis and Religion.* New Haven, Conn.: Yale University Press.

Fromm, E. (1951). *The Forgotten Language: An Intro-*

duction to the Understanding of Dreams, Fairy Tales and Myths. New York: Rinehart.

Fromm, E. (1956). *The Art of Loving.* New York: Harper & Brothers.

Fromm, E. (1960). Psychoanalysis and Zen Buddhism. In D. T. Suzuki, E. Fromm, and R. De Martino, *Zen Buddhism and Psychoanalysis.* London: George Allen & Unwin, pp. 77–141.

Fromm, E. (1966). *You Shall Be As Gods: A Radical Reinterpretation of the Old Testament and Its Tradition.* New York: Holt, Rinehart and Winston.

Fromm, E. (1968). *The Revolution of Hope: Toward a Humanized Technology.* New York: Harper & Row.

Fromm, E. (1976). *To Have or To Be?* New York: Harper & Row.

Fromm, E. (1980). *Greatness and Limitations of Freud's Thought.* New York: Harper & Row.

Fromm, E. (1994). *On Being Human.* New York: Continuum.

Fromm-Reichmann, F. (1927). Das judische Speiseritual. *Imago,* 13, 235–246.

Fuchs, A., and Oppermann, R. (1975). Dimensionen der Religiösitat und Bedeutungsstruktur religiöser Konzepte. *Archiv für Religionspsychologie,* 11, 260–266.

Fukuyama, Y. (1961). The Major Dimensions of Church Membership. *Review of Religious Research,* 2, 154–161.

Fuller, A. R. (1990). *Insight into Value: An Exploration of the Premises of a Phenomenological Psychology.* Albany: State University of New York Press.

Funderburk, J. (1977). *Science Studies Yoga: A Review of Physiological Data.* Glenville, Ill.: Himalayan International Institute.

Furst, P. T. (Ed.). (1972). *Flesh of the Gods: The Ritual Use of Hallucinogens.* New York: Praeger.

Galanter, M. (1989). *Cults: Faith, Healing, and Coercion.* New York: Oxford University Press.

Gallemore, J. L., Wilson, W. P., and Rhoads, J. M. (1969). The Religious Life of Patients with Affective Disorders. *Diseases of the Nervous System,* 30, 483–486.

Gallup, G., Jr. (1995). *The Gallup Poll: Public Opinion 1994.* Wilmington, Del.: Scholarly Resources.

Galton, F. (1869). *Hereditary Genius: An Inquiry into Its Laws and Consequences* (2nd, unrevised ed.). London: Macmillan, 1892. (First published 1869)

Galton, F. (1872). Statistical Inquiries into the Efficacy of Prayer. *Fortnightly Review,* 12 (N.S.), 125–135. (Reprinted with minor changes as, Objective Efficacy of Prayer, in F. Galton, *Inquiries into Human Faculty and Its Development* [1st ed.]. London: Macmillan, 1883. Later editions omit this essay.)

Galton, F. (1889). *Natural Inheritance.* New York: Macmillan, 1894. (First published 1889)

Galton, F. (1908). *Memories of My Life* (3rd ed.). London: Methuen, 1909. (First edition 1908)

Garanzini, M. J. (1988). *The Attachment Cycle: An Object Relations Approach to the Healing Ministries.* Mahwah, N.J.: Paulist Press.

Gardiner, M. (Ed.). (1971). *The Wolf-Man,* by the Wolf-Man; with "The Case of the Wolf-Man," by S. Freud; "A Supplement," by R. M. Brunswick; and notes, an introduction, and chapters by the editor. New York: Basic Books.

Gardner, J. (1995). Jung at Heart. *National Review,* 47(13), 60, 62–63.

Gartner, J. (1996). Religious Commitment, Mental Health, and Prosocial Behavior: A Review of the Empirical Literature. In E. P. Shafranske, *Religion and the Clinical Practice of Psychology,* pp. 187–214. (Largely based on Gartner, Larson, and Allen, 1991)

Gartner, J., Larson, D. B., and Allen, G. D. (1991). Religious Commitment and Mental Health: A Review of the Empirical Literature. *Journal of Psychology and Theology,* 19, 6–25.

Gay, P. (1987). *A Godless Jew: Freud, Atheism, and the Making of Psychoanalysis.* New Haven, Conn.: Yale University Press.

Gay, P. (1988). *Freud: A Life for Our Time.* New York: W. W. Norton.

Gay, V. P. (1979). *Freud on Ritual: Reconstruction and Critique.* Missoula, Mont.: Scholar's Press. (Doctoral dissertation, University of Chicago, 1976)

Gazzaniga, M. S. (1967). The Split Brain in Man. *Scientific American,* 217(2), 24–29. (Reprinted in Ornstein, 1973)

Gazzaniga, M. S. (1970). *The Bisected Brain.* New York: Appleton-Century-Crofts.

Gellhorn, E., and Kiely, W. F. (1972). Mystical States of Consciousness: Neurophysiological and Clinical Aspects. *Journal of Nervous and Mental Disease,* 154, 399–405.

Gellhorn, E., and Loofbourrow, G. N. (1963). *Emotions and Emotional Disorders: A Neurophysiological Study.* New York: Hoeber.

Gellner, E. (1992). *Postmodernism, Reason and Religion.* London: Routledge.

Genia, V. (1996). I, E, Quest, and Fundamentalism as Predictors of Psychological and Spiritual Well-Being. *Journal for the Scientific Study of Religion,* 35, 56–64.

Genia, V., and Shaw, D. G. (1991). Religion, Intrinsic-Extrinsic Orientation, and Depression. *Review of Religious Research,* 32, 274–283.

Gergen, K. J. (1991). *The Saturated Self: Dilemmas of Identity in Contemporary Life.* New York: Basic Books.

Gergen, K. J., and Davis, K. E. (1985). *The Social Construction of the Person.* New York: Springer.

Gerrard, N. L. (1968). The Serpent-Handling Religions of West Virginia. *Trans-action,* (May), 22–28.

Geschwind, N. (1983). Interictal Behavior Changes in Epilepsy. *Epilepsia,* 24 (Suppl. 1), S23–S30.

Geschwind, N., and Galaburda, A. M. (1987). *Cerebral Lateralization: Biological Mechanisms, Associations, and Pathology.* Cambridge: The MIT Press.

Geschwind, N., Shader, R. I., Bear, D., North, B., Levin, K., and Chetham, D. (1980). Behavioral

Changes with Temporal Lobe Epilepsy: Assessment and Treatment. *Journal of Clinical Psychiatry,* 41, 89–95.

Giarman, N. J. (1967). The Pharmacology of LSD. In R. C. DeBold and R. C. Leaf, *LSD, Man & Society,* pp. 143–158.

Gibb, L. L. (1968). Home Background and Self-Actualization Attainment. *Journal of College Student Personnel,* 9, 49–53.

Gibbons, D., and DeJarnette, J. (1972). Hypnotic Susceptibility and Religious Experience. *Journal for the Scientific Study of Religion,* 11, 152–156.

Gibbs, J. O., and Crader, K. W. (1970). A Criticism of Two Recent Attempts to Scale Glock and Stark's Dimensions of Religiosity: A Research Note. *Sociological Analysis,* 31, 107–114.

Gill, M., and Brenman, M. (1959). *Hypnosis and Related States: Psychoanalytic Studies in Regression.* New York: International Universities Press.

Gillespie, J. M., and Allport, G. W. (1955). *Youth's Outlook on the Future: A Cross-National Study.* Garden City, N.Y.: Doubleday.

Gilligan, C. (1982). *In a Different Voice: Psychological Theory and Women's Development.* Cambridge, Mass.: Harvard University Press.

Gins, K. (1961). Studien zur Mystik: "Vormystische Erscheinungen." Experimenteller Beitrag zum Frühstadium mystischer Erlebnisweise. *Zeitschrift für Menschenkunde,* 25, 15–41.

Gins, K. (1967). Experimentell untersuchte Mystik—fragwürdig? Ein Beitrag zur methodischen Problematik. *Archiv für Religionspsychologie,* 9, 213–253.

Gins, K. (1982). Analyse von Mystiker—Aussagen zur Unterscheidung christlicher und ekstatischer Erlebnisweise. *Archiv für Religionspsychologie,* 15, 155–194.

Gins, K. (1992). *Experimentell-meditative Versenkung in Analogie zur klassischen christlichen Mystik: Religionspsychologie Untersuchung auf introspektiver Grundlage.* Frankfurt am Main: Peter Lang.

Girgensohn, K. (1921). *Der seelische Aufbau des religiösen Erlebens: Eine religionspsychologische Untersuchung auf experimenteller Grundlage* (2nd ed.). Corrected and supplemented by W. Gruehn. Gütersloh: C. Bertelsmann, 1930. (First edition 1921)

Girgensohn, K. (1923a). Die Erscheinungsweisen religiöser Gedanken. *Zeitschrift für systematische Theologie,* 1, 335–347.

Girgensohn, K. (1923b). *Religionspsychologie, Religionswissenschaft und Theologie.* Leipzig: A. Deichert (Dr. Werner Scholl).

Girgensohn, K. (1924). *Grundriß der Dogmatik.* Leipzig: A. Deichert (Dr. Werner Scholl).

Girgensohn, K. (1926). [Autobiography]. In E. Stange (Ed.), *Die Religionswissenschaft der Gegenwart in Selbstdarstellungen.* Leipzig: Félix Meiner, pp. 41–76.

Glassl, A. (1970). The Psychology of Religion: The Present Soviet Stand. *Bulletin, Institute for the Study of the USSR,* 17, 24–27.

Glaze, J. A. (1928). Psychological Effects of Fasting. *American Journal of Psychology,* 40, 236–253.

Gleason, J. J., Jr. (1975). *Growing Up to God: Eight Steps in Religious Development.* Nashville, Tenn.: Abingdon Press.

Glock, C. Y. (1962). On the Study of Religious Commitment. *Religious Education, Research Supplement,* 57(4), S98–S110.

Glock, C. Y., and Hammond, P. E. (Eds.). (1973). *Beyond the Classics? Essays in the Scientific Study of Religion.* New York: Harper & Row.

Glock, C. Y., and Stark, R. (1966). *Christian Beliefs and Anti-Semitism.* New York: Harper & Row.

Glover, E. (1950). *Freud or Jung?* London: George Allen & Unwin.

Glueck, B. C., and Stroebel, C. F. (1975). Biofeedback and Meditation in the Treatment of Psychiatric Illnesses. *Comprehensive Psychiatry,* 16, 303–321.

Godin, A. (Ed.). (1959). *Research in Religious Psychology: Speculative and Positive.* Brussels: Lumen Vitae.

Godin, A. (Ed.). (1961). *Child and Adult Before God.* Chicago: Loyola University Press, 1965. (First published 1961)

Godin, A. (Ed.). (1964). *From Religious Experience to a Religious Attitude.* Chicago: Loyola University Press, 1965. (First published 1964)

Godin, A. (Ed.). (1968). *From Cry to Word: Contributions Toward a Psychology of Prayer.* Brussels: Lumen Vitae.

Godin, A. (Ed.). (1972). *Death and Presence: The Psychology of Death and the After-Life.* Brussels: Lumen Vitae.

Godin, A., and Hallez, M. (1964). Parental Images and Divine Paternity. In A. Godin, *From Religious Experience to a Religious Attitude,* pp. 65–96.

Goldberg, B. Z. (1930). *The Sacred Fire: The Story of Sex in Religion.* New York: Liveright.

Goldbrunner, J. (1949). *Individuation: A Study of the Depth Psychology of Carl Gustav Jung.* Translated by S. Godman. Notre Dame, Ind.: University of Notre Dame Press, 1964. (Original German edition 1949)

Goldenberg, N. (1979). *Changing of the Gods: Feminism and the End of Traditional Religions.* Boston: Beacon Press.

Goldenberg, N. R. (1990). *Returning Words to Flesh: Feminism, Psychoanalysis, and the Resurrection of the Body.* Boston: Beacon Press.

Goldman, R. (1964). *Religious Thinking from Childhood to Adolescence.* London: Routledge & Kegan Paul.

Goldman, R. (1965). *Readiness for Religion: A Basis for Developmental Religious Education.* London: Routledge and Kegan Paul.

Goldman, R. (1967). *Education for Uncertainty: The Essex Hall Lecture 1967.* London: Lindsey Press.

Goleman, D. (1988). *The Meditative Mind: The Varieties of Meditative Experience.* Los Angeles: J. P. Tarcher.

Goleman, D. J., and Schwartz, G. E. (1976). Meditation as an Intervention in Stress Reactivity. *Journal of Consulting and Clinical Psychology,* 44, 456–466.

Gómez, L. O. (1995). Oriental Wisdom and the Cure of Souls: Jung and the Indian East. In D. S. Lopez, Jr. (Ed.), *Curators of the Buddha: The Study of Buddhism Under Colonialism.* Chicago: University of Chicago Press, pp. 197–250.

Goodenough, E. R. (1965). *The Psychology of Religious Experiences.* New York: Basic Books.

Goodman, F. D. (1972). *Speaking in Tongues: A Cross-Cultural Study of Glossolalia.* Chicago: University of Chicago Press.

Goodman, F. D. (1986). Body Posture and the Religious Altered State of Consciousness: An Experimental Investigation. *Journal of Humanistic Psychology,* 26(3), 81–118.

Goodman, F. D. (1988). *Ecstasy, Ritual, and Alternate Reality: Religion in a Pluralistic World.* Bloomington: Indiana University Press.

Gordon, L. V. (1972). A Typological Assessment of "A Study of Values" by Q-methodology. *Journal of Social Psychology,* 86, 55–67.

Gorlow, L., and Schroeder, H. E. (1968). Motives for Participating in the Religious Experience. *Journal for the Scientific Study of Religion,* 7, 241–251.

Gorlow, L., Simonson, N. R., and Krauss, H. (1966). An Empirical Investigation of the Jungian Typology. *British Journal of Social and Clinical Psychology,* 5, 108–117.

Gorsuch, R. L. (1968). The Conceptualization of God as Seen in Adjective Ratings. *Journal for the Scientific Study of Religion,* 7, 56–64.

Gorsuch, R. L. (1984). Measurement: The Boon and Bane of Investigating Religion. *American Psychologist,* 39, 228–236.

Gorsuch, R. L. (1988). Psychology of Religion. *Annual Review of Psychology,* 39, 201–221.

Gorsuch, R. L. (1990). Measurement in Psychology of Religion Revisited. *Journal of Psychology and Christianity,* 9, 82–92.

Gorsuch, R. L. (1995). Religious Aspects of Substance Abuse and Recovery. *Journal of Social Issues,* 51, 65–83.

Gorsuch, R. L., and Aleshire, D. (1974). Christian Faith and Ethnic Prejudice: A Review and Interpretation of Research. *Journal for the Scientific Study of Religion,* 13, 281–307.

Gorsuch, R. L., and McPherson, S. E. (1989). Intrinsic/Extrinsic Measurement: I/E-Revised and Single-Item Scales. *Journal for the Scientific Study of Religion,* 28, 348–354.

Graff, R. W., and Ladd, C. E. (1971). POI Correlates of a Religious Commitment Inventory. *Journal of Clinical Psychology,* 27, 502–504.

Grasmick, H. G., Bursik, R. J., and Kimpel, M. (1991). Protestant Fundamentalism and Attitudes Toward Corporal Punishment of Children. *Violence and Victims,* 6, 283–298.

Grass, K. (1915). Men of God. In J. Hastings, *Encyclopedia of Religion and Ethics,* Vol. 8, pp. 544–546.

Grass, K. (1920). Sects (Russian). II. Other Sects. In J. Hastings, *Encyclopedia of Religion and Ethics,* Vol. 11, pp. 339–343.

Graumann, C. F. (1988). Phenomenological Analysis and Experimental Method in Psychology—The Problem of Their Compatibility. *Journal for the Theory of Social Behaviour,* 18, 33–50.

Graves, R. (1960). *The Greek Myths ,* Vol. 1 (rev. ed.). Baltimore: Penguin.

Gray, E. D. (Ed.). (1988). *Sacred Dimensions of Women's Experience.* Wellesley, Mass.: Roundtable Press.

Gray, J. A. (Ed.). (1964). *Pavlov's Typology: Recent Theoretical and Experimental Developments from the Laboratory of B. M. Teplov.* Oxford: Pergamon Press.

Greeley, A. M. (1972). Comment on Hunt's "Mythological-Symbolic Religious Commitment: The LAM Scales." *Journal for the Scientific Study of Religion,* 11, 287–289.

Greeley, A. M. (1975). *The Sociology of the Paranormal: A Reconnaissance.* Sage Research Papers in the Social Sciences, vol. 3, series no. 90–023 (Studies in Religion and Ethnicity Series). Beverly Hills, Calif., and London: Sage Publications.

Green, C. W., and Hoffman, C. L. (1989). Stages of Faith and Perceptions of Similar and Dissimilar Others. *Review of Religious Research,* 30, 246–254.

Green, E. E., and Green, A. M. (1986). Biofeedback and States of Consciousness. In B. B. Wolman and M. Ullman, *Handbook of States of Consciousness,* pp. 553–589.

Green, E. E., Green, A. M., and Walters, E. D. (1970a). Self-Regulation of Internal States. In J. Rose (Ed.), *Progress of Cybernetics: Proceedings of the International Congress of Cybernetics, London, 1969.* London: Gordon & Breach, pp. 1299–1317.

Green, E. E., Green, A. M, and Walters, E. D. (1970b). Voluntary Control of Internal States: Psychological and Physiological. *Journal of Transpersonal Psychology,* 2, 1–26.

Greenberg, D., and Witztum, E. (1994). The Influence of Cultural Factors on Obsessive Compulsive Disorder: Religious Symptoms in a Religious Society. *Israeli Journal of Psychiatry and Related Sciences,* 31, 211–220.

Greenberg, J. R., and Mitchell, S. A. (1983). *Object Relations in Psychoanalytic Theory.* Cambridge, Mass.: Harvard University Press.

Greenwald, A. G. (1975). Does the Good Samaritan Parable Increase Helping? A Comment on Darley and Batson's No-Effect Conclusion. *Journal of Personality and Social Psychology,* 32, 578–583.

Greisheimer, E. M., and Wiedeman, M. P. (1972). *Physiology and Anatomy* (9th ed.). Philadelphia: J. B. Lippincott.

Grensted, L. W. (1952). *The Psychology of Religion.* London: Oxford University Press.

Gresser, M. (1994). *Dual Allegiance: Freud as a Modern Jew.* Albany: State University of New York Press.

Greven, P. (1991). *Spare the Child: The Religious Roots of Punishment and the Psychological Impact of Physical Abuse.* New York: Alfred A. Knopf.

Greyson, B. (1981). Near-Death Experiences and Attempted Suicide. *Suicide and Life-Threatening Behavior,* 11, 10–16.

Greyson, B. (1990). Near-Death Encounters With and Without Near-Death Experiences: Comparative NDE Scale Profiles. *Journal of Near-Death Studies,* 8, 151–161.

Greyson, B., and Bush, N. E. (1992). Distressing Near-Death Experiences. *Psychiatry,* 55, 95–110.

Griffin, G. A. E., Gorsuch, R. L., and Davis, A.-L. (1987). A Cross-Cultural Investigation of Religious Orientation, Social Norms, and Prejudice. *Journal for the Scientific Study of Religion,* 26, 358–365.

Grinspoon, L., and Bakalar, J. B. (1979). *Psychedelic Drugs Reconsidered.* New York: Basic Books.

Grinstein, A. (Ed.). (1956–1973). *The Index of Psychoanalytic Writings* (13 vols.). New York: International Universities Press.

Grof, S. (1972). Varieties of Transpersonal Experiences: Observations from LSD Psychotherapy. *Journal of Transpersonal Psychology,* 4, 45–80.

Grof, S. (1975). *Realms of the Human Unconscious: Observations from LSD Research.* New York: Viking.

Grof, S. (1985). *Beyond the Brain: Birth, Death, and Transcendence in Psychotherapy.* Albany: State University of New York Press.

Grof, S. (1988). *The Adventure of Self-Discovery.* Albany: State University of New York Press.

Grof, S. (1993). *The Holotropic Mind: The Three Levels of Human Consciousness and How They Shape Our Lives.* San Francisco: HarperSanFrancisco.

Grof, S., and Valier, M. L. (Eds.). (1988). *Human Survival and Consciousness Evolution.* Albany: State University of New York Press.

Grolnick, S. A., Barkin, L., and Muensterberger, W. (1978). *Between Reality and Fantasy: Transitional Objects and Phenomena.* New York: Jason Aronson.

Grom, B. (1981). Gottesvorstellung, Elternbild und Selbstwertgefühl. *Stimmen der Zeit,* 106, 697–711.

Grom, B. (1986). *Religionspädagogische Psychologie des Kleinkind-, Schul- und Jugenalters.* Düsseldorf: Patmos.

Grom, B. (1992). *Religionspsychologie.* Munich: Kösel; Göttingen: Vandenhoeck & Ruprecht.

Grønbaek, V. (1958). *Religionspsykologi. Forskere og forskning.* Copenhagen: Forlag Arnold Busck.

Grønbaek, V. (1964). Das religiöse Bilderlebnis bei 4– bis 7 jahrigen Kindern. *Archiv für Religionspsychologie,* 8, 85–98.

Grønbaek, V. (1967). *Seelsorge an alten Menschen.* Translated by E. Harbsmeier. Göttingen: Vandenhoeck & Ruprecht, 1969. (First Swedish edition 1967)

Grønbaek, V. (1969). Visuelle Vorstellungen im Gebetsleben alter Menschen. In C. Hörgl, K. Krenn, and F. Rauh (Eds.), *Wesen und Weisen der Religion.* Munich: Max Hueber, pp. 115–131.

Grønbaek, V. (1970). Die heutige Lage der Religionspsychologie. *Theologische Literaturzeitung,* 95, 321–327

Grønbaek, V. (1974). *Nogle linier i religionspsykologiens udvikling: Edwin D. Starbuck og William James i religionspsykologiens historie og nutid.* Lund: Studentlitteratur.

Grossmann, E. (1958). *Beiträge zur psychologischen Analyse der Reformatoren Luther und Calvin.* Basel: S. Karger.

Gruehn, W. (1924). *Das Werterlebnis: Eine religionspsychologische Studie auf experimenteller Grundlage.* Leipzig: S. Hirzel.

Gruehn, W. (1930). Forschungsmethoden und Ergebnisse der exakten empirischen Religionspsychologie seit 1921. In K. Girgensohn, *Der seelische Aufbau des religiösen Erlebens* (2nd ed.), pp. 703–898.

Gruehn, W. (1960). *Die Frömmigkeit der Gegenwart: Grundtatsachen der empirischen Psychologie* (2nd ed.). Konstanz: Friedrich Bahn. (First edition 1956)

Gründler, O. (1922). *Elemente zu einer Religionsphilosophie auf phänomenologischer Grundlage.* Munich: Josef Kösel & Friedrich Pustet.

Grzymala-Moszczynska, H. (1991). The Psychology of Religion in Poland. *International Journal for the Psychology of Religion,* 1, 243–247.

Guntrip, H. (1956). *Mental Pain and the Cure of Souls.* London: Independent Press.

Guntrip, H. (1961). *Personality Structure and Human Interaction.* London: Hogarth Press.

Guntrip, H. (1969a). Religion in Relation to Personal Integration. *British Journal of Medical Psychology,* 42, 323–333.

Guntrip, H. (1969b). *Schizoid Phenomena, Object Relations and the Self.* New York: International Universities Press.

Guntrip, H. (1971). *Psychoanalytic Theory, Therapy, and the Self.* New York: Basic Books, 1973. (First published 1971)

Guntrip, H. (1975). My Experience of Analysis with Fairbairn and Winnicott. *International Review of Psycho-Analysis,* 2, 145–156.

Gupta, M. N. (1897–1932). *The Gospel of Sri Ramakrishna.* Translated by Swami Nikhilananda. New York: Ramakrishna-Vivekananda Center, 1942. (Original Bengali edition 1897–1932)

Gussler, J. D. (1973). Social Change, Ecology, and Spirit Possession Among the South African Nguni. In E. Bourguignon (Ed.), *Religion, Altered States of Consciousness, and Social Change.* Columbus: Ohio State University Press, pp. 88–126.

Guth, J. L., Kellstedt, L. A., Smidt, C. E., and Green, J. C. (1993). Theological Perspectives and Environmentalism Among Religious Activists. *Journal for the Scientific Study of Religion,* 32, 373–382.

Guthrie, E. R. (1952). *The Psychology of Learning* (rev. ed.). New York: Harper & Row.

Guthrie, E. R. (1959). Association by Contiguity. In S. Koch (Ed.), *Psychology: A Study of a Science* (Vol. 2). New York: McGraw-Hill, pp. 158–195.

Habegger, A. (1994). *The Father: A Life of Henry James, Sr.* New York: Farrar, Straus and Giroux.

Haerich, P. (1992). Premarital Sexual Permissiveness

and Religious Orientation: A Preliminary Investigation. *Journal for the Scientific Study of Religion,* 31, 361–365.

Haile, H. G. (1980). *Luther: An Experiment in Biography.* Princeton, N.J.: Princeton University Press.

Hale, N. G., Jr. (Ed.). (1971). *James Jackson Putnam and Psychoanalysis.* Cambridge, Mass.: Harvard University Press.

Hall, C. S., and Lindzey, G. (1978). *Theories of Personality* (3rd ed.). New York: John Wiley & Sons.

Hall, G. S. (1882). The Moral and Religious Training of Children. *The Princeton Review,* 9, 26–48. (Reprinted in *Pedagogical Seminary,* 1891, 1, 196–210)

Hall, G. S. (1900). The Religious Content of the Child-Mind. In N. M. Butler et al., *Principles of Religious Education.* New York: Longmans, Green, pp. 161–189.

Hall, G. S. (1901). Some Fundamental Principles of Sunday School and Bible Teaching. *Pedagogical Seminary,* 8, 439–468.

Hall, G. S. (1904). *Adolescence: Its Psychology and Its Relations to Physiology, Anthropology, Sociology, Sex, Crime, Religion, and Education* (2 vols.). New York: D. Appleton.

Hall, G. S. (1917). *Jesus, the Christ, in the Light of Psychology.* New York: D. Appleton, 1923. (Reprint, with revised Introduction, of the original, two-volume edition by Doubleday, Page, 1917)

Hall, G. S. (1923). *Life and Confessions of a Psychologist.* New York: D. Appleton.

Hallesby, O. (1940). *Temperament and the Christian Faith.* Minneapolis: Augsburg Publishing House, 1962. (Original Norwegian edition 1940)

[Hallstrom], L. L. Marlin (1987). Embodied Truth: The Life and Presence of a Hindu Saint. *Harvard Divinity Bulletin,* 17(2), 5–6.

Hand, C. M., and Van Liere, K. D. (1984). Religion, Mastery-Over-Nature, and Environmental Concern. *Social Forces,* 63, 555–570.

Handy, R. T. (1984). *A Christian America: Protestant Hopes and Historical Realities* (rev. ed.). New York: Oxford University Press.

Hanna, J. L. (1988). The Representation and Reality of [Divinity] in Dance. *Journal of the American Academy of Religion,* 66, 281–306.

Hannah, B. (1976). *Jung, His Life and Work: A Biographical Memoir.* New York: G. P. Putnam's Sons.

Hansen, G. L. (1992). Religion and Marital Adjustment. In J. F. Schumaker, *Religion and Mental Health,* pp. 189–198.

Harding, M. E. (1935). *Women's Mysteries, Ancient and Modern* (rev. ed.). New York: Pantheon, 1955. (First edition 1935)

Hardy, A. (1975). *The Biology of God: A Scientist's Study of Man the Religious Animal.* New York: Taplinger, 1976. (First, British edition 1975)

Hardy, A. (1979). *The Spiritual Nature of Man: A Study of Contemporary Religious Experience.* Oxford: Oxford University Press.

Harms, E. (1944). The Development of Religious Experience in Children. *American Journal of Sociology,* 50, 112–122.

Harner, M. J. (Ed.). (1973). *Hallucinogens and Shamanism.* New York: Oxford University Press.

Harré, R. (Ed.). (1986). *The Social Construction of Emotions.* Oxford: Basil Blackwell.

Harris, M. (1977). *Cannibals and Kings: The Origins of Cultures.* New York: Vintage.

Harrison, J. E. (1927). *Themis: A Study of the Social Origins of Greek Religion* (2nd ed.). Published with *Epilegomena to the Study of Greek Religion.* New Hyde Park, N. Y.: University Books, 1962. (Originally published in this edition 1927)

Hartland, E. S. (1917). Phallism. In J. Hastings, *Encyclopedia of Religion and Ethics,* Vol. 9, pp. 815–831.

Hartmann, E. von. (1882). *Das religiöse Bewusstsein der Menschheit im Stufengang seiner Entwickelung.* Berlin: Carl Buncker.

Hartz, G. W. (1987). *Clinical Issues Raised by Fundamentalists Anonymous.* Paper presented at the convention of the American Psychological Association, New York, August.

Harvey, M. L., and Bell, P. A. (1995). The Moderating Effect of Threat on the Relationship Between Population Concern and Environmental Concern. *Population and Environment: A Journal of Interdisciplinary Studies,* 17, 123–133.

Harvey, V. A. (1995). *Feuerbach and the Interpretation of Religion.* Cambridge: Cambridge University Press.

Hastings, J. (Ed.). (1908–1926). *Encyclopaedia of Religion and Ethics* (13 vols.). Edinburgh: T. & T. Clark.

Haub, E. (1992). Die Messung der Religiosität: Empirische Grundlagen und Methode. In E. Schmitz, *Religionspsychologie,* pp. 263–279.

Havens, J. (Ed.). (1968). *Psychology and Religion: A Contemporary Dialogue.* Princeton, N.J.: Van Nostrand.

Hawkins, D., and Pauling, L. (Eds.). (1973). *Orthomolecular Psychiatry: Treatment of Schizophrenia.* San Francisco: W. H. Freeman.

Hawley, J. S. (Ed.). (1994). *Fundamentalism and Gender.* New York: Oxford University Press.

Hay, D., and Morisy, A. (1978). Reports of Ecstatic, Paranormal, or Religious Experience in Great Britain and the United States—A Comparison of Trends. *Journal for the Scientific Study of Religion,* 17, 255–268.

Haynes, C. T., Hebert, J. R., Reber, W., and Orme-Johnson, D. W. (1977). The Psychophysiology of Advanced Participants in the Transcendental Meditation Programme: Correlations of EEG Coherence, Creativity, H-Reflex Recovery, and Experience of Transcendental Consciousness. In D. W. Orme-Johnson and J. T. Farrow, *Scientific Research on the Transcendental Meditation Program,* pp. 208–212.

Healy, W., Bronner, A. F., and Bowers, A. M. (1930). *The Structure and Meaning of Psychoanalysis.* New York: Alfred A. Knopf.

Heath, D. H. (1969). Secularization and Maturity of Religious Beliefs. *Journal of Religion and Health*, 8, 335–358.

Hecker, J. F. C. (1837). *The Dancing Mania of the Middle Ages*. Translated by B. G. Babington. New York: Burt Franklin, 1970. (Originally published, 1837)

Heiler F. (1914). Die Entwicklung der Religionspsychologie. *Das Neue Jahrhundert: Wochenschrift für religiöse Kultur*, 6, 318–321, 326–330, 341–342, 352–355.

Heiler, F. (1918). *Das Gebet: Eine religionsgeschichtliche und religionspsychologische Untersuchung* (reprint of the 5th edition 1923, with literature supplement). Munich: Ernst Reinhardt, 1969. (First edition 1918)

Heiler, F. (1932). *Prayer: A Study in the History and Psychology of Religion*. Translated by S. McComb. New York: Oxford University Press. (Abridged translation of the 5th edition of Heiler, 1918)

Heiler, F. (1961). *Erscheinungsformen und Wesen der Religion*. Stuttgart: Kohlhammer.

Heim, A. (1892). Remarks on Fatal Falls. Translated by R. Noyes and R. Kletti. *Omega*, 1972, 3, 45–52. (Original German edition 1892)

Heimbrock, H.-G. (1977). *Phantasie und christlicher Glaube: Zum Dialog zwischen Theologie und Psychoanalyse*. Kaiser: Grünewald.

Heimbrock, H.-G. (1984). *Lern-Wege religiöser Erziehung: Historische, systematische und praktische Orientierung für eine Theorie religiöse Lernens*. Göttingen: Vandenhoeck & Ruprecht.

Heisig, J. W. (1973). Jung and Theology: A Bibliographical Essay. *Spring: An Annual of Archetypal Psychology and Jungian Thought*, 204–255.

Heisig, J. W. (1979). *Imago Dei: A Study of C. G. Jung's Psychology of Religion*. Lewisburg, Pa.: Bucknell University Press.

Heist, P., and Yonge, G. (1968). *Omnibus Personality Inventory, Form F: Manual*. New York: Psychological Corporation.

Heller, J. B. (1956). Freud's Mother and Father. *Commentary*, 21, 418–421. (Reprinted in Ruitenbeek, 1973)

Hellpach, W. (1907a). Zur "Formenkunde" der Beziehungen zwischen Religiosität und Abnormität. *Zeitschrift für Religionspsychologie*, 1, 97–110.

Hellpach, W. (1907b). Religiöse Wahnbildung bei thyreogener Erregung. Eine psychopathologische Analyse. *Zeitschrift für Religionspsychologie*, 1, 360–382.

Helson, R. (1971). Women Mathematicians and the Creative Personality. *Journal of Consulting and Clinical Psychology*, 36, 210–220.

Heltsley, M. E., and Broderick, C. B. (1969). Religiosity and Premarital Sexual Permissiveness: Reexamination of Reiss's Traditionalism Proposition. *Journal of Marriage and the Family*, 31, 441–443.

Helve, H. (1993). *The World View of Young People: A Longitudinal Study of Finnish Youth Living in a Suburb of Metropolitan Helsinki*. Helsinki: Suomalainen Tiedeakatemia.

Henderson, J. L. (1967). *Thresholds of Initiation*. Middleton, Conn.: Wesleyan University Press.

Henderson, L. A., and Glass, W. J. (Eds.). (1994). *LSD: Still With Us After All These Years*. New York: Lexington.

Henney, J. H. (1974). Spirit-Possession Belief and Trance Behavior in Two Fundamentalist Groups in St. Vincent. In F. D. Goodman, J. H. Henney, and E. Pressel, *Trance, Healing, and Hallucination: Three Field Studies in Religious Experience*. New York: John Wiley & Sons, pp. 1–111.

Herik, G. M. (1987). Religious Orientation and Prejudice: A Comparison of Racial and Sexual Attitudes. *Personality and Social Psychology Bulletin*, 13, 34–44.

Hermann, B. P., and Riel, P. (1981). Interictal Personality and Behavioral Traits in Temporal Lobe and Generalized Epilepsy. *Cortex*, 17, 125–128.

Hermans, H. J. M., and Kempen, H. J. G. (1993). *The Dialogical Self: Meaning as Movement*. San Diego, Calif.: Academic Press.

Herr, M. D. (1971). Day of Atonement. *Encyclopaedia Judaica*, 5, 1376–1384.

Hetherington, R. (1975). *The Sense of Glory: A Psychological Study of Peak-Experiences*. London: Friends Home Service Committee.

Hibben, J. G. (1903). [Review of] *The Varieties of Religious Experience*. *Psychological Review*, 10, 180–186.

Hicks, R. E., Fink, R. J., and Hammett, V. B. O. (Eds.). (1969). *Psychedelic Drugs*. New York: Grune & Stratton.

Higgins, N. C., Pollard, C. A., and Merkel, W. T. (1992) Relationship Between Religion-Related Factors and Obsessive Compulsive Disorder. *Current Psychology Research and Reviews*, 11, 79–85.

Hilgard, E. R. (1987). *Psychology in America: A Historical Survey*. San Diego: Harcourt Brace Jovanovich.

Hill, R. K. (1935). *Measurable Changes in Attitude Resulting from the Use of Drama in Worship*. A part of a doctoral dissertation, University of Chicago Divinity School, 1933. Chicago: Private edition, distributed by the University of Chicago Libraries.

Hillman, J. (1975). *Re-Visioning Psychology*. New York: Harper & Row.

Hilty, D. M., and Stockman, S. J. (1986). A Covariance Structure Analysis of the DeJong, Faulkner, and Warland Religious Involvement Model. *Journal for the Scientific Study of Religion*, 25, 483–493.

Himmelfarb, H. S. (1975). Measuring Religious Involvement. *Social Forces*, 53, 606–618.

Hine, V. M. (1969). Pentecostal Glossolalia: Toward a Functional Interpretation. *Journal for the Scientific Study of Religion*, 8, 211–266.

Hinkelman, E. A., and Aderman, M. (1968). Apparent Theoretical Parallels Between G. Stanley Hall and Carl Jung. *Journal of the History of the Behavioral Sciences*, 4, 254–257.

Hirai, T. (1974). *Psychophysiology of Zen.* Tokyo: Igaku Shoin.

Hirai, T. (1989). *Zen Meditation and Psychotherapy.* Tokyo and New York: Japan Publications.

Hirschi, T., and Stark, R. (1969). Hellfire and Delinquency. *Social Problems,* 17, 202–213.

Hjelle, L. A. (1974). Transcendental Meditation and Psychological Health. *Perceptual and Motor Skills,* 39, 623–628.

Hjelle, L. A. (1975). Relationship of a Measure of Self-Actualization to Religious Participation. *Journal of Psychology,* 89, 179–182.

Hocking, W. E. (1912). *The Meaning of God in Human Experience: A Philosophic Study of Religion.* New Haven, Conn.: Yale University Press.

Hodges, H. A. (1952). *The Philosophy of Wilhelm Dilthey.* London: Routledge & Kegan Paul.

Hoeller, S. A. (1982). *The Gnostic Jung and the Seven Sermons to the Dead.* Wheaton, Ill.: Theosophical Publishing House.

Höffding, H. (1901). *The Philosophy of Religion.* Translated from the German edition by B. E. Meyer. London: Macmillan, 1906. (First Danish edition 1901)

Höffding, H. (1918). *Erlebnis und Deutung. Eine vergleichende Studie zur Religionspsychologie.* Translated by E. Magnus. Stuttgart: Fr. Frommanns Verlag (H. Kurtz), 1923. (Original Danish edition 1918)

Hoffer, A., and Osmond, H. (1967). *The Hallucinogens.* New York: Academic Press.

Hogan, R. (1972). [Review of Study of Values]. In O. K. Buros (Ed.), *The Seventh Mental Measurements Yearbook,* Vol. 1. Highland Park, N.J.: Gryphon Press, pp. 355–356.

Hoge, D. R. (1974). *Commitment on Campus: Changes in Religion and Values Over Five Decades.* Philadelphia: Westminster.

Hoge, D. R., and Carroll, J. W. (1973). Religiosity and Prejudice in Northern and Southern Churches. *Journal for the Scientific Study of Religion,* 12, 181–187.

Hoge, D. R., and Carroll, J. W. (1975). Christian Beliefs, Nonreligious Factors and Anti-Semitism. *Social Forces,* 53 581–594.

Hole, G. (1977). *Der Glaube bei Depressiven: Religionspathologische und klinisch-statistische Untersuchung.* Stuttgart: Ferdinand Enke.

Holl, A., and Fischer, G. H. (1968). *Kirche auf Distanz: Eine religionspsychologische Untersuchung ber die Einstellung Österreichischer Soldaten zu Kirche und Religion.* Wien: Wilhelm Braumller.

Hollingworth, H. L. (1926). *The Psychology of Thought, Approached Through Studies of Sleeping and Dreaming.* New York: D. Appleton.

Holm, N. G. (Ed.). (1982). *Religious Ecstasy.* Stockholm: Almqvist & Wiksell.

Holm, N. G. (1987a). *Scandinavian Psychology of Religion.* Åbo: Åbo Akademi.

Holm, N. G. (1987b). Sundén's Role Theory and Glossolalia. *Journal for the Scientific Study of Religion,* 26, 383–389.

Holm, N. G., and Belzen, J. A. (Eds.). (1995). *Sundén's Role Theory—An Impetus to Contemporary Psychology of Religion.* Åbo: Åbo Akademi.

Holmes, A. (1929). *The Mind of St. Paul: A Psychological Study.* New York: Macmillan.

Holmes, D. S. (1987). The Influence of Meditation Versus Rest on Physiological Arousal: A Second Examination. In M. A. West (Ed.), *The Psychology of Meditation.* Oxford: Oxford University Press, pp. 81–103.

Holmyard, E. J. (1957). *Alchemy.* Baltimore: Penguin.

Homans, P. (1970). *Theology after Freud: An Interpretive Inquiry.* Indianapolis, Ind.: Bobbs-Merrill.

Homans, P. (1979). *Jung in Context: Modernity and the Making of a Psychology.* Chicago: University of Chicago Press.

Hong, K. M. (1978). The Transitional Phenomena: A Theoretical Integration. *The Psychoanalytic Study of the Child,* 33, 47–79.

Hood, R. W., Jr. (1970). Religious Orientation and the Report of Religious Experience. *Journal for the Scientific Study of Religion,* 9, 285–291.

Hood, R. W., Jr. (1971). A Comparison of the Allport and Feagin Scoring Procedures for Intrinsic/Extrinsic Religious Orientation. *Journal for the Scientific Study of Religion,* 10, 370–374.

Hood, R. W., Jr. (1972). Normative and Motivational Determinants of Reported Religious Experience in Two Baptist Samples. *Review of Religious Research,* 13, 192–196.

Hood, R. W., Jr. (1973). Religious Orientation and the Experience of Transcendence. *Journal for the Scientific Study of Religion,* 12, 441–448.

Hood, R. W., Jr. (1975). The Construction and Preliminary Validation of a Measure of Reported Mystical Experience. *Journal for the Scientific Study of Religion,* 14, 29–41.

Hood, R. W., Jr. (1976). Mystical Experience as Related to Present and Anticipated Future Church Participation. *Psychological Reports,* 39, 1127–1136.

Hood, R. W., Jr. (1977). Differential Triggering of Mystical Experience as a Function of Self Actualization. *Review of Religious Research,* 18, 264–270.

Hood, R. W., Jr. (1978). Anticipatory Set and Setting: Stress Incongruities as Elicitors of Mystical Experience in Solitary Nature Situations. *Journal for the Scientific Study of Religion,* 17, 279–287.

Hood, R. W., Jr. (Ed.). (1995). *Handbook of Religious Experience.* Birmingham, Ala.: Religious Education Press.

Hood, R. W., Jr., and Morris, R. J. (1985). Conceptualization of Quest: A Critical Rejoinder to Batson. *Review of Religious Research,* 26, 391–397.

Hood, R. W., Jr., Spilka, B., Hunsberger, B., and Gorsuch, R. (1996). *Psychology of Religion: An Empirical Approach* (2nd ed.). New York: Guilford.

Hood, R. W., Morris, R. J., and Watson, P. J. (1986).

Maintenance of Religious Fundamentalism. *Psychological Reports,* 59, 547–559.

Horne, J. (1988). *Why We Sleep: The Functions of Sleep in Humans and Other Mammals.* Oxford: Oxford University Press.

Horton, A. L., and Williamson, J. A. (Eds.). (1988). *Abuse and Religion: When Praying Isn't Enough.* New York: Lexington Books.

Horton, P. C. (1974). The Mystical Experience: Substance of an Illusion. *Journal of the American Psychoanalytic Association,* 22, 364–380.

Horton, W. M. (1924). The Origin and Psychological Function of Religion According to Pierre Janet. *American Journal of Psychology,* 35, 16–52.

Hostie, R. (1955). *Religion and the Psychology of Jung.* Translated by G. R. Lamb. London: Sheed and Ward, 1957. (Original French edition 1955)

Houston, J. (1987). *The Search for the Beloved.* Los Angeles: Jeremy P. Tarcher.

Houston, J., and Masters, R. E. L. (1972). The Experimental Induction of Religious-Type Experiences. In J. White, *The Highest State of Consciousness,* pp. 303–321.

Howard, G. S. (1993). On Certain Blindnesses in Human Beings: Psychology and World Overpopulation. *Counseling Psychologist,* 21, 560–581.

Howard, G. S. (1994). Reflections on Change in Science and Religion. *International Journal for the Psychology of Religion,* 4, 127–143.

Howden, J. C. (1873). The Religious Sentiment in Epileptics. *Journal of Mental Science,* 18, 482–497.

Huckaby, P. (1975). Survey of the Response to Behavioral Psychology in Recent Religious Literature. *Journal of Pastoral Care,* 29, 262–270.

Hufford, D. J. (1985). Commentary: Mystical Experience in the Modern World. In G. W. Foster, *The World Was Flooded with Light,* pp. 87–183.

Hume, D. (1757). *The Natural History of Religion.* Edited by H. E. Root. Stanford, Calif.: Stanford University Press, 1956. (First published 1757)

Humphreys, C. (1935). *Concentration and Meditation: A Manual of Mind Development* (rev. ed.). London: Watkins, 1968. (First edition 1935)

Hunsberger, B. (1992). The Psychology of Religion in Canada. *International Journal for the Psychology of Religion* 2, 47–55.

Hunsberger, B. (1995). Religion and Prejudice: The Role of Religious Fundamentalism, Quest, and Right-Wing Authoritarianism. *Journal of Social Issues,* 51, 113–129.

Hunsberger, B., and Platonow, E. (1986). Religion and Helping Charitable Causes. *Journal of Psychology,* 120, 517–528.

Hunt, R. A. (1968). The Interpretation of the Religious Scale of the Allport-Vernon-Lindzey Study of Values. *Journal for the Scientific Study of Religion,* 7, 65–77.

Hunt, R. A. (1972a). Mythological-Symbolic Religious Commitment: The LAM Scales. *Journal for the Scientific Study of Religion,* 11, 42–52.

Hunt, R. A. (1972b). Reply to Greeley. *Journal for the Scientific Study of Religion,* 11, 290–292.

Hunt, R. A., and King, M. (1971). The Intrinsic-Extrinsic Concept: A Review and Evaluation. *Journal for the Scientific Study of Religion,* 10, 339–356.

Hutsebaut, D. (1996a). Post-critical Belief: A New Approach to the Religious Attitude Problem. *Journal of Empirical Theology,* 9(2), 48–66.

Hutsebaut, D. (1996b). Personal communication, June 13.

Huxley, A. (1954). *The Doors of Perception.* New York: Harper.

Huxley, A. (1956). *Heaven and Hell.* London: Chatto & Windus.

Huxley, A. (1961). Visionary Experience. In J. White, *The Highest State of Consciousness.,* 1972, pp. 34–57. (From a speech delivered in 1961)

Huxley, J. (Organizer). (1966). A Discussion on Ritualization of Behavior in Animals and Man. *Philosophical Transactions of the Royal Society of London; Series B. Biological Sciences,* 251 (No. 772), 247–526.

Hyde, K. E. (1990). *Religion in Childhood and Adolescence: A Comprehensive Review of the Research.* Birmingham, Ala.: Religious Education Press.

Hyers, C. (1983). Once-born, Twice-born Zen: William James and the Rinzai and Soto Schools of Japanese Buddhism. In P. Slater and D. Wiebe (Eds.), *Traditions in Contact and Change.* Waterloo: Wilfred Laurier University Press, pp. 187–199.

Iannaccone, L. R. (1994). Why Strict Churches Are Strong. *American Journal of Sociology,* 99, 1180–1211.

Ideler, K. W. (1848–1850). *Versuch einer Theorie des religiösen Wahnsinns. Ein Beitrag zur Kritik der religiösen Wirren der Gegenwart* (2 vols.). Halle: Schwetschke & Sohn.

Imbens, A., and Jonker, I. (1985). *Christianity and Incest.* Translated by P. McVay. Minneapolis: Fortress Press, 1991. (Original Dutch edition 1985)

Ishill, J. (1940). Theodore Schroeder. In J. Ishill (Ed.), *A New Concept of Liberty, From an Evolutionary Psychologist: Theodore Schroeder: Selections from His Writings.* Berkeley Heights, N.J.: Oriole Press, pp. ix–xxx.

Jackson, D. N., and Messick, S. (Eds.). (1967). *Problems in Human Assessment.* New York: McGraw-Hill.

Jackson, L. E., and Coursey, R. D. (1988). The Relationship of God Control and Internal Locus of Control to Intrinsic Religious Motivation, Coping and Purpose in Life. *Journal for the Scientific Study of Religion,* 27, 399–410.

Jacobs, B. L. (1984). Postsynaptic Serotonergic Action of Hallucinogens. In B. L. Jacobs (Ed.), *Hallucinogens: Neurochemical, Behavioral, and Clinical Perspectives.* New York: Raven Press, pp. 183–202.

Jacobs, H. (1961). *Western Psychotherapy and Hindu-Sâdhanâ: A Contribution to Comparative Studies in Psychology and Metaphysics.* London: George Allen & Unwin.

Jacoby, H. J. (ca. 1939). *Changes of Character Produced*

by *Religious Conversions, as Shown in Changes of Handwriting* (Guild Lecture No. 6). London: Guild of Pastoral Psychology, n.d.

Jacquet, C. H., Jr. (Ed.). (1986). *Yearbook of American and Canadian Churches 1986*. Nashville, Tenn.: Abingdon Press.

Jaffe, L. W. (1990). *Liberating the Heart: Spirituality and Jungian Psychology*. Toronto: Inner City Books.

Jaffé, A. (Ed.). (1979). *C. G. Jung: Word and Image*. Princeton, N.J.: Princeton University Press.

Jahoda, M. (1958). *Current Concepts of Positive Mental Health*. New York: Basic Books.

Jahoda, M. (1977). *Freud and the Dilemmas of Psychology*. New York: Basic Books.

James, H. (Ed.). (1920). *The Letters of William James* (2 vols.). Boston: Little, Brown.

James, W. (1882). On Some Hegalisms. In *The Will to Believe*, 1897, pp. 196–221. (First published 1882)

James, W. (1890). *The Principles of Psychology* (3 vols.). Cambridge, Mass.: Harvard University Press, 1981. (Original edition 1890)

James, W. (1896). Louis Agassiz. In *Essays, Comments, and Reviews*. Cambridge, Mass.: Harvard University Press, 1987, pp. 1–16. (Addressed given in 1896)

James, W. (1897). *The Will to Believe and Other Essays in Popular Philosophy*. Cambridge, Mass.:: Harvard University Press, 1979. (Original edition 1897)

James, W. (1899). *Talks to Teachers On Psychology and To Students On Some of Life's Ideals*. Cambridge, Mass.: Harvard University Press, 1983. (Original edition 1899)

James, W. (1901). Frederick Myers' Services to Psychology. In *Essays in Psychical Research*. Cambridge, Mass.: Harvard University Press, 1986, pp. 192–202. (First published 1901)

James, W. (1902). *The Varieties of Religious Experience: A Study in Human Nature*. Cambridge, Mass.: Harvard University Press, 1985. (Original edition 1902)

James, W. (1907a). The Energies of Men. In *Essays in Religion and Morality*. Cambridge, Mass.: Harvard University Press, 1982, pp. 129–146. (First published 1907)

James, W. (1907b). *Pragmatism*. Cambridge, Mass.: Harvard University Press, 1976. (Original edition 1907)

Janet, P. (1926–1928). *De l'angoisse a l'extase, études sur les croyances et les sentiments* (2 vols.). Paris: Félix Alcan.

Jarrell, H. R. (1985). *International Meditation Bibliography, 1950–1982*. London: Scarecrow Press.

Jaynes, J. (1976). *The Origin of Consciousness in the Breakdown of the Bicameral Mind*. Boston: Houghton Mifflin.

Jelik, W. G. (1982). Altered States of Consciousness in North American Indian Ceremonials. *Ethos*, 10, 326–343.

Jelke, R. (1948). *Grundzüge der Religionspsychologie*. Heidelberg: Jedermann.

Jésus-Marie, B. de. (Ed.). (1948). *Satan*. London: Sheed and Ward, 1951. (Based on the French edition 1948)

Jésus-Marie, B. de. (Ed.). (1954). *Nos sens et Dieu*. Paris: Descleé de Brouwer.

Jevning, R., Wilson, A. F., and O'Halloran, J. P. (1982). Muscle and Skin Blood Flow and Metabolism During States of Decreased Activation. *Physiology and Behavior*, 29, 343–348.

Johnson, P. E. (1953). A Psychological Understanding of Prayer. *Pastoral Psychology*, 4(36), 33–39.

Johnson, P. E. (1959). *Psychology of Religion* (rev. ed.). New York: Abingdon Press. (First edition 1945)

Johnson, R. A. (Ed.). (1977). *Psychohistory and Religion: The Case of Young Man Luther*. Philadelphia: Fortress Press.

Johnson, R. A. (1979). *Congregations as Nurturing Communities: A Study of Nine Congregations of the Lutheran Church in America*. [Philadelphia]: Lutheran Church in America.

Johnson, R. W., George, D. T., and Saine, K. C. (1993). The Christian Orthodoxy Scale: A Validity Study. *Psychological Reports*, 72, 537–538.

Jonas, H. (1963). *The Gnostic Religion: The Message of the Alien God and the Beginnings of Christianity* (2nd ed.). Boston: Beacon Press.

Jones, B. H., and McNamara, K. (1991). Attitudes Toward Women and Their Work Roles: Effects of Intrinsic and Extrinsic Religious Orientations. *Sex Roles*, 24, 21–29.

Jones, E. (1913). The God Complex. In E. Jones, *Essays*, 1951, pp. 244–265. (First published, in German, in 1913)

Jones, E. (1914). The Madonna's Conception through the Ear. In E. Jones, *Essays*, 1951, pp. 266–357. (Published in a briefer German version 1914)

Jones, E. (1923). A Psycho-Analytic Study of the Holy Ghost Concept. In E. Jones, *Essays*, 1951, pp. 358–373. (First published, in German, in 1923)

Jones, E. (1927). The Psychology of Religion. In E. Jones, *Essays*, 1951, pp. 190–197. (First published 1927)

Jones, E. (1930). Psycho-Analysis and the Christian Religion. In E. Jones, *Essays*, 1951, pp. 198–211. (Lecture given in 1930)

Jones, E. (1951). *Essays in Applied Psycho-Analysis, Vol. 2: Essays in Folklore, Anthropology, and Religion*. London: Hogarth Press.

Jones, E. (1953). *The Life and Work of Sigmund Freud, Vol. 1: 1856–1900, The Formative Years and the Great Discoveries*. New York: Basic Books.

Jones, E. (1955). *The Life and Work of Sigmund Freud, Vol. 2: 1901–1919: Years of Maturity*. New York: Basic Books.

Jones, E. (1957). *The Life and Work of Sigmund Freud, Vol. 3: The Last Phase*. New York: Basic Books.

Jones, M. B. (1958). Religious Values and Authoritarian Tendency. *Journal of Social Psychology*, 48, 83–89.

Jones, R. M. (1947). *A Call to What Is Vital.* New York: Macmillan.

Jones, S. L. (1994). A Constructive Relationship for Religion With the Science and Profession of Psychology. *American Psychologist,* 49, 184–199. (Reprinted in Shafranske, 1996)

Jones, V. (1970). Attitudes of College Students and Their Changes: A 37-Year Study. *Genetic Psychology Monographs,* 81, 3–80.

Jonte-Pace, D. (1987). Object Relations Theory, Mothering, and Religion: Toward a Feminist Psychology of Religion. *Horizons,* 14, 310–327.

Jordan, G. R., Jr. (1963). LSD and Mystical Experiences. *Journal of Bible and Religion,* 31, 114–123. (Reprinted in J. White, 1972)

Jordan, G. R., Jr. (1971). Psychedelics and Zen: Some Reflections. *The Eastern Buddhist,* 4, 138–140.

Josselson, R., and Lieblich, A. (Eds.). (1995). *Interpreting Experience: The Narrative Study of Lives,* Vol. 3. Thousand Oaks, Calif.: Sage.

Jourard, S. M. (1974). *Healthy Personality: An Approach from the Viewpoint of Humanistic Psychology.* New York: Macmillan.

Joy, D. M. (1983). *Moral Development Foundations: Judeo-Christian Alternatives to Piaget/Kohlberg.* Nashville, Tenn.: Abingdon Press.

Juan, I. R., Raiva, R. E. A., Haley, H. B., and O'Keefe, R. D. (1974). High and Low Levels of Dogmatism in Relation to Personality Characteristics of Medical Students: A Follow-up Study. *Psychological Reports,* 34, 303–315.

Julian of Norwich. (1901). *Revelations of Divine Love.* Edited by G. Warrack. London: Methuen.

Jung, C. G. (1953–1979). *The Collected Works of C. G. Jung* (20 vols.). Edited by H. Read, M. Fordham, and G. Adler; translated by R. F. C. Hull (except for Vol. 2, translated by L. Stein and D. Riviere). Princeton, N.J.: Princeton University Press.

Jung, C. G. (1921). *Psychological Types.* In *Collected Works,* Vol. 6, 1971. (German edition 1921)

Jung, C. G. (1929). Freud and Jung: Contrasts. In *Collected Works,* Vol. 4, 1961, pp. 333–340. (First German edition 1929)

Jung, C. G. (1931a). Basic Postulates of Analytical Psychology. In *Collected Works,* Vol. 8 (2nd ed.), 1969, pp. 338–357. (First German edition 1931)

Jung, C. G. (1931b). The Spiritual Problem of Modern Man. In *Collected Works,* Vol. 10 (2nd ed.), 1969, pp. 74–94. (Revised German edition 1931)

Jung, C. G. (1931c). The Stages of Life. In *Collected Works,* Vol. 8 (2nd ed.), 1969, pp. 387–403. (Revised German edition 1931)

Jung, C. G. (1932). Psychotherapists or the Clergy. In *Collected Works,* Vol. 11 (2nd ed.), 1969, pp. 327–347. (First German edition 1932)

Jung, C. G. (1933). *Modern Man in Search of a Soul.* New York: Harcourt, Brace.

Jung, C. G. (1934). A Review of the Complex Theory. In *Collected Works,* Vol. 8 (2nd ed.), 1969, pp. 92–104. (First German edition 1934)

Jung, C. G. (1935). The Relations Between the Ego and the Unconscious. In *Collected Works,* Vol. 7 (2nd ed.), 1966, pp. 121–241. (Second German edition 1935)

Jung, C. G. (1936). The Concept of the Collective Unconscious. In *Collected Works,* Vol. 9, Part I (2nd ed.), 1968, pp. 42–53. (Originally published in English, 1936)

Jung, C. G. (1938). Psychology and Religion. In *Collected Works,* Vol. 11 (2nd ed.), 1969, pp. 3–105. (Originally published in English, 1938)

Jung, C. G. (1943a). On the Psychology of the Unconscious. In *Collected Works,* Vol. 7 (2nd ed.), 1966, pp. 1–119. (Fifth German edition 1943)

Jung, C. G. (1943b). The Psychology of Eastern Meditation. In *Collected Works,* Vol. 11 (2nd ed.), 1969, pp. 558–575. (First German edition 1943)

Jung, C. G. (1948a). The Phenomenology of the Spirit in Fairytales. In *Collected Works,* vol. 9, Part I (2nd ed.), 1968, pp. 207–254. (Revised German edition 1948)

Jung, C. G. (1948b). A Psychological Approach to the Dogma of the Trinity. In *Collected Works,* Vol. 11 (2nd ed.), 1969, pp. 107–200. (Revised German edition 1948)

Jung, C. G. (1949). The Father in the Destiny of the Individual. In *Collected Works,* Vol. 4, 1961, pp. 301–323. (Third German edition 1949)

Jung, C. G. (1951a). *Aion: Researches into the Phenomenology of the Self.* In *Collected Works,* Vol. 9, Part II (2nd ed.), 1968. (First German edition 1951)

Jung, C. G. (1951b). The Psychological Aspects of the Kore. In *Collected Works,* Vol. 9, Part I (2nd ed.), 1968, pp. 182–203. (Fourth German edition 1951)

Jung, C. G. (1951c). The Psychology of the Child Archetype. In *Collected Works,* Vol. 9, Part I (2nd ed.), 1968, pp. 149–181. (Fourth German edition 1951)

Jung, C. G. (1952a). Answer to Job. In *Collected Works,* Vol. 11 (2nd ed.), 1969, pp. 355–470. (First German edition 1952)

Jung, C. G. (1952b). *Psychology and Alchemy.* In *Collected Works,* Vol. 12 (2nd ed.), 1968. (Revised German edition 1952)

Jung, C. G. (1952c). *Symbols of Transformation: An Analysis of the Prelude to a Case of Schizophrenia.* In *Collected Works,* Vol. 5 (2nd ed.), 1967. (Fourth German edition 1952)

Jung, C. G. (1952d). Synchronicity: An Acausal Connecting Principle. In *Collected Works,* Vol. 8 (2nd ed.), 1969, pp. 417–519. (First German edition 1952)

Jung, C. G. (1954a). Archetypes of the Collective Unconscious. In *Collected Works,* Vol. 9, Part I (2nd ed.), 1968, pp. 3–41. (Revised German edition 1954)

Jung, C. G. (1954b). Concerning the Archetypes, with Special Reference to the Anima Concept. In *Col-*

lected Works, Vol. 9, Part I (2nd ed.), 1968, pp. 54–72. (Revised German edition 1954)

Jung, C. G. (1954c). The Philosophical Tree. In Collected Works, Vol. 13, 1967, pp. 251–349. (Revised German edition 1954)

Jung, C. G. (1954d). On the Psychology of the Trickster Figure. In Collected Works, Vol. 9, Part I (2nd ed.), 1968, pp. 255–272. (First German edition 1954)

Jung, C. G. (1954e). Psychological Aspects of the Mother Archetype. In Collected Works, Vol. 9, Part I (2nd ed.), 1968, pp. 73–110. (Revised German edition 1954)

Jung, C. G. (1954f). Transformation Symbolism in the Mass. In Collected Works, Vol. 11 (2nd ed.), 1969, pp. 201–296. (Revised German edition 1954)

Jung, C. G. (1954g). The Visions of Zosimos. In Collected Works, Vol. 13, 1967, pp. 57–108. (Revised German edition 1954)

Jung, C. G. (1955–1956). Mysterium Coniunctionis: An Inquiry into the Separation and Synthesis of Psychic Opposites in Alchemy. In Collected Works, Vol. 14 (2nd ed.), 1970. (First German edition 1955–1956)

Jung, C. G. (1957). The Undiscovered Self (Present and Future). In Collected Works, Vol. 10 (2nd ed.), 1969, pp. 245–305. (First German edition 1957)

Jung, C. G. (1958). The Transcendent Function. In Collected Works, Vol. 8 (2nd ed.), 1969, pp. 67–91. (Revised German edition 1958)

Jung, C. G. (1962). Memories, Dreams, Reflections. Recorded and edited by A. Jaffé and translated by R. and C. Winston. New York: Pantheon, 1963. (German edition 1962)

Jung, C. G. (1969). Psychology and Religion: West and East (2nd ed.). In Collected Works, Vol. 11.

Jung, E. (1934). On the Nature of the Animus. Translated by C. F. Baynes. In E. Jung, Animus and Anima. New York: Spring, 1972, pp. 1–43. (Original German edition 1934)

Jung, E., and von Franz, M.-L. (1960). The Grail Legend. Translated by A. Dykes. New York: G. P. Putnam's Sons, 1970. (Original German edition 1960)

Jurji, E. D. (1975). Psychoanalytic Anthropology: Orthodox Psychoanalysis in American Anthropology as Found in the Work of Géza Róheim, Weston La Barre and George Devereux (University of Washington, 1974). Dissertation Abstracts International, 36, 3831a-3832a. (University Microfilms No. 75-28,370)

Kabat-Zinn, J. (1994). Wherever You Go There You Are: Mindfulness Meditation in Everyday Life. New York: Hyperion.

Källstad, T. (1974). John Wesley and the Bible: A Psychological Study. Stockholm: Nya Bokförlags Aktiebolaget.

Källstad, T. (Ed.). (1978). Psychological Studies on Religious Man. Stockholm: Almqvist & Wiksell.

Kagan, J. (1984). The Nature of the Child. New York: Basic Books.

Kahoe, R. D. (1974a). Personality and Achievement Correlates of Intrinsic and Extrinsic Religious Orientations. Journal of Personality and Social Psychology, 29, 812–818.

Kahoe, R. D. (1974b). The Psychology and Theology of Sexism. Journal of Psychology and Theology, 2, 284–290.

Kahoe, R. D. (1975). Authoritarianism and Religion: Relationships of F Scale Items of Intrinsic and Extrinsic Religious Orientations. JSAS Catalog of Selected Documents in Psychology, 5, 284–285. (Ms. No. 1020)

Kahoe, R. D. (1992). A birthday for psychology of religion? Newsletter of Division 36, American Psychological Association, 17(3), 9.

Kahoe, R. D., and Dunn, R. F. (1975). The Fear of Death and Religious Attitudes and Behavior. Journal for the Scientific Study of Religion, 14, 379–382.

Kakar, S. (1978). The Inner World: A Psycho-analytic Study of Childhood and Society in India (2nd ed.). Delhi: Oxford University Press, 1981. (First edition 1978)

Kaldestad, E. (1991). Intrinsic, Extrinsic, and Quest Scales: Development of Norwegian Versions. In O. Wikström (Ed.), Klinisk religions psykologi. Uppsala: Uppsala Universitet, Teologiska institutionen, pp. 85–101.

Kales, A. (Ed.). (1969). Sleep: Physiology and Pathology: A Symposium. Philadelphia: J. B. Lippincott.

Kamiya, J. (1969). Operant Control of the EEG Alpha Rhythm and Some of Its Reported Effects on Consciousness. In C. T. Tart, Altered States of Consciousness, pp. 600–611. (First published in the 1969 edition)

Kane, S. M. (1987). Appalachian Snake Handlers. In J. C. Cobb and C. R. Wilson (Eds.), Perspectives on the American South, Vol. 4. New York: Gordon and Breach, pp. 115–127.

Kantrowitz, B. (1994). In Search of the Sacred. Newsweek, November 28, pp. 53–55.

Karlins, M., and Andrews, L. M. (1972). Biofeedback: Turning on the Power of Your Mind. Philadelphia: J. B. Lippincott.

Kasamatsu, A., and Hirai, T. (1966). An Electroencephalographic Study on the Zen Meditation (Zazen). Folio Psychiatrica Neurologica Japonica, 20, 315–336. (Reprinted without figures in Tart, 1990)

Kassel, M. (1980). Biblische Urbilder: Tiefenpsychologische Auslegung nach C. G. Jung. Munich: J. Pfeiffer.

Katz, M. M., Waskow, I. E., and Olsson, J. (1968). Characterizing the Psychological State Produced by LSD. Journal of Abnormal Psychology, 73, 1–14.

Katz, S. T. (1978). Language, Epistemology, and Mysticism. In S. T. Katz (Ed.), Mysticism and Philosophical Analysis. New York: Oxford University Press, pp. 22–74.

Kaufmann, W. (1958). Critique of Religion and Philoso-

phy. Garden City, N.Y.: Anchor, 1961. (First published in 1958)

Kaye, H. L. (1986). *The Social Meaning of Modern Biology: From Social Darwinism to Sociobiology*. New Haven, Conn.: Yale University Press.

Keintzel, R. (1991). *C. G. Jung: Retter der Religion? Auseinandersetzung mit Werk und Wirkung*. Mainz: Matthais-Grünewald-Verlag.

Kelley, D. M. (1972). *Why Conservative Churches Are Growing: A Study in Sociology of Religion* (2nd ed.). New York: Harper & Row, 1977. (First edition 1972)

Kelsey, M. T. (1974). *God, Dreams, and Revelation: A Christian Interpretation of Dreams* Minneapolis: Augsburg Publishing House.

Kelsey, M. T. (1982). *Christo-Psychology*. New York: Crossroad.

Kemp, C. G. (1960). Changes in Values in Relation to Open-Closed Systems. In M. Rokeach, *The Open and Closed Mind: Investigations into the Nature of Belief Systems and Personality Systems*. New York: Basic Books, pp. 335–346.

Kendler, H. H. (1981). *Psychology: A Science in Conflict*. New York: Oxford University Press.

Kendler, H. H. (1987). A Good Divorce is Better Than a Bad Marriage. *Annals of Theoretical Psychology*, 5, 55–89.

Keniston, K. (1965). *The Uncommitted: Alienated Youth in American Society*. New York: Harcourt, Brace, and World.

Kennedy, E. C. (1974). *Believing*. Garden City, N. Y.: Doubleday.

Kennedy, E. C., and Heckler, V. J. (1972). *The Catholic Priest in the United States: Psychological Investigations*. Washington, D.C.: United States Catholic Conference.

Kennedy, E. C., Heckler, V. J., Kobler, F. J., and Walker, R. E. (1977). Clinical Assessment of a Profession: Roman Catholic Clergymen. *Journal of Clinical Psychology*, 33, 120–128.

Kerr, J. (1993). *A Most Dangerous Method: The Story of Jung, Freud, and Sabina Spielrein*. New York: Alfred A. Knopf.

Kerr, J. (1994). Madnesses. *London Review of Books*, 17 (March 23), 3, 5–6.

Keys, A., Brozek, J., Henschel, A., Mickelsen, O., and Taylor, H. L. (1950). *The Biology of Human Starvation* (2 vols.). Minneapolis: University of Minnesota Press.

Kieval, H. (1971). Kol Nidrei. *Encyclopaedia Judaica*, 10, 1166–1167.

Kildahl, J. (1972). *The Psychology of Speaking in Tongues*. New York: Harper & Row.

Kilpatrick, D. G., Sutker, L. W., and Sutker, P. B. (1970). Dogmatism, Religion, and Religiosity, a Review and Re-evaluation. *Psychological Reports*, 26, 15–22.

King, M. [B.] (1967). Measuring the Religious Variable: Nine Proposed Dimensions. *Journal for the Scientific Study of Religion*, 6, 173–190.

King, M. B., and Hunt, R. A. (1969). Measuring the Religious Variable: Amended Findings. *Journal for the Scientific Study of Religion*, 8, 321–323.

King, M. B., and Hunt, R. A. (1972a). Measuring the Religious Variable: Replication. *Journal for the Scientific Study of Religion*, 11, 240–251.

King, M. B., and Hunt, R. A. (1972b). *Measuring Religious Dimensions: Studies of Congregational Involvement*. Dallas: Southern Methodist University.

King, M. B., and Hunt, R. A. (1975a). Measuring the Religious Variable: National Replication. *Journal for the Scientific Study of Religion*, 14, 13–22.

King, M. B., and Hunt, R. A. (1975b). Religious Dimensions: Entities or Constructs? *Sociological Focus*, 8, 57–63.

King, M.B., and Hunt, R. A. (1990). Measuring the Religious Variable: Final Comment. *Journal for the Scientific Study of Religion*, 29, 531–535.

King, S. (1988). Two Epistemological Models for the Interpretation of Mysticism. *Journal of the American Academy of Religion*, 56, 257–279.

King, U. (1993). *Women and Spirituality: Voices of Protest and Promise* (2nd ed.). University Park, Pa.: Pennsylvania State University Press.

King, W. P. (Ed.). (1930). *Behaviorism—A Battle Line*. Nashville, Tenn.: Cokesbury Press.

Kirk, G. S. (1970). *Myth: Its Meaning and Functions in Ancient and Other Cultures*. London: Cambridge University Press.

Kirkpatrick, C. (1949). Religion and Humanitarianism: A Study of Institutional Implications. *Psychological Monographs*, 63, No. 9 (Whole No. 304).

Kirkpatrick, C., and Stone, S. (1935). Attitude Measurement and the Comparison of Generations. *Journal of Applied Psychology*, 5, 564–582.

Kirkpatrick, L. A. (1989). A Psychometric Analysis of the Allport-Ross and Feagin Measures of Intrinsic-Extrinsic Religious Orientation. *Research in the Social Scientific Study of Religion*, 1, 1–31.

Kirkpatrick, L. A. (1992). An Attachment-Theory Approach to the Psychology of Religion. *International Journal for the Psychology of Religion*, 2, 3–28.

Kirkpatrick, L. A. (1995a). Attachment Theory and Religious Experience. In R. W. Hood, Jr., *Handbook of Religious Experience*, pp. 446–475.

Kirkpatrick, L. A. (1995b). On the Use and Misuse of Quantitative Methods in the Psychology of Religion. *Newsletter of Division 36, American Psychological Association*, 20(1), 1–3.

Kirkpatrick, L. A., and Hood, R. W., Jr. (1990). Intrinsic-Extrinsic Religious Orientation: The Boon or Bane of Contemporary Psychology of Religion? *Journal for the Scientific Study of Religion*, 29, 442–462.

Kirkpatrick, L. A., and Spilka, B. (1989). *The Treatment of Religion in Psychology Textbooks: A Review and Analysis of Past and Current Trends*. Paper presented at the convention of the American Psychological Association, New Orleans, August.

Kirscht, J. P., and Dillehay, R. C. (1967). *Dimensions*

of Authoritarianism: A Review of Research and Theory. Lexington: University of Kentucky Press.

Klages, L. (1927). Die "religiöse Kurve" in der Handschrift. *Zeitschrift für Menschenkunde, 2, 1–8.*

Klein, D. B. (1981). *Jewish Origins of the Psychoanalytic Movement.* New York: Praeger.

Klein, M. (1928). Early Stages of the Oedipus Conflict. In *Love, Guilt and Reparation & Other Works 1921–1945.* New York: Delacorte Press, 1975, pp. 186–198. (First published 1928)

Klein, M. (1932). *The Psychoanalysis of Children.* (rev. ed.). Translated by A. Strachey and revised by H. A. Thorner in collaboration with A. Strachey. New York: Delacorte Press. (Original German edition 1932)

Klünker, W.-U. (1985). *Psychologische Analyse und theologische Wahrheit: Die religionspsychologische Methode Georg Wobbermins.* Göttingen: Vandenhoeck & Ruprecht.

Knapp, R. R. (1990). *Handbook for the Personal Orientation Inventory* (2nd ed.). San Diego: Edits.

Knapp, T. J. (1985). Who's Who in American Introductory Psychology Textbooks: A Citation Study. *Teaching of Psychology, 12, 15–17.*

Knöpfelmacher, F., and Armstrong, D. B. (1963). The Relation Between Authoritarianism, Ethnocentrism and Religious Denomination among Australian Adolescents. *American Catholic Sociological Review, 24, 99–114.*

Knutsson, D. E., and Selinus, R. (1970). Fasting in Ethiopia; An Anthropological and Nutritional Study. *American Journal of Clinical Nutrition, 23, 956–969.*

Koch, E. (1896). *Die Psychologie in der Religionswissenschaft.* Freiburg: J. C. B. Mohr (Paul Siebeck).

Koch, S., and Leary, D. E. (Eds.). (1985). *A Century of Psychology as Science.* New York: McGraw Hill.

Köhler, W. (1921). *The Mentality of Apes* (2nd ed.). Translated by E. Winter. New York: Harcourt, Brace, 1927. (Second German edition 1921)

Koella, W. P. (1970). Central Nervous Effects of LSD-25. In B. Aaronson and H. Osmond, *Psychedelics,* pp. 198–213.

Koenig, H. G. (1990). Research on Religion and Mental Health in Later Life: A Review and Commentary. *Journal of Geriatric Psychiatry, 23, 23–53.*

Koenig, H. G. (1993). Religion and Aging. *Reviews in Clinical Gerontology, 3, 195–203.*

Koenig, H. G., Kvale, J. N., and Ferrel, C. (1988). Religion and Well-Being in Later Life. *Gerontologist, 28, 18–28.*

Koepp, W. (1920). *Einführung in das Studium der Religionspsychologie.* Tübingen: J. C. B. Mohr (Paul Siebeck).

Köster, F. (1986). *Religiöse Erziehung in den Weltreligionen. Hinduismus, Buddhismus, Islam.* Darmstadt: Wissenschaftliche Buchgesellschaft.

Kohlberg, L. (1981). *The Philosophy of Moral Development: Moral Stages and the Idea of Justice.* San Francisco: Harper & Row.

Kohut, H. (1966). Forms and Transformations of Narcissism. *Journal of the American Psychoanalytic Association, 14, 243–272.*

Kohut, H. (1971). *The Analysis of the Self.* New York: International Universities Press.

Kohut, H. (1977). *The Restoration of the Self.* New York: International Universities Press.

Kojetin, B. A., McIntosh, D. N., Bridges, R. A., and Spilka, B. (1987). Quest: Constructive Search or Religious Conflict? *Journal for the Scientific Study of Religion, 26, 111–115.*

Kolbanovskii, V. N. (1969). Soveshchanie po problemain psikhologii religii. *Voprosy Psikhologii, 15(4),* 178–182.

Kollar, E. J., Slater, G. R., Palmer, J. O., Docter, R. F., and Mandell, A. J. (1964). Measurement of Stress in Fasting Man: A Pilot Study. *Archives of General Psychiatry, 11, 113–125.*

Kotre, J. (1984). *Outliving the Self: Generativity and the Interpretation of Lives.* Baltimore: Johns Hopkins University Press.

Kovel, J. (1974). Erik Erikson's Psychohistory. *Social Policy, 4(5), 60–64.*

Kovel, J. (1990). Beyond the Future of an Illusion: Further Reflections on Freud and Religion. *Psychoanalytic Review, 77, 69–87.*

Kraft, W. A., Litwin, W. J., and Barber, S. E. (1987). Religious Orientation and Assertiveness: Relationship to Death Anxiety. *Journal of Social Psychology, 127, 93–95.*

Kretschmer, E. (1961). *Körperbau und Charakter: Untersuchungen zum Konstitutionsproblem und zur Lehre von den Temperamenten* (23rd and 24th ed.). Berlin: Springer.

Kretschmer, W. (1955). *Psychologische Weisheit der Bibel: Urbilder des Seins und Werdens im biblischen Schöpfungsbericht.* Munich: Lehnen.

Krippner, S. (Ed.). (1972). The Plateau Experience: A. H. Maslow and Others. *Journal of Transpersonal Psychology, 4, 107–120.*

Kroeger, O., and Thuesen, J. M. (1988). *Type Talk: The 16 Personality Types That Determine How We Live, Love, and Work.* New York: Delta.

Krüll, M. (1979). *Freud and His Father.* Translated by A. J. Pomerans. New York: W. W. Norton, 1986. (Original German edition 1979)

Kryvelev, I. A. (1961). Overcoming the Vestiges of Religion in the Lives of the Peoples of the USSR. *Soviet Anthropology and Archaeology, 1(2), 11–21.* (Original Russian edition 1961)

Kubose, S. K. (1976). An Experimental Investigation of Psychological Aspects of Meditation. *Psychologia, 19, 1–10.*

Kühnholz, W. (1978). Sexualitt—Eine uralte Geschichte (Gen 3). In Y. Spiegel, *Doppeldeutlich,* pp. 35–43.

Küng, H. (1979). *Freud and the Problem of God.* Translated by E. Quinn. New Haven, Conn.: Yale University Press.

Kuhre, B. E. (1971). The Religious Involvement of

the College Student from a Multi-Dimensional Perspective. *Sociological Analysis,* 32, 61–69.

Kushner, H. I. (1993). Taking Erikson's Identity Seriously: Psychoanalyzing the Psychohistorian. *The Psychohistory Review,* 22, 7–34.

Kvale, S. (1992). *Psychology and Postmodernism.* London: Sage.

Kwilecki, S. (1986). Religious Orientation and Personality: A Case Study. *Review of Religious Research,* 28, 16–28.

La Barre, W. (1938). *The Peyote Cult* (enlarged edition). New York: Schocken, 1969. (Original edition 1938)

La Barre, W. (1958). The Influence of Freud on Anthropology. *American Imago,* 15, 275–328.

La Barre, W. (1962). *They Shall Take Up Serpents: Psychology of the Southern Snake-Handling Cult.* Minneapolis: University of Minnesota Press.

La Barre, W. (1966). Géza Róheim: Psychoanalysis and Anthropology. In F. Alexander, S. Eisenstein, and M. Grotjahn (Eds.), *Psychoanalytic Pioneers.* New York: Basic Books, pp. 272–281.

La Barre, W. (1972). *The Ghost Dance: The Origins of Religion* (rev. ed.). New York: Delta, 1972. (First edition 1970)

Lacroze, R. (1970). *Maine de Biran.* Paris: Presses Universitaires de France.

Laforgue, R. (1956). Personal Memories of Freud. In H. M. Ruitenbeek, *Freud as We Knew Him,* 1973, pp. 341–349.

Lajoie, D. H., and Shapiro, S. I. (1992). Definitions of Transpersonal Psychology: The First Twenty-Three Years. *Journal of Transpersonal Psychology,* 24, 79–98.

Lambert, W. W., Triandis, L. M., and Wolf, M. (1959). Some Correlates of Beliefs in the Malevolence and Benevolence of Supernatural Beings: A Cross-Societal Study. *Journal of Abnormal and Social Psychology,* 58, 162–169.

Lammers, A. C. (1994). *In God's Shadow: The Collaboration of Victor White and C. G. Jung.* New York: Paulist Press.

Lancaster, E. G. (1895). The Psychology and Pedagogy of Adolescence. *Pedagogical Seminary,* 5, 61–128.

Landis, B., and Tauber, E. S. (Eds.). (1971). *In the Name of Life: Essays in Honor of Erich Fromm.* New York: Holt, Rinehart and Winston.

Landsborough, D. (1987). St. Paul and Temporal Lobe Epilepsy. *Journal of Neurology, Neurosurgery, and Psychiatry,* 50, 659–664.

Lang, A. (1957). *Wesen und Wahrheit der Religion.* Munich: Max Hueber.

Lange, A. (1971). *De autoritaire persoonlijkheid en zijn godsdienstige wereld.* Assen: Van Gorcum.

Langer, G. (1928). Zur Funktion der jüdischen Türpfostenrolle. *Imago,* 14, 457–468.

Langer, G. (1930). Die jüdischen Gebetsriemen. *Imago,* 16, 435–485.

Langer, S. K. (1942). *Philosophy in a New Key: A Study in the Symbolism of Reason, Rite, and Art* (3rd ed.). Cambridge, Mass.: Harvard University Press, 1957. (First edition 1942)

Langer, S. K. (1972). *Mind: An Essay on Human Feeling,* Vol. 2. Baltimore: Johns Hopkins University Press.

Langfeld, H. S. (1914). On the Psycho-Physiology of a Prolonged Fast. *Psychological Monographs,* 16(5, Whole No. 71).

Lans, J. M. van der. (Ed.). (1979). *Proceedings of the Colloquy of European Psychologists of Religion at Nijmegen, August, 20–23, 1979.* Nijmegen: Department for the Psychology of Culture and Religion, Catholic University.

Lans, J. M. van der. (Ed.). (1982). *Proceedings of the Second Symposion on the Psychology of Religion at Nijmegen, August 23–26, 1982.* Nijmegen: Department for the Psychology of Culture and Religion, Catholic University.

Lans, J. M. van der. (1987). The Value of Sundén's Role-Theory Demonstrated and Tested with Respect to Religious Experiences in Meditation. *Journal for the Scientific Study of Religion,* 26, 401–412.

Lans, J. M. van der. (1991). Interpretation of Religious Language and Cognitive Style: A Pilot Study With the LAM Scale. *International Journal for the Psychology of Religion,* 1, 107–123.

Larsen, L., and Knapp, R. H. (1964). Sex Differences in Symbolic Conceptions of the Deity. *Journal of Projective Techniques and Personality Assessment,* 28, 303–306.

Larson, D. B., Sherrill, K. A., and Lyons, J. S. (1994). Neglect and Misuse of the *R* Word: Systematic Reviews of Religious Measures in Health, Mental Health, and Aging. In J. S. Levin, *Religion in Aging and Health,* pp. 178–195.

Laski, M. (1961). *Ecstasy: A Study of Some Secular and Religious Experiences.* London: Cresset Press.

Leahey, T. H. (1980). The Myth of Operationism. *Journal of Mind and Behavior,* 1, 127–143.

Leak, G. K. (1992). Religiousness and Social Interest: An Empirical Assessment. *Individual Psychology,* 48, 288–301.

Leak, G. K., and Fish, S. (1989). Religious Orientation, Impression Management, and Self-Deception: Toward a Clarification of the Link Between Religiosity and Social Desirability. *Journal for the Scientific Study of Religion,* 28, 355–359.

Leak, G. K., and Randall, B. A. (1995). Clarification of the Link Between Right-Wing Authoritarianism and Religiousness: The Role of Religious Maturity. *Journal for the Scientific Study of Religion,* 34, 245–252.

Leary, D. E. (1990). *Metaphors in the History of Psychology.* Cambridge: Cambridge University Press.

Leary, T. (1964). The Religious Experience: Its Production and Interpretation. *Psychedelic Review,* 1, 324–346. (Reprinted in Weil, Metzner, and Leary, 1965)

Leary, T., and Clark, W. H. (1963). Religious Implications of Consciousness Expanding Drugs. *Religious Education*, 58, 251–256.

Le Clair, R. C. (Ed.). (1966). *The Letters of William James and Thodore Flournoy.* Madison: University of Wisconsin Press.

Lee, R. B. (1968). The Sociology of !Kung Bushman Trance Performances. In R. Prince, *Trance and Possession States*, pp. 35–54.

Lee, R. S. (1949). *Freud and Christianity*. London: James Clark.

Lee, R. S. (1963). *Your Growing Child and Religion: A Psychological Account.* New York: Macmillan.

Lee, R., and Piercy, F. P. (1974). Church Attendance and Self-Actualization. *Journal of College Student Personnel*, 15, 400–403.

Lehman, E. C., Jr., and Shriver, D. W., Jr. (1968). Academic Discipline as Predictive of Faculty Religiosity. *Social Forces*, 47, 171–182.

Lehman, H. C., and Witty, P. A. (1931). Scientific Eminence and Church Membership. *Scientific Monthly*, 33, 544–549.

Lehmann, H. (1915). Über die Disposition zum Gebet und zur Andacht. Vorschälge und Materialien zu einer religionspsychologischen Untersuchung nach der Erhebungsmethode. *Zeitschrift für angewandte Psychologie*, 10, 1–61.

Lehr, E., and Spilka, B. (1989). Religion in the Introductory Psychology Textbook: A Comparison of Three Decades. *Journal for the Scientific Study of Religion*, 28, 366–371.

Lenski, G. (1961). *The Religious Factor: A Sociological Study of Religion's Impact on Politics, Economics, and Family Life.* Garden City, N. Y.: Doubleday.

Lepp, I. (1963). *Atheism in Our Time.* New York: Macmillan.

Le Rider, J. (1993). "Great is Diana of the Ephesians": Masculine-Feminine-Jewish Triangle from Goethe to Freud. *The Psychohistory Review*, 22, 267–293.

LeShan, L. (1974). *How to Meditate: A Guide to Self-Discovery.* Boston: Little, Brown.

Leuba, J. H. (1896). A Study in the Psychology of Religious Phenomena. *American Journal of Psychology*, 7, 309–385.

Leuba, J. H. (1897). The Psycho-Physiology of the Moral Imperative. *American Journal of Psychology*, 8, 528–559.

Leuba, J. H. (1904). Professor William James' Interpretation of Religious Experience. *International Journal of Ethics*, 14, 322–329.

Leuba, J. H. (1912). *A Psychological Study of Religion: Its Origin, Function, and Future.* New York: Macmillan.

Leuba, J. H. (1916). *The Belief in God and Immortality: A Psychological, Anthropological and Statistical Study* (2nd ed.). Chicago: Open Court, 1921. (First edition 1916)

Leuba, J. H. (1925). *The Psychology of Religious Mysticism.* New York: Harcourt, Brace.

Leuba, J. H. (1933). *God or Man? A Study of the Value of God to Man.* New York: Henry Holt.

Leuba, J. H. (1934). Religious Beliefs of American Scientists. *Harper's Magazine*, 169, 291–300.

Leuba, J. H. (1937). The Making of a Psychologist of Religion. In V. Ferm, *Religion in Transition*, pp. 173–200.

Leuba, J. H. (1950). *The Reformation of the Churches.* Boston: Beacon Press.

Levin, J. S. (1994a). Religion and Health: Is There an Association, Is It Valid, and Is It Causal? *Social Science and Medicine*, 38, 589–600.

Levin, J. S. (Ed.). (1994b). *Religion in Aging and Health: Theoretical Foundations and Methodological Frontiers.* Thousand Oaks, Calif.: Sage.

Levin, J. S., and Schiller, P. L. (1987). Is There a Religious Factor in Health? *Journal of Religion and Health*, 26, 9–36.

Levin, J. S., and Vanderpool, H. Y. (1987). Is Frequent Religious Attendance *Really* Conducive to Better Health? Toward an Epidemology of Religion. *Social Science and Medicine*, 24, 589–600.

Levin, R. (1990). Psychoanalytic Theories on the Function of Dreaming: A Review of the Empirical Dream Research. In J. Masling (Ed.), *Empirical Studies of Psychoanalytic Theories*, Vol. 3. Hillsdale, N.J.: Analytic Press, pp. 1–53.

Levy, J. (1974). Psychobiological Implications of Bilateral Asymmetry. In S. Dimond and J. G. Beaumont (Eds.), *Hemisphere Function in the Human Brain.* London: Paul Elek, pp. 121–183.

Levy, L. (1917). Sexualsymbolik in der biblischen Paradiesgeschichte. *Imago*, 5, 16–30.

Levy, L. W. (1960). *Legacy of Suppression: Freedom of Speech and Press in Early American History.* Cambridge, Mass.: Harvard University Press.

Lewis, A. J. (1962). *Zinzendorf, The Ecumenical Pioneer: A Study of the Moravian Contribution to Christian Mission and Unity.* Philadelphia: Westminster Press.

Lewis, C. A. (1994). Religiosity and Obsessionality: The Relationship Between Freud's "Religious Practices." *Journal of Psychology*, 128, 189–196.

Lex, B. W. (1979). The Neurobiology of Ritual Trance. In E. G. d'Aquili et al., *The Spectrum of Ritual*, pp. 117–151.

Leys, W. (1932). *The Religious Control of Emotion.* New York: Ray Long & Richard R. Smith.

Lhermitte, J. (1956). *True and False Possession.* Translated by P. J. Hepburne-Scott. New York: Hawthorn, 1963. (Original French edition 1956)

Lindenthal, J. J., Myers, J. K., Pepper, M. P., and Stern, M. S. (1970). Mental Status and Religious Behavior. *Journal for the Scientific Study of Religion*, 9, 143–149.

Lindskoog, D., and Kirk, R. E. (1975). Some Life-History and Attitudinal Correlates of Self-Actualization Among Evangelical Seminary Students. *Journal for the Scientific Study of Religion*, 14, 51–55.

Link, A. S., and McCormick, R. L. (1983). *Progressivism.* Arlington Heights, Ill.: Harlan Davidson.

Linn, M., Fabricant, S., and Linn, D. (1988). *Healing the Eight Stages of Life.* Mahwah, N.J.: Paulist Press.

Loeb, J. (1912). *The Mechanistic Conception of Life.* Chicago: University of Chicago Press.

Long, E. L., Jr. (1952). *Religious Beliefs of American Scientists.* Philadelphia: Westminster Press.

Lorand, S. (1957). Dream Interpretation in the Talmud (Babylonian and Graeco-Roman Period.). *International Journal of Psychoanalysis,* 38, 92–97.

Lorenz, K. (1949). *King Solomon's Ring: New Light on Animal Ways.* Translated by M. K. Wilson. New York: Thomas Y. Crowell, 1952. (Original German edition 1949)

Lowry, R. J. (1973). *A. H. Maslow: An Intellectual Portrait.* Monterey, Calif.: Brooks/Cole.

Lowry, R. J. (Ed.). (1979). *The Journals of A. H. Maslow* (2 vols.). Monterey, Calif.: Brooks/Cole.

Lubin, A. J. (1958). A Feminine Moses: A Bridge Between Childhood Identifications and Adult Identity. *International Journal of Psycho-Analysis,* 39, 535–546.

Lubin, A. J. (1959). A Boy's View of Jesus. *Psychoanalytic Study of the Child,* 14, 155–168.

Lubin, M. (1969). Study of the High Rate of Male Jewish Membership in the Profession of Psychoanalysis. *Proceedings of the 77th Annual Convention of the American Psychological Association,* 4(Pt. 2), 527–528.

Luce, T. S., Briggs, S. R., and Francis, J. C. (1987). *Religiosity and Rokeach's Value Survey: A Comparison in Three Samples.* Paper presented at the convention of the American Psychological Association, New York, N.Y., August.

Lundahl, C. R. (Ed.). (1982). *A Collection of Near-Death Research Readings.* Chicago: Nelson-Hall.

Lurie, W. (1937). A Study of Spranger's Value Type by the Method of Factor Analysis. *Journal of Social Psychology,* 8, 17–38.

Lyall, S. (1995). Schools Stumble Over a Tough Commandment. *The New York Times* (May 2), p. A4.

MacCulloch, J. A. (1912). Fasting (Introductory and non-Christian). In J. Hastings, *Encyclopedia of Religion and Ethics,* Vol. 5, pp. 759–765.

Mackenzie, B. D. (1977). *Behaviourism and the Limits of Scientific Method.* Atlantic Highlands, N.J.: Humanities Press.

MacLeod, R. B. (1952). Experimental Psychology. In H. N. Fairchild et al., *Religious Perspectives in College Teaching.* New York: Ronald Press, pp. 262–285.

MacLeod, R. B. (1964). Phenomenology: A Challenge to Experimental Psychology. In T. W. Wann (Ed.), *Behaviorism and Phenomenology: Contrasting Bases for Modern Psychology.* Chicago: University of Chicago Press, pp. 47–74.

MacLeod, R. B. (1969). *William James: Unfinished Business.* Washington, D.C.: American Psychological Association.

Macmurray, J. (1936). *The Structure of Religious Experience.* New Haven, Conn.: Yale University Press.

MacRae, D. R. (1977). The Relationship of Psychological Needs to God Concept and Religious Perceptions (Rosemead Graduate School of Psychology, 1977). *Dissertation Abstracts International,* 38, 1954B–1955B. (University Microfilms No. 77–21,528)

Madden, M. C., and Madden, E. H. (1979). The Psychosomatic Illnesses of William James. *Thought: Fordham University Quarterly,* 54, 376–392.

Mahgoub, O. M., and Abdel-Hafeiz, H. B. (1991). Pattern of Obsessive-Compulsive Disorder in Eastern Saudi Arabia. *British Journal of Psychiatry,* 158, 840–842.

Maidenbaum, A., and Martin, S. A. (Eds.). (1991). *Lingering Shadows: Jungians, Freudians, and Anti-Semitism.* Boston: Shambhala.

Maier, N. R. F. (1949). *Frustration: A Study of Behavior Without a Goal.* New York: McGraw-Hill.

Makarec, K., and Persinger, M. A. (1985). Temporal Lobe Signs: Electroencephalographic Validity and Enhanced Scores in Special Populations. *Perceptual and Motor Skills,* 60, 831–842.

Malan, J. (1932). The Possible Origin of Religion as a Conditioned Reflex. *American Mercury,* 25, 314–317.

Malleus Maleficarum of Heinrich Kramer and James Sprenger. (1487). Translated with supplementary material by M. Summers. New York: Dover, 1971. (First published in 1928; original Latin edition ca. 1487)

Malone, M. T. (1983). Traditionalist-Renewalist Tensions: William James and a Modest Conciliatory Proposal. *Anglican Theological Review,* 65, 167–176.

Malony, H. N., and Lovekin, A. A. (1985). *Glossolalia: Behavioral Science Perspectives on Speaking in Tongues.* New York: Oxford University Press.

Mann, U. (1973). *Einführung in die Religionspsychologie.* Darmstadt: Wissenschaftliche Buchgesellschaft.

Manuel, F. E. (1983). *The Changing of the Gods.* Hanover, N.H.: University Press of New England.

Maranell, G. M. (1967). An Examination of Some Religious and Political Attitude Correlates of Bigotry. *Social Forces,* 45, 356–362.

Maranell, G. M. (1968). A Factor Analytic Study of Some Selected Dimensions of Religious Attitude. *Sociology and Social Research,* 52, 430–437.

Maranell, G. M. (1974). *Responses to Religion: Studies in the Social Psychology of Religious Belief.* Lawrence: University Press of Kansas.

Maranell, G. M., and Razak, W. N. (1970). A Comparative Study of the Factor Structure Among Professors and Clergymen. *Journal for the Scientific Study of Religion,* 9, 137–141.

Marchal, J. (1924). *Studies in the Psychology of the Mystics.* Translated by A. Thorold. London: Burns, Oates, and Washbourne, 1927. (Original French edition 1924)

Margreth, J. (1909). Amerikanische Religionspsychologie, in ihrer Grundlage geprüft. *Der Katholik:*

Zeitschrift für katholische Wissenschaft und kirchliches Leben, 40, 223–229.

Martin, J., and Westbrook, M. (1973). Religion and Sex in a University Sample: Data Bearing on Mol's Hypothesis. *Australian Journal of Psychology,* 25, 71–79.

Martin, L. H., and Goss, J. (Eds.). (1985). *Essays on Jung and the Study of Religion.* Lanham, Md.: University Press of America.

Martindale, C. (1978). Hemispheric Asymmetry and Jewish Intelligence Test Patterns. *Journal of Consulting and Clinical Psychology,* 46, 1299–1301.

Marty, M. E., and Appleby, R. S. (1991). Conclusion: An Interim Report on a Hypothetical Family. In M. E. Marty and R. S. Appleby (Eds.), *Fundamentalisms Observed.* Chicago: University of Chicago Press, pp. 814–842.

Marty, M. E., and Appleby, R. S. (1992). *The Glory and the Power: The Fundamentalist Challenge to the Modern World.* Boston: Beacon Press.

Maslow, A. H. (1964). *Religions, Values, and Peak-Experiences.* Columbus: Ohio State University Press.

Maslow, A. H. (1966). *The Psychology of Science: A Reconnaissance.* New York: Harper & Row.

Maslow, A. H. (1968). *Toward a Psychology of Being* (2nd ed.). New York: Van Nostrand Reinhold.

Maslow, A. H. (1970). *Motivation and Personality* (2nd ed.). New York: Harper & Row. (First edition 1954)

Maslow, A. H. (1971). *The Farther Reaches of Human Nature.* New York: Viking.

Masson, J. M. (1984). *The Assault on Truth: Freud's Suppression of the Seduction Theory.* New York: Farrar, Straus and Giroux.

Masters, R. E. L. (1974). Consciousness and Extra-Ordinary Phenomena. *Journal of Altered States of Consciousness,* 1, 153–167.

Masters, R. E. L., and Houston, J. (1966). *The Varieties of Psychedelic Experience.* New York: Holt, Rinehart and Winston.

Masters, R.E. L., and Houston, J. (1972). *Mind Games.* New York: Viking Press.

Masters, R. E. L., and Houston, J. (1973). Subjective Realities. In B. Schwartz (Ed.), *Human Connection and the New Media.* Englewood Cliffs, N. J.: Prentice-Hall, pp. 88–106.

Mathes, E. W., Zevon, M. A., Roter, P. M., and Joerger, S. M. (1982). Peak Experience Tendencies: Scale Development and Theory Testing. *Journal of Humanistic Psychology,* 22(3), 92–108.

Matlock, D. T. (1973). The Social Psychology of Prejudice: The Religious Syndrome and a Belief in Free will (University of Texas, Austin, 1972). *Dissertation Abstracts International,* 33, 3775A-3776A. (University Microfilms No. 73–480)

May, Robert (1980). *Sex and Fantasy: Patterns of Male and Female Development.* New York: W. W. Norton.

May, Rollo. (1939). *The Art of Counseling: How to Gain and Give Mental Health.* New York: Abingdon-Cokesbury Press.

May, Rollo. (1940). *The Springs of Creative Living: A Study of Human Nature and God.* New York: Abingdon-Cokesbury Press.

May, Rollo. (1953). *Man's Search for Himself.* New York: W. W. Norton.

May, Rollo. (1957). The Relation Between Psychotherapy and Religion. In J. E. Fairchild (Ed.), *Personal Problems & Psychological Frontiers: A Cooper Union Forum.* New York: Sheridan House, pp. 168–187.

May, Rollo. (1973). *Paulus: Reminiscences of a Friendship.* New York: Harper & Row.

May, Rollo, Angel, E., and Ellenberger, H. F. (Eds.). (1958). *Existence: A New Dimension in Psychiatry and Psychology.* New York: Basic Books.

Mayer, R. W. (1959). Religious Attitudes of Scientists (Ohio State University, 1959). *Dissertation Abstracts International,* 20, 2412–2413. (University Microfilms No. 59–5921)

McCann, R. V. (1962). *The Churches and Mental Health.* New York: Basic Books.

McClain, E. W. (1979). Religious Orientation the Key to Psychodynamic Differences between Feminists and Nonfeminists. *Journal for the Scientific Study of Religion,,* 18, 40–45.

McCrae, R. R., and Costa, P. T., Jr. (1989). Reinterpreting the Myers-Briggs Type Indicator from the Perspective of the Five-Factor Model of Personality. *Journal of Personality,* 57, 17–40.

McDargh, J. (1983). *Psychoanalytic Object Relations Theory and the Study of Religion: On Faith and the Imaging of God.* Lanham, Md.: University Press of America. (Doctoral dissertation, Harvard University, 1981)

McDermott, J. J. (Ed.). (1967). *The Writings of William James: A Comprehensive Edition.* New York: Random House.

McDougall, W. (1908). *An Introduction to Social Psychology.* London: Methuen.

McFarland, S. G. (1989). Religious Orientations and the Targets of Discrimination. *Journal for the Scientific Study of Religion,* 28, 324–336.

McHugh, P. R. (1995). Jung at Heart. *American Scholar,* 64, 617–618, 620, 622.

McIntosh, D. (1979). The Empirical Bearing of Psychoanalytic Theory. *International Journal of Psycho-Analysis,* 60, 405–431.

McKenna, R. [J.] (1976). Good Samaritanism in Rural and Urban Settings: A Nonreactive Comparison of Helping Behavior of Clergy and Control Subjects. *Representative Research in Social Psychology,* 7, 58–65.

McKenzie, J. L. (1954). The Literary Characteristics of Genesis 2–3. *Theological Studies,* 15, 541–572.

McKinney, D. W., Jr. (1973). *The Authoritarian Personality Studies: An Inquiry into the Failure of Social Science Research to Produce Demonstrable Knowledge.* The Hague: Mouton.

McLaughlin, S. A., and Malony, H. N. (1984). Near-Death Experiences and Religion: A Further Investigation. *Journal of Religion and Health,* 23, 149–159.

Meadow, M. J., and Kahoe, R. D. (1984). *Psychology of Religion: Religion in Individual Lives.* New York: Harper & Row.

Meckel, D. J., and Moore, R. L. (Eds.). (1992). *Self and Liberation: The Jung/Buddhism Dialogue.* New York: Paulist Press.

Meduna, L. J. (1958). *Carbon Dioxide Therapy: A Neurophysiological Treatment of Nervous Disorders* (2nd ed.). Springfield, Ill.: Charles C. Thomas.

Mehta, V. (1976). *Mahatma Gandhi and His Apostles.* New York: Viking.

Meiler, W. (1967). *Grundformen und Fehlformen der Religiosität und Gläubigkeit des Kindes.* Würzburg: Echter.

Meissner, W. W. (1961). *Annotated Bibliography in Religion and Psychology.* New York: Academy of Religion and Mental Health.

Meissner, W. W. (1984). *Psychoanalysis and Religious Experience.* New Haven, Conn.: Yale University Press.

Meissner, W. W. (1987). *Life and Faith: Psychological Perspectives on Religious Experience.* Washington, D. C.: Georgetown University Press.

Menashe, A. (1983). *The Face of Prayer.* New York: Alfred A. Knopf.

Meng, H., and Freud, E. L. (Eds.). (1963). *Psychoanalysis and Faith: The Letters of Sigmund Freud and Oskar Pfister.* Translated by E. Mosbacher. New York: Basic Books, 1963. (Original German edition 1963)

Meredith, G. M. (1968). Personality Correlates to Religious Belief Systems. *Psychological Reports,* 23, 1039–1042.

Merriam, T. W. (1935). Religion in the College Curriculum Today. *Journal of Religion,* 15, 462–470.

Merton, T. (1966). [Comments on Prince and Savage's Mystical States and the Concept of Religion (1966)]. *The R. M. Bucke Memorial Society Newsletter,* 1(1), 4–5.

Merton, T. (1968). The Wild Places. In R. Disch (Ed.), *The Ecological Conscience: Values for Survival.* Englewood Cliffs, N.J.: Prentice-Hall, 1970, pp. 37–43. (First published 1968)

Messer, S. B., Sass, L. A., and Woolfolk, R. L. (Eds.). (1988). *Hermeneutics and Psychological Theory: Interpretive Perspectives on Personality, Psychotherapy, and Psychopathology.* New Brunswick, N.J.: Rutgers University Press.

Metzner, R. (Ed.). (1968). *The Ecstatic Adventure.* New York: Macmillan.

Metzner, R. (1971). *Maps of Consciousness.* New York: Macmillan.

Meyer, D. H. (1971). The Scientific Humanism of G. Stanley Hall. *Journal of Humanistic Psychology,* 11, 201–213.

Michael, C. P., and Norrisey, M. C. (1984). *Prayer and Temperament: Different Prayer Forms for Different Personality Types.* Charlottesville, Va.: Open Door.

Michaelson, R. (1964). *The Scholarly Study of Religion in College and University.* New Haven, Conn.: The Society for Religion in Higher Education.

Mickley, J. R., Carson, V., and Soeken, K. L. (1995). Religion and Adult Mental Health: State of the Science in Nursing. *Issues in Mental Health Nursing,* 16, 345–360.

Mickley, J. R., Soeken, K., and Belcher, A. (1992). Spiritual Well-Being, Religiousness and Hope Among Women With Breast Cancer. *Journal of Nursing Education,* 24, 267–272.

Middleton, E. (1779–1786). *Biographia Evangelica; or, An Historical Account of the Lives and Deaths of the Most Eminent and Evangelical Authors or Preachers, Both British and Foreign, in the Several Denominations of Protestants . . . .* (4 vols.). London: Printed by J. W. Pasham for the author.

Middleton, R. (1973). Do Christian Beliefs Cause Anti-Semitism? *American Sociological Review,* 38, 33–52.

Middleton, R., and Putney, S. (1962). Religion, Normative Standards, and Behavior. *Sociometry,* 25, 141–152.

Miike, D. (1968). Psychological Study on the Individual Differences of Electroencephalography. In Y. Akishige, *Psychological Studies on Zen,* Vol. 1, 1977, pp. 207–224. (First published in 1968)

Mikulas, W. L. (1981). Buddhism and Behavior Modification. *Psychological Record,* 31, 331–342.

Milanesi, G., and Aletti, M. (1973). *Psicologia della religione.* Torino: Elle Di Ci.

Miles, W. R. (1964). Oxygen Consumption During Three Yoga-Type Breathing Patterns. *Journal of Applied Physiology,* 19, 75–82.

Milgram, S. (1974). *Obedience to Authority.* New York: Harper & Row.

Miller, D. H. (1959). *Ghost Dance.* New York: Duell, Sloan and Pearce.

Miller, D. L. (1981). *The New Polytheism: Rebirth of the Gods and Goddesses.* Dallas: Spring.

Miller, D. L. (Ed.). (1995). *Jung and the Interpretation of the Bible.* New York: Continuum.

Miller, W. R., and Martin, J. E. (Eds.). (1988). *Behavior Therapy and Religion: Integrating Spiritual and Behavioral Approaches to Change.* Newbury Park, Calif.: Sage.

Mills, G. K., and Campbell, K. (1974). A Critique of Gellhorn and Kiely's Mystical States of Consciousness. *Journal of Nervous and Mental Disease,* 159, 191–195.

Minton, B., and Spilka, B. (1976). Perspectives on Death in Relation to Powerlessness and Form of Personal Religion. *Omega,* 7, 261–268.

Moacanin, R. (1986). *Jung's Psychology and Tibetan Buddhism: Western and Eastern Paths to the Heart.* London: Wisdom.

Moller, H. (1965). Affective Mysticism in Western Civilization. *Psychoanalytic Review,* 52, 259–274.

Moller, H. (1971). The Social Causation of Affective Mysticism. *Journal of Social History,* 4, 305–338.

Moltmann, J. (1973). *The Crucified God: The Cross of*

Christ as the Foundation and Criticism of Christian Theology. Translated by R. A. Wilson and J. Bowden. New York: Harper & Row, 1974. (Second German edition 1973)

Monaghan, R. R. (1967). Three Faces of the True Believer: Motivations for Attending a Fundamentalist Church. *Journal for the Scientific Study of Religion,* 6, 236–245.

Money-Kyrle, R. (1929). *The Meaning of Sacrifice.* London: Hogarth Press.

Monick, E. (1987). *Phallos: Sacred Image of the Masculine.* Toronto: Inner City Books.

Montmorand, M. de. (1920). *Psychologie des mystiques catholiques orthodoxes.* Paris: Félix Alcan.

Moody, R. A., Jr. (1975). *Life After Life.* Harrisburg, Pa.: Stackpole Books, 1976. (First published 1975)

Moody, R. A., Jr. (1977). *Reflections on Life After Life.* Covington, Ga.: Mockingbird Books.

Moore, J. M. (1938). *Theories of Religious Experience, with Special Reference to James, Otto, and Bergson.* New York: Round Table Press.

Moore, R. L. (1979). *John Wesley and Authority: A Psychological Perspective.* Missoula, Mont.: Scholars Press.

Moore, R. L. (Ed.). (1988). *Carl Jung and Christian Spirituality.* Mahwah, N.J.: Paulist Press.

Moore, R. L., and Meckel, D. J. (Eds.). (1990). *Jung and Christianity in Dialogue: Faith, Feminism, and Hermeneutics.* New York: Paulist Press.

Moore, T. W. (1980). James Hillman: Psychology With Soul. *Religious Studies Review,* 6, 278–285.

Moore, T. (1992). *Care of the Soul: A Guide for Cultivating Depth and Sacredness in Everyday Life.* New York: HarperCollins.

Moraleda, M. (1977). *La actitud religiosa de los adolescentes: Bases para una interpretación psicológica.* Madrid: Editorial Bruño.

Morel, F. (1918). *Essai sur l'introversion mystique: étude psychologique de Pseudo-Denys l'Areopagite et de quelques autres cas de mysticisme.* Geneva: Albert Kundig.

Moreno, A. (1970). *Jung, Gods, and Modern Man.* Notre Dame: University of Notre Dame Press.

Moretti, G. (1952). *The Saints Through Their Handwriting.* Translated by S. Hughes. New York: Macmillan, 1964. (Original Italian edition 1952)

Morgulis, S. (1923). *Fasting and Undernutrition: A Biological and Sociological Study of Inanition.* New York: E. P. Dutton.

Morin, A. J. (1980). Sociobiology and Religion: Conciliation or Confrontation? *Zygon,* 15, 295–306.

Morris, R. J., Hood, R. W., and Watson, P. J. (1989). A Second Look at Religious Orientation, Social Desirability, and Prejudice. *Bulletin of the Psychonomic Society,* 27, 81–84.

Morse, M. (1990). *Closer to the Light: Learning from the Near-Death Experiences of Children.* New York: Villard Books.

Morse, W. H., and Skinner, B. F. (1957). A Second Type of "Superstition" in the Pigeon. *The American Journal of Psychology,* 70, 308–311. (Reprinted in Skinner, 1972)

Moxon, C. (1922). Epileptic Traits in Paulus of Tarsus. *Psychoanalytic Review,* 9, 60–66.

Mudge, E. L. (1923). *The God-Experience: A Study in the Psychology of Religion.* Cincinnati: Caxton Press.

Muelder, W. G. (1957). The Efficacy of Prayer. In S. Doniger (Ed.), *Healing: Human and Divine.* New York: Association Press, pp. 131–143.

Müller, F. M. (1898). *Râmakrishna, His Life and Sayings.* London: Longmans, Green.

Müller-Pozzi, H. (1979). Die Religionspsychologie im zwanzigsten Jahrhundert. In *Die Psychologie des 20. Jahrhunderts,* Vol. 15. Zurich: Kindler, pp. 76–84.

Muensterberger, W. (Ed.). (1969). *Man and His Culture: Psychoanalytic Anthropology after "Totem and Taboo."* New York: Taplinger.

Mulholland, T. B. (1972). Occipital Alpha Revisited. *Psychological Bulletin,* 78, 176–182.

Mullen, J. J. (1927). Psychological Factors in the Pastoral Treatment of Scruples. *Studies in Psychology and Psychiatry,* 1(3).

Mundkur, B. (1983). *The Cult of the Serpent: An Interdisciplinary Survey of Its Manifestations and Origins.* Albany: State University of New York Press.

Mungas, D. (1982). Interictal Behavior Abnormality in Temporal Lobe Epilepsy: A Specific Syndrome or Nonspecific Psychopathology? *Archives of General Psychiatry,* 39, 108–111.

Munroe, R. L. (1955). *Schools of Psychoanalytic Thought: An Exposition, Critique, and Attempt at Integration.* New York: Holt, Rinehart and Winston.

Murisier, E. (1892). *Maine de Biran, esquisse d'une psychologie religieuse.* Paris: Henri Jouve.

Murisier, E. (1901). *Les Maladies du sentiment religieux.* Paris: Félix Alcan.

Murphy, G. (1928). A Note on Method in the Psychology of Religion. *Journal of Philosophy,* 25, 337–345. (Reprinted in Strunk, 1959b)

Murphy, G. (1957). The Current Impact of Freud on American Psychology. In B. Nelson, *Freud and the 20th Century,* pp. 102–122.

Murphy, G., and Ballou, R. O. (Eds.). (1960). *William James on Psychical Research.* New York: Viking.

Murphy, G., and Dale, L. A. (1961). *Challenge of Psychical Research: A Primer of Parapsychology.* New York: Harper.

Murphy, G., and Kovach, J. K. (1972). *Historical Introduction to Modern Psychology* (3rd ed.). New York: Harcourt Brace Jovanovich.

Murphy, M., and Donovan, S. (1996). *The Physical and Psychological Effects of Meditation: A Review of Contemporary Research with a Comprehensive Bibliography, 1931–1996* (2nd ed.). Edited with an Introduction by E. I. Taylor. Sausalito, Calif.: Institute of Noetic Sciences.

Murray, H. A. et al. (1938). *Explorations in Personality.* New York: Oxford University Press.

Murray, H. A., and Morgan, C. D. (1945). A Clinical

Study of Sentiments. *Genetic Psychology Monographs,* 32, 3–311.

Myers, G. E. (Ed.). (1961). *Self, Religion, and Metaphysics: Essays in Memory of James Bissett Pratt.* New York: Macmillan.

Myers, G. E. (1986). *William James, His Life and Thought.* New Haven, Conn.: Yale University Press.

Myers, I. B., and McCaulley, M. H. (1985). *Manual: A Guide to the Development and Use of the Myers-Briggs Type Indicator.* Palo Alto: Consulting Psychologists Press.

Mysticism in the Laboratory. (1970). *Time,* October 5, pp. 72–74.

Nagendra, H. R., and Nagarathna, R. (1986). An Integrated Approach of Yoga Therapy for Bronchial Asthma: A 3–54-Month Prospective Study. *Journal of Asthma,* 23, 123–137.

Nagy, M. (1991). *Philosophical Issues in the Psychology C. G. Jung.* Albany: State University of New York.

Naranjo, C. (1973). *The Healing Journey: New Approaches to Consciousness.* New York: Pantheon.

Naranjo, C., and Ornstein, R. E. (1971). *On the Psychology of Meditation.* New York: Viking.

Nase, E., and Scharfenberg, J. (Eds.). (1977). *Psychoanalyse und Religion.* Darmstadt: Wissenschaftliche Buchgesellschaft.

Neher, A. (1961). Auditory Driving Observed with Scalp Electrodes in Normal Subjects. *Electroencephalography and Clinical Neurophysiology,* 13, 449–451.

Neher, A. (1962). A Physiological Explanation of Unusual Behavior in Ceremonies Involving Drums. *Human Biology,* 34, 151–160.

Nelson, B. (Ed.). (1957). *Freud and the 20th Century.* New York: Meridan.

Nelson, L. D., and Dynes, R. R. (1976). The Impact of Devotionalism and Attendance on Ordinary and Emergency Helping Behavior. *Journal for the Scientific Study of Religion,* 15, 47–59.

Nelson, M. O. (1971). The Concept of God and Feelings Toward Parents. *Journal of Individual Psychology,* 27, 46–49.

Nelson, M. O., and Jones, E. M. (1957). An Application of the Q-Technique to the Study of Religious Concepts. *Psychological Reports,* 3, 293–297.

Nelson, P. B. (1989). Ethnic Differences in Intrinsic/Extrinsic Religious Orientation and Depression in the Elderly. *Archives of Psychiatric Nursing,* 3, 199–204.

Nelson, P. B. (1990). Intrinsic/Extrinsic Religious Orientation of the Elderly: Relationship to Depression and Self-Esteem. *Journal of Gerontological Nursing,* 16, 29–35.

Neufeld, K. (1979). Child-rearing, Religion, and Abusive Parents. *Religious Education,* 74, 234–244.

Neumann, E. (1955). *The Great Mother: An Analysis of the Archetype* (2nd ed.). Translated by R. Manheim. New York: Pantheon, 1963. (German edition 1956; first English edition 1955)

Newman, F. W. (1852). *The Soul, Its Sorrows and Its Aspirations: An Essay Towards the Natural History of the Soul, as the True Basis of Theology* (3rd ed.). London: J. Chapman.

Nidich, S., Seeman, W., and Dreskin, T. (1973). Influence of Transcendental Meditation: A Replication. *Journal of Counseling Psychology,* 20, 565–566.

Niederland, W. G. (1974). *The Schreber Case: Psychoanalytic Profile of a Paranoid Personality.* New York: Quadrangle/New York Times.

Nikhilananda, Swami (1942). Introduction. In M. N. Gupta, *The Gospel of Sri Ramakrishna,* 1942, pp. 3–73.

Nivedita, Sister (1897). *Kali the Mother.* Mayavati, Almora: Advaita Ashrama, 1950. (Written in 1897)

Nolan, E. G., Bram, P., and Tillman, K. (1963). Attitude Formation in High-School Seniors: A Study of Values and Attitudes. *Journal of Educational Research,* 57, 185–188.

Noll, R. (1994). *The Jung Cult: Origins of a Charismatic Movement.* Princeton, N.J.: Princeton University Press.

Noyes, R., Jr. (1980). Attitude Change Following Near-Death Experiences. *Psychiatry,* 43, 234–242.

Noyes, R., Jr., and Kletti, R. (1976). Depersonalization in the Face of Life-Threatening Danger: An Interpretation. *Omega,* 7, 103–114.

Nunn, J. F. (1987). *Applied Respiratory Physiology* (3rd ed.). London: Butterworths.

Nunnally, J. C. (1978). *Psychometric Theory* (2nd ed.). New York: McGraw-Hill.

Nyanaponika Thera. (1962). *The Heart of Buddhist Meditation: A Handbook of Mental Training Based on the Buddha's Way of Mindfulness.* New York: Samuel Weiser.

O'Brien, T. C. (Ed.). (1979). *New Catholic Encyclopedia, Vol. 17: Supplement: Changes in the Church.* New York: McGraw-Hill.

O'Connell, D. F., and Alexander, C. N. (Eds.). (1994). *Self-Recovery: Treating Addiction Using Transcendental Meditation and Maharishi Ayur-Veda.* Binghampton, N.Y.: Haworth Press.

O'Connor, K. V. (1991). The Psychology of Religion in Australia. *International Journal for the Psychology of Religion,* 1, 41–57.

Oesterreich, T. K. (1917). *Einführung in die Religionspsychologie als Grundlage für Religionsphilosophie und Religionsgeschichte.* Berlin: Ernst Siegried Mittler und Sohn.

Oesterreich, T. K. (1921). *Possession, Demoniacal and Other, Among Primitive Races, in Antiquity, the Middle Ages, and Modern Times.* Translated by D. Ibberson. Seacaucus, N.J.: University Books, 1966. (First published 1930; original German edition 1921)

O'Flaherty, W. D. (1984). *Dreams, Illusion, and Other Realities.* Chicago: University of Chicago Press.

Oksanen, A. (1994). *Religious Conversion: A Meta-Analytical Study.* Lund: Lund University Press.

Olds, L. E. (1992). *Metaphors of Interrelatedness: Toward a Systems Theory of Psychology.* Albany: State University of New York Press.

Oliner, S. P., and Oliner, P. M. (1988). *The Altruistic Personality: Rescuers of Jews in Nazi Europe.* New York: Free Press.

Olney, J. (1972). *Metaphors of Self: The Meaning of Autobiography.* Princeton, N.J.: Princeton University Press.

O'Neil, W. M., and Levinson, D. J. (1954). A Factorial Exploration of Authoritarianism and Some of Its Ideological Correlates. *Journal of Personality, 22,* 449–463.

O'Neill, M. (1990). *Women Speaking, Women Listening: Women in Interreligious Dialogue.* Maryknoll, N.Y.: Orbis Books.

Orme-Johnson, D. W. (1973). Autonomic Stability and Transcendental Meditation. *Psychosomatic Medicine, 35,* 341–349.

Orme-Johnson, D. W., and Farrow, J. T. (Eds.). (1977). *Scientific Research on the Transcendental Meditation Program: Collected Papers,* Vol. I (2nd ed.). Weggis, Switzerland: Maharishi European Research University Press.

Ornstein, R. E. (Ed.). (1973). *The Nature of Human Consciousness: A Book of Readings.* New York: Viking Press.

Ornstein, R. E. (1986). *The Psychology of Consciousness* (3rd ed.). New York: Penguin.

Oser, F. (1980). Stages of Religious Judgment. In C. Brusselmans (Ed.), *Toward Moral and Religious Maturity.* Morristown, N.J.: Silver Burdett, pp. 277–315.

Oser, F., and Gmünder, P. (1984). *Religious Judgment: A Developmental Approach.* Translated by N. F. Hahn. Birmingham, Ala.: Religious Education Press, 1991. (Original German edition 1984)

Osis, K., and Haraldsson, E. (1986). *At the Hour of Death* (2nd ed.). New York: Hastings.

Osmond, H., and Smythies, J. (1959). The Significance of Psychotic Experience: A Reply to Professor Zaehner. *Hibbert Journal, 57,* 236–243.

Ostow, M. (1958). Biologic Basis of Religious Symbolism. *International Record of Medicine, 171,* 709–717.

Ostow, M. et al. (1968). *The Psychic Function of Religion in Mental Illness and Health.* New York: Group for the Advancement of Psychiatry.

Ostow, M., and Scharfstein, B. A. (1954). *The Need to Believe: The Psychology of Religion.* New York: International Universities Press.

Oswald, R. M., and Kroeger, O. (1988). *Personality Type and Religious Leadership.* Washington, D.C.: Alban Institute.

Otto, R. (1917). *The Idea of the Holy: An Inquiry into the Non-Rational Factor in the Idea of the Divine and Its Relation to the Rational.* Translated by J. W. Harvey. London: Oxford University Press, 1923; 2nd ed., 1950. (First German Edition, 1917)

Owen, O. E., Morgan, A. P., Kemp, H. G., Sullivan, J. M., Herrera, M. G., and Cahill, G. F. (1967). Brain Metabolism during Fasting. *Journal of Clinical Investigation, 46,* 1589–1595.

Owens, C. M. (1967). The Mystical Experience: Facts and Values. In J. White, *The Highest State of Consciousness,* 1972, pp. 135–152. (First published 1967)

Ozment, S. (1980). *The Age of Reform 1250–1550: An Intellectual and Religious History of Late Medieval and Reformation Europe.* New Haven, Conn.: Yale University Press.

Ozorak, E. W. (1996). The Power, But Not the Glory: How Women Empower Themselves Through Religion. *Journal for the Scientific Study of Religion, 35,* 17–29.

Pacheu, J. (1911). *L'experience mystique et l'activité subconsciente.* Paris: Perrin.

Packer, M. J., and Addison, R. B. (Eds.). (1989). *Entering the Circle: Hermeneutic Investigation in Psychology.* Albany: State University of New York Press.

Pagels, E. (1979). *The Gnostic Gospels.* New York: Random House.

Pagels, E. (1988). *Adam, Eve, and the Serpent.* New York: Random House.

Pahnke, W. N. (1963). *Drugs and Mysticism: An Analysis of the Relationship between Psychedelic Drugs and the Mystical Consciousness.* Unpublished doctoral dissertation, Harvard University.

Pahnke, W. N. (1966). Drugs and Mysticism. *International Journal of Parapsychology, 8,* 295–314. (Reprinted in L. B. Brown, 1973, and J. White, 1972)

Pahnke, W. N. (1967). The Mystical and/or Religious Element in the Psychedelic Experience. In D. H. Salman and R. H. Prince (Eds.), *Do Psychedelics Have Religious Implications?* Montreal: R. M. Bucke Memorial Society, pp. 41–56. (Reprinted, with modifications, in E. M. Pattison (Ed.), *Clinical Psychiatry and Religion.* Boston: Little, Brown, 1969, pp. 149–162)

Pahnke, W. N., and Richards, W. A. (1966). Implications of LSD and Experimental Mysticism. *Journal of Religion and Health, 5,* 175–208. (Reprinted in Tart, 1990)

Paiva, R. E. A., and Haley, H. B. (1971). Intellectual, Personality, and Environmental Factors in Career Specialty Preferences. *Journal of Medical Education, 46,* 281–289.

Palmer, R. (1969). *Hermeneutics.* Evanston, Ill.: Northwestern University Press.

Paloutzian, R. F. (1996). *Invitation to the Psychology of Religion* (2nd ed.). Boston: Allyn and Bacon.

Paloutzian, R. F., and Kirkpatrick, L. A. (Eds.). (1995). Religious Influences on Personal and Societal Well-Being. *Journal of Social Issues, 51*(2).

Pals, D. (1986). Reductionism and Belief: An Appraisal of Recent Attacks on the Doctrine of Irreducible Religion. *Journal of Religion, 66,* 18–36.

Papadopoulos, R. K. (1992). *Carl Gustav Jung: Critical Assessments* (4 vols.). London: Routledge.

Pargament, K. I. (1990). God Help Me: Toward a Theoretical Framework of Coping for the Psychology of Religion. *Research in the Social Scientific Study of Religion, 2,* 195–224.

Pargament, K. I. (1996). Religious Methods of Coping: Resources for the Conservation and Transformation of Significance. In E. P. Shafranske, *Religion and the Clinical Practice of Psychology*, pp. 215–239.

Pargament, K. I., and Park, C. L. (1995). Merely a Defense? The Varieties of Means and Ends. *Journal of Social Issues*, 51, 13–32.

Park, C., Cohen, L. H., and Herb, L. (1990). Intrinsic Religiousness and Religious Coping as Life Stress Moderators for Catholics Versus Protestants. *Journal of Personality and Social Psychology*, 59, 562–574.

Parker, W. R., and St. Johns, E. (1957). *Prayer Can Change Your Life: Experiments and Techniques in Prayer Therapy*. Carmel, N. Y.: Guideposts Associates.

Paul, R. A. (1996). *Moses and Civilization: The Meaning Behind Freud's Myth*. New Haven: Yale University Press.

Pauly, P. J. (1987). *Controlling Life: Jacques Loeb and the Engineering Ideal in Biology*. New York: Oxford University Press.

Payne, I. R., Bergin, A. E., Bielema, K. A., and Jenkins, P. H. (1991). Review of Religion and Mental Health: Prevention and the Enhancement of Psychosocial Functioning. *Prevention in Human Services*, 9, 11–40.

Payne, W. D. (1972). Conceptual Problems in the Correlation of Delinquency and Religiosity. In G. M. Vernon, *Types and Dimensions of Religion*, pp. 35–48.

Peabody, D. (1961). Attitude Content and Agreement Set in Scales of Authoritarianism, Dogmatism, Anti-Semitism and Economic Conservatism. *Journal of Abnormal and Social Psychology*, 63, 1–11.

Pearson, K. (1924). *The Life, Letters and Labours of Francis Galton*, Vol. 2. London: Cambridge University Press.

Pearson, K. (1930). *The Life, Letters and Labours of Francis Galton*, Vol. 3A. London: Cambridge University Press.

Pempel, A. M. (1978). Altered States of Consciousness and Mystical Experience: An Anatomy of Inner Space (Fordham University, 1978). *Dissertation Abstracts International*, 38, 7397A–7398A. (University Microfilms No. 78–07882)

Penfield, W. (1975). *The Mystery of the Mind: A Critical Study of Consciousness and the Human Brain*. Princeton, N.J.: Princeton University Press.

Penner, W. J., Zingle, H. W., Dyke, R., and Truch, S. (1973). Does an In-Depth Transcendental Meditation Course Effect Change in the Personalities of the Participants? *Western Psychologist*, 4, 104–111.

Perkins, H. W. (1992). Student Religiosity and Social Justice Concerns in England and the United States: Are They Still Related? *Journal for the Scientific Study of Religion*, 31, 353–360.

Perry, R. B. (1935). *The Thought and Character of William James* (2 vols.). Boston: Atlantic-Little, Brown.

Perry, W. G., Jr. (1970). *Forms of Intellectual and Ethical Development in the College Years*. New York: Holt, Rinehart and Winston.

Persinger, M. A. (1983). Religious and Mystical Experiences as Artifacts of Temporal Lobe Function: A General Hypothesis. *Perceptual and Motor Skills*, 57, 1255–1262.

Persinger, M. A. (1987). *Neuropsychological Bases of God Beliefs*. New York: Praeger.

Persinger, M. A. (1993). Vectorial Cerebral Hemisphericity as Differential Sources for the Sensed Presence, Mystical Experiences and Religious Conversions. *Perceptual and Motor Skills*, 76, 915–930.

Persinger, M. A. (1994). Near Death Experiences: Determining the Neuroanatomical Pathways by Experiential Patterns and Simulation in Experimental Settings. In L. Bessette (Ed.), *Healing: Beyond Suffering or Death*. Beauport, Quebec: Publications MNH, pp. 277–285.

Persinger, M. A., and Makarec, K. (1987). Temporal Lobe Epileptic Signs and Correlative Behaviors Displayed by Normal Populations. *Journal of General Psychology*, 114, 179–195.

Persinger, M. A., Bureau, Y. R. J., Peredery, O. P., and Richards, P. M. (1994). The Sensed Presence as Right Hemispheric Intrusions into the Left Hemispheric Awareness of Self: An Illustrative Case Study. *Perceptual and Motor Skills*, 78, 999–1009.

Peters, R. S. (Ed.). (1962). *Brett's History of Psychology* (rev. ed.). London: George Allen & Unwin.

Peterson, B. E., Doty, R. M., and Winter, D. G. (1993). Authoritarianism and Attitudes Toward Contemporary Social Issues. *Personality and Social Psychology Bulletin*, 19, 174–184.

Pettersson, O., and Åkerberg, H. (Eds.). (1980). *William James då och nu: Några religionspsykologiska studier*. Lund: Doxa.

Pfeifer, S. (1993). *Glaubensvergiftung—Ein Mythos? Analyse und Therapie religiöser Lebenskonflikte*. Moers: Brendow.

Pfennigsdorf, D. E. (1927). *Der religiöse Wille. Ein Beitrag zum psychologischen Verständnis des Christentums und seiner praktischen Aufgaben* (2nd ed.). Leipzig: A. Deichert. (First edition 1910)

Pfister, O. (1910a). *Die Frömmigkeit des Grafen Ludwig von Zinzendorf: Ein psychoanalytischer Beitrag zur Kenntnis der religiösen Sublimierungsprozesse und zur Erklärung des Pietismus*. Leipzig: Franz Deuticke. (Reprinted with minor changes and a new foreword, 1925)

Pfister, O. (1910b). Zur Psychologie des hysterischen Madonnenkultus. *Zentralblatt für Psychoanalyse*, 1, 30–37.

Pfister, O. (1913). *The Psychoanalytic Method*. Translated by C. R. Payne. New York: Moffat, Yard & Co., 1917. (First German edition 1913)

Pfister, O. (1922). Die Religionspsychologie am Scheidewege. *Imago*, 8, 368–400.

Pfister, O. (1928). The Illusion of a Future: A Friendly

Disagreement with Prof. Sigmund Freud. Translated by S. Abrams. *International Journal of Psycho-Analysis,* 1993, 74, 557–579. (Original German edition 1928)

Pfister, O. (1931). Aus der Analyse eines Buddhisten. Eine Studie zum psychologischen Verständnis des Buddhismus. *Psychoanalytische Bewegung,* 3, 307–328.

Pfister, O. (1944). *Christianity and Fear: A Study in History and in the Psychology and Hygiene of Religion.* Translated by W. H. Johnston. London: George Allen & Unwin, 1948. (Original German edition 1944)

Philp, H. L. (1956). *Freud and Religious Belief.* London: Rockliff.

Philp, H. L. (1958). *Jung and the Problem of Evil.* London: Rockliff.

Piaget, J. (1922). La psychologie et les valeurs religieuses. In *Sainte-Croix 1922* (Récit de la conférence de l'Association Chrétienne d'Étudiants de la Suisse Romande). Lausanne: Imprimerie La Concorde.

Piaget, J. (1930). *Immanentisme et foi religieuse.* Édité par le Groupe romand des Anciens Membres de l'Associaton Chrétienne d'Étudiants. Geneva: H. Robert.

Piaget, J. (1952). [Autobiography]. In E. G. Boring et al. (Eds.), *A History of Psychology in Autobiography,* Vol. 4. Worcester, Mass.: Clark University Press, pp. 237–256.

Piaget, J., and de la Harpe, J. (1928). *Deux types d'attitude religieuse: Immanence et Transcendance.* Éditions de l'Association Chrétienne d'Étudiants de Suisse Romande. Dépt: Geneva: Labor. (Piaget's contribution encompasses pages 7–40)

Pirani, A. (Ed.). (1991). *The Absent Mother: Restoring the Goddess to Judaism and Christianity.* London: Mandala.

Platonov, K. K. (1975). Psikhologii religii i ateisticheskoe vospitanie. *Voprosy Psikhologii,* 22(3), 18–25.

Pöll, W. (1965). *Religionspsychologie: Formen der religiösen Kenntnisnahme.* Munich: Kösel.

Pöll, W. (1974). *Das religiöse Erlebnis und seine Strukturen.* Munich: Kösel.

Pohl, R. (1968). *Die religiöse Gedankenwelt bei Volks- und Hilfsschulkindern.* Munich: Ernst Reinhardt.

Poling, T. H., and Kenney, J. F. (1986). *Hare Krishna Character Type: A Study of the Sensate Personality.* Lewiston, N.Y.: Edwin Mellen.

Polkinghorne, D. (1983). *Methodology for the Human Sciences: Systems of Inquiry.* Albany: State University of New York Press.

Polkinghorne, D. E. (1988). *Narrative Knowing and the Human Sciences.* Albany: State University of New York Press.

Poloma, M. M. (1995). *The "Toronto Blessing": Charisma, Instititionalization and Revival.* Paper presented at the annual meeting of the Society for the Scientific Study of Religion, St. Louis.

Poloma, M. M., and Gallup, G. H., Jr. (1991). *Varieties*

of Prayer: A Survey Report. Philadelphia: Trinity Press International.

Pomper, P. (1970). Review of *Gandhi's Truth,* by E. H. Erikson. *History and Theory,* 9, 202–209.

Pomper, P. (1985). *The Structure of Mind in History: Five Major Figures in Psychohistory.* New York: Columbia University Press.

Ponton, M. O., and Gorsuch, R. L. (1988). Prejudice and Religion Revisited: A Cross-Cultural Investigation with a Venezuelan Sample. *Journal for the Scientific Study of Religion,* 27, 260–271.

Potempa, P. R. (1958). *Persönlichkeit und Religiosität: Versuch einer psychologischen Schau.* Göttingen: Verlag für Psychologie.

Powell, F. C., and Thorson, J. A. (1991). Constructions of Death Among Those High in Intrinsic Religious Motivation: A Factor-Analytic Study. *Death Studies,* 15, 131–138.

Poythress, N. G. (1975). Literal, Antiliteral, and Mythological Religious Orientations. *Journal for the Scientific Study of Religion,* 14, 271–284.

Pratt, J. B. (1907). *The Psychology of Religious Belief.* New York: Macmillan.

Pratt, J. B. (1908). The Psychology of Religion. *Harvard Theological Review,* 1, 435–454. (Reprinted in Strunk, 1959 and 1971)

Pratt, J. B. (1915). *India and Its Faiths.* New York: Macmillan.

Pratt, J. B. (1920). *The Religious Consciousness: A Psychological Study.* New York: Macmillan.

Pratt, J. B. (1923). Religion and the Younger Generation. *The Yale Review,* 12, 594–613.

Pratt, J. B. (1926). Objective and Subjective Worship. *Religionspsychologie: Veröffentlichungen des Wiener Religionspsychologischen Forschungs-Institutes,* 1, 42–48.

Pratt, J. B. (1928). *The Pilgrimage of Buddhism and a Buddhist Pilgrimage.* New York: Macmillan.

Pratt, J. B. (1936). Liberal Religion and the Function of Unitarianism. In *Unitarians Face a New Age: The Report of The Commission of Appraisal to the American Unitarian Association.* Boston: The Commission, pp. 53–60.

Pratt, J. B. (1950). *Eternal Values in Religion.* New York: Macmillan.

Prince, R. (Ed.). (1968). *Trance and Possession States.* Montreal: R. M. Bucke Memorial Society.

Prince, R. (1982). Shamans and Endorphins: Hypotheses for a Synthesis. *Ethos,* 10, 409–423.

Prince, R., and Savage, C. (1966). Mystical States and the Concept of Regression. *Psychedelic Review,* No. 8, 59–75. (Reprinted in J. White, 1972)

Prince, R., Goodwin, A., and Engelsmann, F. (1976). Transcendental Meditation and Stress: An Evaluative Study. *R. M. Bucke Memorial Society Newsletter-Review,* 8, 10–27.

Principe, W. (1983). Toward Defining Spirituality. *Sciences Religieuses/Studies in Religion,* 12, 127–141.

Proctor, T. H. (1945). James Bissett Pratt's Philosophy of Religion. *Review of Religion,* 9, 137–152.

Progoff, I. (1966). The Idea of Eranos. *Journal of Religion and Health,* 5, 307–313.

Prothro, E. T., and Jensen, J. A. (1950). Interrelations of Religious and Ethnic Attitudes in Selected Southern Populations. *Journal of Social Psychology,* 32, 45–49.

Proudfoot, W. (1985). *Religious Experience.* Berkeley: University of California Press.

Proudfoot, W., and Shaver, P. (1975). Attribution Theory and the Psychology of Religion. *Journal for the Scientific Study of Religion,* 14, 317–330.

Pruyser, P. W. (1967). Anton T. Boisen and the Psychology of Religion. *Journal of Pastoral Care,* 21, 209–219.

Pruyser, P. W. (1968). *A Dynamic Psychology of Religion.* New York: Harper & Row.

Pruyser, P. W. (1971). A Psychological View of Religion in the 1970s. *Bulletin of the Menninger Clinic,* 35, 77–97.

Pruyser, P. W. (1974). *Between Belief and Unbelief.* New York: Harper & Row.

Pruyser, P. W. (1977). The Seamy Side of Current Religious Beliefs. *Bulletin of the Menninger Clinic,* 41, 329–348.

Pruyser, P. W. (1978). Narcissism in Contemporary Religion. *Journal of Pastoral Care,* 32, 219–231.

Pruyser, P. W. (1983). *The Play of the Imagination: Toward a Psychoanalysis of Culture.* New York: International Universities Press.

Pulver, M. (1942). Jesus' Round Dance and Crucifixion According to the Acts of St. John. Translated by R. Manheim. In J. Campbell (Ed.), *The Mysteries.* Vol. 2 of *Papers from the Eranos Yearbooks,* 1955, pp. 169–193. (Original German edition 1942)

Purpura, D. P. (1967). Neurophysiological Actions of LSD. In R. C. DeBold and R. C. Leaf, *LSD, Man & Society,* pp. 159–185.

Rabinowicz, H. (1971). Dietary Laws. *Encyclopaedia Judaica,* 6, 26–45.

Rabinowitz, L. I. (1971a). Mezuzah. *Encyclopaedia Judaica,* 11, 1474–1477.

Rabinowitz, L. I. (1971b). Tefillin. *Encyclopaedia Judaica,* 15, 898–904.

Radant, N., Blackford, R., Porch, T., Shahbaz, P., and Butman, R. E. (1985). From Jerusalem to Jericho Revisited: A Study in Helping Behavior. *Journal of Psychology and Christianity,* 4, 48–55.

Rahn, C. (1928). *Science and the Religious Life: A Psycho-Physiological Approach.* New Haven, Conn.: Yale University Press.

Rainey, R. M. (1975). *Freud as Student of Religion: Perspectives on the Background and Development of His Thought.* Missoula, Mont.: Scholars Press, 1975.

Raitz von Frentz, E. (1925). Das religiöse Erlebnis im psychologischen Laboratorium. Berechtigung und Ergebnisse der experimentellen Religionspsychologie. *Stimmen der Zeit,* 109, 200–214.

Ramanujan, A. K. (1973). *Speaking of Śiva.* Baltimore: Penguin.

Ramsès le Grand. (1976). Paris: Galeries Nationales du Grand Palais.

Randall, R. L. (1976). Religious Ideation of a Narcissistically Disturbed Individual. *Journal of Pastoral Care,* 30, 35–45.

Randall, R. L. (1984). The Legacy of Kohut for Religion and Psychology. *Journal of Religion and Health,* 23, 106–114.

Rank, O. (1909). *The Myth of the Birth of the Hero: A Psychological Interpretation.* Translated by F. Robbins and S. E. Jelliffe. New York: Robert Brunner, 1952. (First published in 1914; Original German edition 1909)

Rank, O. (1924). *The Trauma of Birth.* New York: Harcourt, Brace, 1929. (Original German edition 1924)

Raschke, V. (1973). Dogmatism and Committed and Consensual Religiosity. *Journal for the Scientific Study of Religion,* 12, 339–344.

Ray Chaudhuri, A. K. (1956). A Psycho-Analytic Study of the Hindu Mother Goddess (Kali) Concept. *American Imago,* 13, 123–146.

Reed, L. A., and Meyers, L. S. (1991). A Structural Analysis of Religious Orientation and Its Relation to Sexual Attitudes. *Educational and Psychological Measurement,* 51, 943–952.

Reich, K. H. (1990). Beliefs of German and Swiss Children and Young People about Science and Religion. *British Journal of Religious Education,* 13, 65–73.

Reich, K. H. (1992). Religious Development Across the Life Span: Conventional and Cognitive Developmental Approaches. In D. L. Featherman, R. M. Lerner, and M. Permutter (Eds.), *Life-Span Development and Behavior,* Vol. 11. Hillsdale, N.J.: Lawrence Erlbaum, pp. 145–188.

Reichelt, K. L. (1947). *Meditation and Piety in the Far East: A Religious-Psychological Study.* Translated by S. Holth. New York: Harper, 1954. (Original Norwegian edition 1947)

Reik, T. (1917). Das Kainszeichen. Ein psychoanalytischer Beitrag zur Bibelerklärung. *Imago,* 5, 31–42.

Reik, T. (1919a). Psychoanalytic Studies of Bible Exegesis. In T. Reik, *Dogma and Compulsion,* 1951, pp. 229–275. (Original German edition 1919)

Reik, T. (1919b). *Ritual: Psycho-Analytic Studies.* Translated by D. Bryan. New York: International Universities Press, 1946. (First German edition 1919)

Reik, T. (1921a). The Science of Religion. *International Journal of Psycho-Analysis,* 2, 80–93.

Reik, T. (1921b). Mysticism and Occultism. *International Journal of Psycho-Analysis,* 2, 225–230.

Reik, T. (1930). The Prayer Shawl and the Phylacteries of the Jews. In T. Reik, *Dogma and Compulsion,* 1951, pp. 181–228. (Original German edition 1930)

Reik, T. (1951). *Dogma and Compulsion: Psychoanalytic Studies of Myths and Religions.* Translated by B. Miall. New York: International Universities Press.

Reik, T. (1957). *Myth and Guilt*. New York: George Braziller.

Reik, T. (1961). *The Temptation*. New York: George Braziller.

Reinert, D. F., and Stifler, K. R. (1993). Hood's Mysticism Scale Revisited: A Factor-Analytic Replication. *Journal for the Scientific Study of Religion, 32*, 383–388.

Reiser, O. L. (1932). The Biological Origins of Religion. *Psychoanalytic Review, 19*, 1–22.

Reynolds, V. (1967). *The Apes*. London: Cassell.

Reynolds, V., and Tanner R. (1983). *The Biology of Religion*. London: Longman.

Ribot, T. (1884). *The Diseases of the Will*. Translated by M.-M. Snell. Chicago: Open Court, 1894. (Original French edition 1884)

Ribot, T. (1896). *The Psychology of the Emotions*. New York: Charles Scribner's Sons, 1903. (Original French edition 1896)

Rice, E. (1990). *Freud and Moses: The Long Journey Home*. Albany: State University of New York Press.

Richards, P. S. (1991). Religious Devoutness in College Students: Relations with Emotional Adjustment and Psychological Separation from Parents. *Journal of Counseling Psychology, 38*, 189–196.

Richardson, J. T. (1973). Psychological Interpretations of Glossolalia: A Reexamination of Research. *Journal for the Scientific Study of Religion, 12*, 199–207.

Ricketts, M. L. (1970). The Nature and Extent of Eliade's "Jungianism." *Union Seminary Quarterly Review, 25*, 211–234.

Rickman, H. P. (1979). *Wilhelm Dilthey: Pioneer of the Human Studies*. London: Paul Elek.

Ricoeur, P. (1960). *The Symbolism of Evil*. Translated by E. Buchanan. New York: Harper & Row, 1967. (Original French edition 1960)

Ricoeur, P. (1965). *Freud and Philosophy: An Essay on Interpretation*. Translated by D. Savage. New Haven, Conn.: Yale University Press, 1970. (Original French edition 1965)

Ricoeur, P. (1966). The Atheism of Freudian Psychoanalysis. *Concilium, 16*, 59–72.

Ricoeur, P. (1969). *The Conflict of Interpretations: Essays on Hermeneutics*. Edited by D. Ihde. Evanston, Ill.: Northwestern University Press. 1974. (Original French edition 1969)

Rieff, P. (1959). *Freud: The Mind of the Moralist* (3rd ed.). Chicago: University of Chicago Press, 1979. (First edition 1959)

Rieff, P. (1966). *The Triumph of the Therapeutic: Uses of Faith After Freud*. New York: Harper & Row.

Ring, K. (1980). *Life at Death: A Scientific Investigation of the Near-Death Experience*. New York: Coward, McCann & Geoghenan.

Ring, K., and Franklin, S. (1981–1982). Do Suicide Survivors Report Near-Death Experiences? *Omega, 12*, 191–208. (Reprinted in Lundahl, 1982)

Ring, K., and Rosing, C. J. (1990). The Omega Project: An Empirical Study of the NDE-Prone Personality. *Journal of Near-Death Studies, 8*, 211–239.

Ritter, H. (1933). Der Reigen der "tanzenden Derwische." *Zeitschrift für vergleichende Musikwissenschaft, 1*, 28–40.

Ritter, H. (1962). Die Mevlânafeier in Konya vom 11–17 Dezember 1960. *Oriens, 15*, 249–270.

Rizzo, R., and Vinacke, E. (1975). Self-Actualization and the Meaning of Critical Experience. *Journal of Humanistic Psychology, 15*(3), 19–30.

Rizzuto, A.-M. (1974). Object Relations and the Formation of the Image of God. *British Journal of Medical Psychology, 47*, 83–99.

Rizzuto, A.-M. (1979). *The Birth of the Living God: A Psychoanalytic Study*. Chicago: University of Chicago Press.

Rizzuto, A.-M. (1980). The Psychological Foundations of Belief in God. In C. Brusselmans, *Toward Moral and Religious Maturity*, pp. 115–135.

Rizzuto, A.-M. (1992) Afterword. In M. Finn and J. Gartner, *Object Relations Theory and Religion*, pp. 155–175.

Roazen, P. (1993). Erik Erikson as a Teacher. *The Psychohistory Review, 22*, 101–117.

Roback, A. A. (1918). Freudian Psychology and Jewish Commentators of the Bible. *Jewish Forum, 1*, 528–533.

Roback, A. A. (1923). *Behaviorism and Psychology*. Cambridge, Mass.: University Bookstore.

Roback, A. A. (1929). *Jewish Influence in Modern Thought*. Cambridge, Mass.: Sci-Art Publishers.

Roback, A. A. (1942). *William James: His Marginalia, Personality and Contribution*. Cambridge, Mass.: Sci-Art.

Roback, A. A. (1957). *Freudiana*. Cambridge, Mass.: Sci-Art Publishers.

Robert, M. (1974). *From Oedipus to Moses: Freud's Jewish Identity*. Translated by R. Manheim. Garden City, N.Y.: Anchor/Doubleday, 1976. (Original French edition 1974)

Roberts, G., and Owen, J. (1988). The Near-Death Experience. *British Journal of Psychiatry, 153*, 607–617.

Robinson, P. A. (1969). *The Freudian Left: Wilhelm Reich, Geza Roheim, Hebert Marcuse*. New York: Harper & Row.

Robinson, T. N. (1990). Eysenck Personality Measures and Religious Orientation. *Personality and Individual Differences, 11*, 915–921.

Rochedieu, E. (1948). *Psychologie et vie religieuse*. Geneva: Roulet.

Rheim, G. (1925). *Australian Totemism*. London: Allen & Unwin

Rheim, G. (1930). *Animism, Magic, and the Divine King*. New York: Alfred A. Knopf.

Rheim, G. (1940). The Garden of Eden. *Psychoanalytic Review, 27*, 1–26, 177–199.

Rheim, G. (1945). *The Eternal Ones of the Dream: A Psychoanalytic Interpretation of Australian Myth and Ritual*. New York: International Universities Press.

Rohrbaugh, J., and Jessor, R. (1975). Religiosity in Youth: A Personal Control Against Deviant Behavior. *Journal of Personality, 43,* 136–155.

Roitblat, H. L. (1987). *Introduction to Comparative Cognition.* New York: W. H. Freeman.

Roith, E. (1987). *The Riddle of Freud: Jewish Influences on His Theory of Female Sexuality.* London: Tavistock.

Rokeach, M. (1956). Political and Religious Dogmatism: An Alternative to the Authoritarian Personality. *Psychological Monographs, 70,* No. 18 (Whole No. 425).

Rokeach, M. (1960). *The Open and Closed Mind: Investigations into the Nature of Belief Systems and Personality Systems.* New York: Basic Books.

Rokeach, M. (1969). Religious Values and Social Compassion. *Review of Religious Research, 11,* 24–39.

Rokeach, M. (1973). *The Nature of Human Values.* New York: The Free Press.

Roland, A. (1988). *In Search of Self in India and Japan: Toward a Cross-Cultural Psychology.* Princeton, N.J.: Princeton University Press.

Rolffs, E. (1938). *Die Phantasie in der Religion.* Berlin: Hans Bott.

Rollins, W. G. (1983). *Jung and the Bible.* Atlanta: John Knox Press.

Roman, K. G. (1952). *Handwriting: A Key to Personality.* New York: Pantheon.

Roof, W. C. (1982). America's Voluntary Establishment: Mainline Religion in Transition. *Daedalus, 111,* 165–184.

Roof, W. C. (1993). *A Generation of Seekers: The Spiritual Journeys of the Baby Boom Generation.* San Francisco: HarperSanFrancisco.

Roof, W. C., Carroll, J. W., and Roozen, D. A. (Eds.). (1995). *The Post-War Generation and Establishment Religion: Cross-Cultural Perspectives.* Boulder, Colo.: Westview Press.

Rorschach, H. (1927). Zwei Schweizerische Sektenstifter. *Imago, 13,* 395–441.

Rosenzweig, S. (1992). *Freud, Jung and Hall the King-Maker: The Expedition to America (1909).* Seattle: Hogrefe & Huber.

Rosmarin, T. W. (1939). *The Hebrew Moses: An Answer to Sigmund Freud.* New York: Jewish Book Club.

Ross, C. (1992). The Intuitive Function and Religious Orientation. *Journal of Analytical Psychology, 37,* 83–103.

Ross, C. (1993). Type Patterns Among Active Members of the Anglican Church: Comparisons with Catholics, Evangelicals, and Clergy. *Journal of Psychological Type, 26,* 28–36.

Ross, C., Wiess, D., and Jackson, L. (1996). Relationship of Jungian Psychological Type to Religious Orientation and Practices. *International Journal for the Psychology of Religion, 6,* in press.

Ross, D. G. (1972). *Stanley Hall: The Psychologist as Prophet.* Chicago: University of Chicago Press.

Ross, M. (1950). *Religious Beliefs of Youth.* New York: Association Press.

Ross, M. E., and Ross, C. L. (1983). Mothers, Infants, and the Psychoanalytic Study of Ritual. *Signs: Journal of Women in Culture and Society, 9,* 26–39.

Roth, P. A. (1987). *Meaning and Method in the Social Sciences: A Case for Methodological Pluralism.* Ithaca: Cornell University Press.

Rouget, G. (1980). *Music and Trance: A Theory of the Relations between Music and Possession.* Translation revised by B. Biebuyck. Chicago: University of Chicago Press, 1985. (Original French edition 1980)

Royce, J. R. (1962). Psychology, Existentialism, and Religion. *Journal of General Psychology, 66,* 3–16.

Rudolph, S. H. (1970). [Review of *Gandhi's Truth*]. *Contemporary Psychology, 15,* 484–486.

Ruf, F. J. (1991). *The Creation of Chaos: William James and the Stylistic Making of a Disorderly World.* Albany: State University of New York Press.

Ruitenbeek, H. M. (Ed.). (1973). *Freud as We Knew Him.* Detroit: Wayne State University Press.

Ruppel, H. J. (1969). Religosity and Premarital Sexual Permissiveness: A Methodological Note. *Sociological Analysis, 30,* 176–188.

Russell, D. E. H. (1986). *The Secret Trauma: Incest in the Lives of Girls and Women.* New York: Basic Books.

Ryan, R. M., Rigby, S., and King, K. (1993). Two Types of Religious Internalization and Their Relations to Religious Orientations and Mental Health. *Journal of Personality and Social Psychology, 65,* 586–596.

Ryce-Menuhin, J. (Ed.). (1994). *Jung and the Monotheisms: Judaism, Christianity and Islam.* London: Routledge.

Sabatier, A. (1897). *Outlines of a Philosophy of Religion Based on Psychology and History.* New York: James Pott, 1897. (Original French edition 1897)

Sabom, M. B. (1981). *Recollections of Death: A Medical Investigation.* New York: Harper & Row.

Samarin, W. J. (1972). *Tongues of Men and Angels: The Religious Language of Pentecostalism.* New York: Macmillan.

Sanford, J. A. (1968). *Dreams: God's Forgotten Language.* Philadelphia: J. B. Lippincott.

Sanford, J. A. (1981a). *Evil: The Shadow Side of Personality.* New York: Crossroad.

Sanford, J. A. (1981b). *The Man Who Wrestled With God: Light from the Old Testament on the Psychology of Individuation.* Ramsey, N.J.: Paulist Press.

Sankey-Jones, N. E. (1921). A Unique Heathen. *The Freethinker,* London, April 17.

Sankey-Jones, N. E. (1934). *Bibliography of Theodore Schroeder on the Psychology of Religion and the Erotogenetic Interpretation of Mysticism.* Cos Cob, Conn.: the author.

Sapp, G. L., and Jones, L. (1986). Religious Orientation and Moral Judgment. *Journal for the Scientific Study of Religion, 25,* 208–214.

Saradananda, Swami (1911–1918). *Sri Ramakrishna, the Great Master.* (2 vols.). Translated by Swami

Jagadananda. Madras: Sri Ramakrishna Math, 1952. (Original Bengali edition 1911–1918)

Sarbin, T. R. (1986). *Narrative Psychology*. New York: Praeger.

Sargant, W. (1957). *Battle for the Mind: A Physiology of Conversion and Brain-Washing*. Garden City, N.Y.: Doubleday.

Sargant, W. (1969). The Physiology of Faith. *British Journal of Psychiatry*, 115, 505–518.

Sargant, W. (1973). *The Mind Possessed: A Physiology of Possession, Mysticism and Faith Healing*. Philadelphia: J. B. Lippincott, 1974. (British edition 1973)

Schachter, S., and Singer, J. E. (1962). Cognitive, Social, and Physiological Determinants of Emotional State. *Psychological Review*, 69, 379–399.

Schär, H. (1943). Die Bedeutung der Religionspsychologie. *Schweizerische Zeitschrift für Psychologie und ihre Anwendungen*, 2, 175–185, 255–265.

Schaer, H. (1946). *Religion and the Cure of Souls in Jung's Psychology*. Translated by R. F. C. Hull. London: Routledge & Kegan Paul, 1951. (Original German Edition, 1946)

Schär, H. (1950). *Erlösungsvorstellungen und ihre psychologischen Aspekte*. Zurich: Rascher.

Schaetzing, E. (1955). Die ekklesiogenen Neurosen. *Wege zum Menschen*, 7, 97–108.

Schafer, R. (1976). *A New Language for Psychoanalysis*. New Haven: Yale University Press.

Schafer, W. E., and King, M. (1990). Religiousness and stress among college students: A survey report. *Journal of College Student Development*, 31, 336–341.

Scharfenberg, J. (1968). *Sigmund Freud and His Critique of Religion*. Translated by O. C. Dean, Jr. Philadelphia: Fortress Press, 1988. (Original German edition 1968)

Schaub, E. L. (1921). A Noteworthy Interpretation of Religious Experience. *Journal of Religion*, 1, 210–217.

Schaub, E. L. (1926). The Psychology of Religion in America During the Past Quarter-Century. *Journal of Religion*, 6, 113–134.

Scheler, M. (1921). *On the Eternal in Man*. Translated by B. Noble. New York: Harper & Brothers, 1960. (First German edition 1921)

Scheler, M. (1928). *Man's Place in Nature*. Translated by H. Meyerhoff. Boston: Beacon Press, 1961. (Original German edition 1928)

Schimmel, A. (1968). Friedrich Heiler (1892–1967). *History of Religion*, 7, 269–272.

Schjelderup, H., and Schjelderup, K. (1932). *Über drei Haupttypen der religisen Erlebnisformen und ihre psychologische Grundlage*. Berlin: de Gruyter.

Schjelderup, K. (1928). *Die Askese: Eine religionspsychologische Untersuchung*. Berlin: de Gruyter.

Schleiermacher, F. (1799). *On Religion: Speeches to Its Cultured Despisers*. Translated by J. Oman. London: Kegan Paul, Trench, Trbner, 1893. (Original German edition 1799)

Schmidt, R. P., and Wilder, B. J. (1968). *Epilepsy*. Philadelphia: F. A. Davis.

Schmidt, W. E. (1908). *Die verschiedenen Typen religiöser Erfahrung und die Psychologie*. Gütersloh: Bertelsmann.

Schmitz, E. (Ed.). (1992). *Religionspsychologie: Eine Bestandsaufnahme des gegenwärtigen Forschungsstandes*. Göttingen: Hogrefe Verlag für Psychologie.

Schneewind, K. A. (1984). *Persönlichkeitstheorien II*. Darmstadt: Wissenschaftliche Buchgesellschaft.

Schneider, C. (1926). Gibt es einen religiösen Menschen? *Christentum und Wissenschaft*, 2, 97–109, 139–146.

Schneider, C. (1929). Studien zur Mannigfaltigkeit des religiösen Erlebens. *Archiv für Religionspsychologie und Seelenfuhrung*, 4, 19–42.

Schneider, C. (1930). *Die Erlebnisechtheit der Apokalypse des Johannes*. Leipzig: Dörffling & Franke.

Schneider, K. (1928). *Zur Einführung in die Religionspsychopathologie*. Tübingen: J. C. B. Mohr (Paul Siebeck).

Scholem, G. G. (1960). *On the Kabbalah and Its Symbolism*. Translated by R. Manheim. New York: Schocken, 1965. (Original German edition 1960)

Schroeder, T. (1908). The Sex-Determinant in Mormon Theology. A Study in the Erotogenesis of Religion. *Alienist and Neurologist*, 29, 208–222.

Schroeder, T. (1914). Wildisbuch Crucified Saint. *Psychoanalytic Review*, 1, 128–148.

Schroeder, T. (1922). Prenatal Psychisms and Mystical Pantheism. *International Journal of Psycho-Analysis*, 3, 445–466.

Schroeder, T. (1929). The Psychoanalytic Approach to Religious Experience. *Psychoanalytic Review*, 16, 361–376.

Schroeder, T. (1932). A "Living God" Incarnate. *Psychoanalytic Review*, 19, 36–46.

Schubart, W. (1941). *Religion und Eros*. Edited by F. Seifert. Munich: C. H. Beck, 1966. (Originally published, 1941)

Schüttler, G. (1971). *Die letzten Tibetischen Orakelpriester: Psychiatrisch-neurologische Aspekte*. Wiesbaden: Franz Steiner.

Schultes, R. E., and Hoffmann, A. (1980). *The Botany and Chemistry of Hallucinogens*. (2nd ed.). Springfield, Ill.: Charles C. Thomas.

Schultz, A. H. (1969). *The Life of Primates*. New York: Universe Books.

Schultz, P. W., and Stone, W. F. (1994). Authoritarianism and Attitudes Toward the Environment. *Environment and Behavior*, 26, 25–37.

Schumaker, J. F. (Ed.). (1992). *Religion and Mental Health*. New York: Oxford University Press.

Schur, M. (1972). *Freud: Living and Dying*. New York: International Universities Press.

Schwartz, B. (1960). Ordeal by Serpents, Fire and Strychnine. *Psychiatric Quarterly*, 34, 405–429.

Scobie, G. E. W. (1975). *Psychology of Religion*. New York: Halsted Press.

Scott, C. E. (1972). An Existential Perspective on B. F. Skinner. *Soundings*, 55, 335–346.

Scrivener, L. (1995). Spiritual Experience Puts

Church on the Map. *The Toronto Star,* October 8, 1995, p. A2.

Scroggs, R. (1982). Psychology as a Tool to Interpret the Text. *Christian Century,* 99, 335–338.

Seberhagen, L. W., and Moore, M. H. (1969). A Note on Ranking the Important Psychologists. *Proceedings of the 77th Annual Convention of the American Psychological Association,* 849–850.

Seeman, W., Nidich, S., and Banta, T. (1972). Influence of Transcendental Meditation on a Measure of Self-Actualization. *Journal of Counseling Psychology,* 19, 184–187.

Segal, R. A. (Ed.). (1992). *The Gnostic Jung.* Princeton, N.J.: Princeton University Press.

Segal, R. A., Singer, J., and Stein, M. (Eds.). (1995). *The Allure of Gnosticism: The Gnostic Experience in Jungian Psychology and Contemporary Culture.* Chicago: Open Court.

Selbie, W. B. (1924). *The Psychology of Religion.* London: Oxford University Press.

Seltzer, W. J. (1984). Conversion Disorder in Childhood and Adolescence: A Familial/Cultural Approach: I. *Family Systems Medicine,* 3, 261–280.

Serafetinides, E. A. (1965). The Effects of LSD-25 on Alpha Blocking and Conditioning in Epileptic Patients Before and After Temporal Lobectomy. *Cortex,* 1, 485–492.

Sethi, S., and Seligman, M. E. P. (1993). Optimism and Fundamentalism. *Psychological Science,* 4, 256–259.

Sethi, S., and Seligman, M. E. P. (1994). The Hope of Fundamentalists. *Psychological Science,* 5, 58.

Shafranske, E. P. (Ed.). (1996). *Religion and the Clinical Practice of Psychology.* Washington, D.C.: American Psychological Association.

Shah, I. (1964). *The Sufis.* Garden City, N.Y.: Doubleday.

Shand, J. D. (1961). *A Factorial Analysis of Clergymen's Ratings of Concepts Regarding What It Means to be "Religious."* Ann Arbor, Mich.: University Microfilms. (No. 61-1980; an extension of the author's unpublished doctoral dissertation, University of Chicago, 1953)

Shapiro, D. H., Jr. (1980). *Meditation: Self-Regulation Strategy and Altered State of Consciousness.* New York: Aldine.

Shapiro, D. H., Jr., and Walsh, R. N. (Eds.). (1984). *Meditation: Classic and Contemporary Perspectives.* New York: Aldine.

Sharma, A. (Ed.). (1987). *Women in World Religions.* Albany: State University of New York Press.

Shaver, P., Lenauer, M., and Sadd, S. (1980). Religiousness, Conversion, and Subjective Well-Being: The "Healthy-Minded" Religion of Modern American Women. *American Journal of Psychiatry,* 137, 1563–1568.

Shaw, C. G. (1917). The Content of Religion and Psychological Analysis. In *Studies in Psychology: Contributed by Colleagues and Former Students of Edward Bradford Titchener.* Worcester, Mass.: Louis N. Wilson, pp. 30–42.

Shaw, M. E., and Wright, J. M. (1967). *Scales for the Measurement of Attitudes.* New York: McGraw-Hill.

Shelburne, W. A. (1988). *Mythos and Logos in the Thought of Carl Jung: The Theory of the Collective Unconscious in Scientific Perspective.* Albany: State University of New York Press.

Sheldon W. H. (1936). *Psychology and the Promethean Will.* New York: Harper & Brothers.

Sheldon, W. H. (1942) *The Varieties of Temperament: A Psychology of Constitutional Differences.* New York: Harper & Brothers.

Shinert, G., and Ford, E. E. (1958). The Relation of Ethnocentric Attitudes to Intensity of Religious Practice. *Journal of Educational Sociology,* 32, 157–162.

Shipley, M. (1933). A Maverick Psychologist. *The New Humanist,* 6(2), 37–40.

Shostrom, E. L. (1966). *Personal Orientation Inventory: An Inventory for the Measurement of Self-Actualization.* San Diego: Educational and Industrial Testing Service.

Shupe, A. (1995). *In the Name of All That's Holy: A Theory of Clergy Malfeasance.* Westport, Conn.: Praeger.

Siegel, R. K. (1980). The Psychology of Life After Death. *American Psychologist,* 35, 911–931.

Siegmund, G. (1942). Die Bedeutung des psychologischen Versuches für die Religionspsychologie. *Philosophisches Jahrbuch,* 55, 389–415.

Sierksma, F. (1950). *Phaenomenologie der Religie en Complexe Psychologie.* Assen: Van Gorcum. (Also published as *Freud, Jung en de Religie,* 1951)

Siggins, I. (1981). *Luther and His Mother.* Philadelphia: Fortress Press.

Silva, P. de. (1984). Buddhism and Behaviour Modification. *Behaviour Research and Therapy,* 22, 661–678.

Simons, R. C., Ervin, F. R., and Prince, R. H. (1988). The Psychobiology of Trance, I: Training for Thaipusam. *Transcultural Psychiatric Research,* 25, 249–266.

Singh, R. H., Shettiwar, R. M., and Udupa, K. N. (1982). Physiological and Therapeutic Studies on Yoga. *The Yoga Review,* 2, 185–209.

Siwek, P. (1950). *The Riddle of Konnersreuth: A Psychological and Religious Study.* Translated by I. McCormick. Milwaukee: Bruce, 1953. (French edition 1950)

Skinner, B. F. (1948a). "Superstition" in the Pigeon. *Journal of Experimental Psychology,* 38, 168–172. (Reprinted in Skinner, 1972)

Skinner, B. F. (1948b). *Walden Two.* New York: Macmillan.

Skinner, B. F. (1953). *Science and Human Behavior.* New York: Macmillan.

Skinner, B. F. (1969). *Contingencies of Reinforcement: A Theoretical Analysis.* New York: Appleton-Century-Crofts.

Skinner, B. F. (1971). *Beyond Freedom and Dignity.* New York: Alfred A. Knopf.

Skinner, B. F. (1972). *Cumulative Record: A Selection of Papers* (3rd ed.). New York: Appleton-Century-Crofts.

Skinner, B. F. (1974). *About Behaviorism.* New York: Alfred A. Knopf.

Skinner, B. F. (1976). *Particulars of My Life.* New York: Alfred A. Knopf.

Skrupskelis, I. K. (1977). *William James: A Reference Guide.* Boston: G. K. Hall.

Slonim, N. B., and Hamilton, L. H. (1971). *Respiratory Physiology* (2nd ed.). Saint Louis, Mo.: C. V. Mosby.

Slotkin, J. S. (1956). *The Peyote Religion.* Glencoe, Ill.: Free Press.

Slusser, G. H. (1986). *From Jung to Jesus: Myth and Consciousness in the New Testament.* Atlanta: John Knox Press.

Smith, A. J. (1951). *Religion and the New Psychology.* Garden City, N.Y.: Doubleday.

Smith, C. D. (1990). *Jung's Quest for Wholeness: A Religious and Historical Perspective.* Albany: State University of New York Press.

Smith, H. (1964). Do Drugs Have Religious Import? *Journal of Philosophy*, 61, 517–530. (Reprinted in Solomon, 1964)

Smith, H. (1967). Psychedelic Theophanies and the Religious Life. *Christianity and Crisis*, 27, 144–147.

Smith, H. (1976). *Forgotten Truth: The Primordial Tradition.* New York: Harper & Row.

Smith, H. (1991). *The World's Religions: Our Great Wisdom Traditions.* San Francisco: HarperSanFrancisco. (Revised edition of *The Religions of Man*, 1958)

Smith, H. S., Handy, R. T., and Loetscher, L. A. (1963). *American Christianity: An Historical Interpretation with Representative Documents, Vol. 2. 1820–1960.* New York: Charles Scribner's Sons.

Smith, J. C. (1975). Meditation as Psychotherapy: A Review of the Literature. *Psychological Bulletin*, 82, 558–564.

Smith, J. C. (1992). *Spiritual Living for a Skeptical Age: A Psychological Approach to Meditative Practice.* New York: Plenum.

Smith, R. E., Wheeler, G., and Diener, E. (1975). Faith Without Works: Jesus People, Resistance to Temptation, and Altruism. *Journal of Applied Social Psychology*, 5, 320–330.

Smith, W. C. (1959). Comparative Religion: Whither—and Why? In M. Eliade and J. M. Kitagawa (Eds.), *The History of Religions: Essays in Methodology.* Chicago: University of Chicago Press, pp. 31–58.

Smith, W. C. (1963). *The Meaning and End of Religion: A New Approach to the Religious Traditions of Mankind.* New York: Macmillan.

Smith, W. C. (1971). A Human View of Truth. *Studies in Religion*, 1, 6–24.

Smith, W. C. (1979). *Faith and Belief.* Princeton, N.J.: Princeton University Press.

Smith, W. C. (1988). Transcendence: The Ingersoll Lecture. *Harvard Divinity School Bulletin*, 18(3), 10–15.

Smith, W. R. (1894). *Lectures on the Religion of the Semites* (rev. ed.). London: Adam and Charles Black. (Original edition 1889)

Sneck, W. J. (1981). *Charismatic Spiritual Gifts: A Phenomenological Analysis.* Washington, D.C.: University Press of America.

Snyder, S. H. (1986). *Drugs and the Brain.* New York: Scientific American Books.

Solomon, D. (Ed.). (1964). *LSD—The Consciousness-Expanding Drug.* New York: G. P. Putnam's Sons.

Solomon, P., Kubzansky, P. E., Leiderman, P. H., Mendelson, J. H., Trumbull, R., and Weler, D. (Eds.). (1961). *Sensory Deprivation: A Symposium Held at Harvard Medical School.* Cambridge, Mass.: Harvard University Press.

Sorokin, P. A. (Ed.). (1954). *Forms and Techniques of Altruistic and Spiritual Growth: A Symposium.* Boston: Beacon Press.

Soyland, A. J. (1994). *Psychology as Metaphor.* London: Sage.

Sparrow, N. H., and Ross, J. (1964). The Dual Nature of Extraversion: A Replication. *Australian Journal of Psychology*, 16, 214–218.

Spence, D. P. (1982). *Narrative Truth and Historical Truth: Meaning and Interpretation in Psychoanalysis.* New York: W. W. Norton.

Spiegel, Y. (Ed.). (1972). *Psychoanalytische Interpretationen biblischer Texte.* Munich: Chr. Kaiser.

Spiegel, Y. (Ed.). (1978). *Doppeldeutlich, Tiefendimensionen biblischer Texte.* Munich: Chr. Kaiser.

Spiegelberg, H. (1965). *The Phenomenological Movement: A Historical Introduction* (2 Vols., 2nd ed.). The Hague: Martinus Nijhoff.

Spiegelberg, H. (1972). *Phenomenology in Psychology and Psychiatry.* Evanston, Ill.: Northwestern University Press.

Spiegelberg, H. (1975). *Doing Phenomenology: Essays On and In Phenomenology.* The Hague: Martinus Nijhoff.

Spiegelman, J. M. (1993). *Judaism and Jungian Psychology.* Lanham, Md.: University Press of America.

Spiegelman, J. M. (Ed.). (1994). *Catholicism and Jungian Psychology.* Tempe, Ariz.: New Falcon.

Spiegelman, J. M. (Ed.). (1995). *Protestantism and Jungian Psychology.* Tempe, Ariz.: New Falcon.

Spiegelman, J. M., and Miyuki, M. (1985). *Buddhism and Jungian Psychology.* Phoenix: Falcon Press.

Spiegelman, J. M., and Vasavada, A. U. (1987). *Hinduism and Jungian Psychology.* Phoenix: Falcon Press.

Spiegelman, J. M., Khan, P. V. I., and Fernandez, T. (Eds.). (1991). *Sufism, Islam and Jungian Psychology.* Scottsdale, Ariz.: New Falcon.

Spies, D. (1984). *Das Weltbild der Psychologie C. G. Jungs: Die philosophische und religionswissenschaftliche Bedeutung der Analytischen Psychologie.* Fellbach-Oeffingen: Adolf Bonz.

Spilka, B., Addison, J., and Rosensohn, M. (1975). Parents, Self, and God: A Test of Competing Theories of Individual-Religion Relationships. *Review of Religious Research,* 16, 154–165.

Spilka, B., Armatas, P., and Nussbaum, J. (1964). The Concept of God: A Factor-Analytic Approach. *Review of Religious Research,* 6, 28–36.

Spilka, B., Comp, G., and Goldsmith, W. M. (1981). Faith and Behavior: Religion in Introductory Psychology Texts of the 1950s and 1970s. *Teaching of Psychology,* 8, 158–160.

Spilka, B., Kojetin, B., and McIntosh, D. (1985). Forms and Measures of Personal Faith: Questions, Correlates and Distinctions. *Journal for the Scientific Study of Religion,* 24, 437–442.

Spilka, B., and McIntosh, D. N. (1995). Attribution Theory and Religious Experience. In R. W. Hood, Jr., *Handbook of Religious Experience,* pp. 421–445.

Spilka, B., Shaver, P., and Kirkpatrick, L. A. (1985). A General Attribution Theory for the Psychology of Religion. *Journal for the Scientific Study of Religion,* 24, 1–20.

Spilka, B., Stout, L., Minton, B., and Sizemore, D. (1977). Death and Personal Faith: A Psychometric Investigation. *Journal for the Scientific Study of Religion,* 16, 169–178.

Spilka, B., and Werme, P. H. (1971). Religion and Mental Disorder: A Research Perspective. In M. P. Strommen, *Research on Religious Development,* pp. 461–481.

Spiro, M. E., and D'Andrade, R. G. (1958). A Cross-Cultural Study of Some Supernatural Beliefs. *American Anthropologist,* 60, 456–466.

Spitz, L. W. (1977). Psychohistory and History: The Case of Young Man Luther. In R. A. Johnson, *Psychohistory and Religion,* pp. 57–87.

Spitz, R. (1946). Anaclitic Depression. *The Psychoanalytic Study of the Child,* 2, 313–342.

Spranger, E. (1969–1980). *Gesammelte Schriften* (11 vols.). Edited by H. W. Bähr et al. Tübingen: Max Niemeyer.

Spranger, E. (1914). *Lebensformen: Geisteswissenschaftliche Psychologie und Ethik der Persönlichkeit* (8th ed.; reprint of 5th ed.). Tübingen: Neomarius, 1950. (Fifth edition 1925; first, much shorter edition, 1914)

Spranger, E. (1924). *Psychologie des Jugendalters.* Leipzig: Quelle und Meyer.

Spranger, E. (1925). *Types of Men: The Psychology and Ethics of Personality.* Translated by P. J. W. Pigors. Halle: Max Niemeyer, 1928. (Translation of the 5th edition of *Lebensformen,* 1925)

Spranger, E. (1929). Der Sinn der Voraussetzungslosigkeit in den Geisteswissenschaften. In *Gesammelte Schriften,* Vol. 6, 1980, pp. 151–183. (First published in 1929)

Spranger, E. (1941). Weltfrömmigkeit. In *Gesammelte Schriften,* Vol. 9, 1974, pp. 224–250. (First published 1941)

Spranger, E. (1942). Zur Psychologie des Glaubens. In *Gesammelte Schriften,* Vol. 9, 1974, pp. 251–270. (First published in 1942)

Spranger, E. (1947). Die Schicksale des Christentums in der modernen Welt. In *Gesammelte Schriften,* Vol. 9, 1974, , pp. 15–74. (First published in 1947)

Spranger, E. (1954). Der unbekannte Gott. In *Gesammelte Schriften,* Vol. 9, 1974, pp. 75–100. (First published in 1954)

Spranger, E. (1964). Kurze Selbstdarstellungen. In H. W. Bähr and H. Wenke (Eds.), *Eduard Spranger: Sein Werk und sein Leben.* Heidelberg: Quelle & Meyer, pp. 13–21.

Spranger, E. (1974). Gibt es eine "religiöse Entwicklung"? In *Gesammelte Schriften,* Vol. 9, 1974, pp. 1–14. (Previously unpublished; written in 1945)

Spring, H., Moosbrugger, H., Zwingmann, C., and Frank, D. (1993). Kirchlicher Dogmatismus und ecclesiogene Neurosen. *Zeitschrift für Klinische Psychologie, Psychopathologie und Psychotherapie,* 41, 31–42.

Springer, S. P., and Deutsch, G. (1995). *Left Brain, Right Brain* (4rd ed.). San Francisco: W. H. Freeman.

Staal, F. (1975). *Exploring Mysticism: A Methodological Essay.* Berkeley: University of California Press.

Staats, A. W. (1987). Unified Positivism: Philosophy for the Revolution in Unity. *Annals of Theoretical Psychology,* 5, 11–54.

Stace, W. T. (1960). *Mysticism and Philosophy.* Philadelphia: J. B. Lippincott.

Stählin, W. (1912). Die Verwendung von Fragebogen in der Religionspsychologie. *Zeitschrift für Religionspsychologie,* 5, 394–408.

Stählin, W. (1914). Experimentelle Untersuchungen über Sprachpsychologie und Religionspsychologie. *Archiv für Religionspsychologie,* 1, 117–194.

Starbuck, E. D. (1897). A Study of Conversion. *American Journal of Psychology,* 8, 268–308.

Starbuck, E. D. (1899). *The Psychology of Religion: An Empirical Study of the Growth of Religious Consciousness.* New York: Charles Scribner's Sons.

Starbuck, E. D. (1904). The Varieties of Religious Experience. *The Biblical World,* NS 24, 100–111.

Starbuck, E. D. (1921). The Intimate Senses as Sources of Wisdom. *Journal of Religion,* 1, 129–145.

Starbuck, E. D. (1924). Life and Confessions of G. Stanley Hall: Some Notes on the Psychology of Genius. *Journal of Philosophy,* 21, 141–154.

Starbuck, E. D. (1925). G. Stanley Hall as a Psychologist. *Psychological Review,* 32, 103–120.

Starbuck, E. D. (1937). Religion's Use of Me. In V. Ferm, *Religion in Transition,* pp. 201–260.

Stark, R. (1971). Psychopathology and Religious Commitment. *Review of Religious Research,* 12, 165–176.

Stark, R., Foster, B. D., Glock, C. Y., and Quinley, H. E. (1971). *Wayward Shepherds: Prejudice and the Protestant Clergy.* New York: Harper & Row.

Stark, R., and Glock, C. Y. (1968). *American Piety: The*

Nature of Religious Commitment. Berkeley: University of California Press.

Staude, J.-R. (1981). *The Adult Development of C. G. Jung*. Boston: Routledge & Kegan Paul.

Stavenhagen, K. (1925). *Absolute Stellungsnahmen: Eine ontologische Untersuchung über das Wesen der Religion*. Erlangen: Verlag der Philosophischen Akademie.

Stein, M. (1985). *Jung's Treatment of Christianity: The Psychotherapy of a Religious Tradition*. Wilmette, Ill.: Chiron.

Stein, M., and Moore, R. L. (Eds.). (1987). *Jung's Challenge to Contemporary Religion*. Wilmette, Ill.: Chiron.

Steinberg, L. (1983). *The Sexuality of Christ in Renaissance Art and in Modern Oblivion* (2nd ed.). Chicago: University of Chicago Press, 1996. (First edition 1983)

Steinfels, P. (1994). Female Concept of God Is Shaking Protestants. *The New York Times*, May 14, p. 28.

Stern, A. (1957). Zum Problem der Epilepsie des Paulus. *Monatsschrift für Psychiatrie und Neurologie*, 133, 276–284.

Stern, D. N. (1985). *The Interpersonal World of the Infant: A View from Psychoanalysis and Developmental Psychology*. New York: Basic Books.

Stern, P. J. (1976). *C. G. Jung: The Haunted Prophet*. New York: Braziller.

Stern, W. (1935). *General Psychology from the Personalistic Standpoint*. Translated by H. D. Spoerl. New York: Macmillan, 1938. (Original German edition 1935)

Stevens, A. (1982). *Archetypes: A Natural History of the Self*. New York: William Morrow.

Stevens, J. (1987). *Storming Heaven: LSD and the American Dream*. New York: Harper & Row.

Stevenson, I. (1975). *Cases of the Reincarnation Type: I. Ten Cases in India*. Charlotteville, Va.: University Press of Virginia.

Stevenson, I. (1977a). The Explanatory Value of the Idea of Reincarnation. *Journal of Nervous and Mental Diseases*, 164, 305–326.

Stevenson, I. (1977b). Research into the Evidence of Man's Survival After Death: A Historical and Critical Survey with a Summary of Recent Developments. *Journal of Nervous and Mental Disease*, 165, 152–170.

Stevenson, J. G. (1913). *Religion and Temperament: A Popular Study of Their Relations, Actual and Possible*. London: Cassell.

Stewin, L. L. (1976). Integrative Complexity: Structure and Correlates. *Alberta Journal of Educational Research*, 22, 226–236.

Strandberg, V. (1981). *Religious Psychology in American Literature: A Study in the Relevance of William James*. Madrid: Jose Porrua Turanzas; Potomac, Md.: Studia Humanitatis.

Stratton, G. M. (1911). *Psychology of the Religious Life*. London: George Allen & Unwin.

Stratton, G. M. (1923) *Anger: Its Religious and Moral Significance*. New York: Macmillan.

Straus, E. (1956). *The Primary World of Senses: A Vindication of Sensory Experience*. Translated by J. Needleman. New York: Free Press of Glencoe, 1963. (Second German edition 1956)

Streeter, B. H., and Appasamy, A. J. (1921). *The Message of Sadhu Sundar Singh*. New York: Macmillan.

Streib, H. (1991). *Hermeneutics of Metaphor, Symbol and Narrative in Faith Development Theory*. Frankfurt am Main: Peter Lang.

Strelau, J. (1983). *Temperament, Personality and Arousal*. London: Academic Press.

Strenger, C. (1991). *Between Hermeneutics and Science: An Essay on the Epistemology of Psychoanalysis*. Madison, Conn.: International Universities Press.

Strickland, B. R., and Shaffer, S. (1971). I-E, I-E, & F. *Journal for the Scientific Study of Religion*, 10, 366–369.

Strickland, B. R., and Weddell, S. C. (1972). Religious Orientation, Racial Prejudice and Dogmatism: A Study of Baptists and Unitarians. *Journal for the Scientific Study of Religion*, 11, 395–399.

Strommen, M. P. (Ed.). (1971). *Research on Religious Development: A Comprehensive Handbook*. New York: Hawthorn.

Strouse, J. (Ed.). (1974). *Women and Analysis: Dialogues on Psychoanalytic Views of Femininity*. New York: Grossman.

Strout, C. (1968a). Ego Psychology and the Historian. *History and Theory*, 7, 218–297.

Strout, C. (1968b). William James and the Twice-Born Sick Soul. *Daedalus*, 97, 1062–1082.

Strout, C. (1971). The Pluralistic Identity of William James: A Psychohistorical Reading of *The Varieties of Religious Experience*. *American Quarterly*, 23, 135–152.

Strozier, C. B. (1994). *Apocalypse: On the Psychology of Fundamentalism in America*. Boston: Beacon Press.

Struening, E. L. (1963). Anti-Democratic Attitudes in Midwest University. In H. H. Remmers (Ed.), *Anti-Democratic Attitudes in American Schools*. Evanston, Ill.: Northwestern University Press, pp. 210–258.

Strunk, O., Jr. (1959a). Perceived Relationships Between Parental and Deity Concepts. *Psychological Newsletter*, 10, 222–226.

Strunk, O., Jr. (Ed.). (1959b). *Readings in the Psychology of Religion*. New York: Abingdon Press.

Strunk, O., Jr. (1962). *Religion: A Psychological Interpretation*. New York: Abingdon Press.

Strunk, O., Jr. (1965). *Mature Religion: A Psychological Study*. New York: Abingdon Press.

Strunk, O., Jr. (Ed.). (1971). *The Psychology of Religion: Historical and Interpretive Readings*. Nashville, Tenn.: Abingdon Press. (A revision and enlargement of Part I of Strunk, 1959)

Stubblefield, H. W., and Richard, W. C. (1965). The Concept of God in the Mentally Retarded. *Religious Education*, 60, 184–188.

Suedfeld, P. (1980). *Restricted Environmental Stimulation*. New York: John Wiley & Sons.

Suedfeld, P., and Mocellin, J. S. P. (1987). The

"Sensed Presence" in Unusual Environments. *Environment and Behavior,* 19, 33–52.

Sulloway, F. J. (1979). *Freud, Biologist of the Mind: Beyond the Psychoanalytic Legend.* New York: Basic Books.

Sundén, H. (1959). *Die Religion und die Rollen. Eine psychologische Untersuchung der Frömigkeit.* Berlin: Alfred Töpelmann, 1966. (Original Swedish edition 1959)

Sundén, H. (1969). Die Rollenpsychologie und die Weisen des Religions-Erlebens. In C. Hörgl, K. Krenn, and F. Rauh (Eds.), *Wesen und Weisen der Religion.* Munich: Max Hueber, pp. 132–144.

Sutker, P. B., Sutker, L. W., and Kilpatrick, D. G. (1970). Religious Preference, Practice, and Personal Sexual Attitudes and Behavior. *Psychological Reports,* 26, 835–841.

Suttie, I. D. (1932). Religion: Racial Character and Mental and Social Health. *British Journal of Medical Psychology,* 12, 289–314.

Suttie, I. D. (1935). *The Origins of Love and Hate.* New York: Julian Press, 1952. (First published 1935)

Sutula, T., Cascino, G., Cavazos, J., Parada, I., and Ramirez, L. (1989). Mossy Fiber Synaptic Reorganization in the Epileptic Human Temporal Lobe. *Annals of Neurology,* 26, 321–330.

Swartz, P. (1969). Fourth Force Psychology: A Humanist Disclaimer. *Psychological Record,* 19, 557–559.

Swedenborg, E. (1749). *Arcana Cœlestia. The Heavenly Arcana Contained in the Holy Scriptures or Word of the Lord . . . ,* Vol. 1. New York: American Swedenborg Printing and Publishing Society, 1853. (Original Latin edition 1749)

Sykes, G. (1962). *The Hidden Remnant.* New York: Harper.

Szentágothai, J. (1984). Downward Causation? *Annual Review of Neuroscience,* 7, 1–11.

Tafel, R. L. (Ed.). (1877). *Documents Concerning the Life and Character of Emanuel Swedenborg* (Vol. 2, Part 1). London: Swedenborg Society.

Tamminen, K. (1991). *Religious Development in Childhood and Youth: An Empirical Study.* Helsinki: Suomalainen Tiedeakatemia.

Tapp, R. B. (1971). Dimensions of Religiosity in a Post-Traditional Group. *Journal for the Scientific Study of Religion,* 10, 41–47.

Tart, C. T. (Ed.). (1975). *Transpersonal Psychologies.* New York: Harper & Row.

Tart, C. T. (Ed.). (1990). *Altered States of Consciousness* (3rd ed.). San Francisco: HarperSanFrancisco.

Tate, E. D., and Miller, G. R. (1971). Differences in Value Systems of Persons with Varying Religious Orientations. *Journal for the Scientific Study of Religion,* 10, 357–365.

Taylor, C., and Fontes, L. A. (1995). Seventh Day Adventists and Sexual Child Abuse. In L. A. Fontes (Ed.), *Sexual Abuse in Nine North American Cultures: Treatment and Prevention.* Thousand Oaks, Calif.: Sage, pp. 176–199.

Taylor, E. (1983). *William James on Exceptional Mental States: The 1896 Lowell Lectures.* New York: Charles Scribner's Sons.

Taylor, G. (1978). Demoniacal Possession and Psychoanalytic Theory. *British Journal of Medical Psychology,* 51, 53–60.

Taylor, M. J. (Ed.). (1960). *Religious Education: A Comprehensive Survey.* New York: Abingdon Press.

Temkin, O. (1971). *The Falling Sickness: A History of Epilepsy from the Greeks to the Beginning of Modern Neurology* (2nd ed.). Baltimore: John Hopkins University Press.

Tennison, J. C., and Snyder, W. O. (1968). Some Relationships Between Attitudes Toward the Church and Certain Personality Characteristics. *Journal of Counseling Psychology,* 15, 187–189.

Tenzler, J. (1975). *Selbstfindung und Gotteserfahrung: Die Persönlichkeit C. G. Jungs und ihr zentraler Niederschlag in seiner "Komplexen Psychologie."* Munich: Ferdinand Schöningh.

Terrill, J., Savage, C., and Jackson, D. D. (1962). LSD, Transcendence and the New Beginning. *Journal of Nervous and Mental Disease,* 135, 425–439. (Reprinted in Solomon, 1964)

Terwee, S. J. S. (1990). *Hermeneutics in Psychology and Psychoanalysis.* Berlin: Springer-Verlag.

Thomas, D. (1979). *The Face of Christ.* Garden City, N.Y.: Doubleday.

Thomas, K. (1964). *Handbuch der Selbstmordverhütung.* Stuttgart: Enke.

Thomas, K. (1971). Die Bedeutung der halluzinogenen Drogen für die Religionspsychologie. *Archiv fr Religionspsychologie,* 10, 100–118.

Thomas, K. (1973). *Meditation in Forschung und Erfahrung in weltweiter Beobachtung und praktischer Anleitung.* Stuttgart: Steinkopf-Thieme.

Thompson, A. D. (1974). Open-Mindedness and Indiscriminat[e] Antireligious Orientation. *Journal for the Scientific Study of Religion,* 13, 471–477.

Thompson, N. H. (Ed). (1988). *Religious Pluralism and Religious Education.* Birmingham, Ala.: Religious Education Press.

Thouless, R. H. (1924). *The Lady Julian: A Psychological Study.* London: S.P.C.K.

Thouless, R. H. (1935). The Tendency to Certainty in Religious Belief. *British Journal of Psychology,* 26, 16–31.

Thouless, R. H. (1971). *An Introduction to the Psychology of Religion* (3rd ed.). London: Cambridge University Press. (First edition 1923)

Thun, T. (1959). *Die Religion des Kindes* (2nd ed.). Stuttgart: Ernst Klett, 1964. (First edition 1959)

Thun, T. (1963). *Die religiöse Entscheidung der Jugend.* Stuttgart: Ernst Klett.

Thun, T. (1969). *Das religiöse Schicksal des alten Menschen.* Stuttgart: Ernst Klett.

Thurston, H. (1952). *The Physical Phenomena of Mysticism.* Edited by J. H. Crehan. London: Burns Oates.

Thurstone, L. L. (1934). The Vectors of Mind. *Psychological Review*, 41, 1–32.

Thurstone, L. L. (1952). [Autobiography.] In E. G. Boring et al., *A History of Psychology in Autobiography*, Vol. 4. Worcester, Mass.: Clark University Press, pp. 295–321.

Thurstone, L. L., and Chave, E. J. (1929). *The Measurement of Attitude: A Psychophysical Method and Some Experiments with a Scale for Measuring Attitude toward the Church*. Chicago: University of Chicago Press.

Tillich, P. (1952). *The Courage to Be*. New Haven, Conn.: Yale University Press.

Tisdale, J. R. (1966). Selected Correlates of Extrinsic Religious Values. *Review of Religious Research*, 7, 78–84.

Tizard, B. (1962). The Personality of Epileptics: A Discussion of the Evidence. *Psychological Bulletin*, 59, 196–210.

Toksvig, S. (1948). *Emanuel Swedenborg: Scientist and Mystic*. New Haven, Conn.: Yale University Press.

Tosi, D. J., and Hoffman, S. (1972). A Factor Analysis of the Personal Orientation Inventory. *Journal of Humanistic Psychology*, 12(1), 86–93.

Travis, F. T., and Orme-Johnson, D. W. (1990). EEG Coherence and Power During Yogic Flying. *International Journal of Neuroscience*, 54, 1–12.

Trillhaas, W. (1953). *Die innere Welt: Religionspsychologie*. Munich: Chr. Kaiser.

Trimingham, J. S. (1971). *The Sufi Orders in Islam*. London: Oxford University Press.

Troeltsch, E. (1904). [Review of] William James, *The Varieties of Religious Experience*. *Deutsche Literaturzeitung*, 25, 3021–3027.

Trout, D. M. (1931). *Religious Behavior: An Introduction to the Psychological Study of Religion*. New York: Macmillan.

Tumarkin, A. (1929). *Die Methoden der psychologische Forschung*. Leipzig: B. G. Teubner.

Tuzin, D. (1984). Miraculous Voices: The Auditory Experience of Numinous Objects. *Current Anthropology*, 25, 579–596.

Tweedie, D. F., Jr. (1961). *Logotherapy and the Christian Faith: An Evaluation of Frankl's Existential Approach to Psychotherapy*. Grand Rapids, Mich.: Baker Book House.

Ugrinovitch, D. M. (1986). *Psichologia religii*. Moscow: Izdatielstvo Politichieskoi Literatury.

Ulanov, A. B. (1971). *The Feminine in Jungian Psychology and in Christian Theology*. Evanston, Ill.: Northwestern University Press.

Ulanov, A. B. (1981). *Receiving Woman: Studies in the Psychology and Theology of the Feminine*. Philadelphia: Westminster Press.

Ulanov, B. (1992). *Jung and the Outside World*. Wilmette, Ill.: Chiron.

Ullman, C. (1989). *The Transformed Self: The Psychology of Religious Conversion*. New York: Plenum.

Underhill, E. (1911). *Mysticism: A Study in the Nature and Development of Man's Spiritual Consciousness* (rev. ed.). London: Methuen, 1930. (First edition 1911)

Unger, S. M. (1963). Mescaline, LSD, Psilocybin, and Personality Change: A Review. *Psychiatry*, 26, 111–125. (Reprinted in Solomon, 1964)

Uren, A. R. (1928). *Recent Religious Psychology: A Study in the Psychology of Religion*. New York: Charles Scribner's Sons.

Utsch, M. (1995). *Grundmerkmale wissenschaftlicher Religionspsychologie und Entwurf einer Synopse*. Bonn: Rheinischen Friedrich-Wilhelms-Universität. (Inaugural dissertation)

Vande Kemp, H. (1976). Teaching Psychology/Religion in the Seventies: Monopoly or Cooperation? *Teaching of Psychology*, 3, 15–18.

Vande Kemp, H. (1984). *Psychology and Theology In Western Thought, 1672–1965: A Historical and Annotated Bibliography*. In collaboration with H. N. Malony. Millwood, N.Y.: Kraus.

Vande Kemp, H. (1985). Theodore Schroeder's Proposed Institute of Religious Psychology. *Newsletter of Division 36, American Psychological Association*, 10(1), 5.

Vande Kemp, H. (1992). G. Stanley Hall and the Clark School of Religious Psychology. *American Psychologist*, 47, 290–298.

Vandendriessche, G. (1965). *The Parapraxis in the Haizmann Case of Sigmund Freud*. Louvain: Publications Universitaires.

Vander Goot, M. (1985). *Piaget as a Visionary Thinker*. Bristol, Ind.: Wyndham Hall Press.

van der Leeuw, G. (1926). Ueber einige neuere Ergebnisse der psychologischen Forschung und ihre Anwendung auf die Geschichte, insonderheit der Religionsgeschichte. *Studi e materiali di storie della religioni*, 2, 1–43.

van der Leeuw, G. (1928). Strukturpsychologie und Theologie. *Zeitschrift für Theologie und Kirche*, N.F. 9, 321–349.

van der Leeuw, G. (1933). *Religion in Essence and Manifestation: A Study in Phenomenology*. Translated by J. E. Turner. London: George Allen & Unwin, 1938. (Original German edition 1933)

van der Post, L. (1975). *Jung and the Story of Our Time*. New York: Vintage.

Van Haitsma, K. (1986). Intrinsic Religious Orientation: Implications in the Study of Religiosity and Personal Adjustment in the Aged. *Journal of Social Psychology*, 126, 685–687.

Van Herik, J. (1982). *Freud on Femininity and Faith*. Berkeley: University of California Press.

van Manen, M. (1990). *Researching Lived Experience: Human Science for an Action Sensitive Pedagogy*. Albany: State University of New York Press.

Van Ormer, E. B. (1931). Behavioristic Psychology: Its Meaning and Its Influence on Morals and Religion. *Lutheran Church Quarterly*, 4, 261–283.

Van Teslaar, J. S. (1915). Religion and Sex: An Account of the Erotogenetic Theory of Religion as

Formulated by Theodore Schroeder. *Psychoanalytic Review*, 2, 81–92.

Vaughan, F., Wittine, B., and Walsh, R. (1996). Transpersonal Psychology and the Religious Person. In E. P. Shafranske, *Religion and the Clinical Practice of Psychology*, pp. 483–509.

Vaughan, G. M., and Mangan, G. L. (1963). Conformity to Group Pressure in Relation to the Value of the Task Material. *Journal of Abnormal and Social Psychology*, 66, 179–183.

Vercruysse, G. (1972). The Meaning of God: A Factoranalytic Study. *Social Compass*, 19, 347–364.

Vergote, A., and Tamayo, A. (Eds.). (1981). *The Parental Figures and the Representation of God: A Psychological and Cross-Cultural Study*. The Hague: Mouton.

Vernon, G. M. (1962). Measuring Religion: Two Methods Compared. *Review of Religious Research*, 3, 159–165.

Vernon, G. M. (1968). The Religious "Nones": A Neglected Category. *Journal for the Scientific Study of Religion*, 7, 219–229.

Vernon, G. M. (Ed.). *Types and Dimensions of Religion: Readings in the Sociology of Religion*. Salt Lake City: Association for the Study of Religion.

Vernon, G. M., and Cardwell, J. D. (1972). Males, Females, and Religion. In G. M. Vernon, *Types and Dimensions of Religion*, pp. 103–132.

Veroff, J., Douvan, E., and Kulka, R. A. (1981). *The Inner American: A Self-Portrait from 1957 to 1976*. New York: Basic Books.

Veszy-Wagner, L. (1966). Ernest Jones: The Biography of Freud. In F. Alexander, S. Eisenstein, and M. Grotjahn (Eds.), *Psychoanalytic Pioneers*. New York: Basic Books, pp. 87–141.

Vetter, G. B. (1958). *Magic and Religion: Their Psychological Nature, Origin, and Function*. New York: Philosophical Library.

Vetter, G. B., and Green, M. (1932). Personality and Group Factors in the Making of Atheists. *Journal of Abnormal and Social Psychology*, 27, 179–194.

Vidal, F. (1987). Jean Piaget and the Liberal Protestant Tradition. In M. G. Ash and W. R. Woodward (Eds.), *Psychology in Twentieth-Century Thought and Society*. Cambridge: Cambridge University Press, pp. 271–294.

Vinacke, W. E., Eindhoven, J., and Engle, J. (1949). Religious Attitudes of Students at the University of Hawaii. *Journal of Psychology*, 28, 161–179.

Vine, I. (1978). Facts and Values in the Psychology of Religion. *Bulletin of the British Psychological Society*, 31, 414–417.

Vitz, P. C. (1977). *Psychology as Religion: The Cult of Self-Worship* (rev. ed.). Grand Rapids, Mich.: William B. Eerdmans, 1994. (First edition 1977)

Vitz, P. C. (1988). *Sigmund Freud's Christian Unconscious*. New York: Guilford.

Voeks, V. W. (1950). Formalization and Clarification of a Theory of Learning. *Journal of Psychology*, 30, 341–362.

Vogel, P. (1936). Ein Beitrag zur Religionspsychologie des Kindes. *Archiv für die gesamte Psychologie*, 96, 311–466.

Von Grünebaum, G. E. (1951). *Muhammadan Festivals*. New York: Henry Schuman.

Von Hügel, F. (1908). *The Mystical Element of Religion, as Studied in Saint Catherine of Genoa and Her Friends*, Vol. 1. (2nd ed.). London: J. M. Dent & Sons, 1923. (First edition 1908)

von Knorre, H. (1991). Ein Beitrag aus psychoanalytischer Sicht. In M. Dieterich (Ed.), *Wenn der Glaube krank macht: Psychische Strungen und religiöse Ursachen*. Wuppertal: R. Brockhaus, pp. 46–56.

von Rad, G. (1972). *Genesis: A Commentary* (rev. ed.). Translated by J. H. Marks. Philadelphia: Westminster Press, 1972. (Ninth German edition 1972)

von Weizacker, V. (1954). Reminiscences of Freud and Jung. In B. Nelson, *Freud and the 20th Century*, 1957, pp. 59–75. (Original German edition 1954)

Vorbrodt, G. (1895). *Psychologie des Glaubens. Zugleich ein Appell an die Verachter des Christentums unter den wissenschaftlich interessirten Gebildeten*. Göttingen: Vandenhoeck und Ruprecht.

Vorbrodt, G. (1904). *Beiträge zur religisen Psychologie: Psychobiologie und Gefühl*. Leipzig: A. Deichert.

Vorbrodt, G. (1911). [Introduction and commentary.] In T. Flournoy, *Beiträge zur Religionspsychologie*. Translated by M. Regel. Leipzig: Fritz Eckardt.

Vorwahl, H. (1933). Die Religion der Jugend. *Viertaljahrschrift für Jugendkunde*, 3, 143–152.

Voutsinas, D. (1975). *La Psychologie de Maine de Biran*. Paris: Société d'Imprimerie Périodiques et d'Édition.

Wach, J. (1951). *Types of Religious Experience, Christian and Non-Christian*. Chicago: University of Chicago Press.

Wahba, M. A., and Bridwell, L. G. (1976). Maslow Reconsidered: A Review of Research on the Need Hierarchy Theory. *Organizational Behavior and Human Performance*, 15, 212–240.

Wallace, E. R., IV. (1984). Freud and Religion: A History and Reappraisal. *Psychoanalytic Study of Society*, 10, 115–161.

Wallace, R. K. (1970a). The Physiological Effects of Transcendental Meditation: A Proposed Fourth Major State of Consciousness (University of California, Los Angeles, 1970). *Dissertation Abstracts International*, 1971, 31, 4303B. (University Microfilms No. 71-735). (Reproduced by MIU Press, 1970)

Wallace, R. K. (1970b). Physiological Effects of Transcendental Meditation. *Science*, 167, 1751–1754.

Wallace, R. K. (1986). *The Neurophysiology of Enlightenment*. Fairfield, Ia.: MIU Press.

Wallace, R. K., and Benson, H. (1972). The Physiology of Meditation. *Scientific American*, 226(2), 84–90.

Wallace, R. K., Benson, H., and Wilson, A. F. (1971). A Wakeful Hypometabolic Physiologic State. *American Journal of Physiology*, 221, 795–799.

Wallace, R. K., Orme-Johnson, D. W., and Dillbeck, M. C. (Eds.). (1990). *Scientific Research on Maharishi's Transcendental Meditation Program: Collected Papers*, Vol. 5. Fairfield, Ia.: MIU Press.

Wallach, M. A., and Wallach, L. (1983). *Psychology's Sanction for Selfishness: The Error of Egoism in Theory and Therapy*. San Francisco: W. H. Freeman.

Walle, A. H. (1992). William James's Legacy to Alcoholics Anonymous: An Analysis and a Critique. *Journal of Addictive Diseases*, 11, 91–99.

Waller, N. G., Kojetin, B. A., Bouchard, T. J., Jr., Lykken, D. T., and Tellegen, A. (1990). Genetic and Environmental Influences on Religious Interests, Attitudes, and Values: A Study of Twins Reared Apart and Together. *Psychological Science*, 1, 138–142.

Wallis, C. (1996). Faith and Healing. *Time*, June 24, pp. 58–62, 64.

Wallis, J. H. (1988). *Jung and the Quaker Way*. London: Quaker Home Service.

Wallulis, J. (1990). *The Hermeneutics of Life History: Personal Achievement and History in Gadamer, Habermas, and Erikson*. Evanston, Ill.: Northwestern University Press.

Walsh, R. (1984). *Staying Alive: The Psychology of Human Survival*. Boulder, Colo.: Shambhala.

Walsh, R. (1993). The Transpersonal Movement: A History and State of the Art. *Journal of Transpersonal Psychology*, 25, 123–139.

Walsh, R. N., and Shapiro, D. H. (Eds.). (1983). *Beyond Health and Normality: Explorations of Exceptional Psychological Well-Being*. New York: Van Nostrand Reinhold.

Walsh, R., and Vaughan, F. (Eds.). (1993). *Paths Beyond Ego: The Transpersonal Vision*. Los Angeles: Jeremy P. Tarcher.

Wann, D. L. (1993). Sexual Permissiveness and Religious Orientation. *Psychological Reports*, 73, 562.

Ward, D. J. H. (1888). *How Religion Arises: A Psychological Study*. Boston: Geo. H. Ellis.

Warren, J. R., and Heist, P. A. (1960). Personality Attributes of Gifted College Students. *Science*, 132, 330–337.

Washburn, M. (1995). *The Ego and the Dynamic Ground: A Transpersonal Theory of Human Development* (2nd ed.). Albany: State University of New York.

Wasson, R. G. (1961). The Hallucinogenic Fungi of Mexico: An Inquiry into the Origins of the Religious Idea among Primitive Peoples. *Harvard Botanical Museum Leaflets*, 19, No. 7. (Reprinted in Weil, Metzner, and Leary, 1965)

Wasson, R. G. (1969). *Soma: Divine Mushroom of Immortality*. New York: Harcourt Brace Jovanovich.

Watson, G. B. (1929). An Approach to the Study of Worship. *Religious Education*, 24, 849–858.

Watson, J. B. (1928). *The Ways of Behaviorism*. New York: Harper & Brothers.

Watson, P. J. (1993). Apologetics and Ethnocentrism: Psychology and Religion. *The International Journal for the Psychology of Religion*, 3, 1–20.

Watson, P. J., Hood, R. W., Jr., Morris, R. J., and Hall, J. R. (1984). Empathy, Religious Orientation, and Social Desirability. *Journal of Psychology*, 117, 211–216.

Watson, P. J., Howard, R., Hood, R. W., Jr., and Morris, R. J. (1988). Age and Religious Orientation. *Review of Religious Research*, 29, 271–280.

Watson, P. J., Morris, R. J., and Hood, R. W., Jr. (1987). Antireligious Humanistic Values, Guilt, and Self Esteem. *Journal for the Scientific Study of Religion*, 26, 535–546.

Watson, P. J., Morris, R. J., and Hood, R. W., Jr. (1989). Interactional Factor Correlations with Means and End Religiousness. *Journal for the Scientific Study of Religion*, 28, 337–347.

Watson, P. J., Morris, R. J., and Hood, R. W. (1994). Religion and Rationality: I. Rational-Emotive and Religious Understandings of Perfectionism and Other Irrationalities. *Journal of Psychology and Christianity*, 13, 356–372.

Watson, P. J., Morris, R. J., Hood, R. W., and Biderman, M. D. (1990). Religious Orientation Types and Narcissism. *Journal of Psychology and Christianity*, 9, 40–46.

Watts, A. W. (1962). *The Joyous Cosmology: Adventures in the Chemistry of Consciousness*. New York: Pantheon.

Wearing, A. J., and Brown, L. B. (1972). The Dimensionality of Religion. *British Journal of Social and Clinical Psychology*, 11, 143–148.

Weaver, A. J., Berry, J. W., and Pittel, S. M. (1994). Ego Development in Fundamentalist and Nonfundamentalist Protestants. *Journal of Psychology and Theology*, 22, 215–225.

Webb, S. C. (1965). An Exploratory Investigation of Some Needs Met Through Religious Behavior. *Journal for the Scientific Study of Religion*, 5, 51–58.

Webster, A. C., and Stewart, R. A. C. (1973). Theological Conservatism. In G. D. Wilson (Ed.), *The Psychology of Conservatism*. London: Academic Press, pp. 129–147.

Wehr, D. (1987). *Jung and Feminism: Liberating Archetypes*. Boston: Beacon Press.

Wehr, G. (1975). *C. G. Jung und das Christentum*. Olten: Walter.

Wehr, G. (1985). *Jung: A Biography*. Translated by D. M. Weeks. Boston: Shambhala, 1987. (Original German edition 1985)

Weigert, A. J., and Thomas, D. L. (1969). Religiosity in 5–D: A Critical Note. *Social Forces*, 48, 260–263.

Weil, G. M., Metzner, R., and Leary, T. (Eds.). (1965). *The Psychedelic Reader*. New Hyde Park, N.Y.: University Books.

Weima, J. (1965). Authoritarianism, Religious Conservatism and Sociocentric Attitudes in Roman Catholic Groups. *Human Relations*, 18, 231–239.

Weima, J. (1986). Batson's Three-Dimensional Model of Religious Orientations. Some Critical Notes and a Partial Replication. In J. A. van Belzen and J. M. van der Lans, *Current Issues in the Psychology of Religion*, pp. 215–224.

Weintraub, W., and Aronson, H. (1974). Patients in Psychoanalysis: Some Findings Related to Sex and Religion. *American Journal of Orthopsychiatry*, 44, 102–108.

Weisner, W. N., and Riffel, P. A. (1960). Scrupulosity: Religion and Obsessive Compulsive Behavior in Children. *American Journal of Psychiatry*, 117, 314–318.

Weitbrecht, H. J. (1948). *Beiträge zur Religionspsychopathologie, insbesondere zur Psychopathologie der Bekehrung.* Heidelberg: Scherer.

Welford, A. T. (1971). *Christianity: A Psychologist's Interpretation.* London: Hodder and Stoughton.

Wellek, A. (1957). The Phenomenological and Experimental Approaches to Psychology and Characterology. In H. P. David and H. von Bracken (Eds.), *Perspectives in Personality Theory.* New York: Basic Books, pp. 278–299.

Wellisch, E. (1954). *Isaac and Oedipus: A Study in Biblical Psychology of the Sacrifice of Isaac, the Akedah.* London: Routledge & Kegan Paul.

Wells, H. G. (1934). *Experiment in Autobiography: Discoveries and Conclusions of a Very Ordinary Brain (Since 1866).* New York: Macmillan.

Wells, H. K. (1962). Religious Attitudes at a Small Denominational College as Compared with Harvard and Radcliffe. *Journal of Psychology*, 53, 349–382.

Wells, W. R. (1917). *A Behavioristic Study of Religious Values.* Unpublished doctoral dissertation, Harvard University.

Wells, W. R. (1921). *The Biological Foundations of Belief.* Boston: R. G. Badger.

Wenger, M. A., and Bagchi, B. K. (1961). Studies of Autonomic Functions in Practitioners of Yoga in India. *Behavioral Science*, 6, 312–323.

Wenger, M. A., Bagchi, B. K., and Anand, B. (1961). Experiments in India on "Voluntary" Control of the Heart and Pulse. *Circulation*, 24, 1319–1325.

West, M. A. (Ed.). (1987). *The Psychology of Meditation.* Oxford: Oxford University Press.

Wheeler, H. (Ed.). (1973). *Beyond the Punitive Society; Operant Conditioning: Social and Political Aspects.* San Francisco: W. H. Freeman.

White, J. (Ed.). (1972). *The Highest State of Consciousness.* Garden City, N.Y.: Doubleday Anchor.

White, J. (Ed.). (1974). *What is Meditation?* Garden City, N.Y.: Doubleday Anchor.

White, L., Jr. (1967). The Historical Roots of Our Ecological Crisis. *Science*, 155, 1203–1207.

White, V. (1952). *God and the Unconscious.* London: Harvill Press.

White, V. (1960). *Soul and Psyche: An Enquiry into the Relationship of Psychotherapy and Religion.* New York: Harper & Brothers.

Whitehead, A. N. (1926). *Religion in the Making.* New York: Macmillan.

Whitehead, E. E., and Whitehead, J. D. (1979). *Christian Life Patterns: The Psychological Challenges and Religious Invitations of Adult Life.* Garden City, N.J.: Doubleday.

Whitmont, E. C. (1982). *Return of the Goddess.* New York: Crossroad.

Whybrow, P. C., Prange, A. J., Jr., and Treadway, C. R. (1969). Mental Changes Accompanying Thyroid Gland Dysfunction. *Archives of General Psychiatry*, 20, 48–63.

Whyte, A. (1895). *The Four Temperaments.* London: Hodder and Stoughton.

Wiehe, V. R. (1990). Religious Influence on Parental Attitudes Toward the Use of Corporal Punishment. *Journal of Family Violence*, 5, 173–186.

Wieman, H. N. (1926). *Religious Experience and Scientific Method.* New York: Macmillan.

Wieman, H. N., and Westcott-Wieman, R. (1935). *Normative Psychology of Religion.* New York: Thomas Y. Crowell.

Wikström, O. (1993). The Psychology of Religion in Scandinavia. *International Journal for the Psychology of Religion*, 3, 47–65.

Wilber, K. (1977). *The Spectrum of Consciousness* (2nd ed). Wheaton, Ill.: Quest, 1993. (First edition 1977)

Wilber, K. (1981). *Up from Eden: A Transpersonal View of Human Evolution.* Garden City, N.Y.: Anchor Press/Doubleday.

Wilber, K. (1995). *Sex, Ecology, Spirituality: The Spirit of Evolution.* Boston: Shambala.

Williams, D. L., and Kremer, B. J. (1974). Pastoral Counseling Students and Secular Counseling Students: A Comparison. *Journal of Consulting Psychology*, 21, 238–242.

Williams, D. R. (1994). The Measurement of Religion in Epidemiologic Studies: Problems and Prospects. In J. S. Levin, *Religion in Aging and Health*, pp. 125–148.

W[ilson], B. (1957). When A.A. Came of Age. In *Alcoholics Anonymous Comes of Age: A Brief History of A.A.* New York: Alcoholics Anonymous World Services, pp. 1–48.

W[ilson], B., and Jung, C. G. (1963). The Bill W.–Carl Jung Letters. *Grapevine*, 24(8), 16–21.

Wilson, E. O. (1978). *On Human Nature.* Cambridge, Mass.: Harvard University Press.

Wilson, G. D. (Ed.). (1973). *The Psychology of Conservatism.* London: Academic Press.

Wilson, G. D., and Lillie, F. J. (1972). Social Attitudes of Salvationists and Humanists. *British Journal of Social and Clinical Psychology*, 11, 220–224.

Wilson, W. C. (1960). Extrinsic Religious Values and Prejudice. *Journal of Abnormal and Social Psychology*, 60, 286–288.

Wilson, W., and Kawamura, W. (1967). Rigidity, Adjustment, and Social Responsibility as Possible Correlates of Religiousness: A Test of Three Points of View. *Journal for the Scientific Study of Religion*, 6, 279–280.

Windholz, G. (1986). Pavlov's Religious Orientation. *Journal for the Scientific Study of Religion,* 25, 320–327.

Winnicott, D. W. (1953). Transitional Objects and Transitional Phenomena. *International Journal of Psycho-Analysis,* 34, 89–97. (Edited version reprinted in Winnicott, 1971)

Winnicott, D. W. (1971). *Playing and Reality.* London: Tavistock.

Witelson, S. F., and Kristofferson, A. B. (Eds.). (1986). McMaster-Bauer Symposium on Consciousness. *Canadian Psychology,* 27, 123–182.

Wittels, F. (1931). *Freud and His Time.* New York: Liveright.

Witztum, E., Greenberg, D., and Buchbinder, J. T. (1990). "A Very Narrow Bridge": Diagnosis and Management of Mental Illness Among Bratslav Hasidim. *Psychotherapy,* 27, 124–131.

Wobbermin, G. (1907). Vorwort des übersetzers. In W. James, *Die Religiöse Erfahrung in ihrer Mannigfaltigkeit.* Translated by G. Wobbermin. Leipzig: J. C. Hinrichs. (Translation of James, 1902)

Wobbermin, G. (1921). *Das Wesen der Religion,* Vol. 2 of *Systematische Theologie nach religionspsychologischer Methode.* Leipzig: J. C. Hinrichs.

Wobbermin, G. (1928). Die Methoden der religionspsychologischen Arbeit. In E. Abderhalden (Ed.), *Handbuch der biologischen Arbeitsmethoden,* Abt. 6, Teil C/1. Berlin: Urban und Schwarzenberg, pp. 1–44.

Wobbermin, G. (1933). *The Nature of Religion.* Translated by T. Menzel and D. S. Robinson. New York: Thomas Y. Crowell. (Translation of Wobbermin, 1921)

Wolman, B. B., and Ullman, M. (Eds.). (1986). *Handbook of States of Consciousness.* New York: Van Nostrand Reinhold.

Wood, E. (1959). *Yoga.* Baltimore: Penguin.

Woodburne, A. S. (1920). *The Relation Between Religion and Science: A Biological Approach.* Chicago: University of Chicago Press.

Woodroof, J. T. (1985). Premarital Sexual Behavior and Religious Adolescents. *Journal for the Scientific Study of Religion,* 24, 343–366.

Woodrum, E., and Hoban, T. (1994). Theology and Religiosity Effects on Environmentalism. *Review of Religious Research,* 35, 193–206.

Woodward, K. (1994). On the Road Again. *Newsweek,* November 28, pp. 61–62.

Woodward, K. L. (1989). Heaven. *Newsweek,* March 27, pp. 52–55.

Wosien, M.-G. (1974). *Sacred Dance: Encounter with the Gods.* New York: Avon Books.

Wright, D. (1971). *The Psychology of Moral Behaviour.* Harmondsworth: Penguin.

Wright, D., and Cox, E. (1967). Religious Belief and Co-education in a Sample of Sixth-Form Boys and Girls. *British Journal of Social and Clinical Psychology,* 6, 23–31.

Wright, J. E., Jr. (1982). *Erikson: Identity and Religion.* New York: Seabury Press.

Wulff, D. M. (1970). Varieties of Temporal Orientation and Their Measurement (University of Michigan, 1969). *Dissertation Abstracts International,* 31, 907B–908B. (University Microfilms No. 70-14,688)

Wulff, David M. (1982). Prolegomenon to a Psychology of the Goddess. In J. S. Hawley and Donna M. Wulff (Eds.), *The Divine Consort: Radha and the Goddesses of India.* Berkeley, Calif.: Religious Studies Series, pp. 283–297.

Wulff, D. M. (1985a). Experimental Introspection and Religious Experience: The Dorpat School of Religious Psychology. *Journal of the History of the Behavioral Sciences,* 21, 131–150.

Wulff, D. M. (1985b). Psychological Approaches. In F. Whaling (Ed.), *Contemporary Approaches to the Study of Religion,* Vol. 2, *The Social Sciences.* Berlin: Mouton, pp. 21–88.

Wulff, D. M. (1992). Reality, Illusion, or Metaphor? Reflections on the Conduct and Object of the Psychology of Religion. *Journal of the Psychology of Religion,* 1, 25–51.

Wulff, D. M. (1995a) An Annotated Bibliography on William James's *The Varieties of Religious Experience,* with a List of English-language Editions, Audio Recordings, and Translations. In D. Capps and J. L. Jacobs, *The Struggle for Life,* pp. 281–305.

Wulff, D. M. (1995b). Phenomenological Psychology and Religious Experience. In R. W. Hood, Jr., *Handbook of Religious Experience,* pp. 183–199.

Wunderle, G. (1922). *Einführung in die moderne Religionspsychologie.* Munich: Josef Kösel & Friedrich Pustet.

Wunderle, G. (1947). *Zur Psychologie des hesychastischen Gebets* (2nd ed.). Würzburg: Augustinus, 1949. (First edition 1947)

Wundt, W. (1905–1909). *Mythus und Religion* (3 vols., 2nd ed.), Vols. 4–6 of *Völkerpsychologie: Eine Untersuchung der Entwicklungsgesetze von Sprache, Mythus und Sitte.* Leipzig: Alfred Kröner, 1910–1915. (First edition 1905–1909)

Wundt, W. (1911). *Probleme der Völkerpsychologie* (2nd ed.). Stuttgart: Alfred Kröner, 1921. (First edition 1911)

Wurtman, R. J. (1975). The Effects of Light on the Human Body. *Scientific American,* 233, 68–77.

Wuthnow, R. (1978). Peak Experiences: Some Empirical Tests. *Journal of Humanistic Psychology,* 18(3), 59–75.

Wyke, B. (1963). *Brain Function and Metabolic Disorders: The Neurological Effects of Changes in Hydrogen Ion Concentration.* London: Butterworths.

Wyss, D. (1961). *Depth Psychology: A Critical History.* Translated by G. Onn. London: George Allen & Unwin, 1966. (Original German edition 1961)

Wyss, D. (1991). *Psychologie und Religion: Untersuchungen zur Ursprünglichkeit religiösen Erlebens.* Würzburg: Königshausen & Neumann.

Yankelovich, D., and Barrett, W. (1970). *Ego and Instinct: The Psychoanalytic View of Human Nature— Revised.* New York: Random House.

Yao, R. (1987). *An Introduction to Fundamentalists Anonymous*. New York: Fundamentalists Anonymous.

Yerushalmi, Y. H. (1991). *Freud's Moses: Judaism Terminable and Interminable*. New Haven: Yale University Press.

Yinger, J. M. (1969). A Structural Examination of Religion. *Journal for the Scientific Study of Religion*, 8, 88–99.

Yinger, J. M. (1977). A Comparative Study of the Substructures of Religion. *Journal for the Scientific Study of Religion*, 16, 67–86.

Yockelson, S., and Samenow, S. E. (1976). *The Criminal Personality: Vol. 1. A Profile for Change*. New York: Jason Aronson.

Young, K. (1926). The Psychology of Hymns. *Journal of Abnormal and Social Psychology*, 20, 391–406.

Young, R. K., Benson, W. M., and Holtzman, W. H. (1960). Change in Attitudes Toward the Negro in a Southern University. *Journal of Abnormal and Social Psychology*, 60, 131–133.

Zacharias, G. P. (1954). *Psyche und Mysterium. Die Bedeutung der Psychologie C. G. Jungs für die christliche Theologie und Liturgie*. Zurich: Rascher.

Zaehner, R. C. (1957). *Mysticism, Sacred and Profane: An Inquiry into Some Varieties of Praeternatural Experience*. London: Oxford University Press.

Zaehner, R. C. (1959). A New Buddha and a New Tao. In R. C. Zaehner (Ed.), *The Concise Encyclopedia of Living Faiths*. New York: Hawthorn Books, pp. 402–412.

Zaehner, R. C. (1972). *Zen, Drugs and Mysticism*. New York: Pantheon. (British edition published as *Drugs, Mysticism and Makebelieve*)

Zaidel, E. (1985). Language in the Right Hemisphere. In D. F. Benson and E. Zaidel (Eds.), *The Dual Brain: Hemispheric Specialization in Humans*. New York: Guilford Press, pp. 205–231.

Zaleski, C. (1987). *Otherworld Journeys: Accounts of Near-Death Experience in Medieval and Modern Times*. New York: Oxford University Press.

Zaleski, C. (1993–94). Speaking of William James to the Cultured Among His Despisers. *Journal of the Psychology of Religion*, 2–3, 127–170. (Reprinted in Capps and Jacobs, 1995)

Zeligs, D. F. (1974). *Psychoanalysis and the Bible: A Study in Depth of Seven Leaders*. New York: Bloch.

Zilboorg, G. (1962). *Psychoanalysis and Religion*. Edited by M. S. Zilboorg. New York: Farrar, Straus and Cudahy.

Zock, H. (1990). *A Psychology of Ultimate Concern: Erik H. Erikson's Contribution to the Psychology of Religion*. Amsterdam: Rodopi.

Zubek, J. P. (Ed.). (1969). *Sensory Deprivation: Fifteen Years of Research*. New York: Appleton-Century-Crofts.

Zuckerman, M., Klorman, R., Larrance, D. T., and Spiegel, N. H. (1981). Facial, Autonomic, and Subjective Components of Emotion: The Facial Feedback Hypothesis Versus the Externalizer-Internalizer Distinction. *Journal of Personality and Social Psychology* 41, 929–944.

Zunini, G. (1954). Sulle "attitudini" religiose di studenti universitari. *Archivio di Psicologia, Neurologia, Psichiatria e Psicoterapia*, 15, 205–249.

Zuriff, G. E. (1985). *Behaviorism: A Conceptual Reconstruction*. New York: Columbia University Press.

Zwingmann, C. (1991). *Religiosität und Lebenszufriedenheit: Empirische Untersuchungen unter besonderer Berücksichtigung der religiösen Orientierung*. Regensburg: S. Roderer.

Zwingmann, C., Hellmeister, G., and Ochsmann, R. (1994). Intrinsische und extrinsische religiöse Orientierung: Fragebogenskalen zum Einsatz in der empirisch-religionspsychologischen Forschung. *Zeitschrift für Differentielle und Diagnostische Psychologie*, 15, 131–139.

Zwingmann, C., Moosbrugger, H., and Frank, D. (1991) Religiöse Orientierung und ihre Bedeutung für den Zusammenhang zwischen Religiosität und Lebenszufriedenheit. *Zeitschrift für Pädagogische Psychologie*, 5, 285–294.

PHOTO CREDITS

Chapter 9   Page 372: Jon Erikson, courtesy Clark-Stewart. Page 388 (left): From Köstlin, *Luthers Leben*, p. 8. Page 388 (right): From Köstlin, *Luthers Leben*, p. 9. Page 391 (left): From P. J. Reiter, *Martin Luthers Umwelt, Charakter, und Psychose: Vol. 2. Luthers Persönlichkeit, Seelenleben und Krankheiten* (Copenhagen: Ejnar Munksgaard, 1941), p. 219. Page 391 (right): From Reiter, *Martin Luthers Umwelt, Charakter, und Psychose*, p. 218. Page 393: Courtesy Religious News Service. Page 399: Courtesy Trustees of the British Museum. Page 411: DPA/Vithalbhai/ The Image Works.

Chapter 10   Page 415: Corbis-Bettmann. Pages 421-422: Courtesy Fritz Bernhard. Page 429: David Wulff. Page 431: Museum of Art, Rhode Island School of Design. Page 441: From M. Maier, *Tripus aureus, hoc est, Tres tractatus chymici selectissimi.* Frankfort on the Main, 1618. Reprinted from Jung (1952b), p.290. Page 443: From *Mutus liber in quo tamen tota philosophia hermetica, figuris hieroglyphicis depingitur.* La Rochelle, 1677. Reprinted from Jung (1952b), p. 66. Page 444: From A. Watts, *Myth and Ritual in Christianity* (London: Thames and Hudson, 1954), p. 155. Page 446: Courtesy Museo del Prado. Page 448: From the Collections of the Library of Congress. Page 449: ©Group 2 by Ernest A. Myette. Page 452: From Strauss, *Dürer,* p. 179. Page 453: From Strauss, *Dürer,* p. 187.

Chapter 11   Page 474: By permission of the Houghton Library, Harvard University. Page 476: By permission of the Houghton Library, Harvard University, and Alexander R. James. Page 491: From the Collections of the Library of Congress. Page 496: Courtesy John Forasté, Brown University. Page 506: From G. E. Myers (1961), frontispiece. Pages 515 and 518: Courtesy William MacQuitty. Page 519: From W. Simpson, *The Buddhist Praying-Wheel* (New York: Macmillan, 1896), p. 19. Page 520: Courtesy Religious News Service. Page 521: Photograph by Bob Thayer for Brown University. Courtesy University Relations Photo Library.

Chapter 12   Page 534: Courtesy Marburg University Library. Page 537: Courtesy Japanese Information Center, Consulate General of Japan, New York. Page 539: Courtesy Donna M. Wulff. Page 540: From the Collections of the Library of Congress. Page 546: Erich-Retzlaff-Foto, from H. Wenke (Ed.), *Eduard Spranger: Bildnis eines geistigen Menschen unserer Zeit* (Heidelberg: Verlag Quelle & Meyer, 1957), frontispiece. Page 550: By permission of the Andover-Harvard Theological Library, Harvard University, and Matri Satsang. Page 558: From J. Frey (Ed.), *Die Theologische Fakultät der Kais. Universität Dorpat-Jurjew, 1802-1903* (Reval: Franz Kluge's Verlag, 1905). Courtesy Tonu Lehtsaar, University of Tartu. Page 566: From Strauss, *Dürer,* p. 185. Page 571: From *Archiv für Religionspsychologie und Seelenführung,* 1929, 4, frontispiece.

Chapter 13   Page 584: Courtesy Harvard University News Office©. Page 595: Rene Burri/ Magnum Photos, Inc. Page 600: From M. Geisberg, *The German Single-Leaf Woodcut: 1500-1550,* Vol. 2. Revised and edited by W. L. Strauss (New York: Hacker Art Books, 1974), p. 503. Page 605: Courtesy Brandeis University. Page 606: Topham/The Image Works. Page 607: Capital Features/The Image Works. Page 619: Giraudon/Art Resource. Page 625: Courtesy Dr. Rollo May. Page 627: Courtesy Dr. Viktor E. Frankl.

AUTHOR INDEX

SUBJECT INDEX